PHILOSOPHY OF EDUCATIONAL RESEARCH

American Educational Research Association
READINGS IN EDUCATIONAL RESEARCH

Merlin C. Wittrock, EDITOR OF THE SERIES

PHILOSOPHY OF EDUCATIONAL RESEARCH
Harry S. Broudy | Robert H. Ennis | Leonard I. Krimerman

INTELLECTUAL DEVELOPMENT
Pauline S. Sears

SOCIAL DEVELOPMENT AND PERSONALITY
George G. Thompson | Francis J. DiVesta | John E. Horrocks

LEARNING AND INSTRUCTION
Merlin C. Wittrock

EDUCATIONAL ORGANIZATION AND ADMINISTRATION
Donald A. Erickson

RESEARCH DESIGN AND ANALYSIS
Raymond O. Collier, Jr.

EVALUATION AND CURRICULUM DEVELOPMENT
William W. Cooley

PHILOSOPHY OF EDUCATIONAL RESEARCH

Harry S. Broudy

PROFESSOR OF PHILOSOPHY OF EDUCATION

University of Illinois, Urbana-Champaign Campus

Robert H. Ennis

PROFESSOR OF PHILOSOPHY OF EDUCATION

University of Illinois, Urbana-Champaign Campus

Leonard I. Krimerman

ASSOCIATE PROFESSOR OF PHILOSOPHY

University of Connecticut

JOHN WILEY & SONS, INC.

New York • London • Sydney • Toronto

Library of Congress Cataloging in Publication Data:

Broudy, Harry S   comp.
  Philosophy of educational research.

  (Readings in educational research)
  Bibliography: p.
  1. Educational research.   I. Ennis, Robert Hugh,
1927-   joint comp.   II. Krimerman, Leonard I.,
joint comp.   III. Title.

LB1028.B755   370'.72   72-2332
ISBN 0-471-10625-9

Printed in the United States of America

10-9 8 7 6 5 4 3 2 1

Preface

Since education is one of the most important human enterprises, it is understandable that efforts to comprehend its nature and to use it for the control of behavior go back to the beginnings of history. Every culture has its educational lore that includes a testament to the importance of education and advice on how to carry it on. However, every culture deplores the fact that generation after generation has fallen short in its program of inducting the young into the best elements of personal and social life. Clearly, the control of human behavior in some ways depends on education, but the manner in which education itself is to be controlled is not at all clear.

Such an important undertaking obviously should be founded on knowledge. What is needed is a science of education—a body of lawlike generalizations founded on facts about educational behavior, from which testable predictions can be made. How reasonable is the expectation that this need can be met?

In our attempt to control the physical environment we have been spectacularly successful in using technology based on scientific knowledge, but it is notoriously plain that we have had no such success in controlling the cultural environment. Can this lack of success be blamed on a lack of research? Hardly. The volume of research in psychology, economics, sociology, and anthropology—to mention a few of the behavioral sciences—has been expanding rapidly. In the last half-century a huge library of research studies in education has been accumulating; our faith in research has been stimulated and nurtured by sharp increases in financial support. And yet, the impact of this research on either the theory or the practice of education is diffuse, episodic, and uneven. It is almost as difficult to arrive at a dependable generalization on the effects of educational research as it is to arrive at a reliable generalization about education itself.

This raises questions. Is educational research being done properly? Is education a proper field for scientific scrutiny? Will the methods that have worked so brilliantly in the physical sciences be equally fruitful in the social and behavioral domains? Recent years have witnessed a widespread revolt among the young against the very idea of "controlling" human beings, and the computer has become the symbol of robotism, of dehumanization, of depersonalization. The apparent inability or unwillingness of our society to attack the problems of race, war, and poverty has embittered many thoughtful people even against the undeniable success of scientific technology. The methods that enabled us to land explorers on the moon, it is alleged, are not the methods by which we can decide whether we should go to the moon at all.

Stated another way, the chief question for educational research is how "scientific" such research can and ought to be. Can educational researchers meet the necessary conditions for an inquiry to qualify as being scientifically valid? This point is vital because if the answer is "No," then research may not be the most useful way of improving education; trial and error, proverbial wisdom, common sense, or tradition may be more reasonable alternatives.

How can we who are interested in these questions become oriented with respect to them? Clearly, one way is to become knowledgeable about the necessary conditions of being scientific and performing scientific experiments. What are scientific statements like? Are they like statements we ordinarily make in telling a story, describing a landscape, ordering a meal, persuading the multitude to vote for our candidate? How are scientific statements warranted? How do we show them to be true? What does it mean to have a "theory"? What does it mean to say that a theory "explains," that we can predict from a theory, and that we can test it? What suppositions do we make when we predict the future from events in the past?

These questions are dealt with in the philosophy of science. Sometimes the contents of the philosophy of science are called metascience because they are not themselves examples of scientific inquiry, but rather discussions about the methods and reasonings involved in such inquiries. Philosophers of science do not "do" science; instead, they talk about what scientists do when they do science. The value of talking about scientific methods in general (as distinct from a discussion of the methods used in such fields as physics, psychology, chemistry, and biology, on the one hand, and from *doing* science, on the other) is still being debated. There has always been a fairly strong sentiment in favor of teaching everybody in school how to think, on the grounds that there was a single scientific method that could be transferred to the methods of the several sciences. Dewey's *How We Think* had a great deal to do with the pedagogical popularity of this notion. Practicing scientists, on the other hand, seem less optimistic about the transfer value of formal instruction in scientific method or scientific thinking.

The scholarly study of education includes many types of inquiry. Although, generally, they could all be designated as "educational research," it is useful to distinguish between scholarly work on educational problems in general and that which purports to be scientific.

In a broad sense, scholarly work in the study of education consists of describing or explaining educational phenomena systematically in the context, or with the concepts, of some intellectual discipline. History provides one such context; others are provided by psychology, sociology, anthropology, economics, political science, philosphy, and physiology. Indeed, it is difficult to find a discipline that is not relevant to some aspect of education.

Insofar as educational investigators use the distinctive methods and canons of these disciplines, the field of educational scholarship is distinguished from other fields only by the fact that its problems have something to do with education or, more particularly, schooling.

Within this general field of educational scholarship, there are (or can be) inquiries that aim at discovering empirical generalizations or laws that not only purport to explain educational phenomena but also claim to meet certain logical and methodological criteria. These inquiries can be called, appropriately, scientific. If these generalizations or laws yield operational hypotheses of the form, "If we do A, B, and C, we can expect consequences P, Q, and R," then we are in a position to formulate rules of educational practice based on science; and we can claim to have an educational technology, that is, an art rationalized by knowledge.

Without denying the scholarly character of many inquiries into problems of education, this book is concerned primarily with research that is or claims to be empirical in character. The readings in Part I have been selected because they shed light on the conditions that would have to be met if such educational research were to make good its claims of being scientific. The readings in Part II deal with the theoretical issues involved in a science of education, assuming that there can be such a science.

The distinction between empirical research and other scholarly, but not empirical, studies of education is not absolute, and few if any inquiries are purely one or the other. Nevertheless, it is important to distinguish between an inquiry into the degree of correlation between family income and the level of schooling and one that discusses the proper role of the school in society in terms of some theory of the good life. There is an important difference between a theory of aesthetics that says "All aesthetic experience is expressive" and a piece of research designed to determine the frequency with which certain "expressive" words are used by first-graders confronted with a specified set of paintings. Many of the readings in this book deal with this distinction; here it is sufficient to point out that empirical knowledge is about matters of fact, about events and entities that have particular locations in time, and often in space. The other type of studies to which we have alluded are concerned directly with the relation between concepts and meanings, and only indirectly, if at all, to existing events. Philosophy in all its branches, political theory, and history represent dimensions on which scholarly work in education may be done, but these inquiries are not empirical in the sense explained above. Nevertheless, some of these scholarly inquiries are relevant to the empirical ones. Thus the philosophy of science contains materials that are concerned with the logical and methodological criteria of empirical activity, but are not themselves empirical truths.

Although the study of the philosophy of science is valuable to anyone who wishes to understand his world, the field has special relevance for the educational researcher who wishes to employ the methods of empirical science. This is true because in education—as well as in many of the behavioral sciences—the questions of method are not yet settled. Unlike the worker in physics or chemistry who can conduct his research with methods that he need not question, the educational researcher cannot assume that his approaches to data gathering and interpretation are logically or methodologically sound. Accordingly, the readings in Part II, which deal with such topics as observation, inference, testability, causation, and models are especially relevant to all scholarly workers in education. For much of the scholarly writing on educational problems, although not empirical, is concerned with the evaluation of findings and methods of empirical research.

Other volumes in this series present readings that describe actual educational researches; this book concentrates on the nature and conditions of scientific inquiry in general and of educational research in particular. Part I deals with the scope, nature, and strategy of educational research, and Part II deals with specific conceptual issues in educational research as well as those found in research in general.

This order of presentation may seem odd because one might argue that the student should first deal with general problems of scientific inquiry and then study the problems of strategy in educational research. Or, it could be argued that the student might profitably study the other, more specific books in this series and become immersed in samples of educational research before examining the more abstract considerations of research in general.

There is nothing wrong with these arguments, and in each case the user of this series must decide on the best strategy. For students already steeped in educational research the more abstract materials could be introduced at an early stage; for those innocent of educational research, the reverse procedure might be more advisable. Part II might be presented ahead of Part I or apposite selections from both parts might be presented together. The reason for the order that we have chosen for this book is that although the questions dealt with in Part I depend logically on those raised in Part II, the materials in Part II are more abstract, more technical, and more theoretical than those of Part I. It is our hope that the student, intrigued or provoked by the issues discussed and raised in Part I, will wish to plunge into Part II for more precise and rigorous lines of arguments and discussion.

There is an abundance of material on many of the topics, and we regret that space limitations required the omission of many good articles. Some could not be used because of the difficulty of securing permission from the authors or publishers. For further study of these topics, we suggest these starting points: 1) H. S. Broudy, M. J. Parsons, I. A. Snook, and R. D. Szoke, *Philosophy of Education: An Organization of Topics and Selected Sources*, Urbana: University of Illinois Press, 1967, and *Supplement*, 1969; 2) Paul Edwards, ed., *The Encyclopedia of Philosophy*, New York: The Macmillan Company and the Free Press, 1967; and 3) the bibliography at the end of this book.

In the preparation and organization of this volume we were helped by many individuals to whom we are deeply grateful, including Ruth Lewis, Wook Park, Hugh Petrie, Christiana M. Smith, Bruce Suttle, and Ronald D. Szoke.

The division of labor among us was approximately as follows: Harry S. Broudy, general supervision and the editing of Part I; Robert H. Ennis, the editing of Part II; and Leonard I. Krimerman, overall reactions to the work and the initial preparation of the bibliography.

Harry S. Broudy
Robert H. Ennis
Leonard I. Krimerman

Contents

PHILOSOPHY OF EDUCATIONAL RESEARCH

PART I

Nature and Scope of Educational Research

Educational Research and Science

As indicated in the Preface, this book has two major divisions. The first has to do with the nature of educational research, its goals, its scope, and its strategy—questions that would be less urgent if the methodology of educational research were unquestionably scientific and not subject to controversy. However, there is controversy, and what that controversy is about will be indicated in the selections that follow. We begin with an article that deals with the need and the possibility of disciplined inquiry for education; this is followed by a selection from Edward L. Thorndike that is now a classic in the effort to make the study of education scientific.

However, the question remains as to whether, or to what extent, there can really be a social "science"—whether the lack of spectacular success in the behavioral sciences is owing merely to the complexity of the data or the relative youthfulness of the field, or whether there is a more fundamental reason for the lack of success.

These questions have elicited many different answers. Those skeptical of the possibility of social sciences have appealed to what they regard as an important difference between human acts and physical objects as data for scientific inquiry. To be sure, this view concedes that human beings are ultimately composed of atoms and molecules in motion, or tissues, hormones, and bony structures; therefore, there is a sense in which the laws of physics, chemistry, and biology help us understand human behavior. But once this concession is made, it is apparent that what the laws of motion tell us about an attractive young person striding down the street or about a banker hurrying to catch a plane is about the last thing we care to know about these phenomena.

No, the data about the young person and the banker that make an inquiry into what they are "doing" interesting are not the states of their molecules or their tissues, but rather their intentions, their plans, their goals, their values, their beliefs, and their expectations.[1] Hence, it is held that to "understand" the activities of men singly or in groups one must reconstruct imaginatively and sympathetically the inner life of the actors; observation of their outward movements will be insufficient for understanding them.

To introduce this view we present a few excerpts from an early champion of it, Wilhelm Dilthey, a German philosopher whose principal writings appeared between 1870 and 1911. Many of these dealt with the difference between the natural sciences and what he called the "human studies." In the latter, he notes, the units are individual minds, known to us as they exist, whereas to get to the nature of physical objects science must develop elaborate constructs such as atoms, electrons, and so on, from which the nature of the object is inferred.

Dilthey concludes that our knowledge of historical and social phenomena has a peculiar limitation: we can understand them but we cannot explain them. The forces at work in society are intelligible (*verständlich*), because we can reconstruct them in our own experience, for we, too, are human. But of the laws that govern these phenomena—if indeed, there can be any—we are almost wholly ignorant; and this because the units of these phenomena are unique individuals, whose differences are the most important things about them, whereas in the natural sciences, the units are homogeneous. Furthermore, to explain human activities one needs to be sure of the motives of the actors, but, as Dilthey notes, the relative strengths of human motives change from one period to another, so that present experience is an unsafe guide to interpret the behavior of previous eras.

"How can subjective meanings be objictified for the purpose of scientific investigation?" The article by G. H. Bantock addresses itself to this question in its attempt to deal with the class of problems raised by Dilthey. The concept of *Verstehen* as a mode of comprehension appropriate to social phenomena is discussed in some detail and its relevance for education research is illustrated.[2]

[1] Cf. Charles Taylor, *The Explanation of Behavior* (London: Routledge and Kegan Paul, 1964) and Richard Taylor, *Action and Purpose* (Englewood Cliffs, N.J.: Prentice-Hall, Inc., 1966).

[2] For further reading on the notion of *Verstehen* and the related notion of methodological individualism, see Ludwig von Mises, *Theory and History* (New Haven: Yale University Press, 1957) and F. A. Hayek, *The Counter Revolution in Science* (Glencoe, Ill.: The Free Press, 1955). Also G. H. Bantock, "Educational Research: A Criticism," *Harvard Educational Review*, **31**, 3:264–280 (Summer, 1961).

A belief that social science (and, therefore, educational science) is possible is expressed in the article by Israel Scheffler. Included in the portion of the article reproduced here is a concise summary of the arguments pro and con on the possibility of assimilating social science to natural science. Scheffler's position is amplified by many philosophers of science, notably Ernest Nagel. See, for example, Ernest Nagel's *The Structure of Science* (New York: Harcourt, Brace and World, 1961), Chapters 13 and 14 of which might be consulted for further study.

Some specific differences in the approaches of the natural sciences and educational research are discussed in the article by J. A. Easley, Jr. He notes, for example, the "strong tendency to confuse an experimental approach in the general sense with statistical methods and models that go under the name of experimental design." He then examines the possibility of some new approaches to research in curriculum and instruction with special emphasis on what he calls "exploratory method," a phase of scientific activity that is often overlooked.[3]

---

[3] It might be profitable to refer to Chapter 6, "Value Judgments in Science," in Part II of this volume because the relation of science to value judgments is of prime importance to educational research and, indeed, to all research into human behavior.

1. DISCIPLINED INQUIRY

Lee J. Cronbach

In discussing disciplined inquiry and its relation to the improvement of education, we give no narrow definition to the term. Too many writers seem to limit the term "research" to quantitative empirical inquiry. While much has been and will be learned from social surveys, measurements, and controlled experiments, the study of education requires nonquantitative as well as quantitative techniques. Naturalistic observation, for example, has tended to fall into disuse, though it is a significant form of disciplined inquiry, as is illustrated by Newcomb's observations of the Bennington College community out of which emerged the ideas represented in today's "cluster colleges."

Inquiry is not restricted to the "scientific." Historical studies provide perspective on current proposals. An excellent case in point is the light cast on debates about public aid for church schools by scholarly studies on the origin and meaning of the first amendment to the Constitution. The philosopher adds to the clarity of educational discussions by helping in the statement and evaluation of goals and by sharpening educational theories. Logical analysis of the school's "subject matter" also can contribute to better instruction.

An inquiry generally sets out to answer a rather narrowly defined question. The specific findings of such inquiries are usually less important than the conceptualizations they generate.

Broadly applicable concepts raise the level of intelligence with which

SOURCE. Reprinted with permission of the Macmillan Company from *Research for Tomorrow's Schools* by Lee J. Cronbach and Patrick J. Suppes. Copyright © 1969 by National Academy of Education.

educational matters can be analyzed. There was a time, for example, when economists conceived of the economy as an occupational arena in which individuals competed for individual rewards; similarly, education was something the individual purchased as a personal capital investment. On the grand account, society's contribution to education was an expense item. In the economist's present view, individual abilities constitute a natural resource. Society reaps an economic reward when abilities are properly developed and deployed, and its educational outlay is a capital investment to be returned with interest. This conception has required planners to devise "manpower policies;" these in turn have raised the priority assigned to education in both the advanced and the developing nations.

Critical Processes. Disciplined inquiry has a quality that distinguishes it from other sources of opinion and belief. The disciplined inquiry is conducted and reported in such a way that the argument can be painstakingly examined. The report does not depend for its appeal on the eloquence of the writer or on any surface plausibility. The argument is not justified by anecdotes or casually assembled fragments of evidence. Scholars in each field have developed traditional questions that serve as touchstones to separate sound argument from incomplete or questionable argument. Among other things, the mathematician asks about axioms, the historian about the authenticity of documents, the experimental scientist about verifiability of observations. Whatever the character of a study, if it is disciplined the investigator has anticipated the traditional questions that are pertinent. He institutes controls at each step of information collection and reasoning to avoid the sources of error to which these questions refer. If the errors cannot be eliminated, he takes them into account by discussing the margin for error in his conclusions. Thus the report of a disciplined inquiry has a texture that displays the raw materials entering the argument and the logical processes by which they were compressed and rearranged to make the conclusion credible.

It is easiest to see the meaning of "discipline" when a study arises strictly within one of the established academic fields such as mathematics or sociology. In each such field there has evolved a consistent system of concepts, techniques, and critical questions, together with a prescribed form for presenting completed arguments. Each has a style well suited to investigate a certain range of problems. But disciplined inquiry can scarcely be mapped into the traditional disciplines, as disciplines themselves evolve.

Subdisciplines branch off within a field, and new hybrid disciplines emerge. Even fields that now have a tradition were new disciplines, or not accepted as disciplines at all, a century ago; this is true of genetics, psychology, even history. Just the past few years have seen new departures: quantitative studies in history, mathematical studies in sociology, and a psychology that uses the computer instead of the animal as an analogue to man. There is an attempt to develop an all-purpose form of disciplined inquiry under such a label as operations research, where the effort is to find a way of asking and answering questions that will generate insight into and control over virtually any complex process.

Disciplined inquiry does not necessarily follow well-established, formal procedures. Some of the most excellent inquiry is free-ranging and speculative in its initial stages, trying what might seem to be bizarre combinations of ideas and procedures, or restlessly casting about for ideas. There was nothing systematic, for instance, in Ventris' procedure for breaking the code of the Mycenaean script Linear B; the style of the inquiry was one of following hunches. But there was discipline in the checking of the hunches and in organizing the report so that any qualified reader could accept or reject the argument. Binet's inquiry into intelligence was not greatly different. He had some vagues ideas about the nature of intellect, but the indicators whose possible usefulness he explored ranged from rote memory to palmistry. His success came both from this openmindedness and from his relentless self-criticism, together with his convincing exposition of the reasons for the scale he finally proposed.

Not all the writings of academic men are scholarly reports. The person who completes a systematic inquiry will perhaps prepare an account of it in a freer style for the general public or for policy-makers. Such general writings may offer views on aspects of education the scholar has not studied intensively. They may extrapolate beyond the relatively limited conclusions strictly warranted by his research. Though essays, polemics, and statements of belief are outside the category of disciplined inquiry, they too can be important. In such writings the academic scholar speaks as a citizen joining the discussions of the community. He wins adherents by persuasive language, like any lawyer or executive who addresses the same audience. His specialized studies have given him a special perspective and, one hopes, some wisdom. His general writings are likely to offer fresh ideas. But a society that regards these essays as the academic man's chief work will not care properly for the headwaters from which the stream of ideas flows.

It is scarcely necessary to remark that not all conclusions of disciplined inquiry are true. Each investigation is limited by its methods, and the consensus of the best-informed members of a discipline is limited by the state of the art. In the most traditional academic fields conceptualizations and theories are continually being debated, and even factual conclusions are altered from time to time.

A disciplined inquiry does have an internal consistency that requires colleagues to take the findings seriously, even when they disagree with them. A scholarly report is considerably more than a printout of speculations, preconceptions, and wish-fulfilling observations. It nourishes thought. Indeed, the fact that it invites and rewards close examination is the mark of worthy inquiry. The detail of the argument, whether it is describing methods of data collection or the derivation of practical recommendations, is lucid, specific, and pertinent. With such a presentation there is something to learn from *explication de texte*, whereas in an undisciplined discussion the summary message is all that can be taken seriously.

The success of academic men in breaking old intellectual molds and inventing fresh concepts results from the fact that they value the process of inquiry at least as much as they value its fruits. They are trained in specialized techniques of observation and analysis. Instruments to refine the judgment of the observer, statistical models to weed out chance effects, mathematical models, canons of documentation, and formal criteria of acceptable definition, constitute the technology of inquiry. But far more fundamental to disciplined inquiry is its central attitude, which places a premium on objectivity and evidential test.

Discipline in Educational Inquiry.   Studies of education can share fully in this attitude. Anyone undertaking educational research can hold himself to the highest standards of careful observation and systematic reasoning. Admittedly, social processes are complex and ever-changing, and can rarely be experimentally controlled or comprehensively observed. Studying a classroom is at least as difficult as studying a hurricane. Even so, given sufficient effort, talent, and self-discipline, systematic inquiry can be expected to give a far more dependable explanation than will come from casual reflection upon casual observations.

Our interest is not confined to encouraging inquiry that advances one of the traditional disciplines. There are important studies to be done that will simultaneously increase knowledge about an aspect of education and understanding about a basic problem in a discipline such as sociology. There are worthwhile analyses to be made of practical educational situations, where techniques of one or more disciplines are employed solely to serve the educator. Other needed educational studies can scarcely be identified with any particular discipline. An example is the construction of the *Taxonomy of Educational Objectives*. The work was rigorous and subject to disciplined criticism. Though it was influenced by psychology, psychometrics, and philosophy, the statement of the problem and the critical questions applied were to some extent unique. Studies of education often have to assemble their own method and rationale, using bits and pieces of statistics, economics, philosophy, etc. to construct a suitably controlled inquiry.

This diversity implies that there is no uniform "method of educational research," and indeed each of the numerous textbooks on how to do educational research is a potpourri. This diversity presents serious problems in the preparation of research workers. The graduate faculty in Education must have extremely varied backgrounds if the faculty is to contain at least one individual well qualified in each important method of inquiry and criticism.

CONCLUSION-ORIENTED AND DECISION-ORIENTED INQUIRY

In the absence of well-understood categories, discussion of the contribution and promotion of various kinds of inquiry is not easy. An enthusiast for an investigatory activity affixes to it whatever label is likely to win favor from his particular audience at a given time. The popular labels "basic research" and "applied research" seem especially hard to employ precisely. It is extremely difficult to tell whether a research study is basic or applied: the cross-fertilization of peas by a curious monk does not differ in its operations from a cross-fertilization carried out on the plantings of a seed company in the hope of direct profit. Storer[1] decided that the main difference between the two approaches to inquiry is the proposed audience:

> Basic research is that which is carried out by a scientist who hopes his findings will be primarily of interest to his scientific colleagues, while applied research is intended to produce findings which will be of greater interest to the investigator's employer or to the lay public.

Marvin Reagan[2] offers the Storer quotation, and a dozen others, to show that the ambiguity of the basic-applied distinction obscures policy recommendations in any field. And when writers use it to categorize studies all of which are significant for education, it becomes extraordinarily troublesome.

Inquiries do need to be categorized, as a rhetorical device to point up contrasts between kinds of study that affect the school in different ways or that flourish in response to somewhat different environments. A distinction of this sort has to be taken lightly, however, for not only are there borderline cases, but a single program of investigation may cross the dividing line as the work progresses. The categories we use emphasize not the topics under study or the motivations of the investigators, but the conditions under which the studies take place.

We propose to distinguish *decision-oriented* from *conclusion-oriented* investigations.[3] In a decision-oriented study the investigator is asked to provide information wanted by a decision-maker: a school administrator, a governmental policy-maker, the manager of a project to develop a new biology textbook, or the like. The decision-oriented study is a commissioned study. The decision-maker believes that he needs information to guide his actions and he poses the question to the investigator. The conclusion-oriented study, on the other hand, takes its direction from the investigator's commitments and hunches. The educational decision-maker can, at most, arouse the investigator's interest in a problem. The latter formulates his own question, usually a general one rather than a question about a particular institution. The aim is to conceptualize and understand the chosen phenomenon; a particular finding is only a means to that end. Therefore, he concentrates on persons and settings that he expects to be enlightening.

The conclusion-oriented investigator is free to reframe his questions as he goes along, taking advantage of each partial insight to redirect his inquiry. Seaborg[4] has said,

> If the investigator is not free to make radical changes in his program or to pursue some unexpected question which has arisen in his work and which excites his curiosity as to why and how, the program is probably not too basic.

We would use the term "conclusion-oriented" rather than "basic," because this freedom for exploration and self-direction can be present in research on (e.g.) practices in school administration or on the effects of educational television—topics that many people would not consider basic.

Freedom is present in a decision-oriented inquiry to only a very limited degree. The investigator can decline the commission. He can recommend that the decision be made without the proposed study, on the ground that the study would not be valuable enough to repay its cost. He can seek to persuade the decision-maker that the wrong question is being asked, and that some different inquiry, perhaps one that will be much slower to arrive at an answer, will be a wiser undertaking. But unless such negotiations cause the decision-maker to sponsor a frankly conclusion-oriented and openended inquiry, the investigator undertakes to deliver an answer to the practical question, more or less on a stated schedule. He is not free to wander down interesting by-paths or to burrow into deeper questions, if that will delay telling the decision-maker what the latter wants to know.

Because of borderline instances our distinction can be puzzling. Two side comments may contribute to greater clarity. First, we acknowledge that often conclusion-oriented research is also commissioned; but the sponsor has a very different understanding of the research than the decision-maker who asks for direct help. Commissioning a conclusion-oriented study is like commissioning a composer to produce a symphony. One does not assign the theme, the key, or the mood; one asks only that he spend the resources on composing for the orchestra rather than on writing songs or writing an autobiography. When a School of Education appoints a research professor, it expects him to do research that can be seen as potentially interesting for education but it does not lay out the questions he is to answer. A slight extension applies to the mission-oriented agency that sponsors conclusion-oriented research. The head of the agency may need to direct the total program so that delivery dates for certain products are met, and yet he may engage investigators to do wide-ranging studies on topics within the agency's area of concern. The classification as conclusion-oriented or decision-oriented applies to a type of study, not to a program or an agency.

The conclusion-decision dichotomy has only a weak correspondence to the basic-applied distinction. Decision-oriented research no doubt is applied. Conclusion-oriented research, however, may also be concerned directly with educational institutions and instructional activities, and in that sense it too may be "applied research." We are not alone in recognizing that some studies of practically important matters should properly be categorized as basic or conclusion-oriented. We note that Frederick Seitz, as President of the National Academy of Sciences, spoke of *"true basic scientific* research of a pure or *applied* nature" (italics ours) in contrast to that spent for "engineering development, testing, and evaluation in preparation for possible production."[5]

The distinction between decision-oriented and conclusion-oriented research lies in the origination of the inquiry and the constraints imposed by its institutional setting, not in topic or technique, nor in the interests held by the investigator. The investigator in a decision-oriented study contracts to deliver the information that a particular school officer, program planner, or curriculum developer has requested. Once the decision-oriented study is undertaken, the investigator is expected to stay with the plan until he has a report on the question selected for study.

The conclusion-oriented study is not planned with an eye to a definite and useful result. The main benefit is in the unforeseen ideas it adds to society's intellectual capital. Hence the gain from a line of work can be judged only after the study has been completed and interpreted. The faith is that with a good many studies in progress, some of them will generate conceptual advances significant enough to offset the cost of the whole enterprise. As Lederberg has put it in a testimony before a Senate Committee,

> It is fair to say that society exploits the poetic fascination that motivates many academic scientists, eventually capitalizing on applications that no one could have foreseen. It may even be that research work loses rigor and sharpness of focus if the research worker himself is too sensitive to the unpredictable implications of what he is doing.
>
> It is important that such utilities be discovered as soon as they can be useful. This discovery, though, is a function of a whole community of basic and applied scientific effort. To place the burden [of practical justification, in advance] on individual projects would be the surest possible way of stifling the most creative and the least predictable advances in scientific understanding.[6]

The conclusion-oriented investigator does not promise to answer a particular question by a particular date. Pressure from a donor or superior to do so reduces him to the status of a technician for the duration of the study.

We warn the reader against reading a value judgment into our distinction. Neither type of inquiry is preferred over the other. The two have distinctive functions, but each needs the stimulus of the other, and neither alone can do the needed job. T. R. McConnell has put it well:

> Experience in other fields has shown that many processes intervene between research and production. . . . There is abundant testimony that the flow from research to development and innovation is neither unidimensional nor unidirectional. At any stage in the process the researcher, the developer, or the evaluator may have to cope with unanticipated variables. Furthermore, "feedback" occurs at various stages of the research-development-evaluation continuum. One stage enriches others; one phase may require adaptation in previous ones, or even an entirely new start.[7]

A particular set of data might be collected with either decision-making or conclusion-drawing in view. A decision-oriented study very often plays a role in the development of broad conclusions. An example is the study *Equality of Educational Opportunity*,[8] conducted for the U.S. Office of Education under a mandate from the Congress. The mandate circumscribed the questions to be asked about the education of minorities, the procedures to be used, and the time schedule for completing the report. The report placed the Congress and the Administration in a position to review their legislative plans. Being thus constrained, the study did not collect the data or follow the research strategy that might have appealed to a scientist seeking primarily to understand the effects of segregation and other differences among schools. The data are good enough, however, that sociologists and educational specialists have started to re-examine them in an effort to extract general conclusions. In addition to studying the published tables and summaries, these investigators are making further tabulations of the original data and trying to enrich the interpretation by direct observation in schools. Questions suggested by the survey inevitably lead to more direct, more intensive studies, some of them decision-oriented and some conclusion-oriented.

Conclusion-oriented research is intended to have a general significance, whereas decision-oriented research is designed for its relevance to a particular institution at a particular time. Occasionally the "institution" is a sprawling one, as in the study mentioned above, on how minorities fare within the American system as a whole. Most decision-oriented studies, however, have a local reference; it is not their aim to be suggestive for other institutions.

The conclusion-oriented study, even when carried out in a single setting, is intended to produce broadly applicable concepts and generalizations.

Thus Newcomb studied Bennington to gain insight into civic education in general. The specific data on Bennington were only incidental to the broader concepts reported, and if the investigator had been forced to move to a different setting he still could have carried on his study. In the decision-oriented study, however, the setting studied is of central interest and transferrable insights, while welcome, are not the aim. Because of its specificity, the decision-oriented study is likely to be carried out by an employee of a school system or another operating agency. Because of its generality, the conclusion-oriented study is normally directed by a university professor or a member of a research laboratory. But this is not a necessary division of labor. A case can be made for a certain amount of conclusion-oriented, publishable research carried out in school systems; this can contribute to the professional thinking of all who participate. And the scholar who joins a decision-oriented investigation comes to see his speciality differently in this value-laden context; the experience can make his subsequent thinking richer and more realistic.

Because conceptualization is the aim in conclusion-oriented work, the results are likely to be relevant to many human activities. A finding that adds to the base of knowledge about education is likely to add to knowledge about other social institutions. It is not especially important to decide whether a study is or is not directly concerned with education. What is vital is that the knowledge be developed with the encouragement and assistance of any of the agencies whose mission could eventually profit from such knowledge.

Types of Decision-Oriented Study. We find it useful to distinguish two kinds of decision-oriented research: (1) operational or institutional research; and (2) product or developmental research. The former is illustrated by the typical work of a research bureau in a city school system, the latter by the work of investigators developing programmed instructional materials for sale to schools. Operational studies are conducted in universities, state educational systems, national agencies such as the Joint Commission on Mental Health in Children, and various other private and public agencies of all sizes. Product research includes not only development of text materials but also the design and evaluation of school buildings and equipment, visual aids, and systems for administrative control such as scheduling by computer.

Operational research is obviously decision-oriented. The research office in the school system or the institutional research office in a university establishes routine procedures for monitoring certain aspects of the system, and uses them to identify trouble spots deserving administrative attention (e.g., dropout rates for various schools and various types of students). The office also conducts *ad hoc* studies of questions that arise in administrative planning

—for example, of the ways district lines could be redrawn to improve racial balance.

The role of each study is to provide the decision-maker with information, not to tell him what to do. The study gives an organized account of relevant facts, and may forecast the probable outcome of each of the possible alternative actions. The choice of action is the responsibility of the school executive rather than the investigator; only the executive or his advisory board is in a position to weigh the political, economic, and educational aspects of the choice.

Decision-oriented "product research" is part of an effort to develop an educational procedure that can be followed systematically in the future, ordinarily in many localities. Such product research is often called "development." Too often, especially in education, the word "development" refers simply to the construction of some procedure or material on the basis of general notions as to what will be effective. Deliberate inquiry, however, is an essential component in true developmental research. This inquiry is directed, first, to collecting information needed to design the product; then to testing the pilot versions in order to identify and explain remediable faults, and eventually to appraising the final product.

For the sake of completeness, we mention one type of inquiry that does not fit neatly into either the conclusion-oriented or decision-oriented category. This is the routine, continuous collection of facts that is often called social accounting. The best-known example of this is the United States census, which compiles facts thought likely to be useful for many different purposes. More mundane examples of social statistics are the compilations of data on enrollment and faculty salary for American schools and colleges. Studies of this sort produce data banks to which persons with diverse questions may turn. Some of them will use the facts as a basis for decision and some will use them in pursuing general conclusions. Although we shall not discuss this type of research at length, its social function is obvious.

Notes

1. Storer, N. W., *Basic Versus Applied Research: The Conflict Between Means and Ends in Science.* Cambridge: Harvard University Press, 1964.

2. Reagan, Marvin D., "Basic and Applied Research: A Meaningful Distinction?" *Science,* Vol. 155 (1967), pp. 1383–1386.

3. Tukey, J. W., "Conclusions vs. Decisions," *Technometrics,* Vol. 2 (1960), pp. 423–433; Merton, Robert B., "Basic Research and Potentials of Relevance," *The American Behavioral Scientist,* Vol. 6 (1963), pp. 86–90.

4. Seaborg, Glenn T., in *Federal Research and Development Programs*. Select Committee on Government Research. Washington, D.C.: Government Printing Office, 1964, Part 1, pp. 65–73.

5. Seitz, Frederick, *ibid.*, pp. 56–65.

6. Ledeberg, Joshua, "Some Problems of Instant Medicine," *Saturday Review*, Vol. 50 (March 6, 1967), pp. 66–70.

7. McConnell, T.R., *Research or Development: A Reconciliation*. Chicago: Phi Delta Kappa, 1967. p. 30.

8. Coleman, James, and others, *Equality of Educational Opportunity*. Washington, D.C.: Government Printing Office, 1968.

2. MEASUREMENT

Edward L. Thorndike

"Whatever exists, exists in some amount. To measure it is simply to know its varying amounts."

The assumption that specific, objective measurement is possible in the study of educational problems was crucial to the argument for a science of education. In 1904 Thorndike published the first complete theoretical exposition and statistical handbook in the new area of measurement in the social sciences. This book, *An Introduction to the Theory of Mental and Social Measurements*, became the standard reference. The brief excerpt printed here is from the introduction to the 1913 edition.

AN INTRODUCTION TO THE THEORY OF MENTAL AND SOCIAL MEASUREMENTS[1]

The Special Difficulties of Mental Measurement.   In the mental sciences, as in the physical, we have to measure things, differences, changes and relations. The psychologist thus measures the acuity of vision, the changes in it due to age, and the relation between acuity and vision and ability to learn to spell. The economist thus measures the wealth of a community, the changes due to certain inventions and perhaps the dependence of the wealth of communities upon their tariff laws or labor laws or poor laws. Such measurements, which involve human capacities and acts, are subject to certain special difficulties, due chiefly to (1) the *absence or imperfection of units* in which to

SOURCE. Reprinted with the permission of the publisher from Geraldine M. Joncich, ed., *Psychology and the Science of Education: Selected Writings of Edward L. Thorndike.* Copyright © 1962 by Teachers College Press, New York.
[1] New York: Teachers College, Columbia University, 1913.

17

measure, (2) the *lack of constancy in the facts* measured, and (3) the *extreme complexity* of the measurements to be made.

If, for instance, one attempts to measure even so simple a fact as the spelling ability of ten-year-old boys, one is hampered at the start by the fact that there exist no units in which to measure. One may, of course, arbitrarily make up a list of ten or fifty or a hundred words, and measure ability by the number spelled correctly. But if one examines such a list, for instance the one used by Dr. J. M. Rice in his measurements of the spelling ability of some eighteen thousand children, one is, or should be, at once struck by the inequality of the units. Is "to spell *certainly* correctly" equal to "to spell *because* correctly"? In point of fact, I find that of a group of about one hundred and twenty children, thirty missed the former and only one the latter. . . .

Economists have not yet agreed upon a system of units of measurement of consuming power. Is an adult man to be scored as twice or two and a half or three times as great a consumer as a ten-year-old boy? If an adult man's consuming power equals 1.00, what is the value of that of an adult woman?

If we measure a school boy's memory or a school system's daily attendance or a working man's daily productiveness or a family's daily expenditures, we find in any case, not a single result, but a set of varying results. The force of gravity, the ratio of the weight of oxygen to the weight of hydrogen in water, the mass of the H atom, the length of a given wire—these are, we say, constants; and though in a series of measures we get varying results, the variations are very slight and can be attributed to the process of measuring. But with human affairs, not only do our measurements give varying results; the thing itself is not the same from time to time, and the individual things of a common group are not identical with each other. If we say that the mass of the O atom is sixteen times the mass of the H atom, we mean that it always is that or very, very near it. But if we say that the size of the American sibling-group is two children, we do not mean that it is that alone; we mean that it is sometimes zero, sometimes one, etc.

Even a very elaborate chemical analysis would need only a score or so of different substances in terms of which to describe and measure its object, but even a very simple mental trait—say, arithmetical ability, or superstition or respect for law—is, compared with physical things, exceedingly complex. The attraction of children toward certain studies can be measured, but not with the ease with which we can measure the attraction of iron to the magnet. The rise and fall of stocks is due to law, but not to any so simple a law as explains the rise and fall of mercury in a thermometer.

The problem for a quantitative study of the mental sciences is thus to devise means of measuring things, differences, changes and relationships for which standard units of amount are often not at hand; which are variable, and so unexpressible in any case by a single figure; and which are so complex that, to represent any one of them, a long statement in terms of different sorts of quantities is commonly needed. This last difficulty of mental measurements is not, however, one which demands any form of statistical procedure essentially different from that used in science in general.

●   ●   ●

THE NATURE, PURPOSES, AND GENERAL METHODS OF MEASUREMENTS OF EDUCATIONAL PRODUCTS[2]

Whatever exists at all exists in some amount. To know it thoroughly involves knowing its quantity as well as its quality. Education is concerned with changes in human beings; a change is a difference between two conditions; each of these conditions is known to us only by the products produced by it—things made, words spoken, acts performed, and the like. To measure any of these products means to define its amount in some way so that competent persons will know how large it is, better than they would without measurement. To measure a product well means so to define its amount that competent persons will know how large it is, with some precision, and that this knowledge may be conveniently recorded and used. This is the general *Credo* of those who, in the last decade, have been busy trying to extend and improve measurements of educational products.

We have faith that whatever people now measure crudely by mere descriptive words, helped out by the comparative and superlative forms, can be measured more precisely and conveniently if ingenuity and labor are set at the task. We have faith also that the objective products produced, rather than the inner condition of the person whence they spring, are the proper point of attack for the measurer, at least in our day and generation.

This is obviously the same general creed as that of the physicist or chemist or physiologist engaged in quantitative thinking—the same, indeed, as that of modern science in general. And, in general, the nature of educational measurements is the same as that of all scientific measurements.

In detail, however, there are notable differences. An educational product, such as a composition written, a solution of a problem in arithmetic, an answer to a question about history, a drawing of a house or the performance of an errand, is commonly a complex of many sorts of things. The task of measuring it seems more like measuring a house or an elephant than it is like

[2] *The Measurement of Educational Products*, Seventeenth Yearbook of the National Society for the Study of Education, Part II (Bloomington, Illinois: Public School Publishing Company, 1918).

measuring a length or a volume or a weight. A complete measurement of, say, a composition might include an exact definition of its spelling, its usage of words, its usage of word forms, its wit, its good sense and so on and on; and each of these might again be subdivided into a score or more of component elements.

What we do, of course, is to make not such a complete measurement of the total fact, but to measure the amount of some feature, *e.g.*, the general merit of the composition or the richness of its vocabulary, just as physical science does not measure the elephant, but his height, or his weight, or his health, or his strength of pull. Every measurement represents a highly partial and abstract treatment of the product. This is not understood by some of our critics who object to tests and scales because of their limited point of view. The critic's real point should be that an educational product commonly invites hundreds of measurements, as we all well know. It should be noted also that single measurements are still in a sense complex, being comparable to volume, wattage or the opsonic index, rather than to length, weight or temperature.

In the second place, the zeros of the scales for the educational measures and the equivalence of their units are only imperfectly known. As a consequence, we can add, subtract, multiply and divide educational quantities with much less surety and precision than is desirable. Indeed, in any given case, the sense in which one educational product is twice as good or as desirable as another, or in which one task is twice as hard as another, or in which one improvement is twice as great as another, is likely to be a rather intricate and subtle matter, involving presuppositions which must be kept in mind in any inferences from the comparison.

In some cases so little is known of units of amount that we do not even try to equate distances along the scale, but simply express relative size in terms of arbitrarily chosen units and reference points. This is the case, for example, with the most commonly used measurement in psychology and education, that due to applying the Binet-Simon tests.

Nobody need be disturbed at these unfavorable contrasts between measurements of educational products and measurements of mass, density, velocity, temperature, quantity of electricity, and the like. The zero of temperature was located only a few years ago, and the equality of the units of the temperature-scale rests upon rather intricate and subtle presuppositions. At least, I venture to assert that not one in four of, say, the judges of the supreme court, bishops of our churches, and governors of our states could tell clearly and adequately what these presuppositions are. Our measurements of educational products would not at present be entirely safe grounds on which to extol or condemn a system of teaching reading or arithmetic, but many of them are far superior to the measurements whereby our courts of law decide that one trademark is an infringement on another. . . .

The purpose of measurements of educational products is in general to provide somebody with the knowledge that he needs of the amount of some thing, difference or relation. The "somebody" may be a scientific worker, a superintendent of schools, a teacher, a parent or a pupil. He may need a very precise or only an approximate measure, according to the magnitude of the difference which he has to determine. He may need it for guidance in many different sorts of decisions and actions.

Some of the most notable uses concern the value of studies in terms of the changes produced by them, the effects of different methods of teaching, and the effects of various features of a school system, such as the salary scale, the length of the school day and year, the system of examining and promoting pupils, or the size of class. There are many problems under each of these heads, and each of these problems is multifarious according to the nature, age, home life and the like of the pupils, and according to the general constitution of the educational enterprise, some small feature of which is being studied.

Another important group of uses concerns inventories of the achievements of certain total educational enterprises such as our educational surveys must become if they are to carry authority with scientific men. The total educational enterprise may be the work of a teacher, of a school, of an orphanage, of a prison, of a system of schools, or the like.

Another important group of uses centers around the problem of giving the individual pupil the information about his own achievement and improvement which he needs as a motive and a guide. It is interesting to note that the first of the newer educational scales, which was expected to be used chiefly by scientific investigators of the teaching of handwriting, now hangs on the wall of thousands of classrooms as a means for pupils to measure themselves. There are many other purposes, and important ones, such as the detection and removal of gross prejudices on the part of teachers in their own evaluations of certain educational aims and products. These, however, cannot be described here.

The superintendents, supervisors, principals and teachers directly in charge of educational affairs have been so appreciative of educational measurements and so sincere in their desire to have tests and scales devised which they can themselves apply, that the tendency at present is very strong to provide means of measurement which are concerned somewhat closely with school achievements, and which can be used by teachers and others with little technical training. There is also a tendency, because of this need for a large number of measurements in the case of educational problems, to try to devise tests which can be scored by persons utterly devoid of judgment concerning the products in question.

It would ill become the present writer to protest against these two tendencies; and they are intrinsically healthy. There is, however, a real danger in sacrificing soundness and principle and precision of result to the demand that we measure matters of importance and measure them without requiring elaborate technique or much time of the measurer. The danger is that the attention of investigators will be distracted from the problems of pure measurement for measurement's sake, which are a chief source of progress in measuring anything. Perhaps not even one person in a million need feel this passion, but for that one to cherish it and serve it is far more important than for him to devise a test which thousands of teachers will employ. Opposition, neglect, and misunderstanding will be much less disastrous to the work of quantitative science in education than a vast output of mediocre tests for measuring this, that and the other school product, of which a large percent are fundamentally unsound.

We have seen that educational measurements vary from an assignment of a certain amount of some clearly defined thing, the zero, or "just not any," of which is fairly accurately known, to a mere assignment of a certain position in a series of products themselves only similarly defined. They vary also from measurements in the most unimpeachable of units, such as time, to measurements where the unit is "that difference in quality which 75 percent of a certain sort of observers succeed in observing" or is even more crudely and hypothetically defined. They include measures in the form of how well a certain task is performed, and of how hard a task can be performed with a certain degree of success. Consequently, the methods of devising and using educational measurements also vary widely—too widely for any unified exposition. What will be said about methods here will, in fact, comprise only certain recommendations and cautions which are likely to be often appropriate.

Consider first certain principles of method designed to ensure reliable measures, or at least measures whose degree of unreliability is known and can be allowed for. These are:

At least two specimens or samples should be taken of any fact about which a statement is to be made. If any individual's achievement in drawing is to be reported, use at least two drawings. If the achievement of a class in addition is to be reported, use at least two tests, preferably on two days. If the effect of a method is to be estimated, test the method with at least two classes taught by different teachers. If the quality of a specimen of handwriting is to be reported, have at least two judges rate it independently. It will often appear from the comparison of two samplings of a fact that many more samplings are needed to permit a statement that is precise enough for the purpose in view.

No fixed rules can be given, since the purpose in view determines the degree of precision that is required, but it may be noted that a test which gives, for a single pupil, an approximation so rough as to be almost useless, gives for a class of thirty-six a result which is six times as precise, and for a group of nine classes a result which is eighteen times as precise. Ten times as large a sampling of the product in question is required to measure a single pupil as to measure the average of a hundred pupils (to the same degree of precision). In general, eight tests of 15 minutes each are superior to four tests of 30 minutes each, and still more superior to two tests of 60 minutes each, since the accidents of particular temporary circumstances are thus reduced in influence.

Consider next certain principles of method that need to be observed if we are to secure measures whose significance is certain.

Great care should be taken in deciding anything about the fate of pupils, the value of methods, the achievement of school systems and the like from the scores made in a test, unless the significance of the test has been determined from its correlations. For example, it cannot be taken for granted that a high score in checking letters or numbers is significant of a high degree of accuracy and thoroughness in general. Letter-checking tests have been so used, but with very little justification. Courtis has given reason to believe that a test with stock problems from text-books in arithmetic may be a very inadequate test of ability to reason with quantitative facts and relations, this ability being in such a test complicated by, and perhaps even swamped by, the ability to understand the verbal description of the facts and relations.

A pupil's score in a test signifies first, such and such a particular achievement, and second, *only whatever has been demonstrated by actual correlations to be implied by it.* Nothing should be taken for granted.

The significance of one *ability* (A) for another (B), is given by the correlation coefficient r_{AB} corrected for attenuation. The significance of a *particular test sampling* (A) for the ability (B) is given by the raw correlation coefficient r_{AB}. Thus, arithmetical ability itself is significant to a high degree of promise of ability with algebra and geometry, but a five-minute test in arithmetic would be much less so.

It is unfortunately the case that we do not at present know at all well the significance of any school ability or of any of the tests which we have devised as convenient means of sampling abilities. We need not blame ourselves for this; the educational measurements now in use are much better than none at all. They do excellent service, provided inferences are made with proper caution. They will do still better service in proportion as the correlations of each are determined. This work is extremely laborious, but sound method requires it.

Consider next certain principles of method designed to free measurements from certain pernicious disturbing factors, notably unfair preparation for the test, inequalities in interest and effort, and inequalities in understanding what the task is.

The best protection against unfair preparation is the provision of many alternative tasks of demonstrated equality in difficulty. This again means extremely laborious and uninteresting work, which nevertheless requires expert talent. It should be subsidized.

There is and can be no absolute assurance of equality in interest and effort. Any educational product is a product of ability conditioned by interest. All that we can do is to choose such conditions for the test as are found to reduce inequalities in interest and effort to a minimum (that is, to show high correlations with the composite of results obtained with a sampling of all conditions likely to influence interest). There is reason to believe that, when the test is taken as a part of school work, the appeal to group competition, as in "We wish to find out whether you can do as well as the sixth-grade children in Boston did," and a promise to report the results to each individual, are useful. In the case of high-school and college students a small payment in money or release from tasks, together with the promise of a full report to each individual, seems a useful method.

Inequalities in understanding what the task is, may be reduced by a preliminary trial, identical in form with the test itself, but with very easy content, and by giving special tuition to any pupil who fails in this preliminary trial. Instructions should be in simple language and should always be accompanied by at least three concrete samples of the task.

One who is eager to find imperfections can find many in present measurements of educational products. Nor is it a hard task to make constructive suggestions for improvement. An intelligent student of education could probably in a single day note a score of sure ways of improving the scales and tests which we now use. That is really child's play. The hard thing is the actual expert work of remedying the imperfection, for this involves hundreds of hours of detailed expert planning, experimenting and computing. What is needed in educational measurement is not the utterance by onlookers of criticisms and suggestion with which the men actually at work with measurements are as familiar as they are with their own names, but expert assistance in overcoming the defect.

If those who object to quantitative thinking in education will set themselves at work to understand it; if those who criticise its presuppositions and methods will do actual experimental work to improve its general logic and detailed procedure; if those who are now at work in devising and in using means of measurement will continue their work, the next decade will bring sure gains in both theory and practice. Of the gains made in the past decade, we may well be proud.

3. HUMAN STUDIES

Wilhelm Dilthey

THE PECULIAR NATURE OF THE HUMAN STUDIES

(From *The Construction of the Historical World in the Human Studies,*
chapter 1, *Delimitation of the Human Studies. G.S.,* VII, 86–7)

We can now mark off the human studies from the natural sciences by quite
clear criteria. These lie in the attitude of mind described above, by which, in
contrast with natural-scientific knowledge, the object of the human studies is
constituted. Mankind, if apprehended only by perception and perceptual
knowledge, would be for us a physical fact, and as such it would be accessible only to natural-scientific knowledge. It becomes an object for the human
studies only in so far as human states are consciously lived, in so far as they
find expression in living utterances, and in so far as these expressions are
understood. Of course this relationship of life, expression, and understanding
embraces not only the gestures, looks, and words in which men communicate,
or the enduring mental creations in which the depths of the creator's mind
open themselves to the spectator, or the permanent objectifications of mind
in social structures, through which the common background of human nature
shines and is permanently visible and certain to us. The mind-body unit of
life is known to itself through the same double relationship of lived experience and understanding, it is aware of itself in the present, it rediscovers

SOURCE. Reprinted from *Wilhelm Dilthey: An Introduction* by H. A. Hodges, 1944, International Library of Sociology and Social Reconstruction Series. Copyright © 1944 by
Routledge & Kegan Paul Ltd., the publishers.

itself in memory as something that once was; but when it tries to hold fast and to apprehend its states, when it turns its attention upon itself, the narrow limits of such an introspective method of self-knowledge make themselves felt. Only from his actions, his fixed utterances, his effects upon others, can man learn about himself; thus he learns to know himself only by the round-about way of understanding. What we once were, how we developed and became what we are, we learn from the way in which we acted, the plans which we once adopted, the way in which we made ourselves felt in our vocation, from old dead letters, from judgments on us which were spoken long ago. In short, it is through the process of understanding that life in its depths is made clear to itself, and on the other hand we understand ourselves and others only when we transfer our own lived experience into every kind of expression of our own and other people's life. Thus everywhere the relation between lived experience, expression, and understanding is the proper procedure by which mankind as an object in the human studies exists for us. The human studies are thus founded on this relation between lived experience, expression, and understanding. Here for the first time we reach a quite clear criterion by which the delimitation of the human studies can be definitively carried out. A study belongs to the human studies only if its object becomes accessible to us through the attitude which is founded on the relation between life, expression, and understanding.

From this common nature of the studies in question follow all the peculiarities which have been emphasized in discussions on the human studies, or cultural studies, or history, as constituting their nature. Thus the peculiar relation in which the unique, singular, individual stands here to universal regularities. Then the combination which takes place here of statements of fact, judgments of value, and ideas of purpose. Again, "the apprehension of the singular or individual is in them as much an ultimate end as is the development of abstract uniformities."[1] But still more will result from this; all the leading concepts with which this group of studies operates are different from the corresponding ones in the field of natural science.

THREE CLASSES OF STATEMENTS IN THE HUMAN STUDIES

(Chapter VI of the *Introduction to the Human Studies. G.S.,* I, 26–7)

The human studies as they exist and operate, by virtue of that logic of facts which was at work in their history (not according to the wishes of the rash architects who desire to rebuild them), combine in themselves three distinct classes of statements. One class of them assert a reality which is given in perception; they include the historical component in knowledge.

[1] Quoted from Dilthey's own *Introduction to the Human Studies.*

Another class unfold the uniform relations between parts of this reality which are singled out by abstraction: they form the theoretical component. The third class express value-judgments and prescribe rules: in them the practical component in the human studies is comprised. Facts, theorems, value-judgments and rules: of these three classes of propositions the human studies are composed. And the relation between the historical, the abstract theoretical, and the practical tendencies in the conception of the human studies is a common basic relationship pervading them all. The apprehension of the singular or individual is in them (since they are the standing refutation of Spinoza's principle, *omnis determinatio est negatio*) [all determination is negation] as much an ultimate end as is the development of abstract uniformities. From the first root in consciousness up to the highest peak the system of value-judgments and imperatives is independent of that of the first two classes. The relation between these three tasks for the thinking consciousness can only be developed in the course of the epistemological analysis. . . . In any case statements about reality remain radically separate from value-judgments and imperatives, and thus arise two kinds of propositions which are different in principle. And at the same time it must be recognized that this difference within the human studies has for its consequence a duality in their structure. As they have grown up, the human studies include, along with the knowledge of what is, the consciousness of value-judgments and imperatives as forming a system in which values, ideals, rules, the tendency towards shaping the future, are bound up together. A political judgment which condemns an institution is not true or false, but right or wrong, in so far as its tendency or aim is estimated; on the other hand, a political judgment which discusses the relations between this institution and other institutions can be true or false. Only when this insight becomes a guiding principle for the theory of statements, assertions, and judgments, can there arise an epistemological groundwork which does not compress the actually existing human studies into the narrow frame of a knowledge of uniformities on the analogy of natural science, and in that way mutilate them, but comprehends and upholds them as they have grown up.

INDIVIDUUM EST INEFFABILE

(From the *Introduction to the Human Studies.   G.S.*, I, 28–9)

The datum which is the starting-point of enquiry in the natural sciences is the sensible appearance of bodies of various sizes, which move in space, extend and expand, shrink and diminish, in which changes of character take place. Only by degrees have these sciences made their way to more correct views of the constitution of matter. In this respect our intelligence stands in a much more advantageous relation to the reality of history and society. The unit which is the element in the very complicated structure of society is given immediately to the intelligence—it is itself—while in the natural sciences it has to be inferred. The subjects to which thought, according to its invariable law, attaches the predications through which all knowledge comes about, are in the natural sciences elements which are obtained by a division of external reality, a breaking and splitting up of things, and then only as hypotheses; in the human studies they are real units given as facts in inner experience. Natural science builds matter up out of small elementary particles incapable of independent existence and only conceivable as components of molecules; the units which interact in the marvelously complex whole of history and society are individuals, wholes composed of mind and body, each of which is distinct from every other, each of which is a world. Indeed, the world is nowhere else but in the consciousness of such individuals. This immensity of a mind-body whole, in which in the last resort the immensity of nature is contained, can be illustrated by the analysis of the world of ideas, where from sensations and ideas an individual intuition is built up, which then, whatever wealth of elements it may comprise, enters as only one element into the conscious combination and separation of ideas. And this singularity of each and every such individual who operates at any point in the immense cosmos of mind can be followed out into his several components, according to the principle, *individuum est ineffabile,* and only so does it become known in its full significance.

4. EDUCATIONAL RESEARCH: A CRITICISM

G. H. Bantock

1.

In recent years research in the psychosocial sciences has come in for considerable criticism. Adverse comment has been directed against the philosophical preconceptions in terms of which empirical research in these fields has been carried on, against particular imperfections in methodology, and on the grounds of the comparative triviality of both the matters which have received attention and of the results which have accrued. In so far as certain sorts of research in education employ procedures characteristic of research in the social sciences (and although the two fields are obviously by no means co-extensive, there is some overlap in that certain educational problems involve sociological or socially psychological factors), many of the criticisms directed against what goes on in the psychosocial sciences have their relevance in the educational field also. The nature of these criticisms, therefore, must be carefully examined. I must state straight away that it is with research in education of this kind that I shall be almost exclusively concerned in this article.

In education, as in the study of society generally, the claim is often made that investigation involves methods of research analagous to those employed in the natural sciences and that the findings can be established with a similar

SOURCE. Bantock, G. H., "Educational Research: A Criticism," *Harvard Educational Review*, **31**, Summer 1961, 264–280. Copyright © 1961 by President and Fellows of Harvard College.

degree of certainty. Thus, for example, the Director of the National Foundation of Educational Research in England has said:

> Over the last sixty years or so, we have come to see that there are
> . . . educational *sciences* which, within their scope, are as susceptible
> to scientific rigour as are the so-called exact and natural sciences.[1]

Yet Dr. Wall notes, in the fields susceptible to scientific investigation, the importance of large scale enterprises undertaken by a team of researchers:

> The complexity of the variables with which we are faced in any real
> problem, coupled with the facts that the variation of one factor at
> a time and the destruction of experimental material, are impossible,
> make the educational sciences extremely precarious if they are not
> pursued by a well equipped team. Moreover exact replication of
> experiments is impossible. Hence we are obliged to rely upon
> carefully chosen large samples, upon the closest possible estimates of
> statistical probability (rather than on exact demonstration) and
> upon a sufficient awareness of sources of error so that they can be
> randomised if not controlled or eliminated.[2]

Here he seems to be admitting that the educational sciences are not, in fact, "as susceptible to scientific rigour as are the so-called exact and natural sciences." But it is interesting to note the grounds on which he admits this. They are based on the complexity ("the variables") of the situations involved and on the fact that in many cases it is not possible to arrange experimental situations involving human beings. There is no suggestion that the nature of the basic "material" of the educational or social sciences may often be different *in kind* from that investigated by the physical sciences. Yet it is on such grounds that the attack on current modes of research in the social sciences has been mounted. The attempt to assimilate the natural and the social sciences, it is urged, is fundamentally a mistake.

The situation has been admirably analysed recently by Mr. P. Winch:

> . . . the notion of a human society involves a scheme of concepts
> which is logically incompatible with the kinds of explanation offered
> in the natural sciences.[3]

---

[1] W. D. Wall, *Educational Research and the Needs of the Schools*. An address delivered at the Annual Conference of the National Association of Inspectors of Schools and Educational Organisers, October 2, 1959 (London: National Association of Inspectors of Schools and Educational Organisers, 1959), p. 3.

[2] *Ibid.*, p. 5.

[3] P. Winch, *The Idea of a Social Science* (London: Routledge and Kegan Paul, 1958), p. 72.

Winch analyses a classical exposition of this view that social phenomena are of the same order as physical, only very much more complicated and involving more variables. He demonstrates its falsity by showing that the natural scientist is governed by only one set of rules, those relevant to scientific investigation, whereas the social scientist has to take into account another set of rules as well, those involved in the "phenomenon" he is investigating; for this phenomenon is itself a manifestation of social activity which will normally be subject to human purposes and meaning in a manner in which natural phenomena are not. This implies that the understanding of social phenomena involves a qualitatively different approach to that needed with natural, in that such understanding implies something more than simply external observation: it necessitates at least an imaginative projection into what the phenomena concerned mean, a meaning which can only come fully from inside the activity to be studied:

> . . . a historian or sociologist of religion must himself have some religious feeling if he is to make sense of the religious movement he is studying. . . . A historian must have some aesthetic sense if he is to understand the problems confronting the artists of his period; and without this he will have left out of his account precisely what would have made it a history of *art*, as opposed to a rather puzzling external account of certain motions which certain people have been perceived to go through.[4]

Mr. Winch's analysis of social phenomena[5] has been considerably influenced by the concept of *Verstehen* adopted by Max Weber and other German social theorists. Quentin Gibson, in his recent book,[6] refers to this concept as involving "a sympathetic understanding of our fellowmen, of finding a meaning in their activities, of grasping intuitively how they feel, what their plans are, what they are driving at." He denies, however, that such "sympathetic understanding" can provide us "with any evidence of an alternative kind" to that supplied empirically, i.e., that "obtained from our sensory observations of the world around us or from our awareness of our own mental processes."[7] He does not deny that participating in a social process may be valuable as a means to understanding; but to do so, he considers, simply places the investigator in a "peculiarly favourable position to give evidence"; it does not open up to him sources of evidence different in *kind* from that available to others:

---

[4] *Ibid.*, p. 88.

[5] He has other important points to make about the possibilities of prediction and the role of generalisation.

[6] Cf. Quentin Gibson, *The Logic of Social Enquiry* (London: Routledge and Kegan Paul, 1960).

[7] *Ibid.*, pp. 47–48.

Unless the anthropologist becomes accepted by the members of the tribe, there are many things he will not hear about. Unless he is in a position to observe the daily round of inconspicuous activities, he will not have the material from which to infer beliefs and attitudes.[8]

But, surely, it is not simply a matter of the "things he will not hear about"; it is a question of the meanings that are to be attached to what he does know about. A social act takes on meaning from the subjective understanding of a personality participating within a specific framework and may differ in significance in accordance with depth of penetrative comprehension. Even when the general character of certain religious practices is recognized as such, the "meaning" that may have to the believer can play a quite different role in the life of that believer from what they can in that of a non-believer. In the same way, the act of sex can "mean" anything from the semi-clinical ("relief of tension") to the semi-mystical ("She is all States, and all Princes, I. . . .").[9]

It may be urged that, even so, our knowledge would still ultimately rest on observation or awareness of our own mental processes.

This may be so; but it is not the point at issue. The significance of the notion of *Verstehen* lies in the way it helps us to appreciate how understanding the social and the natural world may differ. In the case of the latter, we only need to impose our concepts on the regularities observed; in the case of the former, such regularities as are observed take on meaning in relation not to the concepts *we* employ to distinguish them but to the social meanings they already have independently of our observation. It is so that we may arrive at the second order of meaning that "sympathetic understanding" is important. It might, of course, still be argued that the "true" participant understands things which the social scientist who participates only to understand misses—that in the very act of our self-awareness of our own mental activities, we separate ourselves from the unself-conscious experience. And, of course, in what follows I certainly do not wish to deny that much knowledge may be gained by purely external observation, or that there are, for instance, "psychosocial phenomena which are repeated in time and space and lend themselves to statistical mass observation"—such as "the ever-repeated mass phenomena of births, deaths, marriages, divorces" and so on.

The above quotation is from Professor P. Sorokin's recent attack on cur-

---

[8] *Ibid.*, p. 51.

[9] Indeed, one of the difficulties about social investigation is that certain sorts of experience belong, socially, only to a few, though there may be elements within the experience common to mankind—as in sex relationships. Hence the tendency, in so much social investigation, to treat experience at a comparatively crude level; the act of sex, in such investigations, is usually reduced to its common physiological element.

rent methods in sociology.[10] This is a book which obviously needs to be treated with a great deal of caution, as it is frequently intemperate and unbalanced. Nevertheless it contains numerous acute criticisms of modern techniques of psychosocial investigation. Sorokin, indeed, divides social phenomena into two broad categories: what he terms "congeries," chance collocations of unrelated social phenomena similar in kind to the mass phenomena cited above, and "systems," in which the relationships of the parts are of a qualitatively different nature, corresponding to the organic meaning structure implicit in the phenomenon concerned. Such "systems" are understood not through external observation but through "direct cofeeling and coexperiencing":

> Only through direct empathy . . . can one grasp the essential nature
> and difference between a criminal gang and a fighting battalian;
> between a harmonious and a broken family. . . . The same can be
> said of the nature and differences of religious, scientific, aesthetic,
> ethical, legal, economic, technological, and other cultural value-systems
> and their subsystems. Without the direct living experience of
> these cultural values, they will remain *terra incognita* for our outside
> observer and statistical analyst.[11]

In support of his views on intuition he even cites current practice in the natural sciences themselves, where intuition has an important part to play; and concludes that "the anti-intuitional and anti-rational position of our psycho-social empiricists is obsolescent."

Yet, of course, reliance on "intuition" has its grave dangers; one is reminded of Karl Popper's tart comment: "By their intuition some people are prevented from even imagining that anybody can possibly dislike chocolate." And certainly, intuition works better when controlled by the known facts; the intuition of the *natural* scientist, which plays its part in the formation of hypotheses, nevertheless works within the framework created by the discipline of investigation involved. The question now arises as to how the social

[10] P. A. Sorokin, *Fads and Foibles in Modern Sociology* (Chicago: Henry Regnery, 1956).

[11] *Ibid.*, pp. 159–160. Sorokin has many other criticisms to offer—notably about the basis of mental testing (cf. his "Testomania," *Harvard Educational Review*, XXV (Fall, 1955) 199–213.), the emphasis on quantitative methods, the deficiencies of supposedly "experimental methods" and the use of controls, and the drawbacks inherent in questionnaire methods. He is particularly contemptuous of "speech-reactional operations," the lack of adequate definition of terms, the deficiencies of investigations into group behavior, where some of the studies at least are "more dull and vague than a description of the case by a competent novelist or an imaginative participant-observer," and the fallacy of expecting precise prediction in this field. All of these have their relevance to the sorts of techniques, methods and expectations arising from research in the educational fields.

scientist, in view of the complexity of the situation by which he is faced—a complexity, be it noted, which is not reducible simply to a question of "variables" in the sense in which that word would be applicable in the physical sphere—can manipulate his concepts. He cannot simply "arrange" the external world so as to accord with the traditions of his undertaking, for that part of the external world in which he is interested has its own set of meanings, and without some cognisance of those meanings in and for themselves, his undertaking would be fruitless. Further, such concepts may involve problems of value, about which agreement is likely to be difficult to achieve.

One of the most interesting solutions to the problem of how meaning-structures which contain a subjective or evaluative element can be made in some measure objective for scientific investigation is that suggested by the late Alfred Schutz (Schuetz). Schutz accepts the difference between the physical and social worlds and urges that the task of the social sciences is "to develop methodological devices for attaining objective and verifiable knowledge of a subjective meaning structure." His aim methodologically is not to rely exclusively on "empathy" or intuitive understanding but to clarify conceptually how the interpretative subjective understanding men practice in their daily lives in the common sense world can be harnessed to the requirements of what he insists is a *science*. Hence he refers to the "erroneous conclusion that the social sciences are *toto coelo* different from the natural sciences, a view which disregards the fact that certain procedural rules relating to correct thought organisation are common to all empirical sciences."[12] And he refutes the doctrine of what he terms "sensationalistic empiricism . . . which identifies experience with sensory observation and which assumes that the only alternative to controllable and, therefore, objective sensory observation is that of subjective and, therefore, uncontrollable and unverifiable introspection."[13]

Schutz derives much of his positive theory from a refinement of this concept of *Verstehen*, which he translates as "Interpretative Understanding." He begins by considering in some detail how in common sense experience we arrive, in the world of intersubjectivity which is the social world, at an "understanding" of each other. He considers that *Verstehen* simply refers to that understanding of each other at which we arrive by common sense and social acculturation in the ordinary course of events. Furthermore, there are many social situations where what appears to be the privacy of the individual is subject to the publicly verifiable and accountable rules of procedure con-

[12] Alfred Schuetz, "Common-sense and Scientific Interpretation of Human Action," *Philosophy and Phenomenological Research*, XIV (September, 1953), p. 4. I am grateful to Dr. Asher Tropp for drawing my attention to the work of Schutz.

[13] Alfred Schutz, "Concept and Theory Formation in the Social Sciences," *The Journal of Philosophy*, LI (April 29, 1954), p. 261.

trolling the nature of the experience concerned. In illustration he offers the discussions of a trial jury, where the "rules of procedure" are furnished by the "rules of evidence," as controlling elements. It is this "exploration of the general principles according to which man in daily life organises his experiences, and especially those of the social world" which "is the first task of the methodology of the social sciences."[14] Central to the solution of this task is the notion of typicality, with the opportunity it affords for some degree of generalisation.

"Typification" involves an abstraction from the concrete world around one made for the particular purpose in hand. "Objects" are invested with meaning in accordance with these purposes. These meanings are in the last resort only known to the actors. But in so far as their actions form part of the social world, they are open to the same sort of common sense interpretation as has been noted above—something which in daily life we all accomplish frequently. It may therefore be impossible to understand fully the subjective meanings people infuse into their actions (a point which, incidentally, a reading of Joseph Conrad would reinforce), but they can be understood in their typicality; thus:

> . . . the social scientist replaces the thought objects of common sense
> thought relating to unique events and occurrences by constructing
> a model of a sector of the social world within which merely those
> typified events occur that are relevant to the scientist's particular
> problem under scrutiny. [In order to do this, he constructs] typical
> patterns of the actors' motives and ends, even of their attitudes and
> personalities, of which their actual conduct is just an instance or
> example.[15]

These are the first level constructs, involving the notion of subjective interpretation, on which the second level constructs of the social sciences have been built up. The difficulty now is: all scientific explanations of the social world must involve these subjective meanings; but, to be scientific, their propositions must be subject to verification and not refer simply to private uncontrollable experience. In other words, how is it possible "to form objective concepts and an objectively verifiable theory of subjective meaning-structure?"[16]

The answer lies in the construction of models—"homunculi—in terms of which the social situation can be "interpreted."[17]

---

[14] *Ibid.*, p. 267.

[15] *Ibid.*, p. 268.

[16] *Ibid.*, p. 270.

[17] This notion of "homunculi" has, of course, been much influenced by Max Weber's concept of the Ideal Type.

The basic insight that the constructs formed by the social scientist
are constructs of the constructs formed in common-sense thinking
by the actors on the social scene offers an answer.[18]

These scientific constructs are "ideal typical constructs" created as part of
the scientist's procedural rules with regard to relevance, thus ensuring the
objectivity of the investigation. How are they arrived at? The social scientist

... observes certain facts and events within social reality which refer
to human action patterns from what he has observed. Thereupon he
co-ordinates to these typical course-of-action patterns models of an
ideal actor or actors, whom he imagines as being gifted with
consciousness. Yet it is a consciousness restricted so as to contain
nothing but the elements relevant to the performing of the
course-of-action patterns observed. He thus ascribes to this fictitious
consciousness a set of typical notions, purposes, goals, which are
assumed to be invariant in the specious consciousness of the imaginary
actor-model. This homunculus or puppet is supposed to be interrelated
in interaction patterns to other homunculi or puppets constructed
in a similar way. Among these homunculi with which the social
scientist populates his model of the social world of everyday life, sets
of motives, goals, roles—in general, systems of relevances—are
distributed in such a way as the scientific problems under scrutiny
require. Yet . . . these constructs are by no means arbitrary. They
are subject to the postulate of logical consistency and to the
postulate of adequacy. The latter means that each term in such a
scientific model of human action must be constructed in such a way
that a human act performed within the real world by an individual
actor as indicated by the typical construct would be understandable
to the actor himself as well as to his fellowmen in terms of
common-sense interpretation of every-day life. Compliance with the
postulate of logical consistency warrants the objective validity of the
thought objects constructed by the social scientist; compliance
with the postulate of adequacy warrants their compatibility with
the constructs of everyday life.[19]

Thus can subjective meanings be objectified for the purpose of scientific
investigation.

[18] Schutz, op. cit., p. 270.

[19] Further detailed account of these "homunculi" will be found in "Common-sense and
Scientific Interpretation," pp. 31–33. And the criteria operative in their creation—relevance, adequacy, logical consistency and compatibiilty—are discussed in Alfred Schuetz
"The Social World and the Theory of Social Action," Research, XXVII (Summer, 1960),
pp. 220–221.

In the creation of homunculi I can add a refinement on my own account. A training in literature is of great assistance in the sensitising of the intelligence to the complexities of social life and to the psychological reactions of individuals in social situatons, in that literature uniquely affords the feel of the "whole man alive," as D. H. Lawrence pointed out. The literary intelligence can do much to refine the comparatively crude notions of personalities employed in educational research by affording the subjective element in the creation of homunculi width and depth and at the same time by admitting that notion of universality which is an acknowledged criterion of great literature. Researchers, indeed, could do worse than to study the *Notebooks* of Henry James or *The Art of the Novel*. To be specific, what I have in mind is the sort of sensibility cultivated by the artist in relation to his "characters" —represented, for instance, by Turgenev's desire, quoted by James,

> . . . to show my people, to exhibit their relations with each other; for that is all my measure. If I watch them long enough, I see them come together. I see them *placed*, I see them engaged in this or that act, in this or that difficulty. How they look and move and speak and behave, always in the setting I have found for them, is my account of them . . .

together with James' subsequent comments in the preface to *The Portrait of a Lady*. Such insight, controlled by Schutz's postulates of relevance, adequacy, logical consistency and compatibility, offers a step in the direction of a refinement of type creation.[20]

Before I attempt to illustrate by the actual examination of some pieces of educational research how some of the foregoing principles might be applied, there is one final methodological point to be made. Despite some attempts in that direction, the discipline of social research has not succeeded in creating a specialized language of its own; indeed, in view of the nature of its subject matter which, as I have emphasized, is unlike that of the physical sciences in that it deals with what already has meaning apart from that assigned to it by the scientist, it is possible that the social sciences will never succeed in creating a fully technical vocabulary. Since, then, the statement of research topics usually involves the use of words common in every-day usage, the prime requisite in the consideration of research problems is the conceptual clarification of the terms employed, at least to the extent that possible ambiguities are cleared up or that ostensive definitions are offered. Extended clarifications of the type I have in mind can be found in R. S. Peters' *The Concept of Motivation* and in other books in the valuable series of "Studies in Philo-

---

[20] On the role of the literary intelligence in education see my "Education and the Literary Intelligence" in *Education for Teaching*, XXXVIII (November, 1955).

sophical Psychology" to which Mr. Peters' book belongs. A recent article in the *Harvard Educational Review* on research into the relative effectiveness of teacher- and learner-centred methods in education reveals the immense wastage which springs from a failure to analyse adequately the concepts of "democratic" and "authoritarian" teaching respectively.[21] It is disturbing to find how little modern philosophical techniques of linguistic analysis and clarification have affected our thinking about social science research; yet as a preliminary to any such research it is important at least to decide what questions involved are really conceptual and what empirical. As Winch observes:

> . . . many of the more important theoretical issues which have been raised in [social science studies] belong to philosophy rather than to science and are, therefore, to be settled by a priori conceptual analysis rather than by empirical research. For example, the question of what constitutes social behaviour is a demand for an elucidation of the *concept* of social behaviour. In dealing with questions of this sort there should be no question of 'waiting to see' what empirical research will show us; it is a matter of tracing the implications of the concepts we use.[22]

2.

It is necessary to see how the methodological notions we have been examining might affect our assessment of some contemporary educational research. I will take most of my examples from the English Journal, *Educational Research*, though the articles concerned draw extensively on research undertaken in the United States as well as in England.

One omission which can frequently be noted lies in the neglect of an adequate clarification of the concepts employed. Thus Dr. Kellmer Pringle, in the article, "Social Learning and Its Measurement"[23] becomes involved with the extremely difficult conceptual problem as to what constitutes "social maturity." She opens her article with the surprising remark that "The adult who is socially mature is not hard to recognize," and proceeds to list five broad characteristics, each of which merits further analysis on its own account. She then comes to appreciate that "the general concept of social maturity and the more specific one of social competence, are crucial for

---

[21] Richard C. Anderson, "Learning in Discussions: A Resume of the Authoritarian-Democratic Studies," *Harvard Educational Review*, XXIX (Summer, 1959), pp. 201–215.

[22] Cf. P. Winch, *op cit.*, p. 17.

[23] M. L. Kellmer Pringle, "Social Learning and its Measurement," *Educational Research*, II (June, 1960), pp. 194–206.

psychological study" and proceeds to offer a tentative definition in terms of conformity to social custom and of constructive participation in community affairs, a definition which she admits "begs fundamental questions." She shrugs off criticism with the remark that further "argument would lead into moral and philosophical realms outside the scope of this article" and continues as if conformity to the standards laid down by society were the sole mark of the mature personality, though she does admit that these standards may vary from social group to social group.

Obviously, from what she says in the rest of the article, she favors attempts to measure levels of social "competence" which she considers essential elements in the development of social maturity.

> By this term is meant the ability to carry out social tasks normally achieved by children of a given age as there are some fields in which all children are expected to reach eventually certain minimum standards. Examples of such fields are habits of eating, cleanliness, dressing, the attainment of personal and economic independence.[24]

This represents an entirely arbitrary selection from a possible range of characteristics as measuring instruments; moreover, some of these characteristics are themselves subject to wide possibilities of interpretation. What, for instance, constitutes "personal and economic independence"?

The fact is, that research along these lines is impossible given the vagueness of the concepts to be "measured"; and there is a further danger that what will be produced will simply be a number of stereotypes of behaviour which will militate against the recognition of children who, perhaps because of superior ability, demonstrate certain social oddities. As Dr. Wall puts it in the previous number of *Educational Research*, in talking of "Highly Intelligent Children":

> Some of the problems of these children . . . arise from deeply-rooted attitudes in our society, stereotypes of what is and is not acceptable from children and adolescents.[25]

A further example will reinforce the necessity for such conceptual analysis and, at the same time, indicate how Schutz's approach may be of assistance as a technique of research. In an article by Dr. K. M. Evans, it is concluded that, though

> . . . there is a great deal of information available about teachers and teaching efficiency. . . . Some of it is contradictory and some of it

---

[24] *Ibid.*, pp. 199–200.
[25] W. D. Wall, "Highly Intelligent Children," *Educational Research*, II (February, 1960), p. 109.

inconclusive. Differences between results obtained appear to be more marked than similarities. . . .[26]

This is not an impressive result in a matter as fundamental to the process of education as the effectiveness of the teacher, particularly in view of the "very large number of investigations which have been carried out." When one has read Dr. Evans' article, however, it is not difficult to see where some, at least, of the trouble has arisen. She stresses the importance of agreement about the criteria in terms of which what constitutes "good" teaching is to be judged. What, however, she, and those whose work she considers, fail to recognize is that before the question of criteria can even be raised it is necessary to undertake a conceptual clarification of what it means to teach, what, in fact, is involved in the concept of "teaching." The search for criteria all too often rests purely on empirical grounds, as Dr. Evans herself makes clear when she introduces her own search for criteria by asking: "How do we, in fact, assess teaching ability, and are our methods satisfactory?" But the question of what constitutes the process of teaching someone something is not in itself an empirical question; it is a request for a clarification of what is involved, conceptually, in the activity of teaching. Furthermore, of course, the elucidation of what it means when we speak of "teaching" implies that the teaching has been successful, for it is not possible at the same time both to teach someone something and to fail to teach someone something. The notion of teaching unsuccessfully involves a contradiction in terms, though, of course, it is possible to talk of "having tried to teach"; and it is possible to distinguish degrees of success.[27]

When we speak of "teaching" we imply, as part of the grammar of the concept, both a direct and an indirect object—we teach something to someone; no process just of "teaching" is possible. To summarise what should, by rights, be argued at some length, it would be reasonable to conclude that, by such a concept, we imply the conscious bringing about in others of certain desirable mental or dispositional changes by morally acceptable means. It is necessary to insist on the moral reputableness of the means in order to cut out changes brought about by torture, brain-washing, etc. It is also necessary to insist that the changes shall be desirable, as otherwise teachers like Fagin would qualify. Of course, it would be possible to dispute the adequacy of the definition—conceptual questions are not ones that can be "settled" in the

---

[26] K. M. Evans, "Research on Teaching Ability," *Educational Research*, II (June, 1959), p. 33.

[27] Dr. Israel Scheffler, in his recent *The Language of Education* (Illinois: Thomas, 1960), distinguishes between the "success" and the "intentional" use of the word "teaching." Even if one were to accept this rather than a distinction between "teaching" and "teaching" (i.e., an elliptical form implying "trying to teach") it is obvious that, in considering teaching ability, one has the "success" meaning in mind.

way in which, frequently, empirical ones can. Nevertheless, the analysis has
been carried out far enough to make clear some, at least, of the logic of the
concept of "teaching."

For the sake of argument, then, let it be agreed that the success of a teacher
is to be measured in terms of the degree of desirable change he can bring
about in the understanding or dispositional abilities of his pupils. The point
now arises as to how these changes are to be measured. And here it becomes
obvious that there is no possibility of setting up any general test of competence. The tests must take account of the nature of the change involved. In
the same way, it is only possible to construct a model of successful teaching
in relation to the teaching of a particular "subject" in terms of insight into
the *nature* of that particular "subject" and of the particular sorts of demands
that the nature of the "subject" makes in relation to the stage of development of the pupils concerned. For, if the successful teacher is he who makes
those specific changes in his charges which relate most closely to the fundamental structure of the "subject" concerned, taking into account their particular stage of development, it is obvious that "subjects" differ immensely
in the nature of the demands which they are likely to make on the teacher's
capacity. Hence the model of the successful teacher, the "homunculus" in
Schutz's terminology, must differ according to subject and pupils. Thus, to
give an example, it is no good even setting up the possession of a good voice
as a universal requisite for all types of teaching. Even apart from the ambiguity as to what constitutes a "good" voice, it is clear that voice, in the teacher
of poetry with its demands on reading and dramatic ability, is likely to be
more important than it is in, say, a teacher of woodwork; and clarity of
enunciation is likely to be much more vital in a teacher of foreign languages
than it is in one of history.

My point is that there are no universally applicable criteria of what constitutes a good teacher; and the attempt to lay down such general criteria is,
in part, an explanation of the unproductiveness of much of the research on
the subject which has been done. What, then, is required as a preliminary to
research is an initial clarification of the basic concepts employed. Once
teaching is seen as an interactive process in a context, it is relevant to
demand insight into the particular nature of the interactions involved in
different sorts of context. It is useless to draw up lists of "characteristics"
and then to try to measure how important each is. Some of these characteristics may enter into all the contexts where good teaching takes place,[28] but

[28] For example, intelligence. As soon as one begins to look at what is involved in
teaching contexts in the way I have suggested, one comes to see how complex the situation usually is. For instance, what for many years has appeared to be a fairly mechanical
job, that of teaching the first steps in arithmetic, is shown, if the theories of Piaget and
Dr. Dienes are correct, to be a much more complicated matter than was thought; in that

the emphasis to be placed on each will vary with the nature of the specific kind of teaching situation involved; furthermore, such characteristics will be analysable only in relation to a total configuration which will bring into prominence now one aspect, now another. The only way to scientific understanding of such a complex situation lies in the creation of a series of models based in some measure on subjective assessments of objective situations— what it *means* to teach this in this sort of context. There can be no general answer to the question "What makes a good teacher?" because a good teacher is always acting in concrete situations which will vary the demands made upon his skill; at best, there can be a number of particular requirements to meet broadly assessed similarities of situation. Built into the very notion of teaching is the need to consider: "Who is teaching what to whom?" Here, Schutz's conceptual apparatus of the "homunculus" is of the first importance[29] —as, even in general terms, it helped in seeing what is wrong with so many attempts to define the nature of the "good teacher." At the very least one needs to create "homunculi" called "the French teacher," "the history teacher" or the "nursery school teacher," and to assess typically how these conceive of their job.

Something of the same way of looking at the situation, involving a more strongly marked appreciation of the subjective element, may be shown to have its uses in relation to Dr. C. M. Fleming's study of "Class Size as a Variable in the Teaching Situation."[30] Fleming points out that, contrary to expectation,

The benefits of small classes, though commonly taken for granted

what is really necessary is not simply the drilling of mechanical steps but a series of explanations which will clarify not only the processes at stake but help to make clear to the child the very nature of the mathematical concepts involved. Yet Dr. Evans informs us that "Results of statistical studies . . . leave the question of the importance of intelligence in some doubt. In many studies correlations between the results of intelligence tests and assessments of teaching efficiency are small." But this surely simply raises doubts about the relevance of intelligence tests in relation to intelligent behaviour. For "intelligence" is not a quality we can have apart from the ability to act intelligently. When we say that a human being shows intelligence, we don't mean that he applies something called "intelligence" and then behaves; we mean that he displays intelligence by his ability to act successfully (whatever that may mean in the context) in situations requiring a complex interplay of understanding and judgment. When teaching situations are analysed in the way I have suggested this surely is likely to be characteristic of most.

[29] It should be said that Dr. Evans is by no means unaware of some of these difficulties (cf. Section II, "The assessment of teaching"). But she points to general difficulties resting on empirical grounds; she fails to see the initial need for conceptual analysis, and she suggests no conceptual tool by means of which the difficulties may be in some measure overcome.

[30] C. M. Fleming, "Class Size As a Variable in The Teaching Situation," *Educational Research*, I (February, 1959), pp. 35–48.

by theorists, are as yet largely undemonstrated in the pages of accredited research reports. This conclusion has been reached at every level from infant-school to University lecture-theatre. It has been formulated in relation to many subjects; and it is supported both by test results and by assessments of various types.[31]

The interesting thing about the researches that Dr. Fleming analyses is the small amount of attention that appears to be paid to what could reasonably be predicted concerning the subjective interpretation the teachers concerned are likely to place on the nature of their job. Implicit in every effort, it can reasonably be assumed, is a certain interpretation of what each one was about, i.e., that implicit in the concept of teaching which we have already examined above. In other words, whatever the "variables" might seem to be, the total situation is likely to be controlled by the teacher's realisation that it is his function to teach something to a set, large or small, of somebodies. This, at least, is the unspoken assumption of his enterprise. That being so, it is not expecting too much to suggest that the teacher, in various small ways, would adapt himself to the nature of the task in front of him, particularly when he would know he was in a test situation. Adaptations of voice, vigour, clarity of enunciation, and so on would take place—anyone who has taught or lectured to both small and large groups knows how different the "feel" of the two situations is and how that difference of "feel" affects the actual "teaching" in a number of subtle ways, even though superficially the "methods" adopted in the two cases may appear on the surface exactly similar.[32] Thus the element of size cannot simply be regarded as a "variable" in the sense in which a physical phenomenon can be so regarded in a physical experiment, where the "subjective" response of the other "variables" is nonexistent; it is a "variable" which leads to a qualitative difference among the other "variables," a "variable," that is, which alters the "meaning" of the situation in ways which affect conduct qualitatively; and this is quite frequent in the consideration of "variables" in psychosocial phenomena, for the variables themselves are invested with subjective meaning and cannot be treated simply as "factors" with their monolithic implications. In one experiment Fleming reports on, the clue to the situation is perhaps there; but its implications seem to have been missed. Fleming first attempts to treat the mechanical "variables" involved:

[31] *Ibid.*, p. 38.

[32] This is a different matter from those "subtleties of interpersonal relationships" which Dr. Fleming notes at the end of her article, which seem only to involve differences of approach—teacher- or learner-centred—not a difference of the "feel" of a situation springing from a similarity of subjective assessment of the task involved within the *same* approach. (It is stressed in some of the reports that the same methods had to be used in the various test situations.)

In extensive interviews in which an attempt was made to discover the opinions of the students on such matters as vision, hearing, ventilation, opportunities for questions, the large groups appeared to have been as satisfactory as the small except for some complaints as to overcrowding. . . .[33]

However, a crucial element in the situation is hinted at but not taken up—or so the report would seem to signify:

The teachers, on interview, expressed awareness of greater effort in establishing informality with large groups, in enlisting participation in discussion and in discussing special difficulties among students. . . .[34]

The situation, indeed, is analogous to the famous Hawthorne experiment when two groups of girls were chosen for an investigation into factory conditions; the physical conditions of the experimental group were altered in order to assess the importance of a variety of variables in working conditions, whilst those of the control group remained constant. It was discovered that, in these circumstances, such physical variables were unimportant; what mattered was the attention paid to the girls, so that output in both control and experimental groups advanced equally. In other words, the girls' subjective interpretation of the importance of their work had altered: by asking their help and co-operation, the company had made the girls feel important, and their whole attitude to work had changed. This factor of subjective interpretation proved much more important than all the physical variables involved.

Another situation in which it is possible to employ Schutz's conception of the homunculus is in the assessment of the adequacy of questionnaire techniques and in the criticism of specific questions in particular pieces of social and educational research, as well as in the initial refinement of question-setting techniques. One social phenomenon who merits investigation but who has not received the attention he deserves is the question-answerer. A good deal of attention has been focused on the refinement of questioning techniques—avoidance of ambiguities, development of multiple-choice or "open-ended" questions, inventories—and so on. Attention has been paid to lay-out, clarity of instructions, attractiveness of appearance, etc. But much less attempt has been made to analyse the processes implicit in the actual undertaking of questionnaire-solving—the sort of psychic expectations with which it is approached, the nature of the attention which is likely to be given to the question; what, in fact, it is likely to *mean* to a typical questionnaire-solver to be faced by questions of the conventional type for information-finding.

[33] Fleming, *op. cit.*, p. 45.
[34] *Ibid.*

One point which might become clear as a result of an attempt to create such an image of an answerer is the fact that question-answering is a largely rational activity, one which, by the very nature of the demands it makes, the sort of attention it invites, involves only certain aspects of the personality— those associated with "thinking things out," "giving careful consideration to" and the like. This approach would imply the shutting-off of the less disciplined, more emotionally oriented aspects of human personality which, in the conventions of question-answering, are not likely to have much of a look in.

Let me try to illustrate my point by reference to a large-scale piece of research carried out by the Nuffield Foundation in England on the effects television viewing has on children.[35] The researchers attempted to discover something of the effect television had on children's values—the views of society, conceptions of adult life, ideas about foreigners and so on. One of their fields of interest was the ideas about marriage children imbibed from the T.V. screen, especially from the plays:

> We also tried to find out whether television affected the child's ideas
> as to what makes a good husband or wife. The children were
> asked to complete the following two sentences: *A good husband is*
> *a man who . . .* and *A good wife is a woman who. . . .*[36]

In so far as a great deal of popular culture is concerned with love and marriage, the effect which the presentation of marital themes has on the young is one of the profoundest importance. Yet the questions barely skim the surface of the sort of interest which is likely to be aroused about the relations between the sexes. Furthermore, and of greater significance for the point I am making, the very nature of the questions asks for an abstract, "rational," common sense type of answer remote from precisely that sort of affective impact that television is likely to make. Symptomatically, the investigators ask "whether television affected the child's *ideas* as to what makes. . . ." They surely should have recognised the nature of television drama's appeal, an appeal which is remote from the rationalistic-moralistic ("good" wife) interest of the question asked. The sort of information that is needed here cannot be got at by questioning in this way, precisely because the whole psychic atmosphere in which such questions are answered is inimical to obtaining it. In other words, one's appreciation of the mental and psychological preconceptions of question-answering, one's re-creation, as it were, of the typical subjective responses of someone in the questionnaire-answering situation, makes one appreciate that questionnaires are only suit-

[35] H. T. Himmelweit *et al.*, *Television and the Child* (London: Oxford University Press, 1958).

[36] *Ibid.*, p. 247. The treatment is, in fact, very perfunctory for so important an aspect of the investigation.

able for finding certain sorts of information ("for how long did you watch television last evening") and are not likely to elicit useful results when affectively based responses are called for. The answer to the question *"A good husband is a man who . . ."* can probably only be superficially verbalised by adolescents anyway; and when the aim of the questions is to discover the effect of experiences which are themselves emotional in origin, the information gleaned is of only a very limited sort of interest.

Questionnaire-setters have usually assumed that their questions *can* be answered provided they are unambiguous, clearly phrased, etc. What they have insufficiently defined are the limitations involved in the very activity of question-answering which is, in fact, a very particular kind of undertaking. We need, that is, to know much more about the subjective attitudes and expectations of question-answerers. One wonders in how many pieces of research the neglect of similar subjective interpretation of the situation is not commented on or even remarked. At least, the fuller realisation of its importance might do something to amend the present unsatisfactory state of research in education.

5. SCIENCE, MORALS, AND EDUCATIONAL POLICY[1]

Israel Scheffler

INTRODUCTION

To recognize that education is a practical art is not merely to acknowledge the triviality that it is an activity or process, but more significantly,
to class it among those undertakings with dominant objectives, capable of
indefinite refinement through increasing grasp of underlying principles.
While the single instance always involves intuitive judgment in applying
appropriate principles, as well as in coping with features whose governing
principles are yet unknown, the promise of progress in arts like medicine,
psychiatry, engineering, communication, and education lies in research
into underlying principles, i.e. in a scientific understanding of the phenomena in question, their conditions, relations, and outgrowths. This importance of science as a systematic basis for the educator's art does not,
however, exhaust its relevance for education. For a significant part of the
content of education, i.e. what the educator wishes to transmit to learners,
consists precisely of scientific information and scientific modes of thought
and understanding. Science may, then, be adjudged a vital ingredient in both
method and content in educational practice.

SOURCE. Scheffler, Israel, "Science, Morals, and Educational Policy," *Harvard Educational Review*, **26**, Winter 1956, 1–16. Copyright © 1956 by President and Fellows of
Harvard College.
1 This paper was prepared originally, in substantially its present form, for the Faculty
Committee on Curriculum Exploration of the Harvard Graduate School of Education. It
embodies some comments of the writer presented at the Harvard Summer School Conference on *Science and Educational Policy*, 1954.

Since it is thus doubly important to the educator, it would seem imperative that he have a clear grasp of its functions, uses, and limits. Yet the interpretation of science is generally so fraught with confusion that such understanding is not easy to attain, and educational discussions are consequently often misled at crucial points by pseudo-issues. Perhaps the prime example concerning educational method is the lingering dispute between "scientists" and "humanists," in the very formulation of which lurk crucial confusions between scientific modes of inference, scientific techniques, and scientifically grounded technology, usually ignored by both parties. The "scientific" side thus often exaggerates its case by arguing for the universal relevance of some limited technique or technology, while the "humanist" side feels pushed into denying that educational results have conditions which can be studied systematically and, in effect, that education can be rationally planned, while it simultaneously advances (contradictory) claims for some preferred educational program as calculated to lead most efficiently to desired objectives. This dispute lacks logical substance because it rests on insufficiently analyzed notions of science.

An equally familiar example concerning content rather than method is the problem of objectives in science education. Once it is granted that some more general aim is involved than the acquisition of current scientific information, the problem of delimiting it precisely begins, and the inevitable complexity of this inquiry is quite often needlessly magnified by confusions over "scientific method." Those favoring scientific method as the *general* aim of science instruction often confuse it with the temporal order of a good many inquiries in the sciences, e.g. from problem to hypothesis to testing, etc., or with some technique, e.g. experiment or measurement. Those who (rightly) point out that the latter are limited and by no means universally applicable often go on to reject inductive, empirical modes of inference altogether in favor of intuition, inertia, or dogma. At bottom, there is again a failure to make relevant distinctions in the analysis of science. In view of the educational importance of such analysis, it is hoped that the following sections, devoted to selected issues in the interpretation of science, bearing on education, may be of some use.

CAN SCIENCE BE APPLIED TO EDUCATION?

This question ostensibly cuts to the roots of issues of educational method. If science is applicable to human teaching and learning, both can be increasingly understood and improved by well-known modes of investigation and control. If not, we must either resign ourselves to current levels of educational insight and practice or call in a totally new approach to learning phenomena. As a matter of fact, the question may be viewed as part of a more general dispute as to whether social subject-matter requires a radically different method of inquiry from that used in the natural sciences, or not.

Yet, as just stated in general form, the issue between "differentists" and "uniformists" is hopelessly muddled. For in some sense methods of inquiry differ even *within* the natural sciences, and indeed, from problem to problem within any given science. It will be quickly argued, however, that this is not the sense in which differentists intend their claim for a radically new method in social inquiry, nor that in which uniformists deny it. The former affirm some *radical* difference in the two realms, relative to which internal differences are slight, while the latter affirm a radical uniformity, overshadowing undeniable differences in approach and technique. But how radical must a difference be to be a *radical* difference, and how basic must a uniformity be to qualify as *really* basic? If the issue is not to degenerate into a mere verbal quibble as to whether to include or exclude social studies in the application of the term "science," uniformists and differentists must specify *in advance* just those aspects of method relative to which their respective claims of uniformity and difference are intended.

Reconstructing the issue most plausibly in some such terms, we may distinguish in specified ways between *logical method* and *technique* within the natural sciences and ask whether the former is or is not applicable to social studies as well. By *logical method* we may understand, e.g.:

1. Formulation of assertions in logically coherent, objectively testable systems of hypotheses.

2. Observational control of the acceptance and rejection of assertions.

3. Inductive or probabilistic interpretation of observational evidence.

4. Theoretical reversibility of all decisions on acceptance and rejection of assertions.

5. Use of general hypotheses and singular statements to explain and predict occurrences.

By *technique* we may understand any features of scientific work but these, e.g. apparatus, modes of observation or data-collection. Uniformists may now be construed as claiming that the above characteristics of method apply equally to social sciences, while differentists deny this claim.

Even with this reconstruction, however, the issue may be wrongly understood, since it is surely not of the same order as the verbally similar question, "Does glue apply equally well to glass as to paper?," or "Does this statute apply equally to minors?." The latter are relatively easy to answer by gathering and validly interpreting easily attainable empirical evidence. The issue of logical method, on the other hand, concerns the range of the very standards governing valid empirical inference. Past successes in employing such inference in natural science cannot be taken as evidence for success in social studies without begging the question. Past successes in the social studies may constitute partial evidence only if we grant the validity of these principles in determining such successes, and such evidence is often disputed in detail. The important point here, however, is that prior evidence of success is not necessary as a justification of social science, just as prior evidence of success is unnecessary and indeed impossible, as a justification of induction generally in the natural sciences. What sufficiently justifies our presumption to abide by given norms of logical method is the fact that they adequately codify our accumulated store of accepted inferences and our intuitive conceptions of acceptable inferences. That the principles above listed do so for these inferences irrespective of social or non-social content is, then, the minimal sufficient claim of uniformists. Differentists, on the other hand, have generally offered specific reasons for limiting the scope of these principles to non-social subject-matter.

So interpreted, the issue rests on the validity of the latter reasons, since the very fact that differentists feel it necessary to advance such special arguments for limiting the scope of the above principles means that they recognize the general claim of the latter on our acceptance. Once we examine these special differentist arguments in detail, it becomes clear, I think, that they have no force at all and that they present no convincing reasons for limiting the scope of logical method, as above defined, to non-social subject-matter. An exhaustive analysis is, of course, out of place here, but a short survey of some typical arguments follows, together with comments on what I conceive to be their fatal weaknesses in each case.

a. *Uniqueness*—social sciences deal with unique occurrences; hence objective test by different investigators at different positions in space or time is impossible, while general hypotheses are excluded by the same token, thus making it theoretically impossible to predict. [Every occurrence, however, is unique in some sense, while for any two occurrences, some property is common to both.]

b. *Historicity*—social sciences aim to achieve historical knowledge, not general laws; hence explanation and prediction in a scientific sense are impossible. [But geology and astronomy are directly historical in part, physics rests on historical evidence embodied in particular reports, while all three employ general principles in arguing from and reconstructing historical material. Even cultural history must use general principles in interpreting data; unless it did it could not e.g., weight relevance of historical factors and construct a "historically explanatory" account.]

c. *Value-character*—social subject-matter is value-impregnated; hence objectivity is theoretically impossible. [But to study values, we need neither to espouse nor reject them any more than to study the law of falling bodies we need to jump from the Tower of Pisa. In any event, scientific objectivity means not lack of values or interests, but rather their frank exposure and tentative espousal, and the institutionalizing of procedures for submitting valued hypotheses to test by investigators with counter-interests.]

d. *Selective focus*—social scientists, especially historians, select their material, thus precluding objectivity. [But selection, on the level of choice of problem, is unavoidable even in the natural sciences; only selection in the sense of arbitrary avoidance of relevant evidence is pernicious. But why is *such* selection inevitable in the social sciences?]

e. *Social bias*—social class position of social scientist must bias his findings and render them subjective. [But bias, in the sense of selective observation is inevitable everywhere, e.g. physical and physiological status of observer biases his perceptual perspective. The very distinction between biased and unbiased observation allows theoretical possibility of correction for biases by specific devices in each case. Only bias in the sense of arbitrary repudiation of counter-evidence is bad, but why is this an inevitable concomitant of social study, in view of the fact that it is *logically possible* for a social bias and counter-opinion to co-occur? Finally, what is the status of this argument itself, if we accept it; is it merely a function of social class?]

f. *Need for intuitive empathy*—study of human motivations, passions, and needs requires empathy, "verstehen," intuitive insight, rather than projection of tentative hypotheses with subsequent public confirmation. [But intuitive insights do not in themselves constitute adequate justifications for acceptance of beliefs, since they are often in mutual conflict. They are at best *sources* of hypotheses, and as such occur equally in the natural sciences, but in this role require rather than preclude subsequent public test. Finally, we may hypothesize without prior sympathetic insight; few of us can empathize with Hitler, yet we might be reasonably said to understand and explain his behavior.[2]]

g. *Impossibility of experiment or measurement*—no controlled experiments or measurement can be made in the social studies, thus precluding objectivity. [But this is surely false for some areas in social study, while no controlled experiments are conducted in geology or astronomy and measurement is of little importance in e.g., branches of biology, geology. Controlled experiment and measurement are techniques logically independent of method as above defined, and surely unnecessary for objectivity.]

h. *Complexity*—social phenomena are much more complex than natural

[2] I am indebted for certain of my comments in this and the preceding few paragraphs to Professor Ernest Nagel, "The Logic of Historical Analysis," in Feigl and Brodbeck, *Readings in Philosophy of Science*, Appleton-Century-Crofts, 1953. Those who want a more extended treatment of related issues should consult Professor Nagel's excellent discussion.

phenomena; hence cannot be studied by above logical method at all. [But prior to Galileo, physical subject-matter was thought complex, since its principles were unknown. Is the point of this argument perhaps that physics cannot explain social phenomena? But neither can social study explain physical phenomena. Is it rather that physical assumptions and controls enter into social investigations? But analogous assumptions about the observer must be made in physical investigations. Is the point that while physical things are completely explained by physics, social objects are not? But not all aspects of physical things are explained by current physics, unless we trivially redefine "physical things" to mean just those aspects so explained, or trivially reinterpret the claim so as to mean by "physics" whatever does explain physical things completely.]

To reject these and analogous differentist arguments does not, of course, necessitate denying that the current state of social study is in a much more primitive state than physical science, but it does mean that there is no theoretical barrier to the advance of scientific study of social phenomena, and in particular, of education. There are, to be sure, practical problems to overcome, devices of control and correction to be invented, and much theoretical ingenuity required to extend such study, but these are obstacles very like the ones to be met everywhere in scientific research. Theoretically, science *can* be applied to education.

[*Remainder of article omitted*]

6. THE NATURAL SCIENCES AND EDUCATIONAL RESEARCH—A COMPARISON*

J. A. Easley, Jr.

It has been noted that while science (meaning the natural sciences) is continually being revised, it retains its ability to carry on its normal functions such as explanation and prediction. The Viennese philosopher Moritz Schlick likened science to an imaginary ship at sea which its crew rebuilds while it remains afloat. A more true-to-life metaphor of science might be an urban renewal project. A city can and must continue to function as a city in order for rebuilding to go on—which means, for example, that not everything can be torn down at once. In science, as in cities, no feature is fixed absolutely for all time; yet, whenever any features are being rebuilt, other parts of science must support the operation. No one seriously questions the practical value of the natural sciences nor the overall validity of the picture of the universe they present. However, people do not always understand how scientific theories can have such powers and yet be vulnerable at every point—vulnerable to the possibility of criticism in the light of new evidence and to eventual replacement. Reflection on the metaphors just given may be of some help to the reader if this epistemological problem has puzzled him.

More serious is the problem of how it is that useful theories develop. His-

SOURCE. Easley, J. A. Jr., "The Natural Sciences and Educational Research—A Comparison," *The High School Journal*, 50:1, October, 1966. Copyright © 1966 by University of North Carolina Press.

* This paper is based on a talk presented at the Annual Spring Conference, State University College, Brockport, New York, April 29, 1966. The author is indebted to the UICSM Mathematics Project and the National Science Foundation for research opportunities out of which the ideas of this paper grew.

53

torians of science have traced the development of components of Newton's theory of mechanics

$$\left(F = ma, \text{ and } F = \frac{K\,m_1 m_2)}{d^2}\right.$$

back through hundreds of years. But Newtonian mechanics has had remarkable stability among scientific theories. Even short-lived theories in physics, like the Bohr theory of the atom for example, drew on centuries of previous work. Today, however, in some new sciences, we witness an explosive development of new theories having considerable power. Information theory and communication theory come to mind as prominent examples; mathematical learning theory, input-output analysis in economics, and the theory of the genetic code are also striking new developments. In part, such theories represent an importation of ideas from other fields, but in large measure they codify the results of enormous and protracted indigenous research of a systematic, exploratory nature. Their power, in fact, consists largely in their agreement with the results of such exploration—whether these results were obtained before or after the theories themselves were formulated.

In education, we have now had a half century of so-called scientific research. Yet almost everyone I discuss this research with is convinced that the results are not only vulnerable but mostly useless, or even quite misleading, in relation to recent educational innovations. The puzzle of reconciling power and vulnerability doesn't arise in educational research because there is insufficient strength in this research to contrast with lack of certainty. In the natural sciences, when new evidence arises that casts doubt on accepted theories, the theories can usually be patched up until a completely new structure can be built (just as is done with damages to the structures of a city). However, in education, generally speaking, such a temporary repair is difficult to bring off. Theories rise and fall with great rapidity. Old results become suspect when school practices change. I believe this is so because, when a given proposition is attacked, there is sufficient trust and confidence in surrounding structures needed to sustain a repair job. How then can a science of education ever get off the ground?

Recently, we have begun to hear more about educational technology and educational research for purely administrative purposes. I take this to be a sign of weakening of the hope for scientific understanding in education. However, I see no tendency to give up research itself—it is too tightly woven into university and national structures. Perhaps it would be helpful to revisit the halls of science where we received our first inspiration for scientific research in education. Perhaps a second look, coupled with our frustrating experience, might open our eyes to more promising approaches.

THE VARIETY OF RESEARCH TECHNIQUES
AND METHODOLOGICAL PRINCIPLES

Fifty years ago many philosophers and scientists talked of a single scientific method. In some versions, it proceeded step-wise from problem to conclusion; in others it proceeded from observations to theory. Duhem and Dewey did not view it this way, but they spoke of scientific method forcefully, and the idea of steps involving empirical, hypothesis testing became generally identified as the scientific method. Today, faith in a ubiquitous, step-wise method of scientific inquiry has been badly shattered by careful historical research and philosophical analysis. Instead, a wide variety of techniques and criteria of acceptable research are seen as covering many fields of inquiry.

It is incorrect to say, as some have, that each science has its own method —for methodological principles are shared. However, the relative frequency of use of such principles is quite different in different sciences and varies in time within each science. It is possible to speak of a single scientific method only as an evolving collection of methodological principles—a potential resource for all sciences but, for good reasons or bad, not fully utilized in any.

Methodological principles and criteria govern such matters as these: What are considered promising fields for investigation? What counts as satisfactory evidence for conclusions? and What counts as a scientific explanation? Use of mathematics in formulating theories, use of statistics in analyzing data, use of formal procedures in collecting data, and many other aspects of scientific research vary enormously from one science to another—yet, some use of each is made in most sciences.

METHODOLOGICAL PAROCHIALISM IN EDUCATIONAL RESEARCH

Why is it that nearly every graduate student in education must struggle through statistical calculations and produce his evidence by instruments designed so that their reliability can be computed according to the currently popular model of measurement? Do we not have too narrow a focus on experimental methodology? Of course, historical, survey, and philosophical researches are allowed, but they receive only specialized attention, and few now hope they will contribute to a science of education.

The technology of programmed instruction has offered a new alternative to classical experimental design, but this model appears still to lie within the conception of research as hypothesis testing. An instructional program is said to be satisfactory if it meets its behaviorally defined goals. So a program is only an elaborately formulated hypothesis, and research, on this model, consists of testing it to see if the expected result is obtained. In the new curriculum project movement, efforts at research, both by classical experimental methods and by programmed instruction, have not been particularly illuminating. Comparisons of groups trained in new curricula with control groups receiving the traditional curriculum have not generally shown differences in achievement that would warrant the expenditure of funds. (Such a reaction was recently expressed by Gallagher and Rogge, 1966.) Although not yet measurable, other educational outcomes are suspected which would substantially justify the investment; but, we are still left largely in the dark about them. Achievement via programmed instruction has generally not surpassed that by teachers. Viewed in these ways, we have learned little from these studies.

Experimental methods, e.g., curve fitting or hypothesis testing by manipulative control or by sampling from experimental and control groups (with or without statistics), are quite prominent in the natural sciences. Yet in the history of science right up to the present moment, we find widespread use of exploration as an approach to inquiry in all sciences—usually executed with a great deal of personal discipline and often with spectacular success. We have actually had a lot of exploration in education—laboratory schools and individual teachers trying this and that—but it has not been disciplined by standards of practice and procedures of reporting which would permit a cumulative science to grow.

It is said that educational research emulates the physical sciences in its emphasis on statistics and experimental design. I think that this statement is inaccurate. Rather, it was agronomy which developed statistical methodology, and it was subsequently adopted by psychology, education, and other sciences. Relatively speaking, statistical tests of significance are seldom used in physics, chemistry, and astronomy. Of course, having more reliable instruments, these sciences often get results which do not require statistical computation to demonstrate that a difference has occurred. However, I think we should keep the record straight. The trouble with such a statement is that it blinds us to the very large use that physical sciences make of exploratory, as contrasted with hypothesis-testing, approaches.

There is a strong tendency to confuse an experimental approach in the general sense with statistical methods and models that go under the name of experimental design. These are relatively new and powerful techniques for solving problems in which the effects of well-defined variables are to be determined, but they cannot replace systematic, empirical exploration of unexplained phenomena. It is quite significant, for example, that a very large part of the work of Michael Faraday, one of the greatest of experimental scientists, was an exploration of the properties of electric and magnetic fields and of the chemical properties of substances. Also, one of the most exciting developments in physical science today is the exploration of the earth's magnetic field and radiation belts by means of artificial satellites. Figuring out how and when to launch satellites with magneto-meters aboard in order to map the structure of the earth's field is an operation of exploration, not one of experimental design in the technical sense.

One finds many different approaches to research and many different criteria for acceptable research within any well-developed science. The most important question for a research discipline, however, is how to find the most promising approach for research on a problem that is not being solved satisfactorily by conventional techniques. What are the characteristics of problems, and of the state of knowledge, that speak in favor of one technique or another? What are the means of development (or importation) of new approaches to research? I know of no general solutions to these problems. However, I shall examine instances of these problems that have educational significance and describe some approaches toward solving them.

EDUCATIONAL RESEARCH PROBLEMS AND THE CHOICE OF METHOD

What, then, are the problems in education that we are not able to solve by conventional research design, and what new approaches to these problems are being employed that might be developed into research methodologies? The most urgent educational problem today is, in my estimation, "What should the curriculum be to prepare youth for the (technological) world in which they will have to live and work—i.e., to minimize the retraining effort that will be required just to keep them employed?" A corollary of this problem is, "How should such a curriculum best be taught?" These problems do not lend themselves to satisfactory attack by the classical method of comparison of treatments (adopted from agronomy) nor by the new method of programmed instruction.

Although one may think of instruction as a treatment and the resulting learning by students as production, the means of optimizing learning is not one of controlling the amount of various components as one would control fertilizer, pesticides, and irrigation of crops. The total educational experience is not a simple sum of its parts—nor even an interaction effect of treatment variables independently defined. The situation is analogous to (but much more complex than) what Skinnerian behaviorists call hand shaping. The quickness of learning by a pigeon in a Skinner box is not solely determined by the basic treatment variables (frequently of reinforcement, lighting conditions, prior training, etc.). In hand shaping, it is determined primarily by the experimenter's skill in selecting points in the stream of behavior at which to actuate an appropriate reinforcing stimulus. This requires an exploratory approach on the experimenter's part. In these problems, there is, *a priori*, no theoretically unique way to break instructional treatment down into a small number of variables which can be manipulated independently. Only after much successful exploration can we hope to identify the useful reinforcement contingencies for shaping a particular category of behavior.

How different is the case of the student and the Skinnerian teaching machine! No experimenter watches *his* every move; indeed his moves may be mainly internal and examined only in his written responses. No one explores his predispositions; he is presented with a ready-made sequence of stimuli through which he proceeds. Programs, even when arranged as branched strings of questions, are far too rigid to serve as tools for exploratory research. The fields of knowledge through which optimum paths are to be charted are far too complex to give much hope for success unless one can bring the student and the knowledge field into some more intimate relationship. An exploratory approach seems called for, but what is to be explored is the interaction of the student with the field of knowledge.

It will be objected that programmed instruction is not to be compared with hand shaping of a pigeon because the human learner of complex subject matter has already acquired a language and can be guided by verbal instructions as a pigeon cannot. Since we may reasonably expect most human beings to comply with our instructions, the argument goes, the use of language can save the enormous time it would take a person to discover the subject matter even under the best possible reinforcement contingencies. This argument still presupposes that we know our objectives quite precisely and the route by which we wish to take the student to them. Although the first program produced may fail to reach the objectives and later ones may succeed, there is no provision for guidance of the researcher in making major departures in path between successive revisions, since data are collected only on answers given to questions asked, and spontaneous or free responses are not elicited nor used for research guidance.

Most other new ventures on the curriculum and instruction frontier—e.g., the so-called national curriculum projects, SMSG, CBA, CHEMS, BSCS, and others—have followed this same general strategem. Such projects have generally *not* undertaken to develop and try major departures from their preliminary approaches (Goodlad, 1964). These projects, like programmed instruction research, have concentrated upon getting a particular presentation prepared in usable form and have not dealt seriously with the optimization problem nor with understanding educational processes.

EXPLORATORY METHOD IN RESEARCH ON CURRICULUM AND INSTRUCTION

As I have intimated earlier, an exploratory method will be required to solve optimization problems in curriculum and instruction, and to lay an adequate basis for understanding the processes of teaching and learning complex subject matters.

Physicists have often used a test body of some kind to explore the gradient patterns (topography) of a force field. If a field of knowledge were also structured topographically, the optimization problem would consist in finding a path to strategic high points whose slope is everywhere as low as possible —but which is as short as possible too—thus permitting most students to travel with least effort to the best viewpoints. The student himself would be the ideal test body for exploring the psychological structure of such a field— much as Piaget has employed children to study the genetic relationships of conceptual structures. However, a topographic model may be much too simple for useful guidance in research on curriculum and instruction.

Anthropologists studying a strange culture often use themselves as participant-observers in a community of that culture, in order to get a closer look at social processes such as communication and decision making. In this method, as well as in the test-body method of exploratory research in physics, the effect of injecting a foreign body into the system being studied has to be taken into account. Doing so is part of the discipline of research.

The curriculum and instructional problems seem to require a participant-observer who directs the students' attention first to this and then to that matter and notes their reaction, but he must explore a field that has already been mapped by one well-known logical structure and must seek another psychological one. He must map a kind of psychological gradient of comprehensibility on a logical map of theory, somewhat analogously to a physicist who maps forces on a geometric space.

A research style which combines test-body and participant-observer approaches would seem to be a useful approach to problems of curriculum and instruction. Other approaches are also possible, but let us examine a procedure of this sort in order to discover what problems might be encountered in developing it into a disciplined contribution to a science of education.

Max Beberman has developed a style of curriculum research, having some of the desired characteristics, which a number of other curriculum workers have emulated or discovered independently. One can describe this type of research by saying that the researcher brings students into contact with various portions of a field of knowledge and with various arrangements or presentations of these portions, and that he interacts with the students to try to discover their interaction with the subject matter. Depending on their response, he suggests to them one opening or another as he searches for an optimum path to the regions of greatest vantage. In such research, one cannot afford to adopt specific objectives for individual lessons or portions thereof. One must be constantly on the alert for unexpected moves on the part of students which rule out the anticipated avenues of approach to the "high points" or which open up new avenues for continued exploration.

Specific objectives for each lesson, which current orthodoxy requires, would be a hindrance; however, practitioners of this style of research do need to set their sights on what might be called intermediate-range objectives—the "high points" toward which they guide students. It is precisely with respect to what are the best vantage points for students that mathematics educators have disagreed so strongly in what have been called "the math wars." (De-Mott, 1962; see also Moise and others, 1965) However, such disagreement is a matter to be settled by empirical research. (Easley, 1967) Little controversy has been evidenced on the long-range objectives such as problem-solving ability or enabling the student to be able to "navigate" the field of mathematics as much as possible "under his own steam."

The characteristic of a particular path segment in a lesson that makes it easy or hard (likely to be followed or unlikely to be followed) we may wish to attribute to the conceptual ability of the student and to the properties of the concepts along this path segment. Once this relationship is well described for the entire field, it may be possible to design a near optimum path for a given structure—that is, a path which as many students as possible find passable. Continued study of students moving along such a path, and continued criticism of the proposed organization of the subject-matter field, can help to improve the path and refine the underlying structure. Presumably, once some stability is achieved, many teachers can be trained to guide students along it. But stability can only be reached at all through the cooperation of skilled teachers and creative analysts of the field of study.

However, an even more difficult problem now emerges: What is the optimum path for each individual, and can it be predicted in advance? It is surely one of the most important contributions of the programmed instruction movement that it has brought this question to the fore again and with it the related assumption that, if a student fails to learn from what is presented him, the instruction has failed, not the child. It is clear, however, that programmed instruction provides no procedure for solving this problem. It may be insoluble with present techniques, but a solution may be approached if the students themselves are given choices of path in terms that are meaningful to them. Some approaches to open laboratories in science and a few educational systems using computers offer realistic opportunities for student choice. (See below.)

TOWARD A DISCIPLINE OF EXPLORATION IN CURRICULUM AND INSTRUCTION

The first practical problem with an exploratory procedure is how the results of the exploration are to be recorded for purposes of analysis—for science cannot trust unanalyzed impressions. Even in the hand shaping of a pigeon, the usual cumulative record provides inadequate information for describing the interaction of experimenter and experimental subject. A motion picture record is required in most cases.

Films are increasingly employed by explorers in curriculum innovation. Beberman, Page, Davis, Karplus, and others have employed film or video tape extensively to record their teaching and that of their colleagues in research. However, a change of medium does not resolve the problem completely. A substantial problem remains in directing the camera and sound crew. This becomes a research function, since not enough significant behavior is likely to be recorded by an uninformed crew. Very careful attention was given to this problem by the UICSM film project where the director of a 3-camera crew (with cameras hidden behind partitions) was advised on the spot by Gertrude Hendrix while Max Beberman taught the experimental class. Miss Hendrix reports that director and crew came to know the class well enough to anticipate very much of the action (personal communication, see also Hendrix and Sims, 1960.)

The second practical problem with such a procedure is how it is to be reported. The results need to be contributed to the participants in a growing science of education—for science is a social enterprise. There is no tradition of publication of such explorations in education. Professor Beberman has published textbooks deriving from his research (Beberman and Vaughan, 1964). David Page, Robert Davis, and Robert Karplus have published teacher's guides. Hendrix has edited films for teachers. (Hendrix and Sims, 1962)

These professional releases, however, have their limitations as means of communication with other researchers. Their practical purposes suppress a great deal of the research out of which these releases come—research which was recorded in enormous detail, for example, by Miss Hendrix much as field notes might be recorded by an anthropologist studying the linguistic behavior of a new culture.

How could this research be reported? It is unintelligible to a person who lacks a detailed understanding of the mathematical structures that were explored by these workers as they guided their students through the "terrain" of elementary science, algebra, and mathematical logic. For the team of Beberman and Hendrix, working with mathematics class and camera crew, much of the terrain was familiar, having been partially explored with other classes against a logical structure developed by Vaughan (1961-62). One class was only a week ahead of the class being filmed. But some of the logical terrain was encountered with this class for the first time and navigated with a careful eye for their responses to it.

Such an approach allows an attack on the basic problems of curriculum and instruction. It would also allow the development of a discipline, including a basis for criticism by other researchers who were able to employ a similar background of knowledge, and permitting attempts at replication of a study by such researchers. But it is laborious in the extreme.

An exploratory approach to the problems of instructional research has recently emerged through the application of computers to instruction. Although most such work follows the pattern of programmed instruction, some systems are being used in ways that give the student a great deal more freedom of action and choice. Some uses, in fact, having raised a general problem, require that the student ask questions of the computer (in an appropriate code) and may leave the judgment to him of the relevance which the information obtained has to the general problem.

Work of this sort is now going on with the PLATO system for computer-based instruction at the Coordinated Science Laboratory of the University of Illinois (Bitzer and Easley, 1965) and the SOCRATIC system developed by Bolt, Beranek and Newman in Cambridge, Massachusetts (Feurzeig, 1964; Swets and Feurzeig, 1965). Fields being explored include engineering, mathematical proof, and medical diagnosis and treatment.

At Illinois a number of my colleagues and I are engaged in a related human engineering project which is derivative from the PLATO project. This project is undertaking the development of a system for instructional response analysis—a computer-based retrieval system which will permit researchers to obtain information instantly about the responses students have made to instructional programs.* Sufficient data is recorded by the PLATO system while students are using it, so that the sequence of each student's performance can be completely reconstructed. This will permit, therefore, the exploration of students' explorations of a subject which has been represented for their inquiry on the computer. This exploration should suggest modifications of the subject matter represented which can then be made, and another group of students allowed to explore the subject and their performance studied. Students themselves can also assist the researcher by giving evaluative responses to the information they receive during their explorations. Further analysis and further revision can be continued in this way until one is satisfied that all can learn effectively.

The developing retrieval system should permit researchers to do better and more quickly what programmed instruction research is intended to do. But also, when the student is given maximum control of the interchange (as opposed to giving the control to the machine—the ideal of programmed instruction,) there is real hope, for the first time, for a research technique reasonably adequate to those key problems of educational research—curriculum and instruction.

---

* This research is supported by an Office of Education contract.

As second- and third-generation curriculum projects now come on the scene, and teachers and school superintendents are flooded with new materials and extravagant claims, what hope have we that some order and discipline will emerge out of the growing chaos?

The only hope I see lies in the collaboration of skilled teachers with specially trained educational research workers in extended and systematic exploration of new curriculum possibilities. Many such teachers would welcome the opportunities this research requires to deepen their understanding both of their instructional fields and of children's thinking. The graduate education programs of our universities must encourage students to engage in exploratory approaches to problems of curriculum and instruction, rather than discourage them as so often happens at present. Such work, if adequately disciplined, can provide a basis for critical development of learning maps of subject matter domains for "navigational" (i.e., instructional) purposes, and it can help develop an interest in refining the detailed structure of such maps instead of searching for what I believe is a will o' the wisp—a single structure of a discipline which would determine curriculum design and instructional goals. A careful mapping of the subject matter fields in terms of pupil responsiveness seems to me to be the most valuable step we could make toward a general understanding of the perennial problems of education.

References

Beberman, Max and Vaughan, Herbert E. (1964) *High School Mathematics, Course 1, Teacher's Edition.* Boston: D. C. Heath and Company.

Bitzer, Donald L. and Easley, J. A., Jr. (1965) PLATO: a computer-controlled teaching system. In Margo A. Sass and William D. Wilkinson (eds.) *Computer Augmentation of Human Reasoning.* Washington: Spartan Books, Inc., pp. 89–103.

DeMott, Benjamin (1962) The math wars. In *Hells and Benefits,* by the same author. Basic Books. Originally published in *The American Scholar.* Also in Robert W. Heath (ed.). *New Curricula.* Harper and Row, 1964.

Easley, J. A., Jr. (1967) Logic and heuristic in mathematics curriculum reform in *Problems in the Philosophy of Mathematics.* I. Lakatos (ed.). Amsterdam North Holland Publishing Company.

Feurzeig, Wallace (1964) Conversational teaching machine. *Datamation.* June, 1964.

Gallagher, James J. and Rogge, William (1966) The gifted. *Review of Educational Research.* Vol. 36, No. 1, pp. 37–55.

Goodlad, John I. (1964) *School Curriculum Reform.* New York: The Fund for the Advancement of Education.

Hendrix, Gertrude and Sims, Byrl (1960) The UICSM teacher training films. *American Mathematical Monthly.* Vol. 67, No .7.

Moise, Edwin E.; Calandra, Alexander; Davis, Robert B.; Kline, Morris; and Bacon, Harold M. (1965) Five views of the "new math." *Council for Basic Education Occasional Papers.* No. 8. Washington, D.C.

Swets, J. A. and Feurzeig, Wallace (1965) Computer-based instruction. *Science.* Vol. 150, p. 572.

Vaughan, Herbert (1961, 62) A mathematical description of Units I–II. *UICSM Newsletter.* 1961, No. 6, pp. 17–26. 1962, No. 7, pp. 29–38.

CHAPTER 2

Nature, Scope, and Strategy of Educational Research

We come closer now to questions that specifically concern research into education. First of all, should we think of educational research as laying the foundations of a science in its own right, or should it be considered a search for ways of applying the findings of psychology, sociology, anthropology, and other behavioral sciences?

There is a sense, of course, in which the study of education is basic to all other forms of inquiry, because there is none that does not involve learning and usually some teaching. Yet we must be careful not to suggest too hastily that education is the key science because conceivably one could come to understand *how* one learns physics without thereby understanding physics. The laws of learning are not the laws of physics. One might just as well argue that since all scientists breathe while they are doing science, an understanding of respiration would make one conversant with the sciences. Nevertheless, there seems to be no reason why the process of learning–teaching should not be the object of special study, indeed of systematic scholarly study. The question is rather whether enough valid generalizations and laws and hypotheses about education have been achieved or could reasonably be achieved to give shape to a domain called educational science. If not, can one simply "apply" the generalizations of other sciences to problems of education, or does application involve research of another sort, the sort that translates scientific theories into rules of practice?

This question is not only theoretically challenging, but it has important implications for the training of educational researchers. Should they be trained primarily in one of the behavioral sciences and then transfer their knowledge to educational problems, or should they begin with the problems and work in as many of the behavioral sciences as necessary to understand and research these problems?

In the light of the doubts raised in some of the previous readings about the possibilities of a rigorous social science, and in view of the exceedingly modest results that educational research has achieved thus far, some people say it is futile for education even to aim at becoming a science in the ordinary meaning of that term. Instead of striving for an explanatory system of concepts and relationships, we should concentrate on determining the practices that work best in school and disseminate these findings to the practitioners. To be sure, finding out what works best might involve research of a sort, and methods for carrying on such research could and should be refined, but, by and large, common-sense judgments of values, goals, and achievements would be sufficient to carry the inquiry into practical results. However, subsequent readings in this and the second part of the volume will raise serious doubts as to whether "practical" research not grounded in good theoretical research is really very practical.

Further, one can ask whether educational research should model itself after the natural sciences or should seek methods and approaches that are more suitable to the concrete and somewhat amorphous problems of education.

After discussing the differences between educational research and research in the pure sciences, Frank N. Freeman, in selection 7, addresses himself to their meeting place. He discusses their relation in terms of a familiar problem in education—the relative effectiveness of the subject organization of the curriculum and the integrated curriculum. He proceeds to characterize what to him seem to be the "controlling concepts" of educational research:

> If educational research is practical research, the concepts which control it are practical concepts; that is, they are concerned with procedures and activities. At any rate, these are the *distinctive* concepts of educational research. The core of such a concept is a set of activities centering in some definite part of the whole educational enterprise. The curriculum, for example, is such a center of activities and therefore is one of the basic concepts of education. Hence it is a concept which controls research in education.[1]

The reading by Ausubel clearly advocates research at the applied level as appropriate to education. He distinguishes three approaches: the basic

[1] *Supplementary Educational Monographs*, No. 55, The University of Chicago, May 1942, p. 46.

science approach, the extrapolated basic science approach, and research at the applied level.

The basic science approach, Ausubel argues, does not aim at application, even though the findings of some of the basic researchers into such fields as psychology and biology may well have applications in education. Furthermore, the findings are in the forms of high-level generalizations, so that in and of themselves they give little clue as to the loci of their applicability. The extrapolated basic science approach does aim at practical problems, but the research is done on highly simplified versions of such problems; therefore extrapolating the results to concrete problems becomes difficult and risky. In the applied research approach, the real problems are investigated in the context in which they exist. Only in this way is applicability of the research assured, and only in this way can education develop a body of reliable knowledge to guide its practice. Concerning the possibility of developing such knowledge, Ausubel seems to be optimistic.

The article by C. D. Hardie, an Australian philosopher of education, speaks to the same issues as does the Ausubel selection. He notes, as does Ausubel, the low esteem in which educational research is held. He also agrees that the basic science approach is not useful for education. After sketching briefly the requirements of a scientific theory that would make explanation and prediction possible, he concludes that education neither has, nor in likelihood will come up with, theories of this caliber.

He therefore favors "operational research" that aims not at increasing knowledge, but at facilitating more rational decisions, a "scientific preparation for decision." He notes that the military and industry have used research profitably, and he sees no reason why education cannot do likewise. For example, if a school system has to decide whether to build a new school in section A or B of its district, operations research would dictate a population study that would help the school board arrive at a rational decision. In any event, Hardie believes progress in education comes from "teachers rather than scientists, politicians, administrators or research workers." It is not clear that Ausubel would limit the theoretical potentiality of educational research to the extent envisioned by Hardie. Certainly the theoretical quality of some medical and engineering research holds out some hope that educational knowledge might in time aspire to something more than surveys of facts and simple statistical generalizations about existing situations.

The article by John B. Carroll tries to distinguish between basic and applied research. Although the difficulties of doing this are formidable, he believes a workable distinction between them can be made in terms of the nature of the work, the kind of questions investigated, and the procedures of inquiry. However, he points out that none of these can be invoked as the sole sufficient criterion. He draws the conclusion that a balance between support for applied and basic research is needed, and that there is justification for further support for the basic research component in education.

The Kerlinger reading places the blame for the disappointing results of education research upon its preoccupation with methods of research, statistics, measurement, and practicality—a preoccupation that leads to what he calls The Mythology of Educational Research. The methods to which he seems to object are those that stress research as data gathering and data classifying; these are mischievous, he believes, because they stand in the way of thinking about science as theory building and testing. In this sense, Kerlinger seems to take issue with both Hardie and Ausubel as to the importance of basic science or basic research in education. He deplores the relatively low theoretical level at which prospective teachers are trained.

The Ausubel article was written in 1953, the Kerlinger one in 1960, and the Hardie lecture was delivered in 1965. But in 1957 Sputnik I was launched, and shortly thereafter the amounts of money available for educational research increased enormously. This affluence did not change the nature of the theoretical problems of science or research, but it did make more urgent the need to define the functions and potentialities of educational research. Even more concretely, this expansion of research affected the careers of many members of faculties in schools of education and the patterns of graduate study in these institutions.[2]

The selection by Robert Ebel raises an old issue in an interesting form. Ebel makes the point that basic research is best suited for the investigation of natural phenomena, presumably because they have a stable structure that can yield up to scientific inquiry the kinds of understanding and conceptual clarity we associate with successful science. Now education, he holds, is not a natural phenomenon but rather a human enterprise initiated for carrying out highly variable human intentions. The important thing about education is to improve it, not to get adequate intellectual understandings of it. Ebel seems to imply that we do not need to have a scientific understanding of education to bring it closer to fulfilling our goals, whereas some would insist that real improvement cannot be achieved without such understanding.

On the other hand, learning, Ebel holds, is a natural phenomenon and should be the target for basic research, even though it may not directly or ever contribute to the improvement of education. The importance of the distinction, one might suggest, is that if we could separate out those processes within education that are "natural phenomena" we might make a workable distinction between the domains of basic and applied research.

However, that learning is a natural phenomenon amenable to dispassionate

---

[2] See also L. J. Cronbach, "The Role of the University in Improving Educational Research," *Phi Delta Kappan*, XLVII, 10, June 1966, 539–545.

scientific scrutiny and reportable in neutral data language is challenged by Petrie's paper. He argues that educators and psychologists are not talking about the same phenomenon when they use the term "learning." Psychologists, especially those oriented toward the behavioristic tradition, view the phenomenon from the perspective of a stimulus–response theory, where stimuli and responses are more or less mechanical and predictable. The educator, given the teleological concepts of ordinary language, sees learning in terms of goals and purposive acts, what Ebel refers to as "education."

Now a great deal of writing by philosophers who rely heavily on ordinary language analysis for clues to understanding human behavior has sharpened the distinction between goal-oriented human action and mechanical stimulus–response patterns, and if these are truly incompatible, and if learning primarily involves the former, then it would help explain why behavioristic learning theory for the most part has failed to teach us how to learn.[3]

[3] See for example, the selections by N. Chomsky and R. Chisholm in Part II.

7. CONTROLLING CONCEPTS IN EDUCATIONAL RESEARCH

Frank N. Freeman

DIFFERENCES BETWEEN EDUCATIONAL RESEARCH AND RESEARCH IN PURE SCIENCE

Educational research differs in its motive and emphasis from research in the pure sciences, and this difference grows out of the distinction between a profession or an art and a science. The motive in educational research is practical. Educational research is directed toward the solution of some problem which has arisen in practice or which arises when we attempt to work out some plan of procedure. It may be set in motion by difficulties which are encountered in the course of attaining the ends that we have set out to attain or by differences of opinion concerning the best methods of procedure. It may also be directed to the evaluation of the ends themselves, though some persons would deny that research can contribute to the determination of ends.

The motive in pure science is different. The pure scientist, as pure scientist, is not concerned with the practical consequences of his search for facts or laws. When Michelson set out to increase the accuracy of measurement of the speed of light, he did so merely to satisfy his curiosity and that of his fellow-scientists, and his curiosity had no reference to the practical consequences that such determination might have. At least that is his own statement of his motive, made in a public lecture at Chicago. The fact that he put his dis-

SOURCE. Freeman, Frank N., "Controlling Concepts in Educational Research," *Supplementary Educational Monographs, School Review*, No. 55, May 1942. Copyright © 1942 by The University of Chicago Press.

coveries to practical use, as in measuring the meter in terms of the wave-length of cadmium light, was incidental.

It is not true, as is sometimes thought or implied, that the pure scientist devotes himself mainly to the discovery of separate facts. This may some-times seem to be the case, particularly to the outsider who cannot see the relation of a single fact to the general picture. No doubt some scientists are particularists, for whom a fact is a fact and as good as any other. At the other extreme are the builders of systems, who are interested in such large generalizations that they neglect the facts. But true science is neither facts alone nor theory alone. It consists in facts in a scheme of things, and the scheme of things is made up of relations between facts. When the set of rela-tions becomes sufficiently complete and coherent, we have a science.

A science, then, is a systematic body of facts. The system is possible be-cause the facts which make it up are sufficiently similar in nature to fit together into a set of relations. A consequence of this relationship is that certain of the facts can be explained in terms of other facts within the system. Another way of putting it is to say that one set of facts or conditions may be transformed into another within the system. Within such bodies of facts as are mutually explanatory, we establish sets of relations in terms of concepts which are clearly defined within their own respective fields, such as atom, molecule, electron, valence, momentum, force, gravitation, conservation of energy, growth, evolution. Such concepts are characteristic of a science, which is, then, a body of facts brought into a set of systematic relations with one another.

The aim of research in science is to discover facts and bring them into mutually explanatory relations with one another. This undertaking is pri-marily an intellectual task. Its immediate purpose is to understand the world. It is not, in the first instance, directed toward practical ends. If the research is directed primarily toward practical ends, it does not yield good science, for the reason that facts are differently selected and organized in a science and in a practical enterprise. In a science the facts are selected and organized according to their similarity in nature and their susceptibility to organization into systems. In a practical enterprise the facts are selected according to the light they throw on the consequences of, or implications for, the activities which are being performed or are contemplated, although the facts themselves may be of diverse nature, may have no direct bearing on one another, and may be related only by virtue of their common significance for the practical activity.

This is not to say that science has no practical significance or that the technical skill which is secured in scientific research may not be used to great advantage in practical research. Quite the contrary! The explanatory systems developed in research in pure science have the most profound effect on practice after they have been carried far enough to be relatively complete and conclusive. Furthermore, the techniques of research may frequently be carried over almost bodily from pure to applied research. We go even further and say that, for the final solution of practical problems, we must have resort to the findings of pure research and to the scientific systems which have been built up by it. But this is not to obliterate the distinction between pure research and applied research. It is rather to say that, when they are carried through to the end, they ultimately come together; that, for an understanding of the results of practical research, we must rely on the explanatory systems of pure science.

MEETING-PLACE OF EDUCATIONAL RESEARCH AND RESEARCH IN PURE SCIENCE

There seems to be a contradiction between my opening statement that educational research differs in motive and emphasis from pure research in the fundamental sciences and the statement just made that pure and applied research ultimately come together. I believe, however, that this is not a contradiction but only a paradox. Immediate aims, procedures, and findings which are concerned with the determination of practice in its details are in contrast with broader and more general questions which concern the explanation of procedures and, perhaps, the formation of general policies. The correctness of the analysis will be best tested by discussing some examples.

As far back as we have any record, it has been the practice in schools to organize instruction by subjects. Teachers were specialists in subjects, and pupils learned by subjects. In China pupils learned classic language and literature. In ancient Greece they learned grammar, rhetoric, music, and gymnastics. In the medieval universities they learned law and theology. In modern times the subjects have multiplied, but the instruction has continued to be arranged by subjects. From time to time experiments in the rearrangement of subjects have been made, particularly for younger pupils. Subjects which formerly were treated separately, though they were similar in content, have been combined. Correlation between subjects has been carried on more or less completely and more or less successfully. These experiments have altered the boundary lines and the relations between subjects, but they have not abolished the principle of organization of instruction by subjects.

Recently there has grown up a doctrine which challenges the principle of subject organization itself. The proponents of this doctrine maintain that, in life outside the school, learning takes place by situations rather than by subjects. A person sets out to make something, say, and then seeks such information as may be necessary to enable him to do the job. He does not set out systematically to explore some organized body of knowledge or to acquire some definite form of skill, but he picks up the items of knowledge or skill which he finds necessary to meet his immediate practical need. At least this is assumed, though perhaps without sufficient evidence, to be the way we learn. If in everyday life we learn in this informal way, so the argument runs, it must be the natural and probably the most effective way of learning. Some even say it is the only way. Hence it is obviously the way that should be used in school.

This conclusion seems self-evident to some educational theorists and practitioners, but not at all so to others. In fact, many believe it to be dangerously subversive. In such a case we clearly need evidence that will indicate which doctrine is correct and what practice should be followed. The evidence needed to help us solve such a problem must be gathered by research. This research consists in gathering facts and also in the preliminary thinking which will indicate what facts to gather and the interpretative thinking which will bring out the meaning of the facts after they have been gathered.

One kind of approach—the approach that most readily occurs to us when we face a problem like this—is blanket measurement in terms of some criterion that we set up, of the results of two modes of procedure. For example, we may seek to measure the effectiveness of the subject organization in comparison with that of the integrated curriculum by comparing the attainment in college of students who have been instructed in schools where the two types of instruction were used. Attainment in college is here used as the criterion of evaluation. A whole host of questions at once arises in regard to this kind of blanket comparison. What changes in curriculum have actually been made in the experimental schools? How radically do they differ from the control schools? Is attainment in college a fair measure of the kind of learning that takes place in school? Are there particular respects in which students from the experimental schools are superior and others in which they are inferior? Do the results indicate that the fundamental theory underlying the new practices is right or wrong or merely that the new practices are better or worse in particular details? These questions do not imply that blanket comparison is not useful, but they do suggest that this type of appraisal does not give the final answer.

Other kinds of research, some direct and some collateral, should be carried on. Studies could be planned to seek the answer to the questions raised in the preceding paragraph. Direct observations and measurements could be made of the pupils' learning under the various types of organization of the curriculum, and these studies could take account both of the direct outcomes in knowledge, skill, and ability and of the changes in personality which seemed to be brought about. The outcomes both in ability and in personality would have to be evaluated, and this evaluation would call for further research. Some of the assumptions of both the older and the newer practices should be investigated. For example, there should be a check of the assumption of the newer doctrine that people in everyday life seek knowledge and skill in piecemeal fashion to meet immediate and particular needs. It might turn out that the worker outside the school proceeds in more systematic fashion than we suppose, and also that he might, with advantage, proceed in more systematic fashion than he does.

This example has been pursued far enough to indicate that here, in one issue in the organization of the curriculum, we have a whole series of problems that cry aloud for research. The issue is practical. It is an issue between two modes of procedure that may be taken to promote learning: organization by subjects or organization by life-situations. The problem is not one of pure science, and it would probably not arise in the mind of a person pursuing a pure science. It is, to be sure, mainly psychological in nature, since it concerns the factors in learning, but it is not a part of a systematic search for the factors in learning, nor does it deal with a factor that would be likely to be hit upon in such a search. Such a search would be likely to consist in running down singly one factor after another until a fairly exhaustive list of factors was found. Then these factors would be compared until a similarity could be found running through them, and a generalization, based on this similarity, would be constructed. In a complex practical situation, such as is illustrated by the example above, a variety of factors is almost sure to be found. The answer to the question of what should be done in such a situation does not contribute directly to the theoretical question because it does not isolate single factors. Furthermore, the possession of theoretical knowledge concerning the factors does not, by itself, give the answer to the practical question, because it does not enable us to say how the factors will operate in a particular complex combination. It may give hints, but it cannot give the final answer. Again, the attempt to answer the practical question may lead us on beyond it to investigate the underlying principles or rules, but, when this happens, we have passed beyond the practical field into the science.

Thus far I have dwelt on the difference in aim and procedure between the attempt to answer our question concerning the best way to organize the content of instruction and the aim and procedure of the investigation of learning as a scientific enterprise. Science seeks systems and generalizations. Practical research seeks answers to questions of procedure. But the inquiry into the practical problem may lead the inquirer on to the investigation of more general or abstract problems on the one hand, and the scientific generalizations may explain or illuminate the results of the practical inquiry on the other.

This fact may be illustrated by a return to our example. In comparing the organization by subjects with the organization by situations, we come upon the matter of interest. There are some who maintain that the exploration of situations is more interesting than is the study of systematically organized bodies of knowledge. Others deny this assertion and rejoin that intellectual curiosity is aroused by the presentation of a systematic set of observations and reflections and that intellectual curiosity is a form of interest. Here is a question which may profitably be subjected to searching investigation. In spite of endless discussion of the question, we can answer it only on the basis of observation and personal experience.

The investigator of this question would not find his quest a simple one. He might find, for example, that interest is not a single, uniform experience, as seems to be implied in the common use of the term. There may be two or more varieties of interest, differing markedly in their nature and in their source or origin. They may differ also in their significance for learning or for practical affairs. Again, there may be differences between individuals in their susceptibility to one or another kind of interest. Some may be more interested in situations and in practical dealings with them; others may get more satisfaction from systematic, theoretical, and abstract inquiries. Further, persons of different ages may have different appetites for one or another type of inquiry. Finally, the type of interest may shift from one type to another at different stages in the pursuit of a given subject of study.

It appears that, in our study of the practical problem of the organization of subjects, we have been led into making an analysis. First, we have isolated and fixed our attention on one factor in the problem, that of interest. Second, we have broken up the problem of interest into various types of subdivisions. To answer the practical problem seems to require this breaking-up of the situation.

Observe where this procedure has led us. It has led to a more systematic inquiry into a matter of general import—the matter of interest. In order to pursue this inquiry, we are diverted for the time being from the practical question with which we started, and we turn our attention to the study of sets of phenomena which are coherent and of similar nature. We have been led to attack a psychological problem which is scientific in nature.

We might now pursue this problem far enough to become wholly absorbed in it, forgetting the practical problem which we first set out to attack. On the other hand, we might pursue it only far enough to throw light on the practical problem and then return to attack other aspects of it, for the question of interest is obviously not the only one involved. Or, again, after we had identified the question of interest as one pertinent to our practical problem, we might find that other psychologists had already analyzed and investigated it and that we might appropriate the results of their investigations without having to go into the matter ourselves.

The psychologist's plan of procedure and center of attention would have been different. He would start with a general, theoretical question, not a practical problem. He would seek to find out all he could about interest—its nature, origins, types, and manifestations. He would seek to arrive at some generalizations about interest, about the types of situations which arouse it, its effects on behavior, and so on. He might, because he has practical as well as theoretical concerns, make excursions into the practical field and seek to make applications of his findings. He might, one day, meet the educator who was studying the organization of subject matter in the school and suggest that his research threw some light on this question. The two inquirers might meet, and the two realms of inquiry might meet. The one might assist the other. In fact, the one might be necessary to the other, and yet they would differ from each other.

NATURE OF EDUCATIONAL RESEARCH

If what I have said is correct, we may draw certain conclusions concerning research in education.

Education is a practical enterprise, and the pursuit of this enterprise raises many practical problems.

Research in education consists in the investigation of these practical problems. This research differs from research in a science in that it deals with situations, which may be made up of phenomena of diverse nature not capable of being reduced to systems or generalizations.

After the problem has been broken up, however, it may be seen to contain groups of phenomena, each of which, within itself, is a fragment of a science and may be attacked by scientific methods.

When this analysis has been made, the constituent problems may be studied in the scientific manner, or the results of such study may be used.

When the constituent problems have been solved, the solutions must be brought together to find the answer to the original practical problem.

Educational research, then, starts with practical problems, but in the pursuit of the answers to these problems it must either appropriate the results of research in the sciences or embark on this research itself.

Educational research must start from, and return to, the practical problem. It must be organized about practical issues. It uses theoretical research, but this theoretical research must be carried on because it contributes to the solution of practical problems.

The business of education is to bring about changes in individuals. The nature of these changes and the methods and instrumentalities for bringing them about are the objects of inquiry in educational research. These general objects may be broken up into a number of classes of problems, corresponding to the chief groups of activities carried on in the total enterprise. The chief classes of activities are (1) making a curriculum, (2) carrying on instruction or promoting learning, (3) appraising the results of instruction, (4) carrying on guidance, (5) providing for individual differences, (6) organizing the school, (7) educating and providing teacher personnel, (8) financing the educational enterprise, and (9) providing suitable buildings. The effective conduct of each of these activities requires research—practical research.

CONTROLLING CONCEPTS IN EDUCATIONAL RESEARCH

The foregoing analysis was undertaken to serve as a prelude to the treatment of the specific topic of this paper, namely, the controlling concepts of educational research. It appeared, as the theme was approached, that the controlling concepts are themselves controlled by the nature of educational research. If this can be determined, the nature of the controlling concepts follows.

If educational research is practical research, the concepts which control it are practical concepts; that is, they are concerned with procedures and activities. At any rate, these are the *distinctive* concepts of educational research. The core of such a concept is a set of activities centering in some definite part of the whole educational enterprise. The curriculum, for example, is such a center of activities and therefore is one of the basic concepts of education. Hence it is a concept which controls research in education.

The characteristic of such a concept is that it is a complex of many factors. The characteristic of research dealing with such a concept is that it consists in identifying the factors that bear on the concept and weighing the bearing of each of these factors on the issues which arise in the activity in question. This is all there is to educational research in the strict sense of the term.

When we go beyond this procedure of identifying and weighing the bearing of factors in a practical problem in order to determine a course of action, we enter on a study of the factors themselves. Here we encounter one of the basic sciences, each of which deals with a uniform body of experience, such as biology, psychology, economics, political science, or sociology. The controlling concepts now become the concepts of these sciences themselves. They are no different when the research is done because it is needed to clear up one of the factors in an educational problem from what they are when it is done merely in the interests of the science itself. Such research, as has been said, may be necessary as a means of supplying information about one of the factors, but it has no distinctive features.

In conclusion, educational research is practical research and utilizes practical concepts. It is not, in itself, a science and therefore does not demand the creation of new scientific concepts. It leans heavily on the sciences, chiefly the social and the biological sciences; but no new concepts are used, merely the concepts of the sciences themselves.

Educational research starts with practical problems. In the investigation of these problems it uses practical concepts. As the research proceeds in the analysis of its problems, it comes upon the more abstract and general problems of the sciences. Here it encounters the concepts of these sciences. After getting the needed information from the basic sciences, it returns to the practical problem and finds the solution by bringing this information to bear on the practical problem. The practical concept, which is the only distinctive concept in educational research, serves to define the problem, to guide the analysis of the problem so as to determine the factors which compose it, to indicate where basic scientific information should be sought, and to give the framework in which the items of basic information may be brought into relation to one another in the solution of the original problem. This is the function of the controlling concepts in educational research.

8.   THE NATURE OF EDUCATIONAL RESEARCH

David P. Ausubel

Few persons would take issue with the proposition that education is an applied or engineering science. It is an applied[1] science because it is concerned with the realization of certain practical ends which have social value. The precise nature of these ends is highly controversial, in terms of both substance and relative emphasis. To some individuals the function of education is to transmit the ideology of the culture and a core body of knowledge and intellectual skills. To others, education is primarily concerned with the optimal development of potentiality for growth and achievement—not only with respect to cognitive abilities, but also with respect to personality organization and adjustment. Disagreement with respect to ends, however, neither removes education from the category of science nor makes it any less of an applied branch of knowledge. It might be mentioned in passing that automobile engineers are also not entirely agreed as to the characteristics of the "ideal" car; and physicians disagree violently in formulating a definition of health.

Regardless of the ends it chooses to adopt, an applied discipline only becomes a science when it seeks to ground proposed means to ends on empirically validatable propositions. The operations involved in such an undertaking are

SOURCE. Ausubel, David, "The Nature of Educational Research," *Educational Theory*, 3:4, October, 1953. Copyright © 1953 by Educational Theory.

[1] The term "applied" is used her to distinguish between sciences which are oriented toward practical ends as opposed to "basic" sciences which do not serve this function. *Applied* does not imply that the content of the practical disciplines consists of applications from the "basic" disciplines. The problems rather than the knowledge of applied sciences are "applied."

commonly subsumed under the term "research." The question under discussion relates to the nature of search in applied science, or, more specifically, in education. Is educational research a field in its own right with theoretical problems and a methodology of its own, or does it merely involve the operation of applying knowledge from "pure" scientific disciplines to practical problems of pedagogy?

RESISTANCE TO EDUCATIONAL RESEARCH

It should be noted at the outset that there is both little general acceptance of the need for educational research and little appreciation of the relevance of such research for the improvement of education. A tradition of research does not exist in education as it does, for example, in medicine or in engineering, where both professionals and consumers commonly agree that research and progress are almost synonymous. This much is clearly evident from the marked resistance which educational researchers encounter from school boards, school administrators, teachers and parents.

Generally speaking, educational research institutions and public school systems have not succeeded in working out orderly and systematic procedural machinery providing for long-term research programs in the schools. In most cases, each individual researcher is obligated to conduct his own separate negotiations with school authorities every time he wishes to work on a problem; and more often than not he meets with indifference or outright resistance. He has learned that it is more effective to carry on research activities through personal "contacts" in the schools than to obtain the necessary permission through official channels. This chaotic situation is in marked contrast to the well established working agreements which all medical schools have with hospitals relative to the conducting of clinical research.

In addition to, or perhaps reflective of the lack of, perceived relevance of educational research to educational progress are other frequently encountered resistances to the performance of research in the public schools. It is alleged, for example, that research utilizes time urgently needed for subject matter or other purposes, that children are "exploited" by being cast in the role of "guinea pigs," and that irreparable psychological or educational damage is inflicted on some children to further "experiments" of questionable value. Furthermore, some educators demand to know how such research is going to help them solve their immediate problems.

Satisfactory answers to such questions can easily be given once the importance of educational research itself is accepted. It can be pointed out that research projects are not so demanding of pupil or teacher time that they interfere with the curricular program of the school; that the school spends time on many things of less intrinsic value; that the ethical standards of educational researchers are generally high enough to preclude harmful or dangerous experimentation; that many research programs are educational in themselves and can be made enjoyable to children. Finally it can be shown that the criterion of *immediate* value and utility is unreasonable and is not applied in other engineering sciences.

NON-RESEARCH APPROACHES TO THE IMPROVEMENT OF PEDAGOGY

If so much resistance to educational research exists, how do educators and others commonly propose to further pedagogical methodology? A time-honored method employed by many "successful" teachers is to examine their own practices, to abstract what seems to them the basis for their success, and to advocate that these practices be universally emulated. The weaknesses of this approach are obvious. The claimed success of these teachers is rarely verified by objective means, the factors to which success is attributed are merely subjective impressions which have not been objectively identified or measured, and no control data are available as a basis for comparison. Often such teachers are successful for entirely different reasons than those of alleged superior methodology. Some have good teaching personalities, others have unusually good students, and still others teach under atypically favorable conditions. To remedy these shortcomings, some teachers have conducted crude classroom experiments. But since the vast majority of these experiments fail to control relevant variables (i.e., significant characteristics of the experimental population, of the proposed method, of the teacher, of the school environment), do not utilize reliable measuring instruments, and do not subject results to tests of statistical significance, they contribute little to the science of pedagogy.

Another less rational approach merely relies on the authority of presumed expert opinion. Some educators are convinced that after twenty-five years of experience in the profession they are entitled to make dogmatic pronouncements on pedagogic method which require no rationalization whatsoever and are valid by fiat alone, i.e., because of the wisdom which extended experience or high status in an administrative or university hierarchy presumably confers.

A third approach places greater weight on logic than on experience. Method A is inferred to be superior to Method B because it is more compatible (a) with certain theoretical considerations that have logical or face validity or (b) with indirectly related empirical findings. Such thinking is obviously necessary as a preliminary step in the formulation of hypotheses to be tested, and is probably the only approach possible in deciding upon the ends that education should pursue. Clearly, however, it cannot constitute an adequate approach in itself with respect to providing a scientific basis for the means employed toward such ends.

EMPIRICAL (RESEARCH) APPROACHES TO PEDAGOGIC METHODOLOGY

Three different kinds of research orientations have been adopted by those who are concerned with scientific progress in applied disciplines such as education: (a) basic science research,[2] (b) extrapolated research in the basic sciences, and (c) research at an applied level.

The "basic science" research approach is predicated on the very defensible notion that applied sciences are ultimately related to knowledge in the underlying sciences on which they are based. It can be convincingly demonstrated, for example, that progress in clinical medicine is intimately related to progress in biochemistry and bacteriology; that progress in engineering is intimately related to progress in physics and chemistry; and that progress in education is similarly dependent upon advances in psychology, statistics, sociology and philosophy. However, two important kinds of qualifications have to be placed on the value of basic science research for the applied sciences: qualifications of purpose or orientation, and qualifications of level of applicability.

By definition, basic science research is concerned with the discovery of general laws of physical, biological, psychological and sociological phenomenology as an end in itself. Researchers in these fields have no objection, of course, if their findings are applied to practical problems which have social value; in fact there is reason to believe that they are motivated to some extent by this consideration. But the design of basic science research bears no *intended* relation whatsoever to problems in the applied disciplines, the aim being solely to advance· knowledge. Ultimately, of course, such knowledge is applicable in a very broad sense to practical problems; but since the research design is not oriented to the solution of these problems, this applicability is apt to be quite indirect and unsystematic, and relevant only over a time period which is too long to be meaningful in terms of the short-range needs of the applied disciplines.

The second qualification has to do with the level at which findings in the basic sciences can be applied once their relevancy has been established. It should be self-evident that such findings enjoy a much higher level of generality than the problems to which they can be applied. At the applied level,

---

2 The term "basic" refers to the distinction between "basic" and applied sciences made earlier. It does not mean "fundamental." In the latter sense applied research is just as "basic" as research in the pure sciences.

specific ends and conditions are added which demand additional research to make manifest the precise way in which the general law operates in the specific case. That is, the applicability of general principles to specific problems is *not given* in the statement of the general principle, but must be specifically worked out for each individual problem. Knowledge about nuclear fission for example does not tell us how to make an atomic bomb or an atomic-powered airplane.

In fields such as education the problem of generality is further complicated by the fact that the practical problems often exist at higher levels of complexity with respect to the order of phenomenology involved than the basic science findings requiring application. That is, new variables are added which may qualitatively alter the general principles from the basic science to such an extent that at the applied level they only have substrate validity but no explanatory or predictive value. For example, antibiotic reactions that take place in test tubes do not necessarily take place in living systems, methods of learning employed by animals in mazes do not necessarily correspond to methods of learning children use in grappling with verbal materials in classrooms.

The basic science approach in educational research, therefore, is subject to many serious disadvantages. Its relevancy is too remote and indirect because it is not oriented toward solving educational problems, and its findings, if relevant, are applicable only if much additional research is performed to translate general principles into the more specific form they have to assume in the task-specialized and more complex contexts of pedagogy.

These limitations would not be so serious if they were perceived. If the limitations of this approach were perceived, it would be defensible for educational institutions to set aside a *small* portion of their research funds for basic science research as a long-term investment. But since these limitations are *not* perceived, some bureaus of educational research confidently invest their major resources in such programs, and then complacently expect that the research findings which emerge will be both relevant and applicable in their original form to the problems of education.

Naivete with respect to the second premise, i.e., of immediate applicability, is especially rampant and has led to very serious distortions in our knowledge of the psychology of learning that is relevant for pedagogy. The psychology of learning that teachers study is based on findings in general psychology which have been borrowed wholesale without much attempt to test their applicability to the kinds of learning situations that exist in classrooms. It would be a shocking situation indeed if a comparable procedure were practical in medicine, i.e., if physicians employed therapeutic techniques validated only *in vitro* or by animal experimentation.

The second general research approach in the applied disciplines is "extrapolated basic science research." Unlike pure basic science research it is oriented toward the solution of practical or applied problems. It starts out by identifying significant problems in the applied field, and designs experiments pointed toward their solution on an analogous but highly simplified basic science level. In this way it satisfies the important criterion of relevance, but must still contend with the problem of level of applicability. The rationale of this approach is that many practical problems are to complex that before one can develop fruitful hypotheses leading to their solution they must first be reduced to simpler terms and patterned after simpler models. Thus simplified, problems of control and measurement are rendered more manageable.

Depending on the nature of the problem under investigation, this approach may have genuine merit providing that the resulting research findings are only regarded as "leads" or hypotheses to be tested in the applied situation rather than as definitive answers *per se* to problems in pedagogy. As already noted, however, educational researchers have a tendency to extrapolate basic science findings to pedagogical problems without conducting the additional research necessary to bridge the gap between the two levels of generality involved. Also, when it is necessary to cross levels of phenomenological complexity in extrapolating, this approach has very limited usefulness for the reasons already given above.

The third approach to educational research, research at the applied level, is the most relevant and direct of the three, yet paradoxically is utilized least by professional research workers in the field. When research is performed in relation to the actual problems of education, at the level of complexity in which they exist, that is, *in situ* (under the conditions in which they are to be found in practice), the problems of relevance and extrapolation do not arise.[3] Most rigorous research in applied disciplines other than education is conducted at this level. The research program of a hospital or medical school would be regarded as seriously unbalanced if most of its funds and efforts went into biochemical or bacteriological research instead of into clinical research. The major responsibility for furthering research in the former areas belongs to graduate departments of chemistry and bacteriology. On the other hand, unless medical schools undertake to solve their own clinical problems who else will? And the same analogy obviously holds for education as well.

Although applied research presents greater difficulties with respect to research design, control, and measurement, the rewards are correspondingly greater when these problems are solved. Certainly such problems cannot be solved when they are avoided. If other applied disciplines have been able

---

[3] Applied research is also directed toward the discovery of general laws within the framework of its applied ends. The generalizations it discovers, therefore, exist at a different plane of generality than those of "basic" science research.

to evolve satisfactory research methodologies, there is no reason why education cannot also do so. In fact, if any applied discipline with unique and distinctive problems of its own is to survive as a science it has no choice in the matter—it is obliged to do so.

DIFFERENTIATION BETWEEN PSYCHOLOGICAL AND EDUCATIONAL RESEARCH PROBLEMS

Since both psychology and education deal with the problem of learning, how can we distinguish between the special research interests of each discipline in this area? As an applied science, education is not concerned with the general laws of learning *per se*, but only with those properties of learning that can be related to efficacious ways of deliberately effecting stable changes in individuals which have social value. Education, therefore, refers to guided or manipulated learning deliberately directed toward specific practical ends. These ends may be defined as the long-term acquisition of a stable body of knowledge (ideas, concepts, facts), values, habits, skills, ways of perceiving, adjusting, and aspiring, and of the capacities needed for acquiring them.

The psychologist's interest in learning, on the other hand, is much more general. Many other aspects of learning apart from the efficient achievement of designated competencies and capacities for growth in a directed context concern him. More typically, he investigates the nature of current, fragmentary, or short-term learning experiences rather than the kinds of long-term learning involved in assimilating extensive and organized bodies of knowledge, values, habits and skills.

The following kinds of learning problems, therefore, are particularly indigenous to educational research: (a) discovery of the nature of those aspects of the learning process affecting the long-range stability and meaningfulness of organized bodies of knowledge, skills, etc. in the learner; (b) long-range modification (improvement) of learning capacities; (c) discovery of those personality and cognitive aspects of the learner and of the interpersonal and social aspects of the learning environment that affect motivation for learning and characteristic ways of assimilating material; and (d) discovery of appropriate and maximally efficient practices and ways of organizing and presenting learning materials, of deliberately motivating and directing learning toward specified goals.

CONCLUSION

The failure of education to acquire status as an applied scientific discipline can be largely ascribed to two contrasting approaches to the discovery of pedagogical knowledge. One approach has relied on empirically untested theoretical propositions, on dogmatic assertion, or on the unwarranted generalization of subjective impressions from personal teaching experience. The other approach, going to the opposite extreme, has avoided coming to grips with the fundamental research problem of education as an applied science, i.e., the discovery of how pupils assimilate and grow in ability to assimilate symbolical materials in a social and interpersonal environment, and what the optimal conditions for these processes are. Instead it has become preoccupied with basic science research, failing to recognize important limitations of this approach with respect to relevancy and level of generality and complexity, and uncritically extrapolating finding from one level to another without performing the intervening research operations that are necessary.

If the profession of education is open to attack, it is vulnerable on the grounds of failing to make the progress it could reasonably have been expected to make in providing a scientific basis for pedagogy. It is vulnerable because of its complacency, its resistiveness to applied educational research, its tendency to spend more time and effort on dogmatically disseminating unvalidated hypotheses than on endeavoring to secure validation through painstaking research activity. Unfortunately, criticism of professional education is not directed along these lines, but is usually based on the fallacious notions that a science of pedagogy is unnecessary for teaching, that children are not learning as much as they used to, and that the only proper aim of education is the acquisition of factual knowledge and of intellectual skills.

The best defence that education could make to these latter baseless charges is to admit that a science of pedagogy does not yet exist, and to direct its attention toward formulating a research methodology in pedagogy at the applied level of operations at which it functions.

9. RESEARCH AND PROGRESS IN EDUCATION*

C. D. Hardie

The twentieth century has seen considerable progress in education. It has also witnessed the birth of research in education, and has watched the delicate infant grow into a fair-sized, rather noisy and undisciplined child. But so far the child has contributed very little to the progress, which has come about rather by other means. These other means include improved teaching by better educated teachers, and certain social and political factors. By the latter I mean, in the first place, the spread of democratic ideas which has removed, to some extent, class and sex differences in education; and, in the second place, the increasing complications of life in a modern community, so that governments have been compelled to spend much more public money on education to ensure that there will be enough skilled workers to keep the standard of life rising.

On the other hand, research in education has achieved very little up to the present, and it is fairly true to say that it is taken seriously mainly by those who are engaged in it. The great majority of teachers in schools, and almost all teachers in universities, regard it as of little value. Is this the fault of the research, or is it the fault of the teachers? I should like in this lecture to try to answer this by clarifying what I believe to be the nature

SOURCE. Hardie, C. D., "Research and Progress in Education," *Australian Journal of Education*, 1965. Copyright © C. D. Hardie 1965. First published by the Australian Council for Educational Research, Frederick Street, Hawthorn, Victoria 3122, in Volume 9, Number 3 of *The Australian Journal of Education*.
* This was delivered at the University of Melbourne as the John Smyth Memorial Lecture for 1965.

of educational research. It will then be possible to consider how far, if at all, future progress in education is likely to depend on the results of research.

Those who are seriously engaged in research at present are likely to explain the lack of any notable achievements by the shortness of the time during which research has been taking place. Sixty years or so, they would point out, is a negligible period in the history of any science. It may be true that once a science has become well established and has a continuous tradition of research, then sixty years will see enormous progress, as in physics or biology in the present century. But if we were to return to the pre-Newtonian era, then it is surely true that many a sixty years passed in which research in physics made as little progress as research in education has in the last sixty years. Moreover it is sometimes said that if the study of education could find its Newton, the progress would be rapid. For once some worthwhile results have been obtained, then people of ability are attracted to the work, it becomes easy to obtain strong financial support for research, and what was originally a halting and tentative trickle becomes a powerful and fertilising flood. This, I take it, is the view of most of those who are now pressing for increased private and government financial support for research programmes in education. For example, E. A. Peel has recently written about the development of research in England as follows: "All this needs money—more than we now get through the University Grants Committee, and the contributions to the Foundation. We can make appeals, often successful, to the larger foundations and trusts, but why can't we have something like a Department of Scientific and Industrial Research, or a Medical Research Council with financial power at its elbow? Why not a Department of Educational Research, or an Educational Research Council with power to encourage and promote research?"[1]

I should like to think that this point of view was justified, and that by simply increasing expenditure on research, progress would be guaranteed, but I am afraid it is much too simple-minded a point of view. It can hardly be seriously maintained that the present state of education is comparable to pre-Newtonian physics. For an essential pre-requisite for Newton's achievement was the idea of a deductive system, which had been exemplified in Euclid's geometry for about two thousand years prior to Newton. Thus if there is any analogy with physics at all, it would have to be with pre-Euclidean physics, and once this is realised, the prospects of rapid progress resulting from research in education in the foreseeable future looks somewhat bleak. There is no doubt that what caused the birth of research in education was the realisation of the success which experimentation had brought to the

---

[1] Symposium—Educational Research Today. *The British Journal of Educational Psychology.* XXXII, Part 2, 1962.

sciences in the eighteenth and nineteenth centuries, and it was hoped that similar success would be achieved in education. But experimental methods do not of themselves guarantee success, for they are not the only ingredient in research.

The aim of research in the older sciences can be put in different ways. But these all amount to something like this—that research seeks knowledge that will provide some kind of explanation for our present and past experience, and will enable us to predict, at least to some extent, future experience.

Now it does this in the following way. First of all by means of commonsense observation, aided when necessary by experiments of increasing delicacy, it seeks uniformities amid all the changing phenomena we see around us—uniformities such as the ebb and flow of the tides, the regularities in the appearance of the sky at night, the association of properties in what we call the same chemical substance, and so on. Most of these uniformities are what are technically called statistical generalizations, that is, they are statements of what usually or very nearly happens. For example, the length which a golf ball is driven will correlate closely with the time of flight, but it will not be a perfect correlation. There is about almost all our sense experience a kind of fuzziness. Now an important part of research is not to abolish the fuzziness from our ordinary experience, but to clarify how much of our experience may be regarded as orderly and how much as deviation from this order—deviations which appear as fuzziness. It does this by the construction of what are called theories. One of the earliest theories in physics was Newton's theory of gravitation which showed that the orderly part of our experience of matter in motion could be regarded as due to point masses which possessed both velocity at an instant and acceleration at an instant. Now all these are inherently unobservable concepts, for "point," "velocity at an instant," and "acceleration at an instant" are all concepts arrived at by the method of limits. But by adopting certain postulates about the theoretical concepts, and by linking combinations of these theoretical concepts with observational ones, it is possible to deduce a large number of relations, or "laws of nature," to which the observed generalizations are close approximations, so that, for example, the speed of a falling stone is proportional to the time of descent, the length which a golfball is driven is proportional to the time of flight, and so on.

A theory of this sort then enables us both to explain and to predict. Suppose an event E is observed, such as the height of a projectile at a given time. This can be explained by a set of initial conditions (height and velocity at a previous time) together with a relation of law which connects height with time of flight. Similarly, the height of the projectile at a future time can be predicted from its present height and velocity together with the relation or law connecting height with time of flight. There is indeed a symmetry involving the ideas of explanation and prediction. If the event E belongs to the researcher's present or past, then we use the law to explain E. But if E belongs to the researcher's future we use the law to predict E. As most laws of nature are the same if we alter the direction of time, we can also retrodict an event E from the present, as when we retrodict an eclipse of the sun two thousand years ago from observations of the solar system at the present time.

Other theories have been developed in other branches of physics, and gradually still more powerful theories were developed to link together what had appeared to be independent branches. For example, electromagnetic theory unified the two fields of electricity and optics. Physics has now reached the stage when it might be expected that some development of quantum theory will unify most of the subject, but this is still a matter for the future. Theories thus should be seen as deductive systems whose theorems, when suitably interpreted in observational terms, become laws to which our observational generalizations are approximations. The standard model for all such theories is, of course, Euclidean geometry, which consists of an abstract set of postulates about undefined entities which, when given a suitable interpretation, make the theorems derived in the system a set of laws to which the generalizations that we make about our perceptual space are good approximations.

Thus research in the well-established sciences proceeds in either an experimental or a theoretical direction. In so far as it attempts to discover new uniformities, it will observe and experiment; and in so far as it attempts to clarify the rather untidy uniformities of experience by fitting them into an orderly pattern by means of laws of nature, it will attempt to construct theories. The two activities are dependent on each other. For once a large mass of observational data has accumulated, the detection of further uniformities will, in general, come only as a deduction from some body of theory; and the construction of theories, conversely, needs to be checked and tested by their observational consequences. Most research workers, however, can be classified as being experimental or theoretical "types," although the outstanding scientists have generally made both experimental and theoretical discoveries. From a logical point of view in understanding the structure of any branch of knowledge, it is of the utmost importance to distinguish clearly what is an experimental or observational question from what is a theoretical one.

This is a necessarily rather brief account of the relation between theory and experiment that has become clear as a result of the research that has been done in the older sciences. If research in education is to be understood in a similar sense, then we should expect to find a similar structure of theory and a similar relation between theory and experimental observations. Has such an expectation been justified?

It seems clear to me that it has not. It is true that we have a fair number of statistical generalizations in education, most of which have been obtained by the experience of teachers in the class-room, and some of which have been obtained by deliberate and carefully controlled experimentation. For example, in the former class I would include most of the generalizations that are included in books on learning and teaching—things like "knowledge that a response is correct makes it more likely to recur," "several periods of study of a topic are in general more effective than one long period." In the latter class I would include some of the generalizations about the teaching of specific topics—things like "subtraction is in general taught more efficiently by the equal-additions method than by the decomposition method." But while all those generalizations have the fuzziness that we expect of our ordinary experience, there is no body of theory which enables us to detect an order lying behind the fuzziness. We cannot even guess at what the important variables might be in such a theory. As a result, research in education has completely failed to provide the type of explanation that we have come to expect from research in the sciences.

In the early days of this century, Spearman made a valiant attempt to construct an educational theory with the appropriate logical structure. He supposed that with each individual there could be associated certain variables. These were connected by relations that could be expressed by linear equations, and certain combinations of the variables were to be interpreted as the inter-correlations among a battery of tests. Spearman was then able to deduce a number of theorems from his postulates which led to such observable uniformities as hierarchical order among correlation coefficients and zero tetrad differences. All this exemplified admirably the relations between theory and experimental observations that are characteristic of research. Unfortunately, however, further experiments showed that the theory was inadequate. Tetrad differences were often found to differ from zero by more than the fuzziness permitted as experimental error, and subsequent attempts to explain the experimental results by a more complicated type of theory have not been successful. We must admit therefore that research in education has not produced the kind of knowledge which we can use to explain and to predict, and we must even admit that there have been very few attempts at genuine research in education. This failure is due basically to the fact that it seems to be impossible to construct for even a small section of education a body of theory which is an essential part of research in the established sense of the word.

If this is so, it would appear that the next thing to try would be to consider whether research in education might be defined solely in terms of experimentation. Can we reconcile ourselves to the fact that theory construction has no place, and that doing research is just observing and experimenting? At first sight this view seems attractive, and it would appear to derive support from many books and articles. For articles in such works as *The Journal of Educational Research* and *The Journal of Educational Psychology* are almost all straightforward reports of experiments, and the readers and editors of these Journals certainly think of them as research journals.

A typical situation is where some hypothesis is set up and a piece of research is designed by which it can be refuted. For example, the hypothesis might be that there is no difference in intelligence between students in the Faculty of Arts and students in the Faculty of Science at the University of Melbourne at the present time. An hypothesis of this sort is often called a null hypothesis, and it is tested by comparing the characteristic under consideration (in this case intelligence) in two random samples, one drawn from the Faculty of Arts and one from the Faculty of Science. If the difference between the samples is significant at a previously agreed level, then the null hypothesis is rejected. In less technical language, this just means that if the two samples differ to such an extent that it would be very unlikely for such a difference to arise in two random samples drawn from the same population, then we conclude that the samples could not have come from the same population. Now this is straightforward so far as it goes. But it is important to be clear as to what has been proved. What has been proved, or rather shown to be very probable, is that the population of Arts students at present in the University of Melbourne is more intelligent (let us say) than the population of Science students at present in the University of Melbourne. But no conclusion can be drawn about students in other universities or about students at Melbourne at other times. For the two samples chosen are not random samples from these different populations, and it is legitimate to reject the null hypothesis only if the samples concerned have been selected at random. I do not wish to belabour this rather trivial point, but it is not uncommon for even very reputable researchers to draw conclusions far beyond that to which they are entitled, and even on some occasions to fail to make clear the populations about which they are drawing conclusions. I believe that the tendency to do this arises because these experimenters imagine they are establishing a generalization or law similar to laws of nature in the older sciences.

It is, however, very important to understand that the role played by any such generalization is very different from the role played by generalizations that form part of a theory. For the latter are used, as we saw, to explain our past experience and to predict our future experience. But suppose we have established that students in the Arts Faculty at the University of Melbourne in 1965 are more intelligent than students in the Science Faculty. This is useless as regards explanation and prediction. Let us suppose John Doe is an Arts student and Richard Roe a Science student in 1965. Then the generalization is consistent with John Doe being more intelligent than, less intelligent than, or just as intelligent as Richard Roe. How then do such generalizations function?

It seems clear that if they have any function, or play any role at all, it is in the framing of policy. During most of its sixty years or so of existence, I believe that research in education has suffered just because it has been called "research." As such it could be expected to produce that combination of theory and experiment which has been so successful elsewhere, and so to provide both explanations and predictions. This it has failed to do, and, so far as we can tell at present, will fail to do at least for a very long time. The sooner this is realised the better, for as long as a pretence is kept up that research in education is like ordinary research then it will continue to be despised by workers in other fields. This is the explanation of the fact, which I mentioned at the outset, that few teachers in schools and universities take such research at all seriously. But what can be of value in education is what is called elsewhere "operational research" (or sometimes "operations research"). The aim of this is entirely different from the aim of ordinary research. Its aim is not to acquire knowledge by which we can explain or predict, but to enable us to take more rational decisions. If, for example, it is thought to be important that the more intelligent students in Melbourne should study Science rather than Arts, then an investigation which showed that in 1965 the level of intelligence in Arts is higher than that in Science is of relevance. For it means that decisions may have to be taken to attract abler students into the Science Faculty. Such decisions will be more rational if based on generalizations established as a result of investigations of this sort.

Let us look for a moment at the traditional way by which decisions in education have been made, and very often still are made. This is what may be called "the committee method." Committees are appointed by the decision makers, and are expected to meet, or at the very least to correspond, and to produce after due discussion the solution of a problem or a recommendation for action. It would be unfair to condemn this method too severely. Some committees are of value, particularly when the decision maker wants to postpone a decision, or when he wants a compromise of different points of view, or as has been known to happen when he wants to evade the responsibility of making a decision. But many problems in education are unsuitable for committee solution.

Examples of the harm which has been done by committees in education will be familiar to you all, especially when committees are appointed to represent different interests. For it is then most unlikely that any decision will be reached that is opposed to any of the interests that are represented. But what is perhaps worse than the actual conclusion reached is the reliance on a method which by its very nature is unsuited to the problem. We tend to smile in a superior way at committees in the dim and not-so-distant past that wrote about, for example, Latin and mental discipline. But committees in our own time, composed of leaders in the field, have written about the three types of pupil that can be found at age eleven plus, about the abolition of privilege and the establishment of shared ideals by the common school, about the advantages of the non-graded school, and so on. But it would be most unlikely that problems such as these could be solved by reminiscences exchanged round a table. If they are to be solved—if indeed they are to be given meaning so that we can even be clear what the problem is—they have to be analysed, and data obtained either by observation or deliberate experimentation in the way in which Thorndike, for example, finally exploded the hocus-pocus about mental discipline in high-school studies.

"Operational research" is the name given to this better method for arriving at decisions. Historically, it was, I think, pioneered by Sir Robert Watson-Watt, the inventor of radar, who described it as "The application of the basic scientific methods of measurement, classification, comparison and correlation to the selection of means of attaining, with the least expenditure in effort and time, the maximum operational effect which could be extracted from the available or potentially available resources in personnel and material." Since the early days of the war operational research has established itself not only throughout the fighting services, but in such other fields as economics and industrial management. Now it seems to me that Watson-Watt's account of operational research is a very good description of what we might try to mean by "research" in education. Research in this sense is not the acquisition of knowledge for the purposes of explanation and prediction, but a means of enabling us to take decisions that will lead to the maximum effect from the available resources. It is this which has led to the terse description of operational research as "scientific preparation for decision."

I want now to consider how this conception of research helps to remove the conflict of opinion about the value of research in education, and finally to consider how far future progress in education is likely to depend on it.

I have already referred to the different views that are held about research in education. On the one hand there is the opinion of the professional researchers, who claim that it has been mainly lack of financial support that has prevented worthwhile discoveries being made. On the other hand, there is widespread scepticism among teachers in schools and universities because so far research has been so fruitless. Now this second view is correct if the

test of fruitful research is the establishment of a body of knowledge consisting of laws of nature tidily ordered in a deductive theory. In addition I
am afraid it is true that there is no evidence at all to suggest that if millions
of pounds were made available tomorrow, they would contribute anything
to the discovery of such a body of knowledge. It is therefore unfortunate
that those who are professionally engaged in research always appear to write
as if they are seeking this kind of knowledge. Dr. Radford, for example, has
recently given this account: "Research . . . is asking questions about some
aspect or aspects of the educational system and collecting facts to answer
those questions. The theoretical importance of the research depends upon
the importance of the aspect involved; its practical value depends upon the
quality of the questions asked, and upon the quality of the data obtained."[2]
He adds as a footnote that he thinks I would agree with this description, but
I cannot do so. The reason is simple. No research is of theoretical importance in education, for as yet we have no body of theory. I would accept
the first sentence, but only with a severe restriction—that the questions which
are asked are questions about what should be done. If, as Radford appears
to mean in view of his later references to theoretical importance, they are
questions seeking explanations, then they are useless, and the attempt to
answer them is justifiably attacked in academic circles.

On the other hand, let us see what the position is if we abandon this
traditional view about research and think of it only as operational research.
We can certainly point to a few examples where it has been of great value.
I have already mentioned Thorndike's work in connection with mental discipline in high school studies. A more recent example is the work that was
done by the statistical adviser and research officers to the Robbins Committee
on Higher Education in Great Britain. One of the central tasks of the Robbins
Committee was to make recommendations concerning the scale of higher
education up to about 1980, and it did this by estimating the number of
places required to meet the demand from suitably qualified candidates. This
in turn depended on estimates of:

(1) the size of the age groups relevant to higher education,
(2) the proportions of these age groups likely to reach the particular
levels of attainment considered relevant for entry to higher education,
(3) the proportions of those so qualified that would apply to enter higher
education,
(4) the proportion of those applicants who should be given places.

The calculated estimates showed that the percentage of the age group who

---

[2] Radford, W. C., *A Field for Many Tillings*. Hawthorn: Australian Council for Educational Research, 1964, p. 6.

would obtain, for example, three or more A-level passes in the G.C.E. examinations in 1980 was approximately double the percentage of the corresponding age group in 1961. In other words there is no law of nature which prescribes what percentage of an age group will attain a given standard. This clearly depends on the nature of the curriculum, the skill and supply of teachers, the material resources of families and their attitude to education, and no doubt on a host of other variables. But we can try to raise the percentage steadily by improving the curriculum, the skill and supply of teachers and so on.

Now the aim of the research associated with the Robbins proposals was quite frankly to ensure a better use of the available resources in higher education. It was therefore an excellent example of operational research. Moreover, it was successful, and the proposals have been widely acclaimed for their sanity because they were based on that kind of research. This indicates therefore that research in education can be and will be widely respected if it is clearly operational research and does not claim to be research in the traditional sense of the word. For the Robbins research did not lead to anything by which we could explain what has happened or predict what will happen to John Doe in his progress through school to university.

This is typical of what can be claimed or hoped for in operational research. Even when some hypothesis is established, for example, by disproving the null hypothesis, we have to remember that the hypothesis does not partake of the character of a law of nature and may well be falsified in the future. Without any theory to guide us, we do not know what variables are important and what are irrelevant. But the establishment of hypotheses in this way is a procedure that is sometimes of value in operational research. Let me take as another example one to which I have already referred in the teaching of subtraction. In an extensive experiment on this,[3] 842 pupils were taught by the equal-additions method and 464 by the decomposition method. In a test which afforded 224 possible opportunities for mistakes, the errors were marked and the mean number of errors calculated for each set of scripts. These means were 12·9 for the equal additions method, and 20·9 for the decomposition method. If we consider the hypothesis that the sets of scripts were two random samples from the same population, then we can show that the chance of getting such a large difference between the means is extremely small, and it is therefore reasonable to conclude that the scripts were not random samples from the same population.

Now this may mean that they were random samples from different populations, or that they were from the same population but were not random

[3] Murray, J. "The Relative Merits of the Methods of Teaching Subtraction." *Studies in Arithmetic*, Vol. II.

samples. If the former was true, then we could expect that future results might continue to favour the equal additions method. But the latter may well be true. Indeed in one sense it clearly is true, for the scripts all come from the population of children that were accessible to the experimenter at a given time and place. Because we have no theory to guide us, we cannot say that there is a natural law to the effect that the equal additions method is better than the decomposition method. But we can say the rejection of the null hypothesis in this experiment indicates that a young teacher who seeks guidance on the teaching of subtraction should be recommended to start with the equal additions method. In other words the experiment affords a basis for deciding what to do.

But we must always remember that further experimentation may lead us to alter our recommendations about what to do. Numerous examples of this could be given from the experience of operational research units during the war. Early in the war, for example, it was thought that it would be good policy to bomb German railways and communications. But after some experimentation this was found to be very ineffective. Later on, however, perhaps because of increased accuracy of navigational aids and bomb aiming, it was found to be very effective, and was one of the main reasons German production broke down late in 1944. Moreover, even without further experimentation, our recommendations must always be tentative and not dogmatic. For it must be emphasized that in education we do not know of laws connecting the important variables in a problem—we do not even know what the important variables are. This is the real reason why there is no "best" method of dealing with any educational situation; there is no best method of teaching reading, no best method of teaching arithmetic and so on. Consequently, the teacher in my view must always occupy a crucial position in education, for he has still to get a child to read and to count even when the recommended methods will not work with him.

Here again I must disagree with Dr. Radford in his recent pamphlet on research. At one point he laments the fact that Australia has not produced a Spearman, Bruner, Cuisenaire, Skinner, etc. This sounds, and it is clear that Radford means it to sound, like a recital of the founders of a science in the way that one might wish Australia could produce a Newton, a Maxwell, a Bohr, or an Einstein in Physics. Now in the first place it is quite misleading to group Spearman with the other names. I believe, as I have already said, that Spearman's research was research in the traditional sense, and that it was a brilliant attempt to provide for education a body of theory similar to that of the older sciences. But it ended in failure. The others mentioned by Radford are in an entirely different category. Teachers will have different opinions about the value of what they have achieved, but their work has all been research of the operational kind, and therefore cannot have the kind of permanent value associated with the work of a Newton or a Maxwell. Education has many heroes, but their names do not live long. By all means let us pay tribute to the work of these men admired by Radford, but let us pay even more tribute to the teacher of fifty children who can still get them to count more or less correctly when rods and programmed learning have failed.

The fact that our recommendations have to be tentative and not dogmatic is sometimes urged by the critics of educational research to show how useless it is. "Look," they may say, "after all the work that has been done, no one yet knows the best method of teaching reading or arithmetic." This type of criticism no longer need embarrass us. It would have justification if research in education was research in the traditional sense, but it is entirely mistaken if, as I am arguing, research in education can only be operational research. All it shows in fact is that the critic has not understood the nature of the subject matter and of what we are trying to do. However, the happy reception accorded to the Robbins proposals by most academic people in Britain—proposals, as I have indicated, that were based on the painstaking work of Professor Moser and his colleagues—indicates that when the research does not pretend to be something that it isn't, it is accepted and respected.

What now about future progress in education, and how far is that likely to be determined by research? I believe that if research in education is interpreted in the way I have suggested, its record is not as poor as many of its critics allege, and I am quite sure that with closer association between administrators and research workers much progress will result. I would plead, therefore, for a strengthening of the research sections of the State Departments of Education, for it is there that operational research can clearly be of most use to those responsible for decision making, in precisely the way research was involved in the Robbins proposals. At the same time it is clear that research of the operational kind can never provide either the intellectual satisfaction or lead to the practical achievements of research in the traditional sense. For it is only the latter that leads to that combination of theory and experiment which satisfies our desire for explanation and also provides for control over our future.

I believe, therefore, that those of us who have looked to research to provide the means of progress in education have been, at least to some extent, mistaken. By all means let us derive what progress we can from research, but let us not have misguided hopes. Progress can come in education even if we forget about research, as for example, in a good deal of the progress we have seen this century. I mentioned at the outset what education owes to the gradual spread of democratic practices, and to the growth of science, and we can surely anticipate still further progress from these sources. But to my mind the main source of progress in education must always come from teachers rather than from scientists, politicians, administrators or research workers and I shall end by indicating one way in which it seems to me teachers could now contribute considerably to further progress. In brief this is by obtaining a clearer understanding of the way language functions in communication.

The importance of a symbolism as distinct from what the symbolism symbolises has long been recognised. The most striking example from an educational point of view is a very old one—the Arabic method of symbolising the natural numbers. By means of this, quite dull children in our schools can learn to solve arithmetical problems that would have defeated highly intelligent Greeks who had to struggle with a different symbolism. There have been from time to time speculations about the tremendous benefits which would be derived by the construction of a language which would be able to help children's thinking in the way in which the Arabic symbolism helps children's counting. Leibniz went so far as to predict that a time would come when two human beings who had reached different conclusions would be able to resolve the conflict by saying "Come, let us sit down and calculate." There is not much doubt that these speculations were much too optimistic. Nevertheless, we are now a good deal clearer about the ways in which a language functions, and about the reasons why some combinations of symbols successfully communicate, while other combinations do not. But as yet this has not had as much influence on teachers, and consequently on their pupils, as it deserves. In particular, many words are still used in writing and in talking about education as if they were names of activities that were being performed on a private stage inside the child's mind, words such as understanding, interest, attitude, etc. In so far as they are construed in this way, sentences which involve them will fail to communicate successfully, and it is therefore not surprising that, as long as this goes on, so much of what is written on the child psychology aspect of education appears to float idly by, anchored to nothing and achieving nothing.

The most common uses of language both in teaching and in talk about teaching are three, which we may call the analytic or verbal, the descriptive or factual, and the prescriptive or evaluative uses. It is of the utmost importance that these uses should not be confused with each other. Many years ago William James propounded the problem of the hunter and the squirrel. A hunter walks round a tree while a squirrel hiding in the tree moves round so that the hunter and the squirrel are always face to face but with the tree between them. In the end both hunter and squirrel return to their original positions, and it is obviously correct to say that they have both gone round the tree, the hunter in a large circle, the squirrel in a small circle. But what is the answer to the question has the hunter gone round the squirrel? One would naturally think that this is a factual question to be settled by observation. Yet a little consideration shows that no amount of care in observing, aided by the most accurate optical instruments, can provide an answer. The question is an analytic or verbal one—it is to be answered by deciding what rule we are going to apply for the use of the word "round." Now most of us would have thought that the use of the word "round" was clear enough, but by this example James showed that in certain circumstances this is not so. In asking the question did does the hunter go round the squirrel?, we are not asking for something to be settled by observation of the world but are asking for something to be settled by a verbal rule. Unfortunately this kind of confusion is very common in talk about education. We often think we are asking factual questions when we ask about, for example, children's social co-operation, acceptance of authority, self-expression, experience of causality, social maturity, and so on. But it is not true that in general we need to know more facts about children or about teaching to answer these questions. Quite a number of the questions often proposed for research will indeed never be answered except analytically. That is, some decision has to be made about the criteria for the application of these words; we are really asking for identification marks for things that we are not always able to identify.

Just as confusion between the descriptive or factual use of language and the analytic or verbal use will give rise to unanswerable problems, so will confusion between the descriptive and evaluative uses. Teachers must realise that no amount of factual evidence entails any value judgment. We may try to persuade children to make the value judgements of which we approve by presenting carefully selected facts to them on appropriate occasions, but we should be clear what we are doing. There does not seem to me to be enough awareness among teachers that moral teaching and aesthetic teaching —any teaching whose aim involves the teaching of values—are very different sorts of activity from the teaching of factual or descriptive material. Confusion of the two leads to the kind of artificiality which I think most of us feel infects at times almost all education and which runs riot on occasions such as school assemblies, Speech Nights and Royal Visits. But even in the calm of an author's study it is easy to blunder. For example, Edward Best in his article "A Failure in Communication"[4] has recently provided an excellent detailed analysis of the confusions of this sort into which the late Susan Isaacs fell when she wrote *Social Development in Young Children*.

Closer attention to the different uses of language in communication would make possible a different sense for "theory" in the phrase "theory of education." In this sense a theory of education would not be a deductive pattern correlating different empirical laws, but a collection of sentences that had a variety of functions. Some of them would be analytic, functioning as definitions; others would be empirical generalizations from observations and experiments; still others would be prescriptions leading to evaluative sentences; and so on. In the formation of these sentences logical words such as "if . . . then," "true," "not," "all" would be used as well as extra-logical or empirical words. The latter would be either terms from common sense or technical terms, linked to observation by means of definitions. An educational theory would then be considered satisfactory if it was successful in correlating a wide range of experience. The construction of an educational theory in this sense would make coherent the kind of talk in which we indulge when we write articles or talk about our work either with our colleagues or on more solemn occasions such as lectures and conferences.

If I may now summarize the conclusions that I would draw from all this argumentation, they are these:

1. Research in education, if interpreted in the usual sense of seeking knowledge with which to understand our experience, has been quite unsuccessful, and there is no reason to suppose that it will be successful in the foreseeable future.

2. If research in education, however, accepts the more modest aim of providing reasons for changing some aspect of educational practice, then it has quite a number of achievements to its credit, and may look forward to many more. In particular, administrators should look more and more to their research staffs rather than to committees when seeking advice about what to do. This means, of course, that research staffs should be chosen from people who have some understanding of operational research—even if that understanding has been gained outside the field of education.

3. Progress in education can be expected to result from this kind of research, but other factors are likely to remain more influential, at least in the immediate future. General social and political conditions will always be important, but the most influential source of progress for a long time to come will be the teacher. In particular, a better training for all teachers with special study of the ways in which communication takes place should have top priority.

10. THE MYTHOLOGY OF EDUCATIONAL RESEARCH: THE METHODS APPROACH

Fred N. Kerlinger

The mythology of educational research is a body of legends and beliefs purporting to be the rationale, purpose, and methods of educational research. It has an essentially mystical character which seems to be rooted in the past. To question the mythology amounts to heresy.

The foundations of the mythology are: a general ignorance among educators of science and scientific research; an overwhelming preoccupation with practicality; and a negative and sometimes anti-intellectual attitude toward science and research. Educational research often has been criticized for its triviality, superficiality, and scientific naivete. It has been said that these deficiencies are due to education being a young discipline, to the lack of imagination of educational researchers, to lack of theoretical development, and to general lack of sufficient attention to the canons of science.[1] These points have truth. But more important, perhaps, are the mythology and the knowledge, training, attitudes, and values of people doing, supporting (or not supporting), and consuming educational research—the educators themselves.

The mythology of educational research includes a number of interesting individual myths: methods, statistics, measurement, practicality,[2] "educa-

SOURCE. Kerlinger, Fred N., "The Mythology of Educational Research," *School and Society*, 88: 2171, March 26, 1960. Copyright © 1960 by School and Society, the publisher.

[1] Cf., B. O. Smith, in W. S. Monroe, editor, *Encyclopedia of Educational Research* (New York: Macmillan, 1950), pp. 1145–1152.

[2] The practicality myth has been discussed elsewhere. See the writer's article, "Practicality and Educational Research," *School Review*, 67:281–291, Autumn, 1959. Other myths will be discussed in future articles.

tional research is special and different," action research, etc. The concern of the present essay is the methods myth, one of the more influential of the myths in distorting the research thinking of educators and students of education.

The methods myth seems to be very prevalent in the research thinking of American educators. The teaching of educational research in university schools of education, for example, seems to concentrate largely on "methods of research." Indeed, what is perhaps the most-used text in educational research courses is entitled *Methods of Research*.[3] The methods approach is rather narrowly pragmatic. If you want to investigate an educational problem, you must do some research on it. In order to do the research, you need a method. So find a method, the "right" method. Concomitantly, the way to train students in research is to teach them "methods of research."

An example may help to clarify the point being made. Perhaps the most naive form the methods approach takes is the idea that if you want information on an educational subject, then use the "survey" and/or mail questionnaire. It is difficult to tell which of these is the more hackneyed and misused. Both are usually done poorly. This is *not* to say that the school survey has no useful function. It is an important part of the educational enterprise. But to confuse a school survey—which is basically clerical work of a higher order —with a scientific study of the relations among certain variables is another matter. For example, we might do a survey to determine the success of a new system of school consolidation. This is perfectly legitimate and necessary. But to call such an investigation research, much less scientific research, is misleading. Such a study can be scientific. Needless to say, however, the great difficulties in the way of scientifically studying anything as complex as a drastic change in educational administrative practice and its effects on educational outcomes are hardly appreciated.

A basic aspect of the methods approach is the general idea that gathering data constitutes research. This is closely related to the notion that science is fundamentally concerned with gathering, classifying, and storing facts. It is a confusion of the taxonomic function of science with science itself. In addition, it is a static view of science and research which emphasizes fact-gathering and which reinforces the methods approach, since it leads to a search for the best "methods" for gathering facts.

Part of scientific research activity unquestionably consists of gathering and classifying facts. But a more advanced and fruitful notion of research is a dynamic one which conceives it as an ongoing scientific activity in which hypothetical and theoretical propositions are tested systematically, not neces-

---

[3] C. V. Good and D. E. Scates, *Methods of Research* (New York: Appleton-Century-Crofts, 1954).

sarily and primarily to yield knowledge (although this is, of course, important), but to help refine and formulate theories and to yield further hypotheses for further testing. Few educators seem to have this conception of research. The notion which seems to be held is that the purpose of research is to increase knowledge so that education, particularly school practices, can be somehow improved. This is not necessarily a wrong notion; it is, rather, an incomplete and too narrow one. What it succeeds in doing is to choke off higher-level, theoretically oriented investigations in education.[4] It also distracts attention from the most important part of scientific activity—theory-building and testing—and focuses attention on a less important part of science—so-called methods of research. Thus, education becomes saddled with a methods orientation, and the attention of students of education tends to be distracted from research problems and the theories behind them.

The argument on the other side of the question seems to be that education is not ready for theories, that many more facts are needed, and that the facts gathered must be pertinent to the solution of practical educational problems. But no area of investigation is ever "ready" for theory; facts by themselves are meaningless; and facts gathered only for practical ends tend to throttle scientific activity. Cohen put it nicely:

> . . . There is, however, no genuine progress in scientific insight through . . . accumulating empirical facts without hypotheses or anticipation of nature. Without some guiding idea we do not know what facts to gather. Without something to prove, we cannot determine what is relevant and what is irrelevant.[5]

Education needs both data and fact-gathering *and* the systematic testing of theoretical and hypothetical propositions in a rigorous fashion. But an emphasis on methods leads persuasively to a stereotype of educational research as mere data-gathering, since methods are devised to gather data. This mode of thinking makes it difficult, if not impossible, for the educational scientist to work in a theoretical framework.[6] The scientific purposes of theory, predic-

---

[4] An interesting example of this tendency is the explanatory material for research proposals put out by the U.S. Office of Education, Department of Health, Education, and Welfare, in connection with Public Law 531 on co-operative research projects. Under the heading, "Criteria for the Evaluation of Proposals for Research Under P. L. 531," 13 criteria are given, not one of which says anything directly about basic research or theory in educational research. The first of these is significant: "1. The proposed research, survey, or demonstration is concerned with the development of new knowledge directly applicable to the educational process or with new applications of existing knowledge to the problems in education."

[5] M. R. Cohen, *A Preface to Logic* (New York: Meridian Books, 1956), p. 148.

[6] It is interesting and distressing to note that the large foundations interested in educational problems are channeling huge sums of money into research with rather narrowly

tion, and control are lost with such a viewpoint, and it is probably just these features of science which are the most fruitful stimulants of scientific curiosity and scientific research.

What implications does the methods myth have for educational research? Because of space limitations, only two of these will be discussed. Perhaps most obvious is the effect on graduate curricula. Evidently few schools of education require systematic and thorough study of research design, statistics and statistical inference, and measurement. Courses offered in these fields tend to be practical and "consumer-oriented." They are designed supposedly to help students understand ("consume") rather than to do. When a course in research is offered, it tends to stress the various so-called methods "appropriate to educational research"—the normative-survey, the causal comparative method, the case study, the correlation method, and so on.[7] Little or no stress is put on design of research springing from the adequate statement of a problem or problems, statistical inference and probabilistic thinking are de-emphasized, and the many recent, significant developments in social scientific and other branches of research—multivariate analysis, such as the analysis of variance and factor analysis, the mathematics of sets, matrices, and probability, and the several important developments in measurement—either are ignored or dismissed in a few words.

Judging from the products of doctoral students of education and the understanding of educators of science and scientific research, courses in educational research have been failures. They neither have trained students to do research and to use statistics and measurement, nor have they given students much understanding of these matters. It is not claimed that the methods approach is the cause of the much-bemoaned incompetence of doctoral students of education in handling thesis problems. It is, rather, a symptom of the deeper disease of educational thinking, outlined earlier as the foundations of the mythology, which can be epitomized in three words: ignorance, practicality, anti-intellectualism.

The immediate point is that doctorates are conferred upon methods-oriented doctoral students, some of whom will be the future educational leaders who have to train the next generation of students. The argument often is used that

conceived practical ends. Unfortunately, little of this support seems to go to the theoretically oriented investigations. Apparently one must show that the results of one's research will help make a better educational world, especially according to the foundation's definition of a better educational world.

[7] Good and Scates, *op. cit.* Significantly, the earlier edition of this work carried a whole chapter called "The Classification of Research Methods" in which attempts to categorize educational research were summarized. This chapter is one of the best pieces of evidence of the tendency I am discussing—the tendency to think directly and basically in methods terms. See C. V. Good, A. S. Barr, and D. E. Scates, *The Methodology of Educational Research* (New York: Appleton-Century-Crofts, 1936). Chap. V.

schools of education are and should be basically concerned with turning out practitioners and not "theoreticians" and researchers. But whether this should be so, while pertinent, is not the real issue. The hard fact is that the professors of the next generation are selected from the doctoral students of this generation. If the training now is no better, or even worse, than it was in the past, then we can expect nothing more than a perpetuation of the mythology with, perhaps, a few more, newer, and possibly more defensive rationalizations than have been used in the past. Along with this is the equally devastating thought that the present attitudes of doctoral students tend to become the future attitudes of educators in general. Thus, the relatively narrow methods-centered and even covert anti-intellectual attitudes of present doctoral students —due to their training, the social milieu in which they train, and the mythology—become the attitudes of most educators.

A second implication or consequence of the methods approach in educational research thinking is the cultural lag attendant upon such a conception of research. Educational research is perhaps 10–20 years behind other related fields of research. Psychological research, for instance, has well incorporated into itself the multivariate thinking of Fisher, Thurstone, and others. More important, a large proportion of psychological research is science-oriented and not methods-oriented. The same is more or less true of sociology and sociological research. But not so in education. The school of education which insists that its doctoral students learn to understand science and to use modern scientific analytic tools seems to be rare. The emphasis, instead, is on the vague vagaries of methods which, in the last analysis, help the education doctoral student—or, for that matter, any investigator in education—very little. On the contrary, they seem to be successful only in confusing the student. They confuse him, as hinted earlier, because they lead him to believe that research problems can be solved mainly with their aid. And, generally speaking, this is not so. The graduate student of education needs to learn, among other things, the nature of science and how the scientist thinks and works, modern multivariate approaches *and their rationale*, and modern modes of analysis of data. There are other indispensable ingredients, naturally. For instance, the student also needs to understand modern measurement conceptions, such as the recent advances in thinking on the validity problem.[8] But a good start could be made by simply dropping out of the curriculum of the graduate education school the whole methods approach as it has been preached for decades and by substituting rigorous courses in research design and scientific thinking.

Lest too negative an impression be left with the reader, it should be noted

----

[8] *E.g.*, see E. E. Cureton, in E. F. Lindquist, editor, *Educational Measurement* (Washington, D. C.: American Council on Education, 1951), pp. 621–694.

that there are visible chinks in the educational research armor. Occasional excellent studies always have been published—but they have been too occasional. In the last four or five years, however, there has been an increasing upsurge of significant and well-designed and executed studies.[9] It probably is still true that many or most doctoral theses continue to be poor. But if the present trend toward broader theoretical and methodological thinking continues, educational research will be revolutionized. And it is the business of schools of education to hasten and not to hinder this revolution. Above all, it is the business of schools of education not to create and perpetuate mythologies, but to destroy them.

[9] Four good examples of this upsurge are: N. Gross, W. S. Mason, and A. W. McEachern, *Explorations in Role Analysis: Studies of the School Superintendency Role* (New York: Wiley, 1958) ; E. B. Page, "Teacher Comments and Student Performance: A Seventy-Four Classroom Experiment in School Motivation," *Journal of Educational Psychology*, 49: 173–181, Aug., 1958; D. G. Ryans, "The Investigation of Teacher Characteristics," *Educational Record*, 34: 370–396, Oct., 1953 (general report on a series of studies) ; I. Sarnoff, *et al.*, "A Cross-Cultural Study of Anxiety Among American and English School Children," *Journal of Educational Psychology*, 49: 129–136, June, 1958.

11. BASIC AND APPLIED RESEARCH IN EDUCATION: DEFINITIONS, DISTINCTIONS, AND IMPLICATIONS

John B. Carroll

At a time when questions are being raised with particular poignancy about the value of basic research in the social and behavioral sciences,[1] it seems useful to try to clarify some of the issues as they pertain to research in education. After a period of about ten years during which Federal support of educational research increased markedly—a period in which there was a relative lack of concern as to whether the research being supported was "basic" or "applied," as a result of which a considerable amount of research of a fairly "basic" character was supported—recent Congressional actions and corresponding policy decisions in the Bureau of Research of the U. S. Office of Education[2] have tended to put much more weight on the support

SOURCE. Carroll, John B., "Basic and Applied Research in Education: Definitions, Distinctions, and Implications," *Harvard Educational Review*, **38**, Spring 1968, 263–276. Copyright © 1968 by President and Fellows of Harvard College.

[1] House of Representatives, *The Use of Social Research in Federal Domestic Programs*. Parts I–IV. A staff study for the Research and Technical Programs Subcommittee of the Committee on Government Operations (Washington: U.S. Government Printing Office, 1967).

[2] A leading critic of governmental educational research programs has been Lee J. Cronbach (1966), who states that the U. S. Office of Education Bureau of Research "has thrown its forces heavily on the side of 'practical products' and dissemination." "While the USOE is a passive patron of basic research," he continues, "it has done nothing to formulate and sell to Congress a policy that will promote the healthy development of basic investigation." Further, he points out that the Office "declines to support a research and development center unless it includes a dissemination program from the outset," a fact to which I can personally testify. Nevertheless, there are signs of at least a slight

of "applied" research which would be directed toward the solution of immediately practical problems in education. This state of affairs appears to reflect considerable confusion about the role of basic research in education and what this research may be expected to achieve. This paper will argue not only that it is possible and useful to distinguish between basic and applied research, but also that there is a continuing need for both of these types of research in education. Since funding agencies already give strong support to applied research, an argument in its favor will not be developed.[3] Thus, while recognizing the importance and desirability of applied research, we shall focus attention on the arguments for basic research.

Education is not the only field in which this question has been raised. A spate of articles and editorials in *Science* on basic *versus* applied research is a sign that the issue is one of great concern to scientists in general, particularly where it involves the relative amounts of monetary support given to the two types of research. Many scientists feel that basic science is nowadays being by-passed in favor of large "mission-oriented" programs of applied science such as the man-on-the-moon effort. Some (e.g., Weinberg, 1961) have phrased the issue in terms of an opposition between "little science"—the activities of isolated scientists in their laboratories—and "big science"—the efforts of large, well-funded teams of workers toiling in special-purpose research organizations. Yet Kidd (1959) finds it difficult to arrive at "operational criteria" by which basic and applied science activities can be distinguished. He avers that it may be easy enough to *describe* the differences between clear cases of each, in terms of the nature of the activities or possibly in terms of the motivations of the scientists involved, but that one cannot apply any rigorous and well-established criteria to decide whether any given research project is of a basic or of an applied character. Thus, he contends that statistics compiled by government organizations on the relative amounts of support given to basic and to applied research are inherently meaningless. As a possible criterion, he suggests that an activity is "basic science" to the extent that it has a high probability of yielding a "new scientific finding." But such a criterion is itself problematical: an eminently practical new invention, arising from "applied science" activity, may often represent "new knowledge." A recent article by Reagan (1967) suggests abandoning, for practical political purposes, any distinction between basic and applied science, preserving only a distinction between "research" and "development." Unfortunately, such a

change in USOE policy. In an interview (Robinson, 1966), Richard L. Bright, the Assistant Commissioner for Research in the USOE, voiced his hope that an effective program for "more really *basic* research" could be instituted in the near future.

[3] Indeed, if anything, one might be tempted to argue against the policy of strong support for applied research on the grounds that there are some respects in which its merits are debatable—for example, its tendency towards lack of generalizability.

step could have the effect of inhibiting or jeopardizing support for promising basic research whose direct relevance to a specific practical goal or mission cannot immediately be demonstrated, because politicians could always claim they are still supporting "research" even if all the research is mission-oriented.

There have been few attempts to define basic research in education or to specify its role. Clark (1963) puts forth a number of general arguments for basic research, mostly revolving around the claim that such research will have broad applications in improving the educational process, in introducing new educational technology, and in establishing new curricula. Ausubel (1953), on the other hand, believes that educational research should restrict itself to "applied science"—testing out the application of "extrapolated basic science" to its own practitioners. But now that the support of basic research in education is a "political" issue, it is critical to consider what possible role basic science activities may have in educational research and to what extent they merit fiscal support either from the government or from private sources. Before we can do so, however, it is necessary to re-examine some of the issues raised by Kidd, Reagan, and others in the context of a broader view of the nature of scientific inquiry and the sources of its motivation.

THE GOALS OF SCIENTIFIC INQUIRY

There has been much confusion in the literature about the goals of scientific inquiry. Although it may be difficult to consider the motives of individual scientists in pursuing their work, it remains true that science does have goals and that such goals imply motives to achieve those goals. Indeed, the very notion of inquiry contains the notion of questions needing answers. What some writers have failed to recognize, however, is that motives can be structured in a hierarchy—some goals being more ultimate and others more proximate—and that some of the proximate motives in the hierarchy can be "functionally autonomous," to use Gordon Allport's (1937) phrase. That is to say, from a psychological standpoint, some goals may operate as ends in themselves, without reference to the extent to which they may actually serve still other, more remote goals.

Roughly speaking, the usual goals of scientific inquiry can be arranged in such a hierarchy. The ultimate goal, and the basis of society's general support for science, is usually said to be the solution of utilitarian, practical problems.[4] Ideally, these goals ought to be well defined, e.g., the building of safer automobiles, the reduction of air pollution, or the elimination of cancer; or

---

[4] But, as Professor Israel Scheffler has pointed out to me, perhaps even utilitarian, practical goals may be construed only as instrumental to achieving intrinsically valuable cultural goals such as the attainment of knowledge for its own sake. Thus we would have not a hierarchy but a circular network of goals.

in the field of education, the overcoming of handicaps due to mental retardation or due to "social disadvantage," the nourishment of creativity in gifted children, the facilitation of the learning of foreign languages, etc.

Many scientific research projects are immediately in contact with such well-defined practical problems. But in order to feed necessary basic knowledge into such activities, science can be said to have a more general utilitarian aim—utilitarian in the best Benthamist sense—to produce knowledge and understanding of all natural phenomena that are likely to be relevant to human concerns. This general utilitarian aim is ordinarily conceived to be characteristic of basic science—and indeed of all scientific and scholarly activities. That it can also be regarded as a "functionally autonomous" motive is illustrated by Seaborg's (1963) claim that "the motivating force [for basic research] is not utilitarian goals, but a search for a deeper understanding of the universe and of the phenomena within it."

Some scientists also claim that a basic motive for science is a kind of "curiosity." From the standpoint of the individual scientist, according to Teller (1963), pure research "is a game, is play, led by curiosity, by taste, style, judgment, intangibles." The implication is that the scientist is often motivated not by any ultimate utilitarian aim, not even by some duty to produce new knowledge, but merely by the fun and challenge of unanswered questions (like mountains that must be climbed "just because they're there"). This too—this love of intellectual challenge—is a form of autonomous motive, one that is quite legitimate psychologically as a source of persistent creative effort.[5] As a matter of fact, the public at large may be said to possess curiosity about many questions whose relevance to any utilitarian ends is at best remote. Why does the public support the efforts of linguists endeavoring to decipher Mayan hieroglyphic writing? I can think of no tangible reason other than societal curiosity, except perhaps for the light the results might throw on the nature of human writing systems or on the character of Mayan society. Yet we have little hesitation in supporting this and similar scholarly work with foundation grants, fellowships, and the like. We may equally well support work aimed to satisfy our curiosity about interesting, albeit possibly useless, scientific questions like the nesting habits of the dodo.

Thus, we can exhibit a hierarchy of motives, each imperceptibly merging into the next, as follows:

Curiosity →Better understanding → General, undefined → Well-defined
                of natural phenomena   utilitarian aims   practical goals

[5] See the studies of Rossman (1931) and Roe (1952) for evidence on the role of intrinsic motivation in the creative work of inventors and scientists. In Roe's study, indications of humanitarian motives were found only in some social scientists, and very rarely in natural scientists.

The questions asked in science can arise from either or both of two sources: (1) our lack of understanding of some given set of phenomena; (2) our inability to achieve some practical goal. Basic science receives its justification both from the fact that better understanding of natural phenomena is a legitimate autonomous motive and from the fact that such understanding has the potential of serving utilitarian aims even though it is not usually possible to define those aims. Applied science derives its justification, obviously, from its orientation towards the achievement of well-defined practical goals. Basic and applied science can thus be roughly distinguished by the types of questions to which they are addressed. Of course, it is frequently the case that applied science must address itself to basic science questions, answers to which are needed to facilitate progress towards the achievement of a practical end. And as Pfaffmann (1965) has pointed out, ". . . often practical problems [and the superficial solutions one finds for them] are symptoms of [and engender] deeper problems that require more basic study and research." But there is no reason why an applied-science research project cannot be broken down into those tasks that are of a basic-science nature and those that are more concerned with testing basic-science knowledge in its application to a specific practical goal.[6]

Although I do not believe that motivation can be wholly ruled out of any attempt to distinguish basic from applied science—precisely because (as I have tried to show above) science starts from questions which are themselves motivating—it is nevertheless possible to decide, on a fairly objective basis, whether a given scientific task is more immediately addressed to the better understanding of phenomena or to the achievement of a specific practical goal. Any well-designed scientific inquiry contains a series of explicit problems, defined variables, and stated procedures. I would venture the guess that a group of experienced and knowledgeable scientists, upon examination of the design of a scientific investigation, could reach a high degree of agree-

---

[6] For the purposes of this paper, we must rule out the definition of "applied" which is implied by Revelle's (1965) remark that "because the astronomical and earth sciences do not deal with universals, but only with physical laws acting in particular situations, the physicist tends to think of them as applied rather than fundamental sciences." Even if we believe that all phenomena can be explained, reductionistically, by appeal to a small number of physical laws, there is still a place for "basic science" in determining the way in which these physical laws manifest themselves or interact at the higher levels of physical organization represented by biological cells, nervous systems, or social groups.

We must also rule out the definition that one might derive from McLane's (1965) statement that "25 years ago symbolic logic was the 'purest' branch of mathematics; today it is heavily applied, as in computers." The fact that a science *has* applications or has *been* applied does not make it an applied science, nor does it exclude the possibility that one can do basic science in such a field. Otherwise we would have to say that theoretical physics, because it spawned the atom bomb, is an applied science!

ment on the extent to which it is of a basic or an applied character. It would not be necessary for them to hire a psychologist or a psychiatrist to inquire into the inner motives of the scientist (as Seitz [1963] seems to suggest); the motives of the scientist should be manifest in his statement of hypotheses, procedures and expected results.

Some writers on basic and applied research have attempted to distinguish them with reference to the different reward systems that appear to apply to them. Storer (1964), for example, writes: "Basic research is that which is carried out by a scientist who hopes that his findings will be primarily of interest to his scientific colleagues, while applied research is intended to produce findings which will be of greater interest to the investigator's employer or to the lay public." But Storer's remarks seem simply to point out that there are different ways in which the scientist can, if he chooses, confirm whether his work has the outcomes he himself hopes for it. The basic scientist looks to his scientific colleagues, generally, for affirmation that his work is sound, reasonable, and contributory to the advance of knowledge; the applied scientist gets his signals from his sponsors, who can be expected to reward him in material ways when his discoveries result in useful applications. There will be many scientists, however, for whom these particular reward systems will have little appeal. Fundamentally, the reward system for the scientist or even for a team of scientists is inherent in scientific activity itself. That is, in basic science, effort will be continued until the investigators are rewarded with answers to their questions, while in applied science, efforts will persist until the desired practical ends are achieved.

Public acclaim or disapproval is no criterion either. Both basic and applied scientists will continue their work—as they should, if they are otherwise justified—despite lack of public support. An example of the ridicule that can come from uninformed journalism is to be found in a recent article in the *Reader's Digest* (Schulz, 1967) which holds up to scorn a government-supported research project entitled "Understanding the slump in fourth-grade creativity"—a project that, it happens, was conducted by a well-respected educational researcher (E. P. Torrance) concerning a problem of practical significance to many teachers and parents.

THE DIMENSION OF "RELEVANCE"

Much has been said about the evaluation of research in terms of its "relevance" to utilitarian ends. Most frequently, this question is raised about "basic" research: Is this research even conceivably relevant to *any* kind of utilitarian end? From the point of view expressed here, this question is thoroughly inappropriate for at least three reasons:

(1) The better understanding of phenomena is a legitimate end in itself

which can be justified, if necessary, on the ground of the general experience that at least *some* scientific activity addressed solely to fundamental questions has "paid off" in unexpected practical applications.

(2) The potential applications of many basic-science researches cannot always immediately be anticipated, even when they do in fact result eventually in practical applications. (The long-delayed application of the discovery of penicillin is a classic case in point.) Often a given scientific finding needs to be further investigated or supplemented before a practical application can be perceived.

(3 One can never predict whether a given scientific investigation will be "successful" even in its own terms. We are perhaps unaware of the tremendous amount of scientific activity that is "unsuccessful" in the sense that it fails to yield any new knowledge; further, sometimes a negative result (e.g., the failure to confirm a hypothesis or the failure to find a solution to a problem) is a distinct contribution to knowledge because it informs the scientific community that the hypothesis or methodology tried is apparently of no avail. Thus we should not try to evaluate the relevance of a given scientific investigation in terms of its results. Even in the case of "applied science" investigations, the use of this criterion would not be appropriate, for many such studies fail to achieve practical solutions although they are nonetheless clearly so *directed*. To assess relevance, we must concentrate on evaluating the *process* of scientific investigation—the framing of questions and hypotheses, the research design, the analysis of findings, and so on— and not the results.

In this light, basic-science investigation is *inherently* relevant (at least to the undefined utilitarian aims mentioned above) when it is addressed to questions that the investigator—if he is well-trained and knowledgeable in his field—feels are reasonable and useful to answer, and when in the judgment of his fellow scientists it is properly designed to answer those questions. We shall not insist, however, on the additional qualification that the relevant scientific community also approve the reasonableness of the questions asked because there are a number of cases in the history of science where a lone investigator successfully showed that apparently unreasonable questions were in fact worth pursuing.

We should point out, too, that except for rare cases, a scientist pursues questions *within a fairly well-defined area*—one for which it is possible to specify in a general way the kinds of practical applications that can be foreseen. We know the kinds of applications that have been made of findings in theoretical physics, in chemistry, in biology, in psychology, or in sociology. We could expect, for example, that work on fundamental processes of learning would have applications, if any, mainly in education—and not, say in civil engineering; work in molecular biology could be expected to have applications both in learning and in the control of genetics. Relevance is therefore specifiable in general terms, even for the purest of basic research; and it is on this basis that the public can justify the support of basic research even when specific applications are not immediately foreseen. If society cannot find any area of relevance for an *area* of research, the case might be different. But one must be careful even here: in Galileo's time, society rejected large areas of science, and for a long period the Soviet government rejected work in Mendelian genetics. More recently, the practical relevance of learning theory has been debated, even by learning theorists.

SOME FURTHER, BUT ROUGHER, DISTINCTIONS

If basic and applied research can be distinguished in terms of the nature of the work, the kinds of questions investigated, the procedures, and the like, it will be useful to expand on some of these points. No one of them, however, can be used as a sole criterion.

With respect to the questions asked, basic research tends to differ from applied research in the fact that it is more concerned with "understanding" and the attainment of knowledge about fundamental variables and their relationships; the prediction of socially important phenomena is of secondary concern, arising solely out of the laws and relationships discovered; and control of phenomena is often of only incidental interest except to verify a finding. Applied research, however, is generally concerned with the control of socially significant phenomena, or if control is difficult or impossible, at least their prediction. It is interested in the "understanding" of phenomena in terms of laws and relationships as a basis for prediction and control. Generally it starts with facts and propositions already established in basic science and proceeds to test them in particular situations and/or in particular combinations such that extrapolation from basic science is risky.

Correlated with this difference is the fact that basic science, in order to gain a better understanding of the workings of phenomena, is more often concerned with detailed, fundamental processes, such as chemical reaction mechanisms, nerve impulses, or isolated learnings; applied research, on the other hand, is more often concerned with gross, higher-order macro-processes like wine fermentation, social attitudes, or scholastic achievements, because these are the phenomena one wants to predict or control. In the behavioral sciences, we say that basic research has often to do with a "molecular" level of behavior, while applied research has to do with a "molar" level of behavior. For example, basic research in learning is concerned with the precise combinations of stimulus and response variables that produce certain effects, whereas applied research might be concerned with the effects, say, of massive doses of positive reward, which for certain groups of school learners might *on the average* produce significantly beneficial effects. The applied researcher would not necessarily worry about why positive reward works, or why it does not always work for all students, whereas the basic research scientist—if he is worth his salt—will push for understanding of the total dynamics of the phenomena he is studying. (As soon as the applied researcher starts worrying about deeper questions, he becomes a basic scientist.)

In its concern for processes on a "molecular" level, basic research relies to a greater extent on models of functional relationship that involve relatively small error components, while applied research tends to use models that are more probabilistic and error-laden. It is not an accident that statistical procedures were first developed in applied fields of research like certain branches of economics, agriculture, and psychological testing, even though these procedures are, of course, extensively used in basic research even in theoretical physics.

Basic research is more often conducted in the laboratory, or in highly controlled situations, in order to observe the effects of particular variables independently of other possibly relevant variables. Applied research tends to be done in situations that are identical to, or closely similar to, those in which one wants to apply the findings. On the other hand, some basic research is done in relatively uncontrolled situations, and some applied research employs rigorous controls. It is not necessary to suppose that research cannot be basic when it is done in live field situations. In fact, in education there are many arguments for doing certain types of research in such situations. But discussion of this point would take us too far afield.

Basic research is more concerned with the development of theory and of all-embracing models for the explanation of phenomena, while applied research either takes for granted previously established theory and extrapolates from it, or avoids theoretical problems altogether. In any case, basic science stands in a relation of logical priority to applied science. Applied science usually relies heavily upon findings in basic science. It is less often the case that basic science takes off from a finding of applied science; in the instance where this occurs, the purpose usually is to explore the deeper rationale of the finding. Although the essential priority of basic science is not as clearcut in the behavioral and social sciences as it is in the natural sciences, much is to be gained, I think, by following the model of the natural sciences in giving emphasis to basic research at points where applied research cannot make progress alone.

BASIC EDUCATIONAL RESEARCH

It is thus doubtful, in educational research, that we can move ahead to effective educational engineering without an adequate base in fundamental research in mathematics, computer science, genetics, physiology, psychology, sociology, anthropology, and other relevant disciplines. Particularly where applied research seems to be yielding diminishing dividends, we must turn to basic research on the phenomena in which we are interested. I would propose that such research be called *basic educational research,* and that it be thought of as a part of basic science.

It can be easily demonstrated that many of the most fruitful developments in applied educational technology would have been well-nigh impossible without an adequate foundation in basic research. At the same time, some of these same developments have now reached a point of decreasing returns such that they need a new infusion of results from basic research. A good example is the history of so-called programmed instruction.

Let us consider what has happened in this field since the publication of B. F. Skinner's well-known article, "The Science of Learning and the Art of Teaching" (1954). It was basic research, of an extensive and profound character, that led Skinner to conclude that certain propositions about "reinforcement" (roughly, the reward of responses) and the temporal relationships between stimuli, responses, and reinforcements could be "applied" in a special way to the conduct of instruction. Skinner felt that he needed to make no apologies for proposing to apply results of research with rats and pigeons to teaching human beings. It took Skinner and others about five years of "applied" research, however, to develop instructional materials that would incorporate the principles he had arrived at from animal research. Many of the "programed" courses that resulted from this development phase seemed to be eminently successful, at least under certain conditions. But others, *apparently* using the same principles as the successful ones, were not as effective.

Many investigators who tried to develop programed courses realized that some of Skinner's principles had not been adequately tested in their application to human learnings, and began to investigate them more thoroughly. From the studies that have been conducted over the last ten years, reviewed by such writers as Morrill (1961) and Holland (1965), it can be concluded that many of Skinner's original propositions—deriving from his basic research—were not sufficiently precise to guide the development of programed instruction unfailingly. Where it had been claimed that the student must construct his own response, a selective response was often found to be more efficient. Where it had been claimed that reinforcement must be immediate, it was on occasion found that it could sometimes be delayed, or even omitted entirely, without affecting the success of learning. Where it had been claimed that instruction must proceed in small, carefully sequenced steps, it was found that the steps did not always have to be small and that under some conditions it made no difference whether the steps were presented in a "logical" or in a random sequence.

At the present juncture, therefore, our ideas as to exactly how programed instruction ought to be developed are confused. It is apparent that we must return to some quite basic research and theorizing in order to bring the various apparently conflicting results of applied research into line. Without the necessary basic research into the detailed processes of perception, learning, and forgetting that underlie programed instruction, further "engineering" development will make little headway.

One can cite other instances in which basic research on psychological processes is needed to guide developmental efforts in education. Levin, Gibson, and their associates (Levin, 1966) at Cornell University have recognized such a need in the field of reading and have devoted several years of a concentrated effort to investigating fundamental processes in reading and learning to read. Some of Levin's research draws heavily upon recent findings and formulations in linguistics. Although results of many of the studies have no immediate application, they promise to contribute towards a new theory of the reading process that will guide the development of practical materials. and procedures for the teaching of reading. In another field, Guilford's (1966, 1967) twenty-year program of research on individual differences in cognitive abilities can be regarded as basic educational research that may have far-reaching implications for the design of curricula. In view of the burgeoning of interest in the teaching of creativity, his explorations of the dimensions of "divergent production" are being watched with interest by applied researchers. Basic research investigations into the nature of creativity have also been conducted by Getzels and Jackson (1962), with close relation to the more applied-science work of Torrance (1962). A good deal of this research has been supported by funds from the U. S. Office of Education.

Of course, it may be observed that there is already much basic-research activity in psychology and other behavioral sciences carried on outside the field of education as such. Experimental psychologists, for example, are now engaged in intensive programs of basic research in processes of perception, learning, motivation, and so forth, supported by such diverse federal federal agencies as the National Science Foundation, the National Institutes of Health, the Office of Naval Research, and even the National Aeronautics and Space Administration, as well as by various private foundations. Should educational agencies continue to support basic research in educational psychology when the needs are being fairly well met by support from noneducational sources? I believe they should, on the ground that the mission of educational agencies can have a beneficial effect on directing the attention of basic researchers to the problem areas of education, which in turn will lead them to select basic research problems that will have an appreciable probability of "pay-off" in educational development—not necessarily immediately, but ultimately, after basic scientific development has run its natural course. The history of research in such areas as programed instruction and reading shows that the applied researchers have posed problems for basic research that might never have been posed purely in the context of basic science as such. As has been the case in the natural sciences, applied problems can have a rejuvenating effect on the development of basic science.

Applied research, development, and dissemination programs have a well-recognized place in education. It has been my purpose to argue that basic educational research can be clearly distinguished from applied research, and that it has an equally vital role to play. If the U. S. Office of Education and other funding agencies are to carry out their responsibilities to education, they must support basic educational research in a due proportion. Just what this proportion should be, monetarily, is a complex question involving the availability of research facilities and of qualified researchers, the relative expense of basic and of applied research, the total funding available, and other factors. The answer would probably turn out to be somewhere between 15 and 25 per cent. This figure would include the support not only of basic-research programs themselves, but also of the training of basic-research workers in undergraduate and graduate degree programs that would be distinct from, even though possibly allied with, research operations. A clear mandate for basic research should be given to the universities, either as a part of Research and Development Center programs (which ought not to be constrained within narrow problem areas) or in the form of grants for specific projects. Significant amounts of funds would also be made available to public and private research institutions (both nonprofit and profit-making), including Regional Educational Laboratories if they are appropriately staffed, where concentrated and prolonged efforts could be undertaken.

The establishment and steady pursuit, on the part of funding agencies, of a clear policy that would give adequate recognition to basic educational research would be of enormous benefit to education as well as to the discipline of educational research.

References

Allport, G. W. *Personality*. New York: Holt, Rinehart & Winston, 1937.

Ausubel, D. P. The nature of educational research. *Educational Theory*, 1953, *3*, 314–320.

Clark, D. L. Educational research: A national perspective. In J. A. Culbertson and S. P. Hencley (Eds.), *Educational research: New perspectives*. Danville, Ill.: Interstate, 1963, pp. 7–18.

Cronbach, L. J. The role of the university in improving education. *Phi Delta Kappan*, 1966, *47* (10), 539–545.

Getzels, J. W. & Jackson, P. W. *Creativity and intelligence: Explorations with gifted students.* New York: Wiley, 1962.

Guilford, J. P. Potentiality for creativity and its measurements. In Anne Anastasi (Ed.), *Testing problems in perspective.* Washington: Amer. Council on Educ., 1966, pp. 429–435.

Guilford, J. P. *The nature of intelligence.* New York: McGraw-Hill, 1967.

Holland, J. G. Research on programing variables. In R. Glaser (Ed.), *Teaching machines and programed learning, II: Data and directions.* Washington: Dept. of Audiovisual Instruction. Nat. Educ. Assn., 1965, pp. 66–117.

Kidd, C. V. Basic research—description versus definition. *Science,* 1959, *129,* 368–371.

Levin, H. Reading research: What, why and for whom? *Elementary English,* 1966 (Feb.), 138–147.

McLane, S. In *Basic research and national goals.* Report to the House Committee on Science and Astronautics by the Nat. Acad. of Sci. Washington: U.S. Government Printing Office, 1965, p. 196.

Morrill, C. S. Teaching machines: A review. *Psychol. Bull.,* 1961, *58,* 363–375.

Pfaffmann, C. Behavioral sciences. *Amer. Psychologist,* 1965, *20,* 667–686.

Reagan, M. D. Basic and applied research: A meaningful distinction? *Science,* 1967, *155,* 1383–1386.

Revelle, R. In *Basic research and national goals.* Report to the House Committee on Science and Astronautics by the Nat. Acad. of Sci. Washington: U.S. Government Printing Office, 1965, p. 239.

Robinson, Donald W. The USOE and research in education, an interview with Richard Louis Bright. *Phi Delta Kappan,* 1966, *48* (1), 2–5.

Roe, Anne. *The making of a scientist.* New York: Dodd, Mead, 1952.

Rossman, J. *The psychology of the inventor.* Washington: Inventors Publishing Co., 1931.

Schulz, W. The great research boondoggle. *Reader's Digest,* 1967 (March) 91–96.

Seaborg, G. T. In *Federal research and development programs.* Hearings before the House Select Committee on Government Research, 88th Congress, 1st Session. Washington: U.S. Government Printing Office, 1963, p. 66.

Seitz, F. In *Government and science.* Hearings before the Subcommittee on Science, Research, and Development of the House Committee on Science and Astronautics, 88th Congress, 1st Session. Washington: U.S. Government Printing Office, 1963, p. 283.

Skinner, B. F. The science of learning and the art of teaching. *Harvard Educational Review,* 1954, *24,* 86–97.

Storer, N. W. *Basic versus applied research: The conflict between means and ends in science.* Cambridge, Mass.: Harvard Univer. Press, 1964.

Teller, E. In *Government and science.* Hearings before the Subcommittee on Science, Research, and Development of the House Committee on Science and Astronautics, 88th Congress, 1st Session. Washington: U.S. Government Printing Office, 1963, p. 115.

Torrance, E. P. *Guiding creative talent.* Englewood Cliffs, N. J.: Prentice-Hall, 1962.

Weinberg, A. M. Impact of large-scale science on the United States. *Science,* 1961, *134,* 161–164.

12. SOME LIMITATIONS OF BASIC RESEARCH IN EDUCATION

Robert L. Ebel

The thesis I will try to defend is this:

Basic research in education can promise very little improvement in the process of education, now or in the foreseeable future.

If this is true, and if the primary task of professional educators is to improve the process of education as much as possible, as rapidly as possible, they will do well to direct their efforts, not toward basic research on the conditions of learning or the processes of instruction, but instead toward applied research designed to yield information immediately useful in the solution of contemporary educational problems.

This view is almost diametrically opposed to that recently expressed by Cronbach.[1] He argued that efforts to improve education on the technological level would be largely futile, and that significant improvement could come only out of deep understanding of such basic elements of education as learning and motivation. He may be right. Obviously many educational research workers share the same opinion. But this opinion seems to rest more on faith and hope than on evidence and logic. Hence I invite you to examine its foundations critically. Perhaps they are no more substantial than the Emperor's new clothes.

SOURCE. Reprinted with permission from "Some Limitations of Basic Research in Education," by Robert L. Ebel. Originally printed in *Phi Delta Kappan*, October 1967. Copyright © 1967 by Phi Delta Kappa, Inc.

[1] Lee Cronbach, "The Role of the University in Improving Education," *Phi Delta Kappan*, June, 1966, pp. 539–45.

To begin we must say clearly what the term *basic research* will mean in this discussion. We use it to refer to the activity whose immediate aim is the quantitative formulation of verifiable general laws, and whose ultimate aim is establishment of a system of concepts and relations (the so-called nomothetic net) in which all specific propositions are deducible from a few general principles. Basic research seeks eternal verities. Its hallmark is the carefully designed and well controlled experiment whose conclusions are rigorously tested for statistical significance.

Applied research, on the other hand, refers to the collection of data that promise help in the solution of some immediate practical problem. Experience, not experiment, is the source of most applied research data. The problems, the data, the solutions tend to be ephemeral, not eternal.

The foregoing definition of basic research is not the only one possible, and probably not the one that is currently most popular. Some research workers define basic research negatively, but very inclusively, as any research that does *not* seek to help solve a current problem, that does *not* promise results of practical value. These individuals almost seem to make a virtue of uselessness. No matter how insignificant a study may be, no matter how unrelated to any coherent theoretical structure of concepts and relations, they honor it as basic research so long as it is free from the taint of practical utility. Secure in the belief that whatever they do will add something to the store of human knowledge, they wash their hands of responsibility for showing that it is something of value. It is nice work if you can get it.

Some argue that the term "applied research" involves a contradiction, since all research, properly speaking, is concerned only with understanding and not at all with applications. What we are calling applied research they would call simply development, and distinguish it from research in the same way that technology is sometimes distinguished from science. Others point out that the distinction between basic and applied research is not categorical but rather a distinction between two poles of a continuum. What one man calls basic research another calls applied. An interesting illustration of this situation is that the amount the federal government reported recently it was spending on basic research in the universities was only half the amount the universities reported they were receiving for basic research from the federal government.[2]

But whatever terms we use to describe these activities, it is clear that they are different, if only in degree. What Mr. Cronbach favored is not the same thing that he deplored. Seeking to discover basic laws of learning or instruction is not the same as seeking to work out a solution to some immediate,

---

[2] National Science Foundation, *Basic Research, A National Resource.* Washington, D.C., 1957, p. 25.

specific educational problem. Cronbach and I are in full agreement that the difference between these two kinds of activities is real and important. What we do not agree on is which activity has more to offer toward the improvement of education.

There are three reasons why it seems to me that basic research in education can promise very little improvement in the process of education.

1. Its record of past performance is very poor.

2. The justifiable explanations of that poor performance call attention to serious basic difficulties that are unlikely to be overcome in the foreseeable future.

3. The process of education is not a natural phenomenon of the kind that has sometimes rewarded scientific study in astronomy, physics, chemistry, geology, and biology.

Let us consider each of these in turn.

Almost everyone agrees that basic research in education has not produced many results that excite admiration. Years ago, when the first Encyclopedia of Educational Research appeared, Isaac Kandel recorded his doubts of the extent to which the mountain of material reviewed there would lead to improvement in educational practice.[3] More recently Tom Lamke wrote, ". . . if the research in the previous three years in medicine, agriculture, physics, and chemistry were to be wiped out, our life would be changed materially, but if research in the area of teacher personnel in the same three years were to vanish, educators and education would continue much as usual."[4]

For all his advocacy of basic research in education, Cronbach would be among the last to argue that confidence in it is justified by its past performance. If the educational programs of most schools are inadequate, as he thinks they are, it is not for failure to apply the principles of instruction that basic research has revealed, for he says, ". . . we professionals do not know enough about learning and instruction to design the desired reform." And again, "The tragedy is that there is so small a gap between what we know and what we do." It is revealing to note that in this article of his that urges the value of basic research in education so strongly, there is not even a single example of basic research that has yielded a valuable result. Where are the illustrations of the kinds of rigorous laws of learning, and of teaching, we are supposed to get from such basic research? Where are even the basic, operationally defined quantitative concepts which such laws might relate?

Again, in Mouly's list of 21 outstanding examples of significant educational

---

[3] Isaac L. Kandel, "Educational Research," *School and Society*, October 7, 1950, p. 232.
[4] Tom Lamke, "Introduction," *Review of Educational Research*, June, 1955, p. 192.

research studies,[5] which included Binet's study of the measurement of scholastic aptitude, the Eight Year study of the Progressive Education Association, Hartshorne and May's studies of character, Morphett and Washburne's investigation of the best age to begin reading instruction, studies of reliability of grading examinations by Starch and Elliott, and Wickman's study of teachers' attitudes toward children's behavior problems, not one could be called basic research in terms of the definition given earlier. Either we need a different definition of basic research, or a different perception of the importance of basic research in education.

A great many explanations are offered for the failure of basic research in education to produce many useful results. One is that educational research is much younger than research in other areas, so that it has not had time to develop equally impressive results. But this does not explain why educators should have been so slow to get started. Were not the problems of education apparent to mankind just as soon as the problems of planetary motion, or of the behavior of falling bodies?

Another group of excuses is based on criticism of previous research activities. Too little money was available for research in education. The studies undertaken were too small in scope, too brief in duration, too local in applicability. Too few of the research workers were well trained. But here again the excuses fail to explain why research in the physical and biological sciences has been so much more fortunate in escaping such limitations.

A more plausible set of explanations calls attention to the great complexity of human behavior and the consequent difficulty of doing productive research on it. Each behavioral act is the resultant of very many antecedent and concomitant factors which are complexly interrelated. To identify these factors and to discover their functional relations is an awesome task, whose probable payoff does not begin to promise returns sufficient to justify the efforts that would have to be expended. The very modest level at which basic research in education has usually been supported may be all that its past performance and future prospects warrant.

The "variables" we ordinarily work with in education—such constructs as ability, motivation, success, environment, self-concept, etc.—are so global and encompass such a diversity of specifics as to defy precise definition and exact quantification. The same generality and inclusiveness that makes them useful as verbal concepts ruins them as quantitative scientific constructs. If we were to analyze them into precisely definable and quantifiable specific elements, two things would be likely to happen.

[5] George Mouly, *The Science of Educational Research*. New York: American Book Company, 1963, pp. 429–76.

1. The number of concepts for us to deal with would be enormously increased.

2. The importance of each to us would be sharply reduced.

Nor is the behavior we are attempting to study a stable phenomenon that can be isolated without distortion for scientific study. The very experiment designed to study it changes it. What was true of the naive subject may no longer be true of the sophisticated subject, and there is no assurance that what was discovered in the controlled conditions of an experiment will hold true under more natural nonexperimental conditions.

Controlled experiments on human behavior are difficult not only because of the great variety of factors that must be controlled, but also because human beings are involved. People are not always easy to manipulate. The experimenter must treat his subjects as fellow human beings, not as depersonalized objects of his scientific study. No experimental treatment that is or may be harmful or even disadvantageous is likely to be tolerated.

These and other difficulties of research on human behavior help to explain why little progress has been made in understanding human behavior via basic research. They are justifiable excuses. But since these difficulties are inherent in the situation and are likely to persist, they justify skepticism concerning future progress in this area.

Nomothetic science has been highly successful in some areas, such as mechanics, electromagnetic radiations, and atomic physics. It has been distinctly less successful in other areas, such as weather phenomena, accoustics, and human behavior. The difference seems to lie in the extent to which there is simple structure in the phenomena involved—few variables and simple (often linear) relations among them. If the structure is complex, if the variables are numerous, if they interact complexly, if the lines of relationship have critical regions of nonlinearity or discontinuity, then the nomothetic net is likely to be sketchy or nonexistent.

To question the power of basic research on human behavior it is not necessary to deny, and I do not deny, the predictability *in principle* of every human act. What I do question, in view of the manifold influences (variables) involved, the complexity of the relations, and the inherent plasticity of the response system involved, is the practical feasibility of such predictions. The game is just not worth the candle.

The third reason why basic research in education can promise little improvement in education is that the process of education is not a rewarding subject for scientific study. Science has been defined as the systematic study of natural phenomena for the purpose of understanding them. But formal education (i.e., purposeful instruction), which is what we are trying to improve, is not a natural phenomena. It is a human invention, a construction, a cultural institution designed and built by men. It is not so much in need of analysis and understanding as one of the givens in our universe as it is in need of redesign and reconstruction to serve our human purposes better. And we make a grave mistake, I fear, if we believe that the best way to redesign and reconstruct it is to study its current forms scientifically with a view to understanding them. Is the case for a scientific study of education, as a means of improving education, any stronger than the case for a scientific study of poetry as a means of improving poetry? Of course we can, if we wish, do what appears to be basic research on anything, from the distribution of word lengths in Robert Frost's poems to the symbolism in a particular kindergartener's finger painting. But how basic is it, and to what? Basic research is no more free than any other human activity from the necessity of being worthwhile.

What I have been saying about the limitations of basic research in education is intended to apply to formal education, to schooling, to instruction, not to the psycho-biology of learning. For learning *is* a natural phenomenon. What learning is biologically, how it occurs, what happens to the organism and why—these are fit subjects of scientific study. Here basic research may be rewarding. But an understanding of the psycho-biology of learning is unlikely to contribute much to the improvement of formal education. It will do little to answer either of the two basic educational questions: What shall we try to teach children? And how shall we go about getting them to learn it?

Some defenders of basic research in education, admitting its limitations and the difficulties attending it, still argue that it should be supported generously and pursued energetically because, in their view, there is no other way to improve education. If science can't do it, they seem to say, nothing can. The jig is up. We may as well toss in the sponge. In this they are quite wrong, I think. They greatly overestimate the scope and versatility of nomothetic, experimental science. They greatly underestimate the variety and power of other techniques of gathering data and solving problems. Doing basic research is not the only way, and probably not the best way, for a man to use his head to solve an educational problem.

Human beings were solving problems and making progress in building their culture long ages before experimental science was ever invented or popularized. Even today, when the prestige of science is at its height, most of the world's problems are being solved and most of the progress is being achieved by methods which involve experience and reason and dialogue and consensus. Seldom if ever do the findings of basic research have significant impact on the decision reached. The alternative to basic scientific research is not just traditionalism or mysticism or speculation. There are also empiricism (i.e., experience) and discussion and reasoned decision.

Most of the knowledge with which we guide our lives and solve our problems has come, not from controlled experiments, but from practical experience. The notion that we don't really know a thing is true until basic research has verified its truth is quite unwarranted. The things that experience has taught us about education, the things that Plato, Quintillian, Comenius, Rousseau, Spencer, James, Dewey, and Conant have called to our attention, are far truer on the whole than most of the new things that one reads under the heading of "News from the Research Frontier."

Most of the problems we face in the world today, including our educational problems, involve questions of purposes and values. Hence the decisions we must make in our parliaments and councils, in our school boards and faculty meetings, in our families and private lives, are decisions that science could not possibly make for us. The scientific understanding of what *is* sheds only a little light on what ought to be. To make the decisions that will solve our problems we need in addition to knowledge free exchanges of ideas, open discussions of values, and sympathetic, cooperative search for consensus.

But knowledge is necessary. Seldom do we have as much knowledge as we need to decide wisely the questions before us. Research can give us this knowledge, but it is the kind of research that educational scientists tend to disdain as mere data gathering. For example, should we launch an extensive program to improve the self-concepts of slum children? No doubt we should if slum children don't learn mainly because they think they can't learn. But is it true that they have poor self-concepts? Is it true that they tend to blame themselves, not society, for their difficulties? Is it true that many of them think of themselves as lacking in ability to learn? To find the answers to these questions would involve data gathering, not basic research. But it could contribute substantially to the wisdom of our decision on a serious problem.

Consider another example. Should colleges institute pass-or-fail grading for certain courses in order to encourage the students to broaden the range of their educational experience? It has often been said that even good students are reluctant to take courses outside of their major field, courses in which they would have to compete for grades with students who were majoring in that field. Now, is it in fact true that a significant proportion of good students who want to take a course outside their major, and who feel that they are prepared to study it profitably, are deterred by the prospect of a lower grade? Do they choose instead to take a less valuable course that may give them a higher grade? A well-designed questionnaire could provide solid answers to these questions and thus help the decision makers to act wisely.

This article has contended that basic research in education promises little improvement in the process of education because it has not done so in the past, because it is fraught with serious, inherent limitations, and because the process of education is not a natural phenomenon, and hence not a profitable object of scientific study. In its proper sphere, and for its limited purposes, pure science, and the basic research on which it rests, is a powerful tool. But the problems of the world, and of education, we have argued, require the application of other sources of information and other processes of decision than pure science provides.

Let me not take too much credit for the views expressed in this paper, nor assume too solitary a role as a defender of them. Others, among whom are Morris Cohen,[6] Harold Larrabee[7] and Ernest van den Hoag,[8] seem to hold similar views. Psychologists from James[9] to Estes[10] have warned educators not to expect much help from psychology in the solution of educational problems.

Basic research in education seeks to discover a simple structure of concepts and causal relations that will permit effective control of the process of education and precise prediction of its results. One can hardly doubt that the discovery of such a simple theoretical structure would place a powerful tool in the hands of the educational scientist. But it must be discovered; it can not be invented. And if it does not exist it can not be discovered. That is, if a sparsity of relevant variables and a simplicity of their interrelations are inherent in the process of education, basic research might discover it. If not, no amount of basic research can create it.

The search for a simple structure of basic variables underlying the apparent complexities of human behavior has motivated much of the work in factor analysis for decades. So far the search has not been notably successful. No one can say with certainty that such a simple structure *does not* exist and await discovery, but as of the present moment there is little if any reason to believe that it *does* exist. To persist in searching for something that persists in not being found, and in giving no reason to believe that it even exists, is hardly a profitable way to spend one's time.

Herein, it seems to me, lies one of the reasons for the futility of some research in education. We have persisted in using the techniques of basic research despite persistent failure of those techniques to pay off. Of course there are other weaknesses. Some studies concern themselves with trivial problems, or are inadequate in design, or are incompetently executed. The

[6] Morris R. Cohen, *Reason and Nature.* New York: Harcourt, Brace, 1931, pp. 250–63.

[7] Harold Larrabee, *Reliable Knowledge.* Cambridge, Mass.: Houghton Mifflin, 1945, pp. 473–505.

[8] Ernest van den Hoag, "Man as an Object of Science," *Science,* January 30, 1959, pp. 243–47.

[9] William James, *Talks to Teachers.* New York: Henry Holt, 1913, pp. 7–8.

[10] William K. Estes, "Learning," in *Encyclopedia of Educational Research, Third Edition* (Chester W. Harris, ed.). New York: Macmillan, 1960, p. 752.

room for improvement in educational research is, as many critics have pointed out, almost unlimited.

What are we then to do? Shall we abandon research in education? By no means. Let us even persist in basic research on those psycho-biological problems where basic research has a fighting chance to produce useful results. But let us also push, and rather more strongly, the kind of survey research that provides data crucial to the decisions we must make. Let us not worship pure science and basic research unrealistically and irrationally.

What I have been saying may sound anti-scientific. It may seem to have a mystical humanistic or theistic bias that glories in the limitations of science and fights to preserve some field of activity for the free, undetermined spirit of man, some sphere of influence for a mysterious, powerful God. But this is not my intent. I am a thorough-going rational empiricist. I believe in the power of knowledge, and in the wisdom of decisions solidly based on relevant knowledge. Where I differ from some of my colleagues is not in faith in science, broadly defined as human knowledge, verified and organized. It is rather in my doubts that basic research, as here defined, will ever provide the knowledge we need to solve the educational problems that perplex us.

13. WHY HAS LEARNING THEORY FAILED TO TEACH US HOW TO LEARN?

Hugh G. Petrie

The purpose of this paper is to suggest a novel answer to a tired old question. The question is: Why, despite the almost universally held belief that psychology and especially learning theory are the foundation sciences of education, have these "foundations" given such minimal support and assistance to actual day-to-day educational practice? And the answer which I will suggest is that, paradoxical as it may sound, learning theorists in psychology and practical educators are, for the most part, talking about two entirely different things.

I think it is abundantly evident that psychology, with the possible exception of psychometrics, has contributed little, if anything, to education. At any rate it is clear that learning theory, at once hailed as the best developed of the fields of psychology and at the same time the one field from which the most could reasonably be expected for educational purposes, has contributed next to nothing. For even Ernest Hilgard, one of the most respected learning theorists, and one who is interested in the problems of relating basic research in psychology to educational practice, clearly recognizes the paucity of contribution that learning theory has made. In both the 1964 NSSE yearbook,[1]

SOURCE. Petrie, Hugh G., "Why Has Learning Theory Failed to Teach Us How to Learn?" *Philosophy of Education, 1968; Proceedings of the Twenty-Fourth Annual Meeting of the Philosophy of Education Society.* Copyright © 1968 by Philosophy of Education Society.

[1] E. R. Hilgard (ed.), *Theories of Learning and Instruction,* Yearbook LXIII (Chicago: National Society for The Study of Education, 1964).

of which he is the editor, and in the third edition of his own widely read book on learning theory,[2] Hilgard concludes with an apologetic for the seeming irrelevance of learning theory to education.

It will be instructive to see the kind of reasons Hilgard advances for this lack of relation, in order better to compare them with the answer I am proposing. His reasons for the lack of relation are essentially two. On the one hand is the general problem of development and application of theory which is common to all applied disciplines. On the other hand Hilgard believes that educators have generally not adequately specified the tasks and the criteria of success for these tasks for basic theory to be of much use. And, of course, Hilgard's two answers are commonly accepted by psychologists and educators alike.

Without denying the importance of what Hilgard says, what I wish to do is to point out that problems of development and application and task analysis logically presuppose that the facts of learning are the same for the different learning theorists and for the educator. As Hilgard says, "all the theorists accept all of the facts."[3] That such a presupposition is indeed present is easy to see. We could scarcely begin to concern ourselves with development and application of theoretical results to concrete situations unless the facts of the concrete situations are of the same nature as the facts of laboratory-based theory. Nor would a more precise specification of tasks help in applying theory to practice unless the object domain of the task is the same as that of the theory.

For that matter, the supposition that all the theorists accept all the facts is not a surprising one. It is a fairly common piece of scientific folklore and just a simple restatement of the generally accepted principle that we can always draw a sharp and clear distinction between an observation language which reports the facts of our environment and a theoretical language which interprets those facts. Thus the presupposition is that there is a neutral data language upon which all agree and there are differing theoretical languages to interpret the data and over which there can be disagreement.[4]

And yet, there has recently arisen a serious challenge to such "obvious" presuppositions. It can be found in the writings of such men as N. R. Hanson,[5] W. V. O. Quine,[6] Stephen Toulmin,[7] and, perhaps best known of all, T. S.

---

[2] E. R. Hilgard and G. H. Bower, *Theories of Learning*, 3rd ed. (New York: Appleton-Century-Crofts, 1966).

[3] *Ibid.*, p. 9.

[4] *Ibid.*, p. 9.

[5] N. R. Hanson, *Patterns of Discovery* (London: Cambridge University Press, 1958).

[6] W. V. O. Quine, *Word and Object* (New York: John Wiley and Sons, 1960).

[7] Stephen Toulmin, *Foresight and Understanding* (New York: Harper Torch Books, 1961).

Kuhn.[8] These men have begun to argue that scientific theories are radically underdetermined by experience, and that although scientific theories must have empirical content—be testable by experience—they do not and cannot arise solely out of experience. It has been argued that what even counts as experience is essentially theory-dependent. That is, two scientists may look at the "same" thing and, because of different theoretical perspectives, may literally not *see* the same object. What is relevant for one theory may be totally ignored by another theory and even be logically incapable of being observed.

It should be emphasized at this point what a truly radical conception this is. It might easily be supposed that all that is being claimed here is that any science in fact focuses on certain features of experience to describe and ignores others. For example, classical physics, it has often been said, owed much of its success to having concerned itself with just the right physical properties, position and momentum, ignoring such properties as color and taste. If this is the sort of thing being claimed, then why all the fuss?

But if we stop here we miss the point entirely. For the "focussing" conception of science indicated above logically presupposes a kind of neutral experiential base upon which one may focus, now here, now there. Correlatively, a neutral observation language is also presupposed within which one could in principle describe all the physical properties of situations and events, leaving to the scientific theory the choice of those features to be covered by the theory. The non-favored features are still "there"; they are simply not deemed relevant.

However, it is the position of the view under consideration that no such neutral observation language exists nor can experience be described independently of theory—a radical view indeed.

Psychologists are not unaware of the problems of being constrained in their observations by the use of certain favored approaches and methodologies. For example, Underwood[9] has noted the unimaginativeness of many verbal learning experiments which seem often to return to the basic techniques of paired-associate experiments. However, most psychologists tend to treat such problems of constraint as problems in the psychology of methodology, assuming that with proper care and imagination they can be overcome. Without in the least attempting to minimize the psychological part of this problem, I want to be as clear as possible in suggesting that there may well be a logical and conceptual problem as well. In other words, it may be the case that all the care and imagination in the world may be unable to help

[8] T. S. Kuhn, *The Structure of Scientific Revolutions* (Chicago: The University of Chicago Press, 1962).

[9] B. J. Underwood, "The Representativeness of Rote Verbal Learning" in A. W. Melton (ed.), *Categories of Human Learning* (New York: Academic Press, 1964).

an experimenter see a certain result if such results are not countenanced by the theory he explicitly or implicitly espouses.

If such a theory-dependency thesis of observation is indeed true, then it can easily be seen, at least in outline, how this might give weight to my contention that the major reason learning theory has been of such little help to education is that learning theorists and educators are generally talking about two different things. For most learning theorists, given the general pervasiveness of at least a methodological behaviorism, will see more or less mechanical stimuli and responses; whereas, most educators, given the teleological concepts of ordinary language, see goals and actions as purposive. Such a conception immediately shows the extent to which Hilgard was correct in asserting that a better task analysis is often a good way of bridging the gap between theory and practice. For if the task description can be given an S-R twist it would be easier to make the application. On the other hand, if the general results of learning theory are cast in teleological form, the application would again be easier.

Let me then pursue the theory-dependency thesis a bit further. An extreme form of the thesis would present us with a most radical kind of Whorfianism. For if each of us sees only what the theory we have enables us to see, and it is furthermore granted that everyone's conceptual scheme differs at least slightly from everyone else's, and finally, that our conceptual schemes are, in some sense, our theories of the world, then no one ever sees precisely what anyone else sees, and a rigorous notion of intersubjective confirmation or justification of some one theory is logically out of the question. Such an extreme view often seems to be implied by some of the things Kuhn says.

Fortunately, I do not think that such an extreme view is correct. For one thing it faces all the difficulties which any radical skepticism faces along with some of its own which I shall briefly mention. First of all, if this kind of theory-dependency thesis is even intelligible at all, it will be intelligible *on its own grounds* only in terms of some theory which determines observational categories sufficient for us to see the intelligibility of the theory-dependency thesis. It seems obvious that such an all-embracing metatheory is nothing more nor less than philosophy and thus that philosophical argumentation is appropriate to the theory-dependency thesis. For if the thesis actually asserts that it itself is outside the realm of any justification, even a philosophical justification, then quite clearly we can have no justification for accepting it, and yet equally clearly the thesis is capable of being argued about.

Second, even if we grant the extreme Whorfian version of the theory as a metaphysical possibility, we could not on epistemological grounds ever assert or deny this possibility. For as Quine has so adequately pointed out,[10] there is no way of deciding on the basis of the empirical evidence between

10 W. V. O. Quine, *op. cit.*

someone's looking at the world radically differently and a mistake in transla-tion. To make sense of the differences in conceptualization we do find, we must assume a tremendously large core of common conceptualization as a background.

Having concluded this much, however, we are still left with a reasonably strong version of the thesis. And this version states that there may be logically incompatible observational categories which are, nevertheless, philosophically basic and hence incapable of being decided between on empirical grounds, although philosophical argumentation would be appropriate. There is also a weaker thesis which states that within a single philosophically basic observa-tional category, it is possible to have differing empirical specifications of what falls under that category.

What I would now like to do is to illustrate both the strong and the weak theses with reference to some of the changes which have occurred in the definition of a stimulus as learning theorists have moved from conditioning theory to discrimination learning to conceptual behavior.

Historically, hard-line behaviorists began by taking the definition of a stimulus to be in terms of physical events of some sort or other impinging directly on the organism, e.g., light waves hitting photoreceptors, or auditory nerves being stimulated. And indeed such a definition works well for typical conditioning experiments where it is fairly easy to determine what change in the carefully controlled laboratory environment will count as a stimulus, and it is also fairly easy to generalize on the stimulus.

However, once one enters the field of discrimination learning, not only must the subject be conditioned to some stimulus, but also he must learn in some manner what is to *count* as a stimulus. This involves problems of atten-tion, focussing, stimulus patterning, and stimulus generalization which do not seem to occur at all in classical conditioning experiments. Now is not the time to enter into a detailed discussion of the experimental results of dis-crimination learning. Nor will I discuss whether or not these results can be accommodated within classical conditioning theory by means of some sort of selection and retention of repeated total stimuli defined in physical terms.[11] It will be sufficient for my purposes to note that discrimination-learning re-sults have prompted many psychologists to retreat from the kind of hardline definitional behaviorism exemplified, for example, by Hull to a methodological behaviorism. A "methodological behaviorism," as I shall use the term, allows the introduction of any number of "mentalistic" intermediaries, or representa-tions, or cues, as long as the introduction of such cues can be shown to have genuine explanatory power within the theory and as long as there is some observational test of such cues, no matter how indirect. Even Skinner ver-

---

[11] However, see Charles Taylor, *The Explanation of Behavior* (London: Routledge and Kegan Paul, 1964), for a sustained attack on the possibility that a simple extension of classical conditioning principles can account for the results of discrimination learning.

bally subscribes only to a methodological behaviorism, although he combines this with a further belief that on his system very few, if any, such mentalistic cues need to be introduced.

When one moves to the area of concept formation, the problems become even more acute. In discrimination learning single stimuli need to be discriminated one from another, whereas in concept formation whole classes of stimuli need to be discriminated from other classes. To see the problems involved in attempting to carry over the definition of a stimulus in physical terms as specified in conditioning theory to the physical definition of the class of stimuli which call forth a given concept one need only reflect on the incredibly wide physical dissimilarities involved in all the physical objects falling under the concept of a chair. The possibility of remaining within the bounds of a physical definition of the stimuli seems remote indeed.

As a result, more and more psychologists have tended to introject into the organism larger and larger parts of the environment to which the organism is supposed to be responding in discrimination and concept learning. And this is, of course, to come closer to the position which many philosophers and gestalt psychologists have long urged; namely, that an organism responds to what it *believes* the environment to be and not to what the environment actually is.

And yet, as has been pointed out by Kendler,[12] the whole process of a change in the definition of a stimulus from conditioning to discrimination to concept formation can still be considered to fall under a theoretical stimulus-response associationism. Thus despite the change in definition of the stimulus (and usually corresponding changes in the definition of a response), we still have the notion that any behavioral event can be *analyzed* in terms of an environmental feature (stimulus), some components of total behavior (response), and the association between the two.

In the sense, then, in which human behavior is considered analyzable in an S-R kind of way, we have an illustration of the weak sense of the theory-dependency thesis. For it will be recalled that the weak version of this thesis claimed that there might be differences in empirical specification of a single philosophically basic observational category. Thus we have the philosophical category of an S-R analysis of human behavior, and differing empirical specifications of this observational category ranging from physical definitions to cues internal to the organism. If the basic philosophical category is indeed of the S-R variety, then the criteria for deciding on the empirical specification of this category in different situations are, broadly speaking, empirical in nature. That is, we must await the results of the psychologists' investigations to tell us which ones are correct.

<hr>

[12] H. H. Kendler, "Concept of the Concept," in A. W. Melton (ed.), *Categories of Human Learning* (New York: Academic Press, 1964).

Nevertheless, it is still easy to see how, even under the weak version of the theory-dependency thesis, it might be difficult to translate the results of learning theory into educational practice. For it seems obvious enough that the practicing educator observes the educational process largely in terms which define the stimulus as internal cues; whereas the most reliable, if limited, results in learning theory come from seeing stimuli in terms of physical events—two widely different conceptions.

But now what if the basic philosophical category of a stimulus-response analysis of human behavior is wholly rejected? That is, what happens if the notion of a human action is actually unanalyzable in such terms and is either itself a basic philosophical observational category or at least cannot be analyzed in the causal terms of the S-R conception. Charles Taylor[13] has recently argued the latter while Richard Taylor[14] has argued the former. That is, both have argued on philosophical grounds that human action is essentially teleological in character in so strong a sense that the S-R conception sketched above is wholly inapplicable. What we now have is an illustration of the strong version of the theory-dependency thesis. For the claim by the two Taylors is that no matter how stimuli are defined they cannot, logically cannot, be used as an observational category for human action. And the reason is that human action belongs to a philosophical category different from that embodied in an S-R conception. Note, too, that the criteria for deciding between an S-R conception and a broadly teleological conception of human action are philosophical in character and hence must be decided on philosophical grounds.

Without deciding if ordinary language analyses actually yield the metaphysical results claimed for them, one can grant that the analyses of our ordinary use of action terminology are indeed teleological as claimed by the two Taylors. But if this is granted, and if it is further granted that practicing educators largely make use of ordinary language in describing the educational process, then it will follow that the theory embodied in ordinary language renders it logically impossible to observe human action in the educational process in the categories in which learning theorists state their results. And hence it is logically impossible, as long as ordinary terms are used as the basic philosophical category for the observation of human action, that learning theory as presently constituted could be of any relevance to education. For the basic philosophical categories of the two ways of looking at the world are incompatible and it will require a philosophical argument to settle the issue between them.

In conclusion let me make a few comments on this analysis. First, the framework I have offered gives *prima facie* promise of providing an ex-

13 Charles Taylor, *op. cit.*
14 Richard Taylor, *Action and Purpose* (Englewood Cliffs, N.J.: Prentice-Hall, 1966).

planation of how it is that learning theory has contributed what it has. Under my view one ought to be able to predict that principles of conditioning theory are most applicable in areas where our ordinary language concepts are not teleological, and least successful where such ordinary concepts are teleological, and indeed a glance at Hilgard's summary of just these items reveals a *prima facie* confirmation.[15]

Second, my own opinion is that the two Taylors are wrong in asserting that the teleological character of human action is such as to render it inexplicable in an extended S-R framework. However, this is essentially the philosophical controversy over whether reasons or intentions or motives can be causes, and it cannot be entered into now. However, as I have urged, the solution to this question must necessarily be a philosophical one.

Third, given an extended S-R framework, the isomorphism which has been noted by Suppes and Atkinson[16] between the recent mathematical S-R learning theories and certain cognitive theories is easily understood. The formal isomorphism could be proved because both fell within the broad formal framework of an S-R conception of human action although they may have differed in empirical specification of stimulus and response. A cognitive theory falling under a different basic philosophical conception could probably not be proved isomorphic.

Fourth, I have not argued directly for the theory-dependency thesis, but rather have assumed it to be in broad outline correct. It has seemed to me that such a view has been ably argued by others and has not been conclusively refuted. Thus, I believe it deserves to have some of its implications traced out in detail, and I consider the framework it provides for understanding the problems I have sketched in this paper to be a kind of indirect argument for the theory-dependency thesis.

Finally, despite the sweeping topics I have considered and the sketchy treatment I have offered of them, I believe I have made it at least plausible that there may be philosophical reasons for the seeming irrelevance of learning theory to education. I hope I have also been able to indicate the vast amount of work which remains to be done by philosophers of psychology and philosophers of education in this area.[17]

[15] E. R. Hilgard, *op. cit.*, p. 562–64.

[16] P. Suppes and R. C. Atkinson, *Markov Learning Models for Multiperson Interactions* (Stanford: Stanford University Press, 1960).

[17] The foregoing work has been supported in part by the Office of Education, Contract No. O–8–080023–3669 (010).

CHAPTER 3

Research Ethics

A number of complicated ethical problems arise in the course of any educational research project. Not only is the resolution of any particular problem often controversial, but it is probable that no set of principles, however carefully designed, can dictate answers to problems that were unforeseen at the time of the writing; nor can any set of principles even be expected to imply answers to all the variations of problems that are known about at the time of writing. As Aristotle said in *Nicomachean Ethics*:

> We must be content, then in speaking of such subjects . . . to indicate the truth roughly and in outline, and in speaking about things which are only for the most part true, and with premises of the same kind, to reach conclusions that are no better.

In education, there is the additional problem of distinguishing between "experimentation" with human subjects and introducing practices into classrooms variously labeled as "pilot projects" or "innovations." Inasmuch as the results of "pilot projects" and "innovations" are rarely reversible, one must raise the question as to whether school authorities have the right to introduce such changes without the consent of parents.

We here present two selections: a discussion by M. Brewster Smith of some difficult ethical questions and a guide proposed at Cornell University, Ithaca, New York. Neither is aimed specifically at educational research, but they both certainly apply to educational research with human subjects. The topic is largely unexplored, and we present these selections in order to provide some basis for discussion of these difficult problems.

14. CONFLICTING VALUES AFFECTING BEHAVIORAL RESEARCH WITH CHILDREN[1]

M. Brewster Smith

What limits, if any, should be set on research into children's behavior? Who should set these limits? These, and other questions related to them, are being asked these days by many people in and out of research—parents and lawmakers included.

Only recently, when research on behavior was a marginal activity of a few college professors and their graduate students, carried out with little financial support and that support received mainly from private donors and foundations, such questions hardly arose. From the professor's standpoint, the responsibility for decisions about the nature of the research was solely his—a matter of academic freedom and privilege within the framework of formal or informal codes of professional ethics. Nobody was likely to challenge him: The whole enterprise of research in the behavioral sciences was unimportant and inconspicuous, and public funds were not involved.

Today, however, the behavioral scientist has to pay the penalty for success. Behavioral research is no longer inconspicuous: Even though it is not as affluent as the physical sciences, it is now big business. And since most of its financial support now comes from the Federal Government, its errors of

source. Smith, M. Brewster, "Conflicting Values Affecting Behavioral Research with Children," *American Psychologist*, 22:5, May 1967. Reprinted with permission of American Psychological Association. Copyright © 1967 by American Psychological Association.

[1] I am grateful to colleagues at the Institute of Human Development for comments on an earlier draft of this paper. The article was first published in the March–April issue of *Children* by the United States Department of Health, Education, and Welfare, Welfare Administration, Children's Bureau.

judgment as well as its successful results now attract political attention. Public concern with the methods that scientists use in studying other people is of course warranted on grounds quite apart from the basis of funding.

For perspective on the special problems of controls on research with children, we had best begin with a brief look at the anxieties and misgivings about the political and ethical aspects of the behavioral sciences that figure prominently in the current climate of discussion.

Many people, including United States Congressmen, are worried about many loosely related issues. Do personality questionnaires violate the citizen's right to privacy when used in Government personnel procedures or in research (Testing and Public Policy, 1965)? Is it ever permissible for experimenters to deceive the subjects of their experiments, as some types of investigation seem to require (Kelman, 1967)? If deception is used, how can the "informed consent" of subjects be obtained (Ruebhausen & Brim, 1965)? Do the potentialities for computer retrieval of data collected for administrative purposes (tax returns, census files, and the like) threaten the privacy and perhaps even the liberty of the individual citizen? What of Government-sponsored research in foreign countries—how can the sensitivities of the citizens of other countries, the interests of the United States Government, and the needs of the social sciences for comparative data all be taken into account (Camelot and Psychological Tests, 1966)? How can the Government and the public be assured they are getting their money's worth out of social and behavioral science? Is adequate support available for the study of socially important problems (Carter, 1966)? All these questions and many others have found their way into the legislative hopper. Several Congressional committees have held hearings that bear upon them. Suddenly, the social and behavioral sciences are politically visible.

ISSUES CONCERNING CHILDREN

Each of these issues has its counterpart for research on the behavior of children, though issues concerned with studies of children in foreign countries have not yet received much attention. But the issues look and are different when children are involved.

Personality Questionnaires and the Right to Privacy. When children are questioned for research purposes, the privacy and sensitivity of parents have to be considered in addition to the possible effects of the questioning on the child. Some kinds of questions—those about sexual attitudes, knowledge, and practices, for example—are likely to be regarded as intrinsically inappropriate in questionnaires for use with children; questions about child-rearing practices, on the other hand, may be seen as invading the parents' right to privacy and perhaps even as undermining parent-child relations.

Parents who have little understanding of the methods or objectives or value of behavioral research have objected to their children's being asked about their parents' education and other indicators of socioeconomic status —seemingly incidental information that is often essential in a research project! Very likely only a few parents would be disturbed by the kinds of questions a responsible investigator would find necessary and proper to ask, but their objections have to be taken seriously, not dismissed impatiently as "crackpot." The narrowest interpretation of what is permissible would put many important problems beyond the range of possible research. The most lenient would affront many citizens.

Deception. In this regard, the issues concerning children shape up differently from those concerning deception with college students and adults. In a typical case, the problem under study requires the subjects to undergo a standard sequence of successes and failures on an experimental task. To produce this standard sequence, the subjects are provided with believable false reports about their performances of the task, according to the requirements of the experimental design.

Generally, investigators working with adults or college students attempt to meet the ethical problem in such deception by carefully explaining the reason for the deception to each subject after the experiment is over. When the subjects are students in psychology courses, such a "debriefing" procedure usually makes sense (though it may not balance the harm done to the students by conveying the idea that a manipulative approach to people is acceptable). When "debriefing" is carried out scrupulously, the participant may learn something relevant to his studies, both about psychological research and about his own reactions.

In research with young children, however, no one can argue for "debriefing" as an adequate solution to the ethical problem of deception. A full explanation of procedures to the young child is seldom desirable or possible. In the example that we have been considering, the usual scrupulous practice would be to so contrive matters that by the end of the session every child would leave with a solid experience of success.

Yet such a solution leaves one uneasy. The experimenter who knows that he must subsequently explain to his adult subjects just how he has deceived them may be likely to exercise self-restraint in his procedures. The experimenter with children is under no obligation to explain himself to his subjects, and if he is not required to justify his procedures to others, everything hinges on his private judgment. Can the experimenter's unavoidably self-interested judgment of what is best for the child be trusted?

Consent. The difficult but crucial issue of when the participant in research may be regarded as having given his informed consent appears in a different guise in respect to research with children. Legally, only parents can consent on behalf of children. But when is parental consent "informed"? How much do parents have to know about a particular research project before their consent may be so regarded? When, if at all, may the responsible authorities in schools and other social agencies give consent *in loco parentis?* When, if at all, may implicit consent be assumed? Any call for a rigid enforcement of a requirement for explicit parental consent presents serious obstacles to research studies that hinge on obtaining data from a representative sample of children. This is because, in ways that affect their children, the parents who neglect to return consent forms may differ from those who do return them. A narrow interpretation of the consent issue could very seriously hamper behavioral research with children.

Uses of Information. Whether information collected for administrative purposes that can be retrieved and collated by a high-speed computer for other purposes presents risks to the privacy and liberty of adults is still a matter for conjecture, since such data banks are not yet generally available. However, the cumulative school records of children's psychological tests are already with us and may do real harm.

Useful as ability tests undoubtedly are, they are clearly a mixed blessing (Goslin, 1963; Goslin, Rayner, & Hallock, 1965). The low test scores of a child who gets off to a poor start may exclude him from opportunities to improve his position. Teachers who rely on the predictive power of a poor score help confirm the prediction. On the other hand, without test results, social stereotyping might play a larger part than it does in deciding a child's educational future. Much careful thought and further research are needed to find ways of using ability tests so as to maximize each child's educational opportunities instead of accentuating existing inequalities of opportunity. Because the testing technology is a product of scientific psychology, problems concerned with the administrative use of tests naturally get entangled with the logically distinct problems of their research uses. It is important to keep the issues separate.

Information collected from children for research should never be used to their disadvantage. When the nature of the research permits data to be collected and stored anonymously, the interests of the individual child can be readily protected. When, on the other hand, identification of individual persons is essential to the research—as in "longitudinal" studies that follow the same persons over a period of time—elaborate precautions are essential to safeguard confidentiality. In such research, protecting the anonymity of the persons studied is an absolute about which there can be no compromise.

COMPETING VALUES

As we explore these issues, it is easy to become preoccupied with the dangers of using children as subjects of behavioral research and the safeguards necessary to protect them at the expense of appreciating the actual and potential contributions of behavioral research to child welfare. The cumulative findings of research on child development are just beginning to break the cyclical fashions in child rearing advice (Hoffman & Hoffman, 1964, 1966). In this country we are just launching a host of new and expensive programs in the schools based on extrapolations from current knowledge about behavior that urgently require monitoring and rigorous evaluation through research. Now is not the time to stifle behavioral research with severe restrictions.

In its own interest, the public needs to make some accommodations to the requirements of research. Behavioral scientists and the agencies that support their work should be actively involved in educating the public and its representatives in Government to the characteristics and value of such research.

The beginning of wisdom in this regard, it seems to me, is to recognize that we must come to terms with competing values. Humanitarian values require that we never harm the individual child and always strive to advance child welfare. Libertarian values require us to respect the integrity and privacy of the child and his parents. Scientific values prescribe the extension of knowledge for its own sake, usually with the faith that in the long run knowledge contributes to humanitarian ends. Legal values require us to respect the status of minors and the rights and obligations of parents, though legal rights in relation to behavioral research are still in the process of clarification (Ruebhausen & Brim, 1965). Often these different frames of evaluation point to the same conclusion. The cases in which they do are the simple ones that pose no serious practical or ethical problem. But often they conflict with one another. For example, the child's privacy and perhaps his integrity are violated for the sake of advancing knowledge of a topic that is theoretically and humanly important when, in a study of how moral character develops, he is tempted to cheat and whether he does so or not is surreptitiously observed. In such instances, we need principles and mechanisms for adjudication.

Both principles and mechanisms become indispensable once we grant that decision on these conflicts in values can no longer be left to the unaided conscience of the individual investigator. Now that behavioral science has grown so important that it captures public attention, forces are clearly such that decision will not be left to the individual investigator. Nor should it be. He is likely to be a biased judge, one who will set a higher priority on scientific values than nonscientists are likely to do. He wants so much to conduct research and to advance knowledge that, being human, he may underestimate or rationalize away the costs and risks to his subjects. At any rate, he is open to the legitimate suspicion of being vulnerable to bias. Anyone who has been privy to discussions among tough-minded behavioral scientists about the "trade off" between ethical risks and potential scientific gain will have no doubt that this bias exists.

CODES OF ETHICS

Further codification of ethical principles by the scientific disciplines concerned to help guide decision in the difficult cases is a much needed first step. Existing codes of ethics provide a good start but they stop short of some of the harder issues before us. Thus, the code adopted in 1959 by the American Psychological Association (1959) provides for the confidentiality of research materials and calls upon the psychologist to show "sensible regard for the social codes and moral expectations of the community in which he works. . . ." In what is probably the critical principle, it states:

> Only when a problem is significant and can be investigated in no other way is the psychologist justified in giving misinformation to research subjects or exposing research subjects to physical or emotional stress.
>
> a. When the possibility of serious aftereffects exists, research is conducted only when the subjects or their responsible agents are fully informed of this possibility and volunteer nevertheless.
>
> b. The psychologist seriously considers the possible harmful aftereffects and removes them as soon as permitted by the design of the experiment. . . . [Principle 16. *Harmful aftereffects.*]

Such a code of principles typically contains some absolutes. (Provision a above approaches an absolute requirement for voluntary consent, though the decision about when a "possibility of serious aftereffects exists" remains judgmental.) More of the principles will point to strongly desirable or highly undesirable practices that are nevertheless open to some kind of negotiation.

I would like to see some nearly absolute principles added that, I think, are essential to maintaining a relationship of trust between researcher and human subject, a relationship that is a prerequisite to society's continued tolerance of the behavioral scientist. Under very few circumstances is an investigator justified in violating a pledge of confidentiality given to a research subject, even though the interests of the subject are fully protected. The frequency with which hidden devices are used to identify supposedly anonymous questionnaires is deplorable. I would also like assurance that when an investigator *has* employed deception and subsequently explains his action to his subjects in a "debriefing" session, he presents the literal truth—and does not, as sometimes has been the case, use the session for further experimental manipulation.

However, in general, I would prefer to keep the absolutes to a minimum and would open even the few absolutes proposed to debate and to legitimate exceptions, under safeguards of a sort to be discussed shortly. Thus, I can imagine a research situation in which the covert identification of questionnaires might be an essential and justifiable method for checking on the effects of lack of anonymity on questionnaire responses.

The inherent limitation in ethical codes is the leeway they leave for human judgment and for balancing competing values. Without such leeway, any code would be unworkable; with it, the code is open to evasion. Application of ethical principles to real cases is literally a problem in casuistry and is vulnerable to the abuses that gave casuistry a bad name. In the principle I have quoted, what determines "when a problem is significant"? How much unsuccessful search do we require of an investigator before we allow him to decide that the problem "can be investigated in *no* other way"? How big a probability is a "possibility" of serious aftereffect, and how much does the experimenter have to hurt people for it to be "serious"? And who is to decide all this?

I am not criticizing the ambiguous wording of the principle. Insofar as there is no objective, common measure by which competing values can be "traded off," the fallibility of human judgment cannot be eliminated from decisions about the ethics of research. The question is whose judgment should it be and under what safeguards. What we need, therefore, are mechanisms of responsible "due process."

A DUE-PROCESS MECHANISM

At present, universities throughout the country are having their initial experience with one type of such a due-process mechanism. Through regulations promulgated in February and July 1966, the Surgeon General of the United States Public Health Service requires every institution receiving a USPHS grant to develop principles and procedures governing the use of human subjects in research. A crucial feature of these requirements is a review of the judgment of each principal investigator or program director by a multidisciplinary committee of his institutional associates. Since the procedures became operative only on November 1, 1966, it is too early to report the experience that universities have had in administering these controls. After an era of laissez-faire, an attitude which can no longer be justified, I can safely predict that loud complaints from academic investigators will be heard for some time. Nonetheless, with only slightly less assurance, I also predict that a decentralized system of institutional review on the USPHS model will become the pattern for the social control of Federally financed research on human subjects, including children. I think it is a desirable pattern, for all the nuisance it is creating.

What will this decentralized system accomplish?

1. It will assure the public and its representatives that the welfare of

human subjects is protected by adequate safeguards. The acceptability of an investigator's procedures will be reviewed by others and will be justified to them. The requirement that the review committee be interdisciplinary promotes the development of common ethical standards across disciplines and professions and is likely to have a corrective influence on disciplines or subdisciplines that have become habituated to dubious practices.

2. Because the investigator's possible bias in regard to the ethical acceptability of research procedures is checked by making the judgment a matter of shared public responsibility, it will for the most part obviate the need for rigid and absolute rules and allow flexible judgment that takes the particulars of a research situation into account. The same considerations by which a jury system is a proper device for administering justice "beyond reasonable doubt" make a system of collegial review appropriate to the inherently judgmental issues research deals with.

3. At the cost of some initial confusion and inequity, it will encourage creative and responsible thinking within institutions as they formulate and revise the ethical codes under which the review committees will operate. Some may wish to keep formal principles to a minimum and evolve a kind of common law from the precedents that are established in borderline cases. Others may try to spell out more fully elaborated codes. Through their scientific and professional associations, the disciplines concerned would be well advised to watch these developments closely and to take the lead in preparing statements of principles for the institutional committees that reflect the special problems of their own areas of research.

4. It will avert the stultifying rigidity of Federal centralized administrative or statutory control over research practices.

I think the special problems of research on the behavior of children can best be dealt with in such a framework of decentralized institutional self-monitoring according to explicit principles and procedures, which can and should be modified as we learn from experience in working with them. Reviewing committees will naturally be slow to approve procedures that they are at all dubious about when the subjects of the research are young children.

A SPECIAL PROBLEM

The issue that may demand the closest attention and give the greatest trouble is the one involving explicit parental consent. In regard to this problem, and to many others, behavioral research does not parallel clinical medical research (Ladimer & Newman, 1963) closely enough for the medical research codes to be particularly helpful.

The relationship of physician to patient, involving as it does the highly charged issue of life and death, can when it is diverted to research objectives be perverted to an unspeakable evil (as in the Nazi death camps), unless the strictest controls protect the patient's interests. If patients are to be able to turn confidently to their physicians for help, they must know that they will not be used in medical experimentation without their knowledge and consent. In the case of minors, parental consent is the legally required equivalent of the patient's consent. (Yet matters here are not simple either: Advances in pharmacology that none of us would forgo depend on the use of placebos and "double-blind" designs, practices that are hard to reconcile with the principle of voluntary consent.)

In contrast to medical research, much behavioral research, with children or with adults, is concerned with far less sensitive matters. When the requirement of explicit parental consent would defeat the purpose of an otherwise important behavioral study requiring a representative sample of children *and* no reasonable person would expect the study to harm the child or insult the parents' values, an exception to the requirement seems justifiable.

The sort of responsible review of the investigator's justification of his research procedures that the Public Health Service is now requiring makes it possible to consider such exceptions on their merits. Review groups will have to develop their own guidelines for deciding when the explicit consent of a parent or guardian should be obligatory, when parents should be given the opportunity to consent implicitly by failing to object to an announced research plan that involves their child, and when the responsible head of an institution such as a school system or a school might appropriately consent to the research being done without consulting the parents. School authorities will of course base their decisions to give or withhold permission not only on their own judgment about what is ethical but also on the compatibility of the research with the school's educational objectives for the child. The latter judgments are more appropriately made by superintendents and principals than by investigators, review committees, *or* parents.

RESPECT FOR THE SUBJECT

Lest I give the impression that the due-process mechanism the Public Health Service has decreed for American campuses will of itself fully allay the concern about the proprieties of research with children and other human subjects, which many social and behavioral scientists share with other citizens, I need to draw, by way of conclusion, a distinction between what is ethically permissible and what is ethically desirable. My own view is that the predominant cast of much permissible behavioral research falls short of the desirable in too often adopting a manipulative or condescending attitude toward its human subjects rather than a genuinely respectful, collaborative one.

Much public resentment toward the behavioral sciences arises, I think, from correct perception of this tendency toward manipulation. Review committees and codes of ethics will not directly improve this state of affairs because inevitably they are concerned with ruling out what is not permissible, rather than with making what is desirable prevail. If and as behavioral scientists come more characteristically to grant their subjects the respect they accord to collaborators in an enterprise they understand and accept, they should, by the same token, help create a more favorable atmosphere for behavioral research. The styles of research that prevail may be more important than skill in public relations in creating a favorable "image" of behavioral science.

In research with children, an atmosphere of respect and care is particularly important. Improvement in what is normative practice in research in the behavioral disciplines must be the outgrowth of continued discussion in the professional societies and in the universities and of resultant changes in graduate training.

Such discussions are in process as a by-product of the review procedures the Public Health Service is requiring of the universities. As a result of participating in them, social and behavioral scientists may come increasingly to realize that they have lost their innocence. They can no longer live in a world of simple good and evil in which their research decisions follow unambiguously from academic-scientific values. Like it or not, they are now faced with picking their way among conflicting values and resolving the conflicts as best they can. It comes to many of us as a surprise, though it should not, that the modes of resolving such conflicts are in the broadest sense inherently political.

References

American Psychological Association. *Ethical standards of psychologists.* Washington, D. C.: APA, 1959.

Camelot and psychological tests. (Special issue) *American Psychologist,* 1966, 21, 401–477.

Carter, L. J. Social sciences: Where do they fit in the politics of science? *Science,* 1966, 154, 488–491.

Goslin, D. A. *The search for ability: Standardized testing in social perspective.* New York: Russell Sage Foundation, 1963.

Goslin, D. A., Rayner, R. E., & Hallock, B. The use of standardized tests in elementary schools. New York: Russell Sage Foundation, 1965. (Mimeo)

Hoffman, M., & Hoffman, L. W. (Eds.) *Review of child development research.* Vol. 1. New York: Russell Sage Foundation, 1964.

Hoffman, M., & Hoffman, L. W. (Eds.) *Review of child development research.* Vol. 2. New York: Russell Sage Foundation, 1966.

Kelman, H. C. Human use of human subjects: The problem of deception in social psychological experiments. *Psychological Bulletin,* 1967, 67, 1–11.

Ladimer, I., & Newman, R. W. (Eds.) *Clinical investigation in medicine: Legal, ethical and moral aspects. An anthology and bibliography.* Boston: Boston University, Law-Medicine Institute, 1963.

Ruebhausen, O. M., & Brim, O. G., Jr. Privacy and behavioral research. *Columbia Law Review,* 1965, 65, 1184–1211.

Testing and public policy. (Special issue) *American Psychologist,* 1965, 20, 857–993.

15. CORNELL RESEARCH ETHICS: POLICY GOVERNING RESEARCH AND TEACHING WITH HUMAN BEINGS AS SUBJECTS

INTRODUCTION

The development of information and knowledge concerning man and his environment has long been recognized as both a prime function and a major obligation of educational institutions such as Cornell. Indeed, it has become increasingly well understood that the long run welfare of mankind is dependent upon a firm base of research, both basic and applied.

If man is to understand himself, he himself must be a subject of research. However, as research has moved from the study of man's environment, the classic subject of scientific inquiry, to the study of man himself and man in relation to his environment, new difficulties as well as new benefits can result. While research is capable of untold benefits for human beings, it is not without its hazard for them. There is thus a potential conflict between our desire for the enormously fruitful products of scientific investigations involving people and a particular individual's or group's human and political rights when he is a subject of an experiment.

It is to the resolution of this possible conflict and to the protection of both the Cornell investigator and the person or persons being studied that the following procedures are dedicated. They apply to research and teaching activities carried out under the auspices of Cornell University, Ithaca. (A separate but similar policy exists for Cornell units in New York City.)

SOURCE. "Policy Governing Research and Teaching with Human Beings As Subjects," Ithaca, N.Y.: Cornell University's Office of Vice President for Research and Advanced Study, June 30, 1967. Copyright © 1967 by Cornell University.

151

GENERAL POLICY CONSIDERATIONS

In conducting research and teaching involving human subjects, the primary responsibility for the well-being of the subjects, for ethical behavior and for avoiding legal difficulties lies with the scientific investigator. He must be sensitive, therefore, to the manifold problems which may arise. There is also a Cornell University corporate responsibility arising from its position as employer; the University must therefore always be concerned about the safety of human subjects.

The following list is illustrative of the types of procedures which may involve potentially harmful consequences to human subjects. Investigators shall seek consultation and advice through the mechanism described below whenever their studies with human subjects fall into one of the following categories, or when other difficulties—whether they be legal, medical, biological, ethical, moral, psychological, or sociological—might derive from their programs with human subjects.

a. *Excessive exposure to potentially harmful stimuli via—*

> Drugs
> Ionizing radiation
> Non-ionizing radiation
> > Ultra violet
> > Visible light
> > Infrared radiations
> > Microwaves
> Ambient pressure
> Noise
> Vibration
> Electric shock
> Heat and/or humidity
> Special diets
> Cold and/or wind
> Magnetic fields
> Gravitational fields
> Hypnotic suggestions
> Deceptions
> Mental stresses
> Induced changes in attitudes, values or other
> > enduring psychological characteristics
> Alterations of social structure

b. Excessive deprivation of stimuli through—

Sensory deprivation
Food deprivation
Special diets
Sleep deprivation
Isolation

Human subjects are entitled to and must be given, in advance, full knowledge of all the anticipated risks which characterize the proposed activities. If there is a chance of harm to the subject it is essential that his informed consent be obtained in writing and then kept on file; if the subject is a minor or otherwise legally incompetent the written consent of his parent(s) and/or his legal representative is necessary. However, he need not be told the actual operational details of the investigation or demonstration, if withholding such information will promote the success of the study without harm to the welfare or rights of the subject. In comparing the requirements of the activity against the desirability of candid disclosure of the objectives, the investigator must always give primary and overriding consideration to the welfare of his subjects.

Each faculty member is expected to consider the following questions when setting up his program. These are intended to typify the concerns but should not be considered as all-inclusive.

1. Will the purposes of the experiment and the nature of the subject's participation be explained in terms which the subject can understand?

2. Will unnecessary stress be avoided?

3. Is there significant danger of unduly severe exposure or deprivation?

4. If deception is to be used, is it clearly justified in terms of the purposes of the activity? Is there a later opportunity to explain the deception?

5. Where relevant, have the procedures been tried with animals?

6. Does the investigator possess the necessary scientific qualifications and experiences for research involving human beings as subjects?

7. Will a subject be free to, and capable of, bringing his participation to an end if he so desires?

8. Is the investigator prepared to terminate the experiment if in his judgment a subject should not go on?

9. Will a subject's personal privacy be protected?

10. Have possibilities of ill effects to the subjects been considered on a broad basis and have precautions been taken?

11. Is there a persuasive case that the expected benefits to science clearly outweigh any potential hazards to the subjects?

12. Has the investigator safeguarded the personal integrity of the subject in obtaining his consent, especially if the subject is in a dependent relationship such as that of an employee of Cornell or student of the investigator?

PROCEDURES

All research and teaching with human beings as subjects should be under the supervision of a Cornell University faculty member whose responsibility it is to ensure that no harm comes to the human subjects. Other personnel may of course participate in the experiments but may not assume full responsibility for them.

Whenever a faculty member proposes a new or modified project in which humans are to be subjects, he should discuss it with his department chairman or with a committee elected by the Department (or if this is not applicable, with his Center director or dean) to determine whether there is a significant chance of harm to the subjects. If this discussion reveals a significant chance of harm to a human subject, or if the answer to any of the foregoing 12 questions so indicates, the faculty member is required to review his plans for use of human subjects with an advisory committee as set forth below, which will make recommendations concerning the safety of the procedures and the adequacy of professional attention and facilities to the well-being of the subjects.

The responsibility for review of the proposed procedures and for a determination of their acceptability rests with the Committee on Human Subjects (CHS) which is a university committee appointed by the President upon recommendation of the Faculty Council. The CHS consists of 4 faculty members serving four-year staggered terms and a physician designated by the Director of Student Health Services. This committee normally will convene an *ad hoc* group, usually of three members, for each plan submitted to it for review. The investigator may suggest members of the *ad hoc* group; CHS will consider such suggestions as advisory and will strive in all cases to appoint a committee with knowledge and judgment in the particular field involved. The investigator will make available to the *ad hoc* committee on request whatever materials he has prepared for his contemplated program. The review should occur as early in the development of the program as possible.*

* For research with human subjects which is done either at the Gannett Clinic or Sage Hospital, the Director of University Health Services plans *additionally* to request the advice of his Research Advisory Committee, with final approval by himself. Clinical research under Cornell University auspices will always be carried out within the spirit of and consistent with the 1964 Declaration of Helsinki, which established a code of ethics

The CHS has the responsibility to respond rapidly to requests for review. *Ad hoc* committees may be organized by telephone with the charge to them forwarded by the chairman of CHS. The *ad hoc* committees will be asked to report back within 10 days. If the proposed use of human subjects is approved by the *ad hoc* committee, the chairman of CHS, at his discretion, may directly transmit approval to the requesting faculty member. If approval is denied, the CHS shall meet as soon as feasible to render its final judgment. All decisions will be forwarded in writing with copies to the Department or Center involved and, for record-keeping purposes, to the Office of the Co-ordinator of Research.

The CHS and its *ad hoc* committee are expected to view the plan for the proposed use of human subjects from the standpoint of acceptability in terms of the general policy considerations outlined above. The review shall involve an independent determination of the acceptability of the proposal, with consideration of: (i) the rights and welfare of the individual or individuals involved; (ii) the appropriateness of methods used to secure informed consent; (iii) the risks and potential benefits. CHS and the *ad hoc* committees may also make additional suggestions on alternative methods or procedures but any such additional recommendations will be purely advisory, it being no function of the *ad hoc* committees or the CHS to mandate precisely how research and teaching shall be done. The *ad hoc* committee shall reports its conclusions to the CHS which will make the final determination and communicate it to the scholar and to his department chairman. The scholar may appeal the determination of the CHS to the Faculty Council, whose decision will be final.

If a faculty member plans substantial changes in a project which has already been considered or reviewed, and if those changes might involve an increase of potential risk to a human subject, these changes should be submitted to CHS for review.

The CHS and the *ad hoc* committees shall maintain minutes of all meetings and shall record their findings and recommendations as part of these minutes. These records shall be maintained in the Office of the Coordinator of Research. The CHS shall make an annual report to the President on its activities for the year and shall make its report available to the Faculty Council.

on human experimentation, as well as within the well established code of conduct and the legal and ethical constraints recognized in the orthodox doctor/patient relationship.

Conceptual Issues in Educational Research

Many problems, confusions, and disagreements in educational research are conceptual in nature. Here, in the second part of the book, we present selections relevant to nine major areas of conceptual concern in educational research: observation, inference, testability, causation, models, value judgments, concepts and their interpretation, behaviorism, and programmed instruction. Within each of these areas there are conceptual difficulties, confusions, and disagreements that affect educational research at its roots.

A basic issue running through these areas of concern is the extent to which a radical empirical approach is appropriate. By a radical empirical approach, we mean the view that the only meaningful statements are: (1) those describing sense impressions or observations, and (2) those expressing the results of logical or mathematical operations on statements decribing sense impressions or observations. David Hume essentially took this stance in his classic radical-empiricist volume, *An Enquiry Concerning Human Understanding*:

> When we run over libraries, . . . what havoc must we make? If we take in our hand any volume . . . let us ask, *Does it contain any abstract reasoning concerning quantity or number?* No. *Does it contain any experimental reasoning concerning matter of fact and existence?* No. Commit it then to the flames: for it can contain nothing but sophistry and illusion.[1]

[1] David Hume, *An Enquiry Concerning Human Understanding* (LaSalle, Illinois: The

A popular twentieth-century radical-empiricist view is labeled "logical positivism." Labels attached to sister views include "behaviorism," "operationalism," and "neopositivism."[2]

At the opposite end of the spectrum is an approach we shall label "humanism," by which we mean that view which sees the living intellect and its product as of primary importance. Again mathematics and definitions play an important role, but the attempt to reduce everything to simple indubitable observation statements, which is so characteristic of radical empiricism, is notably absent in humanism. In humanism, intelligent, informed intuition plays an important role in the search for truth. Experience is not ignored, but it is held to have much richer content than can possibly be reported in simple observation statements; experience is not thought to be more important than the faculty of reason. Reason, understanding, insight, and interpretation are emphasized, as opposed to the collection and formal organization of publicly and readily verifiable facts.

Radical empiricism and humanism differ from a third approach, which we could label "irrationalism." This third approach is characterized by a faith in feeling, distrust of any supposedly objective evidence, and distrust of the intellect, logic, and mathematics. "How I feel now" is what matters. This approach is contemptuous of educational research, whatever its form, and therefore has no part in the interplay between radical empiricism and humanism that provides the central drama of this part of the book.

At this point, the reader might be helped by the mention of several more or less popular issues that exemplify (in at least some degree) the conflict between radical empiricism and humanism: behaviorism and operationalism versus their opponents; exclusively correlational validity versus construct validity; viewing human attributes as intervening variables versus viewing them as hypothetical constructs; belief in the reducibility of theoretical concepts versus belief in their irreducibility; viewing causation as constant conjunction or correlation versus viewing it as power; science as data summarization versus science as, at least in part, theory that goes beyond the data; contempt for value judgments unless they are reduced to empirical statements versus willingness to evaluate, without feeling that the result is simply a report; intolerance of nonbehavioral objectives versus intolerance of behavioral objectives; viewing human beings as machines versus viewing human beings as uniquely human; trust in computers versus suspicion of them; and insistence on precision versus tolerance of vagueness.

Open Court Publishing Co., 1907), (a reprint made from the posthumous edition of 1777), p. 176.

[2] But there are nonpositivistic views that attach great importance to behavior and that do endorse a loose form of operational definitions.

The above characterization is deliberately oversimplified in order to facilitate the presentation of a basic issue and is unavoidably sketchy. We invite you to participate in the exploration of the great variety of developments and departures from the basic disagreement as you read the following selections and as you pursue the suggested items in the bibliographies.

CHAPTER 4

Observation

The opening sentence of Francis Bacon's *Novum Organum* (1620) expresses the at that time awakening spirit of empiricism: the demand that we base our scientific knowledge only upon *observation*:

> Man, as the minister and interpreter of nature, does and understands as much as his observations on the order of nature, either with regard to things or the mind, permit him, and neither knows nor is capable of more.[1]

Although it was not always so, this spirit is clearly dominant among twentieth-century scientists, including educational researchers. It is so dominant that most of us simply take it for granted.

A second, fairly well-accepted contemporary doctrine is that we must distinguish our observations from our inferences, placing more reliance on observations than on inferences from them. This doctrine has been incorporated into our research lore and has been included in a number of attempts at curriculum reform, including the process-approach science curriculum backed by the American Association for the Advancement of Science. John Stuart Mill expressed this second doctrine as follows:

> What is needful, in order that the fact, supposed to be observed, may safely be received as true? The answer to this question is very simple, at least in its first aspect. The sole condition is, that what

[1] Joseph Dewey, editor.

is supposed to have been observed shall really have been observed; that it is an observation, not an inference.[2]

A problem arises, however, in deciding just what is an observation and what is an inference. As Mill put it:

> In almost every act of our perceiving faculties, observation and inference are intimately blended. What we are said to observe is usually a compound result, of which one-tenth may be observation, and the remaining nine-tenth inference.
>
> I affirm, for example, that I hear a man's voice. This would pass, in common language, for a direct perception. All however, which is really perception, is that I hear a sound. That the sound is a voice, and that the voice the voice of a man, are not perceptions but inferences. . . .
>
> In every act of what is called observation, there is at least one inference—from the sensations to the presence of the object. . . .[3]

The problem is a thorny one, as shown by the large amount of philosophical ink devoted to attempts to secure for us a firm grounding for the empirical conclusion drawing that we do. It is a problem for the radical empiricist approach[4] because of the dependence of this approach upon the supposedly firm building blocks provided by observation.

In the first selection Norwood Russell Hanson urges that observation is quite theory dependent, implying that observation and inference are closely intertwined. His view casts some doubt on the assumption of the objectivity of science. For, if inter-observer reliability is not achievable, then how can one expect objectivity in conclusions? And inter-observer reliability would, under this view, be hard to achieve, given observers with different theoretical orientations.[5]

One attempt to rescue objectivity utilizes phenomenalistic descriptions (which are put in terms of appearances). Carl Hempel, in Selection 17, objects to this solution and speaks as if the distinction between observations and inferences is not particularly problematic anyway.

Sir Arthur Eddington, a noted physicist, has come up with the view that all observation statements are essentially mistaken, since they ignore the

[2] John Stuart Mill, *System of Logic* (London: Longmans, Green, and Co., 1906), p. 420.
[3] *Ibid.*, pp. 186 and 188.
[4] Described briefly in the introduction to Part II.
[5] Another interesting discussion alleging theory dependence of observation statements is that of P. K. Feyerabend, "Explanation, Reduction, and Empiricism," in Herbert Feigl and Grover Maxwell, eds., *Minnesota Studies in the Philosophy of Science*, Vol. III (Minneapolis: University of Minnesota Press, 1967), pp. 28–97.

physical reality of our universe. He holds, for example, that it is misleading to report that a plank is solid, when in fact it is made up of small particles separated by large spaces. Eddington's approach is quoted and attacked in the selection by L. Susan Stebbing. Her position, to simplify a bit, is that the perfectly serviceable language that we have developed for referring to and commenting on everyday things is made useless by such statements as Eddington's that the floor "has no solidity or substance." She holds that our perfectly plain observational talk with such words as "solid" is quite satisfactory and useful.

Not only is the substance of Stebbing's remarks of interest here, but her strategy as well. Consider the following brief passage from the selection:

> If the plank appears to be *solid*, but is really *non-solid*, what does "solid" mean? If "solid" has no assignable meaning, then "nonsolid" is also without sense.

This kind of move, which attacks attempts to eliminate the distinction between two contrary categories, is called the "excluded-opposite" argument by John Passmore,[6] and is applicable to many universal denials of things or qualities. It applies to the claim that there are really no observations—only inferences; and it might well be applicable to the claims that there is no such thing as mind, that nothing is ever proven, and that there is no such thing as voluntary action. These claims have played a significant role in thinking about the science of education.

In summary, Hempel and Stebbing try to make us feel secure in our ordinary simple observation reports, a security needed by radical empiricism, and Hanson raises doubts about this security.

[6] John Passmore, *Philosophical Reasoning* (New York: Charles Scribner's Sons, 1961), pp. 100–118.

16. OBSERVATION

Norwood Russell Hanson

Were the eye not attuned to the Sun,
The Sun could never be seen by it.
                                GOETHE*

A

Consider two microbiologists. They look at a prepared slide; when asked what they see, they may give different answers. One sees in the cell before him a cluster of foreign matter: it is an artefact, a coagulum resulting from inadequate staining techniques. This clot has no more to do with the cell, *in vivo*, than the scars left on it by the archaeologist's spade have to do with the original shape of some Grecian urn. The other biologist identifies the clot as a cell organ, a "Golgi body." As for techniques, he argues: "The standard way of detecting a cell organ is by fixing and staining. Why single out this one technique as producing artefacts, while others disclose genuine organs?"

The controversy continues. It involves the whole theory of microscopical technique; nor is it an obviously experimental issue. Yet it affects what scientists say they see. Perhaps there is a sense in which two such observers do not see the same thing, do not begin from the same data, though their eyesight is normal and they are visually aware of the same object.

SOURCE. Reprinted with the permission of Cambridge University Press from *Patterns of Discovery* by Norwood Russell Hanson. Copyright © 1965 by Cambridge University Press.
  *

> Wär' nicht das Auge sonnenhaft,
> Die Sonne könnt' es nie erblicken;
Goethe, *Zahme Xenien* (Werke, Weimar, 1887–1918), Bk. 3, 1805.

Imagine these two observing a Protozoon—*Amoeba*. One sees a one-celled animal, the other a non-celled animal. The first sees *Amoeba* in all its analogies with different types of single cells: liver cells, nerve cells, epithelium cells. These have a wall, nucleus, cytoplasm, etc. Within this class *Amoeba* is distinguished only by its independence. The other, however, sees *Amoeba's* homology not with single cells, but with whole animals. Like all animals *Amoeba* ingests its food, digests and assimilates it. It excretes, reproduces and is mobile—more like a complete animal than an individual tissue cell.

This is not an experimental issue, yet it can affect experiment. What either man regards as significant questions or relevant data can be determined by whether he stresses the first or the last term in "unicellular animal."

Some philosophers have a formula ready for such situations: "Of course they see the same thing. They make the same observation since they begin from the same visual data. But they interpret what they see differently. They construe the evidence in different ways." The task is then to show how these data are moulded by different theories or interpretations or intellectual constructions.

Considerable philosophers have wrestled with this task. But in fact the formula they start from is too simple to allow a grasp of the nature of observation within physics. Perhaps the scientists cited above do not begin their inquiries from the same data, do not make the same observations, do not even see the same thing? Here many concepts run together. We must proceed carefully, for wherever it makes sense to say that two scientists looking at x do not see the same thing, there must always be a prior sense in which they do see the same thing. The issue is, then, "Which of these senses is most illuminating for the understanding of observational physics?"

These biological examples are too complex. Let us consider Johannes Kepler: imagine him on a hill watching the dawn. With him is Tycho Brahe. Kepler regarded the sun as fixed: it was the earth that moved. But Tycho followed Ptolemy and Aristotle in this much at least: the earth was fixed and all other celestial bodies moved around it. *Do Kepler and Tycho see the same thing in the east at dawn?*

We might think this an experimental or observational question, unlike the questions "Are there Golgi bodies?" and "Are Protozoa one-celled or non-celled?." Not so in the sixteenth and seventeenth centuries. Thus Galileo said to the Ptolemaist ". . . neither Aristotle nor you can prove that the earth is *de facto* the centre of the universe. . . ." "Do Kepler and Tycho see the same thing in the east at dawn?" is perhaps not a *de facto* question either, but rather the beginning of an examination of the concepts of seeing and observation.

The resultant discussion might run:

"Yes, they do."

"No, they don't."

"Yes, they do!"

"No, they don't!" . . .

That this is possible suggests that there may be reasons for both contentions. Let us consider some points in support of the affirmative answer.

The physical processes involved when Kepler and Tycho watch the dawn are worth noting. Identical photons are emitted from the sun; these traverse solar space, and our atmosphere. The two astronomers have normal vision; hence these photons pass through the cornea, aqueous humour, iris, lens and vitreous body of their eyes in the same way. Finally their retinas are affected. Similar electro-chemical changes occur in their selenium cells. The same configuration is etched on Kepler's retina as on Tycho's. So they see the same thing.

Locke sometimes spoke of seeing in this way: a man sees the sun if his is a normally-formed retinal picture of the sun. Dr Sir W. Russell Brain speaks of our retinal sensations as indicators and signals. Everything taking place behind the retina is, as he says, "an intellectual operation based largely on non-visual experience. . . ."[1] What we *see* are the changes in the *tunica retina*. Dr Ida Mann regards the macula of the eye as itself "seeing details in bright light," and the rods as "seeing approaching motor-cars." Dr Agnes Arber speaks of the eye as itself seeing.[2] Often, talk of seeing can direct attention to the retina. Normal people are distinguished from those for whom no retinal pictures can form: we may say of the former that they can see whilst the latter cannot see. Reporting when a certain red dot can be seen may supply the oculist with direct information about the condition of one's retina.

This need not be pursued, however. These writers speak carelessly: seeing the sun is not seeing retinal pictures of the sun. The retinal images which Kepler and Tycho have are four in number, inverted and quite tiny. Astronomers cannot be referring to these when they say they see the sun. If they are hypnotized, drugged, drunk or distracted they may not see the sun, even though their retinas register its image in exactly the same way as usual.

Seeing is an experience. A retinal reaction is only a physical state—a

---

[1] Brain, *Recent Advances in Neurology* (with Strauss) (London, 1929), p. 88. Compare Helmholtz: "The sensations are signs to our consciousness, and it is the task of our intelligence to learn to understand their meaning" (*Handbuch der Physiologischen Optik* (Leipzig, 1867), vol. III, p. 433).

See also Husserl, "Ideen zu einer Reinen Phaenomenologie," in *Jahrbuch für Philosophie*, vol. I (1913), pp. 75, 79, and Wagner's *Handwörterbuch der Physiologie*, vol. III, section 1 (1846), p. 183.

[2] Mann, *The Science of Seeing* (London, 1949), pp. 48–9. Arber, *The Mind and the Eye* (Cambridge, 1954). Compare Müller: "In any field of vision, the retina sees only itself in its spatial extension during a state of affection. It perceives itself as . . . etc." (*Zur vergleichenden Physiologie des Gesichtesinnes des Menschen und der Thiere* (Leipzig, 1826), p. 54).

photochemical excitation. Physiologists have not always appreciated the differences between experiences and physical states. People, not their eyes, see. Cameras, and eye-balls, are blind. Attempts to locate within the organs of sight (or within the neurological reticulum behind the eyes) some nameable called "seeing" may be dismissed. That Kepler and Tycho do, or do not, see the same thing cannot be supported by reference to the physical states of their retinas, optic nerves or visual cortices: there is more to seeing than meets the eyeball.

Naturally, Tycho and Kepler see the same physical object. They are both visually aware of the sun. If they are put into a dark room and asked to report when they see something—anything at all—they may both report the same object at the same time. Suppose that the only object to be seen is a certain lead cylinder. Both men see the same thing: namely this object—whatever it is. It is just here, however, that the difficulty arises, for while Tycho sees a mere pipe, Kepler will see a telescope, the instrument about which Galileo has written to him.

Unless both are visually aware of the same object there can be nothing of philosophical interest in the question whether or not they see the same thing. Unless they both see the sun in this prior sense our question cannot even strike a spark.

Nonetheless, both Tycho and Kepler have a common visual experience of some sort. This experience perhaps constitutes their seeing the same thing. Indeed, this may be a seeing logically more basic than anything expressed in the pronouncement "I see the sun" (where each means something different by "sun"). If what they meant by the word "sun" were the only clue, then Tycho and Kepler could not be seeing the same thing, even though they were gazing at the same object.

If, however, we ask, not "Do they see the same thing?" but rather "What is it that they both see?", an unambiguous answer may be forthcoming. Tycho and Kepler are both aware of a brilliant yellow-white disc in a blue expanse over a green one. Such a "sense-datum" picture is single and uninverted. To be unaware of it is not to have it. Either it dominates one's visual attention completely or it does not exist.

If Tycho and Kepler are aware of anything visual, it must be of some pattern of colours. What else could it be? We do not touch or hear with our eyes, we only take in light. This private pattern is the same for both observers. Surely if asked to sketch the contents of their visual fields they would both draw a kind of semicircle on a horizon-line. They say they see the sun. But they do not see every side of the sun at once; so what they really see is discoid to begin with. It is but a visual aspect of the sun. In any single observation the sun is a brilliantly luminescent disc, a penny painted with radium.

So something about their visual experiences at dawn is the same for both:

a brilliant yellow-white disc centred between green and blue colour patches. Sketches of what they both see could be identical—congruent. In this sense Tycho and Kepler see the same thing at dawn. The sun appears to them in the same way. The same view, or scene, is presented to them both.

In fact, we often speak in this way. Thus the account of a recent solar eclipse:[3] "Only a thin crescent remains; white light is now completely obscured; the sky appears a deep blue, almost purple, and the landscape is a monochromatic green . . . there are the flashes of light on the disc's circumference and now the brilliant crescent to the left. . . ." Newton writes in a similar way in the *Opticks*: "These Arcs at their first appearance were of a violet and blue Colour, and between them were white Arcs of Circles, which . . . became a little tinged in their inward Limbs with red and yellow. . . ."[4] Every physicist employs the language of lines, colour patches, appearances, shadows. In so far as two normal observers use this language of the same event, they begin from the same data; they are making the same observation. Differences between them must arise in the interpretations they put on these data.

Thus, to summarize, saying that Kepler and Tycho see the same thing at dawn just because their eyes are similarly affected is an elementary mistake. There is a difference between a physical state and a visual experience. Suppose, however, that it is argued as above—that they see the same thing because they have the same sense-datum experience. Disparities in their accounts arise in *ex post facto* interpretations of what is seen, not in the fundamental visual data. If this is argued, further difficulties soon obtrude.

B

Normal retinas and cameras are impressed similarly by fig. 1. Our visual sense-data will be the same too. If asked to draw what we see, most of us will set out a configuration like fig. 1.

Do we all see the same thing? Some will see a perspex cube viewed from

---

[3] From the B.B.C. report, 30 June 1954.

[4] Newton, *Opticks*, Bk. II, part 1. The writings of Claudius Ptolemy sometimes read like a phenomenalist's textbook. Cf. e.g. *The Almagest* (Venice, 1515), VI, section 11, "On the Directions in the Eclipses," "When it touches the shadow's circle from within," "When the circles touch each other from without." Cf. also VII and VIII, IX (section 4). Ptolemy continually seeks to chart and predict "the appearances"—the points of light on the celestial globe. *The Almagest* abandons any attempt to explain the machinery behind these appearances.

Cf. Pappus: "The (circle) dividing the milk-white portion which owes its colour to the sun, and the portion which has the ashen colour natural to the moon itself is indistinguishable from a great circle" (*Mathematical Collection* (Hultsch, Berlin and Leipzig, 1864), pp. 554–60).

below. Others will see it from above. Still others will see it as a kind of polygonally-cut gem. Some people see only criss-crossed lines in a plane. It may be seen as a block of ice, an aquarium, a wire frame for a kite—or any of a number of other things.

FIGURE 1.

Do we, then, all see the same thing? If we do, how can these differences be accounted for?

Here the "formula" re-enters: "These are different *interpretations* of what all observers see in common. Retinal reactions to fig. 1 are virtually identical; so too are our visual sense-data, since our drawings of what we see will have the same content. There is no place in the seeing for these differences, so they must lie in the interpretations put on what we see."

This sounds as if I do two things, not one, when I see boxes and bicycles. Do I put different interpretations on fig. 1 when I see it now as a box from below, and now as a cube from above? I am aware of no such thing. I mean no such thing when I report that the box's perspective has snapped back into the page.[5] If I do not mean this, then the concept of seeing which is natural in this connexion does not designate two diaphanous components, one optical, the other interpretative. Fig. 1 is simply seen now as a box from below, now as a cube from above; one does not first soak up an optical pattern and then clamp an interpretation on it. Kepler and Tycho just see the sun. That is all. That is the way the concept of seeing works in this connexion.

"But," you say, "seeing fig. 1 first as a box from below, then as a cube from above, involves interpreting the lines differently in each case." Then for you and me to have a different interpretation of fig. 1 just *is* for us to see something different. This does not mean we see the same thing and then interpret it differently. When I suddenly exclaim "Eureka—a box from above," I do not refer simply to a different interpretation. (Again, there is a logically prior sense in which seeing fig. 1 as from above and then as from below is seeing the same thing differently, i.e. being aware of the same diagram in different ways. We can refer just to this, but we need not. In this case we do not.)

Besides, the word "interpretation" is occasionally useful. We know where it applies and where it does not. Thucydides presented the facts objectively; Herodotus put an interpretation on them. The word does not apply to every-thing—it has a meaning. Can interpreting always be going on when we see? Sometimes, perhaps, as when the hazy outline of an agricultural machine looms up on a foggy morning and, with effort, we finally identify it. Is this the "interpretation" which is active when bicycles and boxes are clearly seen? Is it active when the perspective of fig. 1 snaps into reverse? There was a time

---

[5] "Auf welche Vorgänge spiele ich an?" (Wittgenstein, *Phil. Inv.* p. 214).

when Herodotus was half-through with his interpretation of the Graeco-Persian wars. Could there be a time when one is half-through interpreting fig. 1 as a box from above, or as anything else?

"But the interpretation takes very little time—it is instantaneous." Instantaneous interpretation hails from the Limbo that produced unsensed sensibilia, unconscious inference, incorrigible statements, negative facts and *Objektive*. These are ideas which philosophers force on the world to preserve some pet epistemological or metaphysical theory.

Only in contrast to "Eureka" situations (like perspective reversals, where one cannot interpret the data) is it clear what is meant by saying that though Thucydides could have put an interpretation on history, he did not. Moreover, whether or not an historian is advancing an interpretation is an empirical question: we know what would count as evidence one way or the other. But whether we are employing an interpretation when we see fig. 1 in a certain way is not empirical. What could count as evidence? In no ordinary sense of "interpret" do I interpret fig. 1 differently when its perspective reverses for me. If there is some extraordinary sense of the word it is not clear, either in ordinary language, or in extraordinary (philosophical) language. To insist that different reactions to fig. 1 *must* lie in the interpretations put on a common visual experience is just to reiterate (without reasons) that the seeing of *x must* be the same for all observers looking at *x*.

"But 'I see the figure as a box' means: I am having a particular visual experience which I always have when I interpret the figure as a box, or when I look at a box. . . ." ". . . if I meant this, I ought to know it. I ought to be able to refer to the experience directly and not only indirectly . . . ."[6]

Ordinary accounts of the experiences appropriate to fig. 1 do not require visual grist going into an intellectual mill: theories and interpretations are "there" in the seeing from the outset. How can interpretations "be there" in the seeing? How is it possible to see an object according to an interpretation? "The question represents it as a queer fact; as if something were being forced into a form it did not really fit. But no squeezing, no forcing took place here."[7]

Consider now the reversible perspective figures which appear in textbooks on Gestalt psychology: the tea-tray, the shifting (Schröder) staircase, the tunnel. Each of these can be seen as concave, as convex, or as a flat drawing. Do I really see something different each time, or do I only interpret what I see in a different way? To interpret is to think, to do something; seeing is an experiential state. The different ways in which these figures are seen are not due to different thoughts lying behind the visual reactions. What could "spontaneous" mean if these reactions are not spontaneous? When the stair-

6 *Ibid.* p. 194 (top).
7 *Ibid.* p. 200.

case "goes into reverse" it does so spontaneously. One does not think of anything special; one does not think at all. Nor does one interpret. One just sees, now a staircase as from above, now a staircase as from below.

The sun, however, is not an entity with such variable perspective. What has all this to do with suggesting that Tycho and Kepler may see different things in the east at dawn? Certainly the cases are different. But these reversible perspective figures are examples of different things being seen in the same configuration, where this difference is due neither to differing visual pictures, nor to any "interpretation" superimposed on the sensation.

Some will see in fig. 2 an old Parisienne, others a young woman (à la Toulouse-Lautrec). All normal retinas "take" the same picture; and our sense-datum pictures must be the same, for even if you see an old lady and I a young lady, the pictures we draw of what we see may turn out to be geometrically indistinguishable. (Some can see

FIGURE 2.

this *only* in one way, not both. This is like the difficulty we have after finding a face in a tree-puzzle; we cannot thereafter see the tree without the face.)

When what is observed is characterized so differently as "young woman" or "old woman," is it not natural to say that the observers see different things? Or must "see different things" mean only "see different objects"? This is a primary sense of the expression, to be sure. But is there not also a sense in which one who cannot see the young lady in fig. 2 sees something different from me, who sees the young lady? Of course there is.

Similarly, in Köhler's famous drawing of the Goblet-and-Faces we "take" the same retinal/cortical/sense-datum picture of the configuration; our drawings might be indistinguishable. I see a goblet, however, and you see two men staring at one another. Do we see the same thing? Of course we do. But then again we do not. (The sense in which we *do* see the same thing begins to lose its philosophical interest.)

I draw my goblet. You say "That's just what I saw, two men in a staring contest." What steps must be taken to get you to see what I see? When attention shifts from the cup to the faces does one's visual picture change? How? What is it that changes? What could change? Nothing optical or sensational is modified. Yet one sees different things. The organization of what one sees changes.

How does one describe the difference between the *juene fille* and the *vieille femme* in fig. 2? Perhaps the difference is not describable: it may just show itself. That two observers have not seen the same things in fig. 2 could show

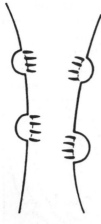

FIGURE 3.

itself in their behaviour. What is the difference between us when you see the zebra as black with white stripes and I see it as white with black stripes? Nothing optical. Yet there might be a context (for instance, in the genetics of animal pigmentation), where such a difference could be important.

A third group of figures will stress further this organizational element of seeing and observing. They will hint at how much more is involved when Tycho and Kepler witness the dawn that "the formula" suggests.

What is portrayed in fig. 3? Your retinas and visual cortices are affected much as mine are; our sense-datum pictures would not differ. Surely we could all produce an accurate sketch of fig. 3. Do we see the same thing?

I see a bear climbing up the other side of a tree. Did the elements "pull together"/cohere/organize, when you learned this?[8] You might even say with Wittgenstein "it has not changed, and yet I see it differently. . . ." Now, does it not have ". . . a quite particular 'organization' "?

Organization is not itself seen as are the lines and colours of a drawing. It is not itself a line, shape, or a colour. It is not an element in the visual field, but rather the way in which elements are appreciated. Again, the plot is not another detail in the story. Nor is the tune just one more note. Yet without plots and tunes details and notes would not hang together. Similarly the organization of fig. 3 is nothing that registers on the retina along with other details. Yet it gives the lines and shapes a pattern. Were this lacking we would be left with nothing but an unintelligible configuration of lines.

How do visual experiences become organized? How is seeing possible?

Consider fig. 4 in the context of fig. 5:

The context gives us the clue. Here, some people could not see the figure as an antelope. Could people who had never seen an antelope, but only birds, see an antelope in fig. 4?

In the context of fig. 6 the figure may indeed stand out as an antelope. It might even be urged that the figure seen in fig. 5 has no similarity to the one in fig. 6 although the two are congruent. Could anything be more opposed to a sense-datum account of seeing?

Of a figure similar to the Necker cube (fig. 1) Wittgenstein writes, "You could imagine [this] appearing in several places in a text-book. In the rele-

---

[8] This case is different from fig. 1. Now I can help a "slow" percipient by tracing in the outline of the bear. In fig. 1 a percipient either gets the perspectival arrangement, or he does not, though even here Wittgenstein makes some suggestions as to how one might help; cf. *Tractatus*, 5. 5423, last line.

FIGURE 4.   FIGURE 5.

vant text something different is in question every time: here a glass cube, there an inverted open box, there a wire frame of that shape, there three boards forming a solid angle. Each time the text supplies the interpretation of the illustration. But we can also see the illustration now as one thing, now as another. So we interpret it, and see it as we interpret it."[9]

Consider now the head-and-shoulders in fig. 7:

The upper margin of the picture cuts the brow, thus the top of the head is not shown. The point of the jaw, clean shaven and brightly illuminated, is

FIGURE 6.

just above the geometric center of the picture. A white mantle . . . covers the right shoulder. The right upper sleeve is exposed as the rather black area at the lower left. The hair and beard are after the manner of a late mediaeval representation of Christ.

The appropriate aspect of the illustration is brought out by the verbal context in which it appears. It is not an illustration of anything determinate

[9] *Ibid.* p. 193. Cf. Helmholtz, *Phys. Optik*, vol. III, pp. 4, 18 and Fichte (*Bestimmung des Menschen*, ed. Medicus (Bonn, 1834), vol. III, p. 326). Cf. also Wittgenstein, *Tractatus*, 2. 0123.

unless it appears in some such context. In the same way, I must talk and gesture around fig. 4 to get you to see the antelope when only the bird has revealed itself. I must provide a context. The context is part of the illustration itself.

FIGURE 7.

Such a context, however, need not be set out explicitly. Often it is "built into" thinking, imagining and picturing. We are set to appreciate the visual aspect of things in certain ways. Elements in our experience do not cluster at random.

A trained physicist could see one thing in fig. 8: an X-ray tube viewed from the cathode. Would Sir Lawrence Bragg and an Eskimo baby see the same

FIGURE 8.

thing when looking at an X-ray tube? Yes, and no. Yes—they are visually aware of the same object. No—the *ways* in which they are visually aware are profoundly different. Seeing is not only the having of a visual experience; it is also the way in which the visual experience is had.

At school the physicist had gazed at this glass-and-metal instrument. Returning now, after years in University and research, his eye lights upon the same object once again. Does he see the same thing now as he did then? Now he sees the instrument in terms of electrical circuit theory, thermodynamic theory, the theories of metal and glass structure, thermionic emission, optical transmission, refraction, diffraction, atomic theory, quantum theory and special relativity.

Contrast the freshman's view of college with that of his ancient tutor. Compare a man's first glance at the motor of his car with a similar glance ten exasperating years later.

"Granted, one learns all these things," it may be countered, "but it all figures in the interpretation the physicist puts on what he sees. Though the layman sees exactly what the physicist sees, he cannot interpret it in the same way because he has not learned so much."

Is the physicist doing more than just seeing? No; he does nothing over and above what the layman does when he sees an X-ray tube. What are you doing over and above reading these words? Are you interpreting marks on a page? When would this ever be a natural way of speaking? Would an infant see what you see here, when you see words and sentences and he sees but marks and lines? One does nothing beyond looking and seeing when one dodges bicycles, glances at a friend, or notices a cat in the garden.

"The physicist and the layman see the same thing," it is objected, "but they do not make the same thing of it." The layman can make nothing of it. Nor is that just a figure of speech. I can make nothing of the Arab word for *cat*, though my purely visual impressions may be indistinguishable from those of the Arab who can. I must learn Arabic before I can see what he sees. The layman must learn physics before he can see what the physicist sees.

If one must find a paradigm case of seeing it would be better to regard as such not the visual apprehension of colour patches but things like seeing what time it is, seeing what key a piece of music is written in, and seeing whether a wound is septic.

Pierre Duhem writes:

Enter a laboratory; approach the table crowded with an assortment of apparatus, an electric cell, silk-covered copper wire, small cups of mercury, spools, a mirror mounted on an iron bar; the experimenter is inserting into small openings the metal ends of ebony-headed pins; the iron oscillates, and the mirror attached to it throws a luminous band upon a celluloid scale; the forward-backward motion of this spot enables the physicist to observe the minute oscillations of the iron bar. But ask him what he is doing. Will he answer 'I am studying the oscillations of an iron bar which carries a mirror'? No, he will say that he is measuring the electric resistance of the spools. If you are astonished, if you ask him what his words mean, what relation they have with the phenomena he has been observing and which you have noted at the same time as he, he will answer that your question requires a long explanation and that you should take a course in electricity.[10]

The visitor must learn some physics before he can see what the physicist sees. Only then will the context throw into relief those features of the objects before him which the physicist sees as indicating resistance.

This obtains in all seeing. Attention is rarely directed to the space between the leaves of a tree, save when a Keats brings it to our notice. (Consider also what was involved in Crusoe's seeing a vacant space in the sand as a footprint.) Our attention most naturally rests on objects and events which dominate the visual field. What a blooming, buzzing, undifferentiated confusion visual life would be if we all arose tomorrow without attention capable of dwelling only on what had heretofore been overlooked.

The infant and the layman can see: they are not blind. But they cannot see what the physicist sees; they are blind to what he sees. We may not hear that the oboe is out of tune, though this will be painfully obvious to the trained musician. (Who, incidentally, will not hear the tones and *interpret* them as being out of tune, but will simply hear the oboe to be out of tune. We simply see what time it is; the surgeon simply sees a wound to be septic; the physicist sees the X-ray tube's anode overheating.) The elements of the visitor's visual field, though identical with those of the physicist, are not organized for him as for the physicist; the same lines, colours, shapes are apprehended by both, but not in the same way. There are indefinitely many ways in which a constellation of lines, shapes, patches, may be seen. *Why* a visual pattern is seen differently is a question for psychology, but *that* it may be seen differently is important in any examination of the concepts of seeing and observation. Here, as Wittgenstein might have said, the psychological is a symbol of the logical.

You see a bird, I see an antelope; the physicist sees an X-ray tube, the child a complicated lamp bulb; the microscopist sees coelenterate mesoglea, his new student sees only a gooey, formless stuff. Tycho and Simplicius see a mobile sun, Kepler and Galileo see a static sun.

It may be objected, "Everyone, whatever his state of knowledge, will see

10 Duhem, *La théorie physique* (Paris, 1914), p. 218.

fig. 1 as a box or cube, viewed as from above or as from below." True; almost everyone, child, layman, physicist, will see the figure as box-like one way or another. But could such observations be made by people ignorant of the construction of box-like objects? No. This objection only shows that most of us—the blind, babies, and dimwits excluded—have learned enough to be able to see this figure as a three-dimensional box. This reveals something about the sense in which Simplicius and Galileo do see the same thing (which I have never denied): they both see a brilliant heavenly body. The schoolboy and the physicist both see that the X-ray tube will smash if dropped. Examining how observers see different things in x marks something important about their seeing the same thing when looking at x. If seeing different things involves having different knowledge and theories about x, then perhaps the sense in which they see the same thing involves their sharing knowledge and theories about x. Bragg and the baby share no knowledge of X-ray tubes. They see the same thing only in that if they are looking at x they are both having some visual experience of it. Kepler and Tycho agree on more: they see the same thing in a stronger sense. Their visual fields are organized in much the same way. Neither sees the sun about to break out in a grin, or about to crack into ice cubes. (The baby is not "set" even against these eventualities.) Most people today see the same thing at dawn in an even stronger sense: we share much knowledge of the sun. Hence Tycho and Kepler see different things, and yet they see the same thing. That these things can be said depends on their knowledge, experience, and theories.

Kepler and Tycho are to the sun as we are to fig. 4, when I see the bird and you see only the antelope. The elements of their experiences are identical; but their conceptual organization is vastly different. Can their visual fields have a different organization? Then they can see different things in the east at dawn.

It is the sense in which Tycho and Kepler do not observe the same thing which must be grasped if one is to understand disagreements within microphysics. Fundamental physics is primarily a search for intelligibility—it is philosophy of matter. Only secondarily is it a search for objects and facts (though the two endeavours are as hand and glove). Microphysicists seek new modes of conceptual organization. If that can be done the finding of new entities will follow. Gold is rarely discovered by one who has not got the lay of the land.

To say that Tycho and Kepler, Simplicius and Galileo, Hooke and Newton, Priestley and Lavoisier, Soddy and Einstein, De Broglie and Born, Heisenberg and Bohm all make the same observations but use them differently is too easy. It does not explain controversy in research science. Were there no sense in which they were different observations they could not be used differently. This may perplex some: that researchers sometimes do not appreciate data in the same way is a serious matter. It is important to realize, however, that sorting out differences about data, evidence, observation, may require more than simply gesturing at observable objects. It may require a comprehensive reappraisal of one's subject matter. This may be difficult, but it should not obscure the fact that nothing less than this may do.

17. THE VOCABULARY OF SCIENCE: TECHNICAL TERMS AND OBSERVATION TERMS

Carl Hempel

Empirical science, we noted earlier, does not aim simply at a description of particular events: it looks for general principles which permit their explanation and prediction. And if a scientific discipline entirely lacks such principles, then it cannot establish any connections between different phenomena: it is unable to foresee future occurrences, and whatever knowledge it offers permits of no technological application, for all such application requires principles which predict what particular effects would occur if we brought about certain specified changes in a given system. It is, therefore, of paramount importance for science to develop a system of concepts which is suited for the formulation of general explanatory and predictive principles.

The vocabulary of everyday discourse, which science has to use at least initially, does permit the statement of generalizations, such as that any unsupported body will fall to the ground; that wood floats on water but that any metal sinks in it; that all crows are black; that men are more intellectual than women; etc. But such generalizations in everyday terms tend to have various shortcomings: (1) their constituent terms will often lack precision and uniformity of usage (as in the case of 'unsupported body', 'intellectual', etc.), and, as a consequence, the resulting statement will have no clear and precise meaning; (2) some of the generalizations are of very limited scope (as, for

SOURCE. Hempel, Carl G., "Fundamentals of Concept Formation in Empirical Science," *International Encyclopedia of Unified Science*, Vol. II, No. 7. Chicago: University of Chicago Press, 1952. Reprinted with permission. Copyright © 1952 by The University of Chicago Press.

example, the statement dealing only with crows) and thus have small predictive and explanatory power (compare in this respect the generalization about floating in water with the general statement of Archimedes' principle) ; (3) general principles couched in everyday terms usually have "exceptions," as is clearly illustrated by our examples.

In order to attain theories of great precision, wide scope, and high empirical confirmation, science has therefore evolved, in its different branches, comprehensive systems of special concepts, referred to by technical terms. Many of those concepts are highly abstract and bear little resemblance to the concrete concepts we use to describe the phenomena of our everyday experience. Actually, however, certain connections must obtain between these two classes of concepts; for science is ultimately intended to systematize the data of our experience, and this is possible only if scientific principles, even when couched in the most esoteric terms, have a bearing upon, and thus are conceptually connected with, statements reporting in "experiential terms" available in everyday language what has been established by immediate observation. Consequently, there will exist certain connections between the technical terms of empirical science and the experiential vocabulary; in fact, only by virtue of such connections can the technical terms of science have any empirical content. Much of the discussion in the present Chapter II will concern the nature of those connections. Before we can turn to this topic, however, we have to clarify somewhat more the notion of experiential term.

The experiential vocabulary is to be used in describing the kind of data which are usually said to be obtainable by direct experience and which serve to test scientific theories or hypotheses. Such experiential data might be conceived of as being sensations, perceptions, and similar phenomena of immediate experience; or else they might be construed as consisting in simple physical phenomena which are accessible to direct observation, such as the coincidence of the pointer of an instrument with a numbered mark on a dial; a change of color in a test substance or in the skin of a patient; the clicking of an amplifier connected with a Geiger counter; etc. The first of these two conceptions of experiential data calls for a phenomenological vocabulary, which might contain such expressions as "blue-perception," "looking brighter than" (applicable to areas of a visual field, not to physical objects), "sour-taste-sensation," "headachy feeling," etc. The second conception requires, for the description of experiential data, a set of terms signifying certain directly observable characteristics of physical objects, i.e., properties or relations whose presence or absence in a given case can be intersubjectively ascertained, under suitable circumstances, by direct observation. A vocabulary of this kind might include such terms as "hard," "liquid," "blue," "coincident with," "contiguous with," etc., all of which are meant here to designate intersubjectively ascertainable attributes of physical objects. For brevity, we will refer to such attributes as *observables*, and to the terms naming them as *observation terms*.

A phenomenalistic conception will appeal to those who hold that the data of our immediate phenomenal experience must constitute the ultimate testing ground for all empirical knowledge; but it has at least two major disadvantages: first, while many epistemologists have favored this view, no one has ever developed in a precise manner a linguistic framework for the use of phenomenalistic terms; and, second, as has been pointed out by Popper, the use of observation reports couched in phenomenalistic language would seriously interfere with the intended objectivity of scientific knowledge: The latter requires that all statements of empirical science be capable of test by reference to evidence which is public, i.e., which can be secured by different observers and does not depend essentially on the observer. To this end, data which are to serve as scientific evidence should be described by means of terms whose use by scientific observers is marked by a high degree of determinacy and uniformity. . . . These considerations strongly favor the second conception mentioned above, and we will therefore assume, henceforth, especially in the context of illustrations, that the vocabulary used in science for the description of experiential evidence consists of observation terms. Nevertheless, the basic general ideas of the following discussion can readily be transferred to the case of an experiential vocabulary of the phenomenalistic kind.

18. "FURNITURE OF THE EARTH"

L. Susan Stebbing

Roused by the shock he started from his trance—
The cold white light of morning, the blue moon
Low in the west, the clear and garish hills,
The distant valley and the vacant woods,
Spread round him where he stood. Whither have fled
The hues of heaven that canopied his bower
Of yesternight? The sounds that soothed his sleep,
The mystery and the majesty of Earth,
The joy, the exultation?

WORDSWORTH

I enter my study and see the blue curtains fluttering in the breeze, for the windows are open. I notice a bowl of roses on the table; it was not there when I went out. Clumsily I stumble against the table, bruising my leg against its hard edge; it is a heavy table and scarcely moves under the impact of my weight. I take a rose from the bowl, press it to my face, feel the softness of the petals, and smell its characteristic scent. I rejoice in the beauty of the graded shading of the crimson petals. In short—I am in a familiar room, seeing, touching, smelling familiar things, thinking familiar thoughts, experiencing familiar emotions.

In some such way might any common reader describe his experiences in the familiar world that he inhabits. With his eyes shut he may recognize a rose from its perfume, stumble against a solid obstacle and recognize it to be a table, and feel the pain from its contact with his comparatively yielding flesh. You, who are reading this chapter, may pause and look around you. Perhaps you are in your study, perhaps seated on the seashore, or in a cornfield, or on board ship. Wherever you may be, you will see objects distinguishable one from another, differing in colour and in shape; probably you are hearing various sounds. You can see the printed marks on this page, and notice that they are black marks on a whitish background. That you are perceiving something coloured and shaped you will not deny; that your body

SOURCE. Reprinted with permission from *Philosophy and the Physicists* by Susan L. Stebbing, Methuen & Co. Ltd., London, 1937. Copyright © 1937 by Methuen & Co., Ltd., London, the publishers.

presses against something solid you are convinced; that, if you wish, you can stop reading this book, you know quite well. It may be assumed that you have some interest in philosophy; otherwise you would not be reading *this*. Perhaps you have allowed yourself to be persuaded that the page is not "really coloured," that the seat upon which you are sitting is not "really solid"; that you hear only "illusory sounds." If so, it is for such as you that this chapter is written.

Imagine the following scene. You are handed a dish containing some apples—rosy-cheeked, green apples. You take the one nearest to you, and realize that you have been "had." The "apple" is too hard and not heavy enough to be really an apple; as you tap it with your finger-nail it gives out a sound such as never came from tapping a "real" apple. You admire the neatness of the imitation. To sight the illusion is perfect. It is quite sensible to contrast this ingenious fake with a "real" apple, for a "real" apple just is an object that *really* is an apple, and not only *seems* to be one. This fake is an object that looks to your eyes to be an apple, but neither feels nor tastes as an apple does. As soon as you pick it up you know that it is not an apple; there is no need to taste it. We should be speaking in conformity with the rules of good English if we were to say that the dish contained real apples and imitation apples. But this mode of speaking does not lead us to suppose that there are two varieties of *apples*, namely real and imitation apples, as there are Bramley Seedlings and Blenheim Pippins. Again, a shadow may be thrown on a wall, or an image may be thrown through a lantern on to a screen. We distinguish the shadow from the object of which it is the shadow, the image from that of which it is the image. Shadow and image are apprehensible only by sight; they really are visual, i.e. *seeable*, entities. I can see a man, and I can see his shadow; but there is not both a *real* man and a *shadow* man; there is just the shadow of the man.

This point may seem to have been unduly laboured. It is, however, of great importance. The words "real" and "really" are familiar words; they are variously used in every-day speech, and are not, as a rule, used ambiguously. The opposition between a *real* object and an *imitation* of a real object is clear. So, too, is the opposition between 'really seeing a man' and having an illusion.[1] We can speak sensibly of the distinction between "the real size" and "the apparent size" of the moon, but we know that both these expressions are extremely elliptical. The significance of the words "real" and "really" can be determined only by reference to the context in which they are used. Nothing but confusion can result if, in one and the same sentence, we mix up language used appropriately for the furniture of earth and our daily dealings with it with language used for the purpose of philosophical and scientific discussion.

---

[1] Cf. "How easy is that bush supposed a bear!"

A peculiarly gross example of such a linguistic mixture is provided by one of Eddington's most picturesque passages:

> I am standing on a threshold about to enter a room. It is a complicated business. In the first place I must shove against an atmosphere pressing with a force of fourteen pounds on every square inch of my body. I must make sure of landing on a plank traveling at twenty miles a second round the sun—a fraction of a second too early or too late, the plank would be miles away. I must do this whilst hanging from a round planet head outward into space, and with a wind of aether blowing at no one knows how many miles a second through every interstice of my body. The plank has no solidity of substance. To step on it is like stepping on a swarm of flies. Shall I not slip through? No, if I make the venture one of the flies hits me and gives me a boost up again; I fall again and am knocked upwards by another fly; and so on. I may hope that the net result will be that I remain steady; but if unfortunately I should slip through the floor or be boosted too violently up to the ceiling the occurrence would be, not a violation of the laws of Nature, but a rare coincidence. (*N.Ph.W.* 342.)

Whatever we may think of Eddington's chances of slipping through the floor, we must regard his usage of language in this statement as gravely misleading to the common reader. I cannot doubt that it reveals serious confusion in Eddington's own thinking about "the nature of the physical world." Stepping on a plank is not in the least like "stepping on a swarm of flies." This language is drawn from, and is appropriate to, our daily intercourse with the familiar furniture of earth. We understand well what it is like to step on to a solid plank; we can also imagine what it would be like to step on to a swarm of flies. We know that two such experiences would be quite different. The plank is solid. If it be securely fixed, it will support our weight. What, then, are we to make of the comparison of stepping on to a plank with stepping on to a swarm of flies? What can be meant by saying that "the plank has no solidity of sustance"?

Again, we are familiar with the experience of shoving against an obstacle, and with the experience of struggling against a strong head-wind. We know that we do not have "to shove against an atmosphere" as we cross the threshold of a room. We can imagine what it would be like to jump on to a moving plank. We may have seen in a circus an equestrian acrobat jump from the back of a swiftly moving horse on to the back of another horse moving with approximately the same speed. We know that no such acrobatic feat is required to cross the threshold of a room.[2]

---

[2] Eddington's words suggest that he is standing on a stationary plank and has to land

I may seem too heavy-handed in my treatment of a picturesque passage, and thus to fall under the condemnation of the man who cannot see a joke and needs to be "in contact with merry-minded companions"[3] in order that he may develop a sense of humour. But the picturesqueness is deceptive; the passage needs serious criticism since Eddington draws from it a conclusion that is important. "Verily," he says, "it is easier for a camel to pass through the eye of a needle than for a scientific man to pass through a door. And whether the door be barn door or church door it might be wiser that he should consent to be an ordinary man and walk in rather than wait until all the difficulties involved in a really scientific ingress are resolved." It is, then, suggested that an ordinary man has no difficulty in crossing the threshold of a room but that "a really scientific ingress" presents difficulties.[4] The suggested contrast is as absurd as the use of the adjective "scientific" prefixed to "ingress," in this context, is perverse. Whatever difficulties a scientist, by reason of his scientific knowledge, may encounter in becoming a member of a spiritual church, these difficulties bear no comparison with the difficulties of the imagined acrobatic feat. Consequently, they are not solved by the consideration that Eddington, no less than the ordinary man, need not hesitate to cross the threshold of his room. The false emotionalism of the picture is reminiscent of Jeans's picture of human beings standing on "a microscopic fragment of a grain of sand." It is open to a similar criticism.

If Eddington had drawn this picture for purely expository purposes, it might be unobjectionable. The scientist who sets out to give a popular exposition of a difficult and highly technical subject must use what means he can devise to convey to his readers what it is all about. At the same time, if he wishes to avoid being misunderstood, he must surely warn his readers that, in the present stage of physics, very little can be conveyed to a reader who lacks the mathematical equipment required to understand the methods by

---

on to another plank that is moving, relatively to himself, with a speed of twenty miles a second. It would be charitable to regard this as a slip, were it not that its rectification would spoil this part of his picture. There is an equally gross absurdity in the statement that he is "hanging head outward into space."

[3] See *N.Ph.W.* 336.

[4] In the article "The Domain of Physical Science" (*Science, Religion and Reality*) a similar passage begins as follows:

"The learned physicist and the man in the street were standing together on the threshold about to enter a room.

The man in the street moved forward without trouble, planted his foot on a solid unyielding plank at rest before him, and entered.

The physicist was faced with an intricate problem." (There follows much the same account of the difficulties as in the passage quoted.)

Eddington here goes on to suggest that the physicist may be "content to follow *the same crude conception* of his task that presented itself to the mind of his unscientific colleague" (my italics).

which results are obtained and the language in which these results can alone find adequate expression. Eddington's picture seems to me to be open to the objection that the image of a swarm of flies used to explain the electronic structure of matter is more appropriate to the old-fashioned classical conceptions that found expression in a model than to the conceptions he is trying to explain. Consequently, the reader may be misled unless he is warned that nothing resembling the spatial relations of flies in a swarm can be found in the collection of electrons. No concepts drawn from the level of common-sense thinking are appropriate to sub-atomic, i.e. microphysical, phenomena. Consequently, the language of common sense is not appropriate to the description of such phenomena. Since, however, the man in the street tends to think in pictures and may desire to know something about the latest developments of physics, it is no doubt useful to provide him with some rough picture.[5] The danger arises when the scientist uses the picture for the purpose of making explicit denials, and expresses these denials in common-sense language used in such a way as to be devoid of sense. This, unfortunately, is exactly what Eddington has done in the passage we are considering, and indeed, in many other passages as well.

It is worth while to examine with some care what exactly it is that Eddington is denying when he asserts that "the plank has no solidity of substance." What are we to understand by "solidity"? Unless we do understand it we cannot understand what the denial of solidity to the plank amounts to. But we can understand "solidity" only if we can truly say that the plank is solid. For "solid" just is the word we use to describe a certain respect in which a plank of wood resembles a block of marble, a piece of paper, and a cricket ball, and in which each of these differs from a sponge, from the interior of a soap-bubble, and from the holes in a net. We use the word "solid" sometimes as the opposite of "empty," sometimes as the opposite of "hollow," sometimes as the opposite of "porous." We may also, in a very slightly technical usage, contrast "solid" with "liquid" or with "gaseous." There is, no doubt, considerable variation in the precise significance of the word "solid" in various contexts. Further, as is the case with all words, "solid" may be misused, and may also be used figuratively. But there could not be a *misuse*, nor a *figurative* use, unless there were some correct and literal usages. The point is that the common usage of language enables us to attribute a meaning to the phrase "a solid plank"; but there is no common usage of language that provides a meaning for the word "solid" that would make sense to say that the plank on which I stand is not *solid*. We oppose the solidity of the walls of a house to the emptiness of its unfurnished rooms; we oppose the solidity of a piece of pumice-stone to the porous loofah sponge. We do not deny that the pumice-

[5] Jeans has a happy gift using such pictures in his purely expository works. See, for example, his image of the postage-stamp, the penny, and Cleopatra's needle, used to illustrate certain proportions of the history of the world—*The Universe Around Us*, p. 342.

stone is to some degree porous, that the bricks of the wall have chinks and crevices. But we do not know how to use a word that has no sensible opposite. If the plank is non-solid, then what does "solid" *mean*? In the companion passage to the one quoted above, and to which reference was made in a preceding footnote, Eddington depicts the physicist, about to enter a room, as reflecting that "the plank is not what it appears to be—a continuous support for his weight." This remark is absurd. The plank appears to be capable of supporting his weight, and, as his subsequent entry into the room showed, it *was* capable of supporting his weight. If it be objected that the plank is "a support for his weight" but not "a *continuous* support," I would reply that the word "continuous" is here used without any assigned meaning. The plank appears *solid* in that sense of the word "solid" in which the plank is, in fact, solid. It is of the utmost importance to press the question: If the plank appears to be *solid*, but is really *non-solid*, what does "solid" mean? If "solid" has no assignable meaning, then "non-solid" is also without sense. If the plank is non-solid, then where can we find an example to show us what "solid" means? The pairs of words, "solid"—"empty," "solid"—"hollow," "solid"— "porous," belong to the vocabulary of common-sense language; in the case of each pair, if one of the two is without sense, so is the other.

This nonsensical denial of solidity is very common in popular expositions of the physicist's conception of material objects. The author of a recently published book says: "A table, a piece of paper, no longer possess that solid reality which they appear to possess; they are both of them porous, and consist of very small electrically charged particles, which are arranged in a peculiar way."[6] How are we to understand the statement that the table *no longer* possesses 'the solid reality' which it appears to possess? The context of the statement must be taken into account. The sentence quoted occurs in a summary of the view of the physical world according to classical physics. It immediately follows the statement: "This picture formed by the physicists has one great drawback as compared with the picture formed by the non-scientific man in the street. It is much more abstract." In a later chapter we shall find reason to consider carefully what is meant by "more abstract." Here we are concerned only with the suggestion that the non-scientific man forms one "picture" of the material world and the scientist another. There are, then, two pictures. Of what, we must ask, are they pictures? Where are we to find application for the words "solid reality," which we may not use with reference to the table? Again we must ask: If the table is non-solid, what does "solid" mean?

[6] Ernst Zimmer: *The Revolution of Physics*, trans. by H. Stafford Hatfield, 1936, p. 51. I have not been able to consult the German original, so I am unable to determine whether 'solid reality' is a good rendering of Zimmer's meaning. Certainly the juxtaposition of the two words is unfortunate, but is evidently judged to be appropriate at least by his translator.

CHAPTER 5

Inference

Even if we agree with Hanson that observation involves theory (and thus inference), there remains a vast area of research operation that properly is called inference. Stated another way, there is generally a step from what we are satisfied to call our observations (whatever their status) to what we offer as a conclusion. Since our interests go beyond the given data to the prediction of ungathered data, our conclusions generally go beyond the data, thus requiring some sort of inference.

It is sometimes thought that the use of statistical tests of significance avoids the introduction of human judgment into this inferential process, with the inference from data to conclusion being a necessary inference determined by the laws of probability. (This feeling is in the spirit of radical empiricism, since it shies away from human judgment.) Now it is true that on the assumption of random sampling from a given population, the chance of getting a given result can be determined with the mathematics of probability and its rather sophisticated recent developments. But in deciding that the sample actually was a random one from the population of interest, human judgment inevitably is introduced into the inference process; further, the decision to reject (or accept) a null hypothesis ("This could not have—or could have—occurred by chance") constitutes an inference that goes beyond the data and requires human judgment; and lastly, an inference is often made to a different population from that from which the supposedly random sample was drawn. This latter inference is clearly not a necessary one; it requires intelligent, informed human judgment.

This problem, a frequently neglected one in treatments of educational statistics, is recognized in the following quotation from C. D. Hardie who, as a radical empiricist, appears to discourage the making of this inference:

A typical situation is where some hypothesis is set up and a piece of research is designed by which it can be refuted. For example, the hypothesis might be that there is no difference in intelligence between students in the Faculty of Arts and students in the Faculty of Science at the University of Melbourne at the present time. An hypothesis of this sort is often called a null hypothesis, and it is tested by comparing the characteristic under consideration (in the case of intelligence) in two random samples, one drawn from the Faculty of Arts and one from the Faculty of Science. If the difference between the samples is significant at a previously agreed level, then the null hypothesis is rejected. In less technical language, this just means that if the two samples differ to such an extent that it would be very unlikely for such a difference to arise in two random samples drawn from the same population, then we conclude that the samples could not have come from the same population. Now this is straightforward so far as it goes. But it is important to be clear as to what has been proved. What has been proved, or rather shown to be very probable, is that the population of Arts students at present in the University of Melbourne is more intelligent (let us say) than the population of Science students at present in the University of Melbourne. But no conclusion can be drawn about students in other universities or about students at Melbourne at other times. For the two samples chosen are not random samples from these different populations, and it is legitimate to reject the null hypothesis only if the samples concerned have been selected at random. I do not wish to belabour this rather trivial point, but it is not uncommon for even very reputable researchers to draw conclusions far beyond that to which they are entitled, and even on some occasions to fail to make clear the populations about which they are drawing conclusions.[1]

The attempt to infer from the results of a test of significance to a generalization about a population not included in the group from which a random sample was drawn thus requires more than a significance test.

The question remains: "What are the criteria for judging whether inferences going beyond the data are legitimate or not?" This question provides the focus for the next set of selections. Because there are a number of approaches to this question, we have set up rough subdivisions in this chapter: Generalization, Strong Inference, Mill's Methods, Hypothetico-Deductivism and Deductive Explanation, Falsifiability and Corroboration, and Bayesian Inference.

---

[1] C. D. Hardie, "Research and Progress in Education," *Australian Journal of Education*, Vol. 9, No. 3 (1965), pp. 229–230.

A. Generalization

"Generalization" is a broad term referring to the process of inferring from statements about one or more cases to the statement that what holds of these cases holds for others as well. Thus the topic "Generalization" overlaps some of the others in this chapter and might be regarded as an introductory topic. P. F. Strawson makes appropriate introductory remarks when he notes that the criteria of deduction are generally not appropriate in this area, that there is an essential lack of precision in our ways of stating conclusions, and that two basic criteria for generalizing require attention to the *number* and *variety* of instances.

19. INDUCTIVE REASONING AND PROBABILITY

P. F. Strawson

SUPPORT AND PROBABILITY

1. Of a piece of deductive reasoning one can inquire: Is it valid or invalid? Do the premises entail the conclusion, or do they not? These are questions to which a "Yes-or-No" answer is possible. If the sense of the argument is clear enough to admit of an answer it admits of a clear-cut answer: the argument is valid; or it is not. This is not to say that we might not hesitate over the question of whether an argument was valid or not. But this is the sort of hesitation which leads, perhaps, to saying: "Well, interpreted in this way, the argument would be valid; interpreted in that way, it

SOURCE. Reprinted with permission from *Introduction to Logical Theory* by P.F. Strawson, Methuen & Co. Ltd., London, 1952. Copyright © 1952 by Methuen & Co., Ltd., London, the publishers.

would be invalid." It could never lead to our assigning an intermediate status to the argument. The phrase "moderately valid argument" has no sense.

Deductive reasoning is not the only kind of reasoning, or even the most common kind. We make deductive steps when we do pure mathematics and, sometimes, when we argue philosophically. We make such steps in less rarified regions as well: when we do the arithmetic of everyday; when we turn one form of words into another, when we make a précis, when we try to show that our opponent in argument has contradicted himself. But a good deal of our reasoning does not proceed by steps of this kind, but of another; though a single train of argument may involve moves of both sorts. Thus the detective and the historian, when they draw conclusions from their premises, their evidence, often draw conclusions which are not entailed by those premises. There would often be nothing self-contradictory in accepting the premises, and rejecting the conclusions, of their arguments. But it does not follow from the fact that an historian's or a detective's argument is, by deductive standards, invalid, that it is in any sense unsound. It may be an argument to which deductive standards are inappropriate: it may make no claim to be deductively valid. Deductive standards are not the only standards of good argument; for deductive reasoning is not the only kind of reasoning. The reasoning of the experimental scientist, like that of the historian and the detective, is, in differing degrees, non-deductive. Of course, the scientist may make many deductive steps; but if these were the only permissible steps, experimental science would be impossible. For it is a part of the scientist's function to establish conclusions which are not entailed by his data, his evidence. An example of a well-established scientific statement might be one giving the melting-point of a certain metal: "Under pressure-conditions x, m always melts at y degrees." The evidence on which such a statement was based might consist of one or two experimental tests, together with the fact that no *known* metal has, *so far as has been observed*, a variable melting-point under constant-pressure conditions. These "premises" do not entail the conclusion that m always melts at y degrees under conditions x. There would be nothing self-contradictory in conjoining them with the prediction that the next piece of m, melted under these conditions, will melt at $y + 50$ degrees. Yet the evidence may be quite conclusive, though the "argument" is not deductively valid. Of course, one could introduce an argument which *would* be deductively valid. We could introduce as a premise the general statement: "All metals have constant melting-points under constant-pressure conditions." This statement, together with that recording the result of just one experimental test, would entail a conclusion of the form: "Under pressure condition x, m always melts at y degrees." The general statement introduced as a premise might itself be a consequence of some other theoretical statement accepted as well established. But at some point we should inevitably come to a theoretical statement based ultimately upon the evidence embodied in statements recording the results of particular observations; statements which did not entail the theoretical statement. No number of statements recording particular observations can ever entail a theoretical statement of this kind; for the theoretical statement is, while the particular observation-statements are not, exposed to the logical risk of refutation by statements recording the results of similar particular observations which may be made in the future.

Examples of this sort are perhaps better avoided. For most of us know little of natural science. Fortunately, we need go to nothing so elevated as history, science, or detection to find examples of non-deductive reasoning. Ordinary life provides enough. Consider

(a) He's been travelling for twenty-four hours, so he'll be very tired.

(b) The kettle's been on the fire for the last ten minutes, so it should be boiling by now.

(c) There's a hard frost this morning: you'll be cold without a coat.

Plainly the statement made by the first clause of each sentence is regarded as a reason for accepting the statement made by the second clause. The second statement in each case is in some sense a *conclusion* from the first; the first can in some sense be called a *premise*. But the premise does not entail the conclusion. It would not be self-contradictory to say: "The kettle has been on the fire for ten minutes, but the water is stone cold." One might be inclined to say that this would be impossible: but the impossibility is not logical. On the other hand, though the premise does not entail the conclusion, it is a perfectly adequate reason for accepting the conclusion in each case. The arguments, though not deductively valid, are perfectly sound arguments.

As before, we might be tempted to explain the apparently non-deductive soundness of the arguments by saying that they were *really* deductive arguments with a suppressed premise. And it certainly is true that we can, for each of the arguments (a)–(c), construct a corresponding and valid deductive argument by introducing a fresh premise: e.g., for (a), "People who travel for twenty-four hours are always tired afterwards"; for (b), "Kettles always boil within ten minutes of being put on the fire"; for (c), "Anyone not wearing a coat is cold on a frosty morning." But by regarding these general statements as suppressed premises of arguments (a)–(c), we do not get rid of the general problem of explaining how we can reasonably draw conclusions from premises that do not entail them. We merely shifts its emphasis to the narrower question: How do we establish general propositions such as these? For these are not logically necessary propositions. If they had been, arguments (a)–(c) would have been deductively valid. It is, of course, common experience that constitutes our grounds for general beliefs like these. But the beliefs go beyond the experience. To inquire by what kind of reasoning we are justified in accepting unrestricted general propositions which are not necessary propositions, is merely to put the general problem in a more specific, and less realistic, form. The form is less realistic because these generalizations based on common experience do not often appear in practice as the conclusions of arguments from particular instances. They are less reflectively adopted. But "*p* so *q*" arguments like (*a*), (*b*), and (*c*) are common.

There seems in fact to be no good reason for limiting the question in this way. We saw earlier that, given a certain *deductive* inference, it was always possible to construct a different inference by introducing, as an additional premise, a necessary statement corresponding to the principle of the original inference. But we saw that the claim that this procedure revealed the real character of the original inference was in general misleading; for our acceptance of the additional premise as logically necessary was the same thing as our acceptance of the original inference as valid. Similarly, in the case of the non-deductive steps in (*a*), (*b*), and (*c*), our acceptance of the corresponding general proposition in each case as true, is the same thing as our acceptance of the particular inference, not as deductively valid, but as somehow sound, or correct, or reasonable. One might say that, as the necessary proposition stands to the principle of the original deductive inference, so the non-necessary general proposition stands to a principle of some other kind of reasoning. We cannot express principles of this kind by the use of the second-order words, like "entails," which belong to deduction; but we might express them by the use of phrases like ". . . makes it certain that . . .", or ". . . is a good ground for concluding that . . . ." Thus our acceptance of the non-necessary proposition that all kettles boil within ten minutes of being put on the fire will be the same as our acceptance of the non-deductive principle that the fact that a kettle has been on the fire for ten minutes is a good ground for concluding that it will be boiling; and both are the same as our acceptance of the step in (*b*) as sound or correct or reasonable.

The problem we are to consider, then, is the nature of that kind of reasoning from one non-necessary statement (or conjunction of statements) to another, in which the first does not entail the second. This kind of reasoning is generally called inductive. Sometimes this title tends to be reserved for those cases in which the conclusion is a general statement. But this we see to be an artificial restriction. For the acceptance of a non-necessary general proposition as established is the same as the acceptance of the general correctness of a class of particular pieces of reasoning from premises to conclusions which they do not entail; just as the acceptance of a certain general statement as necessary is the acceptance of the validity of a class of particular deductive inferences.

2. I want now to draw attention to certain further differences between

inductive and deductive reasoning. For this purpose, I want a general word for the relation between the ground for an inductive conclusion and the conclusion itself. The only thing I have said so far about the relation is that it is not that of entailment. Let us say that in an inductive argument the grounds *support* the conclusion; and let us, instead of speaking of the premises of an inductive argument, speak of the *evidence* for an inductive conclusion. Now we saw, at the beginning of the last section, that the premises of a deductive argument either entail the conclusion or they do not. They cannot entail it more or less; there can be no question of *degrees* of entailment. But there can be, and is, a question of degrees of support; there can be, and is, better or worse evidence for inductive conclusions. Thus suppose that p_1-p_n are statements which support the statement that q. Think, then, of the degrees of support which common speech discriminates: p_1-p_n may make it *certain* that q; they may make it *virtually certain* that q; they may make it *highly probable* or *quite probable* or *quite likely* that q; they may give *some probability* to q. Or again, in terms of the word "evidence": they may constitute *overwhelming* or *conclusive* evidence for q; *pretty conclusive* or *good* evidence, *some* evidence or *slender* evidence. Similarly, they may be conclusive grounds or reasons, good grounds or reasons, slender grounds or poor reasons for holding that q. It is important to notice that where we may speak of conclusive or overwhelming evidence for q, of p_1-p_n making it certain that q, there also we may speak of *proving, establishing,* or *putting it beyond all doubt* that q, although, since the arguments are inductive, we do not produce as grounds anything that entails q. For it is not a question of support falling generally short of entailment; of entailment being the perfection of support. They are not related as the winner to the runner-up and the rest in the same race. The perfection of support is proof, but not deductive proof; it is conclusive evidence.

A way we have, then, of acknowledging, when support for an inductive conclusion is less than overwhelming, that this is so, is the use of the words "probable," "probability," "probably." These words are the source and subject of many confusions. One which need be mentioned only in order to be dismissed emerges in the statement, sometimes made, that the conclusions of inductive arguments are, *as such,* only probable; perhaps very, very probable, but never certain; for they are not entailed by their grounds. This is to make the mistake of thinking that entailment and support are competitors in the same field. But there are other confusions, more difficult to disentangle, for which the misunderstanding of the words "probable," "probably," and "probability" is responsible. Let us observe these words in their role of acknowledging that support for an inductive conclusion is less than overwhelming.

A psycho-analyst might make the following pronouncement: "On the basis of clinical experience over a good many years, it now seems probable that a very strict régime in the nursery is always followed by aggressiveness in later life." Let us express the generalization here said to seem probable in the short form: "All cases of f (very strict nursery-régime) are cases of h (later aggressiveness)." We may suppose that the qualifying phrases are omitted, that someone says simply:

($g1$) It is probable that all cases of f, are cases of h.

Here an inductive generalization is declared to be probable. Consider now how this pronouncement might be applied in a particular case. Someone might say: "Her nursery régime is very strict indeed; so she'll probably develop aggressive tendencies in later life." We may write this shortly as

($s1$) fa, so probably ha.

The word "probably" here acknowledges that fa is less than conclusive support for ha. Let us call support that is less than conclusive, *incomplete support*. Then acknowledging, in ($s1$), that fa incompletely supports ha is indirectly acknowledging the incompleteness of the support for the universal proposition that all cases of f are cases of h.

Now compare the use of "probably" in ($s1$) with its use in the following cases:

($s2$) He's been travelling for seven hours, so probably he's tired.
($s3$) There's a fog to-night, so the train will probably be late.

If someone demurred at ($s2$) or ($s3$) ("I don't see why that should tire him"), the first speaker might back them up with:

($g2$) Well, people generally are tired after travelling for seven hours (or) Most people are tired after seven hours travelling, you know.
($g3$) Trains generally are late when there's a fog.

What we now have to compare is the relations between ($s1$) and ($g1$) with the relations between ($s2$) and ($g2$), and between ($s3$) and ($g3$). The singular sentences ($s2$) and ($s3$) resemble the singular sentence ($s1$) in that they are all of the pattern "p, so probably q." In all three the use of "probably" acknowledges the incompleteness of the support which the statement preceding "so" (the statement that p) gives to the statement following "so" (the statement that q). In ($s1$) acknowledging this is also acknowledging the incompleteness of the support for the universal generalization that all cases of f are cases of h. But in ($s2$) and ($s3$), acknowledging the incompleteness of the support which the statement that p gives to the statement that q is not acknowledging the incompleteness of the support for a universal proposition. We may regard it as beyond question that people are *usually* tired after travelling for seven hours, that trains are *usually* late when there is a fog. If so, what our use of "probably" indirectly acknowledges in these cases is not the incompleteness of the support for a universal proposition, but the fact that the generalization is itself not a universal, but a proportional, generalization. It says, not "all" but "most," not "always" but "generally." Such statements are sometimes called relative frequency generalizations: (g2) for example, asserts that the relative frequency, among people who have just been travelling for seven hours, of people who are tired, is high. In this instance the relative frequency is only vaguely indicated; but it may be given, with more precision, by a numerical ratio.

So while "probably" may be said to have the same role in (s2) and (s3) as it has in (s1), there are differences in the ways in which it comes to have that role. It has the same role in each, in that it acknowledges the incompleteness of the support which the statement that p gives to the statement that q. It has the same role in that, while acknowledging the incompleteness of the support, it nevertheless claims the support to be fairly good. The acceptance of (s1) and (s2) has parallel effects on our actions. If we want only non-aggressive people in our school, we rate low the claims for admission of the person of whom (s1) is said; but we do not rule her out altogether. If we want only non-tired people for the expedition which is about to begin, we rate low the claims of the person of whom (s2) is said; though we do not rule him out altogether. The reason why the candidates for school and expedition respectively are not ruled out altogether is that each may be an exception to a general rule. But the reasons why each may turn out to be an exception to a general rule are different. In the first case the relevant generalization (though universal) was said to be only probable and may therefore turn out to be false, i.e., to have exceptions, of which the candidate may be one. In the second case the relevant generalization (though its truth is unquestioned) is not a universal generalization, and therefore admits of exceptions, of which the candidate may be one.

To sum the matter up rather crudely. We use the word "probably" in one case because there is incomplete support for a "complete" generalization; in the other case, because there is complete support for an "incomplete" generalization. Of course, we might also use it where there was incomplete support for an incomplete generalization.

It must not be supposed that whenever we utter a singular sentence of the form "p so probably q," we can always point to just one generalization, complete or incomplete, so simply related to our argument as (g2) is to (s2), or as the generalization declared to be probable in (g1) is to (s1). For this would by no means be true. It suffices that the simple cases exist, and that, if we understand them, we shall find it easier to understand the more complex ones.

3. A generalization which is, in the above sense, incomplete (as, e.g., one of the form "Most cases of f are cases of g") may be more, or less, incomplete. That is to say, the ratio of $f \cdot g$ cases to f cases affirmed in such a generalization may be more or less high. To indicate this ratio with any precision we have to have recourse to figures; to fractions or percentages. Thus we write: "78% of f-cases are g-cases" or "The ratio of $f \cdot g$ cases to f cases is 78/100."[1] Where our use of the word "probable" or its cognates reflects the incompleteness of a generalization, it will tend to reflect also the *degree* of incompleteness of the generalization. We talk of degrees of probability, and may express these numerically: we might say, for example, "Both parents have fair hair, so the probability of their child having fair hair is x/y." This has encouraged the hope that talk of the probability of something being g, given that it is f (e.g., of a child having fair hair, given that it has fair-haired parents), can be explained simply as talk of the ratio of $f \cdot g$ things to f things (e.g., the ratio of fair-haired children with fair-haired parents to children with fair-haired parents). Up to a point, this is correct. For it is correct, though pedantic, to re-express the generalization "x out of y children of fair-haired parents have fair hair" in the form "The probability of a child of fair-haired parents having fair hair is x/y"; and conversely, the word "probability," in this use, can be eliminated in favour of a statement of relative frequencies. But some have been encouraged to go further, and to suggest that an account in terms of relative frequency ratios may provide a complete elucidation of the notion of probability and, with it, of the notion of support; since variations in degree of support can be expressed by the use of the word "probable" and associated words. This is obviously wrong. Only if observed relative frequency ratios offered strong *support* to the generalization that the ratio of $f \cdot g$ cases to f cases was x/y should we be justified in saying, of a fresh case, as in our example, "Both parents have fair hair, so the probability of their child having fair hair is x/y." The observed relative frequency explains *the degree of support* which "Both parents have fair hair" gives to "Their child will have fair hair"; but only on the assumption that the generalization of the x/y ratio beyond the observed cases is itself *adequately supported* by the evidence of the observed cases. So this second and fundamental sense of support cannot itself be explained in terms of relative frequencies and indeed cannot be expressed in numerical terms at all; it can be characterized only by such expressions as "strong," "adequate," "weak" and so on.

---

[1] Why not "the ratio of g cases to f cases is 78/100"? An example will make the answer clear. "7 out of 10 children under twelve have an I.Q. below 100" does not mean "The ratio of the number of *people* with an I.Q. below 100 to the number of children under twelve is as 7 to 10"; it means "The ratio of the *number of children under twelve* with an I.Q. below 100 to the number of children under twelve is as 7 to 10."

The point is indeed a very obvious one. If we return to our earlier example of the form "*p* so probably *q*" (viz., "He's been travelling for seven hours, so probably he's tired"), it is obvious that the strength of the support which the statement that *p* gives to the statement that *q* is the product of two factors: first, the degree of completeness of the underlying generalization; second, the degree of completeness of the support for the underlying generalization. The first is a matter of relative frequencies; the second is not. The assimilation of the second to the first is perhaps encouraged by the fact that the strength of the support which one singular statement gives to another is a function of both.

4. There is another class of propositions in which we assign numerical probabilities to singular statements; but seemingly not on the basis of statistical generalizations. They may, however, lead to similar confusions to those which we have just discussed. To someone about to cut a pack of cards, one might say that the chances of his cutting an ace or a court-card were $4/13$. To someone about to throw a die we might say that the mathematical probability of his throwing a six was $\frac{1}{6}$. We are in fact more likely to use the language of "chances" than that of "probabilities"; but we may waive this point. Here we might seem to be in the position of being able to assign a probability to a statement simply by doing a little calculating. The first probability-statement seems to be *entailed* by the statement, which we can verify here and now by counting, that there are fifty-two cards in the pack of which sixteen are court-cards or aces; the second probability-statement seems to be *entailed* by the statement, which we can similarly verify here and now, that the die is a cube, of which one side and one side only is marked with six dots. So it might seem that in each case we make an inductive step (for is not the conclusion couched in the language of probability?), and yet a step of which the correctness depends on nothing more problematical than simple arithmetic. Such cases have exercised an undue fascination over some logicians concerned to elucidate the nature of inductive reasoning. If it could be shown that all probabilities were fundamentally similar to these, then to those obsessed with deduction as the model of all reasoning, there seemed to come hope of relief. For it would then seem possible to exhibit induction, not as a special (i.e., non-deductive) kind of reasoning to conclusions which are not entailed by their premises, but as ordinary (i.e., deductive) reasoning to conclusions which *are* entailed by their premises, but which are conclusions of a special kind, i.e., numerical, or quasi-numerical, probability-statements. This hope of interpreting induction as a kind of calculation, a special branch of the deductive science of arithmetic, is illusory. We may grant that the step from the statement that the object before us is a cube of which one side only is marked with six dots, to the statement that the probability of a six

being thrown is $\frac{1}{6}$, is an inductive step. But the fact that the object is a cube provides no logical guarantee of the truth of the statement that there are just six possible ways in which it may lie when it falls. There is nothing self-contradictory in saying that when the cube touches the floor it will explode, disintegrate, or melt. Even the statement that there are just six possible ways in which it may lie when it touches the floor, and that the position in which the six is uppermost is one of these, does not entail the statement that the probability of the six turning up is $\frac{1}{6}$. This is entailed by nothing less than the statement that the six possible ways in which the die may lie are *equally* probable or, as it is sometimes expressed, equally possible. And this will be so only if the cube is a body of a certain kind: of a kind, namely, of which it is true that the number of times that the different surfaces of bodies of that kind turn up in successive throws tend to equality as the number of throws increases. The statement that there are six equally possible ways for the die to fall is an inductive conclusion from the data with which we began; but, although it may be adequately supported by these data, it does not follow from them by a mathematical calculation. The induction is over before the calculation begins. The calculation of chances is not even a species of induction, let alone the whole story about induction. Either the data of the calculation are themselves the conclusions of inductions or induction does not enter into the picture at all.

Of course, we in fact incorporate the relevant provisos about equality of chances in the sense we give to the expression "true die": so that the step from "This is a true die" to "The chance of your throwing a six is $\frac{1}{6}$" is a purely deductive step. But this fact is of no help to anyone who wishes to explain degrees of inductive support in terms of arithmetically calculable chances. It shows only that certain steps which we might be tempted to think of as inductive, since their conclusions contain the word "probability," are not inductive at all.

5. The notion of support and with it, that of degrees of probability, cannot then be explained solely in terms of relative frequencies or numerical chances. On the contrary, the relevance of chance and frequency ratios to our practical assessments of certainties and likelihoods presupposes the existence of a kind of support which cannot itself be analysed in these terms. For their relevance depends upon our having certain general beliefs which may themselves be better or worse grounded, well or poorly supported. It is because we possess, say, a general belief that a certain proportion of As are Bs, that we take this proportion into account in estimating the likelihood of a particular thing being a B. It is in the light of a general belief, say, that certain chances are equal, that we take into account the mathematical ratio of desired cases to possible cases in estimating the likelihood of an event of the desired

kind. General beliefs of this sort, which are the preconditions of particular estimates of probability, need not, however, be explicitly formulated; any more than we need explicitly formulate the principles of particular pieces of deductive reasoning which we unselfconsciously perform. Forming a general belief may be more like forming a mental habit than arriving at a reasoned conclusion. But, however a general belief is arrived at, it will always make sense to ask how strong the evidence for it is, whether it is well or ill supported.

It is this fundamental sense of "support" which must, then, be examined. How do we tell when evidence is good or bad, strong or weak, conclusive or slender, better or worse? This may seem a difficult question. But the kind of difficulty should be noticed. Judges and historians, detectives, biologists, and ourselves every day assess the quality of evidence for conclusions, make judgments of relative probability. The clever do it better than the stupid. But it is not so difficult a matter that some of us cannot do it at all. It is not a specialized skill. The difficulty we are faced with is not the difficulty of doing it, but the difficulty of describing what we do.

The question, then, is: what do we mean by saying of a non-necessary generalization—to the effect, say, that all (or most) As are Bs—that it is well established, or more or less strongly supported by the evidence? Now, in fact, in estimating the evidence for such a generalization, a factor of enormous importance is its relation to the general body of our knowledge and belief: the question of how it fits in with the rest of our everyday general convictions and with accepted scientific theories. The importance of this factor obviously depends on the degree to which the relevant beliefs form a closely knit complex structure. Thus it has maximum importance in the field of physical theory; minimum importance where we are dealing with the unorganized congeries of rule-of-thumb beliefs by which we are guided in our unspecialized transactions with the world. In general, however, its importance is so great that to neglect it in practice would be absurd. But it is no less absurd to refuse to abstract from it in this theoretical inquiry. A generalization might fit in as well as you please with some wider body of beliefs; and yet both it and the general theory might be false. The ultimate test of a generalization which applies directly to instances is to be found in the instances to which it applies.

Having abstracted to this degree from the considerations which we in fact take into account in assessing the evidence for a generalization, we can give our question quite a simple answer. It is this. The evidence for a generalization to the effect that all As are Bs is good (1) in proportion as our observations of instances of As which are B are numerous, and (2) in proportion as the variety of conditions in which the instances are found is wide; always provided that no instance is found of an A which is not B; for such an instance would, of course, suffice to refute the generalization, if the latter were strictly interpreted. Conditions (1) and (2) are commonly contrasted: the mere accumulation of instances favourable to the generalization is called "simple enumeration"; and "induction by simple énumeration" is said to be a relatively weak form of argument. But the contrast is misleading, though it has a point. If all the instances of A observed had in common not only A and B but also a third feature C, then the assumption that (1) was the only relevant condition would lead to the conclusion that we had at our disposal equally strong evidence for the two logically nonequivalent generalizations, viz., "All As are Bs" and "All ACs are Bs." The first of these entails the second, but is not entailed by it: the truth of "All ACs are Bs" is consistent with the falsity of, say, "All ADs are Bs," and hence with the falsity of "All As are Bs." So evidence that supports to a certain degree the claim that all ACs are B supports to a lesser degree the wider claim that all As are B. This is the point of the contrast, the reason why condition (2) is required. But the need for condition (2) does not imply the existence of two fundamentally contrasted kinds of inductive reasoning. Suppose we frame a higher-order generalization to the effect that all generalizations of the form "All A—s are Bs" (e.g., "All ACs are Bs," "All ADs are Bs," &c.) are true. Then the truth of "All ACs are B" constitutes one favourable instance of this generalization, the truth of "All ADs are Bs" constitutes another favourable instance and so on. By condition (1), the greater the number of such generalizations we establish, the better the evidence for the higher-order generalization. But the higher-order generalization and the original generalization ("All As are Bs") have exactly the same force, are logically equivalent. So, if we were to think of conditions (1) and (2) as describing contrasting methods of induction, we should have the paradox that the application of the second method to the original generalization was identical with the application of the first method to a generalization equivalent to the original generalization. This should teach us to think of conditions (1) and (2) not as describing contrasted methods, but as stressing complementary factors to be weighed in assessing the evidence for a generalization. The essential unity of the process of accumulating evidence might be emphasized by writing the generalization, not in the form "All As are Bs," but in the equivalent doubly general form "In all conditions, all As are Bs."

The case of proportional, as opposed to universal, generalizations presents no important difference in principle. Abstracting from the factors we have decided to abstract from, the evidence that a certain more or less exactly specified proportion of As are Bs varies in strength with the variety of kinds of instance in which that proportion is found to hold, and with the numbers of instances of each kind.

6. Now I must emphasize, with all possible force, that the preceding two paragraphs, though they say something fundamental about the nature of evidence for general beliefs, are not to be taken as an accurate description

of some standard and familiar process of inductive inference. Because we can *count* instances, for example, and because the strength of the evidence is said to be related to the number of favourable instances, we might be tempted to think that we could assess the strength of the evidence for a general belief with numerical precision; or we might be tempted to think that every black crow we see should fortify us in our conviction that all crows are black. In fact, we can never describe the strength of evidence more exactly than by the use of such words as "slender," "good," "conclusive," &c.; it is exceptional that a single favourable instance should make any difference to the strength of our conviction; and when a single instance does make a difference, it may take us straight from ignorance to certainty, as when, in the laboratory, a general fact is established by a single test. Such facts are in part explained by the factors, already mentioned, from which we have abstracted: the relevance of the general background of experience, assumption, and explicitly formulated theory against which we make our assessments of the evidence, whether for a general or a particular conclusion. These background presumptions will determine, to mention nothing else, which variations in conditions we shall think it necessary to take account of. We have to remember, too, the great complexity of the ways in which background beliefs may be related to foreground problems; how many general beliefs may bear upon the probability of a single event; how important are the analogies between one case and another, as well as the strictly deductive relations between beliefs; how relatively crude many of our ways of classifying phenomena are. When we bear in mind these things, it will not seem surprising either that no precise rules of general application can be formulated for the assessment of evidence or that no precise vocabulary is available for the description of its degrees. There are techniques of limited application (e.g., for collecting and interpreting statistics), but there is no general technique. We say, of a man who is good at weighing evidence in the ordinary affairs of life, that he has good judgment. The use of this very general, non-specialist, word is revealing. The man who is good at weighing evidence has not mastered the instructions for using some particularly intricate scales. His experience must be wide; but he is not, except incidentally, a specialist.

We must remember, moreover, that our assessment of evidence is an activity undertaken not primarily for its own sake, but for the sake of practical decision and action. Our use of words for grading evidence will in part reflect the degree of caution demanded by the action proposed. Evidence which the general public finds conclusive may not satisfy the judge.

B. Strong Inference

John R. Platt's endorsement of what he calls "strong inference" has received wide notice among educational researchers and is looked upon by Platt himself as neo-Baconian. Platt, a biochemist, recommends the methodical elimination of one or more alternative hypotheses through crucial experiments, and the continued repetition of this operation. In Chapter 6, "Testability," Carl Hempel raises questions about the doctrine of crucial experiments. Norwood Russell Hanson in his comments about observation (see Chapter 4) implies that Platt's views about the given in a science are oversimplified. Regardless, Platt offers a neat system that many find appealing.

---

20. STRONG INFERENCE

John R. Platt

Scientists these days tend to keep up a polite fiction that all science is equal. Except for the work of the misguided opponent whose arguments we happen to be refuting at the time, we speak as though every scientist's field and methods of study are as good as every other scientist's, and perhaps a little better. This keeps us all cordial when it comes to recommending each other for government grants.

But I think anyone who looks at the matter closely will agree that some fields of science are moving forward very much faster than others, perhaps by an order of magnitude, if numbers could be put on such estimates. The discoveries leap from the headlines—and they are real advances in complex and difficult subjects, like molecular biology and high-energy physics. As

SOURCE. Platt, John R., "Strong Inference," *Science*, Vol. 146, pp. 347–353, October 16, 1966. Reprinted with permission. Copyright © 1966 by the American Association for the Advancement of Science.

Alvin Weinberg says (*1*), "Hardly a month goes by without a stunning success in molecular biology being reported in the Proceedings of the National Academy of Sciences."

Why should there be such rapid advances in some fields and not in others? I think the usual explanations that we tend to think of—such as the tractability of the subject, or the quality or education of the men drawn into it, or the size of research contracts—are important but inadequate. I have begun to believe that the primary factor in scientific advance is an intellectual one. These rapidly moving fields are fields where a particular method of doing scientific research is systematically used and taught, an accumulative method of inductive inference that is so effective that I think it should be given the name of "strong inference." I believe it is important to examine this method, its use and history and rationale, and to see whether other groups and individuals might learn to adopt it profitably in their own scientific and intellectual work.

In its separate elements, strong inference is just the simple and old-fashioned method of inductive inference that goes back to Francis Bacon. The steps are familiar to every college student and are practiced, off and on, by every scientist. The difference comes in their systematic application. Strong inference consists of applying the following steps to every problem in science, formally and explicitly and regularly:

1) Devising alternative hypotheses;

2) Devising a crucial experiment (or several of them), with alternative possible outcomes, each of which will, as nearly as possible, exclude one or more of the hypotheses;

3) Carrying out the experiment so as to get a clean result;

4) Recycling the procedure, making subhypotheses or sequential hypotheses to refine the possibilities that remain; and so on.

It is like climbing a tree. At the first fork, we choose—or, in this case, "nature" or the experimental outcome chooses—to go to the right branch or the left; at the next fork, to go left or right; and so on. There are similar branch points in a "conditional computer program," where the next move depends on the result of the last calculation. And there is a "conditional inductive tree" or "logical tree" of this kind written out in detail in many first-year chemistry books, in the table of steps for qualitative analysis of an unknown sample, where the student is led through a real problem of consecutive inference: Add reagent A; if you get a red precipitate, it is subgroup alpha and you filter and add reagent B; if not, you add the other reagent, B′; and so on.

On any new problem, of course, inductive inference is not as simple and certain as deduction, because it involves reaching out into the unknown.

Steps 1 and 2 require intellectual inventions, which must be cleverly chosen so that hypothesis, experiment, outcome, and exclusion will be related in a rigorous syllogism; and the question of how to generate such inventions is one which has been extensively discussed elsewhere (2, 3). What the formal schema reminds us to do is to try to make these inventions, to take the next step, to proceed to the next fork, without dawdling or getting tied up in irrelevancies.

It is clear why this makes for rapid and powerful progress. For exploring the unknown, there is no faster method; this is the minimum sequence of steps. Any conclusion that is not an exclusion is insecure and must be re-checked. Any delay in recycling to the next set of hypotheses is only a delay. Strong inference, and the logical tree it generates, are to inductive reasoning what the syllogism is to deductive reasoning, in that it offers a regular method for reaching firm inductive conclusions one after the other as rapidly as possible.

"But what is so novel about this?" someone will say. This is *the* method of science and always has been; why give it a special name? The reason is that many of us have almost forgotten it. Science is now an everyday business. Equipment, calculations, lectures become ends in themselves. How many of us write down our alternatives and crucial experiments every day, focusing on the *exclusion* of a hypothesis? We may write our scientific papers so that it looks as if we had steps 1, 2, and 3 in mind all along. But in between, we do busywork. We become "method-oriented" rather than "problem-oriented." We say we prefer to "feel our way" toward generalizations. We fail to teach our students how to sharpen up their inductive inferences. And we do not realize the added power that the regular and explicit use of alternative hypotheses and sharp exclusions could give us at every step of our research.

The difference between the average scientist's informal methods and the methods of the strong-inference users is somewhat like the difference between a gasoline engine that fires occasionally and one that fires in steady sequence. If our motorboat engines were as erratic as our deliberate intellectual efforts, most of us would not get home for supper.

MOLECULAR BIOLOGY

The new molecular biology is a field where I think this systematic method of inference has become widespread and effective. It is a complex field; yet a succession of crucial experiments over the past decade has given us a surprisingly detailed understanding of hereditary mechanisms and the control of enzyme formation and protein synthesis.

The logical structure shows in every experiment. In 1953 James Watson and Francis Crick proposed that the DNA molecule—the "hereditary substance" in a cell—is a long two-stranded helical molecule (4). This suggested a number of alternatives for crucial test. Do the two strands of the helix stay together when a cell divides, or do they separate? Matthew Meselson and Franklin Stahl used an ingenious isotope-density-labeling technique which showed that they separate (5). Does the DNA helix always have two strands, or can it have three, as atomic models suggest? Alexander Rich showed it can have either, depending on the ionic concentration (6). These are the kinds of experiments John Dalton would have liked, where the combining entities are not atoms but long macromolecular strands.

Or take a different sort of question: Is the "genetic map" showing the statistical relationship of different genetic characteristics in recombination experiments—a one-dimensional map like the DNA molecule (that is, a linear map), as T. H. Morgan proposed in 1911, or does it have two-dimensional loops or branches? Seymour Benzer showed that his hundreds of fine microgenetic experiments on bacteria would fit only the mathematical matrix for the one-dimensional case (7).

But of course, selected crucial experiments of this kind can be found in every field. The real difference in molecular biology is that formal inductive inference is so systematically practiced and taught. On any given morning at the Laboratory of Molecular Biology in Cambridge, England, the blackboards of Francis Crick or Sidney Brenner will commonly be found covered with logical trees. On the top line will be the hot new result just up from the laboratory or just in by letter or rumor. On the next line will be two or three alternative explanations, or a little list of "What he did wrong." Underneath will be a series of suggested experiments or controls that can reduce the number of possibilities. And so on. The tree grows during the day as one man or another comes in and argues about why one of the experiments wouldn't work, or how it should be changed.

The strong-inference attitude is evident just in the style and language in which the papers are written. For example, in analyzing theories of antibody formation, Joshua Lederberg (8) gives a list of nine propositions "subject to denial," discussing which ones would be "most vulnerable to experimental test."

The papers of the French leaders François Jacob and Jacques Monod are also celebrated for their high "logical density," with paragraph after paragraph of linked "inductive syllogisms." But the style is widespread. Start with the first paper in the *Journal of Molecular Biology* for 1964 (9), and you immediately find: "Our conclusions . . . might be invalid if . . . (i) . . . (ii) . . . or (iii). . . . We shall describe experiments which eliminate these' alternatives." The average physicist or chemist or scientist in any field accustomed to less closely reasoned articles and less sharply stated inferences will find it a salutary experience to dip into that journal almost at random.

RESISTANCE TO ANALYTICAL METHODOLOGY

This analytical approach to biology has sometimes become almost a crusade, because it arouses so much resistance in many scientists who have grown up in a more relaxed and diffuse tradition. At the 1958 Conference on Biophysics, at Boulder, there was a dramatic confrontation between the two points of view. Leo Szilard said "The problems of how enzymes are induced, of how proteins are synthesized, of how antibodies are formed are closer to solution than is generally believed. If you do stupid experiments and finish one a year, it can take 50 years. But if you stop doing experiments for a little while and *think* how proteins can possibly be synthesized there are only about 5 different ways, not 50! And it will take only a few experiments to distinguish these."

One of the young men added: "It is essentially the old question: How *small* and *elegant* an experiment can you perform?"

These comments upset a number of those present. An electron microscopist said, "Gentlemen, this is off the track. This is philosophy of science."

Szilard retorted, "I was not quarreling with third-rate scientists: I was quarreling with first-rate scientists."

A physical chemist hurriedly asked, "Are we going to take the official photograph before lunch or after lunch?"

But this did not deflect the dispute. A distinguished cell biologist rose and said, "No two cells give the same properties. Biology is the science of heterogeneous systems." And he added privately, "You know there are *scientists*; and there are people in science who are just working with these oversimplified model systems—DNA chains and in vitro systems—who are not doing science at all. We need their auxiliary work: they build apparatus, they make minor studies, but they are not scientists."

To which Cy Levinthal replied: "Well, there are two kinds of biologists, those who are looking to see if there is one thing that can be understood and those who keep saying it is very complicated and that nothing can be understood. . . . You must study the *simplest* system you think has the properties you are interested in."

As they were leaving the meeting, one man could be heard muttering, "What does Szilard expect me to do—shoot myself?"

Any criticism or challenge to consider changing our methods strikes of course at all our ego-defenses. But in this case the analytical method offers the possibility of such great increases in effectiveness that it is unfortunate that it cannot be regarded more often as a challenge to learning rather than as a challenge to combat. Many of the recent triumphs in molecular biology have in fact been achieved on just such "oversimplified model systems," very much along the analytical lines laid down in the 1958 discussion. They have not fallen to the kind of men who justify themselves by saying, "No two cells are alike," regardless of how true that may ultimately be. The triumphs are in fact triumphs of a new way of thinking.

HIGH-ENERGY PHYSICS

This analytical thinking is rare, but it is by no means restricted to the new biology. High-energy physics is another field where the logic of exclusions is obvious, even in the newspaper accounts. For example, in the famous discovery of C. N. Yang and T. D. Lee, the question that was asked was: Do the fundamental particles conserve mirror-symmetry or "parity" in certain reactions, or do they not? The crucial experiments were suggested; within a few months they were done, and conservation of parity was found to be excluded. Richard Garwin, Leon Lederman, and Marcel Weinrich did one of the crucial experiments. It was thought of one evening at suppertime; by midnight they had rearranged the apparatus for it; and by 4 a.m. they had picked up the predicted pulses showing the nonconservation of parity (10). The phenomena had just been waiting, so to speak, for the explicit formulation of the alternative hypotheses.

The theorists in this field take pride in trying to predict new properties or new particles explicitly enough so that if they are not found the theories will fall. As the biologist W. A. H. Rushton has said (11), "A theory which cannot be mortally endangered cannot be alive." Murray Gell-Mann and Yuval Ne'eman recently used the particle grouping which they call "The Eightfold Way" to predict a missing particle, the Omega-Minus, which was then looked for and found (12). But one alternative branch of the theory would predict a particle with one-third the usual electronic charge, and it was not found in the experiments, so this branch must be rejected.

The logical tree is so much a part of high-energy physics that some stages of it are commonly built, in fact, into the electronic coincidence circuits that detect the particles and trigger the bubble-chamber photographs. Each kind of particle should give a different kind of pattern in the electronic counters, and the circuits can be set to exclude or include whatever types of events are desired. If the distinguishing criteria are sequential, they may even run through a complete logical tree in a microsecond or so. This electronic preliminary analysis, like human preliminary analysis of alternative outcomes, speeds up progress by sharpening the criteria. It eliminates hundreds of thousands of the irrelevant pictures that formerly had to be scanned, and when it is carried to its limit, a few output pulses, hours apart, may be enough to signal the existence of the antiproton or the fall of a theory.

I think the emphasis on strong inference in the two fields I have mentioned has been partly the result of personal leadership, such as that of the classical geneticists in molecular biology, or of Szilard with his "Midwest Chowder and Bacteria Society" at Chicago in 1948–50, or of Max Delbrück with his summer courses in phage genetics at Cold Spring Harbor. But it is also partly due to the nature of the fields themselves. Biology, with its vast informational detail and complexity, is a "high-information" field, where years and decades can easily be wasted on the usual type of "low-information" observations or experiments if one does not think carefully in advance about what the most important and conclusive experiments would be. And in high-energy physics, both the "information flux" of particles from the new accelerators and the million-dollar costs of operation have forced a similar analytical approach. It pays to have a top-notch group debate every experiment ahead of time; and the habit spreads throughout the field.

INDUCTION AND MULTIPLE HYPOTHESES

Historically, I think, there have been two main contributions to the development of a satisfactory strong-inference method. The first is that of Francis Bacon (*13*). He wanted a "surer method" of "finding out nature" than either the logic-chopping or all-inclusive theories of the time or the laudable but crude attempts to make inductions "by simple enumeration." He did not merely urge experiments, as some suppose; he showed the fruitfulness of interconnecting theory and experiment so that the one checked the other. Of the many inductive procedures he suggested, the most important, I think, was the conditional inductive tree, which proceeded from alternative hypotheses (possible "causes," as he calls them), through crucial experiments ("Instances of the Fingerpost"), to exclusion of some alternatives and adoption of what is left ("establishing axioms"). His Instances of the Fingerpost are explicitly at the forks in the logical tree, the term being borrowed "from the fingerposts which are set up where roads part, to indicate the several directions."

Many of his crucial experiments proposed in Book II of *The New Organon* are still fascinating. For example, in order to decide whether the weight of a body is due to its "inherent nature," as some had said, or is due to the attraction of the earth, which would decrease with distance, he proposes comparing the rate of a pendulum clock and a spring clock and then lifting them from the earth to the top of a tall steeple. He concludes that if the pendulum clock on the steeple "goes more slowly than it did on account of the diminished virtue of its weights . . . we may take the attraction of the mass of the earth as the cause of weight."

Here was a method that could separate off the empty theories!

Bacon said the inductive method could be learned by anybody, just like learning to "draw a straighter line or more perfect circle . . . with the help of a ruler or a pair of compasses." "My way of discovering sciences goes far to level men's wit and leaves but little to individual excellence, because it performs everything by the surest rules and demonstrations." Even occasional mistakes would not be fatal. "Truth will sooner come out from error than from confusion."

It is easy to see why young minds leaped to try it.

Nevertheless there is a difficulty with this method. As Bacon emphasizes, it is necessary to make "exclusions." He says, "The induction which is to be available for the discovery and demonstration of sciences and arts, must analyze nature by proper rejections and exclusions; and then, after a sufficient number of negatives, come to a conclusion on the affirmative instances." "[To man] it is granted only to proceed at first by negatives, and at last to end in affirmatives after exclusion has been exhausted."

Or, as the philosopher Karl Popper says today, there is no such thing as proof in science—because some later alternative explanation may be as good or better—so that science advances only by disproofs. There is no point in making hypotheses that are not falsifiable, because such hypotheses do not say anything: "it must be possible for an empirical scientific system to be refuted by experience" (14).

The difficulty is that disproof is a hard doctrine. If you have a hypothesis and I have another hypothesis, evidently one of them must be eliminated. The scientist seems to have no choice but to be either soft-headed or disputatious. Perhaps this is why so many tend to resist the strong analytical approach—and why some great scientists are so disputatious.

Fortunately, it seems to me, this difficulty can be removed by the use of a second great intellectual invention, the "method of multiple hypotheses," which is what was needed to round out the Baconian scheme. This is a method that was put forward by T. C. Chamberlin (15), a geologist at Chicago at the turn of the century, who is best known for his contribution to the Chamberlin-Moulton hypothesis of the origin of the solar system.

Chamberlin says our trouble is that when we make a single hypothesis, we become attached to it.

"The moment one has offered an original explanation for a phenomenon which seems satisfactory, that moment affection for his intellectual child springs into existence, and as the explanation grows into a definite theory his parental affections cluster about his offspring and it grows more and more dear to him. . . . There springs up also unwittingly a pressing of the theory to make it fit the facts and a pressing of the facts to make them fit the theory. . . .

"To avoid this grave danger, the method of multiple working hypotheses is urged. It differs from the simple working hypothesis in that it distributes the effort and divides the affections. . . . Each hypothesis suggests its own criteria, its own means of proof, its own method of developing the truth, and if a group of hypotheses encompass the subject on all sides, the total outcome of means and of methods is full and rich."

Chamberlin thinks the method "leads to certain distinctive habits of mind" and is of prime value in education. "When faithfully followed for a sufficient time, it develops a mode of thought of its own kind which may be designated the habit of complex thought. . . ."

This charming paper deserves to be reprinted in some more accessible journal today, where it could be required reading for every graduate student —and for every professor.

It seems to me that Chamberlin has hit on the explanation—and the cure —for many of our problems in the sciences. The conflict and exclusion of alternatives that is necessary to sharp inductive inference has been all too often a conflict between men, each with his single Ruling Theory. But whenever each man begins to have multiple working hypotheses, it becomes purely a conflict between ideas. It becomes much easier then for each of us to aim every day at conclusive disproofs—at *strong* inference—without either reluctance or combativeness. In fact, when there are multiple hypotheses which are not anyone's "personal property" and when there are crucial experiments to test them, the daily life in the laboratory takes on an interest and excitement it never had, and the students can hardly wait to get to work to see how the detective story will come out. It seems to me that this is the reason for the development of those "distinctive habits of mind" and the "complex thought" that Chamberlin described, the reason for the sharpness, the excitement, the zeal, the teamwork—yes, even international teamwork—in molecular biology and high-energy physics today. What else could be so effective?

When multiple hypotheses become coupled to strong inference, the scientific search becomes an emotional powerhouse as well as an intellectual one.

Unfortunately, I think, there are other areas of science today that are sick by comparison, because they have forgotten the necessity for alternative hypotheses and disproof. Each man has only one branch—or none—on the logical tree, and it twists at random without ever coming to the need for a crucial decision at any point. We can see from the external symptoms that there is something scientifically wrong. The Frozen Method. The Eternal Surveyor. The Never Finished. The Great Man With a Single Hypothesis.

The Little Club of Dependents. The Vendetta. The All-Encompassing Theory Which Can Never Be Falsified.

Some cynics tell a story, which may be apocryphal, about the theoretical chemist who explained to his class.

"And thus we see that the C-Cl bond is longer in the first compound than in the second because the percent of ionic character is smaller."

A voice from the back of the room said, "But Professor X, according to the Table, the C-Cl bond is shorter in the first compound."

"Oh, is it?" said the professor. "Well, that's still easy to understand, because the double-bond character is higher in that compound."

To the extent that this kind of story is accurate, a "theory" of this sort is not a theory at all, because it does not exclude anything. It predicts everything, and therefore does not predict anything. It becomes simply a verbal formula which the graduate student repeats and believes because the professor has said it so often. This is not science, but faith; not theory, but theology. Whether it is hand-waving or number-waving or equation-waving, a theory is not a theory unless it can be disproved. That is, unless it can be falsified by some possible experimental outcome.

In chemistry, the resonance theorists will of course suppose that I am criticizing *them,* while the molecular-orbital theorists will suppose I am criticizing *them.* But their actions—our actions, for I include myself among them—speak for themselves. A failure to agree for 30 years is public advertisement of a failure to disprove.

My purpose here, however, is not to call names but rather to say that we are all sinners, and that in every field and in every laboratory we need to try to formulate multiple alternative hypotheses sharp enough to be capable of disproof.

SYSTEMATIC APPLICATION

I think the work methods of a number of scientists have been testimony to the power of strong inference. Is success not due in many cases to systematic use of Bacon's "surest rules and demonstrations" as much as to rare and unattainable intellectual power? Faraday's famous diary (16), or Fermi's notebooks (3, 17), show how these men believed in the effectiveness of daily steps in applying formal inductive methods to one problem after another.

Within 8 weeks after the discovery of x-rays, Roentgen had identified 17 of their major properties. Every student should read his first paper (18). Each demonstration in it is a little jewel of inductive inference. How else could the proofs have gone so fast, except by a method of maximum effectiveness?

Organic chemistry has been the spiritual home of strong inference from the beginning. Do the bonds alternate in benzene or are they equivalent?

If the first, there should be five disubstituted derivatives; if the second, three. And three it is (*19*). This is a *strong*-inference test—not a matter of measurement, of whether there are grams or milligrams of the products, but a matter of logical alternatives. How else could the tetrahedral carbon atom or the hexagonal symmetry of benzene have been inferred 50 years before the inferences could be confirmed by x-ray and infrared measurement?

We realize that it was out of this kind of atmosphere that Pasteur came to the field of biology. Can anyone doubt that he brought with him a completely different method of reasoning? Every 2 or 3 years he moved to one biological problem after another, from optical activity to the fermentation of beet sugar, to the "diseases" of wine and beer, to the disease of silkworms, to the problem of "spontaneous generation," to the anthrax disease of sheep, to rabies. In each of these fields there were experts in Europe who knew a hundred times as much as Pasteur, yet each time he solved problems in a few months that they had not been able to solve. Obviously it was not encyclopedic knowledge that produced his success, and obviously it was not simply luck, when it was repeated over and over again; it can only have been the systematic power of a special method of exploration. Are bacteria falling in? Make the necks of the flasks S-shaped. Are bacteria sucked in by the partial vacuum? Put in a cotton plug. Week after week his crucial experiments build up the logical tree of exclusions. The drama of strong inference in molecular biology today is only a repetition of Pasteur's story.

The grand scientific syntheses, like those of Newton and Maxwell, are rare and individual achievements that stand outside any rule or method. Nevertheless it is interesting to note that several of the great synthesizers have also shown the strong-inference habit of thought in their other work, as Newton did in the inductive proofs of his *Opticks* and Maxwell did in his experimental proof that three and only three colors are needed in color vision.

A YARDSTICK OF EFFECTIVENESS

I think the evident effectiveness of the systematic use of strong inference suddenly gives us a yardstick for thinking about the effectiveness of scientific methods in general. Surveys, taxonomy, design of equipment, systematic measurements and tables, theoretical computations—all have their proper and honored place, provided they are parts of a chain of precise induction of how nature works. Unfortunately, all too often they become ends in themselves, mere time-serving from the point of view of real scientific advance, a hypertrophied methodology that justifies itself as a lore of respectability.

We praise the "lifetime of study," but in dozens of cases, in every field, what was needed was not a lifetime but rather a few short months or weeks of analytical inductive inference. In any new area we should try, like

Roentgen, to see how fast we can pass from the general survey to analytical inferences. We should try, like Pasteur, to see whether we can reach strong inferences that encyclopedism could not discern.

We speak piously of taking measurements and making small studies that will "add another brick to the temple of science." Most such bricks just lie around the brickyard (20). Tables of constants have their place and value, but the study of one spectrum after another, if not frequently re-evaluated, may become a substitute for thinking, a sad waste of intelligence in a research laboratory, and a mistraining whose crippling effects may last a lifetime.

To paraphrase an old saying, beware of the man of one method or one instrument, either experimental or theoretical. He tends to become method-oriented rather than problem-oriented. The method-oriented man is shackled; the problem-oriented man is at least reaching freely toward what is most important. Strong inference redirects a man to problem-orientation, but it requires him to be willing repeatedly to put aside his last methods and teach himself new ones.

On the other hand, I think that anyone who asks the question about scientific effectiveness will also conclude that much of the mathematicizing in physics and chemistry today is irrelevant if not misleading.

The great value of mathematical formulation is that when an experiment agrees with a calculation to five decimal places, a great many alternative hypotheses are pretty well excluded (though the Bohr theory and the Schrö-dinger theory both predict exactly the same Rydberg constant!). But when the fit is only to two decimal places, or one, it may be a trap for the unwary; it may be no better than any rule-of-thumb extrapolation, and some other kind of qualitative exclusion might be more rigorous for testing the assumptions and more important to scientific understanding than the quantitative fit.

I know that this is like saying that the emperor has no clothes. Today we preach that science is not science unless it is quantitative. We substitute correlations for causal studies, and physical equations for organic reasoning. Measurements and equations are supposed to sharpen thinking, but, in my observation, they more often tend to make the thinking noncausal and fuzzy. They tend to become the object of scientific manipulation instead of auxiliary tests of crucial inferences.

Many—perhaps most—of the great issues of science are qualitative, not quantitative, even in physics and chemistry. Equations and measurements are useful when and only when they are related to proof; but proof or disproof comes first and is in fact strongest when it is absolutely convincing without any quantitative measurement.

Or to say it another way, you can catch phenomena in a logical box or in a mathematical box. The logical box is coarse but strong. The mathematical box is fine-grained but flimsy. The mathematical box is a beautiful way of wrapping up a problem, but it will not hold the phenomena unless they have been caught in a logical box to begin with.

What I am saying is that, in numerous areas that we call science, we have come to like our habitual ways, and our studies that can be continued indefinitely. We measure, we define, we compute, we analyze, but we do not exclude. And this is not the way to use our minds most effectively or to make the fastest progress in solving scientific questions.

Of course it is easy—and all too common—for one scientist to call the others unscientific. My point is not that my particular conclusions here are necessarily correct, but that we have long needed some absolute standard of possible scientific effectiveness by which to measure how well we are succeeding in various areas—a standard that many could agree on and one that would be undistorted by the scientific pressures and fashions of the times and the vested interests and busywork that they develop. It is not public evaluation I am interested in so much as a private measure by which to compare one's own scientific performance with what it might be. I believe that strong inference provides this kind of standard of what the maximum possible scientific effectiveness could be—as well as a recipe for reaching it.

AIDS TO STRONG INFERENCE

How can we learn the method and teach it? It is not difficult. The most important thing is to keep in mind that this kind of thinking is not a lucky knack but a system that *can* be taught and learned. The molecular biologists today are living proof of it. The second thing is to be explicit and formal and regular about it, to devote a half hour or an hour to analytical thinking every day, writing out the logical tree and the alternatives and crucial experiments explicitly in a permanent notebook. I have discussed elsewhere (3) the value of Fermi's notebook method, the effect it had on his colleagues and students, and the testimony that it "can be adopted by anyone with profit."

It is true that it takes great courtesy to teach the method, especially to one's peers—or their students. The strong-inference point of view is so resolutely critical of methods of work and values in science that any attempt to compare specific cases is likely to sound both smug and destructive. Mainly one should try to teach it by example and by exhorting to self-analysis and self-improvement only in general terms, as I am doing here.

But I will mention one severe but useful private test—a touchstone of strong inference—that removes the necessity for third-person criticism, because it is a test that anyone can learn to carry with him for use as needed. It is our old friend the Baconian "exclusion," but I call it "The Question." Obviously it should be applied as much to one's own thinking as to others'. It consists of asking in your own mind, on hearing any scientific explanation or theory put forward, "But sir, what experiment could *dis*prove your hypothesis?"; or, on hearing a scientific experiment described, "But sir, what hypothesis does your experiment *dis*prove?"

This goes straight to the heart of the matter. It forces everyone to refocus on the central question of whether there is or is not a testable scientific step forward.

If such a question were asked aloud, many a supposedly great scientist would sputter and turn livid and would want to throw the questioner out, as a hostile witness! Such a man is less than he appears, for he is obviously not accustomed to think in terms of alternative hypotheses and crucial experiments for himself; and one might also wonder about the state of science in the field he is in. But who knows?—the question might educate him, and his field too!

On the other hand, I think that throughout most of molecular biology and nuclear physics the response to The Question would be to outline immediately not one but several tests to disprove the hypothesis—and it would turn out that the speaker already had two or three graduate students working on them!

I almost think that government agencies could make use of this kind of touchstone. It is not true that all science is equal, or that we cannot justly compare the effectiveness of scientists by any method other than a mutual-recommendation system. The man to watch, the man to put your money on, is not the man who wants to make "a survey" or a "more detailed study" but the man with the notebook, the man with the alternative hypotheses and the crucial experiments, the man who knows how to answer your Question of disproof and is already working on it.

There are some really hard problems, some high-information problems, ahead of us in several fields, problems of photosynthesis, of cellular organization, of the molecular structure and organization of the nervous system, not to mention some of our social and international problems. It seems to me that the method of most rapid progress in such complex areas, the most effective way of using our brains, is going to be to set down explicitly at each step just what the question is, and what all the alternatives are, and then to set up crucial experiments to try to disprove some. Problems of this complexity, if they can be solved at all, can be solved only by men generating and excluding possibilities with maximum effectiveness, to obtain a high degree of information per unit time—men willing to work a little bit at thinking.

When whole groups of us begin to concentrate like that, I believe we may see the molecular-biology phenomenon repeated over and over again, with order-of-magnitude increases in the rate of scientific understanding in almost every field.

References and Notes

1. A. M. Weinberg. *Minerva* 1963, 159 (winter 1963) ; *Phys. Today* 17, 42 (1964).

2. G. Polya, *Mathematics and Plausible Reasoning* (Princeton Univ. Press, Princeton N.J., 1954), vol. 1, *Induction and Analogy in Mathematics*; vol. 2, *Patterns of Plausible Inference.*

3. J. R. Platt. *The Excitement of Science* (Houghton Mifflin, Boston, 1962) ; see especially chapters 7 and 8.

4. J. D. Watson and F. H. C. Crick. *Nature* 171, 737 (1953).

5. M. Meselson and F. Stahl. *Proc. Natl. Acad. Sci. U.S.* 44, 671 (1958).

6. A. Rich, in *Biophysical Science: A Study Program*, J. S. Oneley *et al.*, Eds. (Wiley, New York, 1959), p. 191.

7. S. Benzork. *Proc. Natl. Acad. Sci. U.S.* 45, 607 (1959).

8. J. Lederberg, *Science* 129, 1649 (1959).

9. P. F. Davison, D. Freifelder, B. W. Holloway, *J. Mol. Biol.* 8, 1 (1964.)

10. R. L. Garwin, L. M. Lederman, M. Weinrich, *Phys. Rev.* 105, 1415 (1957).

11. W. A. H. Rushton, personal communication.

12. See G. F. Chew, M. Gell-Mann, A. H. Rosenfeld, *Sci. Am.* 210, 74 (Feb. 1964) ; *ibid.* 210, 60 (Apr. 1964) ; *ibid.* 210, 54 (June 1964).

13. F. Bacon, *The New Organon and Related Writings* (Liberal Arts Press, New York, 1969), especially pp. 98, 112, 151, 156, 196.

14. K. R. Popper, *The Logic of Scientific Discovery* (Basic Books, New York, 1959), p. 41. A modified view is given by T. S. Kuhn, *The Structure of Scientific Revolutions* (Univ. of Chicago Press, Chicago, 1962), p. 146; it does not, I believe, invalidate any of these conclusions.

15. T. C. Chamberlin, *J. Geol.* 5, 837 (1897). I am indebted to Professors Preston Cloud and Bryce Crawford, Jr., of the University of Minnesota for correspondence on this article and a classroom reprint of it.

16. M. Faraday, *Faraday's Diary 1820–62* (Bell, London, 1932–36).

17. H. L. Anderson and S. K. Allison, *Rev. Mod. Phys.* 27, 273 (1955).

18. E. C. Watson [*Am. J. Phys.* 13, 281 (1945)] gives an English translation of both of Roentgen's first papers, on x-rays.

19. See G. W. Wheland, *Advanced Organic Chemistry* (Wiley, New York, 1949), chapter 4, for numerous such examples.

20. B. K. Forscher, *Science* 142, 339 (1963).

C. Mill's Methods of Experimental Inquiry

John Stuart Mill's methods of experimental inquiry were designed to determine when one could infer from the data to one particular kind of generalization, a causal generalization. Although the methods are presented as simple sure-fire formulas, Mill himself exhibits reservations about them both in the explanatory material and in the later sections on plurality of causes and intermixture of effects. He concludes, in the material we present here, by stating a general preference for what he calls the "Deductive Method," which incorporates, but differs from, the experimental methods he describes. His comments about his "deductive method" are reproduced in the next section, "Hypothetico-Deductivism and Deductive Explanation."

In the development of his reservations, Mill, interestingly enough, mentions the two rough criteria for induction (bulk and variety of evidence) that were offered by Strawson in the selection under the title "Generalization" presented earlier. Mill says, "It is only when the instances, being indefinitely *multiplied* and *varied,* continue to suggest the same result that this result acquires any high degree of independent value."[1] (Emphasis added.)

Some readily available discussions of Mill's methods are *The Encyclopedia of Philosophy*[2] and Cohen and Nagel's *An Introduction to Logic and Scientific Method.*[3]

[1] John Stuart Mill, *System of Logic* (London: Longman's, Green, and Co., 1906), p. 286.

[2] Paul Edwards (Ed.), *The Encyclopedia of Philosophy*, Volume V (New York: The Macmillan Company and The Free Press, 1967), pp. 324–332.

[3] Morris R. Cohen and Ernest Nagel, *An Introduction to Logic and Scientific Method* (New York: Harcourt Brace and Co., 1934), pp. 249–267.

21. METHODS OF EXPERIMENTAL INQUIRY

John Stuart Mill

§ 1. The simplest and most obvious modes of singling out from among the circumstances which precede or follow a phenomenon those with which it is really connected by an invariable law are two in number. One is, by comparing together different instances in which the phenomenon occurs. The other is, by comparing instances in which the phenomenon does occur, with instances in other respects similar in which it does not. These two methods may be respectively denominated the Method of Agreement and the Method of Difference.

In illustrating these methods, it will be necessary to bear in mind the twofold character of inquiries into the laws of phenomena, which may be either inquiries into the cause of a given effect, or into the effects or properties of a given cause. We shall consider the methods in their application to either order of investigation, and shall draw our examples equally from both.

We shall denote antecedents by the large letters of the alphabet, and the consequents corresponding to them by the small. Let A, then, be an agent or cause, and let the object of our inquiry be to ascertain what are the effects of this cause. If we can either find or produce the agent A in such varieties of circumstances that the different cases have no circumstance in common except A, then whatever effect we find to be produced in all our trials is indicated as the effect of A. Suppose, for example, that A is tried along with B and C, and that the effect is *a b c*; and suppose that A is next

SOURCE. Reprinted from *A System of Logic*, Vol. 1, by John Stuart Mill, Longman's, Green, & Co., London, 1906.

tried with D and E, but without B and C, and that the effect is *a d e*. Then we may reason thus: *b* and *c* are not effects of A, for they were not produced by it in the second experiment; nor are *d* and *e*, for they were not produced in the first. Whatever is really the effect of A must have been produced in both instances; now this condition is fulfilled by no circumstance except *a*. The phenomenon *a* cannot have been the effect of B or C, since it was produced where they were not; nor of D or E, since it was produced where they were not. Therefore it is the effect of A.

For example, let the antecedent A be the contact of an alkaline substance and an oil. This combination being tried under several varieties of circumstances, resembling each other in nothing else, the results agree in the production of a greasy and detersive or saponaceous substance: it is therefore concluded that the combination of an oil and an alkali causes the production of a soap. It is thus we inquire, *by* the Method of Agreement, into the effect of a given cause.

In a similar manner we may inquire into the cause of a given effect. Let *a* be the effect. Here, as shown in the last chapter, we have only the resource of observation without experiment: we cannot take a phenomenon of which we know not the origin, and try to find its mode of production by producing it: if we succeeded in such a random trial it could only be by accident. But if we can observe *a* in two different combinations, *a b c* and *a d e*; and if we know, or can discover, that the antecedent circumstances in these cases respectively were A B C and A D E, we may conclude by a reasoning similar to that in the preceding example, that A is the antecedent connected with the consequent *a* by a law of causation. B and C, we may say, cannot be causes of *a*, since on its second occurrence they were not present; nor are D and E, for they were not present on its first occurrence. A, alone of the five circumstances, was found among the antecedents of *a* in both instances.

For example, let the effect *a* be crystallization. We compare instances in which bodies are known to assume crystalline structure, but which have no other point of agreement; and we find them to have one, and, as far as we can observe, only one, antecedent in common: the deposition of a solid matter from a liquid state, either a state of fusion or of solution. We conclude, therefore, that the solidification of a substance from a liquid state is an invariable antecedent of its crystallization.

In this example we may go farther, and say, it is not only the invariable antecedent, but the cause, or at least the proximate event which completes the cause. For in this case we are able, after detecting the antecedent A, to produce it artificially, and by finding that *a* follows it, verify the result of our induction. The importance of thus reversing the proof was strikingly manifested when by keeping a phial of water charged with siliceous particles undisturbed for years, a chemist (I believe Dr. Wollaston) succeeded in obtaining crystals of quartz; and in the equally interesting experiment in which Sir James Hall produced artificial marble by the cooling of its materials from fusion under immense pressure; two admirable examples of the light which may be thrown upon the most secret processes of Nature by well-contrived interrogation of her.

But if we cannot artificially produce the phenomenon A, the conclusion that it is the cause of *a* remains subject to very considerable doubt. Though an invariable, it may not be the unconditional antecedent of *a*, but may precede it as day precedes night or night day. This uncertainty arises from the impossibility of assuring ourselves that A is the *only* immediate antecedent common to both the instances. If we could be certain of having ascertained all the invariable antecedents, we might be sure that the unconditional invariable antecedent or cause must be found somewhere among them. Unfortunately it is hardly ever possible to ascertain all the antecedents, unless the phenomenon is one which we can produce artificially. Even then, the difficulty is merely lightened, not removed: men knew how to raise water in pumps long before they adverted to what was really the operating circumstance in the means they employed, namely, the pressure of the atmosphere on the open surface of the water. It is, however, much easier to analyse completely a set of arrangements made by ourselves, than the whole complex mass of the agencies which nature happens to be exerting at the moment of the production of a given phenomenon. We may overlook some of the material circumstances in an experiment with an electrical machine; but we shall, at the worst, be better acquainted with them than with those of a thunderstorm.

The mode of discovering and proving laws of nature, which we have now examined, proceeds on the following axiom. Whatever circumstances can be excluded, without prejudice to the phenomenon, or can be absent notwithstanding its presence, is not connected with it in the way of causation. The casual circumstances being thus eliminated, if only one remains, that one is the cause which we are in search of: if more than one, they either are, or contain among them, the cause; and so, *mutatis mutandis*, of the effect. As this method proceeds by comparing different instances to ascertain in what they agree, I have termed it the Method of Agreement; and we may adopt as its regulating principle the following canon:

FIRST CANON.

If two or more instances of the phenomenon under investigation have only one circumstance in common, the circumstance in which alone all the instances agree is the cause (or effect) of the given phenomenon.

Quitting for the present the Method of Agreement, to which we shall almost immediately return, we proceed to a still more potent instrument of the investigation of nature, the Method of Difference.

§ 2. In the Method of Agreement, we endeavoured to obtain instances which agreed in the given circumstance but differed in every other: in the present method we require, on the contrary, two instances resembling one another in every other respect, but differing in the presence or absnce of the phenomenon we wish to study. If our object be to discover the effects of an agent A, we must procure A in some set of ascertained circumstances, as A B C, and having noted the effects produced, compare them with the effect of the remaining circumstances B C, when A is absent. If the effect of A B C is *a b c*, and the effect of B C, *b c*, it is evident that the effect of A is *a*. So again, if we begin at the other end, and desire to investigate the cause of an effect *a*, we must select an instance, as *a b c*, in which the effect occurs, and in which the antecedents were A B C, and we must look out for another instance in which the remaining circumstances, *b c*, occur without *a*. If the antecedents, in that instance, are B C, we know that the cause of *a* must be A: either A alone, or A in conjunction with some of the other circumstances present.

It is scarcely necessary to give examples of a logical process to which we owe almost all the inductive conclusions we draw in early life. When a man is shot through the heart, it is by this method we know that it was the gunshot which killed him: for he was in the fulness of life immediately before, all circumstances being the same, except the wound.

The axioms implied in this method are evidently the following. Whatever antecedent cannot be excluded without preventing the phenomenon, is the cause, or a condition of that phenomenon: Whatever consequent can be excluded, with no other difference in the antecedents than the absence of a particular one, is the effect of that one. Instead of comparing different instances of a phenomenon, to discover in what they agree, this method compares an instance of its occurrence with an instance of its non-occurrence, to discover in what they differ. The canon which is the regulating principle of the Method of Difference may be expressed as follows:—

SECOND CANON.

If an instance in which the phenomenon under investigation occurs, and an instance in which it does not occur, have every circumstance in common save one, that one occurring only in the former; the circumstance in which alone the two instances differ is the effect, or the cause, or an indispensable part of the cause, of the phenomenon.

§ 3. The two methods which we have now stated have many features of resemblance, but there are also many distinctions between them. Both are methods of *elimination*. This term (employed in the theory of equations to denote the process by which one after another of the elements of a question is excluded, and the solution made to depend on the relation between the remaining elements only) is well suited to express the operation, analogous to this, which has been understood since the time of Bacon to be the foundation of experimental inquiry, namely, the successive exclusion of the various circumstances which are found to accompany a phenomenon in a given instance, in order to ascertain what are those among them which can be absent consistently with the existence of the phenomenon. The Method of Agreement stands on the ground that whatever can be eliminated is not connected with the phenomenon by any law. The Method of Difference has for its foundation, that whatever cannot be eliminated is connected with the phenomenon by a law.

Of these methods, that of Difference is more particularly a method of artificial experiment; while that of Agreement is more especially the resource employed where experimentation is impossible. A few reflections will prove the fact, and point out the reason of it.

It is inherent in the peculiar character of the Method of Difference that the nature of the combinations which it requires is much more strictly defined than in the Method of Agreement. The two instances which are to be compared with one another must be exactly similar in all circumstances except the one which we are attempting to investigate: they must be in the relation of A B C and B C, or of *a b c* and *b c*. It is true that this similarity of circumstances needs not extend to such as are already known to be immaterial to the result. And in the case of most phenomena we learn at once, from the commonest experience, that most of the co-existent phenomena of the universe may be either present or absent without affecting the given phenomenon; or, if present, are present indifferently when the phenomenon does not happen and when it does. Still, even limiting the identity which is required between the two instances, *A B C* and *B C*, to such circumstances as are not already known to be indifferent; it is very seldom that nature affords two instances, of which we can be assured that they stand in this precise relation to one another. In the spontaneous operations of nature there is generally such complication and such obscurity, they are mostly either on so overwhelmingly large or on so inaccessibly minute a scale, we are so ignorant of a great part of the facts which really take place, and even those of which we are not ignorant are so multitudinous, and therefore so seldom exactly alike in any two cases, that a spontaneous experiment, of the kind required by the Method of Difference, is commonly not to be found. When, on the contrary, we obtain a phenomenon by an artificial experiment, a pair of instances such as the method requires is obtained almost as a matter of course, provided the process does not last a long time. A certain state of surrounding circumstances existed before we commenced the experiment; this is B C. We then introduce A; say, for instance, by merely bringing an object from another part of the room, before there has been time for any change in the other elements. It is, in short, (as M. Comte observes,) the very nature of an experiment to introduce into the pre-existing state of circumstances a change perfectly definite. We choose a previous state of things with which we are well acquainted, so that no unforeseen alteration in that state is likely to pass unobserved; and into this we introduce, as rapidly as possible, the phenomenon which we wish to study; so that in general we are entitled to feel complete assurance that the pre-existing state, and the state which we have produced, differ in nothing except the presence or absence of that phenomenon. If a bird is taken from a cage, and instantly plunged into carbonic acid gas, the experimentalist may be fully assured (at all events after one or two repetitions) that no circumstance capable of causing suffocation had supervened in the interim, except the change from immersion in the atmosphere to immersion in carbonic acid gas. There is one doubt, indeed, which may remain in some cases of this description; the effect may have been produced not by the change, but by the means employed to produce the change. The possibility, however, of this last supposition generally admits of being conclusively tested by other experiments. It thus appears that in the study of the various kinds of phenomena which we can, by our voluntary agency, modify or control, we can in general satisfy the requisitions of the Method of Difference; but that by the spontaneous operations of nature those requisitions are seldom fulfilled.

The reverse of this is the case with the Method of Agreement. We do not here require instances of so special and determinate a kind. Any instances whatever, in which nature presents us with a phenomenon, may be examined for the purposes of this method; and if all such instances agree in anything, a conclusion of considerable value is already attained. We can seldom, indeed, be sure that the one point of agreement is the only one; but this ignorance does not, as in the Method of Difference, vitiate the conclusion; the certainty of the result, as far as it goes, is not affected. We have ascertained one invariable antecedent or consequent, however many other invariable antecedents or consequents may still remain unascertained. If A B C, A D E, A F G, are all equally followed by a, then a is an invariable consequent of A. If a b c, a d e, a f g, all number A among their antecedents, then A is connected as an antecedent, by some invariable law, with a. But to determine whether this invariable antecedent is a cause, or this invariable consequent an effect, we must be able, in addition, to produce the one by means of the other; or, at least, to obtain that which alone constitutes our assurance of having produced anything, namely, an instance in which the effect, a, has come into existence, with no other change in the pre-existing circumstances than the addition of A. And this, if we can do it, is an application of the Method of Difference, not of the Method of Agreement.

It thus appears to be by the Method of Difference alone that we can ever, in the way of direct experience, arrive with certainty at causes. The Method of Agreement leads only to laws of phenomena, (as some writers call them, but improperly, since laws of causation are also laws of phenomena,) that is, to uniformities, which either are not laws of causation, or in which the question of causation must for the present remain undecided. The Method of Agreement is chiefly to be resorted to as a means of suggesting applications of the Method of Difference, (as in the last example the comparison of A B C, A D E, A F G, suggested that A was the antecedent on which to try the experiment whether it could produce a,) or as an inferior resource in case the Method of Difference is impracticable; which, as we before showed, generally arises from the impossibility of artificially producing the phenomena. And hence it is that the Method of Agreement, though applicable in principle to either case, is more emphatically the method of investigation on those subjects where artificial experimentation is impossible; because on those it is generally our only resource of a directly inductive nature; while, in the phenomena which we can produce at pleasure, the Method of Difference generally affords a more efficacious process, which will ascertain causes as well as mere laws.

§ 4. There are, however, many cases in which, though our power of producing the phenomenon is complete, the Method of Difference either cannot be made available at all, or not without a previous employment of the Method of Agreement. This occurs when the agency by which we can produce the phenomenon is not that of one single antecedent, but a combination of antecedents, which we have no power of separating from each other and exhibiting apart. For instance, suppose the subject of inquiry to be the cause of the double refraction of light. We can produce this phenomenon at pleasure by employing any one of the many substances which are known to refract light in that peculiar manner. But, if, taking one of those substances, an Iceland spar, for example, we wish to determine on which of the properties of Iceland spar this remarkable phenomenon depends, we can make no use for that purpose of the Method of Difference; for we cannot find another substance precisely resembling Iceland spar except in some one property. The only mode, therefore, of prosecuting this inquiry is that afforded by the Method of Agreement; by which, in fact, through a comparison of all the known substances which have the property of doubly refracting light, it was ascertained that they agree in the circumstance of being crystalline substances; and though the converse does not hold, though all crystalline substances have not the property of double refraction, it was concluded, with reason, that there is a real connection between these two properties; that either crystalline structure, or the cause which gives rise to that structure, is one of the conditions of double refraction.

Out of this employment of the Method of Agreement arises a peculiar modification of that method, which is sometimes of great avail in the investigation of nature. In cases similar to the above, in which it is not possible to obtain the precise pair of instances which our second canon requires— instances agreeing in every antecedent except A, or in every consequent except *a*—we may yet be able, by a double employment of the Method of Agreement, to discover in what the instances which contain A or *a* differ from those which do not.

If we compare various instances in which *a* occurs, and find that they all have in common the circumstance A, and (as far as can be observed) no other circumstance, the Method of Agreement, so far, bears testimony to a connection between A and *a*. In order to convert this evidence of connection into proof of causation by the direct Method of Difference, we ought to be able, in some one of these instances, as, for example, A B C, to leave out A, and observe whether by doing so *a* is prevented. Now supposing (what is often the case) that we are not able to try this decisive experiment, yet, provided we can by any means discover what would be its result if we could try it, the advantage will be the same. Suppose, then, that as we previously examined a variety of instances in which *a* occurred, and found them to agree in containing A, so we now observe a variety of instances in which *a* does not occur, and find them agree in not containing A; which establishes, by the Method of Agreement, the same connection between the absence of A and the absence of *a*, which was before established between their presence. As, then, it had been shown that whenever A is present *a* is present, so it being now shown that when A is taken away *a* is removed along with it, we have by the one proposition A B C, *a b c*, by the other B C, *b c*, the positive and negative instances which the Method of Difference requires.

This method may be called the Indirect Method of Difference, or the Joint Method of Agreement and Difference, and consists in a double employment of the Method of Agreement, each proof being independent of the other, and corroborating it. But it is not equivalent to a proof by the direct Method of Difference. For the requisitions of the Method of Difference are not satisfied unless we can be quite sure either that the instances affirmative of *a* agree in no antecedent whatever but A, or that the instances negative of *a* agree in nothing but the negative of A. Now if it were possible, which it never is, to have this assurance, we should not need the joint method; for either of the two sets of instances separately would then be sufficient to prove causation. This indirect method, therefore, can only be regarded as a great extension and improvement of the Method of Agreement, but not as participating in the more cogent nature of the Method of Difference. The following may be stated as its canon:—

THIRD CANON.

If two or more instances in which the phenomenon occurs have only one circumstance in common, while two or more instances in which it does not occur have nothing in common save the absence of that circumstance, the circumstance in which alone the two sets of instances differ is the effect, or the cause, or an indispensable part of the cause, of the phenomenon.

We shall presently see that the Joint Method of Agreement and Difference constitutes, in another respect not yet adverted to, an improvement upon the common Method of Agreement, namely, in being unaffected by a characteristic imperfection of that method, the nature of which still remains to be pointed out. But as we cannot enter into this exposition without introducing a new element of complexity into this long and intricate discussion, I shall postpone it to a subsequent chapter, and shall at once proceed to a statement of two other methods, which will complete the enumeration of the means which mankind possess for exploring the laws of nature by specific observation and experience.

§ 5. The first of these has been aptly denominated the Method of Residues. Its principle is very simple. Subducting from any given phenomenon all the portions which, by virtue of preceding inductions, can be assigned to known causes, the remainder will be the effect of the antecedents which had been overlooked, or of which the effect was as yet an unknown quantity.

Suppose, as before, that we have the antecedents A B C, followed by the consequents *a b c*, and that by previous inductions (founded, we will suppose, on the Method of Difference) we have ascertained the causes of some of these effects, or the effects of some of these causes; and are thence apprised that the effect of A is *a*, and that the effect of B is *b*. Subtracting the sum of these effects from the total phenomenon, there remains *c*, which now, without any fresh experiments, we may know to be the effect of C. This Method of Residues is in truth a peculiar modification of the Method of Difference. If the instance A B C, *a b c*, could have been compared with a single instance A B, *a b*, we should have proved C to be the cause of *c*, by the common process of the Method of Difference. In the present case, however, instead of a single instance A B, we have had to study separately the causes

A and B, and to infer from the effects which they produce separately what effect they must produce in the case A B C where they act together. Of the two instances, therefore, which the Method of Difference requires,—the one positive, the other negative,—the negative one, or that in which the given phenomenon is absent, is not the direct result of observation and experiment, but has been arrived at by deduction. As one of the forms of the Method of Difference, the Method of Residues partakes of its rigorous certainty, provided the previous inductions, those which gave the effects of A and B, were obtained by the same infallible method, and provided we are certain that C is the *only* antecedent to which the residual phenomenon *c* can be referred; the only agent of which we had not already calculated and subducted the effect. But as we can never be quite certain of this, the evidence derived from the Method of Residues is not complete unless we can obtain C artificially and try it separately, or unless its agency, when once suggested, can be accounted for, and proved deductively, from known laws.

Even with these reservations, the Method of Residues is one of the most important among our instruments of discovery. Of all the methods of investigating laws of nature, this is the most fertile in unexpected results: often informing us of sequences in which neither the cause nor the effect were sufficiently conspicuous to attract of themselves the attention of observers. The agent C may be an obscure circumstance, not likely to have been perceived unless sought for, nor likely to have been sought for until attention had been awakened by the insufficiency of the obvious causes to account for the whole of the effect. And *c* may be so disguised by its intermixture with *a* and *b*, that it would scarcely have presented itself spontaneously as a subject of separate study. Of these uses of the method we shall presently cite some remarkable examples. The canon of the Method of Residues is as follows:—

FOURTH CANON.

Subduct from any phenomenon such part as is known by previous inductions to be the effect of certain antecedents, and the residue of the phenomenon is the effect of the remaining antecedents.

§ 6. There remains a class of laws which it is impracticable to ascertain by any of the three methods which I have attempted to characterize, namely, the laws of those Permanent Causes, or indestructible natural agents, which it is impossible either to exclude or to isolate; which we can neither hinder from being present, nor contrive that they shall be present alone. It would appear at first sight that we could by no means separate the effects of these agents from the effects of those other phenomena with which they cannot be prevented from co-existing. In respect, indeed, to most of the permanent causes, no such difficulty exists; since, though we cannot eliminate them as co-existing facts, we can eliminate them as influencing agents, by simply trying our experiment in a local situation beyond the limits of their influence. The pendulum, for example, has its oscillations disturbed by the vicinity of a mountain: we remove the pendulum to a sufficient distance from the mountain, and the disturbance ceases; from these data we can determine by the Method of Difference the amount of effect due to the mountain; and beyond a certain distance everything goes on precisely as it would do if the mountain exercised no influence whatever, which, accordingly, we, with sufficient reason, conclude to be the fact.

The difficulty, therefore, in applying the methods already treated of to determine the effects of Permanent Causes, is confined to the cases in which it is impossible for us to get out of the local limits of their influence. The pendulum can be removed from the influence of the mountain, but it cannot be removed from the influence of the earth: we cannot take away the earth from the pendulum, nor the pendulum from the earth, to ascertain whether it would continue to vibrate if the action which the earth exerts upon it were withdrawn. On what evidence, then, do we ascribe its vibrations to the earth's influence? Not on any sanctioned by the Method of Difference; for one of the two instances, the negative instance, is wanting. Nor by the Method of Agreement: for though all pendulums agree in this, that during their oscillations the earth is always present, why may we not as well ascribe the phenomenon to the sun, which is equally a co-existent fact in all the experiments? It is evident that to establish even so simple a fact of causation as this, there was required some method over and above those which we have yet examined.

As another example, let us take the phenomenon Heat. Independently of all hypothesis as to the real nature of the agency so called, this fact is certain, that we are unable to exhaust any body of the whole of its heat. It is equally certain that no one ever perceived heat not emanating from a body. Being unable, then, to separate Body and Heat, we cannot effect such a variation of circumstances as the foregoing three methods require; we cannot ascertain, by those methods, what portion of the phenomena exhibited by any body is due to the heat contained in it. If we could observe a body with its heat, and the same body entirely divested of heat, the Method of Difference would show the effect due to the heat, apart from that due to the body. If we could observe heat under circumstances agreeing in nothing but heat, and therefore not characterized also by the presence of a body, we could ascertain the effects of heat, from an instance of heat with a body and an instance of heat without a body, by the Method of Agreement; or we could determine by the Method of Difference what effect was due to the body, when the remainder which was due to the heat would be given by the Method of Residues. But we can do none of these things; and without them the application of any of the three methods to the solution of this problem would be illusory. It would be idle, for instance, to attempt to ascertain the effect of heat by subtracting from the phenomena exhibited by a body all that is due to its other properties; for as we have never been able to observe any bodies without a portion of heat in them, effects due to that heat might form a part of the very results which we were affecting to subtract in order that the effect of heat might be shown by the residue.

If, therefore, there were no other methods of experimental investigation than these three, we should be unable to determine the effects due to heat as a cause. But we have still a resource. Though we cannot exclude an antecedent altogether, we may be able to produce, or nature may produce for us, some modification in it. By a modification is here meant a change in it, not amounting to its total removal. If some modification in the antecedent A is always followed by a change in the consequent *a*, the other consequents *b* and *c* remaining the same; or *vice versa*, if every change in *a* is found to have been preceded by some modification in A, none being observable in any of the other antecedents; we may safely conclude that *a* is, wholly or in part, an effect traceable to A, or at least in some way connected with it through causation. For example, in the case of heat, though we cannot expel it altogether from any body, we can modify it in quantity, we can increase or diminish it; and doing so, we find by the various methods of experimentation or observation already treated of, that such increase or diminution of heat is followed by expansion or contraction of the body. In this manner we arrive at the conclusion, otherwise unattainable by us, that one of the effects of heat is to enlarge the dimensions of bodies; or what is the same thing in other words, to widen the distances between their particles.

A change in a thing, not amounting to its total removal, that is, a change which leaves it still the same thing it was, must be a change either in its quantity, or in some of its variable relations to other things, of which variable relations the principal is its position in space. In the previous example, the modification which was produced in the antecedent was an alteration in its quantity. Let us now suppose the question to be, what influence the moon exerts on the surface of the earth. We cannot try an experiment in the absence of the moon, so as to observe what terrestrial phenomena her annihilation would put an end to; but when we find that all the variations in the *position* of the moon are followed by corresponding variations in the time and place of high water, the place being always either the part of the earth which is nearest to, or that which is most remote from, the moon, we have ample evidence that the moon is, wholly or partially, the cause which determines the tides. It very commonly happens, as it does in this instance, that the variations of an effect are correspondent, or analogous, to those of its cause; as the moon moves farther towards the east, the high-water point does the same: but this is not an indispensable condition, as may be seen in the same example; for along with that high-water point there is at the same instant another high-water point diametrically opposite to it, and which, therefore, of necessity, moves towards the west, as the moon, followed by the nearer of the tide-waves, advances towards the east: and yet both these motions are equally effects of the moon's motion.

That the oscillations of the pendulum are caused by the earth is proved by similar evidence. Those oscillations take place between equidistant points on the two sides of a line, which, being perpendicular to the earth, varies with every variation in the earth's position, either in space or relatively to the object. Speaking accurately, we only know by the method now characterized that all terrestrial bodies tend to the earth, and not to some unknown fixed point lying in the same direction. In every twenty-four hours, by the earth's rotation, the line drawn from the body at right angles to the earth coincides successively with all the radii of a circle, and in the course of six months the place of that circle varies by nearly two hundred millions of miles; yet in all these changes of the earth's position, the line in which bodies tend to fall continues to be directed towards it: which proves that terrestrial gravity is directed to the earth, and not, as was once fancied by some, to a fixed point of space.

The method by which these results were obtained may be termed the Method of Concomitant Variations: it is regulated by the following canon:—

FIFTH CANON.

Whatever phenomenon varies in any manner whenever another phenomenon varies in some particular manner, is either a cause or an effect of that phenomenon, or is connected with it through some fact of causation.

The last clause is subjoined because it by no means follows, when two phenomena accompany each other in their variations, that the one is cause and the other effect. The same thing may, and indeed must happen, supposing them to be two different effects of a common cause: and by this method alone it would never be possible to ascertain which of the suppositions is the true one. The only way to solve the doubt would be that which we have so often adverted to, viz. by endeavouring to ascertain whether we can produce the one set of variations by means of the other. In the case of heat, for example, by increasing the temperature of a body we increase its bulk, but by increasing its bulk we do not increase its temperature; on the contrary, (as in the rarefaction of air under the receiver of an air-pump,) we generally diminish it: therefore heat is not an effect, but a cause, of increase of bulk. If we cannot ourselves produce the variations, we must endeavour, though it is an attempt which is seldom successful, to find them produced by nature in some case in which the pre-existing circumstances are perfectly known to us.

It is scarcely necessary to say, that in order to ascertain the uniform concomitants of variations in the effect with variations in the cause, the same precautions must be used as in any other case of the determination of an invariable sequence. We must endeavour to retain all the other antecedents unchanged, while that particular one is subjected to the requisite series of variations; or, in other words, that we may be warranted in inferring causation from concomitance of variations, the concomitance itself must be proved by the Method of Difference.

It might at first appear that the Method of Concomitant Variations assumes a new axiom, or law of causation in general, namely, that every modification of the cause is followed by a change in the effect. And it does usually happen that when a phenomenon A causes a phenomenon a, any variation in the quantity or in the various relations of A is uniformly followed by a variation in the quantity or relations of a. To take a familiar instance, that of gravitation. The sun causes a certain tendency to motion in the earth; here we have cause and effect; but that tendency is *towards* the sun, and therefore varies in direction as the sun varies in the relation of position; and moreover the tendency varies in intensity, in a certain numerical correspondence to the sun's distance from the earth, that is, according to another relation of the sun. Thus we see that there is not only an invariable connection between the sun and the earth's gravitation, but that two of the relations of the sun, its position with respect to the earth and its distance from the earth, are invariably connected as antecedents with the quantity and direction of the earth's gravitation. The cause of the earth's gravitating at all is simply the sun; but the cause of its gravitating with a given intensity and in a given direction is the existence of the sun in a given direction and at a given distance. It is not strange that a modified cause, which is in truth a different cause, should produce a different effect.

Although it is for the most part true that a modification of the cause is followed by a modification of the effect, the Method of Concomitant Variations does not, however, presuppose this as an axiom. It only requires the converse proposition, that anything on whose modifications, modifications of an effect are invariably consequent, must be the cause (or connected with the cause) of that effect; a proposition, the truth of which is evident; for if the thing itself had no influence on the effect, neither could the modifications of the thing have any influence. If the stars have no power over the fortunes of mankind, it is implied in the very terms that the conjunctions or oppositions of different stars can have no such power.

Although the most striking applications of the Method of Concomitant

Variations take place in the cases in which the Method of Difference, strictly so called, is impossible, its use is not confined to those cases; it may often usefully follow after the Method of Difference, to give additional precision to a solution which that has found. When by the Method of Difference it has first been ascertained that a certain object produces a certain effect, the Method of Concomitant Variations may be usefully called in to determine according to what law the quantity or the different relations of the effect follow those of the cause.

§ 7. The case in which this method admits of the most extensive employment is that in which the variations of the cause are variations of quantity. Of such variations we may in general affirm with safety that they will be attended not only with variations, but with similar variations of the effect: the proposition, that more of the cause is followed by more of the effect, being a corollary from the principle of the Composition of Causes, which, as we have seen, is the general rule of causation; cases of the opposite description, in which causes change their properties on being conjoined with one another, being, on the contrary, special and exceptional. Suppose, then, that when A changes in quantity, a also changes in quantity, and in such a manner that we can trace the numerical relation which the changes of the one bear to such changes of the other as take place within our limits of observation. We may then, with certain precautions, safely conclude that the same numerical relation will hold beyond those limits. If, for instance, we find that when A is double, a is double; that when A is treble or quadruple, a is treble or quadruple; we may conclude that if A were a half or a third, a would be a half or a third; and finally, that if A were annihilated, a would be annihilated; and that a is wholly the effect of A, or wholly the effect of the same cause with A. And so with any other numerical relation according to which A and a would vanish simultaneously; as, for instance, if a were proportional to the square of A. If, on the other hand, a is not wholly the effect of A, but yet varies when A varies, it is probably a mathematical function not of A alone, but of A and something else; its changes, for example, may be such as would occur if part of it remained constant, or varied on some other principle, and the remainder varied in some numerical relation to the variations of A. In that case, when A diminishes, a will be seen to approach not towards zero, but towards some other limit; and when the series of variations is such as to indicate what that limit is, if constant, or the law of its variation if variable, the limit will exactly measure how much of a is the effect of some other and independent cause, and the remainder will be the effect of A (or of the cause of A).

These conclusions, however, must not be drawn without certain precautions. In the first place, the possibility of drawing them at all manifestly supposes that we are acquainted not only with the variations, but with the absolute quantities both of A and *a*. If we do not know the total quantities, we cannot, of course, determine the real numerical relation according to which those quantities vary. It is therefore an error to conclude, as some have concluded, that because increase of heat expands bodies, that is, increases the distance between their particles, therefore the distance is wholly the effect of heat, and that if we could entirely exhaust the body of its heat, the particles would be in complete contact. This is no more than a guess, and of the most hazardous sort, not a legitimate induction; for since we neither know how much heat there is in any body, nor what is the real distance between any two of its particles, we cannot judge whether the contraction of the distance does or does not follow the diminution of the quantity of heat according to such a numerical relation that the two quantities would vanish simultaneously.

In contrast with this, let us consider a case in which the absolute quantities are known—the case contemplated in the first law of motion, viz. that all bodies in motion continue to move in a straight line with uniform velocity until acted upon by some new force. This assertion is in open opposition to first appearances; all terrestrial objects, when in motion, gradually abate their velocity and at last stop; which accordingly the ancients, with their *inductio per enumerationem simplicem,* imagined to be the law. Every moving body, however, encounters various obstacles, as friction, the resistance of the atmosphere, &c., which we know by daily experience to be causes capable of destroying motion. It was suggested that the whole of the retardation might be owing to these causes. How was this inquired into? If the obstacles could have been entirely removed, the case would have been amenable to the Method of Difference. They could not be removed, they could only be diminished, and the case therefore admitted only of the Method of Concomitant Variations. This accordingly being employed, it was found that every diminution of the obstacles diminished the retardation of the motion; and inasmuch as in this case (unlike the case of heat) the total quantities both of the antecedent and of the consequent were known, it was practicable to estimate, with an approach to accuracy, both the amount of the retardation and the amount of the retarding causes or resistances, and to judge how near they both were to being exhausted; and it appeared that the effect dwindled as rapidly, and at each step was as far on the road toward annihilation, as the cause was. The simple oscillation of a weight suspended from a fixed point, and moved a little out of the perpendicular, which in ordinary circumstances lasts but a few minutes, was prolonged in Borda's experiments to more than thirty hours, by diminishing as much as possible the friction at the point of suspension, and by making the body oscillate in a space exhausted as nearly as possible of its air. There could therefore be no hesitation in assigning the whole of the retardation of motion to the influence of the obstacles; and since, after subducting this retardation from the total phenomenon, the remainder was an uniform velocity, the result was the proposition known as the first Law of Motion.

There is also another characteristic uncertainty affecting the inference that the law of variation, which the quantities observe within our limits of observation, will hold beyond those limits. There is, of course, in the first instance, the possibility that beyond the limits, and in circumstances therefore of which we have no direct experience, some counteracting cause might develop itself; either a new agent, or a new property of the agents concerned, which lies dormant in the circumstances we are able to observe. This is an element of uncertainty which enters largely into all our predictions of effects; but it is not peculiarly applicable to the Method of Concomitant Variations. The uncertainty, however, of which I am about to speak is characteristic of that method, especially in the cases in which the extreme limits of our observation are very narrow in comparison with the possible variations in the quantities of the phenomena. Anyone who has the slightest acquaintance with mathematics is aware that very different laws of variation may produce numerical results which differ but slightly from one another within narrow limits; and it is often only when the absolute amounts of variation are considerable that the difference between the results given by one law and by another becomes appreciable. When, therefore, such variations in the quantity of the antecedents as we have the means of observing are small in comparison with the total quantities, there is much danger lest we should mistake the numerical law, and be led to miscalculate the variations which would take place beyond the limits; a miscalculation which would vitiate any conclusion respecting the dependence of the effect upon the cause, that could be founded on those variations. Examples are not wanting of such mistakes. "The formulæ," says Sir John Herschel,[1] "which have been empirically deduced for the elasticity of steam (till very recently) and those for the resistance of fluids, and other similar subjects," when relied on beyond the limits of the observations from which they were deduced, "have almost invariably failed to support the theoretical structures which have been erected on them."

In this uncertainty, the conclusion we may draw from the concomitant variations of a and A, to the existence of an invariable and exclusive connection between them, or to the permanency of the same numerical relation between their variations when the quantities are much greater or smaller than those which we have had the means of observing, cannot be considered to rest on a complete induction. All that in such a case can be regarded as proved on the subject of causation is, that there is some connection between

[1] *Discourse on the Study of Natural Philosophy*, p. 179.

the two phenomena; that A, or something which can influence A, must be *one* of the causes which collectively determine *a*. We may, however, feel assured that the relation which we have observed to exist between the variations of A and *a*, will hold true in all cases which fall between the same extreme limits; that is, wherever the utmost increase or diminution in which the result has been found by observation to coincide with the law, is not exceeded.

The four methods which it has now been attempted to describe are the only possible modes of experimental inquiry—of direct induction *a posteriori*, as distinguished from deduction: at least, I know not, nor am able to imagine, any others. And even of these, the Method of Residues, as we have seen, is not independent of deduction; though, as it also requires specific experience, it may, without impropriety, be included among methods of direct observation and experiment.

These, then, with such assistance as can be obtained from Deduction compose the available resources of the human mind for ascertaining the laws of the succession of phenomena. . . .

OF PLURALITY OF CAUSES, AND OF THE INTERMIXTURE OF EFFECTS

§ 1. In the preceding exposition of the four methods of observation and experiment, by which we contrive to distinguish among a mass of co-existent phenomena the particular effect due to a given cause, or the particular cause which gave birth to a given effect, it has been necessary to suppose, in the first instance, for the sake of simplification, that this analytical operation is encumbered by no other difficulties than what are essentially inherent in its nature; and to represent to ourselves, therefore, every effect, on the one hand as connected exclusively with a single cause, and on the other hand as incapable of being mixed and confounded with any other co-existent effect. We have regarded *a b c d e*, the aggregate of the phenomena existing at any moment, as consisting of dissimilar facts, *a*, *b*, *c*, *d*, and *e*, for each of which one, and only one, cause needs be sought; the difficulty being only that of singling out this one cause from the multitude of antecedent circumstances, A, B, C, D, and E. The cause indeed may not be simple; it may consist of an assemblage of conditions; but we have supposed that there was only one possible assemblage of conditions from which the given effect could result.

If such were the fact, it would be comparatively an easy task to investigate the laws of nature. But the supposition does not hold in either of its parts. In the first place, it is not true that the same phenomenon is always produced by the same cause; the effect *a* may sometimes arise from A, sometimes from B. And, secondly, the effects of different causes are often not dissimilar, but homogeneous, and marked out by no assignable boundaries from one another; A and B may produce not *a* and *b*, but different portions of an effect *a*. The obscurity and difficulty of the investigation of the laws of phenomena is singularly increased by the necessity of adverting to these two circumstances—Intermixture of Effects and Plurality of Causes. To the latter, being the simpler of the two considerations, we shall first direct our attention.

It is not true, then, that one effect must be connected with only one cause, or assemblage of conditions; that each phenomenon can be produced only in one way. There are often several independent modes in which the same phenomenon could have originated. One fact may be the consequent in several invariable sequences; it may follow, with equal uniformity, any one of several antecedents, or collections of antecedents. Many causes may produce mechanical motion: many causes may produce some kinds of sensation: many causes may produce death. A given effect may really be produced by a certain cause, and yet be perfectly capable of being produced without it.

§ 2. One of the principal consequences of this fact of Plurality of Causes is, to render the first of the inductive methods, that of Agreement, uncertain. To illustrate that method we supposed two instances, A B C followed by *a b c*, and A D E followed by *a d e*. From these instances it might apparently be concluded that A is an invariable antecedent of *a*, and even that it is the unconditional invariable antecedent or cause, if we could be sure that there is no other antecedent common to the two cases. That this difficulty may not stand in the way, let us suppose the two cases positively ascertained to have no antecedent in common except A. The moment, however, that we let in the possibility of a plurality of causes, the conclusion fails. For it involves a tacit supposition that *a* must have been produced in both instances by the same cause. If there can possibly have been two causes, those two may, for example, be C and E: the one may have been the cause of *a* in the former of the instances, the other in the latter, A having no influence in either case.

Suppose, for example, that two great artists or great philosophers, that two extremely selfish or extremely generous characters, were compared together as to the circumstances of their education and history, and the two cases were found to agree only in one circumstance: would it follow that this one circumstance was the cause of the quality which characterized both those individuals? Not at all; for the causes which may produce any type of character are very numerous; and the two persons might equally have agreed in their character, though there had been no manner of resemblance in their previous history.

This, therefore, is a characteristic imperfection of the Method of Agreement; from which imperfection the Method of Difference is free. For if we have two instances, A B C and B C, of which B C gives *b c*, and A being added converts it into *a b c*, it is certain that in this instance, at least, A was either the cause of *a*, or an indispensable portion of its cause, even though the cause which produces it in other instances may be altogether different. Plurality of Causes, therefore, not only does not diminish the reliance due to the Method of Difference, but does not even render a greater number of observations or experiments necessary: two instances, the one positive and the other negative, are still sufficient for the most complete and rigorous induction. Not so, however, with the Method of Agreement. The conclusions which that yields, when the number of instances compared is small, are of no real value, except as, in the character of suggestions, they may lead either to experiments bringing them to the test of the Method of Difference, or to reasonings which may explain and verify them deductively.

It is only when the instances, being indefinitely multiplied and varied, continue to suggest the same result, that this result acquires any high degree of independent value. If there are but two instances, A B C and A D E, though these instances have no antecedent in common except A, yet, as the effect may possibly have been produced in the two cases by different causes, the result is at most only a slight probability in favour of A; there may be causation, but it is almost equally probable that there was only a coincidence. But the oftener we repeat the observation, varying the circumstances, the more we advance towards a solution of this doubt. For if we try A F G, A H K, &c., all unlike one another except in containing the circumstance A, and if we find the effect *a* entering into the result in all these cases, we must suppose one of two things, either that it is caused by A, or that it has as many different causes as there are instances. With each addition, therefore, to the number of instances, the presumption is strengthened in favour of A. The inquirer, of course, will not neglect, if an opportunity present itself to exclude A from some one of these combinations from A H K for instance, and by trying H K separately, appeal to the Method of Difference in aid of the Method of Agreement. By the Method of Difference alone can it be ascertained that A is the cause of *a*; but that it is either the cause, or another effect of the same cause, may be placed beyond any reasonable doubt by the Method of Agreement, provided the instances are very numerous as well as sufficiently various.

After how great a multiplication, then, of varied instances, all agreeing in no other antecedent except A, is the supposition of a plurality of causes sufficiently rebutted, and the conclusion that *a* is connected with A divested of the characteristic imperfection, and reduced to a virtual certainty? This is a question which we cannot be exempted from answering: but the consideration of it belongs to what is called the Theory of Probability, which will form the subject of a chapter hereafter. It is seen, however, at once, that the conclusion does amount to a practical certainty after a sufficient number of instances, and that the method, therefore, is not radically vitiated by the characteristic imperfection. The result of these considerations is only, in the first place, to point out a new source of inferiority in the Method of Agreement as compared with other modes of investigation, and new reasons for never resting contented with the results obtained by it, without attempting to confirm them either by the Method of Difference, or by connecting them deductively with some law or laws already ascertained by that superior method. And, in the second place, we learn from this the true theory of the value of a mere *number* of instances in inductive inquiry. The Plurality of Causes is the only reason why mere number is of any importance. The tendency of unscientific inquiries is to rely too much on number, without analysing the instances; without looking closely enough into their nature, to ascertain what circumstances are or are not eliminated by means of them. Most people hold their conclusions with a degree of assurance proportioned to the mere *mass* of the experience on which they appear to rest; not considering that by the addition of instances to instances, all of the same kind, that is, differing from one another only in points already recognized as immaterial, nothing whatever is added to the evidence of the conclusion. A single instance eliminating some antecedent which existed in all the other cases is of more value than the greatest multitude of instances which are reckoned by their number alone. It is necessary, no doubt, to assure ourselves, by repetition of the observation or experiment, that no error has been committed concerning the individual facts observed; and until we have assured ourselves of this, instead of varying the circumstances, we cannot too scrupulously repeat the same experiment or observation without any change. But when once this assurance has been obtained, the multiplication of instances which do not exclude any more circumstances is entirely useless, provided there have been already enough to exclude the supposition of Plurality of Causes.

It is of importance to remark, that the peculiar modification of the Method of Agreement, which, as partaking in some degree of the nature of the Method of Difference, I have called the Joint Method of Agreement and Difference, is not affected by the characteristic imperfection now pointed out. For, in the joint method, it is supposed not only that the instances in which *a* is, agree only in containing A, but also that the instances in which *a* is not, agree only in not containing A. Now, if this be so, A must be not only the cause of *a*, but the only possible cause: for if there were another, as, for example, B, then in the instances in which *a* is not, B must have been absent as well as A, and it would not be true that these instances agreed *only* in not containing A. This therefore, constitutes an immense advantage of the joint method over the simple Method of Agreement. It may seem, indeed, that the advantage does not belong so much to the joint method as to one of its two premises (if they may be so called) the negative premise. The Method of

Agreement, when applied to negative instances, or those in which a phenomenon does *not* take place, is certainly free from the characteristic imperfection which affects it in the affirmative case. The negative premise, it might therefore be supposed, could be worked as a simple case of the Method of Agreement, without requiring an affirmative premise to be joined with it. But though this is true in principle, it is generally altogether impossible to work the Method of Agreement by negative instances without positive ones: it is so much more difficult to exhaust the field of negation than that of affirmation. For instance, let the question be, what is the cause of the transparency of bodies; with what prospect of success could we set ourselves to inquire directly in what the multifarious substances which are *not* transparent agree? But we might hope much sooner to seize some point of resemblance among the comparatively few and definite species of objects which *are* transparent; and this being attained, we should quite naturally be put upon examining whether the *absence* of this one circumstance be not precisely the point in which all opaque circumstances will be found to resemble.

The Joint Method of Agreement and Difference, therefore, or, as I have otherwise called it, the Indirect Method of Difference (because, like the Method of Difference properly so called, it proceeds by ascertaining how and in what the cases where the phenomenon is present differ from those in which it is absent) is, after the Direct Method of Difference, the most powerful of the remaining instruments of inductive investigation; and in the sciences which depend on pure observation, with little or no aid from experiment, this method, so well exemplified in the speculation on the cause of dew, is the primary resource, so far as direct appeals to experience are concerned.

§ 3. We have thus far treated Plurality of Causes only as a possible supposition, which, until removed, renders our inductions uncertain; and have only considered by what means, where the plurality does not really exist, we may be enabled to disprove it. But we must also consider it as a case actually occurring in nature, and which, as often as it does occur, our methods of induction ought to be capable of ascertaining and establishing. For this, however, there is required no peculiar method. When an effect is really producible by two or more causes, the process for detecting them is in no way different from that by which we discover single causes. They may (first) be discovered as separate sequences by separate sets of instances. One set of observations or experiments shows that the sun is a cause of heat, another that friction is a source of it, another that percussion, another that electricity, another that chemical action is such a source. Or (secondly) the plurality may come to light in the course of collating a number of instances, when we attempt to find some circumstances in which they all agree, and fail in doing so. We find it impossible to trace, in all the cases in which the effect is met with any common circumstances. We find that we can eliminate *all* the antecedents; that no one of them is present in all the instances, no one of them indispensable to the effect. On closer scrutiny, however, it appears that though no one is always present, one or other of several always is. If, on further analysis, we can detect in these any common element, we may be able to ascend from them to some one cause which is the really operative circumstance in them all. Thus it is now thought that in the production of heat by friction, percussion, chemical action, &c., the ultimate source is one and the same. But if (as continually happens) we cannot take this ulterior step, the different antecedents must be set down provisionally as distinct causes, each sufficient of itself to produce the effect.

We here close our remarks on the Plurality of Causes, and proceed to the still more peculiar and more complex case of the Intermixture of Effects, and the interference of causes with one another: a case constituting the principal part of the complication and difficulty of the study of nature; and with which the four only possible methods of directly inductive investigation by observation and experiment are for the most part, as will appear presently, quite unequal to cope. The Instrument of Deduction alone is adequate to unravel the complexities proceeding from this source; and the four methods have little more in their power than to supply premises for, and a verification of, our deductions.

§ 4. A concurrence of two or more causes, not separately producing each its own effect, but interfering with or modifying the effects of one another, takes place . . . in two different ways. In the one, which is exemplified by the joint operation of different forces in mechanics, the separate effects of all the causes continue to be produced, but are compounded with one another, and disappear in one total. In the other, illustrated by the case of chemical action, the separate effects cease entirely, and are succeeded by phenomena altogether different, and governed by different laws.

Of these cases the former is by far the more frequent, and this case it is which, for the most part, eludes the grasp of our experimental methods. The other and exceptional case is essentially amenable to them. When the laws of the original agents cease entirely, and a phenomenon makes its appearance, which, with reference to those laws, is quite heterogeneous; when, for example, two gaseous substances, hydrogen and oxygen, on being brought together, throw off their peculiar properties, and produce the substance called water—in such cases the new fact may be subjected to experimental inquiry, like any other phenomenon; and the elements which are said to compose it may be considered as the mere agents of its production; the conditions on which it depends, the facts which make up its cause.

The *effects* of the new phenomenon, the *properties* of water, for instance, are as easily found by experiment as the effects of any other cause. But to discover the *cause* of it, that is, the particular conjunction of agents from which it results, is often difficult enough. In the first place, the origin and actual production of the phenomenon are most frequently inaccessible to our observation. If we could not have learned the composition of water until we found instances in which it was actually produced from oxygen and hydrogen, we should have been forced to wait until the casual thought struck some one of passing an electric spark through a mixture of the two gases, or inserting a lighted paper into it, merely to try what would happen. Besides, many substances, though they can be analysed, cannot by any known artificial means be recompounded. Further, even if we could have ascertained, by the Method of Agreement, that oxygen and hydrogen were both present when water is produced, no experimentation on oxygen and hydrogen separately, no knowledge of their laws, could have enabled us deductively to infer that they would produce water. We require a specific experiment on the two combined.

Under these difficulties, we should generally have been indebted for our knowledge of the causes of this class of effects, not to any inquiry directed specifically towards that end, but either to accident, or to the gradual progress of experimentation on the different combinations of which the producing agents are susceptible; if it were not for a peculiarity belonging to effects of this description, that they often, under some particular combination of circumstances, reproduce their causes. If water results from the juxtaposition of hydrogen and oxygen whenever this can be made sufficiently close and intimate, so, on the other hand, if water itself be placed in certain situations, hydrogen and oxygen are reproduced from it: an abrupt termination is put to the new laws, and the agents reappear separately with their own properties as at first. What is called chemical analysis is the process of searching for the causes of a phenomenon among its effects, or rather among the effects produced by the action of some other causes upon it.

Lavoisier, by heating mercury to a high temperature in a close vessel containing air, found that the mercury increased in weight, and became what was then called red precipitate, while the air, on being examined after the experiment, proved to have lost weight, and to have become incapable of supporting life or combustion. When red precipitate was exposed to a still greater heat, it became mercury again, and gave off a gas which did support life and flame. Thus the agents which by their combination produced red precipitate, namely, the mercury and the gas, reappear as effects resulting from that precipitate when acted upon by heat. So, if we decompose water by means of iron filings, we produce two effects, rust and hydrogen: now rust is already known, by experiments upon the component substances, to be an effect of the union of iron and oxygen: the iron we ourselves supplied, but the oxygen must have been produced from the water. The result therefore is that water has disappeared, and hydrogen and oxygen have appeared in its stead: or, in other words, the original laws of these gaseous agents, which had been suspended by the superinduction of the new laws called the properties of water, have again started into existence, and the causes of water are found among its effects.

Where two phenomena, between the laws or properties of which, considered in themselves, no connection can be traced, are thus reciprocally cause and effect, each capable in its turn of being produced from the other, and each, when it produces the other, ceasing itself to exist (as water is produced from oxygen and hydrogen, and oxygen and hydrogen are reproduced from water); this causation of the two phenomena by one another, each being generated by the other's destruction, is properly transformation. The idea of chemical composition is an idea of transformation, but of a transformation which is incomplete, since we consider the oxygen and hydrogen to be present in the water *as* oxygen and hydrogen, and capable of being discovered in it if our senses were sufficiently keen: a supposition (for it is no more) grounded solely on the fact that the weight of the water is the sum of the separate weights of the two ingredients. If there had not been this exception to the entire disappearance in the compound of the laws of the separate ingredients; if the combined agents had not, in this one particular of weight, preserved their own laws, and produced a joint result equal to the sum of their separate results, we should never, probably, have had the notion now implied by the words chemical composition; and, in the facts of water produced from hydrogen and oxygen, and hydrogen and oxygen produced from water, as the transformation would have been complete, we should have seen only a transformation.

In these cases, where the heteropathic effect (as we called it in a former chapter) is but a transformation of its cause, or, in other words, where the effect and its cause are reciprocally such, and mutually convertible into each other, the problem of finding the cause resolves itself into the far easier one of finding an effect, which is the kind of inquiry that admits of being prosecuted by direct experiment. But there are other cases of heteropathic effects to which this mode of investigation is not applicable. Take, for instance, the heteropathic laws of mind, that portion of the phenomena of our mental nature which are analogous to chemical rather than to dynamical phenomena; as when a complex passion is formed by the coalition of several elementary impulses, or a complex emotion by several simple pleasures or pains, of which it is the result without being the aggregate, or in any respect homogeneous with them. The product, in these cases, is generated by its various factors; but the factors cannot be reproduced from the product; just as a youth can grow into an old man, but an old man cannot grow into a youth. We cannot ascertain from what simple feelings any of our complex states of mind are generated, as we ascertain the ingredients of a chemical compound, by making it, in its turn, generate them. We can only, therefore, discover these laws by the slow process of studying the simple feelings themselves, and ascertaining synthetically, by experimenting on the various combinations of which they are susceptible, what they, by their mutual action upon one another, are capable of generating.

§ 5. It might have been supposed that the other, and apparently simpler variety of the mutual interference of causes, where each cause continues to produce its own proper effect according to the same laws to which it conforms in its separate state, would have presented fewer difficulties to the inductive inquirer than that of which we have just finished the consideration. It presents, however, so far as direct induction apart from deduction is concerned, infinitely greater difficulties. When a concurrence of causes gives rise to a new effect, bearing no relation to the separate effects of those causes, the resulting phenomenon stands forth undisguised, inviting attention to its peculiarity, and presenting no obstacle to our recognizing its presence or absence among any number of surrounding phenomena. It admits, therefore, of being easily brought under the canons of Induction, provided instances can be obtained such as those canons require: and the non-occurrence of such instances, or the want of means to produce them artificially, is the real and only difficulty in such investigations; a difficulty not logical, but in some sort physical. It is otherwise with cases of what, in a preceding chapter, has been denominated the Composition of Causes. There, the effects of the separate causes do not terminate and give place to others, thereby ceasing to form any part of the phenomenon to be investigated; on the contrary, they still take place, but are intermingled with, and disguised by, the homogeneous and closely allied effects of other causes. They are no longer a, b, c, d, e, existing side by side, and continuing to be separately discernible; they are $+ a$, a, $- \frac{1}{2} b$, $- b$, $2 b$, &c.; some of which cancel one another, while many others do not appear distinguishably, but merge in one sum: forming altogether a result, between which and the causes whereby it was produced there is often an insurmountable difficulty in tracing by observation any fixed relation whatever.

The general idea of the Composition of Causes has been seen to be, that though two or more laws interfere with one another, and apparently frustrate or modify one another's operation, yet in reality all are fulfilled, the collective effect being the exact sum of the effects of the causes taken separately. A familiar instance is that of a body kept in equilibrium by two equal and contrary forces. One of the forces if acting alone would carry the body in a given time a certain distance to the west, the other if acting alone would carry it exactly as far towards the east; and the result is the same as if it had been first carried to the west as far as the one force would carry it, and then back towards the east as far as the other would carry it, that is, precisely the same distance; being ultimately left where it was found at first.

All laws of causation are liable to be in this manner counteracted, and seemingly frustrated, by coming into conflict with other laws, the separate result of which is opposite to theirs, or more or less inconsistent with it. And hence, with almost every law, many instances in which it really is entirely fulfilled do not, at first sight, appear to be cases of its operation at all. It is so in the example just adduced: a force, in mechanics, means neither more nor less than a cause of motion, yet the sum of the effects of two causes of motion may be rest. Again, a body solicited by two forces in directions making an angle with one another moves in the diagnoal; and it seems a paradox to say that motion in the diagonal is the sum of two motions in two other lines. Motion, however, is but change of place, and at every instant the body is in the exact place it would have been in if the forces had acted during alternate instants instead of acting in the same instant, (saving that if we suppose two forces to act successively which are in truth simultaneous, we must of course allow them double the time). It is evident, therefore, that each force has had, during each instant, all the effect which belonged to it; and that the modifying influence which one of two concurrent causes is said to exercise with respect to the other may be considered as exerted not over the action of the cause itself, but over the effect after it is completed. For all purposes of predicting, calculating, or explaining their joint result, causes which compound their effects may be treated as if they produced simultaneously each of them its own effect, and all these effects co-existed visibly.

Since the laws of causes are as really fulfilled when the causes are said to be counteracted by opposing causes as when they are left to their own undisturbed action, we must be cautious not to express the laws in such terms as would render the assertion of their being fulfilled in those cases a contradiction. If, for instance, it were stated as a law of nature that a body to which a force is applied moves in the direction of the force, with a velocity proportioned to the force directly, and to its own mass inversely; when in point of fact some bodies to which a force is applied do not move at all, and those which do move (at least in the region of our earth) are, from the very first, retarded by the action of gravity and other resisting forces, and at last stopped altogether; it is clear that the general proposition, though it would be true under a certain hypothesis, would not express the facts as they actually occur. To accommodate the expression of the law to the real phenomena, we must say, not that the object moves, but that it *tends* to move, in the direction and with the velocity specified. We might, indeed, guard our expression in a different mode, by saying that the body moves in that manner unless prevented, or except in so far as prevented, by some counteracting cause, but the body does not only move in that manner unless counteracted; it *tends* to move in that manner even when counteracted; it still exerts in the original direction the same energy of movement as if its first impulse had been undisturbed, and produces, by that energy, an exactly equivalent quantity of effect. This is true even when the force leaves the body as it found it, in a state of absolute rest; as when we attempt to raise a body of three tons weight with a force equal to one ton. For if, while we are applying this force, wind or water or any other agent supplies an additional force just exceeding two tons, the body will be raised; thus proving that the force we applied exerted its full effect by neutralizing an equivalent portion of the weight which it was insufficient altogether to overcome. And if while we are exerting this force of one ton upon the object in a direction contrary to that of gravity, it be put into a scale and weighed, it will be found to have lost a ton of its weight, or, in other words, to press downwards with a force only equal to the difference of the two forces.

These facts are correctly indicated by the expression *tendency*. All laws of causation, in consequence of their liability to be counteracted, require to be stated in words affirmative of tendencies only, and not of actual results. In those sciences of causation which have an accurate nomenclature, there are special words which signify a tendency to the particular effect with which the science is conversant; thus *pressure*, in mechanics, is synonymous with tendency to motion, and forces are not reasoned on as causing actual motion, but as exerting pressure. A similar improvement in terminology would be very salutary in many other branches of science.

The habit of neglecting this necessary element in the precise expression of the laws of nature has given birth to the popular prejudice that all general truths have exceptions; and much unmerited distrust has thence accrued to the conclusions of science when they have been submitted to the judgment of minds insufficiently disciplined and cultivated. The rough generalizations suggested by common observation usually have exceptions; but principles of science, or, in other words, laws of causation, have not. "What is thought to be an exception to a principle" (to quote words used on a different occasion) "is always some other and distinct principle cutting into the former; some other force which impinges[2] against the first force, and deflects it from its direction. There are not a law and an exception to that law, the law acting in ninety-nine cases, and the exception in one. There are two laws, each possibly acting in the whole hundred cases, and bringing about a common effect by their conjunct operation. If the force which, being the less con-

---

[2] It seems hardly necessary to say that the word *impinge*, as a general term to express collision of forces, is here used by a figure of speech, and not as expressive of any theory respecting the nature of force.

spicuous of the two, is called the *disturbing* force, prevails sufficiently over the other force in some one case, to constitute that case what is commonly called an exception, the same disturbing force probably acts as a modifying cause in many other cases which no one will call exceptions.

"Thus if it were stated to be a law of nature that all heavy bodies fall to the ground, it would probably be said that the resistance of the atmosphere, which prevents a balloon from falling, constitutes the balloon an exception to that pretended law of nature. But the real law is, that all heavy bodies *tend* to fall; and to this there is no exception, not even the sun and moon; for even they, as every astronomer knows, tend towards the earth, with a force exactly equal to that with which the earth tends towards them. The resistance of the atmosphere might, in the particular case of the balloon, from a misapprehension of what the law of gravitation is, be said to *prevail over* the law; but its disturbing effect is quite as real in every other case, since though it does not prevent, it retards the fall of all bodies whatever. The rule and the so-called exception do not divide the cases between them; each of them as a comprehensive rule extending to all cases. To call one of these concurrent principles an exception to the other, is superficial, and contrary to the correct principles of nomenclature and arrangement. An effect of precisely the same kind, and arising from the same cause, ought not to be placed in two different categories, merely as there does or does not exist another cause preponderating over it."[3]

§ 6. We have now to consider according to what method these complex effects, compounded of the effects of many causes, are to be studied; how we are enabled to trace each effect to the concurrence of causes in which it originated, and ascertain the conditions of its recurrence—the circumstances in which it may be expected again to occur. The conditions of a phenomenon which arises from a composition of causes may be investigated either deductively or experimentally.

The case, it is evident, is naturally susceptible of the deductive mode of investigation. The law of an effect of this description is a result of the laws of the separate causes on the combination of which it depends, and is therefore in itself capable of being deduced from these laws. This is called the method *a priori*. The other, or *a posteriori* method, professes to proceed according to the canons of experimental inquiry. Considering the whole assemblage of concurrent causes which produced the phenomenon as one single cause, it attempts to ascertain the cause in the ordinary manner, by a comparison of instances. This second method subdivides itself into two different varieties. If it merely collates instances of the effect, it is a method

[3] *Essays on Some Unsettled Questions of Political Economy*, Essay V.

of pure observation. If it operates upon the causes, and tries different combinations of them, in hopes of ultimately hitting the precise combination which will produce the given total effect, it is a method of experiment.

In order more completely to clear up the nature of each of these three methods, and determine which of them deserves the preference, it will be expedient (conformably to a favourite maxim of Lord Chancellor Eldon, to which, though it has often incurred philosophical ridicule, a deeper philosophy will not refuse its sanction) to "clothe them in circumstances." We shall select for this purpose a case which as yet furnishes no very brilliant example of the success of any of the three methods, but which is all the more suited to illustrate the difficulties inherent in them. Let the subject of inquiry be the conditions of health and disease in the human body, or (for greater simplicity) the conditions of recovery from a given disease; and in order to narrow the question still more, let it be limited, in the first instance, to this one inquiry, Is or is not some particular medicament (mercury, for instance) a remedy for the given disease?

Now, the deductive method would set out from known properties of mercury and known laws of the human body, and, by reasoning from these, would attempt to discover whether mercury will act upon the body when in the morbid condition supposed, in such a manner as would tend to restore health. The experimental method would simply administer mercury in as many cases as possible, noting the age, sex, temperament, and other peculiarities of bodily constitution, the particular form or variety of the disease, the particular stage of its progress, &c., remarking in which of these cases it was attended with a salutary effect, and with what circumstances it was on those occasions combined. The method of simple observation would compare instances of recovery, to find whether they agreed in having been preceded by the administration of mercury; or would compare instances of recovery with instances of failure, to find cases which, agreeing in all other respects, differed only in the fact that mercury had been administered or that it had not.

§ 7. That the last of these three modes of investigation is applicable to the case, no one has ever seriously contended. No conclusions of value on a subject of such intricacy ever were obtained in that way. The utmost that could result would be a vague general impression for or against the efficacy of mercury, of no avail for guidance unless confirmed by one of the other two methods. Not that the results which this method strives to obtain would not be of the utmost possible value if they could be obtained. If all the cases of recovery which presented themselves, in an examination extending to a great number of instances, were cases in which mercury had been administered, we might generalize with confidence from this experience, and should have obtained a conclusion of real value. But no such basis for generalisation can we, in a case of this description, hope to obtain. The reason is that which we have spoken of as constituting the characteristic imperfection of the Method of Agreement—Plurality of Causes. Supposing even that mercury does tend to cure the disease, so many other causes, both natural and artificial, also tend to cure it, that there are sure to be abundant instances of recovery in which mercury has not been administered: unless, indeed, the practice be to administer it in all cases; on which supposition it will equally be found in the cases of failure.

When an effect results from the union of many causes, the share which each has in the determination of the effect cannot in general be great; and the effect is not likely, even in its presence or absence, still less in its variations, to follow, even approximately, any one of the causes. Recovery from a disease is an event to which, in every case, many influences must concur. Mercury may be one such influence; but from the very fact that there are many other such, it will necessarily happen that although mercury is administered, the patient, for want of other concurring influences, will often not recover, and that he often will recover when it is not administered, the other favourable influences being sufficiently powerful without it. Neither, therefore, will the instances of recovery agree in the administration of mercury, nor will the instances of failure agree in its non-administration. It is much if, by multiplied and accurate returns from hospitals and the like, we can collect that there are rather more recoveries and rather fewer failures when mercury is administered than when it is not; a result of very secondary value even as a guide to practice, and almost worthless as a contribution to the theory of the subject.[4]

[4] It is justly remarked by Professor Bain, that though the Methods of Agreement and Difference are not applicable to these cases, they are not wholly inaccessible to the Method of Concomitant Variations. "If a cause happens to vary alone, the effect will also vary alone; a cause and effect may be thus singled out under the greatest complications. Thus, when the appetite for food increases with the cold, we have a strong evidence of connection between these two facts, although other circumstances may operate in the same direction. The assigning of the respective parts of the sun and moon in the action of the tides may be effected, to a certain degree of exactness, by the variations of the amount according to the positions of the two attractive bodies. By a series of experiments of Concomitant Variations, directed to ascertain the elimination of nitrogen from the human body under varieties of muscular exercise, Dr. Parkes obtained the remarkable conclusion that a muscle grows during exercise, and loses bulk during the subsequent rest."—*Logic*, ii. 83.

It is, no doubt, often possible to single out the influencing causes from among a great number of mere concomitants, by noting what are the antecedents a variation in which is followed by a variation in the effect. But when there are many influencing causes, no one of them greatly predominating over the rest, and especially when some of these are

§ 8. The inapplicability of the method of simple observation to ascertain the conditions of effects dependent on many concurring causes being thus recognized, we shall next inquire whether any greater benefit can be expected from the other branch of the *à posteriori* method, that which proceeds by directly trying different combinations of causes, either artificially produced or found in nature, and taking notice what is their effect: as, for example, by actually trying the effect of mercury, in as many different circumstances as possible. This method differs from the one which we have just examined, in turning our attention directly to the causes or agents, instead of turning it to the effect, recovery from the disease. And since, as a general rule, the effects of causes are far more accessible to our study than the causes of effects, it is natural to think that this method has a much better chance of proving successful than the former.

The method now under consideration is called the Empirical Method; and in order to estimate it fairly, we must suppose it to be completely, not incompletely, empirical. We must exclude from it everything which partakes of the nature not of an experimental but of a deductive operation. If, for instance, we try experiments with mercury upon a person in health, in order to ascertain the general laws of its action upon the human body, and then reason from these laws to determine how it will act upon persons affected with a particular disease, this may be a really effectual method, but this is deduction. The experimental method does not derive the law of a complex case from the simpler laws which conspire to produce it, but makes its experiments directly upon the complex case. We must make entire abstraction of all knowledge of the simpler tendencies, the *modi operandi,* of mercury in detail. Our experimentation must aim at obtaining a direct answer to the specific question, Does or does not mercury tend to cure the particular disease?

Let us see, therefore, how far the case admits of the observance of those rules of experimentation, which it is found necessary to observe in other cases. When we devise an experiment to ascertain the effect of a given agent, there are certain precautions which we never, if we can help it, omit. In the first place, we introduce the agent into the midst of a set of circumstances which we have exactly ascertained. It needs hardly be remarked how far this condition is from being realised in any case connected with the phenomena of life; how far we are from knowing what are all the circumstances which pre-exist in any instance in which mercury is administered to a living being. This difficulty, however, though insuperable in most cases, may not be so in all:

continually changing, it is scarcely ever possible to trace such a relation between the variations of the effect and those of any one cause as would enable us to assign to that cause its real share in the production of the effect.

there are sometimes concurrences of many causes, in which we yet know accurately what the causes are. Moreover, the difficulty may be attenuated by sufficient multiplication of experiments, in circumstances rendering it improbable that any of the unknown causes should exist in them all. But when we have got clear of this obstacle, we encounter another still more serious. In other cases, when we intend to try an experiment, we do not reckon it enough that there be no circumstance in the case the presence of which is unknown to us. We require also that none of the circumstances which we do know shall have effects susceptible of being confounded with those of the agents whose properties we wish to study. We take the utmost pains to exclude all causes capable of composition with the given cause; or if forced to let in any such causes, we take care to make them such that we can compute and allow for their influence, so that the effect of the given cause may, after the subduction of those other effects, be apparent as a residual phenomenon.

These precautions are inapplicable to such cases as we are now considering. The mercury of our experiment being tried with an unknown multitude (or even let it be a known multitude) of other influencing circumstances, the mere fact of their being influencing circumstances implies that they disguise the effect of the mercury, and preclude us from knowing whether it has any effect or not. Unless we already knew what and how much is owing to every other circumstance (that is, unless we suppose the very problem solved which we are considering the means of solving) we cannot tell that those other circumstances may not have produced the whole of the effect, independently or even in spite of the mercury. The Method of Difference, in the ordinary mode of its use, namely, by comparing the state of things following the experiment with the state which preceded it, is thus, in the case of intermixture of effects, entirely unavailing; because other causes than that whose effect we are seeking to determine have been operating during the transition. As for the other mode of employing the Method of Difference, namely, by comparing, not the same case at two different periods, but different cases, this in the present instance is quite chimerical. In phenomena so complicated it is questionable if two cases, similar in all respects but one, ever occurred; and were they to occur, we could not possibly know that they were so exactly similar.

Anything like a scientific use of the method of experiment, in these complicated cases, is therefore out of the question. We can generally, even in the most favourable cases, only discover by a succession of trials that a certain cause is *very often* followed by a certain effect. For, in one of these conjunct effects, the portion which is determined by any one of the influencing agents, is usually, as we before remarked, but small; and it must be a more potent cause than most, if even the tendency which it really exerts is not thwarted by other tendencies in nearly as many cases as it is fulfilled. Some causes indeed there are which are more potent than any counteracting causes to which they are commonly exposed; and accordingly there are some truths in medicine which are sufficiently proved by direct experiment. Of these the most familiar are those that relate to the efficacy of the substances known as Specifics for particular diseases: "quinine, colchicum, lime-juice, cod-liver oil,"[5] and a few others. Even these are not invariably followed by success; but they succeed in so large a proportion of cases, and against such powerful obstacles, that their *tendency* to restore health in the disorders for which they are prescribed may be regarded as an experimental truth.[6]

If so little can be done by the experimental method to determine the conditions of an effect of many combined causes, in the case of medical science; still less is this method applicable to a class of phenomena more complicated than even those of physiology, the phenomena of politics and history. There, Plurality of Causes exists in almost boundless excess, and effects are, for the most part, inextricably interwoven with one another. To add to the embarrassment, most of the inquiries in political science relate to the production of effects of a most comprehensive description, such as the public wealth, public security, public morality, and the like: results liable to be affected directly or indirectly either in *plus* or in *minus* by nearly every fact which exists, or event which occurs in human society. The vulgar notion that the safe methods on political subjects are those of Baconian induction—that the true guide is not general reasoning, but specific experience—will one day be quoted as among the most unequivocal marks of a low state of the speculative faculties in any age in which it is accredited. Nothing can be more ludicrous than the sort of parodies on experimental reasoning which one is accustomed to meet with, not in popular discussion only, but in grave treatises, when the affairs of nations are the theme. "How," it is asked, "can an institution be bad, when the country has prospered under it?" "How can such or such causes have contributed to the prosperity of one country, when another has prospered without them?" Whoever makes use of an argument of this kind, not intending to deceive, should be sent back to learn the elements of some one of the more easy physical sciences. Such reasoners ignore the fact of Plurality of Causes in the very case which affords the most signal example

[5] Bain's *Logic*, ii. 360.

[6] What is said in the text on the inapplicability of the experimental methods to resolve particular questions of medical treatment does not detract from their efficacy in ascertaining the general laws of the animal or human system. The functions, for example, of the different classes of nerves have been discovered, and probably could only have been discovered, by experiments on living animals. Observation and experiment are the ultimate basis of all knowledge; from them we obtain the elementary laws of life, as we obtain all other elementary truths. It is in dealing with the complex combinations that the experimental methods are for the most part illusory, and the deductive mode of investigation must be invoked to disentangle the complexity.

of it. So little could be concluded, in such a case, from any possible collation of individual instances, that even the impossibility, in social phenomena, of making artificial experiments, a circumstance otherwise so prejudicial to directly inductive inquiry, hardly affords, in this case, additional reason of regret. For even if we could try experiments upon a nation or upon the human race, with as little scruple as M. Magendie tried them on dogs and rabbits, we should never succeed in making two instances identical in every respect except the presence or absence of some one definite circumstance. The nearest approach to an experiment in the philosophical sense, which takes place in politics, is the introduction of a new operative element into national affairs by some special and assignable measure of government, such as the enactment or repeal of a particular law. But where there are so many in-fluences at work, it requires some time for the influence of any new cause upon national phenomena to become apparent; and as the causes operating in so extensive a sphere are not only infinitely numerous, but in a state of perpetual alteration, it is always certain that before the effect of the new cause becomes conspicuous enough to be a subject of induction, so many of the other influencing circumstances will have changed as to vitiate the experiment.[7]

Two, therefore, of the three possible methods for the study of phenomena resulting from the composition of many causes, being, from the very nature of the case, inefficient and illusory, there remains only the third,—that which considers the causes separately, and infers the effect from the balance of the different tendencies which produce it: in short, the deductive or *à priori* method. The more particular consideration of this intellectual process re-quires a chapter to itself.

[7] Professor Bain, though concurring generally in the views expressed in this chapter, seems to estimate more highly than I do the scope for specific experimental evidence in politics (*Logic*, ii. 333–337). There are, it is true, as he remarks (p. 336), some cases "when an agent suddenly introduced is almost instantaneously followed by some other changes, as when the announcement of a diplomatic rupture between two nations is followed the same day by a derangement of the money-market." But this experiment would be quite inconclusive merely as an experiment. It can only serve, as any experi-ment may, to verify the conclusion of a deduction. Unless we already knew by our knowledge of the motives which act on business men that the prospect of war tends to derange the money-market, we should never have been able to prove a connection between the two facts, unless after having ascertained historically that the one followed the other in too great a number of instances to be consistent with their having been recorded with due precautions. Whoever has carefully examined any of the attempts continually made to prove economic doctrines by such a recital of instances, knows well how futile they are. It always turns out that the circumstances of scarcely any of the cases have been fully stated; and that cases, in equal or greater numbers, have been omitted, which would have tended to an opposite conclusion.

D. Hypothetico-Deductivism and Deductive Explanation

One prominent contemporary view about the structure of a scientific system is the hypothetico-deductive view, sometimes called (as in Cronbach and Meehl's article on construct validity, which appears in Chapter 10) the "nomological-network" view. According to this view, a scientific body of knowledge is composed of high-level general laws (or theories) and definitions, from which can be deductively derived lower-level laws or theories, which, in turn, imply lower-level subject matter, and so on, given certain assumptions. The whole superstructure rests on its ability to *explain* and *predict* an observational base.

In the first of the following two selections, John Stuart Mill sketches out his views of hypothetico-deductivism and explanation. He calls the method of developing a hypothetico-deductive system the "deductive method," even though more than deduction is involved, as he points out. In Mill's *System of Logic* this selection follows immediately after the one reproduced in the last section, "Methods of Experimental Inquiry."

Unfortunately, successful simple examples of hypothetico-deductive systems are difficult to find, especially in the area of human behavior. This fact is often urged in criticism of hypothetico-deductivism; but the response is that a hypothetico-deductive system is an ideal toward which social scientists should strive. So that one can have a rough idea of what is being advocated by the hypothetico-deductivists, we have included a selection from Richard Braithwaite's *Scientific Explanation*, in which he uses the subject matter area of freely falling bodies to exemplify a hypothetico-deductive system. Clark Hull's reinforcement theory of learning represents an attempt by a behavioral scientist to make a hypothetico-deductive theory. Because it is so long and complex, we have not included it, our purpose being merely to illustrate what is meant by a hypothetico-deductive system.

Hypothetico-deductivism constitutes a step away from radical empiricism, but is still fairly rigorous and objective in approach. Its very rigor and apparent objectivity, leave it open to the charges lodged against it by Wesley Salmon in his paper appearing later in this book under the topic, "Bayesian Inference." Its objectivity is challenged by Hanson's paper on observation (Chapter 4).

22. OF THE DEDUCTIVE METHOD

John Stuart Mill

§ 1. The mode of investigation which, from the proved inapplicability of direct methods of observation and experiment, remains to us as the main source of the knowledge we possess or can acquire respecting the conditions and laws of recurrence of the more complex phenomena, is called, in its most general expression, the Deductive Method, and consists of three operations —the first, one of direct induction; the second, of ratiocination; the third, of verification.

I call the first step in the process an inductive operation, because there must be a direct induction as the basis of the whole, though in many particular investigations the place of the induction may be supplied by a prior deduction; but the premises of this prior deduction must have been derived from induction.

The problem of the Deductive Method is to find the law of an effect from the laws of the different tendencies of which it is the joint result. The first requisite, therefore, is to know the laws of those tendencies—the law of each of the concurrent causes; and this supposes a previous process of observation or experiment upon each cause separately, or else a previous deduction, which also must depend for its ultimate premises on observation or experiment. Thus, if the subject be social or historical phenomena, the premises of the Deductive Method must be the laws of the causes which determine that class of phenomena; and those causes are human actions, together with the gen-

SOURCE. Reprinted from *A System of Logic*, Vol. 1, by John Stuart Mill, Longman's, Green, & Co., London, 1906.

eral outward circumstances under the influence of which mankind are placed, and which constitute man's position on the earth. The Deductive Method applied to social phenomena must begin, therefore, by investigating, or must suppose to have been already investigated, the laws of human action, and those properties of outward things by which the actions of human beings in society are determined. Some of these general truths will naturally be obtained by observation and experiment, others by deduction; the more complex laws of human action, for example, may be deduced from the simpler ones, but the simple or elementary laws will always and necessarily have been obtained by a directly inductive process.

To ascertain, then, the laws of each separate cause which takes a share in producing the effect is the first desideratum of the Deductive Method. To know what the causes are which must be subjected to this process of study may or may not be difficult. In the case last mentioned, this first condition is of easy fulfilment. That social phenomena depend on the acts and mental impressions of human beings never could have been a matter of any doubt, however imperfectly it may have been known either by what laws those impressions and actions are governed, or to what social consequences their laws naturally lead. Neither, again, after physical science had attained a certain development, could there be any real doubt where to look for the laws on which the phenomena of life depend, since they must be the mechanical and chemical laws of the solid and fluid substances composing the organized body and the medium in which it subsists, together with the peculiar vital laws of the different tissues constituting the organic structure. In other cases really far more simple than these, it was much less obvious in what quarter the causes were to be looked for, as in the case of the celestial phenomena. Until, by combining the laws of certain causes, it was found that those laws explained all the facts which experience had proved concerning the heavenly motions, and led to predictions which it always verified, mankind never knew that those *were* the causes. But whether we are able to put the question before or not until after we have become capable of answering it, in either case it must be answered; the laws of the different causes must be ascertained before we can proceed to deduce from them the conditions of the effect.

The mode of ascertaining those laws neither is nor can be any other than the fourfold method of experimental inquiry, already discussed. A few remarks on the application of that method to cases of the Composition of Causes are all that is requisite.

It is obvious that we cannot expect to find the law of a tendency by an induction from cases in which the tendency is counteracted. The laws of motion could never have been brought to light from the observation of bodies kept at rest by the equilibrium of opposing forces. Even where the tendency is not, in the ordinary sense of the word, counteracted, but only modified, by having its effects compounded with the effects arising from some other tendency or tendencies, we are still in an unfavourable position for tracing, by means of such cases, the law of the tendency itself. It would have been scarcely possible to discover the law that every body in motion tends to continue moving in a straight line, by an induction from instances in which the motion is deflected into a curve, by being compounded with the effect of an accelerating force. Notwithstanding the resources afforded in this description of cases by the Method of Concomitant Variations, the principles of a judicious experimentation prescribe that the law of each of the tendencies should be studied, if possible, in cases in which that tendency operates alone, or in combination with no agencies but those of which the effect can, from previous knowledge, be calculated and allowed for.

Accordingly, in the cases, unfortunately very numerous and important, in which the causes do not suffer themselves to be separated and observed apart, there is much difficulty in laying down with due certainty the inductive foundation necessary to support the deductive method. This difficulty is most of all conspicuous in the case of physiological phenomena: it being seldom possible to separate the different agencies which collectively compose an organised body, without destroying the very phenomena which it is our object to investigate:

> Following life, in creatures we dissect,
> We lose it in the moment we detect.

And for this reason I am inclined to the opinion that physiology (greatly and rapidly progressive as it now is) is embarrassed by greater natural difficulties, and is probably susceptible of a less degree of ultimate perfection than even the social science, inasmuch as it is possible to study the laws and operations of one human mind apart from other minds much less imperfectly than we can study the laws of one organ or tissue of the human body apart from the other organs or tissues.

It has been judiciously remarked that pathological facts, or, to speak in common language, diseases in their different forms and degrees, afford in the case of physiological investigation the most valuable equivalent to experimentation properly so called, inasmuch as they often exhibit to us a definite disturbance in some one organ or organic function, the remaining organs and functions being, in the first instance at least, unaffected. It is true that from the perpetual actions and reactions which are going on among all parts of the organic economy there can be no prolonged disturbance in any one function without ultimately involving many of the others; and when once it has done so, the experiment for the most part loses its scientific value. All depends on observing the early stages of the derangement, which, unfortunately, are of necessity the least marked. If, however, the organs and functions not disturbed in the first instance, become affected in a fixed order of succession, some light is thereby thrown upon the action which one organ exercises over another, and we occasionally obtain a series of effects which we can refer with some confidence to the original local derangement; but for this it is necessary that we should know that the original derangement *was* local. If it was what is termed constitutional, that is, if we do not know in what part of the animal economy it took its rise, or the precise nature of the disturbance which took place in that part, we are unable to determine which of the various derangements was cause and which effect; which of them were produced by one another, and which by the direct, though perhaps tardy, action of the original cause.

Besides natural pathological facts, we can produce pathological facts artificially; we can try experiments, even in the popular sense of the term, by subjecting the living being to some external agent, such as the mercury of our former example, or the section of a nerve to ascertain the functions of different parts of the nervous system. As this experimentation is not intended to obtain a direct solution of any practical question, but to discover general laws, from which afterwards the conditions of any particular effect may be obtained by deduction, the best cases to select are those of which the circumstances can be best ascertained: and such are generally not those in which there is any practical object in view. The experiments are best tried, not in a state of disease, which is essentially a changeable state, but in the condition of health, comparatively a fixed state. In the one, unusual agencies are at work, the results of which we have no means of predicting; in the other, the course of the accustomed physiological phenomena would, it may generally be presumed, remain undisturbed, were it not for the disturbing cause which we introduce.

Such, with the occasional aid of the Method of Concomitant Variations (the latter not less encumbered than the more elementary methods by the peculiar difficulties of the subject) are our inductive resources for ascertaining the laws of the causes considered separately, when we have it not in our power to make trial of them in a state of actual separation. The insufficiency of these resources is so glaring, that no one can be surprised at the backward state of the science of physiology in which indeed our knowledge of causes is so imperfect, that we can neither explain, nor could without specific experience have predicted, many of the facts which are certified to us by the most ordinary observation. Fortunately, we are much better informed as to the empirical laws of the phenomena, that is, the uniformities respecting which we cannot yet decide whether they are cases of causation or mere results of it. Not only has the order in which the facts of organization and life successively manifest themselves, from the first germ of existence to death, been found to be uniform, and very accurately ascertainable; but, by a great application of the Method of Concomitant Variations to the entire facts of comparative anatomy and physiology, the characteristic organic structure corresponding to each class of functions has been determined with considerable precision. Whether these organic conditions are the whole of the conditions, and in many cases whether they are conditions at all, or mere collateral effects of some common cause, we are quite ignorant; nor are we ever likely to know, unless we could construct an organized body, and try whether it would live.

Under such disadvantages do we, in cases of this description, attempt the initial or inductive step in the application of the Deductive Method to complex phenomena. But such, fortunately, is not the common case. In general, the laws of the causes on which the effect depends may be obtained by an induction from comparatively simple instances, or, at the worst, by deduction from the laws of simpler causes, so obtained. By simple instances are meant, of course, those in which the action of each cause was not intermixed or interfered with, or not to any great extent, by other causes whose laws were unknown; and only when the induction which furnished the premises to the Deductive Method rested on such instances has the application of such a method to the ascertainment of the laws of a complex effect been attended with brilliant results.

§ 2. When the laws of the causes have been ascertained, and the first stage of the great logical operation now under discussion satisfactorily accomplished, the second part follows; that of determining from the laws of the causes what effect any given combination of those causes will produce. This is a process of calculation, in the wider sense of the term, and very often involves processes of calculation in the narrowest sense. It is a ratiocination; and when our knowledge of the causes is so perfect as to extend to the exact numerical laws which they observe in producing their effects, the ratiocination may reckon among its premises the theorems of the science of number, in the whole immense extent of that science. Not only are the most advanced truths of mathematics often required to enable us to compute an effect the numerical law of which we already know, but, even by the aid of those most advanced truths, we can go but a little way. In so simple a case as the common problem of three bodies gravitating towards one another, with a force directly as their mass and inversely as the square of the distance, all the resources of the calculus have not hitherto sufficed to obtain any general solution but an approximate one. In a case a little more complex, but still one of the simplest which arise in practice, that of the motion of a projectile, the causes which affect the velocity and range (for example) of a cannon-ball may be all known and estimated; the force of the gun-powder, the angle of elevation, the density of the air, the strength and direction of the wind; but it is one of the most difficult of mathematical problems to combine all these, so as to determine the effect resulting from their collective action.

Besides the theorems of number, those of geometry also come in as premises, where the effects take place in space, and involve motion and extension, as in mechanics, optics, acoustics, astronomy. But when the complication increases, and the effects are under the influence of so many and such shifting causes as to give no room either for fixed numbers or for straight lines and regular curves (as in the case of physiological, to say nothing of mental and social phenomena) the laws of number and extension are applicable, if at all, only on that large scale on which precision of details becomes unimportant. Although these laws play a conspicuous part in the most striking examples of the investigation of nature by the Deductive Method, as, for example, in the Newtonian theory of the celestial motions, they are by no means an indispensable part of every such process. All that is essential in it is reasoning from a general law to a particular case, that is, determining by means of the particular circumstances of that case what result is required in that instance to fulfil the law. Thus in the Torricellian experiment, if the fact that air has weight had been previously known, it would have been easy, without any numerical data, to deduce from the general law of equilibrium that the mercury would stand in the tube at such a height that the column of mercury would exactly balance a column of the atmosphere of equal diameter; because, otherwise, equilibrium would not exist.

By such ratiocinations from the separate laws of the causes we may, to a certain extent, succeed in answering either of the following questions: Given a certain combination of causes, what effect will follow? and, What combination of causes, if it existed, would produce a given effect? In the one case, we determine the effect to be expected in any complex circumstances of which the different elements are known: in the other case we learn, according to what law—under what antecedent conditions—a given complex effect will occur.

§ 3. But (it may here be asked) are not the same arguments by which the methods of direct observation and experiment were set aside as illusory when applied to the laws of complex phenomena, applicable with equal force against the Method of Deduction? When in every single instance a multitude, often an unknown multitude, of agencies, are clashing and combining, what security have we that in our computation à priori we have taken all these into our reckoning? How many must we not generally be ignorant of? Among those which we know, how probable that some have been overlooked; and, even were all included, how vain the pretence of summing up the effects of many causes, unless we know accurately the numerical law of each,—a condition in most cases not to be fulfilled; and even when it is fulfilled, to make the calculation transcends, in any but very simple cases, the utmost power of mathematical science with all its most modern improvements.

These objections have real weight, and would be altogether unanswerable, if there were no test by which, when we employ the Deductive Method, we might judge whether an error of any of the above descriptions had been committed or not. Such a test, however, there is; and its application forms, under the name of Verification, the third essential component part of the Deductive Method, without which all the results it can give have little other value than that of conjecture. To warrant reliance on the general conclusions arrived at by deduction, these conclusions must be found, on careful comparison, to accord with the results of direct observation wherever it can be had. If, when we have experience to compare with them, this experience confirms them, we may safely trust to them in other cases of which our specific experience is yet to come. But if our deductions have led to the conclusion that from a particular combination of causes a given effect would result, then in all known cases where that combination can be shown to have existed, and where the effect has not followed, we must be able to show (or at least to make a probable surmise) what frustrated it: if we cannot, the theory is imperfect, and not yet to be relied upon. Nor is the verification complete, unless some of the cases in which the theory is borne out by the observed result, are of at least equal complexity with any other cases in which its application could be called for.

If direct observation and collation of instances have furnished us with any empirical laws of the effect (whether true in all observed cases, or only true for the most part) the most effectual verification of which the theory could be susceptible would be, that it led deductively to those empirical laws; that the uniformities, whether complete or incomplete, which were observed to exist among the phenomena were accounted for by the laws of the causes —were such as could not but exist if those be really the causes by which the phenomena are produced. Thus it was very reasonably deemed an essential requisite of any true theory of the causes of the celestial motions, that it should lead by deduction to Kepler's laws; which, accordingly, the Newtonian theory did.

In order, therefore, to facilitate the verification of theories obtained by deduction, it is important that as many as possible of the empirical laws of the phenomena should be ascertained by a comparison of instances, conformably to the Method of Agreement, as well as (it must be added) that the phenomena themselves should be described, in the most comprehensive as well as accurate manner possible, by collecting from the observation of parts the simplest possible correct expressions for the coresponding wholes: as when the series of the observed places of a planet was first expressed by a circle, then by a system of epicycles, and subsequently by an ellipse.

It is worth remarking, that complex instances which would have been of no use for the discovery of the simple laws into which we ultimately analyse their phenomena, nevertheless, when they have served to verify the analysis, become additional evidence of the laws themselves. Although we could not have got at the law from complex cases, still when the law, got at otherwise, is found to be in accordance with the result of a complex case, that case becomes a new experiment on the law, and helps to confirm what it did not assist to discover. It is a new trial of the principle in a different set of circumstances; and occasionally serves to eliminate some circumstance not previously excluded, and the exclusion of which might require an experiment impossible to be executed. This was strikingly conspicuous in the example formerly quoted, in which the difference between the observed and the calculated velocity of sound was ascertained to result from the heat extricated by the condensation which takes place in each sonorous vibration. This was a trial, in new circumstances, of the law of the development of heat by compression; and it added materially to the proof of the universality of that law. Accordingly any law of nature is deemed to have gained in point of certainty by being found to explain some complex case which had not previously been thought of in connection with it; and this indeed is a consideration to which it is the habit of scientific inquirers to attach rather too much value than too little.

To the Deductive Method, thus characterised in its three constituent parts, Induction, Ratiocination, and Verification, the human mind is indebted for its most conspicuous triumphs in the investigation of nature. To it we owe all the theories by which vast and complicated phenomena are embraced under a few simple laws, which, considered as the laws of those great phenomena, could never have been detected by their direct study. We may form some conception of what the method has done for us from the case of the celestial motions, one of the simplest among the greater instances of the Composition of Causes, since (except in a few cases not of primary importance) each of the heavenly bodies may be considered, without material inaccuracy, to be never at one time influenced by the attraction of more than two bodies, the sun and one other planet or satellite; making with the reaction of the body itself, and the force generated by the body's own motion and acting in the direction of the tangent, only four different agents on the concurrence of which the motions of that body depend; a much smaller number, no doubt, than that by which any other of the great phenomena of nature is determined or modified. Yet how could we ever have ascertained the combination of forces on which the motions of the earth and planets are dependent by merely comparing the orbits or velocities of different planets, or the different velocities or positions of the same planet? Notwithstanding the regularity which manifests itself in those motions, in a degree so rare among the effects of concurrence of causes; and although the periodical recurrence of exactly the same effect affords positive proof that all the combinations of causes which occur at all, recur periodically; we should not have known what the causes were, if the existence of agencies precisely similar on our own earth had not, fortunately, brought the causes themselves within the reach of experimentation under simple circumstances. As we shall have occasion to analyse, farther on, this great example of the Method of Deduction, we shall not occupy any time with it here, but shall proceed to that secondary application of the Deductive Method the result of which is not to prove laws of phenomena, but to explain them.

OF THE EXPLANATION OF LAWS OF NATURE

§ 1. The deductive operation by which we derive the law of an effect from the laws of the causes, the concurrence of which gives rise to it, may be undertaken either for the purpose of discovering the law, or of explaining a law already discovered. The word *explanation* occurs so continually and holds so important a place in philosophy, that a little time spent in fixing the meaning of it will be profitably employed.

An individual fact is said to be explained by pointing out its cause, that is, by stating the law or laws of causation of which its production is an instance. Thus a conflagration is explained when it is proved to have arisen from a spark falling into the midst of a heap of combustibles; and in a similar manner, a law of uniformity in nature is said to be explained when another law or laws are pointed out, of which that law itself is but a case, and from which it could be deduced.

§ 2. There are three distinguishable sets of circumstances in which a law of causation may be explained from, or, as it also is often expressed, resolved into, other laws.

The first is the case already so fully considered; an intermixture of laws, producing a joint effect equal to the sum of the effects of the causes taken separately. The law of the complex effect is explained by being resolved into the separate laws of the causes which contribute to it. Thus the law of the motion of a planet is resolved into the law of the acquired force which tends to produce an uniform motion in the tangent, and the law of the centripetal force which tends to produce an accelerating motion towards the sun; the real motion being a compound of the two.

It is necessary here to remark, that in this resolution of the law of a complex effect, the laws of which it is compounded are not the only elements. It is resolved into the laws of the separate causes, together with the fact of their co-existence. The one is as essential an ingredient as the other; whether the object be to discover the law of the effect, or only to explain it. To deduce the laws of the heavenly motions, we require not only to know the law of a rectilineal and that of a gravitative force, but the existence of both these forces in the celestial regions, and even their relative amount. The complex laws of causation are thus resolved into two distinct kinds of elements: the one, simpler laws of causation, the other (in the aptly selected expression of Dr. Chalmers) collocations; the collocations consisting in the existence of certain agents or powers, in certain circumstances of place and time. We shall hereafter have occasion to return to this distinction, and to dwell on it at such length as dispenses with the necessity of further insisting on it here. The first mode, then, of the explanation of Laws of Causation, is when the law of an effect is resolved into the various tendencies of which it is the result, together with the laws of those tendencies.

§ 3. A second case is when, between what seemed the cause and what was supposed to be its effect, further observation detects an intermediate link; a fact caused by the antecedent, and in its turn causing the consequent; so that the cause at first assigned is but the remote cause, operating through the intermediate phenomenon. A seemed the cause of C, but it subsequently appeared that A was only the cause of B, and that it is B which was the cause of C. For example: mankind were aware that the act of touching an outward object caused a sensation. It was subsequently discovered, that after we have touched the object, and before we experience the sensation, some change takes place in a kind of thread called a nerve, which extends from our outward organs to the brain. Touching the object, therefore, is only the remote cause of our sensation; that is, not the cause, properly speaking, but the cause of the cause;—the real cause of the sensation is the change in the state of the nerve. Future experience may not only give us more knowledge than we now have of the particular nature of this change, but may also interpolate another link: between the contact (for example) of the object with our outward organs, and the production of the change of state in the nerve, there may take place some electric phenomenon, or some phenomenon of a nature not resembling the effects of any known agency. Hitherto, however, no such intermediate link has been discovered; and the touch of the object must be considered, provisionally, as the proximate cause of the affection of the nerve. The sequence, therefore, of a sensation of touch on contact with an object is ascertained not to be an ultimate law; it is resolved, as the phrase is, into two other laws,—the law that contact with an object produces an affection of the nerve, and the law that an affection of the nerve produces sensation.

To take another example: the more powerful acids corrode or blacken organic compounds. This is a case of causation, but of remote causation;

and is said to be explained when it is shown that there is an intermediate link, namely, the separation of some of the chemical elements of the organic structure from the rest, and their entering into combination with the acid. The acid causes this separation of the elements, and the separation of the elements causes the disorganization, and often the charring of the structure. So, again, chlorine extracts colouring matters (whence its efficacy in bleaching) and purifies the air from infection. This law is resolved into the two following laws. Chlorine has a powerful affinity for bases of all kinds, particularly metallic bases and hydrogen. Such bases are essential elements of colouring matters and contagious compounds, which substances, therefore, are decomposed and destroyed by chlorine.

§ 4. It is of importance to remark, that when a sequence of phenomena is thus resolved into other laws, they are always laws more general than itself. The law that A is followed by C, is less general than either of the laws which connect B with C and A with B. This will appear from very simple considerations.

All laws of causation are liable to be counteracted or frustrated by the non-fulfilment of some negative condition: the tendency, therefore, of B to produce C may be defeated. Now the law that A produces B, is equally fulfilled whether B is followed by C or not; but the law that A produces C by means of B, is of course only fulfilled when B is really followed by C, and is therefore less general than the law that A produces B. It is also less general than the law that B produces C. For B may have other causes besides A; and as A produces C only by means of B, while B produces C whether it has itself been produced by A or by anything else, the second law embraces a greater number of instances, covers as it were a greater space of ground, than the first.

Thus, in our former example, the law that the contact of an object causes a change in the state of the nerve, is more general than the law that contact with an object causes sensation, since, for aught we know, the change in the nerve may equally take place when, from a counteracting cause, as, for instance, strong mental excitement, the sensation does not follow; as in a battle, where wounds are sometimes received without any consciousness of receiving them. And again, the law that change in the state of a nerve produces sensation, is more general than the law that contact with an object produces sensation; since the sensation equally follows the change in the nerve when not produced by contact with an object, but by some other cause; as in the well-known case when a person who has lost a limb feels the same sensation which he has been accustomed to call a pain in the limb.

Not only are the laws of more immediate sequence, into which the law of a remote sequence is resolved, laws of greater generality than that law is, but (as a consequence of, or rather as implied in, their greater generality) they are more to be relied on; there are fewer chances of their being ultimately found not to be universally true. From the moment when the sequence of A and C is shown not to be immediate, but to depend on an intervening phenomenon, then, however constant and invariable the sequence of A and C has hitherto been found, possibilities arise of its failure, exceeding those which can effect either of the more immediate sequences, A, B, and B, C. The tendency of A to produce C may be defeated by whatever is capable of defeating either the tendency of A to produce B, or the tendency of B to produce C; it is therefore twice as liable to failure as either of those more elementary tendencies; and the generalization that A is always followed by C, is twice as likely to be found erroneous. And so of the converse generalization, that C is always preceded and caused by A; which will be erroneous not only if there should happen to be a second immediate mode of production of C itself, but, moreover, if there be a second mode of production of B, the immediate antecedent of C in the sequence.

The resolution of the one generalization into the other two not only shows that there are possible limitations of the former, from which its two elements are exempt, but shows also where these are to be looked for. As soon as we know that B intervenes between A and C, we also know that if there be cases in which the sequence of A and C does not hold, these are most likely to be found by studying the effects or the conditions of the phenomenon B.

It appears, then, that in the second of the three modes in which a law may be resolved into other laws, the latter are more general, that is, extend to more cases, and are also less likely to require limitation from subsequent experience, than the law which they serve to explain. They are more nearly unconditional; they are defeated by fewer contingencies; they are a nearer approach to the universal truth of nature. The same observations are still more evidently true with regard to the first of the three modes of resolution. When the law of an effect of combined forces is resolved into the separate laws of the causes, the nature of the case implies that the law of the effect is less general than the law of any of the causes, since it only holds when they are combined; while the law of any one of the causes holds good both then, and also when that cause acts apart from the rest. It is also manifest that the complex law is liable to be oftener unfulfilled than any one of the simpler laws of which it is the result, since every contingency which defeats any of the laws prevents so much of the effect as depends on it, and thereby defeats the complex law. The mere rusting, for example, of some small part of a great machine, often suffices entirely to prevent the effect which ought to result from the joint action of all the parts. The law of the effect of a combination of causes is always subject to the whole of the negative conditions which attach to the action of all the causes severally.

There is another and an equally strong reason why the law of a complex effect must be less general than the laws of the causes which conspire to produce it. The same causes, acting according to the same laws, and differing only in the proportions in which they are combined, often produce effects which differ not merely in quantity, but in kind. The combination of a centripetal with a projectile force, in the proportions which obtain in all the planets and satellites of our solar system, gives rise to an elliptical motion; but if the ratio of the two forces to each other were slightly altered, it is demonstrated that the motion produced would be in a circle, or a parabola, or an hyperbola; and it is thought that in the case of some comets one of these is probably the fact. Yet the law of the parabolic motion would be resolvable into the very same simple laws into which that of the elliptical motion is resolved, namely, the law of the permanence of rectilineal motion and the law of gravitation. If, therefore, in the course of ages, some circumstance were to manifest itself which, without defeating the law of either of those forces, should merely alter their proportion to one another (such as the shock of some solid body, or even the accumulating effect of the resistance of the medium in which astronomers have been led to surmise that the motions of the heavenly bodies take place) the elliptical motion might be changed into a motion in some other conic section; and the complex law that the planetary motions take place in ellipses would be deprived of its universality, though the discovery would not at all detract from the universality of the simpler laws into which that complex law is resolved. The law, in short, of each of the concurrent causes remains the same, however their collocations may vary; but the law of their joint effect varies with every difference in the collocations. There needs no more to show how much more general the elementary laws must be than any of the complex laws which are derived from them.

§ 5. Besides the two modes which have been treated of, there is a third mode in which laws are resolved into one another; and in this it is self-evident that they are resolved into laws more general than themselves. This third mode is the *subsumption* (as it has been called) of one law under another, or (what comes to the same thing) the gathering up of several laws into one more general law which includes them all. The most splendid example of this operation was when terrestrial gravity and the central force of the solar system were brought together under the general law of gravitation. It had been proved antecedently that the earth and the other planets tend to the sun; and it had been known from the earliest times that terrestrial bodies tend towards the earth. These were similar phenomena; and to enable them both to be subsumed under one law, it was only necessary to prove that, as the effects were similar in quality, so also they, as to quantity, conform to the same rules. This was first shown to be true of the moon, which agreed with terrestrial objects not only in tending to a centre, but in the fact that this centre was the earth. The tendency of the moon towards the earth being ascertained to vary as the inverse square of the distance, it was deduced from this, by direct calculation, that if the moon were as near to the earth as terrestrial objects are, and the acquired force in the direction of the tangent were suspended, the moon would fall towards the earth through exactly as many feet in a second as those objects do by virtue of their weight. Hence the inference was irresistible that the moon also tends to the earth by virtue of its weight, and that the two phenomena, the tendency of the moon to the earth and the tendency of terrestrial objects to the earth, being not only similar in quality, but, when in the same circumstances, identical in quantity, are cases of one and the same law of causation. But the tendency of the moon to the earth, and the tendency of the earth and planets to the sun, were already known to be cases of the same law of causation: and thus the law of all these tendencies and the law of terrestrial gravity were recognized as identical, and were subsumed under one general law, that of gravitation.

In a similar manner, the laws of magnetic phenomena have more recently been subsumed under known laws of electricity. It is thus that the most general laws of nature are usually arrived at: we mount to them by successive steps. For, to arrive by correct induction at laws which hold under such an immense variety of circumstances, laws so general as to be independent of any varieties of space or time which we are able to observe, requires for the most part many distinct sets of experiments or observations, conducted at different times and by different people. One part of the law is first ascertained, afterwards another part: one set of observations teaches us that the law holds good under some conditions, another that it holds good under other conditions, by combining which observations we find that it holds good under conditions much more general, or even universally. The general law, in this case, is literally the sum of all the partial ones; it is a recognition of the same sequence in different sets of instances, and may, in fact, be regarded as merely one step in the process of elimination. The tendency of bodies towards one another, which we now call gravity, had at first been observed only on the earth's surface, where it manifested itself only as a tendency of all bodies towards the earth, and might, therefore, be ascribed to a peculiar property of the earth itself: one of the circumstances, namely, the proximity of the earth, had not been eliminated. To eliminate this circumstance required a fresh set of instances in other parts of the universe: these we could not ourselves create; and though nature had created them for us, we were placed in very unfavourable circumstances for observing them. To make these observations fell naturally to the lot of a different set of persons from those who studied terrestrial phenomena, and had, indeed, been a matter of great interest at a time when the idea of explaining celestial facts by terrestrial laws was looked upon as the confounding of an indefeasible distinction. When, however, the celestial motions were accurately ascertained, and the deductive processes performed, from which it appeared that their laws and those of terrestrial gravity corresponded, those celestial observations became a set of instances which exactly eliminated the circumstance of proximity to the earth, and proved that in the original case, that of terrestrial objects, it was not the earth, as such, that caused the motion or the pressure, but the circumstance common to that case with the celestial instances, namely, the presence of some great body within certain limits of distance.

§ 6. There are, then, three modes of explaining laws of causation, or, which is the same thing, resolving them into other laws. First, when the law of an effect of combined causes is resolved into the separate laws of the causes, together with the fact of their combination. Secondly, when the law which connects any two links, not proximate, in a chain of causation, is resolved into the laws which connect each with the intermediate links. Both of these are cases of resolving one law into two or more; in the third, two or more are resolved into one: when, after the law has been shown to hold good in several different classes of cases, we decide that what is true in each of these classes of cases is true under some more general supposition, consisting of what all those classes of cases have in common. We may here remark that this last operation involves none of the uncertainties attendant on induction by the Method of Agreement, since we need not suppose the result to be extended by way of inference to any new class of case different from those by the comparison of which it was engendered.

In all these three processes, laws are, as we have seen, resolved into laws more general than themselves; laws extending to all the cases which the former extended to, and others besides. In the first two modes they are also resolved into laws more certain, in other words, more universally true than themselves; they are, in fact, proved not to be themselves laws of nature, the character of which is to be universally true, but *results* of laws of nature, which may be only true conditionally, and for the most part. No difference of this sort exists in the third case, since here the partial laws are, in fact, the very same law as the general one, and any exception to them would be an exception to it too.

By all the three processes, the range of deductive science is extended; since the laws, thus resolved, may be thenceforth deduced demonstratively from the laws into which they are resolved. As already remarked, the same deductive process which proves a law or fact of causation if unknown, serves to explain it when known.

The word explanation is here used in its philosophical sense. What is called explaining one law of nature by another, is but substituting one mystery for another, and does nothing to render the general course of nature other than mysterious: we can no more assign a *why* for the most extensive laws than for the partial ones. The explanation may substitute a mystery which has become familiar, and has grown to *seem* not mysterious, for one which is still strange. And this is the meaning of explanation, in common parlance. But the process with which we are here concerned often does the very contrary: it resolves a phenomenon with which we are familiar into one of which we previously knew little or nothing; as when the common fact of the fall of heavy bodies was resolved into the tendency of all particles of matter towards one another. It must be kept constantly in view, therefore, that in science, those who speak of explaining any phenomenon mean (or should mean) pointing out not some more familiar, but merely some more general phenomenon, of which it is a partial exemplification; or some laws of causation which produce it by their joint or successive action, and from which, therefore, its conditions may be determined deductively. Every such operation brings us a step nearer towards answering the question which was stated in a previous chapter as comprehending the whole problem of the investigation of nature, viz. What are the fewest assumptions, which being granted, the order of nature as it exists would be the result? What are the fewest general propositions from which all the uniformities existing in nature could be deduced?

The laws, thus explained or resolved, are sometimes said to be *accounted for;* but the expression is incorrect, if taken to mean anything more than what has been already stated. In minds not habituated to accurate thinking, there is often a confused notion that the general laws are the *causes* of the partial ones; that the law of general gravitation, for example, causes the phenomenon of the fall of bodies to the earth. But to assert this would be a misuse of the word cause: terrestrial gravity is not an effect of general gravitation, but a *case* of it; that is, one kind of the particular instances in which that general law obtains. To account for a law of nature means, and can mean, nothing more than to assign other laws more general, together with collocations, which laws and collactions being supposed, the partial law follows without any additional supposition.

23. THE STRUCTURE OF A SCIENTIFIC SYSTEM

Richard Bevan Braithwaite

A scientific system consists of a set of hypotheses which form a deductive system; that is, which is arranged in such a way that from some of the hypotheses as premisses all the other hypotheses logically follow. The propositions in a deductive system may be considered as being arranged in an order of levels, the hypotheses at the highest level being those which occur only as premisses in the system, those at the lowest level being those which occur only as conclusions in the system, and those at intermediate levels being those which occur as conclusions of deductions from higher-level hypotheses and which serve as premisses for deductions to lower-level hypotheses.

Let us consider as an example a fairly simple deductive system with hypotheses on three levels. This example has been selected principally because it illustrates excellently the points that need to be made, and partly because the construction and the establishment of a similar system by Galileo marks a turning-point in the history of science.

The system has one highest-level hypothesis:

I. Every body near the earth freely falling towards the Earth falls with an acceleration of 32 feet per second per second.

From this hypothesis there follows, by simple principles of the integral calculus,[1] the hypothesis:

SOURCE. Reprinted with permission of Cambridge University Press from *Scientific Explanation* by Richard Bevan Braithwaite. Copyright © 1955 by Cambridge University Press.

[1] Hypothesis I can be expressed by the differential equation $d^2s/dt^2 = 32$, whose solution, under the conditions that $s = 0$ and $ds/dt = 0$ when $t = 0$, is $s = 16t^2$.

II. Every body starting from rest and freely falling towards the Earth falls $16t^2$ feet in t seconds, whatever number t may be.

From II there follows in accordance with the logical principle (the *applicative principle*) permitting the application of a generalization to its instances, the infinite set of hypotheses:

III*a*. Every body starting from rest and freely falling for 1 second towards the Earth falls a distance of 16 feet.

III*b*. Every body starting from rest and freely falling for 2 seconds towards the Earth falls a distance of 64 feet.

And so on.

In this deductive system the hypotheses at the second and third levels (II, III*a*, III*b*, etc.) follow from the one highest-level hypothesis (I); those at the third level (III*a*, III*b*, etc.) also follow from the one at the second level (II).

The hypotheses in this deductive system are empirical general propositions with diminishing generality. The empirical testing of the deductive system is effected by testing the lowest-level hypotheses in the system. The confirmation or refutation of these is the criterion by which the truth of all the hypotheses in the system is tested. The establishment of a system as a set of true propositions depends upon the establishment of its lowest-level hypotheses.

The lowest-level hypothesis III*a* is tested by applying it to a particular case. A body is allowed to fall freely for 1 second and the distance it falls measured.[2] If it is found that it falls 16 feet, the hypothesis is confirmed; if it is found that it falls more, or less, than 16 feet, the hypothesis is refuted.

It is convenient to treat the logic of this procedure as consisting of two steps. A case is either observed, or experimentally produced, of a body falling for 1 second. The following proposition is then empirically known:

e_1. This body freely falls for 1 second towards the Earth, starting from rest.

The general hypothesis III*a* is then applied to this case by first deducing from III*a* the proposition:

III*a'*. It is only the case that this body, starting from rest, freely falls for 1 second towards the Earth if it falls a distance of 16 feet.

From this application of the general hypothesis, together with the proposition e_1, there is deduced:

f_1. This body falls 16 feet.

The testing of a scientific hypothesis thus consists in deducing from it a proposition of the form «e_1 only if f_1». Then there follows from the conjunc-

---

[2] The system tested by Galileo was, in fact, more complicated than our example. Galileo was unable to measure times of fall of bodies accurately enough to test III*a*; what he tested empirically was a more elaborate system on which the lowest-level hypotheses were propositions about descents of bodies rolling down grooves in inclined planes.

tion of e_1 with this proposition the third proposition f_1, whose truth or falsity is observed.

If f_1, the logical consequence of e_1 and IIIa′, is observed to be true, the hypothesis IIIa is ordinarily said to be confirmed. The piece of evidence f_1, conjoined with e_1 (which conjunction will be called an *instance* of the hypothesis), is said to support the hypothesis. But it is clear that this one piece of evidence is insufficient to prove the hypothesis. It would only do so if the hypothesis were a logical consequence of the conjunction of f_1 with e_1. This, of course, is not the case. It is perfectly possible for the hypothesis to hold in this one instance, but to be false in some other instance, and consequently false as a general proposition. And, indeed, this is the case however many times the hypothesis is confirmed. However many conjunctions f_1 with e_1, f_2 with e_2, etc., have been examined and found to confirm the hypothesis, there will still be unexamined cases in which the hypothesis might be false without contradicting any of the observed facts.[3] Thus the empirical evidence of its instances never proves the hypothesis: in suitable cases we may say that it *establishes* the hypothesis, meaning by this that the evidence makes it reasonable to accept the hypothesis; but it never *proves* the hypothesis in the sense that the hypothesis is a logical consequence of the evidence.

The situation is different if f_1 is observed to be false. For the conjunction of not-f_1 with e_1 is logically incompatible with the hypothesis being true; the falsity of the hypothesis is a logical consequence of the conjunction of not-f_1 with e_1. Calling this conjunction a *contrary instance* of the hypothesis, we may say that a hypothesis is proved to be false, or refuted, by one known contrary instance.

This asymmetry of confirmation and refutation is a consequence of the fact that all the hypotheses of a science are general propositions of the form «Every A is B». Propositions of the form «Some A's are B's» (existential propositions),[4] which are the contradictories of general propositions, have the reverse asymmetry; they can be proved by one instance, but no number of contrary instances will suffice to disprove them.

It has been said that there is no greater tragedy than the murder of a beautiful scientific hypothesis by one discordant instance. As will be seen, it

[3] Unless, of course, the hypothesis has only a limited number of instances, and not only have all these instances been examined, but it is known that there are no unexamined instances. Generalizations with only a limited number of instances, which can be proved from a knowledge of these instances by what logicians have called *perfect induction*, present no logical problem; since they are of little interest in science, they will not be considered further. All scientific hypotheses will be taken to be generalizations with an unlimited number of instances.

[4] In the terminology of traditional logic my existential propositions would be called "particular propositions" and my general propositions "universal propositions," the term "general proposition" being used to cover both types.

is usually possible to save any particular higher-level hypothesis from this fate by choosing instead to sacrifice some other higher-level hypothesis which is essential to the deduction. But the fact that in principle a scientific hypothesis (or a conjunction of scientific hypotheses, if more than one are required for the deduction of the observable facts) can be conclusively disproved by observation, although it can never be conclusively proved, sharply distinguishes the question of the refutation of a scientific theory from that of its establishment. The former question is a simple matter of deductive logic, if the system of hypotheses is taken as a whole;[5] the latter question involves the justification of inductive inference, a problem which has worried philosophers since the time of Hume. . . .

So far as confirmation is concerned the relation between lowest-level hypotheses and a hypothesis on the next higher level is similar to that between instances of a lowest-level hypothesis and the hypothesis itself. In our examples, the third-level hypotheses IIIa, IIIb, etc., are special cases of the second-level hypothesis II; each of them can be seen to follow from II in accordance with the applicative principle, but II is not a logical consequence of any finite number of hypotheses such as IIIa, IIIb, etc. The formula $s = 16t^2$ can hold for any finite number of values of s and t without being true in general. This is most easily seen by representing the lowest-level hypotheses as points on a graph (fig. 1). The second-level hypothesis is represented by a curve passing through these points. Any number of curves beside the parabola $s = 16t^2$ can be drawn to pass through any finite number of points. Thus a refutation of IIIa serves to refute II, but a proof of IIIa does not prove II. Nevertheless, evidence in favour of IIIa is evidence in favour of II; and if the evidence is good enough for us to regard IIIa, IIIb, etc., as established, it may also be good enough for us to regard II also as established.

A similar relationship holds between II and I as holds between IIIa and II. The difference is that, whereas the method of deducing IIIa from II is merely the logical principle involved in implying a general proposition to a special case of it (the applicative principle), and this is implicit in the use of any general proposition, the deduction of II from I is made by using methods of the integral calculus, either explicitly by using known theorems of the calculus, or implicitly by constructing a special geometrical proof, as Galileo, ignorant of the calculus, had to do. But this difference is irrelevant to the general nature of the procedure. II is just as much a logical consequence of I as IIIa is of II, although to know the former relationship requires a knowledge of mathematics which must be specially learnt, whereas the

[5] So simple that Karl Popper takes the possibility of falsification by experience as the criterion for a system of hypotheses being an empirical scientific system [*Logik der Forschung* (Vienna, 1935), § 6].

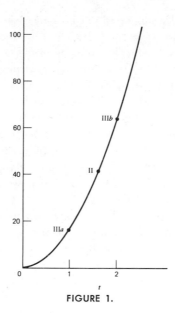

FIGURE 1.

latter relationship we learnt when we were taught how to use the word "every."

The general characteristic of a deductive system is that the logical strength of the hypotheses increases the higher their level. Sometimes, although each of the hypotheses at a certain level is weaker than the one hypothesis at the next higher level from which they are all deducible, yet the conjunction of them all is equivalent to that hypothesis. This will happen when there are a limited number of special cases of the higher-level hypothesis, each of which is asserted by one of the lower-level hypotheses. It should be noted that this situation never arises in the relation of a lowest-level hypothesis to its instances, since no hypothesis is a mere enumerative generalization of a finite set of instances.

There are other important points about scientific deductive systems which are illustrated by our example. Since observed instances of IIIa are evidence for II as well as for IIIa, they are *indirect* evidence[6] for all the logical consequences of II, e.g. IIIb. Thus a hypothesis in a deductive system not at the

---

[6] Observed facts will be said to be *indirect evidence* for a hypothesis p if they are direct evidence for a hypothesis q (or for a set of hypotheses q_1, q_2, etc.) from which p logically follows. A corollary of this definition is that if the observed facts are direct evidence for a set of hypotheses q_1, q_2, . . . , q_n, they are indirect evidence for any one of these hypotheses, since each logically follows from the set.

highest level is empirically supported not only by observation of its instances, or of instances of hypotheses lying below it in the system, but also by observations of instances of other hypotheses in the system. The evidence for a scientific hypothesis is thus frequently much stronger that the *direct* evidence for it of its instances, or of instances of a hypothesis which logically follows from it; it also includes, as indirect evidence, the direct evidence for any higher-level hypothesis from which it logically follows. My reasons for believing that all men are mortal are not confined to knowledge that a great number of men have died; they include also knowledge that a great number of animals have died, which knowledge supports the wider generalization that all animals are mortal. One of the main purposes in organizing scientific hypotheses into a deductive system is in order that the direct evidence for each lowest-level hypothesis may become indirect evidence for all the other lowest-level hypotheses; although no amount of empirical evidence suffices to prove any of the hypotheses in the system, yet any piece of empirical evidence for any part of the system helps towards establishing the whole of the system.

But there is one important point about most scientific deductive systems which our simple example does not illustrate. In our example only one higher-level hypothesis is used as a premiss in deductions to lower-level hypotheses. II logically follows from I alone, III*a*, III*b*, etc., from II alone. In most scientific deductive systems, however, each deduction requires more than one premiss. For instance, the example of Galileo's deductive system was incorporated by Newton into a larger deductive system in which I ceased to be the highest-level hypothesis, but was instead presented as deducible from the conjunction of two higher-level hypotheses, one being that called (in the plural) Newton's Laws of Motion and the other being his Law of Universal Gravitation.[7] Consequently most of the deductive systems used in science are not of the simply branching type exemplified by Galileo's system, but are systems in which there are a number of higher-level hypotheses all of which are required to serve as premisses in one or other of the deductions in the system. Of course if we were to extend our meaning of scientific hypothesis to include conjunctions of generalizations, we could lump all the premisses together into one conjunctive hypothesis, and have only one highest-level hypothesis in every system. Thus any scientific system could be treated as a simply branching system. But to combine disparate hypotheses into one conjunctive hypothesis would confuse thought. And it would have the added disadvantage that we should have to admit as scientific hypotheses propositions which were not themselves generalizations.

Since the consequences of any set of hypotheses are also consequences of

---

[7] I am not stating the hypotheses explicitly, because they make use of the terms *force* and *mass* which are theoretical concepts of the sort to be discussed in Chapter III.

any set of hypotheses which includes this set, the highest-level hypotheses could always be increased by adding any hypothesis to them. But to do this would be to make the observed facts evidence for a set of hypotheses which included one which played no part in their deduction from the set, and would thus make them indirect evidence for the supernumerary hypothesis and for its consequences. Since the supernumerary hypothesis might be any generalization whatever, this would have the undesirable result that any observable fact would be indirect evidence for any generalization whatever.[8] To avoid this result we stipulate that each of the highest-level hypotheses in a system must be necessary for the deduction of the lower-level hypotheses in the system; none must be included which play no part in the system. Similarly, we must treat as two systems, and not conflate into one, two systems whose sets of highest-level hypotheses have no hypothesis in common.

The fact that most scientific deductive systems employ more than one highest-level hypothesis has an important bearing upon the empirical testing of these hypotheses. As has been shown, one contrary instance is sufficient to refute a generalization, and the refutation of this generalization (a lowest-level hypothesis) will be sufficient to refute a higher-level hypothesis from which it logically follows. But suppose, as is frequently the case, that we are considering a deductive system in which there is no one higher-level hypothesis from which this lowest-level hypothesis follows, but instead the system is such that this follows from two or more higher-level hypotheses. Then what will be refuted by the refutation of the lowest-level hypothesis will be the conjunction of these two or more higher-level hypotheses; what will be a logical consequence of the falsity of the lowest-level hypothesis will be that at least one of the higher-level hypotheses is false.

Thus in the case of almost all scientific hypotheses, except the straightforward generalizations of observable facts which serve as the lowest-level hypotheses in the deductive system, complete refutation is no more possible than is complete proof. What experience can tell us is that there is something wrong somewhere, in the system; but we can make our choice as to which part of the system we consider to be at fault. In almost every system it is possible to maintain any one hypothesis in the face of apparently contrary evidence at the expense of modifying the others. Ptolemy was able to save

---

[8] C. G. Hempel [*Mind*, n.s., vol. 54 (1945), p. 104] raises a point similar to this as an objection to defining the 'confirmation' of a hypothesis in terms of what can be deduced from the hypothesis in conjunction with observable propositions. I do not profess to give a precise definition of 'confirmation'; but I believe that the limitation of hypotheses to be themselves general propositions, and the exclusion of supernumerary hypotheses from a scientific system, will avoid the difficulties pointed out by Hempel. There is an elaborate discussion of the whole subject in Rudolf Carnap, *Logical Foundations of Probability* (Chicago, 1950), §§ 87 f.

the geocentric hypothesis by supposing that the planets moved in complicated orbits round the earth. But at some time a point is reached at which the modifications in a system required to save a hypothesis become more unplausible than the rejection of the hypothesis; and then the hypothesis is rejected.

The scientific deductive system which physics has gradually built up by incorporating the original deductive systems of Galileo and his contemporaries has developed by the rejection of hypotheses when the system which included them led to the prediction of observable results which were found not to be observed. But exactly which hypothesis was to be rejected at each point was a matter for the 'hunch' of the physicist. Generally speaking, a hypothesis was not rejected until an alternative hypothesis was available to take its place. Long before Einstein propounded his theory of gravitation it was known that Newton's theory could not account by itself for the observed motion of Mercury's perihelion. But Newton's theory was not dethroned until Einstein's theory was available to take its place. The process of refuting a scientific hypothesis is thus more complicated than it appears to be at first sight.

There is no hard and fast line at the point at which the common-sense synthesis of experience becomes a scientific ordering in a scientific system. Just as in tracing back common-sense thought either in the individual or in the race there is no point at which there were no generalizations believed, so in the history of a science there is rarely any one historical date at which it is possible to say that the first hypothesis was adumbrated. The history of a science is the history of the development of scientific systems from those containing so few generalizations, and these so flimsily established that one might well hesitate to call them systems at all, into imposing structures with a hierarchy of hypotheses. This development takes place by the establishment of some of the original hypotheses, by the replacement of others by better established hypotheses, and by the construction of higher-level hypotheses under which the lower-level hypotheses can be subsumed. The problems raised by this development are of many different kinds. There are historical problems, both as to what causes the individual scientist to discover a new idea, and as to what causes the general acceptance of scientific ideas. The solution of these historical problems involves the individual psychology of thinking and the sociology of thought. None of these questions are our business here. What we are concerned with are the straight logical problems of the internal structure of scientific systems and of the roles played in such systems by the formal truths of logic and mathematics, and also the problems of inductive logic or epistemology concerned with the grounds for the reasonableness or otherwise of accepting well-established scientific systems.

E. Falsifiability and Corroboration

In recent years Karl Popper's views about falsifiability and corroboration have become a popular approach to the problem of the justification of inferences that go beyond the data. He urges that since there are always alternative explanations of any given set of data and since it is always possible that inconsistent data might turn up, we can never prove any conclusions that go beyond the data. The only possibility is that we can falsify them by finding data that are inconsistent with them. Thus, according to Popper, inductive conclusions are not verifiable, only falsifiable.

He does appear to attempt to present a positive position, however, through the use of his notion of corroboration. It is this positive-appearing view that is presented in the following passage. Roughly speaking, he holds that a hypothesis is corroborated to the extent that it is improbable and has withstood severe tests. People have wondered what advantage on Popper's own terms corroboration has over confirmation, an ideal rejected by Popper, since a corroborated hypothesis is still capable of being falsified by inconsistent data, and there are always alternative explanations. Perhaps corroboration is not a positive position after all.

Although this view about corroboration (especially the reference to having "withstood severe tests") is humanistic in flavor, Popper comes from a radical empiricist background. His efforts are one example of an attempt to bridge the gap.

Included in this selection also is Popper's interesting criticism of a variety of views that treat hypotheses as probability statements, making in the course of his criticism the important distinction between the probability of a hypothesis and the probability asserted by a hypothesis.

24. CORROBORATION, OR HOW A THEORY STANDS UP TO TESTS

Sir Karl Popper

Theories are not verifiable, but they can be "corroborated."

The attempt has often been made to describe theories as being neither *true* nor *false*, but instead more or less *probable*. Inductive logic, more especially, has been developed as a logic which may ascribe not only the two values "true" and "false" to statements, but also degrees of probability; a type of logic which will here be called *"probability logic."* According to those who believe in probability logic, induction should determine the degree of probability of a statement. And a principle of induction should either *make it sure* that the induced statement is "probably valid" or else it should *make it probable*, in its turn—for the principle of induction might itself be only "probably valid." Yet in my view, the whole problem of the probability of hypotheses is misconceived. Instead of discussing the "probability" of a hypothesis we should try to assess what tests, what trials, it has withstood; that is, we should try to assess how far it has been able to prove its fitness to survive by standing up to tests. In brief, we should try to assess how far it has been "corroborated."[1]

SOURCE. Reprinted from Chapter X of *The Logic of Scientific Discovery* by Karl R. Popper, copyright © 1959 by Karl Raimund Popper, Basic Books, Inc., Publishers, New York.

[1] I introduced the terms *"corroboration"* (*"Bewährung"*) and especially *"degree of corroboration"* (*"Grad der Bewährung," "Bewährungsgrad"*) in my book because I wanted a *neutral* term to describe the degree to which a hypothesis has stood up to severe tests, and thus "proved its mettle." By "neutral" I mean a term not prejudging the issue whether, by standing up to tests, the hypothesis becomes "more probable," in the sense

CONCERNING THE SO-CALLED VERIFICATION OF HYPOTHESES

The fact that theories are not verifiable has often been overlooked. People often say of a theory that it is verified when some of the predictions derived from it have been verified. They may perhaps admit that the verification is not completely impeccable from a logical point of view, or that a statement can never be finally established by establishing some of its consequences. But they are apt to look upon such objections as due to somewhat unnecessary scruples. It is quite true, they say, and even trivial, that we cannot know for certain whether the sun will rise tomorrow; but this uncertainty may be neglected: the fact that theories may not only be improved but that they can also be *falsified by new experiments* presents to the scientist a serious possibility which may at any moment become actual; but never yet has a theory had to be regarded as falsified owing to the sudden breakdown of a well-confirmed law. It never happens that old experiments one day yield new results. What happens is only that new experiments decide against an old theory. The old theory, even when it is superseded, often retains its validity as a kind of limiting case of the new theory; it still applies, at least with a high degree of approximation, in those cases in which it was successful before. In short, regularities which are directly testable by experiment do not change. Admittedly it is conceivable, or logically possible, that they might change; but this possibility is disregarded by empirical science and does not affect its methods. On the contrary, scientific method presupposes *the immutability of natural processes*, or the "principle of the uniformity of nature."

of the probability calculus. In other words, I introduced the term "degree of corroboration" mainly in order to be able to discuss the problem whether or not "degree of corroboration" could be identified with "probability" (either in a frequency sense or in the sense of Keynes, for example).

Carnap translated my term "degree of corroboration" (*"Grad der Bewährung"*), which I had first introduced into the discussions of the Vienna Circle, as "degree of confirmation." (See his "Testability and Meaning," in *Philosophy of Science* 3, 1936; especially p. 427); and so the term "degree of confirmation" soon became widely accepted. I did not like this term, because of some of its associations ("make firm"; "establish firmly"; "put beyond doubt"; "prove"; "verify": "to confirm" corresponds more closely to *"erhärten"* or *"bestätigen"* than to *"bewähren"*). I therefore proposed in a letter to Carnap (written, I think, about 1939) to use the term "corroboration." (This term had been suggested to me by Professor H. N. Parton.) But as Carnap declined my proposal, I fell in with his usage, thinking that words do not matter. This is why I myself used the term "confirmation" for a time in a number of my publications.

Yet it turned out that I was mistaken: the associations of the word "confirmation" did matter, unfortunately, and made themselves felt: "degree of confirmation" was soon used—by Carnap himself—as a synonym (or "explicans") of "probability." I have therefore now abandoned it in favour of "degree of corroboration."

There is something to be said for the above argument, but it does not affect my thesis. It expresses the metaphysical faith in the existence of regularities in our world (a faith which I share, and without which practical action is hardly conceivable). Yet the question before us—the question which makes the non-verifiability of theories significant in the present context—is on an altogether different plane. Consistently with my attitude towards other metaphysical questions, I abstain from arguing for or against faith in the existence of regularities in our world. But I shall try to show that *the non-verifiability of theories is methodologically important*. It is on this plane that I oppose the argument just advanced.

I shall therefore take up as relevant only one of the points of this argument —the reference to the so-called "principle of the uniformity of nature." This principle, it seems to me, expresses in a very superficial way an important methodological rule, and one which might be derived, with advantage, precisely from a consideration of the non-verifiability of theories.[2]

Let us suppose that the sun will not rise tomorrow (and that we shall nevertheless continue to live, and also to pursue our scientific interests). Should such a thing occur, science would have to try to *explain it, i.e.* to derive it from laws. Existing theories would presumably require to be drastically revised. But the revised theories would not merely have to account for the new state of affairs: *our older experiences would also have to be derivable from them.* From the methodological point of view one sees that the principle of the uniformity of nature is here replaced by the postulate of *the invariance of natural laws*, with respect to both space and time. I think, therefore, that it would be a mistake to assert that natural regularities do not change. (This would be a kind of statement that can neither be argued against nor argued for.) What we should say is, rather, that it is part of our *definition* of natural laws if we postulate that they are to be invariant with respect to space and time; and also if we postulate that they are to have no exceptions. Thus from a methodological point of view, the possibility of falsifying a corroborated law is by no means without significance. It helps us to find out what we demand and expect from natural laws. And the "principle of the uniformity of nature" can again be regarded as a metaphysical interpretation of a methodological rule—like its near relative, the "law of causality."

One attempt to replace metaphysical statements of this kind by principles of method leads to the "principle of induction," supposed to govern the method of induction, and hence that of the verification of theories. But this attempt fails, for the principle of induction is itself metaphysical in character. As I have pointed out in section 1, the assumption that the principle of induc-

---

[2] I mean the rule that any new system of hypotheses should yield, or explain, the old, corroborated, regularities.

tion is empirical leads to an infinite regress. It could therefore only be introduced as a primitive proposition (or a postulate, or an axiom). This would perhaps not matter so much, were it not that the principle of induction would have in any case to be treated as a *non-falsifiable statement*. For if this principle—which is supposed to validate the inference of theories—were itself falsifiable, then it would be falsified with the first falsified theory, because this theory would then be a conclusion, derived with the help of the principle of induction; and this principle, as a premise, will of course be falsified by the *modus tollens* whenever a theory is falsified which was derived from it.[3] But this means that a falsifiable principle of induction would be falsified anew with every advance made by science. It would be necessary, therefore, to introduce a principle of induction assumed not to be falsifiable. But this would amount to the misconceived notion of a synthetic statement which is *a priori* valid, *i.e.* an irrefutable statement about reality.

Thus if we try to turn our metaphysical faith in the uniformity of nature and in the verifiability of theories into a theory of knowledge based on inductive logic, we are left only with the choice between an infinite regress and *apriorism*.

THE PROBABILITY OF A HYPOTHESIS AND THE PROBABILITY OF EVENTS: CRITICISM OF PROBABILITY LOGIC

Even if it is admitted that theories are never finally verified, may we not succeed in making them secure to a greater or lesser extent—more probable, or less so? After all, it might be possible that the question of *the probability of a hypothesis* could be reduced, say, to that of *the probability of events*, and thus be made susceptible to mathematical and logical handling.[4]

Like inductive logic in general, the theory of the probability of hypotheses seems to have arisen through a confusion of psychological with logical questions. Admittedly, our subjective feelings of conviction are of different intensities, and the degree of confidence with which we await the fulfilment of a prediction and the further corroboration of a hypothesis is likely to depend, among other things, upon the way in which this hypothesis has stood up to tests so far—upon its past corroboration. But that these psychological

[3] The premises of the derivation of the theory would (according to the inductivist view here discussed) consist of the principle of induction *and* of observation statements. But the latter are here tacitly assumed to be unshaken and reproducible, so that they cannot be made responsible for the failure of the theory.

[4] The present section contains mainly a criticism of Reichenbach's attempt to interpret *the probability of hypotheses* in terms of *a frequency theory of the probability of events*. . . . Note that Reichenbach is anxious to reduce *the probability of a statement or hypothesis* (what Carnap many years later called "*probability¹*") to a frequency ("*probability²*").

questions do not belong to epistemology is pretty well acknowledged even by the believers in probability logic. They argue, however, that it is possible, on the basis of inductivist decisions, to ascribe degrees of probability to *the hypotheses themselves*; and further, that it is possible to reduce this concept to that of the probability of events.

The probability of a hypothesis is mostly regarded as merely a special case of the general problem of the *probability of a statement*; and this in turn is regarded as nothing but the problem of the *probability of an event*, expressed in a particular terminology. Thus we read in Reichenbach, for example: "Whether we ascribe probability to statements or to events is only a matter of terminology. So far we have regarded it as a case of the probability of events that the probability of 1/6 has been assigned to the turning up of a certain face of a die. But we might just as well say that it is the *statement* 'the face showing the 1 will turn up' which has been assigned the probability of 1/6."[5]

This identification of the probability of events with the probability of statements may be better understood if we recall what was said [previously]. There the concept "event" was defined as a class of singular statements. It must therefore also be permissible to speak of the *probability of statements* in place of the probability of events. So we can regard this as being merely a change of terminology: the reference-sequences are interpreted as sequences of statements. If we think of an "alternative," or rather of its elements, as represented by statements, then we can describe the turning up of heads by the statement "k is heads," and its failure to turn up by the negation of this statement. In this way we obtain a sequence of statements of the form p_j, p_h, p_l, p_m, p_n, . . . , in which a statement p_i is sometimes characterized as "true," and sometimes (by placing a bar over its name) as "false." Probability within an alternative can thus be interpreted as *the relative "truth-frequency"*[6] *of statements within a sequence of statements* (rather than as the relative frequency of a property).

If we like, we can call the concept of probability, so transformed, the "probability of statements" or the "probability of propositions." And we can show a very close connection between this concept and the concept of "truth." For if the sequence of statements becomes shorter and shorter and in the end contains only one element, *i.e.* only *one single* statement, then the probability, or truth-frequency, of the sequence can assume only one of the two values 1 and 0, according to whether the single statement is true or false. The truth or falsity of a statement can thus be looked upon as a limiting case of probability; and conversely, probability can be regarded as a generalization of the

[5] Reichenbach, *Erkenntnis* 1, 1930, pp. 171*f*.

[6] According to Keynes, *A Treatise on Probability*, 1921 p. 101 *ff.*, the expression "truth-frequency" is due to Whitehead; *cf.* the next note.

concept of truth, in so far as it includes the latter as a limiting case. Finally, it is possible to define operations with truth-frequencies in such a way that the usual truth-operations of classical logic become limiting cases of these operations. And the calculus of these operations can be called *"probability logic."*[7]

But can we really identify *the probability of hypotheses* with the probability of statements, defined in this manner, and thus indirectly with the probability of events? I believe that this identification is the result of a confusion. The idea is that the probability of a hypothesis, since it is obviously a kind of probability of a statement, must come under the head of "probability of statements" *in the sense just defined.* But this conclusion turns out to be unwarranted; and the terminology is thus highly unsuitable. Perhaps after all it would be better never to use the expression "probability of statements" if we have the probability of events in mind.[8]

However this may be, I assert that the issues arising from the concept of a *probability of hypotheses* are not even touched by considerations based on probability logic I assert that if one says of a hypothesis that it is not true but "probable," then this statement can under *no* circumstances be translated into a statement about the probability of events.

For if one attempts to reduce the idea of a probability of hypotheses to that of a truth-frequency which uses the concept of a sequence of statements, then one is at once confronted with the question: *with reference to what sequence* of statements can a probability value be assigned to a hypothesis? Reichenbach identifies an "assertion of natural science"—by which he means a scientific hypothesis—itself with a reference-sequence of statements. He says, ". . . the assertions of natural science, which are never singular statements, are in fact sequences of statements to which, strictly speaking, we must assign not the degree of probability 1 but a smaller probability value. It is therefore only probability logic which provides the logical form capable of strictly

---

[7] I am giving here an outline of the construction of the probability logic developed by Reichenbach (*Wahrscheinlichkeitslogik, Sitzungsberichte der Preussischen Akademie der Wissenschaften*, Physik.-mathem. Klasse **29,** 1932, p. 476 *ff.*) who follows E. L. Post (*American Journal of Mathematics* **43,** 1921, p. 184), and, at the same time, the frequency theory of von Mises. Whitehead's form of the frequency theory, discussed by Keynes, *op. cit.* p. 101 *ff.* is similar.

[8] I still think (a) that the so-called "probability of hypotheses" cannot be interpreted by a truth-frequency: (b) that it is better to call a probability defined by a relative frequency—whether a truth-frequency or the frequency of an event—the "probability of an event"; (c) that the so-called "probability of a hypothesis" (in the sense of its acceptability) is *not* a special case of the "probability of statements." And I should now regard the "probability of statements" as one interpretation (the logical interpretation) among several possible interpretations of the formal calculus of probability, rather than as a truth-frequency.

representing the concept of knowledge proper to natural science."[9] Let us now try to follow up the suggestion that the hypotheses themselves are sequences of statements. One way of interpreting it would be to take, as the elements of such a sequence, the various singular statements which can contradict, or agree with, the hypothesis. The probability of this hypothesis would then be determined by the truth-frequency of those among these statements which agree with it. But this would give the hypothesis a probability of $\frac{1}{2}$ if, on the average, it is refuted by every second singular statement of this sequence! In order to escape from this devastating conclusion, we might try two more expedients.[10] One would be to ascribe to the hypothesis a certain probability—perhaps not a very precise one—on the basis of an estimate of the ratio of all the tests passed by it to all the tests which have not yet been attempted. But this way too leads nowhere. For this estimate can, as it happens, be computed with precision, and the result is always that the probability is zero. And finally, we could try to base our estimate upon the ratio of those tests which led to a favourable result to those which led to an indifferent result—i.e. one which did not produce a clear decision. (In this way one might indeed obtain something resembling a measure of the subjective feeling of confidence with which the experimenter views his results.) But this last expedient will not do either, even if we disregard the fact that with this kind of estimate we have strayed a long way from the concept of a truth-frequency, and that of a probability of events. (These concepts are based upon the ratio of the true statements to those which are false, and we must not, of course, equate an indifferent statement with one that is objectively false.) The reason why his last attempt fails too is that the suggested definition would make the probability of a hypothesis hopelessly subjective: the probability of a hypothesis would depend upon the training and skill of the experimenter rather than upon objectively reproducible and testable results.

But I think it is altogether impossible to accept the suggestion that a hypothesis can be taken to be a sequence of statements. It would be possible if universal statements had the form: "For every value of k it is true that at the place k so-and-so occurs." If universal statements had this form, then we could regard basic statements (those that contradict, or agree with, the universal statement) as elements of a sequence of statements—the sequence to be taken for the universal statement. But as we have seen (cf. sections 15 and 28), universal statements do not have this form. Basic statements are never

9 Reichenbach, *Wahrscheinlichkeitslogik* (*op. cit.* p. 488), p. 15 of the reprint.

10 It is here assumed that we have by now made up our minds that whenever there is a clear-cut falsification, we will attribute to the hypothesis the probability zero, so that the discussion is now confined to those cases in which no clear-cut falsification has been obtained.

derivable from universal statements alone.[11] The latter cannot therefore be regarded as sequences of basic statements. If, however, we try to take into consideration the sequence of those negations of basic statements which *are* derivable from universal statements, then the estimate for *every* self-consistent hypothesis will lead to the same probability, namely 1. For we should then have to consider the ratio of the *non-falsified* negated basic statements which can be derived (or other derivable statements) to the *falsified* ones. This means that instead of considering a truth frequency we should have to consider the complementary value of a falsity frequency. This value however would be equal to 1. For the class of derivable statements, and even the class of the derivable negations of basic statements, are both infinite; on the other hand, there cannot be more than at most a finite number of accepted falsifying basic statements. Thus even if we disregard the fact that universal statements, and even if we try to interpret them as something of the kind and to correlate with them sequences of completely decidable singular statements, even then we do not reach an acceptable result.

We have yet to examine another, quite different, possibility of explaining the probability of a hypothesis in terms of sequences of statements. It may be remembered that we have called a given singular occurrence "probable" (in the sense of a 'formally singular probability statement') if it is an *element of a sequence* of occurrences with a certain probability. Similarly one might try to call a hypothesis "probable" if it is an *element of a sequence of hypotheses* with a definite truth-frequency. But this attempt again fails—quite apart from the difficulty of determining the reference sequence (it can be chosen in many ways; *cf.* section 71). For we cannot speak of a truth-frequency within a sequence of hypotheses, simply because we can never know of a hypothesis whether it is true. If we *could* know this, then we should hardly need the concept of the probability of a hypothesis at all. Now we might try, as above, to take the complement of the falsity-frequency within a sequence of hypotheses as our starting point. But if, say, we define the probability of a hypothesis with the help of the ratio of the non-falsified to the falsified hypotheses of the sequence, then, as before, the probability of *every* hypothesis

[11] As explained [previously], the singular statements which *can* be deduced from a theory—the "instantial statements"—are not of the character of basic statements or of observation statements. If we nevertheless decide to take the sequence of these statements and base our probability upon the truth frequency within this sequence, then the probability will be always equal to 1, however often the theory may be falsified; for as has been shown [previously] almost any theory is "verified" by almost all instances (*i.e.* by almost all places *k*.) The discussion following here in the text contains a very similar argument—also based upon "instantial statements" (*i.e.* negated basic statements)—designed to show that the probability of a hypothesis, if based upon these negated basic statements, would always be equal to one.

within *every infinite* reference sequence will be equal to 1. And even if a *finite* reference sequence were chosen we should be in no better position. For let us assume that we can ascribe to the elements of some (*finite*) sequence of hypotheses a degree of probability between 0 and 1 in accordance with this procedure—say, the value 3/4. (This can be done if we obtain the information that this or that hypothesis belonging to the sequence has been falsified.) In so far as these *falsified* hypotheses are elements of the sequence, we thus would have to ascribe to them, *just because of this information*, not the value 0, but 3/4. And in general, the probability of a hypothesis would decrease by $1/n$ in consequence of the information that it is false, where n is the number of hypothesis in the reference sequence. All this glaringly contradicts the programme of expressing, in terms of a *"probability of hypotheses,"* the degree of reliability which we have to ascribe to a hypothesis in view of supporting or undermining evidence.

This seems to me to exhaust the possibilities of basing the concept of the probability of a hypothesis on that of the frequency of true statements (or the frequency of false ones), and thereby on the frequency theory of the probability of events.[12]

[12] One might summarize my foregoing attempts to make sense of Reichenbach's somewhat cryptic assertion that the probability of a hypothesis is to be measured by a truth frequency, as follows. . . .

Roughly, we can try two possible ways of defining the probability of a theory. One is to count the number of experimentally testable statements belonging to the theory, and to determine the relative frequency of those which turn out to be true; this relative frequency can then be taken as a measure of the probability of a theory. We may call this a *probability of the first kind*. Secondly, we can consider the theory as an element of a class of ideological entities—say, of theories proposed by other scientists—and we can then determine the relative frequencies within this class. We may call this a *probability of the second kind*.

In my text I tried, further, to show that each of these two possibilities of making sense of Reichenbach's idea of truth frequency leads to results which must be quite unacceptable to adherents of the probability theory of induction.

Reichenbach replied to my criticism, not so much by defending his views as by attacking mine. In his paper on my book (*Erkenntnis* **5**, 1935, pp. 267–284), he said that "the results of this book are completely untenable," and explained this by a failure of my "method"—by my failure "to think out all the consequences" of my conceptual system.

Section iv of his paper (pp. 274 f.) is devoted to our problem—the probability of hypotheses. It begins: "In this connection, some remarks may be added about the probability of theories—remarks which should render more complete my so far all too brief communications of the subject, and which may remove a certain obscurity which still surrounds the issue." After this follows a passage which forms the second paragraph of the present note, headed by the word "Roughly" (the only word which I have added to Reichenbach's text).

Reichenbach remained silent about the fact that his attempt to remove "the obscurity which still surrounds the issue" is but a summary—a rough one, admittedly—of some

I think we have to regard the attempt to identify the probability of a hypothesis with the probability of events as a complete failure. This conclusion is quite independent of whether we accept the claim (it is Reichenbach's) that *all hypotheses of physics* are "in reality," or "on closer examination" nothing but probability statements (about some average frequencies within sequences of observations which always show deviations from some mean value), or whether we are inclined to make a distinction between two different *types* of natural laws—between the "deterministic" or "precision" laws on the one hand, and the "probability laws" or "hypotheses of frequency" on the other. For both of these types are hypothetical assumptions which in their turn can never become "probable": they can only be corroborated, in the sense that they can "prove their mettle" under fire—the fire of our tests.

How are we to explain the fact that the believers in probability logic have reached an opposite view? Wherein lies the error made by Jeans when he writes—at first in a sense with which I can fully agree—that ". . . we can know nothing . . . *for certain*," but then goes on to say: "At best we can only deal in *probabilities*. [And] the predictions of the new quantum theory agree so well [with the observations] that the odds in favour of the scheme having some correspondence with reality are *enormous*. Indeed, we may say the scheme is *almost certain* to be quantitatively true . . ."?[13]

Undoubtedly the commonest error consists in believing that hypothetical estimates of frequencies, that is to say, hypotheses regarding probabilities, can in their turn be only probable; or in other words, in ascribing to *hypotheses of probability* some degree of an alleged *probability of hypotheses*. We may be able to produce a persuasive argument in favour of this erroneous conclusion if we remember that hypotheses regarding probabilities are, as far as their logical form is concerned (and without reference to our methodological requirement of falsifiability), neither verifiable nor falsifiable. (*Cf.* sections 65 to 68.) They are not verifiable because they are universal statements, and they are not strictly falsifiable because they can never be logically contradicted by any basic statements. They are thus (as Reichenbach puts it)

pages of the very book which he is attacking. Yet in spite of this silence I feel that I may take it as a great compliment from so experienced a writer on probability (who at the time of writing his reply to my book had two books and about a dozen papers on the subject to his credit) that he did accept the results of my endeavours to "think out the consequences" of his "all too brief communications on the subject." This success of my endeavours was due, I believe, to a rule of "method"; that we should always try to clarify and to strengthen our opponent's position as much as possible before criticizing him, if we wish our criticism to be worth while.

[13] Jeans, *The New Background of Science,* 1934, p. 58. (Only the words "for certain" are italicized by Jeans.)

completely undecidable.[14] Now they can, as I have tried to show, *be better, or less well, "confirmed,"* which is to say that they may agree more, or less, with accepted basic statements. This is the point where, it may appear, probability logic comes in. The symmetry between verifiability and falsifiability accepted by classical inductivist logic suggests the belief that it must be possible to correlate with these "undecidable" probability statements some scale of degrees of validity, something like "continuous degrees of probability whose unattainable upper and lower limits are truth and falsity,"[15] to quote Reichenbach again. According to my view, however, probability statements, just because they are completely undecidable, are *metaphysical* unless we decide to make them falsifiable by accepting a methodological rule. Thus the simple result of their non-falsifiability is not that they can be better, or less well corroborated, but *that they cannot be empirically corroborated at all.* For otherwise—seeing that they rule out nothing, and are therefore compatible with every basic statement—they could be said to be "corroborated" by *every arbitrarily chosen basic statement* (of any degree of composition) provided it describes the occurrence of some relevant instance.

I believe that physics uses probability statements only in the way which I have discussed at length in connection with the theory of probability; and more particularly that it uses probability assumptions, just like other hypotheses, as falsifiable statements. But I should decline to join in any dispute about how physicists "in fact" proceed, since this must remain largely a matter of interpretation.

*   *   *

INDUCTIVE LOGIC AND PROBABILITY LOGIC

The probability of hypotheses cannot be reduced to the probability of events. This is the conclusion which emerges from the examination carried out in the previous section. But might not a different approach lead to a satisfactory definition of the idea of a *probability of hypotheses?*

I do not believe that it is possible to construct a concept of the probability of hypotheses which may be interpreted as expressing a "degree of validity" of the hypothesis, in analogy to the concepts "true" and "false" (and which, in addition, is sufficiently closely related to the concept "objective probabil-

---

[14] Reichenbach, *Erkenntnis* I, 1930, p. 169 (*cf.* also Reichenbach's reply to my note in *Erkenntnis* **3,** 1933, pp. 426 *f.*). Similar ideas about the degrees of probability or certainty of inductive knowledge occur very frequently (*cf.* for instance Russell, *Our Knowledge of the External World,* 1926, pp. 225 *f.,* and *The Analysis of Matter,* 1927, pp. 141 and 398).

[15] Reichenbach, *Erkenntnis* I, 1930, p. 186 (*cf.* note 4 to section 1).

ity," *i.e.* to relative frequency, to justify the use of the word "probability").[16] Nevertheless, I will now, for the sake of argument, adopt the *supposition* that such a concept has in fact been successfully constructed, in order to raise the question: how would this affect the problem of induction?

Let us suppose that a certain hypothesis—say Schrödinger's theory—is recognized as "probable" in some definite sense; either as "probable to this or that numerical degree," or merely as "probable," without specification of a degree. The statement that describes Schrödinger's theory as "probable" we may call its *appraisal.*

An appraisal must, of course, be a synthetic statement—an assertion about "reality"—in the same way as would be the statement "Schrödinger's theory is true" or "Schrödinger's theory is false." All such statements obviously say something about the adequacy of the theory, and are thus certainly not tautological.[17] They say that a theory is adequate or inadequate, or that it is adequate in some degree. Further, an appraisal of Schrödinger's theory

---

[16] (Added while the book was in proof.) It is conceivable that for estimating degrees of corroboration, one might find a formal system showing some limited formal analogies with the calculus of probability (*e.g.* with Bayes's theorem), without however having anything in common with the frequency theory. I am indebted to Dr. J. Hosiasson for suggesting this possibility to me. I am satisfied, however, that it is quite impossible to tackle *the problem of induction* by such methods with any hope of success. . . .

Since 1938, I have upheld the view that "to justify the use of the word probability," as my text puts it, we should have to show that the axioms of the formal calculus are satisfied. . . . This would of course include the satisfaction of Bayes's theorem.

[17] The probability statement "$p(S,e) = r$," in words, "Schrödinger's theory, given the evidence e, has the probability r"—a statement of relative or conditional logical probability—may certainly be tautological (provided the values of e and r are chosen so as to fit each other: if e consists only of observational reports, r will have to equal zero in a sufficiently large universe). But the "appraisal," in our sense, would have a different form—for example, the following: $p_k(S) = r$, where k is today's date; or in words: "Schrödinger's theory has *today* (in view of the actual total evidence now available) a probability of r." In order to obtain this assessment, $p_k(S) = r$, from (i) the tautological statement of relative probability $p(S,e) = r$, and (ii) the statement "e is the total evidence available today," we must apply a *principle of inference.* . . . This principle of inference looks very much like the *modus ponens*, and it may therefore seem that it should be taken as analytic. But if we take it to be analytic, then this amounts to the decision to consider p_k as defined by (i) and (ii), or at any rate as meaning *no more* than do (i) and (ii) together; but in this case, p_k cannot be interpreted as being of any practical significance: it *certainly* cannot be interpreted as a practical measure of acceptability. This is best seen if we consider that in a sufficiently large universe, $p_k(t,e)' \approx 0$ for *every* universal theory t, provided e consists only of singular statements. But in practice, we certainly do accept some theories and reject others.

If, on the other hand, we interpret p_k as *degree of adequacy or acceptability*, then the principle of inference mentioned—the "rule of absolution" (which, on this interpretation, becomes a typical example of a "principle of induction")—is simply *false*, and therefore clearly non-analytic.

must be a *non-verifiable* synthetic statement, just like the theory itself. For the "probability" of a theory—that is, the probability that the theory will remain acceptable—cannot, it appears, be deduced from basic statements *with finality*. Therefore we are forced to ask: How can the appraisal be justified? How can it be tested? (Thus the problem of induction arises again. . . .)

As to the appraisal itself, this may either be asserted to be "true," or it may, in its turn, be said to be "probable." If it is regarded as "true" then it must be a *true synthetic statement* which has not been empirically verified— a synthetic statement which is *a priori* true. If it is regarded as "probable," then we need a *new* appraisal: an appraisal of the appraisal, as it were, and therefore an appraisal on a higher level. But this means that we are caught up in an infinite regress. The appeal to the probability of the hypothesis is unable to improve the precarious logical situation of inductive logic.

Most of those who believe in probability logic uphold the view that the appraisal is arrived at by means of a "principle of induction" which ascribes probabilities to the induced hypotheses. But if they ascribe a probability to this principle of induction in its turn, then the infinite regress continues. If on the other hand they ascribe "truth" to it then they are left with the choice between infinite regress and *a priorism*. "Once and for all," says Heymans, "the theory of probability is incapable of explaining inductive arguments; for precisely the same problem which lurks in the one also lurks in the other (in the empirical application of probability theory). In both cases the conclusion goes beyond what is given in the premises."[18] Thus nothing is gained by replacing the word "true" by the word "probable," and the word "false" by the word "improbable." Only if *the asymmetry between verification and falsification* is taken into account—that asymmetry which results from the logical relation between theories and basic statements—is it possible to avoid the pitfalls of the problem of induction.

Believers in probability logic may try to meet my criticism by asserting that it springs from a mentality which is "tied to the framework of classical logic," and which is therefore incapable of following the methods of reasoning employed by probability logic. I freely admit that I am incapable of following these methods of reasoning.

---

[18] Heymans, *Gesetze und Elemente des wissenschaftlichen Denkens* (1890, 1894), pp. 290*f.*; * third edition, 1915, p. 272. Heymans's argument was anticipated by Hume in his anonymous pamphlet. *An Abstract of a Book lately published entitled A Treatise of Human Nature*, 1740. I have little doubt that Heymans did not know this pamphlet which was re-discovered and attributed to Hume by J. M. Keynes and P. Sraffa, and published by them in 1938. I knew neither of Hume's nor of Heymans's anticipation of my arguments against the probabilistic theory of induction when I presented them in 1931 in an earlier book, still unpublished, which was read by several members of the Vienna Circle. The fact that Heymans's passage had been anticipated by Hume was pointed out to me by J. O. Wisdom; *cf.* his *Foundations of Inference in Natural Science*, 1952, p. 218.

THE POSITIVE THEORY OF CORROBORATION: HOW A HYPOTHESIS MAY "PROVE ITS METTLE"

Cannot the objections I have just been advancing against the probability theory of induction be turned, perhaps, against my own view? It might well seem that they can; for these objections are based on the idea of an *appraisal*. And clearly, I have to use this idea too. I speak of the *"corroboration"* of a theory; and corroboration can only be expressed as an appraisal. (In this respect there is no difference between corroboration and probability.) Moreover, I too hold that hypotheses cannot be asserted to be "true" statements, but that they are "provisional conjectures" (or something of the sort); and this view, too, can only be expressed by way of an appraisal of these hypotheses.

The second part of this objection can easily be answered. The appraisal of hypotheses which indeed I am compelled to make use of, and which describes them as "provisional conjectures" (or something of the sort) has the status of a *tautology*. Thus it does not give rise to difficulties of the type to which inductive logic gives rise. For this description only paraphrases or interprets the assertion (to which it is equivalent by definition) that strictly universal statements, *i.e.* theories, cannot be derived from singular statements.

The position is similar as regards the first part of the objection which concerns appraisals stating that a theory is corroborated. The appraisal of the corroboration is not a hypothesis, but can be derived if we are given the theory as well as the accepted basic statements. It asserts the fact that these basic statements do not contradict the theory, and it does this with due regard to the degree of testability of the theory, and to the severity of the tests to which the theory has been subjected, up to a stated period of time.

We say that a theory is "corroborated" so long as it stands up to these tests. The appraisal which asserts corroboration (the corroborative appraisal) establishes certain fundamental relations, *viz.* compatibility and incompatibility. We regard incompatibility as falsification of the theory. But compatibility alone must not make us attribute to the theory a positive degree of corroboration: the mere fact that a theory has not yet been falsified can obviously not be regarded as sufficient. For nothing is easier than to construct any number of theoretical systems which are compatible with any given system of accepted basic statements. (This remark applies also to all "metaphysical" systems.)

It might perhaps be suggested that a theory should be accorded some positive degree of corroboration if it is compatible with the system of accepted basic statements, and if, in addition, part of this system can be derived from the theory. Or, considering that basic statements are not derivable from a purely theoretical system (though their negations may be so derivable), one might suggest that the following rule should be adopted: a theory is to be accorded a positive degree of corroboration if it is compatible with the accepted basic statements and if, in addition, a non-empty sub-class of these basic statements is derivable from the theory in conjunction with the other accepted basic statements.

I have no serious objections to this last formulation, except that it seems to me insufficient for an adequate characterization of the positive degree of corroboration of a theory. For we. wish to speak of theories as being better, or less well, corroborated. But the *degree of corroboration* of a theory can surely not be established simply by counting the number of the corroborating instances, *i.e.* the accepted basic statements which are derivable in the way indicated. For it may happen that one theory appears to be far less well corroborated than another one, even though we have derived very many basic statements with its help, and only a few with the help of the second. As an example we might compare the hypothesis "All crows are black" with the hypothesis "the electronic charge has the value determined by Millikan." Although in the case of a hypothesis of the former kind, we have presumably encountered many more corroborative basic statements, we shall nevertheless judge Millikan's hypothesis to be the better corroborated of the two.

This shows that it is not so much the number of corroborating instances which determines the degree of corroboration as *the severity of the various tests* to which the hypothesis in question can be, and has been, subjected. But the severity of the tests, in its turn, depends upon the *degree of testability*, and thus upon the simplicity of the hypothesis: the hypothesis which is falsifiable in a higher degree, or the simpler hypothesis, is also the one which is corroborable in a higher degree. Of course, the degree of corroboration actually attained does not depend *only* on the degree of falsifiability: a statement may be falsifiable to a high degree yet it may be only slightly corroborated, or it may in fact be falsified. And it may perhaps, without being falsified, be superseded by a better testable theory from which it—or a sufficiently close approximation to it—can be deduced. (In this case too its degree of corroboration is lowered.)

The degree of corroboration of two statements may not be comparable in all cases, any more than the degree of falsifiability: we cannot define a numerically calculable degree of corroboration, but can speak only roughly in terms of positive degrees of corroboration, negative degrees of corroboration, and so forth.[19] Yet we can lay down various rules; for instance the rule

---

19 As far as practical application to existing theories goes, this seems to me still correct; but I think now that it is possible to define "degree of corroboration" in such a way that we can *compare* degrees of corroboration (for example, those of Newton's and of Einstein's theory of gravity). Moreover, this definition makes it even possible to attribute numerical degrees to corroboration to statistical hypotheses, and perhaps even

that we shall not continue to accord a positive degree of corroboration to a theory which has been falsified by an inter-subjectively testable experiment based upon a falsifying hypothesis. (We may, however, under certain circumstances accord a positive degree of corroboration to another theory, even though it follows a kindred line of thought. An example is Einstein's photon theory, with its kinship to Newton's corpuscular theory of light.) In general we regard an inter-subjectively testable falsification as final (provided it is well tested) : this is the way in which the asymmetry between verification and falsification of theories makes itself felt. Each of these methodological points contributes in its own peculiar way to the historical development of science as a process of step by step approximation. A corroborative appraisal made at a later date—that is, an appraisal made after new basic statements have been added to those already . accepted—can replace a positive degree of corroboration by a negative one, but not *vice versa*. And although I believe that in the history of science it is always the theory and not the experiment, always the idea and not the observation, which opens up the way to new knowledge, I also believe that it is always the experiment which saves us from following a track that leads nowhere: which helps us out of the rut, and which challenges us to find a new way.

Thus the degree of falsifiability or of simplicity of a theory enters into the appraisal of its corroboration. And this appraisal may be regarded as one of the logical relations between the theory and the accepted basic statements: as an appraisal that takes into consideration the severity of the tests to which the theory has been subjected.

CORROBORABILITY, TESTABILITY, AND LOGICAL PROBABILITY[20]

In appraising the degree of corroboration of a theory we take into account its degree of falsifiability. A theory can be the better corroborated the better testable it is. Testability, however, is converse to the concept of *logical probability*, so that we can also say that an appraisal of corroboration takes into account the logical probability of the statement in question. And this, in turn, is related to the concept of objective probability—the probability of events. Thus by taking logical probability into account the concept of corroboration is linked, even if perhaps only indirectly and loosely, with that of the probability of events. The idea may occur to us that there is perhaps a connection here with the doctrine of the probability of hypotheses criticized above.

to other statements *provided* we can attribute degrees of (absolute and relative) logical probability to them *and to the evidence statements.*

[20] If the terminology is accepted which I first explained in my note in *Mind*, 1938, then the word "absolute" should be inserted here throughout before "logical probability" (in contradistinction to "relative" or "conditional" logical probability).

When trying to appraise the degree of corroboration of a theory we may reason somewhat as follows. Its degree of corroboration will increase with the number of its corroborating instances. Here we usually accord to the first corroborating instances far greater importance than to later ones: once a theory is well corroborated, further instances raise its degree of corroboration only very little. This rule however does not hold good if these new instances are very different from the earlier ones, that is if they corroborate the theory in a *new field of application*. In this case, they may increase the degree of corroboration very considerably. The degree of corroboration of a theory which has a higher degree of universality can thus be greater than that of a theory which has a lower degree of universality (and therefore a lower degree of falsifiability). In a similar way, theories of a higher degree of precision can be better corroborated than less precise ones. One of the reasons why we do not accord a positive degree of corroboration to the typical prophecies of palmists and soothsayers is that their predictions are so cautious and imprecise that the logical probability of their being correct is extremely high. And if we are told that more precise and thus logically less probable predictions of this kind have been successful, then it is not, as a rule, their success that we are inclined to doubt so much as their alleged logical improbability: since we tend to believe that such prophecies are non-corroborable, we also tend to argue in such cases from their low degree of corroborability to their low degree of testability.

If we compare these views of mine with what is implicit in (inductive) probability logic, we get a truly remarkable result. According to my view, the corroborability of a theory—and also the degree of corroboration of a theory which has in fact passed severe tests, stand both, as it were,[21] in inverse ratio to its logical probability; for they both increase with its degree of testability and simplicity. *But the view implied by probability logic is the precise opposite of this.* Its upholders let the probability of a hypothesis increase in *direct proportion* to its logical probability—although there is no doubt that they *intend* their "probability of a hypothesis" to stand for much the same thing that I try to indicate by "degree of corroboration."[22]

---

[21] I said in the text "*as it were*": I did so because I did not really believe in numerical (absolute) logical probabilities. In consequence of this, I wavered, when writing the text, between the view that the degree of corroborability is *complementary* to (absolute) logical probability and the view that it is inversely proportional; or in other words, between a definition of $C(g)$, *i.e.* the degree of corroborability, by $C(g) = 1 - P(g)$ which would make *corroborability equal to content*, and by $C(g) = 1/P(g)$, where $P(g)$ is the absolute logical probability of g. In fact, definitions may be adopted which lead to either of these consequences, and both ways seem fairly satisfactory on intuitive grounds; this explains, perhaps, my wavering. There are strong reasons in favour of the first method, or else of a logarithmic scale applied to the second method.

[22] The last lines of this paragraph, especially from the italicized sentence on (it was

Among those who argue in this way is Keynes who uses the expression "*a priori* probability" for what I call "logical probability." He makes the following perfectly accurate remark[23] regarding a "generalization" *g* (*i.e.*, a hypothesis) with the "condition" or antecedent or protasis φ and the "conclusion" or consequent or apodosis *f*: "The more comprehensive the condition φ and the less comprehensive the conclusion *f*, the greater *à priori*[24] probability do we attribute to the generalization *g*. With every increase in φ this probability increases, and with every increase in *f* it will diminish." This, as I said, is perfectly accurate, even though Keynes does not draw a sharp distinction[25] between what he calls the "probability of a generalization"— corresponding to what is here called the "probability of a hypothesis"—and its "*a priori* probability." Thus in contrast to my *degree of corroboration*, Keynes's *probability of a hypothesis* increases with its *a priori logical probability*. That Keynes nevertheless intends by his "probability" the same as I do by my "corroboration" may be seen from the fact that his "probability" rises with the number of corroborating instances, and also (most

not italicized in the original) contain the crucial point of my criticism of the probability theory of induction. The point may be summarized as follows.

We want *simple* hypotheses—hypotheses of a high *content*, a high degree of *testability*. These are also the highly *corroborable* hypotheses, for the degree of corroboration of a hypothesis depends mainly upon the severity of its tests, and thus upon its testability. Now we know that testability is the same as high (absolute) logical *improbability*, or low (absolute) logical *probability*.

But if two hypotheses, h_1 and h_2, are comparable with respect to their content, and thus with respect to their (absolute) logical probability, then the following holds: let the (absolute) logical probability of h_1 be smaller than that of h_2. Then, whatever the evidence *e*, the (relative) logical probability of h_1 given *e* can never exceed that of h_2 given *e*. Thus the *better testable and better corroborable hypothesis can never obtain a higher probability, on the given evidence, than the less testable one.* But this entails that *degree of corroboration cannot be the same as probability.*

This is the crucial result. My later remarks in the text merely draw the conclusion from it: if you value high probability, you must say very little—or better still, nothing at all: tautologies will always retain the highest probability.

[23] Keynes, *A Treatise on Probability*, 1921, pp. 224 *f.*

[24] Keynes follows some eminent Cambridge logicians in writing "*à priori*" and "*à posteriori*"; one can only say, *à propos de rien*—unless, perhaps, apropos of "*à propos*".

[25] Keynes does, in fact, allow for the distinction between the *a priori* (or "absolute logical," as I now call it) probability of the "generalization" *g* and its probability with respect to a given piece of evidence *h*, and to this extent, my statement in the text needs correction. (He makes the distinction by assuming, correctly though perhaps only implicitly—see p. 225 of the *Treatise*—that if φ = $φ_1 φ_2$, and $f = f_1 f_2$, then the *a priori* probabilities of the various *g* are: $g(φ, f_1) \geqslant g(φ, f) \geqslant g(φ_1, f)$.) And he correctly *proves* that the *a posteriori* probabilities of these hypotheses *g* (relative to *any* given piece of evidence *h*) change in the same way as their *a priori* probabilities. Thus while his probabilities change like (absolute) logical probabilities, it is my cardinal point that degrees of corroborability (*and* of corroboration) change in the opposite way.

important) with the increase of diversity among them. But Keynes overlooks the fact that theories whose corroborating instances belong to widely different fields of application will usually have a correspondingly high degree of universality. Hence his two requirements for obtaining a high probability— the least possible universality and the greatest possible diversity of instances —will as a rule be incompatible.

Expressed in my terminology, Keynes's theory implies that corroboration (or the probability of hypotheses) *decreases* with testability. He is led to this view by his belief in inductive logic.[26] For it is the tendency of inductive logic to make scientific hypotheses as *certain* as possible. Scientific significance is assigned to the various hypotheses only to the extent to which they can be justified by experience. A theory is regarded as scientifically valuable only because of the close *logical proximity* between the theory and empirical statements. But this means nothing else than that the *content* of the theory must go *as little as possible* beyond what is empirically established.[27] This view is closely connected with a tendency to deny the value of prediction. "The peculiar virtue of prediction" Keynes writes[28] ". . . is altogether imaginary. The number of instances examined and the analogy between them are the essential points, and the question as to whether a particular hypothesis happens to be propounded before or after their examination is quite irrelevant." In reference to hypotheses which have been "*a priori* proposed"—that is, proposed before we had sufficient support for them on inductive grounds— Keynes writes: ". . . if it is a mere guess, the lucky fact of its preceding some or all of the cases which verify it adds nothing whatever to its value." This view of prediction is certainly consistent. But it makes one wonder why we should ever have to generalize at all. What possible reason can there be for constructing all these theories and hypotheses? The standpoint of inductive logic makes these activities quite incomprehensible. If what we value most is the securest knowledge available—and if predictions as such contribute nothing towards corroboration—why then may we not rest content with our basic statements?[29]

[26] In my theory of corroboration—in direct opposition to Keynes's, Jeffreys's, and Carnap's theories of probability—corroboration does not *decrease* with testability, but tends to *increase* with it.

[27] This may also be expressed by the unacceptable rule: 'Always choose the hypothesis which is most *ad hoc!*'

[28] Keynes, *op. cit.*, p. 305.

[29] Carnap, in his *Logical Foundations of Probability*, 1950, believes in the *practical* value of predictions; nevertheless, he draws part of the conclusion here mentioned—that we might be content with our basic statements. For he says that theories (he speaks of "laws") are "not indispensable" for science—not even for making predictions: we can manage throughout with singular statements. "Nevertheless," he writes (p. 575) "it is expedient, of course, to state universal laws in books on physics, biology, psychology,

Another view which gives rise to very similar questions is that of Kaila.[30] Whilst I believe that it is the simple theories, and those which make little use of auxiliary hypotheses which can be well corroborated, just because of their logical improbability, Kaila interprets the situation in precisely the opposite way, on grounds similar to Keynes's. He too sees that we usually ascribe a high probability (in our terminology, a high "probability of hypotheses") to *simple* theories, and especially to those needing few auxiliary hypotheses. But his reasons are the opposite of mine. He does not, as I do, ascribe a high probability to such theories because they are severely testable, or logically improbable; that is to say because they have, *a priori* as it were, *many opportunities of clashing with basic statements*. On the contrary he ascribes this high probability to simple theories with few auxiliary hypotheses because he believes that a system consisting of *few* hypotheses will, *a priori*, have *fewer* opportunities of clashing with reality than a system consisting of many hypotheses. Here again one wonders why we should ever bother to construct these adventurous theories. If we shrink from conflict with reality, why invite it by making assertions? The safest course is to adopt a system *without any* hypotheses. (*"Speech is silvern, silence is golden."*)

My own rule which requires that auxiliary hypotheses shall be used as sparingly as possible (the "principle of parsimony in the use of hypotheses") has nothing whatever in common with considerations such as Kaila's. I am not interested in merely keeping down the number of our statements: I am interested in their *simplicity in the sense of high testability*. It is this interest which leads, on the one hand, to my rule that auxiliary hypotheses should be used as sparingly as possible, and on the other hand, to my demand that the number of our axioms—of our most fundamental hypotheses—should be kept down. For this latter point arises out of the demand that statements of a high level of universality should be chosen, and that a system consisting of many "axioms" should, if possible, he deduced from (and thus explained by) one with fewer "axioms," and with axioms of a higher level of universality.

REMARKS CONCERNING THE USE OF THE CONCEPTS "TRUE" AND "CORROBORATED"

In the logic of science here outlined it is possible to avoid using the concepts "true" and "false."[31] Their place may be taken by logical considerations

---

etc." But the question is not one of expediency—it is one of scientific curiosity. *Some scientists want to explain the world:* their aim is to find satisfactory explanatory theories —well testable, *i.e.* simple theories—and to test them.

[30] Kaila, *Die Principien der Wahrscheinlichkeitslogik* (*Annales Universitatis Aboensis*, Turku 1926), p. 140.

[31] Not long after this was written, I had the good fortune to meet Alfred Tarski who

about derivability relations. Thus we need not say: "The prediction p is true provided the theory t and the basic statement b are true." We may say, instead, that the statement p follows from the (non-contradictory) conjunction of t and b. The falsification of a theory may be described in a similar way. We need not say that the theory is "false," but we may say instead that it is contradicted by a certain set of accepted basic statements. Nor need we say of basic statements that they are "true" or "false," for we may interpret their acceptance as the result of a conventional decision, and the accepted statements as results of this decision.

This certainly does not mean that we are forbidden to use the concepts "true" and "false," or that their use creates any particular difficulty. The very fact that we can avoid them shows that they cannot give rise to any new fundamental problem. The use of the concepts "true" and "false" is quite analogous to the use of such concepts as *"tautology," "contradiction," "conjunction," "implication"* and others of the kind. These are non-empirical

---

explained to me the fundamental ideas of his theory of truth. It is a great pity that this theory—one of the two great discoveries in the field of logic made since *Principia Mathematica*—is still often misunderstood and misrepresented. It cannot be too strongly emphasized that Tarski's idea of truth (for whose definition with respect to formalized languages Tarski gave a method) is the same idea which Aristotle had in mind and indeed most people (except pragmatists): the idea that *truth is correspondence with the facts* (or with reality). But what can we possibly mean if we say of a *statement* that it corresponds with the *facts* (or with reality)? Once we realize that this correspondence cannot be one of structural similarity, the task of elucidating this correspondence seems hopeless; and as a consequence, we may become suspicious of the concept of truth, and prefer not to use it. Tarski solved this apparently hopeless problem (with respect to formalized languages), by reducing the unmanageable idea of correspondence to a simpler idea (that of "satisfaction" or "fulfilment").

As a result of Tarski's teaching, I no longer hesitate to speak of "truth" and "falsity." And like everybody else's views (unless he is a pragmatist), my views turned out, as a matter of course, to be consistent with Tarski's theory of absolute truth. Thus although my views on formal logic and its philosophy were revolutionized by Tarski's theory, my views on science and its philosophy were fundamentally unaffected, although clarified.

Some of the current criticism of Tarski's theory seems to me wide of the mark. It is said that his definition is artificial and complex; but since he defines truth with respect to formalized languages, it has to be based on the definition of a well-formed formula in such a language; and it is of precisely the same degree of "artificiality" or "complexity" as this definition. It is also said that only propositions or statements can be true or false, but not sentences. Perhaps "sentence" was not a good translation of Tarski's original terminology. (I personally prefer to speak of "statement" rather than of "sentence"; see for example my "Note on Tarski's Definition of Truth," *Mind* 64, 1955, p. 388, footnote 1.) But Tarski himself made it perfectly clear that an uninterpreted formula (or a string of symbols) cannot be said to be true or false, and that these terms only apply to interpreted formulae—to *"meaningful* sentences" (as the translation has it). Improvements in terminology are always welcome; but it is sheer obscurantism to criticize a theory on terminological grounds.

concepts, logical concepts.[32] They describe or appraise a statement irrespective of any changes in the empirical world. Whilst we assume that the properties of physical objects (of "genidentical" objects in Lewin's sense) change with the passage of time, we decide to use these logical predicates in such a way that the logical properties of statements become timeless: if a statement is a tautology, then it is a tautology once and for all. This same timelessness we also attach to the concepts "true" and "false," in agreement with common usage. It is not common usage to say of a statement that it was perfectly true yesterday but has become false today. If yesterday we appraised a statement as true which today we appraise as false, then we implicitly assert today that *we were mistaken yesterday*; that the statement was false even yesterday—timelessly false—but that we erroneously "took it for true."

Here one can see very clearly the difference between truth and corroboration. The appraisal of a statement as corroborated or as not corroborated is also a logical appraisal and therefore also timeless; for it asserts that a certain logical relation holds between a theoretical system and some system of accepted basic statements. But we can never simply say of a statement that it is as such, or in itself, "corroborated" (in the way in which we may say that it is "true"). We can only say that it is *corroborated with respect to some system of basic statements*—a system accepted up to a particular point in time. "The corroboration which a theory has received up to yesterday" is *logically not identical* with "the corroboration which a theory has received up to today." Thus we must attach a subscript, as it were, to every appraisal of corroboration—a subscript characterizing the system of basic statements to which the corroboration relates (for example, by the date of its acceptance).

Corroboration is therefore not a "truth value"; that is, it cannot be placed on a par with the concepts "true" and "false" (which are free from temporal subscripts) ; for to one and the same statement there may be any number of different corroboration values, of which indeed all can be "correct" or "true" at the same time. For they are values which are logically derivable from the theory and the various sets of basic statements accepted at various times.

The above remarks may also help to elucidate the contrast between my views and those of the pragmatists who propose to *define "truth" in terms of the success of a theory—and thus of its usefulness, or of its confirmation or of its corroboration*. If their intention is merely to assert that a logical appraisal of the success of a theory can be no more than an appraisal of its corroboration, I can agree. But I think that it would be far from "*useful*" to identify the concept of corroboration with that of truth.[33] This is also

---

[32] (Added in 1934 in proof.) Carnap would probably say "syntactical concepts" (*cf.* his *Logical Syntax of Language*).

[33] Thus if we were to define "true" as "useful" (as suggested by some pragmatists), or

avoided in ordinary usage. For one might well say of a theory that it has hardly been corroborated at all so far, or that it is still uncorroborated. But we should not normally say of a theory that it is hardly true at all so far, or that it is still false.

THE PATH OF SCIENCE

One may discern something like a general direction in the evolution of physics—a direction from theories of a lower level of universality to theories of a higher level. This is usually called the "inductive" direction; and it might be thought that the fact that physics advances in this "inductive" direction could be used as an argument in favour of the inductive method.

Yet an advance in the inductive direction does not necessarily consist of a sequence of inductive inferences. Indeed we have shown that it may be explained in quite different terms—in terms of degree of testability and corroborability. For a theory which has been well corroborated can only be superseded by one of a higher level of universality; that is, by a theory which is better testable and which, in addition, *contains* the old, well corroborated theory—or at least a good approximation to it. It may be better, therefore, to describe that trend—the advance towards theories of an even higher level of universality—as "quasi-inductive."

The quasi-inductive process should be envisaged as follows. Theories of some level of universality are proposed, and deductively tested; after that, theories of a higher level of universality are proposed, and in their turn tested with the help of those of the previous levels of universality, and so on. The methods of testing are invariably based on deductive inferences from the higher to the lower level;[34] on the other hand, the levels of universality are reached, in the order of time, by proceeding from lower to higher levels.

The question may be raised: "Why not invent theories of the highest level of universality straight away? Why wait for this quasi-inductive evolution? Is it not perhaps because there is after all an inductive element contained in it?" I do not think so. Again and again suggestions are put forward—conjectures, or theories—of all possible levels of universality. Those theories which are on too high a level of universality, as it were (that is, too far removed from the level reached by the testable science of the day) give rise, perhaps, to a "metaphysical system." In this case, even if from this system statements should be deductible (or only semi-deductible, as for example in

---

else as "successful" or "confirmed" or "corroborated," we should only have to introduce a new "absolute" and "timeless" concept to play the role of "truth."

[34] The "deductive inferences from the higher to the lower level" are, of course, *explanations*; thus the hypotheses on the higher level are *explanatory* with respect to those on the lower level.

the case of Spinoza's system), which belong to the prevailing scientific system, there will be no *new* testable statement among them; which means that no crucial experiment can be designed to test the system in question.[35] If, on the other hand, a crucial experiment can be designed for it, then the system will contain, as a first approximation, some well corroborated theory, and at the same time also something new—and something that can be tested. Thus the system will not, of course, be "metaphysical." In this case, the system in question may be looked upon as a new advance in the quasi-inductive evolution of science. This explains why a link with the science of the day is as a rule established only by those theories which are proposed in an attempt to meet the current problem situation; that is, the current difficulties, contradictions, and falsifications. In proposing a solution to these difficulties, these theories may point the way to a crucial experiment.

To obtain a picture or model of this quasi-inductive evolution of science, the various ideas and hypotheses might be visualized as particles suspended in a fluid. Testable science is the precipitation of these particles at the bottom of the vessel: they settle down in layers (of universality). The thickness of the deposit grows with the number of these layers, every new layer corresponding to a theory more universal than those beneath it. As the result of this process ideas previously floating in higher metaphysical regions may sometimes be reached by the growth of science, and thus make contact with it, and settle. Examples of such ideas are atomism; the idea of a single physical "principle" or ultimate element (from which the others derive); the theory of terrestrial motion (opposed by Bacon as fictitious); the age-old corpuscular theory of light; the fluid-theory of electricity (revived as the electron-gas hypothesis of metallic conduction). All these metaphysical concepts and ideas may have helped, even in their early forms, to bring order into man's picture of the world, and in some cases they may even have led to successful predictions. Yet an idea of this kind acquires scientific status only when it is presented in falsifiable form; that is to say, only when it has become possible to decide empirically between it and some rival theory.

My investigation has traced the various consequences of the decisions and conventions—in particular of the criterion of demarcation—adopted at the beginning of this book. Looking back, we may now try to get a last comprehensive glimpse of the picture of science and of scientific discovery which has emerged. (What I have here in mind is not a picture of science as a biological phenomenon, as an instrument of adaptation, or as a roundabout method of production: I have in mind its epistemological aspects.)

[35] It should be noted that I mean by a crucial experiment one that is designed to refute a theory (if possible) and more especially one which is designed to bring about a decision between two competing theories by refuting (at least) one of them—without, of course, proving the other.

Science is not a system of certain, or well-established, statements; nor is it a system which steadily advances towards a state of finality. Our science is not knowledge (*epistēmē*) : it can never claim to have attained truth, or even a substitute for it, such as probability.

Yet science has more than mere biological survival value. It is not only a useful instrument. Although it can attain neither truth nor probability, the striving for knowledge and the search for truth are still the strongest motives of scientific discovery.

We do not know: we can only guess. And our guesses are guided by the unscientific, the metaphysical (though biologically explicable) faith in laws, in regularities which we can uncover—discover. Like Bacon, we might describe our own contemporary science—"the method of reasoning which men now ordinarily apply to nature"—as consisting of "anticipations, rash and premature" and of "prejudices."[36]

But these marvellously imaginative and bold conjectures or "anticipations" of ours are carefully and soberly controlled by systematic tests. Once put forward, none of our "anticipations" are dogmatically upheld. Our method of research is not to defend them, in order to prove how right we were. On the contrary, we try to overthrow them. Using all the weapons of our logical, mathematical, and technical armoury, we try to prove that our anticipations were false—in order to put forward, in their stead, new unjustified and unjustifiable anticipations, new "rash and premature prejudices," as Bacon derisively called them.[37]

It is possible to interpret the ways of science more prosaically. One might say that progress can ". . . come about only in two ways: by gathering new perceptual experiences, and by better organizing those which are available already."[38] But this description of scientific progress, although not actually

---

[36] Bacon, *Novum Organum*, I, 26.

[37] Bacon's "anticipation" (*"anticipatio"*; *Novum Organum* I, 26) means almost the same as "hypothesis" (in my usage). Bacon held that, to prepare the mind for the intuition of the true *essence* or *nature* of a thing, it has to be meticulously cleansed of all anticipations, prejudices, and idols. For the source of all error is the impurity of our own minds: Nature itself does not lie. The main function of eliminative induction is (as with Aristotle)to assist the purification of the mind. (*See also* my *Open Society*, Chapter 24; note 59 to chapter 10; note 33 to chapter 11, where Aristotle's theory of induction is briefly described.) Purging the mind of prejudices is conceived as a kind of ritual, prescribed for the scientist who wishes to prepare his mind for the interpretation (the unbiassed reading) of the Book of Nature; just as the mystic purifies his soul to prepare it for the vision of God. [*Cf.* the Introduction to my *Conjectures and Refutations* (1963) 1965.]

[38] P. Frank, *Das Kausalgesetz und seine Grenzen,* 1932. The view that the progress of science is due to the accumulation of perceptual experiences is still widely held (*cf.* my second Preface, 1958). My denial of this view is closely connected with the rejection of the doctrine that science or knowledge is *bound* to advance since our experiences

wrong, seems to miss the point. It is too reminiscent of Bacon's induction: too suggestive of his industrious gathering of the "countless grapes, ripe and in season,"[39] from which he expected the wine of science to flow: of his myth of a scientific method that starts from observation and experiment and then proceeds to theories. (This legendary method, by the way, still inspires some of the newer sciences which try to practice it because of the prevalent belief that it is the method of experimental physics.)

The advance of science is not due to the fact that more and more perceptual experiences accumulate in the course of time. Nor is it due to the fact that we are making ever better use of our senses. Out of uninterpreted sense-experiences science cannot be distilled, no matter how industriously we gather and sort them. Bold ideas, unjustified anticipations, and speculative thought, are our only means for interpreting nature: our only organon, our only instrument, for grasping her. And we must hazard them to win our prize. Those among us who are unwilling to expose their ideas to the hazard of refutation do not take part in the scientific game.

Even the careful and sober testing of our ideas by experience is in its turn inspired by ideas: experiment is planned action in which every step is guided by theory. We do not stumble upon our experiences, nor do we let them flow over us like a stream. Rather, we have to be active: we have to *"make"* our experiences. It is we who always formulate the questions to be put to nature; it is we who try again and again to put these question so as to elicit a clear-cut "yes" or "no" (for nature does not give an answer unless pressed for it). And in the end, it is again we who give the answer; it is we ourselves who, after severe scrutiny, decide upon the answer to the question which we put to nature—after protracted and earnest attempts to elicit from her an unequivocal "no." "Once and for all," says Weyl,[40] with whom I fully agree, "I wish to record my unbounded admiration for the work of the experimenter in his struggle to wrest *interpretable facts* from an unyielding Nature who knows so well how to meet our theories with a decisive *No*—or with an inaudible *Yes*."

The old scientific ideal of *epistēmē*—of absolutely certain, demonstrable knowledge—has proved to be an idol. The demand for scientific objectivity

are *bound* to accumulate. As against this, I believe that the advance of science depends upon the free competition of thought, and thus upon freedom, and that it must come to an end if freedom is destroyed (though it may well continue for some time in some fields, especially in technology). This view is more fully expounded in my *Poverty of Historicism* (section 32). I also argue there (in the Preface) that the growth of our knowledge is unpredictable by scientific means, and that, as a consequence, the future course of our history is also unpredictable.

[39] Bacon, *Novum Organum* I, 123.

[40] Weyl, *Gruppentheorie und Quantenmechanik*, 1931, p. 2. English translation by H. P. Robertson: *The Theory of Groups and Quantum Mechanics*, 1931, p. xx.

makes it inevitable that every scientific statement must remain *tentative for ever*. It may indeed be corroborated, but every corroboration is relative to other statements which, again, are tentative. Only in our subjective experiences of conviction, in our subjective faith, can we be "absolutely certain."[41]

With the idol of certainty (including that of degrees of imperfect certainty or probability) there falls one of the defences of obscurantism which bar the way of scientific advance. For the worship of this idol hampers not only the boldness of our questions, but also the rigour and the integrity of our tests. The wrong view of science betrays itself in the craving to be right; for it is not his *possession* of knowledge, of irrefutable truth, that makes the man of science, but his persistent and recklessly critical *quest* for truth.

Has our attitude, then, to be one of resignation? Have we to say that science can fulfil only its biological task; that it can, at best, merely prove its mettle in practical applications which may corroborate it? Are its intellectual problems insoluble? I do not think so. Science never pursues the illusory aim of making its answers final, or even probable. Its advance is, rather, towards an infinite yet attainable aim: that of ever discovering new, deeper, and more general problems, and of subjecting our ever tentative answers to ever renewed and ever more rigorous tests.

[41] This last remark is of course a psychological remark rather than an epistemological one.

F. Bayesian Inference

Members of a recent movement ("Bayesians") make use of Bayes' Inversion Theorem in inferring from data to a conclusion that goes beyond the data. The operation of this theorem and the personalistic theory of probability that generally accompanies it are sketched out in a selection from a classic article in this area, "Bayesian Statistical Inference for Psychological Research," by Ward Edwards, Harold Lindman, and Leonard J. Savage. Along with this selection, we have included their bibliography for those who want to pursue the subject further, as these authors see their subject.

Henry Kyburg, a philosopher of science, has written a compact critique of personal probability as used by the Bayesians, and we have included this as well. Wesley Salmon, another philosopher of science, supports and explains the use of an adaptation of the Bayes Theorem, but his reservations about personal probability lead him to try to replace it with a frequency-type probability. The selection by Salmon also includes a criticism of hypothetico-deductivism, an approach to scientific inferences sketched out earlier in selections from Mill and Braithwaite.

The acceptance of personal probability by the Bayesians can be viewed as one attempt to avoid the mechanical-appearing strategies of the radical empiricists.

25. BAYESIAN STATISTICAL INFERENCE FOR PSYCHOLOGICAL RESEARCH

Ward Edwards, Harold Lindman, & Leonard J. Savage

Bayesian statistics, a currently controversial viewpoint concerning statistical inference, is based on a definition of probability as a particular measure of the opinions of ideally consistent people. Statistical inference is modification of these opinions in the light of evidence, and Bayes' theorem specifies how such modifications should be made. The tools of Bayesian statistics include the theory of specific distributions and the principle of stable estimation, which specifies when actual prior opinions may be satisfactorily approximated by a uniform distribution. A common feature of many classical significance tests is that a sharp null hypothesis is compared with a diffuse alternative hypothesis. Often evidence which, for a Bayesian statistician, strikingly supports the null hypothesis leads to rejection of that hypothesis by standard classical procedures. The likelihood principle emphasized in Bayesian statistics implies, among other things, that the rules governing when data collection stops are irrelevant to data interpretation. It is entirely appropriate to collect data until a point has been proven or disproven, or until the data collector runs out of time, money, or patience.

The main purpose of this paper is to introduce psychologists to the Bayesian outlook in statistics, a new fabric with some very old threads. Although this purpose demands much repetition of ideas published elsewhere, even Bayesian specialists will find some remarks and derivations

SOURCE. Ward Edwards, Harold Lindman, and Leonard J. Savage, "Bayesian Statistical Inference for Psychological Research," *Psychological Review*, 70:3, 1963. Reprinted with permission of American Psychological Association. Copyright © 1963 by American Psychological Association.

hitherto unpublished and perhaps quite new. The empirical scientist more interested in the ideas and implications of Bayesian statistics than in the mathematical details can safely skip almost all the equations; detours and parallel verbal explanations are provided. The textbook that would make all the Bayesian procedures mentioned in this paper readily available to experimenting psychologists does not yet exist, and perhaps it cannot exist soon; Bayesian statistics as a coherent body of thought is still too new and incomplete.

Bayes' theorem is a simple and fundamental fact about probability that seems to have been clear to Thomas Bayes when he wrote his famous article published in 1763 (recently reprinted), though he did not state it there explicitly. Bayesian statistics is so named for the rather inadequate reason that it has many more occasions to apply Bayes' theorem than classical statistics has. Thus, from a very broad point of view, Bayesian statistics dates back at least to 1763.

From a stricter point of view, Bayesian statistics might properly be said to have begun in 1959 with the publication of *Probability and Statistics for Business Decisions,* by Robert Schlaifer. This introductory text presented for the first time practical implementation of the key ideas of Bayesian statistics: that probability is orderly opinion, and that inference from data is nothing other than the revision of such opinion in the light of relevant new information. Schlaifer (1961) has since published another introductory text, less strongly slanted toward business applications than his first. And Raiffa and Schlaifer (1961) have published a relatively mathematical book. Some other works in current Bayesian statistics are by Anscombe (1961), de Finetti (1959), de Finetti and Savage (1962), Grayson (1960), Lindley (1961), Pratt (1961), and Savage et al. (1962).

The philosophical and mathematical basis of Bayesian statistics has, in addition to its ancient roots, a considerable modern history. Two lines of development important for it are the ideas of statistical decision theory, based on the game-theoretic work of Borel (1921), von Neumann (1928), and von Neumann and Morgenstern (1947), and the statistical work of Neyman (1937, 1938b, for example), Wald (1942, 1955, for example), and others; and the personalistic definition of probability, which Ramsey (1931) and de Finetti (1930, 1937) crystallized. Other pioneers of personal probability are Borel (1924), Good (1950, 1960), and Koopman (1940a, 1940b, 1941). Decision theory and personal probability fused in the work of Ramsey (1931), before either was very mature. By 1954, there was great progress in both lines for Savage's *The Foundations of Statistics* to draw on. Though this book failed in its announced object of satisfying popular non-Bayesian statistics in terms of personal probability and utility, it seems to have been of some service toward the development of Bayesian statistics. Jeffreys

(1931, 1939) has pioneered extensively in applications of Bayes' theorem to statistical problems. He is one of the founders of Bayesian statistics, though he might reject identification with the viewpoint of this paper because of its espousal of personal probabilities. These two, inevitably inadequate, paragraphs are our main attempt in this paper to give credit where it is due. Important authors have not been listed, and for those that have been, we have given mainly one early and one late reference only. Much more information and extensive bibliographies will be found in Savage et al. (1962) and Savage (1954, 1962a).

We shall, where appropriate, compare the Bayesian approach with a loosely defined set of ideas here labeled the classical approach, or classical statistics. You cannot but be familiar with many of these ideas, for what you learned about statistical inference in your elementary statistics course was some blend of them. They have been directed largely toward the topics of testing hypotheses and interval estimation, and they fall roughly into two somewhat conflicting doctrines associated with the names of R. A. Fisher (1925), 1956) for one, and Jerzy Neyman (e.g. 1937, 1938b) and Egon Pearson for the other. We do not try to portray any particular version of the classical approach; our real comparison is between such procedures as a Bayesian would employ in an article submitted to the *Journal of Experimental Psychology*, say, and those now typically found in that journal. The fathers of the classical approach might not fully approve of either. Similarly, though we adopt for conciseness an idiom that purports to define *the* Bayesian position, there must be at least as many Bayesian positions as there are Bayesians. Still, as philosophies go, the unanimity among Bayesians reared apart is remarkable and an encouraging symptom of the cogency of their ideas.

In some respects Bayesian statistics is a reversion to the statistical spirit of the eighteenth and nineteenth centuries; in others, no less essential, it is an outgrowth of that modern movement here called classical. The latter, in coping with the consequences of its view about the foundations of probability which made useless, if not meaningless, the probability that a hypothesis is true, sought and found techniques for statistical inference which did not attach probabilities to hypotheses. These intended channels of escape have now, Bayesians believe, led to reinstatement of the probabilities of hypotheses and a return of statistical inference to its original line of development. In this return, mathematics, formulations, problems, and such vital tools as distribution theory and tables of functions are borrowed from extrastatistical probability theory and from classical statistics itself. All the elements of Bayesian statistics, except perhaps the personalistic view of probability, were invented and developed within, or before, the classical approach to statistics; only their combination into specific techniques for statistical inference is at all new.

The Bayesian approach is a common sense approach. It is simply a set of techniques for orderly expression and revision of your opinions with due regard for internal consistency among their various aspects and for the data. Naturally, then, much that Bayesians say about inference from data has been said before by experienced, intuitive, sophisticated empirical scientists and statisticians. In fact, when a Bayesian procedure violates your intuition, reflection is likely to show the procedure to have been incorrectly applied. If classically trained institutions do have some conflicts, these often prove transient.

ELEMENTS OF BAYESIAN STATISTICS

Two basic ideas which come together in Bayesian statistics, as we have said, are the decision-theoretic formulation of statistical inference and the notion of personal probability.

Statistics and Decisions. Prior to a paper by Neyman (1938a), classical statistical inference was usually expressed in terms of justifying propositions on the basis of data. Typical propositions were: Point estimates; the best guess for the unknown number μ is m. Interval estimates; μ is between m_1 and m_2. Rejection of hypotheses; μ is not 0. Neyman's (1938a, 1957) slogan "inductive behavior" emphasized the importance of action, as opposed to assertion, in the face of uncertainty. The decision-theoretic, or economic, view of statistics was advanced with particular vigor by Wald (1942). To illustrate, in the decision-theoretic outlook a point estimate is a decision to act, in some specific context, as though μ were m, not to assert something about μ. Some classical statisticians, notably Fisher (1956, Ch. 4), have hotly rejected the decision-theoretic outlook.

While Bayesian statistics owes much to the decision-theoretic outlook, and while we personally are inclined to side with it, the issue is not crucial to a Bayesian. No one will deny that economic problems of behavior in the face of uncertainty concern statistics, even in its most "pure" contexts. For example, "Would it be wise, in the light of what has just been observed, to attempt such and such a year's investigation?" The controversial issue is only whether such economic problems are a good paradigm of all statistical problems. For Bayesians, all uncertainties are measured by probabilities, and these probabilities (along with the here less emphasized concept of utilities) are the key to all problems of economic uncertainty. Such a view deprives debate about whether all problems of uncertainty are economic of urgency. On the other hand, economic definitions of personal probability seem, at least to us, invaluable for communication and perhaps indispensable for operational definition of the concept.

A Bayesian can reflect on his current opinion (and how he should revise it on the basis of data) without any reference to the actual economic significance, if any, that his opinion may have. This paper ignores economic considerations, important though they are even for pure science, except for brief digressions. So doing may combat the misapprehension that Bayesian statistics is primarily for business, not science.

Personal Probability. With rare exceptions, statisticians who conceive of probabilities exclusively as limits of relative frequencies are agreed that uncertainty about matters of fact is ordinarily not measurable by probability. Some of them would brand as nonsense the probability that weightlessness decreases visual acuity; for others the probability of this hypothesis would be 1 or 0 according as it is in fact true or false. Classical statistics is characterized by efforts to reformulate inference about such hypotheses without reference to their probabilities, especially initial probabilities.

These efforts have been many and ingenious. It is disagreement about which of them to espouse, incidentally, that distinguishes the two main classical schools of statistics. The related ideas of significance levels, "errors of the first kind," and confidence levels, and the conflicting idea of fiducial probabilities are all intended to satisfy the urge to know how sure you are after looking at the data, while outlawing the question of how sure you were before. In our opinion, the quest for inference without initial probabilities has failed, inevitably.

You may be asking, "If a probability is not a relative frequency or a hypothetical limiting relative frequency, what is it? If, when I evaluate the probability of getting heads when flipping a certain coin as .5, I do not mean that if the coin were flipped very often the relative frequency of heads to total flips would be arbitrarily close to .5, then what do I mean?"

We think you mean something about yourself as well as about the coin. Would you not say, "Heads on the next flip has probability .5" if and only if you would as soon guess heads as not, even if there were some important reward for being right? If so, your sense of "probability" is ours; even if you would not, you begin to see from this example what we mean by "probability," or "personal probability." To see how far this notion is from relative frequencies, imagine being reliably informed that the coin has either two heads or two tails. You may still find that if you had to guess the outcome of the next flip for a large prize you would not lift a finger to shift your guess from heads to tails or vice versa.

Probabilities other than .5 are defined in a similar spirit by one of several mutually harmonious devices (Savage, 1954, Ch. 1–4). One that is particularly vivid and practical, if not quite rigorous as stated here, is this. For you, now, the probability $P(A)$ of an event A is the price you would just be willing to pay in exchange for a dollar to be paid to you in case A is true. Thus, rain tomorrow has probability $1/3$ for you if you would pay just $\$.33$ now in exchange for $\$1.00$ payable to you in the event of rain tomorrow.

A system of personal probabilities, or prices for contingent benefits, is inconsistent if a person who acts in accordance with it can be trapped into accepting a combination of bets that assures him of a loss no matter what happens. Necessary and sufficient conditions for consistency are the following, which are familiar as a basis for the whole mathematical theory of probability:

$$0 \leqq P(A) \leqq P(S) = 1, P(A \cup B) = P(A) + P(B),$$

where S is the tautological, or universal, event; A and B are any two incompatible, or nonintersecting, events; and $A \cup B$ is the event that either A or B is true, or the union of A and B. Real people often make choices that reflect violations of these rules, especially the second, which is why personalists emphasize that personal probability is orderly, or consistent, opinion, rather than just any opinion. One of us has presented elsewhere a model for probabilities inferred from real choices that does not include the second consistency requirement listed above (Edwards, 1962b). It is important to keep clear the distinction between the somewhat idealized consistent personal probabilities that are the subject of this paper and the usually inconsistent subjective probabilities that can be inferred from real human choices among bets, and the words "personal" and "subjective" here help do so.

Your opinions about a coin can of course differ from your neighbor's. For one thing, you and he may have different bodies of relevant information. We doubt that this is the only legitimate source of difference of opinion. Hence the personal in personal probability. Any probability should in principle be indexed with the name of the person, or people, whose opinion it describes. We usually leave the indexing unexpressed but underline it from time to time with phrases like "the probability for you that H is true."

Although your initial opinion about future behavior of a coin may differ radically from your neighbor's, your opinion and his will ordinarily be so transformed by application of Bayes' theorem to the results of a long sequence of experimental flips as to become neatly indistinguishable. This approximate merging of initially divergent opinions is, we think, one reason why empirical research is called "objective." Personal probability is sometimes dismissed with the assertion that scientific knowledge cannot be mere opinion. Yet, obviously, no sharp lines separate the conjecture that many human cancers may be caused by viruses, the opinion that many are caused by smoking, and the "knowledge" that many have been caused by radiation.

Conditional probabilities and Bayes' theorem. In the spirit of the rough definition of the probability $P(A)$ of an event A given above, the conditional probability $P(D|H)$ of an event D given another H is the amount you would be willing to pay in exchange for a dollar to be paid to you in case D is true, with the further provision that all transactions are canceled unless H is true. As is not hard to see, $P(D \cap H)$ is $P(D|H)P(H)$ where $D \cap H$ is the event that D and H are both true, or the intersection of D and H. Therefore,

$$P(D|H) = \frac{P(D \cap H)}{P(H)}, \qquad [1]$$

unless $P(H) = 0$.

Conditional probabilities are the probabilistic expression of learning from experience. It can be argued that the probability of D for you—the consistent you—after learning that H is in fact true is $P(D|H)$. Thus, after you learn that H is true, the new system of numbers $P(D|H)$ for a specific H comes to play the role that was played by the old system $P(D)$ before.

Although the events D and H are arbitrary, the initial letters of Data and Hypothesis are suggestive names for them. Of the three probabilities in Equation 1, $P(H)$ might be illustrated by the sentence: "The probability for you, now, that Russia will use a booster rocket bigger than our planned Saturn booster within the next year is .8." The probability $P(D \cap H)$ is the probability of the joint occurrence of two events regarded as one event, for instance: "The probability for you, now, that the next manned space capsule to enter space will contain three men and also that Russia will use a booster rocket bigger than our planned Saturn booster within the next year is .2." According to Equation 1, the probability for you, now, that the next manned space capsule to enter space will contain three men, given that Russia will use a booster rocket bigger than our planned Saturn booster within the next year is $.2/.8 = .25$.

A little algebra now leads to a basic form of Bayes' theorem:

$$P(H|D) = \frac{P(D|H)P(H)}{P(D)}, \qquad [2]$$

provided $P(D)$ and $P(H)$ are not 0. In fact, if the roles of D and H in Equation 1 are interchanged, the old form of Equation 1 and the new form can be expressed symmetrically, thus:

$$\frac{P(D|H)}{P(D)} = \frac{P(D \cap H)}{P(D)P(H)} = \frac{P(H|D)}{P(H)}, \qquad [3]$$

which obviously implies Equation 2. A suggestive interpretation of Equation 3 is that the relevance of H to D equals the relevance of D to H.

Reformulations of Bayes' theorem apply to continuous parameters or data.

In particular, if a parameter (or set of parameters) λ has a prior probability density function $u(\lambda)$, and if x is random variable (or a set of random variables such as a set of measurements) for which $v(x|\lambda)$ is the density of x given λ and $v(x)$ is the density of x, then the posterior probability density of λ given x is

$$u(\lambda|x) = \frac{v(x|\lambda)\,u(\lambda)}{v(x)}.$$ [4]

There are of course still other possibilities such as forms of Bayes' theorem in which λ but not x, or x but not λ, is continuous. A complete and compact generalization is available and technically necessary but need not be presented here.

In Equation 2, D may be a particular observation or a set of data regarded as a datum and H some hypothesis, or putative fact. Then Equation 2 prescribes the consistent revision of your opinions about the probability of H in the light of the datum D—similarly for Equation 4.

In typical applications of Bayes' theorem, each of the four probabilities in Equation 2 performs a different function, as will soon be explained. Yet they are very symmetrically related to each other, as Equation 3 brings out, and are all the same kind of animal. In particular, all probabilities are really conditional. Thus, $P(H)$ is the probability of the hypothesis H for you conditional on all you know, or knew, about H prior to learning D; and $P(H|D)$ is the probability of H conditional on that same background knowledge together with D.

Again, the four probabilities in Equation 2 are personal probabilities. This does not of course exclude any of them from also being frequencies, ratios of favorable to total possibilities, or numbers arrived at by any other calculation that helps you form your personal opinions. But some are, so to speak, more personal than others. In many applications, practically all concerned find themselves in substantial agreement with respect to $P(D|H)$; or $P(D|H)$ is public, as we say. This happens when $P(D|H)$ flows from some simple model that the scientists, or others, concerned accept as an approximate description of their opinion about the situation in which the datum was obtained. A traditional example of such a statistical model is that of drawing a ball from an urn known to contain some balls, each either black or white. If a series of balls is drawn from the urn, and after each draw the ball is replaced and the urn thoroughly shaken, most men will agree at least tentatively that the probability of drawing a particular sequence D (such as black, white, black, black) given the hypothesis that there are B black and W white balls in the urn is

$$\left(\frac{B}{B+W}\right)^{b}\left(\frac{W}{B+W}\right)^{w}$$

where b is the number of black, and w the number of white, balls in the sequence D.

Even the best models have an element of approximation. For example, the probability of drawing any sequence D of black and white balls from an urn of composition H depends, in this model, only on the number of black balls and white ones in D, not on the order in which they appeared. This may express your opinion in a specific situation very well, but not well enough to be retained if D should happen to consist of 50 black balls followed by 50 whites ones. Idiomatically, such a datum convinces you that this particular model is a wrong description of the world. Philosophically, however, the model was not a description of the world but of your opinions, and to know that it was not quite correct, you had at most to reflect on this datum, not necessarily to observe it. In many scientific contexts, the public model behind $P(D|H)$ may include the notions of random sampling from a well-defined population, as in this example. But precise definition of the population may be difficult or impossible, and a sample whose randomness would thoroughly satisfy you, let alone your neighbor in science, can be hard to draw.

In some cases $P(D|H)$ does not command general agreement at all. What is the probability of the actual seasonal color changes on Mars if there is life there? What is this probability if there is no life there? Much discussion of life on Mars has not removed these questions from debate.

Public models, then, are never perfect and often are not available. Nevertheless, those applications of inductive inference, or probabilistic reasoning, that are called statistical seem to be characterized by tentative public agreement on some model and provisional work within it. Rough characterization of statistics by the relative publicness of its models is not necessarily in conflict with attempts to characterize it as the study of numerous repetitions (Bartlett, in Savage et' al., 1962, pp. 36–38). This characterization is intended to distinguish statistical applications of Bayes' theorem from many other applications to scientific, economic, military, and other contexts. In some of these nonstatistical contexts, it is appropriate to substitute the judgment of experts for a public model as the source of $P(D|H)$ (see for example Edwards, 1962a, 1963).

The other probabilities in Equation 2 are often not at all public. Reasonable men may differ about them, even if they share a statistical model that specifies $P(D|H)$. People do, however, often differ much more about $P(H)$ and $P(D)$ than about $P(H|D)$, for evidence can bring initially divergent opinions into near agreement.

The probability $P(D)$ is usually of little direct interest, and intuition is often silent about it. It is typically calculated, or eliminated, as follows. When there is a statistical model, H is usually regarded as one of a list, or partition, of mutually exclusive and exhaustive hypotheses H_i such that the

$P(D|H_i)$ are all equally public, or part of the statistical model. Since $\Sigma_i P(H_i|D)$ must be 1, Equation 2 implies that

$$P(D) = \Sigma_i P(D|H_i) P(H_i).$$

The choice of the partition H_i is of practical importance but largely arbitrary. For example, tomorrow will be "fair" or "foul," but these two hypotheses can themselves be subdivided and resubdivided. Equation 2 is of course true for all partitions but is more useful for some than for others. As a science advances, partitions originally not even dreamt of become the important ones (Sinclair, 1960). In principle, room should always be left for "some other" explanation. Since $P(D|II)$ can hardly be public when H is "some other explanation," the catchall hypothesis is usually handled in part by studying the situation conditionally on denial of the catchall and in part by informal appraisal of whether any of the explicit hypotheses fit the facts well enough to maintain this denial. Good illustrations are Urey (1962) and Bridgman (1960).

In statistical practice, the partition is ordinarily continuous, which means roughly that H_i is replaced by a parameter λ (which may have more than one dimension) with an initial probability density $u(\lambda)$. In this case,

$$P(D) = \int P(D|\lambda) u(\lambda) d\lambda.$$

Similarly, $P(D)$, $P(D|H_i)$, and $P(D|\lambda)$ are replaced by probability densities in D if D is (absolutely) continuously distributed.

$P(H|D)$ or $u(\lambda|D)$, the usual output of a Bayesian calculation, seems to be exactly the kind of information that we all want as a guide to thought and action in the light of an observational process. It is the probability for you that the hypothesis in question is true, on the basis of all your information, including, but not restricted to, the observation D.

PRINCIPLE OF STABLE ESTIMATION

Problem of Prior Probabilities. Since $P(D|H)$ is often reasonably public and $P(H|D)$ is usually just what the scientist wants, the reason classical statisticians do not base their procedures on Equations 2 and 4 must, and does, lie in $P(H)$, the prior probability of the hypothesis. We have already discussed the most frequent objection to attaching a probability to a hypothesis and have shown briefly how the definition of personal probability answers that objection. We must now examine the practical problem of determining $P(H)$. Without $P(H)$, Equations 2 and 4 cannot yield $P(H|D)$. But since $P(H)$ is a personal probability, is it not likely to be both vague and variable, and subjective to boot, and therefore useless for public scientific purposes?

Yes, prior probabilities often are quite vague and variable, but they are not necessarily useless on that account (Borel, 1924). The impact of actual vagueness and variability of prior probabilities differs greatly from one problem to another. They frequently have but negligible effect on the conclusions obtained from Bayes' theorem, although utterly unlimited vagueness and variability would have utterly unlimited effect. If observations are precise, in a certain sense, relative to the prior distribution on which they bear, then the form and properties of the prior distribution have negligible influence on the posterior distribution. From a practical point of view, then, the untrammeled subjectivity of opinion about a parameter ceases to apply as soon as much data becomes available. More generally, two people with widely divergent prior opinions but reasonably open minds will be forced into arbitrarily close agreement about future observations by a sufficient amount of data. An advanced mathematical expression of this phenomenon is in Blackwell and Dubins (1962). . . .

References

Anscombe, F. J. Bayesian statistics. *Amer. Statist.*, 1961, 15(1), 21–24.

Bahadur, R. R., & Robbins, H. The problem of the greater mean. *Ann math. Statist.*, 1950, 21, 469–487.

Barnard, G. A. A review of "Sequential Analysis" by Abraham Wald. *J. Amer. Statist. Ass.*, 1947, 42, 658–664.

Barnard, G. A., Jenkins, G. M., & Winsten, C. B. Likelihood, inferences, and time series. *J. Roy Statist. Soc.*, 1962, 125(Ser. A), 321–372.

Bayes, T. Essay towards solving a problem in the doctrine of chances. *Phil. Trans. Roy. Soc.*, 1763, 53, 370–418. (Reprinted: *Biometrika*, 1958, 45, 293–315.)

Berkson, J. Some difficulties of interpretation encountered in the application of the chi-square test *J. Amer. Statist. Ass.*, 1938, 33, 526–542.

Berkson, J. Tests of significance considered as evidence. *J. Amer. Statist. Ass.*, 1942, 37, 325–335.

Birnbaum, A. On the foundations of statistical inference. *J. Amer. Statist. Ass.*, 1962, 57, 269–306.

Blackwell, D., & Dubins, L. Merging of opinions with increasing information. *Ann. math. Statist.*, 1962, 33, 882–886.

Borel, E. La théorie du jeu et les équations intégrales à noyau symétrique. *CR Acad. Sci., Paris*, 1921, 173, 1304–1308. (Trans. by L. J. Savage, *Econometrica*, 1953, 21, 97–124.

Borel, E. A propos d'un traité de probabilités. *Rev. Phil.*, 1924, 98, 321–336. (Reprinted: In, *Valeur pratique et philosophie des probabilités*. Paris: Gauthier-Villars, 1939. Pp. 134–146.

Bridgman, P. W. A critique of critical tables. *Proc. Nat. Acad. Sci.*, 1960, 46, 1394–1401.

Cramér, H. *Mathematical methods of statistics.* Princeton: Princeton Univer. Press, 1946.

de Finetti, B. Fundamenti logici del ragionamento probabilistico. *Boll. Un. mat. Ital.*, 1930, 9(Ser. A), 258–261.

de Finetti, B. La prévisian: Ses lois ligoques, ses sources subjectives. *Ann. Inst. Henri Poincaré*, 1937, 7, 1–68.

de Finetti, B. La probabilità e la statistica nei rapporti con l'induzione, secondo i diversi punti da vista. In, *Induzione e statistica*. Rome, Italy: Istituto Matematico dell' Universita, 1959.

de Finetti, B., & Savage, L. J. Sul modo di scegliere le probabilità iniziali. In, *Biblioteca del "metron."* Ser. C. Vol. 1. *Sui fondementi della statistica.* Rome: University of Rome, 1962, Pp. 81–154.

Edwards, W. Dynamic decision theory and probalistic information processing. *Illum. Factors*, 1962, 4, 59–73. (a)

Edwards, W. Subjective probabilities inferred from decisions. *Psychol. Rev.*, 1962, 69, 109–135. (b)

Edwards, W. Probabilistic information processing in command and control systems. Report No. 3780–12-T, 1963, Institute of Science and Technology, University of Michigan.

Fisher, R. A. *Statistical methods for research workers.* (12th ed., 1954) Edinburgh: Oliver & Boyd, 1925.

Fisher, R. A. *Contributions to mathematical statistics.* New York: Wiley, 1950.

Fisher, R. A. *Statistical methods and scientific inference.* (2nd ed., 1959) Edinburgh: Oliver & Boyd, 1956.

Good, I. J. *Probability and the weighing of evidence.* New York: Hafner, 1950.

Good, I. J. Weight of evidence, corroboration, explanatory power, information and the utility of experiments, *J. Roy Statist. Soc.*, 1960, 22(Ser. B), 319–331.

Grant, D. A. Testing the null hypothesis and the strategy and tactics of investigating theoretical models. *Psychol. Rev.* 1962, 69, 54–61.

Grayson, C. J., Jr. *Decisions under uncertainty: Drilling decisions by oil and gas operators.* Boston: Harvard Univer. Press, 1960.

Green, B. J. Jr., & Tukey, J. W. Complex analysis of variance: General problems. *Psychometrika*, 1960, 25, 127–152.

Guilford, J. P. *Fundamental statistics in psychology and education.* (3rd. ed., 1956) New York: McGraw-Hill 1912.

Halmos, P. R., & Savage, L. J. Application of the Radon-Nikodym theorem to the theory of sufficient statistics. *Ann. math. Statist.*, 1949, 20, 225–241.

Hildreth, C. Bayesian statisticians and remote clients. *Econometrica*, 1963, 31.

Hodges, J. L., & Lehmann, E. L. Testing the approximate validity of statistical hypotheses. *J. Roy. Statist. Soc.*, 1954, 16 (Ser. B), 261–268.

Jeffreys, H. *Scientific inference.* (3rd ed., 1957) England: Cambridge Univer. Press, 1931.

Jeffreys, H. *Theory of probability.* (3rd ed., 1961) Oxford, England: Clarendon, 1959.

Koopman, B. O. The axioms and algebra of intuitive probability. *Ann. Math.*, 1940, 41 (Ser. 2), 269–292. (a)

Koopman, B. O. The bases of probability. *Bull. Amer. Math. Soc.*, 1940, 46, 763–774. (b).

Koopman, B. O. Intuitive probabilities and sequences. *Ann. Math.*, 1941, 42 (Sed. 2), 169–187.

Lehmann. E. L. Significance level and power. *Ann. math. Statist.*, 1958, 20, 1167–1176.

Lehmann, E. L. Testing statistical hypotheses. New York: Wiley, 1959.

Lindley, D. V. A statistical paradox. *Biometrika*, 1957, 44, 187–192.

Lindley, D. V. The use of prior probability distributions in statistical inferences and decisions. In, *Proceedings of the fourth Berkeley symposium on mathematics and probability.* Vol. 1. Berkeley: Univer. California Press, 1964. Pp. 453–463.

Neyman, J. Outline of a theory of statistical estimation based on the classical theory of probability. *Phil. Trans. Roy. Soc.* 1937, 236 (Ser. A), 333–380.

Neyman, J. L'estimation statistique traitée comme un probléme classique de probabilité. In, *Actualités scientifiques et industrielles.* Paris, France: Hermann & Cie, 1938. Pp. 25–57. (a)

Neyman, J. *Lectures and conferences on mathematical statistics and probability.* (2nd ed., 1952) Washington, D.C.: United States Department of Agriculture, 1938. (b)

Neyman, J. "Inductive behavior" as a basic concept of philosophy of science. *Rev. Math. Statist. Inst.*, 1957, 25, 7–22.

Pearson, E. S. In L. J. Savage et al., *The foundations of statistical inference: A discussion.* New York: Wiley, 1962.

Pratt, J. W. Review of *Testing Statistical Hypotheses* by E. L. Lehmann. *J. Amer. Statist. Ass.*, 1961, 56, 163–167.

Raiffa, H., & Schlaifer, R. *Applied statistical decision theory.* Boston: Harvard University, Graduate School of Business Administration, Division of Research, 1961.

Ramsey, F. P. "Truth and probability" (1926), and "Further considerations" (1928). In, *The foundations of mathematics and other essays.* New York: Harcourt, Brace, 1931.

Rozedoom, W. W. The fallacy of the null-hypothesis significance test. *Psychol. Bull.*, 1960, 57, 416–428.

Savage, I. R. Nonparametric statistics. *J. Amer. Statist. Ass.*, 1967, 52, 331–344.

Savage, I. R. *Bibliography of nonparametric statistics.* Cambridge: Harvard Univer. Press, 1962.

Savage, L. J. *The foundations of statistics.* New York: Wiley, 1954.

Savage, L. J. The foundations of statistics reconsidered. In, *Proceedings of the fourth Berkeley symposium on mathematices and probability.* Vol. 1. Berkeley: Univer. California Press, 1961. Pp. 575–586.

Savage, L. J. Bayesian statistics. In, *Decision and information processes.* New York: Macmillan, 1962. Pp. 161–194. (a)

Savage, L. J. Subjective probability and statistical practice. In L. J. Savage et al., *The foundations of statistical inferences: A discussion.* New York: Wiley, 1962. (b)

Savage, L. J., et al. *The foundations of statistical inference: A discussion.* New York: Wiley, 1962.

Scheffé, H. *The analysis of variance.* New York: Wiley, 1959.

Schlaifer, R. *Probability and statistics for business decisions.* New York: McGraw-Hill, 1959.

Schlaifer, R. *Introduction to statistics for business decisions.* New York: McGraw-Hill, 1961.

Sinclair, H. Hiawatha's lipid. *Perspect. Biol. Med.*, 1960, 4, 72–76.

Stein, C. A remark on the likelihood principle. *J. Roy. Statist. Soc.*, 1962, 125 (Ser. A), 565–568.

Sterling, T. D. What is so peculiar about accepting the null hypothesis? *Psychol. Rep.*, 1960, 7, 363–364.

Tukey, J. W. The future of data analysis. *Ann. math Statist.*, 1962, 33, 1–67.

Urey, H. C. Origin of tektites. *Science*, 1962, 137, 746.

von Neumann, J. Zur Theorie der Gesellschaftsspiele. *Math. Ann.*, 1928, 100, 295–320.

von Neumann, J., & Morgenstern, O. *Theory of games and economic behavior.* (3rd ed., 1953) Princeton: Princeton Univer. Press, 1947.

Wald, A. On the principles of statistical inference. (Notre Dame Mathematical Lectures, No. 1) Ann Arbor, Mich.: Edwards, 1942. (Litho)

Wald, A. *Selected papers in statistics and probability.* New York: McGraw-Hill, 1955.

Walsh, J. E. *Handbook of nonparametric statistics.* Princeton, N.J.: Van Nostrand, 1962.

Wolfowitz, J. Bayesian inference and axioms of consistent decision. *Econometrica*, 1962, 30, 470–479.

26. THE PERSONALISTIC THEORY OF PROBABILITY

Henry E. Kyburg, Jr.

1. The subjective, or personalistic, theory of probability was first explicitly suggested by Ramsey; it is mentioned in his book of essays, *The Foundations of Mathematics*.[1] It has not been considered very important until recently, and Ramsey himself seems to have considered it only a supplement to a relative frequency or class ratio theory.[2] De Finetti[3] was the first statistician to take it seriously, and in 1954 J. L. Savage published a detailed presentation of the foundations of the theory.[4] Recently certain parts of the personalistic theory have been employed to provide a justification for the axioms conventionally laid down for confirmation functions.[5]

The basic thesis of the theory is that probability statements are statements concerning actual degrees of belief. Some statements are certain, e.g., statements known to be logical or mathematical theorems, while others are be-

SOURCE. Copyright © 1961 by Wesleyan University. Reprinted from *Probability and the Logic of Rational Belief*, by Henry E. Kyburg, Jr., by permission of Wesleyan University Press.

1 Ramsey, *The Foundations of Mathematics*, p. 166 ff.

2 As do Braithwaite (*Scientific Explanations*), von Wright (*The Logical Problem of Induction*), and others, who generally attach even less importance to it than Ramsey did.

3 De Finetti, *La prévision: ses lois logiques, ses sources subjectives. Annales de l'Institut Henri Poincaré* 7, 1937.

4 L. J. Savage, *The Foundations of Statistics*, New York, 1954.

5 Abner Shimony, "Coherence and the Axioms of Confirmation," *Journal of Symbolic Logic* 20, 1955. John Kemeny, "Fair Bets and Inductive Probabilities," *Journal of Symbolic Logic* 20, 1955. R. Sherman Lehman, "On Confirmation and Rational Betting," *Journal of Symbolic Logic* 20, 1955.

lieved only to a certain degree, e.g., the statement, "It will rain tomorrow." I neither completely believe nor completely disbelieve this statement; instead, I partially believe it, or, in the language of the personalistic theory, attach a certain degree of probability to it.

According to Ramsey, it is possible to discover the degree of probability I attach to the proposition that it will rain tomorrow by considering a hypothetical sequence of bets. The actual value of the probability, for me, now, is that indicated by the highest odds I would offer in betting on the occurrence of rain tomorrow. If these odds were 5:2, the probability would be $5/(2+5)$, or 0.7142 . . . Due to the diminishing marginal utility of money, this technique is difficult to apply in practise, although as the sums involved become smaller and smaller it becomes more and more plausible. Savage provides an alternative method of measuring degrees of belief, however, which eliminates the difficulties that crop up in trying to apply Ramsey's technique directly.

Savage begins with a set of *states* (of the world); a set of *consequences; acts*, which are functions from states to consequences; and a relation, "is not preferred to," which holds between acts. In a given context, one of a certain set of states actually obtains, although we may not know which one it is. An act is a function that tells us, for every state, which consequence would result from that act if that state actually obtained. The primitive relation "is not preferred to" provides a simple ordering among acts: for every two acts, f and g, either f is not preferred to g, or g is not preferred to f, or both.

On this basis it is possible to define preference between acts, given B, where B is a subset of the set of states S. It is then possible to define preference between consequences. The definition of probability then proceeds as follows: Let A and B be subsets of the set S of states. We offer a person a choice between two acts. The first of these acts is that he is to receive a prize f in case A obtains, or a prize f' in case A does not obtain. The second of these acts is that he is to receive a prize f in case B obtains, or a prize f' in case B does not obtain. The prize f is definitely preferred to the prize f' by this person. We now say, "A is not more probable than B" if and only if the first act is not preferred to the second act.[6]

This definition yields an ordering among events (subsets of S) with respect to the relation, "is not more probable than." From here to quantitative probabilities is an easy step. A *probability measure* P is defined as a function assigning to every subset B of S a real number $P(B)$ such that:

(1) $P(B) \geqslant 0$, for every B.

(2)   If $B \cap C \equiv 0, P(B \cup C) = P(B) + P(C)$.

(3) $P(S) = 1$.

[6] Savage, *op. cit.*, p. 31 ff.

In order to arrive at quantitative probabilities, now, we merely have to assume some postulate to the effect that there exist partitions of S into arbitrarily many equivalent (equiprobable) subsets. (B and C constitute a partition of S if every element of S belongs to either B or C, and if no element of S belongs to both B and C.) If there is an n-fold partition of S into equivalent subsets, for example, the probability of each of these subsets is $1/n$.

2. It is clear that some probability statements on this theory are empirical. To find out whether A is more probable than B for person Z at time t, we must conduct an inquiry. We must discover whether he would prefer to stake a possible gain on the occurrence of A or on the occurrence of B. This is a problem (and not necessarily a trivial one) in experimental psychology. To find the numerical probability which the person attaches to the occurrence of A, we may take B as a sequence of coin tosses, in which the person is absolutely convinced that the tosses are independent and that the coin is fair, and make comparisons accordingly. If the person would just as soon stake a possible gain on the occurrence of A as on the occurrence of three consecutive heads, the probability of A, for him, at this time, is 0.12500 . . . Now if we have such a coin, we can go down the list of possible events or states in the person's world, and discover the precise degree of probability that he attaches to each possibility; and we may do this to any degree of accuracy we please. We can evaluate the probability, for him, now, that the next president will be a republican, to 1000 decimal places. Every probability statement would then be empirical; it would make an assertion about the actual state of the person's beliefs.

To say, then, that the postulates, theorems, etc., of the theory hold good for these probabilities, would be to advance a psychological theory. This theory would have such consequences as this: If a person has a degree of belief equal to p_1 in A, and a degree of belief equal to p_2 in B, and a degree of belief equal to 0 in the conjunction of A and B, then he will have a degree of belief in the alternation of A *or* B equal to p_1 plus p_2. This psychological theory is clearly false in general, although it may hold approximately, for some people, some of the time, in some areas of belief.

But the subjective theory of probability has never been proposed as a *purely* empirical theory about the relationships among people's beliefs. Instead of this, the personalistic *calculus* of probability has been taken as normative for relations between degrees of belief in related propositions. The theory of probability as a whole is partly normative. According to Savage, a person has certain degrees of confidence in certain propositions; should the person discover empirically that the confidence he has in related propositions violates the rules of the calculus, he will modify his beliefs. A distribution of probabilities (degrees of confidence) is called 'consistent' by Savage if no two related probability statements violate the rules of the calculus. (Ramsey also uses the term 'consistent' in this sense.)

Savage offers the following illustration. A person considers the 32 possible outcomes of tossing a coin five times to be equally probable. He also considers it more probable that there will be four or five heads in the five tosses than that the first two tosses will both be heads. There are straight-forward psychological statements about the degrees of belief that the person actually has in the propositions concerned. Now reference to the rules of the calculus shows that if the tosses are regarded by this person as independent, and if each of the 32 possibilities has a probability of 1/32, then the probability of four or five heads out of the five tosses is 6/32, while the probability of two heads on the first two tosses is 8/32. The person has caught himself in an inconsistency, but, "The theory does not tell him how to resolve the inconsistency; there are literally an infinite number of possibilities among which he must choose."[7]

In general, the most plausible choice seems to be to hold fast to the position that all 32 outcomes of the five tosses are equally probable, and to adjust the other beliefs accordingly. Savage attempts to explain this by distinguishing between "those probability statements about which we feel sure" and "those about which we feel unsure." "When our opinions, as reflected in real or envisaged action, are inconsistent, we sacrifice the unsure opinions to the sure ones."[8] (But perhaps it would be in better conformity with Savage's treatment of 'learning from experience' to abandon the opinion that the tosses are independent and that all 32 outcomes are equally probable.) He admits that the distinction between sure and unsure opinions cannot be explained by reference to his theory of probability.[9]

3. Savage suggests that it is perfectly plausible to suppose that two perfectly rational people, "faced with the same evidence, may have different degrees of confidence in the truth of the same propositions."[10] People do seem to differ in the confidence they have in the same propositions, even when they are presumably faced with the same evidence. But this can occur even in mathematics: Alice was sure that 1 from 365 was 364; Humpty Dumpty preferred to see it done on paper. The interesting point is that there exists a procedure by which (within rather wide limits) a mathematical disagreement can be resolved to the satisfaction of everybody concerned. Savage does not feel that it is possible to formulate such a procedure for probability

[7] *Ibid.*, p. 68.

[8] *Ibid.*, p. 57.

[9] But isn't it precisely *this* distinction that probability statements are often intended to express?

[10] Savage, *op. cit.*, p. 3.

statements. However, he points out that on his theory, as two people accumulate *new* evidence about a proposition they will come closer and closer to agreement about the degree of confidence which is justified. ". . . in certain contexts, any two opinions, provided that neither is extreme in the technical sense, are almost sure to be brought very close to one another by a sufficiently large body of evidence."[11] An *extreme* opinion is one which assigns a probability of 0 or 1 to a proposition. In this case no evidence is relevant. If your prejudices are deepseated enough, it is unreasonable *not* to disregard the evidence.

It is true that people do not have to agree precisely in their assignments of probability in order to arrive at an agreement concerning some future action. But the fact that they agree even approximately seems to be no more than a fortunate psychological quirk; the theory itself regards *no* distribution of beliefs which is in accord with the rules of the calculus as "unreasonable." This includes the 'technically extreme' distributions as well as the more conventional ones. The fundamentalist is being reasonable when he refuses to admit that the evidence in favor of evolution carries any weight. Most people, I think, would balk at calling the extreme positions reasonable; and in spite of the fact that we may wish to allow for some minor differences of opinion about probabilities, we surely do not wish to call *every* non-extreme distribution reasonable merely because it is "consistent." If someone maintains that a certain long shot is "practically certain" to win a given race, but can give me no evidence supporting this hypothesis, I shall decline to call him "reasonable" however consistent his degrees of belief may be.

The personalistic theory of probability cannot be called upon to settle disputes about probability; in fact, there can be no disputes except about whether or not a given person's assignments of probability are consistent. Savage seems to feel that it is asking too much to expect two people having the same information to agree about the probability of a given proposition. Now it may be that he is right in feeling that it is impossible to lay down a plausible set of rules which will guarantee that they will eventually achieve some measure of agreement, in the same sense in which there is a set of rules which will guarantee that Humpty Dumpty and Alice will eventually agree about the result of subtracting 1 from 365. It may not be possible (although I think it is) to offer any more specific explication of "reasonableness of belief" than that provided by the personalistic theory. But there is no *a priori* reason why this should be so, and in fact people do seem to use the word "reasonable" much less lavishly than Savage would allow them to use it.[12]

11 *Ibid.*, p. 58.
12 Shimony, Kemeny, and Lehman are on the side of the angels in this matter; they consider consistency of degrees of belief only a necessary and not a sufficient condition of rationality.

New problems arise when we attempt to apply the personalistic theory of probability to general statements. Braithwaite has pointed this out in connection with Ramsey's theory.[13] How can we interpret, "The probability that the theory T is true is (at least) 0.99?" According to the general scheme of personalistic probability, this should be interpreted as meaning that I would just as soon risk a possible gain on the truth of the theory as on (say) the truth of the hypothesis that the outcome of a hundred tosses of a coin will have a certain character—e.g., exhibit a relative frequency of heads within such and such limits. But the truth of the theory can never be definitively established, and it therefore seems absurd to say that I would prefer to risk a possible gain on the truth of the theory than on any other possible fact at all. If I choose to stake a possible gain on the occurrence of a hundred heads on the next hundred tosses of a coin, at least I stand *some* chance of collecting. On the other hand, even if I am quite sure that the theory is true, I might prefer to stake a possible gain on the falsehood of the theory—or rather, the event of its being falsified during the next two years—than upon (say) the occurrence of a thousand tails in the next thousand tosses of a fair coin. But already I am being inconsistent—since I am expressing a very low degree of belief in the falsity of the theory, and a very low degree of belief in the truth of the theory, in spite of the act that I am certain that the theory is either true or false.

The most plausible way out seems to be to avoid reference to the "probability" of statements that cannot be definitively confirmed in some finite time. This, of course, applies with as much force to statistical statements about indefinitely large classes as to universal generalizations and theories, and it renders the use of Bayes' theorem for induction impossible. To use Bayes' theorem, we must assume that some general statistical statement (e.g., the statement that the proportion of A's which are B's falls between p_1 and p_2) has a finite probability. But to say that such a statement has a finite probability (for me) is to say that I would prefer to risk a possible gain on the truth of this general statement than on the truth of some practically testable statement such as "The next one hundred tosses of this coin will all land heads."

Savage does not attempt to get along without Bayes' theorem; he uses it to show that, as the evidence accumulates, two people will come to agreement about the probable state of the world, even though their initial assignments of probability differ, and also to show that with a large amount of evidence at hand, a non-extreme person will be almost certain that the state s obtains when s is in fact the state that obtains. Both these uses of Bayes' theorem

[13] Braithwaite, *op. cit.*, p. 357 ff.
[14] Nicod, *Foundations of Geometry and Induction*, New York, 1950.

depend on the explicit assumption that the *a priori* probability of the actual state is represented by some definite number greater than zero. (As Nicod has shown[14] it is not sufficient to demand that the probability in question be "greater than 0"—we must demand that it be greater than some definite positive number ε.) But this is precisely what seems questionable on the personalistic theory. To suppose that there are only a finite number of statistical hypotheses to be considered could provide us with our *a priori* probabilities, but it is difficult to see how these probabilities can be interpreted as personalistic ones.

We might get around the difficulty of assigning non-zero probabilities to theories and general statements by having an angel perform our psychological tests for us. Since the angel would presumably know which state of the world obtained, the person would be able to collect even if he voted for the theory. But this begins to seem a little far fetched.

The personalistic theory breaks down altogether with regard to contexts (1) through (5),* even if we suppose that the angelic hypothesis suffices to save contexts dealing with the probability of general statements and theories. In the first place it is obvious that not even an angel would decide whether or not to pay off on the state of the world corresponding to "a toss of this coin will result in heads." The indefinite article here cannot be translated into "some" or "there is a" or "all." We cannot interpret, "The probability that a toss of this coin will result in heads is $1/2$," as a personalistic probability at all. The holders of the personalistic theory are therefore obliged to reject these contexts as containing an improper use of the word "probability." The problem created by these contexts is usually called the problem of "unknown" probabilities; this is somewhat misleading, for the problem is just as great a one when the "probability" in question is supposed to be known.

These contexts are among the most important for science, and they have received much attention from the holders of personalistic views. De Finetti has provided an indirect interpretation of these contexts which does make use of personalistic probability. This is accomplished by introducing a "probability measure" in the abstract mathematical sense. This abstract probability measure, which is merely a species of bounded measure, may or may not correspond to an actual probability. There are, however, certain sequences of events (such as the tossing of a coin) in which this abstract probability measure may be supposed to exist, and in which it may sometimes be interpreted as a personal probability. These interesting sequences are called *symmetric*, which means that with respect to a certain property P, the personal probability that any b members of the sequence have the property, and any c members lack it, depends solely on the integers b and c.[15]

---

* [At the end of the discussion are listed fourteen contexts containing the word "probability" or a cognate.—Ed.]

[15] Savage, *op. cit.*, p. 52.

Savage gives the following example: "If, for example, a statistician were to say, 'I do not know the p of this coin, but I am sure that it is at most one half,' that would mean in personalistic terms, 'I regard the sequence of tosses of this coin as a symmetric sequence, the measure M of which assigns unit measure to the interval $(0, 1/2)$.' "[16] If the statistician were sure that the p of the coin were very close to $1/2$, he would say that the measure M assigns unit measure to a small interval around $1/2$. The first five contexts from Appendix II must therefore be construed as statements about abstract probability measures and symmetric sequences. The first statement will be rendered: "I regard the sequence of tosses of this well-tested coin as a symmetric sequence, the measure M of which assigns unit measure to a small interval about the value $1/2$." Anyone who accepts this statement will assign a personal probability of $1/2$ to the occurrence of heads on a given future toss of the coin, provided he interprets the probability M as a personal probability. (He is not obligated to do so, and since personal probability must be represented by a real number rather than by an interval, he has to use his imagination in any case.)

Much of the apparent objectivity of the first five contexts, as well as the word "probability" itself, seems to disappear in the translation into acceptable personalistic terminology. On the personalistic theory two people may very well reasonably disagree about statements like these, even though they have exactly the same information to go on. In the first place one of them may regard the sequence as symmetric; the other may not. There are quite a number of people who consider the sequence of results of tossing a coin, HTHHTHTTH, more probable than the sequence HHHHHTTTT; for these people the sequence of coin tosses will not be symmetrical. Savage does not discuss the relation of evidence (if any) to the supposed symmetry of a sequence; it appears to be merely another fortunate psychological coincidence that statisticians generally seem to agree that the sequences that concern them are symmetric. In the second place, the assignment of a measure M to the sequence brings up all the problems mentioned earlier in connection with general statements. We may be led to assign very different measures to the sequence (on a given amount of evidence) depending on the *a priori* probabilities with which we start.

To sum up: The personalistic theory does not provide a direct interpretation for "probability" as it occurs in the first five contexts; the holders of personalistic views do attempt to deal with these contexts, but their interpretations, in addition to being very indirect, do not seem to be at all true to life. Contexts (9) through (12), which refer to general statements, cannot be handled by the personalistic theory without recourse to what I have called the angelic hypothesis. The remaining statements, which refer to the prob-

---

[16] *Ibid.*, p. 53.

ability of some definite event, can be handled by the personalistic theory as it stands. But even here the theory has shortcomings. It seems too liberal to be taken as the sole criterion of reasonableness, and too strict when it demands consistency to an arbitrary number of decimal places. It does not provide a framework within which disagreements can be settled: Two people, given the same evidence, are free on this theory to assign any probability whatsoever to the same proposition, provided only that they adjust their other beliefs to avoid inconsistency. Essentially, there *can* be no disagreements about probability between different people. The distinction between sure and unsure opinions, which may have been offered as a means of alleviating the oddity of this situation, is altogether too vague to be of much help. . . .

Contexts

Typical contexts in which the word "probability" occurs:

(1) The probability of getting a head on a toss of this well-tested coin is 1/2.

(2) The probability that a human birth will be the birth of a male is 0.52.

(3) The probability of an alpha ray striking the area A of the target, in experiment E, is 0.3476.

(4) The probability of an American male of the professional class who is alive at 35, being alive at 36, is p.

(5) The probability of 10 heads occurring in 10 tosses of this well-tested coin is $(1/2)^{10}$.

(6) The probability that 10 of the 50 men of age 35, belonging to the professional class, who take out insurance with us this year, will die before next year, is r.

(7) The probability that the next ten tosses of this coin will all yield heads is s.

(8) The probability that the next toss of this coin will result in heads is 1/2.

(9) Given an n-fold random sample of P's, m of which are Q's, the probability is t that between $m/n - d$ and $m/n + d$ of all P's are Q's.

(10) Relative to the evidence that m P's out of n are Q's, the probability is v that the next P to be examined is also a Q.

(11) Given the collective evidence of biology and zoology, the probability is very high that all mammals have hearts.

(12) Given the evidence of experiments performed on heredity, the probability is w that the genetic theory is true.

(13) It is highly probable that Caesar crossed the Rubicon.

(14) If you are wealthy, it is more probable that if you cheat on your income tax you will be caught than it is if you are not wealthy.

27. INQUIRIES INTO THE FOUNDATIONS OF SCIENCE

Wesley C. Salmon

In 1950, L. Ron Hubbard published his book *Dianetics*,[1] which purported to provide a comprehensive explanation of human behavior, and which recommended a therapy for the treatment of all psychological ills. According to Hubbard's theory, psychological difficulties stem from "engrams," or brain traces, that are the results of experiences the individual has undergone while unconscious due to sleep, anesthesia, a blow to the head, or any other cause. Of particular importance are those that occur before birth. Hubbard gives strikingly vivid accounts of life in the womb, and it is far from idyllic. There is jostling, sloshing, noise, and a variety of rude shocks. Any unpleasant behavior of the father can have serious lasting effects upon the child. On a Saturday night, for example, the father comes home drunk and in an ugly mood; he beats the mother and with each blow he shouts, "Take that, take that!" The child grows up and becomes a kleptomaniac.

It is perhaps worth remarking that the author of this work had no training whatsoever in psychology or psychiatry. The basic ideas were first published in an article in *Astounding Science Fiction*. In spite of its origins, this book

SOURCE. Salmon, Wesley C., *Inquiries Into the Foundations of Science*, Chapter 1 (Vistas in Science), University of New Mexico Press, 1968. Originally published in Robert G. Colodny, editor, *Mind and Cosmos* (University of Pittsburgh Press, 1966), and as a separate book, *The Foundations of Scientific Inference* (University of Pittsburgh Press, 1967). Reprinted with permission. Copyright © 1966, 1967 by University of Pittsburgh Press. Copyright © 1968 by The University of New Mexico Press.

[1] L. Ron Hubbard, *Dianetics: The Modern Science of Mental Healing* (Hermitage House, 1950).

was widely read, the theory was taken seriously by many people, and the therapy it recommended was practiced extensively. A psychologist friend of mine remarked at the time, "I can't condemn this theory before it is carefully tested, but afterwards I will."

In the same year—it seems to have been a vintage year for things of this sort—Immanuel Velikovski published *Worlds in Collision*,[2] a book that attempted to account for a number of the miracles alleged in the *Old Testament*, such as the flood and the sun's standing still. This latter miracle, it was explained, resulted from a sudden stop in the earth's rotation about its axis which was brought about, along with the various other cataclysms, by the very close approach to the earth of a giant comet which later became the planet Venus. One of the chief difficulties encountered by Velikovski's explanation is that, on currently accepted scientific theory, the rotation of the earth simply would not stop as a result of the postulated close approach of another large body. In order to make good his explanation, Velikovski must introduce a whole body of physical theory which is quite incompatible with that which is generally accepted today, and for which he can summon no independent evidence. The probability that Velikovski's explanation is correct is, therefore, no greater than the probability that virtually every currently accepted physical theory is false.

Before the publication of the book, parts of Velikovski's theory were published serially in *Harper's Magazine*. When the astounding new theory did not elicit serious consideration from the scientific community, the editors of *Harper's* expressed outrage at the lack of scientific objectivity exhibited by the scientists.[3] They complained, in effect, of a scientific establishment with its scientific orthodoxy, which manifests such overwhelming prejudice against heterodox opinions that anyone like Velikovski, with radically new scientific ideas, cannot even get a serious hearing. They were not complaining that the scientific community rejected Velikovski's views, but rather that they dismissed them without any serious attempt at testing.

The foregoing are but two examples of scientific prejudgment of a theory; many other fascinating cases can be found in Martin Gardner's *Fads and Fallacies in the Name of Science*.[4] Yet, there is a disquieting aspect of this situation. We have been told on countless occasions that the methods of science depend upon the objective observational and experimental testing of

---

[2] Immanuel Velikovski, *Worlds in Collision* (Doubleday and Co., 1950).

[3] *Harper's Magazine*, 202 (June, 1951), 9–11.

[4] Martin Gardner, *Fads and Fallacies in the Name of Science* (Dover Publications, Inc., 1957). Gardner's excellent discussions of Hubbard and Velikovski provide many additional details.

hypotheses; science does not, to be sure, prove or disprove its results absolutely conclusively, but it does demand objective evidence to confirm or
disconfirm them. This is the scientific ideal. Yet scientists in practice do
certainly make judgments of plausibility or implausibility about newly suggested theories, and in cases like those of Hubbard and Velikovski, they
judge the new hypotheses too implausible to deserve further serious consideration. Can it be that the editors of *Harper's* had a point, and that there
is a large discrepancy between the ideal of scientific objectivity and the
actual practice of prejudgment on the basis of plausibility considerations
alone? One could maintain, of course, that this is merely an example of the
necessary compromise we make between the abstract ideal and the practical
exigencies. Given unlimited time, talent, money, and material, perhaps we
should test every hypothesis that comes along; in fact, we have none of these
commodities in unlimited supply, so we have to make practical decisions
concerning the use of our scientific resources. We have to decide which
hypotheses are promising, and which are not. We have to decide which experiments to run, and what equipment to buy. These are all practical decisions
that have to be made, and in making them, the scientist (or administrator)
is deciding which hypotheses will be subjected to serious testing and which
will be ignored. If *every* hypothesis that comes along had to be tested, I
shudder to think how Air Force scientists would be occupied with anti-gravity
devices and refutations of Einstein.

Granted that we do, and perhaps must, make use of these plausibility considerations, the natural question concerns their status. Three general sorts
of answers suggest themselves at the outset. In the first place, they might be
no more than expressions of the attitudes and prejudices of individual scientists or groups of scientists. The editors of *Harper's* might be right in claiming that they are mere expressions of prejudice against ideas that are too
novel—the tool used by the scientific establishment to enforce its own
orthodoxy. If that suggestion is too conspiratorial in tone, perhaps they arise
simply from the personal attitudes of individual scientists. In the second
place, they might be thought to have a purely practical function. Perhaps
they constitute a necessary but undesirable compromise with the ideal of
scientific objectivity for the sake of getting on with the practical work of
science. Or maybe these plausibility considerations have a heuristic value in
helping scientists discover new and promising lines of research, but their
function is solely in relation to the discovery of hypotheses, not to their
justification. In the third place, it might be held that somehow plausibility
arguments constitute a proper and indispensible part of the very logic of the
justification of scientific hypotheses. This is the view I shall attempt to
elaborate and defend. I shall argue that plausibility arguments are objective

in character, and that they must be taken into account in the evaluation of scientific hypotheses on the basis of evidence.[5]

The issue being raised is a logical one. We are asking what ingredients enter into the evaluation of scientific hypotheses in the light of evidence. In order to answer such questions, it is necessary to look at the logical schema that represents the logical relation between evidence and hypotheses in scientific inference. Many scientific textbooks, especially the introductory ones, attempt to give a brief characterization of the process of confirming and disconfirming hypotheses. The usual account is what is generally known as the *hypothetico-deductive method*. As it is frequently described, the method consists in deducing consequences from the hypothesis in question, and checking by observation to determine whether these consequences actually occur. If they do, that counts as confirming evidence for the hypothesis; if they do not, the hypothesis is disconfirmed.

One immediate difficulty with the foregoing characterization of the hypothetico-deductive method is that from a general hypothesis it is impossible to deduce any observational consequences. Consider, for example, Kepler's first two laws of planetary motion: the first states that the orbits of the planets are elliptical, and the second describes the way the speed of the planet varies as it moves through the ellipse. With this general knowledge of the motion of Mars, for instance, it is impossible to deduce its location at midnight, and so to check by observation to see whether it fulfills the predictiton or not. But with the addition of some further observational knowledge, it is possible to make such deductions—for instance, if we know its position and velocity at midnight last night. This additional observational evidence is often referred to as the "initial conditions;" from the hypothesis together with statements about initial conditions it is possible to deduce a concrete prediction that can be checked by observation. With this addition, the hypothetico-deductive method can be represented by the following simple schema:

$$
\begin{array}{ll}
\text{H-D schema:} & \text{H} \quad (\text{Hypothesis}) \\
& \text{I} \quad (\text{initial conditions}) \\
\hline
& \text{O} \quad (\text{observational prediction})
\end{array}
$$

Although it is always possible for errors of observation or measurement to occur, and consequently for us to be mistaken about the initial conditions, I shall assume for purposes of the present discussion that we have correctly ascertained the initial conditions, so that the hypothesis is the only premise whose truth is in question. This is one useful simplifying assumption.

---

[5] In my book, *The Foundations of Scientific Inference* (University of Pittsburgh Press, 1967), I have discussed these issues in greater detail and have argued this case at greater length.

Another very important simplifying assumption is being made. In many cases the observational prediction does not follow from the hypothesis and initial conditions alone, but so-called "auxiliary hypotheses" are also required. For instance, if an astronomical observation is involved, optical theories concerning the behavior of telescopes may be implicitly invoked. In principle, a false prediction can be the occasion to call these auxiliary hypotheses into question, so that the most that can be concluded is that *either* an auxiliary hypothesis *or* the hypothesis up for testing is false, but we cannot say which. For purposes of this discussion, however, I shall assume that the truth of the auxiliary hypotheses is not in question, so that the hypothesis we are trying to test is still the only premise of the argument whose truth is open to question. Such simplifying assumptions are admittedly unrealistic, but things are difficult enough with them, and relinquishing them does not help with the problems we are discussing.

Under the foregoing simplifying assumptions a false prediction provides a decisive result: if the prediction is false the hypothesis is falsified, for a valid deduction with a false conclusion *must* have at least one false premise, and the hypothesis being tested is the only premise about which we are admitting any question. However, if the prediction turns out to be true, we certainly cannot conclude that the hypothesis is true, for to infer the truth of the premises from the truth of the conclusion is an elementary logical fallacy. And this fallacy is not mitigated in the least by rejecting the simplifying assumptions and admitting that other premises might be false. The fallacy, called *affirming the consequent*, is illustrated by the following example: If the patient has chickenpox, he will run a fever; the patient is running a fever; therefore, he has chickenpox. The difficulty is very fundamental and very general. Even though a hypothesis gives rise to a true prediction, there are always other different hypotheses that would provide the same prediction. This is the *problem of the alternative hypotheses*. It is especially apparent in any case in which one wishes to explain data that can be represented by points on a graph in terms of a mathematical function that can be represented by a curve. There are always many different curves that fit the data equally well; in fact, for any finite number of data, there are infinitely many such curves. Additional observations will serve to disqualify some of these (in fact, infinitely many), but infinitely many alternatives will still remain.

Since we obviously cannot claim that the observation of a true consequence establishes the truth of our hypothesis, the usual claim is that such observations tend to support or confirm the hypothesis, or to lend it probability. Thus, it is often said, the inference from the hypothesis and initial conditions to the prediction is deductive, but the inference in the opposite direction, from the truth of the prediction to the hypothesis is inductive. Inductive inferences do not pretend to establish their results with certainty; instead, they confirm them or make them probable. The whole trouble with looking at the matter this way is that it appears to constitute an automatic transformation of deductive fallacies into correct inductive arguments. When we discover, to our dismay, that our favorite deductive argument is invalid, we simply rescue it by saying that we never intended it to be deductive in the first place, but that it is a valid induction. With reference to this situation, the famous American logician Morris R. Cohen is said to have quipped, "A logic book is divided into two parts; in the first (on deduction) the fallacies are explained, and in the second (on induction) they are committed." Surely inductive logic, if it plays a central role in scientific method, must have better credentials than this.

When questions about deductive validity arise, they can usually be resolved in a formal manner by reference to an appropriate logical system. It has not always been so. Modern mathematical logic dates from the early nineteenth century, and it has undergone extraordinary development, largely in response to problems that arose in the foundations of mathematics. One such problem concerned the foundations of geometry, and it assumed critical importance with the discovery of non-Euclidean geometries. Another problem concerned the status of the infinitesimal in the calculus, a concept that was the center of utter confusion for two centuries after the discovery of the "infinitesimal" calculus. Thanks to extensive and fruitful investigations of the foundations of mathematics, we now have far clearer and more profound understanding of many fundamental mathematical concepts, as well as an extremely well-developed and intrinsically interesting discipline of formal deductive logic. The early investigators in this field could never have conceived in their wildest imaginings the kinds of results that have emerged.[6]

It is an unfortunate fact that far less attention has been paid to the foundational questions that arise in connection with the empirical sciences and their logic. When questions of inductive validity arise, there is no well-established formal discipline to which they can be referred for definitive solution. A number of systems of inductive logic have been proposed, some in greater and some in lesser detail, but none is more than rudimentary, and none is widely accepted as basically correct. Questions of inductive correctness are more often referred to scientific or philosophical intuitions, and these are notoriously unreliable guides.

We do have one resource which, although not overlooked entirely, is not exploited as fully as it could be. I refer to the mathematical calculus of probability. The probability calculus will not, by itself, solve all of our foundational problems concerning scientific inference, but it will provide us with a logical schema for scientific inference which is far more adequate than the

---

[6] For a very readable account of recent developments, and a comparison with the earlier situation in the foundations of geometry see Paul J. Cohen and Reuben Hersh, "Non-Cantorian Set Theory," *Scientific American*, December 1967, Vol. 217, no. 6.

H-D schema. And insofar as the probability calculus fails to provide the answers to foundational questions, it will at least help us to pose those problems in intelligible and, hopefully, more manageable form.

In order to show how the probability calculus can illuminate the kinds of questions I have been raising, I should like to introduce a very simple illustrative game. This game is played with two decks of cards composed as follows: deck 1 contains eight red cards and four black cards; deck 2 contains four red cards and eight black cards. A player begins by tossing a standard die; if the side one appears he draws a card from the first deck, and if any other side comes up he draws a card from the second deck. The draw of a red card constitutes a win. There is a simple formula for calculating the probability of a win resulting on a play of this game. Letting "P(A,B)" stand for the probability *from* A *to* B (i.e., the probability of B, given A), and letting "A" stand for tosses of the die, "B" for draws from deck 1 (which occur when and only when an ace is tossed on the die), and "C" for draws of red cards, the following formula, which is a special case of the "theorem on total probability" yields the desired computation:

$$P(A,C) = P(A,B)P(A \& B,C) + P(A,\overline{B})P(A \& \overline{B},C) \tag{1}$$

The ampersand means "and" and the bar above a symbol negates it. Accordingly, the probabilities appearing in the formula are:

P(A,C)—probability of drawing a red card on a play of the game.
P(A,B)—probability of drawing from deck 1 on a play of the game $(= \frac{1}{6})$.
P(A,$\overline{B}$)—probability of drawing from deck 2 on a play of the game $(= \frac{5}{6})$.
P(A&B,C)—probability of drawing a red card if you play and draw from deck 1 $(= \frac{2}{3})$.
P(A&$\overline{B}$,C)—probability of drawing a red card if you play and draw from deck 2 $(= \frac{1}{3})$.

The theorem on total probability yields the result

$$P(A,C) = \frac{1}{6} \times \frac{2}{3} + \frac{5}{6} \times \frac{1}{3} = 7/18$$

Suppose, now, that this game is being played, and you enter the room just in time to see that the player has drawn a red card, but you did not see from which deck it was drawn. Perhaps someone even offers you a wager on whether it came from deck 1 or deck 2. Again, the probability calculus provides a simple formula to compute the desired probability. This time it is a special form of "Bayes' theorem" and it can be written in either of two ways:

$$P(A \& C,B) = \frac{P(A,B)P(A \& B,C)}{P(A,C)} \tag{2}$$

$$= \frac{P(A,B)P(A \& B,C)}{P(A,B)P(A \& B,C) + P(A,\overline{B})P(A \& \overline{B},C)} \tag{3}$$

The theorem on total probability (1) assures us that the denominators of the two fractions are equal; we must, of course, impose the restriction that $P(A,C) \neq 0$ in order to avoid an indeterminate fraction. The expression on the left evidently represents the probability that a draw which produced a red card was made from deck 1. Substituting known values in equation (2) yields

$$P(A \& C, B) = [\frac{1}{6} \times \frac{2}{3}]/[7/18] = 2/7$$

There is nothing controversial about either of the foregoing theorems or their applications to simple games of chance of the type just described.

In order to get at our logical questions about the nature of scientific inference, let me redescribe the game and what we learned about it, and in so doing I shall admittedly be stretching some meanings. It is nevertheless illuminating. We can think of the drawing of a red card as an effect that can be produced in either of two ways, by tossing an ace and drawing from the first deck or by tossing a number other than one and drawing from the second deck. When we asked for the probability that a red card had been drawn from deck 1, we were asking for the probability that the first of the two possible causes rather than the second was operative in bringing about this effect. In fact, there are two causal hypotheses, and we were calculating the probability that was to be assigned to one of them, namely, the hypothesis that the draw came from the first deck. Notice that the probability that the draw came from the first deck is considerably less than one-half, making it much more likely that the draw came from the second deck, even though the probability that you will get a red card if you draw from the first deck is much greater than the probability that you will get a red card if you draw from the second deck. The reason, obviously, is that many more draws are made from the second deck, so even though many more black than red cards are drawn from the second deck, still the preponderance of red cards also comes from the second deck. This point has fundamental philosophical importance.

Continuing with the bizarre use of terms, let us look at the probabilities used to carry out the computation via Bayes' theorem. $P(A,B)$ and $P(A,B)$ are known as *prior probabilities;* they are the probabilities, respectively, that the particular cause is operative or not, regardless of the result of the draw. These probabilities are obviously linked in a simple manner,

$$P(A,B) = 1 - P(A,B),$$

so that knowledge of one of them suffices. $P(A\&B,C)$ and $P(A\&B,C)$ are usually known as *likelihoods.* $P(A\&B,C)$ is the likelihood of the causal hypothesis that the draw came from deck 1 given that the draw was red, while $P(A\&B,C)$ is the likelihood that that hypothesis is false (i.e., the likelihood of an alternative) given the same result. Note, however, that *the likelihood of a hypothesis is not a probability of that hypothesis;* it is, instead, the probability of a result given that the hypothesis holds. Note, also, that the two likelihoods need not add up to one; they are logically independent of one another and both need to be known—knowledge of one only does not suffice. These are the probabilities that appear on the right hand side of the second form of Bayes' theorem (3). In the first form of Bayes' theorem (2) we do not need the second likelihood, $P(A\&B,C)$, but we require $P(A,C)$ instead. This probability has no common name, but it is the probability that the effect in question occurs regardless of which cause is operative. But whichever form of the theorem is used, we need three logically distinct probabilities in order to carry out the calculation. $P(A\&C,B)$, the probability we endeavor to establish, is known as the *posterior probability* of the hypothesis. When we entertain the two causal hypotheses about the draw of the card, we may take the fact that the draw produced a red card as observational evidence relevant to the causal hypotheses. (A rapid calculation will show that the probability that the draw came from deck 1 if it was a black card $= 1/11$.) Thus, we may think of our posterior probability, $P(A\&C,B)$, as the probability of a hypothesis in the light of observational evidence. This is precisely the kind of question which arose in connection with the hypothetico-deductive method, and in connection with our attempt to understand how evidence confirms or disconfirms scientific hypotheses. Bayes' theorem therefore constitutes a logical schema, found in the mathematical calculus of probability, that shows some promise of incorporating the main logical features of the kind of inference the hypothetico-deductive schema is intended to describe.

The striking difference between Bayes' theorem and the H-D schema is the relative complexity of the former compared with the latter. In fact, in some special cases the H-D schema provides just one of the probabilities required in Bayes' theorem, but never does it yield either of the other two required. Thus, the H-D schema is inadequate as an account of scientific inference because it is a gross oversimplification which omits reference to essential logical features of the inference. Bayes' theorem fills these gaps. The H-D schema describes a situation in which an observable result is deducible from a hypothesis (in conjunction with initial conditions, and possibly auxiliary hypotheses, all of which we are assuming to be true); thus, if the hypothesis is correct, the result *must* occur and cannot fail to occur. In this special case, $P(A\&B,C) = 1$, but without two other probabilities, say $P(A,B)$ and $P(A\&B,C)$, no conclusion at all can be drawn regarding the posterior probability. Inspection of Bayes' theorem makes it evident that $P(A\&B,C) = 1$ is completely compatible with $P(A\&C,B) = 0$. At best, the H-D schema yields the likelihood of the hypothesis for that given evidence, but we need a prior probability and the likelihood of an alternative hypothesis on the same evidence.

That these other probabilities are indispensible, and the manner in which they function in scientific reasoning, can be indicated by examples. Consider *Dianetics* once more. As remarked above, this book contained not only a theory to explain behavior, but also it contained recommendations for a therapy to be practiced for the treatment of psychological disturbances. The therapeutic procedure. bears strong resemblances to psychoanalysis; it consists of the elimination of those "engrams" that are causing trouble by bringing to consciousness, through a process of free association, the unconscious experiences that produced the engrams in the first place. The theory, presumably, enables us to deduce that practice of the recommended therapy will produce cures of psychological illness. At the time the theory was in vogue, this therapy was practiced extensively, and there is every reason to believe that "cures" did occur. There were unquestionably cases in which people with various neurotic symptoms were treated, and they experienced a remission of their symptoms. Such instances would seem to count, according to the hypothetico-deductive method, as confirming instances. That they cannot actually be so regarded is due to the fact that there is a far better explanation of these "cures." We know that there is a phenomenon of "faith-healing" that consists in the efficacy of any treatment the patient sincerely believes to be effective. Many neurotic symptoms are emenable to such treatment, so anyone with such symptoms who believed in the soundness of the dianetic approach could be "cured" regardless of the truth or falsity of the theory upon which it is based. The reason, in terms of Bayes' theorem, is that the second likelihood—the probability $P(A\&B,C)$ that the same phenomenon would occur even if the hypothesis were false—is very high. Since this term occurs in the denominator, the value of the whole fraction tends to be small when the term is large.

A somewhat similar problem arises in connection with psychotherapy based upon more serious theoretical foundations. The effectiveness of any therapeutic procedure has to be compared with the so-called "spontaneous remission rate." Any therapy will produce a certain number of cases in which there is a remission of symptoms, but in a group of people with similar problems, but who undergo no therapy of any kind, there will also be a certain percentage who experience remission of symptoms. For a therapy to be judged effective, it has to improve upon the spontaneous remission rate; it is not sufficient that there be some remissions among those who undergo the treatment. In terms of Bayes' theorem, this means that we must look at both likelihoods, $P(A\&B,C)$ and $P(A\&B,C)$, not just the one we have been given in the standard H-D schema. This is just what experimental controls are all about. For instance, vitamin C has been highly touted as a cold remedy, and many cases have been cited of people recovering quickly from colds after taking massive doses. But in a *controlled* experiment in which two groups of people of comparable age, sex, state of general heath, and severity of colds are compared, where one group is given vitamin C and the other is not, no difference in duration or severity of colds is detected.[7] This gives us a way of comparing the two likelihoods.

Let me mention, finally, an example of a strikingly successful confirmation, showing how the comparative likelihoods effect this sort of situation. At the beginning of the nineteenth century, two different theories of light were vying for supremacy: the wave theory and the corpuscular theory. Each had its strong advocates, and the evidence up to that point was not decisive. One of the supporters of the corpuscular theory was the mathematician Poisson, who deduced from the mathematical formulation of the wave theory that, if that theory were true, there should be a bright spot in the center of the shadow of a disk. Poisson declared that this absurd result showed that the wave theory is untenable, but when the experiment was actually performed the bright spot was there. Such a result was unthinkable on the corpuscular theory, so this turned into a triumph for the wave theory, because the probability on any other theory then available was negligible.[8] It was not until about a century later that the need for a combined wave-particle theory was realized. Arithmetically, the force of this dramatic confirmation is easily seen by noting that if $P(A\&B,C) = 0$ in (3), the posterior probability $P(A\&C,B)$ automatically becomes 1.

In addition to the two likelihoods, Bayes' theorem requires us to have a prior probability $P(A,B)$ or $P(\overline{A},B)$ in order to ascertain the posterior probability. These prior probabilities are probabilities of hypotheses without regard to the observational evidence provided by the particular test we are considering. In the card-drawing game described above, the prior probability was the probability of a draw from one particular deck regardless of whether the draw produced a red or black card. In the more serious cases of the attempt to evaluate scientific hypotheses, the probability of a hypothesis without regard to the test is precisely the sort of plausibility considered that was discussed at the outset. How plausible is a given hypothesis; what is its chance of being a successful one? This is the type of consideration that is demanded by Bayes' theorem in the form of a prior probability. The traditional stumbling-block to the use of Bayes' theorem as an account of the logic of scientific inference is the great difficulty of giving a description of what sort of things these prior probabilities could be.

It seems possible, nevertheless, to give many examples of plausibility arguments, and even to classify them into very general types. Such arguments may then be regarded as criteria which are used to evaluate prior probabilities—

---

[7] The Editors of Consumer Reports, *The Medicine Show* (Simon and Schuster, 1961), chapter 2.

[8] See Max Born and Emil Wolf, *Principles of Optics* (Pergamon Press, 1964), p. 375.

criteria that indicate whether a hypothesis is plausible or implausible, whether its prior probability is to be rated high or low. I shall mention three general types of criteria, and give some instances of each.

1. Let us call criteria of the first general type *formal criteria*, for they involve formal logical relations between the hypothesis under consideration and other accepted parts of science. This kind of consideration was illustrated at the outset by Velikovski's theory, which contradicts virtually all of modern physics. Because of this formal relationship we can say that Velikovski's theory must have a very low prior probability, since it is incompatible with so much we accept as correct. Another example of the same type can be found in those versions of the theory of telepathy that postulate the *instantaneous* transference of thought from one person to another, regardless of the distance that separates them. For, the special theory of relativity stipulates that information cannot be transmitted at a speed greater than the speed of light, and so it would preclude instantaneous thought transmission. It would be even worse for precognition, the alleged process of direct perception of future occurrences, for this would involve messages being transmitted backward in time! Such a parapsychological hypotheses must be given extremely low prior probabliities because of their logical incompatibility with well-established portions of physical science. A hypothesis could, of course, achieve a high prior probability on formal grounds by being the logical consequence of a well-established theory. Kepler's laws, for example, are extremely probable (as approximations) because of their relation to Newtonian gravitational theory.

2. I shall call criteria of the second type *pragmatic criteria*. Such criteria have to do with the evaluation of hypotheses in terms of the circumstances of their origin—for example, the qualifications of the author. This sort of consideration has already been amply illustrated by the example of *Dianetics*. Whenever a hypothesis is dismissed as being a "crank" hypothesis, pragmatic criteria are being brought to bear. In his fascinating *Fads and Fallacies in the Name of Science*, Martin Gardner offers some general characteristics by which cranks can be identified.[9]

One might be tempted to object to the use of pragmatic criteria on the ground, as we have all been taught, that it is a serious fallacy to confuse the *origin* of a theory with its *justification*. Having been told the old story about how Newton was led to think of universal gravitation by seeing an apple fall, we are reminded that that incident has nothing to do with the truth or justification of Newton's gravitational theory. That issue must be decided on the evidence.[10] Quite so. But there are factors in the origin of a hypothesis, such

---

[9] See p. 12–14, Reference 4.

[10] An elementary account of the distinction between discovery and justification is given in my *Logic* (Prentice-Hall, Inc., 1963), § 3.

as the qualifications of the author, which have an *objective* probability relationship to the hypothesis and its truth. Crank hypotheses seldom, if ever, turn out to be sound; they are based upon various misunderstandings, prejudices, or sheer ignorance. It is *not* fallacious to conclude that they have low prior probabilities.

3.   Criteria of the third type are by far the most interesting and important; let us call them *material criteria*. They make reference, in one way or another, to what the hypothesis actually says, rather than to its formal relation to other theories, or to the circumstances surrounding its origins. These criteria do, however, depend upon comparisons of various theories or hypotheses; they make reference to analogies or similarities among different ones. Again, a few examples may be helpful.

Perhaps the most frequently cited criterion by which to judge the plausibility of hypotheses is the property of simplicity. Curve drawing illustrates this point very aptly. Given data which can be represented graphically, we generally take the smoothest curve—the one with the simplest mathematical expression—which comes sufficiently near the data points as representing the best explanatory hypothesis for those data. This factor was uppermost with Kepler, who kept searching for the simplest orbits to account for planetary motion, and finally settled upon the ellipse as filling the bill. Yet, we do not *always* insist upon the simplest explanation. We do not take seriously the "hypothesis" that television is solely responsible for the breakdown of contemporary morals, assuming that there is such a breakdown, for it is an obvious oversimplification. It may be that simplicity is more to be prized in the physical than in the social sciences, or in the advanced than in the younger sciences. But it does seem that we need to exercise reasonable judgment as to just what degree of simplicity is called for in any given situation.

Another consideration that may be used in plausibility arguments concerns causal mechanisms. There was a time when all scientific explanation was teleological in character; even the motion of inanimate objects was explained in terms of the endeavor to achieve their natural places. After the physics of Galileo and Newton had removed all reference to purpose from these realms, the remnants of teleological language remained: "Nature abhors a vacuum" and "Water seeks its own level." But though there have been a few attempts to read purpose into such laws as least action ("The Absolute is lazy"), it is for the most part fully conceded that physical explanation is nonpurposive.

The great success of Newtonian physics provided a strong plausibility argument for Darwin's account of the development of the biological species. The major difference between Darwin's evolutionary theory and its alternative contenders is the thoroughgoing rejection of teleological explanation by Darwin. Although teleological sounding language may sometimes creep in when we talk about natural selection, the concept is entirely nonpurposive. We ask,

"Why is the polar bear white?" We answer, "Because that color provides a natural camouflage." It sometimes sounds a bit as if we are saying that the bear thinks the situation over and decides before he is born that white would be the best color, and so he chooses that color. But, of course, we mean no such thing. We are aware that, literally, no choice or planning is involved. There are chance mutations, some favorable to escaping from enemies and finding food. Those animals that have the favorable characteristics tend to survive and reproduce their kind, while those with unfavorable characteristics tend to die out without reproducing. The cause and effect relations in the evolutionary account are just as mechanical and without purpose as are those in Newtonian physics. This non-teleological theory is in sharp contrast to the theory of special creation according to which God created the various species because it somehow fit his plan.

The non-teleological character of Newton's theory surely must lend plausibility to a non-teleological biological theory such as Darwin's. If physics, which was far better developed and more advanced than any other science, got that way by abandoning teleological explanations for efficient causation, then it seems plausible for those sciences that are far less developed to try the same approach. When this approach paid off handsomely in the success of evolutionary theory, how much more plausible it becomes for other branches of science to follow the same line. Thus, for theories in psychology and sociology, for example, higher plausibility and higher prior probability would now attach to those hypotheses that are free from teleological components than to those that retain teleological explanation. When a biological hypothesis comes along that regresses to the pre-Darwinian teleology, such as Lecomte du Noüy's *Human Destiny*, it must be assigned a low prior probability.[11]

Let me give one final example of material criteria. Our investigations of the nature of physical space, extending over many centuries, have led to some rather sophisticated conceptions. To early thinkers, nothing could have been more implausible than to suppose that space is homogeneous and isotropic. Everyday experience seems clearly to demonstrate that there is a preferred direction—down. This view was expressed poetically by Lucretius in *The Nature of the Universe*, in which he describes the primordial state of affairs in which all the atoms are falling downward in space at a uniform speed.[12] On this view, not only was the downward direction preferred, but also, it was possible to distinguish absolute motion from absolute rest. By Newton's time it seemed clear that space had no preferred direction; rather, it was isotropic

---

[11] Pierre Lecomte du Noüy, *Human Destiny* (Longmans, Green and Co., 1947).

[12] Lucretius, *The Nature of the Universe*, trans. Ronald Latham (Penguin Books, 1951). Originally titled *De Rerum Natura*, and usually translated *On the Nature of Things*. The Latham translation is modern, and is far more intelligible than the older ones.

—possessed of the same structure in every direction. This consideration lent considerable plausibility to Newton's inverse square law, for if space is Euclidean and it has no preferred directions, then we should expect any force, such as gravitation, to spread out uniformly in all directions. In Euclidean geometry, the surface of a sphere varies with the square of the radius, so if the gravitational force spreads out uniformly in the surrounding space, it should diminish with the square of the distance.

Newton's theory, though it regards space as isotropic, still makes provision for absolute motion and rest. Einstein, reflecting on the homogeneity of space, enunciated a principle of relativity which precludes distinguishing physically between rest and uniform motion. In the beginning, if we believe Einstein's own autobiographical account, this principle recommended itself entirely on the grounds of its very great plausibility.[13] The matter does not rest there, of course, for it had to be incorporated into a physical theory that could be subjected to experimental test. His special theory of relativity has been tested and confirmed in a wide variety of ways, and it is now a well-established part of physics, but prior to the tests and its success in meeting them, it could be certified as highly plausible on the basis of very general characteristics of space.

Up to this point I have been attempting to establish two facts about prior probabilities: (1) Bayes' theorem shows that they are needed, and (2) scientific practice shows that they are used. But their status has been left very vague indeed. There is a fundamental reason. In spite of the fact that the probability calculus was established early in the seventeenth century, hardly any serious attention was given to the analysis of the meaning of the concept of probability until the latter part of the nineteenth century. There is nothing especially unusual about this situation. Questions about the meanings of fundamental concepts are foundational questions, and foundational investigations usually follow far behind the development of a discipline. Even today there is no real consensus on this question; there are, instead, three distinct interpretations of the probability concept, each with its strong adherents. A fortiori, there is no widely accepted answer to the question of the nature of the prior probabilities, for they seem to be especially problematic in character. Among the three leading probability theories, the *logical theory* regards probability as an *a priori measure* that can be assigned to propositions or states of affairs, the *personalistic theory* regards probability as a *subjective measure* of degrees of belief, and the *frequency* theory regards probability as a *physical characteristic* of types of events.

The logical theory is the direct descendent of the famous classical theory

---

[13] Albert Einstein, "Autobiographical Notes" in *Albert Einstein: Philosopher-Scientist,* ed., Paul Arthur Schilpp (The Library of Living Philosophers, 1949).

of Laplace. According to the classical theory, probability is the ratio of favorable to equally possible cases. The equi-possibility of cases, which is nothing other than the equal probability of these cases, is determined a priori on the basis of a *principle of indifference,* namely, two cases are equally likely if there is no reason to prefer one to the other. This principle gets into deep logical difficulty. Consider, for example, a car that makes a trip around a one mile track in a time somewhere between one and two minutes, but we know no more about it. It seems reasonable to say that the time could have been in the interval from one to one- and one-half minutes, or it could have been in the interval of one-and-one-half to two minutes; we don't know which. Since these intervals are equal, we have no reason to prefer one to the other, and we assign a probability of one-half to each of them. Our information about this car can be put in other terms. We know that the car made its trip at an *average* speed somewhere in the range of 60 to 30 miles per hour. Again, it seems reasonable to say that the speed could have been in the range 60-45 miles per hour, or it could have been in the range 45-30 miles per hour; we don't know which. Since the two intervals are equal, we have no reason to prefer one to the other, and we assign a probability of one-half to each. But we have just contradicted our former result, for a time of one-and-one-half minutes corresponds with an average speed of forty, not forty-five, miles per hour.

This contradiction, known as the Bertrand paradox, brings out the fundamental difficulty with any method of assigning probabilities a priori. Such a priori decisions have an unavoidable arbitrary component to them, and in this case, the arbitrary component gives rise to two equally reasonable, but incompatible, ways of assigning the probabilities. Although the logical interpretation, in its current form, escapes this particular form of paradox, it is still subject to philosophical criticism because of the same general kind of aprioristic arbitrariness.

The personalistic interpretation is the twentieth century successor of an older and more naive subjective concept. According to the crude subjective view, a probability is no more nor less than a subjective degree of belief; it is a measure of our ignorance. If I assign the probability value one-half to an outcome of heads on a toss of the coin, this means that I expect heads just as often as I expect tails, and my uncertainty is equally divided between the two outcomes. If I expect twice as strongly as not that an American will be the first human to set foot on the moon, then that event has a probability of two-thirds.

The major difficulty with the old subjective interpretation arises because subjective states do not always come in sizes that will fit the mathematical calculus of probability. It is quite possible, for example, to find a person who believes to the degree one-sixth that a six will turn up any toss of a given die, and who also believes that the tosses are independent of one another (the degree to which he believes in an outcome of six on a given toss is unaffected by the outcome of the previous toss). This same individual may also believe to the degree one-half, that he will get at least one six in three tosses of that die. There is, of course, something wrong here. If the probability of six on a given toss is one-sixth, and if the tosses are independent, this probability is considerably less than one-half (it is approximately 0.42). For four tosses, the probability of at least one six is well over one-half. This is a trivial kind of error that has been recognized as such for hundreds of years, but it is related to a significant error that led to the discovery of the mathematical calculus of probabliity. In the seventeenth century, the view was held that in 24 tosses of a pair of dice, there should be at least a fifty-fifty chance of tossing at least one double six. In fact, the probability is just under one-half in 24 tosses; in 25 it is just over one-half. The point of these examples is very simple. If probabilities are just subjective degrees of belief, the mathematical calculus of probability is mistaken, because it specifies certain relations among probabilities that do not obtain among degrees of belief.

Modern personalists do not interpret probabilities merely as subjective degrees of belief, but rather, as *coherent* degrees of belief. To say that degrees of belief are coherent means that they are related in such manner as to satisfy the conditions imposed by the mathematical calculus of probability. The personalists have seen that degrees of belief that violate the mathematical calculus involve some sort of error or blunder that is analogous to a logical inconsistency. Hence, when a combination of degrees of belief is incoherent, some adjustment or revision is called for in order to bring these degrees into conformity with the mathematical calculus. The chief objection to the personalist view is that it is not objective; we shall have to see whether and to what extent the lack of objectivity is actually noxious.

The frequency interpretation goes back to Aristotle who characterized the probable as that which happens often. More exactly, it regards a probability as a relative frequency of occurrence in a large sequence of events. For instance, a probability of one-half for heads on tosses of a coin would mean that in the long run the ratio of the number of heads to the number of tosses approaches and remains close to one-half. To say that the probability of getting a head on a particular toss is one-half means that this toss is a member of an appropriately selected large class of tosses within which the overall relative frequency of heads is one-half. It seems evident that there are many contexts in which we deal with large aggregates of phenomena, and in these contexts the frequency concept of probability seems well suited to the use of statistical techniques—e.g., in quantum mechanics, kinetic theory, sociology, and the games of chance, to mention just a few. But it is much more dubious that the frequency interpretation is at all applicable to such matters as the probability of a scientific hypothesis in the light of empirical evidence. In this case where are we to find the large classes and long sequences to which to refer our probabilities of hypotheses? This difficulty has seemed insuperable to most authors who have dealt with the problem. The general conclusion has been that the frequency interpretation is fine in certain contexts, but we need a radically different probability concept if we are to deal with the probability of hypotheses.

Returning to our main topic of concern, we easily see that each of the foregoing three probability theories provides an answer to the question of the nature of plausibility considerations and prior probabilities. According to the logical interpretation, hypotheses are plausible or not on the basis of certain a priori considerations; on this view, reason dictates which hypotheses are to be taken seriously and which not. According to the personalistic interpretation, prior probabilities represent the prior opinion or attitude of the investigator toward the hypothesis before he sets about testing it. Different investigators may, of course, have different views of the same hypothesis, so prior probabilities may vary from individual to individual. According to the frequency interpretation, prior probabilities arise from experience with scientific hypotheses, and they reflect this experience in an objective way. To say that a hypothesis is plausible, or has a high prior probability, means that it is of a type that has proved successful in the past. We have found by experience that hypotheses of this general type have often worked well in science.

From the outset, the personalistic interpretation enjoys a major advantage over the other two. It is very difficult to see how we are to find non-arbitrary a priori principles to use as a basis for establishing prior probabilities of the a priori type for the logical interpretation, and it is difficult to see how we are reasonably to define classes of hypotheses and count frequencies of success for the frequency interpretation. But personal probabilities are available quite unproblematically. Each individual has his degree of belief in the hypothesis, and that's all there is to it. Coherence demands that degrees of belief conform to the mathematical calculus, and Bayes' theorem is one of the important relations to be found in the calculus. Bayes' theorem tells us how, if we are to avoid incoherence, we must modify our degrees of belief in the light of new evidence. The personalists, who constitute an extremely influential school of contemporary statisticians, are indeed so closely wedded to Bayes' theorem that they have even taken its name and are generally known as "bayesians."

The chief objection to the personalist approach is that it injects a purely subjective element into the testing and evaluation of scientific hypotheses; we feel that science should have a more objective foundation. The bayesians have a very persuasive answer. Even though two people may begin with radically different attitudes toward a hypothesis, accumulating evidence will force a convergence of opinion. This is a basic mathematical fact about Bayes' theorem; it is easily seen by an example. Suppose a coin which we cannot examine is being flipped; but we are told the results of the tosses. We know that it is either a fair coin or a two-headed coin, we don't know which, and we have very different prior opinions on the matter. Suppose your prior probability for a two-headed coin is 1/100 while mine is one-half. Then as we learn that various numbers of heads have been tossed (without any tails, of course), our opinions come closer and closer together as follows:

Number of tosses resulting in head	Prior probability that coin has two heads	
	1/100	1/2
	Posterior probability on given evidence	
1	2/101	2/3
2	4/103	4/5
10	$1024/1123 \simeq .91$	$1024/1025 \simeq .99$

After only ten tosses, we both find it overwhelmingly probable that the coin that produced this sequence of results is a two-headed one. This phenomenon is sometimes called "swamping of the priors," for their influence on the ·posterior probabilities becomes smaller and smaller as evidence accumulates. The only qualification is that we must begin with somewhat open minds. If we begin with the certainty that the coin is two-headed or with the certainty that it is not, i.e., with prior probability of zero or one, evidence will not change that opinion. But if we begin with prior probabilities differing ever so little from those extremes convergence will sooner or later occur. As L. J. Savage remarked, it is not necessary to have an open mind, it is sufficient to have one that is slightly ajar.

The same consideration about the swamping of prior probabilities also enables the frequentist to overcome the chief objection to his approach. If it were necessary to have clearly defined classes of hypotheses, within which exact values of frequencies of success had to be ascertained, the situation would be pretty hopeless, but because of the swamping phenomenon, it is sufficient to have only the roughest approximation. All that is really needed is a reasonable guess as to whether the value is significantly different from zero. In the artificial coin tossing example, where there are only two hypotheses, it is possible to be perfectly open-minded and give each alternative a non-negligible prior probability, but in the serious cases of evaluation of scientific hypotheses, there are infinitely many alternative hypotheses; all in conflict with one another, and they cannot all have non-negligible prior probabilities. This is the problem of the alternative hypotheses again. For this reason, it is impossible to be completely open-minded, so we must find some basis for assigning negligible prior probabilities to some possible hypotheses. This is tantamount to judging some hypotheses to be too implausible to deserve further testing and consideration. It is my conviction that this is done on the basis of experience; it is not done by means of purely a priori considerations, nor is it a purely subjective affair. As I tried to suggest by means of the examples of plausibility arguments, scientific experience with the testing, acceptance, and rejection of hypotheses provides an objective basis for deciding which hypotheses deserve serious testing and which do not. I am not suggesting that we proceed on the basis of plausibility considerations to summary dismissal of almost every hypothesis that comes along; on the contrary, the recommendation would be for a high degree of open-mindedness. However, we need not and cannot be completely open-minded with regard to any and every hypothesis of whatever description that happens to be proposed by anyone. This approach shows how we can be reasonably openminded in science without being stupid about it. It provides an answer to the kind of change made by the editors of *Harper's:* Science *is* objective, but its objectivity embraces two aspects, objective testing and objective evaluation of prior probabilities. Plausibility arguments are used in science, and their use is justified by Bayes' theorem. In fact, Bayes' theorem shows that they are indispensable. The frequency interpretation of probability enables us to view them as empirical and objective.

It would be an unfair distortion of the situation for me to conclude without remarking that the view I have been advocating is very definitely a minority view among inductive logicians and probability theorists. There is no well agreed upon majority view. One of the most challenging aspects of this sort of investigation lies in the large number of open questions, and the amount that remains to be done. Whether my view is correct is not the main issue. Of far greater importance is the fact that there are many fundamental problems that deserve extensive consideration, and we cannot help but learn a great deal about the foundations of science by pursuing them.

CHAPTER 6

Testability

Carl Hempel in the next selection, which is from his *Philosophy of Natural Sciences*, presents in clear form a number of the logical considerations bearing on the test of a hypothesis. Among other things, he holds that a truly crucial experiment is not possible, because, instead of rejecting the hypothesis in the face of apparently opposing evidence, one has the logical liberty of modifying or rejecting the assumptions which, together with the hypothesis, were used to make a prediction. If Hempel is right, then Platt's strong inference (Selection 20) is not so strong as it might seem, especially in the behavioral sciences, where assumptions are often rather shaky.

Hempel also develops the contemporary view that a hypothesis must be at least conceivably testable in order to be significant. It is interesting to note that this view is not simply a twentieth-century view, for it appears in Francis Bacon's charge that the content of the science of his time resembled an "empty bladder":

> The admiration of mankind with regard to the arts and sciences, which
> is of itself sufficiently simple and almost puerile, has been increased
> by the craft and artifices of those who have treated the sciences, and
> delivered them down to posterity. For they propose and produce them
> to our view so fashioned, and as it were masked, as to make them pass
> for perfect and complete. For if you consider their method and divisions,
> they appear to embrace and comprise everything which can relate
> to the subject. And although this frame be badly filled up and

351

resemble an empty bladder, yet it presents to the vulgar understanding the form and appearance of a perfect science.[1]

For an example of an attempted application of the testability doctrine to the behavioral sciences, we present an article about psychoanalysis by Alasdair MacIntyre. Following that we present Paul Meehl's attempted defense of the Law of Effect against a charge of untestability. Both articles show that the charge of untestability is not an easy one to establish. Much depends on what the propounder of the allegedly untestable doctrine would say if. . . .

The testability view is one that springs from the radical empiricist camp. Untestable doctrines motivated people like Bacon and Hume to condemn all that was not observational or built up from observational propositions, although in its more sophisticated forms, testability is conducive to considerably more tolerance than shown by Bacon, Hume, and contemporary radical empiricists.

[1] Francis Bacon, *Novum Organum*, edited by Joseph Devey (New York: P. F. Collier & Son, 1902), pp. 65–66.

28. THE TEST OF A HYPOTHESIS: ITS LOGIC AND ITS FORCE

Carl Hempel

EXPERIMENTAL VS. NONEXPERIMENTAL TESTS

Now we turn to a closer scrutiny of the reasoning on which scientific tests are based and of the conclusions that may be drawn from their outcomes. As before, we will use the word "hypothesis" to refer to whatever statement is under test, no matter whether it purports to describe some particular fact or event or to express a general law or some other, more complex, proposition.

Let us begin with a simple remark, to which we will frequently have to refer in the subsequent discussion: the test implications of a hypothesis are normally of a conditional character; they tell us that *under specified test conditions*, an outcome of a certain kind will occur. Statements to this effect can be put into the following explicitly conditional form:

3a]   If conditions of kind C are realized, then an event of kind E will occur.

For example, one of the hypotheses considered by Semmelweis yielded the test implication

> If the patients in the First Division are delivered in lateral position, then their mortality from childbed fever will decrease.

And one of the test implications of his final hypothesis was

> If the persons attending the women in the First Division wash their hands

SOURCE. Hempel, Carl G., *Philosophy of Natural Science*, © 1966. Reprinted by permission of Prentice-Hall, Inc., Englewood Cliffs, N. J.

in a solution of chlorinated lime, then mortality from childbed fever will decrease.

Similarly, the test implications of Torricelli's hypothesis included conditional statements such as

> If a Torricelli barometer is carried to increasing altitudes, then its mercury column will correspondingly decrease in length.

Such test implications are thus implications in a twofold sense: they are implications of the hypotheses from which they are derived, and they have the form of if-then sentences, which in logic are called conditionals or material implications.

In each of the three examples just cited, the specified test conditions C are technologically realizable and can thus be brought about at will; and the realization of those conditions involves some control of a factor (position during delivery; absence or presence of infectious matter; pressure of the atmosphere overhead) that, according to the given hypothesis, affects the phenomenon under study (i.e., incidence of childbed fever in the first two cases; length of the mercury column in the third). Test implications of this kind provide a basis for an *experimental test*, which amounts to bringing about the conditions C and checking whether E occurs as implied by the hypothesis.

Many scientific hypotheses are expressed in quantitative terms. In the simplest case, they will then represent the value of one quantitative variable as a mathematical function of certain other variables. Thus, the classical gas law, $V = c \cdot T/P$, represents the volume of a body of gas as a function of its temperature and pressure (c is a constant factor). A statement of this kind yields indefinitely many quantitative test implications. In our example, these are of the following form: if the temperature of a body of gas is T_1 and its pressure is P_1, then its volume is $c \cdot T_1/P_1$. And an experimental test then consists in varying the values of the "independent" variables and checking whether the "dependent" variable assumes the values implied by the hypothesis.

When experimental control is impossible, when the conditions C mentioned in the test implication cannot be brought about or varied by available technological means, then the hypothesis must be tested nonexperimentally, by seeking out, or waiting for, cases where the specified conditions are realized by nature, and then checking whether E does indeed occur.

It is sometimes said that in an experimental test of a quantitative hypothesis, only one of the quantities mentioned in the hypothesis is varied at a time, while all other conditions are kept constant. But this is impossible. In an experimental test of the gas law, for example, the pressure might be varied while the temperature is kept constant, or vice versa; but many other circumstances will change during the process—among them perhaps the relative humidity, the brightness of the illumination, and the strength of the magnetic field in the laboratory—and certainly the distance of the body of gas from the sun or moon. Nor is there any reason to try to keep as many as possible of these factors constant if the experiment is to test the gas law as specified. For the law states that the volume of a given body of gas is fully determined by its temperature and its pressure. It implies therefore that other factors are "irrelevant to the volume" in the sense that changes in these factors do not affect the volume of the gas. To allow such other factors to vary is therefore to explore a wider range of cases in search of possible violations of the hypothesis under test.

Experimentation, however, is used in science not only as a method of test, but also as a method of discovery; and in this second context, as we will now see, the requirement that certain factors be kept constant makes good sense.

The use of experimentation as a method of test is illustrated by Torricelli's and Péricr's experiments. Here, a hypothesis has been antecedently advanced, and the experiment is performed to test it. In certain other cases, where no ·specific hypotheses have as yet been proposed, a scientist may start with a rough guess and may use experimentation as a guide to a more definite hypothesis. In studying how a metal wire is stretched by a weight suspended from it, he might conjecture that the quantitative increase in length will depend on the initial length of the wire, on its cross section, on the kind of metal it is made of, and on the weight of the body suspended from it. And he may then perform experiments to determine whether those factors do influence the increase in length (here, experimentation serves as a method of test), and if so, just how they affect the "dependent variable"—that is, just what the specific mathematical form of the dependence is (here, experimentation serves as a method of discovery). Knowing that the length of a wire varies also with its temperature, the experimenter will, first of all, keep the temperature constant, to eliminate the disturbing influence of this factor (though later on, he may systematically vary the temperature to ascertain whether the values of certain parameters in the functions connecting the length increase with the other factors are dependent on the temperature). In his experiments at constant temperature, he will vary the factors that he thinks are relevaant, one at a time, keeping the others constant. On the basis of the results thus obtained, he will tentatively formulate generalizations that express the increase in length as a function of the unstretched length, of the weight, and so on; and from there, he may proceed to construct a more general formula representing the increase in length as a function of all the variables examined.

In cases of this kind, then, in which experimentation serves as a heuristic device, as a guide to the discovery of hypotheses, the principle of keeping all but one of the "relevant factors" constant makes good sense. But, of course, the most that can be done is to keep constant all but one of those factors that are believed to be "relevant" in the sense of affecting the phenomenon under study: it is always possible that some other important factors may have been overlooked.

It is one of the striking characteristics, and one of the great methodological advantages, of natural science that many of its hypotheses admit of experimental test. But experimental testing of hypotheses cannot be said to be a distinctive characteristic of all and only the natural sciences. It does not mark a dividing line between natural and social science, for experimental testing procedures are used also in psychology and, if to a lesser extent, in sociology. Also, the scope of experimental testing increases steadily with the advances in the requisite technology. Moreover, not all hypotheses in the natural sciences permit of experimental test. Take, for example, the law formulated by Leavitt and Shapley for the periodic fluctuations in the brightness of a certain type of variable star, the so-called classical Cepheids. The law states that the longer the period P of such a star, i.e., the time interval between two successive states of maximal brightness, the greater is its intrinsic luminosity; in quantitative terms, $M = -(a + b \cdot \log P)$, where M is the magnitude, which by definition varies inversely with the brightness of the star. This law deductively implies any number of test sentences stating what the magnitude of a Cepheid will be if its period has this or that particular value, for example, 5.3 days or 17.5 days. But Cepheids with specific periods cannot be produced at will; hence, the law cannot be tested by experiment. Rather, the astronomer must search the skies for new Cepheids and must then try to ascertain whether their magnitude and period conform to the presumptive law.

THE ROLE OF AUXILIARY HYPOTHESES

We said earlier that test implications are "derived" or "inferred" from the hypothesis that is to be tested. This statement, however, gives only a rough indication of the relationship between a hypothesis and the sentences that serve as its test implications. In some cases, it is indeed possible deductively to infer from a hypothesis certain conditional statements that can serve as test sentences for it. Thus, as we saw, the Leavitt-Shapley law deductively implies sentences of the form: "If star s is a Cepheid with a period of so many days, then its magnitude will be such and such." But often the "derivation" of a test implication is less simple and conclusive. Take, for example, Semmelweis' hypothesis that childbed fever is caused by contamination with infectious matter, and consider the test implication that if the persons attending the patients were to wash their hands in a solution of chlorinated lime, then mortality from childbed fever would be reduced. This statement does not follow deductively from the hypothesis alone, its derivation presupposes the further premiss that unlike soap and water alone, a chlorinated lime solution will destroy the infectious matter. This premiss, which is tacitly taken for granted in the argument, plays the role of what we will call an *auxiliary assumption*, or *auxiliary hypothesis*, in deriving the test sentence from Semmelweis' hypothesis. Hence, we are not entitled to assert here that if the hypothesis H is true then so must be the test implication I, but only that if both H and the auxiliary hypothesis are true then so will be I. Reliance on auxiliary hypotheses, as we shall see, is the rule rather than the exception in the testing of scientific hypotheses; and it has an important consequence for the question whether an unfavorable test finding, i.e., one that shows I to be false, can be held to disprove the hypothesis under investigation.

If H alone implies I and if empirical findings show I to be false, then H must also be qualified as false: this follows by the *modus tollens* argument. But when I is derived from H in conjunction with one or more auxiliary hypotheses A, then the schema must be replaced by the following one:

3b]
> If both H and A are true, then so is I.
> But (as the evidence shows) I is not true.
> _____
> H and A are not both true.

Thus if the test shows I to be false, we can infer only that either the hypothesis or one of the auxiliary assumptions included in A must be false; hence, the test provides no conclusive grounds for rejecting H. For example, if the antiseptic measure introduced by Semmelweis had not been followed by a decline in mortality, Semmelweis' hypothesis might still have been true: the negative test result might have been due to inefficacy of the chloride of lime solution as an antiseptic.

This kind of situation is not a mere abstract possibility. The astronomer Tycho Brahe, whose accurate observations provided the empirical basis for Kepler's laws of planetary motion, rejected the Copernican conception that the earth moves about the sun. He gave the following reason, among others: if the Copernican hypothesis were true, then the direction in which a fixed star would be seen by an observer on the earth at a fixed time of day should gradually change; for in the course of the annual travel of the earth about the sun, the star would be observed from a steadily changing vantage point—just as a child on a merry-go-round observes the face of an onlooker from a changing vantage point and therefore sees it in a constantly changing direction. More specifically, the direction from the observer to the star should vary periodically between two extremes, corresponding to opposite vantage points on the earth's orbit about the sun. The angle subtended by these points is called the annual parallax of the star; the farther the star is from the earth, the smaller will be its parallax. Brahe, who made his observations before the telescope was introduced, searched with his most precise instruments for evidence of such "parallactic motions" of fixed stars—and found none. He therefore rejected the hypothesis of the earth's motion. But the test implication that the fixed stars show observable parallactic motions can be derived from Copernicus' hypothesis only with the help of the auxiliary assumption that the fixed stars are so close to the earth that their parallactic movements are large enough to be detected by means of Brahe's instruments. Brahe was aware of making this auxiliary assumption, and he believed that he had grounds for regarding it as true; hence he felt obliged to reject the Copernican conception. It has since been found that the fixed stars do show parallactic displacements, but that Brahe's auxiliary hypothesis was mistaken: even the nearest fixed stars are vastly more remote than he had assumed, and therefore parallax measurements require powerful telescopes and very precise techniques. The first generally accepted measurement of a stellar parallax was made only in 1838.

The significance of auxiliary hypotheses in testing reaches still further. Suppose that a hypothesis H is tested by checking a test implication, "If C then E," which has been derived from H and a set A of auxiliary hypotheses. The test then ultimately comes to checking whether or not E does occur in a test situation in which, to the best of the investigator's knowledge, the conditions C are realized. If in fact this is not the case—if, for example, the test equipment is faulty or not sufficiently sensitive—then E may fail to occur even if both H and A are true. For this reason, the total set of auxiliary assumptions presupposed by the test may be said to include the supposition that the test arrangement satisfies the specified conditions C.

This point is particularly important when the hypothesis under scrutiny has stood up well in previous tests and is an essential part of a larger system of interconnected hypotheses that is also supported by diverse other evidence. In such a case, an effort will likely be made to account for the nonoccurrence of E by showing that some of the conditions C were not satisfied in the test.

As an example, consider the hypothesis that electric charges have an atomistic structure and are all of them integral multiples of the charge of the atom of electricity, the electron. This hypothesis received very impressive support from experiments conducted by R. A. Millikan in 1909 and later. In these experiments, the electric charges on individual, extremely small drops of some liquid such as oil or mercury were determined by measuring the velocities of the droplets while they were falling in air under the influence of gravity or rising under the influence of a counteracting electric field. Millikan found all the charges either to be equal to, or to be small integral multiples of, a certain basic minimal charge, which he accordingly identified as the charge of the electron. On the basis of numerous careful measurements, he gave its value in electrostatic units as 4.774×10^{-10}. This hypothesis was soon challenged by the physicist Ehrenhaft in Vienna, who announced that he had repeated Millikan's experiment and had found charges that were considerably smaller than the electronic charge specified by Millikan. In his discussion of Ehrenhaft's results,[1] Millikan suggested several likely sources of error (i.e., violations of test requirements) that might account for Ehrenhaft's apparently adverse experimental findings: evaporation during observation, decreasing the weight of a droplet; formation of an oxide film on the mercury droplets used in some of Ehrenhaft's experiments; the disturbing influence of dust particles suspended in the air; the droplet drifting out of focus of the telescope used to observe it; deviation of very small droplets from the requisite spherical shape; inevitable errors in timing the movements of the small particles. In reference to two deviant particles observed and reported on by another investigator, who had experimented with oil drops, Millikan concludes: "The only possible interpretation then which could be put on these two particles . . . was that . . . they were not spheres of oil," but dust particles (pp. 170, 169). Millikan notes further that the results of more precise repetitions of his own experiment were all in essential accord with the result that he had announced earlier. Ehrenhaft continued for many years to defend and further expand his findings concerning subelectronic charges; but other physicists were not generally able to reproduce his results, and the atomistic conception of electric charge was maintained. Millikan's numerical value for the electronic charge, however, was later found to be slightly too small; interestingly, the deviation was traced to an error in one of Millikan's own auxiliary hypotheses: he had used too low a value for the viscosity of air in evaluating his oil drop data!

CRUCIAL TESTS

The preceding remarks are of importance also for the idea of a crucial test, which can be brifly described as follows: suppose that H_1 and H_2 are two rival hypotheses concerning the same subject matter, which have so far stood up equally well in empirical tests, so that the available evidence does not favor one of them over the other. Then a decision between the two may be reached if some test can be specified for which H_1 and H_2 predict conflicting outcomes; i.e., if for a certain kind of test condition, C, the first hypothesis yields the test implication "If C then E_1," and the second hypothesis yields "If C then E_2," where E_1 and E_2 are mutually exclusive outcomes. Performance of the appropriate test will then presumably refute one of the hypotheses and support the other.

A classical example is the experiment performed by Foucault to decide

[1] See Chap. VIII of R. A. Millikan, *The Electron* (Chicago: The University of Chicago Press, 1917). Reprinted, with an introduction by J. W. M. DuMond, 1963.

between two competing conceptions of the nature of light. One of these, proposed by Huyghens and developed further by Fresnel and Young, held that light consists in transverse waves propagated in an elastic medium, the ether; the other was Newton's corpuscular conception, according to which light consists of extremely small particles traveling at high velocity. Either of these conceptions permitted the conclusion that light "rays" should conform to the laws of rectilinear propagation, reflection, and refraction. But the wave conception led to the further implication that light should travel faster in air than in water, whereas the corpuscular conception led to the opposite conclusion. In 1850, Foucault succeeded in performing an experiment in which the velocities of light in air and in water were directly compared. Images of two light-emitting points were produced by means of light rays that passed through water and through air, respectively, and were then reflected in a very rapidly revolving mirror. Depending on whether the velocity of light in air was greater or less than that in water, the image of the first light source would appear to the right or to the left of that of the second light source. The conflicting test implications checked by this experiment may therefore be briefly put as follows: "if the Foucault experiment is performed, then the first image will appear to the right of the second image" and "if the Foucault experiment is performed, then the first image will appear to the left of the second image." The experiment showed the first of these implications to be true.

This outcome was widely regarded as a definitive refutation of the corpuscular conception of light and as a decisive vindication of the undulatory one. But this appraisal, though very natural, overrated the force of the test. For the statement that light travels faster in water than in air does not follow simply from the general conception of light rays as streams of particles; that assumption alone is much too indefinite to yield any specific quantitative consequences. Such implications as the laws of reflection and refraction and the statement about the velocities of light in air and in water can be derived only when the general corpuscular conception is supplemented by specific assumptions concerning the motion of the corpuscles and the influence exerted upon them by the surrounding medium. Newton did specify such assumptions; and in so doing, he set forth a definite *theory* concerning the propagation of light. It is the total set of those basic theoretical principles that leads to experimentally testable consequences such as the one checked by Foucault. Analogously, the wave conception was formulated as a *theory* based on a set of specific assumptions about the propagation of ether waves in different optical media; and again it is this set of theoretical principles that implied the laws of reflection and refraction and the statement that the velocity of light is greater in air than in water. Consequently—granting the truth of all other auxiliary hypotheses—the outcome of Foucault's experiment entitles us to infer only that not all the basic assumptions, or principles, of the corpuscular theory can be true—that at least one of them must be false. But it does not tell us which of them is to be rejected. Hence, it leaves open the possibility that the general conception of particle-like projectiles playing a role in the propagation of light might be retained in some modified form which would be characterized by a different set of basic laws.

And in fact, in 1905, Einstein did propound a modified version of the corpuscular conception in his theory of light quanta or photons, as they came to be called. The evidence he cited in support of his theory included an experiment performed by Lenard in 1903. Einstein characterized it as a "second crucial experiment" concerning the undulatory and corpuscular conceptions, and he noted that it "eliminated" the classical wave theory, in which by then the notion of elastic vibrations in the ether had been replaced by the idea, developed by Maxwell and Hertz, of transverse electromagnetic waves. Lenard's experiment, involving the photoelectric effect, could be regarded as testing two conflicting implications concerning the light energy that a radiating point P can transmit, during some fixed unit of time, to a small screen that is perpendicular to the light rays. On the classical wave theory, that energy will gradually and continuously decrease toward zero as the screen moves away from the point P; on the photon theory, the energy must be at least that carried by a single photon—unless during the given time interval, no photon strikes the screen, in which case the energy received will be zero; hence, there will be no continuous decrease to zero. Lenard's experiment had borne out this latter alternative. Again, however, the wave conception was not definitely refuted; the outcome of the experiment showed only that *some* modification was needed in the system of basic assumptions of the wave theory. Einstein, in fact, endeavored to modify the classical theory as little as possible.[2] In sum, then, an experiment of the kind here illustrated cannot strictly refute one of the two rival hypotheses.

But neither can it "prove" or definitely establish the other; for scientific hypotheses or theories cannot be conclusively proved by any set of available data, no matter how accurate and extensive. This is particularly obvious for hypotheses or theories that assert or imply general laws either for some process that is not directly observable—as in the case of the rival theories of light—or for some phenomenon more readily accessible to observation and measurement, such as free fall. Galileo's law, for example, refers to *all* instances of free fall in the past, present, and future; whereas all the relevant evidence available at any time can cover only that relatively small set of cases—all of them belonging to the past—in which careful measurements have been carried out. And even if Galileo's law were found to be strictly

---

[2] This example is discussed at some length in Chap. 8 of P. Frank, *Philosophy of Science* (Englewood Cliffs, N.J.: Prentice-Hall, Spectrum Books, 1962).

satisfied in all the observed cases, this would obviously not preclude the possibility that some unobserved cases in past or future may not conform to it. In sum, even the most careful and extensive test can neither disprove one of two hypotheses nor prove the other: thus strictly construed, a crucial experiment is impossible in science.[3] But an experiment, such as Foucault's or Lenard's, may be crucial in a less strict, practical sense: it may reveal one of two conflicting theories as seriously inadequate and may lend strong support to its rival; and as a result, it may exert a decisive influence upon the direction of subsequent theorizing and experimentation.

AD HOC HYPOTHESES

If a particular way of testing a hypothesis H *presupposes* auxiliary assumptions $A_1, A_2, \ldots, A_n$—i.e., if these are used as additional premises in deriving from H the relevant test implication I—then, as we saw earlier, a negative test result, which shows I to be false, tells us only that H or one of the auxiliary hypotheses must be false and that a change must be made somewhere in this set of sentences if the test result is to be accommodated. A suitable adjustment might be made by modifying or completely abandoning H or by making changes in the system of auxiliary hypotheses. In principle, it would always be possible to retain H even in the face of seriously adverse test results —provided that we are willing to make sufficiently radical and perhaps burdensome revisions among our auxiliary hypotheses. But science is not interested in thus protecting its hypotheses or theories at all costs—and for good reasons. Consider an example. Before Torricelli introduced his conception of the pressure of the sea of air, the action of suction pumps was explained by the idea that nature abhors a vacuum and that, therefore, water rushes up the pump barrel to fill the vacuum created by the rising piston. The same idea also served to explain several other phenomena. When Pascal wrote to Périer asking him to perform the Puy-de-Dôme experiment, he argued that the expected outcome would be a "decisive" refutation of that conception: "If it happens that the height of the quicksilver is less at the top than at the base of the mountain . . . it follows of necessity that the weight and pressure of the air is the sole cause of this suspension of the quicksilver, and not the abhorrence of a vacuum: for it is quite certain that there is much more air that presses on the foot of the mountain than there is on its summit, and one can-

---

[3] This is the famous verdict of the physicist and historian of science, Pierre Duhem. Cf. Part II, Chap. VI of his book, *The Aim and Structure of Physical Theory*, trans. P. P. Wiener (Princeton: Princeton University Press, 1954), originally published in 1905. In his Foreword to the English translation, Louis de Broglie includes some interesting observations on this idea.

not well say that nature abhors a vacuum more at the foot of the mountain than at its summit."[4] But the last remark actually indicates a way in which the conception of a *horror vacui* could be saved in the face of Périer's findings. Périer's results are decisive evidence against that conception only on the auxiliary assumption that the strength of the horror does not depend upon location. To reconcile Périer's apparently adverse evidence with the idea of a *horror vacui* it suffices to introduce instead the auxiliary hypothesis that nature's abhorrence of a vacuum decreases with increasing altitude. But while this assumption is not logically absurd or patently false, it is objectionable from the point of view of science. For it would be introduced *ad hoc*—i.e., for the sole purpose of saving a hypothesis seriously threatened by adverse evidence; it would not be called for by other findings and, roughly speaking, it leads to no additional test implications. The hypothesis of the pressure of air, on the other hand, does lead to further implications. Pascal mentions, for example, that if a partly inflated balloon were carried up a mountain, it would be more inflated at the mountaintop.

About the middle of the seventeenth century, a group of physicists, the plenists, held that a vacuum could not exist in nature; and in order to save this idea in the face of Torricelli's experiment, one of them offered the *ad hoc* hypothesis that the mercury in a barometer was being held in place by the "funiculus," an invisible thread by which it was suspended from the top of the inner surface of the glass tube. According to an initially very useful theory, developed early in the eighteenth century, the combustion of metals involves the escape of a substance called phlogiston. This conception was eventually abandoned in response to the experimental work of Lavoisier, who showed that the end product of the combustion process has greater weight than the original metal. But some tenacious adherents of the phlogiston theory tried to reconcile their conception with Lavoisier's finding by proposing the *ad hoc* hypothesis that phlogiston had negative weight, so that its escape would increase the weight of the residue.

We should remember, however, that with the benefit of hindsight, it seems easy to dismiss certain scientific suggestions of the past as *ad hoc* hypotheses, whereas it may be quite difficult to pass judgment on a hypothesis proposed in a contemporary context. There is, in fact, no precise criterion for *ad hoc* hypotheses, though the questions suggested earlier provide some guidance: is the hypothesis proposed just for the purpose of saving some current conception against adverse evidence, or does it also account for other phenomena, does it yield further significant test implications? And one further relevant consideration is this: if more and more qualifying hypotheses have to be intro-

[4] From Pascal's letter of November 15, 1647 in I.H.B. and A.G.H. Spiers, trans., *The Physical Treatises of Pascal* (New York: Columbia University Press, 1937), p. 101.

duced to reconcile a certain basic conception with new evidence that becomes available, the resulting total system will eventually become so complex that it has to give way when a simple alternative conception is proposed.

TESTABILITY-IN-PRINCIPLE AND EMPIRICAL IMPORT

As the preceding discussion shows, no statement or set of statements T can be significantly proposed as a scientific hypothesis or theory unless it is amenable to objective empirical test, at least "in principle." This is to say that it must be possible to derive from T, in the broad sense we have considered, certain test implications of the form "if test conditions C are realized, then outcome E will occur"; but the test conditions need not be realized or technologically realizable at the time when T is propounded or contemplated. Take the hypothesis, for example, that the distance covered in t seconds by a body falling freely from rest near the surface of the moon is $s = 2.7\ t^2$ feet. It yields deductively a set of test implications to the effect that the distances covered by such a body in 1, 2, 3, . . . seconds will be 2.7, 10.8, 24.3, . . . feet. Hence, the hypothesis is testable in principle, though it is as yet impossible to perform the test here specified.

But if a statement or set of statements is not testable at least in principle, in other words, if it has no test implications at all, then it cannot be significantly proposed or entertained as a scientific hypothesis or theory, for no conceivable empirical finding can then accord or conflict with it. In this case, it has no bearing whatever on empirical phenomena, or as we will also say, it lacks *empirical import*. Consider, for example, the view that the mutual gravitational attraction of physical bodies is a manifestation of certain "appetites or natural tendencies" closely related to love, inherent in those bodies, which make their "natural movements intelligible and possible."[5] What test implications can be derived from this interpretation of gravitational phenomena? Considering some characteristic aspects of love in the familiar sense, this view would seem to imply that gravitational affinity should be a selective phenomenon: not just any two physical bodies should attract each other. Nor should the strength of the affinity of one body to a second one always equal that of its converse, nor should it depend significantly on the masses of the bodies or on their distance. But since all of the consequences thus suggested are known to be false, the conception we are considering evidently is not meant to imply them. And indeed, that conception claims merely that the natural affinities underlying gravitational attraction are *related* to love. But,

---

[5] This idea is set forth, for example, in J. F. O'Brien, "Gravity and Love as Unifying Principles," *The Thomist*, Vol. 21 (1958), 184–93.

as will now be clear, this assertion is so elusive that it precludes the derivation of *any* test implications. No specific empirical findings of any kind are called for by this interpretation; no conceivable observational or experimental data can confirm or disconfirm it. In particular, therefore, it has no implications concerning gravitational phenomena; consequently, it cannot possible explain those phenomena or render them "intelligible." To illustrate this further, let us suppose someone were to offer the alternative thesis that physical bodies gravitationally attract each other and tend to move toward each other from a natural tendency akin to hatred, from a natural inclination to collide with and destroy other physical objects. Would there by any conceivable way of adjudicating these conflicting views? Clearly not. Neither of them yields any testable implications; no empirical discrimination between them is possible. Not that the issue is "too deep" for scientific decision: the two verbally conflicting interpretations make no assertions at all. Hence, the question whether they are true or false makes no sense, and that is why scientific inquiry cannot possibly decide between them. They are *pseudo-hypotheses:* hypotheses in appearance only.

It should be borne in mind, however, that a scientific hypothesis normally yields test implications only when combined with suitable auxiliary assumptions. Thus Torricelli's conception of the pressure exerted by the sea of air yields definite test implications only on the assumption that air pressure is subject to laws analogous to those for water pressure; this assumption underlies, for example, the Puy-de-Dôme experiment. In judging whether a proposed hypothesis does have empirical import, we should ask ourselves, therefore, what auxiliary hypotheses are explicitly or tacitly presupposed in the given context, and whether in conjunction with the latter, the given hypothesis yields test implications (other than those that may be derivable from the auxiliary assumptions alone).

Moreover, a scientific idea will often be introduced in an initial form that offers only limited and tenuous possibilities for test; and on the basis of such initial tests it will gradually be given a more definite, precise, and diversely testable form.

For these reasons, and for certain others which would lead us too far afield,[6] it is not possible to draw a sharp dividing line between hypotheses and theories that are testable in principle and those that are not. But even though it is somewhat vague, the distinction here referred to is important and illuminating for appraising the significance and the potential explanatory efficacy of proposed hypotheses and theories.

[6] The issue is discussed further in another volume of this series: William Alston, *Philosophy of Language*, Chap. 4. A fuller, technical discussion will be found in the essay, "Empiricist Criteria of Cognitive Significance: Problems and Changes," in C. G. Hempel, *Aspects of Scientific Explanation* (New York: The Free Press, 1965).

29. THE PSYCHO-ANALYSTS

Alasdair MacIntyre

The more that is written about psycho-analysis the more puzzled one can become. On the one hand there are the ever new but all too familiar expositions of the system. Dr. J. A. C. Brown's[1] and Dr. Reuben Fine's[2] are among the most recent to hand. Excellent as expositions, the time has come when defensive exposition is not enough. Taken as we are again and again on the same conducted tour of Freud's views, the intellectual boredom is intensified. Yet there is a whole series of books which excite and illuminate, and could not have been written but for Freud. I do not mean by this simply to assert the truism that there are dull authors and that there are exciting authors. The contrasts between psycho-analysts are far more extreme than that. It is rather that what is at first sight the same Freudian methodology appears capable both of crippling the intellect and of liberating it. How so?

Psycho-analysts, like priests, suffer from an initial disadvantage: they have to take care to keep separate the situations in which they must assume the pose of authority from those in which they themselves must accept the authority of rational argument. The pulpit is no place to debate the existence of God and the couch is for free association not for theoretical objections. And yet— unless the theoretical objections can be answered, the clinical authority of the

SOURCE. MacIntyre, Alasdair, "The Psycho-analysts," *Encounter*, 24:5, 1965. Reprinted with permission. Copyright © 1965 by Encounter Ltd.

[1] J. A. C. Brown, *Freud and the Post-Freudians* (Pelican Books, 3s. 6d.).

[2] Reuben Fine, *Freud: A Critical Re-Evaluation Of His Theories* (Allen & Unwin, 35s.).

analyst is faked. It was Karl Kraus who remarked that psycho-analysis is in fact the disease for which it purports to be the cure. One gets a hint that, as so often with Kraus, what looks like an easy witticism will bear closer scrutiny from the curious tone which infects the answers that some psycho-analysts make to their critics. There is an important difference between their attitude and that of Freud who wrote:

> Looking back, then, over the patchwork of my life's labours, I can say that I have made many beginnings and thrown out many suggestions. Something will come of them in the future, though I cannot myself tell whether it will be much or little. . . .

This underlying caution was always there to temper Freud's flights of speculative enthusiasm. Unfortunately it appears to be mainly the speculative enthusiasm which his heirs have inherited—at least on the occasions when they respond to criticism.

In order to evaluate this response, we must first understand the critics, and in order to understand them we must set out the features of psycho-analytic theory which invite criticism. We can illuminate the logical structure of psycho-analytic theory by remembering that Freud's contentions were made at three different levels. First of all, Freud drew our attention to hitherto un-noticed types of episodes. He reclassified and redescribed our behaviour. He made us aware of what needed to be explained. Secondly, he suggested a correlation between adult episodes and traits and the passions and actions of the world of early childhood. Thirdly, he produced a theory to explain that correlation; or rather he produced a range of theoretical notions, of which the earlier account of the distribution and transformations of libido and the later trinity of id, super-ego, and ego are the most important. It is often difficult in exposition to keep the distinction between these three levels clear, partly because kindred notions rear at all three and more especially when this is so because the explanatory theory helps to provide a vocabulary for the description of the very facts which the theory is designed to explain. One example of this is the way in which the notion of unconscious motivation is often used *both* descriptively to bring out features of goal-directed behaviour in which the agent himself remains unaware of his goals and resists (again without recognising what he is doing) any correct identification of them—and *also* as part of the account of the formation of character which is invoked to explain such behaviour. Another is the way in which adult behaviour may be characterised as Oedipal, an instructive resemblance with childhood behaviour being brought out by a term the use of which already half-commits us to a particular explanation of this resemblance.

This transition from level to level is itself important for at least two reasons. There is perhaps no discipline to compare with psycho-analysis for the way in which the very use of the vocabulary commits the novice—quite unconsciously —to acceptance of a complex theoretical framework. And moreover this is common to all the rival analytic schools, or to all at least which share some sort of Freudian commitment. Melanie Klein differed from Freud about many things, and especially the characterisation of early childhood; Freud himself was always prepared to revise his own theoretical apparatus; but what cannot be revised without loss of the theory altogether is the notion of a set of childhood traits, a corresponding set of adult traits, and a theoretical bridge between them. It is upon the concepts out of which this bridge is to be built that attention can therefore usefully be focused.

Central among them is that of *repression*. Freud's own view both of the cause and of the consequences of repression gradually changed. He came in his later period to see repression as a response above all to anxiety, when he had earlier seen anxiety as an effect of repression. And he came to envisage it as only one of the defensive strategems to which the threatened ego might resort. But it retains a central and characteristic place. In a paper of 1908, *Character and Anal Erotism* Freud wrote that:

> We can at any rate lay down a formula for the way in which character in its final shape is formed out of the constituent instincts: the permanent character traits are either unchanged prolongations of the original instincts, or the sublimations of those instincts, or reaction-formations against them.

To this thought Freud remained faithful; and this required that he remained faithful also to the notion of repression. Dr. Brown has summarised his unchanging view in writing:

> that the unconscious plays a predominant part in mental life, since it takes its energy from the instinctual drives, and its contents are kept out of awareness not because they lack significance but because they may be so significant as to constitute what is felt as a threat to the ego. When this occurs they are actively repressed and can find expression only by devious methods, as in symptoms, certain character traits, and the other phenomena which represent compromise solutions to a conflict between primitive drives seeking an outlet and learned ego and super-ego behaviour patterns which must inhibit them. . . . Repression is itself an unconscious process. . . .

The difficulties which critics have alleged against this position are of at least three kinds. There is the too open texture of the concepts; the apparent falsity and the untested character of certain of the factual claims; and the unfalsifiability of parts of the theoretical apparatus. A concept like "repression," for instance, can only be safely used if we are given criteria for its application, such that we can identify at least central cases of repression taking place. For its full use in psycho-analytic theory we should also need criteria to determine when behaviour evidences the effect of repression and when memories that have been recalled have been recalled as a result of a cessation of repression rather than from some other possible cause.

But we are supplied with no adequate criteria. We are not told how to recognise the response of repression when it is first made; and when later on the analyst interprets his patient's behaviour as manifesting effects of repression, what he will treat as confirmatory of his interpretation is probably a set of further reactions by the patient—dreams, newly recalled memories, changes in attitude to the analyst, and the like. Analysts have discussed with a great deal of care what the criteria of a correct interpretation ought to be.[3] But while they have produced some interesting generalisations about the kind of result that may follow from one sort of interpretation rather than another, what they have not done is to explain how these responses help to confirm the *truth* of the interpretation, as distinct from the effectiveness of it in producing further reactions. To do this successfully we should need the concept of repression and kindred concepts of defence to be defined more sharply in operational terms. More than this we must take care to see that the concepts are not defined in terms of the theory. For if repression is defined or explained in terms of unconscious instinctual drives, as it is in the quotation from Dr. Brown, then the use of the term is already part of our theoretical explanation of what occurs, and we shall still lack an adequate way of characterising and identifying the occurrences which the theory is designed to explain.

At the level of the empirically observable there are much simpler questions to be put to the analyst. What are the alleged facts which the theory explains? What factual generalisations are entailed by the theory and must be true if the theory is true? Experimental psychologists have expended effort and ingenuity in trying to specify the necessary generalisations and confirm or falsify them. The result of this effort is a sifting out from the Freudian amalgam of particular hypotheses concerning the effects of maternal deprivation at different ages, the preferences of children for one parent rather than the other, the formation of character traits, and so on. When these hypotheses are tested, we find that the Freudian doctrine seems to be a mixture of true true and false statements. In so appearing it loses its unity of structure. This loss is further intensified by the separating out in the process of the testable elements in the theory from the untestable.

I am not now referring to the kind of untestability which derives from the too open texture of the key concepts, but to the tendency to specify too many

[3] See especially Susan Isaacs, "Criteria for Interpretation," *International Journal of Psycho-Analysis* (1939) and P. M. Torquet, "The Criteria For a Psycho-Analytic Interpretation," *Aristotelian Society Supplementary Volume* (1962).

ways in which the theory may be confirmed and not enough ways in which it might be falsified. Consider the already quoted statement from *Character and Anal Erotism*. The instinctual drives may be transformed so that they manifest themselves in one way; or it may be that the processes of reaction formation result in their being manifested in a precisely opposite way. The same type of background may result in sadistic aggressive behaviour or in gentle, non-violent behaviour. The hypothesis has become a bet that cannot lose; but by the same token, as Karl Popper has shown, it cannot win. Whatever the behaviour the hypothesis is not falsified, and its unfalsifiability is fatal to its status as a hypothesis.

All this is preliminary to a central argument. The criticisms I have summarised are almost over-familiar to analysts.[4] But what has been inadequately commented upon is the type of answer which is being made by the analysts and their supporters to the critics. I ought in fairness to the reader to stress that I am going to try to set out the analytic case against the critics at its strongest. This is why I want to attend especially to arguments used by Dr. Brown and Dr. Edward Glover.

Begin with Brown's reply to the charge that experimental evidence does not bear out Freud's hypotheses:

> That two American psychologists should ask college students to
> recall at random pleasant and unpleasant experiences on the assumption
> that, if repression were a fact, more of the former than the latter
> would be recalled is bad enough; that, as Professor Eysenck assures
> us, a group of strong and presumably normal individuals were
> persuaded to starve themselves for an appreciable period in order
> to prove that Freud's theory of dreams as wish-fulfilments was false
> because they did not dream of food, strains one's credibility; but that
> an eminent educational psychologist should solemnly "prove" the
> Oedipus complex to be a myth by the simple expedient of asking
> a number of other professional psychologists about the preferences
> of their own children towards one parent or the other baffles
> comprehension. Freud at no time said that unpleasant experiences
> as such were likely to be forgotten; he said that experiences which might
> conflict with other dominant tendencies of the personality were likely
> to be repressed, whether as experiences they were pleasant or not;
> he did not say that for any appreciable period a child showed overt
> preference for the parent of the opposite sex, because the very word
> "complex" refers to *unconscious* attitudes which are unconscious

---

[4] See especially H. J. Eysenck, "What is Wrong with Psychoanalysis?" in *Uses and Abuses of Psychology* and B. A. Farrell, "Psychoanalytic Theory?" in *New Society*, June 20 and 27, 1963.

precisely because they are forbidden; he did not assert that hunger made one dream of food, although explorers and others subjected involuntarily to hunger have said that it did, and he would certainly have seen through the fallacy of supposing that voluntary and experimental subjection to starvation bears any resemblance in its emotional significance to the involuntary situation in which the basic issue is not primarily lack of food but imminent proximity of death.[5]

Let us concede at once the crudity of the experiments referred to; but even that crudity is a testimony to the difficulty of translating Freudian concepts into terms that will yield testable hypotheses. If the experimentalists have, as Brown accuses, mistranslated the concepts, the only adequate rejoinder would be to produce a correct translation and then await the verdict of experiment. But not only does Brown not do this, he does not even seem to admit the suggestion that there is a need for experiment. Yet until and unless such translations and experiments are provided the best available verdict on psycho-analytic theory would be that of "Not Proven." Nonetheless Brown claims that

> Freud alone amongst the founders of analytic schools understood
> and made thorough use of the scientific method in his investigations.
> Freud's approach was as logical and his findings as carefully tested as
> Pavlov's, but he was able to deal successfully with phenomena
> inaccessible to Pavlov. . . .

Yet throughout Brown's book what we are offered are confirmatory observations, not crucial tests of Freudian theory.

It is of course not only the opponents of analysis who have recognized the need for more enquiry at this point. Dr. Edward Glover has subjected both the lack of adequate definition of concepts and the absence of prediction and testing from psycho-analytic work to a critique as fierce as that of any experimentalist. But, so he has argued in two recent papers,[6] we should not therefore arrive at negative conclusions about psycho-analysis. For the carefully devised experiments of the ordinary descriptive psychologist are themselves suspect, since in the experimental study of variations in the behaviour of a particular group compared with a control group, we may ignore the possibility of unconscious factors affecting the behaviour of the chosen control, in such a way that the matching and comparison are unreliable.

From all this follows the somewhat disconcerting conclusion that under

[5] *Freud and The Post-Freudians*, pp. 192–3.
[6] "Psycho-analysis and 'Controlled' Research in Delinquency," *British Journal of Criminology* (1962) and "Research Techniques in Psycho-Analysis and in General Psychology," *Readings in Psychology* (ed. J. Cohen).

present systems of control we have no sound justification for abandoning a causal theory simply because the application of statistical controls appears to show that it is non-specific. When allegedly scientific procedures appear to point conclusively in one direction, the investigator of deep and unconscious factors should not be too perturbed if these conclusions run counter to his own interpretations. Although apparently wrong by the standards of natural science he may yet be right by the standards of depth psychology.

The difficulty with this argument lies in its covert circularity. We cannot trust present experimental techniques because their use neglects the operation of unconscious factors; the only techniques which would be reliable would therefore be those which took account of the operation of such factors. But to admit the existence of the kind of unconscious factors of which Dr. Glover speaks is already to concede substantial truth to the very body of theory which we require to be tested. Dr. Glover's criticism of the experimentalists pre-supposes that the issue which divides him from them has already been funda-mentally settled in his favour. Appearing to concede the need for neutral experiment, he in fact lays down preconditions for the construction of such experiments which ensure that his own positions will remain basically un-scathed. It is this that makes the onus of disproof which he lays upon the experimental critics so unreal.

The inescapable conclusion of this part of the argument is that psycho-analytic theory is in no sense well founded and that it is not science in any recognisable sense. But this is not just because it is inadequately vindicated by experiment. It is much more because, although it clearly is in fact not vindicated, it is presented by its adherents as though its truth were well established. Dr. Brown compares Freud to Newton; Dr. Glover says that "Freud was able to establish some of the most important laws regarding human behaviour"; Dr. Fine asserts that general psychology now accepts the core of Freud's work. Brown and Fine give the impression that the rejection of psycho-analysis is eccentric and restricted to an imperceptive minority. But Professor O. H. Mowrer, a central figure in the development of contempo-rary psychology, by any standards, decided in the end for "the basic un-soundness of Freud's major premises." This kind of conclusion the layman all too seldom has brought to his attention.

But it works, so it will be said. Surely, it will be added, it is unforgivable to have treated psycho-analysis primarily as a body of explanations rather than as a method of therapy. Yet the whole argument so far is intended, above all, to raise a question about the therapy. It has often been asserted that the therapy is ineffective; roughly speaking, such evidence as there is points to an insufficiently dissimilar rate of cure for patients who are not treated at all as for those who are treated by analysis. But the evidence is not very good and about it, once again, the important point is not that the claims of psychoanalysis have been overthrown, but that they have never been vindicated. Yet even this is not what is crucial. What matters is that the practice of the therapy presupposes the truth of the theory. The claim that what the patient acquires is genuine self-knowledge of a past still alive in his present can only be made good if the theoretical bridge between childhood and adult life does not break down. The authority of the analyst in his therapeutic role rests on his supposed theoretical equipment and backing as well as his clinical skills. Yet the theory which the therapy embodies is a theory in which neither analyst nor patient have a right to be confident. But without confidence the therapy could not even begin. So how is the confidence to be engendered? Only in unjustifiable ways.

The larger problem is the sociological one. False or unjustified assertions have been propagated in our time with the power of almost omnipotent states to back them up; beliefs now usually discredited but once plausible have often survived into our own age. But I know of no other example of a system of beliefs, unjustified on the basis of the criteria to which it itself appeals, and unbacked by political power or past tradition, which has propagated itself so successfully as Freudian orthodoxy. How did it do it?

Consider the following vocabulary: adjustment, conflict, integrate, relate, relationship. . . . It is the vocabulary of Jules Feiffer's characters. It is also the vocabulary of Feiffer's readers: the vocabulary of a segment of urban, middleclass intelligentsia whose cultural situation deprived them of large-scale theory at the same time as it made large-scale theory an intense necessity for them. The scepticism of an earlier generation had deprived them of religion. The history of their own time deprived them of Marxism and in so doing of their hold upon the public world of political ends. The intellectual may be socially valued for his functional utility; but otherwise his arena is increasingly that of private life. He needs to make his own experience intelligible: an image of the public world as a mere projection upon a larger screen of the private rages and longings, hopes and fears which circumscribe him. The intolerable character of his condemnation to private life is relieved by an overpersonalisation of that life. The ideology of personal relationships invokes a public sanction in the closed system of psycho-analytic theory. And a whole vocabulary of personal relationships enables psycho-analysis to appear, not as one more questionable theory, but as the unquestionable framework which gives life meaning.

Yet if this suggestion—which amounts to saying that psycho-analysis is the folk religion of one section of the intelligentsia—were not only true, but the whole truth, we should scarcely expect the series of encounters between psycho-analysis and the larger world of society, politics, and history, to be as fruitful as they have been. Two books published since 1958 furnish a record of such encounters. They are Bruno Bettelheim's *The Informed Heart*[7] and Erik H. Erikson's *Young Man Luther: A Study in Psycho-analysis and History*.[8] Both exhibit a certain ambivalence towards the orthodox psycho-analytic tradition. Both return us to Freud himself, but to a different Freud both from the Freud of orthodoxy and from the Freud of each other.

Bettelheim is at once the most striking and the most intelligently radical of Freudian revisionists. He is the most striking because his revisions began in Dachau and Buchenwald. He is intelligently radical in his clear statement of what must be rejected in Freud.

> What struck me first was . . . that those persons who according to
> psycho-analytic theory as I understood it then, should have stood
> up best under the rigour of the camp experience, were often very poor
> examples of human behaviour under extreme stress.

So he began to reflect on the nature of environment and on the apparent irrelevance of the explanation of types of behaviour in terms of their origin.

> It just would not do under conditions prevailing in the camps to view
> courageous, life-endangering actions as an outgrowth of the death
> instinct, aggression turned against the self, testing the indestructibility
> of the body, megalomaniac denial of danger, histrionic feeding of one's
> narcissism or whatever other category the action would have to be
> viewed from in psycho-analysis.

Not only the predictions, but also the values of psycho-analysis were put in question, and a common root was discerned for both errors. This root lay in the attention paid to the pathological, the lack of attention to the normal. Bettelheim stresses how psycho-analytic explanations of genius explain everything but the genius. Work, art, social life: all the normal ends of man evade being treated as the outcrops of infantile patterns.

When Bettelheim discusses his own experience in the camps in detail what is striking is the way in which psycho-analysts' concepts become less and less theoretical, more and more descriptive. The same is true of Erikson's work. Erikson—both in his earlier work, *Childhood and Society*, and in his study of Luther—uses not the Freudian system, but rather Freud's techniques of observation. He pays attention to the facts which Freud discovered rather than to the theoretical entities alleged to be lurking behind these facts. And he works empirically, generalising from instance to instance, and making modest predictions based on such generalisations. So he detects a pattern of

[7] Thames and Hudson (London), Free Press (Glencoe, Illinois, 1961).
[8] Faber & Faber (London) 1959, W. W. Norton (New York).

crises in the development of the child. He makes use of Freud's descriptions to illuminate these crises; but his theory of stages is derived not from the theory so much as from generalisations about the empirical material of a much more modest kind than are some of Freud's own larger statements. The historical material is in his hands not something to which a ready-made psycho-analytic theory is applied. The vindication of Erikson's statements about Luther lies in *the evidence* about Luther, not in the congruence with established psycho-analytic doctrine. In other words psycho-analysis need not become the self-enclosed system which it so often is. But how do we avoid this? What is the difference between Brown and Fine on the one hand and Bettelheim and Erikson on the other?

Part of the answer is surely obtained by considering the strain within Freud's own writings between observation and explanation, between the material he amasses and the theoretical forms into which he cast his presentation of that material. The comparison with Newton misled not only his expositors but Freud himself. What Freud showed us were hitherto unnoticed facts, hitherto unrevealed motives, hitherto unrelated facets of our life. And in doing so his achievement broke all preconceived conceptual schemes— including his own. As a discoverer he perhaps resembles a Proust or a Tolstoy rather than a Dalton or a Pasteur. We could have learnt this from reading Freud himself; but the division among his heirs also reveals the fact clearly.

Yet both sets of heirs are legitimate. The sterility and the perversity are as Freudian as the perceptive fertility of a Bettelheim or an Erikson. Freud, too, was a victim of the need to explain, of the need to be Newton. The paradox of the history of psycho-analysis is that it is those analysts most intent on presenting their subject as a theoretical science who have transformed it into a religion, those most concerned with actual religious phenomena, such as Bettelheim (who has written a monograph on initiation rites) and Erikson, who have preserved it as science. The achievement of Bettelheim and Erikson has been to extend our subjection to the phenomena themselves. But in so doing they have not diminished but increased its complexity.

The outcome of Freud's discoveries is to leave us not with a solution but with more problems, among them the problem of how to understand the analysts themselves, and the differences between them.

30. ON THE CIRCULARITY OF THE LAW OF EFFECT

Paul E. Meehl

In his recent review on "The History and Present Status of the Law of Effect," Postman (19) * lays considerable emphasis on the problem of "circularity" which he sees as crucial in the formulation of the law. He says:

> Whereas some critics were most concerned with the mechanisms meditating effect, others focussed their attention on the nature of the satisfiers and annoyers to which reference is made in Thorndike's law. Although Spencer and Bain, in whose tradition Thorndike continued, frankly invoked pleasure and pain as agents responsible for the fixation and elimination of responses, Thorndike's law has been a law of *effect*. not *affect*. He carefully defines satisfiers and annoyers in terms independent of subjective experience and report. "By a satisfying state of affairs is meant one which the animal does nothing to avoid, often doing such things as to attain and preserve it. By a discomforting state of affairs is meant one which the animal avoids and abandons." Although admittedly free of hedonism, such a definition of satisfiers and annoyers has faced another serious difficulty: the danger of circularity. The critic may easily reword the definition to read: "The animal does what it does because it does it, and it does not do what it does not to because it does not do it." This *reductio ad adsurdum*

SOURCE. Meehl, Paul E., "On the Circularity of the Law of Effect," *Psychological Bulletin*, 47, 1950. Reprinted with permission of American Psychological Association. Copyright © 1950 by American Psychological Association.

* Numbers in parenthesis refer to the bibliography at the end of this article.

is probably not entirely fair, but it points up the danger of the definition
in the absence of an *independent* determination of the nature of
satisfiers and annoyers. The satisfying or annoying nature of a state
of affairs can usually be determined fully only in the course of a learning
experiment and cannot then be invoked as a causal condition of learning
without circularity. In their experimental work Thorndike and his
associates have made no significant attempts to establish the satisfying
or annoying nature of their rewards and punishments independently
of the learning experiment (19, p. 496).

And a little later Postman says:

Stripped of virtually all defining properties and qualifications, the law
does indeed have a very wide range of applicability but only at the
expense of vagueness. The sum and substance of the argument now
is that something happens in the organism (nervous system) after an
act is performed. The fact that something happens influences further
action. This something is, however, so little defined that it has almost no
predictive efficiency. The O.K. reaction has no measurable properties,
the conditions for its occurrence are so general as to embrace almost
every conceivable situation. Hence the operation of O.K. reaction
can be inferred only *ex post facto*, after learning has taken place. But
here we are again impaled on the horns of the dilemma of circularity
(19, p. 497).

And still further:

In attempting to evaluate the controversy which has raged around the
definition of satisfiers one is struck by the key importance of the
hedonistic issue. Certainly hedonism is an immediate ancestor of the
law, and now that the principle of effect has reached an uneasy maturity
it is clear that it cannot deny its origin without sacrificing much of its
vigor. When the law is stripped of hedonistic implications, when effect
is not identified with tension-reduction or pleasure (as by Thorndike),
the law of effect can do no more than claim that the state of affairs
resulting from a response in some way influences future responses.
Such a statement is a truism and hardly lends itself to the rigorous
deduction of hypotheses and experimental tests. If a neohedonistic
position is frankly assumed (as, e.g., by Mowrer) the law becomes an
important tool for research, provided "satisfaction" is independently
defined and not merely inferred from the fact that learning has occurred
(19, p. 501).

Throughout Postman's paper this problem is constantly lurking behind the scenes even when the author does not single it out for specific mention. I am in complete agreement with Postman's final remark that "at the present state of our knowledge the law of effect as a monistic principle explaining all learning has not been substantiated," and Postman performs a service by emphasizing this problem of circularity in his discussion of the "law." I am inclined, however, to think that he has settled the question of circularity somewhat too easily, and that his settlement of it has an effect upon much of his argumentation. I gather from the above quotations that Postman looks upon any definition of effect or reinforcement in terms of the resulting change in response strength as "circular," where that word has a pejorative sense. If he is right in this it is very serious. While the law of effect has many difficulties, I do not believe that "circularity" is among them. To show this is the aim of the present paper.

I shall consider the problem of circularity in the law of effect as identical with the problem of circularity in the definition of *reinforcement* in instrumental conditioning. I take it that Postman does the same, since in the first quotation above he cites a passage from Hilgard and Marquis' *Conditioning and Learning*, where the two problems are considered together and with free interchange of the two terminologies. These authors say:

> It is apparent that no definition of effect provides an independent
> measure of the strength of reinforcement. The degree of satisfaction,
> of complacency, or of tension reduction has not been objectively
> determined. The strength of reinforcement can be given comprehensive
> definition only in terms of the amount of learning resulting from it. This
> is, of course, a circular definition, if strength of reinforcement is to be
> used as a factor determining degree of learning. A partial escape from
> circularity is achieved by the fact that a stimulus such as food which
> is found to be reinforcing in one situation will also be reinforcing
> in other situations, and with other animals (9, p. 83).

Writing in 1948, however, Hilgard states concerning Thorndike's "operational" definition of satisfiers and annoyers:

> These definitions are not circular, so far as the law of effect is
> concerned. That is, the states of affairs characterized as satisfying
> and annoying are specified independently of their influence upon
> modifiable connections. The law of effect then states what may be
> expected to happen to preceding modifiable connections which are
> followed by such specified states. The objection that Thorndike was
> lacking in objectivity in the statement of the law of effect is not a valid
> one (8, p. 24).

Hilgard is willing to let the concept of reinforcement (effect, satisfaction, reward) be introduced on the basis of behavior, but only because there are behavioral criteria of seeking and avoiding other than the effect of reinforcement upon *modifiable* connections. Whether this restriction is necessary needs to be considered carefully.

Skinner dismisses the whole problem in two sentences:

> A reinforcing stimulus is defined as such by its power to produce
> the resulting change. There is no circularity about this; some stimuli
> are found to produce the change, others not, and they are classified
> as reinforcing and nonreinforcing accordingly (22, p. 62).

Spence (23) takes essentially the same tack in his recent discussions of secondary reinforcement. The stimuli which impinge upon an organism may be divided, he says, into two classes: those which produce an increment in response strength, and those which do not. It seems from the several preceding quotations that there is a lack of agreement as to whether or not the law of effect or the principle of reinforcement involves an unavoidable circularity, or, if it does not, how circularity is to be avoided. In what follows, I make no claim to originality, since the essence of my development is contained in the previous quotations, together with the work of Tolman. But I feel it worthwhile to bring the arguments together in one context, and to show that the problem merits somewhat more extended treatment than is usually given it. Without claiming to present a definitive solution, I shall indicate the general direction which I believe the solution might take, and in the process introduce distinctions and terminological proposals which I feel might clarify our discussion and experimentation.

THE MEANING OF CIRCULARITY

It must be pointed out that there are two meanings of the word "circular" in common use. We have on the one hand circularity in *definition*, in which an unfamiliar term is defined by using other terms which are (directly or ultimately) defined by the term in question. There is no question of circularity in this sense in a definition of the Skinner-Spence type. Let us accept as a crude preliminary formulation the following: "A reinforcing stimulus is one which increases the subsequent strength of responses which immediately precede it." The words *stimulus*,[1] *strength*, *increase* and *response* are all definable without any reference to the fact or theory of reinforcement. The definitions of these terms, particularly the term "response," present terrible difficulties; but I do not know of anyone who maintains that they involve the

---

[1] "Stimulus" will be used broadly to include "stimulus change," and stimulus configurations of all degrees of patterning and complexity.

notion of reinforcement. Words such as these are current in the vocabulary of many kinds of psychological theorists who do not accept the Law of Effect as a principle of learning and in the absence of any indications to the contrary, I shall assume that we can tell what we mean by them. We can determine empirically when the strength of a response has increased without knowing anything about reinforcing stimuli, drives, satisfactions, and the like. It seems clear that the definition of a reinforcing stimulus in terms of its effect on response strength does not involve circularity in *this* sense.

The other meaning of the word circularity refers not to meanings (definition of terms) but to the establishment of propositions. We speak of *proofs* as being circular if it can be shown that in the process of establishing (proving) a proposition we have made use of the probandum. I am not aware that any responsible theorist has attempted to "prove" the Law of Effect in this way. It is true that those who look upon the law as fundamental are skeptical when they hear of a case of increase of response strength which does not *seem* to involve any obvious reinforcing consequences so that they begin to invent hypotheses to explain the results. There is no harm in this so long as the proposed explanations are in principle confirmable on the basis of some other experimental consequences, however remote. If an animal learns a response sequence without being given food, water, or any of the usual rewards, I suspect most Hullians would begin to talk about secondary reinforcement present in the situation. One can, of course, be careless with this kind of explanation, but there is nothing intrinsic to the concept that entails non-confirmability. The establishment of secondary reinforcing effects as explanations of a given experimental result consists in combining the facts known about primary reinforcers with facts about the animal's life history, in terms of which we understand how certain stimuli have acquired their secondary reinforcing powers. People on both sides of the present controversy over reinforcement theory, are performing many different sorts of experiments in order to confirm or disconfirm the Law of Effect. It would seem that if the law of effect *were* being treated by anyone as a consequence of definition, or established by some hidden assumption of its truth, the experiments would not be going on.

CAN "REINFORCEMENT" BE INDEPENDENTLY DEFINED?

Nonetheless, when we think about this definition we feel uncomfortable. I do not think we have in mind either a circularity in definition or a begging-the-question fallacy, but some sort of peculiar pseudo-circularity in which it seems to us vaguely that the law *could* be "derived" from the proposed definition, even though no one in fact seems to be trying to do it this way. The problem can be stated very simply: How can we introduce the concept of reinforcement in terms of effect upon strength, and still have a "law of effect" or "principle of reinforcement" which has the empirical content that everybody seems to be taking for granted in experimentation?

1. Suppose we reject the Thorndike-Skinner-Spence procedure of defining reinforcement in terms of response strength, and decide to define the term quite independently of the learning process. The first possibility, which we shall dismiss rather dogmatically, is to do it subjectivistically in terms of pleasure, experiences of satisfaction, and the like. Aside from the general behavioristic objections, and the specific problems of measurement created, this approach is not feasible because it leaves us without any basis for speaking of reinforcing value in the case of that very important class of motivations that are unconscious or at least inadequately verbalized in the human case; and it makes impossible the establishment of reinforcing value in the case of lower organisms. At the present time there are probably very few psychologists who would consider this alternative seriously.

2. Secondly, we might try to define reinforcers in terms of certain physical properties on the stimulus side. I shall attempt to show below that this is a procedure which *follows* the introduction of the generic notion of a reinforcer, and which at a later stage becomes very important. But no one wants to group together an arbitrary class of physical objects or stimuli and call them "reinforcers," since the aim of our concept formation is to make possible the statement of laws. The possibility of identifying common physical properties of that large class of stimuli already grouped together as "rewarding" seems very remote. Besides, we would set up these properties or sets of properties by examining the members of the reinforcing class, which we already have set apart on some basis or other; and the question is: How have we arrived at the members of that class?

3. A third possibility, seen in the work of Hull, is to define reinforcement ultimately in terms of drive reduction, that is, in terms of the inner physiological events involved. Here again, I do not suppose that anyone would be able to give even the vaguest specification of the defining property of all neural events which are reinforcing. Even for the so-called primary physiological needs such as hunger, the evidence as to their exact physiological basis is most incomplete. No psychologist today is willing to equate "hunger" with "stomach contractions," in the light of the experimentation on visceral denervations, specific sub-hungers, and the like. In other cases, we have practically no information on the neurophysiology, e.g., the neurophysiologic basis of the reinforcing effect of the presence of another organism, the turning off of a light in the Skinner box, or the going through of "exploratory" behavior on

the other side of a grill. There is some reason to suppose that certain stimuli retain their secondary reinforcing value in the absence of the primary drive (2, 16), which complicates the problem further.

These considerations force a return to the *effect* of stimuli as a basis for specifying that they are reinforcers, and this leads to the paradox. If we define a reinforcing agent by its effect upon learning, then it seems that whenever learning is effected, we know ("by definition") that we have given a reinforcement. For surely, when the organism behaves, some stimulus change occurs, if nothing else than the proprioceptive effects of responding. If the behavior increases in strength, then these stimulus changes, which were in fact preceded by the response, are reinforcers. Hence, it seems that a definition of reinforcement in terms of an increase of habit strength makes the law tautological and devoid of factual content. This train of thought, which I am sure is familiar to most readers, seems obvious and straightforward. But I believe it can be shown to be mistaken, once the law is stated *explicitly* in the way we all really think of it *implicitly* when we perform experiments or try to explain a given case of learning.

AN EMPIRICAL DERIVATION OF REINFORCEMENT

Let us begin afresh by going to the behavior itself in a situation in which there is little or no disagreement as to what occurs. Consider a bright, inductively inclined Martian, who had never experienced any needs or satisfactions (except perhaps *n Cognizance!*) and who was observing the behavior of a rat in successive runnings in a T-maze. For the moment we shall simply consider a "standard rat," neglecting the individual differences in parameters and the accidents of personal histories that generate special secondary reinforcing properties. These refinements need to be added later, but as is usually the case will have to be added by being integrated into the whole structure of reinforcement theory, since we cannot treat everything at once. At the begining, the Martian observes that the organism turns to the right or left with, let us say, about equal frequency. With further trials, a change occurs until finally the rat is responding close to 100% of the time by turning to the right. A Martian could obviously discover this with no notion of rewards, pleasure and the like. If he is ingenious enough to think of the possibility that the strength of a response might be influenced by the events that follow it in time, he would then proceed to investigate the changes that are contingent on this right turning.[2] He notes that when the rat turns to the right he brings about

---

[2] Actually, no great ingenuity is involved here. Study of the events immediately *preceding* a run, e.g., the manner in which the experimenter handles the rat, what orientation he gives its head in placing it in the entry box, etc., would fail to reveal any

the following states of affairs on the stimulus side which he does not bring about when he turns to the left: He ends up nearer to the right-hand wall, which is painted green; he twists his own body to the right in responding; he ends up in a wooden box having knots in the wood; he ends up nearer the North pole; and to a dynamo on the other side of the campus; and he comes into the presence of a cup of sunflower seeds. These are the stimuli (stimulus changes) which are contingent on right turns. Is it possible that the gradual strengthening of the right turning is dependent upon one, some, or all of these changes following it? Our scientist from Mars would proceed to study a series of standard rats in the situation, altering the above variables systematically by usual inductive procedures. As a matter of empirical fact, he would discover that, within certain very wide limits, alterations in the first five have no effect. The sixth, the sunflower seeds, have a tremendous effect. He finds that he can alter the geographical direction, the direction of the body twist required, the wall color approached, etc.—that he can introduce all manner of modifications in the other factors; and so long as the sunflower seeds are presented, the rat will tend to go to where they are. On the other hand, if the sunflower seeds are omitted, and nothing else put in their place, a preference fails to develop as a function of these remaining differences.

But we have already greatly over-simplified. Actually, the Martian would discover that the effect of finding sunflower seeds in some cases is almost too slight to be detected; furthermore, even after a preference has been acquired, it may on some occasions fail to show itself. Now, it has already been apparent that when he comes upon these sunflower seeds, the rat behaves toward them in a characteristic way, that is, he ingests them. In seeking to understand the variability in the development and manifestation of a preference, one would notice a correlation between the strengthening of a preference and the rate, strength, and consistency of ingestive responses in the presence of the food. Identifying the same rat on successive days, it is found that on those days on which a preference already established broke down, very frequently the ingestive response in the presence of the sunflower seeds was at a very low or even zero strength. Failing to find anything varying in the maze situation itself to account for these differences, one can study the experiences of the animals between runs. Here appears a very striking correlate of both preference strength *and* the ingestive response in the maze: that which a human experimenter would call the "feeding schedule." The Martian would observe that when sunflower seeds were made available to the rats in their cages, they behave with respect to them in the same way as they do when they come upon

systematic factor related to the direction of a preference. Considering this, together with the fact that before any runs have been made no preference exists, the Martian would be led to ask whether it is something that happens *after* the run (or during it) that affects the probability of a similar choice in subsequent runs.

the sunflower seeds in the goal box: namely, with ingestive responses. He would discover, again by systematic variation in these conditions, that such matters as the chemical nature of the substance made available, the periodicity of its availability, the lapse of time between when it was last available and the maze run; the rate of ingestion manifested at the moment of beginning deprivation (i.e., how close the rat was to satiety when interrupted), and so on, all exert an effect upon the maze response. By far the most intimate correlate would be the lapse of time since feeding. To quote Skinner again.

> The problem of drive arises because much of the behavior of an organism shows an apparent variability. A rat does not always respond to food placed before it, and a factor called its "hunger" is invoked by way of explanation. The rat is said to eat only when it is hungry. It is because eating is not inevitable that we are led to hypothesize the internal state to which we may assign the variability. Where there is no variability, no state is needed. . . . In dealing with the kind of behavior that gives rise to the concept of hunger, we are concerned with the strength of a certain class of reflexes and with the two principal operations that affect it—feeding and fasting (22, pp. 341, 343).

For a considerable class of stimuli found to affect choice behavior in the maze, there is a fairly well demarcated class of events in the extramaze activities which exert an effect. Food, water, a female rat, all depend for their efficacy upon a deprivation schedule of some sort. For other stimuli, the rest of the day's activities seem of less relevance. For example, the effects of turning off a light in the Skinner box upon the lever pressing response would not depend upon a schedule of extra box illumination in any such obvious way as the effects of a food pellet depend upon the extra maze operations of feeding and fasting. Even here, at the extremes, it is likely that the schedule has some effect. Although I know of no experimental material on the point, it would be surprising if rats raised and maintained in a dark or extremely bright living cage would show the same response to light-off as a reinforcing agent. In order to keep the discussion quite general, I shall refer to *schedule-reinforcer* combinations, which will be understood to include those combinations in which almost any life-maintaining schedule is adequate. Whether there are any such does not need to be settled here. The stimulus presented is a *reinforcer*, and the presentation of it (an "event") is a *reinforcement*.

We are now in possession of a rather simple set of empirical facts. A certain stimulus, for a rat which has been under a specified schedule, for instance the sunflower seeds for a rat who has not ingested anything for 23 hours, will exert a strengthening effect. We can formulate a "law" stated crudely as follows: "In a rat which has not recently ingested sunflower seeds, bran mash, Purina chow, etc., a response of turning in a given direction in the

T-maze will be increased if the fairly immediate presentation of sunflower seeds, etc., is made contingent upon that response." Similarly, we would find such a specific law to hold for thirst and water, sex and a mate, and so on. The general form of such special laws would be: "On schedule M, the termination of response sequence R, in setting S, by stimulus S^1 is followed by an increment in the strength of S.R." Such a law may be called a *situational-reinforcement* law, where the "reinforcement" is understood to stand for "presentation-of-a-reinforcer-following-a-specified-maintenance-schedule," and the term "situational" covers "response R in situation S."

Actually, in any given case, M, R, S, S^1 are classes. This is indicated by the suspicious-looking "etc." in the first "law" above. There is nothing shady about this "etc.," inasmuch as what is actually involved here is a class of operations and effects which are ultimately to be specified by locating each instance with respect to a whole complex set of dimensions. For example, Guttman (6) shows a relation between concentration of sugar solution used as a reinforcing agent and the strength of the lever pressing response. Heron and Peake (7) have studied protein as a specific component of reinforcement. There is to be discovered a vast number of such rather special laws which are comparable to the myriads of laws in chemistry concerning the solubility of substance Y in substance X and the like.

The next thing to notice is that while the schedule, reinforcement, response, and situation are all classes showing certain relations to one another, in general the schedule and reinforcer are related to one another more intimately than either is to the situation or response. The strength of a response which is maintained by food reinforcement is heavily dependent upon the feeding-fasting schedule, whereas the effect of a food reinforcement upon a response is relatively independent of, say recency of copulatory activity, so that a given schedule-reinforcement pair are "tied" to one another. But the Martian observes that the strengthening effect of a given schedule-reinforcement combination is relatively (not wholly!) neutral with respect to the response we are trying to strengthen and the situation in which we are trying to strengthen it. For a hungry rat, right turning depends heavily upon finding food; for a satiated rat, it depends very little. So the feeding schedule is intimately related to the reinforcing agent's efficacy. However, this "hungry-food" schedule-reinforcement combination seems to be capable of strengthening chain-pulling, lever-pressing, wheel-turning, marble-rolling, gnawing-through-paper, and so on through a very wire range of behaviors differing greatly in their topography and in their stimulus conditions. This leads to the question, will a certain schedule-reinforcer combination increase the strength of *any* response, in *any* setting?" This question turns out empirically to be answered in the negative, since we find at least three limitations upon the generality of a schedule-reinforcer combination as response strengthener. Leaving out the trivial case in which the response is anatomically impossible, e.g., to teach an elephant to thread a needle, we find:

1. No situation-response sequences may involve stimulus dimensions which are not discriminable by the organism. (Tolman's "discriminating capacities").

2. Some response sequences seem on the basis of their sequence, timing, or "complexity" not to be learnable by members of a given species, or subgroups within a species. It appears impossible to teach a rat a quintuple alternation problem, or to teach a human moron integral calculus.

3. There are cases in which the response we wish to strengthen is incompatible with responses at a very high (and relatively unmodifiable) strength under the schedule-stimulus combinations we are employing. For example, it would probably be next to impossible to teach a very hungry cat to carry a piece of fresh liver across the room, deposit it in a box, and return to receive food as a reinforcement. "Defensive" and "anxiety-related" responses are among the most important examples of this case.

How do we discover what responses have these characteristics? Experimentally, as we discover anything else. Let us call a situation-response combination having none of these properties *learnable*. A positive definition will be given below. What we find is that whereas learnable responses seem to differ somewhat in their "readiness" under different schedule-reinforcement combinations, this is a matter of parameters and does not invalidate the following tentative "law," which is stated qualitatively: "Any learnable response will be strengthened by sunflower seeds as a reinforcer." The general form of such a law is "the stimulus S^1 on schedule M will increase the strength of any learnable response." I shall call such a law a *trans-situational reinforcement* law. It must be noted carefully that such a law is still about a *particular* reinforcing agent, having, to be sure, a class character; but the particular reinforcing agent (and its associated necessary schedule, if any) is no longer tied to the response sequence first studied. The reinforcing property of sunflower seeds was noted first in the T-maze. The Martian will discover that white rats *can* learn to pull chains, press levers, and roll marbles. He finds that these learnable responses can also be strengthened by making the feeding of sunflower seeds contingent upon them. He makes the inductive generalization that sunflower seeds would exert this effect upon all learnable responses in the rat.

He now asks the obvious question: Are all schedule-reinforcer combinations like this? That is to say, when we study a new schedule-reinforcer combination and find it strengthens a response, can we assume that it will increase the strength of all learnable responses? Naturally, our confidence in the general reinforcing power of any particular one will increase as we try it out on more and more learnable responses. But we do not know whether a higher-order inductive statement is justified, so long as we study sunflower seeds only or study several kinds of agents but in only one situation each.

Having found a particular reinforcer in a particular situation, we have discovered that it is trans-situational. Next we discover that all of the reinforcers that we have investigated have turned out to be trans-situational. The next induction is, "If a learnable response is followed by a stimulus which is known to be a reinforcer of learnable responses the strength will increase." A shorter way of saying this, having first defined a reinforcer as "a stimulus which will increase the strength of at least one learnable response," is simply: *all reinforcers are trans-situational.* Nothing is said as to the *amount* of strengthing. It is sufficient, in order to demonstrate the trans-situational character of a reinforcing agent, to show that it produces an increment in strength. If equal increments were required, it is probable that very few (if any) reinforcers would be trans-situational because of the varying behavior readinesses and different parameters of habit acquisitions from one drive to another and from one situation to another.

This assertion, that all reinforcers are trans-situational, I propose to call the *Weak Law of Effect.* It is not our problem in this paper to discuss whether the Weak Law of Effect holds or not. A "proof" of the Weak Law of Effect consists, as usual, of establishing inductively many instances of it in a variety of situations with our confidence increasing on the basis of the usual inductive canons. A "disproof" of the Weak Law of Effect would involve showing that a certain stimulus change acts as a reinforcing agent for one response, i.e., that the presentation of this stimulus following the response will increase the latter's strength; but that another response, previously established as learnable, cannot be strengthened by a presentation of this agent. A failure of the Weak Law of Effect to hold strictly would not be particularly serious, since one could (at the very least!) specify the exceptions and would hope to be able to generalize about them, that is, to discover empirically what are the kinds of reinforcers, or kinds of differences among situations, which reveal its invalidity. Actually, here again we have a case in which the law is stated in a qualitative all-or-none form; but the development of a science of behavior would eventually result in substituting a multiplicity of laws indicating the extent to which the reinforcing (strengthening) property generalized over various dimensions of the stimulus side, the reinforcing agent, and the "required" response properties. Assuming the Weak Law of Effect to have been established inductively, where are we now in our development? We have specific situation-reinforcer laws which state that a given stimulus is a reinforcing agent for a specified kind of response in a specified situation. As an example, we discover that for a standard rat, sunflower seeds will strengthen right turning in the T-maze. Having established several such specific situation-reinforcer laws, we find it convenient to introduce a definition, saying that a situational reinforcer is a stimulus which occurs as a term in such a specific situation-reinforcer law. Sunflower seeds are hence situational reinforcers. This definition is "arbitrary" or "conventional" in the usual sense, but clearly leads to no circularity. We cannot tell from the definition whether or not there is such a thing as a situational reinforcer, just as we cannot tell from the definition of a unicorn or of the phrase "King of France" whether such a thing exists. All we stipulate in the definition is that if a thing having certain properties turns out to exist, we will call it by this name. That there are situational reinforcers, that is to say, that we can find stimuli that do increase the strength of responses in a certain situation, is an empirical result. It is obvious that the specific situation-reinforcer laws have a perfectly good factual content (e.g., each such law could be false) in spite of the conventional character of the definition.

If our science contained nothing but a collection of such situational-reinforcer laws, we would still be in possession of valuable information. But we discover inductively that we can actually say more than this. For any given reinforcer, we discover that it can in fact be used to increase the strength of responses differing very greatly in topography from the one which originally led us to infer that it was a reinforcer, and in very different stimulating fields. It is true that there are a few special cases, as our cat with the liver, in which we cannot increase the strength of a *kind* of a response (carrying an object from one place to another) which we know from independent study this species is able to learn. But in all such cases we are able to specify an interfering response at such high strength that the behavior in question does not get a chance to be emitted, and hence cannot be reinforced. With this exception, we are able to say that a given reinforcer will increase the strength of all learnable responses of the species; although there will be quantitative differences which remain to be discovered and generalized about after much painstaking experimentation. We define a reinforcer which is of this sort as trans-situational, and from a study of numerous reinforcers we conclude that they are all of this type. The second order induction that all reinforcers are trans-situational (the Weak Law of Effect) is then made.

This last is certainly a very rich and powerful induction. It is true that to make predictions we must study at least one learnable response in order to find out whether a given stimulus change is reinforcing, and we must know for any contemplated response whether it is learnable. Experience with a given species need not be too extensive in ordr to get a general idea of the kinds of behavior which are possible and learnable; and once having this, we proceed to strengthen responses by means of reinforcing agents which have never been utilized before in connection with these responses. This is so commonplace that we are likely to underestimate its theoretical significance. So far as I know, no animal psychologist has the least hesitation in utilizing any of a very large class of reinforcing objects called "food" in experimentation upon practically any kind of behavior which he is interested in studying. Should he find a failure of response strength to increase, the chances of his asking what is wrong with the food are negligible. His inductive confidence in the Weak Law of Effect is such that he will immediately begin to investigate what is wrong with the stimulus field, or what requirements concerning the response properties he has imposed which transcend the powers of the organism. I am stressing this point because there is a tendency to say that since we have to study the effects upon strength in order to know whether an agent is reinforcing, we do not really "know anything" when we have enunciated the Law of Effect. I think it should be obvious from the diversity of both the class called learnable and the class of agents called reinforcing that to the extent that this law holds almost without exception, when we have enunciated it we have said a great deal.

The man from Mars might be tempted here to take a final step which would be suggested by the ubiquity of the manifestations of the Weak Law of Effect. It might occur to him that the great majority of the instances in which changes in response strength occur seem to involve the operation of the Weak Law, i.e., the presentation of a member of the reinforcing class. Perhaps it is not only true that any learnable response can be strengthened by the presentation of a trans-situational reinforcer but may it not be that this is the *only* way to increase the strength of responses (by learning)? Response strength may be increased by surgical and drug procedures, and also by maturation; but the demarcation of learning as a very general mode of response change, while it presents difficult problems, need not concern us here. Assuming that we have some satisfactory basis for distinguishing an increase in the strength which is based upon "experience" rather than upon interference with the reaction mechanism or biological growth determined by genetic factors given minimal (viable) environments, we may ask whether learning takes place on any *other* basis than the Weak Law of Effect. Certain apparent exceptions to this statement of reinforcement as a necessary condition would appear, but the Martian might ask whether these exceptions are more apparent than real. The formulation of such a law would run something like this: "Every learned increment in response strength requires the operation of a trans-situational reinforcer." I shall designate this rash inductive leap as the *Strong Law of Effect*.

It appears obvious that this also is a statement far from being experimentally empty or in any sense a consequence of definition. I have heard psychologists translate the statement "he learns because he was reinforced" as being tantamount to "he learns because he learns." Postman suggests the same kind of thing in the first quotation above. This is too easy. The expanded form which I suspect everyone has implicitly in mind when he talks about the Strong Law of Effect is: "He learns following the presentation of a stimulus change which for this species has the property of increasing response strength; and, other things being equal in the present setting, if this change had *not* occurred he would not have learned." Such a statement can clearly be false to fact, either because no such trans-situational reinforcer can be shown to have been present, or because the same learning can be shown to be producible without it in the present setting. The claim of the reinforcement theorist to explanation is (at this stage of our knowledge) of exactly the same character as "he developed these symptoms because he was invaded by the Koch bacillus, and we know that the Koch bacillus has these effects." This is not a very *detailed* explanation, because the intermediate or micro-details of the causal sequence are not given; but it is certainly neither factually empty nor trivial.

In our initial quotation from Postman, we find him saying, "The satisfying or annoying nature of a state of affaris can usually be determined fully only in the course of a learning experiment and cannot then be invoked as a causal condition of learning without circularity." The trouble with this remark lies in the ambiguity of the phrase "*a* learning experiment." That we cannot know what is reinforcing without having done *some* experimentation is obvious, and is just as it should be in an empirical science. But once having found that a certain state of affairs *is* reinforcing for a given species, there is no reason why a given case of learning cannot be explained by invoking the occurrence of this state of affairs as a causal condition. The definition of force does not entail the truth of Hooke's law. It is only by an experiment that we find out that strain is proportional to stress. Once having found it out, we are all quite comfortable in utilizing Hooke's law to account for the particular cases we come across. I am confident that Postman would not be disturbed if in answer to the question, "Why does that door close all the time?" someone were to reply, "Because it has a spring attached to it on the other side." There is no more "circularity" in this kind of causal accounting than in any other kind. It is perfectly true that this kind of "lowest-order" explanation is not very intellectually satisfying in some cases, although even here there is a considerable variability depending upon our familiarity with the situation. For a detailed consideration of these problems by more qualified persons I refer the reader to papers by Hospers (10), Feigl (4, 5), and Pratt (20).

I think it is obvious that this is the way we think of the Law of Effect, whatever we may think as to its truth. When an apparent case of learning in the absence of reinforcement occurs, those who are interested in preserving the status of the Law of Effect (in my terminology, in preserving the status of the *Strong* Law of Effect) begin to search for changes following the response which can be shown to be of the reinforcing sort. They do not simply look for *any* stimulus change and insist ("by definition") that it is a rein-forcement. The statement that a given case of apparently non-reinforcement learning is actually based upon secondary reinforcement is essentially a claim that some stimulus change can be shown to have followed the strengthened response, and that this stimulus change has (still earlier) been put in temporal contiguity with a stimulus change of which we know, from a *diversity* of situations, that it exerts a reinforcing effect.

Abandoning the charge of circularity, a critic might offer a "practical" criticism, saying, "What good does it do to know that a reinforcer strengthens, when the only way to tell when something is a reinforcer is to see if it strength-ens?" The trouble here lies in the vagueness, since the *generality* is not in-dicated, and this failure to indicate generality neglects the usual advantages of induction. That a describable state of affairs *is* reinforcing can only be found out, to be sure, by experimenting on some organisms utilizing *some* learnable response. But it is not required (if the Weak Law of Effect is true) that we, so to speak, start afresh with each new organism of the species and each new response. As a matter of fact, after we have considerable experience with a given species, we can generalize about the physical properties of a stimulus class. So that finally "food" means many substances which may never yet have been tried in a learning situation, and may never have been presented in natural circumstances to the members of a particular species. Wild rats do not eat Purina Chow. Here we begin to approach inductively one of the pre-viously rejected bases of defining reinforcement, namely, the physical char-acter of the stimulus change itself. To ask for a definition of reinforcers which will tell us beforehand for a given species which objects or stimuli will exert the reinforcing effect is to ask that a definition should tell us what the world is like before we investigate it, which is not possible in any science. It happens that the psychologist is worse off than others, because species differences, in-dividual hereditary differences, and differences of the reactional biography make a larger mass of facts necessary in order to know whether a given agent will reinforce a particular organism. But at worst the Weak Law of Effect in conjunction with its member laws is far from useless. When I know inductively that all non-toxic substances containing sugar will act as reinforcers for organisms from rat to man and therefore that I can almost certainly strengthen all responses learnable by any of these species on the basis of the presentation of any of these substances, I know a great deal and my science has a very considerable predictive power.

AN ANALOGOUS PROBLEM IN PHYSICS

It is instructive to consider a somewhat analogous problem in physics, in the definition of "force." Once mass has been defined by some such artifice as Mach's acceleration-ratio technique, and acceleration defined in terms of time and distance, Newton's second law is a *definition* of force. I neglect here other attempts to introduce the notion such as the "school of the thread" (18), utilizing Hooke's law in the form of a definition rather than a law, or its modern variants, e.g., Keenan's (13) recent effort. Force is "that which accelerates mass." Mach's introduction of the concept of mass was somewhat disturbing to certain of his contemporaries because of a suggested circularity. Mach saw that it was the *inertial* character of mass, rather than "weight" or "quantity of matter" which was crucial in setting up the definition of force. Accordingly, he proceeds as follows:

a. *Experimental Proposition.* Bodies set opposite each other induce in each other, under certain circumstances to be specified by experimental physics, contrary *accelerations* in the direction of their line of junction. (The principle of inertia is included in this.)

b. *Definition.* The mass-ratio of any two bodies is the negative inverse ratio of the mutually induced accelerations of those bodies.

c. *Experimental Proposition.* The mass-ratios of bodies are independent of the character of the physical states (of the bodies) that condition the mutual accelerations produced, be those states electrical, magnetic, or what not; and they remain, moreover, the same, whether they are mediately or immediately arrived at.

d. *Experimental Proposition.* The accelerations which any number of bodies A, B, C. . . . induce in a body K, are independent of each other. (The principle of the parallelogram of forces follows immediately from this.)

e. *Definition.* Moving force is the product of the mass-value of a body into the acceleration induced in that body. Then the remaining arbitrary definitions of the algebraical expressions "momentum," "vis viva," and the like, might follow. But these are by no means indispensable. The propositions above set forth satisfy the requirements of simplicity and parsimony which on economico-scientific grounds, must be exacted of them. They are, moreover, obvious and clear; for no doubt can exist with respect to any one of them either concerning its meaning or its source; and we always know whether it asserts an experience or an arbitrary convention (17, pp. 243–244).

In the appendix to the second English edition, Mach replies to critics of this procedure as follows:

A special difficulty seems to be still found in accepting my definition of mass. Streintz has remarked in criticism of it that it is based solely upon gravity, although this was expressly excluded in my first formulation of the definition (1868). Nevertheless, this criticism is again and again put forward, and quite recently even by Volkmann. My definition simply takes note of the fact that bodies in mutual relationship, whether it be that of action at a distance, so called, or whether rigid or elastic connexions be considered, determine in one another changes of velocity (accelerations). More than this, one does not need to know in order to be able to form a definition with perfect assurance and without the fear of building on sand. It is not correct as Höfler asserts, that this definition tacitly assumes *one and the same force* acting on both masses. It does not assume even the notion of force, since the latter is built up subsequently upon the notion of mass, and gives then the principle of action and reaction quite independently and without falling into Newton's logical error. In this arrangement one concept is not misplaced and made to rest on another which threatens to give way under it (17, pp. 558–559).

It is obvious that Mach defines mass in the way he does *so that* the definition of force by $F = ma$ will lead to the kinds of laws we want. That is, a previous "knowledge" of the law of gravity based upon a cruder notion of mass is involved historically in the formulation of such a definition. But the crucial point is that it is involved only in the context of discovery, not in the context of justification (21, pp. 6–7). There is nothing wrong with making use of any notions, including vague anthropomorphic experiences of pleasure, in deciding how we shall formulate definitions, since our aim is to erect concepts and constructs which will fit into the most convenient and powerful system of laws. The point is that we wish to come out with explicit notions that are free of this vagueness and which do not require any notions which cannot be finally introduced objectively. There is probably a remnant of hedonism in the thinking of the most sophisticated contemporary reinforcement theorists, and there is no reason why anybody should pretend that when he talks about rewards he does not have some faint component in his thinking which involves the projection of such pleasure-pain experiences. But this does not mean that these notions are made part of the scientific structure he erects, in the sense that either the definitions of terms or the establishment of the laws requires such associated imagery in his readers. I suggest that Thorndike's critics are in the same position as Mach's.

One might ask, why would a physicist be upset should he attend a spiritualist seance and find tumblers leaping off tables and floating through the air? If the concept of force is given simply by the relation $F = ma$, then, if a glass tumbler undergoes an acceleration, a force must act and his definition assures him that the physical world will not surprise him. I do not think the answer to this question is far to seek. While it is admittedly a question of decision, I doubt that most physicists would decide to say that an acceleration occurred in the absence of a force. If the genuineness of the phenomenon were satisfactorily established, I do not think there would be a re-definition of the *concept* of force, but rather that the existence of "forces" on other bases than those previously known would be assumed. That is, the physicist would not say "here is a case of acceleration without a force," but he would rather say "here is a case of force not arising from the usual mechanical, gravitational, or electro-magnetic situations which I have thought, up to now, were the sole bases on which forces came into being." It is certainly no criticism of a Newtonian definition of force (I leave out the fact that Newton, while he defined force in this way, apparently also treated his second law as one of empirical content) to say that having thus defined force you cannot know beforehand what are the conditions in the world under which forces will appear. The mechanical forces involved in direct contact, the force of gravity, and certain electrostatic and magnetic forces were known to Newton. There is nothing about his definition of force which tells us that a peculiarly directed force will exist between a wire carrying an electric current and a compass needle, nor that attracting or repelling forces will exist between parallel wires each of which carries a current. The discovery of these conditions under which forces exist was an empirical contribution of Oersted and Ampere.

Similarly, the psychologist defines what is meant by a reinforcer, and proceeds to search for the agents that fall under this definition. There are undoubtedly kinds of stimulus changes of which we are as yet unaware which will turn out to have the reinforcing property. Dr. Wilse Webb (personal communication) has found in preliminary experiments that at least in one kind of Skinner box the click produced by the operation of an empty magazine will exert a reinforcing effect in an animal whose experience has never given this stimulus an opportunity to acquire secondary reinforcing properties. This is surprising to us. What are the conditions under which this will occur? Suppose it should be found that almost *any* stimulus change within a fairly wide range (avoiding extreme intensities which are anxiety-producing) would exert a slight reinforcing effect in the Skinner box or in any similar apparatus in which there is a considerable stimulus restriction and a marked constancy in the homogeneity of the visual and auditory fields. It might be discovered that when a member of this species has remained in such a homogeneous field for a period of time, stimulus *changes* (not otherwise specified) exert a reinforcing effect. Maybe the rat is "bored" and just likes to make something happen! A difficult notion to nail down experimentally, to be sure. But its complexity and the number of things to be ruled out, does not take it out of the realm of the confirmable.

Let us consider a very extreme case. Suppose in the T-maze situation a systematic increase in the strength of the right turn should be discovered for a standard rat. Suppose that the most thoroughgoing exhaustive manipulation of the external effect of right-turning should fail to reveal any condition necessary for the effect. "No member of the reinforcing class is to be found." I think that at this point we would begin reluctantly to consider a reinforcing property of the response itself. Perhaps turning to the right is inherently reinforcing to this species. It seems, for instance, that "fetching" behavior in certain species of dogs is self-reinforcing (or at least that it has a biologically replenished reserve). The only reason for calling right-turning "self-reinforcing" rather than simply saying that it is a response of innately high strength in the species is that a *change* in strength occurs with successive runs, otherwise "turning to the right" is simply a kind of tropism. Is the "self-reinforcing" idea factually empty? Although many people would disagree with me at this point, I do not think it is. But it has factual meaning only intradermally. There is no reason why we could not study the proprioceptive effects of a right turn and find out whether, if they are cut out, the increase in response strength continues to occur. In principle we could create the proprioceptive effects of a right turn by artificial means and on that basis strengthen a topographically different response such as lifting the fore paw, wiggling the whiskers, or the like. Here there are difficulties, but I would be prepared to argue that in principle the self-reinforcing effect of right-turning is an empirically meaningful notion.

An interesting side-light is that even the Strong Law of Effect is, as stated, compatible with the latent learning experiments. I am not interested in avoiding the consequences of those experiments by shrewd dialectics, but in the interests of clarity it should be pointed out that in, e.g., the Blodgett design, the big drop in errors *does* follow a reinforcement. So long as the Strong Law of Effect is stated qualitatively and does not explicitly mention amounts and times, it would be admittedly difficult to design an experiment in which it could be refuted. A neo-Hullian interested for some reason in preserving the Strong Law of Effect might simply add a quantitative postulate. He might assume that when a response undergoes an increment in strength on the basis of a minimally reinforcing agent (that is, one in which the asymptote of the acquisition of habit strength is relatively low), then, if subsequently a strong reinforcement is introduced, the parameter in the new growth function which determines the rate of approach to the new asymptote is greater than it would have been without the original learning. Since in the Blodgett design there is evidence of acquisition of differential habit strengths during the latent phase, such a postulate would lead to a preservation of the Strong Law of Effect. The main reason that we are concerned to deal with latent learning material of the Blodgett type is that in the reinforcement theory as now formulated, the effect of a reinforcer is implicitly assumed to operate immediately.

RELATIONSHIP OF REINFORCEMENT TO DRIVE

Perhaps a comment is needed on the way in which reinforcement has been treated here as the primary notion whereas drive, need, or demand is defined in terms of it. I do not mean to imply that need or drive is not the more "basic" factor, if by this is meant that what is a reinforcer or what acquires reinforcing properties depends upon a certain relevance to need. But this manner of speaking refers to the causal reconstruction of behavior, and reverses the epistemological order. The needs of an organism are inferred from changes in behavior strength as a function of certain states of affairs. That is to say, we "get a fix" on a need by being able to induce the chief defining properties of those states of affairs to which behavior is shown to tend. I do not see how there is any possibility in proceeding otherwise at the level of molar behavior. Whether it will be feasible or desirable to hypothesize a kind of state called need in the case of all reinforcers is a moot point at present. I gather that Hull would argue it will, whereas Skinner would argue it will not. One can consider a sort of continuum of reinforcing states of affairs at one end of which it is most easy and natural and obviously very useful to speak in terms of a need, e.g., the case of food or water; whereas at the other end, e.g., the reinforcing effects of hearing a click or turning off a light, the notion of needs seems relatively less appropriate. But the *causal* primacy of needs in our final reconstruction of behavior laws must not be confused with the epistemological status of needs, i.e., the operations by which we arrive at a conception of the needs. Whether the reduction of need is a necessary condition for learning is a question that is not involved in my formulation of either the Weak or the Strong Law of Effect since need-reduction is not equated to reinforcement. This independence of the notions of reinforcement and need-reduction is seen not only in the question of whether need-reduction is (for a sophisticated organism) a necessary condition for reinforcing effect, but it is the intention of these definitions to leave it an open question as to whether a kind of event called need-reduction is involved in reinforcing effects at any stage. The alternative to this is to exhaust completely the concept of need by defining an intervening variable via a class of reinforcing agents, i.e., the organism's "need" is not specified in any way except to say that it is "whatever state" within the organism is involved in the reinforcing effect of a stimulus change known experimentally to exert such an effect. In this case, of course, a rat may be said to have a "need" to keep the light off, to be with another rat, to hear a sound, etc. Whether this is a desirable way of speaking we need not consider here.

In the preceding developments, I have avoided consideration of refinements which would be necessary to complete the theoretical picture. The most important of these is the apparent exception to the Weak Law of Effect in which a change in strength does not occur in spite of the presentation of a known reinforcing agent because certain other dominant factors are at work. As an example, we may consider the "fixation" of a response which is followed by anxiety reduction to the point that an opposing response consistently reinforced with food fails to develop an increase in strength. In any particular situation it is the task of experimental analysis to show what the relations are; as a nice example of this I may refer to the recent work of Farber (3). Of course, if the response does not have sufficient opportunity to *occur*, be reinforced, and hence develop strength, the Weak Law of Effect is not violated. Those cases in which this is not an adequate explanation must be dealt with by considering the opposing forces, leaving open the question as to whether these opposing forces can themselves be satisfactorily subsumed under the Strong Law of Effect. The case here is not essentially different from the case in mechanics where we introduce the concept of force as a dynamic concept (that is, by accelerations produced) and subsequently apply the same notions to systems which are in equilibrium. In physics, one makes use of the laws about force which are based upon the dynamical notion of it in order to explain those cases in statics in which no motion results. Whereas the detailed reconstruction of the causal system remains as a task for the future, I do not believe there are any fundamental logical difficulties involved in the notion that a reinforcing state of affairs is initially defined by an increase in strength, and subsequently the failure of such a state of affairs to exert the effect is explained in terms of the occurrence of other operations or states which oppose it.

SUMMARY

Let me conclude by summarizing the development, using Mach as a model. For convenience I neglect here the specification of a schedule:

a. *Experimental Proposition:* In the rat, if turning to the right in the T-maze is followed by the presentation of sunflower seeds, the strength of the right-turning response will increase. (A situational-reinforcer law.)

b. *Definition:* A stimulus or stimulus change which occurs as the strengthening condition in a situational-reinforcer law is a *reinforcer*.

This empirical law together with the above definition enables us now to assert (as an empirical statement) "sunflower seeds are a reinforcer." The empirical content of this is that there is at least one response which the presentation of sunflower seeds will strengthen.

The presentation of a reinforcer is called *reinforcement*.

c. *Definition:* If the strength of a response may be increased as a function of behavior in an exposure to a situation (rather than by surgical, drug, or maturational changes), such a response is *learnable* by the organism. No reference to reinforcement is made here; we simply require that response strength be shown to increase following "experience," of whatever sort.

d. *Experimental Propositions:* Following suitable manipulation of their experiences, rats will show increases in the strength of pressing levers, pulling chains, rolling marbles, turning to the right at certain choice points, gnawing through paper, digging through sawdust, turning wheels, etc. (Expanded, this would consist simply in a long list of specific "laws" asserting the learnability of certain response classes.)

e. *Experimental Propositions:* Sunflower seeds may be used to strengthen lever pressing, chain pulling, etc. In general, sunflower seeds may be used to strengthen all learnable responses in the rat. (This asserts the generality of the reinforcing effect of sunflower seeds and is what I am calling a trans-situational reinforcer law.)

f. *Definition:* A trans-situational reinforcer is a stimulus which will strengthen all learnable responses. (We have already defined reinforcer so that it does not commit us to its generality, that is, a reinforcer is *at least* a situational reinforcer. If there are any reinforcers which exert the reinforcing effect upon all learnable responses, they are trans-situational.) This definition with the immediately preceding experimental propositions enables us to say, "Sunflower seeds are a trans-situational reinforcer."

Such a collection of specific empirical laws in combination with the above general definition leads to a large set of laws such as these last stated ones so that in the end we find the following:

g. *Experimental Proposition:* All reinforcers are trans-situational. (The Weak Law of Effect.)

h. *Experimental Proposition:* Every increment in strength involves a trans-situational reinforcer. (The Strong Law of Effect.)

It seems clear that in the above sequence both the definitional and the factual (empirical) elements are present, and in a simple, commonplace form. The definitional and conventional elements appear in the specification of the circumstances under which a stimulus is to be called "reinforcing." Such a stipulation, however, cannot tell us whether any such stimuli exist. That they do exist, which no one doubts, is an empirical finding; and the numerous statements about them constitute situational-reinforcer laws which are in a sense the special "sub-laws" of effect. These are related to the Weak Law of Effect somewhat in the same way that the particular empirical laws about the properties of bromine, fluorine, chlorine, and so on, are related to the Periodic Law. That the stimuli which occur in the situational-reinforcer laws have a generality of their reinforcing power is also an empirical finding, at present less well established (the Weak Law of Effect). That all cases of learning require certain time relationships to the presentation of such general reinforcers is yet a further factual claim, at present very much in dispute (the Strong Law of Effect).

I can see no reason why any theorist, whatever his position, should find the preceding treatment objectionable as an explication of the Law of Effect. I do not see any way in which the Strong Law of Effect, which is after all the big contemporary issue, has been surreptitiously put into the definitions in such a way that what is intended as an empirical proposition is effectively made a consequence of our use of words. The status of the Strong Law of Effect and even to some extent the Weak Law is presently in doubt. Further, some of the words used in these definitions, e.g., the word "response," are difficult to define in a way that makes them behave in the total system as we wish them to. I have not tried to deal with all these problems at once, but I hope that there are no difficulties springing from the problem of circularity which have not been met. That it is difficult to untangle the learning sequence which has given the reinforcing property to some states of affairs, particularly in the human organism, is admitted by everyone. That a large amount of detailed work of the "botanizing" type, not particularly ego-rewarding, needs to be done before the special sub-laws of effect are stated in terms of quantitative relations is quite clear. Finally, it would be very nice if in some magical way we could *know* before studying a given species exactly what stimulus changes would have the reinforcing property; but I have tried to indicate that this is an essentially irrational demand. In the light of the previous analysis I think the burden of proof is upon those who look upon a sophisticated formulation of the Law of Effect as circular, in either of the ordinary uses of that word.

Bibliography

1. Carr, H. A., *et al*. The Law of Effect: a roundtable discussion. *Psychol. Rev.*, 1938, 45, 191–218.

2. Estes, W. K. A study of motivating conditions necessary for secondary reinforcement. *Amer. Psychologist*, 1948, 3, 240–241. (Abstract.)

3. Farber, I. E. Response fixation under anxiety and non-anxiety conditions. *J. exp. Psychol.*, 1948, 38, 111–131.

4. Feigl, H. Operationism and scientific method. *Psychol. Rev.*, 1945, 52, 250–259.

5. Feigl, H. Some remarks on the meaning of scientific explanation. In H. Feigl & W. Sellars., *Readings in philosophical analysis*. New York: Appleton-Century-Crofts, 1949. Pp. 510–514.

6. Guttman, N. On the relationship between resistance to extinction of a bar-pressing response and concentration of reinforcing agent. Paper presented at the meeting of the Midwestern Psychological Association, Chicago, Ill., April 29, 1949.

7. Heron, W. T., & Peake, E. Qualitative food deficiency as a drive in a

discrimination problem. *J. comp. physiol. Psychol.*, 1949, 42, 143–147.

8. Hilgard, E. R. *Theories of learning.* New York: Appleton-Century-Crofts, 1948.

9. Hilgard, E. R., & Marquis, D. G. *Conditioning and learning.* New York: Appleton-Century, 1940.

10. Hospers, J. On explanation. *J. Philos.*, 1946, 43, 337–356.

11. Hull, C. L. Thorndike's *Fundamentals of learning. Psychol. Bull.*, 1935, 32, 807–823.

12. Hull, C. L. *Principles of behavior.* New York: Appleton-Century, 1943.

13. Keenan, J. Definitions and principles of dynamics. *Sci. Mon., N. Y.*, 1948, 67, 406–414.

14. Lenzen, V. F. *The nature of physical theory.* New York: John Wiley, 1931.

15. Lindsay, R. B., & Margenau, H. *Foundations of physics.* New York: John Wiley, 1936.

16. MacCorquodale, K., & Meehl, P. E. "Cognitive" learning in the absence of competition of incentives. *J. comp. physiol. Psychol.*, 1949, 42, 383–390.

17. Mach, E. *The science of mechanics* (Transl. by T. J. McCormack). Second English Ed. Chicago: Open Court Publishing Co., 1902.

18. Poincaré, H. *The foundations of science.* New York: Science Press, 1913.

19. Postman, L. The history and present status of the Law of Effect. *Psychol. Bull.*, 1947, 44, 489–563.

20. Pratt, C. C. Operationism in psychology. *Psychol. Rev.*, 1945, 52, 262–269.

21. Reichenbach, H. *Experience and prediction.* Chicago: Univ. of Chicago Press, 1938.

22. Skinner, B. F. *The behavior of organisms.* New York: Appleton-Century, 1938.

23. Spence, K. W. Studies on secondary reinforcement. Address given to the Minnesota Chapter of Psi Chi, Minneapolis, April 22, 1948.

24. Taylor, L. W. *Physics, the pioneer science.* New York: Houghton, Mifflin, 1941.

25. Thorndike, E. L. *The fundamentals of learning.* New York: Teachers College, Columbia Univ., 1932.

26. Thorndike, E. L. *Animal intelligence.* New York: Macmillan, 1911.

27. Thorndike, E. L. *The original nature of man.* New York: Teachers College, 1913.

28. Thorndike, E. L., *The psychology of learning.* New York: Teachers College, 1913.

29. Tolman, E. C. *Purposive behavior in animals and men.* New York: Appleton-Century, 1932.

CHAPTER 7

Causation

Causation is a thorny topic for educational researchers, yet one that we must face, and face squarely. We know how easy it is to commit the *post hoc* fallacy: to think that just because something followed or follows something else, it was or is caused by that something else; so we are justifiably cautious about making causal allegations. But sometimes this caution is carried to the extreme: complete avoidance of the use of the word "cause" (often self-defeatingly accompanied by use of terms with similar meaning, like "brings about," or "produces," or accompanied by an ambiguous statement of the conclusion so that it is obvious if noncausal, but not explicitly causal in nature; for example, "Racism is associated with violence.").

We cannot avoid concern with causal relationships, both general and particular. Education is concerned with bringing about changes, with providing general guidelines for so doing (guidelines that must take the form of causal generalizations), and with particular causal analyses of existing or recent occurrences (e.g., parental neglect is responsible for his low motivation; the cause of the riot is simply poverty). Furthermore, a number of educators are interested in knowing when children have developed a concept of causation and/or when they are ready to develop this concept. These practical concerns of the educator require educational researchers to use causal terms. We should be as clear as possible about what we are saying when we make a causal allegation and should have a good idea about what counts as proof and disproof, and support for and opposition to a causal allegation.

The topic is still controversial. In the following selections witness the broad difference in approach of the more humanistic ordinary-language philosophers, Douglas Gasking and Michael Scriven, from that of the radical empiricist May Brodbeck, who carries on in the tradition of David Hume. Hume's presentation of the "constant-conjunction" view of causation, which in essence does not distinguish between correlation and causation, is a classic that has been very influential to this day. It has been developed in twentieth-century terms by Bertrand Russell and applied with modifications by May Brodbeck to education. Hume's alternative notion, the feeling-of-anticipation view, has had considerably less contemporary influence, perhaps because of the subjectivity involved.

John Stuart Mill shared Hume's distaste for volition-ridden animistic notions of causation, but came up with a less radical proposal, one that, in contrast to Russell, does not claim that night causes day (night and day *are* constantly conjoined), but that does assert a complete universalizability of causal statements, in contrast to Scriven, in particular. However, there are in Mill's approach a number of hints of the later, ordinary-language approaches to causation.

It should be observed that Mill noticed that education, as an effect of a a cause, is not itself an observed event but rather a capacity, a "state of preparation in an object for producing an effect." He thus would not want the educational researcher to limit himself to concern with production of particular events (items of behavior), but would want the concern to be with production of capacity for behavior. This issue is discussed further in the sections on behaviorism and concepts.

Douglas Gasking treats causal generalizations roughly as recipes for producing or preventing something. Although the qualifications that Gasking feels obliged to add do give us pause, it appears that if educational researchers seeking causal generalizations think of themselves as searching for general recipes, then there should be less guilt felt about the task than many now feel about seeking causes. This is especially so if we think (along the lines suggested by Michael Scriven) that we are not coming up with broad universals, but rather with context-limited statements.

In focusing on the historian's approach to causation, Scriven evidences concern more with singular causal claims than with general causal claims (although he deals with both), and thus complements Gasking's concern with generalizations. Those educational researchers who do descriptive research, clinical research, and anthropological research will find Scriven's insights directly illuminating. Those researchers who seek causal generalizations, in spite of Scriven's emphasis on singular causal statements, should also find his ideas interesting, partly because his approach can be extended to generalizations (as Scriven himself shows) and partly because those people who do historianlike causal explanations of educational occurrences (whether the occurrence be the present educational crisis or the success of one child on a task) will probably be making use of causal generalizations (if any) produced by the researcher. It is well to note the possible use of the product of one's research.

Many would say that Scriven's concern with history—and thus with people —makes his writing more relevant to the work of an educational researcher than the writing of Gasking and Russell, who think in terms of examples from physics. The applicability to human behavior of the research model provided by physics is controversial, but in any case it is at least interesting and provocative to note what Russell and Gasking say. Furthermore, some would argue that the concept *causation* is an everyday concept that means the same thing to the physicist, lawyer, and historian as it does to the educational researcher and his client, the educator.

In the last selection in this causation series, Donald Davidson addresses himself directly to the question "Are reasons causes?" In dealing with this question, which many feel is a crucial one in the humanist's battle to preserve freedom of choice, Davidson makes heavy use of the distinction between singular and general causal statements and notes, using everyday examples, some things to which causal allegations commit us and some things to which they do not commit us. He avoids talking in terms of necessary and sufficient conditions, presumably because at his level of precision, the use of those terms makes no headway.

This now-classic article of Davidson's is midway between the radical empiricist and humanist camps. To the chagrin of the extreme humanists, he argues for the claim that reasons are causes and thus that all human behavior could be caused—and even describable in physical terms—but he rejects the reductionistic approach so characteristic of the radical empiricists. He does not attempt to reduce causal statements to observation statements.

31. CONNECTIONISM AND CAUSATION

David Hume

We have sought in vain for an idea of power or necessary connexion in all the sources from which we could suppose it to be derived. It appears that, in single instances of the operation of bodies, we never can, by our utmost scrutiny, discover any thing but one event following another, without being able to comprehend any force or power by which the cause operates, or any connexion between it and its supposed effect. The same difficulty occurs in contemplating the operations of mind on body—where we observe the motion of the latter to follow upon the volition of the former, but are not able to observe or conceive the tie which binds together the motion and volition, or the energy by which the mind produces this effect. The authority of the will over its own faculties and ideas is not a whit more comprehensible: So that, upon the whole, there appears not, throughout all nature, any one instance of connexion which is conceivable by us. All events seem entirely loose and separate. One event follows another, but we never can observe any tie between them. They seem *conjoined*, but never *connected*. And as we can have no idea of any thing which never appeared to our outward sense or inward sentiment, the necessary conclusion *seems* to be that we have no idea of connexion or power at all, and that these words are absolutely without any meaning, when employed either in philosophical reasonings or common life.

SOURCE. Reprinted with permission of The Open Court Publishing Company from *An Enquiry Concerning Human Understanding* by David Hume, 2nd ed., 1966. Copyright © 1946, 1966 by The Open Court Publishing Company, La Salle, Illinois. From posthumous edition of 1777.

But there still remains one method of avoiding this conclusion, and one source which we have not yet examined. When any natural object or event is presented, it is impossible for us, by any sagacity or penetration, to discover, or even conjecture, without experience, what event will result from it, or to carry our foresight beyond that object which is immediately present to the memory and senses. Even after one instance or experiment where we have observed a particular event to follow upon another, we are not entitled to form a general rule, or foretell what will happen in like cases; it being justly esteemed an unpardonable temerity to judge of the whole course of nature from one single experiment, however accurate or certain. But when one particular species of event has always, in all instances, been conjoined with another, we make no longer any scruple of foretelling one upon the appearance of the other, and of employing that reasoning which can alone assure us of any matter of fact or existence. We then call the one object, *Cause*; the other, *Effect*. We suppose that there is some connexion between them; some power in the one, by which it infallibly produces the other, and operates with the greatest certainty and strongest necessity.

It appears, then, that this idea of a necessary connexion among events arises from a number of similar instances which occur of the constant conjunction of these events; nor can that idea ever be suggested by any one of these instances, surveyed in all possible lights and positions. But there is nothing in a number of instances, different from every single instance, which is supposed to be exactly similar; except only that after a repetition of similar instances, the mind is carried by habit, upon the appearance of one event, to expect its usual attendant, and to believe that it will exist. This connexion, therefore, which we *feel* in the mind, this customary transition of the imagination from one object to its usual attendant, is the sentiment or impression from which we form the idea of power or necessary connexion. Nothing farther is in the case. Contemplate the subject on all sides; you will never find any other origin of that idea. This is the sole difference between one instance, from which we can never receive the idea of connexion, and a number of similar instances, by which it is suggested. The first time a man saw the communication of motion by impulse, as by the shock of two billiard balls, he could not pronounce that the one event was *connected*: but only that it was *conjoined* with the other. After he has observed several instances of this nature, he then pronounces them to be *connected*. What alteration has happened to give rise to this new idea of *connexion*? Nothing but that he now *feels* these events to be *connected* in his imagination, and can readily foretell the existence of one from the appearance of the other. When we say, therefore, that one object is connected with another, we mean only that they have acquired a connexion in our thought, and give rise to this inference, by which they become proofs of each other's existence: A conclusion which is somewhat extraordinary, but which seems founded on sufficient evidence. Nor will its evidence be weakened by any general diffidence of the understanding, or sceptical suspicion concerning every conclusion which is new and extraordinary. No conclusions can be more agreeable to scepticism than such as make discoveries concerning the weakness and narrow limits of human reason and capacity.

And what stronger instance can be produced of the surprising ignorance and weakness of the understanding than the present? For surely, if there be any relation among objects which it imports to us to know perfectly, it is that of cause and effect. On this are founded all our reasonings concerning matter of fact or existence. By means of it alone we attain any assurance concerning objects which are removed from the present testimony of our memory and senses. The only immediate utility of all sciences, is to teach us, how to control and regulate future events by their causes. Our thoughts and enquiries are, therefore, every moment, employed about this relation: Yet so imperfect are the ideas which we form concerning it, that it is impossible to give any just definition of cause, except what is drawn from something extraneous and foreign to it. Similar objects are always conjoined with similar. Of this we have experience. Suitably to this experience, therefore, we may define a cause to be *an object, followed by another, and where all the objects similar to the first are followed by objects similar to the second.* Or in other words *where, if the first object had not been, the second never had existed.* The appearance of a cause always conveys the mind, by a customary transition, to the idea of the effect. Of this also we have experience. We may, therefore, suitably to this experience, form another definition of cause and call it, *an object followed by another and whose appearance always conveys the thought to that other.* But though both these definitions be drawn from circumstances foreign to the cause, we cannot remedy this inconvenience, or attain any more perfect definition, which may point out that circumstance in the cause, which gives it a connexion with its effect. We have no idea of this connexion, nor even any distinct notion what it is we desire to know, when we endeavour at a conception of it. We say, for instance, that the vibration of this string is the cause of this particular sound. But what do we mean by that affirmation? We either mean *that this vibration is followed by this sound, and that all similar vibrations have been followed by similar sounds:* Or, *that this vibration is followed by this sound, and that upon the appearance of one the mind anticipates the senses, and forms immediately an idea of the other.* We may consider the relation of cause and effect in either of these two lights; but beyond these, we have no idea of it.

To recapitulate, therefore, the reasonings of this section: Every idea is copied from some preceding impression or sentiment; and where we cannot find any impression, we may be certain that there is no idea. In all single instances of the operation of bodies or minds, there is nothing that produces any impression, nor consequently can suggest any idea of power or necessary connexion. But when many uniform instances appear, and the same object is always followed by the same event; we then begin to entertain the notion of cause and connexion. We then *feel* a new sentiment or impression, to wit, a customary connexion in the thought or imagination between one object and its usual attendant; and this sentiment is the original of that idea which we seek for. For as this idea arises from a number of similar instances, and not from any single instance, it must arise from that circumstance, in which the number of instances differ from every individual instance. But this customary connexion or transition of the imagination is the only circumstance in which they differ. In every other particular they are alike. The first instance which we saw of motion communicated by the shock of two billiard balls (to return to this obvious illustration) is exactly similar to any instance that may, at present, occur to us; except only, that we could not, at first, *infer* one event from the other; which we are enabled to do at present, after so long a course of uniform experience. I know not whether the reader will readily apprehend this reasoning. I am afraid that, should I multiply words about it, or throw it into a greater variety of lights, it would only become more obscure and intricate. In all abstract reasonings there is one point of view which, if we can happily hit, we shall go farther towards illustrating the subject than by all the eloquence in the world. This point of view we should endeavour to reach, and reserve the flowers of rhetoric for subjects which are more adapted to them.

32. ON THE NOTION OF CAUSE, WITH APPLICATIONS TO THE FREE-WILL PROBLEM

Bertrand Russell

In the following paper I wish, first, to maintain that the word "cause" is so inextricably bound up with misleading associations as to make its complete extrusion from the philosophical vocabulary desirable; secondly, to inquire what principle, if any, is employed in science in place of the supposed "law of causality" which philosophers imagine to be employed; thirdly, to exhibit certain confusions, especially in regard to teleology and determinism, which appear to me to be connected with erroneous notions as to causality.

All philosophers, of every school, imagine that causation is one of the fundamental axioms or postulates of science, yet, oddly enough, in advanced sciences such as gravitational astronomy, the word "cause" never occurs. Dr. James Ward, in his *Naturalism and Agnosticism*, makes this a ground of complaint against physics: the business of those who wish to ascertain the ultimate truth about the world, he apparently thinks, should be the discovery of causes, yet physics never even seeks them. To me it seems that philosophy ought not to assume such legislative functions, and that the reason why physics has ceased to look for causes is that, in fact, there are no such things. The law of causality, I believe, like much that passes muster among philosophers, is a relic of a bygone age, surviving, like the monarchy, only because it is erroneously supposed to do no harm. . . .

SOURCE. Reprinted with permission of George Allen & Unwin Ltd. from *Logic and Mysticism* by Bertrand Russell. Copyright © 1917 by George Allen & Unwin Ltd., London.

I return now to the question, What law or laws can be found to take the place of the supposed law of causality?

First, without passing beyond such uniformities of sequence as are contemplated by the traditional law, we may admit that, if any such sequence has been observed in a great many cases, and has never been found to fail, there is an inductive probability that it will be found to hold in future cases. If stones have hitherto been found to break windows, it is probable that they will continue to do so. This, of course, assumes the inductive principle, of which the truth may reasonably be questioned; but as this principle is not our present concern, I shall in this discussion treat it as indubitable. We may then say, in the case of any such frequently observed sequence, that the earlier event is the *cause* and the later event the *effect*.

Several considerations, however, make such special sequences very different from the traditional relation of cause and effect. In the first place, the sequence, in any hitherto unobserved instance, is no more than probable, whereas the relation of cause and effect was supposed to be necessary. I do not mean by this merely that we are not sure of having discovered a true case of cause and effect; I mean that, even when we have a case of cause and effect in our present sense, all that is meant is that on grounds of observation, it is probable that when one occurs the other will also occur. Thus in our present sense, A may be the cause of B even if there actually are cases where B does not follow A. Striking a match will be the cause of its igniting, in spite of the fact that some matches are damp and fail to ignite.

In the second place, it will not be assumed that *every* event has some antecedent which is its cause in this sense; we shall only believe in causal sequences where we find them, without any presumption that they always are to be found.

In the third place, *any* case of sufficiently frequent sequence will be causal in our present sense; for example, we shall not refuse to say that night is the cause of day. Our repugnance to saying this arises from the ease with which we can imagine the sequence to fail, but owing to the fact that cause and effect must be separated by a finite interval of time, *any* such sequence *might* fail through the interposition of other circumstances in the interval. Mill, discussing this instance of night and day, says:—

"It is necessary to our using the word cause, that we should believe not only that the antecedent always *has* been followed by the consequent, but that as long as the present constitution of things endures, it always *will* be so."

In this sense, we shall have to give up the hope of finding causal laws such as Mill contemplated; any causal sequence which we have observed may at any moment be falsified without a falsification of any laws of the kind that the more advanced sciences aim at establishing.

In the fourth place, such laws of probable sequence, though useful in daily life and in the infancy of a science, tend to be displaced by quite different laws as soon as a science is successful. The law of gravitation will illustrate what occurs in any advanced science. In the motions of mutually gravitating bodies, there is nothing that can be called a cause, and nothing that can be called an effect; there is merely a formula. Certain differential equations can be found, which hold at every instant for every particle of the system, and which, given the configuration and velocities at one instant, or the configurations at two instants, render the configuration at any other earlier or later instant theoretically calculable. That is to say, the configuration at any instant is a function of that instant and the configurations at two given instants. This statement holds throughout physics, and not only in the special case of gravitation. But there is nothing that could be properly called "cause" and nothing that could be properly called "effect" in such a system.

No doubt the reason why the old "law of causality" has so long continued to pervade the books of philosophers is simply that the idea of a function is unfamiliar to most of them, and therefore they seek an unduly simplified statement. There is no question of repetitions of the "same" cause producing the "same" effect; it is not in any sameness of causes and effects that the constancy of scientific law consists, but in sameness of relations. And even "sameness of relations" is too simple a phrase; "sameness of differential equations" is the only correct phrase. It is impossible to state this accurately in non-mathematical language; the nearest approach would be as follows: "There is a constant relation between the state of the universe at any instant and the rate of change in the rate at which any part of the universe is changing at that instant, and this relation is many-one, i.e. such that the rate of change in the rate of change is determinate when the state of the universe is given." If the "law of causality" is to be something actually discoverable in the practice of science, the above proposition has a better right to the name than any "law of causality" to be found in the books of philosophers.

In regard to the above principle, several observations must be made—

(1) No one can pretend that the above principle is *a priori* or self-evident or a "necessity of thought." Nor is it, in any sense, a premiss of science: it is an empirical generalisation from a number of laws which are themselves empirical generalisations.

(2) The law makes no difference between past and future: the future "determines" the past in exactly the same sense in which the past "determines" the future. The word "determine," here, has a purely logical significance: a certain number of variables "determine" another variable if that other variable is a function of them.

(3) The law will not be empirically verifiable unless the course of events within some sufficiently small volume will be approximately the same in any

two states of the universe which only differ in regard to what is at a considerable distance from the small volume in question. For example, motions of planets in the solar system must be approximately the same however the fixed stars may be distributed, provided that all the fixed stars are very much farther from the sun than the planets are. If gravitation varied directly as the distance, so that the most remote stars made the most difference to the motions of the planets, the world might be just as regular and just as much subject to mathematical laws as it is at present, but we could never discover the fact.

(4) Although the old "law of causality" is not assumed by science, something which we may call the "uniformity of nature" is assumed, or rather is accepted on inductive grounds. The uniformity of nature does not assert the trivial principle "same cause, same effect," but the principle of the permanence of laws. That is to say, when a law exhibiting, e.g. an acceleration as a function of the configuration has been found to hold throughout the observable past, it is expected that it will continue to hold in the future, or that, if it does not itself hold, there is some other law, agreeing with the supposed law as regards the past, which will hold for the future. The ground of this principle is simply the inductive ground that it has been found to be true in very many instances; hence the principle cannot be considered certain, but only probable to a degree which cannot be accurately estimated.

The uniformity of nature, in the above sense, although it is assumed in the practice of science, must not, in its generality, be regarded as a kind of major premiss, without which all scientific reasoning would be in error. The assumption that *all* laws of nature are permanent has, of course, less probability than the assumption that this or that particular law is permanent; and the assumption that a particular law is permanent for all time has less probability than the assumption that it will be valid up to such and such a date. Science, in any given case, will assume what the case requires, but no more. In constructing the *Nautical Almanac* for 1915 it will assume that the law of gravitation will remain true up to the end of that year; but it will make no assumption as to 1916 until it comes to the next volume of the almanac. This procedure is, of course, dictated by the fact that the uniformity of nature is not known *a priori*, but is an empirical generalisation, like "all men are mortal." In all such cases, it is better to argue immediately from the given particular instances to the new instance, than to argue by way of a major premiss; the conclusion is only probable in either case, but acquires a higher probability by the former method than by the latter.

33. CAUSATION

May Brodbeck

I mentioned before that to cite a cause is, implicitly at least, to assert a law connecting the "cause" with other things. In other words, "*A* causes *B*" says the same as the law "Whenever *A* then *B*." Yet we are sometimes reluctant to call certain observed regularities "real" laws or causal connections. What is the difference between a causal connection and a merely regular but noncausal conjunction of events? What is the difference between a true and a spurious correlation? (The terms *true* and *spurious* are used here as in Zeisel, 1957, Ch. 9. The term *spurious* is not being used here in the sense that "something other than the tendency of the two variables to vary concomitantly affects the value [of the correlation coefficient] obtained: e.g., the correlation obtained when one of the variables actually includes the other with which it is correlated," English & English, 1958, p. 519.) Despite immediate appearance to the contrary, these turn out to be quite the same question. Researchers accustomed to working with statistical correlations have developed techniques for distinguishing the true from the spurious correlation. A high correlation, for instance, between female marital status and job absenteeism is said to be true, while that between marital status and candy consumption is called spurious. In the latter case, the introduction of an additional factor, age, leads us to abandon the original correlation. In the true case, on the other hand, the introduction of an additional factor, increased housework, is said to con-

SOURCE. Reprinted from "Logic and Scientific Method in Research on Teaching," by May Brodbeck in N. L. Gage (ed.), *Handbook of Research on Teaching*. Chicago: Rand McNally & Co., 1963. Copyright © 1963 by American Educational Research Association.

firm the correlation (Zeisel, 1957). Why, in each case, do we treat the original correlations differently after introducing the additional factor?

After all, marriage is statistically correlated with age, thus also with candy-eating. Statistically, therefore, in both cases there actually is a correlation and both are explained by the third factor. Married people eat less candy because they are older; married women are absent more from jobs because they have more housework. We justify saying that the former correlation is spurious and the latter is true, because we analyze the notion of a true correlation in terms of a presumed causal connection. Getting married causes more housework, which in turn causes increased absenteeism; therefore, getting married is truly correlated with absenteeism. Getting older, on the other hand, is a common cause both of marriage and eating less candy. All concomitants of age, like gray hair and paunchiness, would give a high correlation with eating less candy, if age does. They have a common cause, but are not causes of each other. Thus, the difference between true and spurious correlations resolves into a difference between causal and noncausal connections.

Nor does the difference between causal and noncausal conjunctions arise only for statistical correlations. Nonstatistical generalizations, asserting for all things of a certain kind that they are uniformly connected with something else, also raise the same problem. "All gases expand when heated" states a true causal connection, while "All the books on my desk are blue" does not. Philosophers have puzzled about how to distinguish the truly causal connections from those which are merely regular. In particular, it has been pointed out that the usual formulation of an empirical law as an "if-then" statement does not reveal this distinction. Both the causal law and the mere conjunction would each be expressed as conditional statements. If anything is a book on my desk, it is blue; if anything is a heated gas, it expands. The conditional states the observed constant conjunction of these characteristics.

The analysis of statements like "A causes B" into statements about a uniform conjunction of events, without using the term "cause," has been, ever since David Hume, basic empiricist doctrine. This analysis follows from the empiricist criterion of meaning, of which operationism is merely an application. All that we observe is the constant conjunction of the events "A" and "B," not a third thing called a cause.

USING THE SUBJUNCTIVE

Idiomatically, we may distinguish between accidental and causal connections by using the subjunctive mood. If this gas were heated, it would expand. On the other hand, if a book in the bookcase were on my desk, it would not have to be blue. It has, therefore, been suggested that only by means of the subjunctive can we distinguish lawful connections from mere generalizations.

"*A* causes *B*" or "If *A* then *B*" is an empirical law only if we can truly assert the corresponding subjunctive, "If anything *were A*, then it *would be B*." To put it differently, if the corresponding subjunctive is true, then we have a real connection; otherwise, we have only an accidental generalization. This seems a rather neat solution. Unfortunately, it has some obvious difficulties.

How are we to *know* the truth or falsity of the corresponding subjunctive? Fundamentally, there are only two alternatives. One is that we know it by inductive generalization from observation. But we observe only that whenever we have *A*, we also have *B*. The subjunctive, therefore, can be asserted only on the basis of prior knowledge of the indicative conditional. But then the subjunctive is superflous, since the evidence for it is no different from the evidence for the corresponding indicative conditional. The alternative is that we know the truth of the subjunctive in some special way. The empirical evidence for both the causal connection, or true empirical law, and the accidental conjunction is never more than a finite number of instances. There are thus no observations distinguishing the truth of the subjunctive from that of the indicative form. If, therefore, the subjunctive says more than the corresponding indicative and if this excess meaning is not further analyzable, we must establish this meaning in some special way.

We must somehow grasp or see that one subjunctive is true while another is false. According to the empiricist analysis, a law of nature is expressed by the indicative "if-then" form. Rejection of this analysis leads us down the path of rationalistic intuition or reason. I mentioned before that one's principle of proper concept-formation or criterion of meaning was fundamental. We see now why this is so. If we adopt the unanalyzable subjunctive view of empirical laws, we are, in effect, taken back to an unanalyzed notion of cause and to rejection of the empiricist criterion of referential meaning. Inductive generalization gives way to intuitive grasp of real connections. Is this really the price we must pay for the ability to distinguish between lawful and accidental uniformities? Clearly, this is a distinction we should like to be able to make. Fortunately, this can be done without sacrificing empiricist views on meaning and knowledge. But the distinction cannot be made simply by considering generalizations in isolation.

LOOKING AT THE CONTEXT

The difference between a law and an accidental conjunction of events is a matter of fact and not of meaning. For matters of fact, it is reasonable to point out that we must look at the context, that is, a the rest of what we know. Let us reanalyze the difference between the spurious correlation between female marital status and candy consumption and the true correlation between female marital status and absenteeism. Why in this latter case does an additional factor, increased housework, confirm the correlation? The answer can be given without the use of cause. Introduction of the third factor, more housework, leads to two new generalizations: When a woman marries, she has more housework, and if housework increases, so does absenteeism. From these two generalizations, the correlation in question between marriage and absenteeism follows as a deductive consequence. It is thus explained by the two generalizations in the only precise meaning "explanation" has in science. Because we can explain the correlation by deducing it from other generalizations, we consider it to be a true one.

On the other hand, in the spurious case, the additional factor, age, does not permit such deduction or explanation. Again we have two new generalizations, namely, age correlates with marriage and age correlates with candy consumption. But from these two generalizations, all that logically follows is that age is correlated both with marriage and with candy consumption. We cannot derive the correlation between marriage and candy consumption. When we define "explain" precisely, we see that the new factor, age, does not explain the correlation. That is why it is abandoned as spurious.

What all this shows is that we more confidently call a generalization a law if it is part of a theory. The generalizations serving as premises are laws because they permit the derivation, hence the prediction and explanation, of other laws. If a generalization either predicts or is predicted by other laws, the evidence for it is more than the mere conjunction of its observed instances. It is for this reason that we state firmly that if a gas were heated, it would expand. We assert the subjunctive because the law about the expansion of gases is not established by mere enumeration of instances. On the other hand, neither is it due to any unanalyzable connection between temperature and expansion. Rather, we believe this to be more than a mere conjunction because it is part of the theory of thermodynamics. It both implies and is implied by many other highly confirmed statements. Until we know more about how an isolated correlation is connected with other facts and generalizations, we cannot tell whether it is true or spurious, to use statistical jargon. The decision about whether we have a law or an accidental conjunction thus depends upon further empirical knowledge and is not a matter of intuitive insight or grasp of real connections among things.

34. UNIVERSAL CAUSAL STATEMENTS

John Stuart Mill

§ 2. The notion of Cause being the root of the whole theory of Induction, it is indispensable that this idea should, at the very outset of our inquiry, be, with the utmost practicable degree of precision, fixed and determined. If, indeed, it were necessary for the purpose of inductive logic that the strife should be quelled which has so long raged among the different schools of metaphysicians respecting the origin and analysis of our idea of causation, the promulgation, or at least the general reception, of a true theory of induction might be considered desperate for a long time to come. But the science of the Investigation of Truth by means of Evidence is happily independent of many of the controversies which perplex the science of the ultimate constitution of the human mind, and is under no necessity of pushing the analysis of mental phenomena to that extreme limit which alone ought to satisfy a metaphysician.

I premise, then, that when in the course of this inquiry I speak of the cause of any phenomenon, I do not mean a cause which is not itself a phenomenon; I make no research into the ultimate or ontological cause of anything. To adopt a distinction familiar in the writings of the Scotch metaphysicians, and especially of Reid, the causes with which I concern myself are not *efficient*, but *physical* causes. They are causes in that sense alone in which one physical fact is said to be the cause of another. Of the efficient causes of phenomena, or whether any such causes exist at all, I am not called upon to give an

SOURCE. Reprinted from *A System of Logic*, Vol. I, by John Stuart Mill, Longman's, Green, & Co., London, 1906.

opinion. The notion of causation is deemed by the schools of metaphysics most in vogue at the present moment to imply a mysterious and most powerful tie, such as cannot, or at least does not, exist between any physical fact and that other physical fact on which it is invariably consequent; and which is popularly termed its cause: and thence is deduced the supposed necessity of ascending higher, into the essences and inherent constitution of things, to find the true cause, the cause which is not only followed by, but actually produces, the effect. No such necessity exists for the purposes of the present inquiry, nor will any such doctrine be found in the following pages. The only notion of a cause which the theory of induction requires is such a notion as can be gained from experience. The Law of Causation, the recognition of which is the main pillar of inductive science, is but the familiar truth that invariability of succession is found by observation to obtain between every fact in nature and some other fact which has preceded it, independently of all considerations respecting the ultimate mode of production of phenomena, and of every other question regarding the nature of "Things in themselves."

Between the phenomena, then, which exist at any instant, and the phenomena which exist at the succeeding instant, there is an invariable order of succession; and, as we said in speaking of the general uniformity of the course of nature, this web is composed of separate fibres; this collective order is made up of particular sequences, obtaining invariably among the separate parts. To certain facts, certain facts always do, and, as we believe, will continue to, succeed. The invariable antecedent is termed the cause; the invariable consequent, the effect. And the universality of the law of causation consists in this, that every consequent is connected in this manner with some particular antecedent or set of antecedents. Let the fact be what it may, if it has begun to exist, it was preceded by some fact or facts with which it is invariably connected. For every event there exists some given concurrence of circumstances, positive and negative, the occurrence of which is always followed by that phenomenon. We may not have found out what this concurrence of circumstances may be; but we never doubt that there is such a one, and that it never occurs without having the phenomenon in question as its effect or consequence. On the universality of this truth depends the possibility of reducing the inductive process to rules. The undoubted assurance we have that there is a law to be found if we only knew how to find it, will be seen presently to be the source from which the canons of the Inductive Logic derive their validity.

§ 3. It is seldom, if ever, between a consequent and a single antecedent that this invariable sequence subsists. It is usually between a consequent and the sum of several antecedents; the concurrence of all of them being requisite to produce, that is, to be certain of being followed by, the consequent. In such cases it is very common to single out one only of the antecedents under the denomination of Cause, calling the others merely Conditions. Thus, if a person eats of a particular dish, and dies in consequence, that is, would not have died if he had not eaten of it, people would be apt to say that eating of that dish was the cause of his death. There needs not, however, be any invariable connection between eating of the dish and death; but there certainly is, among the circumstances which took place, some combination or other on which death is invariably consequent: as, for instance, the act of eating of the dish, combined with a particular bodily constitution, a particular state of present health, and perhaps even a certain state of the atmosphere; the whole of which circumstances perhaps constituted in this particular case the *conditions* of the phenomenon, or, in other words, the set of antecedents which determined it, and but for which it would not have happened. The real Cause is the whole of these antecedents; and we have, philosphically speaking, no right to give the name of cause to one of them exclusively of the others. What, in the case we have supposed, disguises the incorrectness of the expression is this: that the various conditions, except the single one of eating the food, were not *events* (that is, instantaneous changes, or successions of instantaneous changes) but *states* possessing more or less of permanency; and might therefore have preceded the effect by an indefinite length of duration, for want of the event which was requisite to complete the required concurrence of conditions: while as soon as that event, eating the food, occurs, no other cause is waited for, but the effect begins immediately to take place; and hence the appearance is presented of a more immediate and close connection between the effect and that one antecedent, than between the effect and the remaining conditions. But though we may think proper to give the name of cause to that one condition, the fulfilment of which completes the tale, and brings about the effect without further delay; this condition has really no closer relation to the effect than any of the other conditions has. All the conditions were equally indispensable to the production of the consequent; and the statement of the cause is incomplete, unless in some shape or other we introduce them all. A man takes mercury, goes out of doors, and catches cold. We say, perhaps, that the cause of his taking cold was exposure to the air. It is clear, however, that his having taken mercury may have been a necessary condition of his catching cold; and though it might consist with usage to say that the cause of his attack was exposure to the air, to be accurate we ought to say that the cause was exposure to the air while under the effect of mercury.

If we do not, when aiming at accuracy, enumerate all the conditions, it is only because some of them will in most cases be understood without being expressed, or because for the purpose in view they may without detriment be overlooked. For example, when we say, the cause of a man's death was that his foot slipped in climbing a ladder, we omit as a thing unnecessary to be stated the circumstance of his weight, though quite as indispensable a condition of the effect which took place. When we say that the assent of the crown to a bill makes it law, we mean that the assent, being never given until all the other conditions are fulfilled, makes up the sum of the conditions, though no one now regards it as the principal one. When the decision of a legislative assembly has been determined by the casting vote of the chairman, we sometimes say that this one person was the cause of all the effects which resulted from the enactment. Yet we do not really suppose that his single vote contributed more to the result than that of any other person who voted in the affirmative; but, for the purpose we have in view, which is to insist on his individual responsibility, the part which any other person had in the transaction is not material.

In all these instances the fact which was dignified with the name of cause was the one condition which came last into existence. But it must not be supposed that in the employment of the term this or any other rule is always adhered to. Nothing can better show the absence of any scientific ground for the distinction between the cause of a phenomenon and its conditions, than the capricious manner in which we select from among the conditions that which we choose to denominate the cause. However numerous the conditions may be, there is hardly any of them which may not, according to the purpose of our immediate discourse, obtain that nominal pre-eminence. This will be seen by analysing the conditions of some one familiar phenomenon. For example, a stone thrown into water falls to the bottom. What are the conditions of this event? In the first place, there must be a stone and water, and the stone must be thrown into the water; but these suppositions forming part of the enunciation of the phenomenon itself, to include them also among the conditions would be a vicious tautology; and this class of conditions, therefore, have never received the name of cause from any but the Aristotelians, by whom they were called the *material* cause, *causa materialis*. The next condition is, there must be an earth; and accordingly it is often said that the fall of a stone is caused by the earth, or by a power or property of the earth, or a force exerted by the earth; all of which are merely roundabout ways of saying that it is caused by the earth; or, lastly, the earth's attraction, which also is only a technical mode of saying that the earth causes the motion, with the additional particularity that the motion is towards the earth, which is not a character of the cause, but of the effect. Let us now pass to another condition. It is not enough that the earth should exist; the body must be within that distance from it in which the earth's attraction preponderates over that of any other body. Accordingly we may say, and the expression would be confessedly correct, that the cause of the stone's falling is its being *within the sphere* of the earth's attraction. We proceed to a further condition. The stone is immersed in water: it is therefore a condition of its reaching the ground that its specific gravity exceed that of the surrounding fluid, or, in other words, that it surpass in weight an equal volume of water. Accordingly any one would be acknowledged to speak correctly who said that the cause of the stone's going to the bottom is its exceeding in specific gravity the fluid in which it is immersed.

Thus we see that each and every condition of the phenomenon may be taken in its turn, and, with equal propriety in common parlance, but with equal impropriety in scientific discourse, may be spoken of as if it were the entire cause. And in practice that particular condition is usually styled the cause whose share in the matter is superficially the most conspicuous, or whose requisiteness to the production of the effect we happen to be insisting on at the moment. So great is the force of this last consideration, that it sometimes induces us to give the name of cause even to one of the negative conditions. We say for example, The army was surprised because the sentinel was off his post. But since the sentinel's absence was not what created the enemy or put the soldiers asleep, how did it cause them to be surprised? All that is really meant is, that the event would not have happened if he had been at his duty. His being off his post was no producing cause, but the mere absence of a preventing cause: it was simply equivalent to his non-existence. From nothing, from a mere negation, no consequences can proceed. All effects are connected, by the law of causation, with some set of *positive* conditions; negative ones, it is true, being almost always required in addition. In other words, every factor phenomenon which has a beginning invariably arises when some certain combination of positive facts exists, provided certain other positive facts do not exist.

There is, no doubt, a tendency (which our first example, that of death from taking a particular food, sufficiently illustrates) to associate the idea of causation with the proximate antecedent *event*, rather than with any of the antecedent *states*, or permanent facts, which may happen also to be conditions of the phenomenon; the reason being that the event not only exists, but begins to exist immediately previous; while the other conditions may have preexisted for an indefinite time. And this tendency shows itself very visibly in the different logical fictions which are resorted to, even by men of science, to avoid the necessity of giving the name of cause to anything which had existed for an indeterminate length of time before the effect. Thus, rather than say that the earth causes the fall of bodies, they ascribe it to a *force* exerted by the earth, or an *attraction* by the earth, abstractions which they can represent to themselves as exhausted by each effort, and therefore constituting at each successive instant a fresh fact, simultaneous with or only immediately preceding the effect. Inasmuch as the coming of the circumstance which completes the assemblage of conditions, is a change or event, it thence happens that an event is always the antecedent in closest apparent proximity to the consequent: and this may account for the illusion which disposes us to look upon the proximate event as standing more peculiarly in the position of a cause than any of the antecedent states. But even this peculiarity, of being in closer proximity to the effect than any other of its conditions, is, as we have already seen, far from being necessary to the common notion of a cause; with which notion, on the contrary, any one of the conditions, either positive or negative, is found, on occasion, completely to accord.[1]

[1] The assertion that any and every one of the conditions of a phenomenon may be and is, on some occasions and for some purposes, spoken of as the cause, has been disputed by an intelligent reviewer of this work in the *Prospective Review,* (the predecessor of the justly esteemed *National Review,*) who maintains that "we always apply the word cause rather to that element in the antecedents which exercises *force,* and which would *tend* at all times to produce the same or a similar effect to that which, under certain conditions, it would actually produce." And he says, that "every one would feel" the expression, that the cause of a surprise was the sentinel's being off his post, to be incorrect; but that the "allurement or force which *drew* him off his post might be so called, because in doing so it removed a resisting power which would have prevented the surprise." I cannot think that it would be wrong to say that the event took place because the sentinel was absent, and yet right to say that it took place because he was bribed to be absent. Since the only direct effect of the bribe was his absence, the bribe could be called the remote cause of the surprise, only on the supposition that the absence was the proximate cause; nor does it seem to me that any one (who had not a theory to support) would use the one expression and reject the other.

The reviewer observes, that when a person dies of poison, his possession of bodily organs is a necessary condition, but that no one would ever speak of it as the cause. I admit the fact; but I believe the reason to be, that the occasion could never arise for so speaking of it; for when in the accuracy of common discourse we are led to speak of some one condition of a phenomenon as its cause, the condition so spoken of is always one which it is at least possible that the hearer may require to be informed of. The possession of bodily organs is a known condition, and to give that as the answer, when asked the cause of a person's death, would not supply the information sought. Once conceive that a doubt could exist as to his having bodily organs, or that he were to be compared with some being who had them not, and cases may be imagined in which it might be said that his possession of them was the cause of his death. If Faust and Mephistopheles together took poison, it might be said that Faust died because he was a human being, and had a body, while Mephistopheles survived because he was a spirit.

It is for the same reason that no one (as the reviewer remarks) "calls the cause of a leap, the muscles or sinews of the body, though they are necessary conditions; nor the cause of a self-sacrifice, the knowledge which was necessary for it; nor the cause of writing a book, that a man has time for it, which is a necessary condition." These conditions (besides that they are antecedent *states,* and not proximate antecedent *events,* and are therefore never the conditions in closest apparent proximity to the effect) are all of them so obviously implied, that it is hardly possible there should exist that necessity for insisting on them, which alone gives occasion for speaking of a single condition as if it were the cause. Wherever this necessity exists in regard to some one condition, and does not exist in regard to any other, I conceive that it is consistent with usage, when scientific accuracy is not aimed at, to apply the name cause to that one condition. If the only condition which can be supposed to be unknown is a negative condition, the negative condition may be spoken of as the cause. It might be said that a person died for want of

The cause, then, philosophically speaking, is the sum total of the conditions positive and negative taken together; the whole of the contingencies of every description, which being realised, the consequent invariably follows. The negative conditions, however, of any phenomenon, a special enumeration of which would generally be very prolix, may be all summed up under one head, namely, the absence of preventing or counteracting causes. The convenience of this mode of expression is mainly grounded on the fact, that the effects of any cause in counteracting another cause may in most cases be, with strict scientific exactness, regarded as a mere extension of its own proper and sepa-

medical advice, though this would not be likely to be said unless the person was already understood to be ill, and in order to indicate that this negative circumstance was what made the illness fatal, and not the weakness of his constitution, or the original virulence of the disease. It might be said that a person was drowned because he could not swim; the positive condition, namely, that he fell into the water, being already implied in the word drowned. And here let me remark, that his falling into the water is in this case the only positive condition: all the conditions not expressly or virtually included in this (as that he could not swim, that nobody helped him, and so forth) are negative. Yet, if it were simply said that the cause of a man's death was falling into the water, there would be quite as great a sense of impropriety in the expression, as there would be if it were said that the cause was his inability to swim: because, though the one condition is positive and the other negative, it would be felt that neither of them was sufficient, without the other, to produce death.

With regard to the assertion that nothing is termed the cause except the element which exerts active force, I waive the question as to the meaning of active force, and accepting the phrase in its popular sense, I revert to a former example, and I ask, would it be more agreeable to custom to say that a man fell because his foot slipped in climbing a ladder, or that he fell because of his weight? for his weight, and not the motion of his foot, was the active force which determined his fall. If a person walking out on a frosty day stumbled and fell, it might be said that he stumbled because the ground was slippery, or because he was not sufficiently careful but few people, I suppose, would say that he stumbled because he walked. Yet the only active force concerned was that which he exerted in walking: the others were mere negative conditions; but they happened to be the only ones which there could be any necessity to state; for he walked, most likely, in exactly his usual manner, and the negative conditions made all the difference. Again, if a person were asked why the army of Xerxes defeated that of Leonidas, he would probably say, because they were a thousand times the number; but I do not think he would say it was because they fought, though that was the element of active force. To borrow another example, used by Mr. Grove and by Mr. Baden Powell, the opening of floodgates is said to be the cause of the flow of water; yet the active force is exerted by the water itself, and opening the floodgates merely supplies a negative condition. The reviewer adds, "There are some conditions absolutely passive, and yet absolutely necessary to physical phenomena, viz. the relations of space and time; and to these no one ever applies the word cause without being immediately arrested by those who hear him." Even from this statement I am compelled to dissent. Few persons would feel it incongruous to say (for example) that a secret became known because it was spoken of when A. B. was within hearing; which is a condition of space; or that the cause why one of two particular trees is taller than the other is that it has been longer planted; which is a condition of time.

rate effects. If gravity retards the upward motion of a projectile, and deflects it into a parabolic trajectory, it produces, in so doing, the very same kind of effect, and even (as mathematicians know) the same quantity of effect, as it does in its ordinary operation of causing the fall of bodies when simply deprived of their support. If an alkaline solution mixed with an acid destroys its sourness, and prevents it from reddening vegetable blues, it is because the specific effect of the alkali is to combine with the acid, and form a compound with totally different qualities. This property, which causes of all descriptions possess, of preventing the effects of other causes by virtue (for the most part) of the same laws according to which they produce their own,[2] enables us, by establishing the general axiom that all causes are liable to be counteracted in their effects by one another, to dispense with the consideration of negative conditions entirely, and limit the notion of cause to the assemblage of the positive conditions of the phenomenon: one negative condition invariably understood, and the same in all instances (namely, the absence of counteracting causes) being sufficient, along with the sum of the positive conditions, to make up the whole set of circumstances on which the phenomenon is dependent.

§ 4. Among the positive conditions, as we have seen that there are some to which, in common parlance, the term cause is more readily and frequently awarded, so there are others to which it is, in ordinary circumstances, refused. In most cases of causation a distinction is commonly drawn between something which acts, and some other thing which is acted upon; between an *agent* and a *patient*. Both of these, it would be universally allowed, are conditions of the phenomenon; but it would be thought absurd to call the latter the cause, that title being reserved for the former. The distinction, however, vanishes on examination, or rather is found to be only verbal, arising from an incident of mere expression, namely, that the object said to be acted upon, and which is considered as the scene in which the effect takes place, is commonly included in the phrase by which the effect is spoken of, so that if it were also reckoned

---

[2] There are a few exceptions; for there are some properties of objects which seem to be purely preventive; as the property of opaque bodies by which they intercept the passage of light. This, as far as we are able to understand it, appears an instance not of one cause counteracting another by the same law whereby it produces its own effects, but of an agency which manifests itself in no other way than in defeating the effects of another agency. If we knew on what other relations to light, or on what peculiarities of structure, opacity depends, we might find that this is only an apparent, not a real exception to the general proposition in the text. In any case it needs not affect the practical application. The formula which includes all the negative conditions of an effect in the single one of the absence of counteracting causes, is not violated by such cases as this; though if all counteracting agencies were of this description, there would be no purpose served by employing the formula.

as part of the cause, the seeming incongruity would arise of its being supposed to cause itself. In the instance which we have already had, of falling bodies, the question was thus put: What is the cause which makes a stone fall? and if the answer had been "the stone itself," the expression would have been in apparent contradiction to the meaning of the word cause. The stone, therefore, is conceived as the patient, and the earth (or, according to the common and most unphilosophical practice, an occult quality of the earth) is represented as the agent or cause. But that there is nothing fundamental in the distinction may be seen from this, that it is quite possible to conceive the stone as causing its own fall provided the language employed be such as to save the mere verbal incongruity. We might say that the stone moves towards the earth by the properties of the matter composing it; and according to this mode of presenting the phenomenon, the stone itself might without impropriety be called the agent; though to save the established doctrine of the inactivity of matter, men usually prefer here also to ascribe the effect to an occult quality, and say that the cause is not the stone itself, but the *weight* or *gravitation* of the stone.

Those who have contended for a radical distinction between agent and patient, have generally conceived the agent as that which causes some state of, or some change in the state of, another object which is called the patient. But a little reflection will show that the license we assume of speaking of phenomena as *states* of the various objects which take part in them (an artifice of which so much use has been made by some philosophers, Brown in particular, for the apparent explanation of phenomena) is simply a sort of logical fiction, useful sometimes as one among several modes of expression, but which should never be supposed to be the enunciation of a scientific truth. Even those attributes of an object which might seem with greatest propriety to be called states of the object itself, its sensible qualities, its colour, hardness, shape, and the like, are in reality (as no one has pointed out more clearly than Brown himself) phenomena of causation, in which the substance is distinctly the agent or producing cause, the patient being our own organs, and those of other sentient beings. What we call states of objects, are always sequences into which the objects enter, generally as antecedents or causes; and things are never more active than in the production of those phenomena in which they are said to be acted upon. Thus, in the example of a stone falling to the earth, according to the theory of gravitation the stone is as much an agent as the earth, which not only attracts, but is itself attracted by, the stone. In the case of a sensation produced in our organs, the laws of our organisation, and even those of our minds, are as directly operative in determining the effect produced, as the laws of the outward object. Though we call prussic acid the agent of a person's death, the whole of the vital and organic properties of the patient are as actively instrumental as the poison in the chain of effects which so rapidly terminates his sentient existence. In the process of education, we may call the teacher the agent and the scholar only the material acted upon; yet in truth all the facts which pre-existed in the scholar's mind exert either co-operating or counteracting agencies in relation to the teacher's efforts. It is not light alone which is the agent in vision, but light coupled with the active properties of the eye and brain, and with those of the visible object. The distinction between agent and patient is merely verbal: patients are always agents; in a great proportion, indeed, of all natural phenomena, they are so to such a degree as to react forcibly on the causes which acted upon them: and even when this is not the case, they contribute, in the same manner as any of the other conditions, to the production of the effect of which they are vulgarly treated as the mere theatre. All the positive conditions of a phenomenon are alike agents, alike active; and in any expression of the cause which professes to be complete, none of them can with reason be excluded, except such as have already been implied in the words used for describing the effect; nor by including even these would there be incurred any but a merely verbal impropriety.

§ 5. There is a case of causation which calls for separate notice, as it possesses a peculiar feature, and presents a greater degree of complexity than the common case. It often happens that the effect, or one of the effects, of a cause is, not to produce of itself a certain phenomenon, but to fit something else for producing it. In other words, there is a case of causation in which the effect is to invest an object with a certain property. When sulphur, charcoal, and nitre are put together in certain proportions and in a certain manner, the effect is, not an explosion, but that the mixture acquires a property by which, in given circumstances, it will explode. The various causes, natural and artificial, which educate the human body or the human mind, have for their principal effect, not to make the body or mind immediately do anything, but to endow it with certain properties—in other words, to give assurance that in given circumstances certain results will take place in it, or as consequences of it. Physiological agencies often have for the chief part of their operation to *predispose* the constitution to some mode of action. To take a simpler instance than all these: putting a coat of white paint upon a wall does not merely produce in those who see it done the sensation of white; it confers on the wall the permanent property of giving that kind of sensation. Regarded in reference to the sensation, the putting on of the paint is a condition of a condition; it is a condition of the wall's causing that particular fact. The wall may have been painted years ago, but it has acquired a property which has lasted till now and will last longer; the antecedent condition necessary to enable the wall to become in its turn a condition has been fulfilled once for all. In a case like this, where the immediate consequent in the sequence is a property produced in an object, no one now supposes the property to be a substantive entity "inherent" in the object. What has been produced is what, in other language, may be called a state of preparation in an object for producing an effect. The ingredients of the gunpowder have been brought into a state of preparation for exploding as soon as the other conditions of an explosion shall have occurred. In the case of the gunpowder, this state of preparation consists in a certain collocation of its particles relatively to one another. In the example of the wall, it consists in a new collocation of two things relatively to each other—the wall and the paint. In the example of the moulding influences on the human mind, its being a collocation at all is only conjectural; for, even on the materialistic hypothesis, it would remain to be proved that the increased facility with which the brain sums up a column of figures when it has been long trained to calculation, is the result of a permanent new arrangement of some of its material particles. We must, therefore, content ourselves with what we know, and must include among the effects of causes the capacities given to objects of being causes of other effects. This capacity is not a real thing existing in the objects; it is but a name for our conviction that they will act in a particular manner when certain new circumstances arise. We may invest this assurance of future events with a fictitious objective existence, by calling it a *state* of the object. But unless the state consists, as in the case of the gunpowder it does, in a collocation of particles, it expresses no present fact; it is but the contingent future fact brought back under another name.

It may be thought that this form of causation requires us to admit an exception to the doctrine that the conditions of a phenomenon—the antecedents required for calling it into existence—must all be found among the facts immediately, not remotely, preceding its commencement. But what we have arrived at is not a correction, it is only an explanation, of that doctrine. In the enumeration of the conditions required for the occurrence of any phenomenon, it always has to be included that objects must be present, possessed of given properties. It is a condition of the phenomenon explosion that an object should be present, of one or other of certain kinds, which for that reason are called explosive. The presence of one of these objects is a condition immediately precedent to the explosion. The condition which is not immediately precedent is the cause which produced, not the explosion, but the explosive property. The conditions of the explosion itself were all present immediately before it took place, and the general law, therefore, remains intact.

§ 6. It now remains to advert to a distinction which is of first-rate importance both for clearing up the notion of cause, and for obviating a very specious objection often made against the view which we have taken of the subject.

When we define the cause of anything (in the only sense in which the present inquiry has any concern with causes) to be "the antecedent which it invariably follows," we do not use this phrase as exactly synonymous with "the antecedent which it invariably *has* followed in our past experience." Such a mode of conceiving causation would be liable to the objection very plausibly urged by Dr. Reid, namely, that according to this doctrine night must be the cause of day, and day the cause of night; since these phenomena have invariably succeeded one another from the beginning of the world. But it is necessary to our using the word cause that we should believe not only that the antecedent always *has* been followed by the consequent, but that as long as the present constitution of things[3] endures it always *will* be so. And this would not be true of day and night. We do not believe that night will be followed by day under all imaginable circumstances, but only that it will be so *provided* the sun rises above the horizon. If the sun ceased to rise, which, for aught we know, may be perfectly compatible with the general laws of matter, night would be, or might be, eternal. On the other hand, if the sun is above the horizon, his light not extinct, and no opaque body between us and him, we believe firmly that unless a change takes place in the properties of matter, this combination of antecedents will be followed by the consequent day; that if the combination of antecedents could be indefinitely prolonged, it would be always day; and that if the same combination had always existed, it would always have been day, quite independently of night as a previous condition. Therefore is it that we do not call night the cause, nor even a condition, of day. The existence of the sun (or some such luminous body), and there being no opaque medium in a straight line[4] between that body and the part of the earth where we are situated, are the sole conditions; and the union of these, without the addition of any superfluous circumstance, constitutes the cause. This is what writers mean when they say that the notion of cause involves the idea of necessity. If there be any meaning which confessedly belongs to the term necessity, it is *unconditionalness*. That which is necessary, that which *must* be, means that which will be, whatever supposition we may make in regard to all other things. The succession of day and night evidently is not necessary is this sense. It is conditional on the occurrence of other antecedents. That which will be followed by a given consequent when, and only when, some third circumstance also exists, is not the cause, even though

[3] I mean by this expression, the ultimate laws of nature (whatever they may be) as distinguished from the derivative laws and from the collocations. The diurnal revolution of the earth (for example) is not a part of the constitution of things, because nothing can be so called which might possibly be terminated or altered by natural causes.

[4] I use the words "straight line" for brevity and simplicity. In reality the line in question is not exactly straight, for, from the effect of refraction, we actually see the sun for a short interval during which the opaque mass of the earth is interposed in a direct line between the sun and our eyes; thus realising, though but to a limited extent, the coveted desideratum of seeing round a corner.

no case should ever have occurred in which the phenomenon took place without it.

Invariable sequence, therefore, is not synonymous with causation, unless the sequence, besides being invariable, is unconditional. There are sequences, as uniform in past experience as any others whatever, which yet we do not regard as cases of causation, but as conjunctions in some sort accidental. Such, to an accurate thinker, is that of day and night. The one might have existed for any length of time, and the other not have followed the sooner for its existence; it follows only if certain other antecedents exist; and where those antecedents existed, it would follow in any case. No one, probably, ever called night the cause of day; mankind must so soon have arrived at the very obvious generalisation, that the state of general illumination which we call day would follow from the presence of a sufficiently luminous body, whether darkness had preceded or not.

We may define, therefore, the cause of a phenomenon to be the antecedent or the concurrence of antecedents, on which it is invariably and *unconditionally* consequent. Or if we adopt the convenient modification of the meaning of the word cause which confines it to the assemblage of positive conditions without the negative, then instead of "unconditionally," we must say, "subject to no other than negative conditions."

To some it may appear, that the sequence between night and day being invariable in our experience, we have as much ground in this case as experience can give in any case for recognising the two phenomena as cause and effect; and that to say that more is necessary—to require a belief that the succession is unconditional, or, in other words, that it would be invariable under all changes of circumstances—is to acknowledge in causation an element of belief not derived from experience. The answer to this is, that it is experience itself which teaches us that one uniformity of sequence is conditional and another unconditional. When we judge that the succession of night and day is a derivative sequence, depending on something else, we proceed on grounds of experience. It is the evidence of experience which convinces us that day could equally exist without being followed by night, and that night could equally exist without being followed by day. To say that these beliefs are "not generated by our mere observation of sequence,"[5] is to forget that twice in every twenty-four hours, when the sky is clear, we have an *experimentum crucis* that the cause of day is the sun. We have an experimental knowledge of the sun which justifies us on experimental grounds in concluding, that if the sun were always above the horizon there would be day, though there had been no night, and that if the sun were always below the horizon there would be night, though there had been no day. We thus know from

5 *Second Burnet Prize Essay*, by Principal Tulloch, p. 25.

experience that the succession of night and day is not unconditional. Let me add, that the antecedent, which is only conditionally invariable, is not the invariable antecedent. Though a fact may, in experience, have always been followed by another fact, yet if the remainder of our experience teaches us that it might not always be so followed, or if the experience itself is such as leaves room for a possibility that the known cases may not correctly represent all possible cases, the hitherto invariable antecedent is not accounted the cause; but why? Because we are not sure that it *is* the invariable antecedent.

Such cases of sequence as that of day and night not only do not contradict the doctrine which resolves causation into invariable sequence, but are necessarily implied in that doctrine. It is evident, that from a limited number of unconditional sequences, there will result a much greater number of conditional ones. Certain causes being given, that is, certain antecedents which are unconditionally followed by certain consequents, the mere co-existence of these causes will give rise to an unlimited number of additional uniformities. If two causes exist together, the effects of both will exist together; and if many causes co-exist, these causes (by what we shall term hereafter the intermixture of their laws) will give rise to new effects, accompanying or succeeding one another in some particular order, which order will be invariable while the causes continue to co-exist, but no longer. The motion of the earth in a given orbit round the sun is a series of changes which follow one another as antecedent and consequents, and will continue to do so while the sun's attraction, and the force with which the earth tends to advance in a direct line through space, continue to co-exist in the same quantities as at present. But vary either of these causes, and this particular succession of motions would cease to take place. The series of the earth's motions therefore, though a case of sequence invariable within the limits of human experience, is not a case of causation. It is not unconditional.

This distinction between the relations of succession which, so far as we know, are unconditional, and those relations, whether of succession or of co-existence, which, like the earth's motions or the succession of day and night, depend on the existence or on the co-existence of other antecedent facts, corresponds to the great division which Dr. Whewell and other writers have made of the field of science into the investigation of what they term the Laws of Phenomena and the investigation of causes; a phraseology, as I conceive, not philosophically sustainable, inasmuch as the ascertainment of causes, such causes as the human faculties can ascertain, namely, causes which are themselves phenomena, is, therefore, merely the ascertainment of other and more universal Laws of Phenomena. And let me here observe, that Dr. Whewell, and in some degree even Sir John Herschel, seem to have misunderstood the meaning of those writers who, like M. Comte, limit the sphere of scientific investigation to Laws of Phenomena, and speak of the inquiry into causes as vain and futile. The causes which M. Comte designates as inaccessible are efficient causes. The investigation of physical, as opposed to efficient, causes (including the study of all the active forces in Nature, considered as facts of observation) is as important a part of M. Comte's conception of science as of Dr. Whewell's. His objection to the *word* cause is a mere matter of nomenclature, in which, as a matter of nomenclature, I consider him to be entirely wrong. "Those," it is justly remarked by Mr. Bailey,[6] "who, like M. Comte, object to designate *events* as causes, are objecting without any real ground to a mere but extremely convenient generalisation, to a very useful common name, the employment of which involves, or needs involve, no particular theory." To which it may be added, that by rejecting this form of expression, M. Comte leaves himself without any term for marking a distinction which, however incorrectly expressed, is not only real, but is one of the fundamental distinctions in science; indeed, it is on this alone, as we shall hereafter find, that the possibility rests of framing a rigorous Canon of Induction. And as things left without a name are apt to be forgotten, a Canon of that description is not one of the many benefits which the philosophy of Induction has received from M. Comte's great powers.

[6] *Letters on the Philosophy of the Human Mind*, First Series, p. 219.

35. CAUSATION AND RECIPES

Douglas Gasking

We sometimes speak of one thing, or of one sort of thing, causing another —of the second as being the result of or due to the former. In what circumstances do we do so?

If we start with some typical statements of causal connection—"The train-smash was due to a buckled rail"; "Vitamin B deficiency causes beri-beri"— two things are likely to strike us. First, the effect is something that comes into being after the cause, and secondly, we suppose that anyone fully conversant with the circumstances and the relevant causal laws could, from a knowledge of the cause, predict the effect. So it is very natural to suggest, as an answer to our question: We say that A causes B whenever a person with the requisite empirical information could infer from the occurrence of A to the subsequent occurrence of B. Or we might put it: We say that A causes B whenever B regularly follows A.

But this "regular succession" notion will not do. For there are cases where we would speak of A causing B where it is not the case that from the occurrence of A we may infer the subsequent occurrence of B.

An example to illustrate this: Iron begins to glow when its temperature reaches a certain point. I do not know what that temperature is: for the sake of the illustration I will suppose it to be 1,000° C., and will assume that iron never glows except at or above this temperature. Now, if someone saw a bar of iron glowing and, being quite ignorant of the physical facts, asked: What

SOURCE. Gasking, Douglas, "Causation and Recipes," *Mind*, Volume 64, No. 256, pp. 479–487, October 1955. Reprinted with permission. Copyright © 1955 by the author.

makes that iron glow? What causes it to glow?" we should answer: "It is glowing because it is at a temperature of 1,000° C. or more." The glowing, B, is caused by the high temperature, A. And here the B that is caused is not an event subsequent to the cause A. Iron reaches 1,000° C. and begins glowing at the same instant. Another example: current from a battery is flowing through a variable resistance, and we have a voltmeter connected to the two poles of the battery to measure the potential difference. Its reading is steady. We now turn the knob of our variable resistance and immediately the voltmeter shows that the potential difference has increased. If someone now asks: What caused this increase?, we reply: "the increase of the resistance in the circuit." But here again the effect was not something subsequent to the cause, but simultaneous.

So perhaps our account should be emended so as to read: We speak of A as causing B when the occurrence of B may be inferred from the occurrence of A and the occurrence of B is either subsequent to or simultaneous with the occurrence of A.

But this will not do either. For there are, first of all, cases where from the occurrence of A we may infer the subsequent occurrence of B, yet would not speak of A as causing B. And secondly there are cases where from the occurrence of A we may infer the simultaneous occurrence of B, yet would not speak of A as causing B.

Here is an example of the first case. Given (A) that at t_1 a body freely falling *in vacuo* is moving at a speed of 32 feet per second we can infer (B) that at t_2, one second later, it will be moving at 64 feet per second. We might be prepared to say that this inference was in some sense or other a causal inference. But it would be a most unnatural and "strained" use of the word "cause" to say that the body's movement at 64 feet per second at t_2 was caused by its moving at 32 feet per second at t_1. It would be even more unnatural, to take a famous example, to say that the day that will be here in twelve hours time is caused by the fact that it is now night. Yet from the present fact we can certainly infer that in twelve hours' time it will be day.

An example to illustrate the second point. From the fact that a bar of iron is now glowing we can certainly infer (and it will be a causal inference) that it is now at a temperature of 1,000° C. or over. Yet we should not say that its high temperature was caused by the glowing: we say that the high temperature causes the glowing, not *vice-versa*. Another example: watching the voltmeter and battery in the electrical circuit previously described we see that the needle suddenly jumps, showing that the potential difference has suddenly increased. From this we infer that the electrical resistance of the circuit has, at that moment, increased. But we should not say that the rise in potential difference caused the increase in resistance: rather that the rise in resistance caused a rise in the potential difference. Or again, knowing the properties of a certain sort of wax, we infer from the fact that the wax has melted that, at that very moment, it reached such and such a temperature. Yet we should not say that the wax's melting caused it to reach the critical temperature: rather that its reaching that temperature caused it to melt. Why do we speak of "cause" in some cases in which we can infer from A to B, but not in others?

The reason is not always of the same sort. Sometimes in such a case it would be nonsense to speak of A causing B, sometimes it would merely be false. Our very last example is a rather trivial instance of the first sort of reason. It is nonsense to speak of the melting of the wax causing the high temperature of the wax because "x melts" means "high temperature causes x to become liquid." So "the melting of the wax caused the high-temperature of the wax" is equivalent to the absurdity "The high temperature of the wax's causing of the wax to become liquid caused the high temperature of the wax."

But it is not for this sort of reason that we do not say that the glowing of the iron causes the high temperature of the iron. "Melting" is by definition an effect and not a cause of an increase in temperature, but the same is not true of "glowing." It is not logically absurd to say that the glowing of a piece of iron causes its high temperature; it is merely untrue. It is possible to imagine and to describe a world in which it would have been true. Here is an account of such an imaginary world.

"Our early ancestors many millennia ago discovered that you could make a large range of substances (wood, water, leaves, etc.) glow first blue, then purple, then red by a process of alternately covering them so as to exclude light, then rapidly letting light fall on them, then quickly covering them again, and so on. Wood, for instance, starts glowing after about six minutes of this treatment, and reaches the red stage in about ten minutes. If it is then left in constant daylight or in constant darkness it gradually fades through purple to blue and then ceases glowing. A number of other substances behave similarly, though the time needed to produce the glowing effect differs somewhat from substance to substance. None of the things that early man thus learnt to make glow, however, suffered any change of temperature in the process. Then, about 1000 B.C. men got hold of samples of fairly pure iron, for the first time. They tried the covering-uncovering technique on it to see if it too, like wood and water, but unlike certain sorts of rock, would glow if manipulated in this way. They found that it would, but that, unlike other substances, iron began to get hot when it started glowing, got hotter still at the purple stage, and when glowing red was very hot indeed. Precise measurements in modern times showed that on reaching the red stage the temperature of iron was 1,000° C. In other respects this imaginary world is just like our world, except that when you put a poker or other non-combustible object in a fire it does not begin to glow, however hot it gets."

Who can doubt that in this imaginary world we should have said that the glowing of the iron caused its temperature to rise, and not *vice-versa?* What, then, are the essential differences between this world and ours, which would lead us to say one thing in one world and another in another?

Human beings can make bodily movements. They do not move their arms, fingers, mouths and so on by doing anything else; they just move them. By making bodily movements men can manipulate things: can lift them, hold them in certain positions, squeeze them, pull them, rub them against each other, and so on. Men discovered that whenever they manipulated certain things in certain ways in certain conditions certain things happened. When you hold a stone in your hand and make certain complex movements of arm and fingers the stone sails through the air approximately in a parabola. When you manipulate two bits of wood and some dry grass for a long time in a certain way the grass catches fire. When you squeeze an egg, it breaks. When you put a stone in the fire it gets hot. Thus men found out how to produce certain effects by manipulating things in certain ways: how to make an egg break, how to make a stone hot, how to make dry grass catch fire, and so on.

We have a general manipulative technique for making anything hot: we put it on a fire. We find that when we manipulate certain things in this way, such as water in a vessel, it gets hot but does not begin to glow. But we find, too, that certain other things, such as bars of iron, when manipulated in this way do not only get hot, they also, after a while, start to glow. And we have no general manipulative technique for making things glow: the only way to make iron glow is to apply to it the general technique for making things hot. We speak of making iron glow by making it hot, i.e. by applying to it the usual manipulative technique for making things hot, namely, putting it on a fire, which in this special case, also makes it glow. We do not speak of making iron hot by making it glow, for we have no general manipulative technique for making things glow. And we say that the high temperature causes the glowing, not *vice-versa.*

In our imaginary world there is a general manipulative technique for making things glow—namely, rapidly alternating exposure to light and shielding from light. There is no other way of making them glow. In general, things manipulated in this way glow, but do not get hot. Iron, however, glows and gets hot. In this world we speak of making iron hot by making it glow, *i.e.* by applying to it the usual manipulative technique for making things glow which, in this special case, also makes it hot. We do not speak of making iron glow by making it hot, for the general manipulative technique of putting things on fire, which makes them hot, does not, in this world, also make things glow. And in this world, we should say that the glowing causes the high temperature, not *vice-versa.*

What this example shows is the following: When we have a general manipulative technique which results in a certain sort of event A, we speak of producing A by this technique. (Heating things by putting them on a fire.) When in certain cases application of the general technique for producing A also results in B we speak of producing B by producing A. (Making iron glow by heating it.) And in such a case we speak of A causing B, but not *vice-versa*. Thus the notion of causation is essentially connected with our manipulative techniques for producing results. Roughly speaking: "A rise in the temperature of iron causes it to glow" means "By applying to iron the general technique for making things hot you will also, in this case, make it glow." And "The glowing of iron causes its temperature to rise" means "By applying to iron the general technique for making things glow you will also, in this case, make it hot." This latter statement is, as it happens, false, for there is no general technique for making things glow, let alone one which, applied to iron, also makes it hot.

Thus a statement about the cause of something is very closely connected with a recipe for producing it or for preventing it. It is not exactly the same, however. One often makes a remark of the form "A causes B" with the practical aim of telling someone how to produce or prevent B, but not always. Sometimes one wishes to make a theoretical point. And one can sometimes properly say of some particular happening, A, that it caused some other particular event, B, even when no one could have produced A, by manipulation, as a means of producing B. For example, one may say that the rise in mean sea-level at a certain geological epoch was due to the melting of the Polar ice-cap. But when one can properly say this sort of thing it is always the case that people can produce events of the first sort as a means to producing events of the second sort. For example, one can melt ice in order to raise the level of water in a certain area. We could come rather closer to the meaning of "A causes B" if we said: "Events of the B sort can be produced by means of producing events of the A sort."

This account fits in with the principle that an event, A, at time t_2 cannot be the cause of an event B at an earlier time, t_1. It is a logical truth that one cannot alter the past. One cannot, therefore, by manipulations at time t_2 which produce A at t_2 also produce B retrospectively at t_1.

Let us turn now to the cases where, although from a state of affairs A we can infer a later state of affairs B, we nevertheless would not say that A causes B; e.g. to the case where from the speed of a freely falling body at t_1 we can infer its speed at t_2, or infer coming darkness from present daylight. These are cases where a process is taking place whose law we know, so that we can infer from one stage in the process a later stage. Our inference presupposes that nothing happens to interfere with the process; the falling body will not encounter an obstruction, the earth's spinning will not be stopped by, say, our sun becoming a super-nova. The difference between the earth's spinning and the body's falling is that in the latter case we can set the process going and arrange that nothing shall thereafter interfere with it for a certain time; in the former case we cannot. It is the same sort of difference as there is between melting ice in a bucket and the water-level rising in the bucket and melting Polar ice-caps and sea-level rising. We cannot set the earth spinning, but we can set a top spinning.

Imagine a world in which there is an exact correlation between the colour and the temperature of everything. Anything at a certain low temperature is a certain shade of, say, blue. If an object becomes warmer its colour changes to purple, then red, then orange, then yellow and finally to white. Cold (or blue) objects can be made hot (or red) by putting them in a fire; after a long time in a very big fire they become very hot (yellow). In such a world we should very probably not have had two sets of words: "cold," "warm," "hot," "very hot" and also "blue," "purple," "red," "yellow"—but only one set—say the words "blue," "purple," "red," and so on. We should have spoken of things "looking purple," or "being purple to the eyes" and of their "feeling purple" or "being purple to the touch." (In our actual world we talk of things being round or square whether we apprehend their shapes by the eye or by the touch: we do not have a special word meaning "round to the eye" and another quite different word meaning "round to the touch," since there is a correlation between these.)

In such a world we should speak of making purple things red by putting them on a fire, but should not normally speak of making something "red to the eye" (i.e. what we mean by "red") by putting it on a fire; nor of making something "red to the touch" (i.e. what we mean by "hot") by this method. Still less should we speak of making something "red to the eye" by making it "red to the touch" or of making it "red to the touch" by making it "red to the eye." (In our actual world we do not speak of making things "visibly round" by making them "tangibly round," nor *vice-versa*.) When a single manipulation on our part invariably produces two effects A and B, we do not speak of producing one by producing the other, nor do we speak of one as a cause of the other. (The visible roundness is neither cause nor effect of the tangible roundness of a penny.) It is only when we have a technique for producing A which in some circumstances but not in all also produces B that we speak of producing A, and speak of A as causing B.

When we set a process going—drop a stone from a tower, set a top spinning—we set the stage, see that nothing shall interfere (for a certain time at least) with the process we are about to start, and then set things going. After that, things take their own course without further intervention on our part—the stone gathers speed, the top loses it. There are successive stages in the process. At stage A at t_1 the stone is moving fairly fast, at a later stage B at t_2 the stone is going very fast. But, on the presupposition that the process continues undisturbed, the very same initial stage-setting and send-off, C, which will produce fairly fast motion at t_1 (A), will always produce very fast motion at

t_2 (B), and the initial stage-setting and send-off C which will produce very fast motion at t_2 (B) will always produce fairly fast motion at t_1 (A). That is, the process being undisturbed, an initial send-off C will always produce both A and B: there is not a general technique for producing A which in some circumstances also produces B. Hence we do not speak of producing B by producing A. There is not a general technique for bringing it about that, one second after the start, a stone is falling at 32 feet per second, which in some circumstances can also be used to bring it about that two seconds after the start it is falling at 64 feet per second. Hence we do not speak of achieving the latter by means of the former, and do not speak of the former as causing the latter.

Of course one could, by attaching a rocket to the falling body, which fires one second after the start, secure that a body which is moving at 32 feet per second one second after departure is one second later travelling much faster than 64 feet per second. But this would contradict our presupposition that the process, after being started, was left uninterfered with. It is on this presupposition only that C always produces both A and B.

I have made two points:

First: that one says "A causes B" in cases where one could produce an event or state of the A sort as a means to producing one of the B sort. I have, that is, explained the "cause-effect" relation in terms of the "producing-by-means-of" relation.

Second: I have tried to give a general account of the producing-by-means-of relation itself: what it is to produce B by producing A. We learn by experience that whenever in certain conditions we manipulate objects in a certain way a certain change, A, occurs. Performing this manipulation is then called: "producing A." We learn also that in certain special cases, or when certain additional conditions are also present, the manipulation in question also results in another sort of change, B. In these cases the manipulation is also called "producing B," and, since it is in general the manipulation of producing A, in this case it is called "producing B by producing A." For example, one makes iron glow by heating it. And I discussed two sorts of case where one does not speak of "producing B by producing A." (1) Where the manipulation for producing A is the general technique for producing B, so that one cannot speak of "producing B by producing A" but only *vice-versa*. (2) Where the given manipulation invariably produces both A and B, so that the manipulation for producing B is not a special case only of that for producing A.

The notion of "cause" here elucidated is the fundamental or primitive one. It is not the property of scientists; except for those whose work most directly bears on such things as engineering, agriculture or medicine, and who are naturally interested in helping their practical colleagues, scientists hardly ever make use of the notion. A statement about causes in the sense here outlined comes very near to being a recipe for producing or preventing certain effects. It is not simply an inference-licence. Professional scientists, when they are carefully stating their findings, mostly express themselves in functional laws, which are pure inference-licences, with nothing of the recipe about them (explicitly at least). Thus the formula

$$I = \frac{E}{R}$$

tells you how to infer the current in a given circuit, knowing the electro-motive force and the resistance; it tells you how to infer the electro-motive force, knowing the resistance and current; and how to infer the resistance from current and electro-motive force. All these three things it tells you; and no one of them any more specially than any other—it works all ways, as an inference-licence. But while one might say a current of 3 amps. was caused by an e.m.f. of 6 volts across a resistance of 2 ohms, one would hardly say that a resistance of 2 ohms in the circuit was caused by an e.m.f. of 6 volts and a current of 3 amps. Why not? Given an e.m.f. of 6 volts one could make 3 amps. flow by making the resistance equal to 2 ohms. But one could not, given an e.m.f. of 6 volts, make the resistance of the circuit equal to 2 ohms by making a current of 3 amps. flow.

From one point of view the progress of natural science can be viewed as resulting from the substitution of pure inference-licences for recipes.

There is, however, what might be called a "popular science" use of "cause" which may not exactly fit the account given—a use of the word by laymen who know some science and by some scientists in their less strictly professional moments. I have in mind such a locution as "Gravity causes unsupported bodies to fall." Such a statement is not quite on a par, logically with "Great heat causes steel to melt." It would be fair to say, I think, that the use of the word "cause" here is a sophisticated extension from its more primitive and fundamental meaning. It is the root notion that I have been concerned with.

In accounts of causation given by philosophers in the past a specially fundamental role was often played by the motion of bodies. Every kind of change and every kind of natural law was often supposed to be "ultimately reducible to" or to be explicable in terms of it. In this account, too, though in a rather different way, the motion of bodies occupies a special position. Central to this account is the notion of a manipulation to produce A and thereby to produce B. When we manipulate things we control the motion of bodies, e.g. by rubbing sticks together (motion of bodies) men made them hot and thereby caused them to ignite. At least all those causal chains that are initiated by human beings go back to manipulations, that is, to matter in motion.

36. CAUSES, CONNECTIONS AND CONDITIONS IN HISTORY

Michael Scriven

1. AIMS AND JUSTIFICATION

The most important explanatory notion in history is that of causation, although it is by no means the only one. Its importance is not to be gauged by the frequency with which the actual word "cause" occurs; for the notion is very frequently embedded in other terms. Failure to notice this has led some philosophers and historians to believe, quite wrongly, that the notion could easily be eliminated from historiography.

If we examine a passage of historical writing that is intentionally condensed, say for an encyclopedia article, and is presumably thereby pared of the less essential details, we find a combination of purely descriptive narrative and explanatory narrative. The *Encyclopaedia Brittanica* article "English History," 1953 edition, written by Lucy Sutherland and John Holland Rose, provides such an example. The account there given of the history of the period contains both non-causal explanation and non-explanatory narrative; but a sample page also contains almost thirty occurrences of causal claims of which only two involve the term "cause." For example: "While political progress was *checked* by war, economic and social changes were *furthered* by it" (p. 531) (my emphasis on the causal notions). I take it that this could be translated without loss of essential meaning as: "The war *caused* a slowing-down of political progress, but also some advance in economic and social conditions."

SOURCE. Reprinted from "Causes, Connections and Conditions in History," by Michael Scriven in William H. Dray (ed.), *Philosophical Analysis and History*. By permission of Harper & Row, Publishers, Inc. Copyright © 1966 by William H. Dray.

Similar translations of other terminology are equally obvious, some of their phrases being: "resulted partly from," "led to," "stimulated," "increased under the pressure of," "enhanced by," "entailed," "made possible by," "forced," "brought on," "averted," "pauperized," "added to," "gave a sharp stimulus to." (It should be stressed that some of these phrases can be used in other contexts in a non-causal way.)

How can we best analyze the causal element in these common terms of the historian's vocabulary? In everyday contexts, it is sometimes quite easy to use terms like these when describing activities to which one is a witness; for causal claims are not always based on complex inferences. They seem to be easy to understand and easy to use on many occasions. Even on occasions where there is difficulty, its source does not generally lie in the *meaning* of the causal terms. The historian frequently encounters two special problems. On the one hand, he wishes to apply these terms to activities in the past, which he does not witness directly; on the other, he uses them to refer to entities on a scale where direct witness is impossible—for example, he may speak of a political *movement* as having caused certain *social* changes. But neither of these extensions of the use beyond the simplest cases seems to provide any important *logical* difficulties, although both, of course, introduce further practical ones.

The logical difficulty is to offer a satisfactory *analysis* of the concept of cause itself. Such analysis is normally taken to require reduction of the idea to some other simpler ideas. This paper undertakes a more modest type of analysis, the elucidation of the concept in terms of a systematic classification of its types; but the argument also suggests that no analysis of the reductionist kind is possible. Support is provided for the latter contention with particular reference to the frequently proposed analyses in terms of necessary or sufficient conditions.

Despite the ease of applying causal notions in *some* cases, a better understanding of these points can be of considerable assistance to the practitioner of causal notions. For there arise in history certain very complex cases (e.g., the causes of the Civil War) where it does become necessary to examine the evidence in the light of a thorough analysis of cause, and the analyses hitherto employed on such occasions have been much too simple.

2. THE CONTINUUM OF CAUSAL AND NON-CAUSAL LANGUAGE

Before we can analyze causal language, we need to see how it differs from non-causal language. Is there a sharp distinction?

If you are watching people enter a lecture room, you might notice someone who seems to be in a particular hurry doing what you would naturally describe as "forcing his way in." A policeman is sometimes described as "forcing a door," or as "forcing suspects to get into the Black Maria." An investor is sometimes said to have been "forced to sell blue-chip stock" to cover heavy losses on a speculative issue. These uses differ in important ways, but they are all causal notions in that they identify some agent as being responsible for an identified effect. They are miniature explanations of the named effect; and yet it is also reasonable to say that they are simply descriptions of what can be observed. When you see someone force a door or knock over a lamp, you have witnessed something which is correctly described in that way, but which is also a case of cause and effect; there is no sharp line between causal claims and observations. But there are clear cases of each that are not cases of the other, so we are dealing with a continuum and not a confusion.

The fact that it may be witnessed does not make the causal process a simple one logically, for the trained perception is capable of responding to immensely complex configurations and of building a very complex interpretation into the response. Our task is to clarify the kind of interpretation involved in a causal claim by contrast with a simple non-causal description like "He walked down the shorter path"; and yet, as we look carefully at this example, we can see that the term "walked" means "caused to move by the action of his legs, etc." The causal concepts are buried very deep in our language, indeed in our perception. The search for non-causal language is reminiscent of the search for pure sense-data. It would now be held by many that our concepts of physical objects are not built up from and cannot be analyzed in terms of pure sensations or appearances, and the analogous claim can be made here. We can explain the relation between causal and non-causal language, but not by showing that one is built out of the other.

Apart from the continuity and irreducibility claims just made, there is another aspect of causal language which involves a continuum, the continuum between cause and effect. We normally think of these as distinct, and it is often true that they are. But there are occasions where the distinction vanishes and the effect is simply part of the cause. "Opening a door" is a cause-impregnated descriptive phrase referring to an activity which brings about and explains an effect, namely, the door opening or being open. But it is *logically* impossible for this cause to occur without the effect occurring. This kind of example shows the extent to which we build the concept of causal connection into our language, and hence reinforces the original continuum claim. But it does more than this. It also shows how the distinction between cause and effect is itself a limited one, in the sense of being highly context-dependent. What is a cause in one context can be seen as itself a combination of cause and effect in another context. It is partly for this reason that historical narrative is explanatory—it incorporates what we might call micro-explanations in its very texture. In merely describing the course of a war or a reign the historian is constantly choosing language which implicitly identifies some phenomenon or aspect of a phenomenon as a cause and some other as an effect. And we, reading his account, are thus given a picture, an interpretation, which is a chain of causal explanations just as surely as it is when the resources of the language and our trained perception oblige us to use separate descriptions for cause and effect and label the connection between them with some explicitly connecting word.

Historical writing is of other kinds too. The narrative may be explanatory without being causally explanatory, by interpreting historical events as being of certain kinds that we understand well. In a neutral sense, this can be described as "evaluative." Moral evaluation sometimes enters into this process ("treachery," "treason," etc.) and sometimes even into the causal analysis— and it may serve as an end in itself, despite the protestations of the "scientific" historians, for applied social science cannot and should not be divorced from moral evaluation, unless we want psychiatry to be applied to the politically deviant on the grounds of their statistical abnormality, corruption and bribery to be regarded as fringe benefits for power figures, civil rights to be lumped with the short hemline as mere convention, etc. Moral distinctions are not only made, but are important, and part of an historian's task is set by, and hence requires understanding of, the moral distinctions and their relative importance. But these are other stories. This one concludes with a reminder that the absence of a sharp line between causal and non-causal, between cause and effect, between object-descriptions and sensation-descriptions, between names and descriptions, between facts and hypotheses, between fat men and thin men, does not show these distinctions to be unimportant.

3. THE TEMPORAL AND SPATIAL RELATIONS OF CAUSE AND EFFECT

A causal claim connects, though it may not distinguish, two distinguishable but perhaps not wholly separable elements. These elements may be events, processes, states, or the absence of these; they may be separated in time, adjacent, overlapping, or concurrent; and they may or may not have identifiable links between them.

Thus, there is a way of distinguishing the action of opening the door from the door's opening (an event or process)—but the first is not only temporally coextensive with the second, it logically cannot occur without the second. There are indeed important differences between logical entailment and causal connection, but this truth does not entitle one to conclude that cases of the one do not include some cases of the other. Cases like this are to be found throughout historical writing:

At the same time the significance of the City of London as a financial centre was enhanced by the transactions of the business involved in the provision of British subsidies, the supplying of British armies and the raising of government loans as well as by the eclipse of the financial power of Amsterdam. The growth of British exports, . . . was very rapid and entailed a similar growth in merchant shipping. . . .[1]

Notice that the first effect mentioned (an increase in the significance of the City of London) is not only simultaneous with its causes, but is to some extent the same thing as them—viewed from a different standpoint. The same comments apply to the relation between the growth of exports and of shipping. Any account of cause that fails to allow for cases where cause and effect are physically identical and only conceptually distinct will do scant justice to the historian's use.

Proceeding to the other extreme, it is a commonplace to the historian that events at one time may cause entirely different events at a much later time or at a distant place (and yet this has frequently been treated by philosophers as a logical impropriety). It is part of an historian's task to find out the intervening links, when a causal connection is asserted to hold over an interval—indeed, it is usually because they are already in his possession that he asserts the connection: but an historian has a good instinctive understanding of what is *meant* by the causal claim even when he lacks the links (otherwise he could not tell when the claim had been substantiated or disproved by the discovery, or proof of the non-existence, of certain links). However, it seems clear that the presence of the links is the *evidence for* a causal assertion, not the *meaning of* it, since in the experimental sciences it is easy enough to show a causal relationship when we have no idea at all as to the kind of intervening linkage there is, nor even any commitment to the view that there has to be one. (Gravitational effects provide an important historical case.) But the events of history are not so foreign to our understanding, and it might plausibly be argued that, as a matter of fact, there are always linkages of certain recognized kinds between any temporally separated historical cause and effect.

Any general analysis of cause would have to concern itself not only with cases in which there are long intervals between cause and effect, and with cases where they are simultaneous, but also with cases where the cause might plausibly be said to come after the effect (precognition, for example).[2] But since historians seldom assert and have never substantiated the latter, we shall not concern ourselves with such cases here, except to say that they cannot be regarded as non-existent and make one stage of the analysis much harder.

[1] "English History," *Encyclopedia Britannica*, 1953 edition.
[2] Michael Scriven, "Randomness and the Causal Order," *Analysis*, October, 1956.

4. THE ALLEGED CONNECTION BETWEEN CAUSES AND LAWS

The feature of causal assertions usually regarded as the most important, from a logical or philosophical point of view, is their alleged claim to instantiate universal laws. The key argument for such a conclusion goes like this. If C is said to be the cause of E, then more is being said than that C occurred and E occurred, even though those facts may be all that direct observation reveals about C and E.[3] We must therefore be relying on some further knowledge besides the fact of their occurrence to support our claim of a causal connection between C and E. Now that knowledge cannot be simply further observations about the circumstances surrounding C and E, since this would only yield more descriptions of particular events and no combination of these entails a causal claim. Nor can it be simply about the circumstances in *other* cases where E followed C, since that would be irrelevant to a causal claim about *this* case. Yet it seems clear that we have learned *something* from other cases which enables us to see in this one a causal connection between C and E. What we have learned must be some kind of generalization which we apply to this case. In some way, the co-occurrence of C and E must be a particular instance of a general law that connects a type of event of which C is an instance with a type of which E is an instance. This argument allegedly shows that particular causal claims, including those found in historical narrative, can only be analyzed in terms of general laws.

Now the general law might be of the simple form "C's are always accompanied by E's." This form implies that the association has been such that a C is always accompanied by an E, the reverse not having been established. It is usually thought that we can take this generalization to imply that C's always cause E's.

An illicit conclusion is that *whenever* we say C caused E we are committed to the unqualified generalization that C's always cause E's. We are only committed to *some* generalization of which the conjunction of C and E is a consequence. When an historian says that the London Corresponding Society "caused alarm" in the London of 1792 by its sympathy with the French Government,[4] he obviously does not stand committed to the claim that sympathy with France is always a cause of alarm in London. He asserts only that *in the circumstances of that time*, sympathy *by that group* caused alarm.

Logicians espousing the above argument have often said, in order to avoid

---

[3] It is usually assumed by proponents of this argument that C, E, and other circumstances are described in non-causal language and that causal connections cannot be directly observed. We ignore these errors for the moment.

[4] "English History," *Encyclopedia Britannica*, 1953 edition.

the mistake just discussed, that the historian judges those circumstances to be of a kind about which he knows a law like this: "Whenever sympathy is expressed, in certain circumstances, with a foreign power meeting certain conditions, by a group of a certain kind, alarm follows." We may call this a *qualified* (although still *universal*) generalization about C and E. It proposes a general, though very vague, set of conditions of which C is part, that are together *sufficient* for the occurrence of E. Now historians have usually not felt the above to be an accurate reconstruction of their procedures, chiefly because they do not profess knowledge of even such heavily qualified and vague laws. Yet the argument seems to show that we cannot justify the original causal claim, except by claiming it to be an instance of such a law.

I shall claim that only a much weaker kind of general statement, which the historian agrees he *does* have, is enough to satisfy what is sound in the argument. The above argument is invalid at the point where it tries to prove that *universal* laws are required. What it actually shows is only that we must appeal to some general proposition which (a) applies reliably to the present case, and (b) is founded upon other cases. But knowing a universal C-E connection, qualified or not, is only one means to this. Another is knowing a *possible* C-E connection, combined with an *elimination* of other possible connections. And a third is the *trained judgment* of the historian, which requires no knowledge of laws at all.

5. ELIMINATIVE CAUSAL ANALYSIS

My alternative account of causal explanations and their grounds may conveniently be approached through an examination of Professor Ernest Nagel's treatment of an historical example in *The Structure of Science.*[5] The example is Maitland's explanation of Queen Elizabeth's use of "etc." in stating her full title: the Queen is said deliberately to have chosen a vague expression to leave herself freedom of maneuver on the religious question troubling England at a time when Henry's breach with Rome was by no means accepted as final. Nagel rightly points out that the explanation, although it may well be perfectly sound historically, only leads us to see why she would choose *some* ambiguous phrase, of which the one cited was merely one of many open to her. Taking Maitland's explanation to be typical, Nagel generalizes as follows (p. 558): ". . . at best, the historian's explanation shows only that, under the asumptions stated, x's performance of A_1 on occasion t is probable" (where A_1 is the particular action, e.g., the use of the particular term "etc."). He thus concludes that typical historical explanation cannot attain the ideal status of

[5] Nagel, *The Structure of Science*, New York, 1962, pp. 552 ff.

instantiating a precise general law, but only a weak law which asserts a statistical connection between the conditions given and the occurrence of the effect.

The example, however, is actually devastating to the entire theory of explanation which Nagel, like other so-called "covering law" or "deductive model" theorists, accepts. He rightly sees that we could not *deduce*, using known laws and antecedent conditions, that the Queen would use this particular phrase; and he expresses this by saying that the explanation "at best . . . shows only that . . . [her doing this] is probable." But there are surely a *very* large number of alternative phrases or devices that could have been used by Elizabeth to express herself ambiguously; the actual probability that she would choose the one she did is therefore very small; it could surely not be said that it was *likely* that she would; it was only a *possibility*. Yet the basic tenet of Nagel's concept of probabilistic explanation is that "though the premises are logically insufficient to secure the truth of the explicandum, they are said to make the latter 'probable' " (p. 22).

One might suppose that Nagel's reply to this would be that all the historian is "really" explaining is the use of an ambiguous phrase, and not the use of *the particular one* Queen Elizabeth employed. This reply has frequently been suggested by other proponents of the covering law model of explanation (whether deductive or probabilistic), who would thus "reconstruct" the explanation to bring its claims into conformity with their theory of what a good explanation must be like. The historian regards himself as having put forward a reasonable explanation of the precise utterance, which is presumably what his job requires; the philosopher contends that all he has "really" done is explain the Queen's producing an utterance of a certain general type. The distinction is not merely verbal: the alleged connection of explanation and prediction, on covering law theory, is thereby protected at the expense of a slight reflection on the historian's professional achievement. We are told something that, if we had known it in advance, would have shown us that what happened "was to be expected." For Elizabeth's circumstances and intelligence were indeed such that one might have expected, with some confidence, the use of some ambiguous phrase, though not the use of "etc."

Nagel, however, does not take this way out; he has too much respect for the historian. He takes seriously the task of analyzing rather than improving the historian's procedure, up to the point where errors or inconsistencies can conclusively be demonstrated. But having come this far, he seems to hesitate on the brink of producing a really novel account of historical explanation; and this not only cheats him of discovery, but leaves him in an intrinsically awkward position—more vulnerable to counter-examples from historical usage than his more reconstructionist colleagues, yet advocating a type of position which is not sufficiently different from theirs to accommodate these examples satisfactorily.[6] Let us see what sort of logical account emerges from a more sustained attempt to accept the explanation as the historian claims it to be.

We should have to begin by conceding that it does not at all demonstrate that the events to be explained were to be expected. Covering law theorists, Nagel included, have always felt that, if this were not done, we should be left simply with a narrative description of *what* happened, without any explanation of *why* it happened: if we're not shown that what happened *had* to happen (in accordance with a law) given the preceding conditions, then we are just relating a sequence of events, none of which "brings about" its successors. Quite apart from the possibility that descriptions of what happened may be proper answers to the important kind of request for explanations that demand *how* something happened,[7] there is a straightforward way of meeting this very legitimate concern. An explanation tells us why something occurred if it tells us what factor or factors of the type in which we are interested (e.g., economic, motivational, political) actually brought it about, i.e., what factor, in the circumstances, so *tipped the balance of events* as to produce the known outcome. Such a factor need not itself be a sufficient condition for the outcome; it may be simply one element in a set which is jointly sufficient. This far the covering law model can still go. But the crucial point is that the historian *does not need to know* what the other conditions are that make up the sufficient condition. He isn't interested in them, usually, but he couldn't give them even if he were. So he is not in any way capable of showing that the event had to happen or was to be expected. But how then can he know that the factor he does quote *is* part of a sufficient condition for the effect? He knows this because he takes it as axiomatic that there had to be *some* set of conditions present which brought about the effect, i.e., he assumes determinism in the sense of the ever-presence of explanations.

Now of course many of the elements in the antecedent conditions are not causally efficacious. An historian *must* be able to show that the factor he selects is not causally redundant: a condition whose occurrence or non-occurrence would have had no effect whatsoever on the course of events leading to *E*. He must have reasons for supposing that the alleged cause "pulls some weight." One cannot, however, simply say that the cause is an antecedent factor that is a *necessary* condition for the effect—obviously some effects can be brought about in several ways and in such a case no one of these possible causes is necessary for the effect to occur. Professor Nagel strikes out in a

---

[6] For further discussion see *Minnesota Studies in the Philosophy of Science*, Vol. II (ed. H. Feigl, M. Scriven and G. Maxwell, University of Minnesota Press, Minneapolis 1958), pp. 99–102.

[7] There is ultimately a coincidence between the answers to "How did it come about?" and "Why did it happen?", which I believe to be the key types of explanation request in history (cf. "How *could* it have come about?").

more promising direction from talk about causes as sufficient or as necessary conditions when he proposes, as a criterion of causal connection, the idea of a cause as being "contingently necessary"; as being one which, *given the other circumstances*, is necessary for the outcome. In *this* situation, we would be claiming, the outcome would not have occurred had the cause not occurred. But even this improvement is open to possible misinterpretation. For there may be several possible replacements for the non-redundant condition which will causally complete a sufficient set, although they simply happen not to be present. Elizabeth might have had to compress her title on the coin of the realm for space-saving reasons or to avoid some currently vulgar use of terms in the official title. We can make a further improvement and say that a cause is one of several alternative factors the presence of one (any one) of which is necessary in order that a set of conditions actually present be sufficient for the effect. There are a number of possible reasons which might have led Elizabeth to choose an ambiguous phrase; Maitland believes he has identified the one that did—not that *had* to, but just that *did*. He is giving the *explanatory* factor, because in its absence, *and* in the absence of any other possible causes (which we discover by inspection), the effect would not have occurred in the way it did.

Now we could put all of this into the notion of "contingently necessary" which Nagel does not do (*loc. cit.*, p. 559). But *in either case* we shall have to reject his overall claim about the limitations on historical explanation. For in order to establish a causal claim on behalf of a factor what does the historian need? Merely evidence that his candidate was present, that it has on other occasions clearly demonstrated its capacity to produce an effect of the sort here under study (or there might be theoretical grounds for thinking it a possible cause rather than previous direct experience of its actual efficacy), and the *absence* of evidence (despite a thorough search) (a) that its *modus operandi* was inoperative here, and/or (b) that any of the other possible causes were present. If the event studied had a cause at all (which the historian assumes it did), then he may confidently assert that the residual condition is elected. This argument *proves* his claim—and it requires nothing the historian does not possess. The only general proposition that might be involved would be a list of the known possible causes of the kind of effect in question. Explanation proceeds by the elimination of possible causes, not by the application of possible laws.

6. DIAGNOSTIC JUDGMENT AND *VERSTEHEN*

But how does a historian establish the claim of a certain factor to be a "possible" cause? I discuss this in the next section but make one comment here. By refusing to accept a covering law answer to such a question, I do not intend to deny a link between the particular case and our general experience. My analysis instead supports the idea, common among historians, that history teaches us about human nature and our future best choices by teaching us about *possibilities* rather than *regularities*. For the "causal lists" we learn, or learn to apply, on this analysis are backward-looking generalizations from which predictions about particular cases are not normally possible. Nevertheless, they can serve as important guides to individual behavior and social action since, for example, the deliberate and sustained elimination of all the possible causes of something guarantees its non-occurrence, and the attempt to bring about all its possible causes at least *increases* the chance it will occur.

Another question arises about this modest "schematization." Is it realistic to suppose that we are ever or often in possession of a "list of possible causes?" For wars, murders, strikes, and many other effects it is not hard to give such lists. But I do not believe such lists are essential, though possibly desirable. Even an experienced political historian might find it hard to give a comprehensive list of possible causes of the collapse of governments. Yet long training may have given him considerable diagnostic *skill:* he may be extremely good at identifying causes even though he does not know, let alone know how to describe, the perceptual cues he employs. The good mechanic can tell from the sound of the motor that the overheating is almost certainly due to a main bearing failure—but he cannot tell you just what it is about the sound that enables him to tell this. Nor can he tell you the *whole* list of other possible causes of overheating he would have explored had he not spotted this immediately (and which he can now ignore, because—unlike the historian—he knows that there is a negligible probability of overdetermination in such a case). He is like a man who can sing hymns from memory in a congregation but cannot recite them; at the end of each line, he needs the cues provided by the circumstances around him in order to remember the next.

The mechanic in his special field and the historian in his, like each of us in the field of human behavior, has learned to spot causes and motives from the myriad clues of language and context—in objects, documents, or persons —and even though we can rarely give any exhaustive list, we can often be rightly confident that "It must have been this—there's nothing else it *could* have been," because we can be fairly sure we would have spotted any others that were present in the course of our thorough search.

There is no magic about explicit inferences that makes them any more reliable than trained immediate diagnosis, and the empathists and *verstehen* theorists were right to recognize the peculiar virtues of the human instrument in diagnosing human behavior. The human historian can use himself as an extremely versatile model, just as an hydraulics engineer may use a model of a dam site to determine silting rates; neither needs to know exactly what makes the model work as long as they can check that it does on enough occasions to make it reasonable to rely on it.

The special training of the historian (like the anthropologist) in a particular period or field can give him a special "feeling" for the people he studies and hence lead him to better explanations than would come naturally to someone unfamiliar with that culture. Confirmation of his judgments is often possible with the discovery of new material and serves to provide us with grounds for confidence in them when no direct confirmation is possible. It seems to me Nagel is wrong to suppose that empathic insight is heuristically helpful but not of itself a valid basis for the claim of comprehension. One may "see" (or understand) immediately why someone or some group did something, and not require further testing to be justifiably confident that this really is the reason. The internal complexity of the behavior studied may be sufficiently high for it to be entirely reasonable to conclude that one's insight has yielded the only possible explanation. One "sees" the explanation via *verstehen*—but the act of "seeing" is a highly tested skill, as is "seeing" the solution of a bridge or chess problem, or "seeing" that a set of tracks are those of a red fox running. The "seer" is a well-tested instrument, and the historian-reader combination is in an extremely privileged position in that the procedure of explanation only requires the historian to present enough cues to the reader to enable the latter to trigger off his own trained responses and obtain the same insight. This is a process which is most importantly and valuably—and not "unfortunately"—related to that involved in reading a work of literature. It is not in the very least unscientific; indeed it is extremely close to the very efficient way in which engineers or physicists communicate explanations by the use of analogies or jargon whose function is also to set up certain response-patterns.

The other special feature of *verstehen* is the way it explains actions with motives, rather than with a law of the "constant conjunction" sort. The latter may be well understood or accepted, but it cannot in general be any better understood than the former. The *verstehen* theorist does not, I think, maintain the less defensible thesis that we can understand *why* "an insult tends to produce anger" *better* than any physical phenomenon (Nagel, *op. cit.*, p. 483) ; all he needs is to understand *that* it does in order, say, to understand fully why Brutus became angry at Cassius when insulted.

Opponents of the *verstehen* approach often stress the undoubted fact that the presence of a motive or reason in a man's mind does not prove its causal efficacy; they ask how (except in the covering law way) we can *show* that it was the operative factor in the way the man acted. As Nagel points out, the accused in a murder trial may be under grave suspicion because he is "known to have hated the victim"; yet "he may have killed the deceased by accident, because he was paid to do so, or for a number of other reasons" (p. 555). But how *would* the prosecutor go about showing the motive was hatred? He would show that none of the other factors which are possible causes appeared to be present. Antony loved Cleopatra; nevertheless, he may have fled from the battle of Actium not to join her but because of "his ambition to make Egypt a granary of Rome" (p. 555). We look for evidence from his intimates, his diaries and his later actions to support any such alternative hypothesis. If this is not present, we justifiably conclude that the eminently suitable motive which we know about was the operative one. If another factor *is* present, we look for evidence that it had none of the intermediate effects which would be necessary if it were finally to bring about the effect in which we are interested. What could be more reasonable? An account of explanation like Nagel's, however, leaves room for only "one viable answer: the historian can justify his causal imputation only by the assumption that, when the given factor is a circumstance under which men act, they generally conduct themselves in a manner similar to the particular action described in the imputation . . ." (p. 555). Haters *generally* murder; lovers *generally* flee from battles. This is surely an implausible suggestion.

The historian cannot do without some kind of general knowledge about human nature. The truth is, however, that this simply does not need to be of the kind "cited in theoretical treatises" (p. 549). The most abysmal truisms suffice: that people *can* commit murder from hatred and greed; that they *often* want food and clothing; that they *sometimes* value their children's lives before their own, and so on. (It should be noted that no distinction between causes and reasons is being made, for there is no difference in the analysis of their roles in explanations.) The reason these trivialities suffice is simple: historians have *only* to explain, so they have only to choose from the factors present the one(s) most likely to have been the cause(s). To do this they do not even have to know lists of all possible causes of the effect in question; they only need to be good at recognizing its causes when present. *This* can be called knowledge of human nature though not scientific knowledge.

7. CAUSE AND CONTEXT

We must now proceed to a somewhat more careful analysis. In a given explanatory inquiry, there will generally be a number of factors which meet the formal requirement of being a non-redundant member of a sufficient set of conditions; yet we quite often talk of *the* cause of what occurred. A full analysis of causal judgment thus requires reference to further considerations of a pragmatic or contextual sort. Such considerations in fact carry half the weight.

The contextual aspect may be characterized as follows. The search for causes proceeds in a context which indicates two connected features: (a) the *type* of factor which is of interest, and (b) what may be called a "contrast state." For example, given the context, the proper type may be physiological or motivational, characterological or controllable, local or distant. Sometimes the "proximate cause" is of paramount interest, e.g., the assassination at Sarajevo, sometimes a remote one, e.g., childhood experiences. The choice is sometimes dictated by considerations of controllability, but often also by merely analytical considerations, as in astrophysical discussions of the motion and explosion of stars. The function of contrast is shown in the fact that the quetion "Why has this man developed skin cancer?" may mean "Why has he got cancer *now*, whereas a month or so ago he did not?" or it may mean "Why has *he* got cancer whereas his brother, who works in the same job, has not?" In the first case, the implied contrast is between *his* being cancer-free and his present afflicted state. In the second, it is between *another* cancer-free individual and his afflicted state. So the answer to the first question may be "Because he was exposed to a heavy dose of ultra-violet radiation," and to the second, "Because of some (as-yet-unidentified) constitutional factor(s) present in about 20 percent of the population." The considerations of *type* directly bear on selection of the cause, those of *contrast* on the identification of the effect and hence indirectly on selection of cause.

In the Queen Elizabeth case, the contrast that interests the historian is between her using the ambiguous phrase and using her full title, not between using *this* ambiguous phrase and using another one. (For a speech-habit specialist, the latter might well be the contrast of interest.) Hence Maitland produces the factors which explain why Elizabeth used *this* phrase *in so far as the phrase has any historical significance*. It is not that he *doesn't* explain why she used *this* phrase; he does explain it, fully, with regard to the historically appropriate contrast. The difference between this analysis and the reconstructionist approach is still fundamental and not just verbal: for the other approach suggests that more work is needed to get a decent explanation; that all the historian has is just a weak probability explanation of what he is trying to explain.

We have introduced the idea that cause (and, in general, explanation) is essentially a context-dependent notion. This does not mean that we are giving a "psychological" rather than a "logical" analysis (as formalists often claim), or a "subjective" rather than "objective" one. It means that the territory of logic is not terminated by the period at the end of the sentence. The proper analysis of the meaning of some terms—as computer programmers trying to get their machines to translate foreign languages have long known—sometimes requires that one resolve ambiguities in an utterance by consideration of contextual cues, and the relevant context is not always merely further linguistic utterances; it may be the state of knowledge of the reader.[8] When we are looking for causes we are looking for explanations in terms of a few

---

[8] Cf. the "requirement of total evidence" in probability theory and C. G. Hempel's theory of explanation. (See his essay in *Minnesota Studies in the Philosophy of Science*, Vol. III, ed. H. Feigl and G. Maxwell, University of Minnesota Press, Minneapolis, 1962).

factors or a single factor; and what counts as an explanation is whatever fills in the gap in the inquirer's or reader's understanding. If he's puzzled by a certain contrast, then what we need is the factor which accounts for this contrast; and it's often much easier to find this than it would be to find the set of conditions which are sufficient for the total state of affairs which is "the effect." That is a work of supererogation.

It is not wholly adequate but may be somewhat helpful to formulate the preceding point as: "What counts as *the effect* is dependent on the context." The way in which the context focusses the search applies also to the cause itself. It is thus that we get the restriction to factors of a certain type, e.g., economic or political or manipulable.[9]

A common kind of case is the following, though it is not the general case. If one of two causal candidates—otherwise equal—is a standing condition, always present, and known by the inquirer to be present, whereas the other is an unexpected "interfering condition" whose occurrence is a discovery for the inquirer, then it is correct to call the latter *the* cause. For this factor is (a) informative and (b) crucial for the relevant contrast. In these cases the contrast is between the state which actually occurs, and the one which was normal or to be expected; but in other cases the contrast may only be with a state which appears at least *as* likely to have occurred, or whose nonoccurrence is not surprising but especially interesting because it was the rational, proper, prudent, or legal outcome, or an outcome that could easily have been brought about by the agent. (Similarly, the non-occurrence of a certain event may be identified as the cause, because the contrast of interest is with the situation in which the cause occurs and the effect does not.)

When we look for the cause(s) of the war between Napoleonic France and Russia, it is by contrast with the state of peace—it is *not* by contrast with the state of affairs in which the separate political entities of France and Russia do not exist. Thus, although the very possibility of a war between Napoleonic France and Russia, and hence the war itself, *depends* on the historically interesting circumstances which led to the formation of Czarist Russia, that dependence is not adequate ground for asserting that these circumstances are a cause of the war. They are necessary conditions but not the causes of the war. The historian's inquiry about the war begins with—is not *now* concerned with—the existence of those nations and his interest is simply in explaining a *change* in their relations. This contextual focussing can convert the merely

---

[9] In the legal context, as a special example, there is a noticeable tendency to incorporate notions of responsibility into the notion of cause since this is our principle concern. Hence foreseeability-by-a-reasonable-man (of the possibility of something like the effect) becomes a criterion in identifying an action as a cause (see H. L. A. Hart and A. M. Honoré, *Causation in the Law, passim*). One *might* say this is an attributive use rather than an explanatory one, but the distinction is not mandatory.

"causal factor" status of any single item in the usual historical explanation into full causal status as "the cause"—in a given context only.

We may generalize this point to cover cases of sufficient conditions. It is perfectly true that, since all men are mortal, birth is a sufficient condition for death. But this is not an adequate ground for offering to a coroner investigating a murder the suggestion that he need look no further—the victim's death was caused by his birth. For the coroner's inquiry is clearly couched in terms of a contrast state of continued life, and birth is as much a sufficient condition for the continued life (had *it* occurred) as it is for eventual death (which *did* occur). So it does not provide us with a factor which accounts for the *contrast*. We need some factor which occurs only in the *actual* course of events and which (possibly with cooperation from factors common to both courses of events) is a sufficient condition for the difference between that course of events and the contrast state.

Of course, there *might* be circumstances in which the contrast state to death would not be "continued life," but another form of life-ending, say transfiguration. If death occurs only to those who are born and transfiguration occurs only to those whose life-beginning occurs as condensation from an insubstantial spirit, *then* the suggestion that birth was the cause of a particular individual's death, made in an appropriate context, would be sensible. But in our world, poetry and philosophy provide the only contexts where the contrast is not with "continued life," and so it is never appropriate, in practical circumstances, to cite birth as the cause of death.

8. DEFECTS OF THE NECESSARY CONDITION ANALYSIS

The foregoing analysis has represented causes as selected on pragmatic grounds from conditions which are (a) known to be possible causes, (b) known to be present in the case under consideration, and (c) not known to operate in a way contraindicated by known data about the case.

But this only defines "cause" in terms of "possible cause." Can we not proceed further and define "possible cause" in terms of some combination of necessary and sufficient conditions, these being interpreted as simple regularity notions? The answer appears to be that we cannot. The concept of cause is fundamental to our conception of the world in much the same way as the concept of number: we cannot define it in terms of other notions without conceptual or ostensive[10] circularity.

[10] Ostensive circulatory afflicts the Russellian definition of a number, which can only be applied by someone with the capacity to count that number of quantifiers, and hence in an important sense presupposes possession of the concept. (Cf. Tarski's definition of truth.) Neither ostensive nor conceptual circularity are fatal to *all* the purposes of definitions, but generally make their use as eliminative or reductive devices unsatisfactory.

It is probably best to see the notion of cause, like number, as systematically developed from a simple case which we can exhibit, though not define in non-causal terms. The existence of this developmental sequence does not establish the common idea that later members are simply complex combinations of the earlier ones. (Finding the sum of an infinite series is not done by a complex combination of counting procedures even though the calculus is a development from arithmetic.)

8.1. *Basic Experimental Case.* Suppose that whenever and however we produce C, E occurs, and that E never occurs unless C is produced (so that C is in a sense the only handle by means of which we can manipulate E) then C is the cause of E. (We assume a normal experimental context throughout. E may also turn out to be a cause of C, e.g., where C and E are alterations in pressure and temperature of a cylinder of gas.)

8.2. *Basic Observation Case.* Suppose that C just occurs on various occasions and is accompanied by (perhaps followed by) E, and E never occurs on any other occasions. C is the cause of E if (but not only if) we can conclude that C *would* always be accompanied by E, no matter how or when it was produced (i.e., if we can reduce it to Case 8.1). Since we assume that something is responsible for the occurrence of E (determinism) and C is at least always present, the great problem is to eliminate the possibility that some *other* antecedent of C and E, say X, is bringing them both about *independently*.[11] Thus, the correlation between the early and the late symptoms of a disease has often been mistakenly identified as a causal connection until it is discovered both are due to a third factor, the infection itself.

Case 8.1 is immune to this difficulty, since when we experimentally control C we produce it at random moments, i.e., moments not determined by[12] any preceding environmental factor that could possibly determine E (we may use a table of random numbers, dice, a roulette wheel, a decimal clock, or an electronic randomizer).

8.3. *Compound Causes.* Suppose that we need to bring about not only C but also D in order to get E (and that D alone is not sufficient). We may call C and D *causal factors or co-causes* of E. Neither can be called *the* cause, except when the context changes so that one or the other can be regarded as a standing condition or an irrelevant factor.

8.4. *Multiple Causes.* If C and D are *each* sufficient to bring about E, and

---

[11] Of course, even if C is the cause of E, many antecedents of C bring it about and *hence* bring about E. To say X brings about C and E independently means roughly that prevention of C's occurrence will not prevent E's occurrence.

[12] Notice that this definition of "random" itself involves the causal notion of "determined by," just as the Case 8.1 description involves the notion of "producing" C. Both are dispensable only in terms of other causal notions, e.g., those of "independent and dependent variable," "free act" (in a technical sense).

nothing else is, then whichever occurs is the cause. If both occur, one of them may not have had any effect on this occasion, a possibility which we check by examining the situation for the presence of known intermediate links which characterize the *modus operandi* of C and D, i.e., any sets of conditions "C_1 or C_2 or ..." (or "D_1 or D_2 or ...") which are necessary for C (or D) to act as the cause of E. This test does not apply where no such links are known, and since it is not logically necessary that there be any (C and E may be adjacent links in the chain, or differ only from a certain descriptive standpoint, or represent "action at a distance"), the test is not part of the meaning, of course. But it is the historian's and the coroner's key test.

If one has brought about E before the other could, although it would have in time, we have a case of *independent overdetermination* (Case 8.5), but only one cause.

If both occur, both may have been effective, bringing about E simultaneously, or essentially simultaneously for the purpose at hand, which gives the case of *simultaneous overdetermination* (Case 8.6)—for example, a firing squad—and neither factor can be identified as *the* cause (but cf. the compound cause, Case 8.3).

In any case of an effect for which there are multiple causes we are no longer able to infer to C from E, i.e., C is not a necessary condition for E. However, we can infer from C plus the absence of the other possible causes to E, and since the absence of the other causes is part of the surrounding circumstances, we might still regard the cause as "necessary in the circumstances" or what Nagel calls "contingently necessary." But this situation is complicated by the possibility of overdetermination, i.e., any cases of multiple causation where the causes are not mutually exclusive. If a revolution is overdetermined, as such events frequently are, there are several factors present which will ensure its occurrence, one of which we may assume gets in first. It will be quite incorrect to say that this factor is contingently necessary for the effect if, *ex hypothesi*, the remaining circumstances are quite adequate to bring about the effect by themselves.

We might try to save the situation for the contingently necessary analysis by invoking the fact that the other factors would not bring about the effect at the same time, and we might argue that the effect we are trying to explain is a revolution at the particular time it took place (i.e., the contrast state is peace at that moment). Unfortunately, this possibility is undermined by a species of overdetermination which we may call *linked overdetermination* (Case 8.7). There the factors are not independent; the circumstances are such that the very act of preventing C from occurring will bring about D which will itself cause E ("Damned if he does and damned if he doesn't"). Suppose a radical group attempts a *coup d'état*; the effort is watched attentively by the army, which will take action if the coup is unsuccessful, but not otherwise. In such a case, where the political coup may be slower moving than the military, we cannot argue that the government's downfall would occur at a different time.

Suppose we argue that the cause is necessary to explain the way in which the collapse occurred, if not the time. But *many* facts about the way the collapse occurred are, in a particular case, such that the cause is not a necessary condition for *their* occurrence, e.g., whether communication of the crisis details between members of the tottering cabinet was telephonic or telegraphic. The necessary condition analyst replies that these facts are not historically significant, not relevant to the contrast in which he is interested. He *is* explaining the *exact* historical occurrence, but only historically, i.e., not with an equal interest in all aspects of it. How do we determine which details are historically relevant—since, after all, the delay involved in telegraphing could well be crucial in some such cases? The answer must be, it seems, that it depends on its consequences for the occurrence of the item of principal interest. Alas, this is a *causal* consideration and so we have not analyzed cause in terms of necessary condition but in terms of necessary condition and cause. The attempt is not without value, but it is not a reductive analysis. It reflects the good methodological principle of building up a case by finding clues which in their totality can *only* be explained by the hypothesis that C caused E.[13]

In general, then, the search for an acausal definition of "cause" turns out to be ultimately as unsuccessful as the search for an amoral definition of

---

[13] *Technical footnote:* "C is the only possible cause of E in circumstances C'" is not the same as "C is a necessary condition for E in C'" not only for the reasons given (which show the first to include cases the second excludes unless made equivalent by circularity) but because, embarrassingly enough, the second description would identify many an *effect* of E as E's cause. For, with a suitable choice of C', there are many effects of E (call them $G_1, G_2, \ldots$) whose occurrence it is possible to infer from the occurrence of E i.e., the G's must occur if E does—in other words, their occurrence is necessary, given E's occurrence in C'—which makes the G's causes of E on the above proposed definition.

It is possible to salvage the necessary condition analysis here by using a slightly different and possibly more natural definition of necessary condition—unfortunately, it involves a causal notion. An analogous series of difficulties attends the notion of a cause as a non-redundant member of *some* set of conditions which are jointly sufficient for the effect. This handles linked overdetermination nicely but does less well on independent overdetermination, where *it* requires an accessory stipulation about the presence of intervening links, "links" being a causal notion. Nor can causes be distinguished from effects on this definition. It is possible to give a proof of the equivalence of these two notions under certain plausible assumptions, e.g., the assumption of the thesis of detectivism—the converse of determinism—which asserts that different causes have different effects. It seems clear that the distinction between cause and effect is linked to the *range* of warranted counterfactual claims; we can't say flatly that if C hadn't occurred then E wouldn't have, but the weaknesses in this are less than and different from those in the claim that if G (one of E's effects) hadn't occurred, E couldn't (wouldn't?) have occurred.

"moral." It is, however, no less illuminating, and in the present discussion we have uncovered two useful approximations to the notion of cause, formulated in terms of considerations which will at least avoid the common failure to allow for overdetermination. It may also be seen from the discussion how historical and psychological analysis proceeds by the development of knowledge of possible causes and their *modus operandi*—a knowledge very unlike explicit knowledge of scientific laws—which is applied to the explanation of particular cases by the process of evidential, formal and contextual elimination described above.

37. ACTIONS, REASONS, AND CAUSES

Donald Davidson

What is the relation between a reason and an action when the reason explains the action by giving the agent's reason for doing what he did? We may
call such explanations *rationalizations*, and say that the reason *rationalizes*
the action.

In this paper I want to defend the ancient—and common-sense—position
that rationalization is a species of ordinary causal explanation. The defence
no doubt requires some redeployment, but not more or less complete abandonment of the position, as urged by many recent writers.[1]

I

A reason rationalizes an action only if it leads us to see something the
agent saw, or thought he saw, in his action—some feature, consequence, or
aspect of the action the agent wanted, desired, prized, held dear, thought duti-
ful, beneficial, obligatory, or agreeable. We cannot explain why someone did

SOURCE. Davidson, Donald, "Actions, Reasons, and Causes," *Journal of Philosophy*, Vol. 60,
1963. Reprinted with permission. Copyright © 1963 by Journal of Philosophy, Inc.

[1] Some examples: G. E. M. Anscombe, *Intention*, Oxford, 1959; Stuart Hampshire,
Thought and Action, London, 1959; H. L. A. Hart and A. M. Honoré, *Causation in the
Law*, Oxford, 1959; William Dray, *Laws and Explanation in History*, Oxford, 1957; and
most of the books in the series edited by R. F. Holland, *Studies in Philosophical Psychology*, including Anthony Kenny, *Action, Emotion and Will*, London, 1963, and A. I.
Melden, *Free Action*, London, 1961. Page references in parentheses will all be to these
works.

what he did simply by saying the particular action appealed to him; we must indicate what it was about the action that appealed. Whenever someone does something for a reason, therefore, he can be characterized as (*a*) having some sort of pro attitude toward actions of a certain kind, and (*b*) believing (or knowing, perceiving, noticing, remembering) that his action is of that kind. Under (*a*) are to be included desires, wantings, urges, promptings, and a great variety of moral views, aesthetic principles, economic prejudices, social conventions, and public and private goals and values in so far as these can be interpreted as attitudes of an agent directed toward actions of a certain kind. The word "attitude" does yeoman service here, for it must cover not only permanent character traits that show themselves in a lifetime of behaviour, like love of children or a taste for loud company, but also the most passing fancy that prompts a unique action, like a sudden desire to touch a woman's elbow. In general, pro attitudes must not be taken for convictions, however temporary, that every action of a certain kind ought to be performed, is worth performing, or is, all things considered, desirable. On the contrary, a man may all his life have a yen, say, to drink a can of paint, without ever, even at the moment he yields, believing it would be worth doing.

Giving the reason why an agent did something is often a matter of naming the pro attitude (*a*) or the related belief (*b*) or both; let me call this pair the *primary reason* why the agent performed the action. Now it is possible to reformulate the claim that rationalizations are causal explanations, and give structure to the argument as well, by stating two theses about primary reasons:

1. For us to understand how a reason of any kind rationalizes an action it is necessary and sufficient that we see, at least in essential outline, how to construct a primary reason.

2. The primary reason for an action is its cause.

I shall argue for these points in turn.

II

I flip the switch, turn on the light, and illuminate the room. Unbeknownst to me I also alert a prowler to the fact that I am home. Here I do not do four things, but only one, of which four descriptions have been given.[2] I flipped

---

[2] We would not call my unintentional alerting of the prowler an action, but it should not be inferred from this that alerting the prowler is therefore something different from flipping the switch, say just its consequence. Actions, performances, and events not involving intention are alike in that they are often referred to or defined partly in terms of some terminal stage, outcome, or consequence.

The word "action" does not very often occur in ordinary speech, and when it does it is usually reserved for fairly portentous occasions. I follow a useful philosophical practice

the switch because I wanted to turn on the light, and by saying I wanted to turn on the light I explain (give my reason for, rationalize) the flipping. But I do not, by giving this reason, rationalize my alerting of the prowler nor my illuminating of the room. Since reasons may rationalize what someone does when it is described in one way and not when it is described in another, we cannot treat what was done simply as a term in sentences like "My reason for flipping the switch was that I wanted to turn on the light"; otherwise we would be forced to conclude, from the fact that flipping the switch was identical with alerting the prowler, that my reason for alerting the prowler was that I wanted to turn on the light. Let us mark this quasi-intensional[3] character of action descriptions in rationalizations by stating a bit more precisely a necessary condition for primary reasons:

C_1. R is a primary reason why an agent performed the action A under the description d only if R consists of a pro attitude of the agent toward actions with a certain property, and a belief of the agent that A, under the description d, has that property.

How can my wanting to turn on the light be (part of) a primary reason, since it appears to lack the required element of generality? We may be taken in by the verbal parallel between "I turned on the light" and "I wanted to turn on the light." The first clearly refers to a particular event, so we conclude that the second has this same event as its object. Of course it is obvious that the event of my turning on the light can't be referred to in the same way by both sentences, since the existence of the event is required by the truth of "I turned on the light" but not by the truth of "I wanted to turn on the light." If the reference were the same in both cases, the second sentence would entail the first; but in fact the sentences are logically independent. What is less obvious, at least until we attend to it, is that the event whose occurrence makes "I turned on the light" true cannot be called the object, however intensional, of

---

in calling anything an agent does intentionally an action, including intentional omissions. What is really needed is some suitably generic term to bridge the following gap: suppose "A" is a description of an action, "B" is a description of something done voluntarily, though not intentionally, and "C" is a description of something done involuntarily and unintentionally; finally, suppose $A = B = C$. Then A, B, C are the same—what? "Action," "event," "thing done," each have, at least in some contexts, a strange ring when coupled with the wrong sort of description. Only the question "Why did you (he) do A?" has the true generality required. Obviously, the problem is greatly aggravated if we assume, as Melden does (*Free Action*, 85), that an action ("raising one's arm") can be identical with a bodily movement ("one's arm going up").

[3] 'Quasi-intentional' because, besides its intensional aspect, the description of the action must also refer in rationalizations; otherwise it could be true that an action was done for a certain reason and yet the action not have been performed. Compare "the author of *Waverley*" in "George IV knew the author of *Waverley* wrote *Waverley*."

"I wanted to turn on the light." If I turned on the light, then I must have done it at a precise moment, in a particular way—every detail is fixed. But it makes no sense to demand that my want be directed at an action performed at any one moment or done in some unique manner. Any one of an indefinitely large number of actions would satisfy the want, and can be considered equally eligible as its object. Wants and desires often are trained on physical objects. However, "I want that gold watch in the window" is not a primary reason, and explains why I went into the store only because it suggests a primary reason—for example, that I wanted to buy the watch.

Because "I wanted to turn on the light" and "I turned on the light" are logically independent, the first can be used to give a reason why the second is true. Such a reason gives minimal information: it implies that the action was intentional, and wanting tends to exclude some other pro attitudes, such as a sense of duty or obligation. But the exclusion depends very much on the action and the context of explanation. Wanting seems pallid beside lusting, but it would be odd to deny that someone who lusted after a woman or a cup of coffee wanted her or it. It is not unnatural, in fact, to treat wanting as a genus including all pro attitudes as species. When we do this and when we know some action is intentional, it is empty to add that the agent wanted to do it. In such cases, it is easy to answer the question "Why did you do it?" with "For no reason," meaning not that there is no reason but that there is no *further* reason, no reason that cannot be inferred from the fact that the action was done intentionally; no reason, in other words, besides wanting to do it. This last point is not essential to the present argument, but it is of interest because it defends the possibility of defining an intentional action as one done for a reason.

A primary reason consists of a belief and an attitude, but it is generally otiose to mention both. If you tell me you are easing the jib because you think that will stop the main from backing, I don't need to be told that you want to stop the main from backing; and if you say you are biting your thumb at me because you want to insult me, there is no point in adding that you think that by biting your thumb at me you will insult me. Similarly, many explanations of actions in terms of reasons that are not primary do not require mention of the primary reason to complete the story. If I say I am pulling weeds because I want a beautiful lawn, it would be fatuous to eke out the account with "And so I see something desirable in any action that does, or has a good chance of, making the lawn beautiful." Why insist that there is any *step*, logical or psychological, in the transfer of desire from an end that is not an action to the actions one conceives as means? It serves the argument as well that the desired end explains the action only if what are believed by the agent to be means are desired.

Fortunately, it is not necessary to classify and analyse the many varieties of emotions, sentiments, moods, motives, passions, and hungers whose mention may answer the question "Why did you do it?" in order to see how, when such mention rationalizes the action, a primary reason is involved. Claustrophobia gives a man's reason for leaving a cocktail party because we know people want to avoid, escape from, be safe from, put distance between themselves and, what they fear. Jealousy is the motive in a poisoning because, among other things, the poisoner believes his action will harm his rival, remove the cause of his agony, or redress an injustice, and these are the sorts of things a jealous man wants to do. When we learn a man cheated his son out of greed, we do not necessarily know what the primary reason was, but we know there was one, and its general nature. Ryle analyses "he boasted from vanity" into "he boasted on meeting the stranger and his doing so satisfies the lawlike proposition that whenever he finds a chance of securing the admiration and envy of others, he does whatever he thinks will produce this admiration and envy" (*The Concept of Mind*, 89). This analysis is often, and perhaps justly, criticized on the ground that a man may boast from vanity just once. But if Ryle's boaster did what he did from vanity, then something entailed by Ryle's analysis is true: the boaster wanted to secure the admiration and envy of others, and he believed that his action would produce this admiration and envy; true or false, Ryle's analysis does not dispense with primary reasons, but depends upon them.

To know a primary reason why someone acted as he did is to know an intention with which the action was done. If I turn left at the fork because I want to get to Katmandu, my intention in turning left is to get to Katmandu. But to know the intention is not necessarily to know the primary reason in full detail. If James goes to church with the intention of pleasing his mother, then he must have some pro attitude toward pleasing his mother, but it needs more information to tell whether his reason is that he enjoys pleasing his mother, or thinks it right, his duty, or an obligation. The expression "the intention with which James went to church" has the outward form of a description, but in fact it is syncategorematic and cannot be taken to refer to an entity, state, disposition, or event. Its function in context is to generate new descriptions of actions in terms of their reasons; thus "James went to church with the intention of pleasing his mother" yields a new, and fuller, description of the action described in "James went to church." Essentially the same process goes on when I answer the question "Why are you bobbing around that way?" with "I'm knitting, weaving, exercising, sculling, cuddling, training fleas."

Straight description of an intended result often explains an action better than stating that the result was intended or desired. "It will soothe your nerves" explains why I pour you a shot as efficiently as "I want to do something to soothe your nerves," since the first in the context of explanation implies the second; but the first does better, because, if it is true, the facts will justify my choice of action. Because justifying and explaining an action so often go hand in hand, we frequently indicate the primary reason for an action by making a claim which, if true, would also verify, vindicate, or support the relevant belief or attitude of the agent. "I knew I ought to return it," "The paper said it was going to snow," "You stepped on *my* toes," all, in appropriate reason-giving contexts, perform this familiar dual function.

The justifying role of a reason, given this interpretation, depends upon the explanatory role, but the converse does not hold. Your stepping on my toes neither explains nor justifies my stepping on your toes unless I believe you stepped on my toes, but the belief alone, true or false, explains my action.

III

In the light of a primary reason, an action is revealed as coherent with certain traits, long- or short-termed, characteristic or not, of the agent, and the agent is shown in his role of Rational Animal. Corresponding to the belief and attitude of a primary reason for an action, we can always construct (with a little ingenuity) the premises of a syllogism from which it follows that the action has some (as Miss Anscombe calls it) "desirability characteristic."[4] Thus there is a certain irreducible—though somewhat anaemic—sense in which every rationalization justifies: from the agent's point of view there was, when he acted, something to be said for the action.

Noting that nonteleological causal explanations do not display the element of justification provided by reasons, some philosophers have concluded that the concept of cause that applies elsewhere cannot apply to the relation between reasons and actions, and that the pattern of justification provides, in the case of reasons, the required explanation. But suppose we grant that reasons alone justify in explaining actions; it does not follow that the explanation is not also—and necessarily—causal. Indeed our first condition for primary reasons (C_1) is designed to help set rationalizations apart from other sorts of explanation. If rationalization is, as I want to argue, a species of causal explanation, then justification, in the sense given by C_1, is at least one differentiating property. How about the other claim: that justifying is a kind of explaining, so that the ordinary notion of cause need not be brought in? Here it is necessary to decide what is being included under justification. Perhaps it

---

[4] Miss Anscombe denies that the practical syllogism is deductive. This she does partly because she thinks of the practical syllogism, as Aristotle does, as corresponding to a piece of practical reasoning (whereas for me it is only part of the analysis of the concept of a reason with which someone acted), and therefore she is bound, again following Aristotle, to think of the conclusion of a practical syllogism as corresponding to a judgment, not merely that the action has a desirable characteristic, but that the action is desirable (reasonable, worth doing, etc.).

means only what is given by C_1: that the agent has certain beliefs and attitudes in the light of which the action is reasonable. But then something essential has certainly been left out, for a person can have a reason for an action, and perform the action, and yet this reason not be the reason why he did it. Central to the relation between a reason and an action it explains is the idea that the agent performed the action *because* he had the reason. Of course, we can include this idea too in justification; but then the notion of justification becomes as dark as the notion of reason until we can account for the force of that "because."

When we ask why someone acted as he did, we want to be provided with an interpretation. His behaviour seems strange, alien, outré, pointless, out of character, disconnected; or perhaps we cannot even recognize an action in it. When we learn his reason, we have an interpretation, a new description of what he did which fits it into a familiar picture. The picture certainly includes some of the agent's beliefs and attitudes; perhaps also goals, ends, principles, general character traits, virtues or vices. Beyond this, the redescription of an action afforded by a reason may place the action in a wider social, economic, linguistic, or evaluative context. To learn, through learning the reason, that the agent conceived his action as a lie, a repayment of a debt, an insult, the fulfilment of an avuncular obligation, or a knight's gambit is to grasp the point of the action in its setting of rules, practices, conventions, and expectations.

Remarks like these, inspired by the later Wittgenstein, have been elaborated with subtlety and insight by a number of philosophers. And there is no denying that this is true: when we explain an action, by giving the reason, we do redescribe the action; redescribing the action gives the action a place in a pattern, and in this way the action is explained. Here it is tempting to draw two conclusions that do not follow. First, we can't infer, from the fact that giving reasons merely redescribes the action and that causes are separate from effects, that therefore reasons are not causes. Reasons, being beliefs and attitudes, are certainly not identical with actions; but, more important, events are often redescribed in terms of their causes. (Suppose someone was injured. We could redescribe this event "in terms of a cause" by saying he was burned.) Second, it is an error to think that, because placing the action in a larger pattern explains it, therefore we now understand the sort of explanation involved. Talk of patterns and contexts does not answer the question of how reasons explain actions, since the relevant pattern or context contains both reason and action. One way we can explain an event is by placing it in the context of its cause; cause and effect form the sort of pattern that explains the effect, in a sense of "explain" that we understand as well as any. If reason and action illustrate a different pattern of explanation, that pattern must be identified.

Let me urge the point in connexion with an example of Melden's. A man driving an automobile raises his arm in order to signal. His intention, to signal, explains his action, raising his arm, by redescribing it as signaling. What is the pattern that explains the action? Is it the familiar pattern of an action done for a reason? Then it does indeed explain the action, but only because it assumes the relation of reason and action that we want to analyse. Or is the pattern rather this: the man is driving, he is approaching a turn; he knows he ought to signal; he knows how to signal, by raising his arm. And now, in this context, he raises his arm. Perhaps, as Melden suggests, if all this happens, he does signal. And the explanation would then be this: if, under these conditions, a man raises his arm, then he signals. The difficulty is, of course, that this explanation does not touch the question of why he raised his arm. He had a reason to raise his arm, but this has not been shown to be the reason why he did it. If the description "signalling" explains his action by giving his reason, then the signalling must be intentional; but, on the account just given, it may not be.

If, as Melden claims, causal explanations are "wholly irrelevant to the understanding we seek" of human actions (184) then we are without an analysis of the "because" in "He did it because . . . ," where we go on to name a reason. Hampshire remarks, of the relation between reasons and action, "In philosophy one ought surely to find this . . . connection altogether mysterious" (166). Hampshire rejects Aristotle's attempt to solve the mystery by introducing the concept of wanting as a causal factor, on the grounds that the resulting theory is too clear and definite to fit all cases and that "There is still no compelling ground for insisting that the word 'want' *must* enter into every full statement of reasons for acting" (168). I agree that the concept of wanting is too narrow, but I have argued that, at least in a vast number of typical cases, some pro attitude must be assumed to be present if a statement of an agent's reasons in acting is to be intelligible. Hampshire does not see how Aristotle's scheme can be appraised as true or false, "for it is not clear what could be the basis of assessment, or what kind of evidence could be decisive" (167). Failing a satisfactory alternative, the best argument for a scheme like Aristotle's is that it alone promises to give an account of the "mysterious connection" between reason and actions.

IV

In order to turn the first "and" to "because" in "He exercised *and* he wanted to reduce and thought exercise would do it," we must, as the basic move,[5] augment condition C_1 with:

[5] I say "as the basic move" to cancel the suggestion that C_1 and C_2 are jointly

C_2. A primary reason for an action is its cause.

The considerations in favour of C_2 are by now, I hope, obvious; in the remainder of this paper I wish to defend C_2 against various lines of attack and, in the process, to clarify the notion of causal explanation involved.

A. The first line of attack is this. Primary reasons consist of attitudes and beliefs, which are states or dispositions, not events; therefore they cannot be causes.

It is easy to reply that states, dispositions, and conditions are frequently named as the causes of events: the bridge collapsed because of a structural defect; the plane crashed on take-off because the air temperature was abnormally high; the plate broke because it had a crack. This reply does not, however, meet a closely related point. Mention of a causal condition for an event gives a cause only on the assumption that there was also a preceding event. But what is the preceding event that causes an action?

In many cases it is not difficult at all to find events very closely associated with the primary reason. States and dispositions are not events, but the onslaught of a state or disposition is. A desire to hurt your feelings may spring up at the moment you anger me; I may start wanting to eat a melon just when I see one; and beliefs may begin at the moment we notice, perceive, learn, or remember something. Those who have argued that there are no mental events to qualify as causes of actions have often missed the obvious because they have insisted that a mental event be observed or noticed (rather than an observing or a noticing) or that it be like a stab, a qualm, a prick or a quiver, a mysterious prod of conscience or act of the will. Melden, in discussing the driver who signals a turn by raising his arm, challenges those who want to explain actions causally to identify "an event which is common and peculiar to all such cases" (87), perhaps a motive or an intention, anyway "some particular feeling or experience" (95). But of course there is a mental event: at some moment the driver noticed (or thought he noticed) his turn coming up, and that is the moment he signalled. During any continuing activity, like driving, or elaborate performance, like swimming the Hellespont, there are more or less fixed purposes, standards, desires, and habits that give direction and form to the entire enterprise, and there is the continuing input of information about what we are doing, about changes in the environment, in terms of which we regulate and adjust our actions. To dignify a driver's awareness that his turn has come by calling it an experience, much less a feeling, is no doubt exaggerated, but whether it deserves a name or not, it had better be the reason why he raises his arm. In this case, and typically, there may not

sufficient to define the relation of reasons to the actions they explain. I believe C_2 can be strengthened to make C_1 and C_2 sufficient as well as necessary conditions, but here I am concerned only with the claim that both are, as they stand, necessary.

be anything we would call a motive, but if we mention such a general purpose as wanting to get to one's destination safely, it is clear that the motive is not an event. The intention with which the driver raises his arm is also not an event, for it is no thing at all, neither event, attitude, disposition, nor object. Finally, Melden asks the causal theorist to find an event that is common and peculiar to all cases where a man intentionally raises his arm, and this, it must be admitted, cannot be produced. But then neither can a common and unique cause of bridge failures, plane crashes, or plate breakings be produced.

The signalling driver can answer the question "Why did you raise your arm when you did?" and from the answer we learn the event that caused the action. But can an actor always answer such a question? Sometimes the answer will mention a mental event that does not give a reason: "Finally I made up my mind." However, there also seem to be cases of intentional action where we cannot explain at all why we acted when we did. In such cases, explanation in terms of primary reasons parallels the explanation of the collapse of the bridge from a structural defect: we are ignorant of the event or sequence of events that led up to (caused) the collapse, but we are sure there was such an event or sequence of events.

B. According to Melden, a cause must be "logically distinct from the alleged effect" (52); but a reason for an action is not logically distinct from the action; therefore, reasons are not causes of action.[6]

One possible form of this argument has already been suggested. Since a reason makes an action intelligible by redescribing it, we do not have two events, but only one under different descriptions. Causal relations, however, demand distinct events.

Someone might be tempted into the mistake of thinking that my flipping of the switch caused my turning on of the light (in fact it caused the light to go on). But it does not follow that it is a mistake to take "My reason for flipping the switch was that I wanted to turn on the light" as entailing, in part, "I flipped the switch, and this action is further describable as having been caused by my wanting to turn on the light." To describe an event in terms of its cause is not to identify the event with its cause, nor does explanation by redescription exclude causal explanation.

The example serves also to refute the claim that we cannot describe the action without using words that link it to the alleged cause. Here the action is to be explained under the description: "my flipping the switch," and the alleged cause is "my wanting to turn on the light." What possible logical relation is supposed to hold between these phrases? It seems more plausible to

---

[6] This argument can be found, in one or more versions, in Kenny, Hampshire, and Melden, as well as in P. Winch, *The Idea of a Social Science*, London, 1958, and R. S. Peters, *The Concept of Motivation*, London, 1958. In one of its forms, the argument was of course inspired by Ryle's treatment of motives in *The Concept of Mind*.

urge a logical link between "my turning on the light" and "my wanting to turn on the light," but even here the link turned out, on inspection, to be grammatical rather than logical.

In any case there is something very odd in the idea that causal relations are empirical rather than logical. What can this mean? Surely not that every true causal statement is empirical. For suppose "A caused B" is true. Then the cause of $B = A$; so, substituting, we have "The cause of B caused B," which is analytic. The truth of a causal statement depends on *what* events are described; its status as analytic or synthetic depends on *how* the events are described. Still, it may be maintained that a reason rationalizes an action only when the descriptions are appropriately fixed, and the appropriate descriptions are not logically independent.

Suppose that to say a man wanted to turn on the light *meant* that he would perform any action he believed would accomplish his end. Then the statement of his primary reason for flipping the switch would entail that he flipped the switch—"straightway he acts," as Aristotle says. In this case there would certainly be a logical connexion between reason and action, the same sort of connexion as that between "It's water-soluble and was placed in water" and "It dissolved." Since the implication runs from description of cause to description of effect but not conversely, naming the cause still gives information. And, though the point is often overlooked, "Placing it in water caused it to dissolve" does not entail "It's water-soluble"; so the latter has additional explanatory force. Nevertheless, the explanation would be far more interesting if, in place of solubility, with its obvious definitional connexion with the event to be explained, we could refer to some property, say a particular crystalline structure, whose connexion with dissolution in water was known only through experiment. Now it is clear why primary reasons like desires and wants do not explain actions in the relatively trivial way solubility explains dissolvings. Solubility, we are assuming, is a pure disposition property: it is defined in terms of a single test. But desires cannot be defined in terms of the actions they may rationalize, even though the relation between desire and action is not simply empirical; there are other, equally essential criteria for desires—their expression in feelings and in actions that they do not rationalize, for example. The person who has a desire (or want or belief) does not normally need criteria at all—he generally knows, even in the absence of any clues available to others, what he wants, desires, and believes. These logical features of primary reasons show that it is not just lack of ingenuity that keeps us from defining them as dispositions to act for these reasons.

C. According to Hume, "we may define a cause to be an object, followed by another, and where all the objects similar to the first are followed by objects similar to the second." But, Hart and Honoré claim, "The statement that one person did something because, for example, another threatened him, carries no implication or covert assertion that if the circumstances were repeated the same action would follow" (52). Hart and Honoré allow that Hume is right in saying that ordinary singular causal statements imply generalizations, but wrong for this very reason in supposing that motives and desires are ordinary causes of actions. In brief, laws are involved essentially in ordinary causal explanations, but not in rationalizations.

It is common to try to meet this argument by suggesting that we do have rough laws connecting reasons and actions, and these can, in theory, be improved. True, threatened people do not always respond in the same way; but we may distinguish between threats and also between agents, in terms of their beliefs and attitudes.

The suggestion is delusive, however, because generalizations connecting reasons and actions are not—and cannot be sharpened into—the kind of law on the basis of which accurate predictions can reliably be made. If we reflect on the way in which reasons determine choice, decision, and behaviour, it is easy to see why this is so. What emerges, in the *ex post facto* atmosphere of explanation and justification, as *the* reason frequently was, to the agent at the time of action, one consideration among many, *a* reason. Any serious theory for predicting action on the basis of reasons must find a way of evaluating the relative force of various desires and beliefs in the matrix of decision; it cannot take as its starting point the refinement of what is to be expected from a single desire. The practical syllogism exhausts its role in displaying an action as falling under one reason; so it cannot be subtilized into a reconstruction of practical reasoning, which involves the weighing of competing reasons. The practical syllogism provides a model neither for a predictive science of action nor for a normative account of evaluative reasoning.

Ignorance of competent predictive laws does not inhibit valid causal explanation, or few causal explanations could be made. I am certain the window broke because it was struck by a rock—I saw it all happen; but I am not (is anyone?) in command of laws on the basis of which I can predict what blows will break which windows. A generalization like "Windows are fragile, and fragile things tend to break when struck hard enough, other conditions being right" is not a predictive law in the rough—the predictive law, if we had it, would be quantitative and would use very different concepts. The generalization, like our generalizations about behaviour, serves a different function: it provides evidence for the existence of a causal law covering the case at hand.

We are usually far more certain of a singular causal connexion than we are of any causal law governing the case; does this show that Hume was wrong in claiming that singular causal statements entail laws? Not necessarily, for Hume's claim, as quoted above, is ambiguous. It may mean that "*A* caused *B*" entails some particular law involving the predicates used in the descriptions "*A* "and "*B*," or it may mean that "*A* caused *B*" entails that there exists a causal law instantiated by some true descriptions of A and B.[7] Obviously, both versions of Hume's doctrine give a sense to the claim that singular causal statements entail laws, and both sustain the view that causal explanations "involve laws." But the second version is far weaker, in that no particular law is entailed by a singular causal claim, and a singular causal claim can be defended, if it needs defence, without defending any law. Only the second version of Hume's doctrine can be made to fit with most causal explanations; it suits rationalizations equally well.

The most primitive explanation of an event gives its cause; more elaborate explanations may tell more of the story, or defend the singular causal claim by producing a relevant law or by giving reasons for believing such exists. But it is an error to think no explanation has been given until a law has been produced. Linked with these errors is the idea that singular causal statements necessarily indicate, by the concepts they employ, the concepts that will occur in the entailed law. Suppose a hurricane, which is reported on page 5 of Tuesday's *Times*, causes a catastrophe, which is reported on page 13 of Wednesday's *Tribune*. Then the event reported on page 5 of Tuesday's *Times* caused the event reported on page 13 of Wednesday's *Tribune*. Should we look for a law relating events of these *kinds?* It is only slightly less ridiculous to look for a law relating hurricanes and catastrophes. The laws needed to predict the catastrophe with precision would, of course, have no use for concepts like hurricane and catastrophe. The trouble with predicting the weather is that the descriptions under which events interest us—"a cool, cloudy day with rain in the afternoon"—have only remote connexions with the concepts employed by the more precise known laws.

The laws whose existence is required if reasons are causes of actions do not, we may be sure, deal in the concepts in which rationalizations must deal. If the causes of a class of events (actions) fall in a certain class (reasons) and there is a law to back each singular causal statement, it does not follow that there is any law connecting events classified as reasons with events classified as actions—the classifications may even be neurological, chemical, or physical.

D.   It is said that the kind of knowledge one has of one's own reasons in acting is not compatible with the existence of a causal relation between reasons

---

[7] We could roughly characterize the analysis of singular causal statements hinted at here as follows: "A caused B" is true if and only if there are descriptions of A and B such that the sentence obtained by putting these descriptions for "A" and "B" in "A caused B" follows from a true causal law. This analysis is saved from triviality by the fact that not all true generalizations are causal laws; causal laws are distinguished (though of course this is no analysis) by the fact that they are inductively confirmed by their instances and by the fact that they support counterfactual and subjunctive singular causal statements.

and actions: a person knows his own intentions in acting infallibly, without induction or observation, and no ordinary causal relation can be known in this way. No doubt our knowledge of our own intentions in acting will show many of the oddities peculiar to first-person knowledge of one's own pains, beliefs, desires, and so on; the only question is whether these oddities prove that reasons do not cause, in any ordinary sense at least, the actions that they rationalize.

You may easily be wrong about the truth of a statement of the form "I am poisoning Charles because I want to save him pain," because you may be wrong about whether you are poisoning Charles—you may yourself be drinking the poisoned cup by mistake. But it also seems that you may err about your reasons, particularly when you have two reasons for an action, one of which pleases you and one which does not. For example, you do want to save Charles pain; you also want him out of the way. You may be wrong about which motive made you do it.

The fact that you may be wrong does not show that in general it makes sense to ask you how you know what your reasons were or to ask for your evidence. Though you may, on rare occasions, accept public or private evidence as showing you are wrong about your reasons, you usually have no evidence and make no observations. Then your knowledge of your own reasons for your actions is not generally inductive, for where there is induction, there is evidence. Does this show the knowledge is not causal? I cannot see that it does.

Causal laws differ from true but nonlawlike generalizations in that their instances confirm them; induction is, therefore, certainly a good way to learn the truth of a law. It does not follow that it is the only way to learn the truth of a law. In any case, in order to know that a singular causal statement is true, it is not necessary to know the truth of a law; it is necessary only to know that some law covering the events at hand exists. And it is far from evident that induction, and induction alone, yields the knowledge that a causal law satisfying certain conditions exists. Or, to put it differently, one case is often enough, as Hume admitted, to persuade us that a law exists, and this amounts to saying that we are persuaded, without direct inductive evidence, that a causal relation exists.[8]

E.   Finally I should like to say something about a certain uneasiness some philosophers feel in speaking of causes of actions at all. Melden, for example, says that actions are often identical with bodily movements, and that bodily movements have causes; yet he denies that the causes are causes of the actions. This is, I think, a contradiction. He is led to it by the following sort of con-

[8] My thinking on the subject of this section, as on most of the topics discussed in this paper, has been greatly influenced by years of talk with Professor Daniel Bennett, now of Brandeis University.

sideration: "It is futile to attempt to explain conduct through the causal efficacy of desire—all *that* can explain is further happenings, not actions performed by agents. The agent confronting the causal nexus in which such happenings occur is a helpless victim of all that occurs in and to him" (128, 129). Unless I am mistaken, this argument, if it were valid, would show that actions cannot have causes at all. I shall not point out the obvious difficulties in removing actions from the realm of causality entirely. But perhaps it is worth trying to uncover the source of the trouble. Why on earth should a cause turn an action into a mere happening and a person into a helpless victim? Is it because we tend to assume, at least in the arena of action, that a cause demands a causer, agency an agent? So we press the question; if my action is caused, what caused it? If I did, then there is the absurdity of infinite regress; if I did not, I am a victim. But of course the alternatives are not exhaustive. Some causes have no agents. Primary among these are those states and changes of state in persons which, because they are reasons as well as causes, make persons voluntary agents.

CHAPTER 8

Models

This topic has clear implications for the issue "To what extent should educational research be guided by theory?", which received attention in the first part of this book. Here we simply provide a variety of ways in which the term "model" functions within both ordinary and scientific thinking. It is our hope that the distinctions suggested by May Brodbeck and Max Black in the following articles will help the research community avoid the confusion that is often introduced by the ambiguous statement "This is a model of X."[1]

[1] Cf. also Elizabeth and G. S. Maccia, *The Way of Educational Theorizing* (1962); Elizabeth Maccia, *The Conception of Models in Educational Theorizing* (1962), and *An Educational Theory Model* (1963), Columbus, Ohio: The Ohio State University, Occasional Papers, Center for the Construction of Theory in Education.

38. MODELS

May Brodbeck

The term *model* is common in recent social science literature. We encounter models of learning, of rational choice, of communication, of political behavior, of group interaction, and so on, and so on. Yet, what exactly is a model and what purposes does it serve? The fact is that the term model is used most ambiguously. Nor is *mathematical model* any more precise since this term, too, covers different things.

MODELS AS THEORIES

Broadly speaking, there are two major uses of *model*. The most general use is as a synonym for theory. A theory may be well or ill confirmed, narrow or broad in scope, quantified or nonquantified. *Model* is now frequently used for those theories which are either highly speculative or quantified, or, most likely, both. Thus, a guess about the connections between quantified variables of an area like psychology or economics will frequently be called a mathematical model. Such hypotheses are mathematical only in the sense in which physics is mathematical. That is, they are empirical generalizations whose variables are quantified, so that we can say how much one variable changes with changes in others. They share the virtue of all quantified theories in permitting more precise deduction and prediction.

SOURCE. Reprinted from "Logic and Scientific Method in Research on Teaching," by May Brodbeck in N. L. Gage (ed.), *Handbook of Research in Teaching*. Chicago: Rand McNally & Co., 1963. Copyright © 1963 by American Educational Research Association.

Quantification, however, is no guarantee of scope. In areas where behavior depends upon many different variables, we may indeed pay for quantification with triviality. But then, nonquantified guesses at theories, like the doctrines of psychoanalysis or speculations about the physiological concomitants of behavior (which are often broader than quantified theories but lack their precision) are also frequently called models. Such speculative theories, whether quantified or not, are after all just theories. The term *model* serves no particular purpose beyond, perhaps, emphasizing the tentative, unconfirmed nature of the hypotheses in question. This usage would be harmless enough if there were not as unfortunately there is, another, quite different prevalent use of the term.

Strictly speaking, I should have said two further uses. For in this second meaning of the term two different things are really involved though they have a common feature. This feature I shall now explain. A miniature train is a model of a real train if it is isomorphic with it. Isomorphism requires two conditions. First, there must be a one-to-one correspondence between the elements of the model and the elements of the thing of which it is the model. For every chimney stack, there must be a miniature chimney stack; for every window there must be its replica, and the converse must be true. Second, certain relations must be preserved. For instance, if a door is to the left of a window in the original, their replicas must be similarly situated; also, the model is constructed to scale. If the model works on the same principle as the original—if, for instance, a model steam engine is also steam propelled—the isomorphism is complete.

Extending this notion to theories, we may formulate a precise meaning of *model*. The form of a law is given either by the verbal "if-then" formulation or by an equation. Like all other sentences, quantified laws have a certain form. Many other physical properties besides distance vary as the square of some other characteristic, such as time. The linear equation, $y = ax + b$, represents still another quantified form taken by some laws. The variables might stand for many different things, like weight and height or supply and demand, while the form remains the same. But a quantified empirical law such as $d = 16t^2$ differs from an arithmetic statement like $9 = 3^2$. In the empirical law, the latter variables d and t must be given meaning as distance and time before the truth or falsity of the law can be established. No descriptive terms occur in the arithmetic truths. When letters do occur in arithmetic statements, as in $x + y = y + x$, then it is understood that the letters are to be replaced by numbers. It is a logical truth about numbers that the order of addition does not make a difference. As we shall see later, if the letters do not stand for numbers, then the statement may well be false.

Quantified empirical laws, like $d = 16t^2$, are often called "mathematical." But this term is confusing. A quantified law of empirical science is an empirical or synthetic assertion whose truth or falsity depends upon its descriptive terms. Distance varies as the square of time, but demand probably does not. A statement of mathematics, on the other hand, is analytic. In order to stress the distinction between empirical laws and the tautologies of mathematics, I shall continue to use the term *arithmetic* for the latter. Laws, whether quantified or not, have a certain form, as expressed either by the verbal "if . . . then . . ." or by an equation. Theories differ from each other either in their descriptive terms, in which case they are about different things, or in the form of their laws, or both. For instance, theories within physics and those within sociology presumably differ from each other not only in their descriptive terms but also in the form of the statements connecting these concepts. *Time* and *distance*, for example, are descriptive terms or "variables" of physical theory. The parabola $y = ax^2$, or a differential equation of a certain sort, gives the form of the law connecting these terms. Within sociology, the descriptive terms might be, say, *religious preference* and *political attitude*. A law connecting these attributes might have the form of a nonquantified conditional, like "If anyone is a Catholic, then he is also a conservative." Or it might take the form of a quantified linear equation expressing a statistical correlation between the variables.

ISOMORPHIC THEORIES

A model train, we saw, is similar to a real one in being isomorphic with it. The isomorphism is complete if both work on the same principles. When extending this notion to theories, we can formulate a precise meaning of *model*. Two theories whose laws have the same form are isomorphic or *structurally similar* to each other. If the laws of one theory have the same form as the laws of another theory, then one may be said to be a *model* for the other. This is the second most general meaning of the term.

How do we discover whether two theories, or parts of them, are isomorphic to each other? Suppose that one area, as indicated by a set of descriptive concepts, for which a relatively well-developed theory is at hand is said to be a model for another area about which little is as yet known. The descriptive terms in the theory of the better-known area are put into one-to-one correspondence with those of the new area. By means of this one-to-one correspondence, the laws of one area are "translated" into laws of the other area. The concepts of the better-known theory are replaced in the laws by the concepts of the new area. This replacement results in a set of laws or hypotheses about the variables of the new area. If observation shows these hypotheses to be true, then the laws of both areas have the same form. The lawful connections are preserved and the two theories are completely isomorphic to each other.

For example, suppose it is wondered whether rumors spread like diseases. That is, can the laws of epidemiology, about which quite a bit is known, be a model for a theory of rumor-transmission? Or, to say the same thing differently, do the laws about rumors have the same form as the laws about diseases? The descriptive concepts in the laws of epidemiology are first of all replaced by letter variables. This reveals the form of the laws. The concepts referring to diseases are put into one-to-one correspondence with those referring to rumors. The letter variables in the epidemiological laws are replaced by the descriptive terms referring to rumors. This results in a set of hypotheses about rumors, which may or may not be confirmed. If, optimistically, these laws are confirmed, then the two theories have the same form.

The notion of *model* as isomorphism of laws is obviously symmetrical. However, when an area about which we already know a good deal is used to suggest laws for an area about which little is known, then the familiar area providing the form of the laws may be called a model for the new area. But once it is found that the laws of both areas do indeed share a common structure, then of course either is a model for the other.

Where knowledge is scarce, speculation abounds. Social science, not surprisingly, witnesses a plethora of speculative "models" or guesses about isomorphisms. A few illustrations will suffice. The notion of society as an organism, though repeatedly discredited, has a way of cropping up in one form or another. In its Spenglerian form, society is likened to a plant, complete with a seasonal life cycle. Like plants, a society has its vernal and autumnal phases. Society is compared to the growth and physiology of man, having like man its own states of development, its organic interrelatedness of parts, and its homeostatic controls. Evolutionary theory is another favorite model, one in the light of which whole societies are seen as engaged in a struggle for survival and subject to natural selection. Within a society, the various institutions and codes of behavior are viewed in the light of their contribution to adaptation and adjustment. Or individual learning is compared with the process of selective survival among random variations. The human brain is compared to an electronic computer. Servomechanisms like the automatic pilot or thermostat are now frequently evoked models for learning and purposive behavior. How does one go about testing these suggested models?

First, it must be possible to state clearly what is in one-to-one correspondence with what. Organisms grow; they increase in size and weight. What is *social* "growth"? What is the autumnal phase of society corresponding to the autumn of a plant? Relatively precise meaning can be given to adaptive and nonadaptive characteristics of organisms within evolutionary theory. Can we give correspondingly precise meanings to these notions for human institutions? What in learning, fitted to the evolutionary model, corresponds to the role of mutations? Second, once clearly defined empirical concepts in one area are made to correspond to the terms of the model, then formal similarities, if any, are sought. Nutrition is connected with growth in biology. Are the social concepts corresponding to nutrition and to growth similarly connected? In other words, not only must the terms of the two areas correspond, but the connections among these concepts must also be preserved, if the model is to be of any use. One area, either part or all of it, can be a fruitful model for another only if corresponding concepts can be found and if at least some of the laws connecting the concepts of the model also can be shown to connect their corresponding concepts in the second area. This implies that the model is from an area better developed than that for which it is used. If very little is known about either field, then to speak of a "model" is hardly more than loose and pointless talk.

MODELS AND MEASUREMENT

A third prevalent use of *model* also has something to do with isomorphism, but not with that between the laws of empirical theories. *Mathematical model*, as I just said, may simply mean any quantified theory. On the other hand, it may and frequently does mean any arithmetical structure of a kind I must now explain. We saw before that replacing all the descriptive terms or concepts in the theory of one area by those of a different area results in another theory with the same form but different contect from the original. The isomorphic sets of laws, those of the model and of its "translation," are both empirical theories whose truth or falsity depends upon the facts. It is possible, and often highly desirable, to establish another kind of isomorphism, in which the result is not two empirical theories sharing a common structure. Instead, the laws, or some of them, of an empirical theory may have the same form as a set of purely arithmetical truths. If this is the case, then the latter is called an *arithmetical representation* of the empirical theory.

Mathematical model sometimes means just this sort of arithmetical representation of an empirical theory. The laws of arithmetic, rather than those of another empirical theory, may be used as a model. Indeed, only when this is possible can arithmetic be used in empirical science. When laws are quantified, arithmetical tautologies may be used for deducing other laws and facts from them. This is the most important use of such tautologies within science. If, in Galileo's law, $d = 16t^2$, distance is expressed in feet and time in seconds, then from that law in conjunction with the fact that the time of fall was three seconds, we may deduce that the distance was 144 feet. The additional factual premise about the time of fall permits the deduction from the law that the distance is equal to 16 times 3^2. Using the arithmetical tautology $3 \times 3 = 9$ as an additional premise, we deduce that the distance is 16×9. The tautology $16 \times 9 = 144$ permits the final deduction that the distance fallen was 144 feet.

Since the arithmetical statements are tautologies, they may be added as premises without adding any more factual content than is given by the initial empirical premises about distance and time. In such simple calculations or deductions, the arithmetical premises are usually not stated explicitly, but are nevertheless being used. Arithmetic is a subtle and strong logic permitting deductions which, without it, might be quite impossible. What conditions must empirical properties meet before arithmetic can be applied to them?

Consider, first of all, the following three logical truths about numbers. The symbols ">" and "=" have their customary arithmetic meaning.

1. For any three numbers, if $N_1 > N_2$ and $N_2 > N_3$, then $N_1 > N_3$.
2. For any two numbers, at most one of $N_1 > N_2$, $N_1 = N_2$, $N_2 > N_1$ holds.
3. For any two numbers, at least one of $N_1 > N_2$, $N_1 = N_2$, $N_2 > N_1$ holds.

For this set of axioms to be a representation of an empirical theory, a set of descriptive terms must be coordinated to the arithmetic entities and relations. Let the numbers correspond to individual people, the relation ">" to the descriptive relation "higher-in-status" and "=" to "same status." After this coordination, the statements are probably again true, but, if so, they are now empirical truths about the descriptive relation "higher-in-status."

Other descriptive terms can easily be found for which the axioms fail. Let ">" be coordinated to "sibling" and "=" to "same person as." In this case, the second axiom is false. For, of course, if John is Peter's sibling, then Peter is John's sibling and the axiom states that not both of these can hold. The axioms are an arithmetic representation of those descriptive properties which can be ordered. Many other such properties also satisfy the axioms: men and the relationship "taller than," physical bodies and "heavier than," the relative hardness of stones, and students' scores on tests, are a few more candidates for true correspondence with the structure of integers and the relation "greater-than." All true representations of these axioms share a common structure.

The theorems implied by the axioms exhibit still further structure, for instance, irreflexivity and asymmetry. "Irreflexivity" means that an individual cannot have the relation to himself. A person may love himself but he cannot be taller than himself. "Loves" does not satisfy the axioms, so the theorems need not be true of it. "Taller than" does, so it must also be asymmetric and irreflexive.

The axioms and theorems together tell us more than appears at first glance about the structure of whatever satisfies the axioms. Whether or not a descriptive property has this structure is a matter of observable fact. Some things do and, as we have seen, some things do not. Those that do are said to have the structure of what is called a "complete ordering." The possibility of establishing an order of succession among attributes is not an unimportant characteristic, particularly in social science. This possibility is expressed by a set of empirical laws of which these axioms are an arithmetical representation. These empirical laws make ranking possible. There are many descriptive properties which satisfy the first two axioms of order, but not the third. Thus, when the properties of incomparable things are being considered, like food and plays, or musicians and painters, then the relation of "better than" does not satisfy the third axiom. Nor can we order all the people in the world by the relation "ancestor," since, given any two different individuals, one need not be the ancestor of the other. The first two axioms alone therefore express a "partial ordering." Only all three axioms express a completely ordered domain. Insofar as the descriptive concepts of different theories are true representations of some or all of the axioms of order, they share a common structure or form. By virtue of this shared structure, ranking is possible.

For measurement in the strict sense (yielding what Stevens [1951] called *ratio scales*) also to be possible, the descriptive properties must share certain other structural features of arithmetic. In particular, they must also have the same form as axioms like the following three:

4. For any two positive numbers, N_1 and N_2, there is exactly one other, N_3, such that $N_1 + N_2 = N_3$.

5. For any two positive numbers, $N_1 + N_2 = N_2 + N_1$.

6. For any three positive numbers, $(N_1 + N_2) + N_3 = N_1 + (N_2 + N_3)$.

Axiom 4 states that for any two numbers, there is uniquely a third which is their sum. Axiom 5 states that the sum of any two numbers is independent of their order; Axiom 6, that when any three numbers are added, the result is independent of how they are grouped. These axioms state part of the structure of addition. Addition is a binary operation of the elements or members of the set of positive integers, that is, a way of combining two elements of the set to get a third. Note that while these axioms are logical truths about the addition of positive numbers, they are all false when applied to subtraction of the same elements. If we extend the system of elements to include both positive and negative numbers, then Axioms 5 and 6 do not hold for the operation of subtraction. The kind of elements specified and the kind of operations performed on them determines whether the resulting statements will be logically true or false or, in the case of descriptive entities, empirically true or false.

For these arithmetical truths to be a representation of anything, the number-elements and the arithmetical operations performed on them must be coordinated to descriptive entities and to operations on these descriptive entities. Just as the arithmetical relation "greater-than" can be made to correspond to natural or physical relations like "heavier than," "prefers," "loves," or "higher-in-status," so there must be a natural or physical operation corresponding to addition. As numbers can be added, so things can be put into the same container, glued together, or, even, simultaneously responded to. Suppose that our elements are lumps of sugar, each having a specified weight. Though numbers are assigned to the elements, indicating how much of the property it has, the corresponding operation is performed not on these numbers, but on the elements themselves. Only in the arithmetical representation are the elements themselves numbers. Weight is a measurable property of lumps of sugar because given two lumps of specified weight, the weight resulting from putting them both on the same side of a balance is the arithmetical sum of their individual weights. In other words, the operation of weighing two lumps of sugar has the same structure as the laws of arithmetic.

The sweetness of sugar, on the other hand, is not measurable in the strict sense of ratio scales. For measurable descriptive properties are those having the same form as the addition of numbers. Grinding together two lumps of sugar of equal sweetness, as indicated by some index of sweetness, would not give something twice as sweet. Or the order in which two things are mixed together might make a difference. Not only must a corresponding physical operation be found, but it must satisfy the axioms. If no corresponding physical or natural operation can be found or if it does not satisfy the axioms of addition, then the property cannot be measured. It may be ranked, however, if it satisfies the axioms of order. The measurability of descriptive properties is expressed by a set of empirical laws which are isomorphic to the laws of arithmetic. By virtue of this isomorphism, numbers may be assigned to the properties of things, resulting in quantified empirical laws. All the laws of arithmetic may then be applied to these numbers to derive new empirical laws and facts.

Other parts of arithmetic serving as models for empirical properties are, for example, probability theory and the theory of games. A correspondence is established between the descriptive concepts and those of the arithmetical theory. When a model, either empirical or arithmetical, is used as a source of hypotheses about the connections among the variables of another area, it does not explain these hypotheses. It merely suggests their form. If, however, these new hypotheses are confirmed, they may be used to explain and predict new knowledge.

39. MODELS AND ARCHETYPES

Max Black

Scientists often speak of using models but seldom pause to consider the presuppositions and the implications of their practice. I shall find it convenient to distinguish between a number of operations, ranging from the familiar and trivial to the farfetched but important, all of which are sometimes called "the use of models." I hope that even this rapid survey of a vast territory may permit a well-grounded verdict on the value of recourse to cognitive models.

To speak of "models" in connection with a scientific theory already smacks of the metaphorical. Were we called upon to provide a perfectly clear and uncontroversial example of a model, in the literal sense of that word, none of us, I imagine, would think of offering Bohr's model of the atom, or a Keynesian model of an economic system.

Typical examples of models in the literal sense of the word might include: the ship displayed in the showcase of a travel agency ("a model of the *Queen Mary*"), the airplane that emerges from a small boy's construction kit, the Stone Age village in the museum of natural history. That is to say, the standard cases are three-dimensional miniatures, more or less "true to scale," of some existing or imagined material object. It will be convenient to call the real or imaginary thing depicted by a model the *original* of that model.

We also use the word "model" to stand for a type of design (the dress designer's "spring models," the 1959 model Ford)—or to mean some exem-

SOURCE. Reprinted from Max Black: *Models and Metaphors*. Copyright © 1962 by Cornell University. Used by permission of Cornell University Press.

plar (a model husband, a model solution of an equation). The senses in which a model is a type of design—or, on the other hand, something worthy of imitation—can usually be ignored in what follows.

It seems arbitrary to restrict the idea of a model to something *smaller* than its original. A natural extension is to admit magnification, as in a larger-than-life-size likeness of a mosquito. A further natural extension is to admit proportional change of scale in *any* relevant dimension, such as time.

In all such cases, I shall speak of *scale models*. This label will cover all likenesses of material objects, systems, or processes, whether real or imaginary, that preserve relative proportions. They include experiments in which chemical or biological processes are artificially decelerated ("slow motion experiments") and those in which an attempt is made to imitate social processes in miniature.

The following points about scale models seem uncontroversial:

1. A scale model is always a model *of* something. The notion of a scale model is relational and, indeed, asymmetrically so: If *A* is a scale model of *B*, *B* is not a scale model of *A*.

2. A scale model is designed to serve a purpose, to be a means to some end. It is to show how the ship looks, or how the machine will work, or what law governs the interplay of parts in the original; the model is intended to be enjoyed for its own sake only in the limiting case where the hobbyist indulges a harmless fetishism.

3. A scale model is a representation of the real or imaginary thing for which it stands: its use is for "reading off" properties of the original from the directly presented properties of the model.

4. It follows that some features of the model are irrelevant or unimportant, while others are pertinent and essential, to the representation in question. There is no such thing as a perfectly faithful model; only by being unfaithful in *some* respect can a model represent its original.

5. As with all representations, there are underlying conventions of interpretation—correct ways for "reading" the model.

6. The conventions of interpretation rest upon partial identity of properties coupled with invariance of proportionality. In making a scale model, we try on the one hand to make it resemble the original by reproduction of some features (the color of the ship's hull, the shape and rigidity of the airfoil) and on the other hand to preserve the *relative* proportions between relevant magnitudes. In Peirce's terminology, the model is an *icon*, literally embodying the features of interest in the original.[1] It says, as it were: "*This* is how the original is."

---

[1] "An *Icon* is a sign which refers to the Object that it denotes merely by virtue of characters of its own, and which it possesses, just the same, whether any such Object

In making scale models, our purpose is to reproduce, in a relatively manipulable or accessible embodiment, selected features of the "original": we want to see how the new house will look, or to find out how the airplane will fly, or to learn how the chromosome changes occur. We try to bring the remote and the unknown to our own level of middle-sized existence.[2]

There is, however, something self-defeating in this aim, since change of scale must introduce irrelevance and distortion. We are forced to replace living tissue by some inadequate substitute, and sheer change of size may upset the balance of factors in the original. Too small a model of a uranium bomb will fail to explode, too large a reproduction of a housefly will never get off the ground, and the solar system cannot be expected to look like its planetarium model. Inferences from scale model to original are intrinsically precarious and in need of supplementary validation and correction.

Let us now consider models involving *change of medium*. I am thinking of such examples as hydraulic models of economic systems, or the use of electrical circuits in computers. In such cases I propose to speak of *analogue models*.

An analogue model is some material object, system, or process designed to reproduce as faithfully as possible in some new medium the *structure* or web of relationships in an original. Many of our previous comments about scale models also apply to the new case. The analogue model, like the scale model, is a symbolic representation of some real or imaginary original, subject to rules of interpretation for making accurate inferences from the relevant features of the model.

The crucial difference between the two types of models is in the corresponding methods of interpretation. Scale models, as we have seen, rely markedly upon identity: their aim is to imitate the original, except where the need for manipulability enforces a departure from sheer reproduction. And when this happens the deviation is held to a minimum, as it were: geometrical magnitudes in the original are still *reproduced*, though with a constant change of ratio. On the other hand, the making of analogue models is guided by the more abstract aim of reproducing the *structure* of the original.

An adequate analogue model will manifest a point-by-point correspondence

actually exists or not. . . . Anything whatever . . . is an Icon of anything, in so far as it is like that thing and used as a sign of it." *Collected Papers of Charles Sanders Peirce* (Cambridge, Mass., 1931–35), II, 247.

[2] A good example of the experimental use of models is described in Victor P. Starr's article, "The General Circulation of the Atmosphere," *Scientific American*, CXCV (December 1956), 40–45. The atmosphere of one hemisphere is represented by water in a shallow rotating pan, dye being added to make the flow visible. When the perimeter of the pan is heated the resulting patterns confirm the predictions made by recent theories about the atmosphere.

between the relations *it* embodies and those embodied in the original: every incidence of a relation in the original must be echoed by a corresponding incidence of a correlated relation in the analogue model. To put the matter in another way: there must be rules for translating the terminology applicable to the model in such a way as to conserve truth value.

Thus, the dominating principle of the analogue model is what mathematicians call "isomorphism."[3] We can, if we please, regard the analogue model as iconic of its original, as we did in the case of the scale model, but if we do so we must remember that the former is "iconic" in a more abstract way than the latter. The analogue model shares with its original not a set of features or an identical proportionality of magnitudes but, more abstractly, the same structure or pattern of relationships. Now identity of structure is compatible with the widest variety of content—hence the possibilities for construction of analogue models are endless.

The remarkable fact that the same pattern of relationships, the same structure, can be embodied in an endless variety of different media makes a powerful and a dangerous thing of the analogue model. The risks of fallacious inference from inevitable irrelevancies and distortions in the model are now present in aggravated measure. Any would-be scientific use of an analogue model demands independent confirmation. Analogue models furnish plausible hypotheses, not proofs.

I now make something of a digression to consider "mathematical models."[4] This expression has become very popular among social scientists, who will characteristically speak of "mapping" an "object system" upon one or another of a number of "mathematical systems or models."

When used unemphatically, "model" in such contexts is often no more than a pretentious substitute for "theory" or "mathematical treatment." Usually, however, there are at least the following three additional suggestions: The original field is thought of as "projected" upon the abstract domain of sets, functions, and the like that is the subject matter of the correlated mathematical theory; thus social forces are said to be "modeled" by relations between mathematical entities. The "model" is conceived to be *simpler* and *more abstract* than the original. Often there is a suggestion of the model's being a kind of ethereal analogue model, as if the mathematical equations referred to an invisible mechanism whose operation illustrates or even partially explains the operation of the original social system under investigation. This last suggestion must be rejected as an illusion.

---

[3] For a more precise account of isomorphism, see for instance Rudolf Carnap, *Introduction to Symbolic Logic and Its Applications* (New York, 1958), p. 75.

[4] There is now a considerable literature on this subject. See Kenneth J. Arrow, Mathematical Models in the Social Sciences," in D. Lerner, ed., *The Policy Sciences* (Stanford, Calif., 1951), pp. 129–154.

The procedures involved in using a "mathematical model" seem to be the following:

1. In some original field of investigation, a number of relevant variables are identified, either on the basis of common sense or by reason of more sophisticated theoretical considerations. (For example, in the study of population growth we may decide that variation of population with time depends upon the number of individuals born in that time, the number dying, the number entering the area, and the number leaving.[5] I suppose these choices of variables are made at the level of common sense.)

2. Empirical hypotheses are framed concerning the imputed relations between the selected variables. (In population theory, common sense, supported by statistics, suggests that the numbers of births and deaths during any brief period of time are proportional both to that time and to the initial size of the population.)

3. Simplifications, often drastic, are introduced for the sake of facilitating mathematical formulation and manipulation of the variables. (Changes in a population are treated as if they were continuous; the simplest differential equations consonant with the original empirical data are adopted.)

4. An effort is now made to solve the resulting mathematical equations—or, failing that, to study the *global* features of the mathematical systems constructed. (The mathematical equations of population theory yield the so-called "logistic function," whose properties can be specified completely. More commonly, the mathematical treatment of social data leads at best to "plausible topology," to use Kenneth Boulding's happy phrase;[6] i.e., qualitative conclusions concerning distributions of maxima, minima, and so forth. This result is connected with the fact that the original data are in most cases at best *ordinal* in character.)

5. An effort is made to extrapolate to testable consequences in the original field. (Thus the prediction can be made that an isolated population tends toward a limiting size independent of the initial size of that population.)

6. Removing some of the initial restrictions imposed upon the component functions in the interest of simplicity (e.g., their linearity) may lead to some increase in generality of the theory.

The advantages of the foregoing procedures are those usually arising from the introduction of mathematical analysis into any domain of empirical investigation, among them precision in formulating relations, ease of inference via mathematical calculation, and intuitive grasp of the structures revealed

[5] Further details may be found conveniently in V. A. Kostitsyn, *Mathematical Biology* (London, 1939).

[6] "Economics as a Social Science," in *The Social Sciences at Mid-Century: Essays in Honor of Guy Stanton Ford* (Minneapolis, 1952), p. 73.

(e.g., the emergence of the "logistic function" as an organizing and mnemonic device).

The attendant dangers are equally obvious. The drastic simplifications demanded for success of the mathematical analysis entail a serious risk of confusing accuracy of the mathematics with strength of empirical verification in the original field. Especially important is it to remember that the mathematical treatment furnishes no *explanations*. Mathematics can be expected to do no more than draw consequences from the original empirical assumptions. If the functions and equations have a familiar form, there may be a background of pure mathematical research readily applicable to the illustration at hand. We may say, if we like, that the pure mathematics provides the *form* of an explanation, by showing what *kinds* of function would approximately fit the known data. But *causal* explanations must be sought elsewhere. In their inability to suggest explanations, "mathematical models" differ markedly from the theoretical models now to be discussed.[7]

In order now to form a clear conception of the scientific use of "theoretical models," I shall take as my paradigm Clerk Maxwell's celebrated representation of an electrical field in terms of the properties of an imaginary incompressible fluid. In this instance we can draw upon the articulate reflections of the scientist himself. Here is Maxwell's own account of his procedure:

> The first process therefore in the effectual study of the science must be one of simplification and reduction of the results of previous investigation to a form in which the mind can grasp them. The results of this simplification may take the form of a purely mathematical formula or of a physical hypothesis. In the first case we entirely lose sight of the phenomena to be explained; and though we may trace out the consequences of given laws, we can never obtain more extended views of the subject. If, on the other hand, we adopt a physical hypothesis, we see the phenomena only through a medium, and are liable to that blindness to facts and rashness in assumption which a partial explanation encourages. We must therefore discover some method of investigation which allows the mind at every step to lay hold of a clear physical conception, without being committed to any theory founded on the physical science from which that conception is borrowed, so that it is neither drawn aside from the subject in pursuit of analytical subtleties, nor carried beyond the truth by a favourite hypothesis.[8]

[7] It is perhaps worth noting that nowadays logicians use "model" to stand for an "interpretation" or "realization" of a formal axiom system. See John G. Kemeny, "Models of Logical Systems," *Journal of Symbolic Logic*, XIII (March 1948), 16–30.

[8] *The Scientific Papers of James Clerk Maxwell* (Cambridge University Press, 1890), I, 155–156.

Later comments of Maxwell's explain what he has in mind:

> By referring everything to the purely geometrical idea of the motion
> of an imaginary fluid, I hope to attain generality and precision, and to
> avoid the dangers arising from a premature theory professing to explain
> the cause of the phenomena. . . . The substance here treated of . . . is
> not even a hypothetical fluid which is introduced to explain actual
> phenomena. It is merely a collection of imaginary properties which may
> be employed for establishing certain theorems in pure mathematics in
> a way more intelligible to many minds and more applicable to physical
> problems than that in which algebraic symbols alone are used.[9]

Points that deserve special notice are Maxwell's emphasis upon obtaining a
"clear physical conception" that is both "intelligible" and "applicable to
physical problems," his desire to abstain from "premature theory," and,
above all, his insistence upon the "imaginary" character of the fluid invoked
in his investigations. In his later elaboration of the procedure sketched above,
the fluid seems at first to play the part merely of a mnemonic device for grasping mathematical relations more precisely expressed by algebraic equations
held in reserve. The "exact mental image"[10] he professes to be seeking seems
little more than a surrogate for facility with algebraic symbols.

Before long, however, Maxwell advances much farther toward ontological
commitment. In his paper on action at a distance, he speaks of the "wonderful
medium" filling all space and no longer regards Faraday's lines of force as
"purely geometrical conceptions."[11] Now he says forthrightly that they "must
not be regarded as mere mathematical abstractions. They are the directions
in which the medium is exerting a tension like that of a rope, or rather, like
that of our own muscles."[12] Certainly this is no way to talk about a collocation
of imaginary properties. The purely geometrical medium has become very
substantial.

A great contemporary of Maxwell is still more firmly committed to the
realistic idiom. We find Lord Kelvin saying:

> We must not listen to any suggestion that we are to look upon the
> luminiferous ether as an ideal way of putting the thing. A real matter
> between us and the remotest stars I believe there is, and that light
> consists of real motions of that matter. . . . We know the luminiferous
> ether better than we know any other kind of matter in some particulars.

[9] *Ibid.*, I, 159–160.
[10] *Ibid.*, II, 360.
[11] *Ibid.*, II, 322.
[12] *Ibid.*, II, 323.

We know it for its elasticity; we know it in respect to the constancy of the velocity of propagation of light for different periods. . . . Luminiferous ether must be a substance of most extreme simplicity. We might imagine it to be a material whose ultimate property is to be incompressible; to have a definite rigidity for vibrations in times less than a certain limit, and yet to have the absolutely yielding character that we recognize in a wax-like bodies when the force is continued for a sufficient time.[13]

There is certainly a vast difference between treating the ether as a mere heuristic convenience, as Maxwell's first remarks require, and treating it in Kelvin's fashion as "real matter" having definite—though, to be sure, para-doxical—properties independent of our imagination. The difference is be-tween thinking of the electrical field *as if* it were filled with a material medium, and thinking of it *as being* such a medium. One approach uses a detached comparison reminiscent of simile and argument from analogy; the other requires an identification typical of metaphor.

In *as if* thinking there is a willing suspension of ontological unbelief, and the price paid, as Maxwell insists, is absence of explanatory power. Here we might speak of the use of models as *heuristic fictions*. In risking existential statements, however, we reap the advantages of an explanation but are exposed to the dangers of self-deception by myths (as the subsequent history of the ether[14] sufficiently illustrates.

The *existential use of models* seems to me characteristic of the practice of the great theorists in physics. Whether we consider Kelvin's "rude mechanical models,"[15] Rutherford's solar system, or Bohr's model of the atom, we can hardly avoid concluding that these physicists conceived themselves to be describing the atom *as it is*, and not merely offering mathematical formulas in fancy dress. In using theoretical models, they were not comparing two domains from a position neutral to both. They used language appropriate to the model in thinking about the domain of application: they worked not *by* analogy, but *through* and by means of an underlying analogy. Their models were conceived to be more than expository or heuristic devices.

Whether the fictitious or the existential interpretation be adopted, there is one crucial respect in which the sense of "model" here in question sharply diverges from those previously discussed in this paper. Scale models and

[13] Sir William Thomson, *Baltimore Lectures* (London, 1904), pp. 8–12.
[14] See Sir Edmund Whittaker, *A History of the Theories of Aether and Electricity* (2nd ed.; London, 1951), I. especially chapter 9: "Models of the Aether." For further discussion of Maxwell's position, see Joseph Turner, "Maxwell on the Method of Physical Analogy," *British Journal for the Philosophy of Science*, VI (1955–56), 226 238.
[15] Thomson, *op. cit.*, p. 12.

analogue models must be actually put together: a merely "hypothetical" architect's model is nothing at all, and imaginary analogue models will never show us how things work in the large. But theoretical models (whether treated as real or fictitious) are not literally constructed: the heart of the method consists in *talking* in a certain way.

It is therefore plausible to say, as some writers do, that the use of theoretical models consists in introducing a new language or dialect, suggested by a familiar theory but extended to a new domain of application. Yet this suggestion overlooks the point that the new idiom is always a description of some definite object or system (the model itself). If there is a change in manner of expression and representation, there is also the alleged depiction of a specific object or system, inviting further investigation.

The theoretical model need not be built; it is enough that it be *described*. But freedom to describe has its own liabilities. The inventor of a theoretical model is undistracted by accidental and irrelevant properties of the model object, which must have just the properties he assigns to it; but he is deprived of the controls enforced by the attempt at actual construction. Even the elementary demand for self-consistency may be violated in subtle ways unless independent tests are available; and what is to be meant by the reality of the model becomes mysterious.

Although the theoretical model is described but not constructed, the sense of "model" concerned is continuous with the senses previously examined. This becomes clear as soon as we list the conditions for the use of a theoretical model.

1. We have an original field of investigation in which *some* facts and regularities have been established (in any form, ranging from disconnected items and crude generalizations to precise laws, possibly organized by a relatively well-articulated theory).

2. A need is felt, either for explaining the given facts and regularities, or for understanding the basic terms applying to the original domain, or for extending the original corpus of knowledge and conjecture, or for connecting it with hitherto disparate bodies of knowledge—in short, a need is felt for further scientific mastery of the original domain.

3. We describe some entities (objects, materials, mechanisms, systems, structures) belonging to a relatively unproblematic, more familiar, or better-organized secondary domain. The postulated properties of these entities are described in whatever detail seems likely to prove profitable.

4. Explicit or implicit rules of correlation are available for translating statements about the secondary field into corresponding statements about the original field.

5. Inferences from the assumptions made in the secondary field are trans-

lated by means of the rules of correlation and then independently checked against known or predicted data in the primary domain.

The relations between the "described model" and the original domain are like those between an analogue model and its original. Here, as in the earlier case, the key to understanding the entire transaction is the identity of structure that in favorable cases permits assertions made about the secondary domain to yield insight into the original field of interest.

Reliance upon theoretical models may well seem a devious and artificial procedure. Although the history of science has often shown that the right way to success is to "go round about" (as the Boyg advised Peer Gynt), one may well wonder whether the detour need be as great as it is in the use of models. Is the leap from the domain of primary interest to an altogether different domain really necessary? Must we really go to the trouble of using half-understood metaphors? Are the attendant risks of mystification and conceptual confusion unavoidable? And does not recourse to models smack too much of philosophical fable and literary allegory to be acceptable in a rational search for the truth? I shall try to show that such natural misgivings can be allayed.

The severest critic of the method will have to concede that recourse to models yields results. To become convinced of this, it is unnecessary to examine the great classical instances of large-scale work with models. The pragmatic utility of the method can be understood even more clearly in the simpler examples.

Consider, for instance, a recently published account of investigations in pure mathematics.[16] The problem to be solved was that of finding some method for dissecting any rectangle into a set of unequal squares—a problem of no practical importance, to be sure, and likely to interest only those who enjoy playing with "mathematical recreations." According to the authors' own account of their investigations, the direct path seemed to lead nowhere: trial and error (or "experiment," as they call it) and straightforward computation produced no results. The decisive breakthrough came when the investigators began to "go round about." As they put the matter: "In the next stage of the research we abandoned experiment for theory. We tried to represent rectangles by diagrams of different kinds. The last of these diagrams . . . suddenly made our problem part of the theory of electrical networks."[17]

Here we notice the deliberate introduction of a point-for-point model. Geometrical lines in the original figure were replaced by electrical terminals,

[16] Martin Gardner (ed.), "Mathematical Games," *Scientific American,* CXCIX (November 1958), 136–142. The mathematicians were William T. Tutte, C. A. B. Smith, Arthur H. Stone, and R. L. Brooks.

[17] *Ibid.*, p. 136.

squares by connecting wires through which electrical currents are imagined to flow. By suitable choices of the resistances in the wires and the strengths of the currents flowing through them, a circuit was described conforming to known electrical principles (Kirchoff's Laws). In this way, the resources of a well-mastered theory of electrical networks became applicable to the original geometrical problem. "The discovery of this electrical analogy," our authors say, "was important to us because it linked our problem with an established theory. We could now borrow from the theory of electrical networks and obtain formulas for the currents . . . and the sizes of the corresponding component squares."[18] This fascinating episode strikingly illustrates the usefulness of theoretical models.

It is sometimes said that the virtue of working with models is the replacement of abstractions and mathematical formulas by *pictures*, or any other form of representation that is readily visualized. But the example just mentioned shows that this view emphasizes the wrong thing. It is not easier to visualize a network of electrical currents than to visualize a rectangle dissected into component squares: the point of thinking about the electric currents is not that we can see or imagine them more easily, but rather that their properties are *better known* than those of their intended field of application. (And thus it makes perfectly good sense to treat something abstract, even a mathematical calculus, as a theoretical model of something relatively concrete.) To make good use of a model, we usually need intuitive grasp ("Gestalt knowledge") of its capacities, but so long as we can freely *draw inferences* from the model, its picturability is of no importance. Whereas Maxwell turned away from the electrical field to represent it by a better-known model, subsequent progress in electrical theory now permits us to use the electrical field itself as a model for something else relatively unknown and problematical.

It has been said that the model must belong to a more "familiar" realm than the system to which it is applied. This is true enough, if familiarity is taken to mean belonging to a well-established and thoroughly explored theory. But the model need not belong to a realm of common experience. It may be as recondite as we please, provided we know how to use it. A promising model is one with implications rich enough to suggest novel hypotheses and speculations in the primary field of investigation. "Intuitive grasp" of the model means a ready control of such implications, a capacity to pass freely from one aspect of the model to another, and has very little to do with whether the model can literally be seen or imagined.

The case for the use of theoretical models is that the conditions favoring their success are sometimes satisfied; that sometimes it does prove feasible to invent models "better known" than the original subject matter they are in-

18 *Ibid.*, p. 138.

tended to illuminate; and that it is often hard to conceive how the research in question could have been brought to fruition without recourse to the model. But there is also a formidable case against the use of theoretical models, which must now be heard.

Nobody has attacked the use of models more eloquently or more savagely than the great French physicist Pierre Duhem. Here is a characteristic criticism:

> The French or German physicist conceives, in the space separating two conductors, abstract lines of force having no thickness or real existence, the English physicist materializes these lines and thickens them to the dimensions of a tube which he will fill with vulcanized rubber. In place of a family of ideal forces, conceivable only by reason, he will have a bundle of elastic strings, visible and tangible, firmly glued at both ends to the surfaces of the two conductors, and, when stretched, trying both to contract and to expand. When the two conductors approach each other, he sees the elastic strings drawing closer together, then he sees each of them bunch up and grow large. Such is the famous model of electro-static action designed by Faraday and admired as a work of genius by Maxwell and the whole English School.[19]

Behind such passages as this is a conviction that the nineteenth-century English physicists were corrupting the ideals of science by abandoning clear definitions and a taut system of principles in logical array. "Theory is for him [the English physicist] neither an explanation nor a rational classification, but a model of these laws, a model not built for the satisfying of reason but for the pleasure of the imagination. Hence, it escapes the domination of logic."[20] Duhem might have tolerated, with a grimace, "those disparities, those incoherencies,"[21] he disliked in the work of his English contemporaries could he have believed that models were fruitful. But he held them to be useless.

Oddly enough, Duhem applauds "the use of physical analogues" as "an infinitely valuable thing" and an altogether respectable "method of discovery." He is able to reconcile this approval with his strictures against models by purging reliance upon analogy of all its imaginative power. The two domains to be brought into relation by analogy must *antecedently* have been formulated as "abstract systems," and then, as he says, the demonstration of "an exact

---

[19] *The Aim and Structure of Physical Theory*, trans. Philip P. Wiener (Princeton University Press, 1954), p. 70.

[20] *Ibid.*, p. 81.

[21] *Ibid.* Duhem took preference for working with models to be an expression of the English character. He thought the English, unlike the French, typically manifested "l'esprit de finesse" rather than "l'esprit géométrique."

correspondence" will involve nothing "that can astonish the most rigorous logician."[22]

This is a myopic conception of scientific method; if much in scientific investigation offends the "rigorous logician," the truth may be that the rigor is out of place. To impose upon the exercise of scientific imagination the canons of a codified and well-ordered logical system is to run the risk of stifling research. Duhem's allegations of lack of coherence and clarity in the physical theories he was attacking must not be taken lightly. But this does not require us to treat the use of models as an aberration of minds too feeble to think about abstractions without visual aids.

It is instructive to compare Duhem's intemperate polemic with the more measured treatment of the same topic by a recent writer. In his valuable book, *Scientific Explanation*, Professor R. B. Braithwaite allows that "there are great advantages in thinking about a scientific theory through the medium of thinking about a model for it," but at once adds as his reason that "to do this avoids the complications and difficulties involved in having to think explicitly about the language or other form of symbolism by which the theory is represented."[23] That is to say that he regards the use of models as a *substitute* for the available alternative of taking the scientific theory "straight." The dominating notion in Braithwaite's conception of scientific theory is that of a "deductive scientific system" defined as "a set of hypotheses . . . arranged in such a way that from some of the hypotheses as premises all the other hypotheses logically follow."[24] The ideal form of scientific theory, for Braithwaite as for Duhem, is essentially that of Euclid's *Elements*—or, rather, Euclid as reformed by Hilbert. It is natural, accordingly, for Braithwaite to agree with Duhem in attaching little value to the use of models in science.

Braithwaite says that "the price of the employment of models is eternal vigilance";[25] yet as much could be said for the employment of deductive systems or anything else. The crucial issue is whether the employment of models is to be regarded as a prop for feeble minds (as Duhem thought) or a convenient short cut to the consideration of deductive systems (as Braithwaite seems to think)—in short, as surrogate for some other procedure—or as a rational method having its own canons and principles. Should we think of the use of models as belonging to psychology—like doodles in a margin—or as having its proper place in the logic of scientific investigation? I have been arguing that models are sometimes not epiphenomena of research, but play a distinctive and irreplaceable part in scientific investigation: models are not disreputable understudies for mathematical formulas.

[22] *Ibid.*, pp. 96–97.
[23] *Scientific Explanation* (Cambridge, 1953), p. 92.
[24] *Ibid.*, p. 12.
[25] *Ibid.*, p. 93.

It may be useful to consider this central issue from another point of view. To many, the use of models in science has strongly resembled the use of metaphors. One writer says, "We are forced to employ models when, for one reason or another, we cannot give a direct and complete description in the language we normally use. Ordinarily, when words fail use, we have recourse to analogy and metaphor. The model functions as a more general kind of *metaphor*."[26]

Certainly there is some similarity between the use of a model and the use of metaphor—perhaps we should say, of a sustained and systematic metaphor. And the crucial question about the autonomy of the method of models is paralleled by an ancient dispute about the translatability of metaphors. Those who see a model as a mere crutch are like those who consider metaphor a mere decoration or ornament. But there are powerful and irreplaceable uses of metaphor not adequately described by the old formula of "saying one thing and meaning another."

A memorable metaphor has the power to bring two separate domains into cognitive and emotional relation by using language directly appropriate to the one as a lens for seeing the other; the implications, suggestions, and supporting values entwined with the literal use of the metaphorical expression enable us to see a new subject matter in a new way. The extended meanings that result, the relations between initially disparate realms created, can neither be antecedently predicted nor subsequently paraphrased in prose. We can comment *upon* the metaphor, but the metaphor itself neither needs nor invites explanation and paraphrase. Metaphorical thought is a distinctive mode of achieving insight, not to be construed as an ornamental substitute for plain thought.

Much the same can be said about the role of models in scientific research. If the model were invoked *after* the work of abstract formulation had already been accomplished, it would be at best a convenience of exposition. But the memorable models of science are "speculative instruments," to borrow I. A. Richards' happy title.[27] They, too, bring about a wedding of disparate subjects, by a distinctive operation of transfer of the *implications* of relatively well-organized cognitive fields. And as with other weddings, their outcomes are unpredictable. Use of a particular model may amount to nothing more than a strained and artificial description of a domain sufficiently known otherwise. But it may also help us to notice what otherwise would be overlooked, to shift the relative emphasis attached to details—in short, to *see new connections*.

---

[26] E. H. Hutten, "The Role of Models in Physics," *British Journal for the Philosophy of Science,* IV (1953–54), 289.

[27] *Speculative Instruments* (London, 1955).

A dissenting critic might be willing to agree that models are useful in the ways I have stated, and yet still harbor reservations about their rationality. "You have compared the use of models in science to the use of metaphors," I imagine him saying, "yet you cannot seriously contend that scientific investigation *requires* metaphorical language. That a model may lead to insight not otherwise attainable is just a fact of psychology. The *content* of the theory that finally emerges is wholly and adequately expressed by mathematical equations, supplemented by rules for co-ordination with the physical world. To count the model as an intrinsic part of the investigation is as plausible as including pencil sharpening in scientific research. Your inflated claims threaten to debase the hard-won standards of scientific clarity and accuracy."

This objection treats the relation between the model and the formal theory by which it is eventually replaced as *causal*; it claims that the model is no more than a *de facto* contrivance for leading scientists to a deductive system. I cannot accept this view of the relation between model and theory. We have seen that the successful model must be isomorphic with its domain of application. So there is a rational basis for using the model. In stretching the language by which the model is described in such a way as to fit the new domain, we pin our hopes upon the existence of a common structure in both fields. If the hope is fulfilled, there will have been an objective ground for the analogical transfer. For we call a mode of investigation rational when it has a rationale, that is to say, when we can find reasons which justify what we do and that allow for articulate appraisal and criticism. The putative isomorphism between model and field of application provides such a rationale and yields such standards of critical judgment. We can determine the validity of a given model by checking the extent of its isomorphism with its intended application. In appraising models as good or bad, we need not rely on the sheerly pragmatic test of fruitfulness in discovery; we can, in principle at least, determine the "goodness" of their "fit."

We may deal with any residual qualms about the propriety of condoning metaphorical description in scientific research by stressing the limitation of any comparison between model and metaphor. The term "metaphor" is best restricted to relatively brief statements, and if we wished to draw upon the traditional terms of rhetoric we might better compare use of models with allegory or fable. But none of these comparisons will stand much strain.

Use of theoretical models resembles the use of metaphors in requiring analogical transfer of a vocabulary. Metaphor and model-making reveal new relationships; both are attempts to pour new content into old bottles. But a metaphor operates largely with *commonplace* implications. You need only proverbial knowledge, as it were, to have your metaphor understood; but the maker of a scientific model must have prior control of a well-knit scientific theory if he is to do more than hang an attractive picture on an algebraic formula. Systematic complexity of the source of the model and capacity for analogical development are of the essence. As Stephen Toulmin says:

> It is in fact a great virtue of a good model that it does suggest further questions, taking us beyond the phenomena from which we began, and tempts us to formulate hypotheses which turn out to be experimentally fertile. . . . Certainly it is this suggestiveness, and systematic deployability, that makes a good model something more than a simple metaphor.[28]

I have tried to consider various senses of "model" in a systematic order, proceeding from the familiar construction of miniatures to the making of scale models in a more generalized way, and then to "analogue models" and "mathematical models," until we reached the impressive but mysterious uses of "theoretical models," where mere description of an imaginary but possible structure sufficed to facilitate scientific research. Now I propose to take one last step by considering cases where we have, as it were, an implicit or submerged model operating in a writer's thought. What I have in mind is close to what Stephen C. Pepper meant by "root metaphors." This is his explanation of the notion:

> The method in principle seems to be this: A man desiring to understand the world looks about for a clue to its comprehension. He pitches upon some area of common-sense fact and tries if he cannot understand other areas in terms of this one. The original area becomes then his basic analogy or root metaphor. He describes as best he can the characteristics of this area, or, if you will, discriminates its structure. A list of its structural characteristics becomes his basic concepts of explanation and description. We call them a set of categories. In terms of these categories he proceeds to study all other areas of fact whether uncriticized or previously criticized. He undertakes to interpret all facts upon his categories, he may qualify and readjust the categories, so that a set of categories commonly changes and develops. Since the basic analogy or root metaphor normally (and probably at least in part necessarily) arises out of common sense, a great deal of development and refinement of a set of categories is required if they are to prove adequate for a hypothesis of unlimited scope. Some root metaphors prove more fertile than others, have greater power of expansion and adjustment. These survive in comparison with the others and generate the relatively adequate world theories.[29]

---

[28] *The Philosophy of Science* (London, 1953), pp. 38–39.
[29] *World Hypotheses* (University of California Press, 1942), pp. 91–92.

Pepper is talking about how metaphysical systems ("world hypotheses," as he calls them) arise; but his remarks have wider application. Use of a dominating system of concepts to describe a new realm of application by analogical extension seems typical of much theorizing:

> Any area for investigation, so long as it lacks prior concepts to give it structure and an express terminology with which it can be managed, appears to the inquiring mind inchoate—either a blank, or an elusive and tantalizing confusion. Our usual recourse is, more or less deliberately, to cast about for objects which offer parallels to dimly sensed aspects of the new situation, to use the better known to elucidate the less known, to discuss the intangible in terms of the tangible. This analogical procedure seems characteristic of much intellectual enterprise. There is a deal of wisdom in the popular locution for "what is its nature?" namely: "What's it *like*?" We tend to describe the nature of something in similes and metaphors, and the vehicles of these recurrent figures, when analyzed, often turn out to be the attributes of an implicit analogue through which we are viewing the object we describe.[30]

Here no *specific* structure or system is postulated by the theorist—there is not even a suppressed or implicit model. A system of concepts is used analogically, but there is no question of a definite explanation of given phenomena or laws. For reasons already given, I shall not follow Pepper in speaking of "metaphors." For want of a better term, I shall speak of "conceptual archetypes" or, more briefly, of "archetypes."[31] Others have perhaps had a similar idea in mind when they spoke of "ultimate frames of reference" or "ultimate presuppositions."

By an *archetype* I mean a systematic repertoire of ideas by means of which a given thinker describes, by *analogical extension*, some domain to which those ideas do not immediately and literally apply. Thus, a detailed account of a particular archetype would require a list of key words and expressions, with statements of their interconnections and their paradigmatic meanings in the field from which they were originally drawn. This might then be supplemented by analysis of the ways in which the original meanings become extended in their analogical uses.

A striking illustration of the influence of an archetype upon a theorist's work is to be found in the writings of Kurt Lewin. Ironically enough, he formally disclaims any intention of using models, "We have tried," he says, "to avoid developing elaborate 'models'; instead we have tried to represent

---

[30] M. H. Abrams, *The Mirror and the Lamp* (Oxford University Press, 1953), pp. 31–32.
[31] The term is used in a rather different sense by literary critics as, for example, in Maud Bodkin's well-known *Archetypal Patterns in Poetry* (Oxford, 1934).

the dynamic relations between the psychological facts by mathematical constructs at a sufficient level of generality."[32] Well, there may be no specific models envisaged; yet any reader of Lewin's papers must be impressed by the degree to which he employs a vocabulary indigenous to *physical* theory. We repeatedly encounter such words as "field," "vector," "phase-space," "tension," "force," "boundary," "fluidity"—visible symptoms of a massive archetype awaiting to be reconstructed by a sufficiently patient critic.

In this I see nothing to be deplored on the ground of general principles of sound method. Competent specialists must appraise the distinctive strengths and weaknesses of Lewin's theories; but an onlooker may venture to record his impression that Lewin's archetype, confused though it may be in detail, is sufficiently rich in implicative power to be a useful speculative instrument. It is surely no mere coincidence that Lewin's followers have been stimulated into making all manner of interesting empirical investigations that bear the stamp of their master's archetype. Now if an archetype is sufficiently fruitful, we may be confident that logicians and mathematicians will eventually reduce the harvest to order. There will always be competent technicians who, in Lewin's words, can be trusted to build the highways "over which the streamlined vehicles of a highly mechanized logic, fast and efficient, can reach every important point on fixed tracks."[33] But clearing intellectual jungles is also a respectable occupation. Perhaps every science must start with metaphor and end with algebra; and perhaps without the metaphor there would never have been any algebra.

Of course, there is an ever-present and serious risk that the archetype will be used metaphysically, so that its consequences will be permanently insulated from empirical disproof. The more persuasive the archetype, the greater the danger of its becoming a self-certifying myth. But a good archetype can yield to the demands of experience; while it channels its master's thought, it need not do so inflexibly. The imagination must not be confused with a strait jacket.

If I have been on the right track in my diagnosis of the part played in scientific method by models and archetypes, some interesting consequences follow for the relations between the sciences and the humanities. All intellectual pursuits, however different their aims and methods, rely firmly upon such exercises of the imagination as I have been recalling. Similar archetypes may play their parts in different disciplines; a sociologist's pattern of thought may also be the key to understanding a novel. So perhaps those interested in excavating the presuppositions and latent archetypes of scientists may have something to learn from the industry of literary critics. When the understanding of scientific models and archetypes comes to be regarded as a reputable

[32] Kurt Lewin, *Field Theory in Social Science* (New York, 1951), p. 21.
[33] *Ibid.*, p. 3.

part of scientific culture, the gap between the sciences and the humanities will have been partly filled. For exercise of the imagination, with all its promise and its dangers, provides a common ground. If I have so much emphasized the importance of scientific models and archetypes, it is because of a conviction that the imaginative aspects of scientific thought have in the past been too much neglected. For science, like the humanities, like literature, is an affair of the imagination.

Value Judgments in Science

It is standardly assumed that factual and value statements can be distinguished and that scientists, as scientists, cannot make value judgments but can only make descriptive (which includes theoretical) statements. The sociologist Max Weber expresses this view in his discussion of the editorial policy of the journal *Archiv für Sozialwissenschaft und Sozialpolitick*. Charles L. Stevenson, also maintaining that scientists, as scientists, cannot make value judgments, nevertheless argues that educational scientists, because of their special knowledge of the means for achieving educational ends, still have an obligation to participate in the formulation and defense of aims and value judgments in education because they are better informed than most people.

Problems involved in the attempted separation of factual statements and value judgments are raised in the selections by the philosophers John Passmore and Richard Rudner. Rudner's view is especially crucial since his position that science involves value judgments is based on the lack of objectivity in scientists' decisions of whether there is (or is not) "enough evidence now." Thus, for Rudner, *questions about the justification of scientific inferences are inseparable from questions concerning value judgments.*

Another common view is that social scientists, in contrast to physical scientists, are unable to avoid making value judgments. Ernest Nagel describes and argues against this position, maintaining that social scientists are just as able (or unable) as physical scientists to avoid making value judgments in the course of their work.

In general, attempts to expunge value judgments from science per se (attempted by Weber and Nagel and assumed by Stevenson) are, in that respect, in the radical empiricist camp. Attempts (like those of Passmore and Rudner) to see science as inevitably involving value judgments are in the humanist camp.

40. THE SCIENTIST AS SCIENTIST CANNOT MAKE VALUE JUDGMENTS

Max Weber

When a social science journal which also at times concerns itself with a social policy, appears for the first time or passes into the hands of a new editorial board, it is customary to ask about its "line."* We, too, must seek to answer this question and following up the remarks in our "Introductory Note" we will enter into the question in a more fundamental theoretical way. Even though or perhaps because, we are concerned with "self-evident truths," this occasion provides the opportunity to cast some light on the nature of the "social sciences" as we understand them, in such a manner that it can be useful, if not to the specialist, then to the reader who is more remote from actual scientific work.

In addition to the extension of our knowledge of the "social conditions of all countries," i.e., the facts of social life, the express purpose of the *Archiv* ever since its establishment has been the education of judgment about practical social problems—and in the very modest way in which such a goal can be furthered by private scholars—the criticism of practical social policy, extending even as far as legislation. In spite of this, the *Archiv* has firmly adhered, from the very beginning, to its intention to be an exclusively scientific

SOURCE. Reprinted with permission of The Macmillan Company from *On The Methodology of the Social Sciences*, by Max Weber, edited by Edward A. Shils and Henry A. Finch. Copyright © 1949 by The Macmillan Company.

* This essay was published when the editorship of the *Archiv für Sozialwissenschaft und Sozialpolitik* was transferred to Edgar Jaffé, Werner Sombart and Max Weber. Its form was influenced by the occasion for which it was written and the content should be considered in this light.—Marianne Weber.

journal and to proceed only with the methods of scientific research. Hence arises the question of whether the purpose stated above is compatible in principle with self-confinement to the latter method. What has been the meaning of the value-judgments found in the pages of the *Archiv* regarding legislative and administrative measures, or practical recommendations for such measures? What are the standards governing these judgments? What is the validity of the value-judgments which are uttered by the critic, for instance, or on which a writer recommending a policy founds his arguments for that policy? In what sense, if the criterion of scientific knowledge is to be found in the "objective" validity of its results, has he remained within the sphere of *scientific* discussion? We will first present our own attitude on this question in order later to deal with the broader one: in what sense are there in general "objectively valid truths" in those disciplines concerned with social and cultural phenomena? This question, in view of the continuous changes and bitter conflict about the apparently most elementary problems of our discipline, its methods, the formulation and validity of its concepts, cannot be avoided. We do not attempt to offer solutions but rather to disclose problems—problems of the type to which our journal, if it is to meet its past and future responsibilities, must turn its attention.

We all know that our science, as is the case with every science treating the institutions and events of human culture, (with the possible exception of political history) first arose in connection with *practical* considerations. Its most immediate and often sole purpose was the attainment of value-judgments concerning measures of State economic policy. It was a "technique" in the same sense as, for instance, the clinical disciplines in the medical sciences are. It is now become known how this situation was gradually modified. This modification was not, however, accompanied by a formulation of the logical (*prinzipielle*) distinction between "existential knowledge," i.e., knowledge of what "is," and "normative knowledge," i.e., knowledge of what "should be." The formulation of this distinction was hampered, first, by the view that immutably invariant natural laws,—later, by the view that an unambiguous evolutionary principle—governed economic life and that accordingly, *what was normatively right* was identical—in the former case—with the immutably *existent*—and in the latter—with the inevitably *emergent*. With the awakening of the historical sense, a combination of ethical evolutionism and historical relativism became the predominant attitude in our science. This attitude sought to deprive ethical norms of their formal character and through the incorporation of the totality of cultural values into the "ethical" (*Sittlichen*) sphere tried to give a *substantive content* to ethical norms. It was hoped thereby to raise economics to the status of an "ethical science" with empirical foundations. To the extent that an "ethical" label was given to all possible cultural ideals, the particular autonomy of the ethical imperative was obliterated, without however increasing the "objective" validity of those ideals. Nonetheless we can and must forego a discussion of the principles at issue. We merely point out that even today the confused opinion that economics does and should derive value-judgments from a specifically "economic point of view" has not disappeared but is especially current, quite understandably, among men of practical affairs.

Our journal as the representative of an empirical specialized discipline must, as we wish to show shortly, reject this view in principle. It must do so because, in our opinion, it can never be the task of an empirical science to provide binding norms and ideals from which directives for immediate practical activity can be derived.

What is the implication of this proposition? It is certainly not that value-judgments are to be withdrawn from scientific discussion in general simply because in the last analysis they rest on certain ideals and are therefore "subjective" in origin. Practical action and the aims of our journal would always reject such a proposition. Criticism is not to be suspended in the presence of value-judgments. The problem is rather: what is the meaning and purpose of the scientific criticism of ideals and value-judgments? This requires a somewhat more detailed analysis.

All serious reflection about the ultimate elements of meaningful human conduct is oriented primarily in terms of the categories "end" and "means." We desire something concretely either "for its own sake" or as a means of achieving something else which is more highly desired. The question of the appropriateness of the means for achieving a given end is undoubtedly accessible to scientific analysis. Inasmuch as we are able to determine (within the present limits of our knowledge) which means for the achievement of a proposed end are appropriate or inappropriate, we can in this way estimate the chances of attaining a certain end by certain available means. In this way we can indirectly criticize the setting of the end itself as practically meaningful (on the basis of the existing historical situation) or as meaningless with reference to existing conditions. Furthermore, when the possibility of attaining a proposed end appears to exist, we can determine (naturally within the limits of our existing knowledge) the consequences which the application of the means to be used will produce in addition to the eventual attainment of the proposed end, as a result of the interdependence of all events. We can then provide the acting person with the ability to weigh and compare the undesirable as over against the desirable consequences of his action. Thus, we can answer the question: what will the attainment of a desired end "cost" in terms of the predictable loss of other values? Since, in the vast majority of cases, every goal that is striven for does "cost" or can "cost" something in this sense, the weighing of the goal in terms of the incidental consequences of the action which realizes it cannot be omitted from the deliberation of persons who act with a sense of responsibility. One of the most important functions of the *technical criticism* which we have been discussing thus far is to make this sort of analysis possible. To apply the results of this analysis in the making of a decision, however, is not a task which science can undertake: it is rather the task of the acting, willing person: he weighs and chooses from among the values involved according to his own conscience and his personal view of the world. Science can make him realize that all action and naturally, according to the circumstances, inaction imply in their consequences the espousal of certain values—and herewith—what is today so willingly overlooked—the rejection of certain others. The act of choice itself is his own responsibility.

We can also offer the person, who makes a choice, insight into the significance of the desired object. We can teach him to think in terms of the context and the meaning of the ends he desires, and among which he chooses. We do this through making explicit and developing in a logically consistent manner the "ideas" which actually do or which can underlie the concrete end. It is self-evident that one of the most important tasks of every science of cultural life is to arrive at a rational understanding of these "ideas" for which men either really or allegedly struggle. This does not overstep the boundaries of a science which strives for an "analytical ordering of empirical reality," although the methods which are used in this interpretation of cultural (*geistiger*) values are not "inductions" in the usual sense. At any rate, this task falls at least partly beyond the limits of economics as defined according to the conventional division of labor. It belongs among the tasks of social philosophy. However, the historical influence of ideas in the development of social life has been and still is so great that our journal cannot renounce this task. It shall rather regard the investigation of this phenomenon as one of its most important obligations.

But the scientific treatment of value-judgments may not only understand and empathically analyze (*nacherleben*) the desired ends and the ideals which underlie them; it can also "judge" them critically. This criticism can of course have only a dialectical character, i.e., it can be no more than a formal logical judgment of historically given value-judgments and ideas, a testing of the ideals according to the postulate of the internal *consistency* of the desired end. It can, insofar as it sets itself this goal, aid the acting, willing person in attaining self-clarification concerning the final axioms from which his desired ends are derived. It can assist him in becoming aware of the ultimate standards of value which he does not make explicit to himself or, which he must presuppose in order to be logical. The elevation of these ultimate standards, which are manifested in concrete value-judgments, to the level of explicitness is the utmost that the scientific treatment of value-judgments can do without entering into the realm of speculation. As to whether the person expressing these value-judgments *should* adhere to these ultimate standards is his personal affair; it involves will and conscience, not empirical knowledge.

An empirical science cannot tell anyone what he *should* do—but rather what he *can* do—and under certain circumstances— what he wishes to do. It is true that in our sciences, personal value-judgments have tended to influence scientific arguments without being explicitly admitted. They have brought about continual confusion and have caused various interpretations to be placed on scientific arguments even in the sphere of the determination of simple causal interconnections among facts according to whether the results increased or decreased the chances of realizing one's personal ideals, i.e., the possibility of desiring a certain thing. Even the editors and the collaborators of our journal will regard "nothing human as alien" to them in this respect. But it is a long way from this acknowledgement of human frailty to the belief in an "ethical" science of economics, which would derive ideals from its subject matter and produce concrete norms by applying general ethical imperatives. It is true that we regard as *objectively* valuable those innermost elements of the "personality," those highest and most ultimate value-judgments which determine our conduct and give meaning and significance to our life. We can indeed espouse these values only when they appear to us as valid, as derived from our highest values and when they are developed in the struggle against the difficulties which life presents. Certainly, the dignity of the "personality" lies in the fact that for it there exist values about which it organizes its life;— even if these values are in certain cases concentrated exclusively within the sphere of the person's "individuality," then "self-realization" in *those* interests for which it claims *validity* as *values* is the idea with respect to which its whole existence is oriented. Only on the assumption of belief in the validity of values is the attempt to espouse value-judgments meaningful. However, to *judge* the *validity* of such values is a matter of *faith*. It may perhaps be a task for the speculative interpretation of life and the universe in quest of their meaning. But it certainly does not fall within the province of an empirical science in the sense in which it is to be practised here. The empirically demonstrable fact that these ultimate ends undergo historical changes and are debatable does not affect this distinction between empirical science and value-judgments, contrary to what is often thought. For even the knowledge of the most certain proposition of our theoretical sciences—e.g., the exact natural sciences or mathematics, is, like the cultivation and refinement of the conscience, a product of culture. However, when we call to mind the practical problems of economic and social policy (in the usual sense), we see that there are many, indeed countless, practical questions in the discussion of which there seems to be general agreement about the self-evident character of certain goals. Among these we may mention emergency credit, the concrete problems of social hygiene, poor relief, factory inspection, industrial courts, employment exchanges, large sections of protective labor legislation—in short, all those issues in which, at least in appearance, only the *means* for the attainment of the goal are at issue. But even if we were to mistake the illusion of self-evidence for truth—which science can never do without damaging itself—and wished to view the conflicts immediately arising from attempts at practical realization as purely technical questions of expediency—which would very often be incorrect—even in this case we would have to recognize that this illusion of the self-evidence of normative standards of value is dissipated as soon as we pass from the concrete problems of philanthropic and protective social and economic services to problems of economic and social policy. The distinctive characteristic of a problem of social *policy* is indeed the fact that it cannot be resolved merely on the basis of purely technical considerations which assume already settled ends. Normative standards of value can and must be the objects of *dispute* in a discussion of a problem of social policy because the problem lies in the domain of general *cultural* values. And the conflict occurs not merely, as we are too easily inclined to believe today, between "class interests" but between general views on life and the universe as well. This latter point, however, does not lessen the truth that the particular ultimate value-judgment which the individual espouses is decided among other factors and certainly to a quite significant degree by the degree of affinity between it and his class interests—accepting for the time being this only superficially unambiguous term. One thing is certain under all circumstances, namely, the more "general" the problem involved, i.e., in this case, the broader its cultural *significance*, the less subject it is to a single unambiguous answer on the basis of the data of empirical sciences and the greater the role played by value-ideas (*Wertideen*) and the ultimate and highest personal axioms of belief. It is simply naive to believe, although there are many specialists who even now occasionally do, that it is possible to establish and to demonstrate as scientifically valid "a principle" for practical social science from which the norms for the solution of practical problems can be unambiguously derived. However much the social sciences need the discussion of practical problems in terms of fundamental principles, i.e., the reduction of unreflective value-judgments to the premises from which they are logically derived and however much our journal intends to devote itself specially to them—certainly the creation of a lowest common denominator for our problems in the form of generally valid ultimate value-judgments cannot be its task or in general the task of any empirical science. Such a thing would not only be impracticable; it would be entirely meaningless as well. Whatever the interpretation of the basis and the nature of the validity of the ethical imperatives, it is certain that from them, as from the norms for the concretely conditioned conduct of the *individual, cultural values* cannot be unambiguously derived as being normatively desirable; it can do so the less, the more in-clusive are the values concerned. Only positive religions—or more precisely expressed: dogmatically bound *sects*—are able to confer on the content *of cultural values* the status of unconditionally valid *ethical* imperatives. Outside these sects, cultural ideals which the individual wishes to realize and ethical obligations which he *should* fulfil do not, in principle, share the same status. The fate of an epoch which has eaten of the tree of knowledge is that it must know that we cannot learn the *meaning* of the world from the results of its analysis, be it ever so perfect; it must rather be in a position to create this meaning itself. It must recognize that general views of life and the universe can never be the products of increasing empirical knowledge, and that the highest ideals, which move us most forcefully, are always formed only in the struggle with other ideals which are just as sacred to others as ours are to us.

Only an optimistic syncretism, such as is, at times, the product of evolu-tionary-historical relativism, can theoretically delude itself about the profound seriousness of this situation or practically shirk its consequences. It can, to be sure, be just as obligatory subjectively for the practical politician, in the individual case, to mediate between antagonistic points of view as to take sides with one of them. But this has nothing whatsoever to do with scientific "objectivity." *Scientifically the "middle course" is not truer even by a hair's breadth*, than the most extreme party ideals of the right or left. Nowhere are the interests of science more poorly served in the long run than in those situa-tions where one refuses to see uncomfortable facts and the realities of life in all their starkness. The *Archiv* will struggle relentlessly against the severe self-deception which asserts that through the synthesis of several party points of view, or by following a line between them, practical norms of *scientific validity* can be arrived at. It is necessary to do this because, since this piece of self-deception tries to mask its own standards of value in relativistic terms, it is more dangerous to the freedom of research than the former naive faith of parties in the scientific "demonstrability" of their dogmas. The capacity to distinguish between empirical knowledge and value-judgments, and the fulfill-ment of the scientific duty to see the factual truth as well as the practical duty to stand up for our own ideals constitute the program to which we wish to adhere with ever increasing firmness.

There is and always will be—and this is the reason that it concerns us—an unbridgeable distinction among (1) those arguments which appeal to our capacity to become enthusiastic about and our feeling for concrete practical aims or cultural forms and values, (2) those arguments in which, once it is a question of the validity of ethical norms, the appeal is directed to our con-science, and finally (3) those arguments which appeal to our capacity and need for *analytically ordering* empirical reality in a manner which lays claim to *validity* as empirical truth. This proposition remains correct, despite, as we shall see, the fact that those highest "values" underlying the practical interest are and always will be decisively significant in determining the focus of attention of analytical activity (*ordnende Tätigkeit des Denkens*) in the sphere of the cultural sciences. It has been and remains true that a systematically correct scientific proof in the social sciences, if it is to achieve its purpose, must be acknowledged as correct even by a Chinese—or—more precisely stated—it must constantly *strive* to attain this goal, which perhaps may not be completely attainable due to faulty data. Furthermore, the successful *logical* analysis of the content of an ideal and its ultimate axioms and the discovery of the consequences which arise from pursuing it, logically and practically, must also be valid for the Chinese. At the same time, our Chinese can lack a "sense" for our ethical imperative and he can and certainly often will deny the ideal itself and the concrete value-judgments derived from it. Neither of these two latter attitudes can affect the scientific value of the analysis in any way. Quite certainly our journal will not ignore the ever and inevitably recurrent attempts to give an unambiguous interpretation to culture. On the contrary, these attempts themselves rank with the most important producs of this cultural life and, under certain circumstances, among its dynamic forces. We will therefore constantly strive to follow with care the course of these discussions of "social philosophy" (as here understood). We are furthermore completely free of the prejudice which asserts that reflections on culture which go beyond the analysis of empirical data in order to interpret the world metaphysically can, because of their metaphysical character fulfill no useful cognitive tasks. Just what these cognitive tasks are is primarily an epistemological question, the answer to which we must and can, in view of our purpose, disregard at this point. There is one tenet to which we adhere most firmly in our work, namely, that a social science journal, in our sense, to the extent that it is *scientific* should be a place where those truths are sought, which—to remain with our illustration—can claim, even for a Chinese, the validity appropriate to an analysis of empirical reality.

Of course, the editors cannot once and for all deny to themselves or their contributors the possibility of expressing in value-judgment the ideals which motivate them. However, two important duties arise in connection with this. First, to keep the readers and themselves sharply aware at every moment of the standards by which they judge reality and from which the value-judgment is derived, instead of, as happens too often, deceiving themselves in the conflict of ideals by a value mélange of values of the most different orders and types, and seeking to offer something to everybody. If this obligation is rigorously heeded, the practical evaluative attitude can be not only harmless to scientific interests but even directly useful, and indeed mandatory. In the scientific criticism of legislative and other practical recommendations, the motives of the legislator and the ideals of the critic in all their scope often can not be clarified and analyzed in a tangible and intelligible form in any other way than through the confrontation of the standards of value underlying the ideas criticized with others, preferably the critic's own. Every meaningful *value-judgment* about someone else's *aspirations* must be a criticism from the standpoint of one's own *Weltanschauung*; it must be a struggle against *another's* ideals from the standpoint of one's *own*. If in a particular concrete case, the ultimate value-axioms which underlie practical activity are not only to be designated and scientifically analyzed but are also to be shown in their relationship to *other* value-axioms, "positive" criticism by means of a systematic exposition of the latter is unavoidable.

In the pages of this journal, especially in the discussion of legislation, there will inevitably be found social *policy*, i.e., the statement of ideals, in addition to social *science*, i.e., the analysis of facts. But we do not by any means intend to present such discussions as "science" and we will guard as best we can against allowing these two to be confused with each other. In such discussions, *science* no longer has the floor. For that reason, the second fundamental imperative of scientific freedom is that in such cases it should be constantly made clear to the readers (and—again we say it—above all to one's self!) exactly at which point the scientific investigator becomes silent and the evaluating and acting person begins to speak. In other words, it should be made explicit just where the arguments are addressed to the analytical understanding and where to the sentiments. The constant confusion of the scientific discussion of facts and their evaluation is still one of the most widespread and also one of the most damaging traits of work in our field. The foregoing arguments are directed against this confusion, and not against the clear-cut introduction of one's own ideals into the discussion. An *attitude of moral indifference* has no connection with *scientific* "objectivity." The *Archiv*, at least in its intentions, has never been and should never be a place where polemics against certain currents in politics or social policy are carried on, nor should it be a place where struggles are waged for or against ideals in politics or social-policy. There are other journals for these purposes. The peculiar characteristic of the journal has rather been from the very beginning and, insofar as it is in the power of the editors, shall continue to be that political antagonists can meet in it to carry on scientific work. It has not been a "socialist" organ hitherto and in the future it shall not be "bourgeois." It excludes no one from its circle of contributors who is willing to place himself within the framework of scientific discussion. It cannot be an arena for "objections," replies and rebuttals, but in its pages no one will be protected, neither its contributors nor its editors, from being subjected to the sharpest factual, scientific criticism. Whoever cannot bear this or who takes the viewpoint that he does not wish to work, in the service of scientific knowledge, with persons whose other ideals are different from his own, is free not to participate.

41. THE SCIENTIST'S ROLE AND THE AIMS OF EDUCATION

C. L. Stevenson

I'd like to begin with an example that may seem to have little to do with education, but will tie up with it presently. It has to do with the aims of *economics*; and since I have heard the example used in connection with at least three different economists—which entitles you, by the way, to suspect that the example belongs to fiction—I shall play safe and refer to the economist in question simply as "Professor X."

Back in the 30's when England was about to go off the gold standard, the government asked Professor X to give them economic advice. "Will you tell us," he was asked, "in your capacity as an economist, whether we really ought to go off the gold standard?" Now the trouble with the question was that it combined the word "ought" with the phrase "in your capacity as an economist." This unfortunate combination immediately put Professor X on his professional dignity, and led him to reply: "Gentlemen, I cannot answer this question as an economist. I can, as an economist, predict that *if* you go off the gold standard you will in effect be taking money out of these people's pockets and putting it in those people's pockets. It's well known that a change in the value of the pound will have a different effect on creditors than it will on debtors. But whether you *ought* to take money out of these people's pockets and put it in those people's pockets—well, that is an *ethical* question, and as a mere economic scientist I am not qualified to answer it."

SOURCE. Stevenson, C. L., "The Scientist's Role and the Aims of Education," *Harvard Educational Review*, **24**, 231–238. Copyright © 1954 by President and Fellows of Harvard College.

You are free, I repeat, to doubt whether this statement was ever actually made; but even so, it typifies the stand that scientists are often inclined to take. Ethics, with its judgments of value, seems to the special scientist to be outside his field of competence, and being reluctant to leave his field of competence, he decides that ethics is not for him. Nor is this more typical of economics than of many other sciences.

Consider, for instance, the recent book by Robert Hall, a student of language, under the arresting title, *Leave Your Language Alone*. Mr. Hall protests against those who want to *reform* people's way of talking. It's all right for a philologist to study how people *do* talk. Very interesting to see that so many percent of the people use "ain't," and so many don't. Very interesting to predict whether using "ain't" will prevent your getting a white-collar job, and so on. But as to whether you *should* or you *shouldn't*—that's an evaluative problem, and not for the pure philologist to meddle with. I feel there is a secret evaluation behind all this: philologists oughtn't to evaluate. But at least Hall evaluates only on a second level. He only moralizes *against* moralists, so to speak, and not *with* them.

Well, maybe a scientist, when speaking as a scientist, oughtn't to make value judgments. No doubt value judgments do take one outside his special field. But I do wish to make this simple protest: it seems to me a great pity that a scientist should be reluctant, whether in teaching or in doing something else, to talk beyond his special professional interests. If he won't risk making value judgments, then I'd like to ask who *is* going to make them. There's always the possibility that those who aren't reluctant to make them will turn out to be (in a technical and non-offensive sense, to be sure) complete asses. Take the sort of thing which is done in linguistic reform by those who don't understand the science of language at all. Take the example that my colleague at Michigan, Charles Fries, is so fond of—that of a school teacher who carefully trained all her students to pronounce l-a-u-g-h-t-e-r as "lawter," on the ground that d-a-u-g-h-t-e-r was pronounced "dawter" and s-l-a-u-g-h-t-e-r was pronounced "slawter." (I wonder what happened when she said, "Now children, suppress this unseemly lawter.")

In general, those who don't know, scientifically, how things are and how they came to be are likely to make reforms no less absurd than this one. The most exciting economic reforms (if you go in for that kind of excitement) are proposed by those who don't know economics at all; the most exciting political reforms are proposed by those who know nothing of government; and so on. But perhaps, you will say, the *philosophers* must be called upon to save us from these ignorant reformers. Perhaps the philosophers have the last word about the right direction of reform, and the practical men have only to consult them. Well, *if* that's what you think, I am compelled to remind you (squelching my own professional dignity for the moment) that things don't always go well in that subject. I am reminded of Hartmann's ethics. Hartmann had more intuitions than most of us; he readily intuited that in the realms of value chastity stood above brotherly love, or—and somehow I always forget—perhaps it was the other way round. At any rate, ever so much philosophy, when it reaches these evaluative regions, impresses me as mere dogmatism in fancy clothes. Nor have I been able to find, in philosophy, any royal road to a sense of values. I can't persuade myself to trust any philosopher, when he tells us how things ought to be, unless I find that he has a good scientific knowledge of what they now are; and most philosophers, I regret to say, are rather bad amateurs at the sciences. So here's my point: if scientists don't make evaluations about topics near their special interests, then heaven only knows who will!

Let me now attempt to connect this with my topic about the aims of education. When we ask about these aims we may sometimes be asking a factual question: what have people actually aimed at in education, in the course of its history? Well, the aims of one century are not the aims of another, and so on. But sometimes we speak of aims in a quite different way. A man who asks, "What are the *real* aims of education (or the *true* aims, etc.)?" and then proceeds to tell us the answer, is not telling us what such and such people have in fact aimed at: he is dealing with an evaluative question. He is telling us what education *ought* to aim at. And clearly, there is a difference between what is and what ought to be—that, if you will, being the main difficulty about life in general. Now it's the latter way of talking about the aims of education that interests me here. And my homely point has so far been just this: I hope that those who have studied education as scientists will not feel that they should restrain themselves (like my economist dealing with the gold standard) when asked to evaluate the aims of education—to say what they *ought* to be. Scientists have to evaluate, else they abdicate in favor of the uninformed. On the other hand, it is perfectly true that *if* they do they will be getting beyond their specialized scientific interests. So the question that remains is this: When a scientist, speaking as a man rather than in his professional capacity, makes evaluations, how can he *make use* of his special knowledge? He will not, of course, still be conducting *just* his usual professional inquiries; but if he is to be more trustworthy than the uninformed, he must not turn his back on his professional inquiries either. So how can his training help him in his evaluations?

That's the question that I'll try to answer in the rest of my limited time. It's not easy, so bear with me. I'll have to start by showing how evaluative problems in general differ from the problems that scientists, in their strictly professional capacity, are accustomed to deal with.

If you examine an evaluative problem—the sort of thing that arises, say, when some of you think that the classics are poor stuff for our present-day students and others think that they aren't—the first thing you can profitably notice is that they involve a special sort of disagreement. I like to call it *disagreement in attitude*, as distinct from *disagreement in belief*. We have a disagreement in belief—and hence *not* the sort of thing typical of an evaluative problem—when you think Caesar is read in such and such a Latin course and I think Caesar isn't read in it. But suppose we are discussing whether Caesar *ought* to be read in the course—or suppose we are discussing whether the school ought to teach Latin at all. Now we have an evaluative problem. And if we disagree it won't be *just* a matter of your having one set of beliefs about alleged facts and my having another set. We may do that too, of course; but the main thing is that one of us is *for* teaching Latin and the other is *against* it. We have divergent *attitudes*—that is to say, divergent likings, approvals, or wants—and each of us is recommending (not of course without wanting a recommendation in turn) that his attitude be shared by the other. That's what disagreement in attitude amounts to, and in my opinion it's the chief thing to notice if we are to handle evaluative problems in a way that's free from confusion.

Just see how little is left of an evaluative issue when attitudes are left out of it. Suppose, for instance, that you think a training in Latin is something that every student *ought* to have, and that in a long argument you lead a friend to make this remark: "You've finally convinced me; I do think every student ought to have a training in Latin." So far you feel successful in the argument. But now suppose he adds this to his remark: "And just because they ought to have that training, I'm going to try to prevent them from having it. I fully disapprove of its being taught at all." You are now completely puzzled, and say, "But you just said they *ought* to have it." Whereupon he replies, "O yes, as an intellectual apprehension I 'see' they ought to, but so far as my attitudes are concerned I am inclined to work against it; in fact I feel altogether lofty and noble in my resolve to put an end to all Latin teaching." Clearly, this "intellectual apprehension" is nothing at all in this context. If you haven't made him *favor* teaching Latin—if you haven't made a dent in his *attitudes*—you haven't ended your disagreement with him. To end the disagreement in the way you hope for—to get him to take a new evaluative stand —you must change his attitudes, and no intellectual apprehension of an ought, devoid of an impulse to be *for* what ought to be, will content you.

The next thing to see, in examining an evaluative issue, is that the moral terms have a kind of emotional charge, and have it intimately and in their own right. Just as "alas" expresses sorrow and "hurrah" enthusiasm, so "good" and "right" express approval. What's more, "good" and "right" tend to evoke approval, quasi-imperatively. Compare "hurrah" with "enthusiasm." The latter names an emotion, but the former directly expresses it and makes it contagious. Mr. Richards calls the force of "hurrah" an "emotive meaning" of the word. Anyone who finds difficulty in distinguishing it from the sort of meaning that "enthusiasm" has need only try saying "enthusiasm" at a football game, in the same tone of voice as he would normally say "hurrah!" It's one thing to name an emotion and another thing to give direct vent to it; and emotive meaning permits a word to do the latter. Now I am suggesting that "right," "good," and the other evaluative terms have a meaning of this emotive kind. And that ties up with disagreement in attitude. If the resolution of disagreement in attitude depends on someone's changing his attitude (as distinct from merely changing a belief) then we may expect the terms that are used to talk directly to attitudes, and not to beliefs alone.

When I say, "That's wrong!" you tend to feel a little intimidated, don't you? And if, seeing that you have stage-fright, I say, "Go ahead, you'll certainly do a magnificent job!" you're likely to feel more encouraged. A word like "magnificent," in such a context, isn't used to make a prediction but rather to build up an attitude. It gives an emotional push. And there's also an emotional push in "good," "right," and the other evaluative terms.

And the push has its uses. Note that a moralist is either a reformer—i.e., a person who is encouraging people's attitudes (and consequent actions) to go in a different direction from the usual one—or else he's a conservative—i.e., a person who wants to *prevent* people's attitudes from going in a different direction from the usual one. In either case it's not merely a change of beliefs that's sought, but a change in attitudes—a change in what people yearn for. And how can a moralist initiate that sort of change without using words that have a push? In science, which talks to beliefs and not to attitudes, the emotional push is carefully avoided; but in evaluations (if they are to be more than *private* yearnings) any attempt to avoid it would simply conceal the nature of what is being attempted.

Now let me use two analogies, which I hope will make my contrast between a scientific problem and an evaluative problem, or between a scientist and a moralist (in a broad sense of the term) a little clearer. Suppose that two people are looking out the window at a parade, one a scientist and the other a moralist. The scientist says, "Of course I don't have all my evidence in, but it looks to me now, unless something very quickly happens, that the parade is going to turn right." The moralist replies, "Your prediction may be well-founded, so I'm going to do something about it." So he runs out, gets in front of the parade, shouts, gesticulates, and *gets* it to turn left. To complete the analogy—a scientist who studies attitudes only surveys them; it's not his business to change them. But a moralist has exactly that business, and to that extent is going beyond what a scientist does.

Or again, suppose two men are looking at a tug of war. A scientist, calculating the stresses and strains, may venture to predict who will win. He doesn't join in, but simply observes. But the moralist does join in, pulling with whatever side he wants to win. Here the analogy is completed just as it was above. And I think you will easily see why I want to distinguish between a scientist's function, who deals with attitudes, if at all, only as topics for study, and a moralist's function, who tries to alter attitudes. For the moralist, both disagreement in attitude and emotive meaning are essentials; he cannot, like the scientist, feel that they must be put to one side as beyond the needs of his special studies.

So far, though, I have emphasized the *difference* between science and evaluation. But what I want to show, primarily, is something else. I want to show that a scientist, in spite of this, may be the very person who can most help us in making evaluations. As I began by saying, if the scientists refuse to help us, it's hard to see where *we can* get help. And that leads us to the third point (the first two being disagreement in attitude and emotive meaning) that must be noticed in examining an evaluative problem, namely, that an evaluative conclusion can be backed up, in some sense, by factual *reasons*, even though these reasons have not quite the Q-E-D-ishness, so to speak, of logic. And the scientist, who is in a better position than most of us to give true reasons rather than false ones, can help us with evaluations on that account.

Let me return to my former example. Suppose that you think that the classical languages *ought* to be taught. One of your reasons—or in other words, one of your answers to the question, "Why?"—might be that a discipline with these languages will transfer to other things. Now I myself don't know whether that transference takes place or not; but in any case that much of the issue belongs to psychology, and a well-founded scientific answer to it would be welcome. It would contribute to the evaluative question indirectly, to be sure, but it would not be irrelevant to it; and no scientifically uninformed person could make just this sort of contribution.

We have, then, scientific statements serving as *reasons* for evaluative statements. They can serve in this way simply because our attitudes, which are central to the evaluative problems, are not compartmentalized from our beliefs, but are causally dependent on them. A child ceases to *want* to touch a live coal when he comes to believe that the coal will burn him. To be sure, his *want* to avoid being burned is also in question here; but his *belief* is important as an intermediary, as it were, that enables him to connect his want to avoid being burned with his want to touch the coal, and to change the latter want accordingly. It is by that mechanism that all factual reasons for evaluative statements become relevant; and since science determines which of the beliefs, acting as intermediaries, are true, science has its place in guiding our evaluative judgments one way or another.

We have reasons for *overt imperatives* that back them up in much the same way—and the comparison of evaluative statements to imperatives, by the way, is an illuminating one. Thus if I should say, "Close the door," and you should ask, "Why?" I might give as a *reason*, "Because if you don't we'll both catch cold." Here your "Why?" indicated your reluctance to obey, and my reason backed up my imperative in just this way: if you believed the reason, you would grow more willing to obey—my reason serving to express a belief that would become an intermediary between your desire to avoid catching cold and your desire to close the door. If I had said not "Close the door," but rather, "It would be a *good* thing for you to close the door," the situation would have been much the same, as I need scarcely say.

We have, then, in a connection with value judgments, a situation where attitudes are in the course of being altered; and since one of the ways of altering attitudes is *via* an alteration of beliefs, all of science, with its careful attention to the truth of beliefs, has a bearing on what value judgments we will make and accept. And that, in essentials, is why it seems to me that scientists, so far from backing away from evaluations, should be particularly insistent on making them.

This is not to say, of course, that a scientist can altogether "prove" his evaluative contentions. He can't, any more than I can "prove" that it would be a good thing for you to close the door. When I say, "If you don't, we'll both catch cold" you are free to say "I don't care whether we catch cold or not." And if I add, "But besides that, if you don't close the door there'll be so much noise that you won't hear what I'm saying," you're always free to say that you don't *want* to hear what I'm saying. In other words, between the reasons I give and the evaluative judgment I'm trying to back up there's not a logical connection but only a psychological one. And the same is true on all evaluative issues. If someone says scientifically that a discipline in Latin transfers to other things, we are always free to say that we don't give a hang about this transfer. But it remains the case that very often we *don't* elect to exercise this freedom—that the psychological, rather than logical, connection is quite enough for us. We aren't so different, psychologically, that an appeal to these not-quite-logical reasons is always unavailing; and that's why evaluations illuminated by science have a point to them.

You might still feel, however, that a scientist needn't actually *make* evaluations—and that you, approaching the study of education in a scientific spirit, can also be absolved from them. "Let us," you may say, "be content to have our scientists as pure scientists. Let us have them write up their results in encyclopedic form, and leave it to others to select from the encyclopedia the established beliefs which, as intermediaries, will guide people in evaluating. The scientists needn't do the selecting at all."

I think that's impractical. It's like saying, "Since all the data for biographies is already in the Library of Congress, let's don't worry too much about the selection of this material for any one biography, for the important thing is to have the data available." Not at all. There's a fulltime job in *selecting* the data. And similarly for evaluative judgments, and in particular for deciding what education *ought* to aim at. The scientists best know their way among the factual beliefs; *they* must certainly be *among* those who select them, and adduce them as reasons that, serving as intermediaries, will get our attitudes straightened out under the guidance of beliefs that are well verified.

I think it would be a great pity, then, if those studying education should become so enamoured of pure science that they should suppose that value judgments were only for "others." But at the same time, I think it would be a great pity to fail to distinguish between value judgments and scientific conclusions. When a man goes from a scientific conclusion to a value judgment it seems to me that he should carefully give notice that the value judgment is *more* than a scientific conclusion, and that his repute as a scientist does not entitle him to an evaluation that purports to be the last word of adequacy. For the reasons that back up evaluations are not only less than logically related to the evaluation, but are often rebellious of being limited to any one special field of science. In making evaluations about education, for instance, many of the reasons that back them up will fall within psychology. But many of the reasons will also fall within sociology, and all the other social sciences. So the timorous stand, "I'm only a psychologist, so I can't do the whole job for you," or "I'm only a sociologist, so I can't know about the other things," is in its way understandable. But until the old high school subject, "General Science," becomes a discipline cultivated in its own right, we're going to have that situation. Meanwhile, somebody has go to do the evaluating; and I don't know who else will—or rather, I can guess, and am frightened at the prospect—unless the scientists do, even though, over certain areas, they may have to commit themselves on scientific points that fall outside their special field, and speak as amateurs.

I am reminded of a little couplet with which I should like to end, which I believe is from Hilaire Belloc's *Cautionary Tales for Children:*

> *Always keep a-hold of Nurse*
> *For fear of finding something worse.*

And in the present case the nurse, as I see it, is that unselfconscious willingness to evaluate, on educational as on all matters, that we find so congenial to our habits in common life, and which I should like to see disseminated, as a kind of half-professional interest, among all those who make a scientific study of human affairs, and in particular, among all those who make a scientific study of education.

42. CAN THE SOCIAL SCIENCES BE VALUE-FREE?

J. A. Passmore

Most of the criticisms which have been levelled against positivism leave it quite untouched, at the vital points. First, it is asserted that the positivist cannot help having social preferences. This is obviously true; an interest in social policy is what first leads him to the social field and it is bound to determine, very largely, the kind of problem on which he concentrates. This will seem a fatal objection only if we think that physical science is an exercise in pure reason, in which the scientist lays aside all human passions. This would simply be bad psychology. It is his special interests which lead a man to physics and to particular problems in that field. Certainly, antitheoretical passions are more likely to be stirred up in the social than in the purely physical field. This makes social science difficult, but not impossible.

Secondly, the anti-positivist asserts that positivism is often used as a mask for the propagation of particular social policies. This must be admitted (cf. the "scientific ethics" of the Darwinians). Scientific-sounding words like "efficiency" disguise value-judgments; and factual-seeming statements like "the State is . . ." are often highly misleading ways of formulating social policies. It is certainly better to state social policies openly than to cover them over with pseudo-science. It is part of the task of the social sciences to expose subterfuges of this sort; the mere fact that they are known to exist shows that the contrast can be made between fact and policy—in other words, that a positive social science is not impossible.

SOURCE. Passmore, John A., "Can the Social Sciences Be Value-Free?" *Proceedings of the Tenth International Congress of Philosophy, 1949*, Reprinted with permission. Copyright © 1949 by North-Holland Publishing Company, Amsterdam.

Thirdly, anti-positivists argue that a positivistic social science must distort the fact, because values, aspirations, principles are part of the substance of social life. This the positivist need not at all deny, but only that in order to study morality it is necessary to moralise about it.

The vital point for the positivist is to show that there are non-trivial theoretical problems in the social sciences. We may distinguish, as a first approximation, theoretical problems, technical problems and problems of policy. Theoretical (including historical) problems can be settled by finding out what happens. We propose hypotheses, make observations, and thus, if we are lucky, solve our problem. Not everybody may agree with us, but if our facts and our hypotheses are accepted, there are objective ways of showing that the problem has been solved.

A problem of policy (e.g., "Ought we to abolish class distinctions?") is not solved in this way. Two disputants might agree that the abolition of class distinctions would decrease servility but diminish cultural variety. One concludes: "It follows that we ought to abolish them," the other, that we ought not to do so. How can we decide which is right? In a way, neither; for nothing follows from observations of this sort about what ought to be done. We have still our decision to make after the theoretical work is finished. Our policy is determined in the light of the facts, but it is not deduced from them. If all questions in the social field were problems of policy, then a positive social science cannot answer them; but also, unless there are theoretical issues problems of policy would be quite undiscussable. To discuss a policy is to make testable assertions about its character and consequences. But that there are such testable assertions is all that the positivist account of social science is concerned to assert. Anti-positivists have really to deny the possibility of social discussion; but it clearly takes place, even if often in a rather muddled sort of way, with no clear distinction between what is discussable and what is not.

Technical problems are of the form: "How can something be constructed to such-and-such specifications?" A technical question is only a particularised theoretical question, but serious confusion may be caused because problems of policy are often framed as if they were merely technical. Take the question: "How can child-delinquency be prevented in wartime?" If this were simply a technical question it would be answerable by naming a method. But suppose we answer: "By devoting one third of the total manpower to child-care." We would be told: "That's no solution." What is really being asked is: "How ought we to deal with child-delinquency?" To give a "satisfactory" answer, we should not only have to solve the theoretical question "What social changes would prevent child-delinquency?" but also to find changes which would not conflict with an unstated social policy. Scientists sometimes profess to be giving "merely technical advice" when in fact they are tacitly assuming a particular social policy. This gives encouragement to the view that "positive social sciences" are a sham. But, of course, genuine technical problems can also be found, they are contained within the sham sort; what the sham sort does is to include in the technical specifications factors which it does not mention. It has still to settle certain technical problems even if they are not quite the ones it pretends to be deciding.

The last refuge of the anti-positivist is that although there are theoretical problems in the social sciences these are all of a trivial kind and that the actual effect of positivism in the social sciences is to lead to the production of a vast quantity of work which boasts of being scientific but is empty and commonplace. Now, "trivial" has two senses: a question like "Where will that bomb land?" is methodologically trivial because the answer to it will (usually) have no effect on the theoretical structure of physics, but it can none the less be a question we are tremendously anxious to answer.

When the social sciences are called trivial, sometimes all that is meant is that they fail to tell us many of the things we should particularly like to know. This, of course, is not a serious objection. But a good deal of positivistically-inspired social science is also trivial in a methodological sense. This is sometimes because the scientist wrongly believes that science is the collection of information, sometimes because he thinks that to be a scientist he must leave moral issues alone, in the sense of avoiding any question which involves them, or which might stir up the passions of the investigator. Since these are usually the facts of central importance to the understanding of social life, the natural result of this panic-stricken approach is triviality. Unfortunately, positivists have sometimes held very simple-minded views about morality; they have thought it is just a matter of taste and have grossly under-estimated its social importance. The positivist needs a better understanding of his own position. Then he will see that it is not positivism but cowardice which leads him into trivialities. What he has to do is to produce theories about the structure of morality which are genuinely theories and do not involve the advocacy of any particular social policy. Unless he is prepared to face the central issues, he can abandon the hope of a positive social science which is anything but a collection of commonplaces. A positive social science must be value-free in the sense that it is not social advocacy in disguise, but not in the sense that it has nothing to say about values. Such a theory will have the limitations characteristic of the physical sciences. It will not tell us what we ought to do any more than physics tells us whether to build a bridge or to be content with a ferry. It will not (usually), any more than physics, tell us when a particular event is going to occur, but it will not be trivial, any more than physics is trivial.

43. THE SCIENTIST *QUA* SCIENTIST MAKES VALUE JUDGMENTS*

Richard Rudner

The question of the relationship of the making of value judgments in a typically ethical sense to the methods and procedures of science has been discussed in the literature at least to that point which e. e. cummings somewhere refers to as "The Mystical Moment of Dullness." Nevertheless, albeit with some trepidation, I feel that something more may fruitfully be said on the subject.

In particular the problem has once more been raised in an interesting and poignant fashion by recently published discussions between Carnap (1) and Quine (3) on the question of the ontological commitments which one may make in the choosing of language systems.

I shall refer to this discussion in more detail in the sequel; for the present, however, let us briefly examine the current status of what is somewhat loosely called the "fact-value dichotomy."

I have not found the arguments which are usually offered, by those who believe that scientists do essentially make value judgments, satisfactory. On the other hand the rebuttals of some of those with opposing viewpoints seem to have had at least a *prima facie* cogency although they too may in the final analysis prove to have been subtly perverse.

SOURCE. Rudner, Richard, "The Scientist *Qua* Scientist Makes Value Judgments, *"Philosophy of Science*, Vol. 20, No. 1, January, 1953. Reprinted with permission. Copyright © 1953 by Philosophy of Science.

* The opinions or assertions contained herein are the private ones of the writer and are not to be construed as official or reflecting the views of the Navy Department or the Naval Establishments at large.

Those who contend that scientists do essentially make value judgments generally support their contentions by either

A. pointing to the fact that our having a science at all somehow "involves" a value judgment, or

B. by pointing out that in order to select, say among alternative problems, the scientist must make a value judgment; or (perhaps most frequently)

C. by pointing to the fact that the scientist cannot escape his quite human self—he is a "mass of predilections" and these predilections must inevitably influence all of his activities not expecting his scientific ones.

To such arguments, a great many empirically oriented philosophers and scientists have responded that the value judgments involved in our decisions to have a science, or to select problem A for attention rather than problem B are, *of course*, extra-scientific. If (they say) it is necessary to make a decision to have a science before we can have one, then this decision is literally pre-scientific and the act has thereby certainly not been shown to be any part of the *procedures* of science. Similarly the decision to focus attention on one problem rather than another is extra-problematic and forms no part of the procedures involved in dealing with the problem *decided* upon. Since it is *these* procedures which constitute the method of science, value judgments, so they respond, have not been shown to be involved in the scientific method as such. Again, with respect to the inevitable presence of our predilections in the laboratory, most empirically oriented philosophers and scientists agree that this is "unfortunately" the case; but, they hasten to add, if science is to progress toward objectivity the influence of our personal feelings or biases on experimental results must be minimized. We must try not to let our personal idiosyncrasies affect our scientific work. The perfect scientist—the scientist *qua* scientist does not allow this kind of value judgment to influence his work. However much he may find doing so unavoidable *qua* father, *qua* lover, *qua* member of society, *qua* grouch, *when* he does so he is not behaving *qua* scientist.

As I indicated at the outset, the arguments of neither of the protagonists in this issue appear quite satisfactory to me. The empiricists' rebuttals, telling prima facie as they may against the specific arguments that evoke them, nonetheless do not appear ultimately to stand up, but perhaps even more importantly, *the original arguments* seem utterly too frail.

I believe that a much stronger case may be made for the contention that value judgments are essentially involved in the procedures of science. And what I now propose to show is that scientists as scientists *do* make value judgments.

Now I take it that no analysis of what constitutes the method of science would be satisfactory unless it comprised some assertion to the effect that the scientist as scientist accepts or rejects hypotheses.

But if this is so then clearly the scientist as scientist does make value judgments. For, since no scientific hypothesis is ever completely verified, in accepting a hypothesis the scientist must make the decision that the evidence is *sufficiently* strong or that the probability is *sufficiently* high to warrant the acceptance of the hypothesis. Obviously our decision regarding the evidence and respecting how strong is "strong enough", is going to be a function of the *importance*, in the typically ethical sense, of making a mistake in accepting or rejecting the hypothesis. Thus, to take a crude but easily managable example, if the hypothesis under consideration were to the effect that a toxic ingredient of a drug was not present in lethal quantity, we would require a relatively high degree of confirmation or confidence before accepting the hypothesis—for the consequences of making a mistake here are exceedingly grave by our moral standards. On the other hand, if say, our hypothesis stated that, on the basis of a sample, a certain lot of machine stamped belt buckles was not defective, the degree of confidence we should require would be relatively not so high. *How sure we need to be before we accept a hypothesis will depend on how serious a mistake would be.*

The examples I have chosen are from scientific inferences in industrial quality control. But the point is clearly quite general in application. It would be interesting and instructive, for example, to know just how high a degree of probability the Manhattan Project scientists demanded for the hypothesis that no uncontrollable pervasive chain reaction would occur, before they proceeded with the first atomic bomb detonation or first activated the Chicago pile above a critical level. It would be equally interesting and instructive to know why they decided that *that* probability value (if one was decided upon) was high enough rather than one which was higher; and perhaps most interesting of all to learn whether the problem in this form was brought to consciousness at all.

In general then, before we can accept any hypothesis, the value decision must be made in the light of the seriousness of a mistake, that the probability is *high enough* or that, the evidence is *strong enough*, to warrant its acceptance.

Before going further, it will perhaps be well to clear up two points which might otherwise prove troublesome below. First I have obviously used the term "probability" up to this point in a quite loose and pre-analytic sense. But my point can be given a more rigorous formulation in terms of a description of the process of making statistical inference and of the acceptance or rejection of hypotheses in statistics. As is well known, the acceptance or rejection of such a hypothesis presupposes that a certain level of significance or level of confidence or critical region be selected.[1]

---

[1] "In practice three levels are commonly used: 1 percent, 5 percent and 0.3 of one

It is with respect at least to the *necessary* selection of a confidence level or interval that the necessary value judgment in the inquiry occurs. For, "the size of the critical region (one selects) is related to *the risk one wants to accept* in testing a statistical hypothesis" (4: 435).

And clearly how great a risk one is willing to take of being wrong in accepting or rejecting the hypothesis will depend upon how seriously in the typically ethical sense one views the consequences of making a mistake.

I believe, of course, that an adequate rational reconstruction of the procedures of science would show that every scientific inference is properly construable as a statistical inference (i.e. as an inference from a set of characteristics of a sample of a population to a set of characteristics of the total population) and that such an inference would be scientifically in control only in so far as it is statistically in control. But it is not necessary to argue this point, for even if one believes that what is involved in some scientific inferences is not statistical probability but rather a concept like strength of evidence or degree of confirmation, one would still be concerned with making the decision that the evidence was *strong enough* or the degree of confirmation *high enough* to warrant acceptance of the hypothesis. Now, many empiricists who reflect on the foregoing considerations agree that acceptances or rejections of hypotheses do essentially involve value judgments, but they are nonetheless loathe to accept the conclusion. And one objection which has been raised against this line of argument by those of them who are suspicious of the intrusion of value questions into the "objective realm of science," is that actually the scientist's task is only to *determine* the degree of confirmation or the strength of the evidence which *exists* for an hypothesis. In short, they object that while it may be a function of the scientist *qua member of society* to decide whether a degree of probability associated with the hypothesis is high enough to warrant its acceptance, *still* the task of the scientist *qua* scientist is *just the determination* of the degree of probability or the strength of the evidence for a hypothesis and not the acceptance or rejection of that hypothesis.

But a little reflection will show that the plausibility of this objection is apparent merely. For the determination that the degree of confirmation is say, *p*, or that the strength of evidence is such and such, which is on this view being held to be the indispensable task of the scientist *qua* scientist, is clearly nothing more than *the acceptance by the scientist of the hypothesis that the*

---

percent. There is nothing sacred about these three values; *they have become established in practice without any rigid theoretical justification.*" (my italics) (4:435). To establish significance at the 5 percent level means that one is willing to take the risk of accepting a hypothesis as true when one will be thus making a mistake, one time in twenty. Or in other words, that one will be wrong, (over the long run) once every twenty times if one employed an .05 level of significance. See also (2: ch. V) for such statements as "which of these two errors is most important to avoid (it being necessary to make such a decision in order to accept or reject the given hypothesis) is a *subjective matter* . . ." (p. 262) (my italics).

degree of confidence is p or that the strength of the evidence is such and such; and as these men have conceded, acceptance of hypotheses does require value decisions. The second point which it may be well to consider before finally turning our attention to the Quine-Carnap discussion, has to do with the nature of the suggestions which have thus far been made in this essay. In this connection, it is important to point out that the preceding remarks do *not* have as their import that an empirical description of every present day scientist ostensibly going about his business would include the statement that he made a value judgment at such and such a juncture. This is no doubt the case; but it is a hypothesis which can only be confirmed by a discipline which cannot be said to have gotten extremely far along as yet; namely, the Sociology and Psychology of Science, whether such an empirical description is warranted, cannot be settled from the armchair.

My remarks have, rather, amounted to this: any adequate analysis or (if I may use the term) rational reconstruction of the method of science must comprise the statement that the scientist *qua* scientist accepts or rejects hypotheses and further that an analysis of that statement would reveal it to entail that the scientist *qua* scientist makes value judgments.

I think that it is in the light of the foregoing arguments, the substance of which has, in one form or another, been alluded to in past years by a number of inquiries (notably C. W. Churchman, R. L. Ackoff, and A. Wald) that the Quine-Carnap discussion takes on heightened interest. For, if I understand that discussion and its outcome correctly, although it apparently begins a good distance away from any consideration of the fact-value dichotomy, and although all the way through it both men touch on the matter in a way which indicate that they believe that questions concerning that dichotomy are, if anything merely tangential to their main issue, yet it eventuates with Quine by an independent argument apparently in agreement with at least the conclusion here reached and also apparently having forced Carnap to that conclusion. (Carnap, however, is expected to reply to Quine's article and I may be too sanguine here).

The issue of ontological commitment between Carnap and Quine has been one of relatively long standing. In this recent article (1), Carnap maintains that we are concerned with two kinds of questions of existence relative to a given language system. One is what *kinds* of entities it would be permissable to speak about as existing when that language system is used; i.e. what kind of *framework* for speaking of entities should our system comprise. This, according to Carnap, is an *external* question. It is the *practical* question of what sort of linguistic system we want to choose. Such questions as "are there abstract entities?," or "are there physical entities?" thus are held to belong to the category of external questions. On the other hand, having made the decision regarding which linguistic framework to adopt, we can then raise questions like "are there any black swans?" "What are the factors of 544?" etc. Such questions are *internal* questions.

For our present purposes, the important thing about all of this is that while for Carnap *internal* questions are theoretical ones, i.e., ones whose answers have cognitive content, external questions are not theoretical at all. They are *practical questions*—they concern our decisions to employ one language structure or another. They are of the kind that face us when for example we have to decide whether we ought to have a Democratic or a Republican administration for the next four years. In short, though neither Carnap nor Quine employ the epithet, they are *value questions*.

Now if this dichotomy of existence questions is accepted Carnap can still deny the essential involvement of the making of value judgments in the procedures of science by insisting that concern with *external* questions, admittedly necessary and admittedly axiological, is nevertheless in some sense a prescientific concern. But most interestingly, what Quine then proceeds to do is to show that the dichotomy, as Carnap holds it is untenable. This is not the appropriate place to repeat Quine's arguments which are brilliantly presented in the article referred to. They are in line with the views he has expressed in his "Two Dogma's of Empiricism" essay and especially with his introduction to his recent book, *Methods of Logic*. Nonetheless the final paragraph of the Quine article I'm presently considering sums up his conclusions neatly:

> "Within natural science there is a continuum of gradations, from the statements which report observations to those which reflect basic features say of quantum theory or the theory of relativity. The view which I end up with, in the paper last cited, is that statements of ontology or even of mathematics and logic form a continuation of this continuum, a continuation which is perhaps yet more remote from observation than are the central principles of quantum theory or relativity. The differences here are in my view differences only in degree and not in kind. Science is a unified structure, and in principle it is the structure as a whole, and not its component statements one by one, that experience confirms or shows to be imperfect. Carnap maintains that ontological questions, and likewise questions of logical or mathematical principle, are questions not of fact but of choosing a convenient conceptual scheme or frame work for science; and with this I agree only if the same be conceded for every scientific hypothesis." (3: 71–72).

In the light of all of this I think that the statement that *Scientists qua Scientists* make value judgments, is also a consequence of Quine's position.

Now, if the major point I have here undertaken to establish is correct, then clearly we are confronted with a first order crisis in science & methodology. The positive horror which most scientists and philosophers of science have of the intrusion of value considerations into science is wholly understandable. Memories of the (now diminished but to a certain extent still continuing) conflict between science and, e.g., the dominant religions over the intrusion of religious value considerations into the domain of scientific inquiry, are strong in many reflective scientists. The traditional search for objectivity exemplifies science's pursuit of one of its most precious ideals. But for the scientist to close his eyes to the fact that scientific method *intrinsically* requires the making of value decisions, for him to push out of his consciousness the fact that he does make them, can in no way bring him closer to the ideal of objectivity. To refuse to pay attention to the value decisions which *must* be made, to make them intuitively, unconsciously, haphazardly, is to leave an essential aspect of scientific method scientifically out of control.

What seems called for (and here no more than the sketchiest indications of the problem can be given) is nothing less than a radical reworking of the ideal of scientific objectivity. The slightly juvenile conception of the cold-blooded, emotionless, impersonal, passive scientist mirroring the world perfectly in the highly polished lenses of his steel rimmed glasses,—this stereotype—is no longer, if it ever was, adequate.

What is being proposed here is that objectivity for science lies at least in becoming precise about what value judgments are being and might have been made in a given inquiry—and even, to put it in its most challenging form, what value decisions ought to be made; in short that a science of ethics is a necessary requirement if science's progress toward objectivity is to be continuous.

Of course the establishment of such a science of ethics is a task of stupendous magnitude and it will probably not even be well launched for many generations. But a first step is surely comprised of the reflective self awareness of the scientist in making the value judgments he must make.

References

(1) Carnap, R., "Empiricism, Semantics, and Ontology," *Revue Internationale de Philosophie*, XI, 1950, pp. 20–40.

(2) Newman, J., *First Course in Probability and Statistics*, New York: Henry Holt & Co., 1950.

(3) Quine, W. V., "On Carnap's Views on Ontology," *Philosophical Studies*, II, No. 5, 1951.

(4) Rosander, A. C., *Elementary Principles of Statistics*. New York: D. Van Nostrand Co., 1951.

44. THE ALLEGED SPECIAL SUBJECTIVITY OF THE SOCIAL SCIENCES

Ernest Nagel

THE VALUE-ORIENTED BIAS OF SOCIAL INQUIRY

We turn, finally, to the difficulties said to confront the social sciences because the social values to which students of social phenomena are committed not only color the contents of their findings but also control their assessment of the evidence on which they base their conclusions. Since social scientists generally differ in their value commitments, the "value neutrality" that seems to be so pervasive in the natural sciences is therefore often held to be impossible in social inquiry. In the judgment of many thinkers, it is accordingly absurd to expect the social sciences to exhibit the unanimity so common among natural scientists concerning what are the established facts and satisfactory explanations for them. Let us examine some of the reasons that have been advanced for these contentions. It will be convenient to distinguish four groups of such reasons, so that our discussion will deal in turn with the alleged role of value judgments in (1) the selection of problems, (2) the determination of the contents of conclusions, (3) the identification of fact, and (4) the assessment of evidence.

1. The reasons perhaps most frequently cited make much of the fact that the things a social scientist selects for study are determined by his conception of what are the socially important values. According to one influential view,

SOURCE. Reprinted with permission of Harcourt Brace Jovanovich from *The Structure of Science* by Ernest Nagel. Copyright © 1961 by Harcourt Brace Jovanovich, Inc., New York.

for example, the student of human affairs deals only with materials to which he attributes "cultural significance," so that a "value orientation" is inherent in his choice of material for investigation. Thus, although Max Weber was a vigorous proponent of a "value-free" social science—i.e., he maintained that social scientists must appreciate (or "understand") the values involved in the actions or institutions they are discussing but that it is not their business as objective scientists to approve or disapprove either those values or those actions and institutions—he nevertheless argued that

> The concept of culture is a *value-concept*. Empirical reality becomes "culture" to us because and insofar as we relate it to value ideas.
> It includes those segments and only those segments of reality which have become significant to us because of this value-relevance. Only a small portion of existing concrete reality is colored by our value-conditioned interest and it alone is significant to us. It is significant because it reveals relationships which are important to us due to their connection with our values. Only because and to the extent that this is the case is it worthwhile for us to know it in its individual features. We cannot discover, however, what is meaningful to us by means of a "presuppositionless" investigation of empirical data. Rather perception of its meaningfulness to us is the presupposition of its becoming an *object* of investigation.[1]

It is well-nigh truistic to say that students of human affairs, like students in any other area of inquiry, do not investigate everything, but direct their attention to certain selected portions of the inexhaustible content of concrete reality. Moreover, let us accept the claim, if only for the sake of the argument, that a social scientist addresses himself exclusively to matters which he believes are important because of their assumed relevance to his cultural values.[2] It is not clear, however, why the fact that an investigator selects the materials he studies in the light of problems which interest him and which seem to him to bear on matters he regards as important, is of greater moment for the logic of social inquiry than it is for the logic of any other branch of inquiry. For example, a social scientist may believe that a free economic market embodies a cardinal human value, and he may produce evidence to show that certain kinds of human activities are indispensable to the perpetuation of a free market. If he is concerned with processes which maintain this type of economy rather than some other type, how is this fact more pertinent to the question whether he has adequately evaluated the evidence for his conclusion, than is the bearing upon the analogous question of the fact that a physiologist may

---

[1] Max Weber, *The Methodology of the Social Sciences*, Glencoe, Ill., 1947, p. 76.
[2] This question receives some attention below in the discussion of the fourth difficulty.

be concerned with processes which maintain a constant internal temperature in the human body rather than with something else? The things a social scientist *selects for study* with a view to determining the conditions or consequences of their existence may indeed be dependent on the indisputable fact that he is a "cultural being." But similarly, were we not human beings though still capable of conducting scientific inquiry, we might conceivably have an interest neither in the conditions that maintain a free market, nor in the processes involved in the homeostasis of the internal temperature in human bodies, nor for that matter in the mechanisms that regulate the height of tides, the succession of seasons, or the motions of the planets.

In short, there is no difference between any of the sciences with respect to the fact that the interests of the scientist determine what he selects for investigation. But this fact, by itself, represents no obstacle to the successful pursuit of objectively controlled inquiry in any branch of study.

2. A more substantial reason commonly given for the value-oriented character of social inquiry is that, since the social scientist is himself affected by considerations of right and wrong, his own notions of what constitutes a satisfactory social order and his own standards of personal and social justice do enter, in point of fact, into his analyses of social phenomena. For example, according to one version of this argument, anthropologists must frequently judge whether the means adopted by some society achieves the intended aim (e.g., whether a religious ritual does produce the increased fertility for the sake of which the ritual is performed) ; and in many cases the adequacy of the means must be judged by admittedly "relative" standards, i.e., in terms of the ends sought or the standards employed by that society, rather than in terms of the anthropologist's own criteria. Nevertheless, so the argument proceeds, there are also situations in which

> we must apply absolute standards of adequacy, that is evaluate the end-results of behavior in terms of purposes we believe in or postulate. This occurs, first, when we speak of the satisfaction of psycho-physical 'needs' offered by any culture; secondly, when we assess the bearing of social facts upon survival; and thirdly, when we pronounce upon social integration and stability. In each case our statements imply judgments as to the worthwhileness of actions, as to 'good' or 'bad' cultural solutions of the problems of life, and as to 'normal' and 'abnormal' states of affairs. These are basic judgments which we cannot do without in social enquiry and which clearly do not express a purely personal philosophy of the enquirer or values arbitrarily assumed. Rather do they grow out of the history of human thought, from which the anthropologist can seclude himself as little as can anyone else. Yet as the history of human thought has led not to one

philosophy but to several, so the value attitudes implicit in our ways of thinking will differ and sometimes conflict.[3]

It has often been noted, moreover, that the study of social phenomena receives much of its impetus from a strong moral and reforming zeal, so that many ostensibly "objective" analyses in the social sciences are in fact disguised recommendations of social policy. As one typical but moderately expressed statement of the point puts it, a social scientist

> cannot wholly detach the unifying social structure that, as a scientist's theory, guides his detailed investigations of human behavior, from the unifying structure which, as a citizen's ideal, he thinks ought to prevail in human affairs and hopes may sometimes be more fully realized.
> His social theory is thus essentially a program of action along two lines which are kept in some measure of harmony with each other by that theory—action in assimilating social facts for purposes of systematic understanding, and action aiming at progressively molding the social pattern, so far as he can influence it, into what he thinks it ought to be.[4]

It is surely beyond serious dispute that social scientists do in fact often import their own values into their analyses of social phenomena. It is also undoubtedly true that even thinkers who believe human affairs can be studied with the ethical neutrality characterizing modern inquiries into geometrical or physical relations, and who often pride themselves on the absence of value judgments from their own analyses of social phenomena, do in fact sometimes make such judgments in their social inquiries.[5] Nor is it less evident that students of human affairs often hold conflicting values; that their disagreements on value questions are often the source of disagreements concerning ostensibly factual issues; and that, even if value predications are assumed to be inherently capable of proof or disproof by objective evidence, at least some of the differences between social scientists involving value judgments are not in fact resolved by the procedures of controlled inquiry.

In any event, it is not easy in most areas of inquiry to prevent our likes,

---

[3] S. F. Nadel, *The Foundations of Social Anthropology*, Glencoe, Ill., 1951, pp. 53–54. The claim is sometimes also made that the exclusion of value judgments from social science is undesirable as well as impossible. "We cannot disregard all questions of what is socially desirable without missing the significance of many social facts; for since the relation of means to ends is a special form of that between parts and wholes, the contemplation of social ends enables us to see the relations of whole groups of facts to each other and to larger systems of which they are parts."—Morris R. Cohen, *Reason and Nature*, New York, 1931, p. 343.

[4] Edwin A. Burtt, *Right Thinking*, New York, 1946, p. 522.

[5] For a documented account, see Gunnar Myrdal, *Value in Social Theory*, London, 1958, pp. 134–52.

aversions, hopes, and fears from coloring our conclusions. It has taken centuries of effort to develop habits and techniques of investigation which help safeguard inquiries in the natural sciences against the intrusion of irrelevant personal factors; and even in these disciplines the protection those procedures give is neither infallible nor complete. The problem is undoubtedly more acute in the study of human affairs, and the difficulties it creates for achieving reliable knowledge in the social sciences must be admitted.

However, the problem is intelligible only on the assumption that there is a relatively clear distinction between factual and value judgments, and that however difficult it may sometimes be to decide whether a given statement has a purely factual content, it is in principle possible to do so. Thus, the claim that social scientists are pursuing the twofold program mentioned in the above quotation makes sense, only if it is possible to distinguish between, on the one hand, contributions to theoretical understanding (whose factual validity presumably does not depend on the social ideal to which a social scientist may subscribe), and on the other hand contributions to the dissemination or realization of some social ideal (which may not be accepted by all social scientists). Accordingly, the undeniable difficulties that stand in the way of obtaining reliable knowledge of human affairs because of the fact that social scientists differ in their value orientations are practical difficulties. The difficulties are not necessarily insuperable, for since by hypothesis it is not impossible to distinguish between fact and value, steps can be taken to identify a value bias when it occurs, and to minimize if not to eliminate completely its perturbing effects.

One such countermeasure frequently recommended is that social scientists abandon the pretense that they are free from all bias, and that instead they state their value assumptions as explicitly and fully as they can.[6] The recommendation does not assume that social scientists will come to agree on their social ideals once these ideals are explicitly postulated, or that disagreements over values can be settled by scientific inquiry. Its point is that the question of how a given ideal is to be realized, or the question whether a certain institutional arrangement is an effective way of achieving the ideal, is on the face of it not a value question, but a factual problem—to be resolved by the objective methods of scientific inquiry—concerning the adequacy of proposed means for attaining stipulated ends. Thus, economists may permanently disagree on the desirability of a society in which its members have a guaranteed security against economic want, since the disagreement may have its source in inarbitrable preferences for different social values. But when sufficient evi-

---

[6] See, e.g., S. F. Nadel, *op. cit.*, p. 54; also Gunnar Myrdal, *op. cit.*, p. 120, as well as his *Political Element in the Development of Economic Theory*, Cambridge, Mass., 1954, esp. Chap. 8.

dence is made available by economic inquiry, economists do presumably agree on the factual proposition that, *if* such a society is to be achieved, then a purely competitive economic system will not suffice.

Although the recommendation that social scientists make fully explicit their value commitments is undoubtedly salutary, and can produce excellent fruit, it verges on being a counsel of perfection. For the most part we are unaware of many assumptions that enter into our analyses and actions, so that despite resolute efforts to make our preconceptions explicit some decisive ones may not even occur to us. But in any event, the difficulties generated for scientific inquiry by unconscious bias and tacit value orientations are rarely overcome by devout resolutions to eliminate bias. They are usually overcome, often only gradually, through the selfcorrective mechanisms of science as a social enterprise. For modern science encourages the invention, the mutual exchange, and the free but responsible criticisms of ideas; it welcomes competition in the quest for knowledge between independent investigators, even when their intellectual orientations are different; and it progressively diminishes the effects of bias by retaining only those proposed conclusions of its inquiries that survive critical examination by an indefinitely large community of students, whatever be their value preferences or doctrinal commitments. It would be absurd to claim that this institutionalized mechanism for sifting warranted beliefs has operated or is likely to operate in social inquiry as effectively as it has in the natural sciences. But it would be no less absurd to conclude that reliable knowledge of human affairs is unattainable merely because social inquiry is frequently value-oriented.

3. There is a more sophisticated argument for the view that the social sciences cannot be value-free. It maintains that the distinction between fact and value assumed in the preceding discussion is untenable when purposive human behavior is being analyzed, since in this context value judgments enter inextricably into what appear to be "purely descriptive" (or factual) statements. Accordingly, those who subscribe to this thesis claim that an ethically neutral social science is in principle impossible, and not simply that it is difficult to attain. For if fact and value are indeed so fused that they cannot even be distinguished, value judgments cannot be eliminated from the social sciences unless all predications are also eliminated from them, and therefore unless these sciences completely disappear.

For example, it has been argued that the student of human affairs must distinguish between valuable and undesirable forms of social activity, on pain of failing in his "plain duty" to present social phenomena truthfully and faithfully:

> Would one not laugh out of court a man who claimed to have written a sociology of art but who actually had written a sociology of trash?

The sociologist of religion must distinguish between phenomena which have a religious character and phenomena which are a-religious. To be able to do this, he must understand what religion is. . . . Such understanding enables and forces him to distinguish between genuine and spurious religion, between higher and lower religions; these religions are higher in which the specifically religious motivations are effective to a higher degree. . . . The sociologist of religion cannot help noting the difference between those who try to gain it by a change of heart. Can he see this difference without seeing at the same time the difference between a mercenary and nonmercenary attitude? . . . The prohibition against value-judgments in social science would lead to the consequence that we are permitted to give a strictly factual description of the overt acts that can be observed in concentration camps, and perhaps an equally factual analysis of the motivations of the actors concerned: we would not be permitted to speak of cruelty. Every reader of such a description who is not completely stupid would, of course, see that the actions described are cruel. The factual description would, in truth, be a bitter satire. What claimed to be a straightforward report would be an unusually circumlocutory report. . . . Can one say anything relevant on public opinion polls . . . without realizing the fact that many answers to the questionnaires are given by unintelligent, uninformed, deceitful, and irrational people, and that not a few questions are formulated by people of the same caliber—can one say anything relevant about public opinion polls without committing one value-judgment after another?[7]

Moreover, the assumption implicit in the recommendation discussed above for achieving ethical neutrality is often rejected as hopelessly naive—this is the assumption, it will be recalled, that relations of means to ends can be established without commitment to these ends, so that the conclusions of social inquiry concerning such relations are objective statements which make *conditional* rather than categorical assertions about values. This assumption is said by its critics to rest on the supposition that men attach value only to the ends they seek, and not to the means for realizing their aims. However, the supposition is alleged to be grossly mistaken. For the character of the

---

[7] Leo Strauss, "The Social Science of Max Weber," *Measure*, Vol. 2 (1951), pp. 211–14. For a discussion of this issue as it bears upon problems in the philosophy of law, see Lon Fuller, "Human Purpose and Natural Law," *Natural Law Forum*, Vol. 3 (1958), pp. 68–76; Ernest Nagel, "On the Fusion of Fact and Value: A Reply to Professor Fuller," *op. cit.*, pp. 77–82; Lon L. Fuller, "A Rejoinder to Professor Nagel," *op. cit.*, pp. 83–104; Ernest Nagel, "Fact, Value, and Human Purpose," *Natural Law Forum*, Vol. 4 (1959), pp. 26–43.

means one employs to secure some goal affects the nature of the total outcome; and the choice men make between alternative means for obtaining a given end depends on the values they ascribe to those alternatives. In consequence, commitments to specific valuations are said to be involved even in what appear to be purely factual statements about means-ends relations.[8]

We shall not attempt a detailed assessment of this complex argument, for a discussion of the numerous issues it raises would take us far afield. However, three claims made in the course of the argument will be admitted without further comment as indisputably correct: that a large number of characterizations sometimes assumed to be purely factual descriptions of social phenomena do indeed formulate a type of value judgment; that it is often difficult, and in any case usually inconvenient in practice, to distinguish between the purely factual and the "evaluative" contents of many terms employed in the social sciences; and that values are commonly attached to means and not only to ends. However, these admissions do not entail the conclusion that, in a manner unique to the study of purposive human behavior, fact and value are fused beyond the possibility of distinguishing between them. On the contrary, as we shall try to show, the claim that there is such a fusion and that a value-free social science is therefore inherently absurd, confounds two quite different senses of the term "value judgment": the sense in which a value judgment expresses *approval or disapproval* either of some moral (or social) ideal, or of some action (or institution) because of a commitment to such an ideal; and the sense in which a value judgment expresses *an estimate* of the degree to which some commonly recognized (and more or less clearly defined) type of action, object, or institution is embodied in a given instance.

It will be helpful to illustrate these two senses of "value judgment" first with an example from biology. Animals with blood streams sometimes exhibit the condition known as "anemia." An anemic animal has a reduced number of red blood corpuscles, so that, among other things, it is less able to maintain a constant internal temperature than are members of its species with a "normal" supply of such cells. However, although the meaning of the term "anemia" can be made quite clear, it is not in fact defined with complete precision; for example, the notion of a "normal" number of red corpuscles that enters into the definition of the term is itself somewhat vague, since this number varies with the individual members of a species as well as with the state of a given individual at different times (such as its age or the altitude of its habitat). But in any case, to decide whether a given animal is anemic, an investigator must judge whether the available evidence *warrants* the conclusion that the specimen is anemic.[9] He may perhaps think of anemia as being of several

---

[8] Cf. Gunnar Mydral, *Value in Social Theory*, London, 1958, pp. xxii, 211–13.

[9] The evidence is usually a count of red cells in a sample from the animal's blood. How-

distinct kinds (as is done in actual medical practice), or he may think of anemia as a condition that is realizable with greater or lesser completeness (just as certain plane curves are sometimes described as better or worse approximations to a circle as defined in geometry); and, depending on which of these conceptions he adopts, he may decide either that his specimen has a certain kind of anemia or that it is anemic only to a certain degree. When the investigator reaches a conclusion, he can therefore be said to be making a "value judgment," in the sense that he has in mind some standardized type of physiological condition designated as "anemia" and that he *assesses* what he knows about his specimen with the measure provided by this assumed standard. For the sake of easy reference, let us call such evaluations of the evidence, which conclude that a given characteristic is in some degree present (or absent) in a given instance, "characterizing value judgments."

On the other hand, the student may also make a quite different sort of value judgment, which asserts that, since an anemic animal has diminished powers of maintaining itself, anemia is an undesirable condition. Moreover, he may apply this general judgment to a particular case, and so come to deplore the fact that a given animal is anemic. Let us label such evaluations, which conclude that some envisaged or actual state of affairs is worthy of approval or disapproval, "appraising value judgments."[10] It is clear, however, that an investigator making a characterizing value judgment is not thereby logically bound to affirm or deny a corresponding appraising evaluation. It is no less evident that he cannot consistently make an appraising value judgment about a given instance (e.g., that it is undesirable for a given animal to continue being anemic), unless he can affirm a characterizing judgment about that instance independently of the appraising one (e.g., that the animal is anemic). Accordingly, although characterizing judgments are necessarily entailed by many appraising judgments, making appraising judgments is not a necessary condition for making characterizing ones.

Let us now apply these distinctions to some of the contentions advanced in the argument quoted above. Consider first the claim that the sociologist of religion must recognize the difference between mercenary and nonmercenary

---

ever, it should be noted that "The red cell count gives only an estimate of the *number of cells per unit quantity of blood*," and does not indicate whether the body's total supply of red cells is increased or diminished.—Charles H. Best and Norman B. Taylor, *The Physiological Basis of Medical Practice*, 6th ed., Baltimore, 1955, pp. 11, 17.

10 It is irrelevant to the present discussion what view is adopted concerning the ground upon which such judgments supposedly rest—whether those grounds are simply arbitrary preferences, alleged intuitions of "objective" values, categorical moral imperatives, or anything else that has been proposed in the history of value theory. For the distinction made in the text is independent of any particular assumption about the foundations of appraising value judgments, "ultimate" or otherwise.

attitudes, and that in consequence he is inevitably committing himself to certain values. It is certainly beyond dispute that these attitudes are commonly distinguished; and it can also be granted that a sociologist of religion needs to understand the difference between them. But the sociologist's obligation is in this respect quite like that of the student of animal physiology, who must also acquaint himself with certain distinctions—even though the physiologist's distinction between, say, anemic and nonanemic may be less familiar to the ordinary layman and is in any case much more precise than is the distinction between mercenary and nonmercenary attitudes. Indeed, because of the vagueness of these latter terms, the scrupulous sociologist may find it extremely difficult to decide whether or not the attitude of some community toward its acknowledged gods is to be characterized as mercenary; and if he should finally decide, he may base his conclusion on some inarticulated "total impression" of that community's manifest behavior, without being able to state exactly the detailed grounds for his decision. But however this may be, the sociologist who claims that a certain attitude manifested by a given religious group is mercenary, just as the physiologist who claims that a certain individual is anemic, is making what is primarily a characterizing value judgment. In making these judgments, neither the sociologist nor the physiologist is necessarily committing himself to any values other than the values of scientific probity; and in this respect, therefore, there appears to be no difference between social and biological (or for that matter, physical) inquiry.

On the other hand, it would be absurd to deny that in characterizing various actions as mercenary, cruel, or deceitful, sociologists are frequently (although perhaps not always wittingly) asserting appraising as well as characterizing value judgments. Terms like "mercenary," "cruel," or "deceitful" as commonly used have a widely recognized pejorative overtone. Accordingly, anyone who employs such terms to characterize human behavior can normally be assumed to be stating his disapprobation of that behavior (or his approbation, should he use terms like "nonmercenary," "kindly," or "truthful"), and not simply characterizing it.

However, although many (but certainly not all) ostensibly characterizing statements asserted by social scientists undoubtedly express commitments to various (not always compatible) values, a number of "purely descriptive" terms as used by natural scientists in certain contexts sometimes also have an unmistakably appraising value connotation. Thus, the claim that a social scientist is making appraising value judgments when he characterizes respondents to questionnaires as uninformed, deceitful, or irrational can be matched by the equally sound claim that a physicist is also making such judgments when he describes a particular chronometer as inaccurate, a pump as inefficient, or a supporting platform as unstable. Like the social scientist in this example, the physicist is characterizing certain objects in his field of research; but, also like the social scientist, he is in addition expressing his disapproval of the characteristics he is ascribing to those objects.

Nevertheless—and this is the main burden of the present discussion—there are no good reasons for thinking that it is inherently impossible to *distinguish* between the characterizing and the appraising judgments implicit in many statements, whether the statements are asserted by students of human affairs or by natural scientists. To be sure, it is not always easy to make the distinction formally explicit in the social sciences—in part because much of the language employed in them is very vague, in part because appraising judgments that may be implicit in a statement tend to be overlooked by us when they are judgments to which we are actually committed though without being aware of our commitments. Nor is it always useful or convenient to perform this task. For many statements implicitly containing both characterizing and appraising evaluations are sometimes sufficiently clear without being reformulated in the manner required by the task; and the reformulations would frequently be too unwieldy for effective communication between members of a large and unequally prepared group of students. But these are essentially practical rather than theoretical problems. The difficulties they raise provide no compelling reasons for the claim that an ethically neutral social science is inherently impossible.

Nor is there any force in the argument that, since values are commonly attached to means and not only to ends, statements about means-ends relations are not value-free. Let us test the argument with a simple example. Suppose that a man with an urgent need for a car but without sufficient funds to buy one can achieve his aim by borrowing a sum either from a commercial bank or from friends who waive payment of any interest. Suppose further that he dislikes becoming beholden to his friends for financial favors, and prefers the impersonality of a commercial loan. Accordingly, the comparative values this individual places upon the alternative means available to him for realizing his aim obviously control the choice he makes between them. Now the *total* outcome that would result from his adoption of one of the alternatives is admittedly different from the *total* outcome that would result from his adoption of the other alternative. Nevertheless, irrespective of the values he may attach to these alternative means, each of them would achieve a result—namely, his purchase of the needed car—that is common to both the total outcomes. In consequence, the validity of the statement that he could buy the car by borrowing money from a bank, as well as of the statement that he could realize this aim by borrowing from friends, is unaffected by the valuations placed upon the means, so that neither statement involves any special appraising evaluations. In short, the statements about means-ends relations are value-free.

4. There remains for consideration the claim that a value-free social science is impossible, because value commitments enter into the very *assessment of*

evidence by social scientists, and not simply into the content of the conclusions they advance. This version of the claim itself has a large number of variant forms, but we shall examine only three of them.

The least radical form of the claim maintains that the conceptions held by a social scientist of what constitute cogent evidence or sound intellectual workmanship are the products of his education and his place in society, and are affected by the social values transmitted by this training and associated with this social position; accordingly, the values to which the social scientist is thereby committed determine which statements he *accepts* as well-grounded conclusions about human affairs. In this form, the claim is a *factual* thesis, and must be supported by detailed empirical evidence concerning the influences exerted by a man's moral and social values upon what he is ready to acknowledge as sound social analysis. In many instances such evidence is indeed available; and differences between social scientists in respect to what they accept as credible can sometimes be attributed to the influence of national, religious, economic, and other kinds of bias. However, this variant of the claim excludes neither the possibility of recognizing assessments of evidence that are prejudiced by special value commitmnts, nor the possibility of correcting for such prejudice. It therefore raises no issues that has not already been discussed when we examined the second reason for the alleged value-oriented character of social inquiry.

Another but different form of the claim is based on recent work in theoretical statistics dealing with the assessment of evidence for so-called "statistical hypotheses"—hypotheses concerning the probabilities of random events, such as the hypothesis that the probability of a male human birth is one-half. The central idea relevant to the present question that underlies these developments can be sketched in terms of an example. Suppose that, before a fresh batch of medicine is put on sale, tests are performed on experimental animals for its possible toxic effects because of impurities that have not been eliminated in its manufacture, for example, by introducing small quantities of the drug into the diet of one hundred guinea pigs. If no more than a few of the animals show serious after-effects, the medicine is to be regarded as safe, and will be marketed; but if a contrary result is obtained the drug will be destroyed. Suppose now that three of the animals do in fact become gravely ill. Is this outcome significant (i.e., does it indicate that the drug has toxic effects), or is it perhaps an "accident" that happened because of some peculiarity in the affected animals? To answer the question, the experimenter must *decide* on the basis of the evidence between the hypothesis H_1: the drug is toxic, and the hypothesis H_2: the drug is not toxic. But how is he to decide, if he aims to be "reasonable" rather than arbitrary? Current statistical theory offers him a rule for making a reasonable decision, and bases the rule on the following analysis.

Whatever decision the experimenter may make, he runs the risk of committing either one of two types of errors: he may reject a hypothesis though in fact it is true (i.e., despite the fact that H_1 is actually true, he mistakenly decides against it in the light of the evidence available to him); or he may accept a hypothesis though in fact it is false. His decision would therefore be eminently reasonable, were it based on a rule guaranteeing that no decision ever made in accordance with the rule would commit either type of error. Unhappily, there are no rules of this sort. The next suggestion is to find a rule such that, when decisions are made in accordance with it, the relative frequency of each type of error is quite small. But unfortunately, the risks of committing each type of error are not independent; for example, it is in general logically impossible to find a rule so that decisions based on it will commit each type of error with a relative frequency not greater than one in a thousand. In consequence, before a reasonable rule can be proposed, the experimenter must compare the relative importance to himself of the two types of error, and state what risk he is willing to take of committing the type of error he judges to be the more important one. Thus, were he to reject H_1 though it is true (i.e., were he to commit an error of the first type), all the medicine under consideration would be put on sale, and the lives of those using it would be endangered; on the other hand, were he to commit an error of the second type with respect to H_1, the entire batch of medicine would be scrapped, and the manufacturer would incur a financial loss. However, the preservation of human life may be of greater moment to the experimenter than financial gain; and he may perhaps stipulate that he is unwilling to base his decision on a rule for which the risk of committing an error of the first type is greater than one such error in a hundred decisions. If this is assumed, statistical theory can specify a rule satisfying the experimenter's requirement, though how this is done, and how the risk of committing an error of the second type is calculated, are technical questions of no concern to us. The main point to be noted in this analysis is that the rule presupposes certain appraising judgments of value. In short, if this result is generalized, statistical theory appears to support the thesis that value commitments enter decisively into the rules for assessing evidence for statistical hypotheses.[11]

However, the theoretical analysis upon which this thesis rests does not entail the conclusion that the rules actually employed in every social inquiry for assessing evidence necessarily involve some *special* commitments, i.e., commitments such as those mentioned in the above example, as distinct from those

---

[11] The above example is borrowed from the discussion in J. Neymann, *First Course in Probability and Statistics*, New York, 1950, Chap. 5, where an elementary technical account of recent developments in statistical theory is presented. For a nontechnical account, see Irwin D. J. Bross, *Design for Decision*, New York, 1953, also R. B. Braithwaite, *Scientific Explanation*, Cambridge, Eng., 1953, Chap. 7.

generally implicit in science as an enterprise aiming to achieve reliable knowledge. Indeed, the above example illustrating the reasoning in current statistical theory can be misleading, insofar as it suggests that alternative decisions between statistical hypotheses must invariably lead to alternative actions having immediate practical consequences upon which different special values are placed. For example, a theoretical physicist may have to decide between two statistical hypotheses concerning the probability of certain energy exchanges in atoms; and a theoretical sociologist may similarly have to choose between two statistical hypotheses concerning the relative frequency of childless marriages under certain social arrangements. But neither of these men may have any *special* values at stake associated with the alternatives between which he must decide, other than the values, to which he is committed as a member of a scientific community, to conduct his inquiries with probity and responsibility. Accordingly, the question whether any special value commitments enter into assessments of evidence in either the natural or social sciences is not settled one way or the other by theoretical statistics; and the question can be answered only by examining actual inquiries in the various scientific disciplines.

Moreover, nothing in the reasoning of theoretical statistics depends on what particular subject matter is under discussion when a decision between alternative statistical hypotheses is to be made. For the reasoning is entirely general; and reference to some special subject matter becomes relevant only when a definite numerical value is to be assigned to the risk some investigator is prepared to take of making an erroneous decision concerning a given hypothesis. Accordingly, if current statistical theory is used to support the claim that value commitments enter into the assessment of evidence for statistical hypotheses in social inquiry, statistical theory can be used with equal justification to support analogous claims for all other inquiries as well. In short, the claim we have been discussing establishes no difficulty that supposedly occurs in the search for reliable knowledge in the study of human affairs which is not also encountered in the natural sciences.

A third form of this claim is the most radical of all. It differs from the first variant mentioned above in maintaining that there is a necessary *logical* connection, and not merely a contingent or causal one, between the "social perspective" of a student of human affairs and his standards of competent social inquiry, and in consequence the influence of the special values to which he is committed because of his own social involvements is not eliminable. This version of the claim is implicit in Hegel's account of the "dialectical" nature of human history and is integral to much Marxist as well as non-Marxist philosophy that stresses the "historically relative" character of social thought. In any event, it is commonly based on the assumption that, since social institutions and their cultural products are constantly changing, the intellectual apparatus required for understanding them must also change; and every idea employed for this purpose is therefore adequate only for some particular stage in the development of human affairs. Accordingly, neither the substantive concepts adopted for classifying and interpreting social phenomena, nor the logical canons used for estimating the worth of such concepts, have a "timeless validity"; there is no analysis of social phenomena which is not the expression of some special social standpoint, or which does not reflect the interests and values dominant in some sector of the human scene at a certain stage of its history. In consequence, although a sound distinction can be made in the natural sciences between the origin of a man's views and their factual validity, such a distinction allegedly cannot be made in social inquiry; and prominent exponents of "historical relativism" have therefore challenged the universal adequacy of the thesis that "the genesis of a proposition is under all circumstances irrelevant to its truth." As one influential proponent of this position puts the matter,

> The historical and social genesis of an idea would only be irrelevant
> to its ultimate validity if the temporal and social conditions of its
> emergence had no effect on its content and form. If this were the case,
> any two periods in the history of human knowledge would only be
> distinguished from one another by the fact that in the earlier period
> certain things were still unknown and certain errors still existed which,
> through later knowledge were completely corrected. This simple
> relationship between an earlier incomplete and a later complete period
> of knowledge may to a large extent be appropriate for the exact
> sciences. . . . For the history of the cultural sciences, however, the
> earlier stages are not quite so simply superseded by the later stages,
> and it is not so easily demonstrable that early errors have subsequently
> been corrected. Every epoch has its fundamentally new approach and
> its characteristic point of view, and consequently sees the "same" object
> from a new perspective. . . . The very principles, in the light of which
> knowledge is to be criticized, are themselves found to be socially and
> historically conditioned. Hence their application appears to be limited
> to given historical periods and the particular types of knowledge then
> prevalent.[12]

---

[12] Karl Mannheim, *Ideology and Utopia*, New York, 1959, pp. 271, 288, 292. The essay from which the above excerpts are quoted was first published in 1931, and Mannheim subsequently modified some of the views expressed in it. However, he reaffirmed the thesis stated in the quoted passages as late as 1946, the year before his death. See his letter to Kurt H. Wolff, dated April 15, 1946, quoted in the latter's "Sociology of Knowledge and Sociological Theory," in *Symposium on Sociological Theory* (ed. by Llewellyn Gross), Evanston, Ill., 1959, p. 571.

Historical research into the influence of society upon the beliefs men hold is of undoubted importance for understanding the complex nature of the scientific enterprise; and the sociology of knowledge—as such investigations have come to be called—has produced many clarifying contributions to such an understanding. However, these admittedly valuable services of the sociology of knowledge do not establish the radical claim we have been stating. In the first place, there is no competent evidence to show that the principles employed in social inquiry for assessing the intellectual products are *necessarily* determined by the social perspective of the inquirer. On the contrary, the "facts" usually cited in support of this contention establish at best only a contingent causal relation between a man's social commitments and his canons of cognitive validity. For example, the once fashionable view that the "mentality" or logical operations of primitive societies differ from those typical in Western civilization—a discrepancy that was attributed to differences in the institutions of the societies under comparison—is now generally recognized to be erroneous, because it seriously misinterprets the intellectual processes of primitive peoples. Moreover, even extreme exponents of the sociology of knowledge admit that most conclusions asserted in mathematics and natural science are neutral to differences in social perspective of those asserting them, so that the genesis of these propositions is irrelevant to their validity. Why cannot propositions about human affairs exhibit a similar neutrality, at least in some cases? Sociologists of knowledge do not appear to doubt that the truth of the statement that two horses can in general pull a heavier load than can either horse alone, is logically independent of the social status of the individual who happens to affirm the statement. But they have not made clear just what are the inescapable considerations that allegedly make such independence inherently impossible for the analogous statement about human behavior, that two laborers can in general dig a ditch of given dimensions more quickly than can either laborer working alone.

In the second place, the claim faces a serious and frequently noted dialectical difficulty—a difficulty that proponents of the claim have succeeded in meeting only by abandoning the substance of the claim. For let us ask what is the cognitive status of the thesis that a social perspective enters essentially into the content as well as the validation of every assertion about human affairs. Is this thesis meaningful and valid only for those who maintain it and who thus subscribe to certain values because of their distinctive social commitments? If so, no one with a different social perspective can properly understand it; its acceptance as valid is strictly limited to those who can do so, and social scientists who subscribe to a different set of social values ought therefore dismiss it as empty talk. Or is the thesis singularly exempt from the class of assertions to which it applies, so that its meaning and truth are not inherently related to the social perspectives of those who assert it? If so, it is not evident why the thesis is so exempt; but in any case, the thesis is then a conclusion of inquiry into human affairs that is presumably "objectively valid" in the usual sense of this phrase—and, if there is one such conclusion, it is not clear why there cannot be others as well.

To meet this difficulty, and to escape the self-defeating skeptical relativism to which the thesis is thus shown to lead, the thesis is sometimes interpreted to say that, though "absolutely objective" knowledge of human affairs is unattainable, a "relational" form of objectivity called "relationism" can nevertheless be achieved. On this interpretation, a social scientist can discover just what his social perspective is; and if he then formulates the conclusions of his inquiries "relationally," so as to indicate that his findings conform to the canons of validity implicit in his perspective, his conclusions will have achieved a "relational" objectivity. Social scientists sharing the same perspective can be expected to agree in their answers to a given problem when the canons of validity characteristic of their common perspective are correctly applied. On the other hand, students of social phenomena who operate within different but incongruous social perspectives can also achieve objectivity, if in no other way than by a "relational" formulation of what must otherwise be incompatible results obtained in their several inquiries. However, they can also achieve it in "a more roundabout fashion," by undertaking "to find a formula for translating the results of one into those of the other and to discover a common denominator for these varying perspectivistic insights."[13]

But it is difficult to see in what way "relational objectivity" differs from "objectivity" without the qualifying adjective and in the customary sense of the word. For example, a physicist who terminates an investigation with the conclusion that the velocity of light in water has a certain numerical value when measured in terms of a stated system of units, by a stated procedure, and under stated experimental conditions, is formulating his conclusion in a manner that is "relational" in the sense intended; and his conclusion is marked by "objectivity," presumably because it mentions the "relational" factors upon which the assigned numerical value of the velocity depends. However, it is fairly standard practice in the natural sciences to formulate certain types of conclusions in this fashion. Accordingly, the proposal that the social sciences formulate their findings in an analogous manner carries with it the admission that it is not in principle impossible for these disciplines to establish conclusions having the objectivity of conclusions reached in other domains of inquiry. Moreover, if the difficulty we are considering is to be resolved by the suggested translation formulas for rendering the "common denominators" of conclusions stemming from divergent social perspectives,

13 Karl Mannheim, *op. cit.*, pp. 300–01.

those formulas cannot in turn be "situationally determined" in the sense of this phrase under discussion. For if those formulas were so determined, the same difficulty would crop up anew in connection with them. On the other hand, a search for such formulas is a phase in the search for invariant relations in a subject matter, so that formulations of these relations are valid irrespective of the particular perspective one may select from some class of perspectives on that subject matter. In consequence, in acknowledging that the search for such invariants in the social sciences is not inherently bound to fail, proponents of the claim we have been considering abandon what at the outset was its most radical thesis.

In brief, the various reasons we have been examining for the intrinsic impossibility of securing objective (i.e., value-free and unbiased) conclusions in the social sciences do not establish what they purport to establish, even though in some instances they direct attention to undoubtedly important practical difficulties frequently encountered in these disciplines.

CHAPTER 10

Concepts and Their Delineation

One of the thorniest problems facing educational researchers is determining the nature of the concepts with which they work. Although this problem most immediately is one of defining our terms, it is intimately related to test validity, significance of research findings, specification of educational objectives (for purposes of programming, etc.), and behaviorism. We have included chapters on behaviorism and programmed learning later in this book because of their special interest to educational researchers. However, many of the basic issues will be discussed in this chapter.

One can trace the current emphasis on operationism and behaviorism at least as far back[1] as the trenchant writings of C. S. Peirce, an early American pragmatist, who said in "How to Make Our Ideas Clear":

> Consider what effects, that might conceivably have practical bearings, we conceive the object of our conception to have. Then our conception of these effects is the whole of our conception of the object.[2]

The basic problem in this chapter is the conflict between two frequently opposing tendencies: that of eliminating excess baggage from our concepts (illustrated by the Peirce quote above) and that of maintaining general concepts that fit a variety of situations.

---

[1] Some would go back to the empiricists David Hume and John Locke.

[2] C. S. Peirce, "How to Make Our Ideas Clear," in Collected Papers, Vol. 5 *Pragmatism and Pragmaticism*, edited by Charles Hartshorne and Paul Weiss (Cambridge: Harvard University Press, 1934), paragraph 402.

This section starts out with Kenneth MacCorquodale and Paul Meehl's attempt to distinguish between hypothetical constructs and intervening variables, the latter (roughly speaking) having no surplus meaning beyond observables.[3] Lee Cronbach and Paul Meehl in their paper on construct validity suggest a notion of test validity for use with hypothetical constructs. Harold Bechtoldt's sharp criticisms of the approach of these papers then follows. In contrast to MacCorquodale, Meehl, and Cronbach, Bechtoldt seeks the reduction of our theoretical terms to basic observation terms—with no excess baggage.

Philosopher May Brodbeck methodically develops and defends the radical empiricist view presented by Bechtoldt. Brodbeck's paper is valuable not only for this reason, but also because it sets the issue in terms of the grand concerns of educational research: significance, explanation, and prediction. She sees little difference between intervening variables and hypothetical constructs, treating them both essentially as intervening variables. Her criticism of partial specification of meaning on the ground that it would make science tautologous is a strong one; it forces philosophers to rethink the analytic–synthetic distinction, which Brodbeck presents as the distinction between "statements of fact" and "tautologies."

A development of the radical empiricist approach to operational definition is next presented in an excerpt from the writing of B. F. Skinner who says that "operationism may be defined as the practice of talking about (1) one's observations, (2) the manipulative and calculational procedures involved in making them, (3) the logical and mathematical steps which intervene between earlier and later statements, and (4) *nothing else*." Next, Skinner's and Brodbeck's approaches to operational definitions is challenged by psychologists Wendell R. Garner, Harold W. Hake, and Charles W. Eriksen who, writing in collaboration, object to radical operationist reduction of the concept *perception*. Following this, Robert H. Ennis makes a broad attack on the reductionism of radical operationism, but expresses sympathy with what he takes to be the operationist spirit and suggests some forms for constructing nonreductionist operational definitions. Friedrich Waismann, in his article "Verifiability," challenges Bechtoldt's, Brodbeck's, and Skinner's basic assumption that significant empirical concepts can be closed in meaning. He maintains that many (or all) are "open-textured," and thus exhibits the tolerance of vagueness characteristic of the humanistic approach.

---

[3] The word "observable" here is chosen with the awareness that it is vague. Actually the controversy might well focus on what is to count as observable: i.e., Is a behavior observable? Is a capacity for a behavior observable, or describable in terms of observables? Is an observation term applicable without reference to the raw, uninterpreted world?

See Chapter 4 of this book for some items discussing the notion, *observation*.

45. ON A DISTINCTION BETWEEN HYPOTHETICAL CONSTRUCTS AND INTERVENING VARIABLES

Kenneth MacCorquodale & Paul E. Meehl

As the thinking of behavior theorists has become more sophisticated and self-conscious, there has been considerable discussion of the value and logical status of so-called "intervening variables." Hull speaks of "symbolic constructs, intervening variables, or hypothetical entities" (5, p. 22)[*] and deals with them in his theoretical discussion as being roughly equivalent notions. At least, his exposition does not distinguish among them explicitly. In his presidential address on behavior at a choice point, Tolman inserts one of Hull's serial conditioning diagrams (11, p. 13) between the independent variables (maintenance schedule, goal object, etc.) and the dependent variable ("behavior ratio") to illustrate his concept of the intervening variable. This would seem to imply that Tolman views his "intervening variables" as of the same character as Hull's. In view of this, it is somewhat surprising to discover that Skinner apparently feels that his formulations have a close affinity to those of Tolman, but are basically dissimilar to those of Hull (10, p. 436, 437). In advocating a theoretical structure which is "descriptive" and "positivistic," he suggests that the model chosen by Hull (Newtonian mechanics) is not the most suitable model for purposes of behavior theory; and in general is critical of the whole postulate-deductive approach.

[*] Numbers in parenthesis refer to the references at the end of this article.
SOURCE. MacCorquodale, Kenneth and Meehl, Paul E., "Hypothetical Constructs and Intervening Variables," *Psychological Review*, **55**, 1948. Reprinted with permission of American Psychological Association. Copyright © 1948 by The American Psychological Association.

Simultaneously with these trends, one can still observe among "tough-minded" psychologists the use of words such as "unobservable" and "hypothetical" in an essentially derogatory manner, and an almost compulsive fear of passing beyond the direct colligation of observable data. "Fictions" and "hypothetical entities" are sometimes introduced into a discussion of theory with a degree of trepidation and apology quite unlike the freedom with which physicists talk about atoms, mesons, fields, and the like. There also seems to be a tendency to treat all hypothetical constructs as on the same footing merely because they are hypothetical; so that we find people arguing that if neutrons are admissible in physics, it must be admissible for us to talk about, *e.g.*, the damming up of libido and its reversion to earlier channels.

The view which theoretical psychologists take toward intervening variables and hypothetical constructs will of course profoundly influence the direction of theoretical thought. Furthermore, what *kinds* of hypothetical constructs we become accustomed to thinking about will have a considerable impact upon theory creation. The present paper aims to present what seems to us a major problem in the conceptualization of intervening variables, without claiming to offer a wholly satisfactory solution. Chiefly, it is our aim here to make a distinction between two subclasses of intervening variables, or we prefer to say, between "intervening variables" and "hypothetical constructs" which we feel is fundamental but is currently being neglected.

We shall begin with a common-sense distinction, and proceed later to formulations of this distinction which we hope will be more rigorous. Naively, it would seem that there is a difference in logical status between constructs which involve the hypothesization of an *entity, process,* or *event* which is not itself observed, and constructs which do not involve such hypothesization. For example, Skinner's "reflex reserve" is definable in terms of the total available responses without further conditioning, whereas Hull's "afferent neural interaction" involves the notion of processes within the nervous system which presumably occur within the objective physical system and which, under suitable conditions, we might observe directly. To take examples from another science in which we psychologists may have less stake in the distinction, one might contrast the notion of "resistance" in electricity to the notion of "electron." The resistance of a piece of wire is what Carnap has called a *dispositional concept,* and is defined by a special type of implication relation. When we say that the resistance of a wire is such-and-such, we mean that "so-and-so-volts will give a current of so-and-so amperes." (For a more precise formulation of this see Carnap, 3, p. 440.) Resistance, in other words, is "operational" in a very direct and primitive sense. The electron, on the other hand, is supposedly an *entity* of some sort. Statements about the electron are, to be sure, supported by means of observational sentences. Nevertheless, it is no longer maintained even by positivists that this set of supporting sentences exhaust the entire *meaning* of the sentences about the electron. Reichenbach, for example, distinguishes *abstracta* from *illata* (from Lat. *infero*). The latter are "inferred things," such as molecules, other people's minds, and so on. They are believed in on the basis of our impressions, but the sentences involving them, even those asserting their existence, are not reducible to sentences about impressions. This is the epistemological form, at rock bottom level, of the distinction we wish to make here.

The introduction of the word "entity" in our discussion has served merely to indicate the distinction, but in any crucial case there could be dispute as to whether a stated hypothesis involved the positing of an entity. For instance, is Hull's "habit strength" an entity or not? Is "drive" an entity? Is "super-ego"?

Previous analyses of this difference may enable us to give a somewhat more precise formulation. These two kinds of concepts are variously distinguished by writers on philosophy of science. Feigl (personal communication) refers to *analytic* versus *existential* hypotheses. Benjamin (1) distinguishes between *abstractive* and *hypothetical* methods. In the abstractive or analytic method we merely neglect certain features of experience and group phenomena by a restricted set of properties into classes; relations between such classes can then be discovered empirically, and nothing has been added to the observed in the process. The hypothetical method, on the other hand, relates experiences "by inventing a fictitious substance or process or idea, in terms of which the experiences can be expressed. A hypothesis, in brief, correlates observations by adding something to them, while abstraction achieves the same end by subtracting something" (1, p. 184).

This quotation suggests to us at least three ways of stating the distinction we have in mind. First, it may be pointed out that in the statement of a hypothetical construction, as distinguished from an abstractive one, there occur words (other than the construct name itself) which are not explicitly defined by (or reduced to) the empirical relations. Once having set up sentences (postulates) containing these hypothetical words, we can arrive by deduction at empirical sentences which can themselves be tested. But the words themselves are not defined directly by or reducible to these empirical facts. This is not true of abstractive concepts, such as resistance or solubility or, say, "drive" as used by Skinner. (We may neglect wholly non-committal words such as *state*, which specify nothing except that the conditions are internal.)

A second apparent difference between abstractive and hypothetical concepts is in their logical relation to the facts, *i.e.*, the observation-sentences and empirical laws which are the basis for believing them. In the case of sentences containing only abstractive concepts, the truth of the empirical laws constitutes *both the necessary and sufficient conditions* for the truth of the abstractive sentences. For sentences involving hypothetical concepts, this is well known to be false. The empirical laws are necessary for the truth of the hypothetical sentences, since the latter imply them; but they are not sufficient. All scientific hypothesizing is in the invalid "third figure" of the implicative syllogism. We neglect here the impossibility, emphasized by Reichenbach and others, of equating even an abstractive sentence or empirical "law" to a *finite* number of particular observation sentences; this is of importance to philosophers of science but for help in the understanding of theories is of no particular consequence. We shall be assuming the trustworthiness of induction throughout and hence will treat 'direct' observational laws as universal sentences or as sentential functions. One can deduce empirical laws from sentences involving hypothetical constructs, but not conversely. Thus, beginning with the hypothesis that gases are made up of small particles which obey the laws of mechanics, plus certain approximating assumptions about the relation of their sizes to their distances, their perfect elasticity, and their lack of mutual attraction, one can apply mathematical rules and eventually, by direct substitution and equation, lead without arbitrariness to the empirical equation $PV = K$. However, one cannot rigorously reverse the process. That is, one cannot commence with the empirical gas law $PV = K$ and arrive at the full kinetic theory. The mathematics is reversible, granted that certain arbitrary breakups of constants etc., are permitted; but beginning with the empirical law itself there is no basis for these arbitrary breakups. Furthermore, aside from the equations themselves, there are coordinated with these equations certain existence propositions, and assertions about the properties of the entities hypothesized. We state that there exist certain small particles, that they collide with the walls of the container, that the root mean square of their velocities is proportional to the temperature, etc. These assertions can of course not be deduced from the empirical law relating pressure and volume.

This suggests a third distinction between concepts of the two kinds. In the case of abstractive concepts, the quantitative form of the concept, *e.g.*, a measure of its "amount," can be derived directly from the empirical laws simply by grouping of terms. In the case of hypothetical concepts, mere grouping of terms is not sufficient. We are less assured of this distinction than of the other two, but we have not been able to think of any exceptions. It seems to us also that, in the case of Hull, this is the point which makes our distinction between hypothetical constructs and intervening variables most obvious. Let us therefore consider Hull's equations as an example.

In *Principles of Behavior*, the influence of certain independent variables such as number of reinforcements, delay in reward, stimulus-response asynchronism, etc., upon response strength is experimentally investigated. In the study of the influence of each of these, the other independent variables are held constant. The experimental findings lead to the formulation of the separate laws of dependence as a set of growth and decay functions. We shall neglect for the moment the complication of drive and of all other variables which intervene between the construct $_sH_r$ and the empirical measure of response. That is to say, we shall deal only with the variables introduced in Hull's Postulate 4. The mathematical statement of Postulate 4 is

$$_sH_r = M(1 - e^{-kw})e^{-ft}e^{-ut'}(1 - e^{-iN}).\ (5,\ p.\ 178)$$

This equation asserts that habit strength is a certain joint function of four variables which refer to direct empirical quantities—number of reinforcements, delay in reinforcement, amount of reinforcement, and asynchronism between the discriminative stimuli and the response. It is important to see that in this case Hull does not distinguish the four experimentally separated laws combined in the equation by separate concept-names; the only intervening variable introduced is habit strength, which is written as an explicit function of four empirical variables w, t, t', and N. It would be quite possible to introduce an intervening variable referring to, say, the last bracket only; it might be called "cumulative reinforcement" and it would be a function of only one empirical variable, N. This would be the most reasonable breakdown of habit strength inasmuch as the other three growth functions (two negative) serve merely to modify the asymptote M (5, p. 181). That is to say, given a certain (maintained) rule for the amount of reinforcement given and two time-specifications concerning the constant relation of the response to two other operations, we have determined a parameter m for a dynamic curve describing the course of acquisition of habit strength. The quantity $(1-e^{-iN})$ (which we are here calling "cumulative reinforcement") is then an intervening variable which is multiplied by the parameter m in order to determine the value of habit strength after N reinforcements have occurred.

Suppose now that a critic asks us whether our "cumulative reinforcement" really *exists*. This amounts to asking whether we have formulated a "correct statement" concerning the relation of this intervening variable to the anchoring (empirical) variables. For since the statement of "existence" for the intervening variable is so far confined to the equations above, the "existence" of cumulative reinforcement reduces strictly to the second question. And this second question, as to whether the statement about the intervening variable's relation to the facts is correct, is in turn equivalent to the question, "Are the empirical variables related in such-and-such a way?" In other words, to confirm the equation for habit strength, it is merely necessary to state that (as Hull assumes in his earlier chapters) with drive, etc., constant, some empirical measure of response strength R is a linear function of habit strength. Then we can write directly,

$$R = C(_sH_r) = C \cdot F(w)G(t)H(t')J(N) = Q(w, t, t', N).$$

To confirm or disconfirm this equation is a direct empirical matter. It is possible to multiply out the bracketed quantities in various combinations, so as to make the arbitrary groupings disappear; what will mathematically persist through all such regroupings will be the rather complicated joint function Q of the four empirical variables w, t, t', and N. By various arbitrary groupings and combinations we could define 15 alternative and equivalent sets of intervening variables. Thus, we might multiply out three of the four brackets in the basic equation but for some reason choose to put $e^{-ut'}$ separately into the denominator. This would give us

$$R = \frac{F(w, t, N)}{e^{ut'}}$$

as the particular form for our empirical relation. $F(w, t, N)$ could then be given an appropriate "intervening variable" name, and the stimulus-response asynchronism t' would then define an intervening variable $e^{ut'}$.

It may be objected that "habit strength" presumably refers to some state of the organism which *is* set up by reinforcing N times under specified conditions; whereas $e^{ut'}$ cannot refer to any such state. This seems plausible; but the point is that to establish it as a state, it would be necessary to coordinate to the groupings within equations certain existence propositions, *i.e.*, propositions that do *more* than define a term by saying "Let the quantity $G(x, y, z)$, where x, y, z are empirical variables, be designated by the phrase so-and-so." This setting up of existence propositions could presumably be done even for a quantity such a $e^{ut'}$, by referring to such hypothetical processes as, say, diminishing traces in the neural reverberation circuits activated by a certain discriminative stimulus.

In the above example we have considered the fractionation of the intervening variable $_sH_r$ into others. This reasoning can also be extended in the upward direction, *i.e.*, in the direction of fusion rather than fractionation. Let us treat "habit strength" as Hull would treat our "cumulative reinforcement," by not giving it a name at all. It is still possible to set up equations to fit the Perin-Williams data (5, p. 229, 255) without referring to habit strength, writing merely

$$n = F(N, h),$$

where N and h are again both purely empirical variables.

We do not mean to imply that the divisions made by Hull (or Tolman) are of no value. It is convenient to have some term to refer to the result of a certain maintenance schedule, instead of having to say "that part of the general multivariable equation of response strength which contains *"hours since eating to satiety"* as an independent variable." We merely wish to emphasize that in the case of Hull's intervening variables, it is both necessary and sufficient for the truth of his "theory" about the intervening variables that the empirical facts should be as his equations specify. The latter are merely names attached to certain convenient groupings of terms in his empirically fitted equations. It is always possible to coordinate to these quantities, which as written mathematically contain parameters and experimental variables only, certain existence propositions which would automatically make the construct "hypothetical" rather than "abstractive." This giving of what Reichenbach calls "surplus meaning" automatically destroys the equivalence between the empirical laws and the theoretical construct. When habit strength *means* the product of the four functions of w, t, t' and N, then if the response strength is related to these empirical variables in the way described, habit strength "exists" in the trivial sense that the law holds. Our confidence in the "correctness" of the intervening variable formulation is precisely as great as our confidence in the laws. When, however, habit strength means not merely this product of empirical functions but something more of a neural or other physiological nature, then the theory could be false even if the empirical relations hold.

It seems to us that Tolman himself, in using one of Hull's serial conditioning diagrams as a set of intervening variables (11, p. 13), departs from his original definition. He has first described the situation which the "behavior ratio" is a complex function f_1 of the independent experimental variables. He goes on to say,

> A theory, as I shall conceive it, is a set of intervening variables. These to-be-inserted intervening variables are 'constructs' which we, the theorists, evolve as a useful way of breaking down into more manageable form the original complete f_1 function (11, p. 9).

His reason for introducing intervening variables does not seem to us very cogent as he states it. He says that empirically establishing the form of f_1 to cover the effects on behavior of all the permutations and combinations of the independent variables would be a "humanly endless task." If this means that all of the verifying instances of a continuous mathematical function cannot be empirically achieved it is true; but that is equally true for a function of one variable only. In order to utilize the proposed relationship between Tolman's function f_3 (11, p. 10) which describes the relation of the behavior to the intervening variables, it is still necessary to establish empirically that the relationship holds—which amounts essentially to trying several of the infinitely many permutations and combinations (as in the Perin-Williams study) until we are inductively satisfied by ordinary scientific standards.

However cogent the arguments for intervening variables may be, it seems clear from Tolman's description that they are what we are calling *abstractive* rather than *hypothetical*. His notion of them involves nothing which is not in the empirical laws that support them. (We may speak of "laws" here in the plural in spite of their being just the single function f_1, just as Boyle's and

Charles' laws are distinguished in addition to the more general gas law ($PV/T = R$.) For Tolman, the merit of an intervening variable is of a purely "summarizing" character. One can determine the function f_1 by parts, so to speak (11, p. 17), so that the effect of a given maintenance schedule upon one part of f_1 may be referred to conveniently as *drive*. For a given drive, we can expect such-and-such behavior ratios in a diversity of situations defined by various combinations of the other independent variables.

It has been observed earlier that in introducing one of Hull's well-known serial conditioning diagrams as an example of intervening variables outside Tolman's own system, we see a departure from the definition Tolman gives. The Hull diagrams contain symbols such as r_g (fractional anticipatory goal response) and s_g (the proprioceptive impulses produced by the movements constituting r_g). These symbols refer to hypothetical processes within the organism, having an allegedly real although undetermined neuromuscular locus. These events are in principle directly observable. In fact, here the case for speaking of an objective reality is even stronger than Reichenbach's examples of electrons, molecules, etc.; since even the criterion of *technical* verifiability, admitted by all positivists to be too strong a restriction, would not exclude these hypotheses as empirically meaningless. Even without penetrating the organism's skin we have some direct observational evidence of r_g in the work of Miller (7). Whether r_g occurs and actually plays the role described is not relevant here; the point is that the diagrams and verbal explanations of Hull involve the supposition that it does. He assumes the existence of certain processes which are not logically implied by the empirical laws in the sense of strict equivalence. Even if, by using the nation of fractional anticipatory goal response, Hull deduced all of the empirical laws relating independent and dependent variables, alternative hypotheses could be offered. Because of the "surplus meaning" contained in concepts like r_g and s_g, these concepts are not really "anchored" to the facts in the sense implied by Tolman's definition of intervening variables or by Hull's diagram on page 22 of the *Principles*. Hull states in reference to this diagram,

> When an intervening variable is thus securely anchored to observables on both sides it can be safely employed in scientific theory (5, p. 22).

We presume that Hull means in this statement that the anchoring in question is not only a sufficient but a necessary condition for scientific admissibility. We feel that the criterion is too strong, assuming that the structure of modern physical science is to be allowed. This sort of anchoring makes the intervening variable strictly reducible to the empirical laws, which is, to be sure, what Tolman's original definition implied. But it excludes such extremely fruitful hypotheses as Hull's own fractional anticipatory goal responses, for which the strict reducibility does not exist.

It occurs to us also in this connection that Hull seems to have moved in the direction of Skinner and Tolman in his treatment of intervening variables. The use of the postulate-theorem approach is maintained more as a form in the *Principles* than as an actual instrument of discovery. In this respect, the *Principles* is much less like Hull's Newtonian model than was the *Mathematico-deductive theory of rote learning*. The justification of "postulates" in the usual sense is their ability to mediate deductions of empirical laws which are then verified. In the *Principles*, the "postulates" are verified directly, by the experimental device of holding all variables constant except the one for which we want to find a law. This is quite unlike the derivation of the gas law in physics. The only sense in which any postulates are "assumed" is in the assumption, referred to by Hull on page 181 of the *Principles*, that the separately verified parts of Postulate 4 will in fact operate according to his equation 16 when combined. This is certainly a "postulate" only in a very attenuated sense, since it amounts essentially to an empirical extrapolation which can be verified directly, as Hull suggests.

At this point any distinction between the type of theory advocated by Hull and that advocated by Skinner or Tolman would seem to disappear, except for the relatively non-contributory "neural" references contained in the verbal statement of Hull's postulates. Insofar as this neural reference is taken seriously, however, we are still dealing with concepts of a hypothetical rather than abstractive character. These are various places in Hull's *Principles* where the verbal accompaniment of a concept, which in its mathematical form is an intervening variable in the strict (Tolman) sense, makes it a hypothetical construct. Thus, the operational definition of a *pav* of inhibition (5, p. 281) would seem merely to mean that when we know from the independent variables that the combined habit strength and drive, together with a discriminative stimulus located so many j.n.d.'s from the original, would yield a reaction potential of so many wats, it requires an equal number of pavs of inhibition to yield an effective reaction potential of zero. However, in the accompanying verbal discussion (5, p. 281) Hull refers to the removal of the inhibitory substance by the blood stream passing through effector organs as determining the quantitative law of spontaneous loss of inhibition as a function of time. "Afferent neural interaction" is another example of a concept which is mathematically represented as a relation of intervening variables in Tolman's sense, but to which are coordinated verbal statements that convey the surplus meaning and make it an hypothesis.

The question might be raised, whether this is not always the difference— that the mathematical assertions are definitive of intervening variables but the verbal additions lend the hypothetical character to such concepts. We do not believe this is the essential difference. There are mathematical expressions whose meaning is not defined in the absence of verbal existential accompaniment, because the quantities involved refer to non-observational (*i.e.*, hypothetical) processes or entities. There are other mathematical expressions for which this is not true, since their component symbols have direct observational reference. In the case of our "cumulative reinforcement" term $(1 - e^{-iN})$, no coordinated existential proposition is required. We simply say, "Response probability is such-and-such a multivariate function of such-and-such experimental variables. Within this function can be isolated a simple growth function of one variable, whose value as a function of N is referred to as *cumulative reinforcement.*" This may be taken as an adequate reference for $(1 - e^{-iN})$. On the other hand, in the derivation of the law $PV = K$ there occur statements such as "When the gas is maintained at the same temperature, $mv^2/2$ does not change." Neither m nor v is an empirical variable. This statement does not tell us anything *until* we are informed that v refers to the velocity which each molecule of the gas could be assumed to have in order that their mean kinetic energy should be what it is. In other words, in the derivation of the gas laws from kinetic theory there occur mathematical assertions whose meaning is unclear without the accompanying existence assertions, and *which cannot be utilized to take the subsequent mathematical steps in the chain of inferences unless these assertions are included.* Thus, to get from a purely mathematical statement that a molecule on impact conserves all of its momentum, to a mathematical statement whose terms refer to the empirical concept of "pressure on the walls," it is necessary to know (from the accompanying verbal description) that in the equations of derivation, m refers to the mass of a hypothetical particle that strikes the wall, v to its velocity, and so on. This example shows that some mathematical formulations are themselves incomplete in the sense that they cannot mediate the desired deductions unless certain existential propositions are stated alongside, so as to render certain necessary substitutions and equations legitimate. Therefore it is not merely the matter of mathematical form that distinguishes a "pure" intervening variable from a hypothesis.

In the second place, it seems to us that the use of verbal statements without mathematical formulations does not guarantee that we are dealing with a hypothetical construct rather than an intervening variable. Consider Skinner's definition of emotion as a "state of the organism" which alters the proportionality between reserve and strength. This is not defined as a direct proportionality, and in fact Skinner nowhere deals with its quantitative form. No mathematical statement is given by him; yet we would contend that the use of the word "state" does not in any way make the notion of emotion existential, any more than drive is existential in Skinner's usage. The "state" of emotion is not to be described in any way except by specifying (a) The class of stimuli which are able to produce it and (b) The effects upon response strength. Hence emotion for Skinner is a true intervening variable, in

Tolman's original sense. We conclude from these examples that whether a given concept is abstractive or hypothetical is not merely a matter of whether it is an equation with or without accompanying verbal exposition.

On the basis of these considerations, we are inclined to propose a linguistic convention for psychological theorists which we feel will help to clarify discussion of these matters. We suggest that the phrase "intervening variable" be restricted to the original use implied by Tolman's definition. Such a variable will then be simply a quantity obtained by a specified manipulation of the values of empirical variables; it will involve no hypothesis as to the existence of nonobserved entities or the occurrence of unobserved processes; it will contain, in its complete statement for all purposes of theory and prediction, no words which are not definable either explicitly or by reduction sentences in terms of the empirical variables; and the validity of empirical laws involving only observables will constitute both the necessary and sufficient conditions for the validity of the laws involving these intervening variables. Legitimate instances of such "pure" intervening variables are Skinner's *reserve*, Tolman's *demand*, Hull's *habit strength*, and Lewin's *valence*. These constructs are the behavioral analogue of Carnap's "dispositional concepts" such as solubility, resistance, inflammability, etc. It must be emphasized that the setting up of a definition or reduction for an intervening variable is not a wholly arbitrary and conventional matter. As Carnap has pointed out, it often happens that we give alternative sets of reduction sentences for the same dispositional concept; in these cases there is empirical content in our statement even though it has a form that suggests arbitrariness. The reason for this is that these separate reductions for a given dispositional concept imply that the empirical events are themselves related in a certain way. The notion of amount of electric current can be introduced by several different observations, such as deposition of silver, deflection of a needle, hydrogen separated out of water, and so on. Such a set of reductions has empirical content because the empirical statements together with the reductions must not lead to contradictions. It is a contingent fact, not derivable from definitions alone, that the deposition of silver will give the same answer for "amount of current" as will the deflection of a needle. A similar problem exists in Hull, when he sets up "momentary effective reaction potential" as the last intervening variable in his chain. In the case of striated muscle reactions, it is stated that latency, resistance to extinction, and probability of occurrence of a response are all functions of reaction potential. Neglecting behavior oscillation, which does not occur in the formulation for the second two because they involve many repetitions of the situation, this means that the empirical variables must be perfectly correlated (non-linearly, of course). The only possible source of variation which could attenuate a perfect correlation between probability of occurrence and resistance to extinction would be actual errors of experimental measurement, since there are no sources of uncontrolled variation left within the organism. If we consider average latency instead of momentary latency (which is a function of *momentary* effective reaction potential and hence varies with behavioral oscillation), latency and resistance to extinction should also be perfectly correlated. It remains to be seen whether the fact will support Hull in giving simultaneously several reductions for the notion of reaction potential.

As a second linguistic convention, we propose that the term "hypothetical construct" be used to designate theoretical concepts which do *not* meet the requirements for intervening variables in the strict sense. That is to say, these constructs involve terms which are not wholly reducible to empirical terms; they refer to processes or entities that are not directly observed (although they need not be in principle unobservable); the mathematical expression of them cannot be formed simply by a suitable grouping of terms in a direct empirical equation; and the truth of the empirical laws involved is a necessary but not a sufficient condition for the truth of these conceptions. Examples of such constructs are Guthrie's M.P.S.'s, Hull's r_g's, S_d's, and *afferent neural interaction*, Allport's *biophysical traits*, Murray's *regnancies*, the notion of 'anxiety' as used by Mowrer, Miller, and Dollard and others of the Yale-derived group, and most theoretical constructs is psychoanalytic theory. Skinner and Tolman seem to be almost wholly free of hypothetical constructs, although when Skinner invokes such notions as the "strain on the reserve" (10, p. 289) it is difficult to be sure.

We do not wish to seem to legislate usage, so that if the broader use of "intervening variable" has become stuck in psychological discourse, we would propose alternatively a distinction between intervening variables of the "abstractive" and of the "hypothetical" kind. Since our personal preference is for restricting the phrase *intervening variables* to the pure type described by Tolman, we shall follow this convention in the remainder of the present paper.

The validity of intervening variables as we define them cannot be called into question except by an actual denial of the empirical facts. If, for example, Hull's proposed "grand investigation" of the Perin-Williams type should be carried out and the complex hyperspatial surface fitted adequately over a wide range of values (5, p. 181), it would be meaningless to reject the concept of "habit strength" and still admit the empirical findings. For this reason, the only consideration which can be raised with respect to a given proposed intervening variable, when an initial defining or reduction equation is being written for it, is the question of convenience.

In the case of hypothetical constructs, this is not so clear. Science is pursued for many reasons, not the least of which is *n Cognizance*. Since hypothetical constructs assert the existence of entities and the occurrence of events not reducible to the observable, it would seem to some of us that it is the business of a hypothetical construct to be "true." It is possible to advance scientific knowledge by taking a completely "as if" attitude toward such matters, but there are always those whose theoretical-cognitive need dictates that existential propositions should correspond to what is in fact the case. Contemporary philosophy of science, even as represented by those who have traditionally been most cautious about discussing "truth" and most highly motivated to reduce it to the experiential, gives psychologists no right to be dogmatic about the "as if" interpretation of theoretical knowledge (*cf.* especially Carnap, 4, p. 598, Kaufmann, 6, p. 35, Russell, 9, Introduction and Chapter XXI, and Reichenbach, 8, passim). We would find it rather difficult to defend the ingenious conditioning hypotheses developed in Hull's series of brilliant papers (1929–) in the PSYCHOLOGICAL REVIEW on the ground that they merely provide a "convenient shorthand summarization of the facts" or are of value in the "practical manipulation" of the rat's behavior. We suspect that Professor Hull himself was motivated to write these articles because he considered that the hypothetical events represented in his diagrams may have actually *occurred* and that the occurrence of these events represents the underlying truth about the learning phenomena he dealt with. In terms of practical application, much (if not most) of theoretical psychology is of little value. If we exclude the interesting anecdotes of Guthrie, contemporary learning theory is not of much use to school teachers. As a *theoretical* enterprise, it may fairly be demanded of a theory of learning that those elements which are "hypothetical" in the present sense have some probability of being in correspondence with the actual events underlying the behavior phenomena, *i.e.*, that the assertions about hypothetical constructs be true.[1]

Another consideration may be introduced here from the standpoint of future developments in scientific integration. Even those of us who advocate the pursuit of behavioral knowledge on its own level and for its own sake must recognize that some day the "pyramid of the sciences" will presumably catch up with us. For Skinner, this is of no consequence, since his consistent use of intervening variables in the strict sense genuinely frees him from neurophysiology and in fact makes it possible for him to impose certain conditions upon neurophysiological explanations (10, pp. 429–431). Since he hypothesizes

---

[1] It is perhaps unnecessary to add that in adopting this position we do not mean to defend any form of metaphysical realist thesis. The ultimate "reality" of the world in general is not the issue here; the point is merely that the reality of hypothetical constructs like the atom, from the standpoint of their logical relation to grounds, is not essentially different from that attributed to stones, chairs, other people, and the like. When we say that hypothetical constructs involve the notion of "objective existence" of actual processes and entities within the organism, we mean the same sort of objective existence, defined by the same ordinary criteria, that is meant when we talk about the objective existence of Singapore. The present discussion operates within the common framework of empirical science and common sense and is intended to be metaphysically neutral.

nothing about the character of the inner events, no finding about the inner events could prove disturbing to him. At most, he would be able to say that a given discovery of internal processes must not be complete because it cannot come to terms with his (empirical) laws. But for those theorists who do not confine themselves to intervening variables in the strict sense, neurology will some day become relevant. For this reason it is perhaps legitimate, even now, to require of a hypothetical construct that it should not be manifestly unreal in the sense that it assumes inner events that cannot conceivably occur. The "as if" kinds of argument sometimes heard from more sophisticated exponents of psychoanalytic views often seem to ignore this consideration. A concept like *libido* or *censor* or *super-ego* may be introduced initially as though it is to be an intervening variable; or even less, it is treated as a merely conventional designation for a class of observable properties or occurrences. But somewhere in the course of theoretical discussion, we find that these words are being used as hypothetical constructs instead. We find that the libido has acquired certain hydraulic properties, or as in Freud's former view, that the "energy" of libido has been converted into "anxiety." What began as a name for an intervening variable is finally a name for a "something" which has a host of causal properties. These properties are not made explicit initially, but it is clear that the concept is to be used in an explanatory way which requires that the properties exist. Thus, libido may be introduced by an innocuous definition in terms of the "set of sexual needs" or a "general term for basic strivings." But subsequently we find that certain puzzling phenomena are *deduced* ("explained") by means of the various properties of libido, *e.g.*, that it flows, is dammed up, is converted into something else, tends to regress to earlier channels, adheres to things, makes its "energy" available to the ego, and so on. It is naive to object to such formulations simply on the ground that they refer to unobservables, or are "hypothetical," or are not "statistical." None of these objections is a crucial one for any scientific construct, and if such criteria were applied a large and useful amount of modern science would have to be abandoned. The fundamental difficulty with such theories is twofold. First, as has been implied by our remarks, there is the failure explicitly to announce the postulates concerning existential properties, so that these are introduced more or less surreptitiously and *ad hoc* as occasion demands. Secondly, by this device there is subtly achieved a transition from admissible intervening variables to inadmissible hypothetical constructs. These hypothetical constructs, unlike intervening variables, are inadmissible because they require the existence of entities and the occurrence of processes which cannot be seriously believed because of other knowledge.

In the case of libido, for instance, we may use such a term legitimately as a generic name for a class of empirical events or properties, or as an intervening variable. But the allied sciences of anatomy and physiology impose restrictions upon our use of it as a hypothetical construct. Even admitting the immature state of neurophysiology in terms of its relation to complex behavior, it must be clear that the central nervous-system does not in fact contain pipes or tubes with fluid in them, and there are no known properties of nervous tissue to which the hydraulic properties of libido could correspond. Hence, this part of a theory about "inner events" is likely to remain metaphorical. For a genuine intervening variable, there is no metaphor because all is merely shorthand summarization. For hypothetical constructs, there is a surplus meaning that is existential. We would argue that dynamic explanations utilizing hypothetical constructs ought not to be of such a character that they *have* to remain only metaphors.

Of course, this judgment in itself involves a "best guess" about the future. A hypothetical construct which seems inherently metaphorical may involve a set of properties to which hitherto undiscovered characteristics of the nervous system correspond. So long as the propositions about the construct are not stated in the *terms* of the next lower discipline, it is always a possibility that the purely formal or relational content of the construct will find an isomorphism in such characteristics. For scientific theories this is enough, since here, as in physics, the associated mechanical imagery of the theorist is irrelevant. The tentative rejection of libido would then be based upon the belief that no neural process is likely to have the *combination* of formal properties required. Strictly speaking, this is always problematic when the basic science is incomplete.[2]

SUMMARY

1. At present the phrases "intervening variable" and "hypothetical construct" are often used interchangeably, and theoretical discourse often fails to distinguish what we believe are two rather different notions. We suggest that a failure to separate these leads to fundamental confusions. The distinction is between constructs which merely abstract the empirical relationships (Tolman's original intervening variables) and those constructs which are "hypothetical" (*i.e.*, involve the supposition of entities or processes not among the observed).

2. Concepts of the first sort seem to be identifiable by three characteristics. First, the statement of such a concept does not contain any words which are not reducible to the empirical laws. Second, the validity of the empirical laws is both necessary and sufficient for the "correctness" of the statements about the concept. Third, the quantitative expression of the concept can be obtained without mediate inference by suitable groupings of terms in the quantitative empirical laws.

[2] We are indebted to Dr. Herbert Feigl for a clarification of this point.

3. Concepts of the second sort do not fulfil any of these three conditions. Their formulation involves words not wholly reducible to the words in the empirical laws; the validity of the empirical laws is not a sufficient condition for the truth of the concept, inasmuch as it contains surplus meaning; and the quantitative form of the concept is not obtainable simply by grouping empirical terms and functions.

4. We propose a linguistic convention in the interest of clarity: that the phrase *intervening variable* be restricted to concepts of the first kind, in harmony with Tolman's original definition; and that the phrase *hypothetical construct* be used for those of the second kind.

5. It is suggested that the only rule for proper intervening variables is that of convenience, since they have no factual content surplus to the empirical functions they serve to summarize.

6. In the case of hypothetical constructs, they have a cognitive, factual reference in addition to the empirical data which constitute their support. Hence, they ought to be held to a more stringent requirement in so far as our interests are theoretical. Their actual existence should be compatible with general knowledge and particularly with whatever relevant knowledge exists at the next lower level in the explanatory hierarchy.

References

1. Benjamin, A. C. *An introduction to the philosophy of science.* New York: Macmillan, 1937.
2. Carnap, R. Testability and meaning, Parts I–III. *Phil. Sci.,* 1936, 3, 419–471.
3. ——. Testability and meaning, Part IV, *Phil. Sci.,* 1937, 4, 1–40.
4. ——. Remarks on induction and truth. *Phil. & phenomenol. res.,* 1946, 6, 590–602.
5. Hull, C. L. *Principles of behavior.* New York: Appleton-Century, 1943.
6. Kaufmann, F. *Methodology in the social sciences.* London: Oxford University Press, 1944.
7. Miller, N. E. A reply to 'Sign-Gestalt or conditioned reflex.' *Psychol. Rev.,* 1935, 42, 280–292.
8. Reichenbach, H. *Experience and prediction.* Chicago: University of Chicago Press, 1938.
9. Russell, B. *Inquiry into meaning and truth.* New York: Norton, 1940.
10. Skinner, B. F. *Behavior of organisms.* New York: Appleton-Century, 1938.
11. Tolman, E. C. The determiners of behavior at a choice point. *Psychol. Rev.,* 1938, 45, 1–41.

46. CONSTRUCT VALIDITY IN PSYCHOLOGICAL TESTS

Lee J. Cronbach & Paul E. Meehl

Validation of psychological tests has not yet been adequately conceptualized, as the APA Committee on Psychological Tests learned when it undertook (1950–54) to specify what qualities should be investigated before a test is published. In order to make coherent recommendations the Committee found it necessary to distinguish four types of validity, established by different types of research and requiring different interpretation. The chief innovation in the Committee's report was the term *construct validity*.[1] This idea was first formulated by a subcommittee (Meehl and R. C. Challman) studying how proposed recommendations would apply to projective techniques, and later modified and clarified by the entire Committee (Bordin, Challman, Conrad, Humphreys, Super, and the present writers). The statements agreed upon by the Committee (and by committees of two other associations) were published in the *Technical Recommendations* (59). The present interpretation of construct validity is not "official" and deals with some areas where the Committee would probably not be unanimous. The present writers are solely responsible for this attempt to explain the concept and elaborate its implications.

Identification of construct validity was not an isolated development. Writers on validity during the preceding decade had shown a great deal of dissatisfaction with conventional notions of validity, and introduced new terms and

SOURCE. Cronbach, Lee J. and Meehl, Paul E., "Construct Validity in Psychological Tests," *Psychological Bulletin*, **52**:4, July 1955. Reprinted with permission of the American Psychological Association. Copyright © 1955 by The American Psychological Association.

[1] Referred to in a preliminary report (58) *as congruent validity.*

ideas, but the resulting aggregation of types of validity seems only to have stirred the muddy waters. Portions of the distinctions we shall discuss are implicit in Jenkins' paper, "Validity for what?" (33), Gulliksen's "Intrinsic validity" (27), Goodenough's distinction between tests as "signs" and "samples" (22), Cronbach's separation of "logical" and "empirical" validity (11), Guilford's "factorial validity" (25), and Mosier's papers on "face validity" and "validity generalization" (49, 50). Helen Peak (52) comes close to an explicit statement of construct validity as we shall present it.

FOUR TYPES OF VALIDATION

The categories into which the *Recommendations* divide validity studies are: predictive validity, concurrent validity, content validity, and construct validity. The first two of these may be considered together as *criterion-oriented* validation procedures.

The pattern of a criterion-oriented study is familiar. The investigator is primarily interested in some criterion which he wishes to predict. He administers the test, obtains an independent criterion measure on the same subjects, and computes a correlation. If the criterion is obtained some time after the test is given, he is studying *predictive validity*. If the test score and criterion score are determined at essentially the same time, he is studying *concurrent validity*. Concurrent validity is studied when one test is proposed as a substitute for another (for example, when a multiple-choice form of spelling test is substituted for taking dictation), or a test is shown to correlate with some contemporary criterion (e.g., psychiatric diagnosis).

Content validity is established by showing that the test items are a sample of a universe in which the investigator is interested. Content validity is ordinarily to be established deductively, by defining a universe of items and sampling systematically within this universe to establish the test.

Construct validation is involved whenever a test is to be interpreted as a measure of some attribute or quality which is not "operationally defined." The problem faced by the investigator is, "What constructs account for variance in test performance?" Construct validity calls for no new scientific approach. Much current research on tests of personality (9) is construct validation, usually without the benefit of a clear formulation of this process.

Construct validity is not to be identified solely by particular investigative procedures, but by the orientation of the investigator. Criterion-oriented validity, as Bechtoldt emphasizes (3, p. 1245), "involves the *acceptance* of a set of operations as an adequate definition of whatever is to be measured." When an investigator believes that no criterion available to him is fully valid, he perforce becomes interested in construct validity because this is the only way to avoid the "infinite frustration" of relating every criterion to some more ultimate standard (21). In content validation, *acceptance* of the universe of content as defining the variable to be measured is essential. Construct validity must be investigated whenever no criterion or universe of content is accepted as entirely adequate to define the quality to be measured. Determining what psychological constructs account for test performance is desirable for almost any test. Thus, although the MMPI was originally established on the basis of empirical discrimination between patient groups and so-called normals (concurrent validity), continuing research has tried to provide a basis for describing the personality associated with each score pattern. Such interpretations permit the clinician to predict performance with respect to criteria which have not yet been employed in empirical validation studies (cf. 46, pp. 49–50, 110–111).

> We can distinguish among the four types of validity by noting that each involves a different emphasis on the criterion. In predictive or concurrent validity, the criterion behavior is of concern to the tester, and he may have no concern whatsoever with the type of behavior exhibited in the test. (An employer does not care if a worker can manipulate blocks, but the score on the block test may predict something he cares about.) Content validity is studied when the tester *is* concerned with the type of behavior involved in the test performance. Indeed, if the test is a work sample, the behavior represented in the test may be an end in itself. Construct validity is ordinarily studied when the tester has no definite criterion measure of the quality with which he is concerned, and must use indirect measures. Here the trait or quality underlying the test is of central importance, rather than either the test behavior or the scores on the criteria (59, p. 14).

Construct validation is important at times for every sort of psychological test: aptitude, achievement, interests, and so on. Thurstone's statement is interesting in this connection:

> In the field of intelligence tests, it used to be common to define validity as the correlation between a test score and some outside criterion. We have reached a stage of sophistication where the test-criterion correlation is too coarse. It is obsolete. If we attempted to ascertain the validity of a test for the second space-factor, for example, we would have to get judges [to] make reliable judgments about people as to this factor. Ordinarily their [the available judges'] ratings would be of no value as a criterion. Consequently, validity studies in the cognitive functions now depend on criteria of internal consistency . . . (60, p. 3).

Construct validity would be involved in answering such questions as: To what extent is this test of intelligence culture-free? Does this test of "interpretation of data" measure reading ability, quantitative reasoning, or response sets? How does a person with A in Strong Accountant, and B in Strong CPA, differ from a person who has these scores reversed?

Example of Construct Validation Procedure.   Suppose measure X correlates .50 with Y, the amount of palmar sweating induced when we tell a student that he has failed a Psychology I exam. Predictive validity of X for Y is adequately described by the coefficient, and a statement of the experimental and sampling conditions. If someone were to ask, "Isn't there perhaps another way to interpret this correlation?" or "What other kinds of evidence can you bring to support your interpretation?", we would hardly understand what he was asking because no interpretation has been made. These questions become relevant when the correlation is advanced as evidence that "test X treasures anxiety proneness." Alternative interpretations are possible; e.g., perhaps the test measures "academic aspiration," in which case we will expect different results if we induce palmar sweating by economic threat. It is then reasonable to inquire about other *kinds* of evidence.

Add these facts from further studies: Test X correlates .45 with fraternity brothers' ratings on "tenseness." Test X correlates .55 with amount of intellectual inefficiency induced by painful electric shock, and .68 with the Taylor Anxiety scale. Mean X score decreases among four diagnosed groups in this order: anxiety state, reactive depression, "normal," and psychopathic personality. And palmar sweat under threat of failure in Psychology I correlates .60 with threat of failure in mathematics. Negative results eliminate competing explanations of the X score; thus, findings of negligible correlations between X and social class, vocational aim, and value-orientation make it fairly safe to reject the suggestion that X measures "academic aspiration." We can have substantial confidence that X does measure anxiety proneness if the current theory of anxiety can embrace the variates which yield positive correlations, and does not predict correlations where we found none.

KINDS OF CONSTRUCTS

At this point we should indicate summarily what we mean by a construct, recognizing that much of the remainder of the paper deals with this question. A construct is some postulated attribute of people, assumed to be reflected in test performance. In test validation the attribute about which we make statements in interpreting a test is a construct. We expect a person at any time to possess or not possess a qualitative attribute (amnesia) or structure, or to possess some degree of a quantitative attribute (cheerfulness). A construct has certain associated meanings carried in statements of this general character: Persons who possess this attribute will, in situation X, act in manner Y (with a stated probability). The logic of construct validation is invoked whether the construct is highly systematized or loose, used in ramified theory or a few simple propositions, used in absolute propositions or probability statements. We seek to specify how one is to defend a proposed interpretation of a test; *we are not recommending any one type of interpretation.*

The constructs in which tests are to be interpreted are certainly not likely to be physiological. Most often they will be traits such as "latent hostility" or "variable in mood," or descriptions in terms of an educational objective, as "ability to plan experiments." For the benefit of readers who may have been influenced by certain eisegeses of MacCorquodale and Meehl (40), let us here emphasize: Whether or not an interpretation of a test's properties or relations involves questions of construct validity is to be decided by examining the entire body of evidence offered, together with what is asserted about the test in the context of this evidence. Proposed identifications of constructs allegedly measured by the test with constructs of other sciences (e.g., genetics, neuroanatomy, biochemistry) make up only *one* class of construct-validity claims, and a rather minor one at present. Space does not permit full analysis of the relation of the present paper to the MacCorquodale-Meehl distinction between hypothetical constructs and intervening variables. The philosophy of science pertinent to the present paper is set forth later in the section entitled, "The nomological network."

THE RELATION OF CONSTRUCTS TO "CRITERIA"

Critical View of the Criterion Implied

An unquestionable criterion may be found in a practical operation, or may be established as a consequence of an operational definition. Typically, however, the psychologist is unwilling to use the directly operational approach because he is interested in building theory about a generalized construct. A theorist trying to relate behavior to "hunger" almost certainly invests that term with meanings other than the operation "elapsed-time-since-feeding." If he is concerned with hunger as a tissue need, he will not accept time lapse as *equivalent* to his construct because it fails to consider, among other things, energy expenditure of the animal.

In some situations the criterion is no more valid than the test. Suppose, for example, that we want to know if counting the dots on Bender-Gestalt figure five indicates "compulsive rigidity," and take psychiatric ratings on this trait as a criterion. Even a conventional report on the resulting correlation will say something about the extent and intensity of the psychiatrist's contacts and should describe his qualifications (e.g., diplomate status? analyzed?).

Why report these facts? Because data are needed to indicate whether the criterion is any good. "Compulsive rigidity" is not really intended to mean "social stimulus value to psychiatrists." The implied trait involves a range of behavior-dispositions which may be very imperfectly sampled by the psychiatrist. Suppose dot-counting does not occur in a particular patient and yet we find that the psychiatrist has rated him as "rigid." When questioned the psychiatrist tells us that the patient was a rather easy, free-wheeling sort; however, the patient *did* lean over to straighten out a skewed desk blotter, and this, viewed against certain other facts, tipped the scale in favor of a "rigid" rating. On the face of it, counting Bendor dots may be just as good (or poor) a sample of the compulsive-rigidity domain as straightening desk blotters is.

Suppose, to extend our example, we have four tests on the "predictor" side over against the psychiatrist's "criterion," and find generally positive correlations among the five variables. Surely it is artificial and arbitrary to impose the "test-should-predict-criterion" pattern on such data. The psychiatrist samples verbal content, expressive pattern, voice, posture, etc. The psychologist samples verbal content, perception, expressive pattern, etc. Our proper conclusion is that, from this evidence, the four tests and the psychiatrist all assess some common factor.

The asymmetry between the "test" and the so-designated "criterion" arises only because the terminology of predictive validity has bcome a commonplace in test analysis. In this study where a construct is the central concern, any distinction between the merit of the test and criterion variables would be justified only if it had already been shown that the psychiatrist's theory and operations were excellent measures of the attribute.

INADEQUACY OF VALIDATION IN TERMS OF SPECIFIC CRITERIA

The proposal to validate constructual interpretations of tests runs counter to suggestions of some others. Spiker and McCandless (57) favor an operational approach. Validation is replaced by compiling statements as to how strongly the test predicts other observed variables of interest. To avoid requiring that each new variable be investigated completely by itself, they allow two variables to collapse into one whenever the properites of the operationally defined measures are the same: "If a new test is demonstrated to predict the scores on an older, well-established test, then an evaluation of the predictive power of the older test may be used for the new one." But accurate inferences are possible only if the two tests correlate so highly that there is negligible reliable variance in either test, independent of the other. Where the correspondence is less close, one must either retain all the separate variables operationally defined or embark on construct validation.

The practical user of tests must rely on constructs of some generality to make predictions about new situations. Test X could be used to predict palmar sweating in the face of failure without invoking any construct, but a counselor is more likely to be asked to forecast behavior in diverse or even unique situations for which the correlation of test X is unknown. Significant predictions rely on knowledge accumulated around the generalized construct of anxiety. The *Technical Recommendations* state:

> It is ordinarily necessary to evaluate construct validity by integrating evidence from many different sources. The problem of construct validation becomes especially acute in the clinical field since for many of the constructs dealt with it is not a question of finding an imperfect criterion but of finding any criterion at all. The psychologist interested in construct validity for clinical devices is concerned with making an estimate of a hypothetical internal process, factor, system, structure, or state and cannot expect to find a clear unitary behavioral criterion. An attempt to identify any one criterion measure or any composite as *the* criterion aimed at is, however, usually unwarranted (59, p. 14–15).

This appears to conflict with arguments for specific criteria prominent at places in the testing literature. Thus Anastasi (2) makes many statements of the latter character: "It is only as a measure of a specifically defined criterion that a test can be objectively validated at all . . . To claim that a test measures anything over and above its criterion is pure speculation" (p. 67). Yet elsewhere this article supports construct validation. Tests can be profitably interpreted if we "know the relationships between the tested behavior . . . and other behavior samples, none of these behavior samples necessarily occupying the preeminent position of a criterion" (p. 75). Factor analysis with several partial criteria might be used to study whether a test measures a postulated "general learning ability." If the data demonstrate specificity of ability instead, such specificity is "useful in its own right in advancing our knowledge of behavior; it should not be construed as a weakness of the tests" (p. 75).

We depart from Anastasi at two points. She writes, "The validity of a psychological test should not be confused with an analysis of the factors which determine the behavior under consideration." We, however, regard such analysis as a most important type of validation. Second, she refers to "the will-o'-the-wisp of psychological processes which are distinct from performance" (2, p. 77). While we agree that psychological processes are elusive, we are sympathetic to attempts to formulate and clarify constructs which are evidenced by performance but distinct from it. Surely an inductive inference based on a pattern of correlations cannot be dismissed as "pure speculation."

Specific Criteria Used Temporarily: The "Bootstraps" Effect

Even when a test is constructed on the basis of a specific criterion, it may ultimately be judged to have greater construct validity than the criterion. We start with a vague concept which we associate with certain observations. We then discover empirically that these observations covary with some other observation which possesses greater reliability or is more intimately correlated with relevant experimental changes than is the original measure, or both. For example, the notion of temperature arises because some objects feel hotter to the touch than others. The expansion of a mercury column does not have face validity as an index of hotness. But it turns out that (*a*) there is a statistical relation between expansion and sensed temperature; (*b*) observers employ the mercury method with good interobserver agreement; (*c*) the regularity of observed relations is increased by using the thermometer (e.g., melting points of samples of the same material vary little on the thermometer; we obtain nearly linear relations between mercury measures and pressure of a gas). Finally, (*d*) a theoretical structure involving unobservable microevents—the kinetic theory—is worked out which explains the relation of mercury expansion to heat. This whole process of conceptual enrichment begins with what in retrospect we see as an extremely fallible "criterion"—the human temperature sense. That original criterion has now been relegated to a peripheral position. We have lifted ourselves by our bootstraps, but in a legitimate and fruitful way.

Similarly, the Binet scale was first valued because children's scores tended to agree with judgments by schoolteachers. If it had not shown this agreement, it would have been discarded along with reaction time and the other measures of ability previously tried. Teacher judgments once constituted the criterion against which the individual intelligence test was validated. But if today a child's IQ is 135 and three of his teachers complain about how stupid he is, we do not conclude that the test has failed. Quite to the contrary, if no error in test procedure can be argued, we treat the test score as a valid statement about an important quality, and define our task as that of finding out what other variables—personality, study skills, etc.—modify achievement or distort teacher judgment.

EXPERIMENTATION TO INVESTIGATE CONSTRUCT VALIDITY

Validation Procedures

We can use many methods in construct validation. Attention should particularly be drawn to Macfarlane's survey of these methods as they apply to projective devices (41).

Group Differences. If our understanding of a construct leads us to expect two groups to differ on the test, this expectation may be tested directly. Thus Thurstone and Chave validated the Scale for Measuring Attitude Toward the Church by showing score differences between church members and nonchurchgoers. Churchgoing is not *the* criterion of attitude, for the purpose of the test is to measure something other than the crude sociological fact of church attendance; on the other hand, failure to find a difference would have seriously challenged the test.

Only coarse correspondence between test and group designation is expected. Too great a correspondence between the two would indicate that the test is to some degree invalid, because members of the groups are expected to overlap on the test. Intelligence test items are selected initially on the basis of a correspondence to age, but an item that correlates .95 with age in an elementary school sample would surely be suspect.

Correlation Matrices and Factor Analysis. If two tests are presumed to measure the same construct, a correlation between them is predicted. (An exception is noted where some second attribute has positive loading in the first test and negative loading in the second test; then a low correlation is expected. This is a testable interpretation provided an external measure of either the first or the second variable exists.) If the obtained correlation departs from the expectation, however, there is no way to know whether the fault lies in test A, test B, or the formulation of the construct. A matrix of intercorrelations often points out profitable ways of dividing the construct into more meaningful parts, factor analysis being a useful computational method in such studies.

Guilford (26) has discussed the place of factor analysis in construct validation. His statements may be extracted as follows:

"The personnel psychologist wishes to know 'why his tests are valid.' He can place tests and practical criteria in a matrix and factor it to identify 'real dimensions of human personality.' A factorial description is exact and stable; it is economical in explanation; it leads to the creation of pure tests which can be combined to predict complex behaviors." It is clear that factors here function as constructs. Eysenck, in his "criterion analysis" (18), goes farther than Guilford, and shows that factoring can be used explicitly to test hypotheses about constructs.

Factors may or may not be weighted with surplus meaning. Certainly when they are regarded as "real dimensions" a great deal of surplus meaning is implied, and the interpreter must shoulder a substantial burden of proof. The alternative view is to regard factors as defining a working reference frame, located in a convenient manner in the "space" defined by all behaviors of a given type. Which set of factors from a given matrix is "most useful" will depend partly on predilections, but in essence the best construct is the one around which we can build the greatest number of inferences, in the most direct fashion.

Studies of Internal Structure. For many constructs, evidence of homogeneity within the test is relevant in judging validity. If a trait such as *dominance* is hypothesized, and the items inquire about behaviors subsumed under this label, then the hypothesis appears to require that these items be generally intercorrelated. Even low correlations, if consistent, would support the argument that people may be fruitfully described in terms of a generalized tendency to dominate or not dominate. The general quality would have power to predict behavior in a variety of situations represented by the specific items. Item-test correlations and certain reliability formulas describe internal consistency.

It is unwise to list uninterpreted data of this sort under the heading "validity" in test manuals, as some authors have done. High internal consistency may *lower* validity. Only if the underlying theory of the trait being measured calls for high item intercorrelations do the correlations support construct validity. Negative item-test correlations may support construct validity, provided that the items with negative correlations are believed irrelevant to the postulated construct and serve as suppressor variables (31, p. 431–436; 44).

Study of distinctive subgroups of items within a test may set an upper limit to construct validity by showing that irrelevant elements influence scores. Thus a study of the PMA space tests shows that variance can be partially accounted for by a response set, tendency to mark many figures as similar (12). An internal factor analysis of the PEA Interpretation of Data Test shows that in addition to measuring reasoning skills, the test score is strongly influenced by a tendency to say "probably true" rather than "certainly true," regardless of item content (17). On the other hand, a study of item groupings in the DAT Mechanical Comprehension Test permitted rejection of the hypothesis that knowledge about specific topics such as gears made a substantial contribution to scores (13).

Studies of Change Over Occasions. The stability of test scores ("retest reliability," Cattell's "N-technique") may be relevant to construct validation. Whether a high degree of stability is encouraging or discouraging for the proposed interpretation depends upon the theory defining the construct.

More powerful than the retest after uncontrolled intervening experiences is the retest with experimental intervention. If a transient influence swings test scores over a wide range, there are definite limits on the extent to which a test result can be interpreted as reflecting the typical behavior of the individual. These are examples of experiments which have indicated upper limits to test validity: studies of differences associated with the examiner in projective testing, of change of score under alternative directions ("tell the truth" vs. "make yourself look good to an employer"), and of coachability of mental tests. We may recall Gulliksen's distinction (37): When the coaching is of a sort that improves the pupil's intellectual functioning in school, the test which is affected by the coaching has validity as a measure of intellectual functioning; if the coaching improves test taking but not school performance, the test which responds to the coaching has poor validity as a measure of this construct.

Sometimes, where differences between individuals are difficult to assess by any means other than the test, the experimenter validates by determining whether the test can detect induced intra-individual differences. One might hypothesize that the Zeigarnik effect is a measure of ego involvement, i.e., that with ego involvement there is more recall of incomplete tasks. To support such an interpretation, the investigator will try to induce ego involvement on some task by appropriate directions and compare subjects' recall with their recall for tasks where there was a contrary induction. Sometimes the intervention is drastic. Porteus finds (53) that brain-operated patients show disruption of performance on his maze, but do not show impaired performance on conventional verbal tests and argues therefrom that his test is a better measure of planfulness.

Studies of Process. One of the best ways of determining informally what accounts for variability on a test is the observation of the person's process of performance. If it is supposed, for example, that a test measures mathematical competence, and yet observation of students' errors shows that erroneous reading of the question is common, the implications of a low score are altered. Lucas in this way showed that the Navy Relative Movement Test, an aptitude test, actually involved two different abilities: spatial visualization and mathematical reasoning (39).

Mathematical analysis of scoring procedures may provide important negative evidence on construct validity. A recent analysis of "empathy" tests is perhaps worth citing (14). "Empathy" has been operationally defined in many studies by the ability of a judge to predict what responses will be given on some questionnaire by a subject he has observed briefly. A mathematical argument has shown, however, that the scores depend on several attributes of the judge which enter into his perception of *any* individual, and that they therefore cannot be interpreted as evidence of his ability to interpret cues offered by particular others, or his intuition.

The Numerical Estimate of Construct Validity

There is an understandable tendency to seek a "construct validity coefficient." A numerical statement of the degree of construct validity would be a statement of the proportion of the test score variance that is attributable to the construct variable. This numerical estimate can sometimes be arrived at by a factor analysis, but since present methods of factor analysis are based on linear relations, more general methods will ultimately be needed to deal with many quantitative problems of construct validation.

Rarely will it be possible to estimate definite "construct saturations," because no factor corresponding closely to the construct will be available. One can only hope to set upper and lower bounds to the "loading." If "creativity" is defined as something independent of knowledge, then a correlation of .40 between a presumed test of creativity and a test of arithmetic knowledge would indicate that at least 16 per cent of the reliable test variance is irrelevant to creativity as defined. Laboratory performance on problems such as Maier's "hatrack" would scarcely be an ideal measure of creativity, but it would be somewhat relevant. If its correlation with the test is .60, this permits a tentative estimate of 36 per cent as a lower bound. (The estimate is tentative because the test might overlap with the irrelevant portion of the laboratory measure.) The saturation seems to lie between 36 and 84 per cent; a cumulation of studies would provide better limits.

It should be particularly noted that rejecting the null hypothesis does not finish the job of construct validation (35, p. 284). The problem is not to conclude that the test "is valid" for measuring the construct variable. The task is to state as definitely as possible the degree of validity the test is presumed to have.

THE LOGIC OF CONSTRUCT VALIDATION

Construct validation takes place when an investigator believes that his instrument reflects a particular construct, to which are attached certain meanings. The proposed interpretation generates specific testable hypotheses, which are a means of confirming or disconfirming the claim. The philosophy of science which we believe does most justice to actual scientific practice will now be briefly and dogmatically set forth. Readers interested in further study of the philosophical underpinning are referred to the works by Braithwaite (6, especially Chapter III), Carnap (7; 8, pp. 56–69), Pap (51), Sellars (55, 56), Feigl (19, 20), Beck (4), Kneale (37, pp. 92–110), Hempel (29; 30, Sec. 7).

The Nomological Net

The fundamental principles are these:

1. Scientifically speaking, to "make clear what something *is*" means to set forth the laws in which it occurs. We shall refer to the interlocking system of laws which constitute a theory as a *nomological network*.

2. The laws in a nomological network may relate (*a*) observable properties or quantities to each other; or (*b*) theoretical constructs to observables; or (*c*) different theoretical constructs to one another. These "laws" may be statistical or deterministic.

3. A necessary condition for a construct to be scientifically admissible is

that it occur in a nomological net, at least *some* of whose laws involve observables. Admissible constructs may be remote from observation, i.e., a long derivation may intervene between the nomologicals which implicitly define the construct, and the (derived) nomologicals of type *a*. These latter propositions permit predictions about events. The construct is not "reduced" to the observations, but only combined with other constructs in the net to make predictions about observables.

4. "Learning more about" a theoretical construct is a matter of elaborating the nomological network in which it occurs, or of increasing the definiteness of the components. At least in the early history of a construct the network will be limited, and the construct will as yet have few connections.

5. An enrichment of the net such as adding a construct or a relation to theory is justified if it generates nomologicals that are confirmed by observation or if it reduces the number of nomologicals required to predict the same observations. When observations will not fit into the network as it stands, the scientist has a certain freedom in selecting where to modify the network. That is, there may be alternative constructs or ways of organizing the net which for the time being are equally defensible.

6. We can say that "operations" which are qualitatively very different "overlap" or "measure the same thing" if their positions in the nomological net tie them to the same construct variable. Our confidence in this identification depends upon the amount of inductive support we have for the regions of the net involved. It is not necessary that a direct observational comparison of the two operations be made   we may be content with an intranetwork proof indicating that the two operations yield estimates of the same network-defined quantity. Thus, physicists are content to speak of the "temperature" of the sun and the "temperature" of a gas at room temperature even though the test operations are nonoverlapping because this identification makes theoretical sense.

With these statements of scientific methodology in mind, we return to the specific problem of construct validity as applied to psychological tests. The preceding guide rules should reassure the "toughminded," who fear that allowing construct validation opens the door to nonconfirmable test claims. *The answer is that unless the network makes contact with observations, and exhibits explicit, public steps of inference, construct validation cannot be claimed.* An admissible psychological construct must be behavior-relevant (59, p. 15). For most tests intended to measure constructs, adequate criteria do not exist. This being the case, many such tests have been left unvalidated, or a finespun network of rationalizations has been offered as if it were validation. Rationalization is not construct validation. One who claims that his test reflects a construct cannot maintain his claim in the face of recurrent negative results because these results show that his construct is too loosely defined to yield verifiable inferences.

A rigorous (though perhaps probabilistic) chain of inference is required to establish a test as a measure of a construct. To validate a claim that a test measures a construct, a nomological net surrounding the concept must exist. When a construct is fairly new, there may be few specifiable associations by which to pin down the concept. As research proceeds, the construct sends out roots in many directions, which attach it to more and more facts or other constructs. Thus the electron has more accepted properties than the neutrino; *numerical ability* has more than *the second space factor*.

"Acceptance," which was critical in criterion-oriented and content validities, has now appeared in construct validity. Unless substantially the same nomological net is accepted by the several users of the construct, public validation is impossible. If A uses *aggressiveness* to mean overt assault on others, and B's usage includes repressed hostile reactions, evidence which convinces B that a test measures *aggressiveness* convinces A that the test does not. Hence, the investigator who proposes to establish a test as a measure of a construct must specify his network or theory sufficiently clearly that others can accept or reject it (cf. 41, p. 406). A consumer of the test who rejects the author's theory cannot accept the author's validation. He must validate the test for himself, if he wishes to show that it represents the construct as *he* defines it.

Two general qualifications are in order with reference to the methodological principles 1–6 set forth at the beginning of this section. Both of them concern the amount of "theory," in any high-level sense of that word, which enters into a construct-defining network of laws or lawlike statements. We do not wish to convey the impression that one always has a very elaborate theoretical network, rich in hypothetical processes or entities.

Constructs as Inductive Summaries.   In the early stages of development of a construct or even at more advanced stages when our orientation is thoroughly practical, little or no theory in the usual sense of the word need be involved. In the extreme case the hypothesized laws are formulated entirely in terms of descriptive (observational) dimensions although not all of the relevant observations have actually been made.

The hypothesized network "goes beyond the data" only in the limited sense that it purports to *characterize* the behavior facets which belong to an observable but as yet only partially sampled cluster; hence, it generates predictions about hitherto unsampled regions of the phenotypic space. Even though no unobservables or high-order theoretical constructs are introduced, an element of inductive extrapolation appears in the claim that a cluster including some elements not-yet-observed has been identified. Since, as in any sorting or abstracting task involving a finite set of complex elements, several nonequivalent bases of categorization are available, the investigator may choose a hypothesis which generates erroneous predictions. The failure of a supposed, hitherto untried, member of the cluster to behave in the manner said to be characteristic of the group, or the finding that a nonmember of the postulated cluster does behave in this manner, may modify greatly our tentative construct.

For example, one might build an intelligence test on the basis of his background notions of "intellect," including vocabulary, arithmetic calculation, general information, similarities, two-point threshold, reaction time, and line bisection as subtests. The first four of these correlate, and he extracts a huge first factor. This becomes a second approximation of the intelligence construct, described by its pattern of loadings on the four tests. The other three tests have negligible loading on any common factor. On this evidence the investigator re-interprets intelligence as "manipulation of words." Subsequently it is discovered that test-stupid people are rated as unable to express their ideas, are easily taken in by fallacious arguments, and misread complex directions. These data support the "linguistic" definition of intelligence and the test's claim of validity *for* that construct. But then a block design test with pantomime instructions is found to be strongly saturated with the first factor. Immediately the purely "linguistic" interpretation of Factor I becomes suspect. This finding, taken together with our initial acceptance of the others as relevant to the background concept of intelligence, forces us to reinterpret the concept once again.

If we simply *list* the tests or traits which have been shown to be saturated with the "factor" or which belong to the cluster, no construct is employed. As soon as we even *summarize the properties* of this group of indicators—we are already making some guesses. Intensional characterization of a domain is hazardous since it selects (abstracts) properties and implies that new tests sharing those properties will behave as do the known tests in the cluster, and that tests not sharing them will not.

The difficulties in merely "characterizing the surface cluster" are strikingly exhibited by the use of certain special and extreme groups for purposes of construct validation. The P_d scale of MMPI was originally derived and cross-validated upon hospitalized patients diagnosed "Psychopathic personality, asocial and amoral type" (42). Further research shows the scale to have a limited degree of predictive and concurrent validity for "delinquency" more broadly defined (5, 28). Several studies show associations between P_d and very special "criterion" groups which it would be ludicrous to identify as "*the* criterion" in the traditional sense. If one lists these heterogeneous groups and tries to characterize them intensionally, he faces enormous conceptual difficulties. For example, a recent survey of hunting accidents in Minnesota showed that hunters who had "carelessly" shot someone were significantly elevated on P_d when compared with other hunters (48). This is in line with one's theoretical expectations; when you ask MMPI "experts" to predict for such a group they invariably predict P_d or M_a or both. The finding seems therefore to lend some slight support to the construct validity of the P_d scale. But of course it would be nonsense to *define* the P_d component "operationally" in terms of, say, accident proneness. We might try to subsume the original phenotype and the hunting-accident proneness under some broader category, such as "Disposition to violate society's rules, whether legal, moral, or just *sensible*." But now we have ceased to have a neat operational criterion, and are using instead a rather vague and wide-range class. Besides, there is worse to come. We want the class specification to cover a group trend that (non-delinquent) high school students judged by their peer group as least "responsible" score over a full sigma higher on P_d than those judged most "responsible" (23, p. 75). Most of the behaviors contributing to such sociometric choices fall well within the range of socially permissible action; the proffered criterion specification is still too restrictive. Again, any clinician familiar with MMPI lore would predict an elevated P_d on a sample of (nondelinquent) professional actors. Chyatte's confirmation of this prediction (10) tends to support *both*: (*a*) the theory sketch of "what the P_d factor is, psychologically"; and (*b*) the claim of the P_d scale to construct validity for this hypothetical factor. Let the reader try his hand at writing a brief phenotypic criterion specification that will cover both trigger-happy hunters and Broadway actors! And if he should be ingenious enough to achieve this, does his definition also encompass Hovey's report that high P_d predicts the judgments "not shy" and "unafraid of mental patients" made upon nurses by their supervisors (32, p. 143)? And then we have Gough's report that *low* P_d is associated with ratings as "good-natured" (24, p. 40), and Roessell's data showing that high P_d is predictive of "dropping out of high school" (54). The point is that all seven of these "criterion" dispositions would be readily guessed by any clinician having even superficial familiarity with MMPI interpretation; but to mediate these inferences explicitly requires quite a few hypotheses about dynamics, constituting an admittedly sketchy (but far from vacuous) network defining the genotype *psychopathic deviate*.

Vagueness of Present Psychological Laws. This line of thought leads directly to our second important qualification upon the network schema. The idealized picture is one of a tidy set of postulates which jointly entail the desired theorems; since some of the theorems are coordinated to the observation base, the system constitutes an implicit definition of the theoretical primitives and gives them an indirect empirical meaning. In practice, of course, even the most advanced physical sciences only approximate this ideal. Questions of "categoricalness" and the like, such as logicians raise about pure calculi, are hardly even statable for empirical networks. (What, for example, would be the desiderata of a "well-formed formula" in molar behavior theory?) Psychology works with crude, half-explicit formulations. We do not worry about such advanced formal questions as "whether all molar-behavior statements are decidable by appeal to the postulates" because we know that no existing theoretical network suffices to predict even the *known* descriptive laws. Nevertheless, the sketch of a network is there; if it were not, we would not be saying *anything* intelligible about our constructs. We do not have the rigorous implicit definitions of formal calculi (which still, be it noted, usually permit of a multiplicity of interpretations). Yet the vague, avowedly incomplete network still gives the constructs whatever meaning they do have. When the network is very incomplete, having many strands missing entirely and some constructs tied in only by tenuous threads, then the "implicit definition" of these constructs is disturbingly loose; one might say that the meaning of the constructs is underdetermined. *Since the meaning of theoretical constructs is set forth by stating the laws in which they occur, our incomplete knowledge of the laws of nature produces a vagueness in our constructs* (see Hempel, 30; Kaplan, 34; Pap, 51). We will be able to say "what anxiety is" when we know all of the laws involving it; meanwhile, since we are in the process of discovering these laws, we do not yet know precisely what anxiety is.

CONCLUSIONS REGARDING THE NETWORK AFTER EXPERIMENTATION

The proposition that x per cent of test variance is accounted for by the construct is inserted into the accepted network. The network then generates a testable prediction about the relation of the test scores to certain other variables, and the investigator gathers data. If prediction and result are in harmony, he can retain his belief that the test measures the construct. The construct is at best adopted, never demonstrated to be "correct."

We do not first "prove" the theory, and then validate the test, nor conversely. In any probable inductive type of inference from a pattern of observations, we examine the relation between the total network of theory and observations. The system involves propositions relating test to construct, construct to other constructs, and finally relating some of these constructs to observables. In ongoing research the chain of inference is very complicated. Kelly and Fiske (36, p. 124) give a complex diagram showing the numerous inferences required in validating a prediction from assessment techniques, where theories about the criterion situation are as integral a part of the prediction as are the test data. A predicted empirical relationship permits us to test all the propositions leading to that prediction. Traditionally the proposition claiming to interpret the test has been set apart as the hypothesis being tested, but actually the evidence is significant for all parts of the chain. If the prediction is not confirmed, any link in the chain may be wrong.

A theoretical network can be divided into subtheories used in making particular predictions. All the events successfully predicted through a subtheory are of course evidence in favor of that theory. Such a subtheory may be so well confirmed by voluminous and diverse evidence that we can reasonably view a particular experiment as relevant only to the test's validity. If the theory, combined with a proposed test interpretation, mispredicts in this case, it is the latter which must be abandoned. On the other hand, the accumulated evidence for a test's construct validity may be so strong that an instance of misprediction will force us to modify the subtheory employing the construct rather than deny the claim that the test measures the construct.

Most cases in psychology today lie somewhere between these extremes. Thus, suppose we fail to find a greater incidence of "homosexual signs" in the Rorschach records of paranoid patients. Which is more strongly disconfirmed —the Rorschach signs or the orthodox theory of paranoia? The negative finding shows the bridge between the two to be undependable, but this is all we can say. The bridge cannot be used unless one end is placed on solider ground. The investigator must decide which end it is best to relocate.

Numerous successful predictions dealing with phenotypically diverse "criteria" give greater weight to the claim of construct validity than do fewer predictions, or predictions involving very similar behaviors. In arriving at diverse predictions, the hypothesis of test validity is connected each time to a subnetwork largely independent of the portion previously used. Success of these derivations testifies to the inductive power of the test-validity statement, and renders it unlikely that an equally effective alternative can be offered.

Implications of Negative Evidence

The investigator whose prediction and data are discordant must make strategic decisions. His result can be interpreted in three ways:

1. The test does not measure the construct variable.
2. The theoretical network which generated the hypothesis is incorrect.
3. The experimental design failed to test the hypothesis properly. (Strictly speaking this may be analyzed as a special case of 2, but in practice the distinction is worth making.)

For Further Research. If a specific fault of procedure makes the third a reasonable possibility, his proper response is to perform an adequate study, meanwhile making no report. When faced with the other two alternatives, he may decide that his test does not measure the construct adequately. Following that decision, he will perhaps prepare and validate a new test. Any rescoring or new interpretative procedure for the original instrument, like a new test, requires validation *by means of a fresh body of data.*

The investigator may regard interpretation 2 as more likely to lead to eventual advances. It is legitimate for the investigator to call the network defining the construct into question, if he has confidence in the test. Should the investigator decide that some step in the network is unsound, he may be able to invent an alternative network. Perhaps he modifies the network by splitting a concept into two or more portions, e.g., by designating types of *anxiety*, or perhaps he specifies added conditions under which a generalization holds. When an investigator modifies the theory in such a manner, he is now required to *gather a fresh body of data* to test the altered hypotheses. This step should normally precede publication of the modified theory. If the new data are consistent with the modified network, he is free from the fear that his nomologicals were gerrymandered to fit the peculiarities of his first sample of observations. He can now trust his test to some extent, because his test results behave as predicted.

The choice among alternatives, like any strategic decision, is a gamble as to which course of action is the best investment of effort. Is it wise to modify the theory? That depends on how well the system is confirmed by prior data, and how well the modifications fit available observations. Is it worth while to modify the test in the hope that it will fit the construct? That depends on how much evidence there is—apart from this abortive experiment—to support the hope, and also on how much it is worth to the investigator's ego to salvage the test. The choice among alternatives is a matter of research planning.

For Practical Use of the Test.   The consumer can accept a test as a measure of a construct only when there is a strong positive fit between predictions and subsequent data. When the evidence from a proper investigation of a published test is essentially negative, it should be reported as a stop sign to discourage use of the test pending a reconciliation of test and construct, or final abandonment of the test. If the test has not been published, it should be restricted to research use until some degree of validity is established (1). The consumer can await the results of the investigator's gamble with confidence that proper application of the scientific method will ultimately tell whether the test has value. Until the evidence is in, he has no justification for employing the test as a basis for terminal decisions. The test may serve, at best, only as a source of suggestions about individuals to be confirmed by other evidence (15, 47).

There are two perspectives in test validation. From the viewpoint of the psychological practitioner, the burden of proof is on the test. A test should not be used to measure a trait until its proponent establishes that predictions made from such measures are consistent with the best available theory of the trait. In the view of the test developer, however, both the test and the theory are under scrutiny. He is free to say *to himself privately*, "If my test disagrees with the theory, so much the worse for the theory." This way lies delusion, unless he continues his research using a better theory.

Reporting of Positive Results

The test developer who finds positive correspondence between his proposed interpretation and data is expected to report the basis for his validity claim. Defending a claim of construct validity is a major task, not to be satisfied by a discourse without data. The *Technical Recommendations* have little to say on reporting of construct validity. Indeed, the only detailed suggestions under that heading refer to correlations of the test with other measures, together with a cross reference to some other sections of the report. The two key principles, however, call for the most comprehensive type of reporting. The manual for any test "should report all available information which will assist the user in determining what psychological attributes account for variance in test scores" (59, p. 27). And, "The manual for a test which is used primarily to assess postulated attributes of the individual should outline the theory on which the test is based and organize whatever partial validity data there are to show in what way they support the theory" (59, p. 28). It is recognized, by a classification as "very desirable" rather than "essential," that the latter recommendation goes beyond present practice of test authors.

The proper goals in reporting construct validation are to make clear (a) what interpretation is proposed, (b) how adequately the writer believes this interpretation is substantiated, and (c) what evidence and reasoning lead him to this belief. Without a the construct validity of the test is of no use to the consumer. Without b the consumer must carry the entire burden of evaluating the test research. Without c the consumer or reviewer is being asked to take a and b on faith. The test manual cannot always present an exhaustive statement on these points, but it should summarize and indicate where complete statements may be found.

To specify the interpretation, the writer must state what construct he has in mind, and what meaning he gives to that construct. For a construct which has a short history and has built up few connotations, it will be fairly easy to indicate the presumed properties of the construct, i.e., the nomologicals in which it appears. For a construct with a longer history, a summary of properties and references to previous theoretical discussions may be appropriate. It is especially critical to distinguish proposed interpretations from other meanings previously given the same construct. The validator faces no small task; he must somehow communicate a theory to his reader.

To evaluate his evidence calls for a statement like the conclusions from a program of research, noting what is well substantiated and what alternative interpretations have been considered and rejected. The writer must note what portions of his proposed interpretation are speculations, extrapolations, or conclusions from insufficient data. The author has an ethical responsibility to prevent unsubstantiated interpretations from appearing as truths. A claim is unsubstantiated unless the evidence for the claim is public, so that other scientists may review the evidence, criticize the conclusions, and offer alternative interpretations.

The report of evidence in a test manual must be as complete as any research report, except where adequate public reports can be cited. Reference to something "observed by the writer in many clinical cases" is worthless as evidence. Full case reports, on the other hand, may be a valuable source of evidence so long as these cases are representative and negative instances receive due attention. The report of evidence must be interpreted with reference to the theoretical network in such a manner that the reader sees why the author regards a particular correlation or experiment as confirming (or throwing doubt upon) the proposed interpretation. Evidence collected by others must be taken fairly into account.

VALIDATION OF A COMPLEX TEST "AS A WHOLE"

Special questions must be considered when we are investigating the validity of a test which is aimed to provide information about several constructs. In one sense, it is naive to inquire "Is this test valid?" One does not validate a test, but only a principle for making inferences. If a test yields many different types of inferences, some of them can be valid and others invalid (cf. Technical Recommendation C2: "The manual should report the validity of each type of inference for which a test is recommended"). From this point of view, every topic sentence in the typical book on Rorschach interpretation presents a hypothesis requiring validation, and one should validate inferences about each aspect of the personality separately and in turn, just as he would want information on the validity (concurrent or predictive) for each scale of MMPI.

There is, however, another defensible point of view. If a test is purely empirical, based strictly on observed connections between response to an item and some criterion, then of course the validity of one scoring key for the test does not make validation for its other scoring keys any less necessary. But a test may be developed on the basis of a theory which in itself provides a linkage between the various keys and the various criteria. Thus, while Strong's Vocational Interest Blank is developed empirically, it also rests on a "theory" that a youth can be expected to be satisfied in an occupation if he has interests common to men now happy in the occupation. When Strong finds that those with high Engineering interest scores in college are preponderantly in engineering careers 19 years later, he has partly validated the proposed use of the Engineer score (predictive validity). Since the evidence is consistent with the theory on which all the test keys were built, this evidence alone increases the presumption that the *other* keys have predictive validity. How strong is this presumption? Not very, from the viewpoint of the traditional skepticism of science. Engineering interests may stabilize early, while interests in art or management or social work are still unstable. A claim cannot be made that the whole Strong approach is valid just because one score shows predictive validity. But if thirty interest scores were investigated longitudinally and all of them showed the type of validity predicted by Strong's theory, we would indeed be caviling to say that this evidence gives no confidence in the long-range validity of the thirty-first score.

Confidence in a theory is increased as more relevant evidence confirms it, but it is always possible that tomorrow's investigation will render the theory obsolete. The Technical Recommendations suggest a rule of reason, and ask for evidence for each *type* of inference for which a test is recommended. It is stated that no test developer can present predictive validities for all possible criteria; similarly, no developer can run all possible experimental tests of his proposed interpretation. But the recommendation is more subtle than advice that a lot of validation is better than a little.

Consider the Rorschach test. It is used for many inferences, made by means of nomological networks at several levels. At a low level are the simple un-rationalized correspondences presumed to exist between certain signs and psychiatric diagnoses. Validating such a sign does nothing to substantiate Rorschach theory. For other Rorschach formulas an explicit a priori rationale exists (for instance, high $F\%$ interpreted as implying rigid control of impulses). Each time such a sign shows correspondence with criteria, its rationale is supported just a little. At a still higher level of abstraction, a considerable body of theory surrounds the general area of *outer control*, interlacing many different constructs. As evidence cumulates, one should be able to decide what specific inference-making chains within this system can be depended upon. One should also be able to conclude—or deny—that so much of the system has stood up under test that one has some confidence in even the untested lines in the network.

In addition to relatively delimited nomological networks surrounding *control* or *aspiration*, the Rorschach interpreter usually has an overriding theory of the test as a whole. This may be a psychoanalytic theory, a theory of perception and set, or a theory stated in terms of learned habit patterns. Whatever the theory of the interpreter, whenever he validates an inference from the system, he obtains some reason for added confidence in his overriding system. His total theory is not tested, however, by experiments dealing with only one limited set of constructs. The test developer must investigate far-separated, independent sections of the network. The more diversified the predictions the system is required to make, the greater confidence we can have that only minor parts of the system will later prove faulty. Here we begin to glimpse a logic to defend the judgment that the test and its whole interpretative system is valid at some level of confidence.

There are enthusiasts who would conclude from the foregoing paragraphs that since there is some evidence of correct, diverse predictions made from the Rorschach, the test as a whole can now be accepted as validated. This conclusion overlooks the negative evidence. Just one finding contrary to expectation, based on sound research, is sufficient to wash a whole theoretical structure away. Perhaps the remains can be salvaged to form a new structure. But this structure now must be exposed to fresh risks, and sound negative evidence will destroy it in turn. There is sufficient negative evidence to prevent acceptance of the Rorschach and its accompanying interpretative structures as a whole. So long as any aspects of the overriding theory stated for the test have been disconfirmed, this structure must be rebuilt.

Talk of areas and structures may seem not to recognize those who would interpret the personality "globally." They may argue that a test is best validated in matching studies. Without going into detailed questions of matching methodology, we can ask whether such a study validates the nomological network "as a whole." The judge does employ some network in arriving at his conception of his subject, integrating specific inferences from specific data. Matching studies, if successful, demonstrate only that each judge's interpretative theory has some validity, that it is not completely a fantasy. Very high consistency between judges is required to show that they are using the same network, and very high success in matching is required to show that the network is dependable.

If inference is less than perfectly dependable, we must know which aspects of the interpretative network are least dependable and which are most dependable. Thus, even if one has considerable confidence in a test "as a whole" because of frequent successful inferences, one still returns as an ultimate aim to the request of the Technical Recommendation for separate evidence on the validity of each type of inference to be made.

RECAPITULATION

Construct validation was introduced in order to specify types of research required in developing tests for which the conventional views on validation are inappropriate. Personality tests, and some tests of ability, are interpreted in terms of attributes for which there is no adequate criterion. This paper indicates what sorts of evidence can substantiate such an interpretation, and how such evidence is to be interpreted. The following points made in the discussion are particularly significant.

1. A construct is defined implicitly by a network of associations or pro-

positions in which it occurs. Constructs employed at different stages of research vary in definiteness.

2. Construct validation is possible only when some of the statements in the network lead to predicted relations among observables. While some observables may be regarded as "criteria," the construct validity of the criteria themselves is regarded as under investigation.

3. The network defining the construct, and the derivation leading to the predicted observation, must be reasonably explicit so that validating evidence may be properly interpreted.

4. Many types of evidence are relevant to construct validity, including content validity, interitem correlations, intertest correlations, test-"criterion" correlations, studies of stability over time, and stability under experimental intervention. High correlations and high stability may constitute either favorable or unfavorable evidence for the proposed interpretation, depending on the theory surrounding the construct.

5. When a predicted relation fails to occur, the fault may lie in the proposed interpretation of the test or in the network. Altering the network so that it can cope with the new observations is, in effect, redefining the construct. Any such new interpretation of the test must be validated by a fresh body of data before being advanced publicly. Great care is required to avoid substituting a posteriori rationalizations for proper validation.

6. Construct validity cannot generally be expressed in the form of a single simple coefficient. The data often permit one to establish upper and lower bounds for the proportion of test variance which can be attributed to the construct. The integration of diverse data into a proper interpretation cannot be an entirely quantitative process.

7. Constructs may vary in nature from those very close to "pure description" (involving little more than extrapolation of relations among observation-variables) to highly theoretical constructs involving hypothesized entities and processes, or making identifications with constructs of other sciences.

8. The investigation of a test's construct validity is not essentially different from the general scientific procedures for developing and confirming theories.

Without in the least *advocating* construct validity as preferable to the other three kinds (concurrent, predictive, content), we do believe it imperative that psychologists make a place for it in their methodological thinking, so that its rationale, its scientific legitimacy, and its dangers may become explicit and familiar. This would be preferable to the widespread current tendency to engage in what actually amounts to construct validation research and use of constructs in practical testing, while talking an "operational" methodology which, if adopted, would force research into a mold it does not fit.

References

1. American Psychological Association. *Ethical standards of psychologists.* Washington, D.C.: American Psychological Association, Inc. 1953.

2. Anastasi, Anne. The concept of validity in the interpretation of test scores. *Educ. psychol. Measmt.*, 1950, **10**, 67–78.

3. Bechtoldt, H. P. Selection. In S. S. Stevens (Ed.), *Handbook of experimental psychology.* New York: Wiley, 1951. Pp. 1237–1267.

4. Beck, L. W. Constructions and inferred entities. *Phil. Sci.*, 1950, 17. Reprinted in H. Fegl and M. Brodbeck (Eds.), *Readings in the philosophy of science.* New York: Appleton-Century-Crofts, 1953. Pp. 368–381.

5. Blair, W. R. N. A comparative study of disciplinary offenders and non-offenders in the Canadian Army. *Canad. J. Psychol.*, 1950, **4**, 49–62.

6. Braithwaite, R. B. *Scientific explanation.* Cambridge: Cambridge Univer. Press, 1953.

7. Carnap, R. Empiricism, semantics, and ontology. *Rév. int. de Phil.*, 1950, II, 20–40. Reprinted in P. P. Wiener (Ed.), *Readings in philosophy of science,* New York: Scribner's, 1953. Pp. 509–521.

8. Carnap, R. *Foundations of logic and mathematics. International encyclopedia of unified science,* I, No. 3. Pages 56–69 reprinted as "The interpretation of physics" in H. Feigl and M. Brodbeck (Eds.), *Readings in the philosophy of science.* New York: Appleton-Century-Crofts, 1953. Pp. 309–318.

9. Child, I. L. Personality. *Annu. Rev. Psychol.*, 1954, **5**, 149–171.

10. Chyatte, C. Psychological characteristics of a group of professional actors. *Occupations*, 1949, **27**, 245–250.

11. Cronbach, L. J. *Essentials of psychological testing.* New York: Harper, 1949.

12. Cronbach, L. J. Further evidence on response sets and test design. *Educ. psychol. Measmt*, 1950, **10**, 3–31.

13. Cronbach, L. J. Coefficient alpha and the internal structure of tests. *Psychometrika*, 1951, **16**, 297–335.

14. Cronbach, L. J. Processes affecting scores on "understanding of others" and "assumed similarity." *Psychol. Bull.*, 1955, **52**, 177–193.

15. Cronbach, L. J. The counselor's problems from the perspective of comunication theory. In Vivian H. Hewer (Ed.), *New perspectives in counseling.* Minneapolis: Univ. of Minnesota Press, 1955.

16. Cureton, E. E. Validity. In E. F. Lindquist (Ed.), *Educational measurement.* Washington, D. C.: American Council on Education, 1950. Pp. 621–695.

17. Damrin, Dora E. A comparative study of information derived from a diagnostic problem-solving test by logical and factorial methods of scoring. Unpublished doctor's dissertation, Univer. of Illinois, 1952.

18. Eysenck, H. J. Criterion analysis—an application of the hypothetico-deductive method in factor analysis. *Psychol. Rev.* 1950, **57**, 38–53.

19. Feigl, H. Existential hypotheses. *Phil. Sci.*, 1950, **17**, 35–62.

20. Feigl, H. Confirmability and confirmation. *Rév. int. de Phil.*, 1951, 5, 1–12. Reprinted in P. P. Weiner (Ed.), *Readings in philosophy of science.* New York: Scribner's, 1953. Pp. 522–530.

21. Gaylord, R. H. Conceptual consistency and criterion equivalence: a dual approach to criterion analysis. Unpublished manuscript (PRB Research Note No. 17). Copies obtainable from ASTIA-DSC, AD-21 440.

22. Goodenough, Florence L. *Mental testing.* New York: Rinehart, 1950.

23. Gough, H. G., McClosky, H., & Meehl, P. E. A personality scale for social responsibility. *J. abnorm. soc. Psychol.*, 1952, **47**, 73–80.

24. Gough, H. G., McKee, M. G., & Yandell, R. J. Adjective check list analyses of a number of selected psychometric and assessment variables. Unpublished manuscript. Berkeley: IPAR, 1953.

25. Guilford, J. P. New standards for test evaluation. *Educ. psychol. Measmt.* 1946, **6**, 427–439.

26. Guilford, J. P. Factor analysis in a test-development program. *Psychol. Rev.*, 1948, **55**, 79–94.

27. Gulliksen, H. Intrinsic validity. *Amer. Psychologist*, 1950, **5**, 511–517.

28. Hathaway, S. R., & Monachesi, E. D. *Analyzing and predicting juvenile delinquency with the MMPI.* Minneapolis: Univer. of Minnesota Press, 1953.

29. Hempel, C. G. Problems and changes in the empiricist criterion of meaning. *Rév. int. de Phil.*, 1950, **4**, 41–63. Reprinted in L. Linsky, *Semantics and the philosophy of language.* Urbana: Univer. of Illinois Press, 1952. Pp. 163–185.

30. Hempel, C. G. *Fundamentals of concept formation in empirical science.* Chicago: Univer. of Chicago Press, 1952.

31. Horst, P. The prediction of personal adjustment. *Soc. Sci. Res. Council Bull.*, 1941, No. 48.

32. Hovey, H. B. MMPI profiles and personality characteristics. *J. consult. Psychol.*, 1953, **17**, 142–146.

33. Jenkins, J. G. Validity for what? *J. consult. Psychol.*, 1946, **10**, 93–98.

34. Kaplan, A. Definition and specification of meaning. *J. Phil.*, 1946, **43**, 281–288.

35. Kelly, E. L. Theory and techniques of assessment. *Annu. Rev. Psychol.*, 1954, **5**, 281–311.

36. Kelly, E. L., & Fiske, D. W. *The prediction of performance in clinical psychology*. Ann Arbor: Univer. of Michigan Press, 1951.

37. Kneale, W. *Probability and induction*. Oxford: Clarendon Press, 1949. Pages 92–110 reprinted as "Induction, explanation, and transcendent hypotheses" in H. Feigl and M. Brodbeck (Eds.), *Readings in the philosophy of science*. New York: Appleton-Century-Crofts, 1953. Pp. 353–367.

38. Lindquist, E. F. *Educational measurement*. Washington, D.C.: American Council on Education, 1950.

39. Lucas, C. M. Analysis of the relative movement test by a method of individual interviews. *Bur. Naval Personnel Res. Rep.*, Contract Nonr-694 (00), NR 151-13, Educational Testing Service, March 1953.

40. MacCorquodale, K., & Meehl, P. E. On a distinction between hypothetical constructs and intervening variables, *Psychol. Rev.*, 1948, **55**, 95 107.

41. Macfarlane, Jean W. Problems of validation inherent in projective methods. *Amer. J. Orthopsychiat.*, 1942, **12**, 405–410.

42. McKinley, J. C., & Hathaway, S. R. The MMPI: V. Hysteria, hypomania, and psychopathic deviate. *J. appl. Psychol.* 1944, **28**, 153–174.

43. McKinley, J. C. Hathaway, S. R., & Meehl, P. E. The MMPI: VI. The K scale. *J. consult. Psychol.*, 1948, **12**, 20–31.

44. Meehl, P. E. A simple algebraic development of Horst's suppressor variables. *Amer. J. Psychol.*, 1945, **58**, 550–554.

45. Meehl, P. E. An investigation of a general normality or control factor in personality testing. *Psychol. Monogr.*, 1945, **59**, No. 4 (Whole No. 274).

46. Meehl, P. E. *Clinical vs. statistical prediction*. Minneapolis: Univer. of Minnesota Press, 1954.

47. Meehl, P. E., & Rosen, A. Antecedent probability and the efficiency of psychometric signs, patterns or cutting scores. *Psychol. Bull.*, 1955, **52**, 194–216.

48. *Minnesota Hunter Casualty Study*. St. Paul: Jacob Schmidt Brewing Company, 1954.

49. Mosier, C. I. A critical examination of the concepts of face validity. *Educ. psychol. Measmt*, 1947, **7**, 191–205.

50. Mosier, C. I. Problems and designs of cross-validation. *Educ. psychol. Measmt*, 1951, **11**, 5–12.

51. Pap, A. Reduction-sentences and open concepts. *Methodos*, 1953, **5**, 3–30.

52. Peak, Helen. Problems of objective observation. In L. Festinger and

D. Katz (Eds.), *Research methods in the behavioral sciences.* New York: Dryden Press, 1953. Pp. 243–300.

53. Porteus, S. D. *The Porteus maze test and intelligence.* Palo Alto: Pacific Books, 1950.

54. Roessel, F. P. MMPI results for high school drop-outs and graduates. Unpublished doctor's dissertation, Univer. of Minnesota, 1954.

55. Sellars, W. S. Concepts as involving laws and inconceivable without them. *Phil. Sci.,* 1948, **15**, 287–315.

56. Sellars, W. S. Some reflections on language games. *Phil. Sci.,* 1954, **21**, 204–228.

57. Spiker, C. C., & McCandless, B. R. The concept of intelligence and the philosophy of science. *Psychol. Rev.,* 1954, **61**, 255–267.

58. Technical recommendations for psychological tests and diagnostic techniques: preliminary proposal. *Amer. Psychologist,* 1952, **7**, 461–476.

59. Technical recommendations for psychological tests and diagnostic techniques. *Psychol. Bull. Supplement,* 1954, **51**, 2, Part 2, 1–38.

60. Thurstone, L. L. The criterion problem in personality research. *Psychometric Lab. Rep.,* No. 78. Chicago: Univer. of Chicago, 1952.

47. CONSTRUCT VALIDITY: A CRITIQUE

Harold P. Bechtoldt

In order to accomplish more effective communication between test publishers and test users, a series of "essential," "very desirable," and "desirable" characteristics of the content of test manuals was provided in 1954 by the APA Committee on Psychological Tests (APA, 1954). In the following year two members of the committee, L. J. Cronbach and P. E. Meehl (1955), prepared an extended statement on the topic of construct validity, a term introduced in the *Technical Recommendations* to refer to one of the several distinctions noted in the use of the term validity. It should be emphasized that these distinctions refer only to ways of talking about tests and test performances and not to empirical questions. However, the conclusions, generalizations, or predictions arising from empirical investigations are involved since such statements influence both the design of subsequent experiments and the development of theoretical formulations. It is, therefore, appropriate to take note of the way psychologists speak about "construct validity."

Methods of protecting test consumers from a laissez-faire business philosophy are not being considered at the moment. While the *Technical Recommendations* are clearly restricted to commercial nonresearch devices, the concept of construct validity has been presented as of fundamental importance to many psychologists. It has been said that "Construct validation is important at times for every sort of psychological test: aptitude, achievement, interest, and so

SOURCE. Bechtoldt, Harold P., "Construct Validity: A Critique," *American Psychologist*, **14**, 1959. Reprinted with permission of American Psychological Association. Copyright © 1959 by The American Psychological Association.

on. . . . Much current research on tests of personality is construct validation . . ." (Cronbach & Meehl, 1955, pp. 282–283). The article dealing with the elaboration of the notion of construct validity has been termed "one of the most important papers for the differential psychologist appearing during the span of this [1954–1956] review" (Jenkins & Lykken, 1957, p. 81). In further support of this position, we find another writer stating: "since predictive, and content validities are all essentially *ad hoc*, construct validity is the whole of validity from a scientific point of view" (Loevinger, 1957, p. 636). Still a fourth very favorable comment states: "Construct validity is an important new concept which has immediate implications for both psychometrician and experimentalist" (Jessor & Hammond, 1957, p. 161).

The primary concern of this paper is with the formulation of construct validity as presented in the several articles noted above. A major objective is to consider critically, but necessarily incompletely, the suggestion that psychologists make a place for the notion of construct validity in their methodological thinking. Some of the "dangers" associated with the concept will be discussed as well as the implication that an "operational methodology" is less appropriate for research involving test data, at least in practical testing[1] (Cronbach & Meehl, 1955, p. 300).

Since this is a type of philosophical treatment by a psychologist who is not a philosopher, the philosophical orientation of this analysis must be made clear. The philosophical position taken here is that of one of the branches of logical positivism, sometimes termed logical empiricism, logical behaviorism, or neobehaviorism. Most psychologists are probably familiar with this philosophical point of view as presented by Bergmann (1943, 1951, 1953, 1954, 1955, 1956, 1957), by Bergmann and Spence (1941), and by Brodbeck (1957, 1958a, 1958b) and from articles by psychologists such as Spence (1944, 1948, 1957, 1958) or Spiker and McCandless (1954). It must also be pointed out that this philosophical position differs, with respect to several central issues, from that taken by Cronbach and Meehl who have used the writings of Beck (1950), Carnap (1953), Feigl (1950, 1951), Hempel (1952), Pap (1953), and Sellars (1948) among others in presenting their formulation of construct validity. The marshaling of references and appeal to authority, however, are of limited value in science and perhaps even in the philosophy of science. The crucial question in science is the matter of empirical laws and the relations among them. The appraisal of a philosophical analysis of science would be in terms of the success achieved in the clarification of the knowledge and methods used by scientists.

---

[1] Cronbach and Meehl explicitly state they are not advocating construct validation over other methods (1955, p. 284, 300), but their treatment is somewhat inconsistent on this point. The other papers noted above are definitely favorable toward construct validity as the preferred concept.

Specifically, it is proposed to use the terms of one branch of logical positivism in analyzing what has been said and done about construct validity in terms of two questions:

1. How are tests and testing used in psychology?
2. What relation, if any, does the use of tests and testing have to the notion of construct validity?

TESTS AND TESTING

Although neither the *Technical Recommendations* nor subsequent elaborations specify a definition of the term "test," a statement from representatives of the APA to the Congress of the United States is available (APA, 1958). In a discussion of aptitudes and abilities, it is stated that "Psychological tests are nothing more than careful observations of actual performance under standard conditions." Testing, then, would refer to the process of obtaining these observations. The distinguishing phrase ("careful observations of performance under standard conditions" will, therefore, be substituted for the possibly more emotionally toned words "psychological tests."

As given, this definition of tests is a very general one. The definition carries no implication as to the use to be made of the observations as would terms such as aptitude, diagnostic, or achievement. The statement further specifies nothing about the classification of content. No restrictions are stated as to method of responding nor of classifying responses as to any of their many conceivable properties such as presence or absence, rate, style or quality, persistence, intensity or amplitude, accuracy or relative probability of occurrence. Conceivably, the careful observations could be obtained with complete mechanical control of the stimuli, the time intervals, the feedback or reinforcements, and the recording of responses.

This definition of "psychological test" states the basic preliminary point of this discussion. "Careful observations of performance under standard conditions" are used by psychologists everywhere: in the laboratory, in the clinic, in the schools, and in industry. There are no fundamental distinctions between "psychological test" observations per se and any other equally systematic controlled observations of performance used by psychologists.

The first question can, therefore, be phrased as: "How are careful observations of performance under standard conditions used in psychology?" The work of nearly all psychologists represents two distinctive ways in which observations of performance are used. Stated in the language of the logical behaviorists, these uses are, first, in the definition of psychological concepts of varying degree of abstractness and, second, in the statement of laws about concepts and of relations among such laws. The laws, or generalizations, are statements about how the referents of some concepts affect other concepts. Each such law in psychology regularly involves one concept referring to properties of behavior and one or more other concepts which may refer to features, past and/or present, of the organism's physical environment, to physiological states or events within their bodies, or to other concepts defined by experimentally independent observations of behavior (Bergmann, 1951, 1953, 1957; Brodbeck, 1957, 1958a; Spence, 1957).

In the terminology of the philosophy of science being used, sets of these laws or generalizations relating defined concepts, if deductively connected, are called theories with some of the laws called the axioms, logically implying other laws, termed theorems. As a goal for psychology, the development of systems of deductively connected empirical laws is generally accepted, and the quantitative comprehensive theories of physics have been held up as prototypes of those for psychology. However, it is also generally agreed that in psychology we have no comprehensive theories as the term is used in physics—certainly no axiomatized system like that used in atomic physics, nor even a start in the development of the very general laws required for comprehensive theories (Cronbach & Meehl, 1955; Spence, 1957, 1958).

An answer to the first question of how psychological tests are used in psychology has now been indicated. Psychological tests like any other "careful observations of performance" are used in the definition of concepts varying in abstractness; in the development of psychological laws, i.e., those concerned with the prediction of behavior and of changes in behavior; and in the development of limited sets of deductively interrelated empirical laws. It is contended that this formulation of how observations of performance are *currently* used, and will be used for some time, is inclusive, logically sound, experimentally useful, and sufficient.

CONSTRUCT VALIDITY AND TESTS

Consider now the second question which deals with the relation between the careful observations of performance obtained by the use of tests on the one hand and the formulation of construct validity on the other. From the viewpoint of logical positivism sketched in outline form above, what can be said about construct validity?

Although no explicit definition of construct validity is offered by any of the writers dealing with this topic, a number of statements are made from which one is to induce the class characteristics:

> Construct validation is involved whenever a test is to be interpreted as a measure of some attribute or quality which is not "operationally defined." The problem faced by the investigator is, "What constructs

account for variance in test performance?" . . . Construct validity is not to be identified solely by particular investigative procedures, but by the orientation of the investigator (Cronbach & Meehl, 1955, p. 282).

Construct validity is ordinarily studied when the tester has no definite criterion measure of the quality with which he is concerned, and must use indirect measures. Here the trait or quality underlying the test is of central importance, rather than either the test behavior or the scores on the criteria (APA, 1954, p. 14).

An answer to the second question will involve consideration, among others, of the above illustrative statements.

Operational Definitions

Construct validation is introduced by Cronbach and Meehl as being involved whenever a test is to be interpreted as a measure of some attribute or quality which is not operationally defined, with considerable emphasis placed on the rejection of the necessity for operationally defined concepts or constructs. From the view here taken, there either are no cases to which construct validity would apply in an embryonic empirical science, excepting only the simple characters being named by "undefined descriptive terms" (Bergmann, 1957, p. 14); or a different definition of "operationally defined" is used; or the discussion is not germane to an empirical science of psychology.

Can the discrepancy be a matter of the simple notion of an operational definition? An operational definition is simply a verbal statement of the *if-then* type specifying the observable conditions or rules of procedure under which the term is to be applied in the definition of descriptive or empirical concepts or variables (Bergmann, 1957; Brodbeck, 1957). The only contributions made by operational definitions to an empirical science are those of clarity, objectivity, and precision or accuracy of statement; such definitions enable one to determine, and eventually eliminate, the "ignorance" and "error" represented in any "imperfect" formulation. Terms like hostility, aggression, psychopathic deviate, intelligence, and mechanical ability have some referents and some rules for their use. They are operationally defined in any empirical study, but the specification for their use may change with time. Without specification of rules, or changes therein, for using such defined terms, neither accurate communication nor precise experimentation is possible in any science.

The process of developing definitions for a concept is, in actual practice, neither simple nor unerring. Any creative investigator "breaking ground" will usually have one or more hunches or guesses about the way two or more things in which he is interested might influence one another. As long as the notion remains so personal, so private, and so imprecise that the referents of terms cannot be designated nor the necessary conditions considered as achieved, the guesses are outside the realm of empirical science. When, however, an investigator states explicitly a set of rules or conditions for the application of his terms, the statements are of scientific interest. The explicit statement constitutes an initial definition of the concept; but like any formulation, the initial one may well be useless, somewhat useful, or entirely satisfactory. Those definitions that are of limited usefulness will be re-examined in terms of the available empirical evidence. One common course of action taken in experimental psychology to increase the usefulness of a concept involves redefining the notion by a second, but different, explicit statement (Spence & Ross, 1959). After several experimental studies have resulted in one or more changes of definition, one might say the early concepts were imprecise, incomplete, vague, or of limited usefulness. But, strictly speaking, each change of definition introduces a new concept. These definitions are *not* alternative definitions of the same concept.

The term "vague" so often applied to "imprecise" concepts requires further comment. Vague may refer to that which has not been defined, to the ambiguous, or to the "private" and "subjective." Or the term may refer to an incomplete explicit definition used in an early statement of a concept. These referents are not identical. Dissatisfaction expressed by investigators with an initial "rough," incomplete definition is a reaction against ignorance and error rather than against a strategy of investigation. To admit ignorance as a temporary state of science is one thing. To raise vagueness or lack of definition to the central status of a methodological principle is another. The "constructs" of construct validity appear to be "vague," open, and "not explicitly defined" as a matter of principle rather than as a matter of ignorance.

The statement that changes in the rules properly imply the use of a new word or a subscript to the old word has met with definite objection when applied to the area of intelligence tests (Jenkins & Lykken, 1957, p. 88). However, the fear that such practice prevents the gradual evolution of ideas is baseless; the logical empiricists recognize the gradual and continuous replacement by scientists of less useful concepts with more useful ones (Bergmann, 1943). At each stage of development of a concept, however, the rules for the current usage of the term are to be stated.

In the *Technical Recommendations* (APA, 1954, p. 15), it is stated with emphasis that "*behavior-relevance* in a construct is not logically the same as *behavior-equivalence*" and that psychological constructs need not be *equivalent* to any direct operational behavior measure. Since concepts and, for the moment, constructs may vary in degree of abstractness or length of the definitional chains, there may indeed be many steps between the undefined basic terms, possibly including direct or immediate observations of behavior, and highly abstract defined concepts.

The distinction between undefined and defined descriptive terms is technically based on the principle of (direct) acquaintance, undefined terms naming characters or properties with which the person is directly acquainted. All other descriptive terms are defined (Bergmann, 1957, p. 14–15). The definition, i.e., the conditional features of the *if-then* statement, is reasonably simple for the case of the "response time" property of the eyelid reflex, of a finger withdrawal, or of some vocalization. The definitional operations are somewhat different, perhaps more complex, but still expressed in terms of manifest behavior, when the W, $F+$, or d responses among others to each Rorschach card are evaluated. Meehl (1956) has reported how Halbower used fairly complex and involved procedures to define a few objective personality descriptions in terms of the observed responses of patients to the MMPI. Other "response defined" and rather "abstract" concepts of interest to psychologists include most of the "psychological qualities" or "attributes" or traits presented in the discussions of construct validity (Cronbach, 1957; Cronbach & Meehl, 1955).

Since nearly all defined psychological concepts require very complicated definitional chains, the concepts are indeed not "behaviorally equivalent" if we restrict "behavior-equivalence," for example, to speed or accuracy of any one response. The concepts are, however, defined in terms of properties of observable behavior under specified conditions and in accordance with specified procedures. If the APA test committee were restricting the definition of terms to the "immediately, or almost immediately, observable" characters or properties of manifest behavior, its dissatisfaction with "operational definitions" would be understandable. This condition would imply a definition of "operationally defined" which is far more restrictive and limited than that recommended by the logical behaviorists (Bergmann, 1955). However, if the advocates of construct validity are contending that explicit definitions of terms in empirical science are not essential, then the issue is basic; such disagreement is one that has both "philosophical" and scientific overtones.

Characteristics of Constructs

Although the matter of requiring single explicit definitions of concepts or terms may, or may not, be a point of basic disagreement, an issue does seem to arise in connection with the term "construct." That the notion of "construct" is fundamental to the discussion of construct validity seems indicated (APA, 1954; Cronbach & Meehl, 1955; Jenkins & Lykken, 1957; Jessor & Hammond, 1957). A construct is presented by Cronbach and Meehl as involving at least three characteristics. First, it is a *postulated attribute* assumed to be reflected in test performances; second, it has *predictive* properties; and third, the *meaning* of a construct is given by the laws in which it occurs with the result that clarity of knowledge of the construct is a positive function of the completeness of that set of laws, termed the nomological net.

Meaning.   The third of these characteristics uses the term "meaning" which has at least two technical interpretations. On this point, disagreement among philosophers of science again will be found. The logical empiricists have distinguished between two technical usages of the term: one to refer to the operational definition or empirical referent of a concept, i.e., the "meaning" of a concept, and the second usage to refer to the usefulness or "significance" of a concept as indicated by the theoretical or empirical laws into which it enters (Bergmann, 1951, 1957; Brodbeck, 1957). The logical behaviorists say that a defined concept may be without significance, but significant concepts must be defined. From the logical behaviorists' point of view, the third characteristic above states that concepts vary in usefulness or significance with the greater significance associated with both the number and theoretical or empirical implications of the laws into which they enter.

The development and use of the Taylor Manifest Anxiety Scale (MAS) provides an example of the distinction between meaning and significance. The "meaning" of "manifest anxiety" is given by the procedures for presenting the selected verbal statements or items and for combining the weighted responses of each subject. The resulting score then defines (is the meaning of) the variable "manifest anxiety." Implicit in the defining procedures are such requirements as: to be used with English-speaking adults having a United States cultural background, etc. The usefulness or significance of the MAS score depends on the relations of the MAS with other variables. Two kinds of relations involving the MAS scores have been investigated: one deals with certain drive properties of the MAS variable in experimental studies of simple learning phenomena, and the other involves the congruence of two or more response defined variables both including in the title the word "anxiety." Since both types of relations have been shown to be statistically significant in two or more studies, the MAS can be said to have some degree of usefulness or significance (Spence, 1958; Taylor, 1951, 1953). If no theoretical or empirical relation could be demonstrated between the MAS and any other variable, the MAS would be said to be well defined or meaningful but without significance.

Significance and Validity.   For a number of years one aspect of the "significance" of a variable has been fairly precisely expressed by the notion of "empirical validity." Empirical validity refers to the results of empirical tests of relations between a dependent or predictor measures. There will, of course, be as many indices of validity of a variable as there are dependent variables with which it can be paired (Anastasi, 1950; Bechtoldt, 1951; Cronbach, 1949). A determination of the usefulness or empirical validity of the MAS as a predictor of some other variable also entitled "anxiety" and defined by psychiatric ratings or by responses to other sets of stimuli can be made. But such an appraisal is not an index of the significance of the MAS as a drive variable in Spence's (1958) theory of performance in simple learning situations.

Yet, the "meaning" of the concept of manifest anxiety, according to the formulation of construct validity, is to be given by the laws into which it enters. Which of the many laws, or sets of laws, are to be used? All of them or only those related by a "theory," a theory some writer may prefer, for example, to the one initially formulated? In construct validity terms the concept may have no "meaning" or some "meaning," the appraisal depending on an arbitrary or even capricious selection of a "theory" and of the dependent variables with which the given variable or concept is paired. The logical empiricists would simply say the defined concept is related to some variables but not to others or that the concept enters into some laws but not others. The confusion resulting from the use of the single word "meaning" for both definition and significance seems unnecessary and undesirable.

Constructs and "the Criterion." The meaning-significance confusion also occurs in the statements of the relation of constructs to "criteria." It is suggested (APA, 1954, p. 14; Cronbach & Meehl, 1955, p. 282) that construct validity is to be investigated whenever no criterion or universe of content is accepted as entirely adequate to define the quality to be measured. A failure to separate the defining operations, including content restrictions, from the empirical matter of relations with other variables is evident. In accordance with the construct validity notion, a quality or variable can be defined, when a criterion is available, by the relation of the test to the criterion rather than by the operations of the test itself. But when no criterion is available, the quality is not defined; instead, the construct validity of the test is to be investigated. Three points need to be made with regard to the central position of the "criterion" in this decision making process. First, a criterion measure is a behavioral or response defined variable used as the dependent variable in an investigation. As a behavioral measure, some sequence of operations involving "careful observations of performance" is selected or developed at some (usually earlier) time as the conditional features of the definition. Second, the defining operations are in no way intrinsically different from those used to define any other behavioral variable such as one utilized, for example, as an independent variable. Third, if a variable is *accepted* as the dependent variable, i.e., as the criterion, then indeed a status difference may be created which is reflected in several technical procedures such as the assignment of errors of prediction to the dependent variable and the weighting of the independent variables so as to minimize the errors of prediction. But in no other way is a criterion variable any different from any other test or response defined variable.

Differences among experimenters in the types of prediction they wish to make and in the problems of interest to them are reflected in the emphasis placed on the criterion. In situations where the experimenter is task oriented or problem oriented, as is the case in most applied studies and in "practical testing," the dependent variable would be *defined first* and perhaps given status by *naming* it "the criterion," whether intermediate or final. In such admittedly practical problems, the criterion-orientation seems entirely reasonable. The question asked is of the form: "What defined variables of any kind can be used to predict performance on the criterion?" Those variables that show significant relations with the criterion are said to be "valid" (useful) predictors. No claim to theoretical usefulness is involved; the demonstration of one or more stable empirical relations is both necessary and sufficient (Bechtoldt, 1951). In other experimental situations in which the experimenter is interested in a variable per se or as a part of some theoretical formulation, i.e., when he can be said to be variable oriented, no special status is given to the dependent variable of behavior. In this second case the dependent variable, in fact, is usually selected or developed *after* the independent variable is defined. A "criterion" or behavioral measure will be selected in the second case so that the effect of the independent or experimental variable may be exhibited if the variable enters into the theory or nomological net as hypothesized. The term validity properly could also be applied to such cases in precisely the same sense as in the problem oriented situation. However, the experimental psychologists, who have long used this variable oriented approach and research procedure, have not found the naming of such relations necessary.

Prediction.   The second characteristic of a construct appears at first glance to give no occasion for concern. Cronbach and Meehl state (1955, p. 284):

> A construct has certain associated meanings carried in statements of this general character: Persons who possess this attribute will, in situation X, act in manner Y (with a stated probability).

The "associated meanings" appear to include the class of "test interpretations," i.e., various predictions, as well as whatever "accounts for variance in test performance." The form of the statement is that of the common predictive model. Such statements are laws. The second characteristic asserts that constructs must enter into laws.

Now the notion of explanation in science is often presented, in part, in terms of such a predictive model. If the predictions are logically deduced from other laws and are sustained experimentally, the new observations are said to be "understandable," to be explained by the "axioms" or premises of the set (Bergmann, 1957). However, many predictions in psychology are not deduced from a set of premises but are essentially statements of the reproducibility of previous empirical results. For such "predictions" as well as for "deduced" statements, an empirical test of the accuracy of the prediction regarding behavior Y requires only rules, operations, or procedures for determining, first, whether "manner Y" occurs; second, whether situation X is present; and, third, whether the persons with whom we are dealing have the attribute.

For these empirical checks, the concepts must be defined. Every example used by Cronbach and Meehl to elucidate how construct validation can be accomplished requires some definition of the attribute in behavioral terms. The well-known procedures for evaluating changes in a dependent variable as a function of one or more independent variables are exemplified by their illustrations. In fact, the several recommended validation procedures of construct validity are those regularly used by research psychologists investigating hypotheses involving psychological concepts. It is, therefore, considered that, *in practice*, the second characteristic of lawful relations is empirically sound; nothing new or confusing is involved.

Postulated Attributes.   The first of the three characteristics of a construct, however, is considered as a serious source of confusion. The statement is that a construct is a postulated attribute assumed to be reflected in test performance. This notion also appears in such statements as: the trait or quality underlying the test is of central importance, rather than either the test behavior or the scores on the criteria (APA, 1954, p. 14) ; or "the" or the "real" trait is being "indirectly" or "not really" measured by the test performance (Campbell & Fiske, 1959; Loevinger, 1957). The "postulation"and "assumption" features of this characteristic are more accurately labeled hunches, guesses, or working hypotheses about relations among concepts, i.e., about laws or sets of laws termed theories. The third characteristic states that a hypothesis or even a theory about test behavior has been formulated.

As postulated attributes assumed to be reflected in test performance, many possible sets of words or symbols, often referred to as "theories" or "models" (Brodbeck, 1958b) may be generated by an ingenious, talented, and persistent writer. As literary or mathematical exercises, they may indeed be accurate, elegant, and internally consistent. The question, however, is the relevance of these formulations to behavior and to experimental investigation of the statements. If the constructs or psychological attributes are response defined, either by a simple or complicated series of *if-then* statements, and if the behaviors involved in these definitions are the performances under consideration, then the statements are not hypotheses about empirical relations but are definitions (Bergmann, 1957). Essentially, such statements apply new names and/or transformations to old things. A "construct," in such cases, is a defined concept or variable, values of which are assigned to an individual on the basis of "careful observations of his performance under standard conditions." That "ability" is so defined has been noted by Lord (1952) who states:

> Since, in the final analysis, the only observable variables under
> consideration are the item responses, any operational definition of ability

for present purposes must consist of a statement of a relationship between ability and item responses (p. 4).

Nearly all postulated constructs listed in the papers on construct validity are also of the defined type. It is here suggested that a considerable number, if not all, of the so-called theoretical formulations in psychology dealing with postulated attributes simply use complex definitional transformations of a person's performance as a substitute for an empirical theory. Such transformations indeed may prove to be useful in "practical" situations involving communications with clients and employers. The new names and related hunches (surplus meanings) also may reduce (or increase) the transformations as such are neither theories nor laws. The transformations provide only definitions of concepts.

The possibility of psychologists confusing tautologies with empirical or theoretical relations was recognized by the APA test committee (1954) and by Cronbach and Meehl (1955). In several statements dealing with the nomological net, they insist upon "explicit public steps of inference," upon "contact with observations," and upon "accuracy of prediction" as the final test of a theory. It is also clear that both Cronbach and Meehl favor testing directly or indirectly the hypotheses of the network. However, more than earnest requests for logically correct deductions having some contact with empirical observations is necessary in extending the important but difficult process of building an empirical theory of behavior that will indicate how certain variables may account for variance in test performance. As shown below, the formulation of construct validity can be interpreted as making less of a contribution to the development of such a theory than does an empirically oriented methodology using explicit operational definitions of the variables.

Variables Affecting Behavior

What can be said as to the variables affecting any given behavior, including test performance? It has been demonstrated empirically that behavior is influenced by the amount of formal or informal practice or training or similar materials or methods of response. Strong response tendencies and habits of acquiescence or of avoidance of painful or noxious stimuli would be expected to affect behavior in many given situations. Characteristics of the examiner, of the cultural setting, or of the physiological states of the organism may lead to temporary or persistent behaviors under specified conditions. Surely the formulation of the basic concepts assumed to be reflected in test performance must include reference to such conditions and to other concepts defined by various experimental manipulations or operations. Such empirical concepts are appropriate answers to the question: "What constructs account for variance in test performance?" (Cronbach & Meehl, 1955, p. 282). That response defined variables, such as traits, are emphasized in the papers on construct validity as examples of the basic explanatory concepts probably is a reflection of the lack of control and of knowledge of the experiential history of the subjects used in studies involving human behavior. This lack of knowledge and lack of control of the subjects makes the task of developing laws and theories difficult, but probably not impossible.

As practical devices for the prediction of behavior, traits are clearly useful. That they may also be introduced into theoretical formulations of behavior has been shown by Taylor, Spence, and their associates in terms of the Manifest Anxiety Scale (Spence, 1958; Taylor. 1951). That the theoretical use of response defined variables is not widely understood is clear from several discussions dealing with the validity of the A scale (Bechtoldt, 1953b; Jenkins & Lykken, 1957; Jessor & Hammond, 1957; Kausler & Trapp, 1959; Spence, 1958). The confusion attendant upon the notion of construct validity will be obvious to the readers of these papers.

Traits in Psychological Theorizing

The chief difficulty of the trait or response defined variable approach in the development of theoretical formulations is the fact that a given behavior can arise from many different combinations of experimental conditions. These different conditions involve different concepts and different sets of explanatory laws. Any one of dozens of so-called theories or sets of explanatory constructs can be postulated or assumed and be "correct" in terms of the agreement between prediction and observation. Cronbach (1958) has recently added a valuable postscript to this point in a paper dealing with social-perception scores. He says:

> To interpret a score as a reflection of subtle interpersonal relations, or of covert attitudes about another person, may be to force complex meanings into a very simple phenomena (p. 353).

And then he adds:

> . . . if a behavior which looks like "projection" can arise out of many different processes, there is little point in trying to formulate hypotheses using the concept of "projection" (p. 375).

The point at issue is the development of a theory, or nomological net, using response defined variables which will have explanatory, predictive properties in specified situations. The theory would consist of a set of meaningful concepts and statements about how each given concept enters into specified laws. With such a theory, it is possible to determine whether a given concept, as defined, actually does enter into those laws. To the degree to which the predictions are sustained under the specified boundary conditions of the theory, the concept has significance and, apparently, "construct validity." Extending the hypotheses to include other concepts represents the process of "elaborating the nomological network" (Cronbach & Meehl, 1955, p. 290). Tests of the accuracy of the hypotheses will utilize, among others, the several experimental "validation" procedures of "construct validity." However, as a theory develops and achieves some limited successes, the number of inappropriate and irrelevant "tests" of stated hypotheses can be expected to grow also. Although labeled as "tests of the theory," such studies often represent unwarranted generalizations or improper extensions of the hypotheses or serious misconceptions about the concepts or the structure of the theory itself (Spence, 1958).

It must be emphasized that the private, inductive process involved in the invention of hypotheses, of ideas, or of concepts is not being questioned. There are neither rules nor deductive or inductive principles for the invention of fruitful hypotheses or the definition of significant concepts or the formulation of comprehensive theories. There are no logical reasons why some "theory" of behavior must *a priori* contain defined concepts expressing currently popular "common sense" notions or explanations. Nor are there any reasons to specify some test form or method of test (apparatus) construction as inherently useful or logically necessary in order for the test to be consistent with the procedures of construct validation or with the principles of logical behaviorism (for an opposing view, see Jessor & Hammond, 1957, p. 162).

Neither is there any justification for proposing the techniques of empirical, or "classical," validity as the sole methods to be used in selecting test items. The "adequacy" of any technique as a basis for test construction is a matter of the usefulness of the resulting test for empirical or theoretical purposes (for a contrary view, see Loevinger, 1957, p. 637). However, it is generally recognized that tests developed by utilizing relations with a "criterion" have at least some empirical significance, although they may, or may not, enter into any set of theoretical relations.

What is being questioned is the tendency to consider as a part of a public empirical science hunches involving "vague," ill-defined variables and relations between such variables, these hunches being derived primarily from the observed performance. The extent to which this activity is common in so-called "theorizing" in psychology can perhaps be judged from the frequency with which one encounters "deductions" involving sufficient, but not necessary, conditions such as the following taken from Johnson (1954):

> If "Old Dog Tray" was run through a large and powerful sausage-grinder, he is dead; he is dead, therefore, he was sausaged (p. 723).

Amusing? But what about this one?

> If a person has an over-compensated inferiority complex, he blusters,

is aggressive, domineering, and dogmatic; this man blusters, is aggressive, domineering and dogmatic; therefore, he has an inferiority complex.

The weaknesses and dangers of the postulational technique used *without* explicit definitions or empirical referents or "interpretations" for the premises can perhaps be even more clearly seen in the "valid" deduction and "contact with observations" implicit in this old syllogism: "Bread is made of stone, stone is good to eat; therefore, bread is good to eat." The conclusion is "true to fact," but the usual interpretations of the premises are not fulfilled.

Other instances of the postulation of explanatory constructs from behavior in a circular way are often found in discussions of mental abilities and of personality traits. Although frequent reference is made in the literature on construct validity to factor analysis, we find Thurstone quite clear on the point that an ability is *defined* by a specific test procedure and the method of scoring (Thurstone, 1947). Each test defines a separate ability; several tests involving the "same content" but different methods of presenting the stimuli or of responding likewise define different abilities. Thurstone also clearly *names* the "reference or common abilities" as those used to express the scores on the remaining tests in terms of an assumed linear function. The factors, for all experimental purposes, are literally defined as composite scores on specified subsets of tests in such batteries as the Primary Mental Abilities Tests (L. L. Thurstone & T. G. Thurstone, 1950) or the Educational Testing Service Kit of Reference Tests (French, 1954).

It is well to note, in connection with statements about factors, that the "interpretation" of the common source of variance of a "factor" and the "identification" of a "factor" in two different sets of tests as the "same factor" are both statements of hypotheses. Some "empirical generalization" of response tendencies over a variety of stimulus or treatment conditions which can be experimentally varied is implicit in both of these formulations. And, as for any other hypotheses, empirical tests of the predictions are called for. Such tests require unambiguous definitions of the "factors." That the empirical results may not sustain such predictions or "hypotheses" is logically sound and empirically consistent with observations (Bechtoldt, 1953a).

The danger of circularity of a formulation involving the notion of an "ability" or a "factor" as a concept can easily be eliminated; the "ability" variable can be defined in advance of an experiment through the use of observations experimentally independent of the behavior and hypothesis to be investigated. This "operational methodology" principle has been extended to some types of factor analysis investigations themselves with a restatement of the factor problem (Bechtoldt, 1958).

RELATIONS OF TESTS TO CONSTRUCT VALIDITY

An answer to the second question dealing with the relation between the use of tests and the notion of construct validity now can be stated. The relation is simply the linguistic one between any set of empirical observations on the one hand and any philosophy of science formulation on the other, and logically nothing more. The formulation of construct validity as a way of speaking is not restricted to, nor dependent upon, test concepts or performances; rather, the presentation is that of a general methodological viewpoint. For example, recent articles dealing, in part, with construct validity (Campbell & Fiske, 1959; Loevinger, 1957) have mentioned the correspondence between the construct validity formulation and that of "convergent operationalism" advocated for the definition of properties or characteristics of perception (Garner, Hake, & Eriksen, 1956). The use of multiple and implicit, rather than single explicit, definitions of terms and the meaning-significance confusion indeed are common to the two notions.

There is, however, a historical accident or coincidence that may account for the identification of construct validity with the area of psychological tests. General dissatisfaction has been expressed from time to time with the usefulness of empirical and statistical concepts of tests and testing; such concepts have been considered inadequate for professional psychological testing activities. Statements of such views tend to create a climate favorable to the acceptance of a new formulation, like construct validity, which emphasizes the language and problems of the practicing counselor or clinician. And the inception and development of the methodological viewpoint of construct validity, in addition, represents a laudable attempt to introduce into clinical and counseling testing activities some integration and understanding of the kind represented by the term theory. That construct validity was the creation of psychologists "interested in and sympathetic to constructs evidenced by performance but distinct from it" is the historical accident.

CONCLUSION

A major objective of this paper has been to consider critically the suggestion that psychologists make a place for the notion of construct validity in their methodological thinking. This suggestion is rejected for the several reasons given above. The renaming of the process of building a theory of behavior by the new term "construct validity" contributes nothing to the understanding of the process nor to the usefulness of the concepts. The introduction into discussions of psychological theorizing of the aspects of construct validity discussed in some detail above creates, at best, unnecessary confusion and, at the worst, a nonempirical, nonscientific approach to the study of behavior.

A supplementary objective has been to consider also the relative merits of construct validity and of logical behaviorism plus an operational methodology for the development of psychology as a science. It is suggested here that the terminology of logical behaviorism and the techniques of an "operational methodology" are to be preferred for the formulation and investigation of an empirical, deductive theory of (test) behavior. The statement that an " 'operational' methodology . . . would force research into a mold it does not fit" (Cronbach & Meehl, 1955, p. 300) is rejected as not consistent with published evidence. Considerable space has been devoted to showing how an "operational methodology" can be used in psychological research to improve both the "understanding" and the "prediction" of behavior.

It is, therefore, recommended that the formulation of construct validity, as presented in the several papers noted in this critique, be eliminated from further consideration as a way of speaking about psychological concepts, laws, and theories.

References

American Psychological Association, Committee on Psychological Tests. *Technical recommendations for psychological tests and diagnostic techniques.* Washington, D. C.: APA, 1954.

American Psychological Association. Report of testimony at a congressional hearing. *Amer. Psychologist*, 1958, **13**, 217–223.

Anastasi, Anne. The concept of validity in the interpretation of test scores. *Educ. psychol. Measmt.*, 1950, **10**, 67–78.

Bechtoldt, H. P. Selection. In S. S. Stevens (Ed.), *Handbook of experimental psychology.* New York: Wiley, 1951. Pp. 1237–1267.

Bechtoldt, H. P. Factor analysis of the Airman Classification Battery with civilian reference tests. *HRRC res. Bull.*, 1953, No. 53–59. (a)

Bechtoldt, H. P. Response defined anxiety and MMPI variables. *Iowa Acad. Sci.*, 1953, **60**, 495–499. (b)

Bechtoldt, H. P. Statistical tests of hypotheses in confirmatory factor analysis. *Amer. Psychologist*, 1958, **13**, 380. (Abstract)

Beck, L. W. Constructions and inferred entities. *Phil. Sci.*, 1950, **17**, (Reprinted: In H. Feigl & M. Brodbeck (Eds.), *Readings in the philosophy of science.* New York: Appleton-Century-Crofts, 1953. Pp. 368–381.)

Bergmann, G. Outline of an empiricist philosophy of physics. *Amer. J. Physics*, 1943, **11**, (Reprinted: In H. Feigl & M. Brodbeck (Eds.), *Readings in the philosophy of science.* New York: Appleton-Century-Crofts, 1953. Pp. 262–287.)

Bergmann, G. The logic of psychological concepts. *Phil. Sci.*, 1951, **18**, 93–110.

Bergmann, G. Theoretical psychology. *Annu. Rev. Psychol.*, 1953, **4**, 435–458.

Bergmann, G. Sense and nonsense in operationism. *Scient. Mon.*, 1954, **79**, 210–214. (Reprinted: In Ph. Frank (Ed.), *The validation of scientific theories*. Boston: Beacon, 1956. Pp. 41–52.)

Bergmann, G. Psychoanalysis and the unity of science: Else Frenkel-Brunswik: A review. *J. Phil.*, 1955, **52**, 692–695.

Bergmann, G. The contribution of John B. Watson. *Psychol. Rev.*, 1956, **63**, 265–276.

Bergmann. G. *Philosophy of science*. Madison; Univer. Wisconsin Press, 1957.

Bergmann, G., & Spence, K. W. Operationism and theory in psychology. *Psychol. Rev.*, 1941, **48**, 1–14.

Brodbeck, M. The philosophy of science and educational research. *Rev. educ. Res.*, 1957, **27**, 427–440.

Brodbeck, M. Methodological individualisms: Definition and reduction. *Phil. Sci.*, 1958, **25**, 1–22. (a)

Brodbeck, M. Models, meaning, and theories. In L. Gross (Ed.), *Symposium on sociological theory*. Evanston: Row Peterson, 1958. (b)

Campbell, D. T., & Fiske, D. W. Convergent and discriminant validation by the multitrait-multimethod matrix. *Psychol. Bull.*, 1959, **56**, 81–105.

Carnap, R. Foundations of logic and mathematics. In *International encyclopedia of unified science*. Vol. I, No. 3. Pp. 56–59. (Reprinted: The interpretation of physics. In H. Feigl & M. Brodbeck (Eds.), *Readings in the philosophy of science*. New York: Appleton-Century-Crofts, 1953. Pp. 309–318.)

Cronbach, L. J. *Essentials of psychological testing*. New York: Harper, 1949.

Cronbach, L. J. The two disciplines of scientific psychology. *Amer. Psychologist*, 1957, **12**, 671–684.

Cronbach, L. J. Proposals leading to analytic treatment of social perception scores. In R. Tagiuri & L. Petrullo (Eds.), *Person perception and interpersonal behavior*. Stanford: Stanford Univer. Press, 1958, Pp. 353–379.

Cronbach, L. J., & Meehl, P. E. Construct validity in psychological tests. *Psychol. Bull.*, 1955, **52**, 281–302.

Feigl, H. Existential hypotheses. *Phil. Sci.*, 1950, **17**, 35–62.

Feigl, H. Confirmability and confirmation. *Rev. int. Phil.*, 1951, **5**, 1–12. (Reprinted: In P. P. Wiener (Ed.), *Readings in philosophy of science*. New York: Scribner, 1953. Pp. 522–530.

French, J. W. *Manual for kit of selected tests for reference aptitude and achievement factors*. Princeton: Educ. Testing Service, 1954.

Garner, W. R., Hake, H. H., & Eriksen, C. W. Operationism and the concept of perception. *Psychol. Rev.* 1956, **63**, 149–159.

Hempel, C. G. *Fundamentals of concept formation in empirical science.* Chicago: Univer. Chicago Press, 1952.

Jenkins, J. J., & Lykken, D. T. Individual differences. *Annu. Rev. Psychol.*, 1957, **8**, 79–112.

Jessor, R., & Hammond, K. R. Construct validity and the Taylor Anxiety Scale. *Psychol. Bull.*, 1957, **54**, 161–170.

Johnson, H. M. On verifying hypotheses by verifying their implicates. *Amer. J. Psychol.*, 1954, **67**, 723–727.

Kausler, D. J., & Trapp, E. P. Methodological considerations in the construct validation of drive-oriented scales. *Psychol. Bull.*, 1959, **56**, 152–157.

Loevinger, Jane. Objective tests as instruments of psychological theory. *Psychol. Rep.*, 1957, **3**, 635–694.

Lord, F. A. Theory of test scores. *Psychometr. Monogr.*, 1952, No. 7.

Meehl, P. E. Wanted: A good cookbook. *Amer. Psychologist*, 1956, **11**, 263–272.

Pap, A. Reduction-sentences and open concepts. *Methodos*, 1953, **5**, 3–30.

Sellars, W. S. Concepts as involving laws and inconceivable without them. *Phil. Sci.*, 1948, **15**, 287–315.

Spence, K. W. The nature of theory construction in contemporary psychology. *Psychol. Rev.* 1944, **51**, 47–68.

Spence, K. W. The postulates and methods of behaviorism. *Psychol. Rev.*, 1948, **55**, 67–78.

Spence, K. W. The empirical basis and theoretical structure of psychology. *Phil. Sci.*, 1957, **24**, 97–108.

Spence, K. W. A theory of emotionally based drive (*D*) and its relation to performance in simple learning situations. *Amer. Psychologist*, 1958, **13**, 131–141.

Spence, K. W., & Ross, L. E. A methodological study of the form and latency of eyelid responses in conditioning. *J. exp. Psychol.*, 1959.

Spiker, C. C., & McCandless, B. R. The concept of intelligence and the philosophy of science. *Psychol. Rev.*, 1954, **61**, 255–266.

Taylor, J. A. The relationship of anxiety to the conditioned eyelid response. *J. exp. Psychol.*, 1951, **41**, 81–92.

Taylor, J. A. A personality scale of manifest anxiety. *J. abnorm. soc. Psychol.*, 1953, **48**, 285–290.

Thurstone, L. L., *Multiple-factor analysis.* Chicago: Univer. Chicago Press, 1947.

Thurstone, L. L. & Thurstone, T. G. *Primary mental abilities.* (Manual and tests) Chicago: Science Research Associates, 1950.

48. LOGIC, LANGUAGE, DEFINITION, AND CONCEPTS

May Brodbeck

THE LANGUAGE OF SCIENCE

Language consists of words and sentences. To the *words* of ordinary speech correspond the *concepts* of science; to the *sentences* its *definitions*, its *statements of individual fact* and *of laws*. Certain sets of sentences constitute the *theories* of science. The distinction between a word and a sentence is so fundamental that it impinges on almost all issues that can be raised within the philosophy or methodology of science. For on the linguistic distinction between words and sentences hangs also the distinction, much more than a matter of language only, between meaning and truth. If the former distinction is blurred, so is the latter; and if the difference between meaning and truth is blurred, then intelligibility itself is forfeit. "Meaning" and "truth" are ponderous yet equivocal terms, for words mean in different ways and there is more than one kind of truth. Language contains two kinds of words and, corresponding to them, two kinds of truth.

The language of science, devoid of greetings, exclamations, questions, and commands, consists wholly of declarative sentences. By means of them, the scientist talks about the world. These sentences may be as simple and qualitative as the statement that ice is cold or as complicated and quantitative as the Newtonian law of attraction. In either case, all such general sentences consist

SOURCE. Reprinted from "Logic and Scientific Method in Research on Teaching," by May Brodbeck in N. L. Gage (ed.), *Handbook of Research on Teaching*. Chicago: Rand McNally & Co., 1963. Copyright © 1963 by American Educational Research Association.

of certain arrangements of two kinds of words. Some of the words in a sentence refer to individual things, either simple or complex, like "John" or "Minnesota." Others refer to the characters or attributes of individual things or to relations among them. All such words are called *descriptive* terms. Those which name not individual things, but their characters and relations, are the *concepts* of science. They may name characters of inanimate physical things, of organisms, or of societies. Thus green is a character of some physical objects, notably grass. Hunger at some time or other belongs to the state of an organism, while totalitarianism is an attribute of some societies. A relation is any attribute requiring two or more individuals for its exemplification, like older, between, more populous, or smarter. These names for characters of things, whether relational or nonrelational, distinguish one area from another —psychology, say, from physics. The subject matter or *content* of an area is thus indicated by its descriptive terms or concepts.

Descriptive terms are connected with each other to form statements of individual fact, like "John is blond" or "John runs." As the last example suggests, the "is" or copula of predication is logically superfluous and can always be omitted, as it is in many natural languages, with no more untoward effect than grammatical oddity. "John blond" may be pidgin English, but it says the same as "John is blond." However, when one wants to assert more than a single statement of individual fact, attributing a property to an individual thing or person, certain other kinds of words become indispensable. Sentences are connected with each other to form compound sentences, like "John is blond and Jim is redheaded." These compound sentences express connections among individual facts. The words that permit us to express these connections, like "and," "or," "if-then," and "not," are called *logical* words or connectives. ("All" and "some," though not connectives, are also logical words.) Unlike descriptive words, these do not themselves name or denote anything. Logical words give language its *form* or structure by connecting sentences made up of descriptive words. For example, the sentences "He is a scholar *and* he is an athlete" and "He is a scholar *or* he is an athlete" are alike in that they have the same content or subject matter. But their *form* is different. On the other hand, "*If* this is silver, *then* its melting point is p" is like "*If* anyone is frustrated, *then* he will be aggressive" in that they share a common form. Their subject matter differs but both statements are conditionals. The logical words are common to all sciences.

The meaning of the descriptive words is given by specifying the individuals, or their properties, or the relations among them to which they refer. The meaning of the logical words is specified by giving the conditions for the truth or falsity of the compound sentences formed by means of the logical words. The truth of the simple component sentences containing no logical words, like "John is an athlete," are determined by observation. The truth of a compound sentence is then specified as a function of the truth of its constituents. A conjunction, for instance, is true if and only if both conjuncts are true. Once such conditions are specified for all the connectives, it turns out that, corresponding to the two kinds of words, logical and descriptive, there are also two kinds of sentences, those which are logically true and those which are factually or empirically true. This distinction and its broader implications will be more forcefully seen if we strip compound sentences of their content or descriptive meaning and retain only their form. This may be done by replacing all the simple component statements with letters. Thus "P or Q," "P and Q," "If P then Q," "not-P," are the form of a disjunction, conjunction, conditional, and negation, respectively. As they stand, there is no way to distinguish "P or Q" from "S or T." If, however, each letter-variable is replaced by a sentence containing different descriptive words, then the statements say different things though they have the same form. And logic is exclusively concerned with form.

Having stripped the sentences down to their bones or structure, we can then completely specify the meaning of the connectives by Truth Table 1, in which "T" and "F" stand for "true" and "false."

TRUTH TABLE 1

Sentential Letter-variables		Logical Constants					
P	Q	and	or	if-then	if and only if	not-P	not-Q
T	T	T	T	T	T	F	F
F	T	F	T	T	F	T	F
T	F	F	T	F	F	F	T
F	F	F	F	T	T	T	T

In words, the table tells us that the conjunction of P and Q will be true if and only if both conjuncts are true; the disjunction will be false if and only if both disjuncts are false; the conditional will be false if and only if the antecedent is true and the consequent is false; the biconditional or "if and only if" will be true if both components are true or both components are false; and the negation of a sentence will always take the opposite truth-value from the sentence itself. Thus, for all these compound sentences, once we are given the truth-value of the constituent sentences, we know the truth or falsity of the compound. But we must independently know the truth-values of the component sentences. This of course requires observation. Compound sentences, whose truth or falsity depends in this manner upon the truth or falsity of their component parts, are called factual, empirical, contingent, or synthetic, sentences. Their truth depends upon their *content*.

But now let us replace "*Q*" by "not-*P*." We then get Truth Table 2 for conjunction and disjunction:

TRUTH TABLE 2

Sentential Letter-variable	Logical Constants		
P	not-*P*	*P* and not-*P*	*P* or not-*P*
T	*F*	*F*	*T*
F	*T*	*F*	*T*

In words, "*P* and not-*P*" is false while "*P or* not-*P*" is true, no matter whether "*P*" is true or false. That is, in order to know that "*P* or not-*P*" is true, we do not have to know independently the truth-value of its constituents, and similarly for the falsehood of "*P* and not-*P*." "If *P* then *P*," it can be easily seen, will also be true regardless of whether "*P*" is true or false. If "*P*" stands for the statement that a judge is elected, then the whole sentence says "If a judge is elected, then a judge is elected," which is something less than controversial. All such statements are called logical truths or, also, tautological or analytic. They are also said to be "necessary truths," since they are true no matter what substitutions are made for their component parts, represented by the letter-variables. Their truth depends only on their *form*.

"Either it will rain or we will go swimming." If this statement, of the form "*P* or *Q*," is asserted truly, then we have some factual information, though perhaps it is not as definite as we would like. It will be true if at least one (possibly both) of its disjuncts is true. Appropriate observations will determine its truth or falsity. "Either it will rain or it will not rain." This statement, of the form "*P* or not-*P*," is true regardless of what happens. No observations are required, for its truth is determined by its form alone. Its descriptive words occur vacuously rather than essentially; that is, they make no difference to the truth of the statement. Yet it is a perfectly meaningful and indeed, in its way, an important statement, as are all tautologies or logical truths.

Among other things, they are, as we shall see, indispensable in carrying out logical deductions. Their importance can be assessed by considering that one important subclass of logical or analytic truths is that of mathematics. All arithmetical concepts, like numbers and operations upon them, such as addition, are ultimately definable in terms of logical words alone. The definition is cumbrous and need not concern us here. But, once carried through, it turns out that statements such as $5 + 7 = 12$, as well as those of more abstruse mathematics, are all true by virtue of their form alone. They contain no symbols referring to descriptive properties and relations, and these are irrelevant to the truths of arithmetic. Yet, though they are uninformative about empirical facts, they are clearly both meaningful and remarkably useful assertions.

Some tautologies are as obvious as "*P* or not *P*," or "If *P* then *P*." Others are far from obvious and need long manipulation to reveal their tautological character. Given the structure of our language, as specified by the truth tables for the connectives, the tautologies or logical truths are found—not made—by us.

Definitions are an apparent exception. Since definitions, and the difference between them and factual assertions, are important both in science and in many of the methodological issues discussed in this study, it will be well to be very clear about the logical structure of definitions.

Every science contains a great many defined terms. A definition, no matter how simple or complicated its form, is always a statement about the use of words. It asserts that one or more words may be used as an abbreviation for some combination of several others. Strictly speaking, therefore, definitions are *about* language rather than *within* language. However, it is sometimes useful, particularly for purposes of deduction, to assert the definition as a statement in the language. That is, any *rule about language*, about the use of words, such as " '*A*' means by definition '*B and C*,' " may have a corresponding *sentence within language*, namely, "*A* if and only if *B* and *C*." Because the rule or definition says that "*A*" is just abbreviatory for "*B and C*," both the left- and right-hand side of the "—if and only if—" sentence refer to the same thing. This statement therefore has the logical form of "*A* if and only if *A*" or "*B* and *C* if and only if *B* and *C*."

Within the language, therefore, definitions may be treated as if they were tautologies. They are true by definition, i.e., merely verbal. *Unlike* ordinary tautologies, such as "*P* or not-*P*," their truth is a matter of convention or stipulation. If this convention had not been adopted, then the corresponding tautology would not occur in our language. Moreover, they are, strictly speaking, logically superfluous, since the defined term can always be replaced by its defining ones. That indeed is why the statement takes the form of a tautology. Ordinary tautologies, however, cannot be eliminated from language. This circumstance is sometimes expressed by saying that tautologies express or reflect the logical structure of the world. *Like* ordinary tautologies, definitions are factually empty and their truth is a matter of their form alone. Both their similarities to and differences from tautologies are crucial for understanding the role of definitions in science.

CONCEPTS, FACTS, AND LAWS

Some features of the world *stand out*, almost begging for names. Concepts of clouds, thunder, dog, wealth, hunger, child, colors, tastes, and the like, name differentiated slices of reality that willy-nilly impinge on all of us. The concepts of common sense name these obtrusive daily experiences. Other features of the world have to be *cut out*, as it were. They are discerned only by a more subtle and devious examination of nature, man, and society than is made in everyday life. These more covert aspects of experience are named by the concepts of science. Concepts like mass and momentum, IQ and reaction potential, primary group and totalitarianism, name attributes of things that do not stand out as do love and hunger, colors, tastes, and odors.

Much of the language of common sense consists of names for objects of direct experience that need no definition. Anyone who has learned to speak the language and is not born blind knows the meaning of the concept "blue." But even in everyday language many terms occur that must be defined before we know what they denote. One who has never seen a gnu must have the term explained to him. We explain it by listing the observable attributes of gnus. "Gnu" means "a mammal with an oxlike head, short mane, downward-curved horns, and long tail." This typical, so-called "nominal" definition tells us by what combination of attributes we shall know a gnu when we see one. It states that one word, gnu, is shorthand for a combination of other words that together denote a certain kind of object. To say that a particular animal is a gnu is the same as saying that the animal is an instance of the concept "gnu."

What is "momentum" or "bureaucracy" or "hysteria"? The question in each case is not: What does the concept "really" mean? For it means what we say it does. The question is one of words and is answered in the same way. Words themselves do not "mean." We "mean" by their use. We stipulate what we mean by them by definitions. "Momentum" means "mass times velocity." But what is "mass" and what is "velocity"? We keep exchanging one word for others. On pain of infinite regress or circularity, definition must stop somewhere. It stops where one expects it to, namely, when there is no longer ambiguity or disagreement about the referent of the term.

When is this point reached? In other words, how do we know when we have a good or adequate definition? An adequate definition permits us always to tell when a sentence containing the defined term is true and when it is false. An adequately defined concept is also called "reliable." If a concept is reliable, then different people or the same person at different times always agree about whether or not there is an instance of the concept. "Velocity" is a highly reliable concept, while "anxiety" is much less so. What makes the difference? In part, the difference is that one concept is quantified while the other is not.

The quantified concept "melting point" is a much more reliable defining property of a chemical substance than is "pale yellow." The color concept is vague in a way in which melting point is not. Since colors shade into each other and lighting conditions affect the color seen, the referent of "pale yellow" is hard to pin down precisely. But though quantification has many virtues, it is not quantification as such that distinguishes a good definition from a poor one. A nonquantified concept of, say, "hunger" may be considerably more reliable than the equally nonquantified "anxiety." Moreover, a concept like, for instance, "economic depression," whose definition would undoubtedly contain many quantified terms, is probably no more reliable than "anxiety." Economists are by no means agreed on the defining terms of "depression." A difference in reliability is thus not due to counting and measuring alone.

Operational Definitions

In common sense, the meaning of a term referring to a kind of physical object, like a dog or a chair, is given by listing the observable characters of these objects, like barking or shape. The nominal definition of "gnu" mentioned before is such a definition. In a sense of "abstract" that has no degrees of more or less, both common sense and science use abstract words, that is, concepts or names for properties of things. However, there is a sense in which the character-words of science are more abstract than are the character-words of everyday language. The characteristic abstractness of scientific concepts, like mass or IQ, lies in the fact that these terms cannot be defined by simply listing a cluster of directly observable attributes. Merely by looking at a surface we can tell whether it is red or by looking at an object whether it is a gnu. We cannot so simply tell what the mass of an object or the IQ of a child is. Yet a body has mass as well as color; a child has an IQ as well as blood hair. However, more complicated observations are required to know that a body has a certain mass than to know that it has a certain color. This greater complication is reflected by the way the concepts of science are defined, for scientific definitions are rarely of the simple, dictionary type, illustrated by "gnu." They are not, precisely because they name features of the world that can be discerned only under certain conditions. And these conditions are part of the meaning of the concept. They must therefore be included in the defining properties of it. To do this requires an *operational definition*.

A cow is always a cow, but it is not always hungry. It is so only under certain conditions. A political attitude may be a relatively permanent aspect of a man, but, unlike the color of his eyes, he is not always evincing this attitude. Although a man's height needs no stimulus before it manifests itself, certain conditions, like his standing straight, must be met and measurements must be made before we can ascertain this height. At any given moment, a submissive woman need not be submitting, an authoritarian person giving orders, or a malleable piece of iron being bent. Such concepts are called "dispositional," for they refer to the disposition of certain things or kinds of things to behave in certain ways or exhibit certain characters under certain conditions. We cannot tell merely by direct observation of an individual or thing that it has any of these properties, any more than we can directly see the mass of an object or a child's IQ or his precise height. Yet we must know what to look for in order to tell when a statement that an individual has any of these properties is true or false. To achieve this, scientific terms are defined, not in isolation, as in a dictionary, but by stating the observable conditions under which a sentence containing the term is true or false. Instead of defining the word by itself, as "gnu" was defined, it is defined by giving the conditions for the truth of a sentence in which the term occurs. Such definitions are called "operational," for they frequently state what must be done in order to make certain observations. For instance, in order to determine a child's IQ, we must first administer a test of a specified kind, then observe his performance on the test, and finally make certain calculations. *All* of these conditions define the meaning of IQ as it appears in the sentence "John has an IQ of 115."

More generally, the right-hand side of an operational definition has the form of a conditional or "if-then" sentence. The antecedent or *if* clause of this sentence states the test or stimulus conditions, or what must be done in order to make certain observations. The consequent or *then* clause states the truth or response conditions, or what must be observed after the test conditions have been imposed. In the case of quantitative concepts, these antecedent or test conditions consist of certain measuring procedures or *operations*, such as weighing on a balance or giving an examination. The truth conditions state what must be observed after these operations have been carried out. Terms referring to personality traits, attitudes, and abilities must also be defined in terms of behavior that is exhibited under certain conditions. All terms requiring the "if-then" form of definition may be called *dispositional* concepts.

Suppose that a political scientist wishes to introduce the concept "conservative." In order to be quite clear about the kind of individual he is talking about, he defines his term rather than relying upon the vague and varying connotations of common sense to carry his meaning. A conservative, as this political scientist uses the term, is, by definition, an individual who gives a certain pattern of responses to a battery of questions. The questions constitute the antecedent test conditions. The pattern of responses constitutes the consequent truth condition, or what must be observed after the test is given to make the sentence "*X* is a conservative" true. The entire conditional sentence, stating a connection between antecedent and consequent conditions, defines the concept. For if a different battery of questions were administered, we would not expect the same pattern of responses. The measuring procedure is part of the meaning of the concept.

A science generally contains both nominal definitions of isolated terms as well as operational definitions of terms as they are used in a sentence. In economics, for instance, the amount of production is defined nominally as the arithmetical sum of the amounts of consumption and accumulation. On the other hand, the concept "rational man" requires the conditional or operational definition. "Jones is a rational man" means by definition "*If* Jones is presented with certain choices, *then* he orders his preferences transitively." The only difference between the two kinds of definition is that in the nominal case the term "production" is eliminated by two other terms and an arithmetical computation, while in the "operational" case, one entire sentence containing the word to be defined is replaced by another sentence not containing this critical word. An operational definition, like any other definition, is thus a statement about the use of words, stating how one term may be eliminated by means of others.

But what others? Definition can proceed indefinitely. As I mentioned before, we can keep on exchanging one word for others. Assuming that we do not run around in a circle, the process must end somewhere. Fortunately, the connection between language and the world is such that we can say where it must end. Language, we recall, is given its content by descriptive or referential words, those that refer to some thing or kind of thing. "Gnu" and "unicorn" are both descriptive words, though there are gnus and there are no unicorns. By their definitions alone we could not know this, for a definition tells us only about words and not about the world. But the defining words must enable us to know an instance of the defined concept when we see one. We must, obviously, know what to look for in order to discover, for instance, whether there are or are not any unicorns. If the defining words do not themselves tell us what to look for, then they must in turn be defined. In this way, a long chain of definitions may be constructed.

Where will this chain stop? Not all descriptive words need be or can be defined. Words that cannot be further defined name directly observable properties of things, like certain colors, tastes, odors, textures, and sounds. Knowledge by direct acquaintance is the kind of knowledge that, for instance, a man born blind cannot have of the meaning of the word "blue." No matter what else he may know by other methods about the physics of color, he does not know the referential meaning of "blue." The names for those characters of things, relational or nonrelational, that we either know by direct acquaintance (or, like the blind man, not at all) cannot be further defined. These are the undefinable descriptive words of our language. At this point, therefore, definition stops. If I have finally defined a concept in terms of what anyone can see, feel, hear, and smell, then I shall know how to identify an instance of it. No one can carry definition further.

But even to carry definition this far is, for most scientific purposes, unnecessary. One can, for example, give the meaning of, say, "table" in terms of objects of direct acquaintance like shape, material, and some further descriptive properties and relations. Generally, the names for physical objects do not require this fine a definition. Science takes over the names of common-sense physical objects. When definition becomes necessary, as of "thermometer," the definition is in terms of common-sense physical-object words, as, in the case of "thermometer," "tube," or "box."

Consider, for another example, the concept "momentum." It is a label for the product of mass and velocity. In order to be able to say that a body has a certain momentum, we must know how to ascertain its mass and its velocity. But these terms must in turn be defined. "Velocity" is defined nominally as the distance traveled per unit time. Again, "distance" and "time," as used here, are quantitative notions. Thus they too must be operationally defined by means of rulers and clocks, what we do to them, and what we observe after having done it. But that is as far as we need go. Once the chain of definition has been carried down to the point where all the defining words are names for common-sense physical objects and their directly observable characters, clearly there is no more defining to do. For when this stage is reached, definition has done its job. We know how to tell whether or not we have an instance of the concept and, if the term is quantitative, how much of it is present.

In general, definition in science stops when all descriptive terms in the definition refer either to physical objects, or to some directly observable properties and relations of and among them. To say the same thing differently, definition ends when the defining words are all part of the basic vocabulary of science. In social science, the "physical objects" are people and the characters, among others, their observed behavior. When this basis has been reached, anyone understanding the basic vocabulary can determine whether any sentence containing defined terms is true or false. The longer the chain of definition before this basis is reached, the more "abstract" is the concept being defined.

49. THE OPERATIONAL ANALYSIS OF PSYCHOLOGICAL TERMS

B. F. Skinner

An answer to Question 6* will define the position to be taken in what follows. Operationism is not regarded as a new theory or mode of definition. The literature has emphasized certain critical or hitherto neglected instances, but no new kind of operation has been discovered and none should be singled out. There is no reason to restrict operational analysis to high-order constructs; the principle applies to all definitions (Question 9). This means, in answer to Question 1 (a), that we must explicate an operational definition for every term unless we are willing to adopt the vague usage of the vernacular.

Operationism may be defined as the practice of talking about (1) one's observations, (2) the manipulative and calculational procedures involved in making them, (3) the logical and mathematical steps which intervene between earlier and later statements, and (4) *nothing else.* So far, the major contribution has come from the fourth provision and, like it, is negative. We have learned how to avoid troublesome references by showing that they are artifacts, which may be variously traced to history, philosophy, linguistics, and so on. No very important positive advances have been made in connection with the first three provisions because operationism has no good answer to Question 10. It has not developed a satisfactory formulation of the effective verbal behavior of the scientist.

SOURCE. Skinner, B. F., "The Operational Analysis of Psychological Terms," *Psychological Review*, Vol. 52, No. 5, 1945. Reprinted with permission of the American Psychological Association. Copyright © 1945 by The American Psychological Association.
* See end of article for the list of questions being discussed. Eds.

The operationist, like most contemporary writers in the field of linguistic and semantic analysis, is on the fence between logical "correspondence" theories of reference and empirical formulations of language in use. He has not improved upon the mixture of logical and popular terms usually encountered in casual or even supposedly technical discussions of scientific method or the theory of knowledge (*e.g.*, Bertrand Russell's recent *An inquiry into meaning and truth*). "Definition" is a key term but is not rigorously defined. Bridgman's original contention that the "concept is synonymous with the corresponding set of operations" cannot be taken literally, and no similarly explicit but satisfactory statement of the relation is available. Instead, a few roundabout expressions recur with rather tiresome regularity whenever this relation is mentioned. We are told that a concept is to be defined *"in terms of"* certain operations, that propositions are to be *"based upon"* operations, that a term denotes something only when there are *"concrete criteria for its applicability,"* that operationism consists in *"referring any concept for its definition* to . . . concrete operations . . . ,"* and so on. We may accept expressions of this sort as outlining a program, but they do not provide a general scheme of definition, much less an explicit statement of the relation between concept and operation.

The weakness of current theories of language may be traced to the fact that an objective conception of human behavior is still incomplete. The doctrine that words are used to express or convey meanings merely substitutes "meaning" for "idea" (in the hope that meanings can then somehow be got outside the skin) and is incompatible with modern psychological conceptions of the organism. Attempts to derive a symbolic function from the principle of conditioning (or association) have been characterized by a very superficial analysis. It is simply not true that an organism reacts to a sign "as it would to the object which the sign supplants" (Stevens, 2, p. 250). Only in a very limited area (mainly in the case of autonomic responses) is it possible to regard the sign as a simple substitute stimulus in the Pavlovian sense. Modern logic, as a formalization of "real" languages, retains and extends this dualistic theory of meaning and can scarcely be appealed to by the psychologist who recognizes his own responsibility in giving an account of verbal behavior.

It is not my intention to attempt a more adequate formulation here. The fundamental revision is too sweeping to be made hastily. I should like, however, to try to make a small but positive contribution to this symposium by considering a few points which arise in connection with the operational definition of psychological terms. Much of the material which follows is adapted from a much longer work now in preparation, in which the necessary groundwork is more carefully prepared.

The operational attitude, in spite of its shortcomings, is a good thing in any science but especially in psychology because of the presence there of a vast vocabulary of ancient and non-scientific origin. It is not surprising that the broad empirical movement in the philosophy of science, which Stevens has shown (2) to be the background of operationism, should have had a vigorous and early representation in the field of psychology—namely, behaviorism. In spite of the differences which Stevens pretends to find, behaviorism has been (at least to most behaviorists) nothing more than a thoroughgoing operational analysis of traditional mentalistic concepts. We may disagree with some of the answers (such as Watson's disposition of images), but the *questions* asked by behaviorism were strictly operational in spirit. I also cannot agree with Stevens that American behaviorism was "primitive." The early papers on the problem of consciousness by Watson, Weiss, Tolman, Hunter, Lashley, and many others, were not only highly sophisticated examples of operational inquiry, they showed a willingness to deal with a wider range of phenomena than do current streamlined treatments, particularly those offered by logicians (*e.g.*, Carnap) interested in a unified scientific vocabulary. But behaviorism, too, stopped short of a decisive positive contribution—and for the same reason: it never finished an acceptable formulation of the "verbal report." The conception of behavior which it developed could not convincingly embrace the "use of subjective terms."

A considerable advantage is gained from dealing with terms, concepts, constructs, and so on, quite frankly in the form in which they are observed—namely, as verbal responses. There is then no danger of including in the concept that aspect or part of nature which it singles out. (Several of the present questions seem to mix concept and referent; at least they seem to become trivial when, in order to make the mixture less likely, "term" is substituted for "concept" or "construct.") Meanings, contents, and references are to be found among the determiners, not among the properties, of response. The question "What is length?" would appear to be satisfactorily answered by listing the circumstances under which the response "length" is emitted (or, better, by giving some general description of such circumstances). If two quite separate sets of circumstances are revealed, then there are two responses having the form "length" (Question 2), since a verbal response-class is not defined by phonetic form alone but by its functional relations. This is true even though the two sets are found to be intimately connected. The two responses are not controlled by the same stimuli, no matter how clearly it is shown that the different stimuli arise from the same "thing."

What we want to know in the case of many traditional psychological terms is, first, the specific stimulating conditions under which they are emitted (this corresponds to "finding the referents") and, second (and this is a much more important systematic question), why each response is controlled by its corresponding condition. The latter is not necessarily a genetic question. The individual acquires language from society, but the reinforcing action of the verbal community continues to play an important rôle in maintaining the specific relations between responses and stimuli which are essential to the proper functioning of verbal behavior. How language is acquired is, therefore, only part of a much broader problem.

We may generalize the conditions responsible for the standard 'semantic' relation between a verbal response and a particular stimulus without going into reinforcement theory in detail. There are three important terms: a stimulus, a response, and a reinforcement supplied by the verbal community. (All of these need more careful definitions than are implied by current usage, but the following argument may be made without digressing for that purpose.) The significant interrelations between these terms may be expressed by saying that the community reinforces the response only when it is emitted in the presence of the stimulus. The reinforcement of the response "red," for example, is contingent upon the presence of a red object. (The contingency need not be invariable.) A red object then becomes a discriminative stimulus, an "occasion," for the successful emission of the response "red" (1).

This scheme presupposes that the stimulus act upon both the speaker and the reinforcing community; otherwise the proper contingency cannot be maintained by the community. But this provision is lacking in the case of many "subjective" terms, which appear to be responses to *private* stimuli. The problem of subjective terms does not coincide exactly with that of private stimuli, but there is a close connection. We must know the characteristics of verbal responses to private stimuli in order to approach the operational analysis of the subjective term.

The response "My tooth aches" is partly under the control of a state of affairs to which the speaker alone is able to react, since no one else can establish the required connection with the tooth in question. There is nothing mysterious or metaphysical about this; the simple fact is that each speaker possesses a small but important private world of stimuli. So far as we know, his reactions to these are quite like his reactions to external events. Nevertheless the privacy gives rise to two problems. The first difficulty is that we cannot, as in the case of public stimuli, account for the verbal response by pointing to a controlling stimulus. Our practice is to *infer* the private event, but this is opposed to the direction of inquiry in a science of behavior in which we are to predict response through, among other things, an independent knowledge of the stimulus. It is often supposed that a solution is to be found in improved physiological techniques. Whenever it becomes possible to say what conditions within the organism control the response "I am depressed," for example, and to produce these conditions at will, a degree of control and prediction characteristic of responses to external stimuli will be made possible. Meanwhile, we must be content with reasonable evidence for the belief that responses to public and private stimuli are equally lawful and alike in kind.

But the problem of privacy cannot be wholly solved by instrumental invasion. No matter how clearly these internal events may be exposed in the laboratory, the fact remains that in the normal verbal episode they are quite private. We have not solved the second problem of how the community achieves the necessary contingency of reinforcement. How is the response "toothache" appropriately reinforced if the reinforcing agent has no contact with the tooth? There is, of course, no question of whether responses to private stimuli are possible. They occur commonly enough and must be accounted for. But why do they occur, what is their relation to controlling stimuli, and what, if any, are their distinguishing characteristics?

There are at least four ways in which a verbal community which has no access to a private stimulus may generate verbal behavior in response to it:

(1) It is not strictly true that the stimuli which control the response must be available to the community. Any reasonably regular accompaniment will suffice. Consider, for example, a blind man who learns the names of a trayful of objects from a teacher who identifies the objects by sight. The reinforcements are supplied or withheld according to the contingency between the blind man's responses and the teacher's visual stimuli, but the responses are controlled wholly by tactual stimuli. A satisfactory verbal system results from the fact that the visual and tactual stimuli remain closely connected.

Similarly, in the case of private stimuli, one may teach a child to say "That hurts" in agreement with the usage of the community by making the reinforcement contingent upon public accompaniments of painful stimuli (a smart blow, tissue damage, and so on). The connection between public and private stimuli need not be invariable; a response may be conditioned with merely periodic reinforcement and even in spite of an occasional conflicting contingency (1). The possibility of such behavior is limited by the degree of association of public and private stimuli which will supply a net reinforcement sufficient to establish and maintain a response.

(2) A commoner basis for the verbal reinforcement of a response to a private stimulus is provided by collateral responses to the same stimulus. Although a dentist may occasionally be able to identify the stimulus for a toothache from certain public accompaniments as in (1), the response 'toothache' is generally transmitted on the basis of responses which are elicited by the same stimulus but which do not need to be set up by an environmental contingency. The community infers the private stimulus, not from accompanying public stimuli, but from collateral, generally unconditioned and at least non-verbal, responses (hand to jaw, facial expressions, groans, and so on). The inference is not always correct, and the accuracy of the reference is again limited by the degree of association.

(3) Some very important responses to private stimuli are descriptive of the speaker's own behavior. When this is overt, the community bases its

instructional reinforcement upon the conspicuous manifestations, but the speaker presumably acquires the response in connection with a wealth of additional proprioceptive stimuli. The latter may assume practically complete control, as in describing one's own behavior in the dark. This is very close to the example of the blind man; the speaker and the community react to different, though closely associated, stimuli.

Suppose, now, that a given response recedes to the level of covert or merely incipient behavior. How shall we explain the vocabulary which deals with this private world? (The instrumental detection of covert behavior is again not an answer, for we are interested in how responses to private stimuli are normally, and non-instrumentally, set up.) There are two important possibilities. The surviving covert response may be regarded as an accompaniment of the overt (perhaps part of it), in which case the response to the private stimulus is imparted on the basis of the public stimulus supplied by the overt response, as in (1). On the other hand, the covert response may be *similar to*, though probably less intense than, the overt and hence supply the *same* stimulus, albeit in a weakened form. We have, then, a third possibility: a response may be emitted in the presence of a private stimulus, which has no public accompaniments, provided it is occasionally reinforced in the presence of the same stimulus occurring with public manifestations.

Terms falling within this class are apparently descriptive only of behavior, rather than of other internal states or events, since the possibility that the same stimulus may be both public and private (or, better, may have or lack public accompaniments) seems to arise from the unique fact that behavior may be both covert and overt.

(4) The principle of transfer or stimulus induction supplies a fourth explanation of how a response to private stimuli may be maintained by public reinforcement. A response which is acquired and maintained in connection with public stimuli may be emitted, through induction, in response to private events. The transfer is not due to identical stimuli, as in (3), but to coinciding properties. Thus, we describe internal states as "agitated," "depressed," "ebullient," and so on, in a long list. Responses in this class are all metaphors (including special figures like metonomy). The term "metaphor" is not used pejoratively but merely to indicate that the differential reinforcement cannot be accorded actual responses to the private case. As the etymology suggests, the response is "carried over" from the public instance.

In summary, a verbal response to a private stimulus may be maintained in strength through appropriate reinforcement based upon public accompaniments or consequences, as in (1) and (2), or through appropriate reinforcement accorded the response when it is made to public stimuli, the private case occurring by induction when the stimuli are only partly similar. If these are the only possibilities (and the list is here offered as exhaustive), then we may understand why terms referring to private events have never formed a stable and acceptable vocabulary of reasonably uniform usage. This historical fact is puzzling to adherents of the "correspondence school" of meaning. Why is it not possible to assign names to the diverse elements of private experience and then to proceed with consistent and effective discourse? The answer lies in the process by which "terms are assigned to private events," a process which we have just analyzed in a rough way in terms of the reinforcement of verbal responses.

None of the conditions that we have examined permits the sharpening of reference which is achieved, in the case of public stimuli, by a precise contingency of reinforcement. In (1) and (2) the association of public and private events may be faulty; the stimuli embraced by (3) are of limited scope; and the metaphorical nature of those in (4) implies a lack of precision. It is, therefore, impossible to establish a rigorous scientific vocabulary for public use, nor can the speaker clearly "know himself" in the sense in which knowing is identified with behaving discriminatively. In the absence of the "crisis" provided by differential reinforcement (much of which is necessarily verbal), private stimuli cannot be analysed. (This has little or nothing to do with the availability or capacity of receptors.)

The contingencies we have reviewed also fail to provide an adequate check against fictional distortion of the relation of reference (e.g., as in rationalizing). Statements about private events may be under control of the drives associated with their consequences rather than antecedent stimuli. The community is skeptical of statements of this sort, and any attempt by the speaker to talk to himself about his private world (as in psychological system making) is fraught with self-deception.

Much of the ambiguity of psychological terms arises from the possibility of alternative or multiple modes of reinforcement. Consider, for example, the response "I am hungry." The community may reinforce this on the basis of the history of ingestion, as in (1), or collateral behavior associated with hunger, as in (2), or as a description of behavior with respect to food, or stimuli previously correlated with food, as in (3). In addition the speaker has (in some instances) the powerful stimulation of hunger pangs, which is private, since the community has no suitable connection with the speaker's stomach. "I am hungry" may therefore be variously translated as "I have not eaten for a long time" (1) or "That food makes my mouth water" (2), or "I am ravenous" (3) (compare the expression "I was hungrier than I thought" which describes the ingestion of an unexpectedly large amount of food), or "I have hunger pangs." While all of these may be regarded as synonymous with "I am hungry," they are not synonymous with each other. It is easy for conflicting psychological systematists to cite supporting instances or to train speakers to emit the response "I am hungry" in conformity with a system. With the balloon technique one might condition the verbal response exclusively to stimulation from stomach contractions. This would be an example of either (1) or (2) above. Or a speaker might be trained to make nice observations of the strength of his ingestive behavior, which might recede to the covert level as in (3). The response "I am hungry" would then describe a tendency to eat, with little or no reference to stomach contractions. Everyday usage reflects a mixed reinforcement. A similar analysis could be made of all terms descriptive of motivation, emotion, and action in general, including (of special interest here) the acts of seeing, hearing, and so on.

When public manifestations survive, the extent to which the private stimulus takes over is never certain. In the case of a toothache, the private event is no doubt dominant, but this is due to its relative intensity, not to any condition of differential reinforcement. In a description of one's own behavior, the private component may be much less important. A very strict external contingency may emphasize the public component, especially if the association with private events is faulty. In a rigorous scientific vocabulary private effects are practically eliminated. The converse does not hold. There is apparently no way of basing a response entirely upon the private part of a complex of stimuli. *A differential reinforcement cannot be made contingent upon the property of privacy.* This fact is of extraordinary importance in evaluating traditional psychological terms.

The response "red" is imparted and maintained (either casually or professionally) by reinforcements which are contingent upon a certain property of stimuli. Both speaker and community (or psychologist) have access to the stimulus, and the contingency may be made quite precise. There is nothing about the resulting response that should puzzle anyone. The greater part of psychophysics rests upon this solid footing. The older psychological view, however, was that the speaker was reporting, not a property of the stimulus, but a certain kind of private event, the sensation of red. This was regarded as a later stage in a series beginning with the red stimulus. The experimenter was supposed to manipulate the private event by manipulating the stimulus. This seems like a gratuitous distinction, but in the case of some subjects a similar later stage could apparently be generated in other ways (by arousing an "image"), and hence the autonomy of a private event capable of evoking the response "red" in the absence of a controllable red stimulus seemed to be proved. An adequate proof, of course, requires the elimination of other possibilities (*e.g.*, that the response is generated by the procedures which are intended to generate the image).

Verbal behavior which is "descriptive of images" must be accounted for in any adequate science of behavior. The difficulties are the same for both behaviorist and subjectivist. If the private events are free, a scientific description is impossible in either case. If laws can be discovered, then a lawful description of the verbal behavior can be achieved, with or without references to images. So much for "finding the referents"; the remaining problem of how such responses are maintained in relation to their referents is also soluble. The description of an image appears to be an example of a response to a private stimulus of class (1) above. That is to say, relevant terms are established when the private event accompanies a controllable external stimulus, but responses occur at other times, perhaps in relation to the same private event. The deficiencies of such a vocabulary have been pointed out.

We can account for the response "red" (at least as well as for the "experience" of red) by appeal to past conditions of reinforcement. But what about expanded expressions like "*I see* red" or "*I am conscious of* red"? Here "red" may be a response to either a public or a private stimulus without prejudice to the rest of the expression, but "see" and "conscious" seem to refer to events which are by nature or by definition private. This violates the principle that a reinforcement cannot be made contingent upon the privacy of a stimulus. A reference cannot be narrowed down to a specifically private event by any known method of differential reinforcement.

The original behavioristic hypothesis was, of course, that terms of this sort were descriptions of one's own (generally covert) behavior. The hypothesis explains the establishment and maintenance of the terms by supplying natural public counterparts in similar overt behavior. The terms are in general of class (3). One consequence of the hypothesis is that each term may be given a behavioral definition. We must, however, modify the argument slightly. To say "I see red" is to react, not to red (this is a trivial meaning of "see"), but to one's reaction to red. "See" is a term acquired with respect to one's own behavior in the case of overt responses available to the community. But according to the present analysis it may be evoked at other times by *any private accompaniment* of overt seeing. Here is a point at which a non-behavioral private seeing may be slipped in. Although the commonest private accompaniment would appear to be the stimulation which survives in a similar covert act, as in (3) it might be some sort of state or condition which gains control of the response as in (1) or (2). The superiority of the behavioral hypothesis is not merely methodological. That aspect of seeing which can be defined behaviorally is basic to the term as established by the verbal community and hence most effective in public discourse. A comparison of cases (1) and (3) will also show that terms which recede to the private level as overt behavior becomes covert have an optimal accuracy of reference, as responses to private stimuli go.

The additional hypothesis follows quite naturally that being conscious, as a form of reacting to one's own behavior, is a social product. Verbal behavior may be distinguished, and conveniently defined, by the fact that the contingencies of reinforcement are provided by other organisms rather than by a mechanical action upon the environment. The hypothesis is equivalent to saying that it is only because the behavior of the individual is important to society that society in turn makes it important to the individual. The individual becomes aware of what he is doing only after society has reinforced verbal responses with respect to his behavior as the source of discriminative stimuli. The behavior to be described (the behavior of which one is to be aware) may later recede to the covert level, and (to add a crowning difficulty) so may the verbal response. It is an ironic twist, considering the history of the behavioristic revolution, that as we develop a more effective vocabulary for the analysis of behavior we also enlarge the possibilities of awareness, so defined. The psychology of the other one is, after all, a direct approach to "knowing thyself."

The main purpose of this discussion has been to answer Question 10 by example. To be consistent the psychologist must deal with his own verbal practices by developing an empirical science of verbal behavior. He cannot, unfortunately, join the logician in defining a definition, for example, as a "rule for the use of a term" (Feigl); he must turn instead to the contingencies of reinforcement which account for the functional relation between a term, as a verbal response, and a given stimulus. This is the "operational basis" for his use of terms; and it is not logic but science.

The philosopher will call this circular. He will argue that we must adopt the rules of logic in order to make and interpret the experiments required in an empirical science of verbal behavior. But talking about talking is no more circular than thinking about thinking or knowing about knowing. Whether or not we are lifting ourselves by our own bootstraps, the simple fact is that we *can* make progress in a scientific analysis of verbal behavior. Eventually we shall be able to include, and perhaps to understand, our own verbal behavior as scientists. If it turns out that our final view of verbal behavior invalidates our scientific structure from the point of view of logic and truth-value, then so much the worse for logic, which will also have been embraced by our analysis.

References

1. Skinner, B. F. *The behavior of organisms: an experimental analysis.* New York: D. Appleton-Century Co., 1938.
2. Stevens, S. S. Psychology and the science of science. *Psychol. Bull.,* 1939, **36,** 221–263.

ELEVEN QUESTIONS*

1. (a) What is the purpose of operational definitions? When are they called for?

Since it is obviously impossible to explicate an operational definition for every construct-term used in scientific discussion, there must be some principle which determines when operational definitions are useful.

(b) Logically, operational definitions could form an infinite regress, since the construct-terms used in describing an operation are themselves in need of definition.

How is this regress limited in scientific practice?

2. When the same construct is defined by two independent operations, should it be said that there are really two constructs? For instance, it has been said that tape-measured distance and triangulated distance are really two kinds of distance and should perhaps have different names.

Against this view it can be argued that these are operations for showing the equivalence of operations, *e.g.*, for demonstrating the identity of taped and surveyed short distances.

3. (a) Are hypothetical operations which are physically impossible with present available techniques, of scientific use? Is the other side of the moon what you would see if you went there?

It is arguable that an unperformable operation has value in stating the conditions by which a construct could be validated. Such a statement shows that the construct is not at the moment valid.

(b) Is there a use for hypothetical operations that would define constructs which are actually at the moment nonexistent?

Red and green are supposed to be derived from yellow in the course of evolution. The discriminatory operations which would establish the existence of two new colors, derived similarly from blue, could be stated, although they could not be performed at the present stage of evolutionary development. The operations which would define a new invisible planet are similar.

(c) Is there a use for hypothetical operations which could never be performed?

The definition of infinity depends on operations which can never be completed.

4. Is *experience* a proper construct for operational definition?

It has been held that experience is ultimate, subject to immediate intuition but not to operational definition.

5. Are there scientifically good and bad operations, and how are operations evaluated if they differ in value?

---

* These are the questions to which Skinner was addressing his remarks. They are referred to in the text by their numbers.

Objectivists hold that the data of experience can always be operationally defined if the data become public, because the operations of publication define the datum. It is, however, argued further that the operations of verbal report are 'poorer' than the operations of discriminatory choice (C.R.; jumping stand) because the verbal response itself involves terms that are less rigorously defined.

6. Is operationism more than a renewed and refined emphasis upon the experimental method (as understood already by Galileo, if not even by Archimedes)—i.e., a formulation of modern scientific empiricism and pragmatism (especially of the Peirce-Dewey variety), mainly of criteria of factual meaningfulness and empirical validity?

7. Must operationists in psychology relegate theorizing of all sorts to the limbo of metaphysics? Bridgman in physics is perfectly aware of the value of theories as long as they are in keeping with his operational requirements. The Gestaltists, particularly Köhler and Koffka, have repeatedly attacked positivism (an identical twin of operationism, reproaching it for its (alleged) opposition to theoretical construction. C. C. Pratt (*Logic of Modern Psychology*, pp. 147–154) on the basis of his operationism maintains that all theoretical explanation is circular or tautological. Köhler (*Dynamics in Psychology*, pp. 107–125) holds a strictly opposite view. Which position is the most adequate for psychological research?

8. Some radical operationists assert that the meaning of a quantitative concept lies exclusively in the set of measuring operations which determine the application of the concept. (*E.g.:* "Intelligence is what the intelligence test tests.") But how can we then know what it is that we are after in constructing tests; and what possible meaning is there in talking about improving or revising tests and measurements if there are no criteria outside the chosen test methods?

9. Are *all* scientifically legitimate definitions operational in character? This is (at least in part) a terminological question, but certainly one that it would pay to settle (not only) among psychologists.

10. What is a definition, operational or otherwise? It is important to know whether one is presupposing a logical apparatus for dealing with the language of science or intending through a psychological analysis to justify such an apparatus.

11. For the purpose of operational definition, what class, or classes of events may be used properly as defining-operations? Specifically, can a phenomenon be identified or its properties be defined in terms of the events (operations) which are effective to produce, or occur as results of, the phenomenon?

50. OPERATIONISM AND THE CONCEPT OF PERCEPTION

Wendell R. Garner, Harold W. Hake, & Charles W. Eriksen

The attitude of contemporary operationists toward perceptual research has been well characterized recently by Allport. He has described their attitude by stating "that a perception can be regarded as nothing more nor less than a discriminatory response" (1, p. 53). In even simpler terms, the "reaction is the perception," and thus the role of the researcher is simply to determine the conditions under which a discriminatory response is obtained. These conditions then define perception. Unfortunately, we have to agree that many psychologists who consider themselves operationists do in fact accept this position toward perception. However, this position is not necessary from the tenets of operationism. In fact, we believe that this viewpoint is a perversion of the fundamentals of operationism as stated by its originators.

The essence of the above position is that a concept of perception is not distinguishable from the operations on which it is based, and thus that perception is indistinguishable from the responses which indicate its existence and character. This idea springs from a restricted interpretation of Bridgman's writings. For example, Bridgman states that "The concept is synonymous with the corresponding set of operations" (4, p. 5). This widely quoted statement has been used by psychologists to justify their unwillingness to distinguish between perceptions and responses, and to support their position that any set

SOURCE. Garner, Wendell R., Hake, Harold W., and Eriksen, Charles W., "Operationism and the Concept of Perception," *Psychological Review*, Vol. 63, No. 3, May 1956. Reprinted with permission of American Psychological Association. Copyright © 1956 by The American Psychological Association.

of responses leads to a concept about the properties of the perceptual system. However, to state that a concept is synonymous with a set of operations is not to state that any operation can produce a concept.

Furthermore, psychologists have ignored the fact that Bridgman is talking about a *set* of operations, not a single experimental operation. He later emphasizes this distinction, stating that

> Operational definitions, in spite of their precision, are in application without significance unless the situations to which they are applied are sufficiently developed so that at least two methods are known of getting to the terminus. Definition of a phenomenon by the operations which produced it, taken naked and without further qualification, has an entirely specious precision, because it is a description of a single isolated event (3, p. 248).

Many operationists accept the sterile point of view described by Allport, and consider perception not to have any operationally determinable properties other than discrimination. It seems to us that the above quotations from Bridgman do not require such a narrow point of view. It is true that if the only operation allowed were the discriminating reaction, then it would be impossible to determine whether the perceptual process had any properties other than discrimination. But it is equally unjustifiable to state that perception is nothing more than the discriminating reaction, since other possibilities have not been excluded. Surely the perceptual process has more richness than simple discrimination.

It seems clear that many operationists who nominally subscribe to the narrow operational position also feel that perception is more than discrimination, since they do in fact ascribe other properties to the perceptual process. It is equally unjustifiable to ascribe such additional properties, when they are ascribed on the basis of single experiments whose designs are inadequate to determine the nature of these additional properties. (It is our contention that additional properties of the perceptual system can and must be considered, but that operational experiments of a particular type are necessary to determine the nature of these properties.)

PERCEPTION AS A CONCEPT

We conceive of perception as an intervening process between stimuli and responses as schematically illustrated in Fig. 1. We can directly observe only stimuli and responses and, therefore, perception can be known only as a concept whose properties are induced from objectively determined relations between stimuli and responses. This statement does not in any sense imply that perception is identical to responses (or to stimuli). Indeed it is the purpose of this paper to indicate the kinds of operations which make it possible to distinguish perception from responses, and to show that these operations are necessary if the concept of perception is to have any use or meaning.

The Discriminating Reaction. We agree with contemporary operationists that the fundamental and prerequisite operation in any experiment on percep-

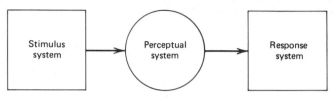

FIGURE 1. A schematic of the perceptual problem. The three systems operate in a causal relationship as indicated, although there may be interdependencies. Each system, however, may have independent properties. The properties of the stimulus and response systems can be directly observed; those of the perceptual system must be inferred.

tion is to demonstrate a discrimination between stimuli on the basis of responses. In other words, it must be demonstrated that there is a contingency relationship between stimuli and responses. If such a relation is demonstrated, we know that a subject can use the same label for the same stimulus within a certain error tolerance.

This operation alone, however, assures us only that we have a system which is operating and which is reliably assigning responses to the various stimuli. This operation provides us with so little information about perception that indeed we cannot distinguish between perceptual and response processes. However, if perception is considered a concept separate from the response system, there are rules for inductively determining the properties of that concept and they are the same as those for determining the properties of any concept.

Converging Operations. The necessary condition which makes possible the determination of particular characteristics of any concept (including the concept of perception) is the use of what have been called converging operations (6). Converging operations may be thought of as any set of two or more experimental operations which allow the selection or elimination of alternative hypotheses or concepts which could explain an experimental result. They are called converging operations because they are not perfectly correlated and thus can converge on a single concept.

To illustrate, let us assume an experiment similar to one reported by McGinnies (11) in which visual thresholds are determined for words with different emotional content. In our hypothetical experiment, we present four alternative stimulus words, tachistoscopically—fire, save, shit, fuck. The responses to these words are the verbal pronunciation of them. We find that the two vulgar words have higher thresholds than the two nonvulgar words.

Such a result has usually been interpreted as indicating that the perceptual system differentially discriminates on the basis of the emotional content of the perceived stimuli. There is, however, at least one other alternative explanation of these results—namely, that the difference in threshold is a result of a characteristic of the response system, which inhibits the verbalizing of some of these words. A converging operation which would discriminate between the two alternative hypotheses would be, to present the same stimuli as before, but to pair these stimuli with responses such that vulgar responses are used for nonvulgar stimuli, and vice versa. This experiment in conjunction with that of the first would allow us to decide which of the two hypotheses is correct, or if some combination of them is. It should be noted that the two operations taken together provide the convergence. One experiment does not converge on the other, but rather the two converge on a mutually acceptable result.

Ideally, converging operations would be orthogonal (completely independent), since such operations are the most efficient. In practice, however, it is difficult to obtain truly orthogonal operations, because the world is so organized that all variables cannot be controlled completely independently. This fact does not seriously change the nature of the problem, because a sufficient number of partially converging operations can still provide precise delimitation of alternative concepts.

Nevertheless sets of operations can be considered more or less efficient in allowing the formation of definitive concepts. One class of operations can be excluded entirely from consideration. This class can be called *parallel operations*. These operations select among alternative hypotheses along the same dimension, and thus cannot converge to a single concept. In our example above, we could do the entire experiment again using different words, but in which two are still vulgar and two nonvulgar. If this experiment produces the same result as the first, we still do not know whether the difference in threshold is due to a characteristic of the perceptual system or of the response system.

There are two special types of parallel operation which deserve mention. One of these is the *repeat operation* in which the same experiment is repeated at another time. Such an experiment does not allow convergence to a single concept unless the concept involves time as a variable. Another special type of parallel operation is the *transform operation*, in which one variable is simply a transformation of another. Again, in the illustration we have been using, suppose we retain the original set of words as the stimuli, but use four synonyms as responses—burn, keep, crap, screw. These synonyms used as responses can be considered transforms of the original words used as responses, and this experiment will not allow us to determine whether the differential effect exists in the perceptual system or in the response system.

It should be obvious from the above discussion that the value of a set of converging operations depends less on the nature of the operations themselves than on the alternative hypotheses or properties which are being considered. For example, we mentioned above the use of synonyms as an example of a transform operation. If, however, the synonyms were used as the stimuli, this experiment in conjunction with the first would converge to determine whether the differential thresholds were due to the letter configurations of the original words, rather than to their meanings. Thus these two experiments would be converging for that purpose, but would not be converging for purposes of determining whether the effect was in the perceptual system or in the response system.

Although a minimum of two converging operations may define a concept, in practice it is rare that two are sufficient. In the first place, there are usually more alternative hypotheses than can be delimited with two converging operations. In the second place, converging operations are rarely orthogonal, but are usually only partially converging. If there are enough partially converging operations, we can still arrive at a single, well-defined concept, but more than two such operations will be necessary.

It is quite legitimate to use assumed converging operations in place of operations actually carried out. We know from previous research that many of the possible converging operations would work in a particular way if we actually tried them, and thus there is little point in trying them again. The fact that we use assumptions, however, should not allow us to lose sight of the fact that the validity of our concepts rests entirely on the validity of the operations, whether carried out or assumed. A concept has no meaning other than that derived from the operations on which it is based, and unless these operations are known, the concept cannot be known either.

OPERATIONAL DISTINCTION BETWEEN RESPONSE AND PERCEPTION

An important use of converging operations is to distinguish effects which exist in the response system from those which exist in the perceptual system. Since the primary function of perceptual research is to determine something about the properties of the perceptual system, a major requirement in such research is to use converging operations which will eliminate the possibility that the outcome of an experiment is due to properties of the response system rather than of the perceptual system.

One of the more important properties of the response system which can affect the outcome of a perceptual experiment (and possible interpretations about properties of the perceptual system) is that of *response differentiation*. For example, if only one response is available to a subject, it is clearly impossible to demonstrate anything about perceptual discrimination. This principle is quite obvious when stated in such an extreme form, but it can also operate in other less obvious ways. For example, if the number of response categories is too small to demonstrate the perceptual discrimination capacity of a subject, then the outcome of the experiment will be limited by a property of the response system rather than by a property of the perceptual system. Thus, a converging operation which is required in many experiments is one which demonstrates that discrimination is invariant with respect to the number of response categories and with respect to the discriminability of differentiation of these categories. Such converging operations must either be carried out or be assumed before we can state anything about the limits of perceptual discrimination; if they are assumed, then the validity of the conclusion is limited by the validity of the assumption.

A second major property of the response system which can affect interpretation of experimental results is that of *response availability*. To some extent this property can be considered as a special case of response differentiation. If a subject fails to use a particular response which is defined as appropriate to a particular stimulus, we cannot state that there was a failure of the perceptual system. The failure of response can be due to sheer motor inability. It can also be due to such things as response inhibition (as in the case of vulgar words). That is to say, the response system can be affected by emotional factors just as well as the perceptual system can.

There are other ways in which response availability can operate. For example, it is known that human subjects (and rats too) have a preference for some responses over others. These preferences can affect the apparent nature of the relation between stimuli and responses, and, unless they are taken into account, can lead to misinterpretations about properties of the perceptual system. Subjects also exhibit sequential effects in their responses and, if preferred sequences of responses conflict with the sequences of stimuli presented, misinterpretations can again occur. This factor is commonly taken into consideration in psychophysical experiments, where truly random sequences of stimuli are rarely used. Rather, modified random sequences are used which prevent long runs, since most subjects do not believe that long runs can occur by chance and thus are unwilling to use them.

In summary, then, there are many ways in which properties of the response system can affect the outcome of a perceptual experiment and, unless converging operations are used to delimit an effect specifically to the perceptual system, properties can be incorrectly ascribed to that system.

CONVERGING OPERATIONS AND SOME CURRENT PROBLEMS IN PERCEPTION

To illustrate more specifically the implications of this discussion for research on perception, we shall discuss three types of experiments in these terms, pointing out the kinds of converging operations which are necessary before the results of experiments can reasonably be ascribed to particular properties of the perceptual system.

Subception. The concept of subception has been introduced by Lazarus and McCleary (10) to explain the results of a certain class of experiments on perception. Typically, in these experiments, subjects make two different but simultaneous responses to stimuli from a set presented one at a time. Usually some of the stimuli have a meaning (frequently anxiety-producing) which is different from that of other stimuli in the set. This different meaning may be inherent in the words, or may be induced by conditioning procedures. One response is overt, usually verbal. The other response is often physiological, nonverbalizable, and presumably indicative of emotion. The GSR has been most frequently used. The result which subception purports to explain is that the nonverbalized response shows discrimination when the verbalized response does not. To explain this result it is assumed that perceptual discrimination occurs subconsciously: thus the term subception, which ascribes a property to the perceptual system.

Underlying this definition of subception is the equation of consciousness with verbal report, a distinction that we are reluctant to accept without more explicit specification of the converging operations on which it rests. But even assuming that these converging operations can be specified, the inference of unconscious perceptual discrimination from the typical subception experiment is not justified. It is not justified because the converging operations are lacking that would permit us to ascribe the results to properties of the perceptual system as opposed to properties of the response system. The fact that the GSR is a nonverbally reportable response, is not sufficient cause for assuming that the perceptual discrimination is also not verbally reportable.

Eriksen (5) has pointed out that the subception result can be looked at basically as the demonstration of a partial correlation between the stimulus and the GSR, with the verbal response held constant. When the subception experiment is conceived this way, many properties of the response system which could produce the subception result become more obvious. For example, Eriksen has noted that such factors as lack of verbal response differentiation, asynchronous response oscillation, and differential response strengths will satisfy the requirements for the partial correlation.

When the problem is looked at this way it becomes obvious that a demonstrated partial correlation as indicated above does not allow us to infer the property of subconscious discrimination to the perceptual system.

Rather, in order to demonstrate that there is perceptual discrimination which cannot be verbally described, it is necessary to show that the first-order correlation of stimuli with nonverbal responses is greater than that between stimuli and verbal responses. But even if a single experiment gave this result, it would still be necessary to use converging operations which demonstrate that the correlation between stimuli and verbal response was not limited by the size or degree of differentiation of the response set. Bricker and Chapanis (2) have shown that more precise discrimination of stimuli can be accomplished verbally if more alternative responses are allowed. If no verbal response system can be found which gives as good a correlation with stimuli as the GSR, then and only then can we conclude that additional perceptual discrimination is operating at a nonverbal level.

Perceptual Set. Many experiments have demonstrated that the nature of the relation between stimuli and responses changes when the response system changes. A common interpretation of such experiments is that the set of responses provided the subject serves to produce a perceptually selective set. In many of these experiments, however, the necessary converging operations have not been undertaken to justify delimitation of the effect to the perceptual system.

Suppose an experiment similar to one by Hyman and Hake (9), in which subjects are required to identify the form of stimuli presented tachistoscopically. In one condition subjects are told prior to the stimulus exposure that the form will be one of two particular alternatives. In another condition they are told that the form will be one of four. When the duration of exposure required for identification of the form is shorter with just two stimuli, a possible conclusion is that subjects adopt a more accurate perceptual set with the smaller number of stimuli.

There is, however, an alternative explanation which requires no assumptions about the accuracy of the perceptual process, namely, that the amount of error in the response system decreases with a decrease in number of response categories. One necessary converging operation, then, is to run another experiment in which four stimuli are presented, but only two response categories are allowed. If the accuracy of identification in this case is identical to the two stimulus-two response case, then we must assume that the effect is due entirely to a characteristic of the response system. To complete the set of converging operations, it would be necessary also to present two stimuli but to allow four response categories. If the responses, however, are direct descriptions of the stimuli, this last operation would be meaningless to carry out.

Actually, there is still another set of converging operations necessary if two responses are used with four stimuli. If the nature of the responses and stimuli are such that the subject can observe one of two aspects of the stimulus, then this operation is parallel to that of using two stimuli and two responses. For example, suppose that the four stimuli were red square, blue square, red circle, blue circle; and the two responses were red, blue. For all practical purposes, there are just two stimuli, not four, and this operation would not allow us to determine where the effect exists. If the responses were abstract, such as letters of the alphabet, and were not assigned to the stimuli by just color or form, the operation would be converging. One system for handling this problem is to use the two responses with all possible pairs of the four stimuli to determine the extent to which meaningful grouping of the stimuli affects discrimination.

Sensory Scales.   One area of perceptual research where these principles of converging operations are most difficult to apply, and have been applied least, is that of sensory magnitude scales. Psychological scales have been produced for pitch, loudness, weight, brightness, length, and many other perceptual attributes. In most cases it is assumed that the resultant scale tells us about a property of the perceptual system, but we believe that very few of the experiments have included the necessary converging operations to insure that the final function truly describes a perceptual process.

To illustrate, let us suppose an experiment similar to one reported by Reese *et al.* (12). We provide a large circular, vertical display on which appears a single line radiating from the center. This line is set to various angular positions, and subjects are asked to estimate the angle, using as responses the whole numbers from 0 to 360. When we have obtained many estimates, and averaged them for given physical settings, we plot the estimated angle against the presented angle. At first glance it would appear that we could call such a function a psychological scale of inclination having interval properties. We have no converging operations, however, to indicate that the subjects actually used the numerical response system in such a way as to reflect the perceived magnitudes of angles. People have had considerable experience with such estimates, particularly with clocks, and in the course of this experience they have learned to identify certain perceptions with certain numbers. The fact that later they can do so in an experiment does not alter the fact that they are using the numbers simply as learned identifying responses. Since the subjects have had experience with the 0 to 12 scale but not with the 0 to 360 scale, it might be argued that the new number system would actually reflect properties of the perceptual system. However, as we pointed out above, one operation which is a transform of another does not satisfy the requirements of converging operations.

There is an operation which would appear to satisfy the requirements of convergence for the property under consideration—an interval property of the perceptual system. This operation would be to have the subjects set series of three radiating lines in such a way that two equal angular intervals are provided. In this case a number system is not used, and thus the chance that the numbers are used simply as identifying labels would seem to be minimized. Subjects are so accustomed to using numbers in this situation, however, that they may very well verbalize the numbers to themselves, and thus once again we have a transform rather than a converging operation.

Actually, in situations where so much learning of objectivity assignable numbers to stimulus attributes has occurred, it is doubtful that we can ever sufficiently satisfy the requirements of converging operations to be sure that we are measuring a metric property of the perceptual system, rather than of the objective stimulus system. It would be necessary to get subjects who have had no previous experience in assigning numbers to the continuum under consideration.

Gibson and Bergman (8) have clearly recognized the nature of this problem in their experiments on estimation of distance. Consistent underestimations of distance can be corrected by one or two correction trials (the correction generalizing to all distances used in the experiment), and the authors feel that the correction has simply changed the subjects' conceptual scale of yards. In other words, they are assuming that the change was not in the perceptual system, but rather in the response system. Given a situation like this, we can make statements about the conceptual scale of numbers which the subject has, and its relation to physically measured distance, but we cannot know anything about the metric properties of the perceptual system.

There are other types of psychological dimension that make the problems more obscure because there is no commonly accepted number system which the usual subject has been trained to use. Of these, the one dimension that has received the greatest attention is loudness. Presumably, subjects have had little or no training in using a number scale to describe the loudness of a tone or noise. So when a subject is asked to assign numbers to the loudnesses of various tones, he should be able to respond only on the basis of the perceived magnitudes. This position has been taken by several psychologists, particularly Stevens (13). However, when subjects are required to use a set of responses which constitute a numerical scale, we have no assurance that they in fact use the response continuum in such a way as to reflect the ratio or interval properties of the perceived loudness correctly. The question is not whether they can use the *number* scale correctly, when using it as an abstract scale, but rather whether they use it in such a way as to reflect a metric property of the perceptual system.

Suppose we have done an experiment in which direct numerical estimates of the loudnesses of tones, or of the relative loudnesses of two different tones, are made. From these estimates we can construct a functional relation which we can tentatively call a psychological scale of loudness. Having no assurance that the number scale was used to reflect the metric properties of the perceptual system—the numbers could have been used as simple identifying responses, or perhaps as ordered responses—we need to carry out one or more operations which converge to allow us to delimit a property of the perceptual system. We could ask our subjects to produce tones which sound half, or a quarter, as loud as other tones which the experimenter provides. Such an operation does not converge with the former, however, since the number system whose use is in doubt is the same in both instances.

A considerably better converging operation is one that does not require the use of numbers at all. If a fractionation or direct estimation has been carried out, and if the resultant function is truly a loudness scale with the properties of a ratio scale, then we should be able to determine a set of equal interval points on our scale. Now if we ask our subject to set a series of tones at intensities which provide a series of equal intervals of loudnesses, these equal intervals should check with those obtained from the fractionation experiments. In the one instance in which such a comparison has been made, Garner (7) showed that the results of the two experiments do not check; the two experimental operations did not converge to a single concept about the metric properties of the perceptual system. Garner also showed that if it is assumed only that the fractionation experiments provided equal ratios—not necessarily with the stated magnitude—the two experiments can converge to a single loudness scale. This scale is quite different from that obtained with numerical estimates, however, and its properties and uses are different from those assumed for "scales" obtained from direct estimates.

The major point of this section is not to prove that psychological magnitude scales are impossible to construct but simply to point out that before we can ascribe a property to the perceptual system as refined as that of a ratio scale, certain minimal converging operations are required—operations that in practice have rarely been carried out. Furthermore, it is not sufficient to carry out the same experiment twice, or to carry out a slightly modified experiment which provides only transform operations. The operations must truly be converging for the pertinent assumed property of the perceptual system. Until these operations are carried out, we can have only functional relations, not magnitude scales.[1]

CONCLUSION

Our emphasis on the use of carefully planned operations in order to isolate properties of perceptual behavior should not be taken to mean that operationism properly used tends to minimize the importance of perception. We believe simply that its proper use rigorously defines those properties which validly can be assigned to perception.

[1] It should be pointed out that there are other scaling techniques for which the ascribed properties of the perceptual system are not at variance with the converging operations carried out. The discriminative scaling techniques, particularly as developed by Thurstone, satisfy these requirements as long as no attempt is made to assume that the resultant scales reflect magnitude of perceptions rather than discriminability of perceptions.

This argument holds for all aspects of behavior which can be described as perceptual. For example, the comparison usually made between the rich, although unreliable, data provided by introspection and the sterile, although rigorous, data provided by operationism is invalid for two reasons: first, because the basic position taken by many operationists does not indicate the real possibilities inherent in this position; second, and more important, because the data produced by introspection can have no meaning independent of the operations used to produce them.

For example, two aspects of the introspective method have been claimed to have special advantages. First, it is claimed that a much more detailed description of experience can be reported by a subject using unrestricted responses. This problem is not unique with introspection. Operationism does not require that responses be restricted in any way; it only points out that with unrestricted response sets, it is difficult or impossible to separate properties of the response system from those of the perceptual system.

A second claimed advantage of introspection is that subjects can be instructed to confine their attention to facts of subjective experience, i.e., the stimulus error can be avoided. There is nothing about operationism which excludes this possibility, either. The effects of the subject's set produced by instruction and training are important experimental problems in perception. We insist, though, that if these effects are in the perceptual system, then operations can be devised to demonstrate this fact. These operations must demonstrate that the effect of instructions is not merely to change the kinds of responses that subjects use, nor simply to decrease the correlation between stimuli and responses by causing subjects to respond to factors other than stimuli. That is to say, the methods of introspection are operations, and as such cannot lead to valid concepts that are independent of these operations. Introspection and the data produced by it do not lie outside the scope of operationism as here conceived.

We also feel that there is no need to minimize experimental questions about "awareness." For humans, at least, awareness is undoubtedly one aspect of perception. We insist, however, that the awareness of a subject can be no more than a property of his perceptual system, and that it can be specified only in terms of a set of converging operations.

In summary, we believe that our position is truly one of operationism. We believe that a concept has no meaning beyond that obtained from the operations on which it is based. This statement does not mean that any set of operations can lead to a concept. Nor does it mean that the complexity and usefulness of concepts derived from operations are necessarily limited in any way. In practice they are limited only by the ingenuity of the individual experimenter to devise appropriate converging operations.

SUMMARY

Perception is conceived as a process intervening between stimuli and responses. As such it can be viewed as a concept whose properties may be delimited by converging operations. Converging operations are any set of experimental operations which eliminate alternative hypotheses and which can lead to a concept which is not uniquely identified with any one of the original operations, but is defined by the results of all operations performed. Thus converging operations can lead to concepts of processes which are not directly observable. For example, converging operations can be used to describe properties of the perceptual process which are distinct from those of the response system directly observed.

Illustrations from current experimental problems in perception indicate how some response characteristics may be isolated from perceptual properties, and vice versa. Some of these properties have been ascribed to perception without supporting converging operations by researchers dissatisfied by the sterility of operationism as it is commonly, but mistakenly, conceived.

References

1. Allport, F. H. *Theories of perception and the concept of structure.* New York: Wiley, 1955.
2. Bricker, P. D., & Chapanis, A. Do incorrectly perceived tachistoscopic stimuli convey some information? *Psychol. Rev.* 1953, **60**, 181–188.
3. Bridgman, P. W. Some general principles of operational analysis. *Psychol. Rev.*, 1945, **52**, 246–249.
4. Bridgman, P. W. *The logic of modern physics.* New York: Macmillan, 1927.
5. Eriksen, C. W. Subception: fact or artifact? *Psychol. Rev.*, 1956, **63**, 74–80.
6. Garner, W. R. Context effects and the validity of loudness scales. *J. exp. Psychol.* 1954, **48**, 218–224.
7. Garner, W. R. A technique and a scale for loudness measurement. *J. acoust. Soc. Amer.*, 1954, **26**, 73–88.
8. Gibson, Eleanor J., & Bergman, R. The effect of training on absolute estimation of distance over the ground. *J. exp. Psychol.*, 1954, **48**, 473–482.
9. Hyman, R., & Hake, H. W. Form recognition as a function of the number of forms which can be presented for recognition. *USAF, WADC Tech. Rep.* 1954, 54–164.

10. Lazarus, R. S., & McCleary, R. A. Autonomic discrimination without awareness: a study of subception. *Psychol. Rev.*, 1951, **58**, 113–122.

11. McGinnies, E. Emotionality and perceptual defense. *Psychol. Rev.*, 1949, **56**, 244–251.

12. Reese, E. P., Reese, T. W., Volkmann, J., & Corbin, H. H. Psychophysical research: summary report 1946–1952. *USN, Spec. Dev. Cent. Tech. Rep.*, 1953, SDC-131–1–5.

13. Stevens, S. S. The direct estimation of sensory magnitudes-loudness. *Amer. J. Psychol.*

51. OPERATIONAL DEFINITIONS

Robert H. Ennis

INTRODUCTION

On all sides we are warned that our results depend on the instruments and procedures used, and we are admonished to define our terms in a manner that takes account of these instruments and procedures (often this admonition specifies that the definition should be operational); yet we want to express our conclusions in terms that are not limited to the particular instruments and procedures. That sets my problem: How can we give operational definitions without unduly restricting the meaning of the terms in which we state our conclusions?

In this paper I shall examine various forms that operational definitions might take and shall develop and defend a set of guides for making these definitions. These guides will enable us to connect our abstract terms to our instruments and procedures without completely limiting the meaning of the terms to these instruments and procedures.

THE SPIRIT OF OPERATIONISM

An early expression of what has come to be called "operationism" is found in P. W. Bridgman's *The Logic of Modern Physics:* "The concept of length involves as much as and nothing more than the set of operations by which

SOURCE. Ennis, Robert H., "Operational Definitions," *American Educational Research Journal*, 1:3, May 1964. Copyright © 1964 by American Educational Research Association.

length is determined. In general, we mean by any concept nothing more than a set of operations; *the concept is synonymous with the corresponding set of operations*" (Bridgman, 1927; p. 5). Although Bridgman, who is regarded as the father of operationism, goes too far in this statement, the focus on instruments and procedures, which is the essence of operationism, comes through clearly. This focus may be viewed as one of the empiricist and pragmatic trends of recent years, as A. C. Benjamin has shown in his interesting summary and appraisal of Bridgman's ideas and their development under criticism (Benjamin, 1955).

As a thesis, the spirit of operationism can be loosely put as follows: *There is an important relationship between the meaning of a term and the instruments and procedures that one would use to see whether the term applies to a particular situation and, if so, how.*

FORMS IN WHICH THIS SPIRIT HAS BEEN EXPRESSED

In the literature on operationism one finds four basic approaches to operational definitions: 1) giving examples; 2) giving a set of operations as the meaning of a concept; 3) equating a phrase or sentence containing the term in question with a phrase or sentence about a combination of operations and observations; and 4) providing implication relationships among operations, observations, and the concept in question. The proposed guides fit under the fourth approach, the description of which has been vague because of the several variations possible.

Since the defense of these guides rests heavily on showing the difficulties of the first three approaches, difficulties that are avoided if one follows the guides, we must look carefully at all four approaches.

1. Giving Examples

Although Bridgman had something more rigorous in mind, the use of examples of abstract concepts sometimes indicates the instruments and procedures involved when using the concepts and, at an unsophisticated level, does provide an empirical interpretation. G. A. Lundberg, the sociologist, indicates endorsement of the example approach in the following statement: "The simplest form of an operational definition of a word is to point to its referent while enunciating the word. Thus we define the word 'cat' to a child by pointing to a certain kind of animal or a succession of animals denoted by the word in our language" (Lundberg, 1942a; p. 730).

Examples are very useful in clarifying terms because they connect them to the concrete world—concreteness is one of the virtues of operational definitions. But in giving an example, one does not necessarily specify a manipulation by an investigator, and thus exemplification misses some of the spirit of operationism. The "cat" example above does not specify a manipulation by an investigator; instead it specifies particular cats.

Nevertheless, it would not be a serious error to treat examples as operational definitions—provided that we have distinct names for what would then be two different kinds of operational definitions. Obvious, though rather wordy, names are "example-type operational definitions" and "manipulative operational definitions." For verbal economy I prefer to mark the distinction with the terms "example" and "operational definition," both of which have established usages. Accordingly, examples would not be operational definitions.

2. Giving a Set of Operations as the Meaning of a Concept
(Form: Concept = Operations)

This approach is suggested by a strict interpretation of Bridgman's statement quoted earlier. According to this approach, *length* means a set of operations, such as putting down a ruler end over end and (presumably) counting the number of times this is done. *Length* means what you do; it is not a property of the thing you do it to. It does not mean what you find out; it means what you do when finding out.

If we apply this approach strictly to a concept often used in social-science research, *IQ* might mean administering and (presumably) scoring the *California Test of Mental Maturity*[1] (henceforth referred to as *CTMM*). An *IQ* would not then be a quality of a child; the child's IQ would mean what you had done to him.

Another feature of this approach is that it implies as many concepts of *length* (*IQ*, etc.) as there are ways of measuring it. According to Bridgman, the concept *length* in *length of a city lot* is different from the concept *length* in *length of a large piece of land* if measuring sticks alone are used for determining the first and measuring sticks plus triangulation for the second, because the sets of operations are different (Bridgman, 1927; p. 14). Similarly, there would be as many concepts of *IQ* as there are tests for IQ and ways of administering them. If meaning is identical with a set of operations, different operations imply different meanings. Bridgman says, "If we have more than one set of operations, we have more than one concept, and strictly there should be a separate name to correspond to each different set of operations" (Bridgman, 1927; p. 10).

Thus, there are these two distinguishing features of this, the second, approach to operationism: (a) the meaning of a concept is limited to the operations, and (b) different operations imply different concepts. I shall criticize each feature.

---

[1] To simplify the presentation, I have not given the form, edition, or level of the tests discussed.

(a) To treat the meaning of a concept (or term) as limited to set of operations seems odd, to say the least. When I say that the length of a bench is five feet, I intend to be talking about the bench—not about what I did. When I say that Johnny has a low IQ, I intend to be talking about Johnny—not about what I did. If one interprets Bridgman's original formula strictly, there seems no way to include the observations that one makes, observations that reveal the qualities measured. One cannot talk about the things measured; one can talk only about what the experimenter does—not about what he perceives.

It may be held that this reading of Bridgman's statements is unfair—that he did not mean them as I have presented them. Perhaps so. I do not see how anyone could really mean them that way although some sociologists and psychologists may appear to have so taken them.[2] An examination of *The Logic of Modern Physics* and the works of these social scientists reveals that it is hard to be sure just what they do mean. However, my purpose here is not to criticize them but to clarify the advantages and disadvantages of various expressions of the operationist spirit. Strictly interpreted, this, the second, approach to operationism neglects the results one gets after doing the operations.

(b) There is no doubt that people (including Bridgman in *The Logic of Modern Physics* and most social scientists that I have read on the subject) have taken seriously the second feature of the second approach to operationism (that different operations imply different concepts), and there has been considerable dispute on this point. I shall not go into it thoroughly here because to do so would require systematic treatment of the nature and content of scientific theories, about which there is a vast literature. I shall only comment on the serious difficulties of this view. These comments are carefully elaborated, however, because they contribute substantially to refuting the third (and most popular) approach to operationism.

The first point to clarify is how to tell if two operations are actually different. Is my administration of the *CTMM* at 9:00 a.m. on Monday, April 6, 1964, in Fall Creek School a different operation from my administration of the *CTMM* at 10:00 a.m. on Monday, April 6, 1964, in Belle Sherman School? The only differences are the time and place of administration. To my knowledge, no satisfactory criterion, operational or otherwise, has been provided by operationists of the concept *different operation*. This is a significant weakness of the thesis that different operations require different concepts. We do not know how different, or in what respects different, the operations have to be to require different concepts.

Let us, however, assume that different times and places do not require a

2 For examples, see Lundberg (1942b, p. 89), Stevens (1951, p. 28), and Marx (1951, p. 11).

judgment of different operations. But presumably the use of measuring sticks and that of measuring sticks plus triangulation would be different operations, as would the use of the *CTMM* and that of the *Lorge-Thorndike Intelligence Tests*. Similarly, using the mercury thermometer, the alcohol thermometer, and the resistance thermometer would be three different operations.

But why should there be two concepts of length, two concepts of IQ, and three concepts of temperature to correspond to the various operations mentioned in the previous paragraph? Why not one concept of length and two ways of measuring it? One concept of IQ and two ways of estimating it? One concept of temperature and three ways of determining it?

Let us consider the concept *temperature*. (Analogous things could be said about *length*, but these things would be considerably more difficult.) What would be the consequences of having three concepts of temperature, say *M-temperature* for the mercury thermometer, *A-temperature* for the alcohol thermometer, and *R-temperature* for the resistance thermometer? Since there are many more ways of measuring temperature, there would, of course, have to be many more concepts.

One difficulty is that people would misunderstand someone who held this view since people think of temperature as one quality, which is measured in various ways. But this is not an insuperable objection. One might stipulate three senses for the word "temperature" that represent qualities highly correlated with one another and hold that these senses should be distinguished for scientists and sloppily merged for laymen. This is a plausible answer; scientists are not bound by ordinary usage in their research.

A second difficulty, however, is that physics itself would become immensely more complicated. The law of thermal expansion would become three laws, one for each concept. (And since there are many more ways of measuring temperature, there would have to be many more laws, where previously we managed with only one.) Furthermore, the law based on *M-temperature* would extend over a different range from that of the law based on *R-temperature* since the two thermometers have different ranges. Not only convenience would be sacrificed, but also simplicity and elegance.

The attempt to explain differences in temperature would run into difficulty. The model provided by the kinetic theory of heat explains them by means of differences in the mean kinetic energy of molecules. There is just this *one* phenomenon, the mean kinetic energy of molecules, to explain differences in temperature. Minor aberrations and inconsistencies between instruments at extreme points have auxiliary explanations, but the fact remains that there is one underlying phenomenon associated with temperature in physical theory, which implies that temperature is just one thing. (This discussion assumes ordinary contexts; later on, we shall consider a special context with somewhat different results.)

Of course, we could conceivably elevate what I have called "auxiliary explanations" to the status of central explanations, in which case we could have a different central explanation for the phenomenon associated with each instrument, but to do so would be inconvenient. The simplest explanation, and the one that suffices in most cases, is the one that refers only to the mean kinetic energy of the molecules.

What about fruitfulness—the ability of theory to generate new predictions and to suggest new ways of looking at other fields? It is difficult to see how the complex structure that is implicit in the requirement that different operations imply different concepts could be a provoker of new ideas or an aid to seeing new applications; it would be so hard to see the structure as a whole, to see it intuitively.

While there is ordinarily only one concept of temperature functioning within our normal range of experience, the concept does become elusive in extreme situations. When we try to measure temperature at points successively farther from the earth's surface, different operations tend to call for different concepts *because different operations produce radically different readings at the same point* and because our interest in hotness and coldness out in space calls for great attention to sources of radiant heat. The reading on a thermometer depends on whether the thermometer is exposed to radiant heat and, if so, on the direction in which the thermometer is aimed. This is something like the dependence of a reading on whether a thermometer is in the sun or in the shade. There are needed, so to speak, a concept, *shade-temperature*, and a concept, *directional-radiant-temperature*. A thermometer suspended in a reflecting sphere would indicate shade-temperature (to the extent that the sphere successfully reflects radiant energy). A thermometer in a reflecting tube *open* at one end (thus admitting radiant energy from one direction) would indicate directional-radiant-temperature. Thus, under conditions that obtain as we leave the earth, it becomes convenient to have two concepts of temperature since different operations give answers that at times are radically different and since our fundamental concern, hotness and coldness, is radically affected by radiant heat.

In summary, once we are willing to bypass the difficulties attendant upon violating the conventions of everyday speech and ordinary technical language, the difficulty with having a different concept for each operation of temperature measurement is the inconvenience. But under certain conditions, given our interests, we have to accept this inconvenience because the results from two different methods of measurement disagree so greatly. The conclusion is that different operations do *not* by themselves imply different concepts although, under certain circumstances for certain purposes, they may call for different concepts.

Now, do the same considerations apply to *IQ*? In ordinary use (among teachers and others who use the concept but who are not scientists), IQ is held to be *one thing*, estimated with varying degrees of validity by the various intelligence tests. But this in itself is not sufficient reason for educational scientists to adopt a unitary concept. They might hold that the matter is not that simple—the measures we have differ so much that, although they contain common elements, they are not enough alike to warrant calling them measures of the same thing. At best, IQ tests correlate around .8. Thus they have much in common, but not *everything* in common, and we know from analyzing them that they emphasize different abilities, such as spatial reasoning, verbal facility, and numerical skill. Furthermore, there is not yet an explanatory theory for IQ comparable to the kinetic theory of heat. In view of these facts, it would be *safest* to develop a number of concepts of IQ, one for each test. (This, in effect, is part of what people are doing who say that "intelligence" means what is measured by a given intelligence test.)

But there still are the arguments for a unitary concept that depend on simplicity, intelligibility, and fruitfulness. In view of these considerations, I treat *IQ* as a single concept for research purposes in the Cornell Critical Thinking Project, with which I am associated. IQ in this sense is measured with some accuracy by the various tests and, in my experience, is well-enough related to the intellectual performance of people who are similarly motivated and whose backgrounds are roughly the same.

This is a matter about which reasonable men can differ. One may argue that the verbal score yielded by the *Lorge-Thorndike Intelligence Tests* emphasizes verbal ability more than does the score yielded by the *CTMM* and therefore we should treat these scores as connected to different concepts, perhaps *verbal IQ* and *general IQ*. If these scores correlate quite differently with the variable in which we are interested at this time—the ability to think critically, we have evidence for treating them as being connected to different concepts. The main point is that this is a question that must be settled by appealing to the circumstances and purposes involved. *Since it makes sense to argue about the question even after it is agreed that the operations are different, it follows that different operations do not by themselves imply different concepts of IQ.*

Again a difference in operations by itself does not imply different concepts, although different concepts are sometimes called for by different operations in conjunction with certain circumstances. In spite of the fact that the second approach to operational definitions is unsatisfactory on the basis of the first feature alone, detailed examination of the second feature was worth while because rejection of the claim that different operations imply different concepts is a central part of the argument against the third approach to operational definitions.

3. Equating a Phrase or Sentence Containing the Term With a Phrase or Sentence About a Combination of Operations and Observations

This appears to be the approach of the radical behaviorists; for example, B. F. Skinner (1953, p. 585). It is May Brodbeck's approach in N. L. Gage's *Handbook of Research on Teaching* (Brodbeck, 1963; p. 50) and may be the approach actually intended by Bridgman in *The Logic of Modern Physics*. A first statement of this form follows:

3.1a. "X has the property T" means the same as "A given operation was performed and a given observation was made,"

where T is, or contains, the term being defined. Example 1 below is an operational definition of IQ according to Form 3.1a.

Example 1: "X has an IQ of n" means the same as "X was given the *CTMM* and received a score of n."

Form 3.1a is limited to cases where T is in a *sentence* that is equated to another sentence. I should like to generalize the form so that T can appear in either a phrase *or* a sentence that is equated to another phrase or sentence:

3.1b. "Tx" means the same as "OPx and $OBSx$,"

where Tx is a phrase or sentence containing the term T to be defined; OPx is a phrase or sentence about the performance of operations; and $OBSx$ is a phrase or sentence about observations. OPx and $OBSx$ may be merged into one phrase or sentence. Example 1 fits Form 3.1b, as does example 2 below.

Example 2: "A person's IQ" means the same as "a person's score resulting from the administration of the *CTMM*" (or, more simply, "a person's score on the *CTMM*").

The term (or concept) IQ is tied down to a particular intelligence test in this, the third, approach to operational definitions; but, in contrast to the second approach, an IQ is a characteristic of a person, not of the operations performed, though it is still dependent on those operations.

An immediate objection presents itself. In example 1, let us assume that X actually has an IQ of, say, 120. If this is not known because he has not yet taken the test, one is obliged to say that it is false that he has an IQ of 120 since the statement alleged to be identical in meaning is false; that is, it is false that X was given the *CTMM*, so it is false that he was given it and got a score of 120. Hence, by this interpretation, it must be false that he has an IQ of 120. No matter what IQ we assume X to have, a contradiction develops. Since he must have some IQ, the definition is faulty.

A similar problem exists for the phrase approach. According to example 2, a person who does not have a score on the *CTMM* does not have an IQ at all since "score on the *CTMM*" and *IQ* mean the same thing. If that were so, it would make no sense for a principal to ask his guidance counselor to ascertain the IQ's for new students who had never before been tested since, by this interpretation, they have no IQ's (because they have no scores on the *CTMM*).

A way out of this difficulty is to use between *OPx* and *OBSx* an implication relationship that is expressed conditionally and can be put in the subjunctive mood. The revised form is:

3.2. "*Tx*" means the same as "If *OPx*, then *OBSx*." Our sentence example becomes:

Example 3: "*X* has an IQ of *n*" means the same as "If *X* is (were) given the *CTMM*, he will (would) get a score of *n*."

Our phrase example becomes:

Example 4: "A person's IQ" means the same as "the score he will (would) get if given the *CTMM*."

There are problems remaining, but the use of implications that can be put in the subjunctive[3] solves this first one. If a person has never taken the *CTMM* —even if he is never going to take it, he nevertheless has an IQ, perhaps never to be known. And if he has taken it and has a score, there still is no inconsistency, for that does not preclude his being given it again.

In future examples, reference to the subjunctive will be omitted for simplicity's sake. But it should be understood that each example is intended to be convertible to the subjunctive—if need be. Furthermore, phrase-type examples will no longer be given; with appropriate modifications, the general points to be made apply also to them.

Let us now consider another difficulty with the third approach. It limits the meaning of a concept to a particular set of operations (in the case discussed above, the administration of the *CTMM*) together with the results of this set of operations. Thus, like the second approach, it implies that different operations require different concepts. As indicated earlier, this view is generally false—although, under certain circumstances and purposes, different operations do require different concepts.

What is needed is a format that will not commit us to having different operations require different concepts in all cases but will permit some leeway.

---

[3] See Chisholm (1949), Goodman (1952), von Wright (1957), and Will (1947) for interesting discussions of counter-factual conditionals. This problem need not bother us here unless we try to reduce all logical relationships to conjunction and negation (or something similar)—an unwise course, in my opinion.

We must replace the relationship, *means the same as*, with one that does not limit the meaning to a particular set of operations. An implication relationship that does not claim equivalence of meaning will meet this requirement. This idea leads us to the fourth approach.

4. Providing Implication Relationships Among Operations, Observations, and the Concept

We can avoid the difficulty caused by the relationship, *means the same as*, by replacing it with the relationship, *if and only if*.[4] The amended form follows:

4.1. Tx; if and only if; if OPx, then $OBSx$.

The use of "if and only if" permits us to have two, or more, different kinds of operations to measure the same thing. The following examples can *both* be operational definitions of the same concept, *temperature:*

Example 5: X has a temperature of t; if and only if; if a mercury thermometer is inserted in X, the thermometer will read t.

Example 6: X has a temperature of t; if and only if; if an alcohol thermometer is inserted in X, the thermometer will read t.

If "means the same as" appeared in these definitions instead of "if and only if," we should be committed to saying that "mercury thermometer" means the same as "alcohol thermometer." In effect, the if-and-only-if formulation allows several accurate ways of measuring the same thing.

If we apply this approach to the measurement of IQ, another problem becomes prominent. There is much less agreement among IQ tests than there is among thermometers. Even the if-and-only-if formulation seems too rigid. Consider these two possible definitions of the concept IQ:

Example 7: X has an IQ of n; if and only if; if the $CTMM$ is administered to X, X will get a score of n.

Example 8: X has an IQ of n; if and only if; if the *Lorge-Thorndike Intelligence Tests* are administered to X, X will get a score of n.

Together these definitions commit us to saying that a person will get the same

---

4 This approach is along the lines recommended by Carl Hempel (1952, 1961), who has applied Rudolph Carnap's (1953) notion of the *reduction sentence* to the formulation of operational definitions. My approach differs from theirs primarily in the interpretation of the if-then relationship, theirs being a truth-functional interpretation and mine being an ordinary-language interpretation. See P. F. Strawson's *Introduction to Logical Theory* (1952) for a discussion of the difference. If the reader who is unacquainted with this difference in approach simply interprets if-then sentences in the way to which he is accustomed, he will be interpreting these sentences as they are here intended.

score on the *CTMM* as on the *Lorge-Thorndike*. For at least two reasons we do not want to be fully committed to this.

First, the conditions of administration may not be standard for both tests in any given pair of situations. If one test is administered under standard conditions and the other is not, we can hardly expect the same scores. This difficulty can be handled by adding some such phrase as "under standard conditions." It is desirable that a list of standard conditions be available, perhaps in the test manual. Incidentally, this same qualification holds for thermometers when precision is necessary.

Second, each instrument has its idiosyncrasies, which inevitably interfere with measurement at some level of precision. If these are large enough to make a practical difference, some word like "approximately" should be added to the operational definition. Since the idiosyncracies of IQ tests do make a practical difference at the level of precision at which they are used, "approximately" should probably be added to operational definitions of *IQ*. I should not ordinarily add it to operational definitions of *temperature* since the idiosyncracies of thermometers do not make a significant difference in the contexts with which I am familiar. However, for certain purposes and situations, some qualifying word should be added for thermometers also.

To remind us of the qualifications, we can add "(WQ)," which stands for "with qualifications," to Form 4.1:

4.2. *Tx*; if and only if; if *OPx*, then *OBSx* (WQ).

An operational definition of *IQ* might look like this:

Example 9: *X* has an IQ of approximately *n*; if and only if; if the *CTMM* is administered to *X* under standard conditions, *X* will get a score of *n*.

In this example, "approximately" was inserted in the clause containing the concept being defined, *IQ*. This is the proper place for the qualifier when we are trying to judge what someone's IQ is; the method of determination gives an approximation. On the other hand, when we are reasoning from an assumption about what someone's IQ is to a predicted score, "approximately" should appear in the clause about the score:

Example 10: *X* has an IQ of n; if and only if; if the *CTMM* is administered to *X* under standard conditions, *X* will get a score of approximately *n*.

Thus, the location of the qualifiers, as well as the decision about whether to make them explicit, depends to some extent on the situation. Henceforth I shall use "(WQ)" in the examples, leaving placement of the qualifiers to be determined by the context.

People who are not adept at dealing with complicated if-then relationships tend to find Form 4.2 hard to understand. Some read into it the suggestion that a person who has not been given the test does not have an IQ. They also are puzzled by the three occurrences of the word "if" so close together. A more understandable formulation follows:

4.3. If OPx; then Tx, if and only if, $OBSx$ (WQ).

Example 11: If the $CTMM$ is administered to X under standard conditions; then X has an IQ of n, if and only if, he gets a score of n (WQ).

Although this new formulation is easier to understand, it does not say quite the same thing as Form 4.2. To see this, consider the situation in which we are trying to make a judgment about an individual's IQ on the basis of his score on the $CTMM$. Using 4.3, we can conclude that X probably has an IQ of approximately n, where n is the score that we have. However, using 4.2, we cannot draw that conclusion without an auxiliary assumption: our conclusion that X has an IQ of approximately n depends on the *generalization* that n is the score he gets *whenever* he takes the test; it does not rest simply on his getting the score of n this time. To make this generalization, one would probably assume that the score we have is typical for him, an assumption we often make in dealing with test scores. Form 4.3 has this assumption built in, so we should not use 4.3 unless we are fairly confident that the scores on which we are basing our judgments are typical.

Neither formulation allows us to escape the problem of typicality. The problem is faced in applying 4.2 and in adopting 4.3. Since we shall want to adopt 4.3 without being completely committed to the belief that all the scores are typical, the word "probably" should be included among the qualifiers referred to by "(WQ)."

Forms 4.2 and 4.3 suffice for the majority of cases calling for an operational definition of a concept (or term). Why do they not suffice for all cases? The trouble is that they commit us to giving the same conditions as both necessary *and* sufficient for the use of the phrase containing the concept. For example, given the administration of the $CTMM$ under standard conditions, a student's getting a score of n is roughly a necessary and sufficient condition for saying that probably his IQ is approximately n. That we sometimes want to avoid such a commitment can be seen in a situation that faced the staff of the Cornell Critical Thinking Project. The discussion will use 4.3 as a springboard, but with appropriate modifications I could say the same things starting from 4.2.

We built a test called *The Cornell Conditional Reasoning Test*, Form X. Among its seventy-two items are six that supposedly test for mastery of the principle that denial of the consequent implies denial of the antecedent; in other words, knowledge that the following form is valid:

> *p implies q*   (*p* is the antecedent; *q* the consequent)
> *q* is false   (denial of consequent)
> therefore, *p* is false   (conclusion: denial of antecedent)

Here is one of the six items:

29. Suppose you know that

If the bicycle in the garage is Bob's, then it is red.
The bicycle in the garage is not red.

Then would this be true?
The bicycle in the garage is not Bob's.

A. YES   It must be true.
B. NO   It can't be true.
C. MAYBE   It may be true or it may not be true. You weren't told
           enough to be *certain* whether the answer is YES or NO.

The correct answer is YES.

The other five items embodying this principle vary in several ways: the valid conclusion is denied (making the answer NO); the content is abstract; the premises are reversed and the antecedent negated; the truth status of the conclusion is obviously different from the validity status of the argument. The six items are numbered 8, 16, 22, 29, 35, and 39.

Our problem, somewhat simplified, was how to give an operational definition of "mastery of the principle that denial of the consequent implies denial of the antecedent." One approach is to change the concept. As stated, it refers to a dichotomous variable, *mastery*, whereas we could shift to a continuous variable, *degree of mastery*. (*IQ* and *temperature* are continuous variables.) The revised question would be: "What is an operational definition of 'degree of mastery of the principle that denial of the consequent implies denial of the antecedent'?" We can answer that question with the following operational definition:

Example 12: If X is given *The Cornell Conditional Reasoning Test*, Form X; then X has mastered to the degree k the principle that denial of the consequent implies denial of the antecedent, if and only if, he gets a score of k right on the following items: 8, 16, 22, 29, 35, and 39 (WQ).

Using this definition, we obtain a score that can vary from zero to six and that indicates *degree of mastery* of the principle. But this score has limitations. It means little to people who are not well acquainted with the test or with the scores of other individuals whose degree of mastery of this principle is known. Yet the audience for our results is likely to consist largely of such people.

Another drawback is that one of our interests is the determination of the percent of students of a given description who have *mastered* the principle. This interest calls for the judgment that a particular student has or has not done so; it does not call for a judgment about his *degree* of knowledge. We need a definition that will fit our attempts to judge with some assurance whether a student has mastered this principle.

One might suppose that these difficulties could be handled by a definition that gave a certain minimum score as a necessary and sufficient condition for having mastered the principle. For example,

Example 13: If X is given *The Cornell Conditional Reasoning Test*, Form X; then X has mastered the principle that denial of the consequent implies denial of the antecedent, if and only if, X answers correctly at least *four* of these items: 8, 16, 22, 29, 35, and 39 (WQ).

In this example, getting at least four items right is a rough necessary-and-sufficient condition for a person's knowing the principle (we assume that he takes the test). However, we do not want to be committed to any one minimum score as both necessary and sufficient; we do not want to draw that sharp a line between mastery and nonmastery. What we should like to say is something to the effect that getting at least *five* right is a probable sufficient condition and getting at least *four* right is a probable necessary condition. That is, we should like to say of a student who gets at least five right that he probably has mastered the principle and of a student who gets fewer than four right that he probably has not mastered it. About the students who get exactly four right, we are not sure what to say. They are borderline cases—and we should like a definition form that will allow us to leave them that way.

The following form permits us to present the sufficient condition:

4.4. If OPx; then, if $OBSx$, then Tx (WQ).[5]

The operational definition corresponding to this sufficient-condition form follows:

Example 14: If X is given *The Cornell Conditional Reasoning Test*, Form X; then, if X answers correctly at least five of items 8, 16, 22, 29, 35, and 39, X has mastered the principle that denial of the consequent implies denial of the antecedent (WQ).

The following form permits us to present the necessary condition:

4.5. If OPx; then, Tx, only if $OBSx$ (WQ).[6]

---

[5] The sufficient-condition form corresponding to 4.2 is Tx; if; if OPx, then $OBSx$ (WQ). This form, with the adjacent "if's," is harder to understand.

[6] The necessary-condition form corresponding to 4.2, which again is harder to understand, is: Tx; only if; if OPx, then $OBSx$ (WQ).

The operational definition corresponding to this necessary-condition form follows:

Example 15: If X is given *The Cornell Conditional Reasoning Test*, Form X; then X has mastered the principle that denial of the consequent implies denial of the antecedent, *only* if X answers correctly at least four of these items: 8, 16, 22, 29, 35, and 30 (WQ).

To give an operational interpretation of the concept, *knowledge that denial of the consequent implies denial of the antecedent*, we supply both operational definitions, each of which provides a partial interpretation. Combined, they still do not provide a complete interpretation of the concept, but they give a basis on which to work and reason.

It is not necessary to agree with our *specific* decisions in the case above to see the need for Forms 4.4 and 4.5. That is, without contradicting my basic thesis, one can hold that answering correctly a minimum of *one* certain number of the items should be considered *both* necessary and sufficient, or one can hold that the number of items in the necessary condition should differ from that in the sufficient condition but that *four* and *five* are not the proper numbers. It is necessary only to see that these forms may sometiimes be needed.

In summary, I recommend that operational definitions start with an if-clause that specifies an operation or a set of operations and that this clause be followed by an implication relationship between a phrase or sentence containing the concept (or term) to be defined and a phrase or sentence specifying an observation or a set of observations. Appropriate qualifications should be implicit or explicit.

OPERATIONAL INTERPRETATION VERSUS OPERATIONAL DEFINITION

Now that all these qualifications have been introduced, one may wonder if the result is a definition at all. It does not exhaust the meaning of a concept; it is loose; and a pair of operational definitions of the same concept sometimes implies an empirical fact. For example, the two definitions of *IQ* using the *CTMM* and the *Lorge-Thorndike* imply a high correlation between the tests; this is certainly an empirical matter. Some people regard the implication of empirical facts as a serious defect, for presumably definitions should give the meaning of concepts, not give facts.

Fortunately, the utility of the guides that I am proposing does not depend on the resolution of this difficult question. If one boggles at calling the examples I have given "operational definitions," call them "operational interpretations." In either case they help indicate the meaning of a concept, and they do so by focusing on concrete things, especially the manipulations of investigators. They help both to delimit and to fill in the meaning of a concept.

What harm is there in calling them "definitions" so long as we remember that they differ from the classical type of definition, which provides expressions that are equivalent in meaning? Since their purpose and function is to indicate *meaning*, the most reasonable term for them, it seems to me, is "operational definitions." But I do not insist on this, for not much turns on the terminology.[7]

THE NECESSITY FOR DELIBERATE MANIPULATION

Carl Hempel, among others, has suggested that a *deliberate manipulation* by an investigator is not really necessary for an operational definition—that all we need is some condition, whether it be a deliberate manipulation or not. He points out that although emphasis on deliberate operations "is of great interest for the practice of scientific research, . . . it is inessential in securing experimental import for the defined term" (Hempel, 1961; p. 59). It is true that a deliberate manipulation is not a necessary condition for experimental import, but there is an important distinction in discussions of the methodology of scientific research between those definitions that specify manipulations and those that specify other conditions.

If we were proceeding on the assumption that all terms must be operationally defined, Hempel's advice should be heeded because not all terms require manipulation by an experimenter as part of their interpretation (unless such activities as *looking* are regarded as manipulations, in which case operationism reduces to empiricism). Perhaps Hempel offered his advice in the context of an assumed recommendation that all terms be operationally definable. If one does not make that recommendation, one can preserve an independent meaning for the term "operationism," a meaning that emphasizes the manipulations of an investigator. In this case, a recommendation that a term be defined operationally would imply that the definition should specify some bona fide manipulations by the research worker.

As with the case in which it was possible (but not preferable) to call examples "operational definitions," I recommend that we preserve the independent meaning of "operational definition" and that some other term, perhaps "conditional definition,"[8] be used to cover both operational defini-

---

[7] The philosopher would say that the sharp distinction between analytic and synthetic statements is blurred by using the term "definitions." The question is a difficult and subtle one, but I might note that the sharpness of this distinction in the area of empirical science has been questioned recently even in the writings of Carl Hempel, who says (1961, p. 66), "It . . . appears doubtful whether the distinction between analytic and synthetic sentences can be effectively maintained in a formal model of the language of empirical science." Keith Donnellan (1962) has provided a valuable discussion of this question.

[8] Rudolph Carnap (1953) has suggested "reduction sentence," a term in widespread

tions and definitions that are similar in form but contain a nonmanipulative condition in the first if-clause. This approach will preserve the necessary distinctions without violating the original spirit of operationism as expressed by Bridgman and recognized for its value by many empirical scientists.

SUMMARY

In this paper I have examined various forms for the operational definition of concepts, or terms, and have formulated the following set of guides:

A.   Operational definitions should
1.   start with an if-clause specifying the nature of the operation performable by the investigator.
2.   contain an implication relationship that holds when a given operation has been performed. This relationship can be necessary (but not sufficient), sufficient (but not necessary), or both necessary and sufficient.
3.   be convertible to the subjunctive mood if they are not already in the subjunctive.
4.   not be taken to require a separate concept for each operational definition. Some concepts will have many operational definitions.
5.   contain, either explicitly or implicitly, qualifying words or phrases like "approximately," "probably," and "under standard conditions."

B.   Three useful forms for operational definitions follow:

Let: Tx represent a phrase or sentence containing the term (or concept) T being defined. For example, "X has an IQ of n," in which IQ is the concept.

OPx represent a phrase or sentence about the performance of an operation or a set of operations. For example, "X is (were) given the $CTMM$."

$OBSx$ represent a phrase or sentence about an observation or a set of observations. For example, "X's score is (will be, would be) n."

WQ indicate that certain qualifications like "approximately" and "probably" should be included in the definition.

Form 1.   In which $OBSx$ is a necessary and sufficient condition, given OPx:

use among philosophers. Because this term is closely associated with truthfunctional logic and suggests that abstract concepts are reduced to concrete terms without loss (this is not Carnap's intent), I prefer "conditional definition." This term is free from these connotations and indicates the conditional aspect of the definition.

If OPx; then Tx, if and only if, $OBSx$ (WQ). (4.3)

Example: If X is given the $CTMM$; then X has an IQ of n, if and only if, X's score is n (WQ).

Form 2. In which $OBSx$ is a sufficient condition, given OPx:

If OPx; then, if $OBSx$, then Tx (WQ). (4.4)

Form 3. In which $OBSx$ is a necessary condition, given OPx:

If OPx; then Tx, only if $QBSx$ (WQ). (4.5)

It was not claimed that all definitions in the empirical sciences should be operational. It was assumed that it is often a good idea to define concepts (or terms) operationally because the specific connections alleged between the concrete world and an abstract concept are important and because an especially important set of these connections involves the particular instruments and procedures used by the investigator.

References

Benjamin, A. Cornelius. *Operationism*. Springfield, Ill.: Charles C Thomas, 1955. 154 pp.

Bergmann, Gustav. "Sense and Nonsense in Operationism." *The Validation of Scientific Theories*. (Edited by Philipp G. Frank.) New York: Collier Books, 1961, pp. 46–56.

Bergmann, Gustav, and Spence, Kenneth W. "Operationism and Theory Construction." *Psychological Theory*. (Edited by Melvin H. Marx.) New York: Macmillan Co., 1951, pp. 54–66.

Bridgman, Percy W. *The Logic of Modern Physics*. New York: Macmillan Co., 1927. 228 pp.

Bridgman, Percy W. "The Present State of Operationalism." *The Validation of Scientific Theories*. (Edited by Philipp G. Frank.) New York: Collier Books, 1961, pp. 75–80.

Brodbeck, May. "Logic and Scientific Method in Research on Teaching." *Handbook of Research on Teaching*. (Edited by Nathaniel L. Gage.) Chicago: Rand McNally and Co., 1963, pp. 44–93.

Carnap, Rudolph, "Testability and Meaning." *Readings in the Philosophy of Science*. (Edited by Herbert Feigl and May Brodbeck.) New York: Appleton-Century-Crofts, 1953, pp. 47–92.

Chapin, F. Stuart. *Contemporary American Institutions*. New York: Harper and Brothers, 1935. 423 pp.

Chapin, F. Stuart. "Definition of Definitions of Concepts." *Social Forces* 18: 153–60; December 1939.

Chisholm, Roderick M. "The Contrary-to-Fact Conditional." *Readings in*

Philosophical Analysis. (Edited by Herbert Feigl and Wilfred Sellars.) New York: Appleton-Century-Crofts, 1949, pp. 482–97.

Coombs, Clyde H. "Theory and Methods of Measurement." *Research Methods in the Behavioral Sciences.* (Edited by Leon Festinger and Daniel Katz.) New York: Dryden Press, 1953, pp. 471–535.

Dodd, Stuart C. "Operational Definitions Operationally Defined." *American Journal of Sociology* 48: 482–89; January 1943.

Dodd, Stuart C. "A System of Operationally Defined Concepts for Sociology. *American Sociological Review* 4: 619–34: October 1939.

Donnellan, Keith, S. "Necessity and Criteria." *Journal of Philosophy* 59: 647–58; October 25, 1962.

Fiegl, Herbert. "Operationism and Scientific Method." *Readings in Philosophical Analysis* (Edited by Herbert Fiegl and Wilfred Sellars.) New York: Appleton-Century-Crofts, 1949, pp. 498–509.

Frank, Philipp G., editor. *The Validation of Scientific Theories.* New York: Colliers Books, 1961. 220 pp.

Goodman, Nelson. "The Problem of Counterfactual Conditionals." *Semantics and the Philosophy of Language.* (Edited by Leonard Linsky.) Urbana, Ill.: University of Illinois Press, 1952, pp. 231–46.

Grünbaum, Adolf. "Operationism and Relativity." *The Validation of Scientific Theories.* (Edited by Philipp G. Frank.) New York: Collier Books, 1961, pp. 83–92.

Hempel, Carl G. *Fundamentals of Concept Formation in Empirical Science.* International Encyclopedia of Unified Science, Vol. 2, No. 7. Chicago: University of Chicago Press, 1952. 93 pp.

Hempel, Carl G. "A Logical Appraisal of Operationism." *The Validation of Scientific Theories.* (Edited by Philipp G. Frank.) New York: Collier Books, 1961, pp. 56–69.

Koch, Sigmund, editor. *Psychology: A Study of a Science,* Vol. 3. New York: McGraw-Hill Book Co., 1959. 837 pp.

Langfeld, Herbert S., editor. "Symposium on Operationism." *Psychological Review* 52: 241–94; September 1945.

Lazarsfeld, Paul F. "Latent Structure Analysis." *Psychology: A Study of a Science,* Vol. 3. (Edited by Sigmund Koch.) New York: McGraw-Hill Book Co., 1959, pp. 476–543.

Lundberg, George A. "Operational Definitions in the Social Sciences." *American Journal of Sociology* 47: 727–43; March 1942a.

Lundberg, George A. *Social Research.* Second edition. London: Longmans, Green and Co., 1942b. 426 pp.

Margenau, Henry. "Interpretations and Misinterpretations of Operationalism." *The Validation of Scientific Theories.* (Edited by Philipp G. Frank.) New York: Collier Books, 1961, pp. 45–46.

Marx, Melvin H. "The General Nature of Theory Construction." *Psycho-

logical Theory. (Edited by Melvin H. Marx.) New York: Macmillan Co., 1951, pp. 4–19.

Schlesinger, G. "P. W. Bridgman's Operational Analysis: The Differential Aspect." *British Journal for the Philosophy of Science* 9: 299–306; February 1959.

Sjoberg, Gideon. "Operationalism and Social Research." *Symposium on Sociological Theory*. (Edited by Llewellyn Gross.) Evanston, Ill.: Row Peterson and Co., 1959, pp. 603–27.

Skinner, Burrhus F. "The Operational Analysis of Psychological Terms." *Readings in the Philosophy of Science*. (Edited by Herbert Feigl and May Brodbeck.) New York: Appleton-Century-Crofts, 1953, pp. 585–95.

Stevens, S. Smith. "Psychology and the Science of Science." *Psychological Theory*. (Edited by Melvin H. Marx.) New York: Macmillan Co., 1951. pp. 21–54.

Strawson, Peter F. *Introduction to Logical Theory*. London: Methuen and Co., 1952. 266 pp.

Valois, A. John. *A Study of Operationism and Its Implications for Educational Psychology*. Washington, D.C.: Catholic University Press, 1960: 162 pp.

Will, Frederick L. "The Contrary-to-Fact Conditional." *Mind* 56: 236–49; July 1947.

Wright, Georg H. von. *Logical Studies*. New York: Humanities Press, 1957. 195 pp.

52. VERIFIABILITY

Friedrich Waismann

I

When we reflect on such a sentence as "The meaning of a statement is the method of its verification," we should, first of all, be quite clear as to what we mean by the term "method of verification." From a logical point of view we are not interested in the various activities that are involved in verifying a statement. What, then, is it we have in mind when we talk of such things? Take an example. Suppose there is a metal ball in front of me, and I have the task of finding out whether the ball is charged with electricity. To do that I connect the ball with an electroscope and watch whether the gold leaves diverge. The statement "The gold leaves of the instrument diverge" (s) describes the verification of the statement "The ball is charged" (p). Now what exactly am I doing when I describe the verification of the statement p? I establish a connection between two statements by declaring that the one (s) is to follow from the other (p). In other words, I lay down a *rule of inference* which allows me to pass from the statement "The ball is charged with electricity" to another that describes an observable situation. By doing this I connect the statement with another one, I make it part of a system of operations, I incorporate it into language, in short, *I determine the way it is to be used*. In this sense giving the verification of a statement is an important part

SOURCE. Reprinted from "Verifiability," by Friedrich Waismann in Antony Flew (ed.), *Logic and Language* (First Series). New York: Doubleday & Company, 1952. Copyright © 1952 by Doubleday & Company, New York.

of giving its use, or, to put it differently, explaining its verification is a contribution to its grammar.

In everyday life we understand sentences without bothering much as to the way they are verified. We understand them because we understand the single words which occur in them and grasp the grammatical structure of the sentence as a whole. The question of the verification arises only when we come across a new sort of combination of words. If, for instance, someone were to tell us that he owned a dog that was able to think, we should at first not quite understand what he was talking about and would ask him some further questions. Suppose he described to us in detail the dog's behaviour in certain circumstances, then we should say "Ah, now we understand you, that's what you call thinking." There is no need to inquire into the verification of such sentences as "The dog barks," "He runs," "He is playful," and so on, as the words are then used as we may say in their *normal* way. But when we say "The dog thinks," we create a new context, we step outside the boundaries of common speech, and then the question arises as to what is meant by such a word series. In such cases explaining the verification is explaining the meaning, and changing the verification is changing the meaning. Obviously meaning and verification *are* connected—so why say they are not?

But when I say that the statement p is connected with the statements s_1, s_2 ... s_n which describes evidences for it, I do *not* say that p is *identical* with s_1, $s_2 \ldots s_n$ or their conjunction.[1] To say this would only be true if s_1, $s_2 \ldots s_n$ or their conjunction entailed p. Now is that so? There *may* be statements which are nothing more than abbreviations for all that which is unfolded in their verification. There are, however, other sorts of statements of which this is certainly not true. Recent discussions on phenomenalism, for example, tend to show that no conjunction or disjunction of sense-datum statements, however complex, entails the existence or the non-existence of a certain material object. If that is so, a material object statement, though it *is* connected with sense-datum statements, is not just an abbreviation for them, rather has it a logical status of its own, and is not equivalent to any truth-function of the latter ones. I think that the result of these discussions is essentially right, and I ask for permission, to make my point quite clear, to add one word more.

The failure of the phenomentalist to translate a material object statement into terms of sense-data is not, as has been suggested, due to the poverty of our language which lacks the vocabulary for describing all the minute details of sense experience, nor is it due to the difficulties inherent in producing an *infinite* combination of sense-datum statements though all these things may contribute to it. In the main it is due to a factor which, though it is very im-

---

[1] This symbolism, and the other symbolism used in this article, is explained as it is introduced, and no knowledge of technical logic is required to understand it.—EDITOR.

portant and really quite obvious, has to my knowledge never been noticed—to the "open texture"[2] of most of our empirical concepts. What I mean is this: Suppose I have to verify a statement such as "There is a cat next door"; suppose I go over to the next room, open the door, look into it and actually see a cat. Is this enough to prove my statement? Or must I, in addition to it, touch the cat, pat him and induce him to purr? And supposing that I had done all these things, can I then be absolutely certain that my statement was true? Instantly we come up against the well-known battery of sceptical arguments mustered since ancient times. What, for instance, should I say when that creature later on grew to a gigantic size? Or if it showed some queer behaviour usually not to be found with cats, say, if, under certain conditions, it could be revived from death whereas normal cats could not? Shall I, in such a case, say that a new species has come into being? Or that it was a cat with extraordinary properties? Again, suppose I say "There is my friend over there." What if on drawing closer in order to shake hands with him he suddenly disappeared? "Therefore it was not my friend but some delusion or other." But suppose a few seconds later I saw him again, could grasp his hand, etc. What then? "Therefore my friend was nevertheless there and his disappearance was some delusion or other." But imagine after a while he disappeared again, or seemed to disappear—what shall I say now? Have we rules ready for all imaginable possibilities?

An example of the first sort tends to show that we can think of situations in which we couldn't be certain whether something was a cat or some other animal (or a *jinni*). An example of the second sort tends to show that we can consider circumstances in which we couldn't be certain whether something was real or a delusion. The fact that in many cases there is no such thing as a conclusive verification is connected with the fact that most of our empirical concepts are not delimited in all possible directions. Suppose I come across a being that looks like a man, speaks like a man, behaves like a man, and is only one span tall—shall I say, it *is* a man? Or what about the case of a person who is so old as to remember King Darius? Would you say he is an immortal? Is there anything like an exhaustive definition that finally and once for all sets our mind at rest? "But are there not exact definitions at least in science?" Let's see. The notion of gold seems to be defined with absolute precision, say by the spectrum of gold with its characteristic lines. Now what would you say if a substance was discovered that looked like gold, satisfied all the chemical tests for gold, whilst it emitted a new sort of radiation? "But such things do not happen." Quite so; but they *might* happen, and that is enough to show

2 I owe this term to Mr. Kneale who suggested it to me as a translation of *Porosität der Begriffe*, a term coined by me in German.

that we can never exclude altogether the possibility of some unforeseen situation arising in which we shall have to modify our definition. Try as we may, no concept is limited in such a way that there is no room for any doubt. We introduce a concept and limit it in *some* directions; for instance, we define gold in contrast to some other metals such as alloys. This suffices for our present needs, and we do not probe any farther. We tend to *overlook* the fact that there are always other directions in which the concept has not been defined. And if we did, we could easily imagine conditions which would necessitate new limitations. In short, it is not possible to define a concept like gold with absolute precision, i.e. in such a way that every nook and cranny is blocked against entry of doubt. That is what is meant by the open texture of a concept.

Vagueness should be distinguished from *open texture*. A word which is actually used in a fluctuating way (such as "heap" or "pink") is said to be vague; a term like "gold," though its actual use may not be vague, is non-exhaustive or of an open texture in that we can never fill up all the possible gaps through which a doubt may seep in. Open texture, then, is something like *possibility of vagueness*. Vagueness can be remedied by giving more accurate rules, open texture cannot. An alternative way of stating this would be to say that definitions of open terms are *always* corrigible or emendable.

Open texture is a very fundamental characteristic of most, though not of all, empirical concepts, and it is this texture which prevents us from verifying conclusively most of our empirical statements. Take any material object statement. The terms which occur in it are non-exhaustive; that means that we cannot foresee completely all possible conditions in which they are to be used; there will always remain a possibility, however faint, that we have not taken into account something or other that may be relevant to their usage; and that means that we cannot foresee completely all the possible circumstances in which the statement is true or in which it is false. There will always remain a margin of uncertainty. Thus the absence of a conclusive verification is directly due to the open texture of the terms concerned.

This has an important consequence. Phenomenalists have tried to translate what we mean by a material object statement into terms of sense experience. Now such a translation would be possible only if the terms of a material object statement were completely definable. For only then could we describe completely all the possible evidences which would make the statement true or false. As this condition is not fulfilled, the programme of phenomenalism falls flat, and in consequence the attempts at analysing chairs and tables into patterns of sense-data—which has become something of a national sport in this country—are doomed to fail. Similar remarks apply to certain psychological statements such as "He is an intelligent person"; here again it is due to the open texture of a term like "intelligent" that the statement cannot be reduced to a conjunction or disjunction of statements which specify the way a man would behave in such-and-such circumstances.

It may have been a dim awareness of this fact that induced Locke to insist on corporeal, and Berkeley on mental substance. Doing away with their metaphysical fog, we may restate what seems to be the grain of truth in their views by saying that a material object statement, or a psychological statement has a logic of its own, and for this reason cannot be reduced to the level of other statements.

But there is a deeper reason for all that, and this consists in what I venture to call the *essential incompleteness* of an empirical description. To explain more fully: If I had to describe the right hand of mine which I am now holding up, I may say different things of it: I may state its size, its shape, its colour, its tissue, the chemical compound of its bones, its cells, and perhaps add some more particulars; but however far I go, I shall never reach a point where my description will be completed: logically speaking, it is always possible to extend the description by adding some detail or other. Every description stretches, as it were, into a horizon of open possibilities: however far I go, I shall always carry this horizon with me. Contrast this case with others in which completeness is attainable. If, in geometry, I describe a triangle, e.g. by giving its three sides, the description is *complete*: nothing can be added to it that is not included in, or at variance with, the data. Again, there is a sense in which it may be said that a melody is described completely in the musical notation (disregarding, for the moment, the question of its interpretation); a figure on a carpet, viewed as an ornament, may be described in some geometrical notation; and in this case, too, there is a sense in which the description may be called complete. (I do not mean the *physical* carpet, but its pattern.) The same applies to a game of chess: it can be described, move by move, from the beginning to the end. Such cases serve merely to set off the nature of an empirical description by the contrast: there is no such thing as completeness in the case in which I describe my right hand, or the character of a person; I can never exhaust all the details nor foresee all possible circumstances which would make me modify or retract my statement. (This was already seen by Leibniz when he said that anything actual is always inexhaustible in its properties and a true image of the Infinite Mind.)

The situation described has a direct bearing on the open texture of concepts. A term is defined when the sort of situation is described in which it is to be used. Suppose for a moment that we were able to describe situations completely without omitting anything (as in chess), then we could produce an exhaustive list of all the circumstances in which the term is to be used so that nothing is left to doubt: in other words, we could construct a *complete definition*, i.e., a thought model which anticipates and settles once for all every possible question of usage. As, in fact, we can never eliminate the possibility of some unforeseen factor emerging, we can never be quite sure that we have included in our definition everything that should be included, and thus the process of defining and refining an idea will go on without ever reaching a final stage. In other words, every definition stretches into an open horizon. Try as we may, the situation will always remain the same: no definition of an empirical term will cover all possibilities. Thus the result is that the incompleteness of our verification is rooted in the incompleteness of the definition of the terms involved, and the incompleteness of the definition is rooted in the incompleteness of empirical description; that is one of the grounds why a material object statement p can *not* be verified conclusively, nor be resolved into statements $s_1, s_2 \ldots s_n$ which describe evidences for it. (In mathematics such a reduction is often possible: thus a statement about rational numbers *can*, without loss of meaning, be translated into statements about integers; but here you have complete description, complete definition and conclusive proof and refutation.)

One word more. Why is it that, as a rule, an experiential statement is not verifiable in a conclusive way? Is it because I can never exhaust the description of a material object or of a situation, since I may always add something to it—something that, in principle, can be foreseen? Or is it because something quite new and unforeseen may occur? In the first case, though I know all the tests, I may still be unable to perform them, say, for lack of time. In the second case I cannot even be sure that I know all the tests that may be required; in other words, the difficulty is to state completely what a verification would be in this case. (Can you foresee all circumstances which would turn a putative fact into a delusion?) Now the answer to the question is that *both factors combine* to prevent a verification from being conclusive. *But they play a very different part.* It is due to the first factor that, in verifying a statement, we can never finish the job. But it is the second that is responsible for the open texture of our terms which is so characteristic of all factual knowledge. To see this more clearly, compare the situation in mathematics: here a theorem, say Goldbach's hypothesis, which says that every even number can be represented as the sum of two primes, may be undecidable as we cannot go through all the integers in order to try it out. But this in no way detracts from the *closed* texture of the mathematical concepts. If there was no such thing as the (always present) possibility of the emergence of something new, there could be nothing like the open texture of concepts; and if there was no such thing as the open texture of concepts, verification would be incomplete only in the sense that it could never be finished (just as in the case of Goldbach).

To sum up: An experiential statement is, as a rule, not conclusively verifiable for two different reasons:

(1) because of the existence of an unlimited number of tests;

(2) because of the open texture of the terms involved.

These two reasons correspond to two different senses of "incompleteness". The first is related to the fact that I can never conclude the description of a material object, or of a situation. I may, for instance, look at my table from ever new points in spaces without every exhausting all the possibilities. The second (and more exciting one) is due to the fact that our factual knowledge is incomplete in another dimension: there is always a chance that something unforeseen may occur. That again may mean two different things:

(*a*) that I should get acquainted with some totally new experience such as at present I cannot even imagine;

(*b*) that some new discovery was made which would affect our whole interpretation of certain facts.

An illustration of the first sort would be supplied by a man born blind who later obtained the experience of seeing. An illustration of the second sort would be the change brought about by the discovery of a new agent of nature, such as electricity. In this case we perceive that the data of observation are connected in a new and unforeseen way, that, as it were, new lines can now be traced through the field of experience. So we can say more exactly that the open texture of concepts is rooted in that particular incompleteness of our factual knowledge which I have just adumbrated.

What I have said modifies to a more or less extent the account I have given of verification. I said that in giving the method of verification we lay down a rule (or rules) of inference. We should, however, feel grave doubts whether that is so. If a material object statement were to entail a sense datum statement, to entail it in a strictly *logical* sense, then the premiss would be cancelled together with the conclusion: or, to put it differently, a single negative instance would suffice to refute the premiss. Suppose someone told me, "Look, there is your friend, he is just crossing the street." Now if I looked in the direction indicated, but failed to perceive the person who is my friend, would I say that the statement was refuted beyond the shadow of a doubt? There may be cases in which I may say that. But there are others in which I would certainly not think that the statement was refuted on the strength of such a single glance (for instance, when I was led to expect my friend at this hour, or received a letter from him saying that he will arrive at that time, and the like). A discrepancy between a material object statement and a single sense experience may always be explained away by some accessory assumption: I haven't looked thoroughly, my friend happened in this very second to be behind someone else, he just stepped into a doorway, and so on, not to mention more fanciful theories. I can never exclude the possibility that, though the evidence was against it, the statement may be true.

Whoever considers these facts with unbiassed eyes will, I trust, assent to the conclusion that a single sense experience, strictly speaking, never excludes a material object statement in the sense in which the negation of p excludes p. That means that no sense-datum statement s can ever come into *sharp logical conflict* with a material object statement p; in other words: $p . \sim s$ never represents a *contradiction* in the sense that $p . \sim p$ does. In the light of this we can no longer adhere to the view that p entails s. How, then, should we formulate the "method of verification"—that is, the connection between a proposition p and the statements $s_1, s_2 \ldots s_n$ which are evidences for it? I propose to say that the evidences $s_1, s_2 \ldots s_n$, *speak for* or *against* the proposition p, that they *strengthen* or *weaken* it, which does not mean that they prove or disprove it strictly.

There is a striking analogy to that in the relation that holds between a law of nature L and certain observational statements $s_1, s_2 \ldots s_n$, an analogy which may help to clarify the situation. It is often said that the statements of observation *follow* from the law (the latter being regarded as a sort of universal premiss). Since an unlimited number of consequences can be derived from a law, the ideal of complete verification is, of course, unattainable; whereas, on the other hand, a single counter observation seems to suffice to overthrow the law. From this it would follow that, while a law cannot be strictly verified, it can be strictly confuted; or that it can be decided only one way.[3] That is unrealistic. What astronomer would abandon Kepler's laws on the strength of a single observation? If, in fact, some anomaly in a planet's behaviour were detected, the most varied attempts at explaining the phenomenon would first be made (such as the presence of unknown heavy masses, friction with rarefied gases, etc.). Only if the edifice of hypotheses thus erected has too little support in experience, if it becomes too complex and artificial, if it no longer satisfies our demand for simplicity, or again if a better hypothesis presents itself to us, such as Einstein's theory, would we resolve to drop those laws. And even then the refutation would not be valid finally and once for all: it may still turn out that some circumstance had escaped our notice which, when taken into consideration, would cast a different light upon the whole. Indeed, the history of science exhibits cases (Olaf Römer, Leverrier) in which the apparent defeat of a theory later turned into complete victory. Who can say that such a situation will not repeat itself?

Here again the view suggests itself strongly that the relationship between a statement and what serves to verify it was too crudely represented in the past; that it was a mistake to describe it in logical terms such as "entailment"; that a law is not a sort of universal statement from which particular statements follow; that its logic is still unexplored, and that it may possibly take the form

[3] See Karl Popper, *Logik der Forschung.*

of rules according to which the law's truth-weight—if I am allowed to use such a term—is increased or lessened by the data of observation. Be that as it may, the mere fact that a single counter observation $\sim s$ can always be reconciled with a general law L by some accessory assumption shows that the true relation between a law and the experiential evidence for it is much more complicated and only superficially in accord with the customary account.

It will be said that this is due to our representing the case in too simple a manner. In reality the observational statement s does not follow from L alone, but from L plus a number of further premisses which are often not expressly stated. So that, if the observation s which we expected fails to materialize, we may say that any of the other premisses is false.

Now this would be perfectly correct if the system of premisses could be stated accurately and completely in every single case. But can it? Can we ever be certain of knowing all, really all the conditions on which the result of even the simplest experiment depends? Plainly not; what is stated is only a *part* of the conditions, viz., those which, e.g., can be isolated in experimental technique and subjected to our will, or which can readily be surveyed, etc. The others merge into one indistinct mass: the vague supposition that "a normal situation subsists," that "no disturbing factors are present" or in whatever way we may hint at the possibility of intervention of some unforeseen conditions. The relation between L and s, then, when exactly stated, is this: Given such-and-such laws $L_1, L_2 \ldots L_m$, given such-and-such initial and boundary conditions $c_1, c_2 \ldots c_n$ and *no other disturbing factors being present*, so-and-so will happen. And here it must be stressed that behind the words italicized a presupposition is concealed which cannot be split up into clear, separate statements. When actually deducing a consequence from a physical law we never make use of this premiss: it never forms part of the body of premisses: it does not enter the process of deduction. But then it should not be termed a premiss at all; what a queer sort of premiss this is, which is never made use of! What is, in fact, conveyed by these words is only that, in case of a conflict between theory and observation, we shall *search* for disturbing factors whilst considering ourselves free to adhere to the theory. The question at issue is *not* whether a certain system of assumption is sufficiently comprehensive—that is a question of fact which may be left to the expert; the question is rather whether there is a *criterion* which assures us that a system of premisses is complete. To this there is no answer; nay, more, we cannot even form any conception of such a criterion; we cannot think of a situation in which a physicist would tell us, "Well, I have finished the job; now I have discovered the last law of nature, and no more is to be found." But if this is devoid of meaning, there is no point in insisting, "*If* all the conditions in the universe, and *if* all the laws governing them were known to us, then—." As the boundary regions of our knowledge are always enveloped in a dust cloud—out of which something new may emerge—we are left with the fact that *s* is not a strict logical consequence of *L* together with the initial conditions. Saying that the class of premises is not "closed" and that *therefore* the conclusion is lacking in stringency comes, in my view, to the same thing as saying that *s* is *not* a logical consequence of the premises as far as they are stated. And that is all I wanted to say.

All this tends to suggest that the relation between a law of nature and the evidences for it, or between a material object statement and a sense-datum statement, or again between a psychological statement and the evidence concerning a person's behaviour is a looser one than had been hitherto imagined. If that is correct, the application of logic seems to be limited in an important sense. We may say that the known relations of logic can only hold between statements which belong to a *homogeneous* domain; or that the deductive nexus never extends beyond the limits of such a domain.

Accordingly we may set ourselves the task of arranging the statements of our language in distinct strata, grouping in the same stratum all those statements linked by clearly apprehended logical relations. It is in this way, for instance, that the theorems of mechanics are organized in a system the elements of which stand in known logical relations with one another and where it is always possible to decide of two theorems in what logical relation they stand —whether one is a consequence of the other, whether they are equivalent, or independent of, or in contradiction with each other. In like manner the statements of a physicist in describing certain data of observation (such as the position of a pointer on his gauges) stand in exactly defined relations to one another. Thus a pointer on a scale cannot possibly be opposite 3 and 5 at the same time: here you have a relation of strict exclusion. On the other hand, no statement of mechanics can ever come into sharp logical conflict with a statement of observation, and this implies that between these two kinds of statements there exist no relations of the sort supplied to us by classical logic. So long as we move only among the statements of a single stratum, all the relations provided by logic remain valid. The real problem arises where two such strata make contact, so to speak; it is the problem of these planes of contact which to-day should claim the attention of the logician. We may, in this context, speak of the looseness of the chains or inference which lead from statements of one stratum to those of another; the connection is no longer coercive—owing to the incompleteness of all our data.

You will find that it is this fact to which the rise of philosophical troubles often can be traced. (Think of how confusing it is to assert or to dispute the statement, "The floor is not solid," as it belongs to two quite distinct strata.) The fracture lines of the strata of language are marked by philosophical problems: the problem of perception, of verification, of induction, the problem of the relation between mind and body, and so on.

You will have noticed that I have used the term "incompleteness" in very different senses. In one sense we may say of a description of a material object that it is incomplete; in another sense we may say that of our knowledge of the boundary conditions in a field of force. There is a sense in which we say that a list of laws of nature is always incomplete, and another sense in which even our knowledge of the agents of nature is so; and you may easily find more senses. They all combine, to a varying degree, to create what I have called the open texture of concepts and the looseness of inferences.

Incompleteness, in the senses referred to, is the mark of empirical knowledge as opposed to *a priori* knowledge such as mathematics. In fact, it is the criterion by which we can distinguish perfectly *formalized* languages constructed by logicians from *natural* languages as used in describing reality. In a formalized system the use of each symbol is governed by a definite number of rules, and further, all the rules of inference and procedure can be stated completely. In view of the incompleteness which permeates empirical knowledge such a demand cannot be fulfilled by any language we may use to express it.

That there is a very close relation between content and verification is an important insight which has been brought to light by empiricists. Only one has to be very careful how to formulate it. Far from identifying the meaning of a statement with the evidences we have for it, the view I tried to sketch leads to a sort of many-level-theory of language in which "every sort of statement has its own sort of logic."

II

In the second part of his paper Mr. MacKinnon is anxious to relate the notions of reality and causality by admitting as real only those objects (or events, or processes) which satisfy the conditions of causality. What he says is "that the manner of discursive thought . . . reveals itself as an obstinate resolve . . . to admit nothing as real that does not manifest some ground of its occurrence." That is part of Kant's doctrine according to which nothing can ever become object of our knowledge which did not conform to certain *a priori* forms of our intuition and our understanding. Such an attempt, if it succeeded, would be of tremendous importance. Think how miraculous it would be, using this method, to deduce from it causality, premises of induction as well as other enjoyable things—I had almost said to *pro*duce them out of the conjuror's hat called the Transcendental Argument. How comforting would be the belief that we know the nature of space and time through and through so that we are able to enunciate the principles of geometry without fear of ever being defeated by experience. How reassuring it would be to say that nature *must* obey causal laws—and so on, you know the tune. The question is only whether Nature will conform to Kant. You will realize that such over-confidence is no longer permissible to-day, in the age of quantum mechanics. We are told by Mr. MacKinnon that "we display an unwillingness to admit the completely random" (by the bye, what does he mean by that?) "and discontinuous as objectively real." But our protest, however strongly worded, would be of no avail if Nature was willing to baffle us. The words Mr. MacKinnon has been using state precisely the sort of situation with which we have come face to face in modern physics: things do happen without ground of their occurrence. May I be allowed to say a few words on this subject?

There are people who think that physicists have just not succeeded in discovering laws which tell us why things happen in the atomic world, in the cheerful hope that someone some day will have a brain-wave which will enable him to fill the gaps in wave mechanics; on this day the latter will turn into a completely deterministic theory. Let these people realize how wide the cleavage is that separates us from the good old days. The hope they cherish is based on an illusion: it has been proved[4] that the structure of quantum mechanics is such that no further laws can be added to it which would make the whole theory deterministic; for if we could, we should, owing to the uncertainty principle, get entangled in contradictions. (The situation is, in fact, more intricate, but this is not the place to go into it.) So we are faced with the dilemma that quantum mechanics is *either* self-consistent *or* deterministic: you can't have it both ways. The crack in the wall of Determinism is definitive, and there is no way out of the situation.

According to Kant causality is an inescapable form which the nature of our understanding imposes on any given material. If this were so, it would be inconceivable—against the conditions of possible experience—ever to come across any events which did not conform to the principle of causality. Quantum phenomena, however, have forced physicists to depart from this principle, or better, to *restrict* it, whilst a torso of it is retained. Though the fate of a single electron is not governed by causal laws, the particle being free to move about, for instance, to "jump" in a collision with light waves however it pleases, the behaviour of millions of electrons is statistically predictable. Not exactly that quantum mechanics confronts us with a mathematician's dream of chaos come true. For, as I said, there is a causal aspect in the new theory, namely this: there are certain waves connected with the motion of particles, the de Broglie waves, which obey rigorous "causal" laws. That is, the propagation of these waves is governed by a differential equation of the respectable old type such as you find in the classical physics of fields. Hence we can, given the initial conditions and the values over the boundary of a region during a certain interval of time, predict with absolute precision the propagation of the waves. That is

---

[4] See, for instance, J. v. Neumann, *Mathematische Grundlagen der Quantenmechanik.*

exactly what any causal theory achieves. What is new, however, is the interpretation we must give to these waves: they are a sort of "probability clouds" the density of which at each point signifies the probability of the occurrence of a particle. So what we can deduce from the theory are only *probability statements* regarding the presence of a particle in a given place at a given time. Such a statement can be tested, not by making a single experiment such as observing a single electron through a microscope, but by repeating the experiment a large number of times, or observing a large number of electrons and forming the mean value of all the data thus obtained. Therefore we cannot say where exactly a certain electron will be, but only with what probability, i.e. in what percentage of cases we may expect to find it at a certain place. In other words, the theory can be used only to predict the *average behaviour* of particles. That is the statistical aspect of the theory.

To sum up: quantum mechanics is neither a theory of the causal, deterministic type nor an indeterministic theory, whatever this may be taken to mean. The new physics combines deterministic and indeterministic features. What is deterministic is the law for the propagation of the de Broglie waves. That is, the propagation of these waves is *causally determined* in much the same way as, e.g., the propagation of electromagnetic waves is in the classical theories. What is indeterministic is the *interpretation* of these waves, that is, their connection with the facts of observation. Such an interpretation can only be given in statistical terms, and any attempt at interpreting it differently so as to reinstate causality would only lead to conflict with other well-established parts of the theory. Thus we have the curious result that causality holds for the de Broglie waves, which are no more than a purely symbolic and formal representation of certain probabilities, whereas the particles themselves obey no causal laws.

To bring home the last point let me add this: If it were possible to repeat exactly the same experiment and to bring about exactly the same conditions, the result would each time be a different one. Therefore the principle "Like causes—like effects" no longer holds. *Lasciate ogni speranza . . .*

But may not quantum mechanics one day be superseded by a better theory that meets our demand for causal explanation? Certainly; no theory is sacrosanct and infallible. This, however, is not the point. What matters is, not whether quantum mechanics draws a true picture of reality, but only whether it draws a *permissible* one. About that there can be little doubt. Kant was of the opinion that if there was no such thing as causality science would simply break down. Now the important thing that has emerged is the *possibility* of constructing a theory along different lines, the *legitimacy* of departing from causality, while science has not died or committed suicide on that account. This suffices to disown any claim on the part of Kant to regard causality as an *indispensable* form of our knowledge of the world. Had he been right, we could not even *entertain* such views as physicists do today; to give up causality, even if in part, would mean robbing ourselves of the very condition for gaining knowledge: which could end in one result only, in complete confusion. But that is not so. Though causality has been severely limited, quantum mechanics is a useful tool. Kant did not foresee the possible forms of physical laws; by laying too much stress on the scheme of causality, by claiming for it an *a priori* status, he unduly narrowed the field of research.

The conclusion to be drawn for the preceding seems to me this: Even if quantum mechanics should one day be found wanting and be superseded by another theory, it still offers a *possible picture* of the material world. This picture is neither self-contradictory nor unintelligible, though it may not be the sort of picture to which we are accustomed; anyhow, it is a working hypothesis which serves its purpose in that it is fruitful, i.e. that it leads to new discoveries. Whether it contains the ultimate truth we cannot tell (nor can we in the case of the deterministic theories). It's only experience that can bring forward evidence against it. But the very fact that we *can* turn to experience is significant: in doing so we grant that quantum mechanics, and consequently the limits of causality, *can* be tested in experiment. Hence every attempt at raising the principle of causality to the status of a necessary truth is irreconcilable with the situation as it has emerged in science. No matter whether quantum mechanics will stand its ground or will have to undergo some modification or other, the mere fact that the construction of such a theory is legitimate should settle the dispute: it proves that Kant's argument is based on a fallacy.

It was indeed an important step when man learnt to ask, Why? But it was also a great step when he learnt to drop this question. But leaving quantum mechanics and turning to the common world of sense, I still fail to see any ground for accepting Kant's position. True, in order to get our bearings in the world we must presuppose that there is some sort of order in it so that we may anticipate the course of events and act accordingly. What I fail to see, however, is why this order should be a strictly *causal* one. Suppose, for the sake of argument, that the objects around us were, *on the average*, to display an orderly behaviour, then the world may still be a liveable place. Suppose, for instance, the behaviour of chairs and the support they give us could be foreseen with much the same accuracy as can the behaviour of Tory and Labour candidates in election times, may we then not make use of them just the same? Or suppose they were to conduct themselves as our best friends do —they won't let us down, no; still, you never know—then, as far as I can see, this would be quite enough for all practical ends. And as to the theoretical ones—well, go to the scientist and you will hear a sorry tale of nature's trickery. I cannot see why such a world should not be possible.

This brings me to the topic in which Mr. MacKinnon is so much interested

—are there any *necessary* conditions which must be fulfilled if we are to attain knowledge of the external world? I propose to drop for the moment the subject of causality and to tackle the problem from a broader angle. Let me begin with some observations on the terms "reality" and "knowledge."

Mr. MacKinnon, in his paper, repeatedly speaks of "the real," "the reality," he asks, for instance, whether "the completely random" can be admitted as "objectively real." He blames Berkeley for having omitted "to face the question of the rules whereby the inclusion in or exclusion from reality was determined; in consequence of which," we are told, "his theory of knowledge flags." In another passage he speaks of "the task of compelling the actual to disclose itself." My impression is that he talks as if there was a clearly bounded domain called "the real" or "the actual" with the implication that it is one of the tasks of the philosopher to define it sharply. Unfortunately the belief that there is such a domain is very slender. Not that I deny for a minute that a word like "reality" is a blessing; it definitely is. Look at such phrases as "A tautology doesn't say anything about reality," "Pure mathematics is not concerned with reality," "In reality it was not Smith I saw but his brother." It would be silly to put such a word on an *Index Prohibitorum Verborum* as though it were a sin to use it. It is very handy—if it were not in use, we should have to invent it. On the other hand, when a philosopher looks closely at it, tears it from the context and asks himself, "Now what *is* reality?" he has successfully manœuvred himself into a fairly awkward position. For it is surprisingly easy to ask a number of questions which are more or less embarrassing; for instance, "Is the elastic force present in a spring something real?" I suppose some people would answer Yes, some No. The fact is that there simply are no fixed rules that govern the use of the word. To go on—"Is a magnetic field something real?" "Is energy? and entropy?" Again, I may ask, "Is the power of my memory real," "Is the genius of a people, is the spirit of an age, is the beauty of a spring day real?" Now we begin to see how the idea is lost in indeterminacy. What we must understand is that such a word is used on many different levels and with many different shades of meaning. It has a *systematic ambiguity*. At the same time there is a sort of family likeness between all these uses, and it is that which makes us denote them by one word.

The same applies to a verb like "to exist." We use the word in many different senses: we may, for instance, say of a memory picture, an after-image, a mirror image, or again of a material object that it "exists"; again, we may say of a wave-motion in a space of many dimensions, or of a law of nature, or of a number satisfying certain conditions that it "exists"; and it is quite obvious that we do use the word in each case according to totally different criteria. So again we have a case of systematic ambiguity.

Next take the term "knowledge." Everyone is familiar with the distinction between knowledge by acquaintance and knowledge by description. This division is not fine enough. When I know something by acquaintance, I may know it in very different senses, as when I say "I know sweetness" (meaning "I am acquainted with the taste of sweetness"), "I know misery," "I know him," "I know his writings." In this series we go progressively farther away from simple acquaintance. In a case like "I know his motives," it is doubtful whether I should say this unless I had experienced some such motive myself. Moreover, there are cases which fall under none of the two groups; so, for instance, when I say "I know French," "I know how to deal with that man." Again, we may speak in different senses of knowledge by description. Compare the case of a reporter who gained knowledge of some hush-hush affair with that of a scientist who claims to possess knowledge of nature. Now is this knowledge in the same sense? And mark, in the latter case there are again subtle differences. Compare knowledge of the history of certain birds as based on observation with knowledge of the history of our solar system as based on some hypothesis; again knowledge of a natural law of the causal type with knowledge of a statistical law. Quantum mechanics, though it is based on the assumption of a randomness in the behaviour of electrons (and other particles), leads to a lot of predictions. On this ground physicists do not hesitate to honour the newly discovered laws by awarding them the degree of knowledge; whereas Mr. MacKinnon thinks "that we do concede the title unintelligible to any field . . . where such (causal) lines have not been traced." Well, I shall not argue about that; my sole object is to call attention to the fact that the actual usage is unsettled, that here are many different types of knowledge, and that, by talking of knowledge *in general*, we are liable to overlook the very important differences between them. Suppose that someone has a vague awareness of the direction in which history moves—shall, or shall I not call this knowledge? Can you draw a clear line to mark where such vague awareness ends and where true knowledge begins? Knowledge as supplied by quantum mechanics was unknown two or three decades ago. Who can tell what forms of knowledge may emerge in the future? Can you anticipate all possible cases in which you may wish to use that term? To say that knowledge is embodied in true propositions does not get you any farther; for there are many different structures that are called "propositions"—different, because they are verified in different senses of the word and governed by different sets of logical rules. (Incidentally speaking, the failure to draw a clear line between the meaningful and the meaningless is due to the fact that these terms have themselves a systematic ambiguity, and so has the term "verifiable.")

There is a group of words such as "fact," "event," "situation," "case," "circumstance," which display a queer sort of behaviour. One might say of such words that they serve as pegs: it's marvellous what a lot of things you can put on them ("the fact that—"). So far they are very handy; but as soon as one focusses on them and asks, e.g., "What *is* a fact?" they betray a tendency of melting away. The peg-aspect is by far the most important of all. It's just as in the case of the word "reality": in reality, e.g., "in reality" is an adverb.

Again, there are many different types of fact; there are many different types of statement which are called "empirical"; there are many different things which are called "experience"; and there are many different senses of communication and clarity.

Now if I am to contribute to the main subject of this symposium, that is, to the question whether there are any *necessary conditions for gaining knowledge of reality*—what am I to reply? Knowledge of reality! Of *what* sort of reality, and *what* sort of knowledge? As a logician I am bound to say that the notions of reality and knowledge have a systematic ambiguity and, moreover, that they are on each level extremely vague and hazy. I am even not quite clear as to what a condition is, let alone a "necessary condition." How questionable all these ideas are! How can I be expected to answer a question which consists only of a series of question marks?

III

So far my criticism was mainly negative. In conclusion I should like to offer some constructive suggestions. Before doing so, I must warn you that I can't see any ground whatever for renouncing one of the most fundamental rights of man, the right of talking nonsense. And now I suppose I may go on.

People are inclined to think that there is a world of facts as opposed to a world of words which describe these facts. I am not too happy about that. Consider an example. We are accustomed to see colour as a "quality" of objects. That is, colour cannot subsist by itself, but must inhere in a thing. This conception springs from the way we express ourselves. When colour is rendered by an adjective, colour is conceived as an attribute of things, i.e. as something that can have no independent existence. That, however, is not the only way of conceiving colour. There are languages such as Russian, German, Italian, which render colour by means of verbs. If we were to imitate this usage in English by allowing some such form as "The sky blues," we should come face to face with the question, Do I mean the same fact when I say "The sky blues" as when I say "The sky is blue"? I don't think so. We say "The sun shines," "Jewels glitter," "The river shimmers," "Windows gleam," "Stars twinkle," etc.; that is, in the case of phenomena of lustre we make use of a verbal mode of expression. Now in rendering colour phenomena by verbs we assimilate them more closely to the phenomena of lustre; and in doing so we alter not only our manner of speaking but our entire way of apprehending colour. We see the blue differently now—a hint that language affects our whole mode of apprehension. In the word "blueing" we are clearly aware of an active, verbal element. On that account "being blue" is not quite equivalent to "blueing," since it lacks what is peculiar to the verbal mode of expression. The sky which "blues" is seen as something that continually brings forth blueness—it radiates blueness, so to speak; blue does not inhere in it as a mere quality, rather is it felt as the vital pulse of the sky; there is a faint suggestion of the operating of some force behind the phenomenon. It's hard to get the feel of it in English; perhaps it may help you to liken this mode of expression to the impressionist way of painting which is at bottom a new way of seeing: the impressionist sees in colour an immediate manifestation of reality, a free agent no longer bound up with things.

There are, then, different linguistic means of rendering colour. When this is done by means of adjectives, colour is conceived as an attribute of things. The learning of such a language involves for everyone who speaks it his being habituated to see colour as a "quality" of objects. This conception becomes thus incorporated into his picture of the world. The verbal mode of expression detaches colour from things: it enables us to see colour as a phenomenon with a life of its own. Adjective and verb thus represent two different worlds of thought.

There is also an adverbial way of talking about colour. Imagine a language with a wealth of expressions for all shades of lustre, but without adjectives for colours; colours, as a rule, are ignored; *when* they are expressed, this is done by adding an adverb to the word that specifies the sort of lustre. Thus the people who use this sort of language would say, "The sea is glittering golden in the sunshine," "The evening clouds glow redly," "There in the depth a shadow greenly gleams." In such phrases colour would lose the last trace of independence and be reduced to a mere modification of lustre. Just as we in our language cannot say "That's very," but only some such thing as "That's very brilliant," so in the language considered we could not say "That's bluish," but only, e.g., "That's shining bluishly." There can be little doubt that, owing to this circumstance, the users of such language would find it very hard to see colour as a quality of things. For them it would not be the *things* that are coloured, rather colour would reside in the lustre as it glows and darkens and changes—evidence that they would see the world with different eyes.

"But isn't it still true to say that I have the same experience whenever I look up at the sky?" You would be less happy if you were asked, "Do you have the same experience when you look at a picture puzzle and see a figure in it as before, when you didn't see it?" You may, perhaps, say you see the same lines, though each time in a different arrangement. Now what exactly corresponds to this different arrangement in the case when I look up at the sky? One might say: we are aware of the blue, but this awareness is itself tinged and coloured by the whole linguistic background which brings into prominence, or weakness and hides certain analogies. In this sense language does affect the whole manner in which we become aware of a fact: the fact articulates itself differently, so to speak. In urging that you *must* have the same experience whenever you look at the sky you forget that the term "experience" is itself ambiguous: whether it is taken, e.g., to include or to exclude all the various analogies which a certain mode of expression calls up.

Again, consider this case: Suppose there is a number of languages *A, B, C* . . . in each of which a proposition is used according to a slightly different logic. Consequently a proposition in the language *A* is not a proposition in exactly the same sense as a proposition in the language *B*, etc. And not only this: what is described by a statement in the language *A*, i.e., if you like, the "fact," is not a fact in the same sense as a fact described in the language *B*, etc.; which tends to show that what is called a fact depends on the linguistic medium through which we see it.

I have observed that when the clock strikes in the night and I, already half asleep, am too tired to count the strokes, I am seized by an impression that the sequence will never end—as though it would go on, stroke after stroke, in an unending measureless procession. The whole thing vanishes as soon as I *count*. Counting frees me, as it were, from the dark formlessness impending over me. (Is this not a parable of the rational?) It seems to me that one could say here that counting alters the quality of the experience. Now is it the same fact which I perceive when counting and when not counting?

Again, suppose there is a tribe whose members count "one, two, three, a few, many." Suppose a man of this tribe looking at a flock of birds said "A few birds" whereas I should say "Five birds"—is it the same fact for him as it is for me? If in such a case I pass to a language of a different structure, I can no longer describe "the same" fact, but only another one more or less resembling the first. What, then, is the objective reality supposed to be described by language?

What rebels in us against such a suggestion is the feeling that the fact is there objectively no matter in which way we render it. I perceive something that exists and put it into words. From this it seems to follow that fact is something that exists independent of, and prior to language; language merely serves the end of communication. What we are liable to overlook here is that the way we see a fact—i.e. what we emphasize and what we disregard—is *our* work. "The sunbeams trembling on the floating tides" (Pope). Here a fact is something that emerges out from, and takes shape against a background. The background may be, e.g., my visual field; something that rouses my attention detaches itself from this field, is brought into focus and apprehended linguistically; that is what we call a fact. A fact is noticed; and by being noticed it becomes a fact. "Was it then no fact before you noticed it?" It was, if I *could* have noticed it. In a language in which there is only the number series "one, two, three, a few, many," a fact such as "There are five birds" is imperceptible.

To make my meaning still clearer consider a language in which description does not take the form of sentences. Examples of such a description would be supplied by a map, a picture language, a film, the musical notation. A map, for instance, should not be taken as a conjunction of single statements each of which describes a separate fact. For what, would you say, is the boundary of a fact? Where does the one end and the other begin? If we think of such types of description, we are no longer tempted to say that a country, or a story told in a film, or a melody must consist of "facts." Here we begin to see how confusing the idea is according to which the world is a cluster of facts—just as if it were a sort of mosaic made up of little coloured stones. Reality is undivided. What we may have in mind is perhaps that *language* contains units, viz. *sentences*. In describing reality, by using sentences, we draw, as it were, lines through it, limit a part and call what corresponds with such a sentence a fact. In other words, language is the knife with which we cut out facts. (This account is over-simplified as it doesn't take notice of *false* statements.)

Reality, then, is not made up of facts in the sense in which a plant is made up of cells, a house of bricks, a stone of molecules; rather, if you want a simile, a fact is present, in much the same sense in which a character manifests itself in a face. Not that I invent the character and read it into the fact; no, the character is somehow written on the face but no one would on that account say that a face is "made up" of features symbolic of such-and-such traits. Just as we have to interpret a face, so we have to interpret reality. The elements of such an interpretation, without our being aware of it, are already present in language—for instance, in such moulds as the notion of thinghood, of causality, of number, or again in the way we render colour, etc.

Noticing a fact may be likened to seeing a face in a cloud, or a figure in an arrangement of dots, or suddenly becoming aware of the solution of a picture puzzle: one views a complex of elements as one, reads a sort of unity into it, etc. Language supplies us with a means of comprehending and categorizing; and different languages categorize differently.

"But surely noticing a face in a cloud is not inventing it?" Certainly not; only you might not have noticed it unless you had already had the experience of human faces somewhere else. Does this not throw a light on what constitutes the noticing of facts? I would not dream for a moment of saying that I *invent* them; I might, however, be unable to perceive them if I had not certain moulds of comprehension ready at hand. These forms I borrow from language. Language, then, *contributes to the formation and participates in the constitution* of a fact; which, of course, does not mean that it *produces* the fact.

So far I have dealt with perceptual situations only. This, I am afraid, will not satisfy Mr. MacKinnon. What he wants to know is whether there are any *general* conditions of the possibility of factual knowledge. We have seen some of the fallacies involved in putting this question. Still we may ask ourselves whether there are any methodological rules which guide us in gaining knowledge. All I can hope to do here is to throw out some hints.

The empiricist has a let-the-facts-speak-for-themselves attitude. Well, this is his faith; what about his works? Remember, a scientific theory is never a slavish imitation of certain features of reality, a dead, passive replica. It is essentially a *construction* which to a more or less degree reflects our own activity. When, for instance, we represent a number of observations made in the laboratory by a corresponding number of dots and connect them by a graph, we assume, as a rule, that the curve is continuous and analytic. Such an assumption goes far beyond any possible experience. There will always be infinitely many other possible curves which accord with the facts equally well; the totality of these curves is included within a certain narrow strip. The ordinary mathematical treatment substitutes an exact law for the blurred data of observation and deduces from such laws strict mathematical conclusions. This shows that there is an element of convention inherent in the formulation of a law. The way we single out one particular law from infinitely many possible ones shows that in our theoretical construction of reality we are guided by certain principles—*regulative principles* as we may call them. If I were asked what these principles are, I should tentatively list the following:

(1) Simplicity or economy—the demand that the laws should be as simple as possible.

(2) Demands suggested by the requirements of the symbolism we use—for instance, that the graph should represent an analytic function so as to lend itself readily to the carrying out of certain mathematical operations such as differentiation.

(3) Aesthetic principles ("mathematical harmony" as envisaged by Pythagoras, Kepler, Einstein) though it is difficult to say what they are.

(4) A principle which so regulates the formulation of our concepts that as many alternatives as possible become decidable. This tendency is embodied in the whole structure of Aristotelian logic, especially in the law of excluded middle.[5]

(5) There is a further factor elusive and most difficult to pin down: a mere tone of thought which, though not explicitly stated, permeates the air of a historical period and inspires its leading figures. It is a sort of field organizing and directing the ideas of an age. (The time from Descartes to Newton, for instance, was animated by an instinctive belief in an Order of Things accessible

---

[5] A more detailed account of this is given in my article on "Alternative Logics" in *Proceedings of the Aristotelian Society,* 1945–6.

to the human mind. Though the thinkers of that time have tried to render this tone of thought into a rationalistic system, they failed: for that which is the living spark of rationalism is irrational.)

Such, I think, are some of the regulative principles. The formulation of some of them is very vague, and advisedly so: it wouldn't be good policy to reduce mathematical harmony, consonance with the whole background of an age, etc., to fixed rules. It's better to have them elastic. Principle (5) should perhaps better be described as a condition for making—and missing—discoveries.

Now none of these principles is *indispensable*, imposed on us by the nature of our understanding. Kant has tried to condense the tone of thought of the Newtonian age into strict rules—into *necessary conditions* of factual knowledge; with what success can be seen from the subsequent development: the belief in synthetic *a priori* judgements soon became something of a brake to research, discouraging such lines of approach as non-Euclidean geometry, and later non-causal laws in physics. Let this be a warning.

Writers on the history of philosophy are inclined to attend too exclusively to one aspect only—to the ideas explicitly stated, canvassing their fabric, but disregarding the tone of thought which gives them their impetus. The deeper significance of rationalism, for instance, lies in the fact that it corresponds to what the scientist *does*, strengthening his belief that, if he only tries hard, he *can* get to the bottom of things. But slowly and gradually the mental climate changes, and then a philosophy may find itself out of tune with its time.

I do not think for a minute that what I have said is a conclusive refutation of Kant. On the other hand—you may confute and kill a scientific theory; a philosophy dies only of old age.

CHAPTER 11

Behaviorism

The previous topic, "Concepts and Their Delineation," develops naturally into (and is difficult to separate from) a discussion of behaviorism. In this chapter, Kenneth Spence leads off with a description of the kind of data acceptable in behavioristic psychology and the sorts of concepts that can legitimately be built upon these data. Next is an article by a behaviorist who probably has had more direct impact upon education than any other—B. F. Skinner, who writes about "Behaviorism at Fifty." Following this is an article by Norman Malcolm, often considered a philosophical behaviorist, who rejects Skinner's views in part and accepts them in part.

Philosophers openly critical of behaviorism are represented in this chapter by H. H. Price, who argues in a simple and straightforward way against the view; Noam Chomsky, who caustically criticizes Skinner's *Verbal Behavior*; Gerald Paske, who sees Skinner's behavioristic views about self-control as trivial or false, but pernicious; Roderick Chisholm, who objects to attempts to behavioristically (or otherwise) eliminate intention from a number of our psychological concepts; and Harry Broudy, who warns against the behavioral objectives movement, which is an outgrowth of behaviorism.

This range of articles, together with the preceding readings about concepts and the next chapter on programmed instruction, touch on what appear to us to be the most important issues in this group of topics, but the issues are so crucial, current, and hotly disputed, that many nuances have inevitably been passed by. In the battle between radical empiricism and humanism, which sets the stage for the particular issues in this part of this book, the behaviorists are clearly on the radical empiricist side, with the others leaning in varying degrees toward humanism.

692

53. THE POSTULATES AND METHODS OF "BEHAVIORISM"

Kenneth W. Spence

There was a time when the term "behaviorism" in the title of a speech required no further specification. Every psychologist at least knew the referent to be that new brand of psychology, introduced by Watson, which proposed to break with tradition and deny that psychology had anything to do either with a mentalistic entity called consciousness or a method known as introspection. Today the situation is not so simple. The term "behaviorism" may, on the one hand, merely imply a very general point of view which has come to be accepted by almost all psychologists and thus does not point to any particular group or theoretical position. Or, on the other hand, it may refer to any one of several varieties of behaviorism which have been offered as supplementations or modifications of the original formulation of Watson (*e.g.*, molecular behaviorism, molar behaviorism, operational behaviorism, purposive behaviorism, logical behaviorism—to mention only some of the varieties). While these current formulations usually acknowledge some debt to Watson, for various reasons which we cannot stop to discuss they almost invariably take great pains to differentiate themselves from what has come to be known as "Watsonian Behaviorism" or "Watsonianism." In fact, so far as I know, there are no proponents today of the original Watsonian version. Proper care should be taken to note, however, that this statement holds true only for the particular pattern of assumptions that Watson advanced. Many of the basic

SOURCE. Spence, Kenneth W., "The Postulates and Methods of Behaviorism," *Psychological Review*, Vol. 55, 1948. Reprinted with permission of the American Psychological Association. Copyright © 1948 by the American Psychological Association.

postulates of his formulation are to be found in the present-day varieties of behaviorism and, what is more important, probably, in the underlying working assumptions of the great majority of present-day American psychologists.

Now that I have taken the precaution to differentiate the behaviorisms of today from the original version of behaviorism, I should like to call attention to the further interesting fact that with the exception possibly of Tolman very few, if any, current psychologists ever seem to think of themselves, or at least explicitly refer to themselves, as behaviorists. Such labeling, when it occurs, is usually the contribution of psychologists who consider themselves opposed to behaviorism. Undoubtedly, one of the reasons underlying this absence or lack of "old-school-tie" spirit is that a large majority of present-day American psychologists just take for granted many of the behavioristic assumptions and, occupied as they have been with the details of developing and applying their specific research tools, they have had little time or inclination to give much thought to the more general methodological and systematic problems of their science.

Even the more theoretical-minded of the behavioristically-oriented psycho-logists seem to have been too preoccupied with matters of detail to get around to the consideration of a more general theoretical framework. Instead of attempting to formulate a complete system of psychology, these theorists have been more concerned with the elaboration of relatively specific hypotheses concerning rather limited realms of data—e.g., theories of simple learning phenomena, motivational theories, theories of personality development, etc. As a consequence we find that instead of being built up around the symbol "behaviorism," allegiances tend to become attached to such labels as associa-tionism, conditioning, reinforcement theory, frustration hypothesis, etc. It seems, in other words, that these psychologists have outgrown the stage of schools.

Under these circumstances, I cannot and I shall not undertake to present a fixed set of articles of faith, articulately and self-consciously held by a group of men calling themselves behaviorists. Instead, I shall attempt to formulate a few methodological principles that are, I believe, exemplified in the work of certain contemporary psychologists who would undoubtedly acknowledge a heavy historical debt to that earlier formulation known as the school of be-haviorism.

The first problem that I shall discuss has to do with the behavior scientist's conception of the nature of psychological events. In the old, classical psycholo-gies, whether of the structural or act varieties, the point of view taken was that psychology, if it was a natural science, was, to say the least, a somewhat unique one. Instead of being conceived like physics, for example, as concerning itself with events mediated by or occurring in the consciousness or immediate experience of the observing scientist, psychology was said to observe and analyze by a kind of inner sense immediate experience *per se*. Sensations, emotions, thoughts were regarded as observable aspects of direct experience rather than systematic constructs which, like the physicist's atoms and electrons, were inferred from immediate experience.

Fortunately, the relationship of immediate experience (consciousness) to the data and constructs of science has been considerably clarified in recent years by the writings of several different groups of thinkers. The philosophers of science, particularly the logical positivists (1, 5, 6, 7), philosophically-minded scientists such as Bridgman (3) and, within psychology, such writers as Boring (2), Pratt (15), and Stevens (18) have succeeded, I believe, in making the point that the data of all sciences have the same origin—namely, the immediate experience of an observing person, the scientist himself. That is to say, immediate experience, the initial matrix out of which all sciences develop, is no longer considered a matter of concern for the scientist qua scientist. He simply takes it for granted and then proceeds to his task of describing the events occurring in it and discovering and formulating the nature of the relationships holding among them.

Boring stated this matter very clearly for psychologists in his book of some years ago, *The Physical Dimensions of Consciousness*. He wrote: "Thus the events of physics, as Wundt said, are mediate to experience, which stands in the background as the dator of scientific data, unrealizable as reality except inductively. In the same way psychology must deal with existential reals which are similarly mediate to experience. There is no way of getting at 'direct experience' because experience gives itself up to science indirectly inferentially, by the experimental method" (2, p. 6).

More recently Pratt, in his *Logic of Modern Psychology* (15), has hammered home this same point with considerable effectiveness. As he points out, the subject matter of psychology is exactly the same in kind as all other sciences; any differentiation among the sciences is merely a matter of convenience, a division of scientific labor resorted to as the amount of detailed knowledge increases beyond the capacity of a single person's grasp.

I think that it is of some historical interest to note in connection with this point that in the first of his articles introducing the behavioristic position, Watson took essentially the same stand. He wrote: "It [psychology] can dispense with consciousness in a psychological sense. The separate observation of 'states of consciousness' is, on this assumption, no more a part of the task of the psychologist than of the physicist. We might call this the return to a nonreflective and naive use of consciousness. In this sense consciousness may be said to be the instrument or tool with which all scientists work" (21, p. 176).

Acknowledging, then, that the psychologist conceives his task as that of bringing order and meaning into the realm of certain events provided by immediate experience, we now turn to the question of what these particular observed events are. In attempting to answer this question, attention should first be directed to the fact that the sense events in the experience of the observing scientist may depend upon or result from two different classes of conditions, intra-organic and extra-organic, the former exciting the interoceptors and the latter, the exteroceptors. The physical sciences, it should be noted, moreover, deal only with events of an extra-organic origin—*i.e.*, those received through the exteroceptors. The data of classical psychology, on the other hand, were regarded as involving primarily sense events initiated through the interoceptors. These latter were regarded as being stimulated by such internal mental activities as thinking, desiring, emotional reactions, perceiving, etc., and hence were thought of as providing primary data concerning them.

It is apparent, however, that these internally initiated experiences differ rather markedly from the externally aroused ones in the extent to which they are publicly controllable and communicable. At least, if we can judge from the interminable disagreements of the introspective psychologists themselves, this class of experiences does not meet too well the requirements of social verification and acceptance demanded by the scientist. It was in the face of this difficulty that Watson made his suggestion that the psychologist, like all other scientists, should confine himself to those segments of his experience which have their origin in extra-organic conditions. In other words, the events studied by the psychologist, Watson held, should consist in observations of the overt behavior of *other* organisms, other persons than the observing scientist himself, and not in the observation of the scientist's own internal activities.

As everyone knows, however, most behavior scientists have continued more or less to make use of this latter type of material in the form of the objectively recordable verbal reports of their subjects. Indeed, the scientist himself, in certain circumstances, may assume a dual role and serve as both subject and experimenter. In this event his own introspective report is recorded as a linguistic response and becomes a part of the objective data. To some critics of the behavioristic viewpoint, this acceptance of the verbal reports of their subjects as a part of the data has seemed to represent an abandonment of the strict behavioristic position and a return to the conception that psychology studies *experiential* events as well as overt behavior.

Such a contention, it seems to me, fails to note a very important difference in the two positions. The introspectionist, it should be recalled, assumed a strict one-to-one relationship between the verbal responses of his subjects and the inner mental processes. Accordingly, he accepted these introspective reports as *facts* or *data* about the inner mental events which they represented. The behavior scientist takes a very different position. He accepts verbal response as just one more form of behavior and he proposes to use this type of data in exactly the same manner as he does other types of behavior variables. Thus he attempts to discover laws relating verbal responses to environmental events of the past or present, and he seeks to find what relations they have to other types of response variables. He also makes use of them as a basis for making inferences as to certain hypothetical or theoretical constructs which he employs. In contrast, then, to the introspectionist's conception of these verbal reports as mirroring directly inner mental events, *i.e.*, facts, the behaviorist uses them either as data in their own right to be related to other data, or as a base from which to infer theoretical constructs which presumably represent internal or covert activities of their subjects. We shall return later to the use made of such language responses in the theorizing of the behaviorist.

From this all too cursory discussion of the initial data of the behavioristic psychologist, I should like now to turn to a consideration of the nature of the concepts which he employs to record and describe these events. I do not believe it is necessary for me to discuss at any length the position of the behaviorist with respect to the movement known as operationism. The insistence of the early behaviorists on a thoroughgoing operational analysis of the traditional mentalistic concepts was really nothing more than an anticipation of this somewhat overemphasized program. That a body of empirical knowledge cannot be built up without providing for veriability of the terms in use is simply taken for granted by the behaviorist. Instead, then, of talking about operational definition of psychological concepts, I should like to discuss certain matters related to a second criterion of acceptability of a scientific concept—namely, its *significance*.

One often hears criticisms to the effect that behavioristic concepts are too elementaristic, too atomistic, or that they fail to portray the real essence or true meaning of man's behavior. These latter critics often complain bitterly about the impoverishment of the mind, and of the lack of warmth and glowing particulars in the behaviorist's picture of psychological events. Some of these criticisms merely reflect, of course, a lack of appreciation on the part of some "psychologists" as to the difference between scientific knowledge of an event on the one hand and everyday knowledge, or the kind of knowledge the novelist or poet portrays, on the other. Either by reason of training or because of their basically non-scientific interests, these critics have never really understood the abstract character of the scientific account of any phenomenon. The only reply that can be made to such a critic is to point out that the scientist's interests are quite different from his. There are, of course, other legitimate interpretations of nature and man than the scientific one and each has its right to be pursued. The behavior scientist merely asks that he be given the same opportunity to develop a scientific account of his phenomena that his colleagues in the physical and biological fields have had. If there are aspects of human or animal behavior for which such an account cannot ever be developed, there are not, so far as I know, any means of finding this out without a try. Unfortunately, the attitudes of too many psychologists with regard to this matter are not such as are likely to lead them to the discovery of such knowledge. The difficulty, I fear is that too many persons whose interests are non-scientific have become psychologists under the mistaken impression that psychology is one of the arts.

As to the criticisms that the behaviorist's concepts are too elementaristic, I must confess to the belief that the term "elementarism" is merely one of those stereotypes, or "rally-round-the-flag" words which the Gestalt psychologist has used in the defense and exposition of his holistic doctrines. However fervently the Gestalt psychologist may claim that he deals only with wholes, with total situations, the fact remains that if he is interested in discovering uniformities or scientific laws he must, of necessity, fractionate or abstract out certain features of the total events he observes. Such uniformities or laws describe ways in which events repeat themselves. Total concrete events, however, are seldom if ever repeated. Only certain features of events are repeated and since this is the case science must always abstract.

The problem here is really one of the size of the "units of description" that the scientist is to employ and this brings us back to the criterion of acceptability of a scientific term which we referred to as *significance*. By the *significance* of a scientific concept is here meant the extent to which a concept or variable aids or enters into the formulation of laws. Significant concepts in science are those which are discovered to have functional relations with other concepts. Unfortunately, there are few if any rules for deciding *a priori* which concepts will and which ones will not be significant. Whether elementaristic concepts or units of description which, like the Gestaltists, are nearer the "meaningful" common sense level, are to be chosen is entirely a pragmatic matter of which ones are most successful—*i.e.*, which ones lead to the discovery of laws. This can be ascertained only by trying them out.

Attention might also be called here to the further fact that it is entirely conceivable that different sizes or levels of descriptive units may be employed for the same set of events. The physical sciences provide us with numerous instances of this sort of thing and we see examples of it in psychology both in the description of behavior and stimulus events. Thus, employing the terms of Brunswik (4) and Heider (8), we may make use of either a proximal or distal account of the stimulus situation, and behavior may be described either in terms of movements (muscular patterns) or in terms of gross achievements. The particular alternative chosen, molecular or molar, depends upon the interest and purpose of the scientist, the kind of law he expects to find or use. As Hull (11) has pointed out in discussing this matter, some of the seeming disagreements among current psychologists are merely that one prefers to use more molar concepts than another.

Such different descriptions, however, do not necessarily represent fundamental disagreements. If the two systems of concepts should each be successful in leading to the discovery and formulation of laws, it should also be possible to discover coordinating definitions which will reveal the interrelations of the two systems. Or, as Hull (11) suggests, the postulates or primary assumptions of those working at a more molar level may ultimately appear as theorems in a more molecular description.

To sum up, then, the position which the behavior scientist takes with respect to the selection of the descriptive concepts to be employed in his science, recognizes (1) that the *significance* of a concept is to be measured in terms of the extent to which it leads to the formulation of laws about the phenomena; (2) that a scientific law is always, in some greater or less degree, abstract in the sense that it refers *only* to certain properties of the events or sequence of events it describes and ignores other properties which are irrelevant to the particular momentary purpose; (3) that the method of elementary abstraction or analysis has been highly successful in all fields of science. While the disentanglement of the great complexes of properties and relations (sequences) among psychological events is undoubtedly much more difficult than in the case of physical phenomena, the difference between them need not be regarded as more than one of degree. On the basis of this assumption thre would seem to be little reason for abandoning the method of abstraction or analysis.

We have said that the primary aim of the behavior scientist is to bring order and meaning into the particular realm of events he studies. Ordering a set of observable events for the scientist consists in discovering relationships between the events or, as we say, in the finding of empirical laws. The scientist seeks to establish laws relating his concepts or variables because they make possible explanation and prediction.

In the case of such areas of science as physics, the finding of empirical laws has involved chiefly the process of inductive generalization from observation and experimentation. In other words, in physics it has been possible to isolate sufficiently simple systems of observation to arrive at such laws in this manner. The situation in psychology and the other behavior sciences in quite different. Primarily because of the greater complexity of psychological as compared with physical phenomena, the psychologist has either been unable to isolate, experimentally, simple systems, or he has not found satisfactory means of measuring all of the relevant variables in the system under observation. In this circumstance he has resorted to guesses or postulations as to the uncontrolled or as yet unmeasurable factors. As a result of this difference the term "theory" has, as I have pointed out elsewhere (17), come to have a very different connotation in psychology from that which it has in physics. Theories in physics are constructions which serve primarily to integrate or organize into a single deductive system sets of empirical laws which previously were unrelated. The classical example is, of course, the Newtonian integration of the previously unconnected areas of mechanics and astronomy by the gravitational theory. Other well-known examples are the electro-magnetic theory of light and the kinetic theory of gases.

In psychology, on the other hand, theories serve primarily as a device to aid in the formulation of the empirical laws. They consist in guesses as to how the uncontrolled or unknown factors in the system under study are related to the experimentally-known variables. To these hypothetical constructs Tolman (20) has applied the very appropriate term "intervening variable" because they are assumed to intervene between the measurable environmental and organic variables, on the one hand, and the measurable behavior properties on the other.

The manner in which the behavior scientist has used these hypothetical, intervening constructs may be shown by considering the various kinds of laws which the psychologist seeks to discover. Confining ourselves for the moment to laws which do not involve any hypothetical components, we find that the variables studied by the behavioristic psychologist fall into two, or possibly three, main groups:

(1) Response variables: measurments of behavior properties.

(2) Stimulus variables: measurements of properties of the physical and social environment.

(3) Organic variables: measurements of neuroanatomical or neurophysiological properties of the organism.

The different types of empirical relationships or laws in which psychologists have been interested are as follows:

$$1. \ \ R = f\,(R)$$
$$2. \ \ R = f\,(S)$$
$$3. \ \ R = f\,(O)$$
$$4. \ \ O = f\,(S)$$

Type 1 laws of association of behavior properties. A great deal of use is made of the statistical constant, the coefficient of correlation, in the formulation of these laws and, as is well known, this type of law is investigated extensively in the field of psychological testing.

Type 2 laws may be concerned with the present environment or with past environmental events. Thus in the case of the typical perception experiments, we are interested in the effects of variation of aspects or features of the environmental stimulus on the perceptual or discrimination responses of the subject. Best examples of laws relating behavior to past events in the environment are laws of learning, laws of secondary motivation, etc.

For the most part the present-day behavioristic psychologists tend to concentrate their energies on these two classes of laws and to a very considerable extent they have favored the use of the molar rather than molecular concepts. A few psychologists whose interests have been in mediational problems have concerned themselves with type 3 and type 4 laws. These latter are obviously in the field of neurophysiological psychology and have in the main been concerned only with the simplest kinds of behavior phenomena—*e.g.*, sensory responses. Indeed, our inability to develop measures of this class of events (*i.e.*, organic variables) in the case of the more complex behavior phenomena has been one of the factors underlying the substitution of the hypothetical intervening constructs in their place.

Figure 1 continues this analysis of the laws of psychology. In this diagram I have attempted to portray, in addition to the four types of empirical laws which we have been discussing, the new hypothetical or guessed-at types of relationships which are involved in the introduction of the hypothetical intervening constructs. These latter are indicated as I_a and I_b and are represented as *hypothetical state variables* (enclosed within the rectangle). The environment or world situation at three different time intervals is represented by $S_t - n$ (past) $S_t = o$ (present) $S_t + n$ (future). These S's and also the R's represent empirical variables. I have also represented the class of experimental neurophysiological variables of the first figure by the symbol O, to the left of the rectangle. The four classes of empirical laws, listed at the right side of the figure, are represented by the solid curved lines. The guessed-at or postulated laws relating to hypothetical state variables (I_a, I_b, etc.) to the various experimental variables are represented by the dotted lines. Thus No. 5 type of "law" defines or introduces the intervening variables in terms of past

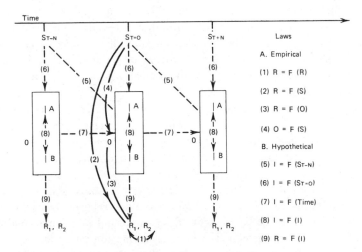

FIGURE 1. Showing different kinds of laws.

events; No. 6 type relates them to the present environmental variables and No. 7 to time; No. 8 "laws" present interrelations assumed between these intervening variables, and, finally, the relations represented by No. 9 relate the intervening variables to the response variables. That is to say, these dotted lines should be thought of as representative of different classes of postulated relationships, not the usual notion of an S–R connection.

Those who are acquainted with the theoretical constructs of Hull (11) will recognize specific examples of these hypothetical laws. Thus his postulate or definition of the construct habit strength, or S^HR, as a function of the number of past reinforcements is a good example of class No. 5 "law." His assumption of the nature of the manner in which H and D interact to determine E falls in Class No. 8 and his postulate as to how the construct of reactive inhibition (I_R) is assumed to change (disintegrate) with time is an instance of No. 7 type of "law." Incidentally, it will be noted that this last relationship is the only one which is similar to the so-called dynamic or process laws of physics. This type of law states or describes the laws governing the changes that occur within a system in time.

A question concerning these theoretical constructs that invariably seems to arise is whether they represent some kind of internal, presumably neurophysiological, process or state. The persistence with which misunderstanding arises on this point is truly surprising. It is probably to be explained in terms of the difficulty and resistance we have in shedding old, familiar meanings of words. In this connection it is not a little amusing to note that whereas Hull is usually accused of stuffing the organism with mythological brain states, Tolman, whose theoretical concepts have exactly the same formal structure as those of Hull—*i.e.*, intervening variables defined in terms of independent environmental events—is often charged with the guilt of dreaming up mentalistic ghosts. The explanation of this situation is readily seen when we recall the terms employed by these two men to designate their intervening variables. Thus Hull used such words as habit, drive, excitatory potential and inhibitory potential while Tolman named his theoretical constructs, demands, sign-Gestalt-expectations, hypotheses, etc.

The only meanings that these theoretical intervening constructs have *at the present time* is provided by the equations which relate them to the known experimental variables—the environmental measurements on the one hand and the behavior measures on the other. Such equations constitute the definitions of these terms.

The present role of these theoretical constructs we have said is to aid the psychologist in his search for the empirical laws relating behavior to the conditions determining it. In this sense they are a kind of calculational device which helps us to write the complete law describing the interrelations between all of the relevant experimental variables. In a recent article (17) on this problem of theory construction in contemporary psychology I called attention to the point that it is possible in the case of the theoretical formulation of simple learning behavior developed by Hull to substitute in the successive equations introducing the intervening theoretical constructs and obtain a single equation which states the response measure as a function of the several antecedent environmental variables. In this equation the intervening theoretical variables are represented among the parameters of the equation.

While both Tolman and I have emphasized the heuristic value of this type of theoretical construction in the formulation of the complete form of the laws, Hull (12) has called attention to another use which these constructs serve. Such constructs as habit and excitatory potential also provide, he claims, convenient, quantitative representations or indices of the particular complex of experimental variables for which they stand. Thus instead of having to state that the subject has had so many reinforcements in the situation under conditions in which the goal was of such-and-such a magnitude and was delayed for such-and-such a period, it is possible to substitute the calculated value of habit strength.

Finally, there remains the possibility, at least, that these intervening constructs may turn out to have their counterparts somewhere under the skin of the organism. Hull in particular has been quite prone to accept this possibility and has not hesitated to add further statements about these constructs which suggest their possible locus and functioning in the nervous system. His justification, however, has always been that such conjectures provide experimental hints to persons interested in making such coordinations of our knowledge. His main theoretical efforts have been primarily at the molar-behavioral level.

In concluding this discussion of the theoretical framework of the behavioristic psychologist, I should like to emphasize that it is as yet only in a very primitive state of development, a fact which has unfortunately been lost sight of by many of the current critics of this position. The theorist in this field apparently has to choose between attempting to lay down the general theoretical framework of the whole range of behavior phenomena or working out the detailed nature of one small realm of data. Tolman has, for the most part, chosen the former alternative with the consequence that his treatment is characterized by an obvious lack of detailed specification of his theoretical constructs. Hull, on the other hand, has elected to follow the second method. His recent book, *Principles of Behavior*, dealt only with the most *simple* instances of laboratory learning phenomena, classical and instrumental conditioning, and he and his students are now engaged in extending the fundamental laws there discovered to the major phenomena of individual behavior.

So far as theoretical constructs are concerned, it is obvious that the simple behavior phenomena dealt with by Hull and other behavioristic-oriented psychologists have not required (to any great extent) a whole class of hypothetical intervening variables that must ultimately be postulated. Thus the theoretical constructs in Hull's recent book—habit, excitatory and inhibitory potential, drive, etc.—are what might be referred to as *state variables*. Each of these constructs represents a hypothetical condition or state of the organism which is assumed to have resulted from and is defined in terms of the past interactions of the organism and its environment. In contrast the new theoretical constructs referred to above will represent, not states, but hypothetical, non-observable responses, implicit processes, occurring in the individual. Thus, in dealing with the more complex types of animal and human behavior, implicit emotional responses, covert verbal responses and not easily observable receptor-exposure and postural adjustments will have to be postulated in addition to these state variables. As yet only a bare beginning has been made in the use of such theoretical constructs—*e.g.*, anxiety reactions and their secondary reinforcing effects (14), fractional anticipatory goal reactions as the basis of purposive behavior (9, 10).

It is in this realm of theorizing that the verbal reports of human subjects are likely to be of most use to the behavior theorist, for presumably these reports can be made the basis on which to postulate the occurrence of these inferred activities. There are, of course, many pitfalls in the use of such verbal reports and considerable caution needs to be exercised in their use. However, careful control and checking in terms of other, non-verbal responses should provide a means of detecting distortions, both deliberate and otherwise, in this source of data (16).

A discussion of behaviorism, especially when it occurs in conjunction with a symposium which includes Gestalt psychology, requires at least some comment on the distinction often made between field and non-field theories in psychology. The Gestalt psychologists, in particular, have been very fond of this contrast and they have not hesitated to imply that their theoretical structures are similar in some respect to the type of field theory in physics represented by the Maxwell electromagnetic theory and Einstein's gravitational theory. In some instances the further implication has been made that behavioristic theories are a mechanical type of theory and as such are just as outmoded as the mechanistic theories of physics. Now I have often wondered what our theoretical brethren from the field of physics would think of these claims if perchance they were ever to take a serious look at these two groups of theories. Certainly the behavioristic theoretical structure I have been talking about uses neither the mechanical models—*i.e.*, particles with their attracting forces—nor the type of mathematical equations that characterize a mechanical theory. Nor do I believe that there is anything even remotely resembling the field equations of Maxwell and Einstein in the theoretical formulations of the Gestalt psychologists. In the sense, then, in which the theoretical physicist understands the dichotomy, mechanical versus field theory, no such distinction, in my opinion, exists in psychology today.

If, on the other hand, the concept of field refers in psychology essentially to the notion of a system of interdependent variables, with its implication that the behavior of an organism at any moment is a resultant of the totality of relevant variables, then there is not to my knowledge any behavioristic theory today which would not also be a field theory. Furthermore, if we accept the additional notion that it is the pattern of interrelationships between the determining variables that is the crucial factor differentiating psychological field theories from non-field theories, I do not believe that the behavior theories which I have been describing would fail to qualify as field theories. The hypothetical equations which Hull (11) postulates in the introduction of his theoretical constructs provide in precise mathematical form these very patterns of interrelationship. Finally, as to the characteristic of field theory emphasized by Lewin (13) under the principle of contemporaneity—namely, that the behavior at any moment is a function of the situation *at that moment only* and not a function of past or future situations,—I find it difficult to believe that any present-day psychologist believes that other conditions than those of the present moment determine the behavior of this moment. Even the psychoanalyst never held, as Lewin sometimes seems to imply, that past events somehow jump through time to determine the present behavior, but, instead, conceived of these past events leaving their effects in the organism and through them determining the behavior of the moment. The behaviorist takes exactly the same view of the matter.

The development of our science has not been helped, in my opinion, by such distinctions as field and non-field theory. A much more useful procedure would be to examine in detail these differing theoretical positions with a view to ascertaining to what extent they differ in the particular variables they believe to be relevant in a particular instance and what differences, if any, exist in their postulation as to the pattern of the interrelationships involved— *i.e.*, in the form of the hypothetical laws they assume. It is my personal belief that if this procedure were followed there would be much less in the way of specific disagreements to settle than is usually thought. I base this prediction not only on the well-known fact that the Gestaltists, psychoanalysts and behaviorists have to a considerable extent been interested in very different realms of psychological phenomena and that hence their theories are not in competition with one another, but also on the fact that very little real theorizing, particularly in the matter of specifying the precise form of the interrelations between the variables, has actually been done. It is most imperative that psychologists attempt to formulate their theories in as precise and articulate a manner as possible, for it is only by means of such theorizing that psychology can hope, finally, to attain fullfledged scientific statehood.

References

1. Bergmann, G. The subject matter of psychology. *Phil Sci.*, 1940, **7**, 415–433.
2. Boring, E. G. *The physical dimensions of consciousness.* New York: The Century Company, 1933.
3. Bridgman, P. W. *The logic of modern physics.* New York: Macmillan Company, 1928.
4. Brunswik, E. The conceptual focus of some psychological systems. *J. Unified Sci. (Erkenntnis)*, 1939, **8**, 36–49.
5. Carnap, R. Testability and meaning. *Phil. Sci.*, 1936, **3**, 419–471; 1937, **4**, 1–40.
6. ———. *Philosophy and logical syntax.* London: Kegan Paul, Trench, Trubner and Co., Ltd., 1935.
7. Feigl, H. Operationism and scientific method. *Psychol. Rev.*, 1945, **52**, 243–246.
8. Heider, F. Environmental determinants in psychological theories. *Psychol. Rev.*, 1939, **46**, 383–410.
9. Hull, C. L. Knowledge and purpose as habit mechanisms. *Psychol. Rev.*, 1930, **37**, 511–525.
10. ———. Goal attraction and directing ideas conceived as habit phenomena. *Psychol. Rev.*, 1931, **38**, 487–506.
11. ———. *Principles of behavior.* New York: D. Appleton-Century Co., 1943.
12. ———. The problem of intervening variables in molar behavior theory. *Psychol. Rev.*, 1943, **50**, 273–291.
13. Lewin, K. Defining the "field" at a given time. *Psychol. Rev.*, 1943, **50**, 292–310.
14. Mowrer, O. H. A stimulus-response analysis of anxiety and its role as a reinforcing agent. *Psychol. Rev.*, 1939, **46**, 553–565.
15. Pratt, C. C. *The logic of modern psychology.* New York: The Macmillan Company, 1939.
16. Skinner, B. F. The operational analysis of psychological terms. *Psychol. Rev.*, 1945, **52**, 270–278.
17. Spence, K. W. The nature of theory construction in contemporary psychology. *Psychol. Rev.*, 1944, **51**, 47–68.
18. Stevens S. S. The operational definition of psychological concepts. *Psychol. Rev.*, 1935, **42**, 517–527.
19. Tolman, E. C. *Purposive behavior in animals and men.* New York: The Century Company, 1932.
20. ———. The determiners of behavior at a choice point. *Psychol. Rev.*, 1938, **45**, 1–41.
21. Watson, J. B. Psychology as the behaviorist views it. *Psychol. Rev.*, 1913, **20**, 158–177.

54. BEHAVIORISM AT FIFTY

B. F. Skinner

Behaviorism, with an accent on the last syllable, is not the scientific study of behavior but a philosophy of science concerned with the subject matter and methods of psychology. If psychology is a science of mental life—of the mind, of conscious experience—then it must develop and defend a special methodology, which it has not yet done successfully. If it is, on the other hand, a science of the behavior of organisms, human or otherwise, then it is part of biology, a natural science for which tested and highly successful methods are available. The basic issue is not the nature of the stuff of which the world is made or whether it is made of one stuff or two but rather the dimensions of the things studied by psychology and the methods relevant to them.

THE INNER MAN

Mentalistic or psychic explanations of human behavior almost certainly originated in primitive animism. When a man dreamed of being at a distant place in spite of incontrovertible evidence that he had stayed in his bed, it was easy to conclude that some part of him had actually left his body. A particularly vivid memory or a hallucination could be explained in the same way. The theory of an invisible, detachable self eventually proved useful for other purposes. It seemed to explain unexpected or abnormal episodes, even

SOURCE. Skinner, B. F., "Behaviorism at Fifty," in T. W. Wann (ed.), *Behaviorism and Phenomenology*, 1964 Phoenix. Chicago: University of Chicago Press. Reprinted with permission. Copyright © 1964 by The University of Chicago Press.

to the person behaving in an exceptional way because he was thus "possessed." It also served to explain the inexplicable. An organism as complex as man often seems to behave capriciously. It is tempting to attribute the visible behavior to another organism inside—to a little man or homunculus. The wishes of the little man become the acts of the man observed by his fellows. The inner idea is put into outer words. Inner feelings find outward expression. The explanation is successful, of course, only so long as the behavior of the homunculus can be neglected.

Primitive origins are not necessarily to be held against an explanatory principle, but the little man is still with us in relatively primitive form. He was recently the hero of a television program called "Gateways to the Mind," one of a series of educational films sponsored by the Bell Telephone Laboratories and written with the help of a distinguished panel of scientists. The viewer learned, from animated cartoons, that when a man's finger is pricked, electrical impulses resembling flashes of lightning run up the afferent nerves and appear on a television screen in the brain. The little man wakes up, sees the flashing screen, reaches out, and pulls a lever. More flashes of lightning go down the nerves to the muscles, which then contract, as the finger is pulled away from the threatening stimulus. The behavior of the homunculus was, of course, not explained. An explanation would presumably require another film. And it, in turn, another.

The same pattern of explanation is invoked when we are told that the behavior of a delinquent is the result of a disordered personality or that the vagaries of a man under analysis are due to conflicts among his superego, ego, and id. Nor can we escape from the primitive features by breaking the little man into pieces and dealing with his wishes, cognitions, motives, and so on, bit by bit. The objection is not that these things are mental but that they offer no real explanation and stand in the way of a more effective analysis.

It has been about fifty years since the behavioristic objection to this practice was first clearly stated, and it has been about thirty years since it has been very much discussed. A whole generation of psychologists has grown up without really coming into contact with the issue. Almost all current textbooks compromise: rather than risk a loss of adoptions, they define psychology as the science of behavior *and* mental life. Meanwhile the older view has continued to receive strong support from areas in which there has been no comparable attempt at methodological reform. During this period, however, an effective experimental science of behavior has emerged. Much of what it has discovered bears on the basic issue. A restatement of radical behaviorism would therefore seem to be in order.

EXPLAINING THE MIND

A rough history of the idea is not hard to trace. An occasional phrase in classic Greek writings that seemed to foreshadow the point of view need not be taken seriously. We may also pass over the early bravado of a La Mettrie who could shock the philosophical bourgeoisie by asserting that man was only a machine. Nor were those who simply preferred, for practical reasons, to deal with behavior rather than with less accessible, but nevertheless acknowledged, mental activities close to what is meant by behaviorism today.

The entering wedge appears to have been Darwin's preoccupation with the continuity of species. In supporting the theory of evolution, it was important to show that man was not essentially different from the lower animals—that every human characteristic, including consciousness and reasoning powers, could be found in other species. Naturalists like Romanes began to collect stories which seemed to show that dogs, cats, elephants, and many other species were conscious and showed signs of reasoning. It was Lloyd Morgan, of course, who questioned this evidence with his Canon of Parsimony. Were there not other ways of accounting for what looked like signs of consciousness or rational powers? Thorndike's experiments at the end of the nineteenth century were in this vein. He showed that the behavior of a cat in escaping from a puzzle-box might seem to show reasoning but could be explained instead as the result of simpler processes. Thorndike remained a mentalist, but he greatly advanced the objective study of behavior which had been attributed to mental processes.

The next step was inevitable: if evidence of consciousness and reasoning could be explained in other ways in animals, why not also in man? And if this was the case, what became of psychology as a science of mental life? It was John B. Watson who made the first clear, if rather noisy, proposal that psychology should be regarded simply as a science of behavior. He was not in a very good position to defend it. He had little scientific material to use in his reconstruction. He was forced to pad his textbook with discussions of the physiology of receptor systems and muscles and with physiological theories which were at the time no more susceptible to proof than the mentalistic theories they were intended to replace. A need for "mediators" of behavior that might serve as objective alternatives to thought processes led him to emphasize sub-audible speech. The notion was intriguing, because one can usually observe oneself thinking in this way; but it was by no means an adequate or comprehensive explanation. He tangled with introspective psychologists by denying the existence of images. He may well have been acting in good faith, for it has been said that he himself did not have visual imagery; but his arguments caused unnecessary trouble. The relative importance of a genetic endowment in explaining behavior proved to be another disturbing digression.

All this made it easy to lose sight of the central argument—that behavior which seemed to be the product of mental activity could be explained in other ways. Moreover, the introspectionists were prepared to challenge it. As late as 1883 Francis Galton could write: "Many persons, especially women and intelligent children, take pleasure in introspection, and strive their very best to explain their mental processes" (5). But introspection was already being taken seriously. The concept of a science of mind in which mental events obeyed mental laws had led to the development of psychophysical methods and to the accumulation of facts which seemed to bar the extension of the principle of parsimony. What might hold for animals did not hold for men, because men could see their mental processes.

Curiously enough, part of the answer was supplied by the psychoanalysts, who insisted that, although a man might be able to see some of his mental life, he could not see all of it. The kind of thoughts Freud called "unconscious" took place without the knowledge of the thinker. From an association, verbal slip, or dream it could be shown that a person must have responded to a passing stimulus, although he could not tell you that he had done so. More complex thought processes, including problem-solving and verbal play, could also go on without the thinker's knowledge. Freud had devised, and never abandoned faith in, one of the most elaborate mental apparatuses of all time. He nevertheless contributed to the behavioristic argument by showing that mental activity did not, at least, *require* consciousness. His proofs that thinking had occurred without introspective recognition were, indeed, clearly in the spirit of Lloyd Morgan. They were operational analyses of mental life—even though, for Freud, only the unconscious part of it. Experimental evidence pointing in the same direction soon began to accumulate.

But that was not the whole answer. What about the part of mental life which a man can see? It is a difficult question, no matter what one's point of view, partly because it raises the question of what seeing means and partly because the events seen are private. The fact of privacy cannot, of course, be questioned. Each person is in special contact with a small part of the universe enclosed within his own skin. To take a non-controversial example, he is uniquely subject to certain kinds of proprioceptive and interoceptive stimulation. Though two people may in some sense be said to see the same light or hear the same sound, they cannot feel the same distention of a bile duct or the same bruised muscle. (When privacy is invaded with scientific instruments, the form of stimulation is changed; the scales read by the scientist are not the private events themselves.)

Mentalistic psychologists insist that there are other kinds of events that are uniquely accessible to the owner of the skin within which they occur but which lack the physical dimensions of proprioceptive or interoceptive stimuli. They are as different from physical events as colors are from wave lengths of light. There are even better reasons, therefore, why two people cannot suffer each other's toothaches, recall each other's memories, or share each other's happinesses. The importance assigned to this kind of world varies. For some, it is the only world there is. For others, it is the only part of the world which can be directly known. For still others, it is a special part of what can be known. In any case, the problem of how one knows about the subjective world of another must be faced. Apart from the question of what "knowing" means, the problem is one of accessibility.

PUBLIC AND PRIVATE EVENTS

One solution, often regarded as behavioristic, is to grant the distinction between public and private events and rule the latter out of scientific consideration. This is a congenial solution for those to whom scientific truth is a matter of convention or agreement among observers. It is essentially the line taken by logical positivism and physical operationism. Hogben (7) has recently redefined "behaviorist" in this spirit. The subtitle of his *Statistical Theory* is "an examination of the contemporary crises in statistical theory from a behaviorist viewpoint," and this is amplified in the following way:

> The behaviourist, as I here use the term, does not deny the convenience
> of classifying *processes* as mental or material. He recognizes the
> distinction between personality and corpse: but he has not yet had the
> privilege of attending an identity parade in which human minds without
> bodies are by common recognition distinguishable from living human
> bodies without minds. Till then, he is content to discuss probability
> in the vocabulary of *events*, including audible or visibly recorded
> assertions of human beings as such. . . .

The behavioristic position, so defined, is simply that of the publicist and "has no concern with structure and mechanism."

The point of view is often called operational, and it is significant that P. W. Bridgman's physical operationism could not save him from an extreme solipsism even within physical science itself. Though he insisted that he was not a solipsist, he was never able to reconcile seemingly public physical knowledge with the private world the scientists (3). Applied to psychological problems, operationism has been no more successful. We may recognize the restrictions imposed by the operations through which we can know of the existence of properties of subjective events, but the operations cannot be identified with the events themselves. S. S. Stevens has applied Bridgman's principle to psychology, not to decide whether subjective events exist, but to determine the extent to which we can deal with them scientifically (9).

Behaviorists have, from time to time, examined the problem of privacy, and some of them have excluded so-called sensations, images, thought processes, and so on from their deliberations. When they have done so not because such things do not exist but because they are out of reach of their methods, the charge is justified that they have neglected the facts of consciousness. The strategy is, however, quite unwise. It is particularly important that a science of behavior face the problem of privacy. It may do so without abandoning the basic position of behaviorism. Science often talks about things it cannot see or measure. When a man tosses a penny into the air, it must be assumed that he tosses the earth beneath him downward. It is quite out of the question to see or measure the effect on the earth, but it must be assumed for the sake of a consistent account. An adequate science of behavior must consider events taking place within the skin of the organism, not as physiological mediators of behavior, but as part of behavior itself. It can deal with these events without assuming that they have any special nature or must be known in any special way. The skin is not that important as a boundary. Private and public events have the same kinds of physical dimensions.

SELF-DESCRIPTIVE BEHAVIOR

In the fify years since a behavioristic philosophy was first stated, facts and principles bearing on the basic issues have steadily accumulated. For one thing, a scientific analysis of behavior has yielded a sort of empirical epistemology. The subject matter of a science of behavior includes the behavior of scientists and other knowers. The techniques available to such a science give an empirical theory of knowledge certain advantages over theories derived from philosophy and logic. The problem of privacy may be approached in a fresh direction by starting with behavior rather than with immediate experience. The strategy is certainly no more arbitrary or circular than the earlier practice, and it has a surprising result. Instead of concluding that man can know only his subjective experiences—that he is bound forever to his private world and that the external world is only a construct—a behavioral theory of knowledge suggests that it is the private world which, if not entirely unknowable, is at least not likely to be known well. The relations between organism and environment involved in knowing are of such a sort that the privacy of the world within the skin imposes more serious limitations on personal knowledge than on scientific accessibility.

An organism learns to react discriminatively to the world around it under certain contingencies of reinforcement. Thus, a child learns to name a color correctly when a given response is reinforced in the presence of the color and extinguished in its absence. The verbal community may make the reinforcement of an extensive repertoire of responses contingent on subtle properties of colored stimuli. We have reason to believe that the child will not discriminate among colors—that he will not see two colors as different—until exposed to such contingencies. So far as we know, the same process of differential reinforcement is required if a child is to distinguish among the events occurring within his own skin.

Many contingencies involving private stimuli need not be arranged by a verbal community, for they follow from simple mechanical relations among stimuli, responses, and reinforcing consequences. The various motions which comprise turning a handspring, for example, are under the control of external and internal stimuli and subject to external and internal reinforcing consequences. But the performer is not necessarily "aware" of the stimuli controlling his behavior, no matter how appropriate and skillful it may be. "Knowing" or "being aware of" what is happening in turning a handspring involves discriminative responses, such as naming or describing, which arise from contingencies necessarily arranged by a verbal environment. Such environments are common. The community is generally interested in what a man is doing, has done, or is planning to do and why, and it arranges contingencies which generate verbal responses which name and describe the external and internal stimuli associated with these events. It challenges his verbal behavior by asking, "How do you know?" and the speaker answers, if at all, by describing some of the variables of which his verbal behavior was a function. The "awareness" resulting from all this is a social product.

In attempting to set up such a repertory, however, the verbal community works under a severe handicap. It cannot always arrange the contingencies required for subtle discriminations. It cannot teach a child to call one pattern of private stimuli "diffidence" and another "embarrassment" as effectively as it teaches him to call one stimulus "red" and another "orange," for it cannot be sure of the presence or absence of the private patterns of stimuli appropriate to reinforcement or lack of reinforcement. Privacy thus causes trouble, first of all, *for the verbal community*. The individual suffers in turn. Because the community cannot reinforce self-descriptive responses consistently, a person cannot describe or otherwise "know" events occurring within his own skin as subtly and precisely as he knows events in the world at large.

There are, of course, differences between external and internal stimuli which are not mere differences in location. Proprioceptive and interoceptive stimuli may have a certain intimacy. They are likely to be especially familiar. They are very much with us: we cannot escape from a toothache as easily as from a deafening noise. They may well be of a special kind: the stimuli we feel in pride or sorrow may not closely resemble those we feel in sandpaper or satin.

But this does not mean that they differ in physical status. In particular, it does not mean that they can be more easily or more directly known. What is particularly clear and familiar to the potential knower may be strange and distant to the verbal community responsible for his knowing.

CONSCIOUS CONTENT

What *are* the private events which, at least in a limited way, a man may come to respond to in ways we call "knowing"? Let us begin with the oldest, and in many ways the most difficult, kind, represented by "the stubborn fact of consciousness." What is happening when a person observes the conscious content of his mind, when he looks at his sensations or images? Western philosophy and science have been handicapped in answering these questions by an unfortunate metaphor. The Greeks could not explain how a man could have knowledge of something with which he was not in immediate contact. How could he know an object on the other side of the room, for example? Did he reach out and touch it with some sort of invisible probe? Or did he never actually come in contact with the object at all but only with a copy of it inside his body? Plato supported the copy theory with his metaphor of the cave. Perhaps a man never sees the real world at all but only shadows of it on the wall of the cave in which he is imprisoned. (The "shadows" may well have been the much more accurate copies of the outside world in a *camera obscura*. Did Plato know of a cave, at the entrance of which a happy super-position of objects admitted only the thin pencils of light needed for a *camera obscura?*) Copies of the real world projected into the body could compose the experience which a man directly knows. A similar theory could also explain how one can see objects which are "not really there," as in hallucinations, afterimages, and memories. Neither explanation is, of course, satisfactory. How a copy may arise at a distance is at least as puzzling as how a man may know an object at a distance. Seeing things which are not really there is no harder to explain than the occurrence of copies of things not there to be copied.

The search for copies of the world within the body, particularly in the nervous system, still goes on, but with discouraging results. If the retina could suddenly be developed, like a photographic plate, it would yield a poor picture. The nerve impulses in the optic tract must have an even more tenuous resemblance to "what is seen." The patterns of vibrations which strike our ear when we listen to music are quickly lost in transmission. The bodily reactions to substances tasted, smelled, and touched would scarcely qualify as faithful reproductions. These facts are discouraging for those who are looking for copies of the real world within the body, but they are fortunate for psychophysiology as a whole. At some point the organism must do more than create duplicates. It must see, hear, smell, and so on, as forms of *action* rather than of *reproduction. It must do some of the things it is differentially reinforced for doing when it learns to respond discriminatively.* The sooner the pattern of the external world disappears after impinging on the organism, the sooner the organism may get on with these other functions.

The need for something beyond, and quite different from, copying is not widely understood. Suppose someone were to coat the occipital lobes of the brain with a special photographic emulsion which, when developed, yielded a reasonable copy of a current visual stimulus. In many quarters this would be regarded as a triumph in the physiology of vision. Yet nothing could be more disastrous, for we should have to start all over again and ask how the organism sees a picture in its occipital cortex, and we should now have much less of the brain available in which to seek an answer. It adds nothing to an explanation of how an organism reacts to a stimulus to trace the pattern of the stimulus into the body. It is most convenient, for both organism and psychophysiologist, if the external world is never copied—if the world we know is simply the world around us. The same may be said of theories according to which the brain interprets signals sent to it and in some sense reconstructs external stimuli. If the real world is, indeed, scrambled in transmission but later reconstructed in the brain, we must then start all over again and explain how the organism sees the reconstruction.

An adequate treatment of this point would require a thorough analysis of the behavior of seeing and of the conditions under which we see (to continue with vision as a convenient modality). It would be unwise to exaggerate our success to date. Discriminative visual behavior arises from contingencies involving external stimuli and overt responses, but possible private accompaniments must not be overlooked. Some of the consequences of such contingencies seem well established. It is usually easiest for us to see a friend when we are looking at him, because visual stimuli similar to those present when the behavior was acquired exert maximal control over the response. But mere visual stimulation is not enough; even after having been exposed to the necessary reinforcement, we may not see a friend who is present unless we have reason to do so. On the other hand, if the reasons are strong enough, we may see him in someone bearing only a superficial resemblance or when no one like him is present at all. If conditions favor seeing something else, we may behave accordingly. If, on a hunting trip, it is important to see a deer, we may glance toward our friend at a distance, see him as a deer, and shoot.

It is not, however, seeing our friend which raises the question of conscious content but "seeing that we are seeing him." There are no natural contingencies for such behavior. We learn to see that we are seeing only because a verbal community arranges for us to do so. We usually acquire the behavior when we are under appropriate visual stimulation, but it does not follow that the thing seen must be present when we see that we are seeing it. The contingencies arranged by the verbal environment may set up self-descriptive responses describing the *behavior* of seeing even when the thing seen is not present.

If seeing does not require the presence of things seen, we need not be concerned about certain mental processes said to be involved in the construction of such things—images, memories, and dreams, for example. We may regard a dream, not as a display of things seen by the dreamer, but simply as the behavior of seeing. At no time during a daydream, for example, should we expect to find within the organism anything that corresponds to the external stimuli present when the dreamer first acquired the behavior in which he is now engaged. In simple recall we need not suppose that we wander through some storehouse of memory until we find an object which we then contemplate. Instead of assuming that we begin with a tendency to *recognize* such an object once it is found, it is simpler to assume that we begin with a tendency to *see* it. Techniques of self-management which facilitate recall—for example, the use of mnemonic devices—can be formulated as ways of strengthening behavior rather than of creating objects to be seen. Freud dramatized the issue with respect to dreaming when asleep in his concept of dreamwork— an activity in which some part of the dreamer played the role of a theatrical producer while another part sat in the audience. If a dream is, indeed, something seen, then we must suppose that it is wrought as such; but if it is simply the behavior of seeing, the dreamwork may be dropped from the analysis. It took man a long time to understand that when he dreamed of a wolf, no wolf was actually there. It has taken him much longer to understand that not even a representation of a wolf is there.

Eye movements which appear to be associated with dreaming are in accord with this interpretation, since it is not likely that the dreamer is actually watching a dream on the undersides of his eyelids. When memories are aroused by electrical stimulation of the brain, as in the work of Wilder Penfield, it is also simpler to assume that it is the behavior of seeing, hearing, and so on, which is aroused rather than some copy of early environmental events which the subject then looks at or listens to. Behavior similar to the responses to the original events must be assumed in both cases—the subject sees or hears—but the reproduction of the events seen or heard is a needless complication. The familiar process of response chaining is available to account for the serial character of the behavior of remembering, but the serial linkage of stored experiences (suggesting engrams in the form of sound films) demands a new mechanism.

The heart of the behavioristic position on conscious experience may be summed up in this way: seeing does not imply something seen. We acquire the behavior of seeing under stimulation from actual objects, but it may occur in the absence of these objects under the control of other variables. (So far as the world within the skin is concerned, it always occurs in the absence of such objects.) We also acquire the behavior of seeing-that-we-are-seeing when we are seeing actual objects, but it may also occur in their absence.

To question the reality or the nature of the things seen in conscious experience is not to question the value of introspective psychology or its methods. Current problems in sensation are mainly concerned with the physiological function of receptors and associated neural mechanisms. Problems in perception are, at the moment, less intimately related to specific mechanisms, but the trend appears to be in the same direction. So far as behavior is concerned, both sensation and perception may be analyzed as forms of stimulus control. The subject need not be regarded as observing or evaluating conscious experiences. Apparent anomalies of stimulus control, which are now explained by appealing to a psychophysical relation or to the laws of perception, may be studied in their own right. It is, after all, no real solution to attribute them to the slippage inherent in converting a physical stimulus into a subjective experience.

The experimental analysis of behavior has a little more to say on this subject. Its techniques have recently been extended to what might be called the psychophysics of lower organisms. Blough's adaptation of the Békésy technique—for example, in determining the spectral sensitivity of pigeons and monkeys—yields sensory data comparable with the reports of a trained observer (1, 2). Hernstein and van Sommers have recently developed a procedure in which pigeons "bisect sensory intervals" (6). It is tempting to describe these procedures by saying that investigators have found ways to get non-verbal organisms to describe their sensations. The fact is that a form of stimulus control has been investigated without using a repertory of self-observation or, rather, by constructing a special repertory the nature and origin of which are clearly understood. Rather than describe such experiments with the terminology of introspection, we may formulate them in their proper place in an experimental analysis. The behavior of the observer in the traditional psychophysical experiment may then be reinterpreted accordingly.

MENTAL WAY STATIONS

So much for "conscious content," the classical problem in mentalistic philosophies. There are other mental states or processes to be taken into account. Moods, cognitions, and expectancies, for example, are also examined introspectively, and descriptions are used in psychological formulations. The conditions under which descriptive repertories are set up are much less successfully controlled. Terms describing sensations and images are taught by manipulating discriminative stimuli—a relatively amenable class of variables. The remaining kinds of mental events are related to such operations as deprivation and satiation, emotional stimulation, and various schedules of reinforcement. The difficulties they present to the verbal community are suggested by the fact that there is no psychophysics of mental states of this sort. That fact has not inhibited their use in explanatory systems.

In an experimental analysis, the relation between a property of behavior and an operation performed upon the organism is studied directly. Traditional mentalistic formulations, however, emphasize certain way stations. Where an experimental analysis might examine the effect of punishment on behavior, a mentalistic psychology will be concerned first with the effect of punishment in generating feelings of anxiety and then with the effect of anxiety on behavior. The mental state seems to bridge the gap between dependent and independent variables and is particularly attractive when these are separated by long periods of time—when, for example, the punishment occurs in childhood and the effect appears in the behavior of the adult.

The practice is widespread. In a demonstration experiment, a hungry pigeon was conditioned to turn around in a clockwise direction. A final, smoothly executed pattern of behavior was shaped by reinforcing successive approximations with food. Students who had watched the demonstration were asked to write an account of what they had seen. Their responses included the following: (1) The organism was conditioned to *expect* reinforcement for the right kind of behavior. (2) The pigeon walked around, *hoping* that something would bring the food back again. (3) The pigeon *observed* that a certain behavior seemed to produce a particular result. (4) The pigeon *felt* that food would be given it because of its action; and (5) the bird came to *associate* his action with the click of the food-dispenser. The observed facts could be stated respectively as follows: (1) The organism was reinforced *when* it emitted a given kind of behavior. (2) The pigeon walked around *until* the food container again appeared. (3) A certain behavior *produced* a particular result. (4) Food was given to the pigeon *when* it acted in a given way; and (5) the click of the food-dispenser *was temporally related* to the bird's action. These statements describe the contingencies of reinforcement. The expressions "expect," "hope," "observe," "feel," and "associate" go beyond them to identify effects on the pigeon. The effect actually observed was clear enough: the pigeon turned more skillfully and more frequently; but that was not the effect reported by the students. (If pressed, they would doubtless have said that the pigeon turned more skillfully and more frequently *because* it expected, hoped, and felt that if it did so food would appear.)

The events reported by the students were observed, if at all, in their own behavior. They were describing what they would have expected, felt, and hoped for under similar circumstances. But they were able to do so only because a verbal community had brought relevant terms under the control of certain stimuli, and this was done *when the community had access only to the kinds of public information available to the students in the demonstration.* Whatever the students knew about themselves which permitted them to infer comparable events in the pigeon must have been learned from a verbal community which saw no more of their behavior than they had seen of the pigeons. Private stimuli may have entered into the control of their self-descriptive repertories, but the readiness with which they applied them to the pigeon indicates that external stimuli had remained important. The extraordinary strength of a mentalistic interpretation is really a sort of proof that in describing a private way station one is, to a considerable extent, making use of public information.

The mental way station is often accepted as a terminal datum, however. When a man must be trained to discriminate between different planes, ships, and so on, it is tempting to stop at the point at which he can be said to *identify* such objects. It is implied that if he can identify an object, he can name it, label it, describe it, or act appropriately in some other way. In the training process he always behaves in one of these ways; no way station called "identification" appears in practice or need appear in theory. (Any discussion of the discriminative behavior generated by the verbal environment to permit a person to examine his conscious content must be qualified accordingly.)

Cognitive theories stop at way stations where the mental action is usually somewhat more complex than identification. For example, a subject is said to *know* who and where he is, what something is, or what has happened or is going to happen—regardless of the forms of behavior through which this knowledge was set up or which may now testify to its existence. Similarly, in accounting for verbal behavior, a listener or reader is said to understand the *meaning* of a passage, although the actual changes brought about by listening to, or reading, the passage are not specified. In the same way, schedules of reinforcement are sometimes studied simply for their effects on the *expectations* of the organism exposed to them, without discussing the implied relation between expectation and action. Recall, inference, and reasoning may be formulated only to the point at which *an experience is remembered or a conclusion reached,* behavioral manifestations being ignored. In practice, the investigator always carries through to some response, if only a response of self-description.

On the other hand, mental states are often studied as causes of action. A speaker thinks of something to say before saying it, and this explains what he says, although the sources of his thoughts cannot be examined. An unusual act is called "impulsive," without inquiring further into the origin of the unusual impulse. A behavioral maladjustment shows anxiety, but the source of anxiety is neglected. One salivates upon seeing a lemon because it reminds one of a sour taste, but why it does so is not specified. The formulation leads directly to a technology based on the manipulation of mental states. To change a man's voting behavior, we change his opinions; to induce him to act, we strengthen his beliefs; to make him eat, we make him feel hungry; to prevent wars, we reduce warlike tensions in the minds of men; to effect psychotherapy, we alter troublesome mental states; and so on. In practice all these ways of changing a man's mind reduce to manipulating his environment, verbal or otherwise.

In many cases we can reconstruct a complete causal chain by identifying the mental state which is the effect of an environmental variable with the mental state which is the cause of action. But this is not always enough. In traditional mentalistic philosophies various things happen at the way station which alter the relation between the terminal events. The effect of the psychophysical function and the laws of perception in distorting the physical stimulus before it reaches the way station has already been mentioned. Once the mental stage is reached, other effects are said to occur. Mental states alter one another. A painful memory may never affect behavior or may affect it in a different way, if another mental state succeeds in repressing it. Conflicting variables may be reconciled before reaching behavior if the subject engages in mental action called "making a decision." Dissonant cognitions generated by conflicting conditions of reinforcement will not be reflected in behavior if the subject can "persuade himself" that one condition was actually of a different magnitude or kind. These disturbances in simple causal linkages between environment and behavior can be formulated and studied experimentally as interactions among variables; but the possibility has not been fully exploited, and the effects still provide a formidable stronghold for mentalistic theories designed to bridge the gap between dependent and independent variables in the analysis of behavior.

METHODOLOGICAL OBJECTIONS

The behavioristic argument is nevertheless still valid. We may object, first, to the predilection for unfinished causal sequences. A disturbance in behavior is not explained by relating it to felt anxiety until the anxiety has in turn been explained. An action is not explained by attributing it to expectations until the expectations have in turn been accounted for. Complete causal sequences might, of course, include references to way stations, but the fact is that the way station generally interrupts the account in one direction or the other. For example, there must be thousands of instances in the psychoanalytic literature in which a thought or memory is said to have been relegated to the unconscious because it was painful or intolerable, but the percentage of those offering even the most casual suggestion as to why it was painful or intolerable must be very small. Perhaps explanations could have been offered, but the practice has discouraged the completion of the causal sequence.

A second objection is that a preoccupation with mental way stations burdens a science of behavior with all the problems raised by the limitations and inaccuracies of self-descriptive repertories. We need not take the extreme position that mediating events or any data about them obtained through introspection must be ruled out of consideration, but we should certainly welcome other ways of treating the data more satisfactorily. Independent variables change the behaving organism, often in ways which survive for many years, and such changes affect subsequent behavior. The subject may be able to describe some of these intervening states in useful ways, either before or after they have affected behavior. On the other hand, behavior may be extensively modified by variables of which, and of the effect of which, the subject is never aware. So far as we know, self-descriptive responses do not alter controlling relationships. If a severe punishment is less effective than a mild one, it is not because it cannot be "kept in mind." (Certain behaviors involved in self-management, such as reviewing a history of punishment, may alter behavior, but they do so by introducing other variables, rather than by changing a given relation.)

Perhaps the most serious objection concerns the order of events. Observation of one's own behavior necessarily follows the behavior. Responses which seem to be describing intervening states alone may embrace behavioral effects. "I am hungry" may describe, in part, the strength of the speaker's on-going ingestive behavior. "I was hungrier than I thought" seems particularly to describe behavior rather than an intervening, possibly causal, state. More serious examples of a possibly mistaken order are to be found in theories of psychotherapy. Before asserting that the release of a repressed wish has a therapeutic effect on behavior, or that when one knows why he is neurotically ill he will recover, we should consider the plausible alternative that a change in behavior resulting from therapy has made it possible for the subject to recall a repressed wish or to understand his illness.

A final objection is that way stations are so often simply invented. It is too easy to say that someone does something "because he likes to do it," or that he does one thing rather than another "because he has made a choice."

The importance of behaviorism as a philosophy of science naturally declines as a scientific analysis becomes more powerful, because there is then less need to use data in the form of self-description. The mentalism that survives in the fields of sensation and perception will disappear as alternative techniques are proved valuable in analyzing stimulus control, and similar changes may be anticipated elsewhere. Cognitive psychologists and others still try to circumvent the explicit control of variables by describing contingencies of reinforcement to their subjects in "instructions." They also try to dispense with recording behavior in a form from which probability of response can be estimated by asking their subjects to evaluate their tendencies to respond. But a person rarely responds to a description of contingencies as he would under direct exposure to them, nor can he accurately predict his rate of responding, particularly the course of the subtle changes in rate which are a commonplace in the experimental analysis of behavior. These attempts to short-circuit an experimental analysis can no longer be justified on grounds of expedience, and there are many reasons for abandoning them. Much remains to be done, however, before the facts to which they are currently applied can be said to be adequately understood.

BEHAVIORISM AND BIOLOGY

Elsewhere, the scientific study of man has scarcely recognized the need for reform. The biologist, for example, begins with a certain advantage in studying the behaving organism, for the structures he analyzes have an evident physical status. The nervous system in somehow earthier than the behavior for which it is largely responsible. Philosophers and psychologists alike have, from time to time, sought escape from mentalism in physiology. When a man sees red, he may be seeing the physiological effect of a red stimulus; when he merely imagines red, he may be seeing the same effect re-aroused. Psychophysical and perceptual distortions may be wrought by physiological processes. What a man feels as anxiety may be antonomic reactions to threatening stimuli. And so on. This may solve the minor problem of the nature of subjective experience, but it does not solve any of the methodological problems with which behaviorism is most seriously concerned. A physiological translation of mentalistic terms may reassure those who want to avoid dualism, but inadequacies in the formulation survive translation.

When writing about the behavior of organisms, biologists tend to be more mentalistic than psychologists. Adrian could not understand how a nerve impulse could cause a thought. A recent article on the visual space sense in *Science* (8) asserts that "the final event in the chain from the retina to the brain is a psychic experience." Another investigator reports research on "the brain and its contained mind." Pharmacologists study the "psychotropic" drugs. Psychosomatic medicine insists on the influence of mind over matter. And psychologists join their physiological colleagues in looking for feelings, emotions, drives, and pleasurable aspects of positive reinforcement in the brain.

The facts uncovered in such research are important, both for their own sake and for their bearing on behavior. The physiologist studies structures and processes without which behavior could not occur. He is in a position to supply a "reductionist" explanation beyond the reach of an analysis which confines itself to terminal variables. He cannot do this well, however, so long as he accepts traditional mentalistic formulations. Only an experimental analysis of behavior will define his task in optimal terms. The point is demonstrated by recent research in psychopharmacology. When the behavioral drugs first began to attract attention, they were studied with impromptu techniques based on self-observation, usually designed to quantify subjective reports. Eventually the methods of an experimental analysis proved their value in generating reproducible segments of behavior upon which effects of drugs could be observed and in terms of which they could be effectively defined and classified. For the same reasons, brain physiology will move forward more rapidly when it recognizes that its role is to account for the mediation of behavior rather than of mind.

BEHAVIORISM IN THE SOCIAL SCIENCES

There is also still a need for behaviorism in the social sciences, where psychology has long been used for explanatory purposes. Economics has had its economic man. Political science has considered man as a political animal. Parts of anthropology and sociology have found a place for psychoanalysis. The relevance of psychology to linguistics has been debated for more than half a century. Studies of scientific method have oscillated between logical and empirical analyses. In all these fields, "psychologizing" has often had disappointing results and has frequently been rejected by turning to an extreme formalism emphasizing objective facts. Economics confines itself to its own abundant data. Political scientists limit themselves to whatever may be studied with a few empirical tools and techniques and confine themselves, when they deal with theory, to formalistic analyses of political structures. A strong structuralist movement is evident in sociology. Linguistics emphasizes formal analyses of semantics and grammar.

Strait-laced commitments to pure description and formal analysis appear to leave no place for explanatory principles, and the short-coming is often blamed on the exclusion of mental activities. For example, a recent symposium on "The Limits of Behavioralism in Political Science" (4) complains of a neglect of subjective experience, ideas, motives, feelings, attitudes, values, and so on. This is reminiscent of attacks on behaviorism. In any case, it shows the same misunderstanding of the scope of a behavioral analysis. In its extension to the social sciences, as in psychology proper, behaviorism means more than a commitment to objective measurement. No entity or process which has any useful explanatory force is to be rejected on the ground that it is subjective or mental. The data which have made it important must, however, be studied and formulated in effective ways. The assignment is well within the scope of an experimental analysis of behavior, which thus offers a promising alternative to a commitment to pure description on the one hand and an appeal to mentalistic theories on the other. To extend behaviorism as a philosophy of science to the study of political and economic behavior, of the behavior of people in groups, of people speaking and listening, teaching and learning— this is not "psychologizing" in the traditional sense. It is simply the application of a tested formulation to important parts of the field of human behavior.

Bibliography

1. Blough, D. S. "Dark Adaptation in the Pigeon," *Journal of Comparative and Physiological Psychology*, XLIX (1956), 425–30.
2. Blough D. S., and Schirer, A. M. "Scotopic Spectral Sensitivity in the Monkey," *Science*, CXXXIX (1963), 493–94.
3. Bridgman, P. W. *The Way Things Are*. Cambridge: Harvard University Press, 1959.
4. Charlesworth, J. C. (ed.). *The Limits of Behavioralism in Political Science*. Philadelphia: American Academy of Political and Social Sciences, 1962.
5. Galton, F. *Inquiries into Human Faculty*. London: J. M. Dent and Company, 1883.
6. Herrnstein, R. J., and Sommers, Peter van. "Method for Sensory Scaling with Animals," *Science*, CXXXV (1962), 40–41.
7. Hogben, L. *Statistical Theory*. London: Allen and Unwin, 1957.
8. Ogle, K. N. "The Visual Space Sense," *Science*, CXXXV (1962), 763–71.
9. Stevens, S. S. "The Operational Basis of Psychology," *The American Journal of Psychology*, XLVII (1935), 323–30.

55. BEHAVIORISM AS A PHILOSOPHY OF PSYCHOLOGY

Norman Malcolm

As a philosopher I have a professional reluctance to make observations about an empirical science and especially so in the presence of some of its distinguished practitioners. I am emboldened by the belief that the dispute over the place of behaviorism in psychology is fundamentally a philosophical issue. In saying this I do not imply that it is an issue which cannot be resolved and with respect to which we must content ourselves with opinions or attitudes. On the contrary, I think that what is right and wrong with the viewpoint and assumptions of behaviorism can be clearly formulated.

A FAILURE TO DISAGREE

Professor Rogers claims that behaviorism has had an unfortunate effect on psychology. It impoverishes psychology by excluding from its data the "private worlds" of people, the "flow of their inner experience," "the whole universe of inner meanings," the purposes, goals, values and choices of people, and their "perceptions of self." He calls all of this "the phenomenal world of the individual" (3, p. 119), and he says that "Not one aspect of this world is open to the strict behaviorist" (3, p. 119). He believes that psychology needs to be enriched by "a science of the inner life" that will attempt to find unlawful relationships between these phenomena and "external behavior." A study

SOURCE. Malcolm, Norman, "Behaviorism as a Philosophy of Psychology," in T. W. Wann (ed.), *Behaviorism and Phenomenology*, 1964 Phoenix. Chicago: University of Chicago Press. Reprinted with permission. Copyright © 1964 by the University of Chicago Press.

which concerns itself with these "inner variables" must be added to empirical psychology if this science is to obtain any deep understanding of human life.

I am willing to bet (a small sum) that Professor Skinner finds this criticism puzzling, because he cannot see in it any specific theoretical issue that divides him and Rogers. Whether Skinner is puzzled or not, I am. I do not see that Skinner's behaviorism commits him to denying or ignoring the existence of the "inner variables" which Rogers thinks are so important. Let me explain.

Skinner is an exponent of a "functional analysis" of human behavior. He holds that every piece of human behavior is a "function" of some condition that is describable in physical terms, as is the behavior itself (4, pp. 35 and 36). The conditions of which behavior is a function are, for the most part, external to the organism, although sometimes they may be "within the organism's skin" (4, p. 257). The physical conditions of which behavior is a function are called "independent variables," and the pieces of behavior are the "dependent variables." A dependent variable is said to be under the "control" of an independent variable. The relations between independent and dependent variables are scientific laws. The aim of behavioristic psychology is to uncover these laws, thus making possible the prediction and control of human behavior. "A synthesis of these laws expressed in quantitative terms yields a comprehensive picture of the organism as a behaving system" (4, p. 35).

Skinner devotes considerable attention to what he calls "explanatory fictions." Some of his examples are being *thirsty*, or *hungry* (4, p. 31), being *absent-minded* or having *confused ideas* (4, p. 30), being *interested* or *discouraged* or having a *sense of achievement* (4, p. 72), having an *incentive* or *goal* or *purpose* (4, pp. 87–88), and the *intent* behind an action or the *meaning* of it (4, p. 36). All of these are examples of what some philosophers call "psychological" or "mental" concepts. I think that anything any philosopher would want to call a "psychological" concept Skinner would consider to be an explanatory fiction. In saying that they are explanatory fictions Skinner means that they are *not* explanatory. Take such an apparent explanation as "He is drinking because he is thirsty." Skinner says that

> If to be thirsty means nothing more than to have a tendency to drink, this is mere redundancy. If it means that he drinks because of a state of thirst, an inner causal event is invoked. If this state is purely inferential—if no dimensions are assigned to it which would make direct observation possible—it cannot serve as an explanation (4, p. 33).

When you speak of a man's "purpose" in doing something or say that he has stopped doing something because he is "discouraged," you are not saying anything worth saying unless you are making a reference, perhaps concealed, to the independent variables which control his behavior (4, e.g., pp. 36, 72).

Skinner's remarks about explanatory fictions are sometimes slightly ambiguous. Sometimes he seems to be saying that there really is not any such thing as, for example, *a sense of achievement.* "We do not give a man a sense of achievement," he says, "we reinforce a particular action" (4, p. 72). When a man is said to be "looking for something," "There is no *current* goal, incentive, purpose, or meaning to be taken into account" (4, pp. 89–90). This would seem to be a denial that the man really has a purpose in doing what he does. But I do not believe that Skinner wants to be in the absurd position of really denying that people are sometimes encouraged or discouraged or that they have goals and purposes, anymore than he wants to deny that they get thirsty. Instead, he is trying to say how these terms are to be understood. Such terms as "meaning" and "intent," he says, "usually conceal references to independent variables" (4, p. 36). "Statements which use such words as 'incentive' or 'purpose' are usually reducible to statements about operant conditioning" (4, p. 87). Skinner will agree that people have purposes, but holds that meaningful statements about purposes are reducible to statements about functional relations between independent and dependent variables.

Let us come back to Rogers' criticism of Skinner. The purposes, goals, values and choices of people, their "private worlds," their "perceptions of self," their "inner experience"—all of those phenomena which, according to him, behaviorism cannot deal with, are examples of Skinner's explanatory fictions. Skinner would willingly accept them as significant phenomena insofar as they can be handled by functional analysis. If you can define them in terms of functional relations between external or internal physical variables and the observable behavior of people, then well and good. If not, then it is not clear what you are talking about.

What I find puzzling is that Rogers himself seems to admit this or at least to go half way toward admitting it. He allows that the study of the "inner variables," of which he speaks—"requires careful definition of observable behaviors which are indexes of these subjective variables. It is recognized that variables of inner experience cannot be measured directly, but it is also realized that the fact that they *are* inner variables does not preclude their scientific study" (3, p. 130). He foresees the development of "operational steps" for the "measurement of the behaviors which represent these inner variables" (3, p. 131). Skinner could retort that the observable behavior and physical conditions which are said by Rogers to "represent" the inner variables, either do or do not define them. If they do, then the "inner" has become "outer," and functional analysis can go full steam ahead. If not, then the expressions which allegedly "represent" inner variables have not been given any meaning.

My conclusion is that Rogers has not shown some theoretical flaw in behaviorism. Skinner could hold that Rogers' "science of the person" would fall, insofar as it has an intelligible subject matter, within the wider domain of functional analysis of behavior. It would be one branch or division of behavioristic science and not an alternative or addition to it.

THE PHILOSOPHICAL BASIS OF BEHAVIORISM

Behaviorism, in my view, is essentially a *philosophical* doctrine. Skinner is agreeing with this when he says that behaviorism is "a philosophy of science concerned with the subject matter and methods of psychology" (5, p. 79). Behaviorism, as a philosophy of psychology, is continuous with the philosophical doctrine of *physicalism*, which was expounded by Rudolf Carnap and other members of the so-called Vienna Circle. I will set forth some of Carnap's views on this topic in order to bring out the close resemblance between Carnap's physicalism and Skinner's behaviorism.

The basic thesis of physicalism, according to Carnap (1), is that "every sentence of psychology may be formulated in physical language" (1, p. 165). When put in "the material mode of speech," the thesis is that "all sentences of psychology describe physical occurrences, namely, the physical behavior of humans and other animals" (1, p. 165). Carnap says: "Our thesis thus states that a definition may be constructed for every psychological concept (i.e., expression) which directly or indirectly derives that concept from physical concepts" (1, p. 167). Psychological laws, too, are translatable into physical language (i.e., into language which describes physical conditions and occurrences), and therefore they are a subclass of physical laws (1, p. 167).

The pure philosophical principle behind this thesis is the so-called Verification Principle: "The meaning of a statement is its method of verification." As Carnap puts it: "A sentence says no more than what is testable about it" (1, p. 174). Thus a statement that I make about another person, e.g., that he is excited or angry, can mean nothing else than that he is behaving in such and such a way, that he will respond in such and such a way to certain stimuli, that his central nervous system is in such and such a state, and so on (1, e.g., p. 172). If we try to claim that over and above, or behind, these physical facts there is an inner state of excitement or anger, which is entirely different from the actual and/or potential behavior and the physiological state and which might or might not be present with these physical facts, then we are claiming something that we do not know how to verify. Our assertion that this person is angry turns out to be "a metaphysical pseudo-sentence" (1, p. 174). It might be objected that the person could *tell* us that he felt angry, and if he was a generally truthful person we should have evidence for the existence of an inner state of anger. Carnap's reply is that the person's statement does not inform us of anything unless we *understand* it, and we do not understand it unless we know what observable phenomena would verify it. As Carnap puts it: "If the sentence 'A was angry yesterday at noon' has no meaning for me —as would be the case if . . . I could not test it—it will not be rendered meaningful by the fact that a sound having the structure of this sentence came from A's own mouth" (1, p. 180). The fact that we rely on the testimony of people as a source of information about them does not relieve us of the necessity of giving a physical interpretation of the sentences they utter, an interpretation which will make those sentences testable. In Carnap's view the psychological concepts of ordinary language are a source of confusion because their reference to physical conditions and behavior is not sufficiently explicit. The clarification of these concepts will consist in "physicalising" them, i.e., in providing explicit behavioristic definitions of them. But, as Carnap says "psychology is a physical science even prior to such a clarification of its concepts—a physical science whose assignment it is to describe systematically the (physical) behavior of living creatures, especially that of human beings, and to develop laws under which this behavior may be subsumed" (1, p. 189).

There is one important respect in which Skinner's behaviorism differs from the physicalism of the Vienna Circle. The question arises as to whether the physicalising of psychological concepts is to be in terms of the inner physiology of the human organism or in terms of its outward behavior. Carnap discusses the example of a sentence which says that a certain person is *excited*. He holds that this sentence has the same "content" as another sentence which asserts that the person's "central nervous system" is in a certain state and also that the person is making "agitated stimuli (1, p. 172). His sample analysis of a psychological sentence refers, therefore, *both* to inner physiology and to outward behavior. This mixed reference is even more explicit in some remarks made by Carl Hempel, also a former exponent of physicalism. Discussing the psychological sentence "Paul has a toothache," Hempel asks "What is the specific content of this proposition, that is to say, what are the circumstances in which it would be verified? He goes on to say that the following are some of the test sentences which describe these circumstances:

a) "Paul weeps and makes gestures of such and such kinds."

b) "At the question, 'What is the matter?' Paul utters the words 'I have a toothache.' "

c) "Closer examination reveals a decayed tooth with exposed pulp."

d) "Paul's blood pressure, digestive processes, the speed of his reactions, show such and such changes."

e) "Such and such processes occur in Paul's central nervous system."

Hempel declares that the proposition about Paul's pain is "simply an abbreviated expression of the fact that all its test sentences are verified" (2, p. 377).

It is evident that the alleged "content" of the sentence about Paul is a very mixed bag, containing references to both the outward behavior of weeping, gestures and utterance, and also to such physiological phenomena as blood pressure, digestive processes, and events in the central nervous system.[1]

Skinner is dissatisfied, rightly I think, with physiological analyses of psychological concepts. For one thing, he says, not enough is known about neural states and events for them to be useful in the prediction and control of specific behavior (4, pp. 28–29). For another thing, he has a "methodological" objection. He believes that holding that the events observed or inferred in an analysis of behavior are basically physiological "does not solve the methodological problems with which behaviorism is most seriously concerned" (5, p. 95). Skinner means, I believe, that behaviorism as a philosophy of psychology is trying to solve a problem that he calls "methodological" and that I should call "philosophical." The problem is, as he puts it, "how one knows about the subjective world of another" (5, p. 83). Now the fact is that we know a great deal about the "subjective worlds" of others. (Here I am formulating a line of thought that I hope Skinner finds acceptable.) That is to say, we know on a great many occasions in ordinary life when someone is *angry, tired, excited,* or *perplexed.* This common knowledge we have of the mental states of others certainly is not a knowledge of physiological processes, about which we are largely ignorant. It is Skinner's view that if behaviorism is to clarify the "testable content" of psychological concepts, it should not concentrate on what lies open to observation, namely, physical circumstances and outward behavior.

Skinner says:

> The practice of looking inside the organism for an explanation of behavior has tended to obscure the variables which are immediately available for a scientific analysis. These variables lie outside the organism, in its immediate environment and in its environmental history (4, p. 31).

Carnap asserted that:

> A sentence about other minds refers to physical processes in the body of the person in question. On any other interpretation the sentence becomes untestable in principle, and thus meaningless (1, p. 191).

Skinner could say, and I should agree with him, that this is a *non sequitur.* If the statement that a certain person is *discouraged* about something refers

---

[1] It should be noted that both Carnap and Hempel subsequently abandoned the view that the "cognitive meaning" of an empirical statement is equivalent to all or some of its test sentences. See Hempel's "The Empiricist Criterion of Meaning" [in *Logical Positivism*, ed. A. J. Ayer (Glencoe: Free Press, 1959)].

to his behavior and also to external circumstances which "control" that behavior, then the statement is testable; and it is far more readily testable than if it referred to processes in his body. Thus Skinner's brand of behaviorism explains psychological concepts in terms of outward behavior and circumstances rather than inner physiology.

Despite Skinner's justified dislike of physicalism's predilection for physiology, the basic aim of his functional analysis is the same as that of physicalism, namely, to achieve a clarification of psychological concepts which will make it evident that psychology is truly a physical science. Like the philosophers of the Vienna Circle, he is attempting to reduce mental concepts to physical concepts, although he has a clearer idea of the form this reduction must take. It may be surprising to some to think of Skinner as engaged in a typically philosophical undertaking of reducing concepts of one kind to concepts of another kind, and therefore I will substantiate this claim by quoting from Skinner. Speaking of occupational therapy he says:

> It is of no advantage to say that such therapy helps the patient by giving him a "sense of achievement" or improves his "morale," builds up his "interest," or removes or prevents "discouragement." Such terms as these merely add to the growing population of explanatory fictions. One who readily engages in a given activity is not showing an interest, he is showing the effect of reinforcement. We do not give a man a sense of achievement, we reinforce a particular action. To become discouraged is simply to fail to respond because reinforcement has not been forthcoming (4, p. 72).

Skinner remarks that it is a "fundamental principal of science" to rule out "final causes." He goes on to say:

> But this principle is violated when it is asserted that behavior is under the control of an "incentive" or "goal" which the organism has not yet achieved or a "purpose" which it has not yet fulfilled. Statements which use such words as "incentive" or "purpose" are usually reducible to statements about operant conditioning, and only a slight change is required to bring them within the framework of a natural science. Instead of saying that a man behaves because of the consequences which *are* to follow his behavior, we simply say that he behaves because of the consequences which *have* followed similar behavior in the past (4, p. 87).

It is fairly evident that in these passages Skinner is trying to give logical analyses, i.e., reductions, of various expressions that, on his view, mislead us. He is trying to tell us what becoming discouraged *is*, what being interested *is*, and what it *is* to do something for a purpose. He pays particular attention to the notion of *looking for something*, which describes an activity in terms of its purpose. He makes this assertion: "In general, looking for something consists of emitting responses which in the past have produced 'something' as a consequence" (4, p. 89). Here he is trying to tell us of what looking for something *consists*. He offers several "translations" of the sentence "I am looking for my glasses." He says that this sentence is "equivalent" to the following: " 'I have lost my glasses,' " 'I shall stop what I am doing when I find my glasses,' or 'When I have done this in the past, I have found my glasses.' " He remarks that these "translations" seem "roundabout," but this is because "expressions involving goals and purposes" are "abbreviations" (4, p. 90).

These remarks I have quoted from Skinner make quite evident his role as a philosopher engaged in translating and reducing the misleading mentalistic expressions of ordinary language. These expressions have a disguised meaning. They are "abbreviations." Skinner's task is to unpack these abbreviations by making explicit the behavioristic variables to which they refer in a "concealed" way and which give them whatever intelligibility and usefulness they have.

I think it is easy to see what makes behaviorism attractive as a philosophy of psychology. It may be conceived of as a reaction against another philosophy of psychology (which I shall call 'introspectionism"), the basic assumption of which is that each of us learns from his own case what pain, anger, fear, purpose, and so on, *are*. Each of us first of all takes note of, and identifies, his own inner experiences and then surmises or infers that others have the same inner experiences. I believe that Wittgenstein has proved this line of thinking to be disastrous (6). It leads to the conclusion that we do not and cannot understand each other's psychological language, which is a form of solipsism. Worse than this (if that is possible), it leads to the result that one's identification of one's own inner experience might be wrong without one's ever being the wiser. Not only might it be the case that what I identify in myself as "anger" is not what others identify in themselves as "anger"; but also it might be that what I identify in myself as "anger" is a *different* something each time, although I *think* it is the same. If it were something different each time then I should not be identifying anything. Whether this were so or not could not be determined, either by myself or anyone else. Introspectionism assumes that each of us makes *correct* identifications of his mental states. But if it makes no sense to determine that my identification is right or wrong, then it does not *have* a right or wrong, and therefore it is not an *identification* of anything. Introspectionism is a self-refuting doctrine, because its assumption that each of us obtains his mastery of psychological concepts from introspection actually leads to the collapse of the notion of inner identification.

One does not have to accept the verification principle "whole hog" in order to acknowledge the strong point of behaviorism. The refutation of intro-spectionism, on purely philosophical grounds, proves that our concepts of mental states and events cannot be divorced from human behavior. As we noted previously, this problem cannot be avoided by the maneuver of holding that *verbal* behavior is a sufficient foundation for our common psychological concepts. Skinner is keenly aware of this point. He says:

> We cannot avoid the responsibility of showing how a private event
> can ever come to be described by the individual or, in the same sense,
> be known to him (4, p. 280).

Skinner puts the point with equal sharpness in his paper for the present colloquium. He talks about a case in which some students applied various psychological terms to the behavior of a pigeon. They said, for example, that the pigeon *hoped* for food, *expected* reinforcement, and so on. Skinner is willing to say that the students were reporting what they themselves "would have expected, felt, and hoped for under similar circumstances" (5, p. 91). But he goes on to emphasize that they must have learned these terms from a "verbal community" which

> *had access only to the kinds of public information available to the*
> *students in the demonstration.* Whatever the students knew about
> themselves which permitted them to infer comparable events in the
> pigeon must have been learned from a verbal community which saw no
> more of their behavior than they had seen of the pigeon's (5, p. 91).

I believe that Skinner has stated here an absolutely decisive objection to introspectionism. The intelligibility of psychological words must be based on something other than the occurrence of those words. That we have a common understanding of them proves that their use has to be logically connected with other public behavior.

THE FALLACY OF BEHAVIORISM

I have been trying to give an account of the hard core of logical truth contained in behaviorism, which gives it toughness as a philosophy of psychology. But now I want to disagree with behaviorism. The Achilles' heel of this doctrine lies in its treatment of psychological sentences in the first-person-present tense. The same error occurs in physicalism. Let me begin to explain this by considering Carnap's sample sentence "I am now excited." Carnap says that the "rational support" for this sentence lies in such sentences as "I feel my hands trembling," "I hear my voice quavering," and so on. He goes on to remark that the sentence "I am now excited" has the "same content" as the "physical" sentence "My body is now in that condition which, both under my own observation and that of others, exhibits such and such characteristics of excitement" (1, p. 191). Carnap is obviously assuming that when a person says, "I am excited," his saying it is based, in part at least, on his observations of the state of his own body. The truth is that it would be a rare case in which a person said that he was excited on the basis of noticing that his hands were trembling or his voice quavering. I do not say that it is impossible for such a case to occur. A man who had narrowly escaped some danger might notice afterwards, perhaps with surprise, that his hands were trembling, and he might conclude that he must be very excited. In the normal case, however, a man does not *conclude* that he is excited. He says that he is, and he is; but his utterance is not the result of self-observation.

The point comes out very strikingly when we consider first-person reports of bodily sensations, e.g., "I have a headache." It would be completely mad if I were to say this on the basis of noticing that my face was flushed, my eyes dull, that I was holding my head, and had just taken some aspirin. If someone were to say, *on that basis*, that he has a headache, either he would be joking or else he would not understand how the words are used. The same is true of a first-person perception sentence, such as "I see a black dog." On the basis of observing that another person's eyes are following a black dog, *I* can say "He sees a black dog." But it would make no sense for *him* to say, on the basis of noticing that his own eyes were following a black dog, that he sees a black dog.

The natural temptation to which behaviorist philosophers have succumbed is to assume that first-person psychological sentences have the same "content," or the same verification, as the corresponding third-person sentences. It looks as if that must be how it is: nevertheless, that is not how it is. I can verify that another man is excited, by the trembling of his hands. But I do not verify in this way that *I* am excited. In the normal case I do not verify it at all. By observing you I can verify that you have a headache. I do not verify that *I* have a headache. I can verify that the animal in the field is a brown cow. I cannot verify, in addition, that I *see* a brown cow. In the case of another person I can verify both that there is a brown cow in the field and that he sees it.

The notion of verification does not apply to a wide range of first-person psychological reports and utterances. Another way to put the point is to say that those reports and utterances are *not based on observations*. The error of introspectionism is to suppose that they are based on observations of inner mental events. The error of behaviorism is to suppose that they are based on observations of outward events or of physical events inside the speaker's skin. These two philosophies of psychology share a false assumption, namely, that a first-person psychological statement is a report of something the speaker has, or thinks he has, observed.

The mistake of assimilating first-person to third-person psychological statements is quite obvious in Skinner's thinking. He refers to an imaginary case
in which we ask a man why he is going down the street and we receive the
reply "I am going to mail a letter." Skinner says:

> We have not learned anything new about his behavior but only about
> some of its possible causes. The subject himself, of course, may be in an
> advantageous position in describing these variables because he has
> had an extended contact with his own behavior for many years.
> But his statement is not therefore in a different class from similar
> statements made by others who have observed his behavior upon fewer
> occasions. . . . [H]e is simply making a plausible prediction in terms
> of his experiences with himself (4, p. 88).

The truth is that normally when a man tells you his purpose in doing something his statement is in a different class from a statement made by somebody
else on the basis of observation of him. If you see someone rummaging about
in the papers on his desk, and remember that when he had done this on
previous occasions the rummaging had come to an end when he grabbed hold
of his spectacles, you might reasonably conclude on these grounds that he is
now looking for his spectacles. But it would be weird if *he* were to reason as
follows: "Here I am rummaging about on my desk. When I have done this in
the past my activity has terminated when I have caught hold of my spectacles.
Therefore, I am probably looking for my spectacles"! If you heard a man
make such a remark and believed that he was not joking, you would thereafter regard him with suspicion, because of the craziness of the remark.

Skinner is puzzled by such utterances as "I was about to go home," "I am
inclined to go home," "I shall go home in half an hour." He says that they
"describe states of affairs which appear to be accessible only to the speaker.
How can the verbal community establish responses of this sort?" He thinks
a possible explanation is that when the language is learned while the individual
is "behaving publicly," "private stimuli" come to be associated with the
"public manifestations." The rest of this possible explanation is that:

> Later when these private stimuli occur alone, the individual may respond
> to them. "I was on the point of going home" may be regarded as the
> equivalent of "I observed events in myself which characteristically
> precede or accompany my going home." What these events are, such
> an explanation does not say (4, p. 262).

For Skinner "private stimuli" would mean, of course, physical events within
the individual's skin. The fact that Skinner regards this hypothesis as a possible explanation of the utterances, even though he does not know what the
private stimuli would be, shows how unquestioningly he assumes that such a

remark as "I am on the point of going home" must be based on the observation of something.

Undoubtedly people sometimes decide to go home because of physical disturbances within their skins. But it is wrong to suppose that the announcement "I am about to go home" is a prediction based on observation. Normally it would be outlandish to ask a man what the observational data are on the basis of which he is predicting that he is about to go home. The announcement "I am about to go home" is normally an announcement of intention. Announcements of intention are not based on the observation of either internal or external variables, despite Skinner's assumption that they must be.

Skinner would reply that surely the announcement or the intention is under the *control* of some variable. Perhaps so, depending on how ambiguously we use the word "control." Normally a man would have some reason for going home, e.g., that it is supper time. We might express this in some cases by saying that the fact it was supper time "determined his decision" to go home, or was the "controlling factor," or some such thing. We usually expect there will be something which controls a man's intention, in this sense. But if we mean "control" in Skinner's technical sense, according to which y is under the control of x if and only if x and y are connected by some *functional relationship*, i.e., by a *law*—if this is what we mean, then I will say (quite dogmatically, because I have not time to go into it) that we have no ground at all for believing that either intentions or announcements of intention are under the "control" of anything.

CONCLUSION

Behaviorism is right in insisting that there must be some sort of conceptual tie between the language of mental phenomena and outward circumstances and behavior. If there were not, we could not understand other people, nor could we understand ourselves. If a small child says "I am hungry" while rejecting food, we consider that he has not quite learned what to say. Or if he says this while rejecting food and going for drink, we think he has confused the words "thirsty" and "hungry." More subtle failures to master the correct use of language may be noted with other psychological terms. But when on several occasions there is the right correlation of behavior and circumstances with the child's utterance of a psychological term, we conclude that he has mastered its correct use. By having behavioral criteria for the truth of some third-person psychological statements, we are able to determine whether someone has a correct understanding of a good many psychological terms.

But then a remarkable development occurs. The person who has satisfied our criteria of understanding those terms begins to use them in first-person statements in the absence of the former behavioral criteria. He says that he is *angry* at someone or *anxious* about something when we should not have supposed so from his demeanor. Probably he will be able to give some reason for his anger or anxiety. The interesting thing, however, is that in a great many cases we accept his testimony. We conclude that he is angry in a case where, if we had been judging solely on the basis of our former behavioral criteria, we should not have supposed it. We use this testimony as a new criterion of what he is feeling and thinking, over and above and even in conflict with the former behavioral criteria.

The first-person psychological sentences must be correlated with behavior up to a point. But they quickly go beyond that point. People tell us things about themselves which take us by surprise, things which we should not have guessed from our knowledge of their circumstances and behavior. A behaviorist philosopher will say that if we had known more about their history, environment, and behavior, we should have been able to infer this same information. I do not believe there are any grounds for thinking so. The testimony that people give us about their intentions, plans, hopes, worries, thoughts, and feelings is by far the most important source of information we have about them. This self-testimony has, one could say, an *autonomous* status. To a great extent we cannot check it against anything else, and yet to a great extent we credit it. I believe we have no reason to think it is even a theoretical possibility that this self-testimony could be supplanted by inferences from external and/ or internal physical variables.

If a study of mankind does not regard man's possession of language as an essential difference between man and the lower animals, then I should not know what was meant by "essential." Within the whole body of language the category of first-person psychological sentences has crucial importance. Man's puzzling status as a subject and a person is bound up with these first-person utterances, having the two striking characteristics I have tried to point out: First, that for the most part, they are not made on the basis of any observation; second, that they are "autonomous" in the sense that, for the most part, they cannot be "tested" by checking them against physical events and circumstances, other than the subject's own testimony. If we want to know what a man wants, what he is thinking about, whether he is annoyed or pleased, or what he has decided, the man himself is our best source of information. We ask *him* and he tells us. He has a privileged status with respect to information about himself, and not "because he has had an extended contact with his own behavior for many years."

In the beginning of my paper I said that Rogers had not, in his contribution to this colloquium, expounded a telling criticism of behaviorism. He does, however, make some remarks which hint at the criticism which I believe to be cogent. For example, he says, by implication, that behaviorism "transforms everything it studies into an object" (3, p. 113). I have argued that behaviorism fails to perceive self-testimony in a true light. It mistakenly assumes that when a man tells you what he wants, intends, or hopes, what he says is based on observation, and, therefore, he is speaking about himself as if he were an *object of observation*. Behaviorism also assumes that these first-person utterances, since they are observational in nature, could theoretically be replaced by the observations of another person, although this might require "technological advances." Behaviorism, in other words, fails to perceive that self-testimony is largely autonomous, not replaceable even in principle by observations of functional relations between physical variables.[2] Perhaps the best way to sum up behaviorism's shortcoming as a philosophy of psychology is to say that it regards man as *solely* an *object*.

Bibliography

1. Carnap, R. "Psychology in Physical Language," *Erkenntnis*, III (1932–33). Reprinted in *Logical Positivism*, ed. A. J. Ayer. Glencoe: Free Press, 1959.
2. Hempel, C. G. "The Logical Analysis of Psychology." In *Readings in Philosophical Analysis*, eds. H. Feigl and W. Sellars. New York: Appleton-Century-Crofts, 1949.
3. Rogers, C. R. "Toward a Science of the Person." In *Behaviorism and Phenomenology: Contrasting Bases for Modern Psychology*, ed. T. W. Wann, Chicago: University of Chicago Press, 1964.
4. Skinner, B. F. *Science and Human Behavior*. New York: Macmillan, 1953.
5. ———. "Behaviorism at Fifty." In *Behaviorism and Phenomenology: Contrasting Bases for Modern Psychology*, ed. T. W. Wann, Chicago: University of Chicago Press, 1964.
6. Wittgenstein, L. *Philosophical Investigations*. New York: Macmillan, 1953.

---

[2] In his brilliant review [*Language*, XXXV (1959), 26–58] of Skinner's *Verbal Behavior*, Noam Chomsky shows conclusively, I think, that Skinner fails to make a case for his belief that "functional analysis" is able to deal with verbal behavior.

56. SOME OBJECTIONS TO BEHAVIORISM

H. H. Price

First, let me say that I have no objections at all to the behavoristic *method*. There is no reason why there should not be a branch of scientific inquiry which confines itself strictly to investigating the publicly observable behavior of human beings and animals. And it has turned out in practice that there is a surprisingly large field of empirical facts which can be profitably studied in this way, especially facts about the behavior of animals. There *is* a science which might be called behavioristics, or the science of behavior, though one may well doubt whether this science should be called psychology. It seems rather to be only one part of psychology, namely that part which can be studied by methods approximating to those used in the physical sciences.

What I do object to is the behavioristic philosophy of mind, which is sometime scalled "reductionist" behaviorism. This is the view that propositions about mental states and happenings of every kind are *reducible* to propositions about publicly observable behavior. On this view, statements containing such words as "seeing," "thinking," "consciousness," "feeling," and "wishing" are only meaningful if and so far as they can be translated into statements about publicly observable bodily happenings. That is the doctrine, or dogma, to which I object, and I do not think it becomes any less objectionable when the term "behavior" is widened so as to include tendencies of dispositions to behave in such-and-such ways.

SOURCE. Reprinted from "Some Objections to Behaviorism," by Henry H. Price in Sidney Hook (ed.), *Dimensions of Mind*, New York: Collier Books, 1961. Reprinted with permission. Copyright © 1961 by Henry H. Price.

The first objection I have is so simple that it may seem naïve. It seems to me to be a fact about human beings that they are *aware* of things, and I find it hard to rid myself of the conviction that at least some of the lower animals are aware of things too, at least sometimes. What I am trying to indicate by the phrase "aware of" is something which cannot be defined or analyzed. It is too fundamental, and if anyone says he cannot understand what I am talking about, I do not know how I can help him. All the same, I do not think he really needs any help. It seems to me that everyone already knows for himself what it is to be aware of something, because he himself is constantly being aware of things. And everyone knows for himself that being aware of something is totally different from any kind of bodily happening, though it may, of course, have all sorts of causal connections with bodily happenings.

My second objection is connected with this first one, and as it is a little more complicated, perhaps it may appear more convincing. It seems to me that there are some serious difficulties about the concept of the *publicly observable*, which I take to be the basic concept of behaviorism.

To begin with, what is observing if it is not a way of being aware of something? What does a behaviorist think he is himself doing when he *observes* a rat running about in a maze? Is he just receiving optical stimuli and responding to those by inscribing black marks in his notebook? If he has a colleague who is also observing the rat, he might perhaps try to maintain that this *is* all that is happening in his colleague. But can he possibly think that this is all that is happening in himself? On the contrary, he is being *aware of*, being *visually conscious of*, the movements of the rat, and the black marks he inscribes in his notebook are a record of what he is being aware. Bodily occurrences, of a pretty complicated kind, are certainly taking place in him. But surely it is obvious—obvious to him if not others—that this is not all that is taking place? He is also being aware of certain events in his environment, and moreover, he is being aware of them in an intelligent or thoughtful manner, and is noticing the relevance they have to some hypothesis concerning rat-behavior.

So my first difficulty about the publicly observable is concerned simply with the notion of "observing" itself. Observing it itself and instance of being aware of something—in that fundamental and unanalyzable sense of the phrase "aware of" to which I drew attention before. My second difficulty about the concept of the publicly observable is concerned with the concept of "publicity." This difficulty too may be stated in a way which may seem naïve. When something, *X*, is described as public, *to whom* is it public?—Presumably to a number of human beings or persons, each of whom either is or can become *aware* of *X*. Lest this should appear too simple, I shall add another argument which is a little more complicated. The word "public" is what one might call a contrast-word. "Public" is contrasted with "private," and gets its whole meaning from that contrast. If nothing is private, nothing is public either. And if we go farther and say, as some behaviorists would, that the term "private" makes no sense, that such expressions as "private experience" or "private mental occurrences" are simply devoid of meaning, then the term "public" makes no sense either. To put it crudely: if everything is public, nothing is public, because the term "public" has lost all its meaning. (The same absurdity would result, of course, if one said that *everything* is private. By saying so, one would have abolished the antithesis from which the term "private" derives its meaning.) This is what is wrong with subjective idealism. Extremes meet, and the "reductive" behaviorist is more like the subjective idealist than one might think.

These remarks about privacy and publicity lead naturally to my final topic, which is introspection. When someone maintains, as I want to, that there is such a process as introspection, he is maintaining: (1) that there are private occurrences or experiences which are not accessible to public observation; (2) that such private occurrences can sometimes be attended to or scrutinized by the person who has them; (3) that such introspective scrutiny is a genuine source of information, a way of finding things out about one's own experiences; (4) that though the occurrences one finds out about are private ones, they are nonetheless publicly describable, since the information one gets by means of introspection can be imparted to others, who can *understand* one's introspective reports whether or not they believe them (it is not true that what is private is therefore incommunicable).

In connection with (2) and (3), a good deal of fuss has been made about the difficulty that the introspective scrutinizing of an experience cannot be simultaneous with the experience itself. I cannot see how this matters very much. Introspection may always be *restro*spection; it may always be form of short-range memory. But even if it is always "retro-," the point is that it *is* "intro-." The attention of scrutinizing may always be a scrutinizing of the recent past, not the present; but still what is scrutinized is an experience of one's own.

It is also argued that an experience is altered by the process of introspecting it: for example, that if one attends carefully to a feeling, the feeling thereupon becomes less intense, and may even disappear altogether. But supposing this to be a fact, how is the fact known? Surely it itself can only be ascertained by introspection? This anti-introspective argument only amounts to saying that introspection may be more carefully or less carefully conducted (which is, of course, true) and that the findings of careless or unguarded introspection can sometimes be corrected by introspecting more carefully.

Moreover, if it is also said that all introspection is retrospective, what meaning can we attach to the contention that a *past* experience can be altered by introspecting it? I suppose we should have to represent the situation thus: we should have to divide both the introspecting and the experiences introspected into successive temporal slices

$$I^1 \quad I^2 \quad I^3 \quad I^4$$
$$E^1 \quad E^2 \quad E^3 \quad E^4$$

and the contention should be that I^1, by having the earlier event E^1 for its object, causes the *contemporary* event E^2 to be different from what it would have been otherwise. And consequently I^2 has a different object from the one it would have had if I^1 had not preceded it. But then we must still ask the same question as before: Assuming this to be a fact, how is the fact known, if not by better and more careful introspection?

One must admit, of course, that there has been some excuse for the attacks which have been made on introspection, and even for the attempts which have been made to argue it out of existence. Extravagant claims have been made for introspection in the past, and they have naturally led to an equally extravagant reaction against it. It has sometimes been alleged that introspection is an infallible source of information, and this has led people to say that on the contrary it is not a source of information at all.

I certainly do not want to defend this claim to infallibility. Perhaps it arose from a confusion between the having or living-through of an experience on the one hand, and the introspective scrutiny on the other. (Both alike could be referred to rather loosely as "self-conscious.") Now if I have an experience I do have it. It is just something which happens, and no question of being mistaken arises. That question only arises when I attend to the experience and make judgments about it. The mere having of experiences—just living through them—is something to which the notion of fallibility does not apply. But it does not follow from this that the mere having of experiences is a kind of infallible cognition. It is not a form of cognition at all. It is neither knowing nor believing, neither correct nor erroneous.

Introspecting, on the other hand, the attentive scrutinizing of experiences and the attempt to make judgments about them, to bring them under concepts and to distinguish between one type of experience and another—this certainly *is* a form of cognition, but it is not an infallible one at all. I find it hard to see why anyone should suppose that it is, if he has ever made a real effort to do some introspecting himself. We need only consider how very difficult introspection can be, what trouble one often has in classifying or describing an experience and disentangling the different elements, how doubtful one often is about the most appropriate words to use in describing one's experiences even to oneself, and still more when trying to describe them to others. Let us remember too that some people are masters of introspective description—

William James is the greatest one I know—while others make a very poor job of it, and still others fall somewhere between the two extremes.

Introspection, in short, is something which requires skill and care (and honesty too). It can be done well, or moderately well, or badly, and up to a point one can train oneself to do it better.

So the claim that introspection is an infallible source of information must certainly be abandoned, and ought never to have been made. But this conclusion should not dismay the advocate of introspection. On the contrary, it should encourage him. One of the characteristic marks of a genuine procedure for obtaining information is that mistakes are possible when one uses it. When one can be wrong, one can also be right. And if someone alleges that there is a procedure in which mistakes are impossible one supposes that it is not really a way of obtaining information at all. When one cannot be wrong, one cannot be right either.

I suggest, then, that we must distinguish between having or living-through an exerience and making introspective judgments about it. The first is not infallible, but might mistakenly be thought to be so, because it is something to which the notion of fallibility does not apply. The second, just because it is a genuine source of information, is perfectly capable of being mistaken on occasion, as other means of getting information are.

In this paper I have said nothing about the bearing of para-normal phenomena upon the behaviorist philosophy of mind. It appears to me that what the "reductive" behaviorist is primarily concerned to deny or to argue out of existence is a set of facts so "normal" and so obvious that everyone is familiar with them—for example, the fact that we are aware of things, that each of us has experiences, that each of us can attend to and make judgments about the experiences which he has. His error seems to me the philosophical error of denying the obvious, and not the scientific error of denying new and strange facts which fail to fit in with current scientific theories.

I do, however, find it very difficult to understand how even an epiphenomenalist or a parallelist, and a fortiori a behaviorist, can manage to reconcile the phenomena of para-normal cognition with his conception of human personality. If he were to make a serious attempt to do so, I think he would have to begin by revising his views of the natural world in a pretty radical way by postulating new types of matter and new types of physical energy which are certainly not parts of the publicly observable world as our sense-organs reveal it and as contemporary physics and biology conceive of it. He might find himself obliged to suppose that each of us has a "hyper-physical" organism in addition to the publicly observable physical organism which physiologists can experiment upon and anatomists can dissect, and that the publicly observable physical environment is sometimes interpenetrated by a "hyper-physical" environment obeying causal laws quite different from those which physicists have discovered. What began as a naturalistic theory of human nature would be transformed into a kind of occultism. A return to an old-fashioned dualistic theory would seem to be a more tolerable alternative.

57. A REVIEW OF B. F. SKINNER'S *VERBAL BEHAVIOR*

Noam Chomsky

1. A great many linguists and philosophers concerned with language have expressed the hope that their studies might ultimately be embedded in a framework provided by behaviorist psychology, and that refractory areas of investigation, particularly those in which meaning is involved, will in this way be opened up to fruitful exploration. Since this volume is the first large-scale attempt to incorporate the major aspects of linguistic behavior within a behaviorist framework, it merits and will undoubtedly receive careful attention. Skinner is noted for his contributions to the study of animal behavior. The book under review is the product of study of linguistic behavior extending over more than twenty years. Earlier versions of it have been fairly widely circulated, and there are quite a few references in the psychological literature to its major ideas.

The problem to which this book is addressed is that of giving a "functional analysis" of verbal behavior. By functional analysis, Skinner means identification of the variables that control this behavior and specification of how they interact to determine a particular verbal response. Furthermore, the controlling variables are to be described completely in terms of such notions as stimulus, reinforcement, deprivation, which have been given a reasonably clear meaning in animal experimentation. In other words, the goal of the book is to provide a way to predict and control verbal behavior by observing and manipulating the physical environment of the speaker.

SOURCE. Chomsky, Noam, "A Review of B. F. Skinner's *Verbal Behavior*," *Language*, **35**, January–March, 1959. Copyright © 1959 by Linguistic Society of America, the publisher, and reprinted with permission.

Skinner feels that recent advances in the laboratory study of animal behavior permit us to approach this problem with a certain optimism, since "the basic processes and relations which give verbal behavior its special characteristics are now fairly well understood . . . the results [of this experimental work] have been surprisingly free of species restrictions. Recent work has shown that the methods can be extended to human behavior without serious modification" (3).[1]

It is important to see clearly just what it is in Skinner's program and claims that makes them appear so bold and remarkable. It is not primarily the fact that he has set functional analysis as his problem, or that he limits himself to study of "observables," i.e. input-output relations. What is so surprising is the particular limitations he has imposed on the way in which the observables of behavior are to be studied, and, above all, the particularly simple nature of the "function" which, he claims, describes the causation of behavior. One would naturally expect that prediction of the behavior of a complex organism (or machine) would require, in addition to information about external stimulation, knowledge of the internal structure of the organism, the ways in which it processes input information and organizes its own behavior. These characteristics of the organism are in general a complicated product of inborn structure, the genetically determined course of maturation, and past experience. Insofar as independent neurophysiological evidence is not available, it is obvious that inferences concerning the structure of the organism are based on observation of behavior and outside events. Nevertheless, one's estimate of the relative importance of external factors and internal structure in the determination of behavior will have an important effect on the direction of

---

[1] Skinner's confidence in recent achievements in the study of animal behavior and their applicability to complex human behavior does not appear to be widely shared. In many recent publications of confirmed behaviorists there is a prevailing note of skepticism with regard to the scope of these achievements. For representative comments, see the contributions to *Modern learning theory* (by Estes et al.; New York, 1954); Bugelski, *Psychology of learning* (New York, 1956); Koch, in *Nebraska symposium on motivation* 58 (Lincoln, 1956); Verplanck, Learned and innate behavior, *Psych. rev.* 52.139 (1955). Perhaps the strongest view is that of Harlow, who has asserted (Mice, monkeys, men, and motives, *Psych. rev.* 60.23–32 [1953]) that "a strong case can be made for the proposition that the importance of the psychological problems studied during the last 15 years has decreased as a negatively accelerated function approaching an asymptote of complete indifference." Tinbergen, a leading representative of a different approach to animal behavior studies (comparative ethology), concludes a discussion of "functional analysis" with the comment that "we may now draw the conclusion that the causation of behavior is immensely more complex than was assumed in the generalizations of the past. A number of internal and external factors act upon complex central nervous structures. Second, it will be obvious that the facts at our disposal are very fragmentary indeed"—*The study of instinct* 74 (Oxford, 1951).

research on linguistic (or any other) behavior, and on the kinds of analogies from animal behavior studies that will be considered relevant or suggestive.

Putting it differently, anyone who sets himself the problem of analyzing the causation of behavior will (in the absence of independent neurophysiological evidence) concern himself with the only data available, namely the record of inputs to the organism and the organism's present response, and will try to describe the function specifying the response in terms of the history of inputs. This is nothing more than the definition of his problem. There are no possible grounds for argument here, if one accepts the problem as legitimate, though Skinner has often advanced and defended this definition of a problem as if it were a thesis which other investigators reject. The differences that arise between those who affirm and those who deny the importance of the specific "contribution of the organism" to learning and performance concern the particular character and complexity of this function, and the kinds of observations and research necessary for arriving at a precise specification of it. If the contribution of the organism is complex, the only hope of predicting behavior even in a gross way will be through a very indirect program of research that begins by studying the detailed character of the behavior itself and the particular capacities of the organism involved.

Skinner's thesis is that external factors consisting of present stimulation and the history of reinforcement (in particular the frequency, arrangement, and withholding of reinforcing stimuli) are of overwhelming importance, and that the general principles revealed in laboratory studies of these phenomena provide the basis for understanding the complexities of verbal behavior. He confidently and repeatedly voices his claim to have demonstrated that the contribution of the speaker is quite trivial and elementary, and that precise prediction of verbal behavior involves only specification of the few external factors that he has isolated experimentally with lower organisms.

Careful study of this book (and of the research on which it draws) reveals, however, that these astonishing claims are far from justified. It indicates, furthermore, that the insights that have been achieved in the laboratories of the reinforcement theorist, though quite genuine, can be applied to complex human behavior only in the most gross and superficial way, and that speculative attempts to discuss linguistic behavior in these terms alone omit from consideration factors of fundamental importance that are, no doubt, amenable to scientific study, although their specific character cannot at present be precisely formulated. Since Skinner's work is the most extensive attempt to accommodate human behavior involving higher mental faculties within a strict behaviorist schema of the type that has attracted many linguists and philosophers, as well as psychologists, a detailed documentation is of independent interest. The magnitude of the failure of this attempt to account for verbal behavior serves as a kind of measure of the importance of the factors omitted from consideration, and an indication of how little is really known about this remarkably complex phenomenon.

The force of Skinner's argument lies in the enormous wealth and range of examples for which he proposes a functional analysis. The only way to evaluate the success of his program and the correctness of his basic assumptions about verbal behavior is to review these examples in detail and to determine the precise character of the concepts in terms of which the functional analysis is presented. §2 of this review describes the experimental context with respect to which these concepts are originally defined. §§3–4 deal with the basic concepts "stimulus," "response," and "reinforcement," §§6–10 with the new descriptive machinery developed specifically for the description of verbal behavior. In §5 we consider the status of the fundamental claim, drawn from the laboratory, which serves as the basis for the analogic guesses about human behavior that have been proposed by many psychologists. The final section (§11) will consider some ways in which further linguistic work may play a part in clarifying some of these problems.

2.   Although this book makes no direct reference to experimental work, it can be understood only in terms of the general framework that Skinner has developed for the description of behavior. Skinner divides the responses of the animal into two main categories. *Respondents* are purely reflex responses elicited by particular stimuli. *Operants* are emitted responses, for which no obvious stimulus can be discovered. Skinner has been concerned primarily with operant behavior. The experimental arrangement that he introduced consists basically of a box with a bar attached to one wall in such a way that when the bar is pressed, a food pellet is dropped into a tray (and the bar press is recorded). A rat placed in the box will soon press the bar, releasing a pellet into the tray. This state of affairs, resulting from the bar press, increases the *strength* of the bar-pressing operant. The food pellet is called a *reinforcer*; the event, a reinforcing event. The strength of an operant is defined by Skinner in terms of the rate of response during extinction (i.e. after the last reinforcement and before return to the preconditioning rate).

Suppose that release of the pellet is conditional on the flashing of a light. Then the rat will come to press the bar only when the light flashes. This is called *stimulus discrimination*. The response is called a *discriminated operant* and the light is called the *occasion* for its emission; this is to be distinguished from elicitation of a response by a stimulus in the case of the respondent.[2]

---

[2] In *Behavior of organisms* (New York, 1938), Skinner remarks that "although a conditioned operant is the result of the correlation of the response with a particular reinforcement, a relation between it and a discriminative stimulus acting prior to the response is the almost universal rule" (178–9). Even emitted behavior is held to be produced by some sort of "originating force" (51) which, in the case of operant behavior is not under

Suppose that the apparatus is so arranged that bar-pressing of only a certain character (e.g., duration) will release the pellet. The rat will then come to press the bar in the required way. This process is called *response differentiation*. By successive slight changes in the conditions under which the response will be reinforced it is possible to shape the response of a rat or a pigeon in very surprising ways in a very short time, so that rather complex behavior can be produced by a process of successive approximation.

A stimulus can become reinforcing by repeated association with an already reinforcing stimulus. Such a stimulus is called a *secondary reinforcer*. Like many contemporary behaviorists, Skinner considers money, approval, and the like to be secondary reinforcers which have become reinforcing because of their association with food etc.[3] Secondary reinforcers can be *generalized* by associating them with a variety of different primary reinforcers.

Another variable that can affect the rate of the bar-pressing operant is drive, which Skinner defines operationally in terms of hours of deprivation. His major scientific book, *Behavior of organisms*, is a study of the effects of food-deprivation and conditioning on the strength of the bar-pressing response of healthy mature rats. Probably Skinner's most original contribution to animal behavior studies has been his investigation of the effects of intermittent reinforcement, arranged in various different ways, presented in *Behavior of organisms* and extended (with pecking of pigeons as the operant under investigation) in the recent *Schedules of reinforcement* by Ferster and Skinner (1957). It is apparently these studies that Skinner has in mind when he refers to the recent advances in the study of animal behavior.[4]

---

experimental control. The distinction between eliciting stimuli, discriminated stimuli, and "originating forces" has never been adequately clarified, and becomes even more confusing when private internal events are considered to be discriminated stimuli (see below).

[3] In a famous experiment, chimpanzees were taught to perform complex tasks to receive tokens which had become secondary reinforcers because of association with food. The idea that money, approval, prestige, etc. actually acquire their motivating effects on human behavior according to this paradigm is unproved, and not particularly plausible. Many psychologists within the behaviorist movement are quite skeptical about this (cf. fn. 23). As in the case of most aspects of human behavior, the evidence about secondary reinforcement is so fragmentary, conflicting, and complex that almost any view can find some support.

[4] Skinner's remark quoted above about the generality of his basic results must be understood in the light of the experimental limitations he has imposed. If it were true in any deep sense that the basic processes in language are well understood and free of species restrictions, it would be extremely odd that language is limited to man. With the exception of a few scattered observations (cf. his article, A case history in scientific method, *The American psychologist* 11.221–33 [1956], Skinner is apparently basing this claim on the fact that qualitatively similar results are obtained with bar-pressing of rats and pecking of pigeons under special conditions of deprivation and various schedules of reinforcement. One immediately questions how much can be based on these facts, which

The notions "stimulus," "response," "reinforcement" are relatively well defined with respect to the bar-pressing experiments and others similarly restricted. Before we can extend them to real-life behavior, however, certain difficulties must be faced. We must decide, first of all, whether any physical event to which the organism is capable of reacting is to be called a stimulus on a given occasion, or only one to which the organism in fact reacts; and correspondingly, we must decide whether any part of behavior is to be called a response, or only one connected with stimuli in lawful ways. Questions of this sort pose something of a dilemma for the experimental psychologist. If he accepts the broad definitions, characterizing any physical event impinging on the organism as a stimulus and any part of the organism's behavior as a response, he must conclude that behavior has not been demonstrated to be lawful. In the present state of our knowledge, we must attribute an overwhelming influence on actual behavior to ill-defined factors of attention, set, volition, and caprice. If we accept the narrower definitions, then behavior is lawful by definition (if it consists of responses); but this fact is of limited significance, since most of what the animal does will simply not be considered behavior. Hence the psychologist either must admit that behavior is not lawful (or that he cannot at present show that it is—not at all a damaging admission for a developing science), or must restrict his attention to those highly limited areas in which it is lawful (e.g. with adequate controls, bar-pressing in rats; lawfulness of the observed behavior provides, for Skinner, an implicit definition of a good experiment).

Skinner does not consistently adopt either course. He utilizes the experimental results as evidence for the scientific character of his system of behavior, and analogic guesses (formulated in terms of a metaphoric extension of the technical vocabulary of the laboratory) as evidence for its scope. This creates the illusion of a rigorous scientific theory with a very broad scope, although in fact the terms used in the description of real-life and of laboratory behavior may be mere homonyms, with at most a vague similarity of meaning. To substantiate this evaluation, a critical account of his book must show that with a literal reading (where the terms of the descriptive system have something like the technical meanings given in Skinner's definitions)

are in part at least an artifact traceable to experimental design and the definition of "stimulus" and "response" in terms of "smooth dynamic curves" (see below). The dangers inherent in any attempt to "extrapolate" to complex behavior from the study of such simple responses as bar-pressing should be obvious, and have often been commented on (cf. e.g. Harlow, op. cit.). The generality of even the simplest results is open to serious question. Cf. in this connection Bitterman, Wodinsky, and Candland, Some comparative psychology, *Am. journ. of psych.* **71**.94–110 (1958), where it is shown that there are important qualitative differences in solution of comparable elementary problems by rats and fish.

the book covers almost no aspect of linguistic behavior, and that with a metaphoric reading, it is no more scientific than the traditional approaches to this subject matter, and rarely as clear and careful.[5]

3. Consider first Skinner's use of the notions "stimulus" and "response." In *Behavior of organisms* (9) he commits himself to the narrow definitions for these terms. A part of the environment and a part of behavior are called stimulus (eliciting, discriminated, or reinforcing), and response, respectively, only if they are lawfully related; that is, if the "dynamic laws" relating them show smooth and reproducible curves. Evidently stimuli and responses, so defined, have not been shown to figure very widely in ordinary human behavior.[6] We can, in the face of presently available evidence, continue to maintain the lawfulness of the relation between stimulus and response only by depriving them of their objective character. A typical example of "stimulus control" for Skinner would be the response to a piece of music with the utterance *Mozart* or to a painting with the response *Dutch*. These responses are asserted to be "under the control of extremely subtle properties" of the physical object or event (108). Suppose instead of saying *Dutch* we had said *Clashes with the wallpaper, I thought you liked abstract work, Never saw it before, Tilted, Hanging too low, Beautiful, Hideous, Remember our camping trip last summer?*, or whatever else might come into our minds when looking at a picture (in Skinnerian translation, whatever other responses exist in sufficient strength). Skinner could only say that each of these responses is under the control of some other stimulus property of the physical object. If we look at a red chair and say *red*, the response is under the control of the stimulus "redness"; if we say *chair*, it is under the control of the collection of prop-

---

[5] An analogous argument, in connection with a different aspect of Skinner's thinking, is given by Scriven in *A study of radical behaviorism = Univ. of Minn. studies in philosophy of science*, Vol. 1. Cf. Verplanck's contribution to *Modern learning theory* (283–8) for more general discussion of the difficulties in formulating an adequate definition of "stimulus" and "response." He concludes, quite correctly, that in Skinner's sense of the word, stimuli are not objectively identifiable independently of the resulting behavior, nor are they manipulable. Verplanck presents a clear discussion of many other aspects of Skinner's system, commenting on the untestability of many of the so-called "laws of behavior" and the limited scope of many of the others, and the arbitrary and obscure character of Skinner's notion of "lawful relation"; and, at the same time, noting the importance of the experimental data that Skinner has accumulated.

[6] In *Behavior of organisms*, Skinner apparently was willing to accept this consequence. He insists (41–2) that the terms of casual description in the popular vocabulary are not validly descriptive until the defining properties of stimulus and response are specified, the correlation is demonstrated experimentally, and the dynamic changes in it are shown to be lawful. Thus, in describing a child as hiding from a dog, "it will not be enough to dignify the popular vocabulary by appealing to essential properties of 'dogness' or 'hidingness' and to suppose them intuitively known." But this is exactly what Skinner does in the book under review, as we will see directly.

erties (for Skinner, the object) "chairness" (110), and similarly for any other response. This device is as simple as it is empty. Since properties are free for the asking (we have as many of them as we have nonsynonymous descriptive expressions in our language, whatever this means exactly), we can account for a wide class of responses in terms of Skinnerian functional analysis by identifying the "controlling stimuli." But the word "stimulus" has lost all objectivity in this usage. Stimuli are no longer part of the outside physical world; they are driven back into the organism. We identify the stimulus when we hear the response. It is clear from such examples, which abound, that the talk of "stimulus control" simply disguises a complete retreat to mentalistic psychology. We cannot predict verbal behavior in terms of the stimuli in the speaker's environment, since we do not know what the current stimuli are until he responds. Furthermore, since we cannot control the property of a physical object to which an individual will respond, except in highly artificial cases, Skinner's claim that his system, as opposed to the traditional one, permits the practical control of verbal behavior[7] is quite false.

Other examples of "stimulus control" merely add to the general mystification. Thus a proper noun is held to be a response "under the control of a specific person or thing" (as controlling stimulus, 113). I have often used the words *Eisenhower* and *Moscow*, which I presume are proper nouns if

[7] 253 f. and elsewhere, repeatedly. As an example of how well we can control behavior using the notions developed in this book, Skinner shows here how we would go about evoking the response *pencil*. The most effective way, he suggests, is to say to the subject "Please say *pencil*" (our chances would, presumably, be even further improved by use of "aversive stimulation," e.g. holding a gun to his head). We can also "make sure that no pencil or writing instrument is available, then hand our subject a pad of paper appropriate to pencil sketching, and offer him a handsome reward for a recognizable picture of a cat." It would also be useful to have voices saying *pencil* or *pen and* . . . in the background; signs reading *pencil* or *pen and* . . . ; or to place a "large and unusual pencil in an unusual place clearly in sight." "Under such circumstances, it is highly probable that our subject will say *pencil*." "The available techniques are all illustrated in this sample." These contributions of behavior theory to the practical control of human behavior are amply illustrated elsewhere in the book, as when Skinner shows (113–4) how we can evoke the response *red* (the device suggested is to hold a red object before the subjct and say "Tell me what color this is").

In fairness, it must be mentioned that there are certain nontrivial applications of "operant conditioning" to the control of human behavior. A wide variety of experiments have shown that the number of plural nouns (for example) produced by a subject will increase if the experimenter says "right" or "good" when one is produced (similarly, positive attitudes on a certain issue, stories with particular content, etc.; cf. Krasner, Studies of the conditioning of verbal behavior, *Psych. bull.*, Vol. 55 [1958], for a survey of several dozen experiments of this kind, mostly with positive results). It is of some interest that the subject is usually unaware of the process. Just what insight this gives into normal verbal behavior is not obvious. Nevertheless, it is an example of positive and not totally expected results using the Skinnerian paradigm.

anything is, but have never been "stimulated" by the corresponding objects. How can this fact be made compatible with this definition? Suppose that I use the name of a friend who is not present. Is this an instance of a proper noun under the control of the friend as stimulus? Elsewhere it is asserted that a stimulus controls a response in the sense that presence of the stimulus increases the probability of the response. But it is obviously untrue that the probability that a speaker will produce a full name is increased when its bearer faces the speaker. Furthermore, how can one's own name be a proper noun in this sense? A multitude of similar questions arise immediately. It appears that the word "control" here is merely a misleading paraphrase for the traditional "denote" or "refer." The assertion (115) that so far as the speaker is concerned, the relation of reference is "simply the probability that the speaker will emit a response of a given form in the presence of a stimulus having specified properties" is surely incorrect if we take the words "presence," "stimulus," and "probability" in their literal sense. That they are not intended to be taken literally is indicated by many examples, as when a response is said to be "controlled" by a situation or state of affairs as "stimulus." Thus, the expression *a needle in a haystack* "may be controlled as a unit by a particular type of situation" (116); the words in a single part of speech, e.g. all adjectives, are under the control of a single set of subtle properties of stimuli (121); "the sentence *The boy runs a store* is under the control of an extremely complex stimulus situation" (335); "*He is not at all well* may function as a standard response under the control of a state of affairs which might also control *He is ailing*" (325); when an envoy observes events in a foreign country and reports upon his return, his report is under "remote stimulus control" (416); the statement *This is war* may be a response to a "confusing international situation" (441); the suffix *-ed* is controlled by that "subtle property of stimuli which we speak of as action-in-the-past" (121) just as the *-s* in *The boy runs* is under the control of such specific features of the situation as its "currency" (332). No characterization of the notion "stimulus control" that is remotely related to the bar-pressing experiment (or that preserves the faintest objectivity) can be made to cover a set of examples like these, in which, for example, the "controlling stimulus" need not even impinge on the responding organism.

Consider now Skinner's use of the notion "response." The problem of identifying units in verbal behavior has of course been a primary concern of linguists, and it seems very likely that experimental psychologists should be able to provide much-needed assistance in clearing up the many remaining difficulties in systematic identification. Skinner recognizes (20) the fundamental character of the problem of identification of a unit of verbal behavior, but is satisfied with an answer so vague and subjective that it does not really contribute to its solution. The unit of verbal behavior—the verbal operant—

is defined as a class of responses of identifiable form functionally related to one or more controlling variables. No method is suggested for determining in a particular instance what are the controlling variables, how many such units have occurred, or where their boundaries are in the total response. Nor is any attempt made to specify how much or what kind of similarity in form or "control" is required for two physical events to be considered instances of the same operant. In short, no answers are suggested for the most elementary questions that must be asked of anyone proposing a method for description of behavior. Skinner is content with what he calls an "extrapolation" of the concept of operant developed in the laboratory to the verbal field. In the typical Skinnerian experiment, the problem of identifying the unit of behavior is not too crucial. It is defined, by fiat, as a recorded peck or bar-press, and systematic variations in the rate of this operant and its resistance to extinction are studied as a function of deprivation and scheduling of reinforcement (pellets). The operant is thus defined with respect to a particular experimental procedure. This is perfectly reasonable, and has led to many interesting results. It is, however, completely meaningless to speak of extrapolating this concept of operant to ordinary verbal behavior. Such "extrapolation" leaves us with no way of justifying one or another decision about the units in the "verbal repertoire."

Skinner specifies "response strength" as the basic datum, the basic dependent variable in his functional analysis. In the bar-pressing experiment, response strength is defined in terms of rate of emission during extinction. Skinner has argued[8] that this is "the only datum that varies significantly and in the expected direction under conditions which are relevant to the learning process." In the book under review, response strength is defined as "probability of emission" (22). This definition provides a comforting impression of objectivity, which, however, is quickly dispelled when we look into the matter more closely. The term "probability" has some rather obscure meaning for Skinner in this book.[9] We are told, on the one hand, that "our

[8] Are theories of learning necessary?, *Psych. rev.* 57.193–216 (1950).

[9] And elsewhere. In his paper Are theories of learning necessary?, Skinner considers the problem how to extend his analysis of behavior to experimental situations in which it is impossible to observe frequencies, rate of response being the only valid datum. His answer is that "the notion of probability is usually extrapolated to cases in which a frequency analysis cannot be carried out. In the field of behavior we arrange a situation in which frequences are available as data, but we use the notion of probability in analyzing or formulating instances of even types of behavior which are not susceptible to this analysis" (199). There are, of course, conceptions of probability not based directly on frequency, but I do not see how any of these apply to the cases that Skinner has in mind. I see no way of interpreting the quoted passage other than as signifying an intention to use the word "probability" in describing behavior quite independently of whether the notion of probability is at all relevant.

evidence for the contribution of each variable [to response strength] is based on observation of frequencies alone" (28). At the same time, it appears that frequency is a very misleading measure of strength, since, for example, the frequency of a response may be "primarily attributable to the frequency of occurrence of controlling variables" (27). It is not clear how the frequency of a response can be attributable to anything BUT the frequency of occurrence of its controlling variables if we accept Skinner's view that the behavior occurring in a given situation is "fully determined" by the relevant controlling variables (175, 228). Furthermore, although the evidence for the contribution of each variable to response strength is based on observation of frequencies alone, it turns out that "we base the notion of strength upon several kinds of evidence" (22), in particular (22–8): emission of the response (particularly in unusual circumstances), energy level (stress), pitch level, speed and delay of emission, size of letters etc. in writing immediate repetition, and—a final factor, relevant but misleading—over-all frequency.

Of course, Skinner recognizes that these measures do not co-vary, because (among other reasons) pitch, stress, quantity, and reduplication may have internal linguistic functions.[10] However, he does not hold these conflicts to be very important, since the proposed factors indicative of strength are "fully understood by everyone" in the culture (27). For example, "if we are shown a prized work of art and exclaim *Beautiful!*, the speed and energy of the response will not be lost on the owner." It does not appear totally obvious that in this case the way to impress the owner is to shriek *Beautiful* in a loud, high-pitched voice, repeatedly, and with no delay (high response strength). It may be equally effective to look at the picture silently (long delay), and then to murmur *Beautiful* in a soft, low-pitched voice (by definition, very low response strength).

It is not unfair, I believe, to conclude from Skinner's discussion of response strength, the "basic datum" in functional analysis, that his "extrapolation" of the notion of probability can best be interpreted as, in effect, nothing more than a decision to use the word "probability," with its favorable connotations of objectivity, as a cover term to paraphrase such low-status words as "interest," "intention," "belief," and the like. This interpretation is fully justified by the way in which Skinner uses the terms "probability" and "strength." To cite just one example, Skinner defines the process of confirming an assertion in science as one of "generating additional variables to increase it probability" (425), and more generally, its strength (425–9). If we take this suggestion quite literally, the degree of confirmation of a scientific assertion

---

[10] Fortunately, "In English this presents no great difficulty" since, for example, "relative pitch levels . . . are not important" (25). No reference is made to the numerous studies of the function of relative pitch levels and other intonational features in English.

can be measured as a simple function of the loudness, pitch, and frequency with which it is proclaimed, and a general procedure for increasing its degree of confirmation would be, for instance, to train machine guns on large crowds of people who have been instructed to shout it. A better indication of what Skinner probably has in mind here is given by his description of how the theory of evolution, as an example, is confirmed. This "single set of verbal responses . . . is made more plausible—is strengthened—by several types of construction based upon verbal responses in geology, paleontology, genetics, and so on" (427). We are no doubt to interpret the terms "strength" and "probability" in this context as paraphrases of more familiar locutions such as 'justified belief' or "warranted assertability," or something of the sort. Similar latitude of interpretation is presumably expected when we read that "frequency of effective action accounts in turn for what we may call the listener's 'belief' " (88) or that "our belief in what someone tells us is similarly a function of, or identical with, our tendency to act upon the verbal stimuli which he provides" (160).[11]

I think it is evident, then, that Skinner's use of the terms "stimulus," "control," "response," and "strength" justify the general conclusion stated in the last paragraph of §2 above. The way in which these terms are brought to bear on the actual data indicates that we must interpret them as mere paraphrases for the popular vocabulary commonly used to describe behavior, and as having no particular connection with the homonymous expressions used in the description of laboratory experiments. Naturally, this terminological revision adds no objectivity to the familiar "mentalistic" mode of description.

4. The other fundamental notion borrowed from the description of bar-pressing experiments is "reinforcement." It raises problems which are similar, and even more serious. In *Behavior of organisms*, "the operation of reinforcement is defined as the presentation of a certain kind of stimulus in a temporal relation with either a stimulus or response. A reinforcing stimulus is defined as such by its power to produce the resulting change [in strength]. There is no circularity about this: some stimuli are found to produce the change, others not, and they are classified as reinforcing and non-reinforcing

---

[11] The vagueness of the word "tendency," as opposed to "frequency," saves the latter quotation from the obvious incorrectness of the former. Nevertheless, a good deal of stretching is necessary. If "tendency" has anything like its ordinary meaning, the remark is clearly false. One may believe strongly the assertion that Jupiter has four moons, that many of Sophocles' plays have been irretrievably lost, that the earth will burn to a crisp in ten million years, etc., without experiencing the slightest tendency to act upon these verbal stimuli. We may, of course, turn Skinner's assertion into a very unilluminating truth by defining "tendency to act" to include tendencies to answer questions in certain ways, under motivation to say what one believes is true.

accordingly" (62). This is a perfectly appropriate definition[12] for the study of schedules of reinforcement. It is perfectly useless, however, in the discussion of real-life behavior, unless we can somehow characterize the stimuli which are reinforcing (and the situations and conditions under which they are reinforcing). Consider first of all the status of the basic principle that Skinner calls the "law of conditioning" (law of effect). It reads: "if the occurrence of an operant is followed by presence of a reinforcing stimulus, the strength is increased" (*Behavior of organisms* 21). As "reinforcement" was defined, this law becomes a tautology.[13] For Skinner, learning is just change in response strength.[14] Although the statement that presence of reinforcement is a sufficient condition for learning and maintenance of behavior is vacuous, the claim that it is a necessary condition may have some content, depending on how the class of reinforcers (and appropriate situations) is characterized. Skinner does make it very clear that in his view reinforcement is a necessary condition for language learning and for the continued availability of linguistic responses in the adult.[15] However, the looseness of the term "reinforcement" as Skinner uses it in the book under review makes it entirely pointless to inquire into the truth or falsity of this claim. Examining the instances of what Skinner calls "reinforcement," we find that not even the requirement that a reinforcer be an identifiable stimulus is taken seriously. In fact, the term is used in such a way that the assertion that reinforcement is necessary for learning and continued availability of behavior is likewise empty.

To show this, we consider some example of "reinforcement." First of all, we find a heavy appeal to automatic self-reinforcement. Thus, "a man talks to himself . . . because of the reinforcement he receives" (163); "the child is reinforced automatically when he duplicates the sounds of airplanes, street-

---

[12] One should add, however, that it is in general not the stimulus as such that is reinforcing, but the stimulus in a particular situational context. Depending on experimental arrangement, a particular physical event or object may be reinforcing, punishing, or unnoticed. Because Skinner limits himself to a particular, very simple experimental arrangement, it is not necessary for him to add this qualification, which would not be at all easy to formulate precisely. But it is of course necessary if he expects to extend his descriptive system to behavior in general.

[13] This has been frequently noted.

[14] See, for example, Are theories of learning necessary? 199. Elsewhere, he suggests that the term "learning" be restricted to complex situations, but these are not characterized.

[15] "A child acquires verbal behavior when relatively unpatterned vocalizations, selectively reinforced, gradually assume forms which produce appropriate consequences in a given verbal community" (31) "Differential reinforcement shapes up all verbal forms, and when a prior stimulus enters into the contingency, reinforcement is responsible for its resulting control . . . The availability of behavior, its probability or strength, depends on whether reinforcements *continue* in effect and according to what schedules" (203–4). Elsewhere, frequently.

cars . . ." (164); "the young child alone in the nursery may automatically reinforce his own exploratory verbal behavior when he produces sounds which he has heard in the speech of others" (58); "the speaker who is also an accomplished listener 'knows when he has correctly echoed a response' and is reinforced thereby" (68); thinking is "behaving which automatically affects the behaver and is reinforcing because it does so" (438; cutting one's finger should thus be reinforcing, and an example of thinking); "the verbal fantasy, whether overt or covert, is automatically reinforcing to the speaker as listener. Just as the musician plays or composes what he is reinforced by hearing, or as the artist paints what reinforces him visually, so the speaker engaged in verbal fantasy says what he is reinforced by hearing or writes what he is reinforced by reading" (439); similarly, care in problem solving, and rationalization, are automatically self-reinforcing (442–3). We can also reinforce someone by emitting verbal behavior as such (since this rules out a class of aversive stimulations, 167), by not emitting verbal behavior (keeping silent and paying attention, 199), or by acting appropriately on some future occasion (152: "the strength of [the speaker's] behavior is determined mainly by the behavior which the listener will exhibit with respect to a given state of affairs"; this Skinner considers the general case of "communication" or "letting the listener know"). In most such cases, of course, the speaker is not present at the time when the reinforcement takes place, as when "the artist . . . is reinforced by the effects his works have upon . . . others" (224), or when the writer is reinforced by the fact that his "verbal behavior may reach over centuries or to thousands of listeners or readers at the same time. The writer may not be reinforced often or immediately, but his net reinforcement may be great" (206; this accounts for the great "strength" of his behavior). An individual may also find it reinforcing to injure someone by criticism or by bringing bad news, or to publish an experimental result which upsets the theory of a rival (154), to describe circumstances which would be reinforcing if they were to occur (165), to avoid repetition (222), to "hear" his own name though in fact it was not mentioned or to hear nonexistent words in his child's babbling (259), to clarify or otherwise intensify the effect of a stimulus which serves an important discriminative function (416), etc.

From this sample, it can be seen that the notion of reinforcement has totally lost whatever objective meaning it may ever have had. Running through these examples, we see that a person can be reinforced though he emits no response at all, and that the reinforcing "stimulus" need not impinge on the "reinforced person" or need not even exist (it is sufficient that it be imagined or hoped for). When we read that a person plays what music he likes (165), says what he likes (165), thinks what he likes (438–9), reads what books he likes (163), etc., BECAUSE he finds it reinforcing to do so, or that we write books or inform others of facts BECAUSE we are reinforced by what we hope will be the ultimate behavior of reader or listener, we can only conclude that the term "reinforcement" has a purely ritual function. The phrase "X is reinforced by Y (stimulus, state of affairs, event, etc.)" is being used as a cover term for "X wants Y," "X likes Y," "X wishes that Y were the case," etc. Invoking the term "reinforcement" has no explanatory force, and any idea that this paraphrase introduces any new clarity or objectivity into the description of wishing, liking, etc., is a serious delusion. The only effect is to obscure the important differences among the notions being paraphrased. Once we recognize the latitude with which the term "reinforcement" is being used, many rather startling comments lose their initial effect—for instance, that the behavior of the creative artist is "controlled entirely by the contingencies of reinforcement" (150). What has been hoped for from the psychologist is some indication how the casual and informal description of everyday behavior in the popular vocabulary can be explained or clarified in terms of the notions developed in careful experiment and observation, or perhaps replaced in terms of a better scheme. A mere terminological revision, in which a term borrowed from the laboratory is used with the full vagueness of the ordinary vocabulary, is of no conceivable interest.

It seems that Skinner's claim that all verbal behavior is acquired and maintained in "strength" through reinforcement is quite empty, because his notion of reinforcement has no clear content, functioning only as a cover term for any factor, detectable or not, related to acquisition or maintenance of verbal behavior.[16] Skinner's use of the term "conditioning" suffers from a similar difficulty. Pavlovian and operant conditioning are processes about which psychologists have developed real understanding. Instruction of human beings is not. The claim that instruction and imparting of information are simply matters of conditioning (357–66) is pointless. The claim is true, if we extend the term "conditioning" to cover these processes, but we know no more about them after having revised this term in such a way as to deprive it of its relatively clear and objective character. It is, as far as we know, quite false, if we use "conditioning" in its literal sense. Similarly, when we say that "it is the function of predication to facilitate the transfer of response from one term to another or from one object to another" (361), we have said nothing of any significance. In what sense is this true of the predication *Whales are mammals?* Or, to take Skinner's example, what point is there in saying that the effect of *The telephone is out of order* on the listener is to bring behavior formerly controlled by the stimulus *out of order* under control of the stimulus *telephone* (or the telephone itself) by a process of simple conditioning (362)?

---

16 Talk of schedules or reinforcement here is entirely pointless. How are we to decide, for example, according to what schedules covert reinforcement is "arranged," as in thinking or verbal fantasy, or what the scheduling is of such factors as silence, speech, and appropriate future reactions to communicated information?

What laws of conditioning hold in this case? Furthermore, what behavior is "controlled" by the stimulus *out of order*, in the abstract? Depending on the object of which this is predicated, the present state of motivation of the listener, etc., the behavior may vary from rage to pleasure, from fixing the object to throwing it out, from simply not using it to trying to use it in the normal way (e.g. to see if it is really out of order), and so on. To speak of "conditioning" or "bringing previously available behavior under control of a new stimulus" in such a case is just a kind of play-acting at science. Cf. also footnote 43.

5. The claim that careful arrangement of contingencies of reinforcement by the verbal community is a necessary condition for language learning has appeared, in one form or another, in many places.[17] Since it is based not on actual observation, but on analogies to laboratory study of lower organisms, it is important to determine the status of the underlying assertion within experimental psychology proper. The most common characterization of reinforcement (one which Skinner explicitly rejects, incidentally) is in terms of drive reduction. This characterization can be given substance by defining drives in some way independently of what in fact is learned. If a drive is postulated on the basis of the fact that learning takes place, the claim that reinforcement is necessary for learning will again become as empty as it is in the Skinnerian framework. There is an extensive literature on the question of whether there can be learning without drive-reduction (latent learning). The "classical" experiment of Blodgett indicated that rats who had explored a maze without reward showed a marked drop in number of errors (as compared to a control group which had not explored the maze) upon introduction of a food reward, indicating that the rat had learned the structure of the maze without reduction of the hunger drive. Drive-reduction theorists countered with an exploratory drive which was reduced during the prereward learning, and claimed that a slight decrement in errors could be noted before food reward. A wide variety of experiments, with somewhat conflicting results, have been carried out with a similar design.[18] Few investigators still doubt

[17] See, for example, Miller and Dollard, *Social learning and imitation* 82–3 (New York, 1941), for a discussion of the "meticulous training" that they seem to consider necessary for a child to learn the meanings of words and syntactic patterns. The same notion is implicit in Mowrer's speculative account of how language might be acquired, in *Learning theory and personality dynamics*, Chapter 23 (New York, 1950). Actually, the view appears to be quite general.

[18] For a general review and analysis of this literature, see Thistlethwaite, A critical review of latent learning and related experiments, *Psych. bull.* 48.97–129 (1951). MacCorquodale and Meehl, in their contribution to *Modern learning theory*, carry out a serious and considered attempt to handle the latent learning material from the standpoint of drive-reduction theory, with (as they point out) not entirely satisfactory results. Thorpe reviews the literature from the standpoint of the ethologist, adding also material on

the existence of the phenomenon. Hilgard, in his general review of learning theory,[19] concludes that "there is no longer any doubt but that, under appropriate circumstances, latent learning is demonstrable."

More recent work has shown that novelty and variety of stimulus are sufficient to arouse curiosity in the rat and to motivate it to explore (visually), and in fact, to learn (since on a presentation of two stimuli, one novel, one repeated, the rat will attend to the novel one),[20] that rats will learn to choose the arm of a single-choice maze that leads to a complex maze, running through this being their only "reward";[21] that monkeys can learn object discriminations and maintain their performance at a high level of efficiency with visual exploration (looking out of a window for 30 seconds) as the only reward;[22] and, perhaps most strikingly of all, that monkeys and apes will solve rather complex manipulation problems that are simply placed in their cages, and will solve discrimination problems with only exploration and manipulation as incentives.[23] In these cases, solving the problem is apparently its own

homing and topographical orientation [*Learning and instinct in animals* (Cambridge, 1956)].

[19] *Theories of learning* 214 (1956).

[20] Berlyne, Novelty and curiosity as determinants of exploratory behavior, *Brit. jour. of psych.* 41.68–80 (1950) ; id., Perceptual curiosity in the rat, *Jour. of comp. physiol. psych.* 48.238–46 (1955) ; Thompson and Solomon, Spontaneous pattern discrimination in the rat, ibid. 47.104–7 (1954).

[21] Montgomery, The role of the exploratory drive in learning, ibid. 60–3. Many other papers in the same journal are designed to show that exploratory behavior is a relatively independent primary "drive" aroused by novel external stimulation.

[22] Butler, Discrimination learning by Rhesus monkeys to visual-exploration motivation, ibid. 46.95–8 (1953). Later experiments showed that this "drive" is highly persistent, as opposed to derived drives which rapidly extinguish.

[23] Harlow, Harlow, and Meyer, Learning motivated by a manipulation drive, *Jour. exp. psych.* 40.228–34 (1950), and later investigations initiated by Harlow. Harlow has been particularly insistent on maintaining the inadequacy of physiologically based drives and homeostatic need states for explaining the persistence of motivation and rapidity of learning in primates. He points out, in many papers, that curiosity, play, exploration, and manipulation are, for primates, often more potent drives than hunger and the like, and that they show none of the characteristics of acquired drives. Hebb also presents behavioral and supporting neurological evidence in support of the view that in higher animals there is a positive attraction in work, risk, puzzle, intellectual activity, mild fear and frustration, etc. (Drives and the CNS, *Psych. rev.* 62.243–54 [1955]). He concludes that "we need not work out tortuous and improbable ways to explain why men work for money, why children learn without pain, why people dislike doing nothing."

In a brief note (Early recognition of the manipulative drive in monkeys, *British journal of animal behavior* 3.71–2 [1955]), W. Dennis calls attention to the fact that early investigators (Romanes, 1882; Thorndike, 1901), whose "perception was relatively unaffected by learning theory, did note the intrinsically motivated behavior of monkeys," although, he asserts, no similar observations on monkeys have been made until Harlow's experiments. He quotes Romanes (*Animal intelligence* [1882]) as saying that "much "reward." Results of this kind can be handled by reinforcement theorists only if they are willing to set up curiosity, exploration, and manipulation drives, or to speculate somehow about acquired drives[24] for which there is no evidence outside of the fact that learning takes place in these cases.

There is a variety of other kinds of evidence that has been offered to challenge the view that drive-reduction is necessary for learning. Results on sensory-sensory conditioning have been interpreted as demonstrating learning without drive-reduction.[25] Olds has reported reinforcement by direct stimulation of the brain, from which he concludes that reward need not satisfy a physiological need or withdraw a drive stimulus.[26] The phenomenon of imprinting, long observed by zoologists, if of particular interest in this connection. Some of the most complex patterns of behavior of birds, in particular, are directed toward objects and animals of the type to which they have been exposed at certain critical early periods of life.[27] Imprinting is the most striking evidence for the innate disposition of the animal to learn in a certain direction, and to react appropriately to patterns and objects of certain restricted types, often only long after the original learning has taken place. It is, consequently, unrewarded learning, though the resulting patterns of behavior may be refined through reinforcement. Acquisition of the typical songs of song birds is, in some cases, a type of imprinting. Thorpe reports studies that show "that some characteristics of the normal song have been learnt in the earliest youth, before the bird itself is able to produce any kind of full song."[28] The phenomenon of imprinting

---

the most striking feature in the psychology of this animal, and the one which is least like anything met with in other animals, was the tireless spirit of investigation." Analogous developments, in which genuine discoveries have blinded systematic investigators to the important insights of earlier work, are easily found within recent structural linguistics as well.

[24] Thus J. S. Brown, in commenting on a paper of Harlow's in *Current theory and research in motivation* (Lincoln, 1953), argues that "in probably every instance [of the experiments cited by Harlow] an ingenious drive-reduction theorist could find some fragment of fear, insecurity, frustration, or whatever, that he could insist was reduced and hence was reinforcing" (53). The same sort of thing could be said for the ingenious phlogiston or ether theorist.

[25] Cf. Birch and Bitterman, Reinforcement and learning: The process of sensory integration, *Psych. rev.* 56.292–308 (1949).

[26] See, for example, his paper A physiological study of reward in McClelland (ed.), *Studies in motivation* 134–43 (New York, 1955).

[27] See Thorpe, op. cit., particularly 115–8 and 337–76, for an excellent discussion of this phenomenon, which has been brought to prominence particularly by the work of K. Lorenz (cf. Der Kumpan in der Umwelt des Vogels, parts of which are reprinted in English translation in Schiller (ed.), *Instinctive behavior* 83–128 (New York, 1957).

[28] Op. cit. 372.

has recently been investigated under laboratory conditions and controls with positive results.[29]

Phenomena of this general type are certainly familiar from everyday experience. We recognize people and places to which we have given no particular attention. We can look up something in a book and learn it perfectly well with no other motive than to confute reinforcement theory, or out of boredom, or idle curiosity. Everyone engaged in research must have had the experience of working with feverish and prolonged intensity to write a paper which no one else will read or to solve a problem which no one else thinks important and which will bring no conceivable reward—which may only confirm a general opinion that the researcher is wasting his time on irrelevancies. The fact that rats and monkeys do likewise is interesting, and important to show in careful experiment. In fact, studies of behavior of the type mentioned above have an independent and positive significance that far outweighs their incidental importance in bringing into question the claim that learning is impossible without drive-reduction. It is not at all unlikely that insights from animal behavior studies with this broadened scope may have the kind of relevance to such complex activities as verbal behavior that reinforcement theory has, so far, failed to exhibit. In any event, in the light of presently available evidence, it is difficult to see how anyone can be willing to claim that reinforcement is necessary for learning, if reinforcement is taken seriously as something identifiable independently of the resulting change in behavior.

Similarly, it seems quite beyond question that children acquire a good deal of their verbal and nonverbal behavior by causal observation and imitation of adults and other children.[30] It is simply not true that children can learn

[29] See e.g. Jaynes, Imprinting: Interaction of learned and innate behavior, *Jour. of comp. physiol. psych.* 49.201–6 (1956), where the conclusion is reached that "the experiments prove that without any observable reward young birds of this species follow a moving stimulus object and very rapidly come to prefer that object to others."

[30] Of course it is perfectly possible to incorporate this fact within the Skinnerian framework. If, for example, a child watches an adult using a comb and then, with no instruction, tries to comb his own hair, we can explain this act by saying that he performs it because he finds it reinforcing to do so, or because of the reinforcement provided by behaving like a person who is "reinforcing" (cf. 164). Similarly, an antomatic explanation is available for any other behavior. It seems strange at first that Skinner pays so little attention to the literature on latent learning and related topics, considering the tremendous reliance that he places on the notion of reinforcement; I have seen no reference to it in his writings. Similarly, Keller and Schoenfeld, in what appears to be the only text written under predominantly Skinnerian influence, *Principles of psychology* (New York, 1950), dismiss the latent-learning literature in one sentence as "beside the point," serving only "to obscure, rather than clarify, a fundamental principle" (the law of effect, 41). However, this neglect is perfectly appropriate in Skinner's case. To the drive-

language only through "meticulous care" on the part of adults who shape their verbal repertoire through careful differential reinforcement, though it may be that such care is often the custom in academic families. It is a common observation that a young child of immigrant parents may learn a second language in the streets, from other children, with amazing rapidity, and that his speech may be completely fluent and correct to the last allophone, while the subtleties that become second nature to the child may elude his parents despite high motivation and continued practice. A child may pick up a large part of his vocabulary and "feel" for sentence structure from television, from reading, from listening to adults, etc. Even a very young child who has not yet acquired a minimal repertoire from which to form new utterances may imitate a word quite well on an early try, with no attempt on the part of his parents to teach it to him. It is also perfectly obvious that, at a later stage, a child will be able to construct and understand utterances which are quite new, and are, at the same time, acceptable sentences in his language. Every time an adult reads a newspaper, he undoubtedly comes upon countless new sentences which are not at all similar, in a simple, physical sense, to any that he has heard before, and which he will recognize as sentences and understand; he will also be able to detect slight distortions or misprints. Talk of "stimulus generalization" in such a case simply perpetuates the mystery under a new title. These abilities indicate that there must be fundamental processes at work quite independently of "feedback" from the environment. I have been able to find no support whatsoever for the doctrine of Skinner and others that slow and careful shaping of verbal behavior through differential reinforcement is an absolute necessity. If reinforcement theory really requires the assumption that there be such meticulous care, it seems best to regard this simply as a reductio ad absurdum argument against this approach. It is also not easy to find any basis (or, for that matter, to attach very much content) to the claim that reinforcing contingencies set up by the verbal community are the single factor responsible for maintaining the strength of verbal behavior. The sources of the "strength" of this behavior are almost a total mystery at present. Reinforcement undoubtedly plays a significant role, but so do a variety of motivational factors about which nothing serious is known in the case of human beings.

As far as acquisition of language is concerned, it seems clear that reinforcement, casual observation, and natural inquisitiveness (coupled with a strong

reductionist, or anyone else for whom the notion "reinforcement" has some substantive meaning, these experiments and observations are important (and often embarrassing). But in the Skinnerian sense of the word, neither these results nor any conceivable others can cast any doubt on the claim that reinforcement is essential for the acquisition and maintenance of behavior. Behavior certainly has some concomitant circumstances, and whatever they are, we can call them "reinforcement."

tendency to imitate) are important factors, as is the remarkable capacity of the child to generalize, hypothesize, and "process information" in a variety of very special and apparently highly complex ways which we cannot yet describe or begin to understand, and which may be largely innate, or may develop through some sort of learning or through maturation of the nervous system. The manner in which such factors operate and interact in language acquisition is completely unknown. It is clear that what is necessary in such a case is research, not dogmatic and perfectly arbitrary claims, based on analogies to that small part of the experimental literature in which one happens to be interested.

The pointlessness of these claims becomes clear when we consider the well-known difficulties in determining to what extent inborn structure, maturation, and learning are responsble for the particular form of a skilled or complex performance.[31] To take just one example,[32] the gaping response of a nestling thrush is at first released by jarring of the nest, and, at a later stage, by a moving object of specific size, shape, and position relative to the nestling. At this later stage the response is directed towards the part of the stimulus object corresponding to the parent's head, and characterized by a complex configuration of stimuli that can be precisely described. Knowing just this, it would be possible to construct a speculative, learning-theoretic account of how this sequence of behavior patterns might have developed through a process of differential reinforcement, and it would no doubt be possible to train rats to do something similar. However, there appears to be good evidence that these responses to fairly complex "sign stimuli" are genetically determined and mature without learning. Clearly, the possibility cannot be discounted. Consider now the comparable case of a child imitating new words. At at early stage we may find rather gross correspondences. At a later stage, we find that repetition is of course far from exact (i.e. it is not mimicry, a fact which itself is interesting), but that it reproduces the highly complex configuration of sound features that constitute the phonological structure of the language in question. Again, we can propose a speculative account of how this result might have been obtained through elaborate arrangement of reinforcing contingencies. Here too, however, it is possible that ability to select

[31] Tinbergen (op. cit., Chapter VI) reviews some aspects of this problem, discussing the primary role of maturation in the development of many complex motor patterns (e.g. flying, swimming) in lower organisms, and the effect of an "innate disposition to learn" in certain specific ways and at certain specific times. Cf. also Schiller, *Instinctive behavior* 265–88, for a discussion of the role of maturing motor patterns in apparently insightful behavior in the chimpanzee.

Lenneberg (*Language, evolution, and purposive behavior*, unpublished) presents a very interesting discussion of the part that biological structure may play in the acquisition of language, and the dangers in neglecting this possibility.

[32] From among many cited by Tinbergen, op. cit. (this on page 85).

out of the complex auditory input those features that are phonologically relevant may develop largely independently of reinforcement, through genetically determined maturation. To the extent that this is true, an account of the development and causation of behavior that fails to consider the structure of the organism will provide no understanding of the real processes involved.

It is often argued that experience, rather than innate capacity to handle information in certain specific ways, must be the factor of overwhelming dominance in determining the specific character of language acquisition, since a child speaks the language of the group in which he lives. But this is a superficial argument. As long as we are speculating, we may consider the possibility that the brain has evolved to the point where, given an input of observed Chinese sentences, it produces (by an "induction" of apparently fantastic complexity and suddenness) the "rules" of Chinese grammar, and given an input of observed English sentences, it produces (by, perhaps, exactly the same process of induction) the rules of English grammar; or that given an observed application of a term to certain instances it automatically predicts the extension to a class of complexly related instances. If clearly recognized as such, this speculation is neither unreasonable nor fantastic; nor, for that matter, is it beyond the bounds of possible study. There is of course no known neural structure capable of performing this task in the specific ways that observation of the resulting behavior might lead us to postulate; but for that matter, the structures capable of accounting for even the simplest kinds of learning have similarly defied detection.[33]

Summarizing this brief discussion, it seems that there is neither empirical evidence nor any known argument to support any SPECIFIC claim about the relative importance of "feedback" from the environment and the "independent contribution of the organism" in the process of language acquisition.

6. We now turn to the system that Skinner develops specifically for the description of verbal behavior. Since this system is based on the notions "stimulus," "response," and "reinforcement," we can conclude from the preceding sections that it will be vague and arbitrary. For reasons noted in §1, however, I think it is important to see in detail how far from the mark any analysis phrased solely in these terms must be and how completely this system fails to account for the facts of verbal behavior.

Consider first the term "verbal behavior" itself. This is defined as "behavior

[33] Cf. Lashley, In search of the engram, *Symposium of the Society for Experimental Biology* 4.454–82 (1950). Sperry, On the neural basis of the conditioned response, *British journal of animal behaviour* 3.41–4 (1955), argues that to account for the experimental results of Lashley and others, and for other facts that he cites, it is necessary to assume that high-level cerebral activity of the type of insight, expectancy, etc. is involved even in simple conditioning. He states that 'we still lack today a satisfactory picture of the underlying neural mechanism' of the conditioned response.

reinforced through the mediation of other persons" (2). The definition is clearly much too broad. It would include as "verbal behavior," for example, a rat pressing the bar in a Skinner-box, a child brushing his teeth, a boxer retreating before an opponent, and a mechanic repairing an automobile. Exactly how much of ordinary linguistic behavior is "verbal" in this sense, however, is something of a question: perhaps, as I have pointed out above, a fairly small fraction of it, if any substantive meaning is assigned to the term "reinforced." This definition is subsequently refined by the additional provision that the mediating response of the reinforcing person (the "listener") must itself "have been conditioned *precisely in order to reinforce* the behavior of the speaker" (225, italics his). This still covers the examples given above, if we can assume that the "reinforcing" behavior of the psychologist, the parent, the opposing boxer, and the paying customer are the result of appropriate training, which is perhaps not unreasonable. A significant part of the fragment of linguistic behavior covered by the earlier definition will no doubt be excluded by the refinement, however. Suppose, for example, that while crossing the street I hear someone shout *Watch out for the car* and jump out of the way. It can hardly be proposed that my jumping (the mediating, reinforcing response in Skinner's usage) was conditioned (that is, I was trained to jump) precisely in order to reinforce the behavior of the speaker. Similarly for a wide class of cases. Skinner's assertion that with this refined definition "we narrow our subject to what is traditionally recognized as the verbal field" (225) appears to be grossly in error.

7. Verbal operants are classified by Skinner in terms of their "functional" relation to discriminated stimulus, reinforcement, and other verbal responses. A *mand* is defined as "a verbal operant in which the response is reinforced by a characteristic consequence and is therefore under the functional control of relevant conditions of deprivation or aversive stimulation" (35). This is meant to include questions, commands, etc. Each of the terms in this definition raises a host of problems. A mand such as *Pass the salt* is a class of responses. We cannot tell by observing the form of a response whether it belongs to this class (Skinner is very clear about this), but only by identifying the controlling variables. This is generally impossible. Deprivation is defined in the bar-pressing experiment in terms of length of time that the animal has not been fed or permitted to drink. In the present context, however, it is quite a mysterious notion. No attempt is made here to describe a method for determining "relevant conditions of deprivation" independently of the "controlled" response. It is of no help at all to be told (32) that it can be characterized in terms of the operations of the experimenter. If we define deprivation in terms of elapsed time, then at any moment a person is in countless states of deprivation.[34] It appears that we must decide that the relevant condition of

[34] Furthermore, the motivation of the speaker does not, except in the simplest cases,

deprivation was (say) salt-deprivation, on the basis of the fact that the speaker asked for salt (the reinforcing community which "sets up" the mand is in a similar predicament). In this case, the assertion that a mand is under the control of relevant deprivation is empty, and we are (contrary to Skinner's intention) identifying the response as a mand completely in terms of form. The word "relevant" in the definition above conceals some rather serious complications.

In the case of the mand *Pass the salt*, the word "deprivation" is not out of place, though it appears to be of little use for functional analysis. Suppose however that the speaker says *Give me the book*, *Take me for a ride*, or *Let me fix it*. What kinds of deprivation can be associated with these mands? How do we determine or measure the relevant deprivation? I think we must conclude in this case, as before, either that the notion "deprivation" is relevant at most to a minute fragment of verbal behavior, or else that the statement "X is under Y-deprivation" is just an odd paraphrase for "X wants Y," bearing a misleading and unjustifiable connotation of objectivity.

The notion "aversive control" is just as confused. This is intended to cover threats, beating, and the like (33). The manner in which aversive stimulation functions is simply described. If a speaker has had a history of appropriate reinforcement (e.g. if a certain response was followed by "cessation of the threat of such injury—of events which have previously been followed by such injury and which are therefore conditioned aversive stimuli") then he will tend to give the proper response when the threat which had previously been followed by the injury is presented. It would appear to follow from this description that a speaker will not respond properly to the mand *Your money or your life* (38) unless he has a past history of being killed. But even if the difficulties in describing the mechanism of aversive control are somehow removed by a more careful analysis, it will be of little use for identifying operants for reasons similar to those mentioned in the case of deprivation.

It seems, then, that in Skinner's terms there is in most cases no way to decide whether a given response is an instance of a particular mand. Hence it is meaningless, within the terms of his system, to speak of the *characteristic* consequences of a mand, as in the definition above. Furthermore, even if we extend the system so that mands can somehow be identified, we will have to face the obvious fact that most of us are not fortunate enough to have our requests, commands, advice, and so on characteristically reinforced (they may nevertheless exist in considerable "strength"). These responses could therefore not be considered mands by Skinner. In fact, Skinner sets up a

---

correspond in intensity to the duration of deprivation. An obvious counter-example is what Hebb has called the "salted-nut phenomenon" (*Organization of behavior* 199 [New York, 1949]). The difficulty is of course even more serious when we consider "deprivations" not related to physiological drives.

category of "magical mands" (48–9) to cover the case of "mands which cannot be accounted for by showing that they have ever had the effect specified or any similar effect upon similar occasions" (the word "ever" in this statement should be replaced by "characteristically"). In these pseudo mands, "the speaker simply describes the reinforcement appropriate to a given state of aversive stimulation." In other words, given the meaning that we have been led to assign to "reinforcement" and "deprivation," the speaker asks for what he wants. The remark that "a speaker appears to create new mands on the analogy of old ones" is also not very helpful.

Skinner's claim that his new descriptive system is superior to the traditional one "because its terms can be defined with respect to experimental operations" (45) is, we see once again, an illusion. The statement "X wants Y" is not clarified by pointing out a relation between rate of bar-pressing and hours of food-deprivation; replacing "X wants Y" by "X is deprived by Y" adds no new objectivity to the description of behavior. His further claim for the superiority of the new analysis of mands is that it provides an objective basis for the traditional classification into requests, commands, etc. (38–41). The traditional classification is in terms of the intention of the speaker. But intention, Skinner holds, can be reduced to contingencies of reinforcement, and, correspondingly, we can explain the traditional classification in terms of the reinforcing behavior of the listener. Thus a question is a mand which "specifies verbal action, and the behavior of the listener permits us to classify it as a request, a command, or a prayer" (39). It is a request if "the listener is independently motivated to reinforce the speaker"; a command if "the listener's behavior is . . . reinforced by reducing a threat"; a prayer if the mand "promotes reinforcement by generating an emotional disposition." The mand is advice if the listener is positively reinforced by the consequences of mediating the reinforcement of the speaker; it is a warning if "by carrying out the behavior specified by the speaker the listener escapes from aversive stimulation"; and so on. All this is obviously wrong if Skinner is using the words "request," "command," etc., in anything like the sense of the corresponding English words. The word "question" does not cover commands. *Please pass the salt* is a request (but not a question), whether or not the listener happens to be motivated to fulfill it; not everyone to whom a request is addressed is favorably disposed. A response does not cease to be a command if it is not followed; nor does a question become a command if the speaker answers it because of an implied or imagined threat. Not all advice is good advice, and a response does not cease to be advice if it is not followed. Similarly, a warning may be misguided; heeding it may cause aversive stimulation, and ignoring it might be positively reinforcing. In short, the entire classification is beside the point. A moment's thought is sufficient to demonstrate the impossibility of distinguishing between requests, commands, advice, etc., on the basis of the behavior or disposition of the particular listener. Nor can we do this on the basis of the typical behavior of all listeners. Some advice is never taken, is always bad, etc., and similarly with other kinds of mands. Skinner's evident satisfaction with this analysis of the traditional classification is extremely puzzling.

8. Mands are operants with no specified relation to a prior stimulus. A *tact*, on the other hand, is defined as "a verbal operant in which a response of given form is evoked (or at least strengthened) by a particular object or event or property of an object or event" (81). The examples quoted in the discussion of stimulus control (§3) are all tacts. The obscurity of the notion "stimulus control" makes the concept of the tact rather mystical. Since, however, the tact is "the most important of verbal operants," it is important to investigate the development of this concept in more detail.

We first ask why the verbal community "sets up" tacts in the child—that is, how the parent is reinforced by setting up the tact. The basic explanation for this behavior of the parent (85–6) is the reinforcement he obtains by the fact that his contact with the environment is extended; to use Skinner's example, the child may later be able to call him to the telephone. (It is difficult to see, then, how first children acquire tacts, since the parent does not have the appropriate history of reinforcement.) Reasoning in the same way, we may conclude that the parent induces the child to walk so that he can make some money delivering newspapers. Similarly, the parent sets up an "echoic repertoire" (e.g. a phonemic system) in the child because this makes it easier to teach him new vocabulary, and extending the child's vocabulary is ultimately useful to the parent. "In all these cases we explain the behavior of the reinforcing listener by pointing to an improvement in the possibility of controlling the speaker whom he reinforces" (56). Perhaps this provides the explanation for the behavior of the parent in inducing the child to walk: the parent is reinforced by the improvement in his control of the child when the child's mobility increases. Underlying these modes of explanation is a curious view that it is somehow more scientific to attribute to a parent a desire to control the child or enhance his own possibilities for action than a desire to see the child develop and extend his capacities. Needless to say, no evidence is offered to support this contention.

Consider now the problem of explaining the response of the listener to a tact. Suppose, for example, that B hears A say *fox* and reacts appropriately, looks around, runs away, aims his rifle, etc. How can we explain B's behavior? Skinner rightly rejects analyses of this offered by Watson and Bertrand Russell. His own equally inadequate analysis proceeds as follows (87–8). We assume (1) "that in the history of [B] the stimulus *fox* has been an occasion upon which looking around has been followed by seeing a fox" and (2) "that the listener has some current 'interest in seeing foxes'—that behavior which depends upon a seen fox for its execution is strong, and that the stimulus supplied by a fox is therefore reinforcing." B carries out the appropriate behavior, then, because "the heard stimulus *fox* is the occasion upon which turning and looking about is frequently followed by the reinforcement of seeing a fox"; i.e. his behavior is a discriminated operant. This explanation is unconvincing. B may never have seen a fox and may have no current interest in seeing one, and yet may react appropriately to the stimulus *fox*.[35] Since exactly the same behavior may take place when neither of the assumptions is fulfilled, some other mechanism must be operative here.

Skinner remarks several times that his analysis of the tact in terms of stimulus control is an improvement over the traditional formulations in terms of reference and meaning. This is simply not true. His analysis is fundamentally the same as the traditional one, though much less carefully phrased. In particular, it differs only by indiscriminate paraphrase of such notions as denotation (reference) and connotation (meaning), which have been kept clearly apart in traditional formulations, in terms of the vague concept "stimulus control." In one traditional formulation a descriptive term is said to denote a set of entities and to connote or designate a certain property or condition that an entity must possess or fulfil if the term is to apply to it.[36]

---

[35] Just as he may have the appropriate reaction, both emotional and behavioral, to such utterances as *The volcano is erupting* or *There's a homicidal maniac in the next room* without any previous pairing of the verbal and the physical stimulus. Skinner's discussion of Pavlovian conditioning in language (154) is similarly unconvincing.

[36] Mill, *A system of logic* (1843). Carnap gives a recent reformulation in Meaning and synonymy in natural languages, *Phil. studies* 6.33–47 (1955), defining the meaning (intension) of a predicate "Q" for a speaker X as "the general condition which an object y must fulfill in order for X to be willing to ascribe the predicate 'Q' to y." The connotation of an expression is often said to constitute its "cognitive meaning" as opposed to its "emotive meaning," which is, essentially, the emotional reaction to the expression.

Whether or not this is the best way to approach meaning, it is clear that denotation, cognitive meaning, and emotive meaning are quite different things. The differences are often obscured in empirical studies of meaning, with much consequent confusion. Thus Osgood has set himself the task of accounting for the fact that a stimulus comes to be a sign for another stimulus (a buzzer becomes a sign for food, a word for a thing, etc.). This is clearly (for linguistic signs) a problem of denotation. The method that he actually develops for quantifying and measuring meaning (cf. Osgood, Suci, Tannenbaum, *The measurement of meaning* [Urbana, 1957]) applies, however, only to emotive meaning. Suppose, for example, that A hates both Hitler and science intensely, and considers both highly potent and "active," while B, agreeing with A about Hitler, likes science very much, although he considers it rather ineffective and not too important. Then A may assign to "Hitler" and "science" the same position on the semantic differential, while B will assign "Hitler" the same position as A did, but "science" a totally different position. Yet A does not think that "Hitler" and "science" are synonymous or that they have the same reference, and A and B may agree precisely on the cognitive meaning of "science." Clearly it is the attitude toward the things (the emotive meaning of the words) that is

Thus the term *vertebrate* refers to (denotes, is true of) vertebrates and connotes the property "having a spine" or something of the sort. This connoted defining property is called the meaning of the term. Two terms may have the same reference but different meanings. Thus it is apparently true that the creatures with hearts are all and only the vertebrates. If so, then the term *creature with a heart* refers to vertebrates and designates the property "having a heart." This is presumably a different property (a different general condition) from having a spine; hence the terms *vertebrate* and *creature with a heart* are said to have different meanings. This analysis is not incorrect (for at least one sense of meaning), but its many limitations have frequently been pointed out.[37] The major problem is that there is no good way to decide whether two descriptive terms designate the same property.[38] As we have just seen, it is not sufficient that they refer to the same objects. *Vertebrate* and *creature with a spine* would be said to designate the same property (distinct from that designated by *creature with a heart*). If we ask why this is so, the only answer appears to be that the terms are synonymous. The notion "property" thus seems somehow language-bound, and appeal to "defining properties" sheds little light on questions of meaning and synonymy.

Skinner accepts the traditional account in toto, as can be seen from his definition of a tact as a response under control of a property (stimulus) of some physical object or event. We have found that the notion "control" has no real substance, and is perhaps best understood as a paraphrase of "denote" or "connote" or, ambiguously, both. The only consequence of adopting the new term "stimulus control" is that the important differences between reference and meaning are obscured. It provides no new objectivity. The stimulus controlling the response is determined by the response itself; there is no independent and objective method of identification (see §3 above). Consequently, when Skinner defines "synonymy" as the case in which "the same stimulus leads to quite different responses" (118), we can have no objection. The responses *chair* and *red* made alternatively to the same object are not synonymous, because the stimuli are called different. The responses *vertebrate* and *creature with a spine* would be considered synonymous because they are

---

being measured here. There is a gradual shift in Osgood's account from denotation to cognitive meaning to emotive meaning. The confusion is caused, no doubt, by the fact that the term "meaning" is used in all three senses (and others). [See Carroll's review of the book by Osgood, Suci, and Tannenbaum in this number of LANGUAGE.]

[37] Most clearly by Quine. See *From a logical point of view* (Cambridge, 1953), especially Chapters 2, 3, and 7.

[38] A method for characterizing synonymy in terms of reference is suggested by Goodman, On likeness of meaning, *Analysis* 10.1–7 (1949). Difficulties are discussed by Goodman, On some differences about meaning, ibid. 13.90–6 (1953). Carnap (op. cit.) presents a very similar idea (§6), but somewhat misleadingly phrased, since he does not bring out the fact that only extensional (referential) notions are being used.

controlled by the same property of the object under investigation; in more traditional and no less scientific terms, they evoke the same concept. Similarly, when metaphorical extension is explained as due to "the control exercised by properties of the stimulus which, though present at reinforcement, do not enter into the contingency respected by the verbal community" (92; traditionally, accidental properties), no objection can be raised which has not already been levelled against the traditional account. Just as we could "explain" the response *Mozart* to a piece of music in terms of subtle properties of the controlling stimuli, we can, with equal facility, explain the appearance of the response *sun* when no sun is present, as in *Juliet is [like] the sun.* "We do so by noting that Juliet and the sun have common properties, at least in their effect on the speaker" (93). Since any two objects have indefinitely many properties in common, we can be certain that we will never be at a loss to explain a response of the form *A is like B*, for arbitrary A and B. It is clear, however, that Skinner's recurrent claim that his formulation is simpler and more scientific than the traditional account has no basis in fact.

Tacts under the control of private stimuli (Bloomfield's "displaced speech") form a large and important class (130–46), including not only such responses as *familiar* and *beautiful*, but also verbal responses referring to past, potential, or future events or behavior. For example, the response *There was an elephant at the zoo* "must be understood as a response to current stimuli, including events within the speaker himself" (143).[39] If we now ask ourselves what proportion of the tacts in actual life are responses to (descriptions of) actual current outside stimulation, we can see just how large a role must be attributed to private stimuli. A minute amount of verbal behavior, outside the nursery, consists of such remarks as *This is red* and *There is a man.* The fact that "functional analysis" must make such a heavy appeal to obscure internal stimuli is again a measure of its actual advance over traditional formulations.

9. Responses under the control of prior verbal stimuli are considered under a different heading from the tact. An *echoic operant* is a response which

[39] In general, the examples discussed here are badly handled, and the success of the proposed analyses is overstated. In each case, it is easy to see that the proposed analysis, which usually has an air of objectivity, is not equivalent to the analyzed expression. To take just one example, the response *I am looking for my glasses* is certainly not equivalent to the proposed paraphrases: "When I have behaved in this way in the past, I have found my glasses and have then stopped behaving in this way," or "Circumstances have arisen in which I am inclined to emit any behavior which in the past has led to the discovery of my glasses; such behavior includes the behavior of looking in which I am now engaged." One may look for one's glasses for the first time; or one may emit the same behavior in looking for one's glasses as in looking for one's watch, in which case *I am looking for my glasses* and *I am looking for my watch* are equivalent, under the Skinnerian paraphrase. The difficult questions of purposiveness cannot be handled in this superficial manner.

"generates a sound pattern similar to that of the stimulus" (55). It covers only cases of immediate imitation.[40] No attempt is made to define the sense in which a child's echoic response is "similar" to the stimulus spoken in the father's bass voice; it seems, though there are no clear statements about this, that Skinner would not accept the account of the phonologist in this respect, but nothing else is offered. The development of an echoic repertoire is attributed completely to differential reinforcement. Since the speaker will do no more, according to Skinner, than what is demanded of him by the verbal community, the degree of accuracy insisted on by this community will determine the elements of the repertoire, whatever these may be (not necessarily phonemes). "In a verbal community which does not insist on a precise correspondence, an echoic repertoire may remain slack and will be less successfully applied to novel patterns." There is no discussion of such familiar phenomena as the accuracy with which a child will pick up a second language or a local dialect in the course of playing with other children, which seem sharply in conflict with these assertions. No anthropological evidence is cited to support the claim that an effective phonemic system does not develop (this is the substance of the quoted remark) in communities that do not insist on precise correspondence.

A verbal response to a written stimulus (reading) is called "textual behavior."

Other verbal responses to verbal stimuli are called "intraverbal operants." Paradigm instances are the response *four* to the stimulus *two plus two* or the response *Paris* to the stimulus *capital of France.* Simple conditioning may be

---

[40] Skinner takes great pains, however, to deny the existence in human beings (or parrots) of any innate faculty or tendency to imitate. His only argument is that no one would suggest an innate tendency to read, yet reading and echoic behavior have similar "dynamic properties." This similarity, however, simply indicates the grossness of his descriptive categories.

In the case of parrots, Skinner claims that they have no instinctive capacity to imitate, but only to be reinforced by successful imitation (59). Given Skinner's use of the word "reinforcement," it is difficult to perceive any distinction here, since exactly the same thing could be said of any other instinctive behavior. For example, where another scientist would say that a certain bird instinctively builds a nest in a certain way, we could say in Skinner's terminology (equivalently) that the bird is instinctively reinforced by building the nest in this way. One is therefore inclined to dismiss this claim as another ritual introduction of the word "reinforce." Though there may, under some suitable clarification, be some truth in it, it is difficult to see how many of the cases reported by competent observers can be handled if "reinforcement" is given some substantive meaning. Cf. Thorpe, op. cit. 353 f.; Lorenz, *King Solomon's ring* 85–8 (New York, 1952); even Mowrer, who tries to show how imitation might develop through secondary reinforcement, cites a case, op. cit. 694, which he apparently believes, but where this could hardly be true. In young children, it seems most implausible to explain imitation in terms of secondary reinforcement.

sufficient to account for the response *four* to *two plus two*,[41] but the notion of intraverbal response loses all meaning when we find it extended to cover most of the facts of history and many of the facts of science (72, 129); all word association and "flight of ideas" (73–6); all translations and paraphrase (77); reports of things seen, heard, or remembered (315); and, in general, large segments of scientific, mathematical, and literary discourse. Obviously the kind of explanation that might be proposed for a student's ability to respond with *Paris* to *capital of France*, after suitable practice, can hardly be seriously offered to account for his ability to make a judicious guess in answering the questions (to him new) *What is the seat of the French government?, . . . the source of the literary dialect?, . . . the chief target of the German blitzkrieg?*, etc., or his ability to prove a new theorem, translate a new passage, or paraphrase a remark for the first time or in a new way.

The process of "getting someone to see a point," to see something your way, or to understand a complex state of affairs (e.g. a difficult political situation or a mathematical proof) is, for Skinner, simply a matter of increasing the strength of the listener's already available behavior.[42] Since "the process is often exemplified by relatively intellectual scientific or philosophical discourse," Skinner considers it "all the more surprising that it may be reduced to echoic, textual, or intraverbal supplementation" (269). Again, it is only the vagueness and latitude with which the notions "strength" and "intraverbal response" are used that save this from absurdity. If we use these terms in their literal sense, it is clear that understanding a statement cannot be equated to shouting it frequently in a high-pitched voice (high response strength), and a clever and convincing argument cannot be accounted for on the basis of a history of pairings of verbal responses.[43]

---

41 Though even this possibility is limited. If we were to take these paradigm instances seriously, it should follow that a child who knows how to count from one to 100 could learn an arbitrary 10 × 10 matrix with these numbers as entries as readily as the multiplication table.

42 Similarly, "the universality of a literary work refers to the number of potential readers inclined to say the same thing" (275; i.e. the most "universal" work is a dictionary of clichés and greetings); a speaker is "stimulating" if he says what we are about to say ourselves (272); etc.

43 Similarly, consider Skinner's contention (362–5) that communication of knowledge or facts is just the process of making a new response available to the speaker. Here the analogy to animal experiments is particularly weak. When we train a rat to carry out some peculiar act, it makes sense to consider this a matter of adding a response to his repertoire. In the case of human communication, however, it is very difficult to attach any meaning to this terminology. If A imparts to B the information (new to B) that the railroads face collapse, in what sense can the response *The railroads face collapse* be said to be now, but not previously, available to B? Surely B could have said it before (not knowing whether it was true), and known that it was a sentence (as opposed to *Collapse face railroads the*). Nor is there any reason to assume that the response has

10. A final class of operants, called *autoclitics*, includes those that are involved in assertion, negation, quantification, qualification of responses, construction of sentences, and the "highly complex manipulations of verbal thinking." All these acts are to be explained "in terms of behavior which is evoked by or acts upon other behavior of the speaker" (313). Autoclitics are, then, responses to already given responses, or rather, as we find in reading through this section, they are responses to covert or incipient or potential verbal behavior. Among the autoclitics are listed such expressions as *I recall, I imagine, for example, assume, let X equal . . .*, the terms of negation, the *is* of predication and assertion, *all, some, if, then,* and, in general, all morphemes other than nouns, verbs, and adjectives, as well as grammatical processes of ordering and arrangement. Hardly a remark in this section can be accepted without serious qualification. To take just one example consider Skinner's account of the autoclitic *all* in *All swans are white* (329). Obviously we cannot assume that this is a tact to all swans as stimulus. It is suggested, therefore, that we take *all* to be an autoclitic modifying the whole sentence *Swans are white. All* can then be taken as equivalent to *always*, or *always it is possible to say*. Notice, however, that the modified sentence *Swans are white* is just as general as *All swans are white*. Furthermore, the proposed translation of *all* is incorrect if taken literally. It is just as possible to say *Swans are green* as to say *Swans are white*. It is not always possible to say either (e.g. while you are saying something else or sleeping). Probably what Skinner means is that the sentence can be paraphrased "*X is white* is true, for each swan X." But this paraphrase cannot be given within his system, which has no place for *true*.

Skinner's account of grammar and syntax as autoclitic processes (Chapter 13) differs from a familiar traditional account mainly in the use of the pseudoscientific terms "control" or "evoke" in place of the traditional "refer." Thus in *The boy runs*, the final *s* of *runs* is a tact under control of such "subtle properties of a situation" as "the nature of running as an *activity* rather than an object or property of an object."[44] (Presumably, then, in *The attempt fails, The difficulty remains, His anxiety increases*, etc., we must also say that the *s* indicates that the object described as the attempt is carrying out the activity of failing, etc.) In *the boy's gun*, however, the *s* denotes possession (as, presumably, in *the boy's arrival, . . . story, . . . age*, etc.) and is under the control of this "rational aspect of the situation" (336). The "relational autoclitic of order" (whatever it may mean to call the order of a

increased in strength, whatever this means exactly (e.g. B may have no interest in the fact, or he may want it suppressed). It is not clear how we can characterize this notion of "making a response available" without reducing Skinner's account of "imparting knowledge" to a triviality.

[44] 332. On the next page, however, the *s* in the same example indicates that "the object described as *the boy* possesses the property of running." The difficulty of even maintaining consistency with a conceptual scheme like this is easy to appreciate.

set of responses a response to them) in *The boy runs the store* is under the control of an "extremely complex stimulus situation," namely, that the boy is running the store (335). *And* in *the hat and the shoe* is under the control of the property "pair." *Through* in *the dog went through the hedge* is under the control of the "relation between the going dog and the hedge" (342). In general, nouns are evoked by objects, verbs by actions, and so on.

Skinner considers a sentence to be a set of key responses (nouns, verbs, adjectives) on a skeletal frame (346). If we are concerned with the fact that Sam rented a leaky boat, the raw responses to the situation are *rent, boat, leak,* and *Sam.* Autoclitics (including order) which qualify these responses, express relations between them, and the like, are then added by a process called "composition" and the result is a grammatical sentence, one of many alternatives among which selection is rather arbitrary. The idea that sentences consist of lexical items placed in a grammatical frame is of course a traditional one, within both philosophy and linguistics. Skinner adds to it only the very implausible speculation that in the internal process of composition, the nouns, verbs, and adjectives are chosen first and then are arranged, qualified, etc., by autoclitic responses to these internal activities.[45]

This view of sentence structure, whether phrased in terms of autoclitics, syncategorematic expressions, or grammatical and lexical morphemes, is inadequate. *Sheep provide wool* has no (physical) frame at all, but no other arrangement of these words is an English sentence. The sequences *furiously sleep ideas green colorless* and *friendly young dogs seem harmless* have the same frames, but only one is a sentence of English (similarly, only one of the sequences formed by reading these from back to front). *Struggling artists can be a nuisance* has the same frame as *marking papers can be a nuisance,* but is quite different in sentence structure, as can be seen by replacing *can be* by *is* or *are* in both cases. There are many other similar and equally simple examples. It is evident that more is involved in sentence structure than insertion of lexical items in grammatical frames; no approach to language that fails to take these deeper processes into account can possibly achieve much success in accounting for actual linguistic behavior.

11. The preceding discussion covers all the major notions that Skinner introduces in his descriptive system. My purpose in discussing the concepts one by one was to show that in each case, if we take his terms in their literal meaning, the description covers almost no aspect of verbal behavior, and if

---

[45] One might just as well argue that exactly the opposite is true. The study of hesitation pauses has shown that these tend to occur before the large categories—noun, verb, adjective; this finding is usually described by the statement that the pauses occur where there is maximum uncertainty or information. Insofar as hesitation indicates on-going composition (if it does at all), it would appear that the "key responses" are chosen only after the "grammatical frame." Cf. C. E. Osgood, unpublished paper; Goldman-Eisler, Speech analysis and mental processes, *Language and speech* 1.67 (1958).

we take them metaphorically, the description offers no improvement over various traditional formulations. The terms borrowed from experimental psychology simply lose their objective meaning with this extension, and take over the full vagueness of ordinary language. Since Skinner limits himself to such a small set of terms for paraphrase, many important distinctions are obscured. I think that this analysis supports the view expressed in §1 above, that elimination of the independent contribution of the speaker and learner (a result which Skinner considers of great importance, cf. 311–2) can be achieved only at the cost of eliminating all significance from the descriptive system, which then operates at a level so gross and crude that no answers are suggested to the most elementary questions.[46] The questions to which Skinner had addressed his speculations are hopelessly premature. It is futile to inquire into the causation of verbal behavior until much more is known about the specific character of this behavior; and there is little point in speculating about the process of acquisition without much better understanding of what is acquired.

Anyone who seriously approaches the study of linguistic behavior, whether linguist, psychologist, or philosopher, must quickly become aware of the enormous difficulty of stating a problem which will define the area of his investigations, and which will not be either completely trivial or hopelessly beyond the range of present-day understanding and technique. In selecting functional analysis as his problem, Skinner has set himself a task of the latter type. In an extremely interesting and insightful paper,[47] K. S. Lashley has implicitly delimited a class of problems which can be approached in a fruitful

---

[46] E.g. what are in fact the actual units of verbal behavior? Under what conditions will a physical event capture the attention (be a stimulus) or be a reinforcer? How do we decide what stimuli are in "control" in a specific case? When are stimuli "similar"? And so on. (It is not interesting to be told e.g. that we say *Stop* to an automobile or billiard ball because they are sufficiently similar to reinforcing people [46].)

The use of unanalyzed notions like "similar" and "generalization" is particularly disturbing, since it indicates an apparent lack of interest in every significant aspect of the learning or the use of language in new situations. No one has ever doubted that in some sense, language is learned by generalization, or that novel utterances and situations are in some way similar to familiar ones. The only matter of serious interest is the specific "similarity." Skinner has, apparently, no interest in this. Keller and Schoenfeld (op. cit.) proceed to incorporate these notions (which they identify) into their Skinnerian "modern objective psychology" by defining two stimuli to be similar when "we make the same sort of *response* to them" (124; but when are responses of the "same sort"?). They do not seem to notice that this definition converts their "principle of generalization" (116), under any reasonable interpretation of this, into a tautology. It is obvious that such a definition will not be of much help in the study of language learning or construction of new responses in appropriate situations.

[47] The problem of serial order in behavior, in *Jeffress* (ed.), *Hixon symposium on cerebral mechanisms in behavior* (New York, 1951).

way by the linguist and psychologist, and which are clearly preliminary to those with which Skinner is concerned. Lashley recognizes, as anyone must who seriously considers the data, that the composition and production of an utterance is not simply a matter of stringing together a sequence of responses under the control of outside stimulation and intraverbal association, and that the syntactic organization of an utterance is not something directly represented in any simple way in the physical structure of the utterance itself. A variety of observations lead him to conclude that syntactic structure is "a generalized pattern imposed on the specific acts as they occur," and that "a consideration of the structure of the sentence and other motor sequences will show . . . that there are, behind the overtly expressed sequences, a multiplicity of integrative processes which can only be inferred from the final results of their activity." He also comments on the great difficulty of determining the "selective mechanisms" used in the actual construction of a particular utterance.

Although present-day linguistics cannot provide a precise account of these integrative processes, imposed patterns, and selective mechanisms, it can at least set itself the problem of characterizing these completely. It is reasonable to regard the grammar of a language L ideally as a mechanism that provides an enumeration of the sentences of L in something like the way in which a deductive theory gives an enumeration of a set of theorems. ("Grammar," in this sense of the word, includes phonology.) Furthermore, the theory of language can be regarded as a study of the formal properties of such grammars, and, with a precise enough formulation, this general theory can provide a uniform method for determining, from the process of generation of a given sentence, a structural description which can give a good deal of insight into how this sentence is used and understood. In short, it should be possible to derive from a properly formulated grammar a statement of the integrative processes and generalized patterns imposed on the specific acts that constitute an utterance. The rules of a grammar of the appropriate form can be subdivided into the two types, optional and obligatory; only the latter must be applied in generating an utterance. The optional rules of the grammar can be viewed, then, as the selective mechanisms involved in the production of a particular utterance. The problem of specifying these integrative processes and selective mechanisms is nontrivial and not beyond the range of possible investigation. The results of such a study might, as Lashley suggests, be of independent interest for psychology and neurology (and conversely). Although such a study, even if successful, would by no means answer the major problems involved in the investigation of meaning and the causation of behavior, it surely will not be unrelated to these. It is at least possible, furthermore, that such notions as "semantic generalization," to which such heavy appeal is made in all approaches to language in use, conceal complexities and specific structure of inference not far different from those that can be studied and exhibited in the case of syntax, and that consequently the general character of the results of syntactic investigations may be a corrective to oversimplified approaches to the theory of meaning.

The behavior of the speaker, listener, and learner of language constitutes, of course, the actual data for any study of language. The construction of a grammar which enumerates sentences in such a way that a meaningful structural description can be determined for each sentence does not in itself provide an account of this actual behavior. It merely characterizes abstractly the ability of one who has mastered the language to distinguish sentences from nonsentences, to understand new sentences (in part), to note certain ambiguities, etc. These are very remarkable abilities. We constantly read and hear new sequences of words, recognize them as sentences, and understand them. It is easy to show that the new events that we accept and understand as sentences are not related to those with which we are familiar by any simple notion of formal (or semantic or statistical) similarity or identity of grammatical frame. Talk of generalization in this case is entirely pointless and empty. It appears that we recognize a new item as a sentence not because it matches some familiar item in any simple way, but because it is generated by the grammar that each individual has somehow and in some form internalized. And we understand a new sentence, in part, because we are somehow capable of determining the process by which this sentence is derived in this grammar.

Suppose that we manage to construct grammars having the properties outlined above. We can then attempt to describe and study the achievement of the speaker, listener, and learner. The speaker and the listener, we must assume, have already acquired the capacities characterized abstractly by the grammar. The speaker's task is to select a particular compatible set of optional rules. If we know, from grammatical study, what choices are available to him and what conditions of compatibility the choices must meet, we can proceed meaningfully to investigate the factors that lead him to make one or another choice. The listener (or reader) must determine, from an exhibited utterance, what optional rules were chosen in the construction of the utterance. It must be admitted that the ability of a human being to do this far surpasses our present understanding. The child who learns a language has in some sense constructed the grammar for himself on the basis of his observation of sentences and nonsentences (i.e. corrections by the verbal community). Study of the actual observed ability of a speaker to distinguish sentences from nonsentences, detect ambiguities, etc., apparently forces us to the conclusion that this grammar is of an extremely complex and abstract character, and that the young child has succeeded in carrying out what from the formal point of view, at least, seems to be a remarkable type of theory construction. Furthermore, this task is accomplished in an astonishingly short time, to a large extent independently of intelligence, and in a comparable way by all children. Any theory of learning must cope with these facts.

It is not easy to accept the view that a child is capable of constructing an extremely complex mechanism for generating a set of sentences, some of which he has heard, or that an adult can instantaneously determine whether (and if so, how) a particular item is generated by this mechanism, which has many of the properties of an abstract deductive theory. Yet this appears to be a fair description of the performance of the speaker, listener, and learner. If this is correct, we can predict that a direct attempt to account for the actual behavior of speaker, listener, and learner, not based on a prior understanding of the structure of grammars, will achieve very limited success. The grammar must be regarded as a component in the behavior of the speaker and listener which can only be inferred, as Lashley has put it, from the resulting physical acts. The fact that all normal children acquire essentially comparable grammars of great complexity with remarkable rapidity suggests that human beings are somehow specially designed to do this, with data-handling or "hypothesis-formulating" ability of unknown character and complexity.[48] The study of linguistic structure may ultimately lead to some significant insights into this matter. At the moment the question cannot be seriously posed, but in principle it may be possible to study the problem of determining what the built-in structure of an information-processing (hypothesis-forming) system must be to enable it to arrive at the grammar of a language from the available data in the available time. At any rate, just as the attempt to eliminate the contribution of the speaker leads to a "mentalistic" descriptive system that succeeds only in blurring important traditional distinctions, a refusal to study the

[48] There is nothing essentially mysterious about this. Complex innate behavior patterns and innate "tendencies to learn in specific ways" have been carefully studied in lower organisms. Many psychologists have been inclined to believe that such biological structure will not have an important effect on acquisition of complex behavior in higher organisms, but I have not been able to find any serious justification for this attitude. Some recent studies have stressed the necessity for carefully analyzing the strategies available to the organism, regarded as a complex "information-processing system" (cf. Bruner, Goodnow, and Austin, *A study of thinking* [New York, 1956]; Newell, Shaw, and Simon, Elements of a theory of human problem solving, *Psych. rev.* 65.151–66 [1958]), if anything significant is to be said about the character of human learning. These may be largely innate, or developed by early learning processes about which very little is yet known. (But see Harlow, The formation of learning sets, *Psych. rev.* 56.51–65 (1949), and many later papers, where striking shifts in the character of learning are shown as a result of early training; also Hebb, *Organization of behavior* 109 ff.) They are undoubtedly quite complex. Cf. Lenneberg, op. cit., and Lees, review of Chomsky's *Syntactic structures* in *Lg.* 33.406 f. (1957), for discussion of the topics mentioned in this section.

contribution of the child to language learning permits only a superficial account of language acquisition, with a vast and unanalyzed contribution attributed to a step called "generalization" which in fact includes just about everything of interest in this process. If the study of language is limited in these ways, it seems inevitable that major aspects of verbal behavior will remain a mystery.

58. FUNCTIONAL ANALYSIS AND SELF-CONTROL

Gerald H. Paske

Psychology is relevant to, and important for, educational theory. This is beyond dispute, but the precise manner in which this relevancy is to be manifested is a problem which transcends psychology itself. To illustrate this point I shall consider one of the contentions of a psychologist who has not hesitated to apply his discoveries to the educational enterprise. I shall not question the factual data upon which he bases his educational suggestions, but I shall show that he has seriously misconstrued the logical import of his data; i.e., I shall show that he has drawn conclusions which ostensively rely upon his data but which, in fact, have no logical connection to this data whatsoever.

Lest the reader feel that I am meddling in affairs of which I have no understanding, for I am no psychologist, I hasten to assure him that the error in question is a philosophical one. Just what constitutes a philosophical error is in itself subject matter for at least an extended essay which I have no intention of supplying here. I shall only state that the error that I am here considering, and which I call philosophical, is a result of a misunderstanding of the relationship between facts and the statement of those facts. Perhaps the best way to clarify this point is to present the error. I shall first state what I conceive the error to be, and I shall then show that the error is actually committed.

In his *Science and Human Behavior* B. F. Skinner offers a brief discussion of self-control.[1] He bases his claims upon his method of psychological investigation which he calls "functional analysis." Functional analysis is the procedure of manipulating certain observable factors in an organism's environment and then determining the observable effect of these manipulations. Since all observable factors except one are kept constant, and since all the investigator is concerned with are observable factors, this procedure is a legitimate example of a controlled experiment. This is not to say that the notion of functional analysis presents no philosophic problems, for it does, but these problems are not relevant to this paper.

What I *am* concerned about is the discussion of self-control which Skinner offers. The importance of a concept of self-control can hardly be underestimated, especially if the concept is to be applied in the areas of education and morals. Skinner does not hesitate to make such an application; and I shall show that his discussion of self-control, which he "derives" from his data, is completely inadequate when so applied. Skinner's definition of self-control is legitimate in so far as it is a technical definition, that is, in so far as the term "self-control" is restricted to the precise sense that can be derived from a functional analysis.

However, in so far as the technical sense deviates from the ordinary sense of "self-control," the use of the term is apt to be misleading. Furthermore, if it is maintained, as Skinner maintains, that the technical sense does adequately reflect the ordinary sense of the term, the probability of being misled becomes a certainty. I shall show that Skinner has not adequately analyzed "self-control," and since this notion permeates his educational and moral pronouncements, this demonstration constitutes a serious, if not fatal, objection to both his educational and moral theories.

I wish to make clear that in arguing against Skinner I am *not* arguing that the ordinary *understanding* of self-control, (if there is such a thing) as distinct from the ordinary application of the term "self-control," is correct. I am merely claiming that the usual application of "self-control" has a corresponding distinction in fact which is extremely important to notice. My point against Skinner, then, is that on his analysis one cannot draw some distinctions which are absolutely vital within educational and moral theory.

I shall first offer a rather long quotation which exemplifies Skinner's position on self-control, and I shall then offer an explication and criticism of that position.

> The individual often comes to control part of his own behavior when a response has conflicting consequences—when it leads to both positive and negative reinforcement. Drinking alcoholic beverages, for example,

[1] Skinner, B. F., *Science and Human Behavior*, The Macmillan Co., New York, 1953, pp. 230–231.

is often followed by a condition of unusual confidence in which one is more successful socially and in which one forgets responsibilities, anxieties, and other troubles. Since this is positively reinforcing, it increases the likelihood that drinking will take place on future occasions. But there are other consequences—the physical illness of the "hang-over" and the possibly disastrous effects of over-confident or irresponsible behavior—which are negatively reinforcing and, when contingent upon behavior, represent a form of punishment. If punishment were simply the reverse of reinforcement, the two might combine to produce an intermediate tendency to drink, but we have seen that this is not the case. When a similar occasion arises, the same or an increased tendency to drink will prevail; but the occasion as well as the early stages of drinking will generate conditioned aversive stimuli and emotional responses to them which we speak of as shame or guilt. The emotional responses may have some deterrent effect in weakening behavior—as by "spoiling the mood." A more important effect, however, is that any behavior which weakens the behavior of drinking is automatically reinforced by the resulting reduction in aversive stimulation. We have discussed the behavior of simply "doing something else," which is reinforced because it displaces punishable behavior, but there are other possibilities. The organism may make the punished response less probable by altering the variables of which it is a function. Any behavior which succeeds in doing this will automatically be reinforced. We call such behavior self-control.

The positive and negative consequences generate two responses which are related to each other in a special way: one response, the *controlling response*, affects variables in such a way as to change the probability of the other, the *controlled response*. The controlling response may manipulate any of the variables of which the controlled response is a function; hence there are a good many different forms of self-control."[2]

Apparently the second of the above two paragraphs is meant to be a somewhat general summary of the example discussed in the first. The second paragraph, however, is patently inadequate, while the first is at least not obviously so. I shall first show that the second paragraph is inadequate, and I shall then show that the *prima facie* plausibility of the first is due to a subtle interplay between the technical and non-technical terms found in this paragraph. Since the plausibility of this paragraph relies upon the non-technical terms, and since these terms are totally inadmissible within Skinnerian psy-

[2] *Ibid.*

chology, a careful analysis of this paragraph completely removes its plausibility.

The argument of Paragraph Two is somewhat generalized, so let us apply it to the following hypothetical situation. Let α be an organism faced with the possibility of doing either A or B, where A and B are mutually exclusive and jointly exhaustive, so that α cannot do both A and B, but must do either A or B. (*e.g.* α must either drink or not drink, he cannot do both, but he must do one.) Suppose further that A has negative consequences and B has positive consequences.

Now suppose that α exhibits behavior B, which has positive consequences. Then B is a controlling response, for doing B eliminates the possibility of doing A and *a fortiori* controls the variables of which A is a function. This is then a case of self-control, and if we instantiate to the drinking situation, α exhibited self-control by not taking the drink, which is a reasonable enough result.

Suppose, however, that α exhibits behavior A, which has negative consequences. In this case A is the controlling behavior and B the controlled. Since doing A is again manipulating the variables of which B is a function, we have another case of self control. But when we now instantiate the drinking example, we find that this time α exhibited self-control by *taking* the drink. This leaves α in the rather strange situation of only being able to exhibit self-control, a situation which if actual would be admirable, but which is not in fact the case.

My argument obviously hinges upon an interpretation of "negative consequences" such that the exhibited behavior of α can have negative consequences. Since Skinner has not defined "negative consequences," I take him to be using the term in an ordinary manner; and therefore I feel that this interpretation is justifiable. However, it is just this interpretation that is covertly rejected in the first paragraph, as I shall show. Before directly discussing this paragraph it is necessary, however, to make one general remark, and to also explicate some of the terms found within it.

As we shall see, the concept of reinforcement involves the notion of a change in the frequency of the performance of a certain type of behavior. The first paragraph, however, describes a situation in which self-control is exhibited in *one particular* act. Since the notion of change of frequency is not applicable to single events, it is difficult to see how Skinner's conception of reinforcement, and thus how his notion of self-control, can be applied here at all. This may constitute a real difficulty, but I think that we can overlook this objection and to some extent we can even circumvent it by restricting our view to one possible occurrence of an act and counting its occurrence as an increase in frequency and its nonoccurrence as a decrease. I am not entirely satisfied with this, but I see no other way of being able to apply Skinner's notion of self-control to specific cases; and I wish to emphasize that if we cannot apply his notion to specific cases, that alone constitutes a very serious objection.

I now wish to explicate some of the terms found in the first paragraph.

REINFORCEMENT

> The only way to tell whether or not a given event is reinforcing to a given organism under given conditions is to make a direct test. We observe the frequency of a selected response, then make an event contingent upon it and observe any change in frequency. If there is a change, we classify the event as reinforcing to the organism under the existing conditions. There is nothing circular about classifying events in terms of their effects; the criterion is both empirical and objective. It would be circular, however, if we then went on to assert that a given event strengthens an operant *because* it is reinforcing.[3]

It is clear from the above, and Skinner goes on to admit, that we can only guess, albeit more or less intelligently, that an event *will be* a reinforcer, whereas we can know that that type of event *has been* a reinforcer in past circumstances which seem relevantly similar to the present situation. What Skinner does not discuss is what we are to say when a particular instance of a type of event which has been reinforcing is not now reinforcing. Are we to say then that that type of event is not really reinforcing, or that the present situation is not really relevantly similar, or what? It is obvious that what we say will make an enormous difference in the value of the concept of reinforcement. I shall not speculate as to what Skinner would say, but I shall examine what he apparently says in the first paragraph.

POSITIVE AND NEGATIVE REINFORCEMENT

> We first define a positive reinforcer as any stimulus the *presentation* of which strengthens the behavior upon which it is made contingent. We define a negative reinforcer (an aversive stimulus) as any stimulus the *withdrawal* of which strengthens behavior.[4]

If we remember that the strength of a type of behavior is merely the frequency with which the behavior occurs, the above is self-explanatory.

PUNISHMENT

Skinner offers a technical definition of punishment which is itself somewhat misleading, and which becomes doubly so since it is not clear as to whether

---

[3] *Ibid.*, pp. 72–73.
[4] *Ibid.*, p. 185.

he is using "punishment" in a technical or non-technical sense in the first paragraph. Our ordinary notion of punishment is extremely complex, and I cannot fully treat it here; however, I shall indicate by reference to a simple paradigm example, coupled with some general remarks, that Skinner's technical definition departs from ordinary usage.

We have all undergone secondary education and I assume that we are all familiar with the detention room or with the practice of keeping one after school. It is quite clear that if one is *kept* after school, as distinct from *being allowed* to stay after, that one is being punished—at least it makes perfectly good sense to say so. This sense of punishment I shall hereafter refer to as o-punishment.

The above example of o-punishment involves at least the following:

(1) The behavior which is punished is considered an offense.
(2) The penalty is unpleasant to the person punished.
(3) The punisher has the authority to inflict the punishment.
and (4) The punisher has the intention of at least deterring the punished person from repeating his acts.

An attempt to o-punish can go wrong in a number of ways, for our purposes the most important of which are (1) the penalty is not really unpleasant and (2) the punished person is not deterred. The first possibility is sometimes extremely difficult to detect, but it is clear that sometimes a punishment fails to deter and nevertheless is still unpleasant to the punished person. In such cases we say that the failure is due to such things as resentment and rebellion. I now wish to consider Skinner's technical definition of "punishment."

> In solving the problem of punishment we simply ask: What is the effect of *withdrawing* a *positive* reinforcer or *presenting* a *negative?* . . . Insofar as we are able to give a scientific definition of a lay term, these two possibilities appear to constitute the field of punishment.[5]

Punishment, then, according to Skinner, is the presenting of a negative reinforcer or the withdrawing of a positive one. I shall hereafter call this "t-punishment," and I shall now show that t-punishment does not correspond to o-punishment.

Let us consider a case of o-punishment, e.g., keeping Jimmy after school because he talked out of turn in school. It is quite clear that in giving Jimmy detention time we may have o-punished him. It is not at all clear, however, as to what type of reinforcer we have introduced, for we can know this only after we have observed Jimmy's subsequent behavior. If he talks out of turn less than previously, we have introduced a negative reinforcer, and we have both

[5] *Ibid.*

o-punished and t-punished him. However, if, as is not unheard of, he now talks out of turn more frequently, we have presented him with a positive reinforcer; and thus, while we have o-punished him, we have not t-punished him.

As a matter of fact, although we frequently punish people with the hope of altering their behavior in a somewhat specifiable manner, our hopes are often in vain. While Skinner claims that as far as it is possible to do so he is giving a scientific definition of a lay term, what he has actually done is to present a definition of "punishment" under which punishment is infallible, that is, the punishment must result in a decrease in the frequency of the punished behavior or else we have not punished at all. This infallibility, however, is merely verbal; for if, when we do not succeed, we do not t-punish, what *is* it that we do? We o-punish, of course.

I suspect that this point has escaped Skinner because he, as the casual reader might, tends to equate negative reinforcers with unpleasant factors. In the drinking example the negative reinforcers, according to Skinner, were the "hangover" and the possible disastrous effects of irresponsible behavior. But as Skinner elsewhere recognizes,[6] these factors may very well be positively reinforcing, just as detention was positively reinforcing for Jimmy.

Another result of Skinner's definition of "punishment" is that there is no difficulty in extending the concept to inanimate objects. Whether or not a specific example of behavior is t-punished depends solely upon the consequences, and thus it is irrelevant whether the "punishment" is administered by a person or by a thing. Although we normally extend the concept of punishment to inanimate objects—a "hang-over" is, in a sense, a punishment—this extension requires a certain amount of hedging; and if pressed we might admit that such cases aren't really cases of punishment, or, at least, aren't *just* like cases of human punishment. But for Skinner they are just alike.

I believe that I have sufficiently explicated the terms of the first paragraph and I now wish to consider this paragraph in respect to these explications.

Skinner correctly states that the concept of self-control is relevant to situations in which a possible response has conflicting consequences, but when he adds that "conflicting consequences" means that the response *leads* to both positive and negative reinforcement, he is making a double error.

First, in using the term "leads," he is misleading the reader in two respects. "Leads" seems to imply more than a mere functional relation; it is not too difficult to slip from "drinking *leads* to certain consequences" to "drinking *causes* certain consequences." This, in turn, when combined with the notion that negative reinforcers are unpleasant, leads one to accept the claim that there is a negative reinforcer in this case, for there is, *ex hypothesi*, a hangover. But this is an error, and Skinner's claim that there are both positive and

6 *Ibid.*, pp. 81–82.

negative reinforcers present is unwarranted; for we *cannot* know what type of reinforcers are present in any *particular* case until *after* we have observed subsequent behavior.

The use of "leads" is not crucial to Skinner's argument, and I only point it out as one of many examples of his utilizing terms whose normal connotations lend psychological force to his argument, but whose connotations are at variance with his scientific terminology. Other examples of this are his use of such terms as, "confidence," "irresponsible behavior," "emotional responses," "shame," "guilt," "spoiling the mood," "succeeds," and "may make."

Skinners second error is that he fails to notice that when we observe behavior which is subsequent to a conflict situation, we run into a very serious problem. The problem is that since there are a number of factors which are varied it is impossible to determine, from functional analysis alone, which factors, or which combination of factors, were reinforcing. Suppose, for example, that a person did drink, and suppose that this resulted in the following consequences: (1) a hang-over, (2) a successful social occasion, and (3) a forgetting of troubles and anxieties; and suppose further, that the frequency of drinking is subsequently seen to increase. Skinner, it seems, would want to say that the hang-over was a negative reinforcer while the other two consequences were positively reinforcing. Such a claim, it is clear, is unjustified.

Even if it had been shown by suitable previous experiments that hang-overs were (usually) negatively reinforcing, such results would not be applicable, *in advance*, to this case. The least serious reason why this is so, is that the mere fact that something had been a negative reinforcer is no guarantee, and in fact cannot be a guarantee, that it will continue so to operate. The force of this objection is mitigated by the fact that we can at least make an intelligent guess that it will continue to do so; but, since Skinner frequently claims that his views are rigorously scientific, this objection is somewhat relevant.

A more serious objection is that in the stated case there was only *one* manipulated variable, and that is the complex variable (1 and 2 and 3). Furthermore, this variable, *ex hypothesi* was *positively* reinforcing. To draw the conclusion that one of the factors of this complex variable actually operated as a negative reinforcer requires the assumption that *a component of a complex variable functions in the same manner within that complex as it does by itself.*

This assumption is false and, therefore, Skinner's claim, that a conflict situation is one in which a possible response has both positive and negative reinforcement as a consequence, is demonstrably inadequate. The plausibility of this claim, of course, resulted from the equating of negative reinforcers with unpleasant consequences; for the situation under consideration, i.e. the drinking conflict, does have both pleasant and unpleasant consequences. The fact that Skinner, on his own terms at least, is unable even to state this can only reflect upon the adequacy of functional analysis as a complete account of human behavior.

Let me pursue this just a little further. Skinner says that *since* social success, etc., is positively reinforcing and *since* hang-overs are negatively reinforcing, there is a conflict. What he should have said was *if* social success is positively reinforcing and *if, at the same time*, the hang-over is negatively reinforcing, then there is a conflict. Since this can never be determined by functional analysis alone, it follows that functional analysis is not adequate for the description of a conflict situation.

Although Skinner's analysis of situations of conflict is inadequate, it does not necessarily follow that his notion of self-control is also inadequate, for mistaken reasons do not necessarily yield wrong answers. I shall now show, however, that his analysis of self-control is also inadequate.

In the first paragraph Skinner states:

> When a similar occasion arises, the same or an increased tendency to drink will prevail; but the occasion as well as the early stages of drinking will generate conditioned aversive stimuli and emotional responses to them which we speak of as shame or guilt.

I have a little difficulty as to what is meant by "a similar occasion," but I presume that Skinner means an occasion in which it is possible to drink. Since he claims that the same or an increased tendency to drink will prevail, he apparently is assuming that the total consequence of the last drinking occasion was positively reinforcing or at least was not negatively reinforcing. What is not clear is what is meant by the claim that this occasion will *generate* conditioned aversive stimuli.

In the context of the first paragraph it seems to me that the claim is plausible if we interpret it to mean that a person may feel guilty about being in a situation where he can drink, e.g., he may feel guilty about entering a bar, and he may also feel ashamed of taking a drink. He may know that he should not spend the money, or he may know that his first drink will not be his last.

Such an interpretation, however, is a flagrant violation of Skinnerian psychology, for *shame* and *guilt* are not observable. The only "emotional" responses to which Skinner can refer are such things as blushing, or down-cast eyes, or furtive glances over one's shoulder, etc. But if these are responses, to what are they responses?

According to Skinner, they are responses to conditioned aversive stimuli which are generated in the early stages of drinking. What then is a conditioned aversive stimulus? Conditioned aversive stimuli are to be distinguished from non-conditioned or "natural" stimuli. What this amounts to is the following: If something—A—acts as a negative reinforcer, and if A is always accompanied by something else—B—, where B has not previously been observed to act as a negative reinforcer, then, if B comes to act as a negative reinforcer, B has become a *conditioned* negative reinforcer.[7]

It is quite evident that the element of conditioning is irrelevant to the present problem, unless by "generated" Skinner means that some present stimulus, which is not now a negative reinforcer, will become one. If this is what he means, then he is saying that some present stimulus will become a negative reinforcer for later situations; but such a claim is entirely irrelevant to the present situation.

On the other hand, if Skinner merely means that the early stages of drinking will *present* negative reinforcers, such a claim holds only if these new stimuli actually have the result of reducing the frequency of drinking. If this is what he is claiming, he is claiming that the early stages of drinking *will* have the result of decreasing the amount of drinking. I hardly need add that this is not necessarily so.

Let us now consider the final few assertions in paragraph one. The first of these is, "The organism may make the punished response less probable by altering the variables of which it is a function."

What constitutes "the punished response"? It is obviously either a response which is t-punished or o-punished. If it is t-punished, then it is simply not true that the organism *may* make the response less probable; for in order for the response to be t-punished at all it *must* be made less probable.

But, if it is an o-punished response which is to be avoided, the question arises as to how it is to be avoided. To say, as Skinner does, that any behavior which *succeeds* in avoiding the punished response will be reinforced, is certainly to imply that the organism was *trying* to avoid that response; for one does not succeed in doing what one did not try to do. But *trying* is inadmissible in Skinnerian psychology. From the point of view of a functional analysis, what happens when an organism avoids a punished response is that previous occurrences of the behavior of this type were followed by negative reinforcers. This, however, holds true for any responses and not merely for punishable ones. The "push" for any type of behavior is always from the past, and on the Skinnerian thesis, the push is no less inexorable in the case of self-control than in other cases.

The distinction, then, between a case of self-control and other cases of behavior is merely that in those cases where one of two possible responses is punishable and the other is not, if the organism exhibits the non-punishable behavior, he has exhibited self-control.

This distinction is both too wide and too narrow; that is, it includes behavior as "self-controlled" which is obviously not, and excludes behavior

---

[7] *Ibid.*, p. 76.

which is obviously self-controlled. An example of the former is the case of the neurotic whose neurosis happens to be socially acceptable, e.g., the man who *must* strive to excel and who manages to do so. An example of the latter is the case where one makes a choice between two socially acceptable alternatives but chooses the one which is personally the less desired, e.g., when one who is not obese and who does not tend to obesity chooses the less fattening, but also the less tempting, dessert.

Having worked through the first paragraph, I now wish to consider the locution "positive and negative consequences" found in the second. I have shown that if a negative consequence is not necessarily a negative reinforcer then this paragraph is blatantly erroneous. However, if by "negative consequences" Skinner means "negative reinforcers," my previous argument does not hold. In this case, however, one cannot fail to be self-controlled, for any situation which presents one with negative reinforcers is by definition one that will tend to diminish in frequency. Thus, in the drinking example, if the early stages of drinking present us with negative reinforcers we will, of course, cease drinking. It is quite relevant to point out that if we stop drinking, even though we want to continue, and even though it is to our benefit to continue, we are nonetheless self-controlled on Skinner's view. The result of this is that the teetotaller who has his doctor's orders to drink alcohol and who wants to do so to preserve his health, but who just can't force himself to take his medicine, exhibits self-control.

I have shown that if one divests Skinner's argument of its illegitimate use of connotative terms, what remains is either erroneous or vacuous. Although this is true, his claim is nonetheless vicious; for it enters into his philosophy in such a manner that he can feel at ease in saying:

> Education grown too powerful is rejected as propaganda or "brainwashing" while really effective persuasion is decried as "undue influence," "demagogery," "seduction," and so on.[8]

Surely one difference between education and brainwashing is that the former results in self-controlled individuals while the latter does not; and surely, contrary to Skinner's analysis, this is both a real and an important distinction.

[8] Skinner, B. F., "Freedom and Control of Men," *The American Scholar*, Vol. 25, Winter 1956, p. 56.

59. SENTENCES ABOUT BELIEVING

Roderick M. Chisholm

1. "I can look for him when he is not there, but not hang him when he is not there."[1] The first of these activities, Brentano would have said, is *intentional*; it may take as its object something which does not exist. But the second activity is "merely physical"; it cannot be performed unless its object is there to work with. "Intentionality," he thought, provides us with a mark of what is psychological.

I shall try to reformulate Brentano's suggestion by describing one of the ways in which we need to use language when we talk about certain psychological states and events. I shall refer to this use as the "intentional use" of language. It is a kind of use we can avoid when we talk about non-psychological states and events.

In the interests of a philosophy contrary to that of Brentano, many philosophers and psychologists have tried to show, in effect, how we can avoid intentional language when we wish to talk about psychology. I shall discuss some of these attempts in so far as they relate to the sorts of things we wish to be able to say about *believing*. I believe that these attempts have been so far unsuccessful. And I think that this fact may provide some reason for saying, with Brentano, that "intentionality" is a mark of what is psychological.

SOURCE. Chisholm, Roderick, "Sentences About Believing," *Proceedings of the Aristotelian Society*, Vol. 56, 1955–56, pp. 125–148. Reprinted with permission. Copyright © 1955, 1956 by Aristotelian Society.

[1] L. Wittgenstein. *Philosophical Investigations*, p. 133e (London and New York: Macmillan, 1953).

2. In order to formulate criteria by means of which we can identify the "intentional" use of language, let us classify sentences as simple and compound. For our purposes I think it will be enough to say that a compound sentence is one compounded from two or more sentences by means of propositional connectives, such as "and," "or," "if-then," "although," and "because." A simple sentence is one which is not compound. Examples of simple sentences are "He is thinking of the Dnieper Dam," "She is looking for a suitable husband for her daughter," "Their car lacks a spare wheel," and "He believes that it will rain." I shall formulate three criteria for saying that simple declarative sentences are intentional, or are used intentionally.

(a) A simple declarative sentence is intentional if it uses a substantival expression—a name or a description—in such a way that neither the sentence nor its contradictory implies either that there is or that there isn't anything to which the substantival expression truly applies. The first two examples above are intentional by this criterion. When we say that a man is thinking of the Dnieper Dam, we do not imply either that there is or that there isn't such a dam; similarly when we deny that he is thinking of it. When we say that a lady is looking for a suitable husband for her daughter, we do not commit ourselves to saying that her daughter will, or that she will not, have a suitable husband; and similarly when we deny that the lady is looking for one. But the next sentence in our list of examples—"Their car lacks a spare wheel"—is not intentional. It is true that, if we affirm this sentence, we do not commit ourselves to saying either that there are or that there are not any spare wheels. But if we deny the sentence, affirming "Their car does not lack a spare wheel," then we imply that there is a spare wheel somewhere.

(b) We may describe a second type of intentional use by reference to simple sentences the principal verb of which takes as its object a phrase containing a subordinate verb. The subordinate verb may follow immediately upon the principal verb, as in "He is contemplating killing himself"; it may occur in a complete clause, as in "He believes it will rain"; it may occur in an infinitive, as in "He wishes to speak"; or it may occur in participial form, as in "He accused John of stealing the money" and "He asked John's brother to testify against him." I shall say that such a simple declarative sentence is intentional if neither the sentence nor its contradictory implies either that the phrase following the principal verb is true or that it is false.[2] "He is con-

---

[2] This criterion must be so interpreted that it will apply to sentences wherein the verb phrases following the principal verb are infinitive, prepositional, or participial phrases; hence it must make sense to speak of such phrases as being true or false. When I say of the phrase, following the main verb of "He accused John of stealing the money," that it is true, I mean, of course, that John stole the money. More generally, when I say of such a sentence that the phrase following the principal verb is true, or that it is false, my statement may be interpreted as applying to that new

templating killing himself" is intentional, according to this second criterion, because neither it nor its denial implies either that he does or that he doesn't kill himself; similarly with our other examples. But "He prevented John from stealing the money" is not intentional, because it implies that John did not steal the money. And "He knows how to swim" is not intentional, because its denial implies that he isn't swimming.

Sometimes people use substantival expressions in place of the kind of phrases I have just been talking about. Instead of saying, "I want the strike to be called off," they may say, "The strike's being called off is what I want." The latter sentence could be said to be intentional according to our first criterion, for neither the sentence nor its contradictory implies either that "there is such a thing as" the strike's being called off, or that there isn't—that is to say, neither implies that the strike will be, or that it will not be, called off.

Many intentional sentences of our first type may be rewritten in such a way that they become instances of our second type. Instead of saying "I would like a glass of water," one may say "I would like to have a glass of water." And instead of saying "He is looking for the Fountain of Youth," one may say "He is trying to find the Fountain of Youth." But some sentences of the first type seem to resist such transformation into the second type; for example, "I was thinking about you yesterday."

(c) If we make use of Frege's concept of "indirect reference," which is, of course, closely related to that of "intentionality," we can add another important class of sentence to our list of those which are intentional.[3] "Indirect reference" may be defined, without using the characteristic terms of Frege's theory of meaning, in the following way: a name (or description) of a certain thing has an indirect reference in a sentence if its replacement by a different name (or description) of that thing results in a sentence whose truth-value may differ from that of the original sentence.[4] It is useful to interpret this

sentence which is like the phrase in question, except that the verb appearing in infinitive or participial form in the phrase is the principal verb of the new sentence. I should add a qualification about tenses, but I do not believe that my failure to do so is serious. It should be noted that, in English, when the subject of an infinitive or of a participle is the same as that of the principal verb, we do not repeat the subject; although we say "I want John to go," we do not say "I want me to go" or "John wants himself to go." When I say, then, that the last two words of "I want to go" are true, my statement should be interpreted as applying to "I shall go."

[3] By adopting Frege's theory of meaning—or his terminology—we could make this criterion do the work of our first two. But I have made use of the first two in order that no one will be tempted to confuse what I want to say with what Frege had to say about meaning. The three criteria overlap to a considerable extent.

[4] If E is a sentence obtained merely by putting the identity sign between two names or descriptions of the same thing, if A is a sentence using one of these names or descriptions, if B is like A except that where A uses the one name or description B uses the other, then the one name or description may be said to have an *indirect reference* in A provided that the conjunction of A and E does not imply B.

criterion in such a way that we can say of those names (or descriptions), such as "the Fountain of Youth" and "a building half again as tall as the Empire State," which don't apply to anything, that they are all names of the same thing. Let us add, then, that a simple declarative sentence is intentional if it contains a name (or description) which has an indirect reference in that sentence. We can now say of certain *cognitive* sentences—sentences which use words such as "know," "remember," "see," "perceive," in one familiar way—that they, too, are intentional. I may see that Albert is here and Albert may be the man who will win the prize; but I do not now *see that* the man who will win the prize is here. And we all remember that although George IV knew that Scott was the author of Marmion he did not know that Scott was the author of Waverley.

(d) With respect to the intentionality of compound sentences—sentences constructed by means of propositional connectives from two or more sentences —it is enough to say this: a compound declarative sentence is intentional if and only if one or more of its component sentences is intentional. "1 will be gratified if I learn that Albert wins the prize" is intentional, because the if-clause is intentional. But "The career of Ponce de Leon would have been most remarkable if he had found the Fountain of Youth" is not intentional, because neither of its components is intentional. (In order that this final criterion be applicable to sentences in the subjunctive, we should, of course, interpret it to mean a compound declarative sentence is intentional if and only if one or more of the component sentences of its indicative version is intentional.)

3. We may now formulate a thesis resembling that of Brentano by referring to intentional language. Let us say (1) that we do not need to use intentional language when we describe non-psychological, or "physical," phenomena; we can express all that we know, or believe, about such phenomena in language which is not intentional.[5] And let us say (2) that, when we wish to describe certain psychological phenomena—in particular, when we wish to describe thinking, believing, perceiving, seeing, knowing, wanting, hoping and the like —either (a) we must use language which is intentional or (b) we must use a vocabulary which we do not need to use when we describe non-psychological, or "physical," phenomena.

I shall discuss this linguistic version of Brentano's thesis with reference to sentences about believing. I do not pretend to be able to show that it is true in its application to believing. But I think that there are serious difficulties, underestimated by many philosophers, which stand in the way of showing that it is false.

[5] Certain sentences describing relations of comparison (e.g. "Some lizards look like dragons") constitute exceptions to (1). Strictly speaking, then, (1) should read: "we do not need any intentional sentences, other than those describing relations of comparison, when we describe non-psychological phenomena."

I wish to emphasize that my question does not concern "subsistence" or "the being of objects which don't exist." Philosophers may ask whether it is possible to think about unicorns if there are no unicorns for us to think about. They may also ask whether you and I can believe "the same thing" if there is no proposition or objective toward which each of our beliefs is directed. But I am not raising these questions. Possibly the feeling that the intentional use of language commits us to the assumption that there are such entities is one motive for seeking to avoid such use. But I wish to ask only whether we can avoid such use and at the same time say all that we want to be able to say about believing.

4. The first part of our thesis states that we do not need to use intentional language when we describe non-psychological, or "physical," phenomena. I do not believe that this statement presents any serious difficulty. It is true that we do sometimes use intentional sentences in non-psychological contexts. The following sentences, for example, are all intentional, according to our criteria, but none of them describe anything we would want to call "psychological": "The patient will be immune from the effects of any new epidemics" and "It is difficult to assemble a prefabricated house." But these sentences are not examples counter to our thesis. Anyone who understands the language can readily transform them into conditionals which are not intentional. (A compound sentence, it should be recalled, is intentional only if it has a component which is intentional.) Instead of using intentional sentences, we could have said, "If there should be any new epidemics, the patient would not be affected by them" and "If anyone were to assemble a prefabricated house, he would have difficulties," (Perhaps the last sentence should be rendered as "If anyone were to try to assemble a prefabricated house, he would have difficulties." In this version the sentence is intentional, once again, but since it contains the verb "to try" it can no longer be said to be non-psychological.)

I believe that any other ostensibly non-psychological sentence which is intentional can be transformed, in an equally obvious way, into a sentence conforming to our version of Brentano's thesis. That is to say, it will become a sentence of one of two possible types: either (a) it will be no longer intentional or (b) it will be explicitly psychological. Sentences about probability may be intentional, but, depending upon one's conception of probability, they may be transformed into the first or into the second type. If I say "It is probable that there is life on Venus," neither my sentence nor its denial implies either that there is life on Venus or that there is not. According to one familiar interpretation of probability, my sentence can be transformed into a non-intentional sentence about frequencies—sentences telling about places where there is life and places where there isn't and comparing Venus with such places, etc. According to another interpretation, my sentence can be transformed into a psychological statement about believing—e.g., "It is reasonable for us to believe that there is life on Venus." Intentional sentences about tendencies and purposes in nature may be treated similarly. If we say, non-intentionally, "The purpose of the liver is to secrete bile," we may mean, psychologically, that the Creator made the liver so that it would secrete bile, or we may mean, non-intentionally, that in most live animals having livers the liver does do this work and that when it does not the animal is unhealthy.

There are people who like to ascribe beliefs, perceptions, plans, desires, and the like to robots and computing machinery. A computing machine might be said to believe, truly, that 7 and 5 are 12; when it is out of order, it may be said to make mistakes and possibly to believe, falsely, that 7 and 5 are 11. But such sentences, once again, are readily transformed into other sentences, usually conditionals, which are no longer intentional. If a man says that the machine believes 7 and 5 to be 11, he may mean merely that, if the keys marked "7" and "5" are pressed, the machine will produce a slip on which "11" is marked. Other intentional sentences about the attitudes of machines may be more complex, but I'm sure that, if they have been given any meaning by those who use them, they can be readily transformed into sentences which are not intentional. Indeed the case with which robot sentences may be made either intentional or non-intentional may be one ground, or cause, for believing that sentences about the attitudes of human beings may readily be transformed in ways counter to our version of Brentano's thesis.

It should be noted, with respect to those universal sentences of physics which have no "existential import," that they are not intentional. It is true that the sentence, "All moving bodies not acted upon by external forces continue in a state of uniform motion in a straight line," does not imply either that there are, or that there are not, such bodies. But its contradictory implies that there are such bodies.

5. The second part of our version of Brentano's thesis states that, when we wish to describe anyone's believing, seeing, knowing, wanting, and the like, either (a) we must use language which is intentional or (b) we must use a vocabulary we don't need when we talk about non-psychological facts.

Perhaps the most instructive way of looking at our thesis is to contrast it with one which is slightly different. It has often been said, in recent years, that "the language of physical things" is adequate for the description of psychological phenomena—this language being any language whose vocabulary and rules are adequate for the description of non-psychological phenomena. If we do not need intentional language for describing physical things, then this counter-thesis—the thesis that the language of physical things is adequate for the description of psychological phenomena—would imply that we do not need intentional language for the description of psychological phenomena.

The easiest way to construct a non-intentional language for psychology is to telescope nouns and verbs. Finding a psychological verb, say "expects," and its grammatical object, say "food," we may manufacture a technical term by combining the two. We may say that the rat is "food-expectant" or that he "has a food-expectancy." Russell once proposed that, instead of saying "I perceive a cat," we say "I am cat-perceptive," and Professor Ryle has described a man seeing a thimble by saying that the man "is having a visual sensation in a thimble-seeing frame of mind."[6] Sentences about thinking, believing, desiring, and the like could readily be transformed in similar ways. But this way of avoiding intentional language has one serious limitation. If we wish to tell anyone what our technical terms mean, we must use intentional language again. Russell did not propose a definition of his technical term "cat-perceptive" in familiar non-intentional terms; he told us, in effect, that we should call a person "cat-perceptive" whenever the person *takes* something to be a cat. Our version of Brentano's thesis implies that, if we dispense with intentional language in talking about perceiving, believing, and expecting, we must use a vocabulary we don't need to use when we talk about non-psychological facts. The terms "food-expectancy," "thimble-seeing frame of mind," and "cat-perceptive" illustrate such a vocabulary.

I shall comment upon three general methods philosophers and psychologists have used in their attempts to provide "physical" translations of belief sentences. The first of these methods makes use of the concepts of "specific response" and "appropriate behavior"; references to these concepts appeared in the writings of the American "New Realists" and can still be found in the works of some psychologists. The second method refers to "verbal behavior"; its clearest statement is to be found in Professor Ayer's *Thinking* and *Meaning*. The third refers to a peculiar type of "fulfilment" or "satisfaction"; its classic statement is William James' so-called pragmatic theory of truth. I shall try to show that, if we interpret these various methods as attempts to show that our version of Brentano's thesis is false, then we can say that they are inadequate. I believe that the last of these methods—the one which refers to "fulfilment" or "satisfaction"—is the one which has the best chance of success.

6. When psychologists talk about the behavior of animals, they sometimes find it convenient to describe certain types of response in terms of the stimuli with which such responses are usually associated. A bird's "nesting responses" might be defined by reference to what the bird does in the presence of its nest and on no other occasions. A man's "rain responses," similarly, might be defined in terms of what he does when and only when he is in the rain. I

---

[6] See Russell's *Inquiry into Meaning and Truth* (American edition), p. 142 (New York: Norton & Co., 1940) and Ryle's *Concept of Mind*, p. 230 (London: Hutchinson's Univ. Libr., 1949).

believe we may say that some of the American "New Realists" assumed that, for every object of which a man can be said ever to be conscious, there is some response he makes when and only when he is in the presence of that object—some response which is *specific* to that object.[7] And they felt that the specific response vocabulary—"rain response," "fire response," "cat response" —provided a way of describing belief and the other types of phenomena Brentano would have called "intentional." This "specific response theory" is presupposed in some recent accounts of "sign behavior."

I think Brentano would have said that, if smoke is a *sign* to me of fire, then my perception of smoke causes me to *believe* that there is a fire. But if we have a specific response vocabulary available, we might say this: smoke is a sign to me of fire provided smoke calls up my *fire responses*. We might then say, more generally, that S is a sign of E for O provided only S calls up O's E-responses. But what would O's E-responses be?

What would a man's fire responses be? If smoke alone can call up his fire responses—as it may when it serves as a sign of fire—we can no longer say that his fire responses are the ways he behaves when and *only* when he is stimulated by fire. For we want to be able to say that he can make these responses in the presence of smoke and not of fire. Should we modify our conception of "fire response," then, and say that a man's fire responses are responses which are *like* those—which are *similar* to those—he makes when stimulated by fire? This would be saying too much, for in some respects every response he makes is like those he makes in the presence of fire. *All* of his responses, for example, are alike in being the result of neural and physiological events. But we don't want to say that all of the man's responses are fire responses. It is not enough, therefore, to say that a man's fire responses are *similar* to those he makes, or would make, in the presence of fire; we must also specify the *respect* in which they are similar. But no one, I believe, has been able to do this.

The problem isn't altered if we say that a man's fire responses constitute some *part* of those responses he makes in the presence of fire. More generally, the problem isn't altered if we introduce this definition: S is a sign of E provided only that S calls up *part* of the behavior that E calls up. It is not enough to say that the sign and the object call up some of the same behavior. The books in this room are not a sign to me of the books in that room, but the books in the two rooms call up some of the same behavior. And it is too much to say that S calls up *all* of the behavior that E calls up—that the sign evokes *all* of the responses that the subject makes to the object. The bell is a sign of food to the dog, but the dog, as we know, needn't eat the bell.

[7] See Chapter 9 of E. B. Holt, *The Concept of Consciousness* (London: G. Allen and Co., Ltd., 1914).

We might try to avoid our difficulties by introducing qualifications of another sort in our definition of sign. Charles E. Osgood proposes the following definition in the chapter entitled "Language Behavior," in *Method and Theory in Experimental Psychology* (New York: Oxford Univ. Press, 1953): "A pattern of stimulation which is not the object is a sign of the object if it evokes in an organism a mediating reaction, this (a) being some fractional part of the total behavior elicited by the object and (b) producing distinctive self-stimulation that mediates responses which would not occur without the previous association of nonobject and object patterns of stimulation" (p. 696). The second qualification in this definition—the requirement that there must have been a "previous association of nonobject and object" and hence that the thing signified must at least once have been experienced by the subject provides a restriction we haven't yet considered. But this restriction introduces a new set of difficulties. I have never seen a tornado, an igloo, or the Queen of England. According to the present definition, therefore, nothing can signify to me that a tornado is approaching, that there are igloos somewhere, or that the Queen of England is about to arrive. Hence the definition leaves one of the principal functions of signs and language unprovided for.

We may summarize the difficulties such definitions involve by reference to our attempt to define what a man's "fire responses" might be—those responses which, according to the present type of definition, are evoked by anything that serves as a sign of fire, and by reference to which we had hoped to define *beliefs* about fires. No matter how we formulate our definition of "fire responses," we find that our definition has one or another of these three defects: (1) a man's fire responses become responses that *only* fire can call up—in which case the presence of smoke alone will *not* call them up; (2) his fire responses become responses he sometimes makes when he *doesn't* take anything to be a sign of fire, when he *doesn't* believe that anything is on fire; or (3) our definitions will make use of intentional language.[8]

The "appropriate action" terminology is a variant of the "specific response" terminology. Psychologists sometimes say that, if the bell is a sign of food, then the bell calls up responses *appropriate* to food. And one might say, more generally, that a man *believes* a proposition p provided only he behaves, or is disposed to behave, in a way that is "appropriate to p," or "appropriate to p's being true." But unless we can find a way of defining "appropriate," this way of talking is intentional by our criteria. When we affirm, or when we deny, "The knight is acting in a way that is appropriate to the presence of dragons," we do not imply either that there are, or that there are not, any dragons.[9]

[8] If we say that smoke signifies fire to O provided only that, as a result of the smoke, "there is a fire in O's *behavioral environment*," or "there is a fire *for* O," and if we interpret the words in the quotations in the way in which psychologists have tended to interpret them, our language is intentional.

[9] R. B. Braithwaite, in "Belief and Action," (*Proceedings of the Aristotelian Society,*

7. In the second type of definition we refer to the "verbal behavior" which we would ordinarily take to be symptomatic of belief. This time we try to describe a man's belief—his believing—in terms of his actual uses of words or of his dispositions to use words in various ways.

Let us consider a man who believes that the Missouri River has its source in the northern part of Montana. In saying that he believes this, we do not mean to imply that he is actually doing anything; we mean to say that, if the occasion arose, he would do certain things which he would not do if he did not believe that the Missouri had its source in northern Montana. This fact may be put briefly by saying that when we ascribe a belief to a man we are ascribing a certain set of dispositions to him. What, then, are these dispositions? According to the present suggestion, the man is disposed to use language in ways in which he wouldn't use it if he didn't have the belief. In its simplest form, the suggestion is this: if someone were to ask the man "Where is the source of the Missouri River?" the man would reply by uttering the words, "In the northern part of Montana"; if someone were to ask him to name the rivers having their sources in the northern part of Montana, he would utter, among other things, the word "Missouri"; if someone were to ask "Does the Missouri arise in northern Montana?" he would say "Yes"; and so on.

We should note that this type of definition, unlike the others, is not obviously applicable to the beliefs of animals. Sometimes we like to say such things as "The dog believes he's going to be punished" and "Now the rat thinks he's going to be fed." But if we accept the present type of definition, we cannot say these things (unless we are prepared to countenance such conditions as "If the rat could speak English, he'd now say 'I am about to be fed'"). I do not know whether this limitation—the fact that the definition does not seem to allow us to ascribe beliefs to animals—should be counted as an advantage, or as a disadvantage, of the "verbal behavior" definition. In any case, the definition involves a number of difficulties of detail and a general difficulty of principle.

The if-then sentences I have used as illustrations describe the ways in which our believer would answer certain questions. But surely we must qualify these sentences by adding that the believer has no desire to deceive the man

Supplementary vol. XX, p. 10), suggests that a man may be said to believe a proposition p provided this condition obtains: "If at a time when an occasion arises relevant to p, his springs of action are s, he will perform an action which is such that, if p is true, it will tend to fulfill s, and which is such that, if p is false, it will not tend to satisfy s." But the definition needs qualifications in order to exclude those people who, believing the true proposition p that there are people who can reach the summit of Mt. Everest, and having the desire s to reach the summit themselves, have yet acted in a way which has not tended to satisfy s. Moreover, if we are to use such a definition to show that Brentano was wrong, we must provide a non-intentional definition of the present use of "wish," "desire," or "spring of action."

who is questioning him. To the question "Where is the source of the Missouri?" he will reply by saying "In northern Montana"—provided he wants to tell the truth. But this proviso brings us back to statements which are intentional. If we say "The man wants to tell the truth" we do not imply, of course, either that he does or that he does not tell the truth; similarly, if we assert the contradictory. And when we say "He wants to *tell the truth*"—or, what comes to the same thing, "He doesn't want to *lie*"—we mean, I suppose, he doesn't want to say anything he *believes* to be false. Perhaps we should also add that he has no objection to his questioner *knowing* what it is that he believes about the Missouri.

We should also add that the man speaks English and that he does not misunderstand the questions that are put to him. This means, among other things, that he should not take the other man to be saying something other than what he is saying. If he took the other man to be saying "Where is the source of the *Mississippi?*" instead of "Where is the source of the Missouri?" he might reply by saying "In Minnesota" and not by saying "In Montana." It would seem essential to add, then, that he must not *believe* the other man to be asking anything other than "Where is the source of the Missouri?"

Again, if the man does not speak English, it may be that he will not reply by uttering any of the words discussed above. To accommodate this possibility, we might qualify our if-then statements in some such way as this: "If someone were to ask the man a question which, for him, had the same meaning as 'Where is the source of the Missouri?' has for us, then he would reply by uttering an expression which, for him has the same meaning as 'In the northern part of Montana' has for us."[10] Or we might qualify our original if-then statements by adding this provision to the antecedents: "and if the man speaks English." When this qualification is spelled out, then, like the previous one, it will contain some reference to the meanings of words—some reference to the ways in which the man uses, applies, or interprets words and sentences. These references to the meanings of words and sentences—to their use, application, or interpretation—take us to the difficulty of principle involved in this linguistic interpretation of believing.

The sentences we use to describe the meanings and uses of words are ordinarily intentional. If I say, "The German word *Riese* means giant," I don't mean to imply, of course, either that there are giants or that there aren't any giants; similarly, if I deny the sentence. If we think of a word as a class of sounds or of designs, we may be tempted to say, at first consideration, that intentional sentences about the meanings and uses of words are examples which run counter to our general thesis about intentional sentences. For here

[10] See Alonzo Church's "On Carnap's Analysis of Statements of Assertion and Belief," *Analysis*, Vol. 10 (1950).

we have sentences which seem to be concerned, not with anyone's thoughts, beliefs, or desires, but rather with the properties of certain patterns of marks and noises. But we must remind ourselves that such sentences are elliptical.

If I say, of the noises and marks constituting the German word *Riese*, that they mean giant, I mean something like this: "When people in Germany talk about giants, they use the word *Riese* to stand for giants, or to refer to giants." To avoid talking about things which don't exist, we might use the expression "gigantic" (interpreting it in its literal sense) and say: "People in Germany would call a thing *ein Riese* if and only if the thing were gigantic." And to make sure that the expression "to call a thing *ein Riese*" does not suggest anything mentalistic, we might replace it by a more complex expression about noises and marks. "To say 'A man calls a thing *ein Riese*' is to say that, in the presence of the thing, he would make the noise, or the mark, *ein Riese*."

Let us ignore all of the difficulties of detail listed above and let us assume, for simplicity, that our speakers have a childlike desire to call things as frequently as possible by their conventional names. Let us even assume that everything having a name is at hand waiting to be called. Is it true that people in Germany would call a thing *ein Riese*—in the present sense of "to call"—if and only if the thing were gigantic?

If a German were in the presence of a giant and *took* it to be something else—say, a tower or a monument—he would not call it *ein Riese*. Hence we cannot say that, if a thing were a giant, he would call it *ein Riese*. If he were in the presence of a tower or a monument and *took* the thing to be a giant, then he would call the tower or the monument *ein Riese*. And therefore we cannot say he would call a thing *ein Riese* only if the thing were a giant.

Our sentence "The German word *Riese* means giant" does not mean merely that people in Germany—however we may qualify them with respect to their desires—would call a thing *ein Riese* if and only if the thing were gigantic. It means at least this much more—that they would call a thing by this name if and only if they *took* the thing to be gigantic or *believed* it to be gigantic or *knew* it to be gigantic. And, in general, when we use the intentional locution, "People use such and such a word to mean so-and-so," part of what we mean to say is that people use that word when they wish to express or convey something they *know* or *believe*—or *perceive* or *take*—with respect to so-and-so.

I think we can say, then, that, even if we can describe a man's believing in terms of language, his actual use of language or his dispositions to use language in certain ways, we cannot describe his use of language, or his dispositions to use language in those ways, unless we refer to what he believes, or knows, or perceives.

The "verbal behavior" approach, then, involves difficulties essentially like those we encountered with the "specific response" theory. In trying to define "fire response," it will be recalled, we had to choose among definitions having at least one of three possible defects. We now seem to find that, no matter how we try to define that behavior which is to constitute "using the word *Riese* to mean giant," our definition will have one of these three undesirable consequences: (1) we will be unable to say that German speaking people ever mistake anything for a giant and call something which is *not* a giant *ein Riese*; (2) we will be unable to say that German speaking people ever mistake a giant for something else and refuse to call a giant *ein Riese*; or (3) our definition will make use of intentional language.

The final approach I shall examine involves similar difficulties.

8. One of the basic points in the grammar of our talk about states of consciousness, as Professor Findlay has observed, is that such states always stand opposed to other states which will "carry them out" or "fulfil" them.[11] The final approach to belief sentences I would like to discuss is one based upon this conception of *fulfilment*. I believe that, if we are to succeed in showing that Brentano was wrong, our hope lies here.

Let us consider a lady who reaches for the teakettle, *expecting* to find it full. We can say of her that she has a "motor set" which would be *disrupted* or *frustrated* if the teakettle turns out to be empty and which would be *fulfilled* or *satisfied* if the teakettle turns out to be full. In saying that the empty teakettle would disrupt or frustrate a "motor set," I am thinking of the disequilibration which might result from her lifting it; at the very least, she would be startled or surprised. But in saying that her set would be fulfilled or satisfied if the teakettle turns out to be full, I am not thinking of a positive state which serves as the contrary of disruption or frustration. Russell has introduced the terms "yes-feeling" and "quite-so feeling" in this context and would say, I think, that if the teakettle were full the lady would have a quite-so feeling.[12] Perhaps she would have such a feeling if her expectation had just been challenged—if someone had said, just before she lifted the teakettle, "I think you're mistaken in thinking there's water in that thing." And perhaps expectation always involves a kind of tension, which is relieved, or consummated, by the presence of its object. But we will be on surer ground if we describe the requisite fulfilment or satisfaction, in negative terms. To say that a full teakettle would cause fulfilment, or satisfaction, is merely to say that, unlike an empty teakettle, it would not cause disruption or frustration. The kind of "satisfaction" we can attribute to successful expectation, then, is quite different from the kind we can attribute to successful strivings or "springs of action."

---

[11] "The Logic of *Bewusstseinslagen*," *Philosophical Quarterly*, Vol. 5 (1955).

[12] See *Human Knowledge* (American edition), pp. 148, 125 (New York: Simon and Schuster, 1948); compare *The Analysis of Matter*, p. 184 (New York: Harcourt, Brace, 1927).

Our example suggests the possibility of this kind of definition: "S *expects* that E will occur within a certain period" means that S is in a bodily state which would be frustrated, or disrupted, if and only if E were not to occur within that period. Or, if we prefer the term "fulfil," we may say that S *is* in a bodily state which would be fulfilled if and only if E were to occur within that period. And then we could define "believes" in a similar way, or perhaps define "believes" in terms of "being-disposed-to expect."

I would like to remark, in passing, that in this type of definition we have what I am sure are the essentials of William James' so-called pragmatic theory of truth—a conception which has been seriously misunderstood, both in Great Britain and in America. Although James used the terms "fulfil" and "fulfil- ment," he preferred "satisfy" and "satisfaction." In his terms, our suggested definition of "believing" would read: "S believes that E will occur within a certain period" means that S is in a bodily state which would be *satisfied* if and only if E were to occur within that period. If we say that S's belief is *true*, that he is correct in thinking that E will occur within that period, then we imply, as James well knew, that E is going to occur in that period—and hence that S's belief will be satisfied. If we say that S's belief is false, we imply that E is not going to occur—and hence that S's belief will not be satisfied. And all of this implies that the man's belief is true if and only if he is in a state which is going to be satisfied. But unfortunately James' readers interpreted "satisfy" in its more usual sense, in which it is applicable to strivings and desirings rather than to believings.

Our definitions, as they stand, are much too simple; they cannot be applied, in any plausible way, to those situations for which we ordinarily use the words "believe," "take," and "expect." Let us consider, briefly, the difficulties involved in applying our definition of "believe" to one of James' own ex- amples.

How should we re-express the statement "James believes there are tigers in India"? Obviously it would not be enough to say merely, "James is in a state which would be satisfied if and only if there are tigers in India, or which would be disrupted if and only if there are no tigers in India." We should say at least this much more: "James is in a state such that, if he were to go to India, the state would be satisfied if and only if there are tigers there." What if James went to India with no thought of tigers and with no desire to look for any? If his visit were brief and he happened not to run across any tigers, then the satisfaction, or disruption, would not occur in the manner required by the definition. More important, what if he came upon tigers and took them to be lions? Or if he were to go to Africa, *believing* himself to be in India— or to India, *believing* himself to be in Africa?

I think it is apparent that the definition cannot be applied to the example unless we introduce a number of intentional qualifications into the definiens.

Comparable difficulties seem to stand in the way of applying the terms of this type of definition in any of those cases we would ordinarily call instances of believing. Yet this type of definition may have an advantage the others do not have. It may be that there are simple situations, ordinarily described as "beliefs" or "expectations," which can be adequately described, non-intentionally, by reference to fulfilment, or satisfaction, and disruption, or surprise. Perhaps the entire meaning of such a statement as "The dog expects to be beaten" or "The baby expects to be fed" can be conveyed in this manner. And perhaps "satisfaction" or "surprise" can be so interpreted that our ordinary beliefs can be defined in terms of "being disposed to have" a kind of expectation which is definable by reference to "satisfaction" or "surprise." And if all of these suppositions are true then we may yet be able to interpret belief sentences in a way which is contrary to the present version of Brentano's thesis. But, I believe, we aren't able to do so now.

9. The philosophers and psychologists I have been talking about seem to have felt that they were trying to do something important—that it would be philosophically significant if they could show that belief sentences can be rewritten in an adequate language which is not intentional, or at least that it would be significant to show that Brentano was wrong. Let us suppose for a moment that we *cannot* rewrite belief sentences in a way which is contrary to our linguistic version of Brentano's thesis. What would be the significance of this fact? I feel that this question is itself philosophically significant, but I am not prepared to answer it. I do want to suggest, however, that the two answers which are most likely to suggest themselves are not satisfactory.

I think that, if our linguistic thesis about intentionality is true, then the followers of Brentano would have a right to take some comfort in this fact. But if someone were to say that this linguistic fact indicates that there is a ghost in the machine I would feel sure that his answer to our question is mistaken. (And it would be important to remind him that belief sentences, as well as other intentional sentences, seem to be applicable to animals.)

What if someone were to tell us, on the other hand, that intentional sentences about believing and the like don't really say anything and that, in consequence, the hypothetical fact we are considering may have no philosophical significance? He might say something like this to us: "The intentional sentences of ordinary language have many important tasks; we may use the ones about believing and the like to give vent to our feelings, to influence the behavior of other people, and to perform many other functions which psychiatrists can tell us about. But such sentences are not factual; they are not descriptive; they don't say things about the world in the way in which certain non-psychological sentences say things about the world." I do not feel that this answer, as it stands, would be very helpful. For we would not be able to evaluate it unless the man also (1) gave some meaning to his technical philosophical expressions, "factual," "descriptive," and "they don't say things about the world," and (2) had some way of showing that, although these expressions can be applied to the use of certain non-psychological sentences, they cannot be applied to the use of those psychological sentences which are intentional.

Or suppose something like this were suggested: "Intentional sentences do not say of the world what at first thought we tend to think they say of the world. They are, rather, to be grouped with such sentences as 'The average carpenter has 2.7 children,' 'Charity is an essential part of our obligations,' and 'Heaven forbid,' in that their uses, or performances, differ in very fundamental ways from other sentences having the same grammatical form. We need not assume, with respect to the words which make sentences intentional, such words as 'believe,' 'desire,' 'choose,' 'mean,' 'refer,' and 'signify,' that they stand for a peculiar kind of property, characteristic, or relation. For we need not assume that they stand for properties, characteristics, or relations at all." We could ask the philosopher taking such a stand to give us a positive account of the uses of these words which *would* be an adequate account and which would show us that Brentano was mistaken. But I do not believe that anyone has yet been able to provide such an account.

60. CAN RESEARCH ESCAPE THE DOGMA OF BEHAVIORAL OBJECTIVES?

Harry S. Broudy

The slogan "Down with nonbehavioral objectives" has dominated and still dominates educational research in this country. It is taken to mean that the goals of instruction shall be stated in terms that command agreement as to reference by all who use them. Presumably, goals defined in terms of overt behavior are most likely to meet these criteria. However, it seems to me that objectivity rather than behaviorality carries the basic import of the slogan. For, primarily, the motive of the slogan is to exorcise the evils of fuzziness and idiosyncracy from subjective judgments. Accordingly, language behavior (usage) that employs only terms unambiguous in reference, whose total meaning can be made explicit, would also satisfy the intent of the demand for "behavioral objectives." In this paper I shall so construe the slogan, and my objections will be aimed against the demand for total explicitness as well as against the stricter demand for overt behavioral equivalents of all terms used in educational research.

INFLUENCE OF THE DOGMA

On Curriculum and Teaching

When I say that this slogan dominates educational research, I do not mean to convey the idea that this is all that it dominates. It is also at the heart of

SOURCE. Broudy, Harry S., "Can Research Escape the Dogma of Behavioral Objectives?" *School Review*, Vol. 79, No. 1, November, 1970. Copyright © 1970 by The University of Chicago Press.

the objective-testing movement, which, in turn, has great influence upon curriculum design and teaching method. This is so because if it is argued that only that can be tested which can be stated objectively, and if one conjoins thereto the injunction that only that shall be taught which can be tested, then the curriculum maker's task and the teacher's duty are clearly delimited if not prescribed. Willy-nilly this requirement has put a premium on the teaching of information, the rote recall of definitions, rules and principles, particular operations, and the solution of problems that have only one correct solution. In other words, the slogan when embodied in testing programs puts a high premium on the replicative use of learning which asks the learner to reinstate the original learning pretty much as learned in response to definite cues. Indispensable as this use of learning is, it is not an end in itself, and it is not a sufficient condition for the development of other uses of learning which depend upon it.

On Uses of Schooling

As to research itself, the ideal of operational definitions is understandable. For either in the experimental or the correlational style of research, unambiguous identification of variables, inputs, and outputs is essential. Nevertheless, adherence to this canon has made research loath to seek answers to educational questions about broad outcomes of schooling as well as long-range outcomes of a course of instruction. Thus, the interpretive, the associative, and some forms of the applicative uses of schooling in nonschool situations are not popular fields for research, and yet to the common man and to society these are the important questions.

I have dealt elsewhere in some detail with the four uses of schooling.[1] The replicative use, or what we may call rote recall, needs no further comment. By the *associative* use of schooling or knowledge, I mean responding to a cue or a stimulus by bringing to consciousness ideas, images, analogues, contrasts, and elaborations that are in some way relevant to the stimulus. The relevance may be logical, but I tend to reserve the term for psychological relevance as determined by the "laws of association."

By *interpretive* use is meant the organizing of the situation or task in terms of some categorical scheme. The scheme may be that of one of the sciences, or it may be that found in a system of philosophy, or in some other theoretical system. Synonyms for interpretation are "understanding" and "comprehension," and succesful interpretation serves to order the situation and to disclose its relation to other phenomena. When we interpret problems scientifically, we also disclose the sort of evidence that would be relevant for their solutions.

---

[1] See H. S. Broudy, B. O. Smith, and J. R. Burnett, *Democracy and Excellence in American Secondary Education* (Chicago: Rand McNally & Co., 1964), chaps. 3 and 4.

By the *applicational* use, I mean using a principle, or a theory, or a generalization as a base from which operational hypotheses can be formulated and verified. From these hypotheses, procedural solutions to problems are projected and tried out. Usually, some technology or device is needed to translate a scientific theory into a procedure that will change a concrete problematic situation.

On Theories of Learning

Still another influence of the slogan is on learning theory itself. It is commonly held that the slogan *follows* from certain theories of learning: behavioristic theories, stimulus-response (S-R) connectionist theories, and their variants. I am not at the moment concerned with the adequacy of these theories but rather want to observe that the popularity of learning theories is influenced by the kind of knowledge that is regarded as important at a given time. Today, when the theoretical scientist is the model of intellectual excellence, learning theory has to make the explanation of scientific creativity primary; when precise statements of fact, careful observation, and limited inductions were regarded as the paradigm of knowledge, behaviorist and S-R-bond learning theories found great favor. An age which celebrated strict deductive reasoning would encourage a learning theory and a view of mind that would make these operations central. I believe that current learning theory is trying to accommodate itself to the imaginative, intuitive, and discovery features of modern scientific knowing (witness the rediscovery of Piaget), while "Down with nonbehavioral objectives" expresses an earlier, more positivistic, and, on the whole, a more naïvely inductive view of science. In other words, the slogan is the counterpart of a theory of knowledge that regards learning primarily as the storing and fixing of associations among stimuli or inputs; the slogan serves to reinforce the theory. The use of school learning is then construed as a retrieval or reinstatement of these inputs pretty much as put in. It follows almost inevitably (almost by operational definition) that what cannot be retrieved was never put in. For example, every so often somebody administers tests—usually objective—to samples of the adult population in order to discover how much or little has been retained of such studies as American history, geography, etc. The results almost invariably make good newspaper copy because the testees do so poorly despite their high school and college diplomas. The inference is drawn that either the subject was not taught or not taught well but in any event not adequately learned.

SOME ANOMALIES

I wish now to examine some of the consequences of long, faithful, and sometimes uncritical adherence to the methodological canon reflected in the slogan "Down with nonbehavioral objectives," when it is translated into the principle that the learning is to be measured by the amount of the instructional input that can be reinstated (or the amount of time saved in relearning what cannot be reinstated). This criterion makes a good deal of sense when used to measure the end-of-course outcomes of instruction, when it is reasonable to expect the learner to retain most of that which has been studied. This is not a test of "life use" of what has been taught, and there is good reason why it need not be. But when the criterion is used to evaluate the results of schooling in nonschool situations, it often leads to anomalies.

Quantity and Significance

One of the anomalies is the discrepancy between the amount of educational research and its significance. I seem to recall a former president of the American Educational Research Association writing somewhere that out of 70,000 pieces of educational research resting on one shelf or another, only seventy could be regarded as significant. Of course, the terms "trivial" and "significant" have no obvious, agreed-upon meaning. In education one is inclined to define the significant as that which produces, or in principle could produce, large changes in educational practice. However, whether or not a research finding produces such changes depends on many factors other than the nature of the finding itself. For example, if teachers and administrators do not know about the finding or how to implement it, no great change will occur. I prefer to judge the significance of research in terms of its potential for making the phenomena of education more intelligible. A finding that helps one to understand an educational problem, to see it in a new light, and that generates hypotheses for further research is highly significant even if it does not immediately generate change in practice. Triviality, I would attribute to findings that cannot be generalized or that formalize generalizations obvious to common sense, although as to the last criterion I would hedge a little. A theory in its early stages perforce has to test itself by congruity with common sense, but its value, nevertheless, consists in being able to go on to explain phenomena that are not obvious to common sense and sometimes by constructs that are not obvious to common sense either.

Many reasons are advanced for the alleged triviality of educational research, and not the least frequent is the difficulty of applying the dogma of "behavioral objectives." Another is the difficulty of reducing the clouds of variables that contaminate the atmosphere in which research on any educational problem is undertaken. But in a very ordinary sense, one important reason for triviality is the absence of concern for "life uses" of schooling. On these uses, the vast volume of research has neither thrown light nor reduced much heat.[2]

2 For further estimates of educational research, see Isaac L. Kandell, "Educational

General Education

Consider, as a further example, the persistence of schools and colleges in offering general education, sometimes called liberal education, in the belief that somehow it will do the recipient some good in later life. But when pressed to define this "somehow" in terms of behavioral outcomes, about all one can say is something vague about character, values, outlooks, the finer things, etc. If the claim is couched in behaviorally defined outcomes—for example, frequency of attendance at symphony concerts, amounts donated to the Salvation Army, or changes in the divorce rate—then research finds it virtually impossible to connect these outcomes with even a glimmer of probability to the school input called "general education" or any component of it. For one reason, the input cannot be unambiguously identified in the output; for another, the outcome could be the result of many factors other than schooling. Why then do the proponents of general or liberal education persist? One factor, of course, might be the invincible ignorance that prevents people from accepting the findings of research when strong traditions are threatened by them. A more likely reason is that the difference in the way of life—of thinking, feeling, evaluating—between the cultivated man and the untutored one is too marked to escape notice, and this difference is not measured by the ability to pass examinations in any particular academic subject matter. Moreover, the difference is discernible between educated and uneducated men of the same social class and economic status.

Using "Forgotten" Knowledge

Next we have the case of a physician who in high school and college passed courses in chemistry, perhaps with some distinction. The examinations given at the end of these courses, one can be sure, attempted to correlate the class inputs with outputs. The items on the examination were justified by saying that if the student had mastered this principle or that formula, he could have answered correctly. Thus the inputs and outputs were translated into observable behaviors, and the performance could be quantified, scored, and a grade assigned.

But suppose the same examination were to be given five years later to the now successful practicing physician. The odds that he would score brilliantly or even passingly are fairly low unless he had been teaching chemistry somewhere or was employed in a branch of medicine that necessitated constant rehearsal of his formal studies in chemistry.

Now what is one to infer from the marked reduction in the ability of the physician to do well on an examination that he had once coped with so well? One could say that he had forgotten some or all of his chemistry. But suppose we now place before him an article on a drug that claims to relieve acid in-

Research," *School and Society* 72 (October 1950) :232; and George Mouly, *The Science of Educational Research* (New York: American Book Co., 1963), pp. 429–76.

digestion. The article expatiates on the chemical structure of the drug, on the process of digestion, etc. Does the physician understand the article? The chances are quite good that he will say that he does. If questioned, he might even attempt some sort of "explanation" in terms of chemical principles.

It would take more space and erudition than I possess to develop fully the possible analyses and hypotheses that might account for the situation. However, a few points may be noted without exploring all of them. One is that a witch doctor noted for his success in helping victims of acid indigestion would not respond to the article as did our physician. It would be a waste of time, one must suppose, for pharmaceutical companies to send him articles on their drugs. Another is that the physician is using knowledge that he did not get in the chemistry course but in other courses or from no courses at all; for example, the principle that is controlling what he did retain—the relevance to therapy—was not itself an input of the chemistry course; a lawyer might not retain the same items as did the physician. Finally, the physician might be hard put to make explicit all the factors in his performance. If we are to avoid the paradox of the physician using knowledge that he does not have, then we have to allow the possibility that he "knows" things that he cannot tell, that he knows "tacitly" as well as explicitly.

Simulated Intelligence

Still another anomaly resulting from the demand for total explicitness is the inability of the computer to simulate some aspects of human intelligence. It cannot, for example, decide the relevance of this or that variable for a problem in terms of a unified goal; it cannot evaluate what it cannot count, as humans obviously can. Should we then dismiss this "human" ability as illusory?[3]

The danger to the research enterprise posed by such anomalies is that the relevance of research to educational policy and practice may be seriously jeopardized. As the unexplained anomalies accumulate, an intellectual-practical scandal ensues, and educational research will either have to revise its basic notions radically or stagnate further into triviality.[4]

Tacit Knowing

It is my hunch that these anomalies are bound to plague us as long as we insist on ignoring or belittling the tacit element in the uses of school learning.

[3] Cf. Hubert I. Dreyfus, "Why Computers Must Have Bodies to Be Intelligent," *Review of Metaphysics* 21, no. 1 (September 1967):13–33; and my chapter, "Some Potentials and Hazards of Education Technology," in *Planning for Effective Utilization of Technology in Education*, ed. E. L. Morphet and D. L. Jesser (Denver: Designing Education for the Future Project, 1968), pp. 92–113.

[4] I am, of course, alluding to a notion made familiar by Thomas Kuhn's *The Structure of Scientific Revolutions* (Chicago: University of Chicago Press, 1962).

According to Polanyi, two forms of knowing enter "jointly into any act of knowing a comprehensive entity." There is (1) knowing a thing by attending to *it* in the way we attend to an entity as a whole, and (2) knowing a thing by relying on it as a cue for purposes of attending to an entity to which it contributes. This latter way of knowing he calls "tacit." As one example of the difference between focal and tacit knowing, Polanyi cites the viewing through a stereopticon of two pictures of an object taken from slightly different positions. We see one image, however, and this is at the focus of attention; of the separate images we are aware—if we are aware of them at all—only as "guides to the image on which we focus our attention." But we cannot see both one and two pictures simultaneously.[5] When one is focal, the other is subsidiary (tacit).

It is to be noted that the resultant image is not merely the sum of the two separate two-dimensional pictures. It is an emergent characterized by solidity and three-dimensional space of which the two "inputs" were the necessary but not sufficient conditions. Analogously, we may hypothesize that life uses of schooling are guided by goals, value schemata, and categories of which we are not explicitly aware albeit they may have been studied explicitly.

The example of the physician can stand for a wide variety of instances in which school learnings function tacitly or subsidiarily as well as focally or explicitly. Perhaps all perceptual and judgmental activities, even fairly simple ones, involve a tacit vector. Not only are knowledgeable men and women unable to recall many of the items they once passed on course examinations, but not infrequently they are overcome by the illusion that they never studied these materials at all. Accordingly, they attribute their success—when queried by interviewers—to almost everything except their formal schooling.

INTERPRETATION AS TACIT KNOWING

I am suggesting that the physician's chemistry learnings in school were not wasted even though he cannot now pass an examination in which he is asked to retrieve a large sample of school input. I think it will be granted—if my example is accepted—that his chemistry learnings are functioning but are functioning in an interpretive rather than a replicative way.[6] It is fair to infer, therefore, that some intervening process has transformed the scholastic

---

[5] Michael Polanyi, "Logic and Psychology," *American Psychologist* 23, no. 1 (January 1968) :27–43; also *The Tacit Dimension*, the Terry Lecture, Yale, 1962 (New York: Doubleday & Co., 1966).

[6] One might ascertain the time the physician might save in relearning the chemistry items he no longer can recall. There is good reason to believe that there would be a saving of time, but it would not tell us how or even that the "forgotten" items are functioning in the physician's experience.

inputs—facts, principles, terms, formulas, experiments, problems—into a frame of interpretation, a cognitive net, so to speak, that organizes and makes intelligible certain classes of phenomena. When using the interpretive frame, the physician may or may not be able to recall detailed inputs, but, even if they are recallable, they are not now in the forefront of the physician's attention. Indeed, as Polanyi has insisted, he cannot keep the details and the interpretive frame in the center of his consciousness simultaneously. The same item cannot serve as figure and ground simultaneously to a given percipient.

The notion that the most significant and typical uses of school learning involve a tacit dimension is closely related to the widely accepted view that man's experience of the world is patterned by categories or categorial schema. If it should turn out that in order to form and use such a schematism the pupil's mind must absorb, digest, and transform—perhaps beyond recognition —the details of formal instruction, then the currently popular methods of measuring the efficacy of teaching and learning may go further from the mark the more refined they become. Such schema may function tacitly.[7]

It is sometimes argued that the behavioral criterion can be invoked to test the effectiveness of schooling, not by asking the pupil to recall specific school learnings of inputs, but by "applying" these learnings to the solving of a problem on which no specific instruction has been given. The input being tested here is some theory or principle, and application enables us to rule out the possibility that the response is one of simple recall or random guessing. The "application" can, in this view, be regarded as a "behavior." Whether this interpretation can be sustained, I shall pass over.

When school learnings are used interpretively, they are used to think and feel *with*.

The importance of interpretive use of knowledge is beyond question. For example, writing about "The Crisis of Crises," W. D. McElroy, director of

---

[7] Professor Cyril Burt in discussing Polanyi has noted that this tacit factor in knowing was first clearly explicated by Stout in his *Analytic Psychology* ([1896], bk. 1, chap. 4) and discussed even earlier by Berkeley, Lotze, Burke, Campbell, and Ruskin. The tacit element is also related to the theory of apperception in Herbart, while gestalt psychology is based pretty much on the notion that wholes determine the roles which constituent elements will have in an experience. It may be appropriate to note here a few of Piaget's observations on structure. Structures, he notes, are not observable as such (*Le structuralisme* [Paris: Presses Universitaires de France, 1968], p. 117 [my own rough translation]). No structure exists without a construction, abstract or genetic, but these two types are not so far apart as is usually believed. Citing Gödel, he says that *content* of one structure is the *form* of a lower structure. The invariance of a structure amid diverse operations is provided by a pattern of relations or rules of transformation to conserve the totality and the autoregulation of a system. I (not Piaget) would want to say that it is by virtue of a cognitive or evaluative structure operating tacitly that we use our school learnings to interpret our experience.

the National Science Foundation, said: "We know little about the more subtle effects of pollution. We cannot predict with confidence the behavior of individuals nor that of social groups and institutions. We are not in a position to assess adequately the relative costs and benefits to society of any technology or any course of action. The special crisis that confronts us, as scientists, and that confronts our political leaders, who need and who must support our efforts, is thus one of perspective."[8] Perspective building is another name for the interpretive use of knowledge; so is context building.

To explore the interpretive uses of school learnings we need a test task that on a scale of abstractness falls somewhere between the end-of-course replicative test and the concrete situations of life. Such a test task, it seems to me, would be the reading (or hearing) and discussing of newspapers, magazines, and books. We have devoted some of our most rewarding research to the reading process in children; it would seem as if the techniques for testing reading comprehension could be broadened so that reading "behavior" in nonschool situations could also be studied.

We need studies of the pupil's context-building habits and resources. We need methods of diagnosing failures at interpretation of standardized materials. Ideally, we should be able to test the adequacy of the individual's scientific, mathematical, historical, moral, and aesthetic scheme of categories— indeed every subject studied at school represents a category system that we expect to function in the nonschool situation.

By the construction of diverse sets of such reading and explicating tasks with diverse appropriate samples, one could apply the techniques of research with which we are so familiar, namely, finding measures of correlation and variance among all sorts of variables. However, this is probably a stage of research for which we may not yet be ready. It may be that we must first study the tacit functioning of school learnings phenomenologically and naturalistically in order to reveal variables that are really relevant. For some time, one might expect, fruitful hypotheses will emerge from intuitive hunches rather than from systematic inductions from systematically gathered data. From such hypotheses, or rather suggestions for hypotheses, will come theoretical constructs that may enable us to understand better how various school inputs become frameworks for a wide variety of cognitive and evaluative interpretations. The work already done in semantics, linguistics, the logic of discourse, and on the dynamics of imagery provides promising beginnings for such study.

I shall conclude this foray into research possibility by anticipating the objection that if we succeed in discovering just what input of a biology, or chemistry, or literature course does function later in life, this could be taught

---

[8] Editorial, *Science*, January 2, 1970.

as it is used. Is this not, therefore, just another way of finding an input that can be replicated as an output? The objection would be more cogent if we could assume that, in order to get the desired output, we need only make it an input. This is a bit like saying, "If you want the body to put out muscular energy, equip it with a motor, not food." However, if, as one might suspect, the input is transformed in becoming an effective schema for association and interpretation, then the objection loses much of its force. This transformation takes us into learning theory and research, and I can only think that here too simple S-R connectionism has not proved apt in accounting for the processes that apparently are instated when knowledge is used interpretively or associatively. This may be a fruitful link between research into school learning and curriculum.

SUMMARY

I have argued (1) that the dogma of behavioral objectives has dominated educational research and that as one result we have a dangerous accumulation of anomalies in educational theory and practice. (2) I then hypothesized that one cause of these anomalies lies in ignoring the possibility that there is a tacit dimension of learning and knowing as well as an explicit one and that the dogma of behavioral objectives prevents our taking this into account, thereby rendering much technically fine research trivial or irrelevant to the genuine concerns of the public and of educators. (3) It was then suggested that educational research turn its attention to the interpretive and associative uses of schooling in nonschool life. To make this feasible, test tasks in the form of responding to materials in both the affective and the cognitive domains are needed. (4) However, before we are ready for sophisticated experimental or correctional studies, much phenomenological analysis and description and analysis of cognitive and evaluative interpretation must be done in order to locate and identify the really relevant variables.

CHAPTER 12

Programmed Instruction

One outgrowth of behaviorism (see Chapter 11) is the development of teaching machines and, more broadly, programmed instruction. Although there is fairly general agreement on the potential of programmed instruction for teaching low-level skills and facts, questions have been raised about the use of this approach in promoting higher-level skills and understanding. In the first selection, Lauren Resnick argues that higher-level cognitive processes can, indeed, be promoted by programmed instruction methods.

The selections by Paul Goodman and Harry Broudy express concern about the educational value of, and priorities established by, programmed instruction and other types of educational technology. Additional problems are raised by the general discussions of concepts and of behaviorism (see Chapters 10 and 11).

In the final paper, Bruce Hicks, a physicist who has migrated to the computer-assisted instruction aspects of education, adopts the humanist concerns of Goodman and Broudy, but sees great possibilities in computer-based programmed instruction. This amalgamation of the humanist and radical empiricist views is perhaps a fitting end to this book of readings, though it is by no means an end to the conflict.

61. PROGRAMMED INSTRUCTION AND THE TEACHING OF COMPLEX INTELLECTUAL SKILLS: PROBLEMS AND PROSPECTS

Lauren B. Resnick

It has become commonplace, in discussions of the role of automated instruction in the educational process, to assign to programmed texts and teaching machines the task of teaching routine "rote" or "drill" subjects, while the teacher is freed to handle the truly creative teaching, where "thinking," "understanding," and "problem solving" are involved. To many teachers and educators this is a very attractive idea. On the one hand, programmed instruction offers means of coping with the universally acknowledged teacher overload. On the other hand, its relegation to matters of drill and routine minimizes the threat that automated instruction will eventually replace the teacher. Not only is the teacher viewed as irreplaceable; he is clearly given the most interesting and important tasks. Attractive as it appears, however, this view is based on an essentially narrow understanding of programmed instruction, one that concentrates on its more obvious technical characteristics and does not probe very deeply into the principles of learning underlying it, or into the more subtle techniques used in implementing these principles.

The reasons for such a misunderstanding of the nature of programmed instruction are not far to seek. Popular introductions to the field usually provide only the most surface discussions of the psychological principles on which programmed instruction is based; and more sophisticated works are usually couched in language far too technical for the psychological layman.

SOURCE. Reprinted with permission from Resnick, Lauren B., "Programmed Instruction and the Teaching of Complex Intellectual Skills: Problems and Prospects," *Harvard Educational Review*, **33**, Fall 1963, 439–471. Copyright © 1963 by President and Fellows of Harvard College.

Secondly, almost all of the programs available today—the programs on which teachers are basing their judgments of the field—are concerned with teaching verbal, factual material and not broader concepts or skills. What is more, many of these programs are based on inadequate analysis of subject matter and employ generally unsophisticated techniques of presenting the material and gathering responses. These are, in fact, little more than the glorified workbooks that many teachers take them for. Finally, and perhaps most important, no casual scanning of even a well-constructed program will reveal those subtle qualities of sequencing and prompting that make it a self-sufficient instructional unit, and not simply a series of more or less random exercises. For such an appreciation, a relatively sophisticated understanding of what goes into the construction of a program and of the principles underlying it is necessary.

I propose to examine in this essay the critical theoretical bases of programmed instruction, and to explore their relevance to the problems of teaching complex concepts and problem-solving skills. In so doing, I will seek to define programmed instruction in such a way as to make its theoretical contributions and requirements particularly evident. This will mean minimizing its self-instructional aspects and emphasizing principles of instruction that may have application in a variety of educational contexts. And it will mean, further, treating programmed instruction as a means of experimenting with the educational process, as well as of meeting immediate educational demands.

We can begin with a characterization of programmed instruction as an attempt to approximate, in a non-tutorial setting, certain critical features of fine tutorial instruction. To this extent, there is agreement among virtually all "schools" of programmed instruction, Crowderian and Skinnerian included. The differences among schools of programmed instruction lie largely in the aspects of tutorial instruction they choose to imitate, and the reasons they give for their choices. Crowder, at least as far as one can determine from his published articles on the subject (e.g. 1960, 1962), is concerned largely with the variable progress toward a goal that marks the tutorial process. The tutor, while retaining the right to define the ultimate learning outcome, must adjust his teaching sequence and procedure to the individual student. Thus, Crowder's approach is based on a psychology of individual differences, and is relatively little concerned with the nature of the learning process itself.

Crowder's "intrinsic programs" reflect this priority of concerns. Branching provides for some degree of adaptation to individual differences; but long texts followed by multiple-choice questions—originally introduced to meet the technological demands of branching within a self-instructional system—are used exclusively, regardless of the nature of the subject matter, and without reference to a theory of how learning actually comes about. This is possible within the framework of Crowder's theory because the actual learning process is relegated to the period during which the student reads the text. The overt response is not considered central to learning, but merely a means of monitoring progress through the variable instructional sequence.

For Skinner, the priorities are reversed, and a fairly ambitious theory about the nature of the learning process assumes first place in determining the form that programmed instruction will take. This is "operant conditioning theory," which places primary emphasis on the overt, observable response of the learner and on the external "reinforcements" contingent upon his response. While individual differences among learners are not denied, they are largely ignored, and attention is focused on learning and teaching mechanisms assumed to be more or less universal. Thus, Skinnerian programmers tend to place more emphasis on defining responses and on techniques for eliciting desirable responses, and less on adjustment to individual differences. There is no theoretical objection to branching, but explorations of its effects seem less interesting within this theoretical framework than exploration of sequencing and prompting techniques and of variations in the kinds of responses required.

For practical instructional purposes, each of these schools has something to offer. Certainly the Crowderian emphasis on adaptation to individual differences meets an important educational need—one that, whatever theory may say about the sources of such differences, will always be present in an institutional educational setting. Yet it seems to me that for the development of a general theory of instruction, it is the Skinnerian approach to programmed instruction that offers more. Crowder asks simply *whether* learning has taken place—an important question from a practical point of view; but Skinner raises the psychologically more fundamental question of *how* learning takes place.

With this question as a starting point, it is possible to treat programmed instruction as primarily an attempt to use psychological theory and method in the development of a systematic theory of instruction. Teaching programs may serve not only as practical instruments of instruction, but also as research tools in the study of fundamental processes of learning and teaching. The aim of such research should be to go beyond the intuitively good teacher to a set of systematically defined principles of instruction, principles that will be widely applicable and that can be communicated to those not blessed with the intuition of the "born teacher."

As a starting point for a theory of instruction, operant conditioning seems particularly appropriate; for, more than most psychological theories of learning, it is concerned with deliberately changing behavior—that is, with instruction. In operant conditioning studies the experimenter attempts to gain as complete control as possible over his subjects' behavior, regulating the stimuli to which they respond, the rate of response, and the nature of the response itself. Yet operant-conditioning theory is essentially "contentless." It is not specific as to the kind of behaviors to which it can be applied, and thus cannot in itself prescribe a teaching procedure or sequence for any given subject-matter or skill. It offers merely a general instructional theory, together with a method of behavioral analysis. The instructional theory is applicable only after the behavioral analysis has presented the task in appropriate terms. The situation is somewhat analogous to the use of a computer: it can, at least potentially, solve complex and difficult problems, but only if the data is presented in a certain "language," often different from the language used to describe the same problem in other settings.

That operant analysis and the instructional techniques associated with it work in the laboratory setting can hardly be disputed. By carefully defining the desired responses and relevant stimuli, by controlling the prior history of the organism, often from birth, and by eliminating competing stimulation to a very great extent, psychologists using operant conditioning techniques have succeeded in establishing and maintaining at will some very complex behavioral repertoires in their animal subjects. Our concern here, however, is whether these analytic procedures and techniques of control are appropriate for human instruction, particularly in the conceptual and problem-solving domains. Can the analytic language be applied to intellectual skills; and, if so, is it worth the effort? Are the techniques of instruction applicable outside the rigorously controlled laboratory situation? How does work within the operant conditioning framework tend to limit the kinds of questions asked, and the nature of the instructional procedures tried? Finally, just how well worked out and definitive *is* the theory, when we seek application to educational problems?

Three operations are central to the process of operant conditioning as practiced in the laboratory. These are 1) reinforcement, as a means of controlling the strength of a response; 2) stimulus discrimination training as a means of establishing environmental control over behavior; and 3) the "shaping up" of new behaviors by subtle manipulation of both stimuli and reinforcements. In the following sections of this paper I shall discuss each of these operations in some detail, considering not only their current status in laboratory experiments but also their present and possible relevance in the application of laboratory learning theory to education. Except in the section on reinforcement, which will be treated relatively briefly, particular attention will be devoted to the application of operant conditioning concepts and procedures to the teaching of complex intellectual skills.

REINFORCEMENT

Reinforcement is the central operation in operant conditioning, which is sometimes, in fact, referred to as "reinforcement theory." In the animal laboratory, the defisition and function of reinforcement are relatively clear. To reinforce a response means to strengthen it—that is, to increase its rate, its intensity, its likelihood of occurrence, and so forth. Any response occurring just before a reinforcer is presented will be strengthened in this way. Reinforcement is, therefore, made contingent upon the subject's behavior. It is given after a desired response, withheld after all other responses. Generally, food or water, administered in small doses, serve as reinforcers. The effectiveness of these reinforcers in controlling behavior stands in some fairly regular and predictable relationship to the subject's prior deprivation and to his progress toward satiation as training progresses.

However, the exact effect of reinforcement depends also upon the "schedule" according to which it is administered (cf. Ferster and Skinner, 1957). Is it given after each "correct" response or only after a number of such responses (i.e., on "ratio" schedules)? Or is it given after the passage of a certain fixed or varying amount of time has passed, regardless of what the subject is doing (i.e., on "interval" schedules)? Much of the recent work in operant conditioning has been concerned with the effects of different reinforcement schedules—singly and in combination—on behavior. The effects have been shown to be impressively lawful and regular.

Most of the work on schedules of reinforcement has been concerned less with establishment than with maintenance of behaviors. It is generally thought that reinforcement of each correct response is the most efficient means of actually establishing a new response; but intermittent schedules of various kinds are effective in controlling rate and intensity of a response already learned, and in making it resistant to extinction (i.e., the withdrawal of all reinforcers). Presumably, then, reinforcement schedules should be applicable in education as a means of assuring that what is learned in school will be retained afterwards. In fact, however, there are probably only a limited number of traditional educational problems in which reinforcement schedules, strictly understood, are likely to be of importance. This claim is based upon a consideration of the various possible causes for apparent "forgetting"—i.e., non-maintenance—of learned behaviors and of the relevance of each of these possible causes to school learning.

Operant theorists make a sharp distinction between "extinction" and "forgetting." If a response is repeatedly *made but not reinforced*, the response eventually drops out and is said to be *extinguished*. If, on the other hand, a period of time elapses during which the response is *not made at all*, its subsequent weakening or complete disappearance is attributed to *forgetting*. Operant theory has been greatly concerned with extinction, but very little with strict forgetting in the sense of simple disuse. In fact, operant psychologists have claimed that mere disuse of a conditioned response actually yields very little weakening (e.g., Keller and Schoenfeld, 1950, p. 79), and have proposed, instead, that much apparent "forgetting" actually results either from subsequent learning of competing and incompatible responses or from the student's not having initially learned the entire range of occasions on which a given behavior will later be appropriate. In the former case, several arithmetic procedures, for example, may be confused and jumbled, so that no one of them is adequately "remembered." In the latter, the student may be in full command of a particular procedure, but be quite unaware that the problem he has just encountered is one to which the procedure is applicable.

Reinforcement schedules are effective as a means of maintaining behavior only when the cause of loss or weakening is extinction—i.e., complete withdrawal of reinforcement while the response continues to be made. There are certain important instances where true extinction is likely to interfere with school learning. The act of arguing against a consensus, for example, or of using "good" English in a society used to slang or dialect, may not only go unreinforced but actually be punished outside of school. For behaviors of this kind, the systematic application of appropriate reinforcement schedules in school may indeed prove effective.[1]

For the most part, however, the behaviors we want to teach are ones that, even after school days are over, will be reinforced on appropriate occasions. This reinforcement may come from the community, from economic advantage, or it may be purely "intrinsic"—the pleasure of solving a problem, for example. Thus extinction, strictly speaking, is probably not often the reason that school learning is unavailable or apparently "forgotten" on later occasions. The learning of incompatible responses or inadequate learning of the occasions appropriate to a given behavior are probably much more frequent causes. Operant theory has a good deal to say about how difficulties of this kind might be avoided. But the solutions offered are concerned, technically speaking, with the establishment of effective and appropriate "stimulus control," as will be discussed in the next section, and not at all with the application of reinforcement schedules.

Still another consideration limits the relevance of reinforcement schedules to educational problems. This is the fact that most of the work on schedules has been concerned with maintaining a single response or a small chain of responses. "Maintenance" means repetition of this response or chain *ad infinitum*, under appropriate stimulus conditions. The very notion of a schedule, in fact, applies only when the same response is repeated several times, in the presence of the same stimulus. Only at a very gross level of analysis is such repetition of concern in education. The gross behavior of "studying" or "paying attention" may require keeping at the same task; but learning the actual subject or skill usually means learning many different, though related, re-

---

[1] In addition, reinforcement schedules may have a general area of applicability in dealing with problems of "motivation" for schoolwork.

sponses. Even where the same response is frequently made, it is generally made with reference to different stimuli and so does not qualify as repetition in the sense required for application of a reinforcement schedule. On a teaching machine, for example, only the general behavior of going through frame after frame can be maintained by an appropriate reinforcement schedule. The specific responses made to the material in the frames must each be reinforced in some way, for each is different from the last.

If reinforcement *schedules* as a means of maintaining behavior have only a limited sphere of relevance in education, the basic concept of reinforcement as a means of gaining control over behavior is nevertheless a powerful one. Together with the theory of shaping, to be discussed in a later section, reinforcement provides the means of initially establishing and refining students' behavior. There is, therefore, room for a great deal of investigation and explicit experimentation with reinforcement in education. Such research, however, must from the outset take cognizance of two important conditions. First, the educator can never, in practice, duplicate the controlled conditions of the laboratory. Second, he does not have at his disposal the same kinds of reinforcers that the laboratory scientist has.

In a classroom, the previous experience of students cannot be controlled at will, nor can competing stimulation be so neatly eliminated as in the laboratory. Truly immediate reinforcement is often impossible. What is more, the teacher does not automatically control all reinforcers. Children can provide one another with powerful social reinforcements whose effects may conflict with those of the reinforcements provided by the teacher. Self-instruction represents, in part, an attempt to gain a greater degree of control over behavior. Competing sources of stimulation and reinforcement are to some extent eliminated. In truly automated systems, furthermore, precision of timing may be achieved and immediate reinforcement for appropriate responses provided. It is largely because of the extra measure of control offered that Skinner and certain others have argued in favor of teaching *machines* and against the widespread substitution of programmed texts.

Automation, then, is one approach to the problem of control; but there are some other avenues of investigation that may be equally promising. We actually know very little, for example, about how reinforcement works in group situations. Can verbal behavior in the classroom be controlled by reinforcement as we know it can in individual experimental or therapy sessions (cf. Krasner, 1958)? Does reinforcement of one student's response have any effect on the behavior of other students? How can the teacher utilize the reinforcements of classmates to support rather than hinder his efforts?[2]

---

[2] In this matter, some of the work in group dynamics may provide at least tentative answers.

Answers to questions such as these should prove fruitful for educational practice.

In addition, since we cannot use the primary reinforcers and the deprivation procedures of the laboratory, it is important that the properties of other reinforcers be explored if reinforcement theory is to be systematically applied in education. For example, it is generally assumed that in a teaching machine program, confirmation of the correct answer—success, that is—serves as a reinforcer. If this is so, do many reinforcements with success lead to "satiation" and hence to reduced effectiveness of the reinforcer? Conversely, does prior failure (i.e., deprivation of success) lead to greater effectiveness?

More generally, we need to investigate the question, *"What* reinforcers work, and for *whom?"* This question is hardly a new one for psychology, although it is somewhat foreign to the operant conditioning framework. Most of the work in motivation, while the term "reinforcement" may never be used, is concerned with the *what* part of the question; and when individual differences in motives are studied, the *whom* part of the question is attacked as well. If the findings of investigations along these lines can be integrated into the operant framework, "reinforcement" may become a truly practical concept in many educational settings.

STIMULUS DISCRIMINATION AND CONTROL

Stimulus discrimination and stimulus control are the operations whereby the subject's behavior is brought under environmental "control"—that is, the organism learns when it is appropriate to make certain responses in his repertoire. The laboratory paradigm for stimulus control is simple: reinforce a response when it is made in the presence of one stimulus; extinguish it (provide no reinforcement) in the presence of all others. The subject will quickly come to make the response only to the stimulus that has been the occasion for reinforcement. The response is then said to be under "control" of that stimulus. When the relevant stimuli are complex or unfamiliar, a period of training in which the organism simply learns to distinguish among them is often required. This is called discrimination training. Through such training the organism learns to distinguish red from green, loud from soft, mirror-image from direct image, noun from verb—and so forth. The list of attributes according to which discriminations can be made is virtually endless. Even animals can be taught astonishingly fine and complex discriminations.[3] Stimulus discrimination and stimulus control are intimately bound up with one another; for control without discrimination is impossible, and the only observable evidence of discrimination is that stimuli control different responses.

[3] Skinner (1960), for example, has trained pigeons to guide missiles, a task that required their making fine discriminations among target points.

The concept of "control" does not imply a physically causal relationship: a stimulus comes to control a response only as a result of reinforcement. Nor does "control" necessarily imply a one-to-one stimulus-response relationship or an automatic connection. The same stimulus may control different responses; and several stimuli may control the same response. In the former case, the patterning of stimuli and the surrounding stimulus context determine which response is appropriate. As a very simple example of the role of context in controlling a response, a pigeon with previous conditioning experience can be observed to peck rapidly at a lighted key when the overhead "house lights" are on, but to remain quiescent in the presence of the same lighted key when the house lights go off. This is because in the past he has been reinforced for pecking only when the house lights were on. In the latter case, where different stimuli control the same response, we have a case of concept formation or "abstraction." Here the response is actually under control of only a single attribute of an object, so that, for example, books, glasses, paints, wines and dresses may all be called "red."[4]

It has been pointed out (Chomsky, 1959, p. 30) that there exists some ambiguity within operant theory as to whether the actual stimulus for a response is anything in the environment at a given moment to which the organism is *capable* of reacting, or only that event to which it in fact *does* react. I think that to be consistent, it is necessary to choose the latter alternative; thus, in effect, admitting that it is possible to identify the effective stimulus in a situation only after the response has been identified. This, in turn, means that it will be impossible to predict behavior under given environmental conditions without also knowing something about the individual organism's past history—that is, how it has reacted on previous occasions to similar events. Operant theory cannot, then, predict behavior in general, but only behavior in a given situation for an individual some of whose history is known.

In educational settings, of course, we rarely have complete knowledge of a student's past experience relevant to a given subject-matter or skill. The lack of such knowledge represents one of the greatest stumbling blocks in the development of teaching programs; for without it, we cannot predict how a student will initially react to certain situations and thus often do not know exactly where and how instruction should begin. Because it provides a detailed record of a student's responses, correct and incorrect, under specifiable conditions, programmed instruction itself, based on careful behavioral analysis, can serve as a very powerful tool in identifying strengths and weaknesses of earlier learning. This kind of diagnosis is, in fact, one of the

---

[4] Abstraction and control by contextual stimuli can occur simultaneously, as when the question "What color are they?" sets the occasion on which "red" will be reinforced, and "What shape are they?" sets the occasion on which "round" will be reinforced; but the array of objects remains the same.

major contributions programmed instruction can make to education, even where it is not to be used as a major mode of instruction (see Resnick, 1963b).

Behaviorial Analysis

"Behavioral analysis" within the operant conditioning framework means specification not only of responses, but of the "discriminative," or controlling, stimuli for those responses. For each response, both "S^D's" (appropriate occasions) and "$S\Delta$'s" (inappropriate occasions) must be named. This is the "language" of analysis for operant theory—the terms into which all problems must be translated before operant conditioning procedures can be systematically applied. Properly understood, this language goes far beyond "automatic" connections. It is a system capable of a great deal of flexibility, and yet it preserves the specificity of stimulus-response analysis. Herein lies its great virtue.

In the context of behavioral analysis, knowledge, skill, and ability can be dealt with only insofar as they can be described in terms of performance. This description is not a matter of listing "correlates" of ability or knowledge, but of deciding what observable behaviors will be accepted as evidence of their existence. The behaviorist simply eschews the question of whether knowledge, for instance, exists apart from these observable behaviors (cf. Scheffler, 1962, pp. 212–213). While, in so doing, he may fail to answer to the philosopher's satisfaction the question, "What is knowledge?", he very effectively provides himself with a set of usable goals for instruction. Skinner has stated the case well:

> We can define terms like "information," "knowledge," and "verbal ability" by reference to the behavior from which we infer their presence. *We may then teach the behavior directly.* Instead of "transmitting information to the student" we may simply set up the behavior which is taken as a sign that he possesses information. Instead of teaching a "knowledge of French" we may teach the behavior from which we infer such knowledge. Instead of teaching "an ability to read" we may set up the behavioral repertoire which distinguishes the child who knows how to read from one who does not. (Skinner, 1961, p. 383).

To claim that behavioral definition and analysis of this kind is necessary is not to claim either that the task has already been accomplished or that it will be easy to accomplish. Part of the difficulty lies in finding persons who are at once competent in the subject-matter under consideration and conversant with the requirements of behavioral analysis.[5] Even for those familiar

---

[5] Contrary to Scheffler's (1962, p. 213) implication in his comment on Skinner's article, psychologists who have worked with teachers and professors at the task of analysis have

with the analytic procedure, however, the task remains a complex and demanding one.

Behavioral analysis of any subject or skill involves defining it in terms of responses made to specific discriminative stimuli. Where verbal learning is involved, however, we rarely encounter situations exactly analogous to the simple laboratory paradigm in which a single response is to be made or not, depending upon the presence of a given stimulus. Instead, there is typically an interlocking network of stimuli and responses, in which SΔ's for one response are S^D's for another, and a given statement can serve as either response or stimulus. Furthermore, for discrimination tasks, the critical features of stimuli may be difficult to identify and describe. Such analyses will, therefore, be difficult to perform; but they will offer much in the way of precision, and they will serve to clarify exactly what must be taught.

Operant Analysis of Reading

In few areas of instruction is the central importance of stimulus discrimination and control more clear-cut than in reading. In fact, we can define as "reading" any behavior which is made in response to (i.e., "under control of") a printed or written text (cf. Skinner, 1957, p. 65ff.). The range of responses that can be made to a text is very wide. Naming the letters, then saying the words aloud are the earliest. Later a person may follow printed directions, summarize, restate in other words, take issue with, or answer questions about a text, all without reading it aloud. All of these responses and a number of others will be taken as evidence that he has "read" the text. What is common to them all is their dependence upon and reference to a text. In each case the individual discriminates among marks on a page and then responds appropriately to these discriminated stimuli.

Yet to say that for each of the reading skills described above the stimuli are identical and only the responses vary would be a gross over-simplification. It is true that all involve making discriminations among letters; but for each skill certain features of the ways in which these letters are combined also serve as discriminative stimuli. A complete behavioral analysis of any of the various skills called "reading," therefore, would need to specify in detail the attributes of the stimuli that actually control the response. At the simplest level, it would need to identify likely sources of confusion among the stimuli as purely physical entities. Letters that look alike (*b* and *d* for example) or words only slightly different in spelling (e.g. *rouge* and *rogue*, or *through* and *thorough*) will need special attention in the course of instruction. For "phonics" reading, moreover, the phonetic units must be specified, along with

found that even the most highly competent of content specialists usually has difficulty, at least initially, in applying the concepts of behavioral analysis to his subject.

the responses they control. A complete analysis would seek regularity beyond the obvious: *th*, for example, controls different responses in *thank* and *there*. Are there rules governing the contexts in which *th* is voiced or unvoiced? If so, the contexts as well, and not the letter groups alone, are among the S^D's and $S\Delta$'s to be specified in analysis.

In the case of behaviors beyond mere "reading aloud," characteristics of language and logical organization, as well as physical marks on a page, serve as controlling stimuli. The relevant dimensions of linguistic and logical variation would need to be identified and their relation to responses of various kinds specified. In all of this, it should be noted, operant theory provides only the analytic framework. Much of the analysis itself falls outside the usual province of the psychologist. Although analogous to the red and green lights of the simple laboratory discrimination experiment, the discriminative stimuli for reading are far more complex. Their accurate specification calls for the skills of a linguist and perhaps a logician or rhetorician. The analysis, in short, carries us deep into the realm of "subject-matter."

Operant Analysis of Grammar

One of the most recurrent criticisms of stimulus-response theory in the cognitive realm has been that it could not easily account for the complexities of grammar and the ability of the human to produce grammatical sentences that he has neither spoken nor heard before. Certainly no extensive analysis of grammatical behavior within the operant framework now exists. The most ambitious attempt to account for language in operant terms, Skinner's *Verbal Behavior* (1957), is concerned not so much with the form as with the function of language. The single chapter on grammar is brief and sketchy. The notion of the "autoclitic" (i.e., response to one's own behavior) as a means of accounting for grammar, while essentially promising, is incompletely developed, and the discussion, as a result, often confuses more than it clarifies. Thus, a convincing and usable operant analysis of grammar still remains to be performed.

The initial difficulty for any such analysis is that grammatical behavior is too complex to be explained in terms of simple serial production of individual words. Miller, Galanter and Pribram (1960, ch. 11) have documented quite convincingly the inadequacy of a stimulus-response analysis in which only words already produced and not words *to be* produced serve as stimuli for successive words. Were operant analysis thus limited to simple word chaining, this demonstration would indeed be damaging to any claim that it could account for grammatical behavior. There seems to be no reason, however, why syntactic patterns or grammatical frames, as well as individual words, cannot be treated as discriminative stimuli controlling responses. Thus, the person who says, "Water boils at 212° F" is responding under control of a syntactic pattern as well as under control of various other verbal and non-verbal stimuli in his environment. Under control of the pattern, words produced at the beginning of a sentence are, in effect, influenced by words later to be produced. It is as if the speaker were responding to his own anticipated behavior.

On the assumption that familiar syntactic patterns do in fact function as discriminative stimuli, I have attempted to teach an aspect of English usage in what I think is a novel way. The problem is to use the homonyms *their*, *they're*, and *there* correctly. The instructional procedure is based on a linguistic analysis which identifies the positions that each of the three words can occupy in simple sentences. Using this analysis, a self instructional program has been constructed which uses only position patterns as prompts—no semantic rules for use of a certain word to express a certain idea are given. A special feature of this program is that, in addition to using syntactic patterns as the sole prompts, it uses a system of successive approximation in presentation of the stimuli. That is, the frames are arranged so that there is a progression from relatively simple and clearly "different" patterns for each of the three words to more complex and more similar patterns. In other words, for each individual frame of the program, the whole series of preceding frames serves as the "prompt." This program has been only partially successful thus far, for a number of reasons which I will not attempt to discuss here. Work on the program is continuing, however, and there are indications that the method—both of using syntactic patterns as prompts and of using the technique of successive approximation—will succeed. Even if we should fail in this double venture, however, it may still prove possible to use syntactic patterns as prompts in a more conventional manner.

Operant theory can, thus, handle the learning and use of grammatical patterns rather easily, once the patterns have been identified and described. It should be noted, however, that there are voices that challenge the adequacy of pattern learning as an explanation of grammatical behavior. The challengers represent only a minority among linguists at the moment, but they are vigorous and growing, and above all cogent in their arguments. Chomsky, spokesman for a new "transformational" grammar has argued that the notion of simple "generalization"—i.e., matching a new stimulus with an old one along some dimension, including syntactic structure—is inadequate and that "we understand a new sentence, in part, because we are somehow capable of determining the *process* by which this sentence is *derived* in the grammar." (Chomsky, 1959, p. 56. Italics mine.)

Operant conditioning theory is able to account for such a "transformational grammar" only in terms of fairly complex behavioral "chains," in which an individual's own response serves as stimulus for his next response. "Chaining" as used here is not simply the serial production of words. The responses, which in turn serve as stimuli, are not single words which more or less automatically call forth the next word in the series. Instead, we must imagine the individual as beginning with a simple sentence[6] to which he responds by, for example, inverting subject and verb. The new string of words he has just produced now functions as stimulus for still another response, perhaps inserting the negative "not." Further links in the chain may take him still further from the original sentence pattern. In this way, an entirely new sentence is created—new not only in the specific words that fill each position, but in the sense that a brand new grammatical pattern has been, in effect, constructed for the occasion.

What is troubling to strict behaviorist psychology about this process is that the chain occurs so quickly, in sophisticated speakers of the language, that it is largely covert and thus not observable. In positing extended chains of this kind, therefore, we are, in effect, looking "inside the organism" and attempting to describe, or at least hypothesize, some of its internal processes. Yet chaining is an accepted concept within operant theory, which assumes that many apparently unitary acts begin as chains of separate responses. Similarly, it proposes that covert responses may have begun as overt and observable ones, which, with practice, became speeded up and internalized (See Keller and Schoenfeld, 1950, ch. 7).

The question, then, is not so much whether operant conditioning theory *can* deal with such covert processes, as whether, in so doing, it offers any true measure of superiority over other descriptions of those processes. Is grammatical behavior, in particular, any better "explained" by using stimulus-response terminology than by stating the actual rules of transformation that an individual applies (cf. Chomsky, 1959)? The answer to this question will depend upon what we mean by "explaining." If we wish simply to describe the content of grammatical transformations, then operant language offers little or no advantage.[7] If, on the other hand, we are interested in finding out how individuals learn and can be taught to make linguistic transformations, the translation into operant terms is of distinct value. It puts us in contact with a body of systematic knowledge concerning learning processes in general and helps to generate hypotheses concerning the nature of language learning in particular. It suggests, furthermore, the kinds of teaching procedures that are likely to be appropriate, since whatever we know about the teaching of behavioral chains of other kinds can now be applied to the teaching of language.

Chomsky has argued that, "It is futile to inquire into the causation of verbal behavior until much more is known about the specific character of this be-

[6] I.e., a sentence of an already established pattern—in Chomsky's terms a "kernel string."

[7] In other subject areas, the precision required for translation into operant language is in itself of major importance. Modern-day linguists, however, have been, if anything, more precise than operant theorists in their descriptive endeavors.

havior; and there is little point in speculating about the process of acquisition without much better understanding of what is acquired" (1959, p. 55). As a linguist, in other words, he gives the task of describing the content of grammatical transformations priority over that of accounting for the way the process of transformation is learned. One cannot but agree that no account of linguistic behavior will be complete until a comprehensive grammar is available. But this certainly does not mean that it is inappropriate for the psychologist to direct his attention to the problem of how grammar is learned, even as the grammar itself is simultaneously developed by the linguist.

In fact, it should be noted that whatever the value of a process-oriented transformational grammar as a descriptive linguistic system, it is still by no means certain that the psychological process of understanding or producing a sentence involves such transformations. Miller (1962) has presented some interesting experimental evidence that tends to support Chomsky's claim; but these data are few and collected under very limited circumstances. Thus, psychologically speaking, the question of pattern versus transformation learning in grammar remains open.

Possible implications of the two hypotheses for instruction can be illustrated by discussing some procedures I have been exploring for teaching children to use new or infrequent (for them) syntactic constructions in their writing. Under the pattern hypothesis, my procedure has been something like this. The children are presented with a number of sentences of a given syntactic pattern. By various methods (these are actually a major subject of investigation), they are led to induce the underlying pattern. Having done this, they produce new sentences of the same pattern. In other words, the pattern, induced from existing grammatical English sentences, serves as S^D for a new sentence.

Under the transformation hypothesis, it would be necessary to present pairs of sentences in which one can be derived from the other by certain rules of transformation. By whatever methods turned out to be appropriate, children might be led to induce the rules that relate the sentences. They might then produce new sentences of the same type as the models; but in this case a chain, in which rules for getting from one sentence to another played an important part, would need to be taught. Probably, with persistence, we could teach children to produce grammatical sentences of any form we chose by either method—pattern or transformation learning. Presumably, however, that method will be more effective which matches the natural method by which children learn grammar by themselves.

Operant Analysis and "Understanding"

That a grammatical pattern, or even a transformational rule, can serve as stimulus for a verbal response lends a rather new dimension to classical S-R analysis. It has implications for behavior that are not strictly linguistic; for presumably patterns can in the same way control complex productions of other kinds. For example, the planned "structure" or "organization" of an entire speech or piece or writing can serve as part of the discriminative stimulus for each section as it is produced. Similarly, in scientific hypothesis-testing the individual responses of the skilled investigator are under control of a total "strategy" or pattern for testing. Since both of these are in part temporal patterns, they serve to relate earlier to later behavior.[8] Other kinds of stimulus configurations (purely perceptual, for example), may lack the temporal dimension, but may nevertheless serve as complex S^D's.

By thus treating patterns and configurations as discriminative stimuli, operant analysis is able to account for much of what is meant by the terms "meaningful learning" or learning with "understanding." At its simplest, the notion of patterns as S^D's simply explains how—within the S-R framework—the individual can learn relationships among events and objects, how he can grasp "principles" and "structure" (cf. Bruner, 1961). To maintain its precision, operant analysis demands, simply, that the exact nature of the relationships and configurations that serve as S^D's be specified. It does not allow imprecise terms such as "whole-perception" and "gestalt" to substitute for detailed analysis and identification of the critical relationships. The whole, in short, is still regarded as no greater than the sum of its parts; but relationships and configurations, along with individual elements, make up the parts to be specified and summed.

A second aspect of "meaningful" or non-rote learning is that the student does not simply learn to make automatic responses to set questions. He is able in some way to "transform" the information given, and, by the same token, can give his answers in several forms. As a result, he is not tied to a particular phraseology of either question or answer. He recognizes, for example, that "5 + 3 = 8" and "five and three make eight" are equivalent statements; or that "water boils at ——° F" and "The boiling point of water is ——° F" call for the same response. How can stimulus-response analysis account for this flexibility without claiming that each such equivalence has been separately and explicitly learned?

Here a process of substitution in which patterns often play a critical part is the answer. In the case of arithmetic, for example, the student learns that statements of the *form* "X + Y = Z" and "X and Y make Z" are equivalent. These forms function much as do grammatical patterns; they are abstracted

---

[8] Since these larger structures are not fixed in the way grammatical patterns are, and are often not as well learned, their control over behavior is likely to be weaker. As a result, simple chaining of overt responses, without reference to a general structure, is more likely to occur in such extended productions than in the production of simple sentences. Witness, for example, the behavior of an ill-prepared speaker.

from many statements and, once learned, allow the individual to respond appropriately to (i.e., "comprehend") and formulate statements he has never heard before. What is more, the forms or patterns function as S^D's for one another. Thus, confronted with the statement "$23 + 72 = ?$," the individual can respond (sometimes covertly, sometimes overtly on paper, "$23 + 72$." His own response then functions as an S^D for the final response, "95."

Sometimes only part of a statement needs to be transformed; but the process of substitution is similar. For example, "boils at" and "boiling point of" may function as S^D's for one another. This equivalence need not have been learned directly. It may have been inferred from similar statements, such as "freezes at" and "freezing point," or even more indirectly from a general relationship within English between verb and participial forms. In any case, confronted with an unfamiliar stimulus, "The boiling point of water is ——° F," the individual can make a substitution that transforms it into the familiar "Water boils at ——° F" and thus respond appropriately. By the same token, he can produce a statement of either form.

This process of transforming stimuli and responding to patterns allows operant theory to account for still another evidence of "understanding" in learning—the student's ability to transfer what he has learned, to deal with material that is not exactly like any he has seen before. The traditional S-R account of transfer in terms of "generalization" seems to rely heavily on physical and formal similarity of the stimuli in the learning and transfer problems. For the simplest cases of transfer—where the new problem is of essentially the same form as the old—such an explanation seems to be adequate. But sometimes there is no such simple formal similarity of stimuli, and yet transfer occurs. In these cases, the learner may respond on the basis of similarities in *relationships* among the stimuli (cf. Anderson, 1962b); or he may transform the given stimuli until they match more closely the ones for which he has learned a response. In fact, many instances of "problem-solving" may be less a matter of finding new solutions than of transforming stimuli until it becomes apparent that a response already in one's repertoire is appropriate.

It should be noted that, as in the case of transformational grammar, each of these attempts to account for understanding has involved the assumption of more or less extended "chains" of behavior in which the individual's own responses serve as stimuli for his next response. For the skilled individual, at any rate, these chains occur very quickly and, in large part, covertly. As a result, they are difficult to study by the usual observational methods. Nonetheless, Skinner (1957, ch. 19), defining "thinking" in terms of just such claims, has claimed that this covert behavior is not different from any other kind of behavior and can easily be accounted for within the same analytic system. His treatment of thought as a process of self-stimulation is in the tradition of Mead (1934), who defined thought as "conversation with the generalized other," carried on within oneself, but learned initially in interaction with others. As an hypothesis on which to base an instructional procedure, this notion is attractive, for it suggests the possibility of overt practice leading to covert "thought." In other words, the elements of the chain may be taught overtly and slowly, later to be internalized and perhaps speeded up.[9] This procedure of teaching separately elements that will later be combined into a skilled performance is one application of the principle of shaping, to a discussion of which we now turn.

SHAPING

The process of shaping up new behaviors by reinforcing successively closer approximations to a desired response is perhaps operant conditioning's most unique contribution to learning theory. Using shaping procedures, animals have been taught such complex behaviors as bowling, playing ping pong in modified form, and even guiding missiles. With the notion of shaping, active teaching by the experimenter is substituted for passive observation of the subject's learning. The relevance of such a concept to a theory of instruction is immediately clear. From shaping, which is essentially a process of building new responses on the basis of preceding ones, derives the notion of small steps, which is so central to programmed instructional theory as it now stands. By approximating a desired behavior gradually—that is, in small steps—it is possible to provide reinforcement more frequently. This keeps the learning process more closely under the control of the experimenter and makes it more certain—than under trial and error learning, for instance—that the desired outcome will be achieved.

However, despite its immediately apparent relevance for instruction, the theory of shaping is in certain ways inadequately developed for purposes of cognitive instructional theory. In the first place, the actual steps used in shaping up a new behavior are seldom described in the experimental literature. Probably this lack of descriptive literature is partly due to the fact that shaping is often only a preliminary to experiments on stimulus discrimination or reinforcement schedules. Usually, in any case, the steps to be taken are ill-defined at the outset of a conditioning experiment. The experimenter knows the final behavior he wants to establish. Then he simply watches the organism until it makes some small move in the direction of that behavior. That move and successive ones toward the terminal behavior are reinforced. The ex-

---

[9] It may be noted, incidentally, that teaching of hypothetically effective chains may be a good means of testing the hypothesis that such chains do occur in thinking. Presumably overt practice would be of little advantage if a similar process did not later occur covertly.

perimenter, in other words, does not impose any fixed route on his subject.

On the analogy of such laboratory procedures, some writers on programming technique have urged that the programmer "let the student write the program" (e.g. Green, 1962; cf. Gilbert, 1960). In fact however, programmed instruction, or indeed any "planned" form of instruction, cannot afford to proceed in this way. It cannot simply define terminal behaviors—no matter how precisely—and leave the rest to observation and hazard. Instead, we must go into the instructional session with some guess as to what route will best bring our student to the desired goal. Changes may be made, whole approaches rejected, in the process of finding the best possible teaching sequence. The student's responses do tell us how to modify our procedures, but we never, in fact, leave the process entirely up to him.

Identification of Component Behaviors

In order to derive at least a tentative definition of the steps to be used in shaping, some systematic method of behavorial analysis is necessary. In an earlier paper (Resnick, 1963a), I have discussed a procedure by which "component behaviors" for the terminal behaviors are identified, and a set of "nesting" behavioral specifications derived such that smaller and less complex units of behavior serve as components of the larger ones. Teaching begins with the simpler behaviors, which are gradually combined and modified until they lead to the terminal behaviors. Although its language is somewhat less technical, the process described in that paper is essentially the same as the one discussed by Wells Hively (1962a). Hively also points out that until the route by which a student has come to make a response is specified, it may be unclear exactly what he has learned. Thus, specification of components is sometimes necessary in order to truly define a terminal behavior. Undoubtedly many people working in the field of programmed instruction have been concerned with the development of such analytic procedures, but very little of this concern has, to my knowledge, found its way into the literature on programmed instruction.[10] Specification of terminal behaviors has received considerable attention (e.g., Mager, 1961), but analysis of component behaviors is rarely accorded more than a paragraph in discussions of programming; and it is hardly ever mentioned in the more theoretical operant conditioning literature.

In any case, in the matter of planning for shaping procedures, operant conditioning theory offers little more than a language of analysis and a trial and error research procedure for discovering which sequences work best. For more substantive aid we need to turn elsewhere. The subject-matter, itself, of

[10] The *Journal of Mathetics*, by way of exception, has published articles and reports of work based on a particular form of operant analysis known as "mathetics."

course, is a major source of ideas for sequencing. Behavioral analysis can never stand apart from the subject-matter being taught. It is always concerned to describe responses that constitute appropriate behavior *in* a subject-matter. As a result, behavioral analyses of both terminal and component behaviors must always be specific to a subject-matter. Certain subjects—mathematics comes immediately to mind—seem to have an inherently logical sequence. The identification of such logical sequences or, in less well ordered subjects, their creation, depends upon a very detailed and sophisticated knowledge of the subject-matter.

As we saw in the case of reading, behavioral analysis can rarely be accomplished by the psychologist alone—unless he is also very knowledgeable in the subject-matter being taught. On the other hand, few scholars are used to dealing with their specialties in behavioral terms. They tend to treat their materials as a "body of knowledge" and not as a complex set of responses to definable stimuli. Thus it is unlikely that analysis for instructional purposes can be left up to the content specialist alone. What is needed, instead, is some form of cooperation between psychologist and content specialist. Whether one "trains" the other in his specialty or the two work collaboratively is a matter to be worked out, perhaps differently in every case. But programmed instruction will make no major practical contribution to education without such cooperation in some form.

While analysis of the subject-matter may suggest logical sequences, the body of psychological studies concerned with "cognition" may help in suggesting *psycho*logically valid teaching sequences. A large and growing number of studies in psychology are concerned with identifying and describing the processes involved in perception, thinking, problem-solving and other "cognitive" activities. An important group of studies (e.g., Inhelder and Piaget, 1958) seeks to discover the "natural" sequences through which individuals pass in the course of their cognitive development. While not usually tied to any single curricular subject, these studies are nevertheless concerned with detailed description and explanation of specific mental processes. They represent, as it were, an attempt to give substance to the covert behavior chains postulated by operant conditioning theory to account for thinking. Thus, they make an essentially substantive contribution to a theory of instruction.

While modern studies in cognition are rigorously experimental, they generally do not share either experimental method or analytic language with operant conditioning studies. What is more, since relatively few cognitive studies begin with an instructional concern, their findings are not usually cast in a form that makes them immediately applicable to teaching. Some "translation" and interpretation, therefore, may be necessary if their findings are to be used within a framework that takes operant conditioning as the basis for instructional method. Such translation, or indeed any attempts to integrate these two branches of psychology, should be richly rewarding to those concerned with instructional theory and practice.

Shaping Discriminations

From the instructional point of view, a second shortcoming of laboratory studies of shaping is their almost exclusive concern with establishing new responses, most often motor responses. Very little attention has been given to the problem of how to shape up discriminations or establish stimulus control. In this matter, the learner has usually been left to his own devices, while the experimenter studied learning and acquisition curves. Yet the need for a body of concrete knowledge concerning shaping procedures is, if anything, greater in the area of discrimination learning than in the area of motor responses. This is not only because discrimination and stimulus control are the more pervasive concerns in the curriculum, but also because the shaping of discriminations inevitably requires the experimenter's or teacher's manipulation of stimuli. If it is uneconomical to begin teaching a new response without at least a tentative plan for the steps to be followed, it is simply impossible to proceed without such a plan in teaching a discrimination.

There are a few studies in which techniques of shaping up discriminations have been explored, and these, of course, are of particular interest. In the animal laboratory, Herbert Terrace (1960) has shown that when SΔ (the negative stimulus) is introduced soon after response to S^D (the positive stimulus) is established, *and* when SΔ is, at the time of introduction, different in several dimensions from S^D and gradually changed until it differs in only the single relevant dimension (color), pigeons can learn discriminations without ever responding to the negative stimulus. What is more, the birds that learn the discrimination without errors show essentially more stable performances. Using pre-school children, Wells Hively (1962b) has explored the effects of various manipulations of stimuli on the learning of a discrimination. The task in his experiments was "matching to sample" and the stimuli were rather complex geometric figures. Techniques of "fading" (i.e., SΔ is first presented very faintly, then becomes darker), of making stimuli successively more complex and similar to one another, of withholding SΔ until response to S^D is established, of using position in an array as a prompt, as well as simple length of practice were explored. In an unreported experiment conducted at Harvard, Sidney Bijou taught young children, some of them mentally retarded, to match complex geometric figures even when they appeared in different rotations on a plane surface. Next the children learned to discriminate mirror images of these rotated figures from "direct" images. In terms of a theory of shaping, one of the most interesting aspects of Bijou's work is that he became successful only when he introduced a form of successive approximation in which the mirror images (SΔ's) were gradually built up out of figures that, upon first introduction, were quite different in form from the direct images (S^D's).

In much verbal, as opposed to perceptual programming, the problems are somewhat different. Often discrimination *per se* poses no problem. Rather, the task is one of establishing control of clearly discriminable stimuli. However, as has been pointed out earlier, stimuli and responses are frequently related to one another in complicated ways. A theory of shaping or "programming" for such tasks must consider how the student's attention can best be directed to the critical elements of the total stimulus context; how esablishment of one part of a repertoire affects learning of subsequent parts; how exposure to $S\Delta$'s affects learning of S^D's, and other such questions. In this area, most of the investigation has come from programmers rather than laboratory experimenters; and a growing body of literature is becoming available concerned with techniques of prompting, arranging, and sequencing stimuli, and eliciting responses (e.g., Eigen, 1959; Homme and Glaser, 1960; Klaus, 1961; Mechner, 1961; Resnick, 1962). Many of today's papers on programming techniques represent little more than catalogues of procedures that have worked. Yet through them programmers are communicating with one another; and ultimately, probably with the additional help of some controlled experimentation, a more unified and generalizable theory of shaping in verbal programming may emerge.

PROGRAMMED INSTRUCTION AND THE DISCOVERY METHOD

In its insistence on small steps, current programmed instructional theory is at odds with another widely acclaimed approach to teaching, the "discovery method." In the opposition that is frequently set up between the two, discovery is usually considered the more appropriate method for teaching understanding and problem solving, while programmed instruction is given the job of rote, factual training. This sense of opposition, however, probably derives as much from the kinds of teaching problems the two have chosen to study as from the nature of the methods themselves.

While there is no clear consensus as to exactly what constitutes the "discovery method," it is possible to pick out certain common elements in the various uses of the term. The method as I understand it typically poses a problem for the learner to solve. Often the solution to the problem involves stating some kind of "law," or rule, or formula relating observed or described events and applicable to future problems of the same type. Thus the noting of relationships and the statement of summary principles—both frequent criteria of "understanding" and both known to be conducive to transfer—are highly prominent where discovery is used. In some cases "hints" are offered to those students who need them; but when well used the method does in fact require the student to figure something out for himself—that is, to come up with an answer without continuous prompting and guidance from the instructor.

There are apparently wide differences of opinion concerning how much guidance may be offered the student without destroying the essential character of the discovery method. However, most proponents of discovery teaching would probably agree that, if the method is to be successful in teaching something besides tolerance for frustration, the student must be able to solve the problem. To make it more likely that he will be able to do so, the posing of the problem is often preceded by a certain amount of small step instruction (whether consciously "programmed" or not), designed to provide the child with the information, concepts and skills he will need to discover the final solution. Thus, the discovery method is probably rarely used in its pure form; pure discovery would mean, simply, no instruction at all. Instead we might say that small step, sequential teaching is used to teach the component behaviors; but a large gap is left at the point where the components are to be combined. Pure programmed instruction would not—knowingly—leave this gap. That, I think, is the essence of the difference.

What, then, is the educational value of this gap? Three possibilities come to mind, each worth serious consideration. The first is motivational. Perhaps the large step, the gap bridged by oneself, is more reinforcing than the sum of reinforcements over many small steps. If so, the use of discovery techniques would tend to keep the student more interested in the learning process in general, and might even tend to maintain learning over a longer period of time. To the best of my knowledge, we have no clear evidence of the relative reinforcing power of success on large and small steps. There are hints that good students, at any rate, become bored with too many small steps, come to resent the time spent on such programs, and as a result often do not do them carefully. It is far from clear, however, that this phenomenon of boredom exists for everyone. It may be something that only bright, usually successful students feel. These students are used to a feeling of "working" for their success—and achieving it. Without the sense of work, they are not certain of their achievement. For students with less experience of success in their studies, the success itself, insured by the use of small steps and adequate prompting, may be far more reinforcing than the sense of work and "accomplishment" of the discovery gap. From my own experience with deprived, poorly achieving city youngsters, it is my guess that success itself is sufficient to keep such children at a programmed learning task for long periods of time. In other words, the motivational preference for discovery or programmed techniques may reduce itself to a question of whom we are trying to teach.

A second value of the large gap may lie in the role of the trial and error process of finding a solution. Through trial and error the student may "learn how to learn," that is, how to solve problems he will encounter outside the guided situation of the classroom. Certainly the trial and error discovery process is a far closer approximation to the procedures of workers on the boundaries of any field of knowledge than is a small step program. It is this similarity to true scientific investigation, in fact, that has generated much of the excitement about the method (Bruner, 1962). Yet a question can be raised whether the discovery process *per se* actually insures that the student will learn the important processes of inquiry. Does he necessarily learn, for example, how to evaluate his own responses or to judiciously select the next step in the search procedure? Does he learn how to profit from errors—or simply how to tolerate them?

My point here is that unless something in the teaching situation controls the student's behavior, so that he follows a certain kind of productive search process, there is no guarantee that he will learn anything about that process. He may simply make a series of trials at random, "pot-shotting" as it were, and possibly come up with the right solution. And at each trial he may rely on a nod from the teacher or a check with the back of the book for confirmation of his response. If this happens, no evaluation of errors, no setting of one's own response within a larger context for purposes of proof and justification, will occur. Techniques for controlling behavior, so that the student does actually go through more productive processes, vary. Sometimes, the way in which the problem is formulated, joined with a classroom procedure that requires proof of solutions, may be sufficient. At other times, more elaborate and careful training procedures may be required; and here some of the techniques of programming for guiding and controlling behavior may be applicable.[11]

Finally, the value of the discovery gap may lie in the quality of what is learned. Such a claim is often made by those who feel that the discovery method's emphasis on inclusive relationships and problem-solving processes is enough to automatically justify its use. In the sense of curricular innovation it is certainly true that the discovery method is far more advanced than programmed instruction, which has for the most part concentrated on teaching specific concepts and information, and these not always the newest in their fields. However, rather than deny the relevance of programmed instruction to the teaching of problem-solving processes, I think it is more correct to say that very few attempts to apply its theory and techniques in this area have been made.

Those few attempts that there have been, have for the most part suggested

---

[11] The possibility that guided training in problem-solving procedures can be given is not limited to any particular *kind* of thought process. Intuitive as well as analytic and inductive procedures can be taught, if we can clearly identify what those processes are. Such specification is just as much a necessary preliminary for explicit teaching of problem-solving processes as it is for teaching of more specific skills and facts.

that small step programming techniques are indeed applicable to the teaching of such processes. James Holland, for example, has constructed a program in "inductive reasoning," which produces learning with virtually no errors. Specifically, the task is to generate the next term in a series of geometric figures. These figures vary in color, position, and the number of repetitions without insertion of a different figure. The series become more and more complex as one proceeds through the program. Well educated adults often have difficulty with the last items, although children who have been through the preceding series can solve the later ones quite easily. This is admittedly only a small aspect of what is meant by "inductive reasoning," and I am unaware of any investigation of transfer from this program to other, related tasks. Nevertheless, the program demonstrates that small steps and successive approximation are appropriate for teaching at least certain limited problem solving skills.

In a study of somewhat broader scope, Robert Gagné and Larry Brown (1961) compared three different programs on number series, a "Rule and Example" program, a "Discovery" program and a "Guided Discovery" program. The criterion test required the student to find a formula for the sum of term values in a number series. The formula was not to involve simply adding up the values. The three programs used the same number series, but the Rule and Example program did not even attempt to teach the terminal behavior tested. It simply provided formulas, and then gave the student practice in using them to determine sums.[12] The Discovery program posed a problem— finding a formula—and then provided "hints" which the student used as he found them necessary. Early hints for the most part served to direct attention to the relevant stimuli and suggest that some means of relating them must be found. In later hints the relationship was sometimes actually pointed out. The hints did not necessarily require active response on the part of the student.

In terms of programming technique, the essential difference between the Discovery and the Guided Discovery programs is that in the latter the hints were not optional—all students used them all—and active response was required in each. Furthermore, the hints in the Guided Discovery program were somewhat more directive in suggesting search or checking procedures. Thus, the Guided Discovery program actually provided more in the way of concrete training in *how* to find a solution than did the Discovery program. As might

---

[12] What is more, in most of the frames of the Rule and Example program, there was nothing to prevent the student from getting the answer by simply adding up the term-values. Thus, many students may not have even used the formulas, much less found them for themselves. It may be that administrative procedure provided some check on the student's procedure, for the program seems to have been administered individually with an experimenter present throughout. My comment is based upon a reading of the program itself.

be expected, both Discovery and Guided Discovery groups did far better on the criterion test than subjects who had had the Rule and Example program (i.e., no training at all). But subjects who had had the Guided Discovery program also did slightly better on the test than did subjects who had had the Discovery program. The results of this experiment suggest that small step programming in how to solve problems is indeed possible, and, under certain conditions at least, may be superior to pure discovery.

In a study of a very different kind, Richard C. Anderson (1962b) is attempting to train children in the logic of scientific problem-solving. Specifically, through a graded series of concept-formation games using cards, he hopes to teach them the strategy of search and proof that involves varying only one attribute at a time and holding all others constant. This is not programmed instruction in the usual sense of either self-instruction or an absolutely fixed sequence. In fact, in later games, the experimenter may change the concept he calls "correct" depending upon the child's behavior, in order to provide the reinforcement of locating a positive instance as frequently as possible when the child is showing evidence of using the desired strategy. It is hoped that once children are fluent in solving card-concept problems, they will transfer the strategy to *logically* similar problems of other kinds. While there is no formal data yet available, preliminary experience suggests that both the training procedure and the transfer test will be successful (see Anderson, 1962a). If it is successful, this work will be important in two ways. First, it will demonstrate that small step instruction is indeed applicable to the teaching of investigative *processes*, and secondly that transfer along a dimension of logical similarity is possible, even where there is no formal similarity of the individual stimuli involved—provided that training has concentrated on logical relationships and not on the qualities of the specific stimuli.

These studies are, we may hope, only the beginning of widespread investigation of the relevance of programmed instruction to the teaching of problem solving skills. In addition to strict programming of these skills, however, there are several possibilities for combining the theory and techniques of programming with some form of "discovery" that may be worth exploring. First, after behavioral analysis within the operant framework has identified a likely sequence for shaping up a skill, it might be interesting to try introducing discovery phases into a program at various points. At each such point, the skills and concepts needed for solving the problem, or bridging the gap, would be clear from the analysis. With these components clearly specified, it should be simpler to provide for adequate preliminary small-step instruction, hints of the right kinds, and structuring of the problem, so as to ensure solution only by performance of the relevant operations. In addition, the effects on later learning of having learned some component by small step instruction or by discovery might be investigated.

A second possibility of considerable interest is that of using small step instruction primarily to teach a checking procedure, so that the student would be able to evaluate his subsequent responses by himself. This would be helpful not only in discovery teaching, but also wherever production of relatively long and complex responses is involved and "self-editing" is appropriate. Thus, children might be taught to check mathematical solutions by actually trying formulas with sample sets of numbers; or how to check one set of scientific observations against another. Where complex productions are involved, discrimination training procedures might be used to teach students to judge good from bad work, using the productions of others. Once they were skillful in making these discriminations—and only then—they might be asked to judge their own productions, and perhaps to edit them. The great advantage of any such checking procedure is that it reduces students' dependence on others for evaluation or "reinforcement" of their work. Reinforcement becomes, in effect, "intrinsic" to the subject matter.

Finally, experimentation with forms of programmed instruction that in some way vary the amount of prompting, or size of step, according to the student's needs should be of interest. Such adaptation to the individual, of course, is the major rationale for Crowderian-type branching, which also, through its explanatory material, tries to help students examine and thereby learn from their errors. For these reasons, Crowder's programming method has often seemed attractive to those concerned with teaching reasoning processes and other complex material. Among others, the University of Illinois Committee on School Mathematics (1962) has adopted this kind of branching as one of the major means of programming an essentially process- and concept-oriented mathematics course.[13]

Nevertheless, the Crowderian technique seems to me to be less than ideal for the purpose. The long texts without active responding, and the exclusive reliance on multiple-choice responses as the means of choosing the next frame mean that the program loses some degree of control over the student's behavior. In addition, the method seems to force the student into making a certain number of wrong responses. He is not allowed to simply recognize the inadequacy of his preparation for a problem and ask for assistance. He *must* make an error (often prompted by one of the wrong choices) before the program knows where to send him for help. I am not sure exactly how this pitfall can be avoided. Something more like the optional hints used in Gagné's Discovery program may be one solution. Perhaps, too, instead of providing the student with the correct answer after he has made his response, a program

---

[13] They have also used a modified form of branching in which the student who makes no errors in a linear-type, short step program, is branched *ahead*, skipping frames designed to give further instruction and practice to those who need it.

might present a series of "checking" procedures. For the student with the correct answer these checks would serve as confirmation. For the student with the wrong answer, or no answer, they would function as hints, leading to an appropriate solution. In this way, students capable of "discovering" the solution would be allowed to do so, while those needing help would receive it; and both would learn methods of evaluating their own responses.

CONCLUSION

Programmed instruction has been treated in this essay as an attempt to apply the concepts and procedures of operant conditioning theory to the educational process. Operant conditioning has been emphasized because, among the popular rationales for programmed instruction, it seems most likely to provide a basis for fruitful investigation of fundamental learning processes, rather than simple imitation of the more obvious characteristics of successful teaching as we have known it in the past. Focusing even in the laboratory on problems of instruction, operant conditioning offers to educational theory the possibility of precision, without restricting the kinds of teaching problems it can attack.

The precision of operant theory derives from its insistence upon behavioral definition and analysis as a prerequisite to systematic instruction. However, it must be said again that in this matter of definition and analysis, operant theory provides only a bare framework. To become truly useful for instructional purposes, the framework must be filled out. Operant analysis, in other words, offers precision *only* if both stimuli and responses are carefully described. This is a substantive task, which must be performed separately for everything we undertake to teach. I have tried to show that operant analysis can be flexible at the same time as it is precise. By treating patterns and configurations as discriminative stimuli and by relying on behavioral chains in which the individual's own responses serve as stimuli for further responses, it is able to account for transfer, flexibility in form of expression, and other signs of "meaningful learning." These are complex kinds of analyses, difficult to perform and dependent upon a more than superficial knowledge of content and subject-matter. Insofar as analyses of the more complex cognitive behaviors can be achieved, however, we will be in a much stronger position in our attempts to teach those behaviors, by whatever methods of instruction are ultimately chosen.

Generally speaking, reliance on the operant conditioning framework has tended to limit the kinds of instructional problems to which programmed instruction addressed itself. This was appropriate, perhaps, for the real infancy of the field. It is time now, however, that we attempt to deal with some of the more complex and demanding aspects of the curriculum. In so doing, we may have to call into question certain of the assumptions and orthodoxies that have already developed. If programmed instruction is to contribute effectively to the teaching of problem solving skills, for example, it may have to forget its preoccupation with low error rates and begin to concentrate on how to teach children to profit from those errors they will inevitably make in the course of independent inquiry. Certainly, format and method of presentation will have to be varied to suit the demands of the new learning tasks with which we will be dealing. Further, we may want to investigate applications of operant conditioning's analytic and shaping procedures not only to self-instruction, but to the design of instructional procedures of all kinds, some involving important components of social interaction.

Whatever specific modification may be made, however, there are certain principles to which I think investigations of programmed instruction ought to remain firmly committed. These are the notions, first, that even in the most complex of subjects explicit instruction can be given; and second, that the way to approach an instructional problem is analytically, seeking to build complex behaviors out of simpler ones. These ideas form the hard core of programmed instruction, so to speak, the basic principles that should not be compromised.

By explicit instruction I mean the deliberate modification of the behavior of other human beings. Programmed instruction, in other words, is not interested in the teacher as stimulator of interest, role model or evaluator of progress. It is interested in him as instructor, or controller of behavior. This means that programmed instruction is applicable only where we do in fact want to change behavior in a given direction. There are cases where for political or ethical reasons we do not want to. We do not, for example, want to train all students to be active partisans of a given political or religious viewpoint, or make everyone like the same kind of literature or music. In such cases, when we honestly do not wish to control behavior, neither programmed instruction nor any other kind of instruction is appropriate. "Exposure" is the most we should attempt.

Often, however, we *would* like to bring about changes in a given direction, but we are unable to specify exactly what those changes are. We know, for example, that there is a certain minimal level of "good" writing or "logical thinking," regardless of the particular stand taken, that we would like to see all students demonstrate. Exactly what the elements of such good writing or logical thinking are, however, is difficult to say. These are what are often called the "intangibles" or "unmeasurables" of education. In these areas, as well as those in which we do not wish to impose a particular viewpoint, programmed instruction has usually seemed inapplicable.

One cannot but agree that as long as these skills and abilities remain undefined, and therefore unmeasurable, programmed instruction cannot be successfully used to teach them. Rather than give up in this matter, however,

I think that what we need to do is devote substantial attention to analyzing precisely those skills that have always seemed somehow undefinable. Just what behaviors are involved, for example, in solving a problem "scientifically"? Precisely what are the characteristics of "good" writing? What do we mean by "evaluating the facts" in a political discussion? Because these questions are so difficult to answer, attempts at programmed instruction in these areas have been few and not usually very inspiring. It should be pointed out, however, that these are neglected skills for *all* kinds of teaching, not only programmed. Rarely are they explicitly taught. Instead, there is a kind of extended "practice," in which problems or tasks of undefined characteristics are set, and the teacher evaluates his students' performance. Often the standards of evaluation are so imprecise that agreement among teachers is difficult to achieve.

Programmed instruction would seek, instead, to create complex behaviors out of simpler ones. This is the notion behind shaping. It is the reason that behavioral analysis and identification of component behaviors is so important. If the necessary component behaviors can be identified, they can be explicitly taught; then the more complex behaviors can be built up. With this in mind, the concept of "readiness" reduces to a question of whether a child can at a given time perform those component behaviors that are to be assumed rather than actually taught. Similarly, "individual differences" can be to a large extent viewed as differences in the component behaviors that individuals can already perform. This, rather than "maturation level" or "general ability" seems to be a fruitful way to look at differences among students, whether within or between age groups. Rather than specifying grade or ability level for a learning task, then, one would begin by describing in detail what would constitute skillful adult performance, and then seek to identify component behaviors for that performance.

Only with extensive behavioral analysis of the kind proposed here can the insights of operant conditioning theory be systematically applied to educational problems. Yet even then much work will remain. Examining operant conditioning theory in the light of demands peculiar to education, one is forced to conclude that while the basic concepts of reinforcement, stimulus control and shaping are indeed powerful, the theory is in few areas fully developed in such a way as to be directly applicable to the design of instructional procedures. Substitutes for the primary reinforcers of the laboratory and methods of using reinforcement in relatively uncontrolled educational situations must be found, for example. In the matter of shaping, a more detailed procedure for teaching discriminations should be developed. Attention must be paid to techniques of teaching several related responses or discriminations simultaneously. That these needs and others like them still exist means that those interested in problems of instruction have more than a technological task before them. They cannot simply apply a ready-made theory from the laboratory and expect it to produce astonishing results. There are important questions about learning and teaching processes that still need answering. There is room, in short, for basic research oriented toward the development of a viable instructional theory.

Research with the demands of education in mind, however, is not the same as "action" or "applied" research. Wholesale comparisons of teaching methods—"conventional" versus self-instructional, for example—may prove that one works better than another in a given case, but it will never make clear just what variables account for the superiority of one method over the other. As a result, the findings will not be generalizable to new problems. Such studies may have administrative value but they offer little to a theory of instruction. The point is not to do research *in* an educational setting but to do research that will be valuable *for* education in a broad sense. Such research may be performed in the laboratory as well as in the classroom; but the kinds of questions that receive attention will be different if the impetus for research derives from educational rather than laboratory concerns.

References

Anderson, R. C. Science sequence and the process of inquiry. Mimeographed. East Brunswick (N.J.) Public Schools, 1962 (a).

Anderson, R. C. Shaping logical behavior in six- and seven-year olds. Research proposal submitted to the U.S. Office of Education, 1962 (b).

Bruner, J. S. *The process of education.* Cambridge, Mass.: Harvard University Press, 1961.

Bruner, J. S. *On knowing: Essays for the left hand.* Cambridge, Mass.: Harvard University Press, 1962.

Chomsky, N. Review of Skinner's *Verbal Behavior. Language,* 1959, **35,** 26–58.

Crowder, N. A. Automatic tutoring by intrinsic programming. In A. A. Lumsdaine and R. Glaser (eds.), *Teaching machines and programmed learning: A source book.* Washington, D. C.: National Education Association, 1960, pp. 286–298.

Crowder, N. A. Simple ways to use the student response for program control. In S. Margulies and L. D. Eigen (eds.), *Applied programmed instruction.* New York: Wiley, 1962.

Eigen, L. *The construction of frames of an automated teaching program.* New York: Center for Programmed Instruction, 1959.

Ferster, C. B. & Skinner, B. F. *Schedules of reinforcement.* New York: Appleton-Century-Crofts, 1957.

Gagné, R. M. & Brown, L. T. Some factors in the programming of conceptual learning. *J. exper. Psychol.*, 1961, **62**, 313–321.

Gilbert, T. F. On the relevance of laboratory investigation of learning to self-instructional programming In A. A. Lumsdaine and R. Glaser (eds.), *Teaching machines and programmed learning: A source book.* Washington, D. C.: National Education Association, 1960, pp. 475–485.

Green, E. J. *The learning process and programmed instruction.* New York: Holt, Rinehart and Winston, 1962.

Hively, W. Specifying "Terminal Behavior" in Mathematics. Mimeographed. Harvard University, 1962 (a).

Hively, W. Programming stimuli in matching to sample. *J. exper. anal. Behav.*, 1962, **5**, 279–298 (b).

Homme, L. E. & Glaser, R. Problems in programming verbal learning sequences. In A. A. Lumsdaine and R. Glaser (eds.), *Teaching machines and programmed learning: A source book.* Washington, D. C.: National Education Association, 1960, pp. 486–496.

Inhelder, Bärbel & Piaget, J. (translated by A. Parsons & S. Milgram). *The growth of logical thinking from childhood to adolescence.* New York: Basic Books, 1958.

Keller, F. S. & Schoenfeld, W. N. *Principles of psychology: A systematic text in the science of behavior.* New York: Appleton-Century-Crofts, 1950.

Klaus, D. J. The art of auto-instructional programming. *A-V Communications Rev.*, 1961, **9**, 130–142.

Krasner, L. Studies of the conditioning of verbal behavior. *Psychol. Bull.*, 1958, **55**, 148–170.

Mager, J. *Preparing objectives for programmed instruction.* San Francisco: Fearon, 1961.

Mead, G. H. *Mind, self and society from the standpoint of a social behaviorist.* Chicago: Univ. of Chicago Press, 1934.

Mechner, F. Programming for automated instruction. With Supplements I, II & III. Mimeographed. New York: Basic Systems, Inc., 1961.

Miller, G. A., Galanter, E., & Pribram, K. H. *Plans and the structure of behavior.* New York: Henry Holt, 1960.

Miller, G. Some psychological studies of grammar. *Amer. Psychologist*, 1962, **17**, 748–762.

Resnick, Lauren B. The development of a discrimination program for teaching verb conjugations. Harvard University Committee on Programmed Instruction. Mimeographed. 1962.

Resnick, Lauren B. Programmed instruction and the teaching of social studies skills. 1963 Yearbook of the National Council for the Social Studies, 1963 (a).

Resnick, Lauren B. Use of programmed instructional materials with culturally deprived children. Technical Report # 630626, New York: Center for Programmed Instructions, 1963 (b).

Scheffler, Israel. A note on behaviorism as educational theory. *Harvard Educ. Rev.*, 1962, **32**, 210–213.

Skinner, B. F. *Verbal behavior*. New York: Appleton-Century-Crofts, 1957.

Skinner, B. F. Pigeons in a pelican. *Amer. Psychologist*, 1960, **15**, 28–37.

Skinner, B. F. Why we need teaching machines. *Harvard Educ. Rev.*, 1961, **31**, 378–398.

Terrace, H. S. Discrimination learning with and without errors. Doctor's dissertation. Harvard University, 1960.

University of Illinois Committee on School Mathematics. *UICSM High School Mathematics*, Parts 101, 102, 103, 104, *104,* & 105. Experimental Programmed Edition. University of Illinois, 1962.

62. PROGRAMMED

Paul Goodman

I

Programmed teaching adapted for machine use goes a further step than conforming students to the consensus which is a principal effect of schooling interlocked with the mass media. In this pedagogic method it is *only* the programmer—the administrative decision-maker—who is to do any "thinking" at all; the students are systematically conditioned to follow the train of the *other's* thoughts. "Learning" means to give some final response that the programmer considers advantageous (to the students). There is no criterion of *knowing* it, of having learned it, of Gestalt-forming or simplification. That is, the student has no active self at all; his self, at least as student, is a construct of the programmer.

What does this imply? Let me analyze a very high-level argument for such teaching by Lauren Resnick, "Programmed Instruction of Complex Skills," in *The Harvard Educational Review* of Fall 1963.

In the conclusion of this perspicuous article, Dr. Resnick tells us:

> By explicit instruction I mean the deliberate modification of the
> behavior of other human beings. Programmed instruction is not
> interested in the teacher as stimulator of interest, role model,
> or evaluator of progress. It is interested in him as instructor,

SOURCE. Reprinted by permission of the publisher, Horizon Press, from *Compulsory Mis-Education* by Paul Goodman. Copyright © 1964 by Horizon Press, New York, the publisher.

or controller of behavior. This means that programmed instruction
is applicable only where we do in fact want to change behavior in a
given direction. There are cases where for political or ethical reasons
we do not want to. We do not, for example, want to train all students
to be active partisans of a given political or religious viewpoint, or make
everyone like the same kind of literature or music. In such cases . . .
'exposure' is the most we should attempt. (p. 467)

Let me put this dramatic statement in juxtaposition with an earlier statement in her essay:

In the context of behavioral analysis, knowledge, skill, and ability
can be dealt with only insofar as they can be described in terms
of performance. This description is not a matter of listing 'correlates'
of ability or knowledge, but of deciding what observable behaviors
will be accepted as evidence of their existence. The behaviorist simply
eschews the question of whether knowledge, for instance, exists apart
from observable behaviors. While, in so doing, he may fail to answer
to the philosopher's satisfaction the question, 'What is knowledge?',
he very effectively provides himself with a set of usable goals
for instruction. (p. 448)

I do not much want to discuss the pedagogic relevance of these ideas. The
only evidence of "performance" that school people ever draw on for their
experiments is scoring on academic tests, and it seems to be impossible to
disabuse school people of the notion that test-passers have necessarily learned
anything relevant to their further progress or careers; or of advantage to
the body politic; or indeed anything whatever that will not vanish in a short
time, when the *real* life-incentive, of passing the test, has passed away. But
I want to ask if this kind of *formulation* of teaching does not involve serious
legal difficulties, in terms of civil liberties, especially where schooling is
compulsory, when the child *must* go to school and submit to having his behavior shaped.

It may seem odd that I keep referring to the constitutional question; but
it is a way of asking what kind of democracy we envisage in our curriculum
and methods of schooling. Besides, since the young have become so clearly
both an exploited and an outcast class, we must begin to think of legal rights.

II

Our Bill of Rights guarantees were grounded in a very different epistemological theory from operant-conditioning, the method that Dr. Resnick has
learned from B. F. Skinner. Roughly, the Enlightenment conception was that

intellect, like conscience, was something "inward," and the aim of teaching was to nurture its "growth" by "knowledge." Even more important, behavior was the "external" effect of an initiating or self-moving of the "soul"; therefore the student was or became "responsible." In my opinion, the inner-outer metaphor of this conception is quite useless; there is not much use in a psychological theory for entities that are not observable as behavior. But the Aristotelian emphasis on the self-moving organism is solid gold.

Now compulsory schooling, as I have pointed out, was justified in this theory, e.g. by Jefferson, as necessary to bring children to the point of self-government, of exercising citizenry initiative, as well as the animal and social initiative that they had by "nature" and the moral initiative that they had by "conscience." Democracy required an educated electorate. To this was later added the justification that only by compulsory education could the poor get an equal democratic opportunity with the rich; poor parents were likely to put their children to work too early, and not give them a chance to develop to their full powers.

In turn, any course of the curriculum or detail of method was justified by showing that it nurtured the growth of the inward intellect, encouraged initiative, and fitted the young to take a free part in political society. On this view, school teaching was precisely not "training," though parents were allowed to train minor children and the masters of apprentices were allowed to train their bonded apprentices. School subjects either had to contain values ideal in themselves, as good, true, or beautiful, which were "liberal" by definition; or they strengthened the "logical faculty," which the young citizen would then apply to all kinds of matters (this was the traditional notion of "transfer"); or they gave him orientation in space and time—as I have mentioned, especially History was prized, because its horrible and noble examples inspired youth to preserve freedom.

Of course, the late nineteenth century compulsory education in the mechanical arts, to the degree that they were merely utilitarian, could not so easily be justified in these "inward" ways—it tended to seem like apprentice-training at the public expense. But in an expanding economy with high social mobility, and where there was considerable self-employment and much new enterprise, there was no occasion to cavil; a free soul would want such advantageous skills of its own volition. Few adolescents went to school anyway, and children never did have many rights, though plenty of privileges.

III

Dr. Resnick's system explicitly excludes all notions of "inward" meaning. And she is also unhappy about the sneaking in of any factor of initiative. For example, in discussing Shaping—the approximation of the responses to the final response—she sharply disagrees with those experimenters who wait for the organism to make a small move in the right direction, to reinforce it. "Programmed instruction," she says, "cannot afford to proceed in this way." (But she never does make clear, at least to me, how she gets the beast to move *ab extra*, in order to have something to shape.)

Also, unlike the liberal or "faculty-developing" curriculum of the Enlightenment theory, no particular subject of learning is chosen because of its characteristic appeal to or stimulation of the powers, liberation, or needs of the learner. Operant-conditioning theory, she says, is essentially "contentless"; it is a pure technique that can teach anything to almost anybody. This might be Dr. Conant's "national needs"; it might be the "improved attitudes" of the Continuation branch of Milwaukee Vocational; it might be the vagaries of Big Brother.

In sum, on this view, compulsory schooling, so far as it is programmed, is identical with compulsory training to the goals of the controllers of behavior, and such goals are set by the "we want" of the first paragraph I have cited. Then I am curious to hear from Dr. Resnick the constitutional justification for compulsory schooling in terms of the "we want" and "we do not want" of that paragraph. Who, we? and what limitation is there to "want" or happen to want? The title of her essay, let us remember, is "Instruction of Complex Skills"; she is not restricting behavior-control to rote and drill subjects, but extending it to the higher branches, to criticism, problem-solving, appreciation, except where "we do not want to."

Needless to say, curriculum, methods, and the school-system itself have *always* been determined by social goals and National Goals, parental ambitions, and the need to baby-sit and police the young. But it is one thing to believe—or pretend—that these educate the children, and quite another thing to *say* that they are behavior-controllers.

IV

Our author's indifference to this kind of consideration appears strongly in an otherwise excellent analysis of the "Discovery Method" as contrasted with step-by-step programmed instruction. One advantage claimed for the Discovery Method—for which, we saw, Dr. Zacharias and the National Science Foundation have manifested enthusiasm—is that the leap over the gap is itself exciting and reinforcing, providing stronger motivation. Dr. Resnick agrees that this might be true for bright students; but she wisely points out that culturally-deprived, poorly achieving youngsters get more satisfaction from steady success, without risk of new failure. A second advantage claimed is that the trial and error in the Discovery process fits the student for the kind of learning that he will have to do outside the classroom; but here Dr.

Resnick doubts that the student learns from his errors unless he is trained in what to ask about them, that is, to notice them. (She is right. For example, a good piano teacher will have the student deliberately play the wrong note that he repeats inadvertently.) Finally, it is claimed, the quality of what is learned by Discovery—the synoptic, the law, the solution of the problem—is superior. This, says Dr. Resnick, is because programmed instruction has so far concentrated almost exclusively on teaching mere concepts and information, rather than complex wholes of learning.

What is astonishing in this thoughtful analysis, however, is that she entirely omits the *salient* virtue that most teachers, classical or progressive, have always hoped for in letting the student discover for himself, namely the development of his confidence that he *can*, that he is adequate to the nature of things, can proceed on his own initiative, and ultimately strike out on an unknown path, where there is no program, and assign his own tasks to himself. The classical maxim of teaching is: to bring the student to where he casts off the teacher. Dewey's model for curriculum and method was: any study so pursued that it ends up with the student wanting to find out something further.

Apparently Dr. Resnick cannot even conceive of this virtue, because it is contradictory to the essence of controlled behavior toward a predetermined goal. It is open. From her point of view, it is not instruction at all. In terms of social theory, it posits an open society of independent citizens—but she and Dr. Skinner think there is a special "we" who "want." Also, scientifically, it posits a more open intellectual future than the complex-skill which programming seems to envisage. Is it indeed the case that so much *is* known—so definitely—that we can tightly program methods and fundamental ideas? Much of the program is bound to be out-of-date before the class graduates.

V

This is a fundamental issue. Intellectually, humanly, and politically, our present universal high-schooling and vastly increasing college-going are a disaster. I will go over the *crude* facts still again! A youngster is compelled for twelve *continuous* years—if middle class, for sixteen years—to work on assigned lessons, during a lively period of life when one hopes he might invent enterprises of his own. Because of the school work, he cannot follow his nose in reading and browsing in the library, or concentrate on a hobby that fires him, or get a job, or carry on a responsible love-affair, or travel, or become involved in political action. The school system as a whole, with its increasingly set curriculum, stricter grading, incredible amounts of testing, is already a vast machine to shape acceptable responses. Programmed instruction closes the windows a little tighter and it rigidifies the present departmentalization and dogma. But worst of all, it tends to nullify the one lively virtue that any school does have, that it is a community of youth and of youth and adults.

Dr. Resnick can assert that there are areas where "we do not want" to control behavior—political, religious, esthetic, perhaps social. But the case is that for sixteen years it is precisely docility to training and boredom that is heavily rewarded with approval, legitimacy, and money; whereas spontaneous initiation is punished by interruption, by being considered irrelevant, by anxiety of failing in the "important" work, and even by humiliation and jail. Yet somehow, after this hectic course of conditioning, young men and women are supposed, on commencement, suddenly to exercise initiative in the most extreme matters: to find jobs for themselves in a competitive market, to make long career plans, to undertake original artistic and scientific projects, to marry and become parents, to vote for public officers. But their behavior has been shaped only too well. Inevitably most of them will go on with the pattern of assigned lessons, as Organization Men or on the assembly-line; they will vote Democratic-Republican and buy right brands.

I am rather miffed at the vulgarity of the implication that, in teaching the humanities, we should at most attempt "exposure"—as if appreciation were entirely a private matter, or a matter of unstructured "emotion." (There is no such thing, by the way, as unstructured emotion.) When Dr. Resnick speaks of the unshaped response to the kind of literature of music "they like," she condemns their esthetic life to being a frill, without meaning for character, valuation, recreation, or how one is in the world. Frankly, as a man of letters I would even prefer literature to be programmed, as in Russia.

That is, *even if behavioral analysis and programmed instruction were the adequate analysis of learning and method of teaching, it would still be questionable, for overriding political reasons, whether they are generally appropriate for the education of free citizens.*

VI

To be candid, I think operant-conditioning is vastly overrated. It teaches us the not newsy proposition that if an animal is deprived of its natural environment and society, sensorily deprived, made mildly anxious, and restricted to the narrowest possible spontaneous motion, it will emotionally identify with its oppressor and respond—with low-grade grace, energy, and intelligence—in the only way allowed to it. The poor beast must do something, just to live on a little. There is no doubt that a beagle can be trained to walk on its hind legs and balance a ball on the tip of its nose. But the dog will show much more intelligence, force, and speedy feedback when chasing a rabbit in the field. It is an odd thought that we can increase the efficiency of learning by nullifying *a priori* most of an animal's powers to learn and taking it out of its best field.

It has been a persistent error of behaviorist psychologies to overlook that there are overt criteria that are organically part of *meaningful* acts of an organism in its environment; we can observe grace, ease, force, style, sudden simplification—and some such characteristics are at least roughly measurable. It is not necessary, in describing insight, knowledge, the kind of assimilated learning that Aristotle called "second nature," to have recourse to mental entities. It is not difficult to *see* when a child *knows* how to ride a bicycle; and he never forgets it, which would not be the case if the learning were by conditioning with reinforcement, because that can easily be wiped away by a negative reinforcement. (Kurt Goldstein has gone over this ground demonstratively.)

On the other hand, it is extremely dubious that by controlled conditioning one *can* teach organically meaningful behavior. Rather, the attempt to control *prevents* learnings. This is obvious to anyone who has ever tried to teach a child to ride a bicycle; the more you try, the more he falls. The best one can do is to provide him a bicycle, allay his anxiety, tell him to keep going, and *not* to try to balance. I am convinced that the same is true in teaching reading.

VII

As is common in many (sometimes excellent) modern scientific papers— whether in linguistics or studies of citizen participation or the theory of delinquency—Dr. Resnick asks for more money; and of course, for purposes of more research, the higher investigations that she asks for should be pursued as long as her enthusiasm lasts and should be supported. Any definite hypothesis that is believed in by a brilliant worker is likely to yield useful by-products that can then be reinterpreted; nor is there any other guide for the advancement of science except the conviction and competence of the researchers.

But I am puzzled at what widespread social benefits she has in mind that warrant a *lot* of expense in brains and machinery. She seems to agree that bright children do not learn most efficiently by these extrinsic methods; and for the average the picture is as I have described it: average employment in a highly automated technology requires a few weeks' training on the job and no schooling at all, and for the kind of humane employment and humane leisure that we hopefully look toward, we require a kind of education and habit entirely different from programmed instruction.

But I am more impressed by what is perhaps Dr. Resnick's deepest concern, the possible *psychotherapeutic* use of more complex programming for the remedial instruction of kids who have developed severe blocks to learning and are far behind. For youngsters who have lost all confidence in themselves, there is a security in being able to take small steps entirely at their own pace and entirely by their own control of the machine. Also, though the chief use of schools is their functioning as a community, under present competitive and stratified conditions it is often less wounding for a kid who has fallen behind to be allowed to withdraw from the group and recover. And this time can usefully and curatively be spent in learning the standard "answers" that can put him in the game again.

There is a pathos in our technological advancement, well exemplified by programmed instruction. A large part of it consists in erroneously reducing the concept of animals and human beings in order to make them machine-operable. The social background in which this occurs, meanwhile, makes many people out-caste and in fact tends to reduce them as persons and make them irresponsible. The refined technique has little valid use for the dominant social group for which it has been devised, e.g. in teaching science; but it does prove to have a use for the reduced out-castes, in teaching remedial arithmetic.

63. SOME POTENTIALS AND HAZARDS OF EDUCATIONAL TECHNOLOGY

Harry S. Broudy

In dealing with the potentials and hazards of educational technology we enjoy the advantage of being in on the very early stages of a movement that has had its analogues in other fields: industrial production, communications, and transportation. The knowledge of the effects of technology in these enterprises, with appropiate cautions, should be valuable in estimating the course and impact of technological developments on education.

But will educational technology convert education into a mass-production enterprise? The word "production" is unfortunate here because pupils are not regarded, even by the most tough-minded proponents of autoinstructional devices, as inert products. However, by "mass production" I merely intend to refer to such features as the intense specialization of function consequent to a high degree of division of labor, hierarchical bureaucratic organization of personnel, large concentrations of capital, a high premium on management, and efficiency as the critical criterion of success.

This is a question of some importance because the nature as well as the magnitude of the effects of technology may depend on the number of people directly and indirectly affected. For example, if the automobile had never gone into mass production, it might have remained on the social scene merely as an interesting diversion for the wealthy, much as yachts are today. It would

SOURCE. Broudy, Harry S., "Some Potential Hazards of Educational Technology," Chapter 5 in Edgar L. Morphet and David Jesser (eds.), *Planning for Effective Utilization of Technology in Education.* Designing Education for the Future: An Eight State Project, 1968.

not have resulted in a large percentage of our working force and capital being devoted to the production and maintenance of automobiles, roads, etc. Similarly, if educational technology should go no further than to provide a fine research instrument for the study of teaching, its results might be of enormous theoretical importance, but it might not produce massive changes in school financing or the location of schools. However, should schooling take on the features of a large-scale, mass-production enterprise, the collateral changes it may engender could have far reaching effects on the very nature of education and its role in the social order. What then are the reasons for believing that schooling will develop the characteristics of mass production?

The size of the schooling enterprise is bound to increase. It has been estimated that in the years to come a huge proportion of our population will be either learning or working at something connected with learning. It is not difficult to imagine that within 30 years, the period of compulsory schooling will stretch from the ages of 3 to 30. Add to this all the varieties of advanced and continuing schooling, and we can understand why education has been called the growth industry of the future. More generally, *education must grow in scope and importance because this century has witnessed the triumph of idea power. All other forms of power—military, economic, political—henceforth will depend on the power that knowledge in the form of technology makes available.* This means, for one thing, that the symbolic-conceptual skills must reach a high level in virtually the total population, and this cannot be brought off without formal schooling on a vast scale. To meet such a demand, it seems reasonable to believe, education will have to take on some of the characteristics of mass production.

One of these characteristics, and perhaps the overarching one, is the reduction of unit costs through volume production. The price for this lower unit cost is a loss of flexibility. Thus, no matter how flexible in function a teaching machine will be—and it can be made very flexible—it will have to be manufactured uniformly in very large lots. For the full benefits of mass production are achieved only when the machines are themselves made by machines.

Another consequence of the large investment that makes unit costs low is that changes in the product become very costly and are therefore undertaken with great caution. And because around every great mass-production enterprise there spring up clusters of ancillary production and distribution units, every substantial change is systemic and possibly threatening to multitudes involved in the system.

Finally, it is characteristic of a mass-production enterprise that it starts out by offering man an economical mechanical servant that will reduce his labor and drudgery, but often ends up by making the master so dependent on the new servant that one wonders which is master and which is servant.

The argument of this paper will be organized as follows:

1. Explicitness as central in the rationale for programmed instruction, based on a discussion of B. F. Skinner's views on teaching.

2. Explicitness and the limitation of computers to simulate human intelligence, based on the article by Hubert L. Dreyfus.

3. Polanyi's distinction between explicit and tacit learnings as it applies to the various uses of schooling.

4. A discussion of the tendency to compare programmed instruction to the tutorial relation, in terms of Socratic teaching and the explicit-tacit distinction.

5. Probable effects of the developments of technology on the nature and function of school personnel, and the probability of utilizing gains from educational technology to provide a high order of personalized or tacit education.

I am sure that my documentation will be incomplete, partly because much of what has been written has become common knowledge, so that I cannot recall where I first read or heard it, and partly because I am in no position to evaluate fairly and properly all the research that has been done in the area, even if I had been able to read all of it. About all I can hope is that my major arguments and conclusions have not already been disproved beyond reasonable doubt by research that is to be judged good research beyond all reasonable doubt.

THE EXPLICIT DIMENSION OF TEACHING

B. F. Skinner is one of the acknowledged pioneers in the development of both teaching machines and the rationale for their use.[1] He very perceptively argues that most of the classroom and pupil behavior regarded as signs of good teaching are really short-term gratifications for teachers rather than proofs of instructional efficiency. Handwaving by pupils, the excited classroom, and discovery are among the fashionable signs of pedagogical success that are rightly regarded by Skinner as misleading. So are the cat-and-mouse maneuverings in what passes for Socratic questioning. For Skinner, the Great Conversations between men and other men in the last 2000 years "has not been notably productive of useful information or wisdom."[2]

Instead he argues for efficiency as a criterion of teaching—that is, for a saving of effort and time in reaching specific behavioral objectives. Efficiency

---

[1] Skinner's book, *The Technology of Teaching* (New York: Appleton-Century-Crofts, 1968), is one of his most recent publications, but I shall not try to present an exhaustive analysis of his writings. My purpose will be served by a few references to his recent article, "Teaching Science in High School—What is Wrong?", *Science*, (February, 1968), pp. 704–10.

[2] *Ibid.*, p. 705.

can be achieved by applying the principle of operant conditioning and involves (1) explicit formulation of the desired terminal behavior, (2) devising
a means of eliciting it, and (3) means of reenforcing it according to a schedule that has been tested for efficiency. Hence, "Teachers need to be retrained
as skillful behavioral engineers."

Skinner rejects the distinction between teaching and training and suspects
that "The traditional distinction comes down to this: when we know what we
are doing, we are training; when we do not know what we are doing, we are
teaching."[3]

In the same vein he says elsewhere:

> . . . What positive reason can we give the student for studying? We
> can point to the ultimate advantage of an education—to the ways
> of life which are open only to educated men—and the student himself
> may cite these to explain why he wants an education, but ultimate
> advantages are not contingent on behavior in ways which generate
> action. Many a student can testify to the result. No matter how
> much he may *want* to become a doctor or an engineer, say, he cannot
> force himself to read and remember the page of text in front of him
> at the moment. All notions of ultimate utility . . . suffer from the same
> shortcoming: they do not specify effective contingencies of
> reinforcement.[4]

As one might expect, Skinner has little patience with mentalistic answers
to the question: What is happening when the student learns? Such notions
as acquiring concepts, seeing relations, having ideas, retrieving information,
and the like are "either metaphors which inadequately represent the changes
taking place in the student's behavior or explanatory fictions which really
explain nothing."[5]

The crucial point in the Skinnerian position is the demand for explicitness.
Success in teaching in general—and therefore also in programmed instruction
—depends on how explicitly behavioral objectives can be stated, a view
echoed in the slogan: "Down with non-behavioral objectives." The most explicit objectives, of course, are those which can be translated into publicly
observable behaviors—a mark on paper, a sound that can be recorded, or a
muscular movement that can be seen or measured. It rules out objectives
stated in merely dispositional terms, such as ability to retrieve information
or make judgments, or tell the truth, for the test of a disposition is the be-

---

[3] *Ibid.*, p. 708.

[4] "Why We Need Teaching Machines" in John P. DeCecco, ed., *Educational Technology*, (San Francisco: Holt, Rinehart & Winston, 1964), p. 95.

[5] "Teaching Science in High School—What is Wrong?", *op cit.*, p. 707.

havior it is predisposed to, so that one should either test directly for its presence or absence or stop talking about it.

The need for explicitness also justifies his unflattering remarks about Socratic dialogue, if—as Skinner mistakenly supposes—some definite answer is its desired outcome. If you want a particular answer, says Skinner, reinforce that rather than the cat-and-mouse game that is supposed to lead to the answer. Otherwise, the pupil will learn cat-and-mousing, not the answer. Furthermore, Great Conversations that decide nothing also are poor stuff for programming, precisely because it is impossible to state and formalize perpetual argument and puzzlement.

One may wish to quarrel with Skinner's general psychological theory or the narrow scope he assigns to education, but within that scope, there is little doubt in my mind that human pupils as well as pigeons can be taught an amazing repertoire of responses. If one knows the terminal behavior wanted and can make this explicit, then the method of operant conditioning, with positive reinforcement by scientific or shrewd scheduling, should bring about the desired learning efficiently. Insofar as programmed instruction uses the Skinner rationale, we can conclude that given the conditions of specificity or explicitness and the ability to formalize objectives, the claims of programmed instruction, especially of computer-aided instruction, in principle seem sound.

What are these claims? First and foremost, perhaps, is the promise of individualizing instruction. Next, is the efficiency with which instruction is carried on. Rapid feedback to the student and the teacher is another claim. All of these claims are sometimes bulked together under the notion of the teaching machine as an ever closer approximation to the tutor-pupil relationship. How good are these claims? I shall reserve the last—the claim to approximate the tutor role—for special consideration, because it rests on a confusion of individualized instruction and the tutorial relation. As for the others, one can say in general that in so far as explicit didactics are concerned, there are strong grounds for believing that the claims are justified.

There is little doubt that machines can drill and review materials in the elementary skill subjects, and that they can introduce the pupil to concepts in various subject matters. Of course, if spoken language is incorporated into the machine, the approximation to the conventional tutorial situation will be improved.

There are problems with computer-aided instruction, such as the tendency for the computer to demand fast responses in elementary skills, so that the slower child feels overly pressed. Then there is the counter difficulty when the machine's response is too slow and attention wanders. Finally, there is the problem of the reliability of the system in evaluating what the student has done.[6]

---

[6] I am indebted for the list of items discussed under computer-aided instruction to

However, these latter problems do not constitute impossibilities in principle. Technical improvements may be expected to mitigate or remove them. A more important reservation is the one voiced in the following quotation.

> In programmed instruction the concern with the measurable, behavioral objectives has led programmers into the subject-matter areas where apparently objectives are relatively easy to identify. Mathematics and physics, for example, are two such areas. Indeed, educators have often reacted to this focusing of attention by questioning the value of programmed instruction for subjects other than those involving procedures, physical events, relationships, and principles.[7]

NONEXPLICIT FACTORS IN INTELLIGENCE

Programmed teaching, simple or sophisticated, depends on the theory that human intelligence can be simulated by a machine—in the case of instruction the machine is supposed to simulate the teacher interacting with a pupil. A better view of the potentials and hazards of educational technology, therefore, can be achieved if we ask about the degree to which such simulation can be successful.

Dreyfus, in an interesting article entitled: "Why Computers Must Have Bodies to be Intelligent," points out that:

> All information with which these computers operate must be represented in terms of binary digits, i.e., in terms of a series of yes's and no's of switches being open or closed. The machine must operate on finite strings of these determinate elements as a series of objects related to each other only by rules. Thus, psychologically, the computer is a model of the mind as conceived of by associationists (for the elements) and intellectualists (for the rules). Both associationists and intellectualists share the traditional conception of thinking as data processing—a third person process in which the involvement of the "processor" plays no essential part. Moreover, since all information fed into such machines must be in terms of bits, the belief that such machines can be made to behave intelligently

notes that I was fortunate enough to take at a recent lecture by Professor Patrick Suppes at Stanford University. Cf. also chapters by Edward B. Fry, James D. Finn, and Ralph J. Melaragno in DeCecco, *Educational Technology, op. cit.*

[7] William A. Deterline, "Practical Problems in Programed Instruction," in *Programed Instruction*, The Sixty-Sixth Yearbook of the National Society for the Study of Education, Part II, (Chicago: University of Chicago Press, 1967), p. 191. See also Ralph H. Ojemann, "Should Educational Objectives Be Stated in Behavioral Terms?" *Elementary School Journal*, 68:5, (February, 1968), pp. 223–231; Thomas F. Green, "Teaching, Acting, and Behaving," *Harvard Educational Review*, 34: 507–524, and B. Paul Komisar, "Conceptual Analysis of Teaching," *High School Journal*, 50: (October, 1966), p. 1421.

presupposes that all relevant information about the world must be expressible in an isolable, determinate way.[8]

Computers can deal brilliantly with ideal languages and abstract logical relations. But what happens when we put to the computer the task of recognizing a pattern, for example, the signature on a check? If the recognition depends on a small number of traits that can be checked by the machine against a set of predetermined "definitions," the task can be accomplished, but Dreyfus feels that the number of such traits that can be looked up by the machine in a reasonable length of time has already reached the technological limit.[9]

The difficulty seems to lie in what Dreyfus regards—and I think correctly—as a fact, namely, that when human intelligence recognizes a pattern it does not do so by associating additively individual bits or elements. Gestalt psychologists have argued endlessly that the human mind recognizes the pattern as a whole, and that this whole gives meaning to the individual parts. We are all familiar with the ambiguous figures in which a drawing can be taken for a vase or for two profiles facing each other. Clearly how the individual lines will be perceived depends on which "whole" he has recognized.

What guides pattern recognition in human perception? The answer would seem to be the interests or purposes or the anticipations of the perceiver. Dreyfus, together with Piaget and Merleau-Ponty, among others, holds that it is the total set of anticipations of our bodies that does the guiding.[10] Whether it is the anticipation of the body or not, an anticipation in the form of goals and interests is the rule.

The expectation that 200 yards ahead we shall encounter a red stop-sign makes us slow down our car, even though upon closer viewing it turns out that the sign has been removed, or at least is no longer where it should have been. Once this is noted, our expectations direct us to perceive certain details as connected with the removal, for example, a road barrier across the adjoining street, a trench being dug in the vicinity and so forth. This embodies a sort of information processing that makes possible the open texture of pattern recognition which would seem to be impossible for a system with a finite set of states.[11]

That perception is goal oriented is a fairly familiar doctrine in philosophy and psychology, and goals, of course, are intimately related to the needs and

[8] Hubert I. Dreyfus, *The Review of Metaphysics*, 21:1, (September, 1967), pp. 13–33.

[9] *Ibid.*, p. 17. I am not sure how valid this conclusion is, but it does not seem to be crucial to Dreyfus' argument from principle.

[10] Jean Piaget, *Psychology of Intelligence* (New York: Harcourt, Brace, & World, 1950), p. 82; Maurice Merleau-Ponty, *Phenomenology of Perception* (London; Routledge and Kegan Paul, 1962), p. 142; and Michael Polanyi, "Logic and Psychology," in *American Psychologist*, 23:1, (Jan. 1968), pp. 33–4.

[11] Dreyfus, *op. cit.*, p. 21.

interests of the body, our instrument of action. This relation is so close that for Michael Polanyi:

> To use language in speech, reading and writing, is to extend our bodily equipment and become intelligent human beings. We may say that when we learn to use language, or a probe, or a tool, and thus make ourselves aware of these things as we are of our body, we *interiorize* these things *and make ourselves* dwell in them.[12]

This embodiment makes it unnecessary for us to know explicitly the rules governing our speech behavior. "If human beings had to store and assess an infinity of facts in order to understand a language, they would have as much trouble as machines."[13]

As for problem solving, Dreyfus is pessimistic about machines simulating our ability to distinguish the essential from the inessential elements in a problem. This procedure seems to "be a uniquely human form of information processing, one not amenable to the mechanical search techniques which operate once the distinction has been made."[14] This ability is especially important in the solution of everyday molar problems (as against purely formal ones) in which there is no *a priori* limit to the data that might be relevant.

> If the machine were to examine explicitly each possibly relevant factor as a determinate bit of information, in order to determine whether to consider or ignore it, it could never complete the calculations necessary to predict the outcome of a single [horse] race. If, on the other hand, the machine systematically excluded possibly relevant factors in order to complete its calculations, then it would sometimes be incapable of performing as well as an intelligent human being.[15]

Accordingly, Dreyfus concludes:

> The force of my argument, insofar as it is an impossibility argument, depends on the open texture of pattern recognition, the infinity of facts that may be relevant in problem solving, and the correlative flexibility of bodily skills. If experience really has this open character, then any *specific* human intelligent performance could indeed be simulated on a computer after the fact, but *fully* intelligent behavior would be impossible in principle for a digital machine.[16]

[12] Michael Polanyi, *Personal Knowledge* (Chicago: University of Chicago Press, 1958), quoted by Dreyfus, *op. cit.*, fn. p. 29.

[13] *Ibid.*

[14] *Ibid.*, p. 23.

[15] *Ibid.*, p. 24.

[16] *Ibid.*, p. 31.

I am not sure that I fully understand the notions of "indwelling" and "embodiment" of which Dreyfus makes so much, nor am I sure that this hypothesis is the only one that would explain the difficulties machines have in simulating human intelligent behavior. These difficulties, it seems to me, are real, and I would agree that they are difficulties of principle. It simply does not seem to be the case that we perceive or use tools or understand problems by putting elements together as one builds a wall out of assorted bits of glass, brick and cement. On the contrary, as far as our experience can tell us, we do not have to be aware of all the details to perceive wholes, and the wholes do seem to be of primary importance in selecting the details that we do perceive and characters we attribute to them.

If Dreyfus' argument is sound, then some interesting points for the capacities and limitations of educational technology would seem to follow. One problem is whether the after-the-fact problem solution achieved by the machine is to serve as a model for the pupil's further problem solving. In one sense, the answer would have to be yes. For example, once certain problems in physics or mathematics are solved, the rules for the solution can be abstracted, and the pupil can learn to use the methods or rules on similar problems (e.g., two trains traveling at different speeds, etc.). Educational technology can facilitate such learnings just as it can facilitate more pedestrian rote learnings. Moreover, since the rationale of this or that problem solution in the sciences or mathematics can be formalized in a set of logical statements, there is no reason, in principle, for doubting that computers can simulate human intelligence in performing this kind of task and guide the pupil in doing likewise.

However, everyday problems of action, as Dreyfus has noted, are not so easily formalized, even if they are as game-like in character as horse races. If instruction is to give the pupil experience in the intellectual moves of comprehensive or molar problem solving—that is, experience in the recognition of problems, making judgments of relevance, formulating and assaying hypotheses, and choosing some form of commitment—then this is not the sort of teaching that the computer can be expected to simulate. If, for example, the problem is whether or not there should be laws against the use of marijuana, the expected learning is hardly the memorization of what somebody said about the problem or even a decision of some court or another. To be sure, some educators have said that what is to be learned is the *method* of problem solving, and in this sense, I suppose, a sufficiently simple set of problems might be programmed on the computer so that the rules could be abstracted and tasks devised to train the pupil in applying them. The danger is that this becomes a caricature of problem solving.

Truly human intelligence is determined not only by formal logical rules and the association of discrete bits of information. In addition to the effect of goals, purposes, and the anticipations of the organism in action on perception and judgment, meanings conveyed aesthetically by images in various media also have a determinative influence on every phase of concrete problem solving.

When, for example, a pine tree is perceived as lonely, or when we hear "the murmuring pines and the hemlocks," we are talking in figures of speech. Literally pines are not lonely and neither they nor hemlocks murmur. It would take us too far afield to investigate the peculiar psychological mechanisms by which we apprehend and respond to figurative uses of language or the combinations of tones in music or the juxtapositions of visual images. The relevant point here is that the import (meanings) of images are not explicit, for they are not simple referential symbols, and certainly such meanings as they convey are not unambiguous. Indeed, one of the primary functions of aesthetically interesting images is to introduce a sense of strangeness into familiar experiences. It is well known that the effect of such literary works as James Joyce's *Ulysses* or *Finnegan's Wake* and to some extent the work of Proust depend on the rapid intermingling and overlapping of associations and images by the reader.[17] But take a simpler case. The image of blood is one of our most powerful stimuli. Blood means life, but it also means the loss of life. In one image, it combines multivalent meanings. One gets the feeling that to ask a computer to simulate this kind of behavior is not only inefficient but misguided.

Indeterminate ambiguity is precisely what cannot be programmed, and yet there is an important sense in which to be a person is to be capable of inconsistency and paradox, and this alone has been put forward as a reason for computers not being able to be persons. A machine cannot be in two inconsistent states at once.[18] Yet human decisions and commitments are more often than not the result of the images of feeling and the indeterminate often unverbalized meanings they convey.

Putting together the arguments of Skinner and Dreyfus makes it clear that in assessing the potentials and hazards of educational technology a clear distinction has to be made between those phases of schooling that are formalizable and can be made explicit and those which cannot. There seem to be few limits, in principle, on the machine for the former and very severe limitation on the latter. There is no limit in principle on the sort of efficiency and individuation that technology can achieve in the sort of learning Skinner has

[17] W. Y. Tindall, *The Literary Symbol* (Bloomington, Indiana: Indiana University Press, 1955).

[18] Henry W. Johnstone, Jr., "Persons and Selves," *Philosophy and Phenomenological Research*, 23:2, (December, 1967), pp. 205–12. In a footnote on p. 212, Johnstone refers on this point to J. R. Lucas, "Minds, Machines and Gödel," reprinted in Anderson, ed., *Minds and Machines* (Englewood Cliffs, N.J.: Prentice-Hall, Inc., 1964), pp. 52–3.

described. Limits loom when we regard the learner as a person with a body, sense organs, and imagination as well as with the ability to function as a logical machine.

Accordingly, it is necessary to go a bit deeper into those nonexplicit factors and processes that we regard as a legitimate part of education and perhaps even of instruction. If these processes are legitimate ingredients of schooling, how will development of educational technology affect them?

TACIT DIMENSION OF KNOWING

For a good many years Michael Polanyi, himself a noted scientist, has been waging a battle in behalf of what he calls the "tacit dimension" of all cognition. In a recent article he refers to the "tacit triad", or the three centers of tacit or implied knowledge: first, subsidiary particulars; second, the focal target; and third, the knower who links the first to the second.[19]

Polanyi distinguishes two kinds of awareness—*from-awareness* and *focal-awareness*. From-awareness is awareness of the subsidiary particulars by means of which we are aware of the focal target. Thus in operating a machine, we are *focally* aware of the purpose for which we are operating it, and *subsidiarily* we use the numerous operations and adjustments that keep the machine operating in certain ways. In using a stereo viewer, we are focally aware of the single picture that portrays the scene in "depth," but only subsidiarily are we aware of the two slightly different images by virtue of which we get the stereoscopic effect. It seems, therefore, that these two types of awareness cannot have the same object as focus and subsidiary in the same way at the same time. Thus if we concentrate on the separate motions that we perform in swimming, we are likely to lose the total coordination of the swimming pattern.

Of special interest to us is the distinction Polanyi makes between explicit inference and tacit inference. After referring to Piaget's contrasts between a sensorimotor act like perception and explicit inference,[20] he says:

> Explicit inference is reversible: We can go back to its premises and go
> forward again to its conclusions, and we can rehearse this process
> as often as we like. This is not true for perception. For example, once
> we have seen through a visual puzzle, we cannot return to an ignorance
> of its solution. This holds, with some variations, for all acts of tacit
> knowing. We can go back to the two pictures of a stereo image

---

[19] Michael Polanyi, "Logic and Psychology," in *American Psychologist*, 23:1, (January, 1968), pp. 27–43.

[20] *Psychology of Intelligence* (London: Routledge and Kegan Paul, Ltd., 1950).

by taking them out of the viewer and looking at them directly, but this completely destroys the stereo image.[21]

Inasmuch as Polanyi extends this principle of tacit or implicit knowing to theories about perception, empirical generalization, explanation, and the pursuit of knowledge and science generally, quite a large domain of learning is excluded from machine simulation, if simulation in confined to what is or can be made explicit.

If an item of instruction is ultimately to function in a subsidiary or tacit role, what is the learning criterion of such an item? Our usual way of testing learning is by recall or recognition of items taught. The counterpart of the slogan "Down with non-behavioral objectives" is "What cannot be recalled has not been learned." But if an item functions subsidiarily, then it is beside the point, and perhaps impossible, to test for it by specific recall and recognition. It may not be efficient or even sensible to test subsidiary awareness by focal awareness.

The distinction, therefore, can affect the way we formulate the outcomes of schooling, as we can see if we examine the diverse uses of schooling. I have elsewhere distinguished four uses of learning or schooling: the replicative, associative, interpretive, and applicative.[22] By the *replicative* use of learning or schooling is meant the reproduction of a learned act or item in just about the form it was learned. For example, to the question "When did Columbus discover America?" one repeats what he has learned, viz., "1492." Facts, terms, poetry—anything learned by rote—can be used replicatively on cue. It would seem that even of the replicative use there are explicit and tacit forms. I have just given an example of the explicit form, viz., a specific response to a specific clue. However, the elements of a skill such as writing are learned for replication but to function subsidiarily, so that when we are writing a letter we think of what we want to say and not how the individual finger movements are occurring. Polanyi has said that when subsidiaries are formed they are interiorized and we can be said to dwell in them. Thus in writing we are in our fingers.[23]

The *associative* use of learning also can be thought of as having explicit and tacit forms. In the explicit form we use a cue to rearouse from our experience items that we have learned to connect with it. "Table" elicits "chair," "blue" elicits "sky," the flag elicits images of a parade. In their most stereotyped versions associative responses are replicative, and if I have distinguished the two it is because in replicative schooling the association is usually be-

[21] Polanyi, *op. cit.*, p. 32.

[22] H. S. Broudy, B. O. Smith and Joe R. Burnett, *Democracy and Excellence in American Secondary Education* (Chicago: Rand McNally Co., 1964), Chapters III and IV.

[23] Polanyi, *op. cit.*, p. 32.

tween the question as a cue and a particular answer as the appropriate response. In associative learning we rely on the rearousal of appropriate material to be set off by a cue, but we do not, it seems to me, teach deliberately that the flag shall be associated with the thought of a parade. Free association is a tacit form of this relationship, as is the kind of association that we call imaginative or creatively imaginative. Which subsidiaries in his experience provide the associations engendered in the mind of the artist by the sight of a spring flower we almost never know, and we would hardly call the act creative if we did. If, as is often maintained, much of the artistic imaginative activity has its source in the preconscious or the unconscious, then this kind of associative learning cannot be made fully explicit.[24] There is a sense in which one might regard the replicative use of schooling as the explicit phase of the associative use, but for the present purpose it is not necessary to discuss the propriety of this distinction in any greater detail.

By the *interpretive* use of schooling is meant the use of a categorical scheme to understand an object or a problem or a task. Sometimes this takes the form of an explicit explanation in terms of theory. At other times we use knowledge to clarify, organize and in other ways to make phenomena intelligible. This looser type of intelligibility (often called understanding) relieves puzzlement, although it does not have the logical rigor of an explanation. It might be called the tacit form of interpretation.[25]

Finally, by *applicative knowledge* is meant the combination of theory with techniques to solve a problem, as, for example, when we apply the principle of lasers to eye surgery or the principle of cybernation to the manufacture of thermostats. The history of invention is rich in instances where applications of theory were hit upon in a way that admirably illustrate the tacit theory of knowing. A desire to solve a problem guides the clicking into place of previously learned subsidiary elements. But, of course, after the insight has occurred and the invention made, one can show explicitly how the theory or principle applies to the invention.

We are now ready, I believe, to formulate the distinction between the explicit and the tacit dimensions of education or schooling. Technology can do remarkable things in the explicit dimensions, but only insofar as these explicit learnings become vectors in tacit knowing can technology contribute to the

---

[24] For example, see Lawrence S. Kubie, "The Distortion of the Symbolic Processes in Neurosis and Psychosis." *Journal of the American Psychoanalytic Association*, I (1953), 59–86.

[25] Polanyi, *op. cit.*, p. 37. Among the other works of Polanyi that bear on the topic of tacit knowing are *Science, Faith and Society* (London: Oxford University Press, 1946); *The Tacit Dimension* (New York: Doubleday, 1966); reprinted by Routledge and Kegan Paul, 1967 (London); and "Sense Giving and Sense Reading," *Philosophy,* 17:162, (October, 1967), p. 301.

latter. *The more distinctively human aspect of experience*—as distinguished from the robot aspect—*seems to rely heavily on the tacit forms of knowing*, and the latter will not take place automatically or predictably simply as the consequence of learning this or that set of facts or rules or acquiring this or that set of skills.

The integration of these explicit learnings into meanings depends on human action and therefore on the value hierarchies and norms that the individual has interiorized. These intentions, these norms, these systems of anticipations cannot be simulated in the mechanical "tutor." Explicit learnings are, one might say, necessary but not sufficient conditions for the more global, evaluative, and cognitive acts of the pupil, and indeed, it may be that without these larger schemata of values, goals, and commitments, the explicit learnings will be harder to achieve and to render functional.

In the light of these comments, it may be helpful to look more closely at the tutor analogy so often invoked by advocates of programmed and computer-aided instruction.

SOCRATES AND THE TEACHING MACHINE

The versatility of the programmed course, especially when aided by technologically sophisticated computers, has led writers in the field to refer to the tutor as the model that programmed instruction hopes to approximate.[26] In support of this hope, the potentiality of educational technology for individualizing instruction is cited, especially the development of the two-way tutor— where program and pupil speak to each other. This, it is claimed, would amount to a tutorial dialogue. This claim may account for the frequency with which Socrates is invoked as the model teacher and the Socratic dialogue as the model teaching process.[27]

The previously noted article by Skinner had two references to Socratic teaching. One had to do with the cat-and-mouse tactics by which teachers elicit the desired answers, and the other was a comment that the demonstration in the *Meno* in which a slave boy, allegedly innocent of mathematics, was taught the Pythagorean theorem by this kind of elicitation. As to the latter, Skinner observed that the slave boy learned nothing.[28]

I quite agree with Skinner's appraisal of that oft-cited pedagogical feat, but Skinner and those who invoke Socrates as a paradigm for programmed

[26] James Finn, for example, speaks of the tutorial relationship made possible by programmed instruction: "Teaching Machines: Auto-Instructional Devices for the Teacher," in DeCecco, *op. cit.*, p. 70.

[27] E.g., Ira S. Cohen "Programmed Learning and the Socratic Dialogue" in DeCecco, *op. cit.*, p. 330.

[28] "The Teaching of High-School Science—What is Wrong With It?", *op. cit.*, p. 706.

instruction may be laboring under a misunderstanding of the Socratic teaching, its goal, its methods and its outcomes.

As regards the goal of Socrates' dialogues with the youth of Athens, it was to determine the nature of virtue and whether or not virtue could be taught.

In the *Apology,* Socrates said:

> Men of Athens . . . while I have life and strength, I shall never cease from the practice and teaching of philosophy, exhorting any one whom I meet and saying to him after my manner: You, my friend . . . are you not ashamed of heaping up the greatest amount of money and honor and reputation, and caring so little about wisdom and truth and the greatest improvement of the soul, which you never regard or heed at all?[29]

In the early Platonic dialogues—for example, *Laches, Euthyphro,* and the *Meno*—Socrates is portrayed as trying to arrive at a generic definition of virtue or excellence. Virtue, Socrates argued, was a kind of knowledge, but knowledge of what? It was not like knowledge of the stars or common sense knowledge of the world. To say that it was knowledge about the norms of standards of conduct is not satisfactory either, because it was obvious that men who knew what they ought to do nevertheless often failed to do it, or did what they acknowledged they ought not to have done, and virtue, if it was knowledge, was action-knowledge. In short, more than ordinary cognition was involved. Schooling for virtue meant shaping the whole personality in such a way that the standards of the good, true, and beautiful became a functional part of the individual's decision-making behavior. In short, virtue was not explicit knowledge, and as such was not a good candidate for mechanical simulation.

How could virtue be taught? In the works of Plato four methods can be distinguished: exhorting the learner to become concerned about the importance of his achieving virtue; dialectical self-examination; disciplining one's appetites (self-mastery) ; and a course of intellectual training culminating in dialectics. The first two of these approaches seem to have been characteristic of Socratic teaching; the latter two probably reflect Plato's own elaborate plan for the ideal state and the education of the guardian of that state as set forth in the *Republic.* The real Socrates did not, according to Xenophon, think so highly of mathematical knowledge as did the Platonic Socrates.[30]

The example in the *Meno* is therefore hardly typical of Socrates' educational concerns or his teaching method. Rather, it is a digression from the main theme of that dialogue, which is about virtue. It is used to show not that the Pythagorean theorem could be taught by Socratic questioning, but rather that

---

[29] From *The Dialogues of Plato,* by B. Jowett (4th ed.) 1953, p. 354.

[30] W. W. Jaeger, *Paideia: The Ideals of Greek Culture.* Trans. by G. Highet (New York: Oxford Univ. Press, Vol. II, 1944), p. 304.

the basic concepts of geometry cannot be *imparted* at all—that they can only be recollected by a soul that had known them in a previous incarnation. It is with regard to such basic Ideas that the teacher can be likened to a midwife who can help the pupil bring to birth what he already "knows."

The use of exhortation is illustrated in the *Protagoras* (313 a-c) when Socrates, accompanying Hippocrates to the house of Callias to hear Protagoras, asks the excited young man:

> Well, but are you aware of the danger which you are incurring? If you
> were going to commit your body to some one, who might do good
> or harm to it, would you not carefully consider and ask the opinion
> of your friends and kindred, and deliberate many days as to whether
> you should give him the care of your body? But when the soul is in
> question, which you hold to be of far more value than the body,
> and upon the good or evil of which depends the well-being of your all—
> about this you never consulted either with your father or with your
> brother or with any of us who are your companions. But no sooner does
> this foreigner appear, than you instantly commit your soul to his keeping.

The learner had to be jolted into uneasy anxiety about his soul, just as contemporary man must be scared a bit before he trots off to his periodic medical checkup. To be shown that one really did not know what seemed so certain, that one's common sense definitions led to awkward consequences, and that one was, in short, abysmally ignorant precisely where one thought himself to be wise, elicited chagrin, embarrassment, and often anger—usually with Socrates, but occasionally with oneself. When the latter happened, the time was ripe for the positive side of the method, namely, dialectical self-examination.

This is a far cry from a programmed dialogue involving logical games, yet if one combines Socrates' evangelical search for virtue with Plato's mathematical metaphysics, we get at the notion of education as a preparation for a conversion of the soul toward the Ideas, the absolute norms of the good, the true, and the beautiful. The dialectical self-examination was to disclose these ideas, and the metamorphosis of the individual's whole value schema would follow. How does one teach the learner to apprehend the most general and absolute norms and at the same time to introject them—that is, accept them —as his own imperatives for thought and conduct?

Two methods were urged by Plato. Today we might call the first a kind of conditioning. By consistent reinforcement of certain behaviors and the punishment of others, the child was to grow up "spontaneously" loving what he ought to love and hating what ought to be hated.

After the future ruler had been inducted into adolescence outfitted with sound habits both of body and of soul, he would, if blessed with adequate mentality, enter upon his secondary education. This consisted of arithmetic, geometry, music, and astronomy, all to be studied in their theoretical aspects rather than in their practical applications to industry or war.

In their theoretical phase, music and astronomy also exhibited mathematical structures and therefore qualified as training in abstraction to supplement arithmetic, geometry, and solid geometry.

The highest level of knowledge, however, was reserved for dialectic in which the deductive relations characteristic of mathematics were discovered to obtain among "real" concepts—that is, the scheme of reality itself. If reality were like a mathematical system, and if the basic primitive propositions could be intuited, metaphysics, the study of the nature of being, would acquire the certainty of mathematics. One should not confuse Plato's respect for mathematics as an *educational* tool with our respect for mathematics as a *theoretical* tool. For Plato the study of mathematics was to shape the soul, just as music and literature shape the soul. Harmonious music makes the soul harmonious; mathematical studies make the soul orderly, its thinking clean and precise, and its action just. No such claims are made for the teaching of mathematics today.

The current interest in teaching machines points up an important difference in how the art of teaching was viewed by Socrates and Plato, on the one hand, and the Rhetoricians, on the other. The Rhetoricians regarded teaching pretty much as systematized imitation. By analyzing procedures in great detail and listing numerous alternatives within each class of operations, it was possible to program the "teaching machine" in clearly definable steps for presenting the task, correcting the trial response, and evaluating the test response.

It is quite a different matter with a Socratic dialogue or the Platonic dialectic. The transaction between teacher and pupil and between both of them and a transcendent ideal requires at least two persons; a machine and a person won't do. The outcome of the teaching is not merely a right response but a response plus an attitude with a complex aura of feeling, an attitude, however, which is not formed once for all.

It is for this kind of dialogue that some college students now seem to be clamoring, but students and faculties are discovering that curricula devoted to systematic impartation of systematically organized bodies of knowledge are not easily adapted to the teaching encounters envisioned by the student.

The reinforcement schedule of the programmed text is more like that of the rhetorical exercises than that of the prodding that incited Socrates' pupils to doubt and self-examination. Finally, the Socratic methodology aimed at a new way of thinking and feeling rather than at the mastery of any specific body of content.

The analogy with the tutor therefore can be misleading and is useful only insofar as education is confined to the imparting of explicit skills, knowledge,

and attitudes that can be behaviorally described and programmed. The notion
of the tutor is far broader than this, as the analysis of the Socratic method
indicates, and as the qualifications of tutors as described by Locke and
Montaigne, for example, would confirm. The character-shaping potentials of
the candidate were regarded as far more important than his intellectual attain-
ments or even his skill as a pedagogue. And these were for a long time the
criteria used to select the teachers at the "prestigious" secondary schools
here and in Great Britain. The careless use of this analogy is in itself one
of the more mischievous hazards posed by educational technology. It arouses
unnecessary antagonisms by connoting an unpleasant presumptuousness.
Thereby the genuine contributions and potentials of technology are put out of
focus and the motives of its advocates misconstrued.[31]

EFFECTS OF TECHNOLOGY ON INSTRUCTIONAL ROLES

I now turn to another class of effects of educational technology—on the
assumption that it will result in some form of mass production. These are the
effects of accelerating the division of labor in the schools. I am referring
primarily to elementary and secondary schools, but the effects need not be
confined to the lower levels of schooling. A fairly common prediction is expressed as follows:

> Any introduction of technology, however, with its accompanying higher
> professional status will demand more of the teacher in terms of
> education, experience, and professional growth. Teachers will need to
> understand much more than they do about learning theory and
> communication: and they will have to exercise sound judgment in terms,
> for example, of selecting programs and in determining which educational
> goals can best be reached through programmed instruction and which
> can best be achieved by other methods.[32]

On the face of it, this seems like a plausible development, but it fails to take
adequate account of the strong resistance in many quarters to the professional-
ization of the classroom teacher. The qualities Finn anticipates for the teacher
of the future would call for far more theoretical and technical preservice study
than is now required by certification laws. It would entail a much higher
degree of autonomy, vis à vis their administrators, than teachers now have.

---

[31] Some of the material on Socrates and the Teaching Machine was excerpted from
H. S. Broudy and John R. Palmer, *Exemplars of Teaching Method* (Chicago: Rand
McNally Co., 1965). Chapter III.

[32] James D. Finn, "Teaching Machines: Auto-Instructional Devices for the Teacher"
in DeCecco, *op. cit.*, p. 20. See also Bert Y. Kersh, "Programming Instruction," *Ibid.*,
pp. 307–8.

I see little evidence that classroom teaching will rise above the status of a white-collar craft so long as the preparation required for it remains at the white-collar apprentice level. And there is still less reason to believe that the public will be willing to pay professional salaries to a huge army of classroom teachers. Developments in other mass-production fields would seem to make it more likely that the proportion of high-grade personnel to relatively low-skilled workers will decrease.

Moreover, there is the assumption in this commonly held view that auto-instructional devices, like textbooks and pencils, are mere instruments to be used by the teacher at her discretion.[33] But even textbooks are not used wholly at the discretion of the teacher. And the imperatives of the textbook are nowhere near so stringent as those of a programmed set of materials that, as some producers of educational materials hope, can be "teacher proof." The view that educational technology will upgrade the autonomy of the teacher also overlooks the fact that if the money investment in any system of instruction is large enough, it becomes a major factor in its own preservation, and the amount of discretion allowed the user is limited accordingly.

> More and more decisions on subject-matter location and instructional strategy are being made outside the classroom. Many of these decisions apply regionally or nationally, and when there is the large volume of potential users that this implies, the preparation of costly, expert, pretested, and reproducible instructional sequences become feasible. New media, high-speed communication and information retrieval, increased population, and the expanding market have brought private enterprise into education on a larger scale than ever before. Programmed instruction is one of the technologies in line for exploitation.[34]

For these reasons I shall advance a somewhat different possibility as to the effects of educational technology on instructional personnel. In the first place, one might expect a class of *instructional technicians* to emerge. It would be their responsibility to assign pupils to programs and to reassign them as the demands of individualized instruction dictate. The amount of judgment needed for such decisions can be kept to a minimum, depending on the overall coherence of the total program. Their special competence will lie in the operation and maintenance of the machines and the management of the logistics connected with their efficient use. In accordance with the logic of the division of labor, which fractionates an operation into sub-operations at a lower skill level, these workers would be trained at a highly specialized technician level either in two-year post secondary courses or as apprentices in the plants of

---

[33] "Increasingly, machines will be valued for qualities not possessed by books," says Phil C. Lange, "Future Developments," in *Programmed Instruction*, op. cit., p. 308.
[34] *Ibid.*

the educational materials industries. Other "para-professionals" might be utilized at lower rates of remuneration for housekeeping tasks such as lunch-room supervision, running errands, etc.

Clearly these instructional technicians will not write the programs that are fed into the machines. For this, a higher level of specialist will be needed—the *instructional programmer*. He will be in charge of developing curriculum materials and the packaging of them for teaching purposes. It is unlikely that this research-developer of materials will ever be seen by the pupils or even by the instructional technicians. He or she will have an office in one of the big educational industries enjoying the fruits of a graduate degree and living only a few blocks away from the very best neighborhoods.

In each building or district or region—whatever the unit of instructional administration will turn out to be—*instructional managers* will turn the package or packages bought from the educational industries into instructional schedules to be implemented by the instructional technicians. They will, of course, exercise general supervision over all instruction. The planning needed to meet the needs of, let us say, 1000 school children from day to day seems like a logistical task of frightening proportions, but here also the computer can be counted on to make the task manageable. The instructional manager probably would not be charged with the total administrative responsibility for his unit; his role would seem to be more like that of the manager of the plant or the manager of production, than the president of the corporation.

The instructional manager, one can be sure, will be a substantial professional in terms of training, experience, and responsibility. It would be interesting to explore the types of professional training needed by the instructional research-developers and instructional managers, but there is little doubt that universities will be able to take this problem in stride. One may recall the phrase of Skinner's that as auto-instruction develops, teaching will become a form of behavioral engineering.

Now where is the traditional teacher in this veritable paradise of instruction with each pupil learning at his own rate; with the right rewards metered out promptly after every response; with programs of instruction carefully graded, patiently presented, and even more patiently repeated, instantaneously tested, measured, and evaluated?

As regards imparting knowledge—either of facts or of principles—for rote learning or for problem solving (the didactic phase of schooling) there is reason to believe that the personnel we have listed: instructional research developers, instructional managers, and instructional technicians are sufficient. For this type of explicit instruction the traditional teacher is needed no more than covered wagons are needed for cross-country transportation. If they are needed, it is for the type of teaching encounters that we noted in Socrates' teaching of virtue, or value education. This is the tacit, personalized phase of instruction. I would argue that the chances of providing personnel for this purpose to supplement the instructional technicians, research-developers, and managers are not very good—no better than that of manning the schools with high-grade professionals.

Several objections can be raised to this analysis and prediction. One is that there are many alternative ways of cutting up the instructional complex, and that there is no inevitability about the one I have described. I cannot refute this objection, but I can ask that the grounds on which my thesis is based be carefully considered. Another possible objection is that the analysis is based on the assumption that the schools of 1990 will resemble the enclaves of pupils and teachers gathered in large groups and located in spaces called schools.

Let us look at the last point. What if technology, by bringing down the price of highly sophisticated autoinstructional devices can place one in every home, library, etc. If this should prove possible, and if the developments in educational technology turn out to be what one might reasonably suppose, then *so far as imparting knowledge or skill or attitude* is concerned, pupils —from kindergarten to the university—need not be congregated into school buildings. And let it be reiterated that the amount of time spent in schooling at all levels on this phase of education is enormous. The non-explicit phases play around and through it, to be sure, but yolks can be separated from whites, and educational technology is a way of separating the explicit from the non-explicit factors in education.

It need not be emphasized that removing the explicit or purely didactic function from a centralized space would revolutionize schooling. I introduce the matter here because my analysis would be altered substantially if these developments came to pass.[35] For example, instructional technicians might remain, but one would hardly hire one for each home. They might be employed at learning centers deployed throughout the community or even throughout a region. The instructional research-developer would still have a place, but the instructional manager's role is a bit harder to formulate, if the envisioned decentralization comes about. Given decentralization, the tacit phases of learning might be left to the home or the mass media or even to the cultural pressures of the milieu where, as a matter of fact, most of it goes on anyway. This would render a professional class of personnel for this purpose superfluous. But let us suppose that some recognizable version of the school system remains, what then would be the role of the teacher as distinct from the instructional technician, research-developer, and manager? And what are the chances of our being able to provide schools with such personnel?

[35] Cf. L. M. Stolurow, "Social Impact of Program Instruction," in DeCecco, *op. cit.,* p. 349.

Presumably these teachers will have to be broadly educated themselves and committed to the kind of value education described in the discussion of the Socratic dialogue. The humanities, aesthetic education, molar problem solving, interdisciplinary explorations are a few of the areas in which encounter-teaching rather than didactic teaching is stressed. The human encounter, Buber's I-Thou relation, the imaginative sympathy entailed by such encounters—these will be the characteristics of their teaching styles.

Such encounters cannot take place en masse, and so the per student cost of this type of instruction will be high both in time and money. Moreover, the value of the outcome will never be precisely formulated or measurable. Some of the values will be, from the point of view of many people, negative, especially if such teaching results in criticism of institutions and norms, not to speak of more violent forms of protest.[36]

An optimistic analysis would argue that the savings spun off from mass-production efficiency made possible by educational technology will provide the time, the personnel, and the money needed for just this type of tuition and teacher. This is a familiar argument. It is fair to say that mass production has produced an increase of efficiency and overall quality of the product. For example, automobiles today are better automobiles than their counterparts of 1910 or even 1920.

A more pessimistic outlook is based on the observation that mass production has improved the quality of the product, but not *necessarily* the quality of life of the individual or of the society that uses that product. For example, mass production produces more leisure, but for the leisure to benefit the masses, mass-production methods have to be applied to make certain facilities economically available to large numbers of people. However, the enjoyment of parks, beaches, the open road is seriously impaired if they have to be shared with hordes of people at one time; moreover, the effort needed to get one's share of such facilities increases to the point where the amount of leisure available for the enjoyment of it is diminished to an almost ludicrous degree.

The pressure for efficiency, if applied to education—and there is every reason to believe that it would be—will accelerate the exploitation of educational technology, but it will also invite a jaundiced gaze at expensive types of instruction that the technology cannot manage or does not choose to undertake. The principle of "necessities for all before luxuries for some" will be as importante here as in other forms of collective social service. The more expensive type of instruction will thus be reserved for those who can afford

---

[36] For the sort of emphasis merely mentioned here the reader might wish to consult *Existential Encounters for Teachers*, edited by Maxine Greene (New York: Random House, 1967), and Van Cleve Morris's *Existentialism and Education* (New York: Harper & Row, 1966). Note that I do not include counseling and guidance as teaching functions in this sense.

it, just as custom-made clothes and automobiles are not for the general run of mankind. One should expect this kind of argument to be urged on schools operated by state agencies of one sort or another.

Among the factors that make for pessimism, in addition to the economic ones already mentioned, is a general defection in the academic world from a commitment of schooling—at any level—to the sovereign virtue of wisdom. And by wisdom I mean the disposition of the person to act in accordance with the norms of science, art, religion, and ethics. In this sense, wisdom might be called enlightened cherishing. I say defection not because members of *academia* no longer value enlightened cherishing, but because nowhere in the academic ranks is there a cadre professionally devoted to its cultivation in the schools. In the university, the teaching for wisdom is at best an academic avocation. Professors feel that their success depends on approbation by scholarly cospecialists. *Wisdom is not a field of specialization, and in a mass society what is nobody's speciality is likely to be nobody's concern.* That is the point of Socrates' quoted remark in the *Apology*. He could think of nothing more important to which to devote his life and that of his pupils, but that is precisely what got him into trouble in Athens and would probably prevent his getting tenure in our better universities. He neither acquired wealth nor published.

This mood has had its effects on the common school curriculum where the ideal of the academic specialist has become the criterion of quality or excellence.[37] The push to the explicit and the definite has pervaded the social sciences as well as the physical ones. Even the humanities tend to be converted into fields of specialized scholarship. I am not condemning specialization or scholarship; I am merely pointing out that the vacuum it creates in value education is not necessarily filled by dedicated humanistic teachers. More likely it is filled by substituting the manners of the dominant class for moral reflection—as is done in the lower schools—or by treating values as matters of private taste, as is likely to be done in higher education. Or it will be filled by the omnipotent tastemakers—the mass media.

Combine this situation with the high priority that must be given to efficiency and economy in the considerations of the school administrators and you have my reasons for a mild pessimism about the relative hazards and potentials of the developments of educational technology. It is not that I fear a loss of jobs for teachers; their absolute number will increase, for the services will be expanded enormously. It is not that a high quality of instruction will be sacrificed to the machine, for I believe the quality of *explicit* instruction will be vastly improved. My apprehensions are rather that the tacit or implied

---

[37] This criterion has been challenged in recent years in the name of the humanistic, nonintellectual values.

dimension of schooling will become a luxury that many people might find desirable, but from which the mass of our people must be excluded.

Yet *the salvation of our era depends on making sure that the quality of thought and instruction that goes into value education*—into the shaping of feeling and will—*is of just as high a quality as the scientific thinking which we hope will shape logical thought.*

But *unless we build this emphasis into the design of the school now while we still have a chance to do so, we may find ourselves in the not too distant future with a school system devoted more and more to that which can best be done inexpensively.* This would be unfortunate regardless of how good the products of technology might be. And once such an educational system becomes the nucleus of numerous satellite industries employing vast numbers of people, substantive changes in it will become as much of a threat to our national economy as would a radical change in our means of transportation or communication. Fortunately, we still have a good deal of choice.

We have before us the opportunity for a breakthrough in education comparable to that engendered in transportation by the introduction of the internal combustion engine, but will this opportunity be used to exploit the possibilities of high grade schooling for all the people? Every great technological advance has presented man with options that would improve the quality of human life, but somehow life, liberty, and the pursuit of happiness are in jeopardy all over the world. It would be the pity of the century if we missed the opportunity that educational technology is now holding before us.

64. WILL THE COMPUTER KILL EDUCATION?

Bruce L. Hicks

The computer has become, after sex, the most overworked symbol in North America. For the "have-nots" the computer symbolizes the Establishment and the destruction of human beings and of human values. To urban experts the computer symbolizes a technology that may save the cities.

Similar fears and hopes attend the growing application of computers in education. Will the computer destroy education which, at its best, seeks to maximize the worth of the individual? Or will the computer aid education in this worthwhile but never-ending search?

These questions should soon be asked by everyone who seeks to improve a democratic society, whatever the color of his political and religious ideologies. Modern computer technology makes possible an explosive proliferation of new educational tools. Hundreds of computer terminals are now being used frequently by thousands of students. Within a few years thousands of much more elaborate terminals will be in the schools, and these instructional terminals will begin to appear in the home, for each terminal will cost no more than the best hi-fi and color TV.

Computer-assisted instruction (or "CAI") is the most powerful of the new, automated, educational assistants that have been developed by computer technology. The question "Will the Computer Kill Education?" can therefore be restated as "What will *CAI* do to education?" In answering this more specific question we shall first describe characteristics of the new assistant

SOURCE. Reprinted with permission from Hicks, Bruce L., "Will the Computer Kill Education?" *The Educational Forum*, Vol. 34, No. 3, March, 1970, pp. 307–312. Copyright © 1970 by The Educational Forum.

that are relevant to the quality of its use in education. We shall then discuss the effects of CAI upon the students, teachers, and programmers who work with this assistant. We shall find that it is possible, but by no means certain, that the computer will, through CAI, serve education in a democratic society.

COMPUTER-ASSISTED INSTRUCTION

Let us look at CAI through the eyes of Mike who is in the fourth grade. Mike is playing arithmetic games with his mechanical friend, a CAI terminal named Snoopy by his classmates. The games he is playing are designed to teach him specific arithmetic skills.

The TV screen in front of him looks like the one at home, and the keyset looks like his dad's typewriter. Mike has learned in a few minutes how to use the TV screen and keyset to "talk" to Snoopy. Letters and numbers that he types appear on the screen in front of him. He has also learned how to give commands to Snoopy. By pushing "command" keys he can get a problem on the screen or get the correct answer to a question, erase a mistyped character or get specific directions and help.

As Mike plays the game, he finds Snoopy to be a helpful kind of friend, for Snoopy is always ready to serve him, allows him to go at his own pace, and attends to his requests very patiently and rapidly. Mike "beats" Snoopy in the third game and returns to his regular classroom with a new sense of confidence in his arithmetic skills.

What does Mike's teacher think of the CAI system? She sees the CAI system as her specialized and competent assistant, her junior partner. She knows that it serves many students simultaneously, as individuals, with the same speed, patience, and accuracy that it serves Mike. She makes use of its versatility: in the afternoon, she will send him to Snoopy for introductory French lessons in which he will learn to recognize spoken French words.

There exist today many CAI systems which, controlled by suitable computer programs, can be used for an astonishing variety of educational activities. They can provide instruction in which the lesson-writer, through his CAI program, guides the learner step-by-step through the material. At another extreme, they can provide the opportunity for "inquiry" in which the student chooses the questions he will answer and the educational resources that he can use in finding the answers. Through CAI, many students can make experiments simultaneously on the same real electronic apparatus, or the students may make a variety of "simulated" experiments requiring no real equipment but only a clever job of CAI programming.

A CAI system can aid in the testing of students both before and after a course and also, more easily than in the conventional school, as often as they need during the course. Each student's performance during the course and on the tests is automatically recorded and can be fed back to the teacher so that she can effectively and promptly evaluate his performance and use the evaluation in designing the best teaching strategy for this student. Lesson-writers can improve the course with the help of sophisticated, computer-aided analysis of the student's responses.

CAI thus supplies new aids to conventional classroom teaching and can often replace it. But CAI is an *idiot savant*. It does just what it has been told to do by the lesson-writers and the programmers. Although it is faster and more logical, and also potentially more patient than a "live" teacher, it is both humane and educationally effective only where its superior patience, speed, and rationality have been utilized by skillful and human lesson-writers, programmers, and teachers. If the effects of computer-assisted instruction are malign, then it is they who have failed, not the computer.

The great speed, memory, and logical powers of a computer may, because of programming error, produce entirely unexpected and extraneous results. Even when a computer is used to solve problems in a well-defined field like mathematical physics, it is not easy to avoid programming errors. The best joint efforts of the physicist and the programmers are needed to "check-out" their problem-solving programs. It is almost impossible at present to check exhaustively a fully developed teaching program for a CAI system against the variety of demands that can be made upon it by a large and varied sample of students. In the future perhaps the CAI systems can themselves help perform this task.

ROBOTS AND ZOMBIES

We like to think that educational activities confer benefits upon teachers as well as students. CAI systems introduce a new educational environment for both teacher and student and create a new professional in education, the CAI programmer or lesson-writer. Will the advent of CAI benefit these three participants in the education processes?

Some CAI programmers prepare materials for CAI lessons. Other CAI programmers write computer programs which tell the computer how it should interact with the students. Because the computer is untiring and is tolerant of ambiguity it makes extreme demands upon these programmers. It also responds to each programmer in an impersonal way. As a working partner the computer is fast and reliable, but stupid and cold.

To any CAI programmer whose success in life is limited to his clever programming, the computer will seem to be a virtuous life model. If he then becomes intolerant of ambiguity, of warmth, and of individual differences, his programming style may injure him and, through the lessons he prepares, also the students. Will he become a robot who can work only for computers? Will they become zombies who will only talk to computers and not to people?

It is possible, however, for the interaction between the computer and the programmer to be such that it will enlarge him as a person rather than deform him, for the relationship can lead to a better understanding of ambiguity and of the overlap between the rational and the affective in human beings. If the programmer discovers, in his writing of a CAI lesson, what it is that reason and logic alone cannot accomplish, then he can make use of this understanding in communicating with each of the students who will use the lesson.

The computer can also aid the lesson-writer and the teacher because it is tolerant, in its own peculiar way. It welcomes any and all solutions of a teaching problem (or any other problem) that can be properly presented to it. *My* style of solution of a problem or even my description of it is never the only one that the computer will accept. Thus the computer does not require the programmer to be intolerant of variety in problem-solving. He can, in fact, write CAI lessons that will tolerate the student's mistakes, will encourage him to correct these mistakes, and will allow him to solve a problem in his own way, and will also suggest to him other valid solutions.

The programmer must always remember that his purpose is not to train zombies but to educate human beings. Consider, for example, the CAI lessons which teach student nurses how to care for heart patients. The students practice their diagnostic skills on a computer simulation of the patient. If they occasionally overdose or even kill him, a new "live" patient is available at the touch of a key! The responsible programmer does more than design a clever computer simulation of the patient. His program will also teach the student nurses that they cannot experiment with patients as if they were guinea pigs, and that they must "listen to the patient" as well as test and dose him. Those few student nurses who do not accept these rules will need special instruction or should perhaps choose a different profession.

The importance of the programmer's role in education, and in society generally, is growing even more rapidly than is the number of computer systems. Soon the intellectual, social, and ethical characteristics of programmers will be widely influential. We must somehow make certain that the CAI programmer or lesson-writer maintains his personal integrity, that he seeks to preserve and expand his own individual creativeness and those of the students and teachers he serves, and that he allows the computer to be intolerant only in stubbornly refusing to "give-up" on the faltering student.

IDEOLOGY

One danger in the use of CAI is obvious: we might, by default, allow bigots and demagogues to control course content. A less obvious but more immediate danger is that CAI will reinforce and extend the unfortunate effects of poor social science courses and texts. Both dangers arise from the power of computer technology to afford rapid and easy duplication and distribution of educational materials. We have already noted that careless programming can inadvertently expose students to authoritarian thinking, because the programmer may ape the computer's apparent intolerance and transmit this intolerance to the students through his CAI programs.

The teacher must be able to recognize the dangers attending such misuse of CAI and must act to minimize these dangers. She must know that computers are not of themselves undemocratic nor intolerant, and that they only try to teach what has been programmed into them (and that this is often more than anyone had realized). A proper education for her, for lesson-writers and programmers, and for students clearly must include objective and often renewed examination of a variety of political forms, social institutions, and religions around the world. It must treat the contentious and the controversial, the quiet knowledge of the past, and the booming technology of the present. It must recognize that changes in society do take place, in particular the changes enforced at bewildering speed by technology. And what better place is there to learn about the source of these changes than in the CAI classroom, which will itself be one of the most powerful agents of change?

MONITOR OR MENTOR

Education should cherish the worth of the individual and encourage his creativity. This principle will be denied if CAI is allowed to manufacture identical citizens on an educational assembly line, like Joseph Lancaster's monitorial schools of 150 years ago. CAI programs can easily be written that merely imitate the educational strategies of the monitorial school, but computer-assisted instruction should be and can be designed that will help and inspire each student differently according to his style of growth and the nature of his creativity.

The promise of an education that is individualized for each student inspired the pioneers in programmed instruction and in the use of the mechanical teaching machines that were the precursors of computer-assisted instruction. Today that promise has been realized only in part. More than 500 different CAI courses or partial courses have been taught, but the majority are still in the experimental stages of development. These courses have been programmed in some 35 CAI or computer languages for about 40 different computers in 40 CAI centers. As a consequence, any one fully developed CAI course is generally not available at more than one center nor to more than a few dozen students at any one time. The few CAI courses that have been given to hundreds of students have been fragmented into small units, each unit only ten or twenty minutes long. Although experiments on computer-assisted instruction therefore tend to be parochial and incomplete, the variety of imaginative and individualized CAI courses already developed provide a foundation for a much wider development and use of computer-assisted instruction, and a type of use that truly recognizes the worth and creativity of the individual, whatever his age or educational background.

We can illustrate the power of CAI in catering to the individual student by citing a number of instructional techniques that have already been applied in CAI courses. Students of different ability in the same CAI classroom are given help as they need or request it. "Challenge" problems are available for the student who finishes a CAI lesson before his fellow students. When the student wishes, he can look up the answers he has previously given or the solutions he has found. He can use his own style of proof in mathematics, for it is only the logical accuracy of his proof that is checked by the computer program.

The student is taught not only in a tutorial style, but also by inquiry or discovery methods in which he can choose the path he follows in obtaining a solution with the help of the resources made available to him by the CAI system, such as a table of properties, theorems, and a specialized lexicon. He should learn how to visualize the relationships among the different aspects of his physical and social environment. To develop his powers of visualization he can, on CAI, manipulate models of reality, such as a simulated physics laboratory, for example, or simulated national economies. In using any of these techniques the teacher gives the students access to the CAI system or to classroom experience, whichever appears warranted by the students' current educational needs. More such techniques will appear in CAI courses as the programmers and teachers together find the CAI analogues of the techniques used by a skilled teacher in the classroom.

Of course a CAI system is not a human being. It is not a good friend, a warm teacher, nor a loving parent. But once a computer has been taught how to deal constructively with individual intellectual differences it can deal more rapidly and more patiently with these differences than can a "live" friend or teacher or parent. And the teacher will find, if she is properly prepared to work with CAI as a versatile, educational assistant, that she possesses a new outlet for her creative interest in her students.

EDUCATION CAN SURVIVE

Our discussion has suggested that the computer and computer-assisted instruction can serve education either badly or well. Whether the computer kills education will then not be decided by the nature of the computer but rather by the decisions we make about its use in education. If our applications of computer-assisted instruction embody creativity, patience, tolerance, and objectivity rather than passivity, impatience, bigotry, and irrationality, then the computer will surely serve education rather than kill it.

Bibliography

This bibliography is broken up into three main parts with some subdivisions: the first two parts and their subdivisions correspond to the categorization of articles reprinted in this book. The third part consists of general works in the philosophy of science. On some occasions a work appears more than once in these lists.

PART I

1. Educational Research and Science

Ackoff, Russell L. *Scientific Method: Optimizing Applied Research Decisions.* New York: John Wiley & Sons, Inc., 1962.

Anton, J. P., and G. K. Plochmann (eds.). *Science, Philosophy and Our Educational Tasks.* (Buffalo Series, Vol. 2, No. 2.) Buffalo, New York: University Council for Educational Administration and School of Education, State University of New York at Buffalo, 1966.

Ayer, A. J. *Man as a Subject for Science.* London: Athlone Press, 1964.

Bakan, David. *On Method: Toward a Reconstruction of Psychological Investigation.* San Francisco: Jossey-Bass, 1967.

Beck, L. W. "The 'Natural Science Ideal' in the Social Sciences," *Scientific Monthly*, Vol. 68 (1949), pp. 386–94.

Berger, Robert, and F. Cioffi (eds.). *Explanation in the Behavioral Sciences.* New York: Cambridge University Press, 1970.

Blake, R. M., C. J. Ducasse, and E. H. Madden. *Theories of Scientific Method: The Renaissance through the Nineteenth Century.* Seattle: University of Washington Press, 1960.

Boulding, Kenneth. *The Impact of the Social Sciences.* New Brunswick, New Jersey: Rutgers University Press, 1967.

Braybrooke, David (ed.). *Philosophical Problems of the Social Sciences.* New York: The Macmillan Company, 1965.

Brodbeck, May (ed.). *Readings in the Philosophy of the Social Sciences.* New York: The Macmillan Company, 1968.

Broudy, Harry S., *et al.* (eds.). *Philosophy of Education: Organization of Topics and Selected Sources.* Urbana, Illinois: University of Illinois Press, 1967.

Brown, Robert. *Explanation in Social Science.* Chicago: Aldine Publishing Company, 1963.

Buber, M. *The Knowledge of Man.* New York: Harper & Row, 1965.

Collingwood, R. G. *The Idea of History.* New York: Oxford University Press, 1946.

Cronbach, Lee J. "The Two Disciplines of Scientific Psychology," *American Psychologist,* Vol. 12, No. 11 (December, 1957), pp. 671–84.

Danto, A. C., A. Donagan, and J. W. Meiland. "Symposium: Historical Understanding," *Journal of Philosophy,* Vol. 63, No. 19 (1966), pp. 566–82.

Dilthey, Wilhelm. "Natural and Humanistic Studies." In H. A. Hodges, *Wilhelm Dilthey: An Introduction.* New York: Oxford University Press, 1944. pp. 141–45.

Di Renzo, Gordon J. (ed.). *Concepts, Theory, and Explanation in the Behavioral Sciences.* New York: Random House, Inc., 1966.

Dray, W. H. *Philosophy of History.* Englewood Cliffs, New Jersey: Prentice-Hall, Inc., 1964.

Easley, J. A., Jr. "The Natural Sciences and Educational Research—A Comparison," *The High School Journal,* Vol. 50, No. 1 (October, 1966), pp. 39–50.

Emmet, Dorothy, and A. MacIntyre (eds.). *Sociological Theory and Philosophical Analysis.* London: The Macmillan Company, 1970.

Faris, Robert E. L. "Some Issues of Relevance of Data for Behavioral Science." In E. W. Count, and G. T. Bowles (eds.), *Fact and Theory in Social Science.* Syracuse, New York: Syracuse University Press, 1964. pp. 107–24.

Gibson, Quentin B. *The Logic of Social Inquiry.* London: Routledge and Kegan Paul, Ltd., 1960.

Goldman, Lucien. *The Human Sciences and Philosophy.* London: Jonathan Cape, Ltd., 1969.

Helmer, Olaf, and Nicholas Rescher. "On the Epistemology of the Inexact Sciences," *Management Science,* Vol. 6, No. 1 (October, 1959), pp. 25–52.

Kaplan, A. *The Conduct of Inquiry: Methodology for Behavioral Science.* San Francisco: Chandler Publishing Company, 1964.

Krimerman, Leonard I. (ed.). *The Nature and Scope of Social Science: A Critical Anthology.* New York: Appleton-Century-Crofts, 1969.

Lazarsfeld, P. F., and M. Rosenberg (eds.). *The Language of Social Research: A Reader in the Methodology of Social Research.* New York: Free Press of Glencoe, Inc., 1955.

Machlup, Fritz. "Are the Social Sciences Really Inferior?" *The Southern Economic Journal*, Vol. 27, No. 3 (January, 1961), pp. 173–84.

Marx, M. H. "The General Nature of Theory Construction." In M. H. Marx (ed.), *Theories in Contemporary Psychology*. New York: The Macmillan Company, 1963. pp. 4–46.

Merton, Robert K. *Social Theory and Social Structure*. New York: The Macmillan Company, 1957.

Mill, John Stuart. *A System of Logic*. London: Longmans, Green, and Co., 1906.

Mills, C. Wright. *The Sociological Imagination*. New York: Oxford University Press, 1959.

Morgenbesser, Sidney. "Is It a Science?" *Social Research*, Vol. 33, No. 2 (Summer, 1966), pp. 255–71. Reprinted in Dorothy Emmet, and A. MacIntyre (eds.), *Sociological Theory and Philosophical Analysis*. London: The Macmillan Company, 1970, pp. 20–35.

Nagel, Ernest. "Philosophy in Educational Research." Paper 5 in F. W. Banghart (ed.). *First Annual Phi Delta Kappa Symposium on Educational Research*. Bloomington, Indiana: Phi Delta Kappan, 1960. pp. 71–84.

———. "Philosophy of Science and Educational Theory," *Studies in Philosophy and Education*, Vol. 7, No. 1 (Fall, 1969), pp. 5–27.

Natanson, Maurice (ed.). *Philosophy of the Social Sciences: A Reader*. New York: Random House, Inc., 1963.

Radcliffe-Brown, A. T. "On the Concept of Function in Social Science," *American Anthropologist*, Vol. 37 (1935), pp. 394–402.

Rudner, R. S. *Philosophy of Social Science*. Englewood Cliffs, New Jersey: Prentice-Hall, Inc., 1966.

Scheffler, Israel. "Science, Morals, and Educational Policy," *Harvard Educational Review*, Vol. 26, No. 1 (Winter, 1956), pp. 1–16.

Schutz, A. *Collected Papers*. 3 vols. Edited by M. Natanson. The Hague: Martinus Nijhoff, 1962.

Sills, D. L. (ed.). *International Encyclopedia of the Social Sciences*. 17 vols. New York: The Macmillan Company and the Free Press of Glencoe, 1968.

Skinner, B. F. *Science and Human Behavior*. New York: The Macmillan Company, 1953.

Smith, Christiana M., and Harry S. Broudy (eds.). *Philosophy of Education: An Organization of Topics and Selected Sources*. (Supplement, 1969.) Urbana, Illinois: University of Illinois Press, 1969.

Thorndike, Edward L. "The Nature, Purposes and General Methods of Measurement of Educational Products," in Geraldine M. Joncich (ed.), *Psychology and the Science of Education: Selected Writings of Edward L. Thorndike*. (Classics of Education, No. 12) New York: Teachers College, Columbia University, 1962. pp. 148–58.

White, Leslie A. *The Science of Culture*. New York: Farrar, Straus & Giroux, Inc., 1949.

Winch, Peter. *The Idea of a Social Science*. New York: Humanities Press, Inc., 1958.

Wooten, B. *Testament for Social Science: An Essay in the Application of Scientific Method to Human Problems*. London: George Allen and Unwin, Ltd., 1950.

2. Nature, Scope, and Strategy of Educational Research

Ausubel, David P. "The Nature of Educational Research," *Educational Theory*, Vol. 3, No. 4 (October, 1953), pp. 314–20.

Bloom, Benjamin S. "Twenty-five Years of Educational Research," *American Educational Research Journal*, Vol .3, No. 3 (May, 1966), pp. 211–21.

Brodbeck, May. "Logic and Scientific Method in Research on Teaching." In Nathaniel L. Gage (ed.), *Handbook of Research on Teaching*. Chicago: Rand McNally & Co., 1963.

———. "The Philosophy of Science and Educational Research," *Review of Educational Research*, Vol. 27 (1957), pp. 427–40.

Carroll, John B. "Basic and Applied Research in Education," *Harvard Educational Review*, Vol. 38, No. 2 (Spring, 1968), pp. 263–76.

———. "Research in Education: Where Do We Stand?" *Bulletin of the Harvard Graduate School of Education Association*, Vol. 5 (Winter, 1960).

Charlesworth, James C. (ed.). *Contemporary Political Analysis*. New York: Free Press of Glencoe, 1967.

Cicourel, A. V. *Method and Measurement in Sociology*. New York: Free Press of Glencoe, 1964.

Coladarci, Arthur P. "Towards More Rigorous Educational Research," *Harvard Educational Review*, Vol. 30, No. 1 (1960), pp. 3–11.

Cook, Desmond L. "The Hawthorne Effect in Educational Research," *Phi Delta Kappan*, Vol. 44 (December, 1962), pp. 116–22.

Cronbach, L. J., and P. Suppes (eds.). *Research for Tomorrow's Schools: Disciplined Inquiry for Education*. Report of the Committee on Educational Research of the National Academy of Education. New York: The Macmillan Company, 1969.

Culbertson, Jack A., and Stephen P. Hencley (eds.). *Educational Research: New Perspectives*. Danville, Illinois: Interstate Printers & Publishers, Inc., 1963.

Dewey, John. *The Sources of a Science of Education*. (Kappa Delta Pi Lecture Series.) New York: Liveright Publishing Corp., 1929.

Dubin, Robert. *Theory Building*. New York: Free Press of Glencoe, 1969.

Ebel, Robert L. (ed.). *Encyclopedia of Educational Research*. 4th ed. New York: The Macmillan Company, 1969.

———. "Some Limitations of Basic Research in Education," *Phi Delta Kappan*, Vol. 49, No. 2 (October, 1967), pp. 81–84. (Paper read before the AERA

Symposium on Basic and Applied Research and Public Policy, at New York City, February 16, 1967.)

Festinger, L., and D. Katz (eds.). *Research Methods in the Behavioral Sciences.* New York: Dryden Press, Inc., 1953.

Flower, Elizabeth. "Comments on Philosophy of Science and Educational Theory," *Studies in Philosophy and Education,* Vol. 7, No. 2 (Fall, 1970), pp. 143–53.

Freeman, Frank N. "Controlling Concepts in Educational Research," *Supplementary Educational Monographs* ("The Conceptual Structure of Educational Research," No. 55.) Chicago: University of Chicago Press, May, 1942.

Gage, N. L. (ed.). *Handbook of Research on Teaching.* (A Project of the American Educational Research Association.) Chicago: Rand McNally & Co., 1963.

Gephart, William J., and Robert B. Ingle (eds.). *Educational Research: Selected Readings.* Columbus, Ohio: Charles E. Merrill Publishing Company, 1969.

Glock, C. Y. (ed.). *Survey Research in the Social Sciences.* New York: Russell Sage Foundation, 1967.

Good, Carter V. *Introduction to Educational Research: Methodology of Design in the Behavioral and Social Sciences.* 2nd ed. New York: Appleton-Century-Crofts, 1963.

Gordon, T. J., and M. J. Raffensperger. "Discussion: A Strategy for Planning Basic Research," *Philosophy of Science,* Vol. 36, No. 2 (June, 1969), pp. 205–18.

Gouldner, A. W. "Theoretical Requirements of the Applied Social Sciences," *American Sociological Review,* Vol. 22 (February, 1957), pp. 92–102.

Gowin, D. B., and J. Millman (issue editors). "Methodology of Educational Research," *Review of Educational Research,* Vol. 39 (December, 1969).

Handy, Rollo. *Methodology of the Behavioral Sciences: Problems and Controversies.* Springfield, Illinois: Charles C Thomas, Publisher, 1964.

Hardie, C. D. "Research and Progress in Education," *Australian Journal of Education,* Vol. 9, No. 3 (1965), pp. 225–38. (Paper read at the University of Melbourne for the John Smyth Memorial Lecture for 1965.)

Holt, Robert T., and John E. Turner (eds.). *The Methodology of Comparative Research.* New York: Free Press of Glencoe, 1970.

Kerlinger, Fred N. *Foundations of Behavioral Research.* New York: Holt, Rinehart and Winston, Inc., 1964.

———. "The Mythology of Educational Research: The Methods Approach," *School and Society,* Vol. 88, No. 2171 (March 26, 1960), pp. 149–51.

Klausmeier, Herbert J., and George T. O'Hearn (eds.). *Research and Development Toward the Improvement of Education.* Madison, Wisconsin: Dembar Educational Research Services, 1968.

Larrabee, Harold A. *Reliable Knowledge.* Boston: Houghton Mifflin Company, 1945.

Lazarsfeld, Paul F., and Sam D. Sieber. *Organizing Educational Research: An Exploration.* Englewood Cliffs, New Jersey: Prentice-Hall, Inc., 1964.

Lazarsfeld, Paul F., and M. Rosenberg. *The Language of Social Research.* New York: Free Press of Glencoe, Inc., 1955.

McLeod, R. B. "The Phenomenological Approach to Social Psychology." In R. Tagiuri, and L. Petrullo (eds.). *Person, Perception and Interpersonal Behavior.* Stanford, California: Stanford University Press, 1958. Pp. 33–53.

Mouly, George J. *The Science of Educational Research.* New York: American Book Company, 1963.

Nordberg, Robert B., Donald J. Reitz, and John E. Wise. *Methods of Research in Education.* Boston: D. C. Heath and Company, 1967.

Petrie, Hugh G. "Why Has Learning Theory Failed to Teach Us How to Learn?" In George L. Newsome, Jr. (ed.), *Philosophy of Education 1968: Proceedings of the Twenty-Fourth Annual Meeting.* Lawrence, Kansas: University of Kansas Press. pp. 163–70.

Phillips, Bernard S. *Social Research: Strategy and Tactics.* New York: The Macmillan Company, 1966.

Scheffler, I. *Philosophy and Education.* 2nd ed. Boston: Allyn and Bacon, Inc., 1966.

Shulman, Lee S. "Reconstruction of Educational Research," *Review of Educational Research,* Vol. 40, No. 3 (June, 1970), pp. 371–96.

Skager, Rodney W., and Carl Weinberg. *Research for Beginning Students in Education.* Glenview, Illinois: Scott, Foresman & Company, 1970.

Smith, B. Othanel. "Science of Education." In W. S. Monroe (ed.), *Encyclopedia of Educational Research.* New York: The Macmillan Company. 1950. pp. 1145–52.

Travers, Robert M. W. *An Introduction to Educational Research.* 2nd ed. New York: The Macmillan Company, 1964.

Webb, Eugene J., *et al. Unobtrusive Measures: Nonreactive Research in the Social Sciences.* Chicago: Rand McNally & Co., 1966.

Weirsma, William. *Research Methods in Education: An Introduction.* Philadelphia: J. B. Lippincott Company, 1969.

Weiss, T., and K. Hooker. *Scientific Foundations of Education.* Dubuque, Iowa: William C. Brown Company, 1964.

Young, Roland (ed.). *Approaches to the Study of Politics.* Evanston, Illinois: Northwestern University Press, 1958.

3. Research Ethics

Astin, Alexander W., and Robert F. Boruch. "A 'Link' System for Assuring Confidentiality of Research Data in Longitudinal Studies," *American Educational Research Journal,* Vol. 7, No. 4 (November, 1970), pp. 615–24.

Boruch, R. F. "Educational Research and the Confidentiality of Data," *Sociology of Education*, Vol. 44, No. 1 (1971), pp. 59–85.

Buber, M. *I and Thou*. New York: Charles Scribner's Sons, 1958.

Freund, Paul A., *et al*. "Ethical Aspects of Experimentation with Human Subjects," *Daedalus*, Vol. 98, No. 2 (Spring, 1969), entire issue.

Peters, R. S. *Ethics and Education*. London: George Allen and Unwin, 1966.

Scriven, Michael. "The Values of the Academy (Moral Issues for American Education and Educational Research Arising from the Jensen Case)," *Review of Educational Research*, Vol. 40, No. 4 (October, 1970), pp. 541–49.

Rescher, Nicholas. "The Ethical Dimension of Scientific Research." In R. G. Colodny (ed.), *Beyond the Edge of Certainty: Essays in Contemporary Science and Philosophy*. Englewood Cliffs, New Jersey: Prentice-Hall, Inc., 1965. pp. 261–76.

U.S. Department of Health, Education and Welfare, Public Health Service. *Protection of the Individual as a Research Subject—Grants, Awards, Contracts*. Washington, D. C.: U.S. Government Printing Office, May, 1969.

PART II

4. Observation

Achinstein, Peter. *Concepts of Science*. Baltimore, Maryland: Johns Hopkins Press, 1968.

Agee, James, and E. Walker. *Let Us Now Praise Famous Men*. Boston: Houghton Mifflin Company, 1941.

Beller, Emanuel K. "Direct and Inferential Observations in the Study of Children," *American Journal of Orthopsychiatry*, Vol. 29 (July, 1959), pp. 560–573.

Campbell, Norman B. *An Account of the Principles of Measurement and Calculation*. London: Longmans, Green, and Co., 1928.

Carnap, Rudolph. *Foundations of Logic and Mathematics*. (*Encyclopedia of Unified Science*, Vol. III.) Chicago: University of Chicago Press, 1937.

Churchman, C. W., and P. Ratoosh (eds.). *Measurement: Definitions and Theories*. New York: John Wiley & Sons, 1959.

Dretske, Fred I. *Seeing and Knowing*. Chicago: University of Chicago Press, 1968.

Ellis, Brian. *Basic Concepts of Measurement*. New York: Cambridge University Press, 1966.

Ennis, Robert H. *Logic in Teaching*. Englewood Cliffs, New Jersey: Prentice-Hall, Inc., 1969. (Especially Chapter 20.)

Feyerabend, P. K. "Explanation, Reductionism, and Empiricism." In Herbert Feigl, and Grover Maxwell (eds.), *Minnesota Studies in the Philosophy of*

Science, Vol. III. Minneapolis: University of Minnesota Press, 1962. Pp. 28–97.

Foster, L., and J. W. Swanson (eds.). *Experience and Theory.* Amherst: University of Massachusetts Press, 1970.

Gellert, Elizabeth. "Systematic Observation: A Method in Child Study," *Harvard Educational Review,* Vol. 25 (Summer, 1955), pp. 179–95.

Hanson, Norwood Russell. "Observation and Interpretation." In Sidney Morgenbesser (ed.), *Philosophy of Science Today.* New York: Basic Books, Inc., 1967. Pp. 88–99.

———. *Perception and Discovery: An Introduction to Scientific Inquiry.* San Francisco: Freeman, Cooper, 1969.

———. *Observation and Explanation: A Guide to Philosophy of Science.* New York: Harper Torchbooks, 1971.

Hardie, C. D. *Truth and Fallacy in Educational Theory.* New York: Cambridge University Press, 1942. (Especially pp. 128–47.)

Hays, William L. *Quantification in Psychology.* Belmont, California: Brooks/Cole Pub. Co., 1967.

Hempel, Carl. "Fundamentals of Concept Formation in Empirical Science," *International Encyclopedia of Unified Sciences,* Vol. II, No. 7. Chicago: University of Chicago Press, 1952.

Mehrens, W. A., and R. L. Ebel (eds.). *Principles of Educational and Psychological Measurement: A Book of Selected Readings.* Chicago: Rand McNally & Co., 1967.

Merleau-Ponty, M. *Phenomenology of Perception.* Translated by Colin Smith. New York: Humanities Press, 1962.

Nagel, E., S. Bromberger, and A. Grünbaum. *Observation and Theory in Science.* Baltimore: Johns Hopkins Press, 1971.

Peak, Helen. "Problems of Objective Observation." In Leon Festinger and Daniel Katz (eds.), *Research Methods in the Behavioral Sciences.* New York: Holt, Rinehart and Winston, 1953. Pp. 243–99.

Scheffler, Israel. "Prospects of a Modest Empiricism," *The Review of Metaphysics,* Vol. 10, Nos. 3–4 (1957), pp. 383–400, 602–625.

———. *Science and Subjectivity.* Indianapolis: Bobbs-Merrill, 1967.

Smith, B. Othanel. *Logical Aspects of Educational Measurement.* New York: Columbia University Press, 1938.

Soltis, J. F. *Seeing, Knowing and Believing: A Study of the Language of Perception.* Reading, Massachusetts: Addison-Wesley Publishing Company, Inc., 1966.

Spector, Marshall. "Theory and Observation," *British Journal for the Philosophy of Science,* Vol. 17 (1966), pp. 1–20.

Stebbing, L. Susan. *Philosophy and the Physicists.* London: Methuen & Co., Ltd., 1937.

Vidich, A. J., J. Bensman, and M. R. Stein (eds.). *Reflections on Community Studies.* New York: John Wiley & Sons, 1964.

Woolf, Harry (ed.). *Quantification: A History of the Meaning of Measurement in the Natural and Social Sciences.* Indianapolis: Bobbs-Merrill, 1961.

5. Inference

Ackerman, Robert, *Nondeductive Inference.* London: Routledge & Kegan Paul Ltd., 1966.

Barker, S. F. *Induction and Hypothesis: A Study in the Logic of Confirmation.* Ithaca, New York: Cornell University Press, 1957.

Blalock, H. M., Jr. *Causal Inferences in Nonexperimental Research.* Chapel Hill, North Carolina: University of North Carolina Press, 1964.

Braithwaite, Richard Bevan. *Scientific Explanation.* Cambridge (England): The University Press, 1955.

Buck, Roger C. "Reflexive Predictions," *Philosophy of Science,* Vol. 30, No. 4 (October, 1963), pp. 359–374. With "Comments" by Adolph Grünbaum and "Rejoinder" by Buck.

Churchman, C. W. *Theory of Experimental Inference.* New York: The Macmillan Company, 1948.

Cohen, Morris R., and Ernest Nagel. *An Introduction to Logic and Scientific Method.* New York: Harcourt, Brace and Company, 1934.

Cooley, W. W., and P. R. Lohnes. *Multivariate Procedures for the Behavioral Sciences.* New York: John Wiley & Sons. 1962.

Davidson, D., and P. Suppes. *Decision Making: An Experimental Approach.* Stanford, California: Stanford University Press, 1957.

Edwards, Ward, Harold Lindman, and Leonard J. Savage. "Bayesian Statistical Inference for Psychological Research," *Psychological Review,* Vol. 70, No. 3 (1963), pp. 193–242.

Ennis, Robert H. *Logic in Teaching.* Englewood Cliffs, New Jersey: Prentice-Hall, Inc., 1969. (Especially Part IV.)

Ferguson, T. S. *Mathematical Statistics: A Decision Theoretic Approach.* New York: Academic Press, 1967.

Festinger, Leon and Daniel Katz. *Research Methods in the Behavioral Sciences.* New York: Holt, Rinehart and Winston, 1953.

Fisher, R. A. *The Design of Experiments.* New York: Hafner Publishing Co., Inc., 1935.

Foster, Marguerite H., and Michael L. Martin (eds.). *Probability, Confirmation, and Simplicity: Readings in the Philosophy of Inductive Logic.* New York: The Odyssey Press, Inc., 1966.

Gibson, Quentin. *The Logic of Social Enquiry.* London: Routledge & Kegan Paul Ltd., 1960.

Good, Carter V. *Introduction to Educational Research: Methodology of Design in the Behavioral and Social Sciences*. 2nd ed. New York: Appleton-Century-Crofts, 1963.

Good, Irving John. *The Estimation of Probabilities: An Essay on Modern Bayesian Methods*. (M. I. T. Research Monograph, No. 30.) Cambridge, Massachusetts: The MIT Press, 1965.

Gottschalk, Louis R. (ed.). *Generalization in the Writing of History*. Chicago: University of Chicago Press, 1963.

Hacking, I. *Logic of Statistical Inference*. Cambridge (England): Cambridge University Press, 1965.

Hays, W. L., and R. L. Winkler. *Statistics: Probability, Inference, and Decision*. New York: Holt, Rinehart and Winston, Inc. 1970.

Jeffrey, R. C. *Formal Logic: Its Scope and Limits*. New York: McGraw-Hill Book Company, 1967.

————. *The Logic of Decision*. New York: McGraw-Hill Book Company, 1965.

Jeffreys, Harold. *Scientific Inference*. 2nd ed. Cambridge (England): Cambridge University Press, 1957.

Kerlinger, Fred N. *Foundations of Behavioral Research*. New York: Holt, Rinehart and Winston, Inc., 1964.

Kyburg, Henry E., Jr., and Ernest Nagel (eds.). *Induction*. Middletown, Connecticut: Wesleyan University Press, 1963.

Kyburg, Henry E., Jr. *Probability and the Logic of Rational Belief*. Middletown, Connecticut: Wesleyan University Press, 1961.

Lerner, D. (ed.). *Evidence and Inference*. New York: Free Press of Glencoe, 1959.

Levi, Isaac. *Gambling with Truth*. London: Routledge & Kegan Paul Ltd., 1967.

Marshall, Jon C. "Bayesian Inference," *Journal of Experimental Education*, Vol. 37, No. 2 (Winter, 1968), pp. 71–75.

Meehl, P. E. *Clinical Versus Statistical Prediction*. Minneapolis: University of Minnesota Press, 1954.

Mill, John Stuart. *A System of Logic*. London: Longmans, Green, and Co., 1906.

Novick, Melvin R., and Paul H. Jackson. "Bayesian Guidance Technology," *Review of Educational Research*, Vol. 40, No. 4 (October, 1970), pp. 459–94.

Platt, John Rader. "Strong Inference," *Science*, Vol. 146, No. 3642 (October, 1964), pp. 347–53.

Popper, Karl. *Conjectures and Refutations: The Growth of Scientific Knowledge*. London: Routledge & Kegan Paul Ltd., 1963.

————. *The Logic of Scientific Discovery*. New York: Harper & Row, Inc., 1968.

Raiffa, Howard. *Decision Analysis: Introductory Lectures on Choices under Uncertainty*. Reading, Massachusetts: Addison-Wesley Publishing Company, Inc., 1968.

Riasanovsky, N. V. (ed.). *Generalizations in Historical Writing*. Philadelphia: University of Pennsylvania Press, 1964.

Salmon, Wesley L. *Inquiries into the Foundations of Science.* Albuquerque, New Mexico: University of New Mexico Press, 1968.

———. *Logic.* Englewood Cliffs, New Jersey: Prentice-Hall, Inc., 1963.

Schmitt, S. A. *Measuring Uncertainty: An Elementary Introduction to Bayesian Statistics.* Reading, Massachusetts: Addison-Wesley Publishing Company, 1969.

Scriven, Michael. "Truisms as the Grounds for Historical Explanations." In Patrick Gardiner (ed.), *Theories of History.* New York: The Macmillan Company, 1959. pp. 443–71.

Stebbins, L. Susan. *A Modern Introduction to Logic.* New York: Harper Torchbooks, 1933.

Stouffer, S. S., *et al. Measurement and Prediction.* Princeton, New Jersey: Princeton University Press, 1950.

Strawson, P. F. *Introduction to Logical Theory.* London: Methuen & Co., Ltd., 1952.

Tarski, Alfred. *Introduction to Logic and to the Methodology of the Deductive Sciences.* New York: Oxford University Press, 1946.

Travers, Robert M. W. *An Introduction to Educational Research.* 2nd ed. New York: The Macmillan Company. 1964.

Walker, Helen M., and Joseph Lev. *Statistical Inference.* New York: Holt, Rinehart and Winston, 1953.

Weirsma, William. *Research Methods in Education: An Introduction.* Philadelphia: J. B. Lippincott Company, 1969.

Wisdom, John O. *Foundations of Inference in Natural Science.* London: Methuen & Co., Ltd., 1952.

Yee, A. H., and N. L. Gage. "Techniques for Estimating the Source and Direction of Causal Influence in Panel Data," *Psychological Bulletin,* Vol. 70, No. 2 (1968), pp. 115–26.

6. Testability

Achinstein, Peter and S. F. Barker (eds.). *Legacy of Logical Positivism.* Baltimore: Johns Hopkins Press, 1969.

Ayer, A. J. (ed.). *Logical Positivism.* Glencoe, Illinois: Free Press, 1959.

Brown, Robert. *Explanation in Social Science.* Chicago: Aldine Publishing Company, 1963.

Buck, R. C., and W. Seeman. "Clinical Judges and Clinical Insight in Psychology," *Philosophy of Science,* Vol. 22 (1955), pp. 73–85.

Carnap, R. *Logical Foundations of Probability.* Chicago: University of Chicago Press, 1950.

———. "Testability and Meaning," *Philosophy of Science,* Vol. 3, No. 4 (1936), pp. 420–471; Vol. 4, No. 1 (1937), pp. 2–40.

Ennis, Robert H. *Logic in Teaching.* Englewood Cliffs, New Jersey: Prentice-Hall, Inc., 1969. (Especially Chapter 18.)

Hempel, Carl G. "Empiricist Criteria of Cognitive Significance: Problems and Changes." In *"Aspects of Scientific Explanation" and Other Essays in the Philosophy of Science.* New York: Free Press of Glencoe, 1965. pp. 101–22.

———. *Philosophy of Natural Science.* Englewood Cliffs, New Jersey: Prentice-Hall, Inc., 1966.

Hospers, John. *An Introduction to Philosophical Analysis.* Englewood Cliffs, New Jersey: Prentice-Hall, Inc., 1967. Chapter 14.

Machlup, F. "The Problems of Verification in Economics," *Southern Economic Journal,* Vol. 22 (1955).

MacIntyre, Alasdair. "The Psycho-analysts," *Encounter,* Vol. 24, No. 5 (1965), pp. 38–43.

———. *The Unconscious: A Conceptual Analysis.* London: Routledge & Kegan Paul Ltd., 1962.

Mackie, J. L. "The Paradoxes of Confirmation," *British Journal for the Philosophy of Science,* Vol. 13 (Feb., 1963), pp. 265–77.

———. "The Relevance Criterion of Confirmation," *British Journal for the Philosophy of Science,* Vol. 20 (May, 1969), pp. 27–40.

Malcolm, Norman. *Dreaming.* London: Routledge & Kegan Paul Ltd,. 1962.

Meehl, Paul E. "On the Circularity of the Law of Effect," *Psychological Bulletin,* Vol. 47 (1950), pp. 52–75.

Scheffler, I. *The Anatomy of Inquiry: Philosophical Studies in the Theory of Science.* New York: Alfred A. Knopf, Inc., 1963. (Especially Part 3.)

Schlesinger, G. "Confirmability and Determinism," *Philosophical Quarterly,* Vol. 18 (January, 1968), pp. 29–39.

Skyrms, B. *Choice and Chance.* Belmont, California: Dickenson Publishing Company, Inc., 1966.

7. Causation

Anscombe, G. E. M. *Causality and Determination.* Cambridge: Cambridge University Press, 1971.

Berofsky, Bernard. "Causality and General Laws," *Journal of Philosophy,* Vol. 63, No. 6 (March 17, 1966), pp. 148–57.

Black, Max. "Making Something Happen." In S. Hook (ed.), *Determinism and Freedom.* New York: New York University Press, 1958, pp. 15–30.

Blalock, Hubert M., Jr. *Causal Inferences in Nonexperimental Research.* Chapel Hill: University of North Carolina Press, 1964.

———. *Theory Construction: From Verbal to Mathematical Formulations.* Englewood Cliffs, New Jersey: Prentice-Hall, Inc., 1969.

Boudon, Raymond. "A Method of Linear Causal Analysis: Dependence Analysis," *American Sociological Review*, Vol. 30, No. 3 (June, 1965), pp. 365–74.

Broad, C. D. *Induction, Probability and Causation.* New York: Humanities Press, 1968.

Brodbeck, May. "Logic and Scientific Method in Research on Teaching." In N. L. Gage (ed.), *Handbook of Research on Teaching.* Chicago: Rand McNally & Co., 1963. pp. 44–93.

Bunge, Mario. *Causality: The Place of the Causal Principle in Modern Science.* Cambridge, Massachusetts: Harvard University Press, 1959.

Burks, Arthur W. "The Logic of Causal Propositions," *Mind*, Vol. 60 (1951), pp. 363–82.

Collingwood, Robin G. "On the So-Called Idea of Causation," *Proceedings of the Aristotelian Society*, Vol. 38 (1937–38), pp. 85–112.

Davidson, Donald, "Actions, Reasons, and Causes," *Journal of Philosophy*, Vol. 60 (1963), pp. 685–700. Reprinted in A. R. White (ed.), *The Philosophy of Action.* London: Oxford University Press, 1968, pp. 79–94; and N. S. Care and C. Landesman (eds.). *Readings in the Theory of Action.* Bloomington: Indiana University Press, 1968, pp. 179–98.

———. "Causal Relations," *Journal of Philosophy*, Vol. 64, No. 21 (November 9, 1967), pp. 691–703.

Dray, William. "Some Causal Accounts of the American Civil War," *Daedalus*, Vol. 91, No. 3 (Summer, 1962), pp. 578–92.

Ducasse, C. J. "Critique of Hume's Conception of Causality," *Journal of Philosophy*, Vol. 63, No. 6 (March 17, 1966), pp. 141–48.

Ewing, A. C. "A Defense of Causality," *Proceedings of the Aristotelian Society*, (1932–33), pp. 95–128. Reprinted in W. E. Kennick, and M. Lazerowitz (eds.), *Metaphysics: Readings and Reappraisals.* Englewood Cliffs, New Jersey: Prentice-Hall, Inc., 1966. Pp. 258–75.

———. *The Fundamental Questions of Philosophy.* London: The Macmillan Company, 1951.

Feigl, Herbert. "Notes on Causality." In H. Feigl and May Brodbeck (eds.), *Readings in the Philosophy of Science.* New York: Appleton-Century-Crofts, 1953, pp. 408–18.

Feuer, L. S., and E. M. Albert. "Causality in the Social Sciences," *Journal of Philosophy*, Vol. 51 (1954), pp. 681–706.

Gasking, Douglas. "Causation and Recipes," *Mind*, Vol. 64 (October, 1955), pp. 479–87.

Gorovitz, Samuel. "Causal Judgments and Causal Explanations," *Journal of Philosophy*, Vol. 62, No. 23 (December 2, 1965), pp. 695–711.

Grünbaum, Adolf. "Causality and the Science of Human Behavior," *American Scientists*, Vol. 40, No. 4 (1952), pp. 665–76. Reprinted in H. Feigl and

May Brodbeck (eds.), *Readings in the Philosophy of Science.* New York: Appleton-Century-Crofts, 1953. Pp. 766–78.

Hanson, N. R. *Patterns of Discovery.* Cambridge, England: Cambridge University Press, 1958. Chapter 3.

Hart, H. L. A., and A. M. Honoré. *Causation in the Law.* Oxford: Clarendon Press, 1959.

Hume, David. *An Enquiry Concerning Human Understanding.* LaSalle, Illinois: Open Court Publishing Company, 1946.

Hume, David. *A Treatise of Human Nature.* L. A. Selby-Bigge (ed.). Oxford: 1955.

Johnson, T. J., *et al.* "Some Determinants and Consequences of the Teacher's Perception of Causation," *Journal of Educational Psychology,* Vol. 55 (October, 1964), pp. 237–246.

Kant, Immanuel. *Critique of Pure Reason* (translated by Norman Kemp Smith). Toronto: Macmillan & Co., Ltd., 1929.

Kim, Jaegwon. "Causes and Events: Mackie on Causation," *Journal of Philosophy,* Vol. 68, No. 14 (July 22, 1971), pp. 426–41.

Lacey, J. I., and K. M. Dallenback. "Acquisition by Children of the Cause-Effect Relationship," *American Journal of Psychology,* Vol. 52 (1939), pp. 103–110.

Laurendeau, Monique, and A. Pinard. *Causal Thinking in the Child: A Genetic and Experimental Approach.* New York: International Universities Press, 1963.

Lenzen, Victor F. *Causality in Natural Science.* Springfield, Illinois: Charles C Thomas, Publisher, 1954.

Lerner, Daniel (ed.). *Cause and Effect.* New York: Free Press of Glencoe, 1965.

Lucas, J. R. "Causation." In R. J. Butler (ed.), *Analytical Philosophy.* Oxford: Basil Blackwell and Mott, Ltd., 1962. Pp. 32–65.

MacIntyre, A. "A Mistake About Causality in Social Science." In P. Laslett and W. C. Runciman (eds.), *Philosophy, Politics and Society.* 2nd ser. Oxford: Basil Blackwell and Mott, Ltd., 1962.

MacIver, R. M. *Social Causation.* Boston: Ginn and Company, 1942.

Mackie, J. L. "Causes and Conditions," *American Philosophical Quarterly,* Vol. 2, No. 4 (October, 1965), pp. 245–64.

———. "Counterfactuals and Causal Laws." In R. J. Butler (ed.), *Analytical Philosophy.* Oxford: Basil Blackwell and Mott, Ltd., 1962. Pp. 66–80.

Malcolm, Norman. "The Conceivability of Mechanism," *Philosophical Review,* Vol. 77 (1968), pp. 45–72.

Michotte, Albert Eduard. *The Perception of Causality.* Translated by T. R. Miles and Elaine Miles. New York: Basic Books, Inc., 1963.

Mill, John Stuart. *A System of Logic.* London: Longmans, Green, and Co., 1906.

Nagel, Ernest. "The Causal Character of Modern Physical Theory." In H. Feigl and May Brodbeck (eds.), *Readings in the Philosophy of Science.* New York: Appleton-Century-Crofts, 1953. Pp. 419–37.

———. *The Structure of Science.* New York: Harcourt, Brace, and World, 1961.

Pap, Arthur. *An Introduction to the Philosophy of Science.* New York: Free Press of Glencoe, 1962. Chapter 14.

Peaker, G. F. *The Plowden Children Four Years Later.* Windsor, England: National Foundation for Educational Research, 1971. (Especially Appendix 2.)

Peters, R. S. "Motives and Causes," *Proceedings of the Aristotelian Society,* Vol. 26 (1952), pp. 139–62.

Piaget, Jean. *The Child's Conception of Physical Causality.* Translated by Marjorie Gabain. London: Routledge & Kegan Paul Ltd., 1930.

———. *The Construction of Reality in the Child.* Translated by Margaret Cook. New York: Basic Books, Inc., 1954.

Planck, Max. "The Concept of Causality in Physics." Translated by F. Gaynor. In P. P. Wiener (ed.), *Readings in Philosophy of Science.* New York: Charles Scribner's Sons, 1953. Pp. 77–87.

Russell, Bertrand. "On the Notion of Cause." *Proceedings of the Aristotelian Society,* Vols. 12 and 13 (1912–13), pp. 1–26. Reprinted in Bertrand Russell, *Mysticism and Logic.* Garden City, New York: Anchor Books, Doubleday & Company, Inc., 1957.

Schlick, Moritz. "Causality in Everyday Life and in Recent Science." ("University of California Publications in Philosophy," No. 15.) 1932. Reprinted in H. Feigl and W. Sellars (eds.), *Readings in Philosophical Analysis.* New York: Appleton-Century-Crofts, 1949. Pp. 515–33.

Scriven, Michael. "Causes, Connections and Conditions in History." In William H. Dray (ed.), *Philosophical Analysis and History.* New York: Harper & Row, 1966. Pp. 238–64.

———. "Philosophy of Science in Educational Research," *Review of Educational Research,* Vol. 30 (December 1960), pp. 422–28.

Shannon, J. R. "Cause and Effect in Educational Research," *California Journal of Educational Research,* Vol. 13 (November, 1962), p. 194 and p. 221.

Simon, Herbert A. "Causation." In David L. Sills (ed.), *International Encyclopedia of the Social Sciences.* New York: The Macmillan Company and The Free Press of Glencoe, 1968. Vol. 2. Pp. 350–56.

———. "On the Definition of the Causal Relation," *Journal of Philosophy,* Vol. 49 (July 31, 1952), pp. 517–28. Reprinted in Herbert A. Simon, *Models of Man.* New York: John Wiley & Sons, 1957. Chapter 3. Pp. 50–61.

———. "Spurious Correlation: A Causal Interpretation," *Journal of the American Statistical Association,* Vol. 49 (1954), pp. 467–79.

Skyrms, Brian. *Choice and Chance.* Belmont, Cal.: Dickenson Publishing Company, Inc., 1966.

Taylor, Charles. *The Explanation of Behavior*. London: Routledge & Kegan Paul Ltd., 1964.

Taylor, Richard. "Causation," *The Monist*, Vol. 47 (1963), pp. 287–313.

———. "Causation." In Paul Edwards (ed.), *Encyclopedia of Philosophy* (8 vols). New York: The Macmillan Company and the Free Press of Glencoe, 1967. Vol. 2, pp. 56–66.

Toulmin, Stephen. "Reasons and Causes." In Robert Borger and Frank Cioffi (eds.), *Explanation in the Behavioral Sciences*. Cambridge (England): Cambridge University Press, 1970. Pp. 1–26. Comment by R. S. Peters, pp. 27–41. Reply by Toulmin, pp. 42–48.

Urmson, J. O. "Motives and Causes," *Proceedings of the Aristotelian Society, Supplementary Volume*, Vol. 26 (1952), pp. 179–94.

Vendler, Z. "Symposium: Effects, Results and Consequences." In R. J. Butler (ed.), *Analytical Philosophy*. Oxford: Basil Blackwell and Mott, Ltd., 1962. Pp. 1–15. Comments by S. Bromberger, pp. 15–20; and W. H. Dray, pp. 20–25. "Reactions and Retractions" by Vendler, pp. 25–31.

Waismann, F. "The Decline and Fall of Causality." In A. C. Crombie, *et al.*, *Turning Points in Physics*. New York: Torchbooks, Harper & Row, 1961. Pp. 84–154. Reprinted in F. Waismann, *How I See Philosophy*. Edited by R. Harré. New York: St. Martin's Press, Inc., 1968. Pp. 208–56.

Walsh, W. H. *Metaphysics*. London: Hutchinson, 1963.

Warnock, G. J. "Every Event Has a Cause." In Antony Flew (ed.), *Logic and Language* (Second Series). New York: Philosophical Library, 1953. Pp. 95–111.

Wartofsky, Marx W. *Conceptual Foundations of Scientific Thought: An Introduction to the Philosophy of Science*. New York: The Macmillan Company, 1968.

Wisdom, John Oulton. *Causation and the Foundations of Science*. Paris: Hermann, 1946.

Wold, Herman (ed.). *Econometric Model Building: Essays on the Causal Chain Approach*. Amsterdam: North-Holland, 1964.

Yee, A. H. and N. L. Gage. "Techniques for Estimating the Source and Direction of Causal Influence in Panel Data," *Psychological Bulletin*, Vol. 70, No. 2 (1968), pp. 115–26.

8. Models

Achinstein, P. "Models, Analogies and Theories," *Philosophy of Science*, Vol. 31 (1964), pp. 328–50.

———. "Theoretical Models," *British Journal for the Philosophy of Science*. Vol. 16 (1965), pp. 102–120.

Arrow, K., S. Karlin, and P. Suppes (eds.). *Mathematical Methods in the Social Sciences*. Stanford, California: Stanford University Press, 1960.

Black, Max. *Models and Metaphors.* Ithaca, New York: Cornell University Press, 1962.

Braithwaite, R. B. "Models in the Empirical Sciences." In Ernest Nagel, Patrick Suppes, and Alfred Tarski (eds.). *Logic, Methodolgy and Philosophy of Science.* Proceedings of the International Congress for Logic, Methodology and Philosophy, Stanford, 1960. Stanford, California: Stanford University Press, 1962.

Brodbeck, May. "Logic and Scientific Method in Research on Teaching." In N. L. Gage (ed.), *Handbook of Research on Teaching.* Chicago: Rand McNally & Co., 1963. Pp. 44–93.

Campbell, D. T., and J. C. Stanley. *Experimental and Quasi-Experimental Designs for Research.* Chicago: Rand McNally & Co., 1966.

Campbell, N. R. *Foundations of Science: The Philosophy of Theory and Experiment.* New York: Dover Publications, Inc., 1957.

Carroll, J. B. "A Model of School Learning," *Teachers College Record,* Vol. 64 (1963), pp. 723–33.

Cooney, Thomas J., and Kenneth B. Henderson. "A Model for Organizing Knowledge," *Educational Theory,* Vol. 21, No. 1 (Winter, 1971), pp. 50–58.

Estes, W. K. "Of Models and Men," *American Psychologist,* Vol. 12 (1957), pp. 609–17.

Fattu, N. A., and S. Elam (eds.). *Simulation Models for Education: Fourth Annual Phi Delta Kappa Symposium on Educational Research.* Bloomington, Indiana: Phi Delta Kappa, 1965.

Freudenthal, H. (ed.). *The Concept and the Role of the Model in Mathematics and Natural and Social Sciences.* The Netherlands: D. Reidel Publishing Company, 1962.

Harary, Frank, Robert Z. Norman, and Dorwin Cartwright. *Structural Models: An Introduction to the Theory of Directed Graphs.* New York: John Wiley and Sons, 1965.

Henderson, Kenneth B. "A Logical Model for Conceptualizing and Other Related Activities." In B. Paul Komisar and C. J. B. Macmillan, *Psychological Concepts in Education.* Chicago: Rand McNally & Company, 1967. Pp. 96–105.

Hesse, Mary B. *Models and Analogies in Science.* London: Sheed and Ward Ltd., 1963. Expanded edition: Notre Dame, Indiana: University of Notre Dame Press, 1966.

Jacobson, Milton D., Reynold P. Stimart, and George T. Wren. "Models and Educational Research," *American Educational Research Journal,* Vol. 8 (1971), pp. 311–20.

Light, R. J., and P. V. Smith. "Social Allocation Models of Intelligence: a Methodological Inquiry," *Harvard Educational Review,* Vol. 39 (1969), pp. 484–510.

Luce, R. D., and H. Raiffa. *Games and Decisions.* New York: John Wiley and Sons, 1957.

Maccia, Elizabeth, George S. Maccia, and Robert E. Jewett. *Construction of Educational Theory Models.* Cooperative Research Project No. 1682. Columbus, Ohio: Ohio State University Research Foundation, 1963.

Mullin, E. "What Do Physical Models Tell Us?" in B. van Rootselaar and J. F. Staal (eds.), *Logic, Methodology and Philosophy of Science III.* Proceedings of the Third International Congress for Logic, Methodology and Philosophy of Science. Amsterdam: North Holland Publishing Co., 1968.

Neumann, J., and O. Morgenstern. *Theory of Games and Economic Behavior.* Princeton, New Jersey: Princeton University Press, 1944.

Scheffler, Israel. "Philosophical Models of Teaching," *Harvard Educational Review*, Vol. 35, No. 2 (1965), pp. 131–43.

Shapley, L. S., and Martin Shubik. "A Method for Evaluating the Distribution of Power in a Committee System," *The American Political Science Review*, Vol. 48, No. 3 (September, 1954), pp. 78–92.

Simon, H. A., A. Audo, and F. M. Fisher. *Essays on the Structure of Social Science Models.* Cambridge, Massachusetts: MIT Press, 1963.

Simon, H. A. *Models of Man.* New York: John Wiley & Sons, 1957.

———. "Some Strategic Considerations in the Construction of Social Science Models." In Paul Lazarsfeld (ed.), *Mathematical Thinking in the Social Sciences.* New York: The Macmillan Company, 1954. Pp. 388–406.

Spector, M. "Models and Theories," *British Journal for the Philosophy of Science*, Vol. 16 (1965), pp. 121–42.

Suppes, P. "A Comparison of the Meaning and Uses of Models in Mathematics and the Empirical Sciences," *Synthese*, Vol. 12 (1960), pp. 287–301.

Walberg, Herbert J. "A Model for Research on Instruction," *School Review*, Vol. 78, No. 2 (February, 1970), pp. 185–200.

West, E. H. "Models in Education," *Journal of Negro Education*, Vol. 39 (Fall, 1970), pp. 275–277.

9. Value Judgments by Scientists

Burtt, E. A. "The Value Presuppositions of Science," *Bulletin of the Atomic Scientists*, Vol. 13, No. 3 (March, 1957), pp. 99–106. Reprinted in P. C. Obler, and H. A. Estrin (eds.), *The New Scientist: Essays on the Methods and Values of Modern Science.* New York: Anchor Books, Doubleday & Company, Inc., 1962. Pp. 258–79.

Churchman, C. W. "Science and Decision Making," *Philosophy of Science*, Vol. 23, (1956), pp. 247–49.

Erikson, Erik H. "The Nature of Clinical Evidence." In Daniel Lerner (ed.), *Evidence and Inference.* New York: The Macmillan Company and the Free Press of Glencoe, 1959. Pp. 73–95.

Gorlow, Leon, and Gary A. Noll. "The Measurement of Empirically Determined

Values," *Educational and Psychological Measurement*, Vol. 27 (1967), pp. 1115–18.

Hayek, F. A. *The Counter-Revolution of Science: Studies on the Abuse of Reason.* Glencoe, Illinois: Free Press, 1952.

Jeffrey, R. C. "Valuation and Acceptance of Scientific Hypotheses," *Philosophy of Science*, Vol. 23 (1956), pp. 237–46.

Klappholz, Kurt. "Value Judgments and Economics," *British Journal for the Philosophy of Science*, Vol. 15 (August, 1964), 97–114.

Levi, Isaac. *Gambling with Truth: An Essay on Induction and the Aims of Science.* New York: Alfred A. Knopf, Inc., 1967.

———. "Must the Scientist Make Value Judgments?" *Journal of Philosophy.* Vol. 57, No. 11 (May, 1960), pp. 345–57.

Lundberg, George A. *Can Science Save Us?* 2nd ed. London: Longmans, Green, and Co., 1961.

Lynd, Robert S. *Knowledge For What? The Place of Social Science in American Culture.* Princeton, New Jersey: Princeton University Press, 1939.

Mannheim, Karl. *Ideology and Utopia.* New York: Harcourt, Brace and World, Inc., 1936.

Myrdal, Gunnar. *Value in Social Theory: A Selection of Essays on Methodology.* Edited by Paul Streetan. London: Routledge & Kegan Paul Ltd., 1958.

———. *Objectivity in Social Research.* New York: Pantheon Books, Random House, Inc., 1969.

Nagel, Ernest. *The Structure of Science.* New York: Harcourt, Brace and World, Inc., 1961.

O'Connor, D. J. "Value Judgments and the Social Sciences," *Sociological Review*, Vol. 1 (1953).

Passmore, John A. "Can the Social Sciences Be Value-Free?" *Proceedings of the Tenth Inter-National Congress of Philosophy.* Amsterdam: North-Holland Publishing Co., 1949. Pp. 674–76.

Rescher, N. "Values and the Explanation of Behavior," *Philosophical Quarterly*, Vol. 17 (1967), pp. 130–136.

Rotenstreich, N. "The Value Aspect of Science," *Philosophy and Phenomenological Research*, Vol. 20 (1960), pp. 513–20.

Rudner, Richard. "The Scientist *Qua* Scientist Makes Value Judgments," *Philosophy of Science*, Vol. 20, No. 1 (January, 1953), pp. 1–6.

Scheffler, I. *Science and Subjectivity.* Indianapolis: Bobbs-Merrill Co., Inc., 1967.

Schmidt, P. F. "Ethical Norms in Scientific Method," *Journal of Philosophy*, Vol. 56 (1959), pp. 644–652.

Snow, C. P. "The Moral Un-neutrality of Science." In P. C. Obler, and H. A. Estrin (eds.), *The New Scientist: Essays on the Methods and Values of Modern Science.* New York: Anchor Books, Doubleday & Company, Inc., 1962. Pp. 127–40.

Stevenson, C. L. "The Scientist's Role and the Aims of Education," *Harvard Educational Review*, Vol. 24, No. 4 (Fall, 1954), pp. 231–38.

Weber, Max. *The Methodology of Social Sciences*. Glencoe, Illinois: The Free Press of Glencoe, 1949.

Werkmeister, W. H. "Social Science and the Problem of Value." In H. Schoeck, and J. W. Wiggins (eds), *Scientism and Values*. Princeton, New Jersey: Van Nostrand, 1960. Pp. 1–21.

10. Concepts and Their Delineation

Achinstein, P. *Concepts of Science: A Philosophical Analysis*. Baltimore: Johns Hopkins Press, 1968.

Bechtoldt, Harold P. "Construct Validity: A Critique," *American Psychologist*, Vol. 15 (1959), pp. 619–29.

Bergman, G. and K. W. Spence. "Operationism and Theory in Psychology," *Psychological Review*, Vol. 48 (1941), pp. 1–14. Reprinted in M. H. Marx (ed.), *Psychological Theory: Contemporary Readings*. New York: The Macmillan Company, 1951, pp. 54–66.

Black, Max. *Critical Thinking*. 2nd ed. Englewood Cliffs, New Jersey: Prentice-Hall, Inc., 1952.

———. *Problems of Analysis*. Ithaca, New York: Cornell University Press, 1954.

Bridgman, Percy W. *The Logic of Modern Physics*. New York: The Macmillan Company, 1927.

———. *The Nature of Physical Theory*. Princeton, New Jersey: Princeton University Press, 1936.

———. "The Operational Aspect of Meaning," *Synthese*, Vol. 8 (1950–51), pp. 251–59.

Brodbeck, May. "Logic and Scientific Method in Research on Teaching." In N. L. Gage (ed.), *Handbook of Research on Teaching*. Chicago: Rand McNally & Co., 1963. Pp. 44–93.

———. "Meaning and Action," *The Philosophy of Science*, Vol. 30, No. 4 (October, 1963), pp. 309–24.

Carnap, Rudolph. "Logical Foundations of the Unity of Science." In Otto Neurath (ed.), *International Encyclopedia of Unified Science*. Chicago: University of Chicago Press, 1955. Pp. 42–62.

Chapin, F. Stuart. "Definition of Definitions of Concepts," *Social Forces*, Vol. 18, No. 2 (December, 1939), pp. 153–160.

Cohen, Morris. "Concepts and Twilight Zones," *Journal of Philosophy*, Vol. 24 No. 25 (1927), pp. 673–83.

———, and Ernest Nagel. *An Introduction to Logic and Scientific Method*. New York: Harcourt, Brace and Company, 1934.

Coleman, J. *Introduction to Mathematical Sociology*. New York: The Free Press of Glencoe, 1964.

Copi, I. M. "The Growth of Concepts." In P. Henle (ed.), *Language, Thought, and Culture*. Ann Arbor: University of Michigan Press, 1958. pp. 25–48.

Cronbach, Lee J., and Paul E. Meehl. "Construct Validity in Psychological Tests," *Psychological Bulletin*, Vol. 52, No. 4 (July, 1955), pp. 281–302.

Delgado, R. Rodriguez, and J. M. R. Delgado. "An Objective Approach to Measurement of Behavior," *Philosophy of Science*, Vol. 29 No. 3 (July, 1962), pp. 253–68.

Ennis, Robert H. "Operational Definitions," *American Educational Research Journal*, Vol. 1, No. 3 (May, 1964), pp. 183–201.

Frank, Philipp G. (ed.). *The Validation of Scientific Theories*. New York: Collier Books, 1961.

Garner, Wendell R., Harold W. Hake, and Charles W. Eriksen. "Operationism and the Concept of Perception," *The Psychological Review*, Vol. 63, No. 3 (May, 1956), pp. 149–59.

Gellner, E. A. "Concepts and Society." *Transactions of the Fifth World Conference of Sociology*. Vol. I. Louvain: International Sociology Association, 1962. Pp. 153–83.

Harré, R. "Concepts and Criteria," *Mind*, Vol. 73, No. 291 (July, 1964), pp. 353–63.

Heidelberger, Herbert. "The Mental and the Physical." In Leonard I. Krimerman (ed.), *The Nature and Scope of Social Science: A Critical Anthology*. New York: Appleton-Century-Crofts, 1969. Pp. 409–15.

Hempel, Carl. *Fundamentals of Concept Formation in Empirical Science*. Chicago: University of Chicago Press, 1952.

Hook, Sidney (ed.). *Dimensions of Mind: A Symposium*. New York: New York University Press, 1960.

Hospers, John. *An Introduction to Philosophical Analysis*. Englewood Cliffs, New Jersey: Prentice-Hall, Inc., 1967.

Kaplan, A. "Definition and Specification of Meaning," *Journal of Philosophy*, Vol. 43, No. 11 (May 23, 1946), pp. 281–88. Reprinted in P. F. Lazarsfeld, and M. Rosenberg (eds.). *The Language of Social Research: A Reader in the Methodology of Social Research*. New York: Free Press of Glencoe, 1955, pp. 527–32.

Lazarsfeld, P. F., and M. Rosenberg (eds). *The Language of Social Research*. Glencoe, Illinois: Free Press of Glencoe, 1955.

Lazarsfeld, P. F., and Allen H. Barton. "Qualitative Measurement in the Social Sciences: Classification, Typologies and Indices." In Daniel Lerner and Harold D. Lasswell (eds.), *The Policy Sciences*. Stanford: Stanford University Press, 1951. Pp. 155–92.

MacCorquodale, Kenneth and Paul E. Meehl. "On a Distinction Between Hypothetical Constructs and Intervening Variables," *Psychological Review*, Vol. 55 (1948), pp. 95–107.

Nagel, T. "Physicalism," *The Philosophical Review,* Vol. 74, No. 3 (1965), pp. 339–56.

Petrie, Hugh G. "A Dogma of Operationalism in the Social Sciences," *Philosophy of Social Science,* Vol. I (1971), pp. 145–60.

Robinson, Richard. *Definition.* Oxford: Clarendon Press, 1954.

Ryle, G. *The Concept of Mind.* London: Hutchinson's University Library, 1949.

Scheffler, Israel. *The Language of Education.* Springfield, Illinois: Charles C Thomas, Publisher, 1960.

Schon, Donald A. *The Displacement of Concepts.* London: Tavistock, 1963.

Scriven, Michael. "A Study of Radical Behaviorism." In Herbert Feigl and Michael Scriven (eds.), *Minnesota Studies in the Philosophy of Science.* Vol. I. Minneapolis: University of Minnesota Press, 1956. Pp. 105–30.

Sellars, W. S. "Concepts as Involving Laws and Inconceivable Without Them," *Philosophy of Science,* Vol. 15 (1948), pp. 287–315.

Skinner, B. F. "The Operational Analysis of Psychological Terms," *Psychological Review,* Vol. 52, No. 5 (1945), pp. 270–77.

Smart, J. J. C. "Sensations and Brain Processes," *Philosophical Review,* Vol. 68, No. 2 (1959), 141–56.

Stevens, S. S. "Mathematics, Measurement and Psychophysics." In S. S. Stevens (ed.). *Handbook of Experimental Psychology.* New York: John Wiley and Sons, Inc., 1951. Pp. 1–49.

———. "On the Theories of Scales of Measurement," *Science,* Vol. 103, No. 2684 (1946), pp. 677–80.

———. "Sensation and Psychological Measurement." In E. G. Boring (ed.), *Foundations of Psychology.* New York: John Wiley and Sons, Inc., 1948. Pp. 250–68.

Stewart, L. H. "Non-metric Procedure for Combining Criterion Groups; Interest Assessment Scales," *California Journal of Educational Research,* Vol. 21 (November, 1970), pp. 208–15.

Waismann, Friedrich. "Verifiability." In Antony Flew (ed.), *Logic and Language* (First Series). Garden City, New York: Doubleday & Co., Inc., 1952. Pp. 122–51.

Whorf, Benjamin Lee. *Language, Thought, and Reality.* Cambridge, Mass.: MIT Press, 1956.

Wilson, F. "Definition and Discovery," *British Journal for the Philosophy of Science,* Vol. 19, No. 1 (May, 1968), pp. 43–56.

11. Behaviorism

Anscombe, G. E. M. *Intention.* Oxford (England): Basil Blackwell and Mott Ltd., 1958.

Blanshard, B., and B. F. Skinner. "The Problem of Consciousness, a Debate," *Philosophy and Phenomenological Research,* Vol. 26 (1967), pp. 317–337.

Brand, Myles (ed.). *The Nature of Human Action*. Chicago: Scott, Foresman & Company, 1970.

Broudy, Harry S. "Can Research Escape the Dogma of Behavioral Objectives?" *School Review*, Vol. 79, No. 1 (November, 1970), pp. 43–56.

Charlesworth, J. C. (ed.). *Contemporary Political Analysis*. New York: Free Press of Glencoe, 1967.

Chisholm, Roderick. "Sentences About Believing," *Proceedings of the Aristotelian Society*, Vol. 56 (1955–56), pp. 125–48.

Chomsky, Noam. "A Review of B. F. Skinner's *Verbal Behavior*," *Language*, Vol. 35 (January-March, 1959), pp. 26–58.

Deese, J. "Behavior and Fact," *American Psychologist*, Vol. 24 (1969), pp. 515–22.

Eulau, Heinz. *The Behavioral Persuasion in Politics*. New York: Random House, Inc., 1963.

Fodor, Jerry A. *Psychological Explanation: An Introduction to the Philosophy of Psychology*. New York: Random House, Inc., 1968.

Gustafson, D. F. (ed.). *Essays in Philosophical Psychology*. New York: Anchor Books, Doubleday & Company, Inc., 1964.

Hampshire, Stuart. *Freedom of the Individual*. New York: Harper & Row, 1965.

Hill, Winfred F. "Contemporary Developments Within Stimulus-Response Learning Theory." In Ernest R. Hilgard (ed.), *Theories of Learning and Instruction*. Chicago: National Society for the Study of Education, 1964. pp. 27–53.

Jenkins, J. J. "The Challenge to Psychological Theorists." In T. R. Dixon, and D. L. Morton (eds.). *Verbal Behavior and General Behavior Theory*. Englewood Cliffs, New Jersey: Prentice-Hall, Inc., 1968. Pp. 538–49.

Kariel, Henry S. "The Political Relevance of Behavioral Existential Psychology," *American Political Science Review*, Vol. 61, No. 2 (1967), pp. 334–42.

MacCorquodale, Kenneth. "On Chomsky's Review of Skinner's *Verbal Behavior*," *Journal of the Experimental Analysis of Behavior*, Vol. 13, No. 1 (January, 1970), pp. 83–99.

MacKay, D. M. "Mindlike Behavior in Artifacts," *British Journal for the Philosophy of Science*, Vol. 2 (1951), pp. 105–21.

Malcolm, Norman. "Behaviorism as a Philosophy of Psychology." In T. W. Wann (ed.), *Behaviorism and Phenomenology*. Chicago: University of Chicago Press, 1964. Pp. 141–55.

Malcolm, Norman. "The Conceivability of Mechanism," *The Philosophical Review*, Vol. 77, No. 1 (January, 1968), pp. 45–72.

Mandler, G., and W. Kessen. *The Language of Psychology*. New York: John Wiley & Sons, 1959.

Morick, Harold (ed.). *Introduction to the Philosophy of Mind: Readings from Descartes to Strawson*. Glenview, Illinois: Scott, Foresman and Company, 1970.

Newell, Allen and Herbert A. Simon. "The Simulation of Human Thought." In *Contemporary Trends in Psychological Theory*. Pittsburgh: University of Pittsburgh Press, 1961. Pp. 152–79.

Paske, Gerald. "Functional Analysis and Self-Control," *Educational Theory*, Vol. 14, No. 4 (October, 1964), pp. 314–22.

Peters, R. S., and H. Tajfel. "Hobbes and Hull—Metaphysicians of Behavior," *British Journal for the Philosophy of Science*, Vol. 8, No. 29 (May, 1957), pp. 30–44.

Price, H. H. "Some Objections to Behaviorism." In Sidney Hook (ed.), *Dimensions of Mind*. New York: Collier Books, 1960. Pp. 79–84.

Roscoe, J. T. "Toward a Behavioral Science Approach to Education," *Education*, Vol. 90 (September, 1969), pp. 83–86.

Ryle, G. *The Concept of Mind*. London: Hutchinson, 1949.

Skinner, B. F. "Behaviorism at Fifty." In T. W. Wann (ed.), *Behaviorism and Phenomenology*. Chicago: University of Chicago Press, 1964. Pp. 79–97.

———. *Science and Human Behavior*. New York: The Macmillan Company, 1953.

———. *Verbal Behavior*. New York: Appleton-Century-Crofts, Inc., 1957.

Spence, Kenneth W. *Behavior Theory and Conditioning*. New Haven, Connecticut: Yale University Press, 1956.

———. "The Nature of Theory Construction in Contemporary Psychology," *Psychological Review*, Vol. 51, No. 1 (January, 1944), pp. 417–68.

———. "The Postulates and Methods of 'Behaviorism'," *Psychological Review*, Vol. 55, No. 2 (1948), pp. 67–78.

Taylor, C. *The Explanation of Behavior*. London: Routledge & Kegan Paul Ltd., 1964.

Taylor, R. G. "Comments on a Mechanistic Conception of Purposefulness," *Philosophy of Science*, Vol. 17 (1950), pp. 310–317.

Wann, T. W. (ed.). *Behaviorism and Phenomenology: Contrasting Bases for Modern Psychology*. Chicago: University of Chicago Press, 1964.

Wolman, B. B., and E. Nagel (eds.). *Scientific Psychology: Principle and Approaches*. New York: Basic Books, 1965.

12. Programmed Instruction

Anderson, R. C., *et al. Current Research on Instruction*. Englewood Cliffs, New Jersey: Prentice-Hall, Inc., 1969.

Arnstine, Donald. "Rote and Reasoning: Some Cautions on Programming," *The High School Journal*, Vol. 5 (1968), pp. 353–64.

Borton, Terry. "Dual Audio Television," *Harvard Educational Review*, Vol. 41, No. 1 (February, 1971), pp. 64–78.

Broudy, Harry S. "Some Potentials and Hazards of Educational Technology." In

Egdar L. Morphet, and David L. Jesser (eds.), *Planning for Effective Utilization of Technology in Education.* Denver, Colorado: Eight-State Project, 1968.

Bushnell, Donald D., and Dwight W. Allen. *The Computer in American Education.* New York: John Wiley and Sons, Inc., 1967.

Ellul, Jacques. *The Technological Society.* Translated by John Wilkinson. New York: Alfred A. Knopf, Inc., 1964.

Garner, W. L. *Programmed Instruction.* New York: Center for Applied Research in Education, 1966.

Goodlad, J. I., J. F. O'Toole Jr., and Louise L. Tyler. *Computers and Information Systems in Education.* New York: Harcourt, Brace and World, 1966.

Goodman, Edith H. (ed.). *Automated Education Handbook.* Detroit: Automated Education Center, 1965.

Goodman, Paul. *Compulsory Miseducation.* New York: Horizon Press, 1964.

Hilgard, Ernest R. (ed.). *Theories of Learning and Instruction.* Sixty-third Yearbook, Part I. National Society for the Study of Education. Chicago: University of Chicago Press, 1964.

Holland, J. G. "Research on Programming Variables." In R. Glaser (ed.), *Teaching Machines and Programmed Learning, II: Data and Directions.* Washington, D. C.: Department of Audiovisual Instruction, National Education Association, 1965. Pp. 66–117.

Jackson, Philip W. *The Teacher and the Machine.* Pittsburgh: University of Pittsburgh Press, 1968.

Jones, Rodney M. and Thomas L. Hick. "Two Sequence Factors in Programmed Instruction," *Journal of Experimental Education*, Vol. 38, No. 2 (Winter, 1969), pp. 66–69.

Kay, Harry, *et al. Teaching Machines and Programmed Instruction.* Baltimore: Penguin Books, 1968.

Mager, Robert F. *Preparing Instructional Objectives.* Palo Alto, California: Fearon Publishers, 1962.

Muller, Herbert J. *The Children of Frankenstein—A Primer on Modern Technology and Human Values.* Bloomington, Indiana: Indiana University Press, 1970.

Mumford, L. *The Myth of the Machine: Technics and Human Development.* New York: Harcourt, Brace and World, Inc., 1967.

Oettinger, A. G. *Run, Computer, Run: The Mythology of Educational Innovation.* Cambridge, Mass.: Harvard University Press, 1969.

Raindance Corporation. *Radical Software: The Alternative Television Movement.* Vol. 1, No. 1, 1970. (Available from Raindance Corporation, 24 East 22 St., New York, New York 10016.)

Resnick, Lauren B. "Programmed Instruction and the Teaching of Complex Intellectual Skills," *Harvard Educational Review*, Vol. 33, No. 4 (Fall, 1963), pp. 439–71.

Skinner, B. F. *The Technology of Teaching*. New York: Appleton-Century-Crofts, 1968.

Smith, K. Y., and Margaret F. Smith. *Cybernetic Principles of Learning and Educational Design*. New York: Holt, Rinehart and Winston, 1966.

Spence, K. W. "The Relation of Learning Theory to the Technology of Education," *Harvard Educational Review*, Vol. 29 (1959), pp. 84–95.

Woods, Elinor M. "Recent Applications of Computer Technology to School Testing Programs," *Review of Educational Research*, Vol. 40, No. 4 (October, 1970), pp. 525–39.

GENERAL WORKS IN PHILOSOPHY OF SCIENCE

Achinstein, Peter. *Concepts of Science: A Philosophical Analysis*. Baltimore: Johns Hopkins Press, 1968.

Ackermann, Robert. *The Philosophy of Science: An Introduction*. New York: Pegasus, 1970.

Baumrin, Bernard (ed.). *Philosophy of Science: The Delaware Seminar. 1961–1962*. Vol. I. New York: Interscience Publishers, Inc., 1963.

—— (ed.). *Philosophy of Science: The Delaware Seminar, 1963*. Vol. II. New York: Interscience Publishers, Inc., 1963.

Bergmann, G. *Philosophy of Science*. Madison, Wisc.: University of Wisconsin Press, 1957.

Braybrooke, David (ed.). *Philosophical Problems of the Social Sciences*. New York: The Macmillan Company, 1965.

Brodbeck, May (ed.). *Readings in the Philosophy of the Social Sciences*. New York: The Macmillan Company, 1968.

Brody, Baruch A. (ed.). *Readings in the Philosophy of Science*. Englewood Cliffs, N. J.: Prentice-Hall, Inc., 1970.

—— and Nicholas Capaldi (eds.). *Science: Men, Methods, Goals. A Reader: Methods of Physical Science*. New York: W. A. Benjamin, Inc., 1968.

Brown, G. B. *Science: Its Method and Its Philosophy*. New York: W. W. Norton & Company, 1950.

Bunge, Mario. *Scientific Research*. 2 vols. New York: Springer-Verlag, Inc., 1967.

Campbell, N. R. *What is Science?* New York: Dover Publications, Inc., 1921.

Carnap, Rudolf. *Philosophical Foundations of Physics: An Introduction to the Philosophy of Science*. Edited by Martin Gardiner. New York: Basic Books, Inc., 1966.

Caws, Peter. *The Philosophy of Science: A Systematic Account*. Princeton, N. J.: D. Van Nostrand Co., Inc., 1965.

Cohen, Morris Raphael. *Reason and Nature: An Essay on the Meaning of Scientific Method*. Glencoe, Illinois: Free Press, 1953.

Cohen, Robert H., and Marx W. Wartofsky (eds.). *Boston Studies in the Philosophy of Science.* Vol. II (Proceedings of the Boston Colloquium for the Philosophy of Science, 1962–1964). New York: Humanities Press, 1965.

—— (eds.). *Boston Studies in the Philosophy of Science.* Vol. III (Proceedings of the Boston Colloquium for the Philosophy of Science, 1964–1966). New York: Humanities Press, 1967.

—— (eds.). *Boston Studies in the Philosophy of Science.* Vol. IV (Proceedings of the Boston Colloquium for the Philosophy of Science, 1966–68). New York: Humanities Press, 1969.

—— (eds.). *Boston Studies in the Philosophy of Science.* Vol. V (Proceeding of the Boston Colloquium for the Philosophy of Science, 1966–1968.) New York: Humanities Press, 1969.

Colodny, Robert G. (ed.). *Beyond the Edge of Certainty.* (University of Pittsburgh Series in the Philosophy of Science, Vol. II.) Englewood Cliffs, N. J.: Prentice-Hall, Inc., 1965.

—— (ed.). *Frontiers of Science and Philosophy.* (University of Pittsburgh Series in the Philosophy of Science, Vol. I.) Pittsburgh: University of Pittsburgh Press, 1962.

—— (ed.). *Mind and Cosmos: Essays in Contemporary Science and Philosophy.* (University of Pittsburgh Series in the Philosophy of Science, Vol. III.) Pittsburgh: University of Pittsburgh Press, 1966.

—— (ed.). *The Nature and Function of Scientific Theories: Essays in Contemporary Science.* (University of Pittsburgh Series in the Philosophy of Science, Vol. IV.) Pittsburgh: University of Pittsburgh Press, 1970.

Conant, James B. *On Understanding Science.* New Haven, Conn.: Yale University Press, 1947.

Cornforth, Maurice. *Science versus Idealism.* London: Lawrence & Wishart, 1955.

Danto, Alfred, and Sidney Morgenbesser (eds.). *Philosophy of Science.* Cleveland: Meridian Books, The World Publishing Company, 1960.

Dray, William H. (ed.). *Philosophical Analysis and History.* New York: Harper & Row, 1966.

Duhem, Pierre. *The Aim and Structure of Physical Theory.* Princeton, N. J.: Princeton University Press, 1954.

Edwards, Paul (ed.). *The Encyclopedia of Philosophy.* 8 Vols. New York: The Macmillan Company and the Free Press, 1967.

Feigl, H., and G. Maxwell (eds.). *Current Issues in the Philosophy of Science.* New York: Holt, Rinehart, and Winston, 1961.

Feigl, H., and Wilfrid Sellars (eds.). *Readings in Philosophical Analysis.* New York: Appleton-Century-Crofts, Inc., 1949.

Feigl, H., and May Brodbeck (eds.). *Readings in the Philosophy of Science.* New York: Appleton-Century-Crofts, Inc., 1953.

Feigl, Herbert, Michael Scriven, and Grover Maxwell (eds.). *Concepts, Theories, and the Mind-Body Problem.* Minneapolis, Minnesota: University of Minnesota Press, 1958.

Feigl, Herbert, and Michael Scriven (eds.). *The Foundations of Science and the Concepts of Psychology and Psychoanalysis.* Minneapolis, Minnesota: University of Minnesota Press, 1956.

Feigl, Herbert, and Grover Maxwell (eds.). *Scientific Explanation, Space, and Time.* Minneapolis, Minnesota: University of Minnesota Press, 1962.

Feyerabend, P., and G. Maxwell (eds.). *Mind, Matter and Method.* Minneapolis, Minnesota: University of Minnesota Press, 1966.

Foster, Marguerite H., and Michael L. Martin (eds.). *Probability, Confirmation, and Simplicity.* New York: The Odyssey Press, Inc., 1966.

Frank, Philipp G. (ed.). *The Validation of Scientific Theories.* New York: Collier Books, Crowell-Collier Publishing Company, 1961.

Gardiner, Patrick (ed.). *Theories of History.* Glencoe, Ill.: The Free Press, 1959.

Hanson, Norwood Russell. *Patterns of Discovery.* New York: Cambridge University Press, 1958.

Harré, R. *An Introduction to the Logic of the Sciences.* London: Macmillan Company, 1960.

———. *The Principles of Scientific Thinking.* London: The Macmillan Company, 1970.

Hawkins, D. *The Language of Nature: An Essay in the Philosophy of Science.* New York: Doubleday and Company, 1967.

Hempel, C. G. *"Aspects of Scientific Explanation" and Other Essays in the Philosophy of Science.* New York: The Free Press of Glencoe, 1965.

———. *Philosophy of Natural Science.* Englewood Cliffs, N. J.: Prentice-Hall, Inc., 1966.

Kaplan, Abraham. *The Conduct of Inquiry: Methodology for Behavioral Science.* San Francisco: Chandler Publishing Company, 1964.

Kemeny, J. G. *A Philosopher Looks at Science.* Princeton, N. J.: D. Van Nostrand Co., Inc., 1959.

Kockelmans, J. J. (ed.). *Philosophy of Science: The Historical Background.* New York: The Free Press of Glencoe, 1968.

Korner, Stephan. *Experience and Theory: An Essay in the Philosophy of Science.* New York: International Library of Philosophy and Scientific Method, Humanities Press, 1966.

Krimerman, Leonard I. (ed.). *The Nature and Scope of Social Science: A Critical Anthology.* New York: Appleton-Century-Crofts, Inc., 1969.

Kuhn, Thomas S. *The Structure of Scientific Revolutions.* Chicago: University of Chicago Press, 1962.

Lakatos, Imre, and A. E. Musgrave (eds.). *Problems in the Philosophy of Science.* Amsterdam: North Holland Publishing Co., 1968.

Lerner, Daniel (ed.). *Parts and Wholes: The Hudyn Colloquium on Scientific Method and Concept.* New York: The Free Press of Glencoe, 1962.

Madden, Edward H. (ed.). *The Structure of Scientific Thought. An Introduction to Philosophy of Science.* Boston: Houghton Mifflin, 1960.

Morgenbesser, Sidney (ed.). *Philosophy of Science Today.* New York: Basic Books, Inc., 1967.

Nagel, Ernest, Patrick Suppes, and Alfred Tarski (eds.). *Logic, Methodology and Philosophy of Science.* (Proceedings of the 1960 International Congress.) Stanford, California: Stanford University Press, 1962.

Nagel, Ernest. *The Structure of Science.* New York: Harcourt, Brace and World, 1961.

Nash, Leonard K. *The Nature of the Natural Sciences.* Boston: Little, Brown and Company, 1963.

Nidditch, P. H. (ed.). *The Philosophy of Science.* London: Oxford University Press, 1968.

Pap, Arthur. *An Introduction to the Philosophy of Science.* New York: The Free Press of Glencoe, 1962.

Poincaré, H. *Science and Hypothesis.* New York: Dover Press, 1952.

Popper, Karl. *Conjectures and Refutations: The Growth of Scientific Knowledge.* New York: Harper & Row, 1968.

———. *The Logic of Scientific Discovery.* New York: Basic Books, Inc., 1959.

Radner, Michael, and Stephen Winokur (eds.). *Analyses of Theories and Methods of Physics and Psychology.* Minneapolis, Minnesota: University of Minnesota Press, 1970.

Rosenblueth, Arturo. *Mind and Brain: A Philosophy of Science.* Cambridge, Massachusetts: MIT Press, 1970.

Scheffler, Israel. *The Anatomy of Inquiry: Philosophical Studies in the Theory of Science.* London: Routledge & Kegan Paul Ltd., 1964.

Schwab, J. J. "What Do Scientists Do?" *Behavioral Science*, Vol. 5, No. 1 (January, 1960), pp. 1–27.

Shapere, Dudley (ed.). *Philosophical Problems of Natural Science.* New York: Macmillan, 1965.

Stuewar, Roger H. (ed.). *Historical and Philosophical Perspectives of Science.* Minneapolis, Minnesota: University of Minnesota Press, 1970.

Toulmin, Stephen. *Foresight and Understanding: An Enquiry into the Aims of Science.* New York: Torchbook, Harper & Row Publishers, 1961.

———. *The Philosophy of Science: An Introduction.* New York: Harper & Row, Publishers, 1953.

Wartofsky, Marx W. (ed.). *Boston Studies in the Philosophy of Science.* Vol. I (Proceedings of the Boston Colloquium for the Philosophy of Science, 1961–62.) New York: Humanities Press, 1963.

———. *Conceptual Foundations of Scientific Thought: An Introduction to the Philosophy of Science.* New York: The Macmillan Company, 1968.

Wiener, P. P. (ed.). *Readings in the Philosophy of Science; Introduction to the Foundations and Cultural Aspects of the Sciences.* New York: Scribner, 1953.

Author Index

Subject Index

Actions, 3ff, 137, 459–473
  versus causal explanations, 464ff
  primary reason for, 460ff
    intentions, 463ff
  pro attitude toward, 459f, 462
  rationalization of, 459ff
  redescription of, 465f
  in terms of means and end, 506f
Analytical methodology, 207ff
  resistance to, 207f
Applied research, versus basic research,
    10ff, 79, 82, 108ff, 112f, 115f,123f
  and behavioral sciences, 115f, 117f
  definition of, 109f, 112, 113, 115f,123
  and motivation, 111ff
  no operational distinction, 109, 113
  and relevance, 113ff
  definition of, 123
  education's need for, 122, 128ff
  see also Research; Research approaches

Basic research, versus applied research, 10ff,
    79, 82, 108ff, 112f, 115f, 123f
  and behavioral sciences, 115f, 117f
  definition of, 109f, 112, 113, 115f,123
  and motivation, 111ff
  no operational distinction, 109, 113
  and relevance, 113ff
  and education, 116ff, 122ff

  and learning, 68f
  and motivation, 111ff
  and relevance, 113ff
  see also Research; Research approaches
Bayesian inference, 307ff, 322ff, 331ff
  versus classical approach, 310ff
  and conditional probabilities, 313ff
  and decision-theoretic formulation, 311f
  definition of, 308, 311
  history of, 308ff
  and personalistic theory of probability,
    312ff, 322ff
  and problem of prior probabilities, 317f
Behavioral objectives, 810–819
  and educational research, 810
    curriculum and teaching, 810f
    faults and limitations of, 819
    school uses, 811f
    theories of learning, 812ff
    and knowledge, 712ff, 740f, 814ff
Behavioral research, versus educational
    research, 65ff
  and ethical limits, 140ff, 151ff
  and excessive exposure or deprivation to
    subject, 152f
  procedures of, 154f
  and subjects' well-being, 152f
  and value conflicts, 140ff
Behavioral testing, variables affecting, 606ff